Lerwick

Kirkwall

Wick

Sunderland

COUNTRY

York

Kingston upon Hull

Leeds

Sheffield

THE MIDLANDS

Nottingham
Derby

Leicester

Coventry

Cambridge

Northampton   Ipswich

Luton

Oxford   LONDON

SOUTHEAST ENGLAND

Southampton   Dover
Portsmouth   Brighton

0 kilometres   100

0 miles   50

D0836897

GREAT BRITAIN

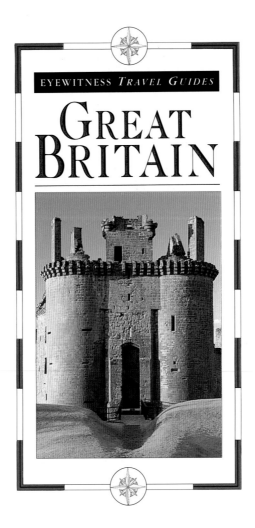

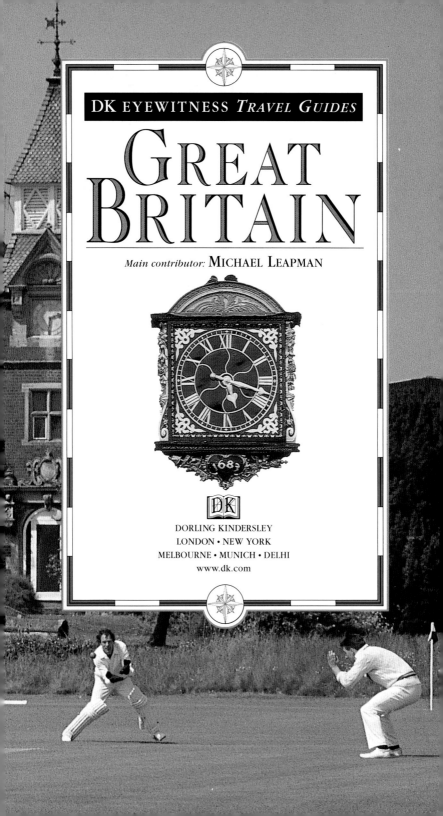

DK EYEWITNESS *TRAVEL GUIDES*

GREAT BRITAIN

Main contributor: MICHAEL LEAPMAN

DORLING KINDERSLEY
LONDON • NEW YORK
MELBOURNE • MUNICH • DELHI
www.dk.com

A DORLING KINDERSLEY BOOK

www.dk.com

ART EDITOR Stephen Bere
PROJECT EDITOR Marian Broderick
EDITORS Carey Combe, Sara Harper, Elaine Harries,
Kim Inglis, Ella Milroy, Andrew Szudek, Nia Williams
DESIGNERS Susan Blackburn, Elly King,
Colin Loughrey, Andy Wilkinson

CONTRIBUTORS
Josie Barnard, Christopher Catling,
Juliet Clough, Lindsay Hunt, Polly Phillimore,
Martin Symington, Roger Thomas

MAPS
Jane Hanson, Phil Rose, Jennifer Skelley (Lovell Johns Ltd)
Gary Bowes (Era-Maptec Ltd)

PHOTOGRAPHERS
Joe Cornish, Paul Harris, Rob Reichenfeld, Kim Sayer

ILLUSTRATORS
Gary Cross, Richard Draper, Jared Gilby (Kevin Jones Assocs),
Paul Guest, Roger Hutchins, Chris Orr & Assocs,
Maltings Partnership, Ann Winterbotham, John Woodcock

Reproduced by Colourscan (Singapore)
Printed and bound by South China Printing Co. Ltd., China

First published in Great Britain in 1995
by Dorling Kindersley Limited
80 Strand, London WC2R 0RL

**Reprinted with revisions 1996, 1997, 1998, 1999, 2000, 2001,
2002**

Copyright 1995, 2002 © Dorling Kindersley Limited, London
A Penguin Company

ISBN 0 7513 4704 3

**The information in every
DK Eyewitness Travel Guide is checked regularly.**
Every effort has been made to ensure that this book is as up-to-
date as possible at the time of going to press. Some details,
however, such as telephone numbers, prices, gallery hanging
arrangements and travel information are liable to change. The
publishers cannot accept responsibility for any consequences
arising from the use of this book, nor for any material on third-
party websites, and cannot guarantee that any website address in
this book will be a suitable source of travel information. We
value the views and suggestions of our readers highly. Please
write to: Senior Publishing Manager, DK Eyewitness Travel Guides,
Dorling Kindersley, 80 Strand, London WC2R 0RL.

CONTENTS

A 14th-century illustration
of two knights jousting

INTRODUCING
GREAT BRITAIN

Beefeater at the Tower of London

LONDON

Eilean Donan Castle on Loch Duich in the Scottish Highlands

Jacobean "Old House"
in Hereford

View of the Usk Valley and the
Brecon Beacons, Wales

How to Use this Guide

This guide helps you to get the most from your holidays in Great Britain. It provides both detailed practical information and expert recommendations. *Introducing Great Britain* maps the country and sets it in its historical and cultural context. The six regional chapters, plus *London*, describe important sights, using maps, pictures and illustrations. Features cover topics from houses and famous gardens to sport. Hotel, restaurant, and pub recommendations can be found in *Travellers' Needs*. The *Survival Guide* has practical information on everything from transport to personal safety.

London

The centre of London has been divided into four sightseeing areas. Each has its own chapter, which opens with a list of the sights described. The last section, *Further Afield*, covers the most attractive suburbs. All sights are numbered and plotted on an area map. The information for each sight follows the map's numerical order, making sights easy to locate within the chapter.

Sights at a Glance lists the chapter's sights by category: Historic Streets and Buildings; Museums and Galleries; Churches and Cathedrals; Shops; Parks and Gardens.

All pages relating to London have red thumb tabs.

A locator map shows where you are in relation to other areas of the city centre.

1 Area Map
For easy reference, the sights are numbered and located on a map. Sights in the city centre are also marked on the Street Finder on pages 133–41.

2 Street-by-Street Map
This gives a bird's-eye view of the key areas in each chapter.

Stars indicate the sights that no visitor should miss.

A suggested route for a walk is shown in red.

3 Detailed information
The sights in London are described individually. Addresses, telephone numbers, opening hours, admission charges, tours, photography and wheelchair access are also provided, as well as public transport links.

THE LOWLANDS

STRATHCLYDE · CENTRAL · TAYSIDE · FIFE
LOTHIAN · DUMFRIES AND GALLOWAY · BORDERS

1 Introduction
The landscape, history and character of each region is outlined here, showing how the area has developed over the centuries and what it has to offer the visitor today.

GREAT BRITAIN AREA BY AREA

Apart from London, Great Britain has been divided into 14 regions, each of which has a separate chapter. The most interesting towns and places to visit have been numbered on a *Pictorial Map*.

Each area of Great Britain can be identified quickly by its colour coding, shown on the inside front cover.

2 Pictorial Map
This shows the main road network and gives an illustrated overview of the whole region. All entries are numbered and there are also useful tips on getting around the region by car, train and other forms of transport.

Exploring the Lowlands

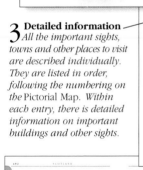

3 Detailed information
All the important sights, towns and other places to visit are described individually. They are listed in order, following the numbering on the Pictorial Map. Within each entry, there is detailed information on important buildings and other sights.

Story boxes explore related topics.

For all the top sights, a Visitors' Checklist provides the practical information you need to plan your visit.

4 The top sights
These are given one or more full pages. Three-dimensional illustrations reveal the interiors of historic buildings. Interesting town and city centres are given street-by-street maps, featuring individual sights.

Edinburgh Castle

INTRODUCING GREAT BRITAIN

Putting Great Britain on the Map

L YING IN NORTHWESTERN EUROPE, Great Britain is bounded by the Atlantic Ocean, the North Sea and the English Channel. The island's landscape and climate are varied, and it is this variety that even today affects the pattern of settlement. The remote shores of the West Country peninsula and the inhospitable mountains of Scotland and Wales are less populated than the relatively flat and fertile Midlands and Southeast, where the vast majority of the country's 58 million people live. Due to this population density, the south is today the most built-up part of the country.

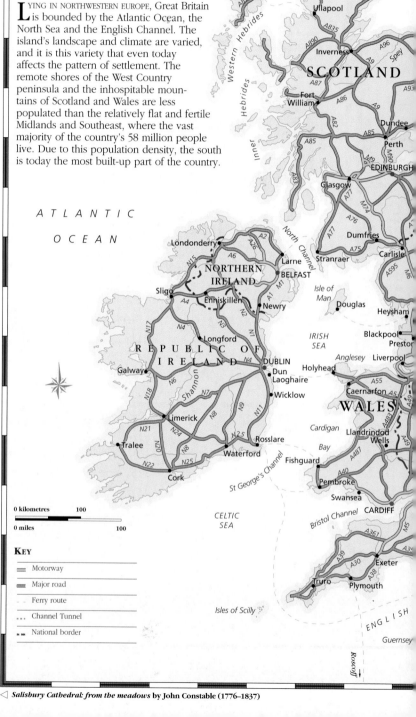

ATLANTIC OCEAN

SCOTLAND

Stornoway
Wick
Ullapool
Inverness
Fort William
Dundee
Perth
EDINBURGH
Glasgow
Dumfries
Carlisle
Stranraer

Western Hebrides
Inner Hebrides
Spey

NORTHERN IRELAND
Londonderry
Larne
BELFAST
Sligo
Enniskillen
Newry
North Channel

Isle of Man
Douglas
Heysham

IRISH SEA
Blackpool
Preston

REPUBLIC OF IRELAND
Longford
DUBLIN
Galway
Dun Laoghaire
Wicklow
Shannon
Limerick
Tralee
Rosslare
Waterford
Cork

Anglesey
Liverpool
Holyhead
Caernarfon

WALES
Cardigan Bay
Llandrindod Wells

St George's Channel
Fishguard
Pembroke
Swansea
CARDIFF

CELTIC SEA

Bristol Channel

Exeter
Truro
Plymouth

Isles of Scilly

ENGLISH

Guernsey

Roscoff

0 kilometres   100
0 miles   100

KEY

▬	Motorway
▬	Major road
- - -	Ferry route
···	Channel Tunnel
▬ ▪	National border

◁ *Salisbury Cathedral: from the meadows* by John Constable (1776–1837)

Europe

Great Britain is situated in the northwest corner of Europe. Its nearest neighbours are Ireland to the west, and the Netherlands, Belgium and France across the Channel. Denmark, Norway and Sweden are also easily accessible.

Shetland and Orkney islands

These islands form the northern-most part of Great Britain, with the Shetlands lying six degrees south of the Arctic Circle. There are transport links to the mainland.

Regional Great Britain: London, the South, the Midlands and Wales

G REAT BRITAIN has airline connections with most cities in the world. London is the main transport hub with two major international airports, including Heathrow, the world's busiest. Southern England, Britain's most populous area, is divided, within this book, into four regions – Southeast England, the West Country, Wales and the Midlands – with a separate chapter for London. Road and rail links to the North and Scotland (*see pp14–15*) are plentiful, as are links between all main towns.

KEY TO COLOUR-CODING

London

Southeast England

The Downs and Channel Coast

East Anglia

Thames Valley

The West Country

Wessex

Devon and Cornwall

Wales

North Wales

South and Mid-Wales

The Midlands

The Heart of England

East Midlands

KEY TO MAP

⛴ Ferry port

✈ Airport

🚌 Long-distance bus terminal

━ Motorway

━ Major road

━ Railway line

⋯ Channel Tunnel

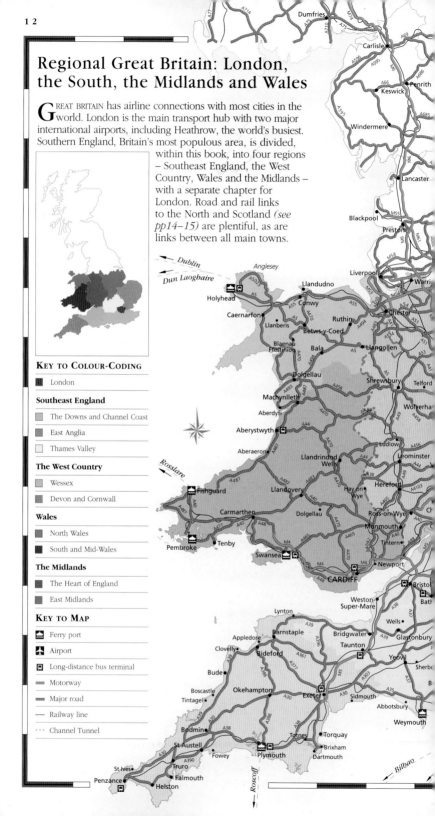

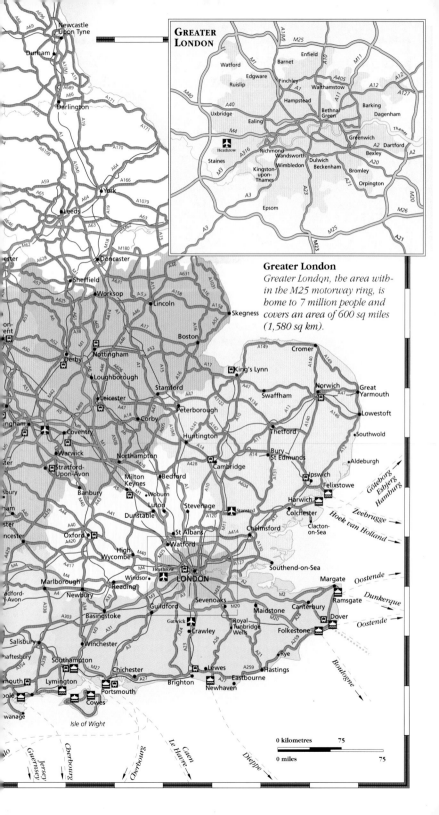

GREATER LONDON

Greater London

Greater London, the area within the M25 motorway ring, is home to 7 million people and covers an area of 600 sq miles (1,580 sq km).

0 kilometres 75

0 miles 75

Regional Great Britain: The North and Scotland

T HIS PART OF GREAT BRITAIN is divided into two sections in this book. Although it is far less populated than the southern sector of the country, there are good road and rail connections, and ferry services link the islands with the mainland.

KEY TO COLOUR-CODING

The North Country

- Lancashire and the Lakes
- Yorkshire and Humber Region
- Northumbria

Scotland

- The Lowlands
- The Highlands and Islands

Isle of Lewis · Stornoway · Tarbert · Ullapool · Western Isles · Lochmaddy · Uig · Isle of Skye · Kyle of Lochalsh · Lochboisdale · Castlebay · Hebrides · Mallaig · Fort William · Arinagour · Tobermory · Scarinish · Craignure · Inner · Oban · Crainlarich · Scalasaig · Jura · Greenock · Kennacraig · Paisley · Ardrossan · Islay · Brodick · Irvine · Port Ellen · Ayr · Campbeltown · Isle of Arran

Isle of Man · Douglas · Larne · Belfast · Cairnryan · Stranraer · Holyhead

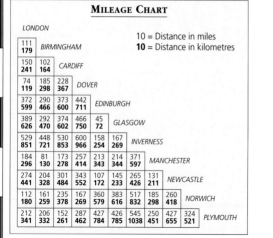

MILEAGE CHART

LONDON

10 = Distance in miles
10 = Distance in kilometres

111 / **179**	BIRMINGHAM									
150 / **241**	102 / **164**	CARDIFF								
74 / **119**	185 / **298**	228 / **367**	DOVER							
372 / **599**	290 / **466**	373 / **600**	442 / **711**	EDINBURGH						
389 / **626**	292 / **470**	374 / **602**	466 / **750**	45 / **72**	GLASGOW					
529 / **851**	448 / **721**	530 / **853**	600 / **966**	158 / **254**	167 / **269**	INVERNESS				
184 / **296**	81 / **130**	173 / **278**	257 / **414**	213 / **343**	214 / **344**	371 / **597**	MANCHESTER			
274 / **441**	204 / **328**	301 / **484**	343 / **552**	107 / **172**	145 / **233**	265 / **426**	131 / **211**	NEWCASTLE		
112 / **180**	161 / **259**	235 / **378**	167 / **269**	360 / **579**	383 / **616**	517 / **832**	185 / **298**	260 / **418**	NORWICH	
212 / **341**	206 / **332**	152 / **261**	287 / **462**	427 / **784**	426 / **785**	545 / **1038**	250 / **451**	427 / **655**	324 / **521**	PLYMOUTH

0 kilometres 100
0 miles 100

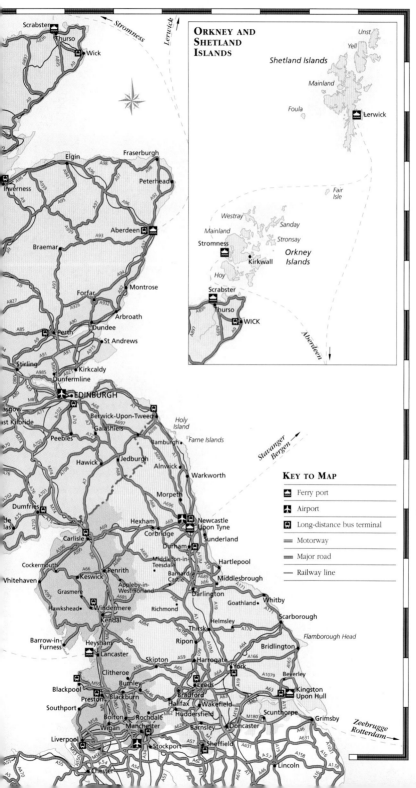

ORKNEY AND SHETLAND ISLANDS

Shetland Islands

Unst

Yell

Mainland

Foula

Lerwick

Fair Isle

Westray

Sanday

Mainland

Stronsay

Stromness

Orkney Islands

Kirkwall

Hoy

Scrabster

Thurso

WICK

Aberdeen

KEY TO MAP

Ferry port

Airport

Long-distance bus terminal

Motorway

Major road

Railway line

A Portrait of Great Britain

BRITAIN HAS BEEN ASSIDUOUS *in preserving its traditions, but offers the visitor much more than stately castles and pretty villages. A diversity of landscape, culture, literature, art and architecture, as well as its unique heritage, results in a nation balancing the needs of the present with those of its past.*

Britain's character has been shaped by its geographical position as an island. Never successfully invaded since 1066, its people have developed their own distinctive traditions. The Roman invasion of AD 43 lasted 350 years but Roman culture and language were quickly overlain with those of the northern European settlers who followed. Ties with Europe were loosened further in the 16th century when the Catholic church was replaced by a less dogmatic established church.

Although today a member of the European Union, Britain continues to delight in its non-conformity, even in superficial ways such as driving on the left-hand side of the road instead of the right. The opening of the rail tunnel to France is a topographical adjustment that does not necessarily mark a change in national attitude.

The British heritage is seen in its ancient castles, cathedrals and stately homes with their gardens and Classical parklands. Age-old customs are renewed each year, from royal ceremonies to Morris dancers performing on village greens.

For a small island, Great Britain encompasses a surprising variety in its regions, whose inhabitants maintain distinct identities. Scotland and Wales are separate countries from England with their own legislative assemblies.

Tudor rose

Walking along the east bank of the River Avon, Bath

◁ Punting, a popular pastime on the River Cam, Cambridge

Widecombe-in-the-Moor, a Devon village clustered round a church and set in hills

They have different customs, traditions, and, in the case of Scotland, different legal and educational systems. The Welsh and Scots Gaelic languages survive and are sustained by their own radio and television networks. In northern and West Country areas, English itself is spoken in a rich variety of dialects and accents, and these areas maintain their own regional arts, crafts, architecture and food.

The landscape is varied, too, from the craggy mountains of Wales, Scotland and the north, through the flat expanses of the Midlands and eastern England to the soft, rolling hills of the south and west. The long, broad beaches of East Anglia contrast with the picturesque rocky inlets along much of the west coast.

Scottish coat of arms at Edinburgh Castle

Despite the spread of towns and cities over the last two centuries, rural Britain still flourishes. Nearly three-quarters of Britain's land is used for agriculture. The main commercial crops are wheat, barley, sugar beet and potatoes, though what catches the eye in early summer are the fields of bright yellow rape or slate-blue flax.

The countryside is dotted with farms and charming villages, with picturesque cottages and lovingly tended gardens – a British passion. A typical village is built around an ancient church and a small, friendly pub. Here the pace of life slows. To drink a pint of ale in a cosy, village inn and relax before a fire is a time-honoured British custom. Strangers will be welcomed cordially, though perhaps with caution; for even if strict formality is a thing of the past, the British have a tendency to be reserved.

In the 19th and early 20th centuries, trade with the extensive British Empire, fuelled by abundant coal supplies, spurred manufacturing and created wealth. Thousands of people moved from the countryside to towns and cities near mines, mills and factories. By 1900 Britain was the world's strongest industrial nation. Now many

Lake and gardens at Petworth House, Sussex

of these old industrial centres have declined, and today manufacturing employs only 22 per cent of the labour force, while 66 per cent work in the growing service sector. These service industries are located mainly in the southeast, close to London, where modern office buildings bear witness to comparative prosperity.

Crowds at Petticoat Lane market in London's East End

SOCIETY AND POLITICS

British cities are melting-pots for people not just from different parts of the country but also from overseas. Irish immigration has long ensured a flow of labour into the country, and since the 1950s hundreds of thousands have come from former colonies in Africa, Asia and the Caribbean, many of which are now members of the Commonwealth. Nearly five per cent of Britain's 58 million inhabitants are from nonwhite ethnic groups – and about half of these were born in Britain. The result

Priest in the Close at Winchester Cathedral

is a multi-cultural society that can boast a wide range of music, art, food and religions. However, prejudice does exist and in some inner-city areas where poorer members of different communities live, racial tensions can occasionally arise. Even though discrimination in housing and employment on the grounds of race is against the law, it does occur in places.

Britain's class structure still intrigues and bewilders many visitors, based as it is on a subtle mixture of heredity and wealth. Even though many of the great inherited fortunes no longer exist, some old landed families still live on their

Bosses in Norwich Cathedral cloisters

large estates, and many now open them to the public. Class divisions are further entrenched by the education system. While more than 90 per cent of children are educated free by the state, richer parents often opt for private schooling, and the products of these private schools are disproportionately represented in the higher echelons of government and business.

The monarchy's position highlights the dilemma of a people seeking to preserve its most potent symbol of national unity in an age that is suspicious of inherited privilege. Without real political power, though still head of the Church of England, the Queen and her family are subject to increasing public scrutiny. Following a spate of personal scandals, some citizens advocate the abolition of the monarchy.

Democracy has deep foundations in Britain: there was even a parliament of sorts in London in the 13th century.

Yet with the exception of the 17th-century Civil War, power has passed gradually from the Crown to the people's elected representatives. A series of Reform Acts between 1832 and 1884 gave the vote to all male citizens, though women were not enfranchised on an equal basis until 1928. Margaret Thatcher – Britain's first woman Prime Minister – held office for 12 years from 1979. During the 20th

Afternoon tea on the back lawn at the Thornbury Castle Hotel, Avon

century, the Labour (left wing) and Conservative (right wing) parties have, during their periods in office, favoured a mix of public and private ownership for industry and ample funding for the state health and welfare systems.

The position of Ireland has been an intractable political issue since the 17th century. Part of the United Kingdom for 800 years, but divided in 1921, it has seen conflict between Catholics and Protestants for many years. The Good Friday Peace Agreement of 1998 was a huge step forward but the path to lasting peace is a rocky one.

CULTURE AND THE ARTS

Britain has a famous theatrical tradition stretching back to the 16th century and William Shakespeare. His plays

The House of Lords, in Parliament

have been performed on stage almost continuously since he wrote them and the works of 17th- and 18th-century writers are also frequently revived. Twentieth-century British playwrights such as Tom Stoppard, Alan Ayckbourn and David Hare draw on this long tradition with their vivid language and by using comedy to illustrate serious themes. British actors such as Vanessa Redgrave, Ian McKellen, Ralph Fiennes and Anthony Hopkins have international reputations.

While London is the focal point of British theatre, fine drama is to be seen in many other parts of the country. The Edinburgh Festival and its Fringe are the high point of Great Britain's cultural calendar with theatre and music to suit all tastes. Other music festivals are held across the country, chiefly in summer, while there are annual

Schoolboys at Eton, the famous public school

festivals of literature at Hay-on-Wye and Cheltenham. Poetry has had an enthusiastic following since Chaucer wrote the *Canterbury Tales* in the 14th century: poems from all eras can even be read on the London Underground, where they are interspersed with the advertisements in the carriages and on the station platforms.

In the visual arts, Britain has a strong tradition in portraiture, caricature, landscape and watercolour. In modern times David Hockney and Francis Bacon, and sculptors Henry Moore and Barbara Hepworth, have enjoyed worldwide recognition. Architects including

Christopher Wren, Inigo Jones, John Nash and Robert Adam all created styles that define British cities; and nowadays, Terry Farrell and Richard Rogers carry the standard for Post-Modernism. Britain is becoming famous for its innovative fashion designers, many of whom now show their spring and autumn collections in Paris.

Reading the newspaper in Kensington Gardens

The British are avid newspaper readers. There are 11 national newspapers published from London on weekdays: the standard of the broadsheets is very high and newspapers such as *The Times* are read the world over because of their reputation for strong international reporting. Most popular, however, are the tabloids packed with gossip, crime and sport, which account for some 80 per cent of the total.

Naomi Campbell, a British supermodel

The indigenous film industry, although squeezed by Hollywood, produces occasional international hits such as *Four Weddings and a Funeral* and *The Full Monty*. British television is famous for the high quality of its serious news, current affairs and nature programmes as well as for its drama. The publicly funded British Broadcasting Corporation, which controls five national radio networks and two television channels, is widely admired.

The British are great sports fans. Soccer, rugby, cricket and golf are popular both to watch and to take part in. An instantly recognizable English image is that of the cricket match on a village green. Nationwide, fishing is the most popular sporting pastime, and the British make good use of their national parks as enthusiastic ramblers and walkers.

British food used to be derided for a lack of imagination. The cuisine relied on a limited range of quality ingredients, plainly prepared. But recent influences from abroad have introduced a wider range of ingredients and more adventurous techniques. Typical English food – plain home cooking and regional dishes – can still be found but they are being supplemented by a tastier modern British cuisine.

In this, as in other respects, the British are doing what they have done for centuries: accommodating their own traditions to influences from other cultures, while leaving the essential elements of their national life and character intact.

Whitby harbour and St Mary's Church, Yorkshire

Gardens Through the Ages

STYLES OF GARDENING in Britain have expanded alongside architecture and other evolving fashions. The Elizabethan knot garden became more elaborate and formal in Jacobean times, when the range of plants greatly increased. The 18th century brought a taste for large-scale "natural" landscapes with lakes, woods and pastures, creating the most distinctively English style to have emerged. In the 19th century, fierce debate raged between supporters of natural and formal gardens, developing into the eclecticism of the 20th century when "garden rooms" in differing styles became popular.

A grotto and cascade brought romance and mystery.

Monumental column

Capability Brown (1715–83) was Britain's most influential garden designer, favouring the move away from formal gardens to man-made pastoral settings.

Blackthorn

Classical temples were a much appreciated feature in 18th-century gardens and were often exact replicas of buildings that the designers had seen in Greece.

Elaborate parterres were a feature of aristocratic gardens of the 17th century, when the fashion spread from Europe. This is the Privy Garden at Hampton Court Palace, restored in 1995 to its design under William III.

IDEAL LANDSCAPE GARDEN

Classical Greece and Rome inspired the grand gardens of the early 18th century, such as Stourhead and Stowe. Informal clumps of trees played a critical part in the serene, manicured landscapes.

Maple

Winding paths were carefully planned to allow changing vistas to open out as visitors strolled around the garden.

DESIGN AND FORMALITY

A flower garden is a work of artifice, an attempt to tame nature rather than to copy it. Growing plants in rows or regular patterns, interspersed with statues and ornaments, imposes a sense of order. Designs change to reflect the fashion of the time and the introduction of new plants.

Medieval gardens usually had a herber (a turfed sitting area) and a vine arbour. A good reconstruction is Queen Eleanor's Garden, Winchester.

Tudor gardens featured edged borders and sometimes mazes. The Tudor House Garden, Southampton, also has beehives and heraldic statues.

Herbaceous borders, *full of lush plants, are the glory of the summer garden. Gertrude Jekyll (1843–1932), was high priestess of the mixed border, with her eye for seductive colour combinations.*

VISITORS' CHECKLIST

The "yellow book", Gardens of England and Wales, *the annual guide to the National Gardens Scheme, lists gardens open to the public.*

DEVELOPMENT OF THE MODERN PANSY

All garden plants derive from wild flowers, bred over the years to produce qualities that appeal to gardeners. The story of the pansy, one of our most popular flowers, is typical.

The wild pansy (*Viola tricolor*) native to Britain is commonly known as heartsease. It is a small-flowered annual which can vary considerably in colour.

The mountain pansy (*Viola lutea*) is a perennial. The first cultivated varieties resulted from crossing it with heartsease in the early 19th century.

The Show Pansy was bred by florists after the blotch appeared as a chance seedling in 1840. It was round in form with a small, symmetrical blotch.

The Fancy Pansy, developed in the 1860s, was much larger. The blotch covered all three lower petals save for a thin margin of colour.

Modern hybrids of pansies, violas and violettas, developed by selective breeding, are varied and versatile in a wide range of vibrant new colours.

Cedar of Lebanon   Yew

Rhododendron

The Palladian bridge was a favourite feature, often decorative rather than practical.

Knot Gardens *were in vogue in the 1500s. Intersecting lines of lavender or box were filled with flowers, herbs or vegetables, as in this restoration at Pitmedden in Scotland.*

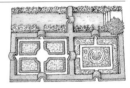

17th-century gardening was more elaborate. Water gardens like those at Blenheim were often combined with parterres of exotic foreign plants.

Victorian gardens, their formal beds a mass of colour, were a reaction to the landscapes of Capability Brown. Alton Towers has a good example.

20th-century gardens mix historic and modern styles, as at Hidcote Manor, Gloucestershire. Growing wild flowers is becoming a popular choice.

Stately Homes

THE GRAND COUNTRY HOUSE reached its zenith in the 18th and 19th centuries, when the old landed families and the new captains of industry enjoyed their wealth, looked after by a retinue of servants. The earliest stately homes date from the 14th century, when defence was paramount. By the 16th century, when the opulent taste of the European Renaissance spread to England, houses became centres of pleasure and showplaces for fine art *(see pp288–9)*. The Georgians favoured chaste Classical architecture with rich interiors, the Victorians flamboyant Gothic. Due to 20th-century social change many stately homes have been opened to the public, some administered by the National Trust.

Adam sketch (c.1760) for ornate panel

The saloon, a domed rotunda based on the Pantheon in Rome, was designed to display the Curzon family's Classical sculpture collection to 18th-century society.

The Drawing Room, the main room for entertaining, contains the most important pictures and some exquisite plasterwork.

The Marble Hall is where balls and other social functions took place among Corinthian columns of pink alabaster.

The Family Wing is a self-contained "pavilion" of private living quarters; the servants lived in rooms above the kitchen. The Curzon family still live here.

The Music Room is decorated with musical themes. Music was the main entertainment on social occasions.

TIMELINE OF ARCHITECTS

1650				1750

Sir John Vanbrugh *(see p384)* was helped by **Nicholas Hawksmoor** (1661–1736) on Blenheim Palace *(see pp214–15)*

Colen Campbell (1676–1729) designed Burlington House *(see p83)*

William Kent (1685–1748) built Holkham Hall *(see p183)* in the Palladian style

Robert Adam (1728–92), who often worked with his brother James (1730–94) was as famous for decorative details as for buildings

John Carr (1723–1807) designed the Palladian Harewood House *(see p396)*

Henry Holland (1745–1806) designed the Neo-Classical south range of Woburn Abbey *(see p216)*

Castle Howard (1702) by Sir John Vanbrugh

Adam fireplace, Kedleston Hall, adorned with Classical motifs

NATIONAL TRUST

National Trust oak leaf design

At the end of the 19th century, there were real fears that burgeoning factories, mines, roads and houses would obliterate much of Britain's historic landscape and finest buildings. In 1895 a group that included the social reformer Octavia Hill formed the National Trust, to preserve the nation's valuable heritage. The first building acquired by the trust was the medieval Clergy House at Alfriston in Sussex, in 1896 (see p166). Today the National Trust is a charity that runs many historic houses and gardens, and vast stretches of countryside and coastline (see p617). It is supported by more than two million members nationwide.

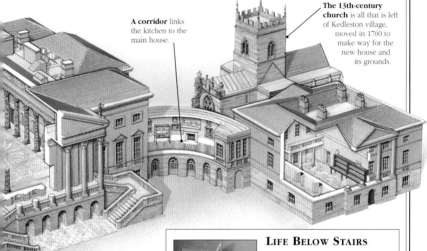

A corridor links the kitchen to the main house.

The 13th-century church is all that is left of Kedleston village, moved in 1760 to make way for the new house and its grounds.

KEDLESTON HALL

This Derbyshire mansion (see p322) is an early work of the influential Georgian architect Robert Adam, who was a pioneer of the Neo-Classical style derived from ancient Greece and Rome. It was built for the Curzon family in the 1760s.

Life Below Stairs by **Charles Hunt (c.1890)**

LIFE BELOW STAIRS

A large community of resident staff was essential to run a country house smoothly. The butler was in overall charge, ensuring that meals were served on time. The housekeeper supervised uniformed maids who made sure the place was clean. The cook ran the kitchen, using fresh produce from the estate. Ladies' maids and valets acted as personal servants.

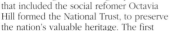

1800	1850

Dining Room, Cragside, Northumberland

Norman Shaw (1831–1912) was an exponent of Victorian Gothic, as in Cragside (above), and a pioneer of the Arts and Crafts movement (see p314)

Philip Webb (1831–1915) was a leading architect of the influential Arts and Crafts movement (see p314), whose buildings favoured the simpler forms of an "Old English" style, instead of flamboyant Victorian Gothic

Sir Edwin Lutyens (1869–1944) designed the elaborate Castle Drogo in Devon (see p281), one of the last grand country houses

Standen, West Sussex (1891–94) by Philip Webb

Heraldry and the Aristocracy

THE BRITISH ARISTOCRACY has evolved over 900 years from the feudal obligations of noblemen to the Norman kings, who conferred privileges of rank and land in return for armed support. Subsequent monarchs bestowed titles and property on their supporters, establishing new aristocratic dynasties. The title of "earl" dates from the 11th century; that of "duke" from the 14th century. Soon the nobility began to choose their own symbols, partly to identify a knight concealed by his armour: these were often painted on the knight's coat (hence the term "coat of arms") and also copied onto his shield.

Order of the Garter medal

The College of Arms, London: housing records of all coats of arms and devising new ones

ROYAL COAT OF ARMS

The most familiar British coat of arms is the sovereign's. It appears on the royal standard, or flag, as well as on official documents and on shops that enjoy royal patronage. Over nearly 900 years, various monarchs have made modifications. The quartered shield in the middle displays the arms of England (twice), Scotland and Ireland. Surrounding it are other traditional images including the lion and unicorn, topped by the crown and the royal helm (helmet).

Edward III (1327–77) was the founder of the chivalric Order of the Garter. The garter, bearing the motto, Honi soit qui mal y pense (evil be to him who thinks of evil), goes round the central shield.

The lion is the most common beast in heraldry.

The red lion is the symbol of Scotland.

The unicorn is a mythical beast, generally regarded as a Scottish royal beast in heraldry.

Henry II (1154–89) formalized his coat of arms to include three lions. This was developed by his son Richard I to become the "Gules three lions passant guardant or" seen on today's arms.

Dieu et mon droit (God and my right) has been the royal motto since the reign of Henry V (1413–22).

The royal helm with gold protective bars was introduced to the arms by Elizabeth I (1558–1603).

Henry VII (1485–1509) devised the Tudor rose, joining the white and red roses of York and Lancaster.

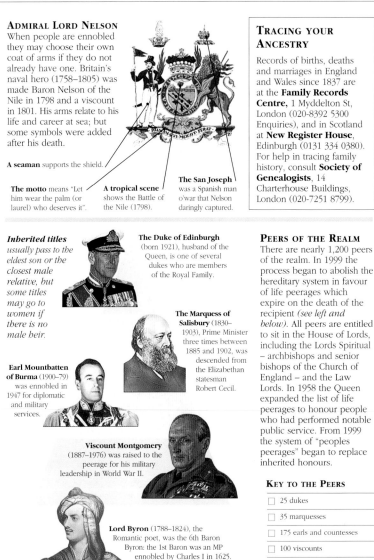

ADMIRAL LORD NELSON

When people are ennobled they may choose their own coat of arms if they do not already have one. Britain's naval hero (1758–1805) was made Baron Nelson of the Nile in 1798 and a viscount in 1801. His arms relate to his life and career at sea; but some symbols were added after his death.

A seaman supports the shield.

The motto means "Let him wear the palm (or laurel) who deserves it".

A tropical scene shows the Battle of the Nile (1798).

The San Joseph was a Spanish man o'war that Nelson daringly captured.

TRACING YOUR ANCESTRY

Records of births, deaths and marriages in England and Wales since 1837 are at the **Family Records Centre**, 1 Myddelton St, London (020-8392 5300 Enquiries), and in Scotland at **New Register House**, Edinburgh (0131 334 0380). For help in tracing family history, consult **Society of Genealogists**, 14 Charterhouse Buildings, London (020-7251 8799).

Inherited titles usually pass to the eldest son or the closest male relative, but some titles may go to women if there is no male heir.

The Duke of Edinburgh (born 1921), husband of the Queen, is one of several dukes who are members of the Royal Family.

Earl Mountbatten of Burma (1900–79) was ennobled in 1947 for diplomatic and military services.

The Marquess of Salisbury (1830–1903), Prime Minister three times between 1885 and 1902, was descended from the Elizabethan statesman Robert Cecil.

Viscount Montgomery (1887–1976) was raised to the peerage for his military leadership in World War II.

Lord Byron (1788–1824), the Romantic poet, was the 6th Baron Byron: the 1st Baron was an MP ennobled by Charles I in 1625.

PEERS OF THE REALM

There are nearly 1,200 peers of the realm. In 1999 the process began to abolish the hereditary system in favour of life peerages which expire on the death of the recipient *(see left and below)*. All peers are entitled to sit in the House of Lords, including the Lords Spiritual – archbishops and senior bishops of the Church of England – and the Law Lords. In 1958 the Queen expanded the list of life peerages to honour people who had performed notable public service. From 1999 the system of "peoples peerages" began to replace inherited honours.

KEY TO THE PEERS

☐	25 dukes
☐	35 marquesses
☐	175 earls and countesses
☐	100 viscounts
☐	800+ barons and baronesses

THE QUEEN'S HONOURS LIST

Twice a year several hundred men and women nominated by the Prime Minister and political leaders for outstanding public service receive honours from the Queen. Some are made dames or knights, a few receive the prestigious OM (Order of Merit), but far more receive lesser honours such as OBEs or MBEs (Orders or Members of the British Empire).

Mother Theresa *received the OM in 1983 for her work in India.*

Terence Conran, *founder of Habitat, was knighted for services to industry.*

The Beatles *were given MBEs in 1965. Paul McCartney was knighted in 1997.*

Rural Architecture

FOR MANY, THE ESSENCE OF BRITISH LIFE is found in villages. Their scale and serenity nurture a way of life envied by those who live in towns and cities. The pattern of British villages dates back some 1,500 years, when the Saxons cleared forests and established settlements, usually centred around a green or pond. Most of today's English villages existed at the time of the *Domesday Book* in 1086, though few actual buildings survive from then. The settlements evolved organically around a church or manor; the cottages and gardens were created from local materials. Today, a typical village will contain structures of various dates, from the Middle Ages onward. The church is usually the oldest, followed perhaps by a tithe barn, manor house and cottages.

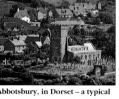

Abbotsbury, in Dorset – a typical village built up around a church

A steep-pitched roof covers the whole house.

Timbers are of Wealden oak.

Eaves are supported by curved braces.

Wealden Hall House in Sussex is a medieval timber-framed house, of a type found in southeast England. It has a tall central open hall flanked by bays of two floors and the upper floor is "jettied", overhanging the ground floor.

A tiled roof keeps the grain dry.

The entrance is big enough for ox-wagons.

Holes let in air – and birds.

Walls and doors are weatherboarded.

The medieval tithe barn stored produce for the clergy – each farmer was required to donate one tenth (tithe) of his annual harvest. The enormous roofs may be supported by crucks, large curved timbers extending from the low walls.

THE PARISH CHURCH

The church is the focal point of the village and, traditionally, of village life. Its tall spire could be seen – and its bells heard – by travellers from a distance. The church is also a chronicle of local history: a large church in a tiny village indicates a once-prosperous settlement. A typical church contains architectural features from many centuries, occasionally as far back as Saxon times. These may include medieval brasses, wall paintings, misericords *(see p327)*, and Tudor and Stuart carvings. Many sell informative guide books inside.

Slender spire from the Georgian era

West elevation

Pinnacled towers dating from the 15th century are situated at the west end.

Bells summon the congregation.

Buttresses support old walls.

Norman arches are rounded.

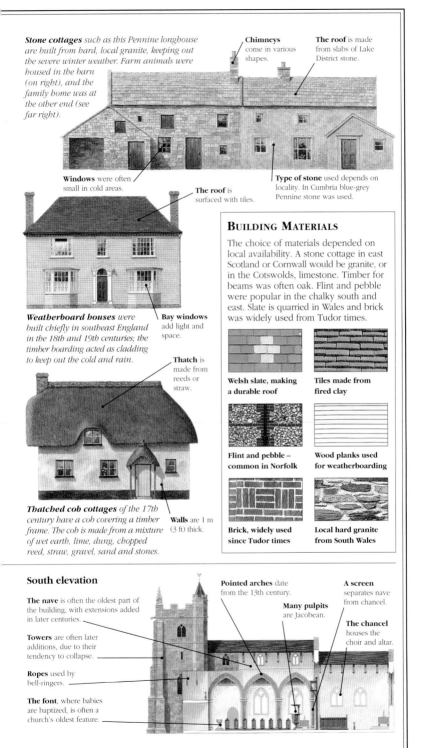

Stone cottages such as this Pennine longhouse are built from hard, local granite, keeping out the severe winter weather. Farm animals were housed in the barn (on right), and the family home was at the other end (see far right).

Chimneys come in various shapes.

The roof is made from slabs of Lake District stone.

Windows were often small in cold areas.

The roof is surfaced with tiles.

Type of stone used depends on locality. In Cumbria blue-grey Pennine stone was used.

Weatherboard houses were built chiefly in southeast England in the 18th and 19th centuries; the timber boarding acted as cladding to keep out the cold and rain.

Bay windows add light and space.

Thatch is made from reeds or straw.

Thatched cob cottages of the 17th century have a cob covering a timber frame. The cob is made from a mixture of wet earth, lime, dung, chopped reed, straw, gravel, sand and stones.

Walls are 1 m (3 ft) thick.

BUILDING MATERIALS

The choice of materials depended on local availability. A stone cottage in east Scotland or Cornwall would be granite, or in the Cotswolds, limestone. Timber for beams was often oak. Flint and pebble were popular in the chalky south and east. Slate is quarried in Wales and brick was widely used from Tudor times.

Welsh slate, making a durable roof

Tiles made from fired clay

Flint and pebble – common in Norfolk

Wood planks used for weatherboarding

Brick, widely used since Tudor times

Local hard granite from South Wales

South elevation

The nave is often the oldest part of the building, with extensions added in later centuries.

Towers are often later additions, due to their tendency to collapse.

Ropes used by bell-ringers.

The font, where babies are baptized, is often a church's oldest feature.

Pointed arches date from the 13th century.

Many pulpits are Jacobean.

A screen separates nave from chancel.

The chancel houses the choir and altar.

The Countryside

Common Blue butterfly

FOR ITS SIZE, Britain contains an unusual variety of geological and climatic conditions that have shaped diverse landscapes, from treeless windswept moorland to boggy marshes and small hedged cattle pastures. Each terrain nurtures its typical wildlife and displays its own charm through the seasons. With the reduction in farming and the creation of footpaths and nature reserves, the countryside is becoming more of a leisure resource.

INDIGENOUS ANIMALS AND BIRDS

There are no large or dangerous wild animals in Britain but a wealth of small mammals, rodents and insects inhabit the countryside, and the rivers and streams are home to many varieties of fish. For bird-watchers there is a great range of songbirds, birds of prey and seabirds.

Livestock graze on low pastures.

Trees provide shelter and protection for wildlife.

Higher land is uncultivated.

Bushes and trees grow between rocks.

Streams flow over a stony bed from mountain springs.

The highest ground is often covered in snow until spring.

WOODED DOWNLAND

Chalk downland, seen here at Ditchling Beacon on the Downs (see p167), has soil of low fertility and is grazed by sheep. However crops are sometimes grown on the lower slopes. Distinctive wild flowers and butterflies thrive here, while beech and yew predominate in the woods.

WILD HILLSIDE

Large tracts of Britain's uplands remain wild terrain, unsuitable for crops or forestry. Purple heather is tough enough to survive in moorland, the haunt of deer and game birds. The highest craggy uplands, such as the Cairngorms (see p530–31) in Scotland, pictured here, are the habitat of birds of prey, such as the golden eagle.

Spear thistle has pink heads in summer that attract several species of butterfly.

Ling, a low-growing heather with tiny pink bell-flowers, adds splashes of colour to peaty moors and uplands.

The dog rose is one of Britain's best-loved wild flowers; its pink single flower is widely seen in hedgerows.

Hogweed has robust stems and leaves with large clusters of white flowers.

Meadow cranesbill is a wild geranium with distinctive purple flowers.

Tormentil has small yellow flowers. It prefers moist, acid soil and is found near water on heaths and moors in summer.

Swallows, swifts and house martins are all summer visitors.

Kestrels are small falcons that prey on mammals such as voles.

Rabbits are often spotted feeding at the edge of fields or near woods.

Robins, common in gardens and hedgerows, have distinctive red breast feathers.

Foxes, little bigger than domestic cats, live in hideaways in woods, near farmland.

Cereal crops ripen in small fields.

Hedgerows provide refuge for wildlife.

Small mixed woods break up the field pattern.

Sheep graze on salty marshes.

Culverts drain water from the field.

Reed beds edge the water.

TRADITIONAL FIELDS

The patchwork fields here in the Cotswolds *(see p290)* reflect generations of small-scale farming. A typical farm would produce silage, hay and cereal crops, and keep a few dairy cows and sheep in enclosed pastures. The tree-dotted hedgerows mark boundaries that may be centuries old.

MARSHLAND

Flat and low-lying wetlands, criss-crossed with dykes and drainage canals, provide the scenery of Romney Marsh *(see also p168)* as well as much of East Anglia. Some areas have rich, peaty soil for crops, or salty marshland for sheep, but there are extensive uncultivated sections, where reed beds shelter wildlife.

The oxeye daisy is a larger relative of the common white daisy, found in grassland from spring to late summer.

Orchids are among the rarer wild flowers. This species is the Common Spotted Orchid.

Cowslips belong to the primrose family. In spring they are often found in the grass on open meadowlands.

Poppies glow brilliant red in cornfields.

Sea lavender is a saltmarsh plant that is tolerant of saline soils. It flowers in late summer.

Buttercups are among the most common wild flowers. They brighten meadows in summer.

Walkers' Britain

The West Highland Way is an arduous 95 mile (153 km) route from Milngavie, near Glasgow, to north of Fort William, across mountainous terrain with fine lochs and moorland scenery *(see p480).*

WALKERS OF ALL LEVELS of ability and enthusiasm are well served in Britain. There is an unrivalled network of long-distance paths through some spectacular scenery, which can be tackled in stages with overnight stays en route, or dipped into for a single day's walking. For shorter walks, Britain is dotted with signposts showing public footpaths across common or private land. You will find books of walk routes in local shops and a large map will keep you on track. Choose river routes for easy walking or take to the hills for a greater challenge.

Walker resting on Scafell Pike, Lake District

The Pennine Way was Britain's first designated long-distance path. The 256 mile (412 km) route from Edale in Derbyshire to Kirk Yetholm on the Scottish border is a challenging upland hike, with long, lonely stretches of moorland. It is only for experienced hill walkers.

Fort William

Glasgow

St Bees Head

Winderr

Offa's Dyke Footpath *follows the boundary between Wales and England. The 168 mile (270 km) path goes through the beautiful Wye Valley* (see p447) *in the Welsh borders.*

Dales Way runs from Ilkley in West Yorkshire to Bowness-on-Windermere in the Lake District, 81 miles (130 km) of delightful flat riverside walking and valley scenery.

Prestatyr

Pembrokeshire Coastal path is 186 miles (229 km) of rugged cliff-top walking from Amroth on Carmarthen Bay to the west tip of Wales at Cardigan.

St Dogmaels

Amroth

Che

Minehead

ORDNANCE SURVEY MAPS

The best maps for walkers are published by the Ordnance Survey, the official mapping agency. Out of a wide range of maps the most useful are the green-covered *Pathfinder* series, on a scale of 1:25,000, and the *Landranger* series at 1:50,000. The *Outdoor Leisure and Explorer* series are maps of the more popular regions and cover a larger area.

The Southwest Coastal Path offers varied scenery from Minehead on the north Somerset coast to Poole in Dorset, via Devon and Cornwall – in all a marathon 600 mile (965 km) round trip.

SIGNPOSTS

Long-distance paths are well signposted, some of them with an acorn symbol (or with a thistle in Scotland). Many shorter routes are marked with coloured arrows by local authorities or hiking groups. Local councils generally mark public footpaths with yellow arows. Public bridleways, marked by blue arrows, are paths that can be used by both walkers and horse riders – remember, horses churn up mud. Signs appear on posts, trees and stiles.

TIPS FOR WALKERS

Be prepared: The weather can change very quickly: dress for the worst. Always take a compass, a proper walking map and get local advice before undertaking any ambitious walking. Pack some food and drink if the map does not show a pub en route.
On the walk: Always keep to the footpath and close gates behind you. Never feed or upset farm animals, leave litter, pick flowers or damage plants.
Where to stay: The International Youth Hostel Federation (see pp616–17) has a network of hostels which cater particularly for walkers. Bed-and-breakfast accommodation is also available near most routes (see p539).
Further information: The Ramblers' Association (tel: 020-7339 8500) is a national organiza-tion for walkers, with a magazine and a guide to accommodation.

The Coast to Coast Walk crosses the Lake District, Yorkshire Dales and North York Moors, on a 190 mile (306 km) route. This demanding walk covers a spectacular range of North Country landscapes. All cross-country routes are best walked from west to east to take advantage of the prevailing wind.

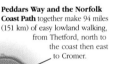

The Ridgeway is a fairly easy path that follows an ancient track once used by cattle drovers. Start-ing near Avebury (see p249) it covers 85 miles (137 km) to Ivinghoe Beacon.

olm

Robin Hood's Bay

Ilkley

Edale

Peddars Way and the Norfolk Coast Path together make 94 miles (151 km) of easy lowland walking, from Thetford, north to the coast then east to Cromer.

Sheringham

Thetford

Icknield Way, the most ancient prehistoric road in Britain, is 105 miles (168 km) long and links the Ridgeway to Peddars Way.

Kemble

Ivinghoe

Avebury

London

Farnham

Dover

Winchester

Eastbourne

The Thames Path follows the river for 213 miles (341 km) from central London to Kemble, its source in Gloucestershire.

e Harbour

The Isle of Wight Coastal Path circles the entire island on an easy 65 mile (105 km) footpath.

The North Downs Way is an ancient route through 141 miles (227 km) of low-lying hills from Farnham in Surrey to Dover or Folkestone in Kent.

The South Downs Way is a varied 106 mile (171 km) walk from Eastbourne on the south coast to Winchester (see p156-7). It can be completed in a week.

The Traditional British Pub

Beer label c.1900

EVERY COUNTRY HAS its bars, but Britain is famous for its pubs or "public houses". Ale was brewed in England in Roman times – mostly at home – and by the Middle Ages there were inns and taverns which brewed their own. The 18th century was the heyday of the coaching inn as stage coaches brought more custom. In the 19th century came railway taverns for travellers and "gin palaces" for the new industrial workers. Today, pubs come in all styles and sizes and many cater to families, serving food as well as drink (see pp608–11).

Early 19th-century coaching inn – also a social centre and post office

THE VICTORIAN PUB

A century ago, many pubs in towns and cities had smart interiors, to contrast with the poor housing of their clients.

Elaborately etched glass is a feature of many Victorian interiors.

Pub games, such as cribbage, bar billiards, pool and dominoes are part of British pub culture. Here some regular customers are competing against a rival pub's darts team.

Pint glasses (containing just over half a litre) are used to serve beer.

The Red Lion pub name is derived from Scottish heraldry (see p26).

Beer gardens outside pubs are a favourite venue for family summer treats.

Old-fashioned cash register contributes to the period atmosphere of the bar.

Pewter tankards, seldom used by drinkers today, add a traditional touch.

WHAT TO DRINK

Draught bitter is the most traditional British beer. Brewed from malted barley, hops, yeast and water, and usually matured in a wooden cask, it varies from region to region. In the north of England the sweeter mild ale is popular, and lagers served in bottles or on tap are also widely drunk. Stout, made from black malt, is another variation.

Beer pump

Draught bitter is drunk at room temperature.

Draught lager is a light-coloured, carbonated beer.

Guinness is a thick, creamy Irish stout.

Pavement tables, crowded with city drinkers during the summer months

A village pub, offering a waterside view and serving drinks in the garden

PUB SIGNS

Early medieval inns used vines or evergreens as signs – the symbol of Bacchus, the Roman god of wine. Soon pubs acquired names that signalled support for monarchs or noblemen, or celebrated victories in battle. As many customers could not read, pub signs had vivid images.

The George *either derives from one of the six English kings of that name, or, as here, from England's patron saint.*

Bottles of spirits, as well as the popular port and sherry, are ranged behind the bar.

Glass lamps imitate the Victorian style.

Wine, once rarely found in pubs, is now increasingly popular.

A deep-toned mahogany bar forms part of the traditional setting.

Draught beer, served from pumps or taps, comes from national and local brewers.

The Bat and Ball *is one of many pubs celebrating the game of cricket, and is often sited near a village green where it is played.*

The Green Man *is a woodland spirit from pagan mythology, possibly the basis for the legend of Robin Hood (see p322).*

The Magna Carta *sign commemorates and illustrates the "great charter" signed by King John in 1215 (see p48).*

Optics dispense spirits in precise measures.

Mild may be served by the pint or in a half-pint tankard (as above).

Top cocktails are gin-and-tonic (right) and Pimm's.

The Bird in Hand *relates to the ancient country sport of falconry, traditionally practised by noblemen.*

A Flavour of British Food

BRITAIN'S UNIQUE contributions to gastronomy include its cooked breakfasts, afternoon teas and satisfying puddings. Fast food and takeaways were pioneered here with fish and chips, the sandwich and the Cornish pasty. Modern British cuisine is innovative and varied, but it is also worth seeking out traditional dishes which use first-rate ingredients: beef, lamb and game figure prominently. As an island, Britain has historically been a fish-eating nation, although shellfish, once cheap, has become pricier.

Fish and chips (French fries) are made from white sea fish, batter-coated and fried in oil, with chipped potatoes, salt and vinegar.

A full English breakfast can include fried bacon and egg, mushrooms, sausage, tomatoes, fried bread and black pudding.

Cockles and whelks remain cheap compared with larger shellfish. They are sold from small stalls outside pubs, and can be awkward to eat.

Laverbread is a Welsh speciality made from dark-coloured seaweed. It is served cold with seafood, or, as here, hot with bacon, toast and tomato.

Cornish pasties are filled with meat and vegetables baked in a pastry crust. They originated as a handy way for farm labourers to take their lunch to work.

TEA TIME

Afternoon tea, taken at around 4pm, is a British tradition enacted daily in homes, tea-shops and grand hotels. The tea is usually from India or Sri Lanka, served with optional milk and sugar; but it could be scented China or herbal tea served with or without lemon. Small, delicately cut sandwiches are eaten first: fish paste and cucumber are traditional fillings. These may be followed by scones, jam and cream, especially in the west of England (see p273). Other options include buttered toast or crumpets, but leave room for a slice of fruit cake or jam sponge, a chocolate éclair or a regional speciality such as Scottish shortbread.

Eccles cake

Bakewell tart

Barra brith or Welsh tea bread

Welsh cakes

Ginger cake

Victoria sponge

Cucumber sandwiches

Ceylon tea

Lapsang Souchong tea

Ploughman's lunch *is served in many pubs. It consists of bread, cheese (often Cheddar), and pickles, garnished with salad. Ham or pâté may be substituted for cheese.*

Horseradish sauce

Gravy

Roast beef

Yorkshire pudding

Broccoli

Roast potatoes

Shepherd's pie *is made from minced lamb baked with a potato topping. If minced (ground) beef is used, the dish is called cottage pie.*

Roast beef *is Britain's traditional Sunday lunch. It usually comes with Yorkshire pudding (savoury batter baked with the meat), roast potatoes and seasonal vegetables. A rich gravy enhances the flavour, and horseradish sauce is a favourite relish.*

Dover sole *is Britain's most prized flat fish. Served on the bone or filleted, it is firm fleshed and delicately flavoured.*

Cumberland sausage, *a regional speciality, is in a coil. Sausages and mashed potatoes are called "bangers and mash".*

Steak and kidney pie *is beef and kidney in thick gravy baked in pastry or in a suet crust, when it is known as a pudding.*

Strawberries and cream *are the delight of early summer, associated with outdoor social occasions of all types. Later, raspberries come into season. Both fruits make excellent jam.*

Cheese *is often served to finish lunch and dinner. Mature Cheddar is one of the most popular regional varieties. Blue-veined cheeses such as Stilton are an acquired taste.*

Stilton

Cheddar

Treacle pudding *is a steamed sponge pudding, topped with syrup and served with custard. It is a popular dessert in winter.*

Cornish Yarg

Sage Derby

Sherry trifle *was originally sponge cake soaked in sweet sherry and served with custard. Modern versions may include sponge fingers covered with fruit, jelly and a layer of cream, and decorated with angelica and cherries.*

Cheshire

Red Leicester

THE HISTORY OF
GREAT BRITAIN

RITAIN BEGAN TO assume a cohesive character as early as the 7th century, with the Anglo-Saxon tribes absorbing Celtic and Roman influences and finally achieving supremacy. They suffered repeated Viking incursions and were overcome by the Normans at the Battle of Hastings in 1066. Over centuries, the disparate cultures of the Normans and Anglo-Saxons combined to form the English nation, a process nurtured by Britain's position as an island. The next 400 years saw English kings involved in military expeditions to Europe, but their control over these areas was gradually wrested from them. As a result they extended their domain over Scotland and Wales. The Tudor monarchs consolidated this control and laid the foundations for Britain's future commercial success. Henry VIII recognized the vital importance of sea power and under his daughter, Elizabeth I, English sailors ranged far across the world, often coming into

Medieval knights, masters of the arts of war

conflict with the Spanish. The total defeat of the Spanish Armada in 1588 confirmed Britain's position as a major maritime power. The Stuart period saw a number of internal struggles, most importantly the Civil War in 1641. But by the time of the Act of the Union in 1707 the whole island was united and the foundations for representative government had been laid. The combination of this internal security with continuing maritime strength allowed Britain to seek wealth overseas. By the end of the Napoleonic Wars in 1815, Britain was the leading trading nation in the world. The opportunities offered by industrialization were seized, and by the late 19th century, a colossal empire had been established across the globe. Challenged by Europe and the rise of the US, and drained by its leading role in two world wars, Britain's influence waned after 1945. By the 1970s almost all the colonies had become independent Commonwealth nations.

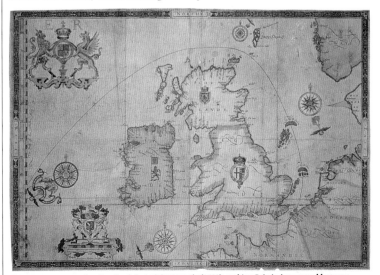

Contemporary map showing the defeat of the Armada (1588), making Britain into a world power

◁ **Henry VIII, founder of the British navy, seen here with his children Edward and Mary**

Kings and Queens

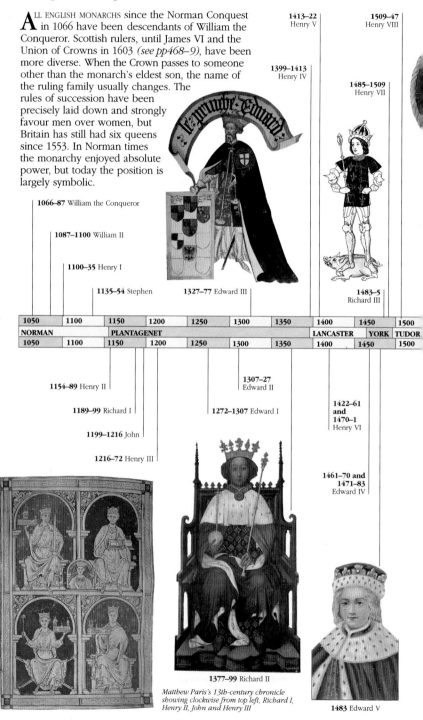

ALL ENGLISH MONARCHS since the Norman Conquest in 1066 have been descendants of William the Conqueror. Scottish rulers, until James VI and the Union of Crowns in 1603 *(see pp468–9)*, have been more diverse. When the Crown passes to someone other than the monarch's eldest son, the name of the ruling family usually changes. The rules of succession have been precisely laid down and strongly favour men over women, but Britain has still had six queens since 1553. In Norman times the monarchy enjoyed absolute power, but today the position is largely symbolic.

1413–22
Henry V

1509–47
Henry VIII

1399–1413
Henry IV

1485–1509
Henry VII

1066–87 William the Conqueror

1087–1100 William II

1100–35 Henry I

1135–54 Stephen

1327–77 Edward III

1483–5
Richard III

1050	1100	1150	1200	1250	1300	1350	1400	1450	1500
NORMAN		PLANTAGENET					LANCASTER	YORK	TUDOR
1050	1100	1150	1200	1250	1300	1350	1400	1450	1500

1154–89 Henry II

1307–27
Edward II

1189–99 Richard I

**1422–61
and
1470–1**
Henry VI

1272–1307 Edward I

1199–1216 John

1216–72 Henry III

**1461–70 and
1471–83**
Edward IV

1377–99 Richard II

Matthew Paris's 13th-century chronicle showing clockwise from top left, Richard I, Henry II, John and Henry III

1483 Edward V

1553–8 Mary I

1660–85 Charles II

1685–8 James II

1689–1702 William III and Mary II

1702–14 Anne

1714–27 George I

1936 Edward VIII

1603–25 James I

1837–1901 Victoria

1901–10 Edward VII

1727–60 George II

1952– Elizabeth II

550	1600	1650	1700	1750	1800	1850	1900	1950	2000
	STUART		HANOVER			SAXE-COBURG	WINDSOR		
550	1600	1650	1700	1750	1800	1850	1900	1950	2000

1830–37 William IV

1649–60 Commonwealth under Lord Protector Oliver Cromwell

1936–52 George VI shown on the George Medal

1820–30 George IV

1910–36 George V

1625–49 Charles I

1558–1603 Elizabeth I

1760–1820 George III

547–53 Edward VI

Prehistoric Britain

BRITAIN WAS PART of the European landmass until the end of the last Ice Age, around 6000 BC, when the English Channel was formed by melting ice. The earliest inhabitants lived in limestone caves: settlements and farming skills developed gradually through the Stone Age. The magnificent wooden and stone henges and circles are masterworks from around 3000 BC, but their significance is a mystery. Flint mines and ancient pathways are evidence of early trading and many burial mounds (barrows) survive from the Stone and Bronze Ages.

Axe Heads
Stone axes, like this one found at Stonehenge, were used by Neolithic men.

Cup and ring marks
were carved on standing stones, such as this one at Ballymeanoch.

MAPPING THE PAST

Monuments from the Neolithic (New Stone), Bronze and Iron Ages, together with artifacts found from these periods, provide a wealth of information about Britain's early settlers, before written history began with the Romans.

Neolithic Tools
Antlers and bones were made into Neolithic leather-working tools. These were found at Avebury (see p249).

Pottery Beaker
The Beaker People, who came from Europe in the early Bronze Age, take their name from these drinking cups often found in their graves.

Gold Breast Plate
Made by Wessex goldsmiths, its spectacular pattern suggests it belonged to an important chieftain.

Pentre Ifan, an impressive Neolithic burial chamber in South Wales, was once covered with a huge earth mound.

Mold Cape
Gold was mined in Wales and Cornwall in the Bronze Age. This intricately worked warrior's cape was buried in a grave at Mold, Clwyd.

This gold cup, found in a Cornish barrow, is evidence of the wealth of Bronze Age tribes.

TIMELINE

6000–5000 As the Ice Age comes to an end, sea levels rise, submerging the land-link between Britain and the Continent

Neolithic flint axes

6000 BC	5500 BC	5000 BC	4500 BC	4000 BC

A gold pendant and button (1700 BC), found in Bronze Age graves

3500 Neolithic Age begins. Long barrows and stone circles built around Britain

Skara Brae is a Neolithic village of about 2500 BC *(see p514)*.

Maiden Castle
An impressive Iron Age hill fort in Dorset, its concentric lines of ramparts and ditches follow the contours of the hill top (see p255).

Iron Age Brochs, round towers with thick stone walls, are found only in Scotland.

Iron Age Axe
The technique of smelting iron came to Britain around 700 BC, brought from Europe by the Celts.

Castlerigg Stone Circle
is one of Britain's earliest Neolithic monuments *(see p347).*

Uffington White Horse
Thought to be 3,000 years old, the shape has to be "scoured" to keep grass at bay (see p207).

A chalk figure, thought to be a fertility goddess, was found at Grimes Graves *(see p180).*

This bronze Celtic helmet (50 BC) was found in the River Thames, London.

Stonehenge was begun around 3,500 years ago *(see pp248–9).*

WHERE TO SEE PREHISTORIC BRITAIN

Wiltshire, with Stonehenge *(p248)* and Avebury *(p249)*, has the best group of Neolithic monuments, and the Uffington White Horse is nearby *(p207)*. The Scottish islands have many early sites and the British Museum *(pp108–9)* houses a huge collection of artefacts.

A circular bank with over 180 stones encloses the Neolithic site at Avebury (see p249).

Snettisham Torc
A torc was a neck ring worn by Celtic men. This one, found in Norfolk, dates from 50 BC and is made from silver and gold.

3000 BC	2500 BC	2000 BC	1500 BC	1000 BC	500 BC

2500 Temples, or henges, are built of wood or stone

1650–1200 Wessex is at the hub of trading routes between Europe and the mines of Cornwall, Wales and Ireland

1000 First farmsteads are settled

550–350 Migration of Celtic people from southern Europe

500 Iron Age begins. Hill forts are built

2100–1650 The Bronze Age reaches Britain. Immigration of the Beaker People, who make bronze implements and build ritual temples

Chieftain's bronze sceptre (1700 BC)

1200 Small, self-sufficient villages start to appear

150 Tribes from Gaul begin to migrate to Britain

Roman Britain

THROUGHOUT the 350-year Roman occupation, Britain was ruled as a colony. After the defeat of rebellious local tribes, such as Boadicea's Iceni, the Romans remained an unassimilated occupying power. Their legacy is in military and civil construction: forts, walls, towns and public buildings. Their long, straight roads, built for easy movement of troops, are still a feature of the landscape.

Roman jasper seal

Cavalry Sports Helmet
Found in Lancashire, it was used in tournaments by horsemen. Cavalry races and other sports were held in amphitheatres near towns.

Silver Jug
This 3rd-century jug, the earliest known silver item with Christian symbols, was excavated near Peterborough.

Exercise corridor

Main baths

Fishbourne Palace was built at the site of a natural harbour and ships could moor here.

Entrance hall

Hadrian's Wall
Started in 120 as a defence against the Scots; it marked the northern frontier of the Roman Empire and was guarded by 17 forts housing over 18,500 foot-soldiers and cavalry.

Mithras
This head of the god Mithras was found on the London site of a temple devoted to the cult of Mithraism. The sect demanded of its Roman followers loyalty and discipline.

TIMELINE

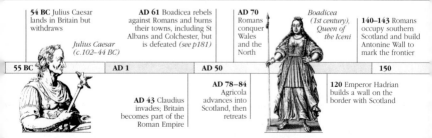

54 BC Julius Caesar lands in Britain but withdraws

Julius Caesar (c.102–44 BC)

AD 61 Boadicea rebels against Romans and burns their towns, including St Albans and Colchester, but is defeated *(see p181)*

AD 70 Romans conquer Wales and the North

Boadicea (1st century), Queen of the Iceni

140–143 Romans occupy southern Scotland and build Antonine Wall to mark the frontier

55 BC   **AD 1**   **AD 50**   **150**

AD 43 Claudius invades; Britain becomes part of the Roman Empire

AD 78–84 Agricola advances into Scotland, then retreats

120 Emperor Hadrian builds a wall on the border with Scotland

Flavian Mosaic
Roman floors of the 1st century used patterns in black and white stone. More mosaics survive at Fishbourne than at any other British site.

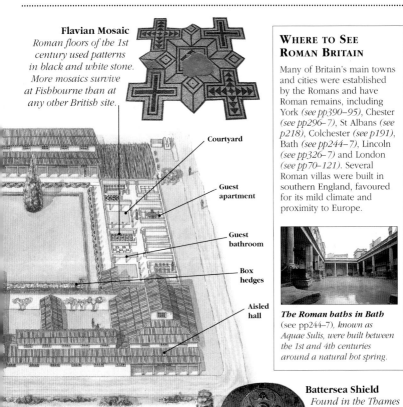

Courtyard

Guest apartment

Guest bathroom

Box hedges

Aisled hall

WHERE TO SEE ROMAN BRITAIN

Many of Britain's main towns and cities were established by the Romans and have Roman remains, including York (see pp390–95), Chester (see pp296–7), St Albans (see p218), Colchester (see p191), Bath (see pp244–7), Lincoln (see pp326–7) and London (see pp70–121). Several Roman villas were built in southern England, favoured for its mild climate and proximity to Europe.

The Roman baths in Bath
(see pp244–7), known as Aquae Sulis, were built between the 1st and 4th centuries around a natural hot spring.

FISHBOURNE PALACE

Built during the 1st century for Togidubnus, a pro-Roman governor, the palace (here reconstructed) had sophisticated functions such as under-floor heating and indoor plumbing for baths (see p157).

Chi-Rho Symbol
This early Christian symbol is from a 3rd-century fresco at Lullingstone Roman villa in Kent.

Battersea Shield
Found in the Thames near Battersea, the shield bears Celtic symbols and was probably made at about the time of the first Roman invasion. Archaeologists suspect it may have been lost by a warrior while crossing the river, or offered as a sacrifice to one of the many river gods. It is now at the British Museum (see pp108–9).

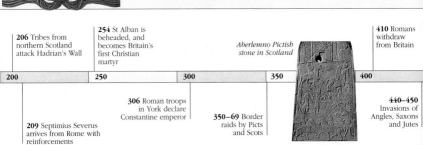

206 Tribes from northern Scotland attack Hadrian's Wall

254 St Alban is beheaded, and becomes Britain's first Christian martyr

Aberlemno Pictish stone in Scotland

410 Romans withdraw from Britain

| 200 | 250 | 300 | 350 | 400 |

306 Roman troops in York declare Constantine emperor

350–69 Border raids by Picts and Scots

440–450 Invasions of Angles, Saxons and Jutes

209 Septimius Severus arrives from Rome with reinforcements

Anglo-Saxon Kingdoms

BY THE MID-5TH CENTURY, Angles and Saxons from Germany had started to raid the eastern shores of Britain. Increasingly they decided to settle, and within 100 years Saxon kingdoms, including Wessex, Mercia and Northumbria, were established over the entire country. Viking raids throughout the 8th and 9th centuries were largely contained, but in 1066, the last invasion of England saw William the Conqueror from Normandy defeat the Anglo-Saxon King Harold at the Battle of Hastings. William then went on to assume control of the whole country.

King Canute (1016–35)

Viking Axe
The principal weapons of the Viking warriors were spear, axe and sword. They were skilled metal-workers with an eye for decoration, as seen in this axe-head from a Copenhagen museum.

Vikings on a Raiding Expedition
Scandinavian boat-building skills were in advance of anything known in Britain. People were terrified by these large, fast boats with their intimidating figureheads, which sailed up the Thames and along the coasts.

ANGLO-SAXON CALENDAR

These scenes from a chronicle of seasons, made just before the Norman invasion, show life in late Anglo-Saxon Britain. At first people lived in small farming communities, but by the 7th century towns began to spring up and trade increased. Saxon kings were supported by nobles but most of the population were free peasants.

TIMELINE

c.470–495 Saxons and Angles settle in Essex, Sussex and East Anglia	**c.556** Saxons move across Britain and set up seven kingdoms		*St Augustine (d.604)*	**730–821** Supremacy of Mercia, whose king, Offa (d.796), builds a dyke along the Mercia–Wales border
			635 St Aidan establishes a monastery on Lindisfarne	

450	500	550	600	650	700	750

450 Saxons first settle in Kent	**563** St Columba lands on Iona	**597** St Augustine sent by Rome to convert English to Christianity	**617–85** Supremacy of Northumbrian kingdom	*Mercian coin which bears the name of King Offa*

Ox-drawn plough for tilling

Alfred Jewel
This 9th-century gold ornament in the Ashmolean Museum (see p210) has the inscription: "Alfred ordered me made". This may refer to the Saxon King Alfred.

WHERE TO SEE ANGLO-SAXON BRITAIN

The best collection of Saxon artefacts is from a burial ship unearthed at Sutton Hoo in Suffolk in 1938 and now on display at the British Museum *(see pp108–9)*. There are fine Saxon churches at Bradwell in Essex and Bosham in Sussex *(see p157)*. In York the Viking town of Jorvik has been excavated *(see p394)* and actual relics are shown alongside models of people and dwellings.

The Saxon church of St Laurence (see p241) was built in the late 8th century.

Minstrels entertaining at a feast

Edward the Confessor
In 1042, Edward – known as "the Confessor" because of his piety – became king. He died in 1066 and William of Normandy claimed the throne.

Hawks, used to kill game

Harold's Death
This 14th-century illustration depicts the victorious William of Normandy after King Harold was killed with an arrow in his eye. The Battle of Hastings (see p167) was the last invasion of Britain.

Legend of King Arthur
Arthur is thought to have been a chieftain who fought the Saxons in the early 6th century. Legends of his knights' exploits appeared in 1155 (see p271).

802–839 After the death of Cenwulf (821), Wessex gains control over most of England

867 Northumbria falls to the Vikings

An invading Norman ship

878 King Alfred defeats Vikings but allows them to settle in eastern England

1016 Danish King Canute *(see p157)* seizes English crown

| 800 | 850 | 900 | 950 | 1000 | 1050 | 1100 |

843 Kenneth McAlpin becomes king of all Scotland

c.793 Lindisfarne sacked by Viking invaders; first Viking raid on Scotland about a year later

926 Eastern England, the Danelaw, is reconquered by the Saxons

1042 The Anglo-Saxon Edward the Confessor becomes king (d.1066)

1066 William of Normandy claims the throne, and defeats Harold at the Battle of Hastings. He is crowned at Westminster

The Middle Ages

Noblemen stag hunting

REMAINS OF Norman castles on English hill tops bear testimony to the military might used by the invaders to sustain their conquest – although Wales and Scotland resisted for centuries. The Normans operated a feudal system, creating an aristo-cracy that treated native Anglo-Saxons as serfs. The ruling class spoke French until the 13th century, when it mixed with the Old English used by the peasants. The medieval church's power is shown in the cathedrals that grace British cities today.

Magna Carta
To protect themselves and the church from arbitrary taxation, the powerful English barons compelled King John to sign a "great charter" in 1215 (see p221). This laid the foundations for an inde-pendent legal system.

Craft Skills
An illustration from a 14th-century manuscript depicts a weaver and a copper-beater – two of the trades that created a wealthy class of artisans.

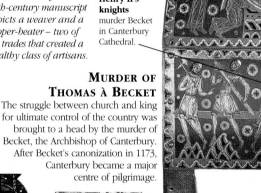

Becket is received into heaven.

Henry II's knights murder Becket in Canterbury Cathedral.

MURDER OF THOMAS À BECKET

The struggle between church and king for ultimate control of the country was brought to a head by the murder of Becket, the Archbishop of Canterbury. After Becket's canonization in 1173, Canterbury became a major centre of pilgrimage.

Ecclesiastical Art
Nearly all medieval art had religious themes, such as this window at Canterbury Cathedral (see pp172–3) depicting Jeroboam.

Black Death
A plague swept Britain and Europe several times in the 14th century, killing mil-lions of people. This illustration, in a religious tract, produced around 100 years later, represents death taking its heavy toll.

TIMELINE

1071 Hereward the Wake, leader of the Anglo-Saxon resistance, defeated at Ely	**1154** Henry II, the first Plantagenet king, demolishes castles, and exacts money from barons instead of military service	**1170** Archbishop of Canterbury, Thomas à Becket, is murdered by four knights after quar-relling with Henry II

1100	1150	1200	1250

1086 The *Domesday Book*, a survey of every manor in England, is compiled for tax purposes

Domesday Book

1215 Barons compel King John to sign the *Magna Carta*

1256 First Parliament to include ordinary citizens

Battle of Agincourt

In 1415, Henry V took an army to France to claim its throne. This 15th-century chronicle depicts Henry beating the French army at Agincourt.

This casket (1190), in a private collection, is said to have contained Becket's remains.

Becket takes his place in Heaven after his canonization.

Two clergymen look on in horror at Becket's murder.

Richard III

Richard, shown in this 16th-century painting, became king during the Wars of the Roses: a bitter struggle for power between two factions of the royal family – the houses of York and Lancaster.

John Wycliffe *(1329–84)*

This painting by Ford Madox Brown (1821–93) shows Wycliffe with the Bible he translated into English to make it accessible to everyone.

WHERE TO SEE MEDIEVAL BRITAIN

The university cities of Oxford *(pp208–13)* and Cambridge *(pp196–201)* contain the largest concentrations of Gothic buildings. Magnificent medieval cathedrals rise high above many historic cities, among them Lincoln *(p326)* and York *(pp390–93)*. Both cities still retain at least part of their ancient street pattern. Military architecture is best seen in Wales *(pp424–5)* with the formidable border castles of Edward I.

All Souls College in Oxford, (see p212), *which only takes graduates, is a superb blend of medieval and later architecture.*

Castle Life

Every section of a castle was allotted to a baron whose soldiers helped defend it. This 14th-century illustration shows the coats of arms (see p26) of the barons for each area.

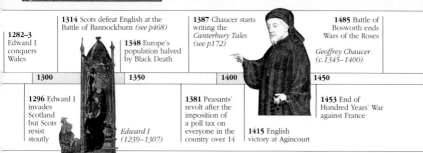

1282–3 Edward I conquers Wales

1314 Scots defeat English at the Battle of Bannockburn *(see p468)*

1348 Europe's population halved by Black Death

1387 Chaucer starts writing the *Canterbury Tales* *(see p172)*

Geoffrey Chaucer (c.1345–1400)

1485 Battle of Bosworth ends Wars of the Roses

1300	1350	1400	1450

1296 Edward I invades Scotland but Scots resist stoutly

Edward I (1239–1307)

1381 Peasants' revolt after the imposition of a poll tax on everyone in the country over 14

1415 English victory at Agincourt

1453 End of Hundred Years' War against France

Tudor Renaissance

AFTER YEARS OF DEBILITATING civil war, the Tudor monarchs established peace and national self-confidence, reflected in the split from the church of Rome – due to Henry VIII's divorce from Catherine of Aragon – and the consequent closure of the monasteries.

Hawking, a popular pastime

Henry's daughter, Mary I, tried to reestablish Catholicism but under her half-sister, Elizabeth I, the Protestant church secured its position. Overseas exploration began, provoking clashes with other European powers seeking to exploit the New World. The Renaissance in arts and learning spread from Europe to Britain, with playwright William Shakespeare adding his own unique contribution.

Curtains behind the queen are open to reveal scenes of the great English victory over the Spanish Armada in 1588.

Sea Power
Henry VIII laid the foundations of the powerful English navy. In 1545, his flagship, the Mary Rose (see p155), sank before his eyes in Portsmouth harbour on its way to do battle with the French.

Theatre
Some of Shakespeare's plays were first seen in purpose-built theatres such as the Globe (see p119) in south London.

The globe signifies that the queen reigns supreme far and wide.

Monasteries
With Henry VIII's split from Rome, England's religious houses, like Fountains Abbey (see pp376–7), were dissolved. Henry stole their riches and used them to finance his foreign policy.

TIMELINE

1497 John Colet denounces the corruption of the clergy, supported by Erasmus and Sir Thomas More

1533–4 Henry VIII divorces Catherine of Aragon and is excommunicated by the Pope. He forms the Church of England

1542–1567 Mary, Queen of Scots rules Scotland

1490	1510	1530

1497 John Cabot *(see p242)* makes his first voyage to North America

1513 English defeat Scots at Flodden *(see p468)*

Henry VIII (1491–1547)

1535 Act of Union with Wales

1536–40 Dissolution of the Monasteries

1549 First Book of Common Prayer introduced

Mary, Queen of Scots

As great-granddaughter of Henry VII, she laid claim to the English throne in 1559. But in 1567, Elizabeth I had her imprisoned for 20 years until her execution for treason in 1587.

Jewels symbolize triumph.

WHERE TO SEE TUDOR BRITAIN

Hampton Court Palace (p159) has been altered over the centuries but remains a Tudor showpiece. Part of Elizabeth I's former home at Hatfield (p217) still survives. In Kent, Leeds Castle, Knole (pp174–5) and Hever Castle (p175) all have connections with Tudor royalty. Burghley House (pp328–9) and Hardwick Hall (p288), both Midlands mansions, retain their 16th-century character.

This astronomical clock *at Hampton Court (see p159), with its intriguing zodiac symbols, was installed in 1540 by Henry VIII.*

DEFEAT OF THE ARMADA

Spain was England's main rival for supremacy on the seas, and in 1588 Philip II sent 100 powerfully armed galleons towards England, bent on invasion. The English fleet – under Lord Howard, Francis Drake, John Hawkins and Martin Frobisher – sailed from Plymouth and destroyed the Spanish navy in a famous victory. This commemorative portrait of Elizabeth I by George Gower (d.1596) celebrates the triumph.

Protestant Martyrs
Catholic Mary I reigned from 1553 to 1558. Protestants who opposed her rule were burned, such as these six churchmen at Canterbury in 1555.

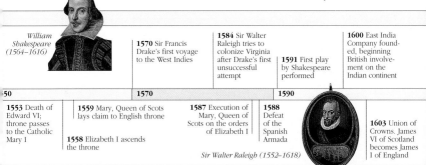

William Shakespeare (1564–1616)

1570 Sir Francis Drake's first voyage to the West Indies

1584 Sir Walter Raleigh tries to colonize Virginia after Drake's first unsuccessful attempt

1591 First play by Shakespeare performed

1600 East India Company founded, beginning British involvement on the Indian continent

50 | **1570** | **1590**

1553 Death of Edward VI; throne passes to the Catholic Mary I

1559 Mary, Queen of Scots lays claim to English throne

1558 Elizabeth I ascends the throne

1587 Execution of Mary, Queen of Scots on the orders of Elizabeth I

1588 Defeat of the Spanish Armada

Sir Walter Raleigh (1552–1618)

1603 Union of Crowns. James VI of Scotland becomes James I of England

Stuart Britain

THE END of Elizabeth I's reign signalled the start of internal turmoil. The throne passed to James I, whose belief that kings ruled by divine right provoked clashes with Parliament. Under his son, Charles I, the conflict escalated into Civil War that ended with his execution. In 1660 Charles II regained the throne, but after his death James II was ousted for Catholic leanings. Protestantism was reaffirmed with the reign of William and Mary, who suppressed the Catholic Jacobites *(see p469)*.

A 17th-century barber's bowl

Science

Sir Isaac Newton (1642–1727) invented this reflecting telescope, laying the foundation for a greater understanding of the universe, including the law of gravity.

Charles I stayed silent at his trial.

Oliver Cromwell

A strict Protestant and a passionate champion of the rights of Parliament, he led the victorious Parliamentary forces in the Civil War. He became Lord Protector of the Commonwealth from 1653 to 1658.

On the way to his death, the king wore two shirts for warmth, so onlookers should not think he was shivering with fright.

Theatre

After the Restoration in 1660 – when Parliament restored the monarchy, theatre thrived. Plays were performed on temporary outdoor stages.

EXECUTION OF CHARLES I

Cromwell was convinced there would be no peace until the king was dead. At his trial for treason, Charles refused to recognize the authority of the court and offered no defence. He faced his death with dignity on 30 January 1649, the only English king to be executed. His death was followed by a republic known as the Commonwealth.

TIMELINE

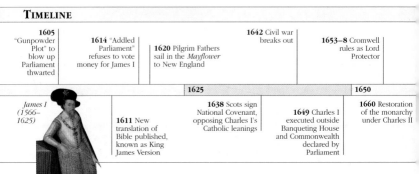

1605 "Gunpowder Plot" to blow up Parliament thwarted	**1614** "Addled Parliament" refuses to vote money for James I	**1620** Pilgrim Fathers sail in the *Mayflower* to New England	**1642** Civil war breaks out	**1653–8** Cromwell rules as Lord Protector	
		1625		1650	
James I (1566–1625)	**1611** New translation of Bible published, known as King James Version	**1638** Scots sign National Covenant, opposing Charles I's Catholic leanings	**1649** Charles I executed outside Banqueting House and Commonwealth declared by Parliament	**1660** Restoration of the monarchy under Charles II	

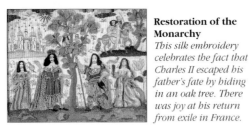

Restoration of the Monarchy

This silk embroidery celebrates the fact that Charles II escaped his father's fate by hiding in an oak tree. There was joy at his return from exile in France.

WHERE TO SEE STUART BRITAIN

The best work of the two leading architects of the time, Inigo Jones and Christopher Wren, is in London, and includes St Paul's Cathedral (pp116–17). In the southeast two classic Jacobean mansions are Audley End (p194) and Hatfield House (p217). The Palace of Holyrood (p496) in Edinburgh, is another example.

The headless body kneels by the block.

The axeman holds the severed head of Charles I.

Plague

Bills of mortality showed the weekly deaths as bubonic plague swept London in 1665. Up to 100,000 Londoners died.

Hatfield House (p217) *is a splendid Jacobean mansion.*

Onlookers soaked up the king's blood with their handkerchiefs to have a memento.

Anatomy

By dissecting corpses, physicians began to gain an understanding of the working of the human body – a crucial step towards modern surgery and medicine.

Pilgrim Fathers

In 1620 a group of Puritans sailed to America. They forged good relations with the native Indians; here they are shown being visited by the chief of the Pokanokets.

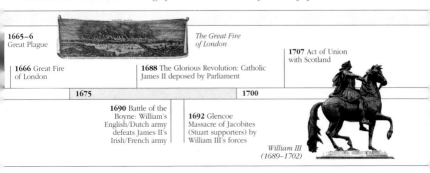

1665–6 Great Plague

The Great Fire of London

1666 Great Fire of London

1688 The Glorious Revolution: Catholic James II deposed by Parliament

1707 Act of Union with Scotland

1675

1700

1690 Battle of the Boyne: William's English/Dutch army defeats James II's Irish/French army

1692 Glencoe Massacre of Jacobites (Stuart supporters) by William III's forces

William III (1689–1702)

Georgian Britain

THE 18TH CENTURY saw Britain, now recovered from the trauma of its Civil War, develop as a commercial and industrial powerhouse. London became a centre of banking, and a mercantile and professional class grew up. Continuing supremacy at sea laid the foundations of an empire; steam engines, canals and railways heralded the Industrial Revolution. Growing confidence was reflected in stately architecture and elegant fashions but, as cities became more crowded, conditions for the underclass grew worse.

Actress Sarah Siddons (1785), Gainsborough

Slate became the preferred tile for Georgian buildings. Roofs became less steep to achieve an Italian look.

A row of sash windows is one of the most characteristic features of a Georgian house.

Battle of Bunker Hill
In 1775 American colonists rebelled against British rule. The British won this early battle in Massachusetts, but in 1783 Britain recognized the United States of America.

Oak was used in the best dwellings for doors and stairs, but pine was standard in most houses.

The saloon was covered in wallpaper, a cheaper alternative to hanging walls with tapestries or fabrics.

The drawing room was richly ornamented and used for entertaining visitors.

The dining room was used for all family meals.

Watt's Steam Engine
The Scottish engineer James Watt (1736–1819) patented his engine in 1769 and then developed it for locomotion.

Lord Horatio Nelson
Nelson (see p27) became a hero after his death at the Battle of Trafalgar fighting the French.

Steps led to the servants' entrance in the basement.

TIMELINE

The Dutch Bubblers

1720 "South Sea Bubble" bursts: many speculators ruined in securities fraud

1746 Bonnie Prince Charlie *(see p521),* Jacobite claimant to throne, defeated at the Battle of Culloden

| 1715 | 1730 | 1745 | 1760 |

1714 George, Elector of Hanover, succeeds Queen Anne, ending the Stuart dynasty and giving Britain a German-speaking monarch

1721 Robert Walpole (1646–1745) becomes the first Prime Minister

1757 Britain's first canal completed

George I (1660–1727)

Satirical engraving about the South Sea Bubble, 1720

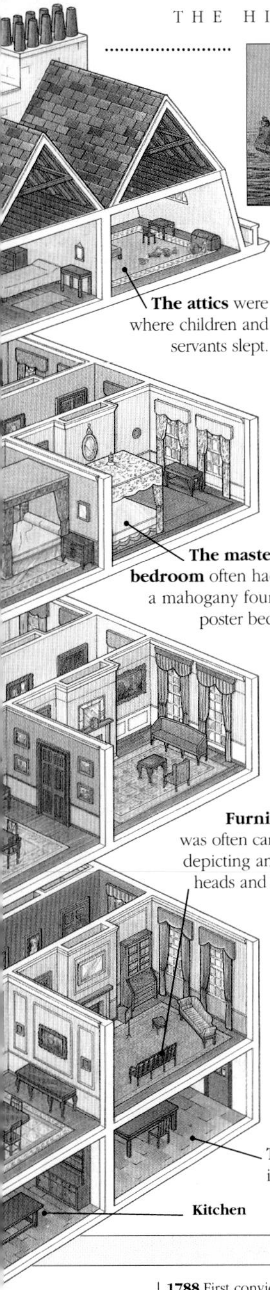

Canal Barge *(1827)*
*Canals were a cheap way
to carry the new indus-
trial goods but were
gradually superseded
by railways during the
19th century.*

The attics were
where children and
servants slept.

**The master
bedroom** often had
a mahogany four-
poster bed.

Furniture
was often carved,
depicting animal
heads and legs.

**Chippendale
Armchair** *(1760)*
*Thomas Chippendale
(1718–79) designed
elegant furniture in a
style still popular today.*

GEORGIAN TOWN HOUSE

Tall, terraced dwellings were
built to house wealthy families.
The main architects of the time
were Robert Adam *(see p24)*
and John Nash *(see p107).*

The servants lived and worked
in the basement during the day.

Kitchen

Silver tureen, 1774

WHERE TO SEE GEORGIAN BRITAIN

Bath *(see pp244–7)* and
Edinburgh *(see pp490–7)*
are two of Britain's best-
preserved Georgian towns.
The Building of Bath Museum
in Bath *(see p247)* has a real
Georgian flavour and
Brighton's Royal Pavilion
(see pp164–5) is a Regency
extravaganza by John Nash.

Charlotte Square (see p490)
*in Edinburgh has fine examples
of Georgian architecture.*

Hogarth's Gin Lane
*Conditions in London's
slums shocked William
Hogarth (1694–1764),
who made prints like this
to urge social reform.*

1776 American
Declaration of
Independence

1788 First convict ships
are sent to Australia

1805 The British, led by Lord
Nelson, beat Napoleon's French
fleet at Battle of Trafalgar

1811–17
Riots
against
growing
unemploy-
ment

1815 Duke of
Wellington beats
Napoleon at
Waterloo

*Caricature of
Wellington
(1769–1852)*

1775	1790	1805	1820

1783 Steam-powered
cotton mill invented
by Sir Richard
Arkwright (1732–92)

1807
Abolition of
slave trade

1811 Prince
of Wales
made Regent
during
George III's
madness

1825
Stockton to
Darlington
railway
opens

1829 Catholic
Emancipation
Act passed

Victorian Britain

WHEN VICTORIA BECAME QUEEN in 1837, she was only 18. Britain was in the throes of its transformation from an agricultural country to the world's most powerful industrial nation. The growth of the Empire fuelled the country's confidence and opened up markets for Britain's manufactured goods. The accelerating growth of cities created problems of health and housing and a powerful Labour movement began to emerge. But by the end of Victoria's long and popular reign in 1901, conditions had begun to improve as more people got the vote and universal education was introduced.

Florence Nightingale *(1820–1910) Known as the Lady with the Lamp, she nursed soldiers in the Crimean War and pioneered many improvements in army medical care.*

Victoria and Disraeli, 1887

Glass walls and ceiling

Prefabricated girders

Newcastle Slum *(1880) Rows of cheap houses were built for an influx of workers to the major industrial cities. The awful conditions spread disease and social discontent.*

UNITED SOCIETY OF BOILERMAKERS AND IRON AND STEEL SHIPBUILDERS ESTD 1834

LONDON DISTRICT COMMITTEE

Union Banner *Trade unions were set up to protect industrial workers against unscrupulous employers.*

As well as silk textiles exhibits included carriages, engines, jewels, glass, plants, cutlery and sculptures.

Ophelia by Sir John Everett Millais *(1829–96) The Pre-Raphaelite painters chose Romantic themes, reflecting a desire to escape industrial Britain.*

TIMELINE

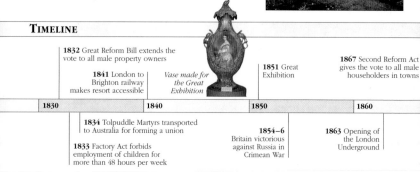

1832 Great Reform Bill extends the vote to all male property owners

1841 London to Brighton railway makes resort accessible

Vase made for the Great Exhibition

1851 Great Exhibition

1867 Second Reform Act gives the vote to all male householders in towns

| 1830 | 1840 | 1850 | 1860 |

1834 Tolpuddle Martyrs transported to Australia for forming a union

1833 Factory Act forbids employment of children for more than 48 hours per week

1854–6 Britain victorious against Russia in Crimean War

1863 Opening of the London Underground

Triumph of Steam and Electricity *(1897)*
This picture from the Illustrated London News *sums up the optimism engendered by the tremendous industrial advances.*

Elm trees were incorporated into the building along with sparrows, and sparrow hawks to control them.

WHERE TO SEE VICTORIAN BRITAIN

The industrial cities of the Midlands and the North are built around grandiose civic, commercial and industrial buildings. Notable Victorian monuments include the Manchester Museum of Science and Industry *(p361)* and, in London, the vast Victoria and Albert Museum *(pp100–101)*.

The Rotunda, Manchester *is a stately Victorian building.*

GREAT EXHIBITION OF 1851

The brainchild of Prince Albert, Victoria's consort, the exhibition celebrated industry, technology and the expanding British Empire. It was the biggest of its kind held up till then. Between May and October, six million people visited Joseph Paxton's lavish crystal palace, in London's Hyde Park. Nearly 14,000 exhibitors brought 100,000 exhibits from all over the world. In 1852 it was moved to south London where it burned down in 1936.

Cycling Craze
The bicycle, invented in 1865, became immensely popular with young people, as illustrated by this etching of 1898.

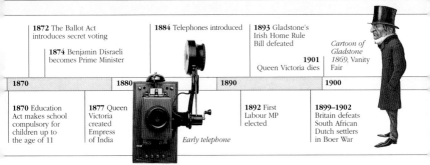

1872 The Ballot Act introduces secret voting

1874 Benjamin Disraeli becomes Prime Minister

1884 Telephones introduced

1893 Gladstone's Irish Home Rule Bill defeated

1901 Queen Victoria dies

Cartoon of Gladstone 1869, Vanity Fair

| 1870 | 1880 | 1890 | 1900 |

1870 Education Act makes school compulsory for children up to the age of 11

1877 Queen Victoria created Empress of India

Early telephone

1892 First Labour MP elected

1899–1902 Britain defeats South African Dutch settlers in Boer War

Britain from 1900 to 1950

Playwright Noel Coward

When Queen Victoria's reign ended in 1901, British society threw off many of its 19th-century inhibitions, and an era of gaiety and excitement began. This was interrupted by World War I. The economic troubles that ensued, which culminated in the Depression of the 1930s, brought misery to millions. In 1939 the ambitions of Germany provoked World War II. After emerging victorious from this conflict, Britain embarked on an ambitious programme of social, educational and health reform.

Welwyn Garden City was based on the Utopian ideals of Sir Ebenezer Howard (1850–1928), founder of the garden city movement.

Suffragettes
Women marched and chained themselves to railings in their effort to get the vote; many went to prison. Women over 30 won the vote in 1919.

The Roaring Twenties
Young flappers discarded the rigid social codes of their parents and instead discovered jazz, cocktails and the Charleston.

New Towns

A string of new towns was created on the outskirts of London, planned to give residents greenery and fresh air. Welwyn Garden City was originally founded in 1919 as a self-contained community, but fast rail links turned it into a base for London commuters.

WE GARD

HOUS
£44 T
OR FOR SALE O
PARTIC
WELWYN
or 64. FI

World War I
British troops in Europe dug into deep trenches protected by barbed wire and machine guns, only metres from the enemy, in a war of attrition that cost the lives of 17 million.

Wireless
Invented by Guglielmo Marconi, radios brought news and entertainment into homes for the first time.

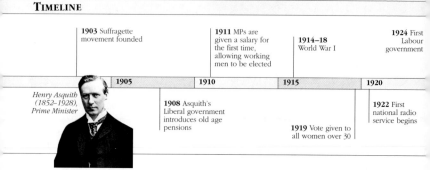

Timeline

	1903 Suffragette movement founded	**1911** MPs are given a salary for the first time, allowing working men to be elected	**1914–18** World War I	**1924** First Labour government
	1905	**1910**	**1915**	**1920**
Henry Asquith (1852–1928), Prime Minister	**1908** Asquith's Liberal government introduces old age pensions		**1919** Vote given to all women over 30	**1922** First national radio service begins

Marching for Jobs
These men were among thousands who marched for their jobs after being put out of work in the 1920s. The stock market crash of 1929 and the ensuing Depression caused even more unemployment.

Garden cities
all had trees, ponds and open spaces.

World War II
German night-time air raids targeted transport, military and industrial sites and cities, such as Sheffield, in what was known as the "Blitz".

WYN N CITY

TO LET
O PER ANNUM
CIAL PURCHASE TERMS
OM ESTATE OFFICE
DEN CITY HERTS
PAVEMENT. E.C.2.

Cheap housing and the promise of a cleaner environment attracted many people to these new cities.

HILLMAN MINX

Family Motoring
By the middle of the century, more families could afford to buy mass-produced automobiles, like the 1950s Hillman Minx pictured in this advertisement.

Modern Homes
Labour-saving devices, such as the vacuum cleaner, invented by William Hoover in 1908, were very popular. This was due to the virtual disappearance of domestic servants, as women took jobs outside the home.

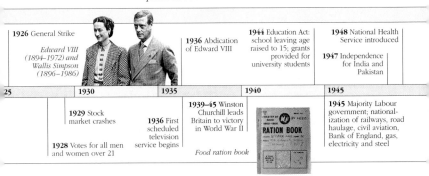

1926 General Strike

Edward VIII (1894–1972) and Wallis Simpson (1896–1986)

1936 Abdication of Edward VIII

1944 Education Act: school leaving age raised to 15; grants provided for university students

1948 National Health Service introduced

1947 Independence for India and Pakistan

25 1930 1935 1940 1945

1929 Stock market crashes

1936 First scheduled television service begins

1939–45 Winston Churchill leads Britain to victory in World War II

Food ration book

MINISTRY OF FOOD
1953-1954
RATION BOOK

1945 Majority Labour government; nationalization of railways, road haulage, civil aviation, Bank of England, gas, electricity and steel

1928 Votes for all men and women over 21

Britain Today

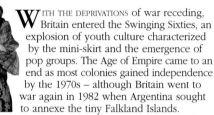

WITH THE DEPRIVATIONS of war receding, Britain entered the Swinging Sixties, an explosion of youth culture characterized by the mini-skirt and the emergence of pop groups. The Age of Empire came to an end as most colonies gained independence by the 1970s – although Britain went to war again in 1982 when Argentina sought to annexe the tiny Falkland Islands.

Designer Vivienne Westwood and Naomi Campbell

People were on the move; immigration from the former colonies enriched British culture – though it also gave rise to social problems – and increasing prosperity allowed millions of people to travel abroad. Britain joined the European Community in 1973, and forged a more tangible link when the Channel Tunnel opened in 1994.

1960s The mini-skirt takes British fashion to new heights of daring – and Flower Power arrives from California

1951 Winston Churchill comes back as Prime Minister as Conservatives win general election

1958 Campaign for Nuclear Disarmament launched, reflecting young people's fear of global annihilation

1965 Death penalty is abolished

1950	1955	1960	1965	1970

1950	1955	1960	1965	1970

1953 Elizabeth II crowned in first televised Coronation

1963 The Beatles pop group from Liverpool captures the spirit of the age with numerous chart-topping hits

1959 First motorway, the M1, built from London to the Midlands

1957 First immigrants arrive from the Caribbean by boat

1951 Festival of Britain lifts postwar spirits

VOTE!

...GET BRITAIN OUT

1973 After years of negotiation, Britain joins the European Community

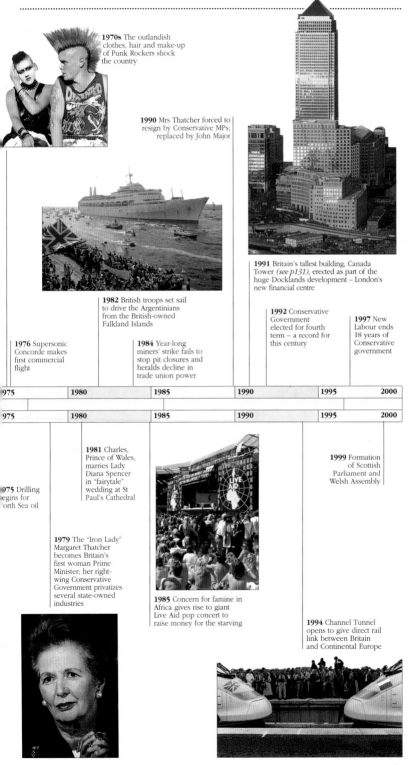

1970s The outlandish clothes, hair and make-up of Punk Rockers shock the country

1990 Mrs Thatcher forced to resign by Conservative MPs; replaced by John Major

1991 Britain's tallest building, Canada Tower (see p131), erected as part of the huge Docklands development – London's new financial centre

1982 British troops set sail to drive the Argentinians from the British-owned Falkland Islands

1992 Conservative Government elected for fourth term – a record for this century

1997 New Labour ends 18 years of Conservative government

1976 Supersonic Concorde makes first commercial flight

1984 Year-long miners' strike fails to stop pit closures and heralds decline in trade union power

975   1980   1985   1990   1995   2000

975   1980   1985   1990   1995   2000

1981 Charles, Prince of Wales, marries Lady Diana Spencer in "fairytale" wedding at St Paul's Cathedral

1999 Formation of Scottish Parliament and Welsh Assembly

975 Drilling egins for orth Sea oil

1979 The "Iron Lady" Margaret Thatcher becomes Britain's first woman Prime Minister; her right-wing Conservative Government privatizes several state-owned industries

1985 Concern for famine in Africa gives rise to giant Live Aid pop concert to raise money for the starving

1994 Channel Tunnel opens to give direct rail link between Britain and Continental Europe

GREAT BRITAIN
THROUGH THE YEAR

EVERY BRITISH SEASON has its particular charms. Most major sights are open all year round, but many secondary attractions may be closed in winter. The weather is changeable in all seasons and the visitor is as likely to experience a crisp, sunny February day as to be caught in a cold, heavy shower in July. Long periods of

Film festival sign

adverse weather and extremes of temperature are rare. Spring is characterized by daffodils and bluebells, summer by roses and autumn by the vivid colours of changing leaves. In wintertime, country vistas are visible through the bare branches of the trees. Annual events and ceremonies, many stemming from age-old traditions, reflect the attributes of the seasons.

Bluebells in spring in Angrove woodland, Wiltshire

SPRING

As THE DAYS get longer and warmer, the countryside starts to come alive. At Easter many stately homes and gardens open their gates to visitors for the first time, and during the week before Whit

Sunday, or Whitsun (the seventh Sunday after Easter), the Chelsea Flower Show takes place. This is the focal point of the gardening year and spurs on the nation's gardeners to prepare their summer displays. Outside the capital, many music and arts festivals mark the middle months of the year.

MARCH

Ideal Home Exhibition *(second week)*, Earl's Court, London. New products and ideas for the home.
Crufts Dog Show *(second week)*, National Exhibition Centre, Birmingham.
International Book Fair *(third week)*, Olympia, London.
St Patrick's Day *(17 March)*. Musical events in major cities celebrate the feast day of Ireland's patron saint.

APRIL

Maundy Thursday (Thursday before Easter), the Queen gives money to pensioners.
St George's Day *(23 April)*, English patron saint's day.
British International Antiques Fair *(last week)*, National Exhibition Centre, Birmingham.

Water garden exhibited at the Chelsea Flower Show

MAY

Furry Dancing Festival *(8 May)*, Helston, Cornwall. Spring celebration *(see p266)*.
Well-dressing festivals *(Ascension Day)*, Tissington, Derbyshire *(see p323)*.
Chelsea Flower Show *(mid-May)*, Royal Hospital, London.
Brighton Festival *(last three weeks)*. Performing arts.
Glyndebourne Festival Opera Season *(mid-May–end Aug)*, near Lewes, East Sussex. Opera productions.
International Highland Games *(last weekend)*, Blair Atholl, Scotland.

Yeomen of the Guard conducting the Maundy money ceremony

SUMMER

LIFE MOVES OUTDOORS in the summer months. Cafés and restaurants place tables on the pavements and pub customers take their drinks outside. The Queen holds garden parties for privileged guests at Buckingham Palace while, more modestly, village fêtes – a combination of a carnival and street party – are organized. Beaches and swimming pools become crowded and office workers picnic in city parks at lunch. The rose, England's national flower, bursts into bloom in millions of gardens. Cultural treats include open-air theatre performances, outdoor concerts, the Proms in London, the National Eisteddfod in Wales, Glyndebourne's opera festival, and Edinburgh's festival of the performing arts.

Glastonbury music festival, a major event attracting thousands of people

Deck chair at Brighton

JUNE

Royal Academy Summer Exhibitions *(Jun–Aug).* Large and varied London show of new work by many artists.
Bath International Festival *(19 May–4 Jun),* various venues. Arts events.
Beaumaris Festival *(27 May–4 Jun),* various venues. Concerts, craft fairs plus fringe activities.
Trooping the Colour *(Sat closest to 10 Jun),* Whitehall,

Assessment of sheep at the Royal Welsh Show, Builth Wells

London. The Queen's official birthday parade.
Glastonbury Festival *(23–25 June),* Somerset.
Aldeburgh Festival *(second and third weeks),* Suffolk. Arts festival with concerts and opera.
Royal Highland Show *(third week),* Ingliston, near Edinburgh. Scotland's agricultural show.
Leeds Castle *(last week).* Open-air concerts.
Glasgow International Jazz Festival *(last weekend).* Various venues.

JULY

Royal Show *(first week),* near Kenilworth, Warwickshire. National agricultural show.
International Eisteddfod *(first week),* Llangollen, North Wales. International music and dance competition *(see p436).*
Hampton Court Flower Show *(early July),* Hampton Court Palace, Surrey.
Summer Music Festival *(third weekend),* Stourhead, Wiltshire.
International Henley Royal Regatta *(first week),* Henley-on-Thames. Rowing regatta on the Thames.
Cambridge Folk Festival *(last weekend).* Music festival with top international artists.
Royal Welsh Show *(last weekend),* Builth Wells, Wales. Agricultural show.
International Festival of Folk Arts *(late Jul–early Aug),* Sidmouth, Devon *(see p275).*

AUGUST

Royal National Eisteddfod *(early in month).* Traditional arts competitions, in Welsh *(see p421).* Various locations.

Reveller in bright costume at the Notting Hill Carnival

Henry Wood Promenade Concerts *(mid-Jul–mid-Sep),* Royal Albert Hall, London. Famous concert series popularly known as the Proms.
Edinburgh International Festival *(mid-Aug–mid-Sep).* The largest festival of theatre, dance and music in the world *(see p495).*
Edinburgh Festival Fringe. Alongside the festival, there are 400 shows a day.
Brecon Jazz *(mid-Aug),* jazz festival in Brecon, Wales.
Beatles Festival *(last weekend),* Liverpool. Music and entertainment related to the Fab Four *(see p363).*
Notting Hill Carnival *(last weekend),* London. West Indian street carnival with floats, bands and stalls.

Boxes of apples from the autumn harvest

AUTUMN

AFTER THE HEADY escapism of summer, the start of the new season is marked by the various party political conferences held in October and the royal opening of Parliament. All over the country on 5 November, bonfires are lit and fireworks let off to celebrate the foiling of an attempt to blow up the Houses of Parliament by Guy Fawkes and his co-conspirators in 1605. Cornfields become golden, trees turn fiery yellow through to russet and orchards

Shot putting at Braemar

are heavy with apples and other autumn fruits. In churches throughout the country, thanksgiving festivals mark the harvest. The shops stock up for the run-up to Christmas, their busiest time of the year.

SEPTEMBER

Blackpool Illuminations *(beg Sep–end Oct)*. A 5 mile (8 km) spectacle of lighting along Blackpool's seafront.
Royal Highland Gathering *(first Sat)*, Braemar, Scotland. Kilted clansmen from all over the country toss cabers, shot putt, dance and play the bagpipes. The royal family usually attends.
International Sheepdog Trials *(14–16 Sep)*, all over Britain, with venues changing from year to year.
Great Autumn Flower Show *(third weekend)*, Harrogate, N Yorks. Displays by nurserymen and national flower organizations.
Horse of the Year Show *(last weekend)*, Wembley, London *(see p67)*.
Oyster Festival *(Sat at beginning of oyster season)*, Colchester. Lunch hosted by the mayor to celebrate the start of the oyster season.

OCTOBER

Harvest Festivals *(whole month)*, all over Britain especially in farming areas.
Nottingham Goose Fair *(second weekend)*. One of Britain's oldest traditional fairs now has a funfair.
Canterbury Festival *(second and third weeks)*. Music, drama and the arts.
Aldeburgh Britten Festival *(third weekend)*. Concerts with music by Britten *(see p189)* and other composers.
Hallowe'en *(31 Oct)*, "trick or treat" games countrywide.

Procession leading to the state opening of Parliament

NOVEMBER

Opening of Parliament *(Oct or Nov)*. The Queen goes from Buckingham Palace to Westminster in a state coach, to open the new parliamentary session.
Lord Mayor's Procession and Show *(second Sat)*. Parade in the City, London.
Remembrance Day *(second Sun)*. Services and parades at the Cenotaph in Whitehall, London, and all over Britain.
RAC London to Brighton Veteran Car Rally *(first Sun)*. A 7am start from Hyde Park, London to Brighton, East Sussex.
Guy Fawkes Night *(5 Nov)*, fireworks and bonfires all over the country.
London Film Festival *(first two weeks)*. Forum for new films, various venues.
Regent Street Christmas Lights *(mid-Nov)*, London.

Fireworks over Edinburgh on Guy Fawkes Night

Winter landscape in the Scottish Highlands, near Glencoe

WINTER

BRIGHTLY COLOURED fairy lights and Christmas trees decorate Britain's principal shopping streets as shoppers rush to buy their seasonal gifts. Carol services are held in churches across the country, and pantomime, a traditional entertainment for children deriving from the Victorian music hall, fills theatres in major towns.

Brightly lit Christmas tree at the centre of Trafalgar Square

Many offices close between Christmas and the New Year. Shops reopen for the January sales on 27 December – a paradise for bargain-hunters.

DECEMBER

Christmas Tree *(first Thu)*, Trafalgar Square, London. The tree is donated by the people of Norway and is lit by the Mayor of Oslo; this is followed by carol singing.
Carol concerts *(whole month)*, all over Britain.
Grand Christmas Parade *(beg Dec)*, London. Parade with floats to celebrate myth of Santa Claus.
Midnight Mass *(24 Dec)*, in churches everywhere around Britain.
Allendale Baal Festival *(31 Dec)*, Northumberland. Parade by villagers with burning tar barrels on their heads to celebrate the New Year.

Sprig of holly

PUBLIC HOLIDAYS

New Year's Day (1 Jan).
2 Jan (Scotland only).
Easter weekend (March or April). In England it begins on **Good Friday** and ends on **Easter Monday**; in Scotland there is no Easter Monday holiday.
May Day (usually first Mon in May).
Late Spring Bank Holiday (last Mon in May).
Bank Holiday (first Mon in August, Scotland only).
August Bank Holiday (last Mon in August, except Scotland).
Christmas and Boxing Day (25–26 December).

JANUARY

Hogmanay and **New Year** *(31 Dec, 1 Jan)*, Scottish celebrations. **Burns Night** *(25 Jan)*. Scots everywhere celebrate poet Robert Burns' birth with poetry, feasting and drinking.

FEBRUARY

Chinese New Year *(late Jan or early Feb)*. Lion dances, firecrackers and processions in Chinatown, London.

Morris dancing on May Day in Midhurst, Sussex

The Sporting Year

MANY OF THE WORLD'S major competitive sports, including soccer, cricket and tennis, were invented in Britain. Originally devised as recreation for the wealthy, they have since entered the arena of mass entertainment. Some, however, such as the Royal Ascot race meeting and Wimbledon tennis tournament, are still valued as much for their social prestige as for the sport itself. Other delightful sporting events in Britain take place at a local level: village cricket, point-to-point racing and the Highland Games are all popular amateur events.

Ewan Thomas

Royal Ascot *is the four day social highlight of the horse racing year. The high class of the thoroughbreds is matched by the high style of the fashions, with royalty attending.*

Oxford and Cambridge Boat Race, *first held in 1829 at Henley, has become a national event, with the two university eights now battling it out between Putney and Mortlake on the Thames.*

The FA Cup Final *is the apex of the football season.*

Derby Day horse races, Epsom

January	February	March	April	May	June

Cheltenham Gold Cup steeplechase *(see p314)*

Grand National steeple-chase, Aintree *(see p362),* Liverpool

Rugby League Cup Final, Wembley

Embassy World Snooker Championships, Sheffield

Wimbledon Lawn Tennis Tournament *is the world's most prestigious lawn tennis championship.*

Six Nations Rugby Union *is an annual contest between England (right), France, Italy, Ireland, Scotland and Wales (left). This league-based competition runs through winter ending in March.*

London Marathon *attracts thousands of long-distance runners, from the world's best to fancy-dressed fund raisers.*

Henley Royal Regatta *(see p221) is an international rowing event on the Thames (first held in 1839). It is also a glamorous social occasion.*

British Grand Prix, held at Silverstone, is Britain's round of the Formula One World Championship.

TICKETS AND TOUTS

For many big sporting events, the only official source of tickets is the club concerned. Booking agencies may offer hard-to-get tickets – though often at high prices. Unauthorized touts may lurk at popular events but their expensive tickets are not always valid. Check carefully.

Tickets for the Grand Prix

British Open Golf Championship, a major golf event, is held at one of several British courses. Here, Nick Faldo putts.

The Cheltenham and Gloucester Trophy is the final of a season of competition to find the year's county cricket champions. It takes place at Lord's (see p127).

Cowes week *(see p154)*, a yachting festival, covers all classes of racing.

Horse of the Year Show brings together top show-jumpers to compete on a tough indoor course *(see p64)*.

Oxford versus Cambridge rugby union, Twickenham

August	September	October	November	December

European Showjumping Championships at Hickstead

Gold Cup Humber powerboat race, Hull

Braemar Highland Games *(see p64)*

British Figure Skating and Ice Dance Championships are a feast of elegance on ice (various venues).

Winmau World Masters Darts Championships

KEY TO SPORT SEASONS

- Cricket
- River fishing
- Football (soccer)
- Hunting and shooting
- Rugby (union and league)
- Flat racing
- Jump racing
- Athletics – track and field
- Road running and cross-country
- Polo

Cartier International Polo, at the Guards Club, Windsor (see p221), is one of the main events for this peculiarly British game, played mainly by royalty and army officers.

Steven Cousins

The Climate of Great Britain

BRITAIN HAS A TEMPERATE CLIMATE. No region is far from the sea, which exerts a moderating influence on temperatures. Seldom are winter nights colder than -15° C, even in the far north, or summer days warmer than 30° C in the south and west: a much narrower range than in most European countries. Despite Britain's reputation, the average annual rainfall is quite low – less than 100 cm (40 inches) – and heavy rain is rare. The Atlantic coast is warmed by the Gulf Stream, making the west slightly warmer, though wetter, than the east.

LANCASHIRE AND THE LAKES

°C

	19		
11.5	13	13.5	6
5		8	
			1.5

5.5 hrs	6 hrs	3 hrs	1.5 hrs
53 mm	85 mm	104 mm	90 mm
month	Apr	Jul	Oct	Jan

THE HEART OF ENGLAND

°C

	20		
12	12.5	13	
4.5		7.5	5.5
			1.5

4.5 hrs	5.5 hrs	3 hrs	1.5 hrs
53 mm	69 mm	69 mm	74 mm
month	Apr	Jul	Oct	Jan

Average monthly maximum temperature

Average monthly minimum temperature

Average daily hours of sunshine

Average monthly rainfall

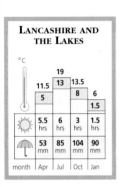

SOUTH AND MID-WALES

°C

	20.5		
13	12.5	14	
5		7.5	7
			2

5.5 hrs	6 hrs	3.5 hrs	1.5 hrs
65 mm	89 mm	109 mm	108 mm
month	Apr	Jul	Oct	Jan

NORTH WALES

°C

	17		
11	11	13.5	
4.5		8	6
			1

3 hrs	3.5 hrs	2.5 hrs	1.5 hrs
144 mm	206 mm	261 mm	252 mm
month	Apr	Jul	Oct	Jan

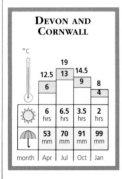

DEVON AND CORNWALL

°C

	19		
12.5	13	14.5	
6		9	8
			4

6 hrs	6.5 hrs	3.5 hrs	2 hrs
53 mm	70 mm	91 mm	99 mm
month	Apr	Jul	Oct	Jan

WEST COUNTRY

°C

	20.5		
13.5	13.5	15	
5.5		8.5	7
			2

5.5 hrs	6.5 hrs	3.5 hrs	2 hrs
49 mm	65 mm	85 mm	74 mm
month	Apr	Jul	Oct	Jan

THAMES VALLEY

°C

	21.5		
13.5	12.5	14.5	
4.5		6.5	6.5
			1

5.5 hrs	6 hrs	3 hrs	1.5 hrs
41 mm	55 mm	64 mm	61 mm
month	Apr	Jul	Oct	Jan

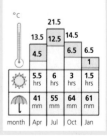

Wick

Inverness

The Highlands and Islands

EDINBURGH

Glasgow

The Lowlands

Lancashire and the Lakes

Liverpo

North Wales

Caernarfon

South and Mid-Wales

CARDIFF

B

West Coun

Exeter

Devon and Cornwall

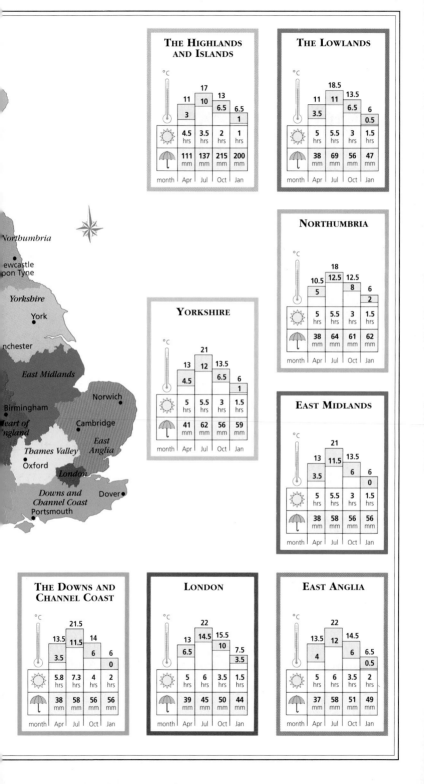

THE HIGHLANDS AND ISLANDS

°C	Apr	Jul	Oct	Jan
	11	17	13	
		10	6.5	6.5
	3			1
☀	4.5 hrs	3.5 hrs	2 hrs	1 hrs
☂	111 mm	137 mm	215 mm	200 mm
month	Apr	Jul	Oct	Jan

THE LOWLANDS

°C	Apr	Jul	Oct	Jan
	11	18.5	13.5	
		11	6.5	6
	3.5			0.5
☀	5 hrs	5.5 hrs	3 hrs	1.5 hrs
☂	38 mm	69 mm	56 mm	47 mm
month	Apr	Jul	Oct	Jan

YORKSHIRE

°C	Apr	Jul	Oct	Jan
	13	21	13.5	
		12	6.5	6
	4.5			1
☀	5 hrs	5.5 hrs	3 hrs	1.5 hrs
☂	41 mm	62 mm	56 mm	59 mm
month	Apr	Jul	Oct	Jan

NORTHUMBRIA

°C	Apr	Jul	Oct	Jan
	10.5	18	12.5	
		12.5	8	6
	5			2
☀	5 hrs	5.5 hrs	3 hrs	1.5 hrs
☂	38 mm	64 mm	61 mm	62 mm
month	Apr	Jul	Oct	Jan

EAST MIDLANDS

°C	Apr	Jul	Oct	Jan
	13	21	13.5	
		11.5	6	6
	3.5			0
☀	5 hrs	5.5 hrs	3 hrs	1.5 hrs
☂	38 mm	58 mm	56 mm	56 mm
month	Apr	Jul	Oct	Jan

THE DOWNS AND CHANNEL COAST

°C	Apr	Jul	Oct	Jan
	13.5	21.5	14	
		11.5	6	6
	3.5			0
☀	5.8 hrs	7.3 hrs	4 hrs	2 hrs
☂	38 mm	58 mm	56 mm	56 mm
month	Apr	Jul	Oct	Jan

LONDON

°C	Apr	Jul	Oct	Jan
	13	22	15.5	
		14.5	10	7.5
	6.5			3.5
☀	5 hrs	6 hrs	3.5 hrs	1.5 hrs
☂	39 mm	45 mm	50 mm	44 mm
month	Apr	Jul	Oct	Jan

EAST ANGLIA

°C	Apr	Jul	Oct	Jan
	13.5	22	14.5	
		12	6	6.5
	4			0.5
☀	5 hrs	6 hrs	3.5 hrs	2 hrs
☂	37 mm	58 mm	51 mm	49 mm
month	Apr	Jul	Oct	Jan

Northumbria

ewcastle pon Tyne

Yorkshire

York

nchester

East Midlands

Birmingham

eart of ngland

Norwich

Cambridge

East Anglia

Thames Valley

Oxford

London

Downs and Channel Coast

Portsmouth

Dover

LONDON

London at a Glance

THE LARGEST CITY IN EUROPE, London is home to about seven million people and covers 625 sq miles (1,600 sq km). The capital was founded by the Romans in the first century AD as a convenient administrative and communications centre and a port for trade with Continental Europe. For a thousand years it has been the principal residence of British monarchs as well as the centre of business and government, and it is rich in historic buildings and treasures from all periods. In addition to its diverse range of museums, galleries and churches, London is an exciting contemporary city, packed with a vast array of entertainments and shops. The attractions on offer are virtually endless but this map highlights the most important of those described in detail on the following pages.

Buckingham Palace *(pp88–9) is London home and office to the monarchy. The Changing of the Guard takes place on the palace forecourt.*

REGENT'S PARK AND BLOOMSBURY
(see pp104–109)

WEST EN AND WESTMINS
(see pp78–

SOUTH KENSINGTON AND HYDE PARK
(see pp96–103)

Hyde Park *(p77), the largest central London park, boasts numerous sports facilities, restaurants, an art gallery and Speakers' Corner. The highlight is the Serpentine Lake.*

```
0 kilometres          1
0 miles        0.5
```

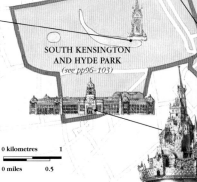

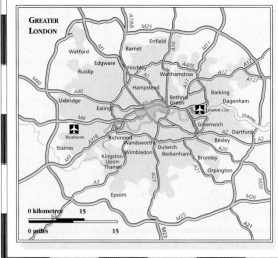

GREATER LONDON

The Victoria and Albert Museum *(pp100–101) is the world's largest museum of decorative arts. This German cup is 15th century.*

KEY

▨	Main sightseeing area

The British Museum's (pp108–9) *vast collection of antiquities from all over the world includes this Portland Vase from the 1st century BC.*

The National Gallery's (pp84–5) *world-famous collection of paintings includes works such as* Christ Mocked (c.1495) *by Hieronymus Bosch.*

THAMES

THE CITY AND SOUTHWARK (see pp110–121)

St Paul's (pp116–17) *huge dome is the cathedral's most distinctive feature. Three galleries around the dome give spectacular views of London.*

Westminster Abbey (pp94–5) *has glorious medieval architecture and is crammed with impressive tombs and monuments to some of Britain's greatest public figures.*

Tate Britain (p93) *displays an outstanding collection of British art ranging from stylized Elizabethan portraiture, such as* The Cholmondeley Sisters, *to cutting edge installation and film.*

The Tower of London (pp120–21) *is most famous as the prison where enemies of the Crown were executed. The Tower houses the Crown Jewels, including the Imperial State Crown.*

A River View of London

THE RIVER THAMES was the artery for much of the country's commerce from Roman times until the 1950s. Today the river is one of London's foremost leisure amenities, with wharves and warehouses converted into riverside marinas, bars and restaurants. One of the most enjoyable ways to see the capital is by boat, and the most popular river trips travel downstream from the Houses of Parliament to Tower Bridge. This 30-minute cruise gives a different perspective on some of London's historic buildings and sights.

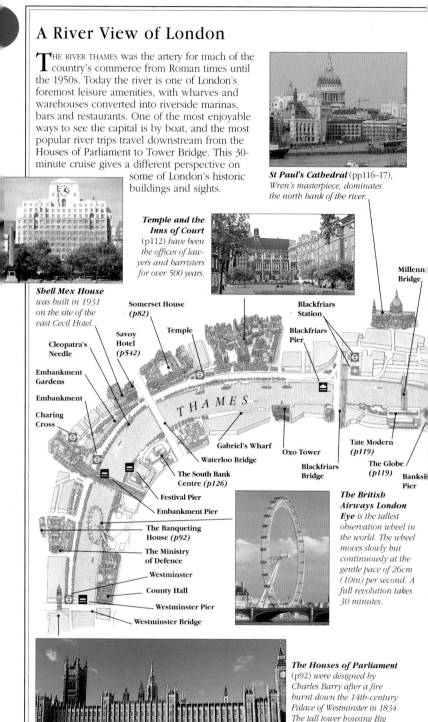

St Paul's Cathedral (pp116–17), *Wren's masterpiece, dominates the north bank of the river.*

Temple and the Inns of Court (p112) *have been the offices of lawyers and barristers for over 500 years.*

Shell Mex House was built in 1931 on the site of the vast Cecil Hotel.

Cleopatra's Needle

Embankment Gardens

Embankment

Charing Cross

Savoy Hotel (p542)

Somerset House (p82)

Temple

Millennium Bridge

Blackfriars Station

Blackfriars Pier

THAMES

Gabriel's Wharf

Waterloo Bridge

The South Bank Centre (p126)

Festival Pier

Embankment Pier

The Banqueting House (p92)

The Ministry of Defence

Westminster

County Hall

Westminster Pier

Westminster Bridge

Oxo Tower

Blackfriars Bridge

Tate Modern (p119)

The Globe (p119)

Bankside Pier

The British Airways London Eye is the tallest observation wheel in the world. The wheel moves slowly but continuously at the gentle pace of 26cm (10in) per second. A full revolution takes 30 minutes.

The Houses of Parliament (p92) *were designed by Charles Barry after a fire burnt down the 14th-century Palace of Westminster in 1834. The tall tower housing Big Ben dominates the skyline.*

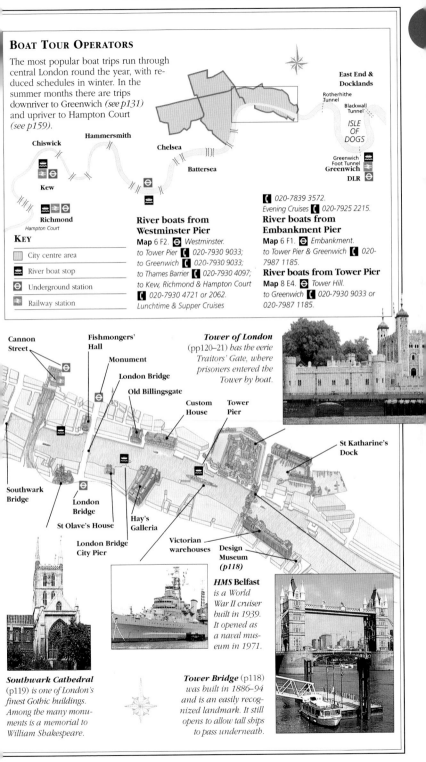

BOAT TOUR OPERATORS

The most popular boat trips run through central London round the year, with reduced schedules in winter. In the summer months there are trips downriver to Greenwich *(see p131)* and upriver to Hampton Court *(see p159)*.

KEY

▦	City centre area
⯐	River boat stop
⊖	Underground station
⯏	Railway station

Chiswick

Hammersmith

Chelsea

Battersea

Kew

Richmond

Hampton Court

East End & Docklands

Rotherhithe Tunnel

Blackwall Tunnel

ISLE OF DOGS

Greenwich Foot Tunnel

Greenwich

DLR

River boats from Westminster Pier
Map 6 F2. ⊖ *Westminster.*
to Tower Pier [020-7930 9033;
to Greenwich [020-7930 9033;
to Thames Barrier [020-7930 4097;
to Kew, Richmond & Hampton Court
[020-7930 4721 or 2062.
Lunchtime & Supper Cruises

[020-7839 3572.
Evening Cruises [020-7925 2215.
River boats from Embankment Pier
Map 6 F1. ⊖ *Embankment.*
to Tower Pier & Greenwich [020-7987 1185.
River boats from Tower Pier
Map 8 E4. ⊖ *Tower Hill.*
to Greenwich [020-7930 9033 or
020-7987 1185.

Cannon Street

Fishmongers' Hall

Monument

London Bridge

Old Billingsgate

Custom House

Tower Pier

Tower of London
(pp120–21) has the eerie Traitors' Gate, where prisoners entered the Tower by boat.

St Katharine's Dock

Southwark Bridge

London Bridge

St Olave's House

Hay's Galleria

London Bridge City Pier

Victorian warehouses

Design Museum *(p118)*

***HMS* Belfast** *is a World War II cruiser built in 1939. It opened as a naval museum in 1971.*

Southwark Cathedral
(p119) is one of London's finest Gothic buildings. Among the many monuments is a memorial to William Shakespeare.

Tower Bridge (p118) *was built in 1886–94 and is an easily recognized landmark. It still opens to allow tall ships to pass underneath.*

London's Parks and Gardens

Camellia japonica

LONDON HAS ONE OF THE WORLD'S greenest city centres, full of tree-filled squares and large expanses of grass, some of which have been public land since medieval times. From the elegant terraces of Regent's Park to the botanic gardens of Kew, every London park and garden has its own charm and character. Some are ancient crown or public land, while others were created from the grounds of private houses or disused land. Londoners make the most of these open spaces: for exercise, listening to music, or simply escaping the bustle of the city.

Holland Park (see pp128–9) *offers acres of peaceful woodland, an open-air theatre (see p125) and a café.*

Kew Gardens (see p132) *are the world's premiere botanic gardens. An amazing variety of plants from all over the world is complemented by an array of temples, monuments and a landscaped lake.*

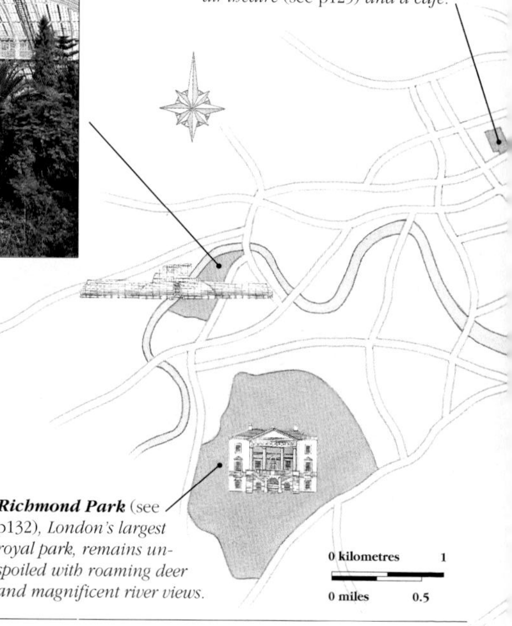

Richmond Park (see p132), *London's largest royal park, remains unspoiled with roaming deer and magnificent river views.*

0 kilometres 1

0 miles 0.5

SEASONAL BEST

As winter draws to a close, spectacular drifts of crocuses, daffodils and tulips are to be found peeping above the ground in Green Park and Kew. Easter weekend marks the start of outdoor events with funfairs on many commons and parks. During the summer months the parks are packed with picnickers and sunbathers and you can often catch a free open-air concert in St James's or Regent's parks. The energetic can play tennis in most

Winter in Kensington Gardens, adjoining Hyde Park

parks, swim in Hyde Park's Serpentine or the ponds on Hampstead Heath, or take rowing boats out on the lakes in Regent's and Battersea parks. Autumn brings a different atmosphere, and on 5 November firework displays and bonfires celebrate Guy Fawkes Night *(see p64)*. Winter is a good time to visit the tropical glasshouses and the colourful outdoor winter garden at Kew. If the weather gets really cold, the Round Pond in Kensington Gardens may be fit for ice-skating.

Hampstead Heath *(see p130)* is a breezy open space embracing a variety of landscapes.

Regent's Park (see p105) *has a large boating lake, an open-air theatre (see p125) and London Zoo. Surrounded by Nash's graceful buildings, it is one of London's most civilized retreats.*

St James's Park, *in the heart of the city, is a popular escape for office workers. It is also a reserve for wildfowl.*

THAMES

Green Park, *with its shady trees and benches, offers a cool, restful spot in the heart of London.*

Battersea Park is a pleasant riverside site with a man-made boating lake.

Greenwich Park (see p131) *is dominated by the National Maritime Museum. There are fine views from the Old Royal Observatory on the hill top.*

Hyde Park and Kensington Gardens (see p103) *are both popular London retreats. There are sporting facilities, a lake and art gallery in Hyde Park. This plaque is from the ornate Italian Garden in Kensington Gardens.*

HISTORIC CEMETERIES

In the late 1830s, a ring of private cemeteries was established around London to ease the pressure on the monstrously overcrowded and unhealthy burial grounds of the inner city. Today the cemeteries, notably **Highgate** *(see p130)* and **Kensal Green,** are well worth visiting for their flamboyant Victorian monuments.

Kensal Green cemetery on the Harrow Road

WEST END AND WESTMINSTER

THE WEST END is the city's social and cultural centre and the London home of the royal family. Stretching from the edge of Hyde Park to Covent Garden, the district bustles all day and late into the night. Whether you're looking for art, history, street- or café-life, it is the most rewarding area in which to begin an exploration of the city.

Westminster has been at the centre of political and religious power for a thousand years. In the 11th century, King Canute founded Westminster Palace and Edward the Confessor built Westminster Abbey, where all English monarchs have been crowned since 1066. As modern government developed, the great offices of state were established in the area.

Horse Guard on Whitehall

SIGHTS AT A GLANCE

Historic Streets and Buildings

Banqueting House ⑱
Buckingham Palace pp88–9 ⑬
Cabinet War Rooms ⑯
Downing Street ⑰
Houses of Parliament pp92–3 ⑲
Piccadilly Circus ⑧
Ritz Hotel ⑩
Royal Mews ⑮
The Mall ⑫
The Piazza and Central Market ❶

Museums and Galleries

London Transport Museum ❷
National Gallery pp84–5 ❻
National Portrait Gallery ❼
Queen's Gallery ⑭
Royal Academy ❾
Somerset House ❹
Tate Britain ㉑
Theatre Museum ❸

Churches

Queen's Chapel ⑪
Westminster Abbey pp94–5 ⑳

Attractions

British Airways London Eye ❺

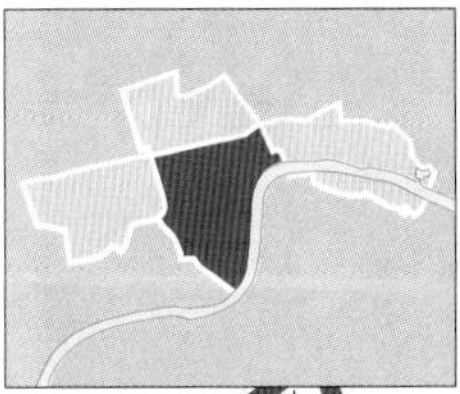

KEY

	Street-by-Street map *pp80–81*
	Street-by-Street map *pp86–7*
	Street-by-Street map *pp90–91*
⊖	Underground station
⇌	Railway station
P	Parking
	River boat boarding point

GETTING THERE

This area is the hub of the city's public transport system, served by virtually all tube lines and scores of buses (*see pp642–3*). The most convenient tube and railway station is Charing Cross.

0 metres 500
0 yards 500

◁ **Big Ben and the Houses of Parliament**

Street-by-Street: Covent Garden

U NTIL 1973, COVENT GARDEN was an area of decaying streets and warehouses, which only came alive after dark when the fruit and vegetable market traders packed up for the day. Since then the Victorian market and elegant buildings nearby have been converted into stylish shops, restaurants, bars and cafés, creating an animated district which attracts a lively young crowd, night and day.

Seven Dials is a replica of a 17th-century monument marking the crossroads.

Covent Garden

Neal Street and Neal's Yard are lined with many specialist shops converted from former warehouses.

St Martin's Theatre (see pp124–5) is home to the world's longest running play, *The Mousetrap*.

Stanfords map shop

The Lamb and Flag, built in 1623, is one of London's oldest pubs.

New Row is lined with little shops and cafés.

St Paul's Church was designed in 1633 by Inigo Jones (see p53), in the style of the Italian Renaissance architect, Andrea Palladio. Jones also designed the original Covent Garden Piazza.

Theatre Museum
This houses a collection of theatrical memorabilia ❸

The Royal Opera House
(see p126) is where many of the greatest opera singers and ballet dancers have performed.

LOCATOR MAP
See Street Finder map 4

KEY

– – – Suggested route

| 0 metres | 100 |
| 0 yards | 100 |

London Transport Museum
This museum's intriguing collection brings to life the history of the city's tubes, buses and trains. It also displays examples of 20th-century commercial art ❷

Jubilee Market

★ **Piazza and Central Market**
Street performers entertain passers-by in the square ❶

STAR SIGHTS

★ **Piazza and Central Market**

The Piazza and Central Market ❶

Covent Garden WC2. **Map** 4 F5.
⊖ *Covent Garden.* ♿ *cobbled streets.* **Street performers in Piazza:** *10am–dusk daily.*

THE 17TH-CENTURY ARCHITECT
Inigo Jones *(see p53)* planned the Piazza in Covent Garden as an elegant residential square, modelled on the piazza in the Tuscan town of Livorno, which he had seen under construction during his travels in Italy. For a brief period, the Piazza became one of the most fashionable addresses in London, but it was superseded by the even grander St James's Square *(see pp86–7)* which lies to the southwest.

Decline accelerated when a fruit and vegetable market developed. By the mid-18th century, the Piazza had become a haunt of prostitutes and most of its houses had turned into seedy lodgings, gambling dens, brothels and taverns.

A mid-18th-century view of Covent Garden's Piazza

Meanwhile the wholesale produce market became the largest in the country and in 1828 a market hall was erected to ease congestion. The market, however, soon outgrew its new home and despite the construction of new buildings, such as Floral and Jubilee halls, the congestion grew worse. In 1973 the market moved to a new site in south London, and over the last two decades Covent Garden has been redeveloped. Today only St Paul's remains of Inigo Jones's buildings, and Covent Garden, with its many small shops, cafés, restaurants, market stalls and street entertainers, is one of central London's liveliest districts.

London Transport Museum ❷

The Piazza, Covent Garden WC2.
Map 4 F5. 020-7379 6344.
Covent Garden. 10am–6pm
Sat–Thu; 11am–6pm Fri (last adm
5:15pm). 24–26 Dec.
phone in advance.

THIS COLLECTION of buses, trams and underground trains ranges from the earliest horse-drawn omnibuses to a present-day Hoppa bus. Housed in the iron, glass and brick Victorian Flower Market of Covent Garden, which was built in 1872, the museum is particularly good for children, who can put themselves in the driver's seat of a bus or an underground train, operate signals and chat to one of the actors playing the part of a 19th-century tube-tunnel miner.

London's bus and train companies have long been prolific patrons of artists, and the museum holds a fine collection of 19th- and 20th-century commercial art. Copies of some of the best posters and works by distinguished artists such as Paul Nash and Graham Sutherland – are on sale at the museum shop.

Poster by Michael Reilly (1929), London Transport Museum

Theatre Museum ❸

7 Russell St WC2. **Map** 4 F5. 020-7943 4700. Covent Garden.
10am–6pm Tue–Sun. public hols.

CHILDREN CAN BE MADE UP with gruesome wounds in this museum, and find out how Cyrano de Bergerac's nose was created for the film. An exhibition reveals how a theatre production is mounted, from cast readings of the author's original script, through videoed rehearsals and backstage procedures, to the first staged performance.

More conventionally, the intriguing history of show business is traced through a collection of memorabilia – playbills, programmes, props and costumes, such as a slinky silver jumpsuit worn by the rock singer Mick Jagger.

Somerset House ❹

Strand WC2. **Map** 4 F5. 020-7438 6622. Temple, Embankment, Charing Cross. 10am–6pm
Mon–Sat, noon–6pm Sun.
24–26 Dec, 1 Jan.
Courtauld Gallery 020-7848 2526. **The Gilbert Collection** 020-7240 4080.

DESIGNED IN 1770 by William Chambers, Somerset House is today home to two great collections of art, the **Courtauld Gallery** and **The Gilbert Collection**. The courtyard has recently been cleared, as part of a major

Somerset House: Strand façade

restoration scheme, to make way for an attractive piazza (which is turned into an ice rink for a few weeks in the winter), and the new riverside development includes a summer café and access to the South Bank. Located in Somerset House but famous in its own right is the Courtauld Gallery. Its exquisite collection of paintings includes major Impressionist and Post-Impressionist works. The Gilbert Collection is London's most recently acquired museum of decorative arts, made up of 800 pieces dating from the 16th to the 19th

SOHO AND CHINATOWN

Soho has been renowned for pleasures of the table, the flesh and the intellect ever since it was first developed in the late 17th century. At first a fashionable residential area, it declined when high society shifted west to Mayfair and immigrants from Europe moved into its narrow streets. Furniture-makers and tailors set up shop here and were joined in the late 19th century by pubs, nightclubs, restaurants and brothels. In the 1960s, Hong Kong Chinese moved into the area around Gerrard and Lisle streets and they created an aromatic Chinatown, packed with many restaurants and food shops. Soho's raffish reputation has long attracted artists and writers, ranging from the 18th-century essayist Thomas de Quincey to poet Dylan Thomas and painter Francis Bacon. Although strip joints and peep shows remain, Soho has enjoyed something of a renaissance, and today is full of stylish and lively bars and restaurants.

Lion dancer in February's Chinese New Year celebrations

The opulent Palm Court of the Ritz Hotel

century, including gold snuff boxes, Italian pietra dura (hard stone) mosaics and European silverware.

British Airways London Eye **5**

Jubilee Gardens, South Bank SE1. **Map** 6 F2. ☎ 0870 5000 600. ☻ Waterloo, Westminster. ◯ Apr–May: 10am–8pm; June–beg. Sep: 10am–10pm; Sep: 10am–8pm; Oct–Mar: 10am–7pm. ● 25, 31 Dec, 1 Jan. ♿ 🎦 ⓦ www.ba-londoneye.com

Tʜᴇ ʙʀɪᴛɪsʜ ᴀɪʀᴡᴀʏs London Eye is a 135-m (443-ft) observation wheel that was installed on the South Bank to mark the Millennium. Its enclosed passenger capsules offer a gentle, 30-minute ride as the wheel makes a full turn, with breathtaking views over London and for up to 42 km (26 miles) around. Towering over one of the world's most familiar riverscapes, it has understandably captured the hearts of Londoners and visitors alike, and is one of the city's most popular attractions. Advance reservations can be made by phone (but must be three days in advance) or in person at the ticket office in County Hall. "Flights" are on the hour and half-hour, and specific times can be booked.

National Gallery **6**

See pp84–5.

National Portrait Gallery **7**

2 St Martin's Place WC2. **Map** 6 E1. ☎ 020-7306 0055. ☻ Leicester Sq. ◯ 10am–6pm Mon–Wed & Sat, 10am–9pm Thu & Fri, 10am–6pm Sun. ● 24–25 Dec, 1 Jan, Good Fri, May Day. ♿ 🎦 Aug. 🖥 📷 🍴 ⓦ www.npg.org.uk

Tʜɪs ᴍᴜsᴇᴜᴍ celebrates Britain's history through portraits, photographs and sculptures; subjects range from Elizabeth I to Margaret Thatcher. The 20th-century section contains paintings and photographs of the royal family, politicians, rock stars, designers, artists and writers.

Piccadilly Circus **8**

W1. **Map** 6 D1. ☻ Piccadilly Circus.

Dᴏᴍɪɴᴀᴛᴇᴅ ʙʏ garish neon advertising hoardings, Piccadilly Circus is a hectic traffic junction surrounded by shopping malls. It began as an early 19th-century crossroads between Piccadilly and John Nash's (see p107) Regent Street. It was briefly an elegant space, edged by curving stucco façades, but by 1910 the first electric advertisements had been installed. For years people have congregated at its centre, beneath the delicately poised figure of Eros, erected in 1892.

Royal Academy **9**

Burlington House, Piccadilly W1. **Map** 6 D1. ☎ 020-7300 8000. ☻ Piccadilly Circus, Green Park. ◯ 10am–6pm daily, 10am–10pm Fri. ● 24–25 Dec, Good Fri. 🈴 ♿ 🎦 Tue–Fri. 🖥 📷 🍴

Fᴏᴜɴᴅᴇᴅ ɪɴ 1768, the Royal Academy is best known for its summer exhibition, which has been an annual event for over 200 years and comprises a rewarding mix of around 1,200 new works by established and unknown painters, sculptors and architects. During the rest of the year, the gallery shows prestigious touring exhibitions from around the world, and the courtyard in front of Burlington House, one of the West End's few surviving mansions from the early 18th century, is often filled with people waiting to get in.

Quite apart from its aesthetic delights, the Royal Academy can provide the weary traveller with a little lacuna of tranquillity. Its interior decoration inspires calm, and seems to be cut off from the stresses of modern city life.

The Statue of Eros

Ritz Hotel **10**

Piccadilly W1. **Map** 5 C1. ☎ 020-7493 8181. ☻ Green Park. ♿ See **Where to Stay** p540.

Cᴇsᴀʀ ʀɪᴛᴢ, the Swiss hotelier who inspired the word "ritzy", had virtually settled down to a quiet, modest retirement by 1906 when this hotel was built and named after him. The colonnaded front of the dominant, château-style building was erected in 1906 to suggest just the merest whiff of Paris, where the grandest hotels were to be found at the turn of the century. It still maintains its Edwardian air of *fin de siècle* opulence and sophisticated grandeur and is a popular venue for afternoon tea. Tea dances and fashion parades are held in the Palm Court, and a touch of *soigné* danger may be found in the casino.

National Gallery ❻

THE NATIONAL GALLERY is London's leading art museum, with over 2,200 paintings, most on permanent display. It has flourished since 1824 when George IV persuaded a reluctant government to purchase 38 major paintings. These became the core of a national collection of European art that now ranges from Giotto in the 13th century to 19th century Impressionists. The gallery's particular strengths are in Dutch, Italian Renaissance and 17th-century Spanish painting. In 1991 the Sainsbury Wing was added to the main Neo-Classical building (1834–8) to hold the Early Renaissance collection.

The Adoration of the Kings *(1564)*
This realistic work is by Flemish artist Pieter Brueghel the Elder (1520–1569).

Orange Street entrance ♿

Stairs to lower floor

★ **The Leonardo Cartoon** *(c.1510)*
The genius of Leonardo da Vinci glows through this chalk drawing of the Virgin and Child, St Anne and John the Baptist.

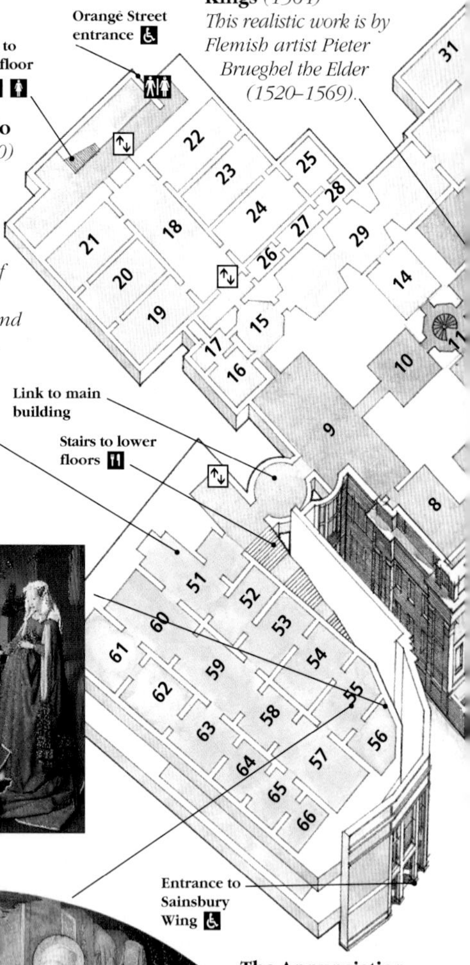

Link to main building

Stairs to lower floors

KEY TO FLOORPLAN

- ☐ Painting 1260–1510
- ☐ Painting 1510–1600
- ☐ Painting 1600–1700
- ☐ Painting 1700–1900
- ▨ Special exhibitions
- ☐ Non-exhibition space

Arnolfini Portrait
Jan van Eyck (1389–1441), one of the pioneers of oil painting, shows his mastery of colour, texture, and minute detail in this portrait of 1434.

Entrance to Sainsbury Wing ♿

The Annunciation
This refined work of 1448, by Fra Filippo Lippi, forms part of the gallery's exceptional Italian Renaissance collection.

★ **Rokeby Venus**
This is Velazquez's only surviving female nude (1649).

Stairs to lower galleries

33

32

34

37

35

36

38

40

41

39

43

42

45

44

46

2 1

Stairs to lower floors 🚻 🛗 🚹

★ **The Haywain** *(1821)*
The great age of 19th-century landscape painting is represented by Constable and Turner (see p93). This picture shows how Constable caught changing light and shadow.

Trafalgar Square entrance

The Neo-Classical façade is made of Portland stone.

The Ambassadors
The strange shape in the foreground of this Hans Holbein portrait (1533) is a foreshortened skull, a symbol of mortality.

GALLERY GUIDE
Most of the collection is housed on the first floor, divided into four wings. The paintings hang chronologically, with the earliest works, notably the Italian Renaissance collection (1260–1510), in the Sainsbury Wing. Lesser paintings of all periods are displayed on the lower floor of the main building. The better of the two restaurants is on the first floor in the Sainsbury Wing.

STAR PAINTINGS

★ **Cartoon by Leonardo da Vinci**

★ **Rokeby Venus by Diego Velazquez**

★ **The Haywain by John Constable**

At the Theatre *(1876–7)*
Renoir was one of the greatest painters to be influenced by the Impressionist movement. The theatre was a popular subject among artists of the time.

Street-by-Street: Piccadilly and St James's

As soon as Henry VIII built St James's Palace in the 1530s, the surrounding area became the centre of fashionable court life. Today Piccadilly forms a contrast between the bustling commercial district full of shopping arcades, eateries and cinemas, with St James's, to the south, which is still the domain of the wealthy and the influential.

St James's Church was designed by Sir Christopher Wren in 1684.

★ **Royal Academy**
The permanent art collection here includes this Michelangelo relief of the Madonna and Child (1505) **9**

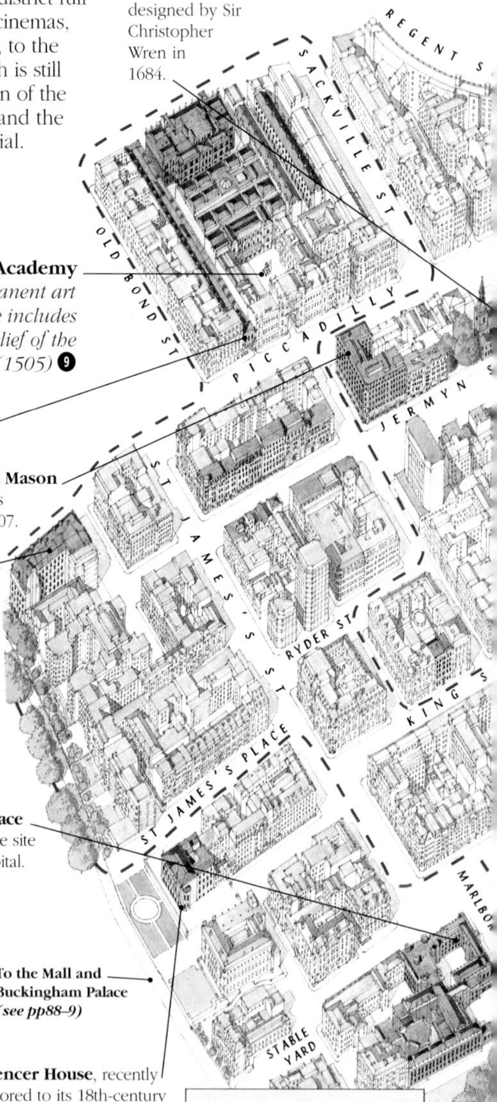

Fortnum and Mason *(see p122)* was founded in 1707.

The Ritz
César Ritz founded one of London's most famous hotels in 1906 **10**

Burlington Arcade, an opulent covered walk, has fine shops and beadles on patrol.

St James's Palace was built on the site of a leper hospital.

To the Mall and Buckingham Palace *(see pp88–9)*

Spencer House, recently restored to its 18th-century splendour, contains fine period furniture and paintings. This Palladian palace was completed in 1766 for the 1st Earl Spencer, an ancestor of the late Princess of Wales.

STAR SIGHTS

★ **Piccadilly Circus**

★ **Royal Academy**

★ Piccadilly Circus
The crowds and dazzling neon lights make this the West End's focal point **8**

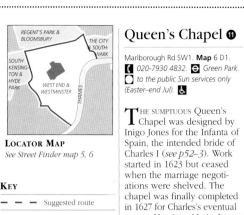

LOCATOR MAP
See Street Finder map 5, 6

KEY

– – – Suggested route

| 0 metres | 100 |
| 0 yards | 100 |

Piccadilly

Jermyn Street has elegant shops selling antiques, unusual gifts and men's clothing.

Pall Mall is a street of gentlemen's clubs, which admit only members and their guests.

St James's Square has long been the most fashionable address in London.

Queen's Chapel
This was the first Classical church in England **11**

Royal Opera Arcade is lined with quality shops. Designed by John Nash, it was completed in 1818.

Queen's Chapel **11**

Marlborough Rd SW1. **Map** 6 D1.
020-7930 4832. ⊖ Green Park.
○ to the public Sun services only (Easter–end Jul). ♿

THE SUMPTUOUS Queen's Chapel was designed by Inigo Jones for the Infanta of Spain, the intended bride of Charles I (*see p52–3*). Work started in 1623 but ceased when the marriage negotiations were shelved. The chapel was finally completed in 1627 for Charles's eventual queen, Henrietta Maria. It was the first church in England to be built in a Classical style, with a coffered ceiling based on a reconstruction by Palladio of an ancient Roman temple.

Interior of Queen's Chapel

The Mall **12**

SW1. **Map** 6 D2. ⊖ Charing Cross, Green Park.

THIS BROAD TRIUMPHAL approach from Trafalgar Square to Buckingham Palace was created by Aston Webb when he redesigned the front of the palace and the Victoria Monument in 1911. The spacious tree-lined avenue follows the course of an old path at the edge of St James's Park. The path was laid out in the reign of Charles II, when it became London's most fashionable and cosmopolitan promenade. The Mall is used for royal processions on special occasions. Flagpoles down both sides fly the national flags of foreign heads of state during official visits. The Mall is closed to traffic on Sundays.

Buckingham Palace ⓲

Queen Elizabeth II

Opened to visitors for the first time in 1993 to raise money for repairing fire damage to Windsor Castle *(see pp222–3)*, the Queen's official London home and office is an extremely popular attraction in August and September. John Nash *(see p107)* began converting the 18th-century Buckingham House into a palace for George IV in 1826 but was taken off the job in 1830 for overspending his budget. The first monarch to occupy the palace was Queen Victoria, just after she came to the throne in 1837. The year 2002 is significant for the monarchy, marking Queen Elizabeth II's Golden Jubilee, 50 years since her accession to the throne.

Music Room
State guests are presented and royal babies christened in this room.

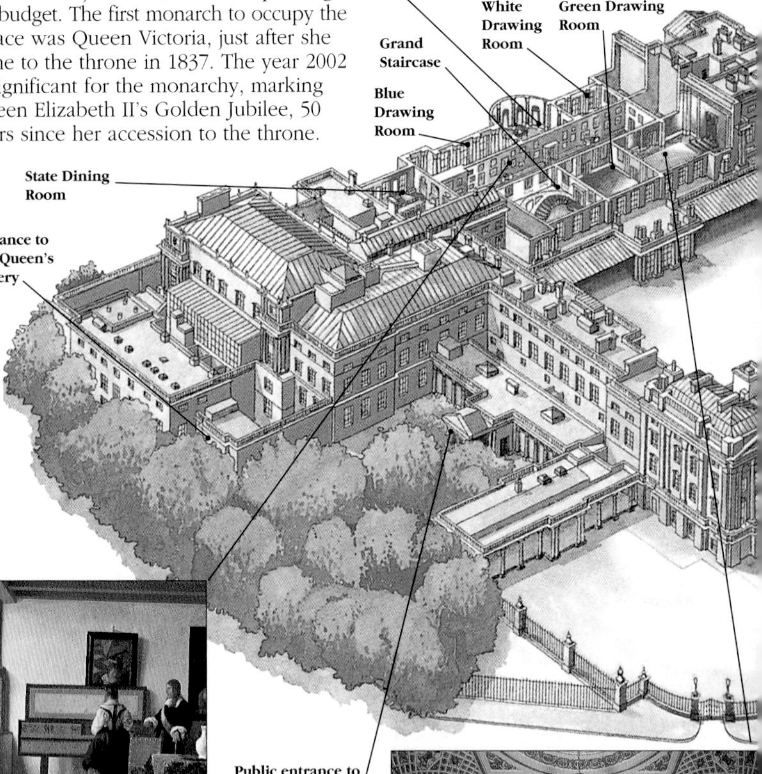

White Drawing Room

Green Drawing Room

Grand Staircase

Blue Drawing Room

State Dining Room

Entrance to The Queen's Gallery

Public entrance to the palace through Ambassadors' Court

Picture Gallery
The valuable collection on display includes this painting by Dutch master Johannes Vermeer: The Music Lesson (c.1660).

Throne Room
The Queen carries out many formal ceremonial duties here, under the richly gilded ceiling.

View over the Mall
On special occasions the Royal Family wave to crowds from the balcony.

VISITORS' CHECKLIST

SW1. **Map** 5 C2. 020-7930 4832. St James's Park, Victoria. 11, 16, 24, 25, 36, 38, 52, 73, 135, C1. Victoria. **State Rooms** 4 Aug– 30 Sep: 9:30am–5:30pm daily (last adm: 4:30pm). The ticket office is located in Green Park by Canada Gate. Each ticket is issued for a set entry time. phone first. **Changing of the Guard**: 11:30am daily or alternate days. Subject to change without notice. 020-7839 1377

The Royal Standard flies while The Queen is in residence.

The East Wing façade was added by Aston Webb in 1913.

The Changing of the Guard takes place on the palace forecourt.

THE CHANGING OF THE GUARD

Dressed in brilliant scarlet tunics and tall furry hats called bearskins, the palace guards stand in sentry boxes outside the Palace. Crowds gather in front of the railings to watch the colourful and musical military ceremony as the guards march down the Mall from St James's Palace, parading for half an hour while the palace keys are handed by the old guard to the new.

Queen's Gallery ⓮

Buckingham Palace Rd SW1. **Map** 5 C2. 020-7839 1377. St James's Park, Victoria. for refurbishment until spring 2002.

THE QUEEN'S ART COLLECTION is one of the finest and most valuable in the world, rich in the works of old masters such as Vermeer and Leonardo. A selection of works is displayed here in themed exhibitions that change once or twice a year. This small building beside Buckingham Palace was used as a conservatory until 1962; part of it is a private chapel screened from the public.

Detail: The Gold State Coach (1762), Royal Mews

Royal Mews ⓯

Buckingham Palace Rd SW1. **Map** 5 C3. 020-7839 1377. Victoria. Oct–Jul: noon–4pm Mon–Thu (last adm 3:30pm); Aug–Sep: 10:30am–4:30pm Mon–Thu (last adm 4pm). 25, 26 Dec.

LOVERS OF HORSES and royal pomp should try to fit in with the restricted opening hours of this working stable and coach house. Designed by John Nash in 1825, it houses horses and state coaches used on official occasions. Among them is the glass coach used for royal weddings and foreign ambassadors. The star exhibit is the ornate gold state coach, built for George III in 1762, with panels by Giovanni Cipriani. The Royal Mews shop sells a selection of interesting merchandise.

Street-by-Street: Whitehall and Westminster

T HE BROAD AVENUES of Whitehall and Westminster are lined with imposing buildings that serve the historic seat of both government and the established church. On weekdays the streets are crowded with civil servants whose work is based here, while at weekends the area takes on a different atmosphere with a steady flow of tourists.

Downing Street
Sir Robert Walpole was the first Prime Minister to live here in 1732 ⓱

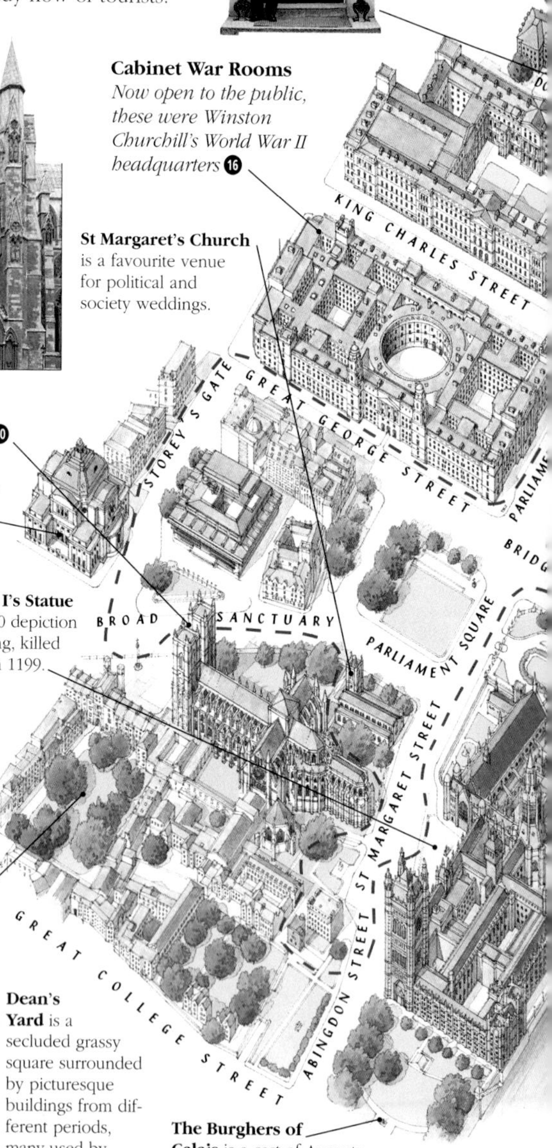

Cabinet War Rooms
Now open to the public, these were Winston Churchill's World War II headquarters ⓰

St Margaret's Church
is a favourite venue for political and society weddings.

★ Westminster Abbey
The abbey is London's oldest and most important church ⓴

Central Hall (1911)
is a florid example of the Beaux Arts style.

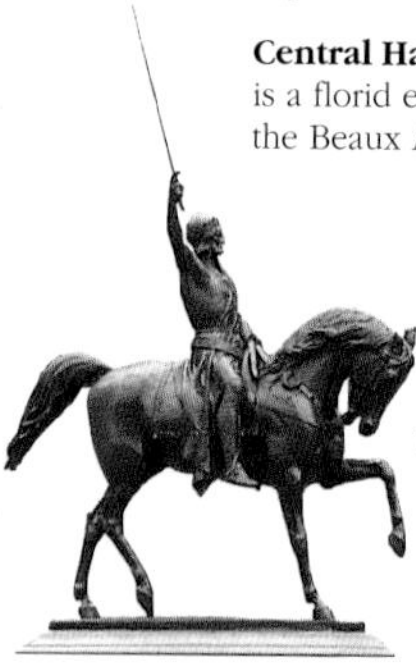

Richard I's Statue
is an 1860 depiction of the king, killed in battle in 1199.

Dean's Yard is a secluded grassy square surrounded by picturesque buildings from different periods, many used by Westminster School.

The Burghers of Calais is a cast of Auguste Rodin's 1886 original in France.

STOREY'S GATE

GREAT GEORGE STREET

KING CHARLES STREET

PARLIAMENT

BRIDG

BROAD

SANCTUARY

PARLIAMENT SQUARE

ST MARGARET STREET

ABINGDON STREET

GREAT COLLEGE STREET

To Trafalgar
Square

**Banqueting
House**
*Inigo Jones
designed
this elegant
building in
1622* **18**

LOCATOR MAP
See Street Finder map 6

The Cenotaph
(1920) is a war
memorial by Sir
Edwin Lutyens.

Horse Guards is a parade
ground protected by a guard,
changed twice each day.

**Westminster
Pier** is the
main starting
point for
river trips
(pp74–5).

Westminster

**★ Houses of
Parliament**
*The seat of
government is
dominated by the
clock tower, holding
the 14-tonne bell Big
Ben, hung in 1858.
Its deep chimes are
broadcast daily on
BBC radio* **19**

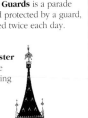

KEY

– – – Suggested route

0 metres   100

0 yards   100

STAR SIGHTS

★ **Westminster Abbey**

★ **Houses of
Parliament**

Cabinet War Rooms **16**

Clive Steps, King Charles St SW1.
Map 6 E2. ☎ 020-7930 6961.
🚇 *Westminster.* ⬜ *Apr–Sep: 9:30am–
6pm; Oct –Mar: 10am–6pm.*
⬛ *24–26 Dec.* 🕮 ♿ 📷

T HIS WARREN OF CELLARS below
 a government office
building is where the War
Cabinet – first under Neville
Chamberlain, then Winston
Churchill from 1940 – met
during World War II when
German bombs were falling
on London. The rooms include
living quarters for ministers
and military leaders and a
sound-proofed Cabinet Room,
where strategic decisions
were taken. All rooms are
protected by a concrete layer
about a metre (3 ft) thick and
are laid out as they were when
the war ended, complete with
Churchill's desk, commun-
ications equipment, and maps
with markers for plotting battles and strategies.

**Telephones in the Map Room,
Cabinet War Rooms**

Downing Street **17**

SW1. **Map** 6 E2. 🚇 *Westminster.*
⬛ *to the public.*

N UMBER 10 Downing Street
 has been the official residence of the British Prime
Minister since 1732. It contains
a Cabinet Room in which government policy is decided, an
impressive State Dining Room
and a private apartment; outside is a well-protected garden.
   Next door at No. 11 is
the official residence of the
Chancellor of the Exchequer,
who is in charge of the nation's
financial affairs. In 1989, iron
gates were erected at the
Whitehall end of Downing
Street for security purposes.

Banqueting House ⑱

Whitehall SW1. **Map** 6 E1. 020-7839 8919. Charing Cross. 10am–5pm Mon–Sat. public hols & for functions.

COMPLETED BY Inigo Jones *(see p53)* in 1622, this was the first building in central London to embody the classical Palladian style of Renaissance Italy. In 1629 Charles I commissioned Rubens to paint the ceiling with scenes exalting the reign of his father, James I. They symbolize a belief in the divine right of kings, disputed by the Parliamentarians, who executed Charles I outside the building in 1649 *(see pp52–3).*

Panels from the Rubens ceiling (1629–34), Banqueting House

Houses of Parliament ⑲

SW1. **Map** 6 E2. 020-7219 3000. Westminster. **Visitors' Galleries** 2:30–10pm Mon, Tue, Thu, 9:30am–10pm Wed, 9:30am–3pm Fri. Question Time (2:30–3:30pm Mon–Thu): apply in advance to your MP or embassy. Easter, late Jul–mid-Oct (summer recess), 3 wks over Christmas, public hols. by appt.

THERE HAS BEEN a Palace of Westminster here since the 11th century, though only Westminster Hall remains from that time. The present Neo-Gothic structure, designed by Sir Charles Barry, was built after the old palace was destroyed by fire in 1834. Since the 16th century it has been the seat of the two Houses of Parliament, the Lords and the Commons. The House of Commons is made up of elected Members of Parliament (MPs) of different parties. The party with most MPs forms the Government, and its leader becomes Prime Minister. The House of Lords is made up of peers *(see p27)*, law lords, bishops and archbishops. Legislation must be debated in both houses before becoming law.

Westminster Abbey ⑳

See pp94–5.

Victoria Tower

Central Lobby

The House of Commons' original chamber was destroyed by fire in 1941.

Royal Gallery

St Stephen's entrance for the public

The House of Lords is a lavishly decorated Gothic Hall designed by Pugin in 1836–7.

Members' entrance

Westminster Hall

Big Ben has kept exact time for the nation almost continuously since 1859.

Portico of Tate Britain

Tate Britain ㉑

Millbank SW1. **Map** 6 E4. ☎ 020-7887 8000. 📠 020-7887 8008. ⊖ Pimlico. 🚌 77a, 88, C10. 🚆 Victoria, Vauxhall. ○ 10am–5.50pm daily. ● 24–26 Dec. 💷 for major exhibitions. 🚫 🚻 Atterbury St. 📷 🍴 🛍 🚻

Formerly the Tate Gallery, Tate Britain is the national gallery of British art, and includes works from the 16th to the 21st century. Displays draw on the enormous Tate Collection, which also includes the international modern art seen at Tate Modern *(p119)*. Located in the adjoining Clore Gallery is the Turner Bequest, left to the nation by the famous landscape painter J M W Turner.

Recumbent Figure (1938) by Henry Moore

The permanent collection displays occupy three-quarters of the main floor. The displays follow a broad chronological sweep from the early 16th century to the present. The size of the collection necessitates some rotation of displays, which are organised in various imaginative and innovative ways. Major themes change on a three yearly basis, solo artists rooms and smaller themed rooms more frequently. Loan exhibitions are installed in the ground floor galleries and part of the main floor.

The section on the years 1500–1800 is dominated by portraiture, as seen in an exquisite portrait of Elizabeth I (c.1575) by the miniaturist Nicholas Hilliard, as well as the lively works of William Hogarth and the grand portraiture of Joshua Reynolds and Thomas Gainsborough. The section concludes with the visionary paintings of William Blake.

The 19th-century section is rich in the great landscape works of John Constable, as well as the vibrant images of the Pre-Raphaelites such as John Everett Millais and Dante Gabriel Rossetti.

The period 1900–1960 includes the war imagery of C R W Nevinson, the landscapes of Paul Nash, and the British modernist works of Henry Moore, Barbara Hepworth and Ben Nicholson.

The Tate Collection is outstanding in its wealth of British art from 1960 to the present, and the displays in this section are changed on a regular basis. Works range from the 1960s Pop artists David Hockney, Richard

***Mr. and Mrs. Clark and Percy* (1970–71) by David Hockney**

Hamilton and Peter Blake, through the works of Gilbert and George and the landscape artist Richard Long, to the 1980s paintings of Lucian Freud, Howard Hodgkin and R B Kitaj. The so-called Young British Artists (YBAs) are well represented by the leading figures Damian Hirst, Tracey Emin and Sarah Lucas, as is the contemporary movement of British artists such as Tacita Dean and Douglas Gordon, who use film and video as their medium.

***Captain Thomas Lee* (1594) by Marcus Gheeraedts**

The Turner Bequest

The Turner Bequest comprises some 300 oil paintings and 20,000 watercolours and drawings, left to the nation by the great landscape painter J M W Turner on his death in 1851. Turner's will had specified that a special gallery be built to house his pictures and this was finally done in 1987 with the opening of the Clore Gallery, a south-east extension of Tate Britain. The oils are on view in the main galleries, and the wonderful watercolours are the subject of changing displays.

***The Scarlet Sunset: A Town on a River* (c.1830–40)**

Westminster Abbey ⑳

WESTMINSTER ABBEY has been the burial place of Britain's monarchs since the 13th century and the setting for many coronations and royal weddings. It is one of the most beautiful buildings in London, with an exceptionally diverse array of architectural styles, ranging from the austere French Gothic of the nave to the astonishing complexity of Henry VII's chapel. Half national church, half national museum, the abbey aisles and transepts are crammed with an extraordinary collection of tombs and monuments honouring some of Britain's greatest public figures, ranging from politicians to poets.

Main Entrance
The mock-medieval stonework is Victorian.

Statesmen's Aisle

Flying buttresses help re-distribute the great weight of the roof.

★ Nave
At a height of 31 m (102 ft), the nave is the highest in England. The ratio of height to width is 3:1.

CORONATION

The coronation ceremony is over 1,000 years old and since 1066, with the crowning of William the Conqueror on Christmas Day, the abbey has been its sumptuous setting. The coronation of Queen Elizabeth II, in 1953, was the first to be televised.

Cloisters
Tombs here include those of several medieval abbots.

STAR FEATURES

★ **Nave**

★ **Henry VII Chapel**

★ **Chapter House**

★ Henry VII Chapel
The chapel, built in 1503–12, has superb late Perpendicular vaultings and choir stalls dating from 1512.

WILLIAM SHAKSPEARE 1564–1616 ERECTED AT STRATFORD-ON-AVON

The Sanctuary, built by Henry III, has been the scene of 38 coronations.

Poets' Corner
A host of great poets are honoured here, including Shakespeare, Chaucer and TS Eliot.

VISITORS' CHECKLIST

Broad Sanctuary SW1. **Map** 6 E2.
📞 020-7222 5152. 🚇 St James's Park, Westminster. 🚌 3, 11, 12, 24, 29, 53, 70, 77, 77a, 88, 109, 159, 170. 🚃 Victoria, Waterloo. 🚤 Westminster Pier.
Cloisters ◯ 8am–6pm daily.
Chapter House, Museum & Pyx Chamber ◯ 10am–4pm daily. **Royal Chapels, Poets' Corner, Choir, Statesmen's Aisle & Nave**
◯ 9am–3:45pm Mon–Fri, 9am–1:45pm Sat. 💷 for Royal Chapels, Poets' Corner, Chapter House Choir, Statesmen's Aisle, Pyx Chamber, Museum & Nave.
✝ Evensong: 5pm Mon–Tue, Thu–Fri, 3pm Sat & Sun. ♿ limited. 📷 for all visitors.

The Museum has many of the abbey's treasures including wood, plaster and wax effigies of monarchs.

★ Chapter House
A beautiful octagonal room, remarkable for its 13th-century tile floor. It is lit by six huge stained glass windows showing scenes from the abbey's history.

The Pyx Chamber is where the coinage was tested in medieval times.

St Edward's Chapel
The Coronation Chair is housed here, along with the tombs of many medieval monarchs.

HISTORICAL PLAN OF THE ABBEY

The first abbey church was established as early as the 10th century, but the present French-influenced Gothic structure was begun in 1245 at the behest of Henry III. Because of its unique role as the coronation church, the abbey escaped Henry VIII's mid-16th-century onslaught on Britain's monastic buildings *(see pp50–51)*.

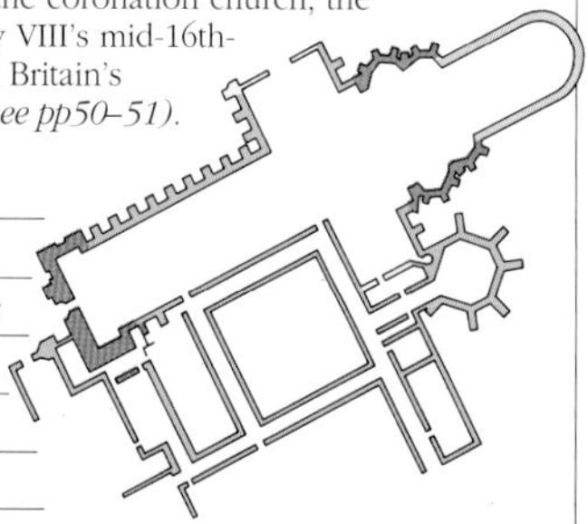

KEY

- Built before 1400
- Added in 15th century
- Built in 1503–19
- Completed by 1745
- Completed after 1850

SOUTH KENSINGTON AND HYDE PARK

THIS EXCLUSIVE district embraces one of London's largest parks and some of its finest museums, shops, restaurants and hotels. Until the mid-19th century it was a genteel, semi-rural backwater of large houses and private schools lying to the south of Kensington Palace. In 1851, the Great Exhibition, until then the largest arts and science event ever staged *(see p56–7)*, was held in Hyde Park, transforming the area into a celebration of Victorian learning and self-confidence.

Peter Pan statue in Kensington Gardens

The brainchild of Queen Victoria's husband, Prince Albert, the exhibition was a massive success and the profits were used to buy 35 ha (87 acres) of land in South Kensington. Here, Prince Albert encouraged the construction of a concert hall, museums and colleges devoted to the applied arts and sciences; most of them survive. The neighbourhood soon became modish, full of flamboyant red-brick mansion blocks, garden squares and the elite shops still to be found in Knightsbridge.

SIGHTS AT A GLANCE

Historic Buildings
Kensington Palace ❼

Churches
Brompton Oratory ❷

Shops
Harrod's ❶

Parks and Gardens
Hyde Park and Kensington Gardens ❻

Museums and Galleries
Natural History Museum ❺
Science Museum ❹
Victoria and Albert Museum pp100–101 ❸

GETTING THERE
South Kensington station (accessible from an entrance on Exhibition Road) is on the Piccadilly, Circle and District lines; only the Piccadilly line passes through Knightsbridge and Hyde Park Corner. The No. 14 bus runs direct from Piccadilly Circus to South Kensington, via Knightsbridge.

0 metres 500
0 yards 500

KEY
Street-by-Street map *pp98–9*
Underground station
Parking

◁ **Ennismore Mews in South Kensington, built 1843–6**

Street-by-Street: South Kensington

THE NUMEROUS MUSEUMS and colleges created in the wake of the Great Exhibition of 1851 *(see pp56–7)* continue to give this neighbourhood an air of leisured culture. Visited as much by Londoners as tourists, the museum area is liveliest on Sundays and on summer evenings during the Royal Albert Hall's famous season of classical "Prom" concerts *(see p126).*

The Royal Albert Hall opened in 1870 and was modelled on Roman amphitheatres.

The Memorial to the Great Exhibition is surmounted by a bronze statue of its instigator, Prince Albert.

The Royal College of Music, founded in 1882, exhibits historic musical instruments such as this harpsichord dating from 1531.

★ **Science Museum**
Visitors can experiment with over a thousand interactive displays ❹

★ **Natural History Museum**
The Creepy Crawlies exhibition has proved highly popular ❺

STAR SIGHTS

★ **Science Museum**

★ **Natural History Museum**

★ **Victoria and Albert Museum**

Entrance to South Kensington tube

KEY

– – – Suggested route

| 0 metres | 100 |
| 0 yards | 100 |

The Albert Memorial was built in memory of Queen Victoria's husband who died in 1861.

LOCATOR MAP
See Street Finder map 2

★ **Victoria and Albert Museum**
The museum has a fine collection of applied arts and photography from around the world ❸

Brompton Oratory
This ornate Baroque church is famous for its splendid musical tradition
❷

Brompton Square (1821)

To Knightsbridge and Harrod's

Harrods Food Hall

Harrods ❶

Knightsbridge SW1. **Map** 5 A3.
📞 020-7730 1234. 🚇 *Knightsbridge.*
🕐 *10am–7pm Mon–Sat.* ♿ *See*
***Shops and Markets** pp122–3.*

IN 1849 HENRY CHARLES HARROD opened a small grocery shop on Brompton Road, which soon became famous for its impeccable service and quality. The store expanded and in 1905 moved into these extravagant premises in Knightsbridge.

Brompton Oratory ❷

Brompton Rd SW7. **Map** 2 F5. 📞
020-7808 0900. 🚇 *South Kensington.*
🕐 *6:30am–8pm daily.* ♿

THE ITALIANATE ORATORY is a lavish monument to the 19th-century English Catholic revival. It was established as a base for a community of priests by John Henry Newman (later Cardinal Newman), who introduced the Oratorian movement to England in 1848. The church was opened in 1884, and the dome and façade added in the 1890s.

The sumptuous interior holds many fine monuments. The 12 huge 17th-century marble statues of the apostles are from Siena Cathedral, the elaborate Baroque Lady Altar (1693) is from the Dominican church at Brescia, and the 18th-century altar in St Wilfred's Chapel is from Rochefort in Belgium.

Victoria and Albert Museum ❸

THE V&A contains one of the world's richest collections of fine and applied arts from all periods and cultures. So broad is the range that it embraces early Christian devotional objects, Doc Marten boots, paintings by Constable, Islamic ceramics and the greatest collection of Indian art outside India. Since 1909 the museum has been housed in a building designed by Sir Aston Webb. Fifteen stunning new galleries – the British Galleries – will see the museum into the 21st century.

Main entrance

Textiles

★ 20th-Century Gallery
This shows modern design such as Daniel Weil's Radio in a Bag *(1983).*

Musical instruments

Stairs to Levels C and D

British Galleries
The elaborate Great Bed of Ware (c.1590) is the V&A's most celebrated piece of furniture.

GALLERY GUIDE

The V&A consists of 7 miles (11 km) of galleries occupying four main floor levels. The galleries are divided between those devoted to art and design, and those concentrating on materials and techniques. In the former, a wide variety of artifacts illustrate the art and design of a particular period or civilization – such as Europe 1600–1800. These galleries occupy most of Level A and Lower A, with British arts on Levels B and C. The materials and techniques galleries contain collections of particular forms of craft, for example, porcelain, tapestries, metalwork, jewellery and glass. Many are situated on Levels C and D. The six-storey Henry Cole Wing holds the museum's collection of paintings, drawings, prints and photographs. A gallery is devoted to architect Frank Lloyd Wright (1867–1959). The British Galleries tell the story of British design from 1500–1900.

Henry Cole Wing
Highlights here include 200 paintings by John Constable and this graceful portrait, A Young Man Among Roses *(1588), by court miniaturist Nicholas Hilliard.*

Exhibition Road entrance

KEY TO FLOORPLAN

- ☐ Lower A
- ☐ Level A
- ☐ Lower B
- ☐ Level B
- ☐ Henry Cole Wing

STAR EXHIBITS

- **★ 20th-Century Gallery**
- **★ Morris, Gamble and Poynter Rooms**
- **★ Medieval Treasury**
- **★ Nehru Gallery of Indian Art**

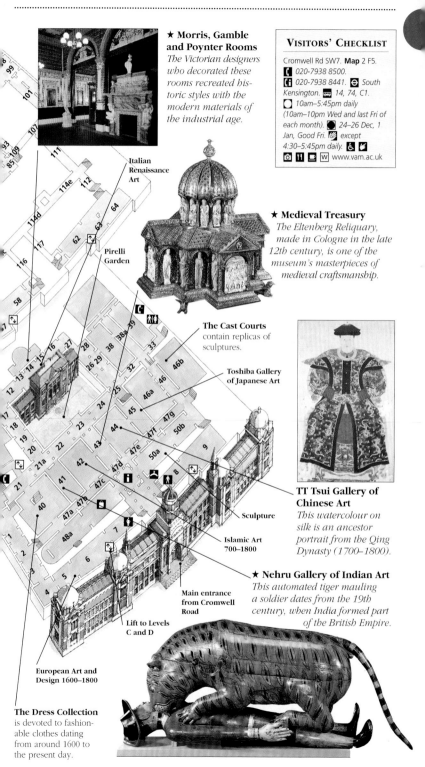

★ **Morris, Gamble and Poynter Rooms**
The Victorian designers who decorated these rooms recreated historic styles with the modern materials of the industrial age.

VISITORS' CHECKLIST

Cromwell Rd SW7. **Map** 2 F5.
020-7938 8500.
020-7938 8441. South Kensington. 14, 74, C1.
10am–5:45pm daily (10am–10pm Wed and last Fri of each month). 24–26 Dec, 1 Jan, Good Fri. except 4:30–5:45pm daily.
www.vam.ac.uk

★ **Medieval Treasury**
The Eltenberg Reliquary, made in Cologne in the late 12th century, is one of the museum's masterpieces of medieval craftsmanship.

Italian Renaissance Art

Pirelli Garden

The Cast Courts contain replicas of sculptures.

Toshiba Gallery of Japanese Art

TT Tsui Gallery of Chinese Art
This watercolour on silk is an ancestor portrait from the Qing Dynasty (1700–1800).

Sculpture

Islamic Art 700–1800

★ **Nehru Gallery of Indian Art**
This automated tiger mauling a soldier dates from the 19th century, when India formed part of the British Empire.

Main entrance from Cromwell Road

Lift to Levels C and D

European Art and Design 1600–1800

The Dress Collection is devoted to fashionable clothes dating from around 1600 to the present day.

Science Museum ❹

Exhibition Rd SW7. **Map** 2 E5. 📞
020 7938 8000. Ⓦ www.nmsi.ac.uk
Ⓔ *South Kensington.* 🕙 *10am–6pm
daily.* ● *24–26 Dec.* 📷 ♿ 🎧

CENTURIES OF continuing
scientific and technolo-
gical development lie at the
heart of the Science Museum,
ranging from Ancient Greek
and Roman medicine to space
exploration and nuclear fission.
The massive and impressive
collection brings entertainment to the process of learning, with many interactive
displays that you do not need

**Newcomen's Steam Engine (1712),
Science Museum**

a science degree to under-
stand. Others are aimed at
children, with staff on hand
to give further explanations.
Of equal importance is the
social context of science: what
discoveries and inventions
mean for day-to-day life, and
the process of discovery itself.
   The best of the displays are
Flight, which gives a chance
to experiment with aeronautical principles, and Launch
Pad, designed to give 7- to
13-year-olds a knowledge of
basic scientific principles. The
Exploration of Space displays
the scarred Apollo 10 space-
craft which carried three
astronauts to the moon and
back in May 1969. There is
also a video of the Apollo 11
moon landing which took
place a few weeks later. More
down-to-earth, but just as
absorbing, is Food for
Thought, which reveals the
impact of science and
technology

on every aspect of food. You
can play shops with a laser
scanner cash register, learn
about additives, with a computer programme, and see how
eating habits have changed
by peering into a series of
larders from 1900 to 1970.
Other popular sections include:
Power and Land Transport,
which displays working steam
engines, vintage trains, cars
and motorbikes; and Optics,
which has holograms, lasers
and colourmixing displays.
   The Wellcome Wing of The
History of Medicine has been
expanded for the new
millennium, and charts medical
practices from ancient times
through to the present day.
Exhibits range from a replica
of an Etruscan dental bridge
to the latest leading edge
biotechnological advances.

Natural History Museum ❺

Cromwell Rd SW7. **Map** 2 E5. 📞 020
7942 5000. Ⓦ www.nhm.ac.uk Ⓔ
South Kensington. 🕙 *10am–5.50pm
Mon–Sat, 11am–5.50pm Sun & public
hols.* ● *23–26 Dec.* 📷 ♿ 🎧

THIS VAST CATHEDRAL-LIKE
building is the most archi-
tecturally flamboyant of the
South Kensington museums.
Its richly sculpted stonework
conceals an iron and steel
frame; this building technique
was revolutionary when the
museum opened in 1881. The
imaginative displays tackle
fundamental issues such as
the ecology and evolution of
the planet, the
origin of species
and the develop-
ment of human
beings – all
explained
through a
dynamic

**Relief from a decorative panel in
the Natural History Museum**

combination of the latest
technology, interactive techniques and traditional displays.
   The museum is divided into
the Life and Earth Galleries. In
the former, the Ecology exhibition begins its exploration
of the complex web of the
natural world, and man's role
in it, through a convincing replica of a moonlit rainforest
buzzing with the sounds of
insects. The most popular exhibit is the Dinosaur Gallery,
which has a new, robotic
Tyrannosaurus rex in the
Dinosaur Pavilion. The state-
of-the-art Earth Galleries
explore the history of Earth
and its wealth of natural
resources, and the Power
Within offers the opportunity
to experience the rumblings
of an earthquake.

**The Tuojiangasaurus
skeleton (about 150
million years old),
Natural History Museum**

Statue of the young Queen Victoria outside Kensington Palace, sculpted by her daughter, Princess Louise

Hyde Park and Kensington Gardens ❻

W2. **Map** 2 F2. ☎ 020-7298 2100.
Hyde Park ⊖ *Hyde Park Corner, Knightsbridge, Lancaster Gate, Marble Arch.* ◻ *dawn–midnight daily.* ♿
Kensington Gardens ☎ 020-7298 2141. ⊖ *Queensway, Lancaster Gate.* ◻ *dawn–dusk daily.* ♿ See **Parks and Gardens** *pp76–7.* **Diana, Princess of Wales Memorial Playground** ⊖ *Queensway, Bayswater.* ◻ *10am–6:45pm daily.* ♿ ▯

T HE ANCIENT MANOR of Hyde was part of the lands of Westminster Abbey seized by Henry VIII at the Dissolution of the Monasteries in 1536 *(see pp50–51)*. James I opened the park to the public in the early 17th century, and it was soon one of the city's most fashionable public spaces. Unfortunately it also became popular with duellists and highwaymen,

and consequently William III had 300 lights hung along Rotten Row, the first street in England to be lit up at night. In 1730, the Westbourne River was dammed by Queen Caroline in order to create the Serpentine, an artificial lake that is today used for boating and swimming, and Rotten Row for horse riding. The park is also a rallying point for political demonstrations, while at Speaker's Corner, in the northeast, anyone has had the right to address the public since 1872. Sundays are particularly lively, with many budding orators and a number of eccentrics reveal-ing their plans for the betterment of mankind.

Adjoining Hyde Park is Kensington Gardens, the former grounds of Kensington Palace. Three great attractions for children are the innovative Diana, Princess of Wales Memorial Playground, the bronze statue of JM Barrie's fictional Peter Pan (1912), by George Frampton, and the Round Pond where people sail model boats. Also worth seeing is the dignified Orangery (1704), once used by Queen Anne as a "summer supper house" and now used as a summer café.

Detail of the Coalbrookdale Gate, Kensington Gardens

Kensington Palace ❼

Kensington Palace Gdns W8.
Map 2 D3. ☎ 020-7937 9561.
⊖ *High St Kensington, Queensway.*
◻ *summer: 10am–6pm daily; winter: 10am–5pm Wed–Sun.* ● *1 Jan, Good Fri, 22–26 Dec.* ▨ ♿ *ground floor.*

K ENSINGTON PALACE was the principal residence of the royal family from the 1690s until 1760, when George III moved to Buckingham Palace. Over the years it has seen a number of import-ant royal events. In 1714 Queen Anne died here from a fit of apoplexy brought on by over-eating and, in June 1837, Princess Victoria of Kent was woken to be told that her uncle William IV had died and she was now queen – the beginning of her 64-year reign. Half of the palace still holds royal apartments, but the other half is open to the public. Among the highlights are the 18th-century state rooms with ceilings and murals by William Kent *(see p24)*. In the days following the death of Princess Diana in 1997, the palace became a focal point for mourners who gathered in their thousands at its gates and turned the surrounding area into a field of bouquets.

REGENT'S PARK AND BLOOMSBURY

Ancient Greek vase, British Museum

CREAM STUCCOED terraces built by John Nash *(see p107)* fringe the southern edge of Regent's Park in London's highest concentration of quality Georgian housing. The park, named for the Prince Regent, was also designed by Nash, as the culmination of a triumphal route from the Prince's house in St James *(see pp86–7)*. Today it is the busiest of the royal parks and boasts a zoo, an open air theatre, boating lake, rose garden, cafés and London's largest mosque. To the northeast is Camden Town *(see p130)* with its popular market, shops and cafés, reached by walking, or taking a boat, along the picturesque Regent's Canal.

Bloomsbury, an enclave of attractive garden squares and Georgian brick terraces, was one of the most fashionable areas of the city until the mid-19th century, when the arrival of large hospitals and railway stations persuaded many of the wealthier residents to move west to Mayfair, Knightsbridge and Kensington. Home to the British Museum since 1753 and the University of London since 1828, Bloomsbury has long been the domain of artists, writers and intellectuals, including the Bloomsbury Group *(see p149)*, George Bernard Shaw, Charles Dickens and Karl Marx. Traditionally a centre for the book trade, it remains a good place for literary browsing.

SIGHTS AT A GLANCE

Historic Streets
Bloomsbury **5**

Museums and Galleries
British Museum pp108–109 **4**

Madame Tussaud's and the Planetarium **1**
Sherlock Holmes Museum **2**
Wallace Collection **3**

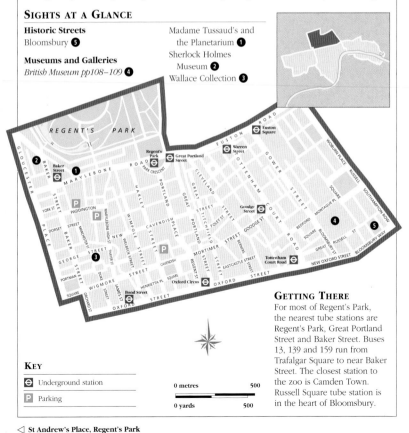

GETTING THERE

For most of Regent's Park, the nearest tube stations are Regent's Park, Great Portland Street and Baker Street. Buses 13, 139 and 159 run from Trafalgar Square to near Baker Street. The closest station to the zoo is Camden Town. Russell Square tube station is in the heart of Bloomsbury.

KEY

🚇 Underground station

🅿 Parking

0 metres   500
0 yards   500

◁ **St Andrew's Place, Regent's Park**

Madame Tussaud's and the Planetarium ❶

Marylebone Rd NW1. **Map** 3 B3.
📞 020-7935 6861. 🚇 Baker St.
Planetarium ○ 10am–5:30pm daily.
Tussaud's ○ 9:30am–5:30pm daily.
● 25 Dec. 📷 📹 ♿

MADAME TUSSAUD began her wax-modelling career making death masks of victims of the French Revolution. She moved to England and in 1835 set up an exhibition of her work in Baker Street, near the present site. Traditional techniques are still used to create figures of royalty, politicians, actors, pop stars, and sporting heroes. The main sections of the exhibition are: the Garden Party, where visitors mingle with life-like models of celebrities; Super Stars, devoted to the giants of the entertainment world; and the Grand Hall, a collection of various royalty, statesmen, world leaders, writers and artists, from Lenin and Martin Luther King to Shakespeare and Picasso.

The Chamber of Horrors is the most renowned part of Madame Tussaud's. Alongside some of the original French Revolution death masks are recreations of murders and

Wax model of Luciano Pavarotti (1990), Madame Tussaud's

Wax figure of Elizabeth II

Conan Doyle's fictional detective Sherlock Holmes

executions. The Spirit of London finale allows visitors travel in stylized taxi-cabs through the city's history, to "witness" events, from the Great Fire of 1666 to the Swinging 1960s. Next door, the Planetarium, built in 1958, has spectacularly exciting star and laser shows.

Sherlock Holmes Museum ❷

221b Baker St NW1. **Map** 3 A3.
📞 020-7935 8866. 🚇 Baker St. ○
9:30am–6pm daily ● 25 Dec. 📷 📹

SIR ARTHUR CONAN DOYLE'S fictional detective was supposed to live at 221B Baker Street, which did not exist. The museum, labelled 221B, actually stands between Nos. 237 and 239, and is the only surviving Victorian lodging house in the street. There is a reconstruction of Holmes' front room, and memorabilia from the stories decorate the walls. Visitors can buy plaques, Holmes hats, Toby jugs and meerschaum pipes.

Wallace Collection ❸

Hertford House, Manchester Sq W1.
Map 3 B4. 📞 020-7935 0687.
🚇 Bond St, Baker St. ○ 10am–5pm
Mon–Sat, 2–5pm Sun. ● 24–26
Dec, 1 Jan, Good Fri, May Day. ♿
phone first. 📷

ONE OF THE WORLD'S finest private collections of art, it has remained intact since 1897.

The product of passionate collecting by four generations of the Seymour-Conway family who were Marquesses of Hertford, it was bequeathed to the state on the condition that it would go on permanent public display with nothing added or taken away. The 25 beautiful galleries are a must for anyone with even a passing interest in European art.

The 3rd Marquess (1777–1842), a flamboyant London figure, used his Italian wife's fortune to build on the rich collection of family portraits he had inherited, buying works by Titian and Canaletto, along with numerous 17th-century Dutch paintings including works by Van Dyck. The collection's particular strength is 18th-century French painting, sculpture, and decorative arts, acquired in France by the 4th Marquess (1800–70) and his natural son, Sir Richard Wallace (1818–90). The Marquess had a taste for lush romanticism rather than realism, a distinct advantage in post-Revolution

A 16th-century Italian majolica dish from the Wallace Collection

France, where most collectors had little time for the dreamy canvases painted for Louis XV and his court. Notable among these are Watteau's *Champs Elysées* (1716–17), Fragonard's *The Swing* (1766) and Boucher's *The Rising and Setting of the Sun* (1753).

Other highlights include Rembrandt's *Titus, the Artist's Son* (1650s), Titian's *Perseus and Andromeda* (1554–6) and Franz Hals's famous *Laughing Cavalier* (1624). There is also an important collection of Renaissance armour, and superb examples of Sèvres porcelain and Italian majolica.

John Nash's Regency London

Statue of John Nash (1752–1835)

JOHN NASH, the son of a Lambeth millwright, was designing houses from the 1780s. However, it was not until the 1820s that he also became known as an inspired town planner, when his "royal route" was completed. This took George IV from his Pall Mall palace, through Piccadilly Circus and up the elegant sweep of Regent Street to Regent's Park, which Nash bordered with rows of beautiful Neo-Classical villas, such as Park Crescent and Cumberland Terrace. Though many of his plans were never completed, this map of 1851, which unusually places the south at the top, shows Nash's overall architectural impact on London. His other work included the revamping of Buckingham Palace *(see pp88–9)*, and the building of several theatres and churches.

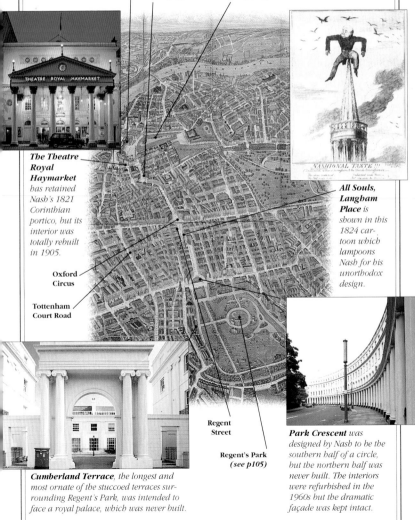

Pall Mall

Piccadilly Circus
(see p83)

St James's Park
(see p76–7)

The Theatre Royal Haymarket *has retained Nash's 1821 Corinthian portico, but its interior was totally rebuilt in 1905.*

Oxford Circus

Tottenham Court Road

All Souls, Langham Place *is shown in this 1824 cartoon which lampoons Nash for his unorthodox design.*

Regent Street

Regent's Park
(see p105)

Park Crescent *was designed by Nash to be the southern half of a circle, but the northern half was never built. The interiors were refurbished in the 1960s but the dramatic façade was kept intact.*

Cumberland Terrace*, the longest and most ornate of the stuccoed terraces surrounding Regent's Park, was intended to face a royal palace, which was never built.*

British Museum ➍

Helmet from Sutton Hoo ship burial

THE OLDEST public museum in the world, the British Museum was established in 1753 to house the collections of the physician Sir Hans Sloane (1660–1753). Sloane's collection has been added to by gifts and purchases from all over the world, and the museum now contains artifacts spanning thousands of years of culture. The main part of the building (1823–50) is by architect Robert Smirke, but the architectural highlight is the modern Great Court, with the Reading Room at its centre.

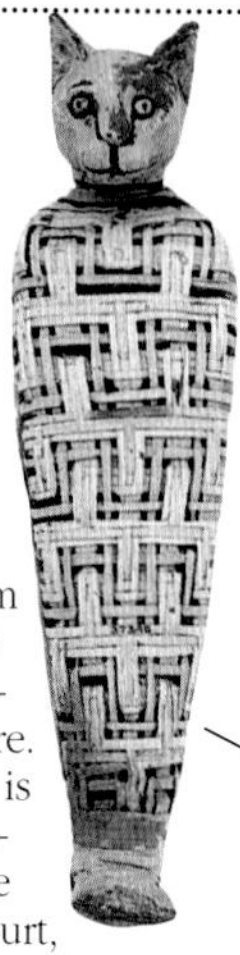

★ Egyptian Mummies
Animals such as this cat (30 BC) were preserved alongside humans by the ancient Egyptians.

Bronze Figure Shiva Nataraja
This statue of the Hindu God Shiva Nataraja (c.1100) from South India forms part of the fine collection of Oriental art.

The Egyptian Gallery on the main floor houses the Rosetta Stone, the inscription that enabled 19th-century scholars to decipher Egyptian hieroglyphs.

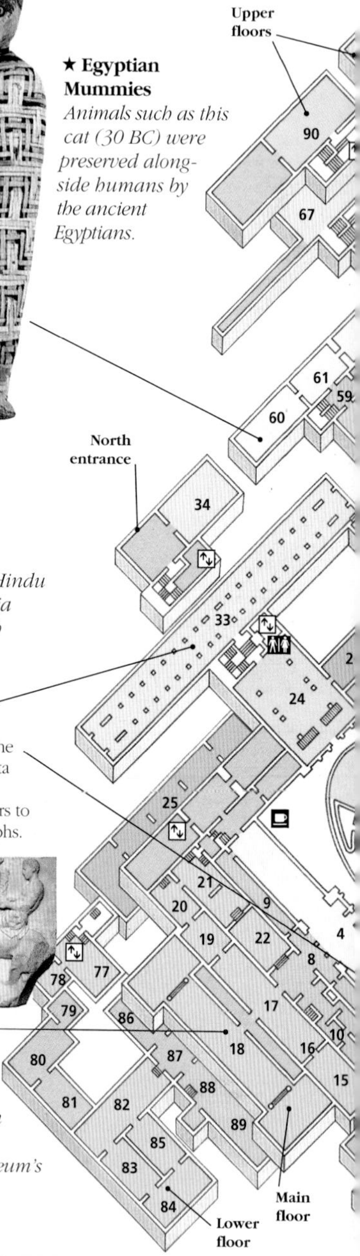

GALLERY GUIDE

The Greek and Roman, and Ancient Near Eastern collections are found on all three levels of the museum, predominantly on the west side. The African collection is located on the lower floor, while Asian exhibits are found on the main and upper floors at the rear of the museum. The Americas collection is located in the northeast corner off the main floor. Egyptian artefacts are found in the large gallery to the west of the Great Court and on the first floor.

★ Elgin Marbles
These 5th-century BC reliefs from the Parthenon in Athens were brought to London by Lord Elgin around 1802 and are the museum's most famous treasure.

Upper floors

North entrance

Main floor

Lower floor

STAR EXHIBITS

★ Egyptian Mummies

★ Elgin Marbles

★ Lindow Man

KEY TO FLOORPLAN

- ☐ Asian collection
- ☐ Americas collection
- ☐ Coins, medals, prints and drawings
- ☐ Greek and Roman collections
- ☐ Egyptian collection
- ☐ Ancient Near Eastern collection
- ☐ Prehistory collection
- ☐ European collection
- ☐ African collection
- ☐ Temporary exhibitions
- ☐ Non-exhibition space

The Great Court is London's largest covered square, with shops, cafés, a restaurant, display areas and educational facilities.

First floor

Private gardens of Bedford Square

Bloomsbury ❺

WC1. **Map** 4 F4. Russell Sq,
Tottenham Court Rd. **Dickens House
Museum** 48 Doughty St WC1.
020-7405 2127. 10am–5pm
Mon–Sat (last adm: 4:30pm).

Mildenhall Treasure
The Great Dish was among the 34 pieces of 4th-century Roman silver tableware ploughed up in Suffolk in 1942.

Reading Room

Main entrance

★ **Lindow Man**
The skin on this 2,000-year-old human body was preserved by the acids of a peat-bog in Cheshire. He was probably killed in an elaborate ritual.

HOME TO numerous writers and artists, Bloomsbury is a traditional centre of the book trade. It is dominated by the British Museum and the University of London and characterized by a number of fine Georgian squares. These include **Russell Square**, where the poet TS Eliot (1888–1965) worked for a publisher for 40 years; **Queen Square** which contains a statue of Queen Charlotte, wife of George III; and **Bloomsbury Square**, laid out in 1661. A plaque here commemorates members of the literary and artistic Bloomsbury Group (*see p149*). One of London's best-preserved 18th-century oases is **Bedford Square**. Charles Dickens (*see p175*) lived at 48 Doughty Street during a brief but critical stage in his career, and it was here that he wrote *Oliver Twist* and *Nicholas Nickleby*, both completed in 1839.

Queen Charlotte (1744–1818)

His former home is now the **Dickens House Museum**, which has rooms laid out as they were in Dickens' time, with miscellaneous objects taken from his other London homes and first editions of many of his works.

THE CITY AND SOUTHWARK

DOMINATED TODAY BY glossy office blocks, the City is the oldest part of the capital. The Great Fire of 1666 obliterated four-fifths of its buildings. Sir Christopher Wren rebuilt much of it and many of his churches survived World War II (see pp58–9). Commerce has always been its lifeblood, and the power of its merchants and bankers secured it a degree of autonomy from state control. Even today the monarch cannot cross its boundaries without permission from the Lord Mayor. Humming with activity in business hours, the City empties at night.

Old bank sign on Lombard Street

In the Middle Ages Southwark, on the south bank of the Thames, was a refuge for pleasure-seekers, prostitutes, gamblers and criminals. Even after 1550, when the area fell under the jurisdiction of the City, its brothels and taverns thrived. There were also several bear-baiting arenas in which plays were staged until the building of theatres such as the Globe (1598), where many of Shakespeare's works were first performed. Relics of old Southwark are mostly on the waterfront, which has been imaginatively redeveloped and provided with a pleasant walkway.

SIGHTS AT A GLANCE

Historic Sights and Buildings
Lloyd's Building ❼
The Old Operating Theatre ⓫
Temple ❶
Tower Bridge ❾

Museums and Galleries
Design Museum ❿
Museum of London ❹
Shakespeare's Globe ⓮
Sir John Soane's Museum ❷
Tate Modern ⓭

Churches and Cathedrals
St Bartholomew-the-Great ❸
St Paul's Cathedral pp116–17 ❺
St Stephen Walbrook ❻
Southwark Cathedral ⓬
Tower of London pp120–21 ❽

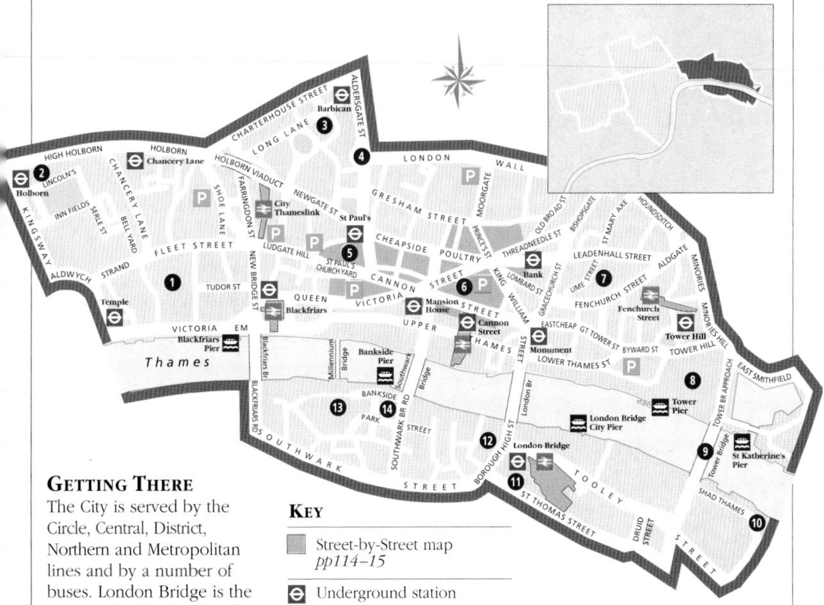

GETTING THERE
The City is served by the Circle, Central, District, Northern and Metropolitan lines and by a number of buses. London Bridge is the main station for Southwark – served by the Northern and Jubilee lines and by trains running from Charing Cross, Cannon Street and Waterloo.

KEY

	Street-by-Street map *pp114–15*
⊖	Underground station
⊠	Railway station
P	Parking
⊠	River boat stop

0 metres   500
0 yards   500

◁ **St Paul's Cathedral in the heart of the City, with the NatWest Tower (1980) to the left**

Wigged and robed barristers, Lincoln's Inn

Temple ❶

Middle Temple Lane EC4. **Map** 7 A3.
🚇 *Temple.* **Middle Temple Hall**
📞 *020-7427 4800.* ⏰ *10am–noon,
3–4pm Mon–Fri (grounds only).*
⬤ *academic hols.* ♿ *phone first.*

A CLUSTER of atmospheric
squares form the Inner
and Middle Temples, two of
London's four Inns of Court,
where law students are trained
(Lincoln's Inn and Gray's Inn

are the other two).
The four Inns fulfil
identical functions
but each remains
conscious of its
separate traditions.
According to an
age-old custom
anyone in Britain
training to be a
barrister has to join
one of the Inns and
must dine there 24
times – as well as
passing exams –
before being offi-
cially qualified.

The name Temple
derives from the
medieval Knights
Templar, a religious
order founded here in 1118 to
protect pilgrims going to the
Holy Land. The Templars
owned this area until 1312
when the order was suppressed on charges of immorality
and heresy. But the real reason
was that they had become very
wealthy, and their power was
seen as a threat to the throne.
Marble effigies of knights lie
on the floor of the circular
Temple church, part of which
dates from the 12th century.

The finest of the Temple's
other ancient buildings is the
opulent Middle Temple Hall,
which retains a wonderful
Elizabethan hammer-beamed
roof that was restored after
bomb damage in World War II.
It is thought that Shakespeare
took part in a performance of
Twelfth Night here in 1601.

St Bartholomew-
the-Great ❸

West Smithfield EC1. **Map** 7 B2.
📞 *020-7606 5171.* 🚇 *Barbican,
St Paul's.* ⏰ *8:30am–5pm Mon–Fri
(mid-Nov–mid-Feb: 8:30am–4pm),
9am–1pm Sat.* ⬤ *25, 26 Dec, 1 Jan.*
📷 ♿ ✉

T HE HISTORIC AREA of Smithfield has witnessed a
number of bloody events over
the years, among them the
execution of rebel peasant
leader Wat Tyler in 1381, and,
in the reign of Mary I (1553–
58), the burning of scores
of Protestant martyrs.

Hidden in a quiet corner
behind Smithfield meat market
(central London's only surviving wholesale food market),

Sir John Soane's
Museum ❷

13 Lincoln's Inn Fields WC2. **Map** 4
F4. 📞 *020-7405 2107.* 🚇 *Holborn.*
⏰ *10am–5pm Tue–Sat, 6–9pm
1st Tue of month.* ⬤ *public hols,
24 Dec.* 📷 *Sat.* 🌐 *www.soane.org*

O NE OF THE MOST eccentric
museums in London, this
house was left to the nation
by Sir John Soane in 1837,
with a stipulation that nothing
should be changed. The son
of a bricklayer, Soane became
one of Britain's leading late
Georgian architects developing a restrained Neo-Classical
style of his own. After marrying the niece of a wealthy
builder, whose fortune he
inherited, he bought and reconstructed No. 12 Lincoln's
Inn Fields. In 1813 he and his
wife moved into No. 13 and
in 1824 he rebuilt No. 14,
adding a picture gallery and
the mock medieval Monk's
Parlour. Today, true to Soane's

wishes, the collections are
much as he left them – an
eclectic gathering of beautiful,
instructional and often simply
peculiar artifacts. There are
casts, bronzes, vases, antique
fragments, paintings and a
selection of bizarre trivia which
ranges from a giant fungus
from Sumatra to a scold-bridle,
a device designed to silence
nagging wives. Highlights
include the sarcophagus of
Seti I, Soanes's own designs,
including those for the Bank
of England, models by leading Neo-Classical sculptors
such as Banks and Flaxman
and the *Rake's Progress* series
of paintings (1734), by
William Hogarth, which Mrs
Soane bought for £520.

The building itself is full of
architectural surprises and
illusions. In the main ground
floor room, cunningly placed
mirrors play tricks with light
and space, while an atrium
stretching from the basement
to the glass-domed roof
allows light onto every floor.

A glass dome lets light
on to all the floors.

A vast sarcophagus
(1300 BC) stands on
the floor of the crypt.

St Bartholomew-the-Great is one of London's oldest churches. It once formed part of a priory founded in 1123 by a monk named Rahere, whose tomb is inside. Rahere was Henry I's court jester until he dreamed that St Bartholomew had saved him from a winged monster. As prior, he would sometimes revert to his former role, entertaining crowds with juggling tricks at the annual Bartholomew Fair.

The 13th-century arch, now topped by a Tudor gatehouse, used to be the entrance to the church until the old nave was pulled down during the Dissolution of the Monasteries (*see pp50–51*).

St Bartholomew's gatehouse

Museum of London **4**

London Wall EC2. **Map** 7 C2.
📞 020-7600 3699. 🚇 Barbican, St Paul's. 🕐 10am–5:50pm Mon–Sat & public hols, noon–5:50pm Sun.
⬤ 24–26 Dec, 1 Jan. 🏷 📷 ♿

THIS MUSEUM traces life in London from prehistoric times to the 20th century. Displays of archaeological finds and original domestic objects alternate with reconstructed street scenes and interiors. A new gallery, World City, charts the birth of modern London from the French

Delft plate made in London 1602, Museum of London

Revolution to World War I. Objects from Roman London include a brightly coloured 2nd-century fresco which came from a Southwark bath house, while from the Tudor city come a Delft plate and costumes, including leather clothes found on a rubbish tip. The 17th-century section holds the shirt Charles I wore on the scaffold (*see pp52–3*), and an audio-visual display recreating the Great Fire of 1666.

A popular exhibit is the Lord Mayor's State Coach, built in 1757 and still used for the colourful Lord Mayor's Show in November (*see pp64–5*).

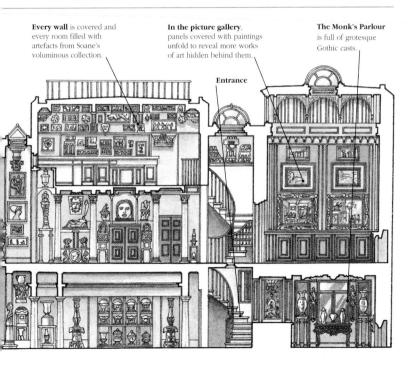

Every wall is covered and every room filled with artefacts from Soane's voluminous collection.

In the picture gallery, panels covered with paintings unfold to reveal more works of art hidden behind them.

The Monk's Parlour is full of grotesque Gothic casts.

Entrance

Street-by-Street: The City

Detail: St Paul's Cathedral

THIS IS THE FINANCIAL HEART of London and has been ever since the Romans set up a trading post here 2,000 years ago. For years it was London's main residential area but today very few people live here. The City was severely bombed in World War II and the main clues to its past are streets named after vanished inns and markets. Its numerous churches, many built after the Great Fire of 1666 by the architect Sir Christopher Wren *(see p116)*, are now dwarfed by lavish banks and post-modern developments.

St Mary-le-Bow takes its name from the bow arches in the Norman crypt. Anyone born within earshot of its bells is said to be a true Cockney.

The Temple of Mithras is an important Roman relic *(see p45)*.

New Change replaces Old Change, a 13th-century street destroyed in World War II.

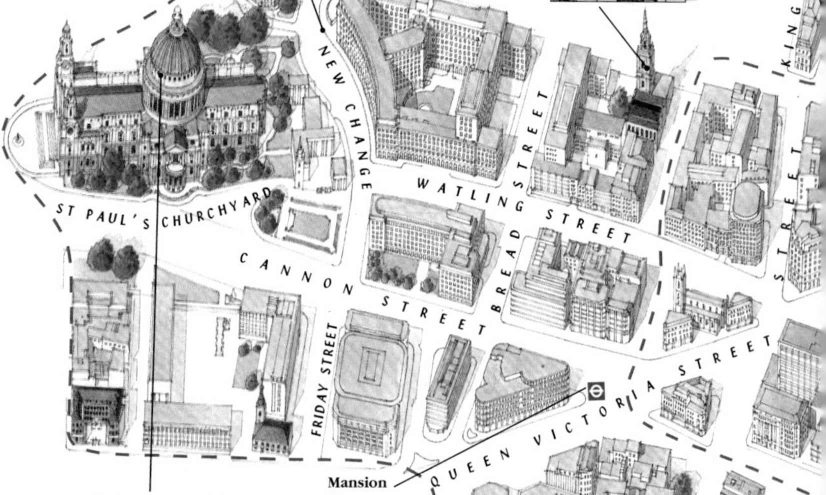

St Paul's

NEW CHANGE

ST PAUL'S CHURCHYARD

CANNON STREET

WATLING STREET

BREAD STREET

FRIDAY STREET

KING ST

STREET

QUEEN VICTORIA STREET

QUEEN

Mansion House

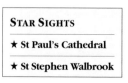

★ **St Paul's Cathedral**
Built after the Great Fire of 1666, Wren's master-piece was funded by a tax on coal ⑤

STAR SIGHTS

★ **St Paul's Cathedral**

★ **St Stephen Walbrook**

KEY

– – – Suggested route

0 metres   100
0 yards   100

Skinners' Hall is an 18th-century Italianate building constructed for the ancient guild that controlled trade in fur and leather.

Lombard Street, named after bankers who came from Lombardy in the 13th century, retains its traditional banking signs.

LOCATOR MAP
See Street Finder map 7, 8

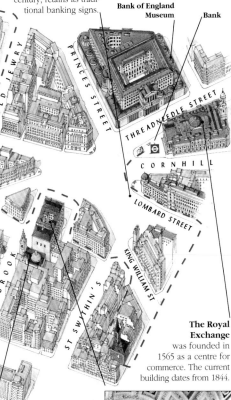

Bank of England Museum

Bank

PRINCES STREET

OLD JEWRY

THREADNEEDLE STREET

CORNHILL

LOMBARD STREET

KING WILLIAM ST

WALBROOK

ST SWITHIN'S

The Royal Exchange was founded in 1565 as a centre for commerce. The current building dates from 1844.

★ **St Stephen Walbrook**
The Walbrook is a tributary of the Thames, now underground ❻

Mansion House (1753), designed by George Dance the Elder, is the official home of the Lord Mayor. One of the most spectacular rooms is the Egyptian Hall.

St Paul's ❺

See pp116–17.

St Stephen Walbrook ❻

39 Walbrook EC4. **Map** 8 D3.
☎ 020-7283 4444. ⊖ *Bank, Cannon St.* ◯ *10am–4pm Mon– Thu, 10am–3pm Fri.* ● *public hols.* ▣

THE LORD MAYOR'S parish church was built by Sir Christopher Wren in the 1670s and is among the finest of all his City churches. The bright, airy interior is flooded with light by a huge dome that appears to float above the eight columns and arches that support it. Original fittings, such as the ornate font and rich pulpit, contrast with the stark simplicity of Henry Moore's massive white stone altar (1987). The best way to see the church is during one of its free organ recitals or lunchtime concerts.

Original 17th-century font

Lloyd's Building ❼

1 Lime St EC3. **Map** 8 E2. ☎ 020-7327 1000. ⊖ *Monument, Bank, Aldgate.* ● *to the public.*

THIS BUILDING, designed by Richard Rogers in 1986 for the world's largest insurance marketplace, echoes his famous Pompidou Centre.
One of London's most interesting modern buildings, it is a vast glass construction, with its functional elements, such as stainless steel pipes, high-tech ducts and lifts, on the exterior.

Tower of London ❽

See pp120–21.

St Paul's Cathedral ❺

T HE GREAT FIRE OF LONDON in 1666 left
the medieval cathedral of St Paul's in
ruins. Wren was commissioned to rebuild
it, but his design for a church on a Greek
Cross plan (where all four arms are equal)
met with considerable resistance. The
authorities insisted on a conventional
Latin cross, with a long nave and short
transepts, which was believed to focus
the congregation's attention on the altar.
Despite the compromises, Wren created
a magnificent Baroque cathedral, which
was built between 1675 and 1710 and
has since formed
the lavish setting
for many state
ceremonies.

★ Dome
*At 113 m (360
ft), the elab-
orate dome
is one of
the highest
in the
world.*

The balustrade
along the top
was added in
1718 against
Wren's wishes.

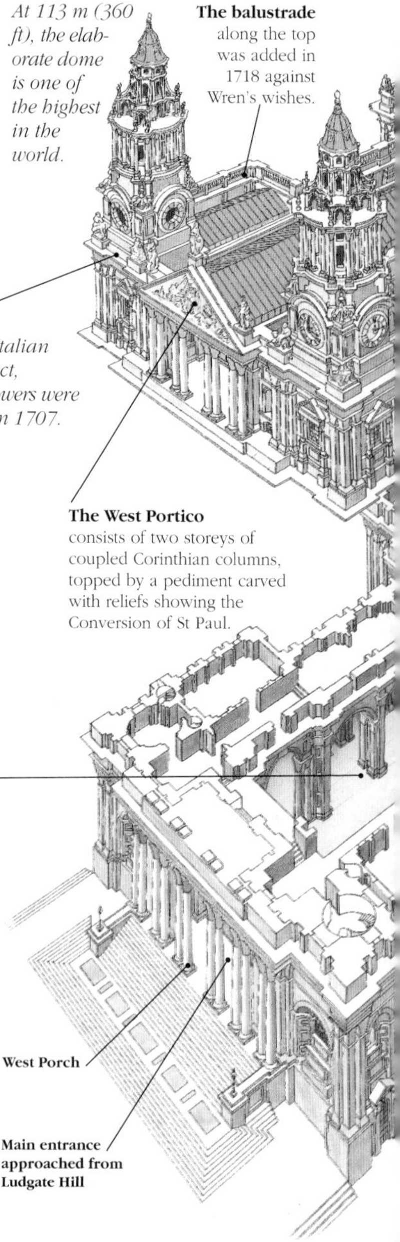

**★ West Front
and Towers**
*Inspired by the Italian
Baroque architect,
Borromini, the towers were
added by Wren in 1707.*

The West Portico
consists of two storeys of
coupled Corinthian columns,
topped by a pediment carved
with reliefs showing the
Conversion of St Paul.

The Nave
*An imposing succession of massive arches
and saucer domes open out into the vast
space below the cathedral's main dome.*

CHRISTOPHER WREN

Trained as a scientist,
Sir Christopher Wren
(1632–1723) began his
impressive architectural
career at the age of 31.
He became a leading
figure in the rebuilding of
London after the Great Fire of
1666, building a total of 52 new churches.
Although Wren never visited Italy, his
work was influenced by Roman, Baroque
and Renaissance architecture, as is apparent in his masterpiece, St Paul's Cathedral.

West Porch

**Main entrance
approached from
Ludgate Hill**

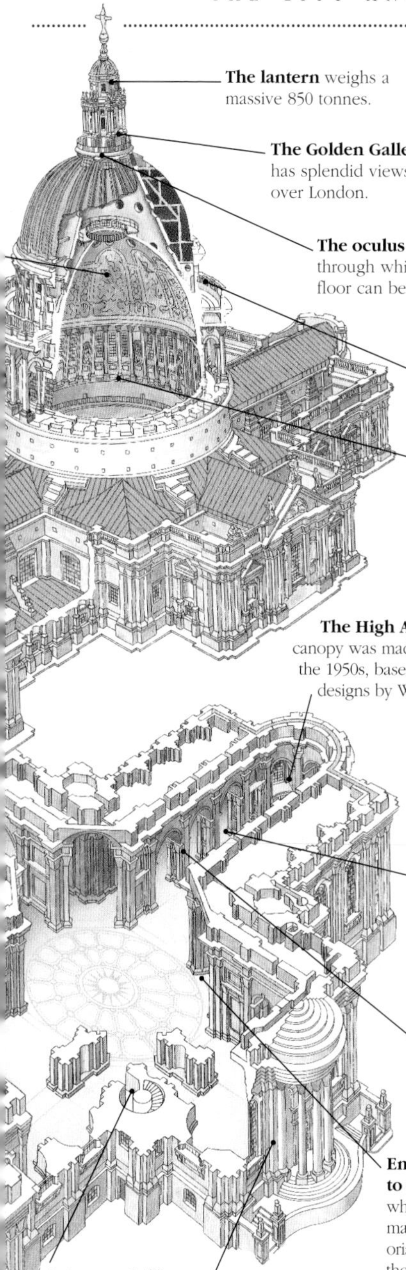

The lantern weighs a massive 850 tonnes.

The Golden Gallery has splendid views over London.

The oculus is an opening through which the cathedral floor can be seen.

Stone Gallery

VISITORS' CHECKLIST

Ludgate Hill EC4. **Map** 7 C2.
☎ 020-7236 4128. ⊖ St Paul's,
Mansion House. 🚌 4, 11, 15, 17,
23, 76, 172. 🚆 City Thameslink.
Cathedral & Crypt ⬚ 8:30am–
4:30pm Mon–Sat (last adm:
4pm); for services only on Sun,
Ash Wed, 25 Dec & Good Fri. 🔊
Galleries ⬚ 9:30am–4:15pm
(last adm: 4pm). 🔊 🎵 Evensong:
5pm Mon–Sat, 3:15pm Sun. 🔊
🍽 💻

The High Altar canopy was made in the 1950s, based on designs by Wren.

★ **Whispering Gallery**
The dome's unusual acoustics mean that words whispered against the wall can be heard clearly on the opposite side.

Choir
Jean Tijou, a Huguenot refugee, created much of the fine wrought iron-work in Wren's time, including these choir screens.

Entrance to crypt, which has many mem-orials to the famous.

Entrance to Golden, Whispering and Stone galleries

The South Portico was inspired by the porch of Santa Maria della Pace in Rome. Wren absorbed the detail by studying a friend's collection of architectural engravings.

STAR SIGHTS

★ **West Front and Towers**

★ **Dome**

★ **Whispering Gallery**

Choir Stalls
The 17th-century choir stalls and organ case were made by Grinling Gibbons (1648–1721), a wood-carver from Rotterdam. He and his team of craftsmen worked on these intricate carvings for two years.

Tower Bridge 9

SE1. **Map** 16 D3. 020-7378 1928.
Tower Hill. **The Tower Bridge
Experience** Apr–Oct: 10am–
6.30pm daily; Nov–Mar: 9.30am–6pm
daily (last adm: 75 mins before closing).
24–26 Dec, 1 Jan.
Video.

THIS FLAMBOYANT piece of
Victorian engineering,
designed by Sir Horace Jones,
was completed in 1894 and
soon became a symbol of
London. Its two Gothic towers
contain the mechanism for
raising the roadway to permit
large ships to pass through.
The towers are made of a
supporting steel framework
clad in stone, and are linked
by two high level walkways
which were closed between
1909 and 1982 due to
their popularity with suicides
and prostitutes. The bridge
now houses The Tower Bridge
Experience, with interactive
displays bringing the bridge's
history to life. There are fine
river views from the walkways, and a look at the steam
engine room that powered the
lifting machinery until
1976, when the system
was electrified.

Walkways, open to the
public, give panoramic views
over the Thames and London.

The roadway, when raised
creates a space 40 m (135 ft)
high and 60 m (200 ft) wide, big
enough for large cargo ships.

Engine room

**Lifts and 300
steps** lead to the
top of the towers.

**The Victorian wind-
ing machinery** was
originally powered
by steam.

Entranc

South Bank

North Bank

Design Museum 10

Butlers Wharf, Shad Thames SE1. **Map**
8 F4. 020-7378 6055. Tower
Hill, London Bridge. 11:30am–6pm
Mon–Fri, 10:30am–6pm Sat–Sun.
24–26 Dec.

THIS MUSEUM was the first in
the world to be devoted
solely to the design of mass-
produced everyday objects.

**Sculpture by Paolozzi (1986)
outside the Design Museum**

The permanent collection
charts technical innovation,
changes in taste and commercial success or failure through
an eclectic range of furniture,
office equipment, cars, radios,
TV sets and household uten-
sils. Elite design classics such
as chairs by GT Rietveld and
a kettle by Philippe Starck
are on show alongside Pyrex
dishes, Tupperware cups and
a Kodak Instamatic camera.
Also worth seeing are proto-
types that disappeared without
trace, such as a television
designed so that people could
watch it lying down.

Temporary exhibitions of
international design held in
the Review and Collections
galleries give a taste of what
may become familiar in the
future, and a chance to catch
up on various new trends.

The Old Operating Theatre 11

9A St Thomas St SE1. **Map** 8 D4.
020-7955 4791. London
Bridge. 10:30am–5pm daily.
15 Dec–5 Jan.

MOST OF the old St Thomas's
hospital was demolished
in 1862 to make room for a
railway. The women's operating theatre (1821) survived
in a garret over the hospital
church, where it lay forgotten
until the 1950s. It has since
been restored and fitted out
exactly as it would have been
in the 19th century, before
the discovery of anaesthetics.
Displays show pre-operative
care: patients were blind-
folded, gagged and bound
to the operating table.

Spectacular downstream view of Tate Modern from Blackfriars

Southwark Cathedral ⑫

Montague Close SE1. **Map** 8 D4.
📞 020-7367 6712. 🚇 London
Bridge. ⬜ 9am–6pm daily.

ALTHOUGH SOME PARTS OF this building date back to the 12th century, it was not until 1905 that it became a cathedral. Many original medieval features remain, notably the superb Gothic choir, and the tomb of John Gower (c.1325–1408), Chaucer's *(see p172)* contemporary and fellow poet.

There is a monument to Shakespeare *(see pp310–11)*, carved in 1912 and a memorial window above, installed in 1954. A chapel commemorates John Harvard, the founder of Harvard University, who was born in Southwark and baptized here in 1607.

Shakespeare window (1954), Southwark Cathedral

Tate Modern ⑬

48 Hopton St SE1. **Map** 7 C3.
📞 020-7401 7302. 🚇 Blackfriars,
Southwark. ⬜ 10am–6pm Mon–Thu,
10am–10pm Fri & Sat. ● 24–26
Dec. 🎟 major exhibitions only. ♿
🍴 🛍 🚻

ONE OF THE WORLD'S most important collections of 20th-century art finally has a home worthy of its status in the decommissioned Bankside Power Station. Its vast spaces are the perfect setting for works by contemporary artists and giants of modern art. The gallery's novel approach to art installation groups works by theme rather than school or era.

Shakespeare's Globe ⑭

New Globe Walk SE1. **Map** 7 C3.
📞 020-7902 1500. 🚇 London
Bridge, Mansion House. ⬜ mid-
May–Sep: 9:15am–12:15pm daily;
Oct–mid-May: 10am–5pm daily.
Exhibition ⬜ 9am–5pm daily.
● 24–25 Dec. 🎟 🚻
Performances mid-May–Sep. 🎟 📷
every 30 mins.

A DETAILED REPRODUCTION of an Elizabethan theatre has been built on the riverside a few hundred metres from the site of the original Globe, Shakespeare's "wooden O" where many of his plays were first performed. Open to the elements (although the seats are protected) the theatre operates only in the summer, and seeing a play here can be a lively experience, with the "groundlings" standing just in front of the stage encouraged to cheer or jeer.

When there is no performance, visitors are taken on an informative tour of the theatre by actors. An exhibition is open all year, featuring the Underglobe, where every aspect of Shakespeare's work is brought to life using a combination of modern technology and traditional crafts. There is also an educational centre nearby, where children can learn all about Shakespeare and the theatre, and may take part in drama workshops.

Shakespeare's *Henry IV* (performed at the Globe Theatre around 1600)

Tower of London ❽

Soon after he became king in 1066, William the Conqueror built a fortress here to guard the entrance to London from the Thames Estuary. In 1097 the White Tower, standing today at the centre of the complex, was completed in sturdy stone; other fine buildings have been added over the centuries. The Tower has served as a royal residence, armoury, treasury and most famously as a prison for enemies of the crown. Many were tortured and among those who met their death there were the "Princes in the Tower", the sons and heirs of Edward IV. Today the tower is a popular attraction, housing the Crown Jewels and other exhibits. Its most celebrated residents are seven ravens whose presence is protected by the legend that the kingdom will fall if they desert the tower.

Beauchamp Tower
Many high-ranking prisoners were held here, often with their own retinues of servants. The tower was built by Edward I around 1281.

"Beefeaters"
Forty Yeoman Warders guard the Tower and live there. Their uniforms hark back to Tudor times.

Two 13th-century curtain walls protect the tower.

Tower Green was the execution site for favoured prisoners, away from crowds on Tower Hill, where many had to submit to public execution. Seven people died here, including two of Henry VIII's eight wives, Anne Boleyn and Catherine Howard.

Queen's House
This Tudor building is the sovereign's official residence at the Tower.

Main entrance from Tower Hill

THE CROWN JEWELS

The world's best-known collection of precious objects, now displayed in a splendid exhibition room, includes the gorgeous regalia of crowns, sceptres, orbs and swords used at coronations and other state occasions. Most date from 1661, when Charles II commissioned replacements for regalia destroyed by Parliament after the execution of Charles I (*see pp52–3*). Only a few older pieces survived, hidden by royalist clergymen until the Restoration – notably, Edward the Confessor's sapphire ring, now incorporated into the Imperial State Crown (*see p73*). The crown was made for Queen Victoria in 1837 and has been used at every coronation since.

The Sovereign's Ring (1831)

The Sovereign's Orb (1661), a hollow gold sphere encrusted with jewels

★ Jewel House
Among the mag-
nificent Crown
Jewels is the
Sceptre with the
Cross (1660),
which now con-
tains the world's
biggest diamond.

VISITORS' CHECKLIST

Tower Hill EC3. **Map** 8 E3.
020-7709 0765. Tower Hill.
15, X15, 25, 42, 78, 100, D1,
D9, D11. Fenchurch Street.
from Westminster to Tower
Pier. **Docklands Light Railway**
Tower Gateway. Mar–Oct:
9am–6pm Mon–Sat, 10am–6pm
Sun; Nov–Feb: 9am–5pm Mon–
Sat, 10am–5pm Sun (last adm: 1
hour before closing). 24–26
Dec, 1 Jan. limited,
except Jewel House. **Ceremony of the Keys**: 9:30pm daily.

★ White Tower
When the tower was finished
in 1097, it was the tallest
building in London at
27 m (90 ft) high.

★ Chapel of St John
This austerely beautiful
Romanesque chapel is a
particularly fine example
of Norman architecture.

Traitors' Gate
The infamous entrance was
used for prisoners brought from
trial in Westminster Hall.

Bloody Tower
Edward IV's two sons were
put here by their uncle,
Richard of Gloucester (subsequently Richard III), after
their father died in 1483.
The princes, depicted here
by John Millais (1829–96),
disappeared mysteriously
and Richard was crowned
later that year. In 1674
the skeletons of two children were found nearby.

STAR SIGHTS

★ Jewel House

★ White Tower

★ Chapel of St John

SHOPS AND MARKETS

Lᴏɴᴅᴏɴ is one of the great shopping cities of Europe, with bustling, lively street markets, world-famous department stores, and a wide variety of eclectic shops selling clothes, crafts and antiques *(see p627)*. The best shopping areas range from elegant, upmarket districts such as Knightsbridge, which sells expensive clothes, porcelain

Bags from two famous West End shops

and jewellery, to the busy, chaotic stretch of Oxford Street, and the colourful, noisy markets of Covent Garden *(see p81)*, Berwick Street and Brick Lane. The city is best known however, for its inexhaustible range of clothes shops selling everything from traditional tweeds to the latest zany designs of an ever changing high-street fashion.

CHAIN AND DEPARTMENT STORES

Façade of Liberty (1925)

Tʜᴇ ᴍᴏsᴛ ғᴀᴍᴏᴜs of London's many department stores is **Harrods**, with some 300 departments, 4,000 staff, and a spectacular Edwardian food hall. Nearby **Harvey Nichols** stocks high fashion and boasts the city's most stylish food hall. Gourmets should make a pilgrimage to **Fortnum and Mason** which has stocked high quality food for nearly 300 years. Traditional teas are available in the top floor café.

Selfridges sells virtually everything from fine cashmeres to household gadgets, while **John Lewis** and its Chelsea partner **Peter Jones** specialize in fabrics, china, glass and household items. **Liberty**, set in a beautiful Tudor-style building, still sells the hand-blocked silks and Oriental goods for which it was famous when it first opened in 1875. **Marks and Spencer**, long known for its good quality own-label clothes,

began as a market stall in Leeds in 1882, and now has some 700 branches worldwide.

The best chain store record shops are **Virgin Megastore**, **Tower Records** and **HMV**.

CLOTHES AND SHOES

Bʀɪᴛɪsʜ ᴅᴇsɪɢɴᴇʀs range from elegant **Jasper Conran** to **Vivienne Westwood**, doyenne of the punkish avant-garde. Somewhere between are **Katharine Hamnett** and **Paul Smith**, while an ever-changing host of adventurous young designers produce outrageous clothes for trendy clubbers. You can find these in shops such as **Urban Outfitters**, while the creations of more established international designers are stocked at places such as **Browns**.

Traditional English clothing – waxed Barbour jackets and Burberry trench coats – are

found in outlets such as **The Scotch House, Burberry** and **Gieves & Hawkes**, while **Laura Ashley** is renowned for its floral print dresses.

Shoes range from Oxfords and traditional brogues from **Church's Shoes** and hand-made footwear from **John Lobb**, to the stylish, more affordable designs at **Hobbs** and **Pied à Terre**.

MARKETS

Lᴏɴᴅᴏɴ's ᴍᴀʀᴋᴇᴛs sell everything from street fashion and vintage clothes to canned food past its sell-by date and cheap household goods. The fashionable markets are **Camden Lock, Greenwich, Portobello Road** and **Covent Garden** where you can find an assortment of handmade crafts, old clothes and antiques. For those more serious about antique collecting, go early

Harrods at night, illuminated by 11,500 lights

on a Friday to **Bermondsey Market** in South London.

The most famous London market is **Petticoat Lane**, worth a visit for the sheer volume of leather goods and the noisy, cheerful atmosphere created by the many Cockney stallholders. **Brick Lane** is another authentic East End market where dubious characters hustle gold watches and jewellery, and sheds are piled high with tatty furniture and bric-a-brac. For a glimpse of spirited costermongers in central London head for **Berwick Street**, which is lined with fruit and vegetables, fabrics and household goods.

Bustling Petticoat Lane market, officially known as Middlesex Street

DIRECTORY

CHAIN AND DEPARTMENT STORES

Fortnum and Mason
181 Piccadilly W1.
Map 6 D1.
☎ 020-7734 8040.

Harrods
87–135 Brompton Rd SW1.
Map 5 A3.
☎ 020-7730 1234.

Harvey Nichols
109–125 Knightsbridge SW1.
Map 5 B2.
☎ 020-7235 5000.

HMV
150 Oxford St W1.
Map 4 D4.
☎ 020-7631 3423.

John Lewis
278–306 Oxford St W1.
Map 3 C5.
☎ 020-7629 7711.

Liberty
210–20 Regent St W1.
Map 3 C5.
☎ 020-7734 1234.

Marks & Spencer
173 & 458 Oxford St W1.
Map 3 C5/3 B5.
☎ 020-7935 7954.
Two of many branches.

Peter Jones
Sloane Square SW1.
Map 5 A4.
☎ 020-7730 3434.

Selfridges
400 Oxford St W1.
Map 3 B5.
☎ 020-7629 1234.

Tower Records
1 Piccadilly Circus W1.
Map 6 D1.
☎ 020-7439 2500.

Virgin Megastore
14–16 Oxford St W1.
Map 4 E4.
☎ 020-7631 1234.

CLOTHES AND SHOES

Browns
23–27 South Molton St W1.
Map 3 B5.
☎ 020-7514 0000.
One of several branches.

Burberry
18–22 Haymarket SW1.
Map 6 D1.
☎ 020-7930 3343.
One of two branches.

Church's Shoes
163 New Bond St W1.
Map 3 C5.
☎ 020-7499 9449.
One of several branches.

Gieves & Hawkes
1 Savile Row W1.
Map 3 C5.
☎ 020-7434 2001.

Hobbs
47 South Molton St W1.
Map 3 C5.
☎ 020-7629 0750.
One of several branches.

Jasper Conran
6 Burnsall St SW3.
Map
☎ 020-7352 3572.

John Lobb
9 St James's St SW1.
Map 6 D1.
☎ 020-7930 3664.

Hamnett at Harvey Nichols
109–125 Knightsbridge SW1. **Map** 5 A3.
☎ 020-7235 5000.

Laura Ashley
256–258 Regent St W1.
Map 4 D5.
☎ 020-7437 9760.
One of several branches.

Paul Smith
40–44 Floral St WC2.
Map 4 E5.
☎ 020-7379 7133.

Pied à Terre
19 South Molton St W1
Map 3 B5.
☎ 020-7493 3637.
One of several branches.

The Scotch House
2 Brompton Rd SW1.
Map 5 A2.
☎ 020-7581 2151.
One of several branches.

Vivienne Westwood
6 Davies St W1.
Map 3 B5.
☎ 020-7629 3757.

Urban Outfitters
36–38 Kensington High St W8. **Map** 1 C4.
☎ 020-7761 1001.

MARKETS

Bermondsey
Long Lane & Bermondsey St SE1.
Map 8 E5.
🕐 5am–2pm Fri.

Berwick Street
Berwick St W1
Map 4 D5.
🕐 9am–6pm Mon–Sat.

Brick Lane
Brick Lane E1.
🚇 Shoreditch, Liverpool St, Aldgate East.
🕐 dawn–1pm Sun.

Camden Lock
Chalk Farm Rd NW1.
🚇 Camden Town, Chalk Farm. 🕐 9:30am–5:30pm daily.

Covent Garden
The Piazza WC2.
Map 4 F5. 🕐 9am–5pm daily (antiques: Mon).

Petticoat Lane
Middlesex St E1.
🚇 Liverpool St, Aldgate, Aldgate East.
🕐 9am–2pm Sun.

Portobello Road
Portobello Rd W10.
🚇 Notting Hill Gate, Ladbroke Grove.
🕐 7am–5:30pm Sat (general market: 9am–5pm Fri–Wed, 9am–1pm Thu).

Greenwich
College Approach SE10.
🚆 Greenwich.
🕐 9am–6pm Sat, Sun.

ENTERTAINMENT IN LONDON

LONDON HAS THE ENORMOUS variety of entertainment that only the great cities of the world can provide. The historical backdrop and the lively bustling atmosphere add to the excitement. Whether dancing the night away at a famous disco or making the most of London's varied arts scene, the visitor has a bewildering choice. A trip to London is not complete without a visit to the theatre which ranges from glamorous West End musicals to experimental Fringe plays. There is world-class ballet and opera in fabled venues such as Sadler's Wells and the Royal Opera House. The musical menu covers everything from classical, jazz and rock to rhythm and

Many London cafés have free live music

blues performed in atmospheric basement clubs, old converted cinemas and outdoor venues such as Wembley. Movie buffs can choose from hundreds of films each night. Sports fans can watch cricket at Lord's or participate in a host of activities from water sports to ice skating.

Time Out, published every Wednesday, is the most comprehensive guide to what's on in London, with detailed weekly listings and reviews. *The Evening Standard*, *The Guardian* (Saturday) and *The Independent* also have reviews and information on events. If you buy tickets from booking agencies rather than direct from box offices, do compare prices – and only buy from ticket touts if you're desperate.

WEST END AND NATIONAL THEATRES

Palace Theatre poster (1898)

THE GLAMOROUS, glittering world of West End theatreland, emblazoned with the names of world-famous performers, offers an extraordinary range of entertainment.

West End theatres (see Directory for individual theatres) survive on their profits and rely on an army of financial backers, known as "angels". Consequently, they tend to stage commercial productions with mass appeal:

musicals, classics, comedies and plays by bankable contemporary playwrights which can, if successful, run for years.

The state-subsidized Royal National Theatre is based in the riverside **South Bank Centre** *(see p126)*. Its three auditoriums – the large, open-staged Olivier, the proscenium-arched Lyttleton, and the small but flexible studio space of the Cottesloe – make a diversity of productions possible.

The Royal Shakespeare Company regularly stages plays by Shakespeare, but its large repertoire includes ancient Greek tragedies, Restoration comedies and modern works. Its main base is at Stratford-upon-Avon *(see pp312–13)* but its major productions also come to its London headquarters at the **Barbican** *(see p126)*, where it performs in the magnificent Barbican Theatre and in the Pit, a more intimate stage in the same complex.

Theatre tickets cost from £5 to £30 and can be bought direct from box offices, by telephone or by post. Many venues sell unclaimed tickets just before a performance. A ticket booth in Leicester Square, open 2:30–6:30pm (from noon for matinées) Monday to Saturday, sells cheap tickets on the day (cash only) for a wide range of shows.

OFF-WEST END AND FRINGE THEATRES

OFF-WEST END THEATRE is a middle category bridging the gap between West End and Fringe theatre. It includes venues that, regardless of location, have a permanent management team and often provide the opportunity for established directors and actors to turn their hands to more adventurous works in a smaller, more intimate, environment. Fringe theatres, on the other hand, are normally venues hired out to visiting companies. Both offer a vast array of innovative productions, serving as an outlet for new, often experimental writing, and for plays by gay, feminist and ethnic minority writers.

The Old Vic, the first home of the National Theatre from 1963

Open-air theatre at Regent's Park

Venues (too numerous to list – see newspaper listings), range from tiny theatres or rooms above pubs such as the Gate, which has a reputation for high quality productions of neglected European classics, to centrally based theatres such as the Donmar Warehouse, which regularly attracts major directors and actors.

OPEN-AIR THEATRE

I<small>N SUMMER</small>, a performance of one of Shakespeare's airier creations such as *Comedy of Errors, A Midsummer Night's Dream* or *As You Like It*, takes on an atmosphere of pure enchantment and magic among the green vistas of Regent's Park or Holland Park. Be sure to take a rug or blanket.

CINEMAS

T<small>HE WEST END</small> abounds with multiplex cinema chains (MGM, Odeon, UCI) which show big budget Hollywood films, usually in advance of the rest of the country, although release dates tend to lag well behind the US and many other European countries.

The Odeon Marble Arch has the largest commercial screen in Europe, while the Odeon Leicester Square boasts London's biggest auditorium with almost 2,000 seats.

Londoners are well-informed cinema-goers and even the larger cinema chains include some low-budget and foreign films in their repertoire. The majority of foreign films are

IMAX Cinema, at Waterloo

subtitled, rather than dubbed. A number of independent cinemas, such as the Metro, Renoir and Prince Charles in central London, and the Curzon in Mayfair, show foreign-language and slightly more offbeat art films.

The largest concentration of cinemas is in and around Leicester Square although there are local cinemas in most areas. Just off Leicester Square, the Prince Charles is the West End's cheapest cinema. Elsewhere in the area you can expect to pay between £6 and £9 for an evening performance – almost twice the price of the local cinemas. Monday and afternoon performances in the West End are often cheaper.

The National Film Theatre (NFT), on the South Bank, is London's flagship repertory cinema. Subsidized by the British Film Institute, it screens a wide range of films, old and new, from all around the world. Nearby at Waterloo is the IMAX, with one of the world's largest screens.

DIRECTORY			
WEST END THEATRES	**Dominion** Tottenham Court Rd. **Map** 4 E4. 📞 020-7416 6060.	**Lyric** Shaftesbury Ave. **Map** 4 D5. 📞 020-7494 5045.	**Savoy** Strand. **Map** 4 F5. 📞 020-7836 8888.
Adelphi Strand. **Map** 4 F5. 📞 020-7344 0055.	**Duchess** Catherine St. **Map** 4 F5. 📞 020-7494 5075.	**New London** Drury Lane. **Map** 4 E5. 📞 020-7405 0072.	**Shaftesbury** Shaftesbury Ave. **Map** 4 E4. 📞 020-7379 5399.
Albery St Martin's Lane. **Map** 4 E5. 📞 020-7369 1730.	**Duke of York's** St Martin's Lane. **Map** 4 E5. 📞 020-7836 5122.	**Palace** Shaftesbury Ave. **Map** 4 E5. 📞 020-7434 0909.	**Strand** Aldwych. **Map** 4 F5. 📞 020-7930 8800.
Aldwych Aldwych. **Map** 4 F5. 📞 020-7379 3367.	**Fortune** Russell St. **Map** 4 F5. 📞 020-7836 2238.	**Phoenix** Charing Cross Rd. **Map** 4 E5. 📞 020-7369 1733.	**St Martin's** West St. **Map** 4 E5. 📞 020-7836 1443.
Apollo Shaftesbury Ave. **Map** 4 E5. 📞 020-7494 5070.	**Garrick** Charing Cross Rd. **Map** 4 E5. 📞 020-7494 5085.	**Piccadilly** Denman St. **Map** 4 D5. 📞 020-7369 1734.	**Theatre Royal:** **–Drury Lane** Catherine St. **Map** 4 F5. 📞 020-7494 5062.
Cambridge Earlham St. **Map** 4 E5. 📞 020-7494 5080.	**Gielgud** Shaftesbury Ave. **Map** 4 D5. 📞 020-7494 5065.	**Prince Edward** Old Compton St. **Map** 4 D5. 📞 020-7447 5400.	**–Haymarket** Haymarket. **Map** 6 E1. 📞 020-7930 8800.
Comedy Panton St. **Map** 6 E1. 📞 020-7369 1731.	**Her Majesty's** Haymarket. **Map** 6 E1. 📞 020-7494 5400.	**Prince of Wales** Coventry St. **Map** 4 D5. 📞 020-7839 5972.	**Vaudeville** Strand. **Map** 4 F5. 📞 020-7836 9987.
Criterion Piccadilly Circus. **Map** 4 D5. 📞 020-7413 1437.	**London Palladium** Argyll St. **Map** 3 C5. 📞 020-7494 5020.	**Queen's** Shaftesbury Ave. **Map** 4 E5. 📞 020-7494 5040.	**Wyndham's** Charing Cross Rd. **Map** 4 E5. 📞 020-7369 1736.

Royal Festival Hall, South Bank Centre

Classical Music, Opera and Dance

London is one of the world's great centres for classical music, with five symphony orchestras, internationally renowned chamber groups such as the Academy of St-Martin-in-the-Fields and the English Chamber Orchestra, as well as a number of contemporary groups. There are performances virtually every week by major international orchestras and artists, reaching a peak during the summer proms season at the **Royal Albert Hall** *(see p63)*. The newly restored **Wigmore Hall** has excellent acoustics and is a fine setting for chamber music, as is the converted Baroque church (1728) of **St John's, Smith Square**.

Although televised and outdoor performances by major stars have greatly increased the popularity of opera, prices at the **Royal Opera House** are still aimed at corporate entertainment but the policy now is to keep a few cheaper seats. The refurbished building is elaborate and productions are often extremely lavish. English National Opera, based at the **London Coliseum**, has more adventurous productions, appealing to a younger audience (nearly all operas are sung in English). Tickets range from £5 to £200 and it is advisable to book well in advance.

The Royal Opera House is also home to the Royal Ballet, and the London Coliseum to the English National Ballet, the two leading classical ballet companies in Britain. Visiting ballets also perform in both. There are numerous young contemporary dance companies that have their own distinctive style, notably the London Contemporary Dance Theatre, based at **The Place Theatre**. Other major dance venues are **Sadler's Wells**, the **ICA**, the **Royalty Theatre** and the **Chisenhale Dance Space**.

The **Barbican** and **South Bank Centre** (comprising the Royal Festival Hall, Queen Elizabeth Hall and Purcell Room) host an impressive variety of events ranging from touring opera performances to free foyer concerts.

Elsewhere in London many outdoor musical events take place in summer *(see p62–3)* at venues such as **Kenwood House**. Events to look out for are: the London Opera Festival (June) with singers from all over the world; the City of London Festival (July) which hosts a range of varied musical events; and contemporary dance festivals Spring Loaded (February–April) and Dance Umbrella (October) – see *Time Out* and newspaper listings.

Kenwood House on Hampstead Heath *(see p130)*

The Hippodrome, Leicester Square

ROCK, POP, JAZZ AND CLUBS

AN ORDINARY WEEKNIGHT in London features scores of concerts, ranging from rock and pop, to jazz, Latin, world, folk and reggae. Artists guaranteed to fill thousands of seats play large venues such as **Wembley Stadium**, **Wembley Arena**, or the **Royal Albert Hall**. However, many major bands prefer to play the **Brixton Academy** and the **Forum**, both former cinemas.

The number of jazz venues has increased over the last few years. Best of the old crop is **Ronnie Scott's**, while of the newcomers the **100 Club**, **Jazz Café** and **Pizza on the Park** have good reputations.

London's club scene is one of the most innovative in Europe, particularly since

1990, when all-night clubbing (though not drinking) was legalized. It is dominated by big-name DJs, who host different nights in different clubs and some of the best clubs are one-nighters (see *Time Out* and newspaper listings). The world-famous mainstream discos **Stringfellows** and the **Hippodrome** are glitzy, expensive and very much part of the tourist circuit, as is the **Limelight** nearby. In contrast the young and trendy **Wag Club**, New York-style **Ministry of Sound**, the camp cabaret of **Madame Jojo's** and a host of other venues ensure that you will never be short of choice. Alternatives are the excellent laser and light shows at **Heaven**, or the fun 1970s

Ticket agency, Shaftesbury Avenue

atmosphere at **Le Scandale** on Saturdays, or the ska, classic soul and R'n'B at **Gossips** on Thursdays. **Heaven** and the **Fridge** are among the most popular of London's gay clubs.

Opening times are usually 10pm–3am, but on weekends many clubs open until 6am.

SPORTS

AN IMPRESSIVE variety of public sports facilities are to be found in London and they are generally inexpensive to use. Swimming pools, squash courts, gyms and sports centres, with an assortment of keep-fit classes, can be found in most districts, and tennis courts hired in most parks. Water sports, ice skating and golf are among the variety of activities on offer. Spectator sports range from football and rugby at various club grounds to cricket at **Lord's** or the **Oval**, and tennis at the **All England Lawn Tennis Club**, Wimbledon. Tickets for the most popular matches can often be hard to come by *(see p67)*. More traditional sports include polo at **Guards**, croquet at **Hurlingham** and medieval tennis at **Queen's Club Real Tennis**. See pages 630 to 631 for more information on sporting activities.

Hippodrome
Leicester Square WC2.
Map 4 E5.
📞 020-7437 4311.

Jazz Café
3-5 Parkway NW1.
🚇 Camden Town.
📞 020-7916 6060.

Le Scandale
53–54 Berwick St W1.
Map 4 D5.
📞 020-7 437 6830.

Limelight
136 Shaftesbury Ave, W1.
Map 4 E5.
📞 020-7 434 0572.

Madame Jojo's
8–10 Brewer St W1.
Map 4 D5.
📞 020-7734 2473.

Ministry of Sound
103 Gaunt St
SE1.
Map 7 C5.
📞 020-7378 6528.

Pizza on the Park
11 Knightsbridge
SW1.
Map 5 B2.
📞 020-7235 5550.

Ronnie Scott's
47 Frith St W1.
Map 4 D5.
📞 020-7439 0747.

Stringfellows
16–19 Upper St Martin's
Lane WC2.
Map 4 E5.
📞 020-7240 5534.

Wag Club
35 Wardour St W1.
Map 4 D5.
📞 020-7437 5534.

SPORTS

General Sports Information Line
📞 020-7222 8000.

All England Lawn Tennis Club
Church Rd, Wimbledon
SW19. 🚇 Southfields.
📞 020-8946 2244.

Guards Polo Club
Windsor Great Park,
Englefield Green, Egham,
Surrey. 🚆 Egham.
📞 01784 434212.

Hurlingham Club
Ranelagh Gdns SW6.
Map 5 B5.
📞 020-7736 8411.

Lord's Cricket Ground
St John's Wood NW8.
🚇 St John's Wood.
📞 020-7289 1611.

Oval Cricket Ground
The Oval, Kennington SE11.
🚇 Oval.
📞 020-7582 6660.

Queen's Club Real Tennis
Palliser Rd W14.
🚇 Barons Court.
📞 020-7385 3421.

FURTHER AFIELD

OVER THE CENTURIES London has steadily expanded to embrace the scores of villages that surrounded it, leaving the City as a reminder of London's original boundaries. Although now linked in an almost unbroken urban sprawl, many of these areas, have maintained their old village atmosphere and character. Hampstead and Highgate are still distinct enclaves, as are artistic Chelsea and literary Islington. Greenwich, Chiswick and Richmond have retained features that hark back to the days when the Thames was an important artery for transport and commerce, while just to the east of the City the wide expanses of the former docks have, in the last 20 years, been imaginatively rebuilt as new commercial and residential areas.

SIGHTS AT A GLANCE

Camden and Islington **7**
Chelsea **1**
Chiswick **10**
East End and Docklands **8**

Greenwich **9**
Hampstead **4**
Hampstead Heath **5**
Highgate **6**

Holland Park **2**
Notting Hill and
   Portobello Road **3**
Richmond and Kew **11**

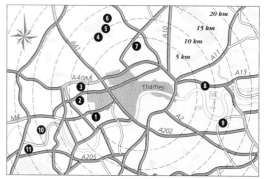

KEY

▨	Main sightseeing areas
☐	Greater London
☐	Parks
═	Motorway
▭	Major road
═	Minor road

10 miles = 15 km

Chelsea **1**

SW3. ⊖ *Sloane Square.*

RIVERSIDE CHELSEA has been fashionable since Tudor times when Sir Thomas More, Henry VIII's Lord Chancellor

Statue of Sir Thomas More (1478–1535), Cheyne Walk

(see p50), lived here. The river views attracted artists and the arrival of the historian Thomas Carlyle and essayist Leigh Hunt in the 1830s began a literary connection. Blue plaques on the houses of **Cheyne Walk** celebrate former residents such as the painter JMW Turner *(see p93)* and writers George Eliot, Henry James and TS Eliot.

  Chelsea's artistic tradition is maintained by its galleries and antique shops, many of them scattered among the clothes boutiques on **King's Road**. This begins at **Sloane Square**, named after the physician Sir Hans Sloane, who bought the manor of Chelsea in 1712. Sloane expanded the **Chelsea Physic Garden** (1673) along Swan Walk to cultivate plants and herbs.

  Wren's **Royal Hospital**, on Royal Hospital Road was built in 1692 as a retirement home for old soldiers and still houses 400 Chelsea Pensioners.

Arab Hall, Leighton House (1866)

Holland Park **2**

W8, W14. ⊖ *Holland Park.*

THIS SMALL but delightful park is more intimate than the large royal parks such as Hyde Park *(see p103)*. It was opened in 1952 on the grounds of **Holland House**, a centre of social and political intrigue in its 19th-century heyday.

  Around the park are some magnificent late Victorian

houses. **Linley Sambourne House** was built about 1870 and has hardly changed since Sambourne furnished it in the cluttered Victorian manner, with china ornaments and heavy velvet drapes. He was a political cartoonist for the satirical magazine *Punch,* and drawings, including a number of his own, cram the walls.

Leighton House, built for the Neo-Classical painter Lord Leighton in 1866, has been preserved as an extraordinary monument to the Victorian Aesthetic movement. The highlight is the Arab Hall, which was added in 1879 to house Leighton's stupendous collection of 13th- to 17th-century Islamic tiles. The best paintings include some by Leighton himself and by his contemporaries Edward Burne-Jones and John Millais.

Georgian house, Hampstead

🏛 **Linley Sambourne House**
18 Stafford Terrace W8. 📞 020-8994 1019. ⊖ High St Kensington. ◯ Mar–Oct: Wed, Sun. 📷
🏛 **Leighton House**
12 Holland Park Rd W14.
📞 020-7602 3316. ⊖ High St Kensington. ◯ Mon–Sat.
⬤ public hols.

Notting Hill and Portobello Road ❸

W11. ⊖ Notting Hill Gate.

IN THE 1950s AND '60s, Notting Hill became a centre for the Caribbean community and today it is a vibrant cosmopolitan part of London. It is also home to Europe's largest street carnival *(see p62–3)* which began in 1966 and takes over the entire area on the August bank holiday weekend, when costumed parades flood through the crowded streets.

Nearby, Portobello Road market *(see p122–3)* has a bustling atmosphere with hundreds of stalls and shops selling a variety of collectables.

Hampstead ❹

NW3, N6. ⊖ *Hampstead.* ⊠ *Hampstead Heath.*

POSITIONED ON A high ridge north of the metropolis, Hampstead has always remained aloof from London. Essentially a Georgian village with many perfectly maintained mansions and houses, it is one of London's most desirable residential areas, home to a community of artists and writers since Georgian times.

Situated in a quiet Hampstead street, **Keats House** (1816), is an evocative and memorable tribute to the life and work of the poet John Keats (1795–1821). Keats lived here for two years before his tragic death from consumption at the age of 25, and was under a plum tree in the garden that he wrote his celebrated *Ode to a Nightingale*.

Original manuscripts and books are among the mementoes of Keats and of Fanny Brawne, the neighbour to whom he was engaged.

The **Freud Museum**, which opened in 1986, is dedicated to the dramatic life of Sigmund Freud (1856–1939), the founder of psychoanalysis. At the age of 82, Freud fled from Nazi persecution in Vienna to this Hampstead house where he lived and worked for the last year of his life. His daughter Anna, pioneer of child psychoanalysis, continued to live here until her death in 1982. Inside, Freud's rich Viennese-style consulting rooms remain unaltered, and 1930s home movies show moments of Freud's life, including scenes of the Nazi attack on his home in Vienna.

🏛 **Keats House**
Keats Grove NW3. 📞 020-7435 2062. ⊖ *Hampstead, Belsize Park.* ◯ noon–5pm Tue & Thu–Sun, noon–8pm Wed.
🏛 **Freud Museum**
20 Maresfield Gdns NW3.
📞 020-7435 2002. ⊖ *Finchley Rd.* ◯ *Wed–Sun.* ♿ *limited.*

Antique shop on Portobello Road

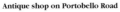

View east across Hampstead Heath to Highgate

Hampstead Heath **❺**

N6. ⊖ *Hampstead, Highgate.* ⇌ *Hampstead Heath.*

Separating the hill-top villages of Hampstead and Highgate, the open spaces of Hampstead Heath are a precious retreat from the city. There are meadows, lakes and ponds for bathing and fishing, and fine views over the capital from **Parliament Hill**, to the east.

Situated in landscaped grounds high on the edge of the Heath is the magnificent **Kenwood House**, where classical concerts *(see p126)* are held by the lake in summer. The house was remodelled by Robert Adam *(see p24)* in 1764 and most of his interiors have survived, the highlight of which is the library. The

mansion is filled with Old Master paintings, including works by Van Dyck, Vermeer, Turner *(see p93)* and Romney. The star attraction of this collection is Rembrandt's self-portrait, painted in 1663.

🏛 **Kenwood House**
Hampstead Lane NW3. 📞 *020-8348 1286.* ◯ *daily.* ● *24–25 Dec.* ♿

Handmade crafts and antiques, Camden Lock indoor market

Highgate **❻**

N6. ⊖ *Highgate, Archway.*

A settlement since the Middle Ages, Highgate, like Hampstead, became a fashionable aristocratic retreat in the 16th century. Today, it still has an exclusive rural feel, aloof from the urban sprawl below, with a Georgian high street and many expensive houses.

Highgate Cemetery *(see p77)*, with its marvellous monuments and hidden overgrown corners, has an extraordinary, magical atmosphere. Tour guides (daily in summer, weekends in winter) tell of the many tales of intrigue, mystery and vandalism connected with the cemetery since it opened in 1839. In the newer eastern section is the tomb of Victorian novelist George Eliot (1819–80) and of the cemetery's most famous incumbent, Karl Marx (1818–83).

🏛 **Highgate Cemetery**
Swains Lane N6. 📞 *020-8340 1834.* ⊖ *Archway, Highgate.* ◯ *daily.* ● *during burials, 25–26 Dec.* 📷

Camden and Islington **❼**

N1, NW1. ⊖ *Angel, Highbury & Islington.*

Camden is a lively area packed with restaurants, shops and a busy **market** *(see p122–3)*. Thousands of people come here each weekend to browse among the wide variety of stalls or simply to soak up the atmosphere of the lively cobbled area around the canal, which is enhanced by the buskers and street performers.

Neighbouring Islington was once a highly fashionable spa but the rich moved out in the late 18th century and the area deteriorated rapidly. In the 20th century, writers such as Evelyn Waugh, George Orwell and Joe Orton lived here. In recent decades, Islington has been rediscovered and is once again fashionable as one of the first areas in London to become "gentrified", with many professionals buying and refurbishing the old houses.

East End and Docklands ❽

E1, E2, E14. **East End** ⊖ *Aldgate East, Bethnal Green.* **Docklands** ⊖ *Canary Wharf.*

IN THE MIDDLE AGES the East End was full of craftsmen practising noxious trades such as brewing, bleaching and vinegar-making, which were banned within the City. The area has also been home to numerous immigrant communities since the 17th century, when French Huguenots, escaping religious persecution moved into Spitalfields, and made it a silk-weaving centre. Even after the decline of the silk industry, textiles and clothing continued to dominate, with Jewish tailors and furriers setting up workshops in the 1880s, and Bengali machinists sewing in cramped premises from the 1950s.

A good way to get a taste of the East End is to explore its Sunday street markets *(see pp122–3)*, and sample freshly baked bagels and spicy Indian food. By way of contrast, anyone interested in contemporary architecture should visit the **Docklands**, an ambitious re-development of disused docks, dominated by the Canada Tower; at 250 m (800 ft) it is London's tallest building. Other attractions include the **Bethnal Green Museum of Childhood,** a toy museum with a good display of dolls' houses and **Dennis Severs' House,** in which Dennis Severs takes you on a historic journey from the 17th to the 19th centuries.

Royal Naval College framing the Queen's House, Greenwich

♛ Dennis Severs' House
18 Folgate St E1. **【** 020-7247 4013. ⏱ *eve performances 1st Mon of month (by appt).* 🦽

🏛 Bethnal Green Museum of Childhood
Cambridge Heath Rd E2. **【** 020-8983 5200. ⏱ *Sat–Thu.* ● *24 Dec, 25 Dec, 1 Jan.*

Greenwich ❾

SE10. ⊜ *Greenwich, Maze Hill.* ⊖ *Cutty Sark DLR.*

THE WORLD'S TIME has been measured from the **Old Royal Observatory** (now housing a museum) since 1884. Greenwich was therefore the obvious setting for the **Millennium Dome**, built to celebrate Britain for the year 2000. The area is full of maritime and royal history, with Neo-Classical mansions, a park, many antique and book shops and various markets *(see pp122–3).* The **Queen's House,** designed by Inigo Jones for James I's wife, was completed in 1637 for Henrietta Maria, Charles I's

Canada Tower, Canary Wharf

queen. It has now been restored to its original state. The highlights include the perfectly cubic main hall and the unusual spiral "tulip staircase".

The adjoining **National Maritime Museum** has exhibits ranging from primitive canoes, through Elizabethan galleons, to modern ships. Anyone interested in naval history should visit the **Royal**

An 18th-century compass, National Maritime Museum

Naval College nearby, which was designed by Christopher Wren *(see p116)* in two halves so the Queen's House could retain its river view. It began as a royal palace, became a hospital in 1692, and in 1873 the Royal Naval College moved here. The Rococo chapel and the 18th-century *trompe l'oeil* Painted Hall, are open to the public.

🏛 Old Royal Observatory
Greenwich Park SE10. **【** 020-8858 4422. ⏱ *daily.* ● *23–26 Dec.* 🦽

🏛 Queen's House and National Maritime Museum
Romney Rd SE10. **【** 020-8858 4422. ⏱ *daily.* ● *24–26 Dec.* 🦽 🔊 *limited.*

♛ Royal Naval College
King William Walk, Greenwich SE10. **【** 020-8269 4747. ⏱ *10am–5pm Mon–Sat; 12:30–5pm Sun.* ● *public hols.*

Chiswick ⑩

W4. 🔵 *Chiswick.*

CHISWICK IS A PLEASANT suburb of London, with pubs, cottages and a variety of birdlife, such as herons, along the picturesque riverside. One of the main reasons for a visit is **Chiswick House**, a magnificent country villa inspired by the Renaissance architecture of Andrea Palladio. It was designed in the early 18th century by the 3rd Earl of Burlington as an annexe to his larger house (demolished in 1758), so that he could display his collection of art and entertain friends. The gardens, with their Classical temples and statues, are now restored to their former glory.

Heron

⛪ Chiswick House
Burlington Lane W4. 📞 020-8995 0508. 🔲 *Apr–Oct: daily; Nov–Mar: Wed–Sun.* ● 24, 25 Dec. ♿

Richmond and Kew ⑪

SW15. 🔵 🚊 *Richmond.*

THE ATTRACTIVE village of Richmond took its name from a palace built by Henry VII (the former Earl of Richmond in Yorkshire) in 1500, the remains of which can be seen off the green. Nearby is the expansive **Richmond Park** (*see p76*), which was once Charles I's royal hunting

ground. In summer, boats sail down the Thames from Westminster Pier, making a pleasant day's excursion from central London (*see pp74–5*).

The nobility continued to favour Richmond after royalty had left, and some of their mansions have survived. The Palladian villa, **Marble Hill House**, was built in 1729 for the mistress of George II and has been restored to its elegant original appearance.

On the opposite side of the Thames, the brooding **Ham House**, built in 1610, had its heyday later that century when it became the home of the Lauderdales. The Countess of Lauderdale inherited the house from her father, who had been Charles I's "whipping boy" – meaning that he was punished whenever the future king misbehaved. He was rewarded as an adult by being given a peerage and the lease of Ham estate.

A little further north along the Thames, **Syon House** has been inhabited by the Dukes and Earls of Northumberland for over 400 years. Numerous attractions here include a butterfly house, a museum of historic cars and a spectacular conservatory built in 1830. The lavish Neo-Classical interiors of the house, created by Robert Adam in the 1760s (*see pp24–5*), remain the highlight.

Brewers Lane, Richmond

On the riverbank to the south, **Kew Gardens** (*see p76*), the most complete botanic gardens in the world, are flawlessly maintained, with examples of nearly every plant that can be grown in Britain. There are also conservatories where thousands of exotic tropical blooms are on display.

⛪ Marble Hill House
Richmond Rd, Twickenham. 📞 020-8892 5115. 🔲 *daily (Nov–Mar: Wed–Sun).* ● 24–26 Dec. ♿ *limited.*

⛪ Ham House
Ham St, Richmond. 📞 020-8940 1950. 🔲 *Apr–Oct: Sat–Wed.* ♿

⛪ Syon House
London Rd, Brentford. 📞 020-8560 0881. **House** 🔲 *mid-Mar–Oct: Wed, Thu, Sun.* **Gardens** 🔲 *daily.* ● *Nov–mid-Mar.* ♿ *gardens only.*

🌿 Kew Gardens
Kew Rd, Richmond. 📞 020-8940 1171. 🔲 *daily.* ● *25 Dec, 1 Jan.* ♿

Chiswick House

STREET FINDER

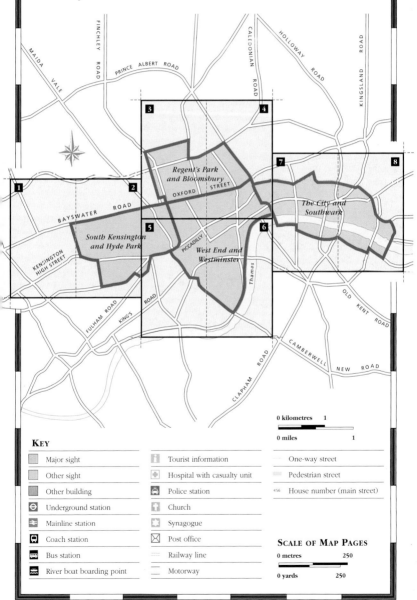

THE MAP REFERENCES given with the sights, hotels, restaurants, shops and entertainment venues based in central London refer to the following four maps. All the main places of interest within the central area are marked on the maps in addition to useful practical information, such as tube, railway and coach stations. The key map below shows the area of London that is covered by the *Street Finder*. The four main city-centre areas (colour-coded in pink) are shown in more detail on the inside back cover.

FINCHLEY ROAD

MAIDA VALE

PRINCE ALBERT ROAD

CALEDONIAN ROAD

HOLLOWAY ROAD

KINGSLAND ROAD

3
4

Regent's Park and Bloomsbury

OXFORD STREET

7
8

The City and Southwark

1
2

BAYSWATER ROAD

KENSINGTON HIGH STREET

5
South Kensington and Hyde Park

PICCADILLY

6
West End and Westminster

Thames

OLD KENT ROAD

FULHAM ROAD

KING'S ROAD

CLAPHAM ROAD

CAMBERWELL NEW ROAD

| 0 kilometres | 1 |
| 0 miles | 1 |

KEY

	Major sight		Tourist information		One-way street
	Other sight		Hospital with casualty unit		Pedestrian street
	Other building		Police station	*56	House number (main street)
⊖	Underground station		Church		
≷	Mainline station		Synagogue		
	Coach station	⊠	Post office	**SCALE OF MAP PAGES**	
	Bus station		Railway line	0 metres	250
	River boat boarding point		Motorway	0 yards	250

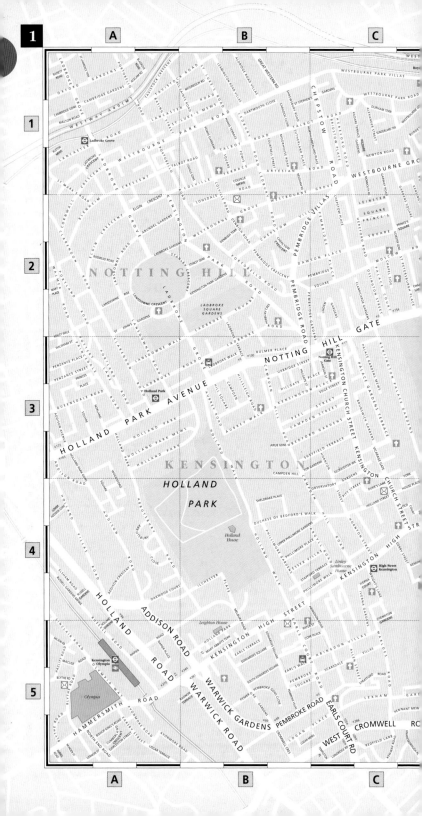

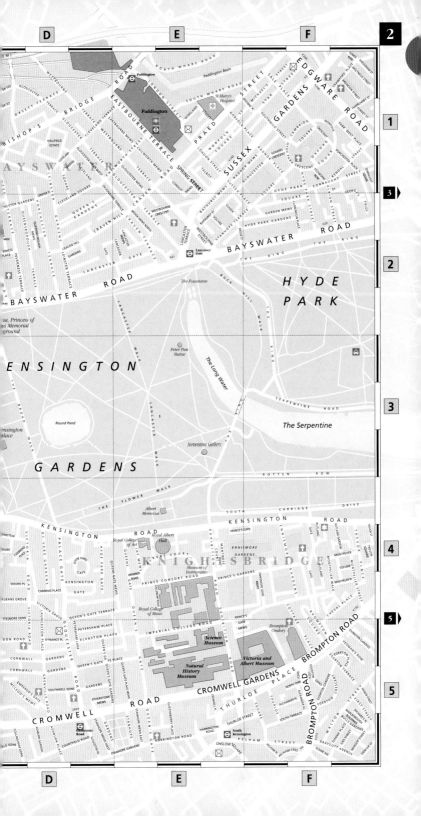

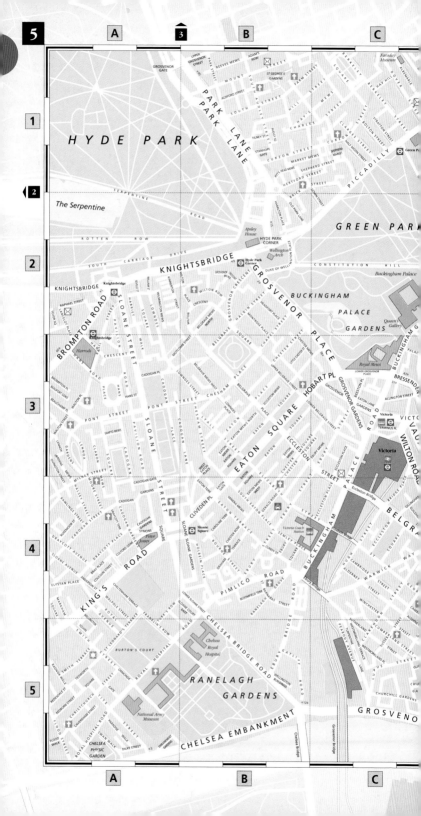

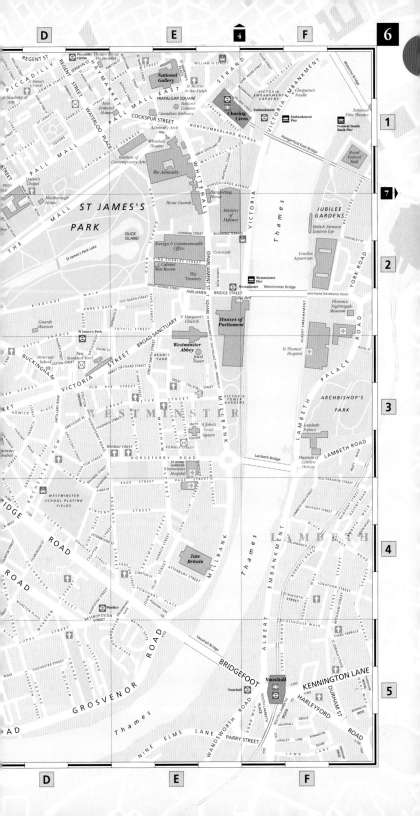

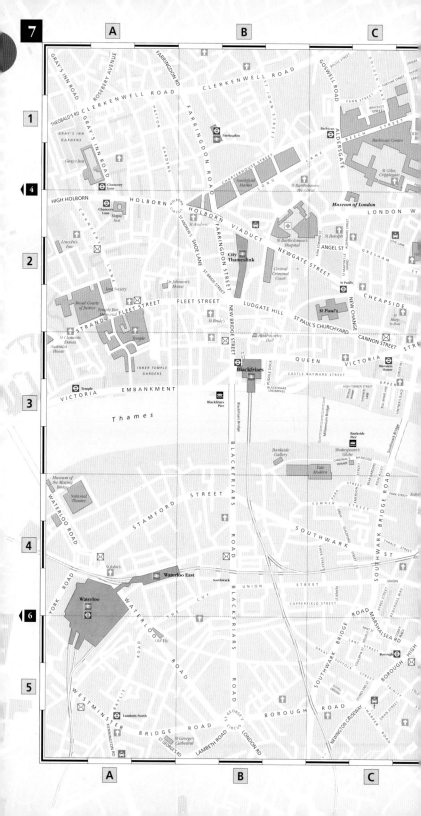

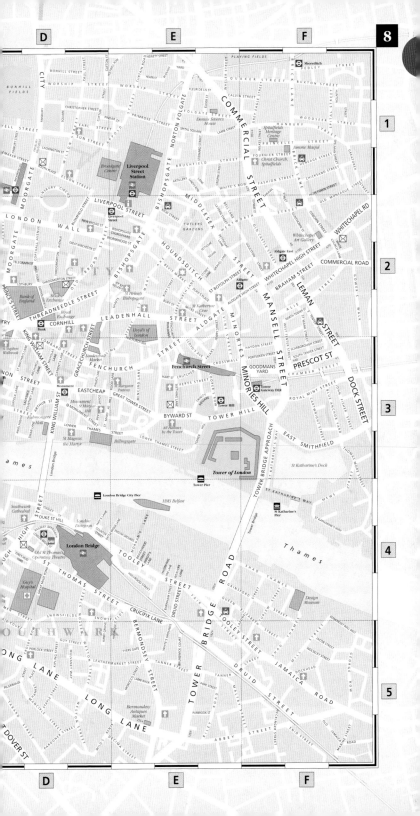

SOUTHEAST
ENGLAND

Southeast England at a Glance

THE OLD SAXON KINGDOMS covered the areas surrounding London, and today, while their accessibility to the capital makes them a magnet for commuters, each region retains a character and history of its own. The attractions include England's oldest universities, royal palaces, castles, stately homes and cathedrals, many of which played critical roles in the nation's early history. The landscape is soft, with the green and rounded hills of the south country levelling out to the flat fertile plains and fens of East Anglia, fringed by broad, sandy beaches.

Blenheim Palace (see pp214–15) is a Baroque masterpiece. The Mermaid Fountain (1892) is part of the spectacular gardens.

Bedfordshire

Hertfor

Buckinghamshire

THAMES VALLEY (see pp202–23)

Oxfordshire

Oxford University's buildings (see pp208–13) amount to a textbook of English architecture from the Middle Ages to the present. Christ Church College (1525) is the largest in the university.

Surrey

Hampshire

West Sussex

Windsor Castle (see pp222–3) is Britain's oldest royal residence. The Round Tower was built in the 11th century when the palace guarded the western approaches to London.

Winchester Cathedral (see pp156–7) was begun in 1097 on the ruins of a Saxon church. The city has been an important centre of Christianity since the 7th century. The cathedral's northwest door is built in a characteristic medieval style.

◁ **The white cliffs of Dover, Kent**

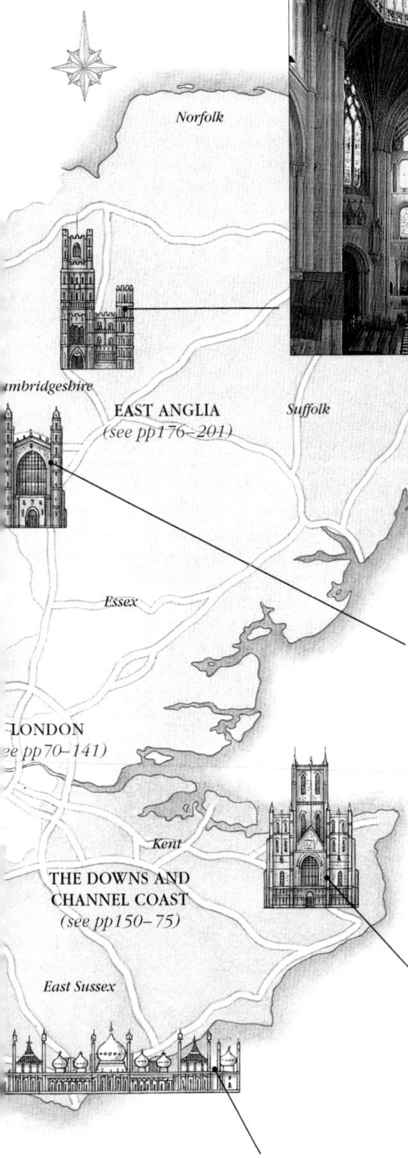

Ely Cathedral's (see pp180–81) *south transept contains some of the finest stone carving in Britain. The octagonal corona was added in the 14th century when the Norman tower collapsed; the replacement tower dominates the surrounding flat fenland.*

Norfolk

ambridgeshire

Suffolk

EAST ANGLIA
(see pp176–201)

Cambridge University's (see pp196–201) *buildings are enhanced by the quiet college gardens, the Backs and the public commons. King's College Chapel is the outstanding example of late medieval architecture in the city.*

Essex

LONDON
ee pp70–141)

Kent

THE DOWNS AND CHANNEL COAST
(see pp150–75)

East Sussex

Canterbury Cathedral (see pp172–3) *is the spiritual home of the Church of England. It contains some of the country's most exquisite medieval stained glass such as the nave's west window. It also has some well-preserved 12th-century wall paintings.*

Brighton's Royal Pavilion (see pp164–5) *was built for the Prince Regent and is one of the most lavish buildings in the land. Its design by John Nash (see p107) is based on Oriental themes and it has recently been restored to its original splendour.*

0 kilometres   25

0 miles   25

The Garden of England

White wine from the southeast

With its fertile soil, mild climate and regular rainfall, the Kentish countryside has flourished as a fruit-growing region ever since its first orchards were planted by the Romans. There has been a recent boom in wine-making, as the vine-covered hillsides around Lamberhurst show, and several vineyards may be visited. The orchards are dazzling in the blossom season, and in the autumn the branches sag with ripening fruit – a familiar sight which inspired William Cobbett (1762–1835) to describe the area as "the very finest as to fertility and diminutive beauty in the whole world". Near Faversham, the fruit research station of Brogdale is open to the public, offering orchard walks, tastings and informative displays.

HOPS AND HOPPING

Hop-picking, a family affair

Oast houses, topped with distinctive angled cowls, are a common feature of the Kentish landscape and many have now been turned into houses. They were original.

SEASONAL FRUIT

This timeline shows the major crops in each month of the farming year. The first blossoms may appear when the fields are still dusted with snow. As the petals fall, fruit appears among the leaves. After ripening in the summer sun, the fruit is harvested in the autumn.

Peach blossom is usually to be found on south-facing walls, as its fruit requires warm conditions.

Orchards are used to grow plums, pears and apples. The latter (blossoming above) remain Kent's most important orchard crop.

Raspberries are a luscious soft fruit. Many growers allow you to pick your own from the fields, and then pay by weigh

MARCH	APRIL	MAY	JUNE	JUL

Sour cherry blossom is the earliest flower. Its fruit is used for cooking.

Pear blossom has creamy white flowers which appear two or three weeks before apple blossom.

Cherry plum blossom is one of the most beautiful blossoms; the plum is grown more for its flowers than its fruit.

Srawberries are Britain's favourite and earliest soft fruit. New strains allow them to be picked all summer.

Gooseberries are not always sweet enough to eat raw, though all types are superb in pies and other desserts.

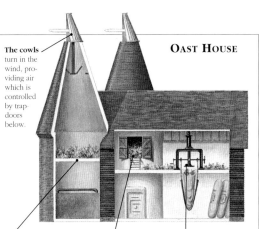

OAST HOUSE

...ilt to dry hops, an ingredient ... brewing beer *(see pp34–5)*. ...any are still used for that, for ...hough imports have reduced ...mestic hop-growing, more ...an four million tonnes are ...roduced in Britain annually, ...ostly in Kent.

...In summer, the fruiting plants ...n be seen climbing the rect-...ngular wire frames in fields by ...e roadside. Until the middle of ...e 20th century thousands of ...milies from London's East End ...ould move to the Kentish hop ...elds every autumn for working ...olidays harvesting the crop and ...mping in barns. That tradition ...as faded, because now the ...ops are picked by machine.

The cowls turn in the wind, providing air which is controlled by trapdoors below.

Hops are dried above a fan which blows hot air from the underlying radiators.

After drying, the hops are cooled and stored.

A press packs the hops into bags, ready for the breweries.

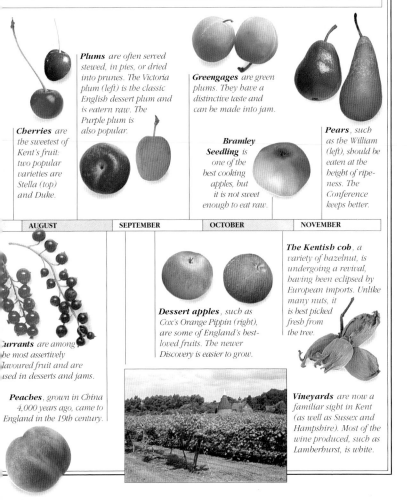

Plums *are often served stewed, in pies, or dried into prunes. The Victoria plum (left) is the classic English dessert plum and is eatern raw. The Purple plum is also popular.*

Greengages *are green plums. They have a distinctive taste and can be made into jam.*

Cherries *are the sweetest of Kent's fruit: two popular varieties are Stella (top) and Duke.*

Bramley Seedling *is one of the best cooking apples, but it is not sweet enough to eat raw.*

Pears, *such as the William (left), should be eaten at the height of ripeness. The Conference keeps better.*

AUGUST	SEPTEMBER	OCTOBER	NOVEMBER

Dessert apples, *such as Cox's Orange Pippin (right), are some of England's best-loved fruits. The newer Discovery is easier to grow.*

The Kentish cob, *a variety of hazelnut, is undergoing a revival, having been eclipsed by European imports. Unlike many nuts, it is best picked fresh from the tree.*

Currants *are among the most assertively flavoured fruit and are used in desserts and jams.*

Peaches, *grown in China 4,000 years ago, came to England in the 19th century.*

Vineyards *are now a familiar sight in Kent (as well as Sussex and Hampshire). Most of the wine produced, such as Lamberhurst, is white.*

Houses of Historical Figures

Visiting the homes of artists, writers, politicians and royalty is a rewarding way of gaining an insight into their private lives. Southeast England, near London, boasts many historic houses that have been preserved as they were when their illustrious occupants were alive. All these houses, from large mansions such as Lord Mountbatten's Broadlands to the more modest dwellings, like Jane Austen's House, contain exhibits relating to the life of the famous people who lived there.

Florence Nightingale *(1820–1910), the "Lady with the Lamp", was a nurse during the Crimean War (see p56). She stayed at Claydon with her sister, Lady Verney.*

Nancy Astor *(1879–1964) was the first woman to sit in Parliament in 1919. She lived at Cliveden until her death and made it famous for political hospitality.*

Claydon House, Winslow, nr Milton Keynes

THAMES VALLEY *(see pp202–23)*

The Duke of Wellington *(1769–1852) was given this house by the nation in 1817, in gratitude for leading the British to victory at Waterloo (see p55).*

Cliveden House, nr Maidenhead

Stratfield Saye, Basingstoke, nr Windsor

Jane Austen *(1775–1817) wrote three of her novels, including* Emma, *and revised the others at this house where she lived for eight years until shortly before her death (see p158).*

Jane Austen's House, Chawton, nr Winchester

Broadlands, nr Southampton

Lord Mountbatten (1900–79), a British naval commander and statesman, was the last Viceroy of India in 1947. He lived here all his married life and remodelled the original house considerably.

Osborne House, Isle of Wight

Queen Victoria (1819–1901) and her husband, Prince Albert, built Osborne House *(see p154)* in 1855 as a seaside retreat for their family because they never truly warmed to the Royal Pavilion in Brighton.

BLOOMSBURY GROUP

A circle of avant-garde artists, designers and writers, many of them friends as students, began to meet at a house in Bloomsbury, London, in 1904 and soon gained a reputation for their Bohemian lifestyle. When Duncan Grant and Vanessa Bell moved to Charleston in 1916, it became a Sussex outpost of the celebrated group. Many of the prominent figures associated with the circle, such as Virginia Woolf, EM Forster, Vita Sackville-West and JM Keynes paid visits here. The Bloomsbury Group was also known for the Omega Workshops, which made innovative ceramics, furniture and textiles.

Vanessa Bell at Charleston **by Duncan Grant (1885–1978)**

Gainsborough's House, Sudbury, nr Ipswich

EAST ANGLIA
(see pp176–201)

Thomas Gainsborough *(1727–88), one of Britain's greatest painters, was born in this house (see p192). He was best known for his portraits, such as this one of* Mr and Mrs Andrews.

Charles Darwin *(1809–82), who developed the theory that man and apes have a common ancestor, wrote his most famous book,* On the Origin of Species, *at the house where he lived.*

Down House, Downe, nr Sevenoaks

THE DOWNS AND CHANNEL COAST
(see pp150–75)

Bleak House, Broadstairs, nr Margate

Charles Dickens (1812–70), the prolific and popular Victorian novelist *(see p175)*, had many connections with Kent. He took holidays at Bleak House, later named after his famous novel.

Chartwell, Westerham, nr Sevenoaks

Batemans, Burwash, nr Hastings

Rudyard Kipling *(1865–1936), the poet and novelist, was born in India, but lived here for 34 years until his death. His most famous works in-clude* Kim, *the two* Jungle Books *and the* Just So Stories.

Winston Churchill (1874–1965), Britain's inspirational Prime Minister in World War II *(see p175)*, lived here for 40 years until his death. He relaxed by rebuilding parts of the house.

Charleston, Lewes

Vanessa Bell (1879–1961), artist and member of the Bloomsbury Group, lived here until her death in 1961. The 18th-century farmhouse reflects her unusual decorative ideas and is filled with murals, paintings and painted furniture.

THE DOWNS AND CHANNEL COAST

HAMPSHIRE · SURREY · EAST SUSSEX · WEST SUSSEX · KENT

W HEN SETTLERS, *invaders and missionaries came from Europe, the southeast coast was their first landfall. The wooded chalk ridges and lower-lying weald beyond them made an ideal base for settlement and proved to be productive farmland.*

The Romans were the first to build major fortifications along the Channel Coast to discourage potential attackers from the European mainland. The remains of many of these can be seen today, and some, like Portchester Castle just outside Portsmouth, were incorporated into more substantial defences in later centuries. There also exists substantial evidence of Roman domestic buildings, such as Fishbourne Palace, in coastal areas and further inland.

The magnificence of cathedrals such as Canterbury and Winchester bear witness to their role as important bases of the medieval church, then nearly as powerful as the state. Many Kent and Sussex ports grew prosperous on trade with the Continent – as did the hundreds of smugglers who operated from them. From Tudor times on, monarchs, noblemen and courtiers acquired estates and built manor houses in the countryside between London and the coast, appreciating the area's moderate climate and proximity to the capital. Many of these survive and are popular attractions for visitors. Today the southeast corner of England is its most prosperous and populous region. Parts of Surrey and Kent, up to 20 miles (32 km) from the capital, are known as the Stockbroker Belt: the area has many large, luxurious villas belonging to wealthy people prominent in business and the professions, attracted by the same virtues that appealed to the Tudor gentry.

The fertile area of Kent has long been known as the Garden of England, and despite the incursion of bricks and mortar, it is still a leading area for growing fruit *(see pp146-7)*, being in a prime position for the metropolitan market nearby.

Aerial view of the medieval and moated Leeds Castle

◁ A lush covering of bluebells in the deciduous woodlands of Kent

Exploring the Downs and Channel Coast

THE NORTH AND SOUTH DOWNS, separated by the lower-lying Weald are ideal walking country as well as being the site of many stately homes. From Tudor times, wealthy, London-based merchants and courtiers built their country residences in Kent, a day's ride from the capital, and many are open to the public. On the coast are the remains of sturdy castles put up to deter invaders from across the Channel. Today, though, the seashore is largely devoted to pleasure. Some of Britain's earliest beach resorts were developed along this coast, and sea bathing is said to have been invented in Brighton.

View of Brighton's Palace Pier from the promenade

Oast houses at Chiddingstone near Royal Tunbridge Wells

Heathrow

Oxford

HAMPTON COURT **11**

Basingstoke Canal

BASINGSTOKE

10 GUILDFORD

Salisbury

SURREY H

Test

A272

A31

A3

Wey

6 WINCHESTER

Arun

PETWORTH HOUSE **9**

SOUTH DOWNS

South Downs Way

4 SOUTHAMPTON

3

NEW FOREST

M27

A35

A3(M)

A27

ARUNDEL **8**

A27

STEY

2 BEAULIEU

Solent

COWES

5

CHICHESTER **7**

A259

PORTSMOUTH

Bournemouth

NEEDLES

A3055

1

ISLE OF WIGHT

0 kilometres 20

0 miles 10

SEE ALSO

- **Where to Stay** pp545–7
- **Where to Eat** pp582–4

GETTING AROUND

The area is well served, with a network of motorways and A roads from London to the major towns. The A259 is a scenic coast road which offers fine views over the English Channel. Bus and rail transport is also good, with a number of coach companies providing regular tours to the major sites. An InterCity train service runs to all the major towns.

SIGHTS AT A GLANCE

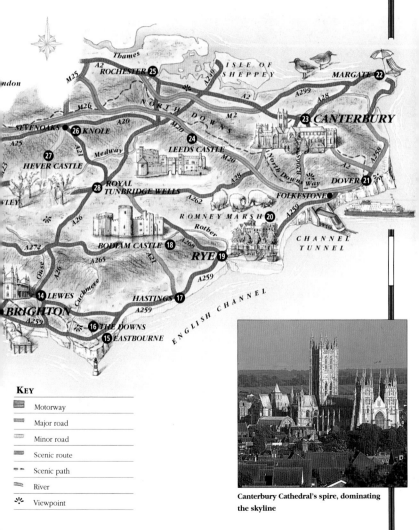

KEY

	Motorway
	Major road
	Minor road
	Scenic route
	Scenic path
	River
☼	Viewpoint

Canterbury Cathedral's spire, dominating the skyline

The Victorian Osborne House, Isle of Wight

Isle of Wight ❶

Isle of Wight. 🏛 *126,000.* 🚢 *from Lymington, Southampton, Portsmouth.* 🅸 *Westridge Centre, Brading Road, Ryde (01983 813818).* Ⓦ *www.islandbreaks.co.uk*

A VISIT TO **Osborne House**, the favoured seaside retreat of Queen Victoria and Prince Albert *(see p148)*, is alone worth the ferry ride from the mainland. Furnished much as they left it, the house provides a marvellous insight into royal life and is dotted with family mementoes.

The **Swiss Cottage** was built for the royal children to play in. It is now a museum attached to Osborne House. Adjacent to it you can see the bathing machine used by the queen to preserve her modesty while taking her to the edge of the sea *(see p383)*.

The other main sight on the island is **Carisbrooke Castle**, built in the 11th century. A walk on its outer wall and the climb to the top of its keep provides spectacular views. It was here that Charles I *(see pp52–3)* was held prisoner in 1647; an attempt to escape was foiled when he got stuck between the bars of a window.

The island is a base for ocean sailing, especially during Cowes Week *(see p67)*. The scenic highlight is the **Needles** – three towers of rock jutting out of the sea at the island's western end. This is only a short walk from

Alum Bay, famous for its multi-coloured cliffs and sand.

🏛 Osborne House
East Cowes. Ⓒ *01983 200022.* ◯ *Apr–Oct: daily; Nov–mid-Dec & Feb–Mar: daily, by* 📷 *only, phone to arrange.* ● *late Dec–Jan.* ♿ limited. ▣ ▢ 🛗

⛪ Carisbrooke Castle
Newport. Ⓒ *01983 522107.* ◯ *daily.* ● *1 Jan, 24–26 Dec.* ♿ limited. 📷 📷 ▢ 🛗

Beaulieu ❷

Brockenhurst, Hampshire. Ⓒ *01590 612345.* 🚇 *Brockenhurst then taxi.* ◯ *daily.* ● *25 Dec.* ♿ 🛗 📷 *by arrangement.* 📷 ▢ 🛗 Ⓦ *www.beaulieu.co.uk*

P ALACE HOUSE, once the gatehouse of Beaulieu Abbey, has been the home of Lord Montagu's family since 1538. It now contains the finest collection of cars in the country. The **National Motor Museum** has over 250 vintage cars ranging from the 1890s to the present.

There is also an exhibition of monastic life in the ruined

ancient **abbey**, founded in 1204 by King John *(see p48)* for Cistercian monks. The original abbey church now serves as the parish church.

ENVIRONS: Just south is the maritime museum at **Buckler's Hard**, telling the story of shipbuilding in the 18th century. The yard employed 4,000 men at its peak but declined when steel began to be used.

🏛 Buckler's Hard
Beaulieu. Ⓒ *01590 616203.* ◯ *daily.* ● *25 Dec.* ♿ limited.

New Forest ❸

Hampshire. 🚇 *Brockenhurst.* 🚌 *Lymington then bus.* 🅸 *main car park, Lyndhurst (023 8028 2269).* Ⓦ *www.thenewforest.co.uk*

T HIS UNIQUE EXPANSE of heath and woodland is, at 145 sq miles (375 sq km), the largest area of unenclosed land in southern Britain.

William the Conqueror's "new" forest, despite its name, is one of the few primeval oak woods in England. It was the popular hunting ground of Norman kings, and in 1100 William II was fatally wounded here in a hunting accident.

Today it is enjoyed by up to seven million visitors a year who share it with the New Forest ponies, unique to the area, and over 1,500 fallow deer.

Southampton ❹

.Hampshire. 🏛 *200,000.* ✈ 🚇 🚌 🚢 🅸 *9 Civic Centre Road (023 808 3333).* 🅰 *Wed–Sat.*

F OR CENTURIES this has been a flourishing port. The *Mayflower* sailed from here to America in 1620 with the

A 1909 Rolls-Royce Silver Ghost at Beaulieu's National Motor Museum

Pilgrim Fathers, as did the *Titanic* on its maiden and ultimately tragic voyage in 1912, when it went down after hitting an iceberg.

The **Maritime Museum** has exhibits about both these ships, along with displays on the huge romantic liners that sailed from the port in the first half of the 20th century.

There is a walk around the remains of the medieval city wall. At the head of the High Street stands the old city gate, **Bargate**, the most elaborate gate to survive in England. It still has its 13th-century drum towers and is decorated

Illustration of the luxurious liner the *Titanic* which sank in 1912

with intricate, 17th-century armorial carvings.

The **Tudor House Museum** has exhibits on Victorian and Edwardian domestic life.

🏛 **Maritime Museum**
Town Quay Rd. [023 8063 5904.
🕐 Tue–Sun (closed 1–2pm). 🌑 25, 26 Dec, 1 Jan & public hols. 👟 limited. 🚻
🏛 **Tudor House Museum**
St Michael's Sq. [023 8033 2513.
🕐 Tue–Sun (closed noon–1pm).
🌑 25, 26 Dec, 1 Jan & public hols.
👟 limited. 🚻

Portsmouth ❺

Hampshire. 🏘 190,000. 🚢 🏢 🛈
The Hard (023 9282 6722). 🛥 Thu–Sat. W www.portsmouthcc.gov.uk/visitor

ONCE A VITAL naval port, with all the nightlife that entails, Portsmouth is today a much quieter town but fascinating for those interested in English naval history.

Under the banner of **Flagship Portsmouth Victorygate**, the city's historic dockyard is the hub of Portsmouth's most important sights. Among these is the hull of the **Mary Rose**, Henry VIII's favourite *(see p50)*, which capsized on its maiden voyage as it left to fight the French in 1545. It was recovered from the sea bed in 1982 along with thousands of 16th-century objects now on display nearby, giving an absorbing insight into life at sea in Tudor times.

Alongside it is HMS **Victory**, the English flagship on which Admiral Nelson was killed at Trafalgar *(see p27)* and now restored to its former glory. You can also visit the **Royal Naval Museum** which deals with naval history from the 16th century to the Falklands War, the 19th-century HMS **Warrior**, and galleries telling the story of Nelson.

Portsmouth's other military memorial is the **D-Day Museum**. This is centred on the *Overlord Embroidery*, a masterpiece of needlework which was commissioned in 1968 from the Royal School

The figurehead on the bow of HMS *Victory* at Portsmouth

of Needlework and took five years to complete. At 83 m (272 ft), its 34 panels are 12 m (41 ft) longer than the *Bayeux Tapestry* in France, and it depicts the World War II Allied landing in Normandy in 1944.

Portchester Castle, on the north edge of the harbour, was fortified in the third century and is the best example of Roman sea defences in northern Europe. The Normans later used the Roman walls to enclose a castle – only the keep survives – and a church. Henry V used the castle as a garrison to assemble his army before the Battle of Agincourt *(see p49)*. In the 18th–19th centuries it was a prisoner-of-war camp and you can still see where the prisoners carved their names on the walls.

Among less warlike attractions is the **Charles Dickens Museum** *(see p175)*. The house where the author was born in 1812 is furnished in the style of that time.

🏛 **Flagship Portsmouth Victorygate**
The Hard. [023 9286 1512.
🕐 daily. 🌑 25 Dec. 📷 👟 🚻 🚻
🏛 **D-Day Museum**
Clarence Esplanade. [023 9282 7261. 🕐 daily. 🌑 24–26 Dec. 📷
👟 📷 📺 🚻
⚔ **Portchester Castle**
Castle St, Porchester. [023 9237 8291. 🕐 daily. 🌑 24–26, 31 Dec & 1 Jan. 📷 📷 by arrangement.
🏛 **Charles Dickens Museum**
393 Old Commercial Rd. [023 9282 7261. 🕐 Apr–Oct, 29 Nov–19 Dec: daily, 7 Feb (Dickens' birthday). 📷

A wild pony and her foal roaming freely in the New Forest

Winchester ⑥

Hampshire. 🏠 *34,000.* 🚉 🚌
ℹ️ *Guildhall, The Broadway (01962
840500).* 🛒 *Thu, Fri, Sat.*
🌐 *www.winchester.gov.uk*

CAPITAL of the ancient kingdom of Wessex, the city
of Winchester was also the
headquarters of the Anglo-
Saxon kings until the Norman
Conquest *(see p47)*.

William the Conqueror built
one of his first English castles
here. The only surviving part
of the castle is the **Great Hall**,
erected in 1235 to replace the

original. It is now home
to the legendary Round
Table. The story
behind the table is a
mix of history and
myth. King Arthur *(see
p271)* had it shaped so
no knight could claim
precedence. It was said
to have been built by the
wizard Merlin but was
actually made in the
13th century.

The **Westgate Museum** is
one of the two surviving 12th-
century gatehouses in the city
wall. The room (once a prison)
above the gate has a 16th-
century painted ceiling. It was
moved here from Winchester
College, England's oldest fee-
paying, or "public school".
Winchester has been an

**The 13th-century Round Table,
Great Hall, Winchester**

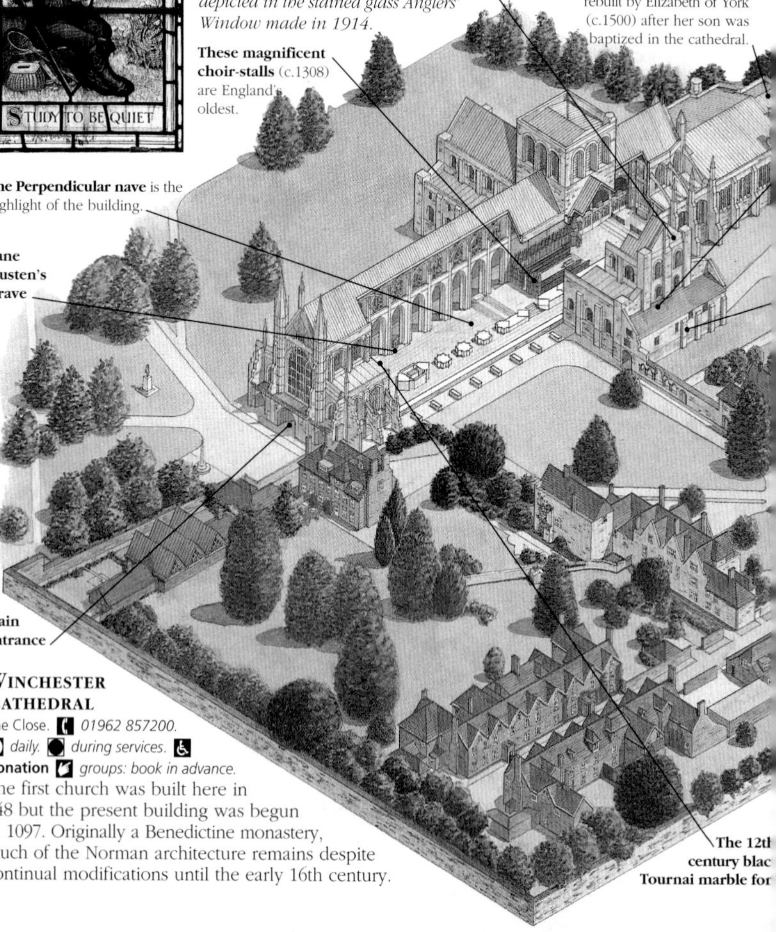

ecclesiastical centre for many
centuries. **Wolvesey Castle**
(built around 1110) was the
home of the **cathedral's**
bishops after the Conquest.
The **Hospital of St Cross** is
an almshouse built in 1446.

*Author Izaac Walton (1593–1683) is
depicted in the stained glass Anglers'
Window made in 1914.*

**These magnificent
choir-stalls** (c.1308)
are England's
oldest.

The Perpendicular nave is the
highlight of the building.

**Jane
Austen's
grave**

**Main
entrance**

The Lady Chapel was
rebuilt by Elizabeth of York
(c.1500) after her son was
baptized in the cathedral.

WINCHESTER
CATHEDRAL

The Close. 📞 *01962 857200.*
🔵 *daily.* 🔴 *during services.* ♿
Donation 📷 *groups: book in advance.*
The first church was built here in
648 but the present building was begun
in 1097. Originally a Benedictine monastery,
much of the Norman architecture remains despite
continual modifications until the early 16th century.

The 12th
century black
Tournai marble for

Weary strangers may claim the "Wayfarer's Dole" a horn (cup) of ale and bread, given out since medieval times.

Great Hall & Visitor Centre Castle Ave. 01962 846476. daily. 25, 26 Dec.

Westgate Museum High St. 01962 848269. Feb, Mar: Tue–Sun; Apr–Oct: Mon–Sun.

Hospital of St Cross St Cross Rd. 01962 851375. Nov–Mar: 10:30am–3:30pm Mon–Sat; Apr–Oct: 9:30am–5pm Mon–Sat. Good Fri, 25 Dec.

The Library has over 4,000 books. This "B" from Psalm 1 is found in the Winchester Bible, an exquisite work of 12th-century illumination.

The Norman chapter house ceased to be used in 1580. Only the Norman arches survive.

Prior's Hall

The Close originally contained the domestic buildings for the monks of the Priory of St Swithun – the name before it became Winchester Cathedral. Most of the buildings, such as the refectory and cloisters, were destroyed during the Dissolution of the Monasteries *(see p50)*.

Chichester ❼

West Sussex. 26,000. 29A South St (01243 775888). Wed, Sat. www.sussexlive.co.uk

Tʜɪs ᴡᴏɴᴅᴇʀꜰᴜʟʟʏ preserved market town, with an elaborate early 16th-century market cross at its centre, is dominated by its **cathedral**, consecrated in 1108. The exterior is a lovely mix of greenish limestone and Caen stone and its graceful spire, said to be the only English cathedral spire visible from the sea, dominates the town. The cathedral still contains much of interest, including a unique detached bell tower dating from 1436.

There are two carved stone panels in the choir, dating from 1140. Modern works include paintings by Graham Sutherland (1903–80), and a stained-glass window by Marc Chagall (1887–1985).

Environs: Just west at Bosham is the Saxon **Holy Trinity Church**, known to have been used by King Canute *(see p46)*. Myth has it that this was where Canute failed to stop the incoming tide and so proved to his courtiers that his powers had limits. The church appears in the *Bayeux Tapestry*, held in France, because Harold heard mass here in 1064 before he was shipwrecked off Normandy and then rescued by William the Conqueror *(see p47)*.

Fishbourne Roman Palace *(see pp44–5)*, further west, is the largest Roman villa in Britain. It covers 3 ha (7 acres) and was discovered in 1960 by a workman digging for drains. Constructed from

Chagall's stained glass window (1978), Chichester Cathedral

AD 75, it had over 100 rooms, but was destroyed by fire in 285. The north wing has some of the finest mosaics in Britain, including one of Cupid.

To the north is the 18th-century **Goodwood House**. Its magnificent art collection features works by Canaletto (1697–1768) and Stubbs (1724–1806). This impressive house, home to the Earl of March, has a racecourse on the Downs.

Chichester Cathedral West St. 01243 782595. daily. during services.

Fishbourne Roman Palace Fishbourne. 01243 785859. mid-Feb–mid-Dec: daily; mid-Dec–mid-Feb (cafeteria closed): Sat, Sun.

Goodwood House Goodwood. 01243 755048. 01243 755040. Apr–Sep: Sun, Mon; Aug: Sun–Thu (pm). special events.

WILLIAM WALKER

At the beginning of the 20th century, the cathedral's east end seemed certain to collapse unless its foundations were underpinned. But because the water table lies only just below the surface, the work had to be done under water. From 1906 to 1911, Walker, a deep-sea diver, worked six hours a day laying sacks of cement beneath the unsteady walls, until the building was safe.

William Walker in his diving suit

The dominating position of Arundel Castle, West Sussex

Arundel Castle ⑧

Arundel, West Sussex. **C** *01903 883136.* ⊒ *Arundel.* ◯ *Apr–Oct: Sun–Fri.* ◗ *Good Fri.* 🅿 ⬛ *by arrangement.* ▯ ▮▮ ⬛
Ⓦ www.arundelcastle.org

Dominating the small riverside town below, this vast, grey hill-top castle, surrounded by castellated walls, was first built by the Normans.

During the 16th century it was acquired by the powerful Dukes of Norfolk, the country's senior Roman Catholic family, whose descendants still live here. They rebuilt it after the original was virtually destroyed by Parliamentarians in 1643 (*see p52*), and restored it again in the 19th century.

In the castle grounds is the parish church of **St Nicholas**. The small Catholic Fitzalan chapel (c.1380) was built into its east end by the castle's first owners, the Fitzalans, and can only be entered from the grounds.

Petworth House ⑨

(NT) Petworth, West Sussex.
C *01798 342207.* ⊒ *Pulborough then bus.* **House** ◯ *Apr–Oct: Sat–Wed & Good Fri; Fri (Jul & Aug only). Closed end Jun for concerts.* **Park** ◯ *daily.* 🅿 🅰 *limited.* ▮▮ ⬛

This late 17th-century house was immortalized in a series of famous views by the painter JMW Turner (*see p93*). Some of his best paintings are on display here and are part of Petworth's outstanding art

collection which also includes works by Titian (1488–1576), Van Dyck (1599–1641) and Gainsborough (*see p149*). Also extremely well represented is ancient Roman and Greek sculpture, such as the 4th-century BC *Leconfield Aphrodite,* widely thought to be by Praxiteles.

The Carved Room is decorated with intricately carved wood panels of birds, flowers and musical instruments, by Grinling Gibbons (1648–1721).

The large deer park includes some of the earliest work of Capability Brown (*see p23*).

The Restoration clock on the Tudor Guildhall, Guildford

Guildford ⑩

Surrey. 🅰 *63,000.* ⊒ 🚌 🚋 **i** *14 Tunsgate (01483 444333).* 🅰 *Fri, Sat.*

The county town of Surrey, settled since Saxon times, incorporates the remains of a small Norman **castle**. The attractive High Street is lined

with buildings of the Tudor period, such as the impressive **Guildhall**. But it is the huge modern red-brick cathedral, completed in 1954, that dominates the town's skyline.

Environs: Guildford stands on the end of the North Downs, a range of chalk hills which are popular for walking (*see p33*). The area also has two famous beauty spots: **Leith Hill** – the highest point in southeast England – and **Box Hill**. The view from the latter is well worth the short, gentle climb from West Humble.

Just to the south of the town is the perfect red brickwork of **Clandon Park**. This 18th-century house has a sumptuous interior, especially the Marble Hall – one of the grandest English interiors of the period. It has an intricate Baroque ceiling, and the hall's side lamps are supported by black ivory forearms jutting from the wall, which represent the Park's West Indian servants.

Southwest is Chawton, where **Jane Austen's House** (*see p148*) is located. This small red-brick house is where she wrote most of her gentle, witty comedies of middle-class manners in Georgian England, such as *Pride and Prejudice*.

🏛 **Clandon Park**
West Clandon, Surrey. **C** *01483 222482.* ◯ *Apr–Oct: Tue–Thu, Sun; Good Fri & public hols.* ◗ *Nov–Mar.* 🅿 🅰 *limited.* ▮▮ ⬛
🏛 **Jane Austen's House**
Alton, Hants. **C** *01420 83262.* ◯ *Jan–Feb: Sat, Sun; Mar–Dec: daily.* ◗ *25, 26 Dec.* 🅿 🅰 *limited.* ▮▮ ⬛

Hampton Court ⑪

East Molesey, Surrey. 📞 020-8781 9500. 🚆 Hampton Court. 🕐 daily. ⬤ 24–26 Dec. 🈺 ♿ ✔ 🍴 📷

THE POWERFUL chief minister and Archbishop of York to Henry VIII *(see p51)*, Cardinal Wolsey, leased a small manor house in 1514 and transformed it into a magnificent country residence. In 1528, to retain royal favour, Wolsey gave it to the king. After the royal takeover, Hampton Court was extended twice, first by Henry himself and then in the 1690s by William and Mary, who used Christopher Wren *(see p116)* as the architect. From the outside the palace is a harmonious blend of Tudor and English Baroque, inside there is a striking contrast between Wren's Classical royal rooms, which include the King's

Ceiling decoration, Hampton Court

Apartments, and Tudor architecture, such as the Great Hall. Many of the state apartments are decorated with furniture, paintings and tapestries from the Royal Collection *(see p223)*. Also from this period are the restored Baroque gardens with their radiating avenues of majestic limes, collections of rare and exotic plants and formal plant beds.

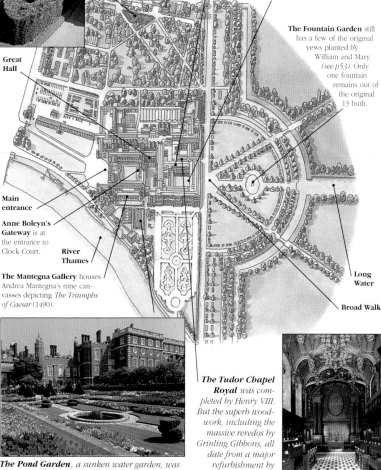

The Baroque maze *is one of the garden's most famous features; visitors often become lost in it.*

The Queen's Apartments, including the Presence Chamber and Bedchamber, are arranged around the the north and east sides of Fountain Court.

Fountain Court

The Fountain Garden still has a few of the original yews planted by William and Mary *(see p53)*. Only one fountain remains out of the original 13 built.

Great Hall

Main entrance

Anne Boleyn's Gateway is at the entrance to Clock Court.

River Thames

The Mantegna Gallery houses Andrea Mantegna's nine canvasses depicting *The Triumphs of Caesar* (1490).

Long Water

Broad Walk

The Tudor Chapel Royal *was completed by Henry VIII. But the superb woodwork, including the massive reredos by Grinling Gibbons, all date from a major refurbishment by Queen Anne (c.1711).*

The Pond Garden, *a sunken water garden, was part of Henry VIII's elaborate designs. The small pond in the middle contains a single-jet fountain.*

Steyning ⑫

West Sussex. ⚐ 5,000 🚉 ℹ️ *9 The Causeway, Horsham (01403 211661).*

THIS LOVELY little town in the lee of the Downs is packed with timber-framed houses from the Tudor period and earlier, with some built of flint and others in sandstone.

In Saxon times, Steyning was an important port and ship-building centre on the River Adur: King Ethelwulf, father of King Alfred *(see p47)*, was buried here in 858; his body was later moved to Winchester. The *Domesday Book (see p48)* records that Steyning had 123 houses, making it one of the largest towns in the south. The 12th-century church is spacious and splendid, evidence of the area's ancient prosperity: the tower, of chequered stone and flint, was added around 1600.

In the 14th century the river silted up and changed course away from the town, putting an end to its days as a port. Later it became an important coaching stop on the south coast road: the **Chequer Inn** recalls this prosperous period, with its unusual 18th-century flint and stone façade.

ENVIRONS: The remains of a **Norman castle** can be visited at Bramber, west of Steyning. This small, pretty village also contains the timber-framed **St Mary's House** (1470). It has fine panelled rooms, including the Elizabethan Painted Room, and one of the oldest trees in the country, a *Ginkgo biloba*.

Chanctonbury Ring and **Cissbury Ring**, on the hills west of Steyning, were Iron Age forts and the latter has the remains of a Neolithic flint mine. Worthing is the resort where Oscar Wilde (1854–1900) wrote *The Importance of Being Earnest*.

🏠 **St Mary's House**
Bramber. 📞 *01903 816205.* ◻
Easter–Sep: Sun, Thu (pm) & public hols. 🗓 ☑ ☐ ☐

Street-by-Street: Brighton ⑬

A stick of Brighton rock

AS THE NEAREST south coast resort to London, Brighton is perennially popular, but has always been more refined than its boisterous rivals further east, such as Margate *(see p169)* and Southend. The spirit of the Prince Regent *(see p165)* lives on, not only in the magnificence of his Royal Pavilion, but in the town's reputation as a venue for adulterous weekends in discreet hotels. Brighton has always attracted actors and artists – Laurence Olivier made his final home here.

KING'S ROAD

BLACK LION

Old Ship Hotel
Built in 1559, it was later bought by Nicholas Tettersells, with the money given to him by Charles II as a reward for taking him to France during the Civil War (see p52).

GRAND JUNCTION ROAD

★ **Palace Pier**
Built in 1899, this typical late-Victorian pier now caters for today's visitors with amusement arcades.

KEY

– – – Suggested route

STAR SIGHTS

★ **Palace Pier**

★ **Royal Pavilion**

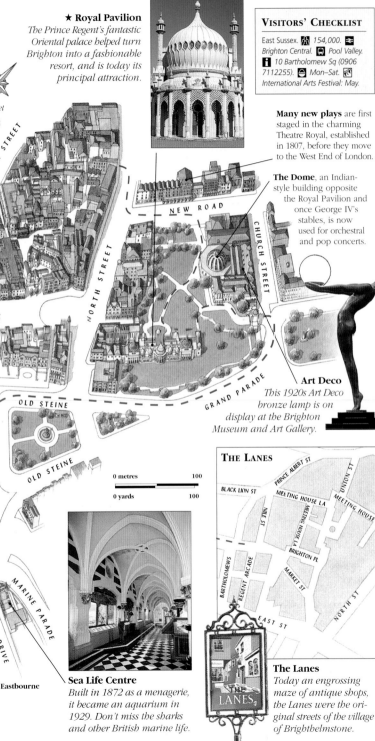

★ Royal Pavilion
The Prince Regent's fantastic Oriental palace helped turn Brighton into a fashionable resort, and is today its principal attraction.

VISITORS' CHECKLIST

East Sussex. 🏠 154,000. 🚉
Brighton Central. 🚌 Pool Valley.
🛈 10 Bartholomew Sq (0906
7112255). 🛍 Mon–Sat. 🎭
International Arts Festival: May.

Many new plays are first staged in the charming Theatre Royal, established in 1807, before they move to the West End of London.

The Dome, an Indian-style building opposite the Royal Pavilion and once George IV's stables, is now used for orchestral and pop concerts.

Art Deco
This 1920s Art Deco bronze lamp is on display at the Brighton Museum and Art Gallery.

THE LANES

Sea Life Centre
Built in 1872 as a menagerie, it became an aquarium in 1929. Don't miss the sharks and other British marine life.

The Lanes
Today an engrossing maze of antique shops, the Lanes were the original streets of the village of Brighthelmstone.

Brighton: Royal Pavilion

As SEA BATHING became fashionable in the mid-18th century, Brighton was transformed into England's first seaside resort. Its gaiety soon appealed to the rakish Prince of Wales, who became George IV in 1820. When, in 1785, he secretly married Mrs Fitzherbert, it was here that they conducted their liaison. He moved to a farmhouse near the shore and had it enlarged by Henry Holland *(see p24)*. As his parties grew more lavish, George needed a suitably extravagant setting for them, and in 1815 he employed John Nash *(see p107)* to transform the house into a lavish Oriental palace. Completed in 1822, the exterior has remained largely unaltered. Queen Victoria sold the Pavilion to the town of Brighton in 1850.

Central Dome
Nash adopted what he called the Hindu Style, as in this delicate tracery on one of the imposing turban domes.

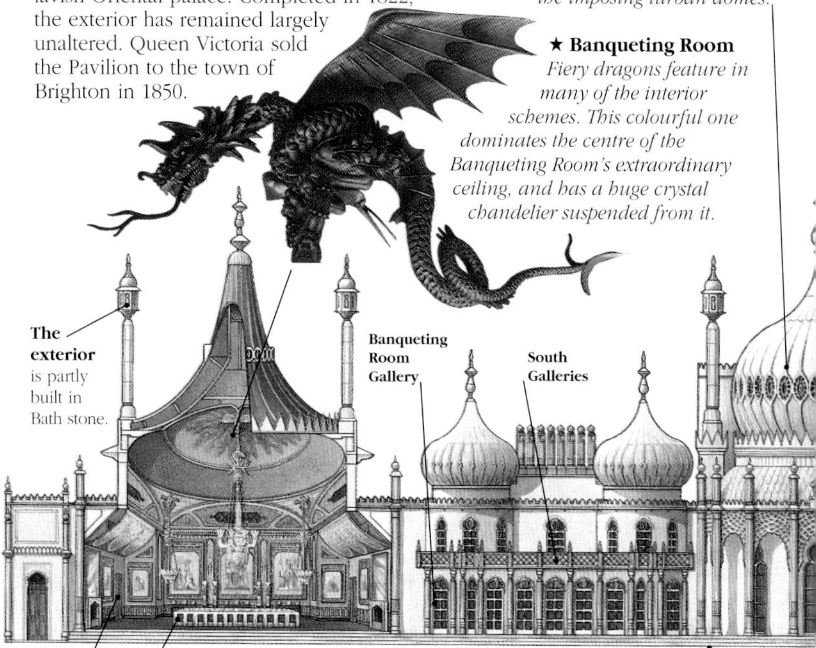

★ **Banqueting Room**
Fiery dragons feature in many of the interior schemes. This colourful one dominates the centre of the Banqueting Room's extraordinary ceiling, and has a huge crystal chandelier suspended from it.

The exterior is partly built in Bath stone.

Banqueting Room Gallery

South Galleries

The banqueting table, which seats 24 people, is laid as for a splendid feast.

The eastern façade of the Pavilion

Standard Lamps
More dragons, along with dolphins and lotus flowers, figure on the Banqueting Room's eight original standard lamps, made of porcelain, ormolu and gilded wood.

★ **Great Kitchen**
The Prince's epic banquets required a kitchen of huge proportions. The vast ranges and long shelves of gleaming copper pans were used by famous chefs of the day.

STAR SIGHTS

★ **Banqueting Room**

★ **Great Kitchen**

◁ Front façade of George IV's extravagant Royal Pavilion, Brighton

Saloon
The gilded wall decorations were designed on Indian themes, but the Chinese wallpaper harks back to an earlier decorative scheme. The long couch mimics an Egyptian river boat.

Long Gallery
Mandarin figures, which can nod their heads, line the pink and blue walls of this 49 m (162 ft) gallery.

Queen Victoria's Bedroom
This reproduction four-poster is on display in the upper floor apartments that were used by Queen Victoria (see p56).

The Music Room, with its crimson and gold murals, was where a 70-piece orchestra played to the Prince's guests.

The domes are made of cast iron.

Music Room Gallery

Bow Rooms

Exit · Entrance · Octagon Hall · Stairs to upper floor · King's Apartments · Shop · Great Kitchen · Banqueting Room · Banqueting Room Gallery · Saloon · Long Gallery · Music Room Gallery · Music Room

PLAN OF THE ROYAL PAVILION
Both Holland and Nash made additions and changes to the original farmhouse. The upper floor contains bedrooms, such as the Bow Rooms, which George's brothers used. The shaded areas represent the artwork above.

PRINCE OF WALES AND MRS FITZHERBERT

The Prince of Wales was only 23 when he fell in love with Maria Fitzherbert, a 29-year-old Catholic widow, and secretly married her. They lived in the farmhouse together and were the toast of Brighton society until George's official marriage took place to Caroline of Brunswick in 1795. Mrs Fitzherbert moved into a small house nearby.

Upstairs interior of Anne of Cleves House, Lewes

Lewes ⑭

East Sussex. 🏘 16,000. 🚂 ℹ️ 187
High St (01273 483448).
W www.lewes.gov.uk

T HE ANCIENT COUNTY TOWN of
Sussex was a vital strategic
site for the Saxons, because of
its high vantage point looking
out over the coastline.

William the Conqueror built
a wooden castle here in 1067
but this was soon replaced by
a large stone structure whose
remains can be visited today.

In 1264 it was the site of a
critical battle in which Simon
de Montfort and his barons
defeated Henry III (see p48),
enabling them to establish the
first English Parliament.

The Tudor **Anne of Cleves
House** is a museum of local
history, although Anne of
Cleves, Henry VIII's fourth
wife, never actually lived here.

On Bonfire Night (see p64)
lighted tar barrels are rolled
to the river and effigies of the
pope are burned instead of
the customary Guy Fawkes.
This commemorates the town's
17 Protestant martyrs burnt at
the stake by Mary I (see p51).

ENVIRONS: Nearby is the 16th-
century **Glynde Place**, a
handsome courtyard house.
It has an extensive display of
early 18th-century needlework and Derby china.

🏛 **Anne of Cleves House**
Lewes. 📞 01273 474610.
⬜ mid-Feb–9 Nov: daily; 10 Nov–
23 Dec: Tues–Sun; 28 Dec–mid-Feb:
Tues, Thu, Sat. 📷 🎫 by
arrangement. 📷
🏰 **Glynde Place**
Lewes. 📞 01273 858224. ⬜ May;
Sun; Jun, Sep: Wed, Sun; Jul; Aug:
Wed, Thu, Sun. 📷 📷 📷

Eastbourne ⑮

East Sussex. 🏘 86,000. 🚂 🚌 ℹ️
Cornfield Rd (01323 411400). 🅿️
Tue, Sat. W www.eastbourne.co.uk

T HIS VICTORIAN SEASIDE resort
is a popular place for
retirement, as well as a first-
rate centre for touring the
Downs. The South Downs
Way (see p33) begins at
Beachy Head, the spectacular
163 m (536 ft) chalk cliff just
on the outskirts of the town.
From here it is a bracing walk
to the cliff top at Birling Gap,
with views to the **Seven
Sisters**, the chalk hills that end
abruptly as they meet the sea.

ENVIRONS: To the west of
Eastbourne is **Seven Sisters
Country Park**, a 285 ha (700
acre) area of chalk cliffs and
Downland marsh. The **Park
Visitor's Centre** contains
information on the local
area, history and geology.

Just north is the pretty
village of **Alfriston**, with an
ancient market cross and a
15th-century inn, **The Star**, in
its quaint main street. Near
the church is the 14th-century
Clergy House that, in 1896,
became the first National
Trust property (see p25). To
the east is the huge prehistoric
chalk carving, the **Long Man
of Wilmington** (see p207).

ℹ️ **Park Visitor's Centre**
Exceat, Seaford. 📞 01323 870280.
⬜ Apr–Oct: daily; Nov–Mar: Sat, Sun.
● 25 Dec. ♿ 🍴 📷
🏰 **Clergy House**
(NT) Alfriston. 📞 01323 870001.
⬜ Apr–Oct: Sat–Mon, Wed, Thu;
Mar: Sat–Sun. 📷 📷

The lighthouse (1902) at the foot of Beachy Head, Eastbourne

The meandering River Cuckmere flowing through the South Downs to the beach at Cuckmere Haven

The Downs ⑯

East Sussex. ⮀ ☒ *Eastbourne.*
🛈 *Cornfield Rd, Eastbourne (01323 411400).*

T HE NORTH and South
Downs are parallel chalk
ridges that run from east to
west all the way across Kent,
Sussex and Surrey, separated
by the lower-lying and fertile
Kent and Sussex Weald.

The smooth Downland hills
are covered with springy turf,
kept short by grazing sheep,
making an ideal surface for
walkers. The hill above the
precipitous **Devil's Dyke**,
just north of Brighton, offers
spectacular views for miles
across the Downs. The legend
is that the Devil cut the gorge
to let in the sea and flood the
countryside, but was foiled
by divine intervention. The
River Cuckmere runs through
one of the most picturesque
parts of the South Downs.

Located at the highest point of
the Downs is **Uppark House**.
This neat square building has
been meticulously restored to
its mid-18th-century appearance after a fire in 1989.

🏛 Uppark House

(NT) Petersfield, West Sussex.
📞 *01730 825857.* ◯ *Apr–Oct:
Sun–Thu.* 🖼 ♿ 🍴 📷

Hastings ⑰

East Sussex. 🏠 *83,000.* ⮀ 🚌
🛈 *Queens Square , Priory
Meadow (01424 781111).*
🌐 *www.hastings.gov.uk*

T HIS FASCINATING seaside
town was one of the first
Cinque Ports *(see p168)* and
is still a thriving fishing port.
The town is characterized by
the unique tall wooden "net
shops" on the beach, where
for hundreds of years fishermen have stored their nets. In

the 19th century, the area to
the west of the Old Town was
built up as a seaside resort,
which left the narrow,
characterful streets of the old

**The wooden net shops, on
Hastings' shingle beach**

fishermen's quarter intact.
There are two cliff railways
and smugglers' caves
displaying where contraband
used to be stored *(see p266).*

ENVIRONS: Seven miles (11
km) from Hastings is Battle.
The centre square of this small
town is dominated by the
gatehouse of **Battle Abbey**.
William the Conqueror built
this on the site of his great
victory, reputedly placing the
high altar where Harold fell,
But the abbey was destroyed
in the Dissolution *(see p50).*
There is an evocative walk
around the actual battlefield.

⋔ Battle Abbey

High St, Battle. 📞 *01424 773792.*
◯ *Easter/Apr-Sep: 10am-6pm; Oct:
10am-5pm; Nov-Mar/Easter: 10am-4pm
daily.* ⬤ *1 Jan, 24–26 Dec.* 🖼 ♿

BATTLE OF HASTINGS

In 1066, William the Conqueror's *(see p47)* invading army
from Normandy landed on the south coast, aiming to take
Winchester and London. Hearing that King Harold and his
army were camped just inland from Hastings, William con-
fronted them. He won the battle after Harold was mortally
wounded by an
arrow in his eye. This
last successful in-
vasion of England is
depicted on the
Bayeux Tapestry in
Normandy, France.

**King Harold's death,
*Bayeux Tapestry***

The fairy-tale 14th-century Bodiam Castle surrounded by its moat

Bodiam Castle ⑱

(NT) Nr Robertsbridge, East Sussex.
☎ *01580 830436.* 🚆 *Robertsbridge
then taxi.* ⬜ *mid-Feb–Oct: daily; Nov–
mid-Feb: Sat–Sun.* ⬤ *24–26 Dec.*
🅿️ 🚻 *limited.* ⬜ 🚽

SURROUNDED BY its wide,
glistening moat, this late
14th-century castle is one of
the most romantic in England.
It was originally built as a
defence against an anticipated
invasion by the French. The
attack never came but the
castle saw action during the
Civil War *(see pp52–3)* when it
was damaged in an assault by
Parliamentary soldiers. They
removed the roof to reduce
its use as a base for Charles I.
It has been uninhabited
since, but its grey stone has
proved indestructible. With the
exception of the roof, it was
restored in 1919 by Lord
Curzon who gave it to the
nation. The round towers offer
fine views of the countryside.

ENVIRONS: To the east is **Great
Dixter**, a 15th-century manor
house restored by Sir Edwin
Lutyens *(see pp24–5)* in 1910
for the Lloyd family. The writer
Christopher Lloyd created a
magnificent garden with an
Edwardian blend of terraces
and borders.

🏛 Great Dixter
Northiam, Rye. ☎ *01797 252878.*
⬜ *Apr–Oct: 2–5:30pm Tue–Sun &
public hols.* 🅿️ 🚽

Rye ⑲

See pp170–71.

Romney Marsh ⑳

Kent. 🚆 *Ashford.* 🚌 *Ashford, Hythe.*
ℹ️ *Magpies Church Approach, New
Romney (01797 364044).*

UNTIL ROMAN TIMES Romney
Marsh and its southern
neighbour Walland Marsh
were entirely covered by the
sea at high tide. The Romans
drained the Romney section,
and Walland Marsh was
gradually reclaimed during
the Middle Ages. Together they
formed a large area of fertile
land, particularly suitable for
the bulky Romney Marsh
sheep bred for the quality
and quantity of their wool.
Dungeness, a desolate and
lonely spot at the southeastern
tip of the area, is dominated
by a lighthouse and two
nuclear power stations that

COASTAL DEFENCE AND
THE CINQUE PORTS

Before the Norman Conquest *(see pp46–7)*,
national government was weak and, with
threats from Europe, it was important for
Saxon kings to keep on good terms with
the Channel ports. So, in return for keeping
the royal fleet supplied with ships and
men, five ports – Hastings, Romney, Hythe,
Sandwich and Dover – were granted the
right to levy taxes; others were added
later. "Cinque" came from the old French
word for five. The privileges were revoked
during the 17th century. In 1803, in
response to the growing threat from France,
74 fixed defences were built along the coast.
Only 24 of these Martello towers still exist.

**The cliff-top position of
Dover Castle**

**A Martello tower,
built as part of the
Channel's defences**

break up the skyline. It is also the southern terminus of the popular **Romney, Hythe and Dymchurch Light Railway** which was opened in 1927. During the summer this takes passengers 14 miles (23 km) up the coast to Hythe on trains a third the conventional size.

The northern edge of the marsh is crossed by the Royal Military Canal, built to serve both as a defence and supply line in 1804, when it was feared Napoleon was planning an invasion (*see p55*).

Dover ㉑

Kent. 🏠 30,000. ✈ 🚌 🚇
ℹ Townwall St (01304 205108).
🏪 Sat. 🆆 www.dover.gov.uk

I TS PROXIMITY to the European mainland makes Dover, with its neighbour Folkestone, now the terminal for the Channel Tunnel (*see p632*), the leading port for cross-Channel travel. Its famous white cliffs exert a strong pull on returning travellers.

Dover's strategic position and large natural harbour mean the town has always had an important role to play in the nation's defences.

Built on the original site of an ancient Saxon fortification, **Dover Castle**, superbly positioned on top of the high cliffs, has helped defend the town from 1198, when Henry II first built the keep, right up to World War II, when it was used as the command post for the Dunkirk evacuation. Exhibits in the castle and in the labyrinth of tunnels beneath made by prisoners in the Napoleonic Wars (*see p55*) cover all these periods.

ENVIRONS: One of the most significant sites in England's early history is the ruin of **Richborough Roman Fort**. Now a large grassy site two miles (3 km) inland, this was where, in AD 43, Claudius's Roman invaders (*see p44*) made their first landing. For hundreds of years afterwards, Rutupiae, as it was known, was one of the most important ports of entry and military bases in the country.

♟ **Dover Castle**
Castle Hill. 📞 01304 211067.
◯ daily. ● 1 Jan, 24–26 Dec. 🏛
🏰 **Richborough Roman Fort**
Richborough. 📞 01304 612013.
◯ Oct–Mar: Sat–Sun; Apr–Nov: daily.
● 24–26 Dec.

Margate ㉒

Kent. 🏠 39,000. 🚌 🚇
ℹ 22 High St (01843 220241).

T RADITIONALLY the most boisterous of the three seaside resorts on the Isle of Thanet (the other two are Ramsgate and Broadstairs), Margate has for a long time been a popular destination for day trippers from London, travelling in Victorian times by steam boat and later by train. The town has theme parks and fairground rides.

ENVIRONS: Just south is a 19th-century gentleman's residence, **Quex House,** which has two unusual towers in its grounds. The adjoining museum has a fine collection of African and Oriental art, as well as unique dioramas of tropical wildlife.

Visitors relaxing on Margate's popular sandy beach

To the west is a Saxon church, built within the remains of the bleak Roman coastal fort of **Reculver**. Dramatic twin towers, known as the Two Sisters, were added to the church in the 12th century – these were luckily saved from destruction in 1809 because they were a useful navigational aid for shipping. The church now stands at the centre of a very pleasant, if rather windy, 37 ha (91 acre) camp site.

🏛 **Quex House**
Birchington. 📞 01843 842168.
◯ Apr–Oct: Tue–Thu, Sun & public holidays (Museum only: Nov–Dec, Mar: Sun). 🏛 🔲 🏛 for groups. 🍴
🏰 **Reculver Fort**
Reculver. 📞 01227 361911 (Herne Bay Tourist Information). ◯ daily.

A drainage dyke running through the fertile plains of Romney Marsh

Street-by-Street: Rye ⑲

THIS ANCIENT and delightful fortified town was added to the original Cinque ports *(see p168)* in the 11th century. A huge storm in 1287 diverted the River Rother so that it met the sea at Rye, and for more than 300 years it was one of the most important channel ports. However,

The Mermaid Inn sign

in the 16th century the harbour began to silt up and the town is now 2 miles (3 km) inland. Rye was frequently attacked by the French, culminating in 1377 when it was burnt to the ground.

★ Mermaid Street
This delightful cobbled street, its huddled houses jutting out at unlikely angles, has hardly altered since it was rebuilt in the 14th century.

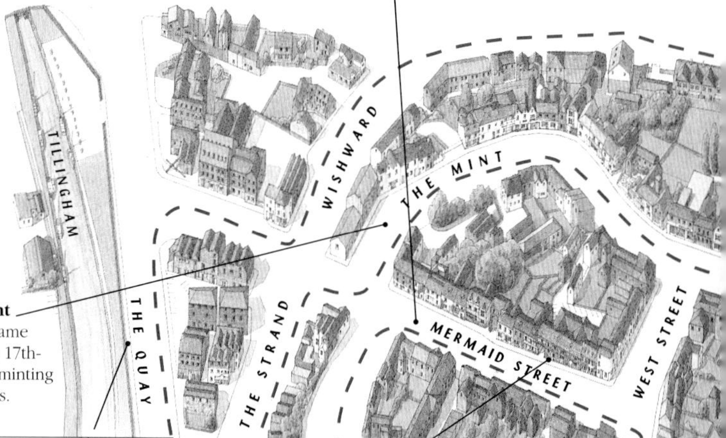

The Mint
got its name from the 17th-century minting of tokens.

The Mermaid Inn, founded in the 11th century, is Rye's largest medieval building. In the 1750s it was the headquarters of a notorious and bloodthirsty smuggling gang called the Hawkhursts.

View over the River Tillingham

Strand Quay
The brick and timber warehouses survive from the prosperous days when Rye was a thriving port.

Lamb House
This fine Georgian house was built in 1722. George I stayed here when stranded in a storm, and author Henry James (1843–1916) lived here.

STAR SIGHTS

★ **Mermaid Street**

★ **Ypres Tower**

St Mary's Church
The 16th-century turret contains the oldest working clock in England. The face was added in 1761.

↑ Hastings and
railway station

QUE PORT STREET

Land Gate
Built in the 14th century this is the only survivor of the old fortified town's four gates.

TOWER STREET
CONDUIT HILL
HIGH STREET
LION STREET
EAST STREET
MARKET STREET
EAST CLIFF

The 16th-century Flushing Inn

This cistern was built in 1735; horse-drawn machinery was used to raise water to the highest part of the town.

Gun Garden,
Ypres Tower

★ **Ypres Tower**
Built as a fort in 1250, it was turned into a house in 1430. It has since been a prison and mortuary.

KEY

– – – Suggested route

0 metres	50
0 yards	50

ENVIRONS: Just 2 miles (3 km) to the south of Rye is the small town of **Winchelsea**. At the behest of Edward I, it was moved to its present position in 1288, when most of the old town on lower land to the southeast, was drowned by the same storm that diverted the River Rother in 1287.

Winchelsea is probably Britain's first coherently planned new town. Although not all of it was built as originally planned, its rectangular grid survives today, as does the **Church of St Thomas Becket** (begun c.1300) at its centre. Several raids during the 14th century by the French damaged the church and burned down scores of houses. The church has three tombs that probably predate it, having been rescued from the old town before it was submerged. There are also two well-preserved medieval tombs in the chantry. The three windows (1928–33) in the Lady Chapel were designed by Douglas Strachan as a memorial to those who died in World War I. Just beyond the edges of present-day Winchelsea are the remains of three of the original gates – showing just how big a town was first envisaged. The beach below is one of the finest on the southeast coast.

Camber Sands, to the east of the mouth of the Rother, is another excellent beach. Once used by fishermen it is now popular with swimmers and edged with seaside bungalows and a holiday camp.

The ruins of **Camber Castle** are west of the sands, between Rye and Winchelsea. This was one of the forts built along this coast by Henry VIII when he feared an attack by the French that never came. When it was first built it was right on the edge of the sea but it was abandoned in 1642 when it became stranded inland as the river silted up.

🏰 **Camber Castle**
Camber, Rye. ☐ for guided tours only: contact Rye tourist office.

Jesus on Christ Church Gate, Canterbury Cathedral

Canterbury ㉓

Kent. ▓ 50,000. ₪ 🖳 🛈 34 St Margaret's St (01227 766567). 🗓 Wed, Fri.

Iᴛs ᴘosɪᴛɪoɴ on the London to Dover route meant Canterbury was an important Roman town even before the arrival of St Augustine in 597, sent by the pope to convert the Anglo-Saxons to Christianity. The town rose in importance, soon becoming the centre of the Christian Church in England.

With the building of the **cathedral** and the martyrdom of Thomas Becket *(see p48)*, Canterbury's future as a religious centre was assured.

Adjacent to the ruins of **St Augustine's Abbey**, destroyed in the Dissolution *(see p50)*, is **St Martin's Church**, the oldest in England. This was where St Augustine first worshipped and it has impressive Norman and Saxon work.

West Gate Museum, with its round towers, is an imposing medieval gatehouse. It was built in 1381 and contains a display of arms and armoury.

The Poor Priests' Hospital, founded in the 12th century, now houses the **Canterbury Heritage Museum**.

🏛 **West Gate Museum**
St Peter's St. ☏ 01227 452747.
◻ Mon–Sat. ● 23 Dec–1 Jan, Good Fri. 🈺 🛈

🏛 **Canterbury Heritage Museum**
Stour St. ☏ 01227 452747.
◻ Jun–Oct: daily; Nov–May: Mon–Sat.
● Christmas wk, Good Fri. 🈺 🛈

Canterbury Cathedral

Tᴏ ᴍᴀᴛᴄʜ ᴄᴀɴᴛᴇʀʙᴜʀʏ's growing ecclesiastical rank as a major centre of Christianity, the first Norman archbishop, Lanfranc, ordered a new cathedral to be built on the ruins of the Anglo-Saxon cathedral in 1070. It was enlarged and rebuilt many times and as a result embraces examples of all styles of medieval architecture. The most poignant moment in its history came in 1170 when Thomas Becket was murdered here *(see p48)*. Four years after his death a fire devastated the cathedral and Trinity Chapel was built to house Becket's remains. The shrine quickly became an important religious site and until the Dissolution *(see p50)* the cathedral was one of Christendom's chief places of pilgrimage.

The nave at 100 m (328 ft) makes Canterbury Europe's longest medieval church.

The South West Porch (1426) may have been built to commemorate the victory at Agincourt *(see p49)*.

Main entrance

★ **Medieval Stained Glass**
This depiction of the 1,000-year-old Methuselah is a detail from the southwest transept window.

GEOFFREY CHAUCER

Considered to be the first great English poet, Geoffrey Chaucer (c.1345–1400), a customs official by profession, wrote a rumbustious and witty account of a group of pilgrims travelling from London to Becket's shrine in 1387 in the *Canterbury Tales*. The pilgrims represent a cross-section of 14th-century English society and the tales remain one of the greatest and most entertaining works of early English literature.

Wife of Bath, *Canterbury Tales*

Bell Harry Tower
The central tower, dominating the skyline, was built in 1496 to house a bell donated by Henry of Eastry 100 years before. The fan vaulting is a superb example of the late Perpendicular style.

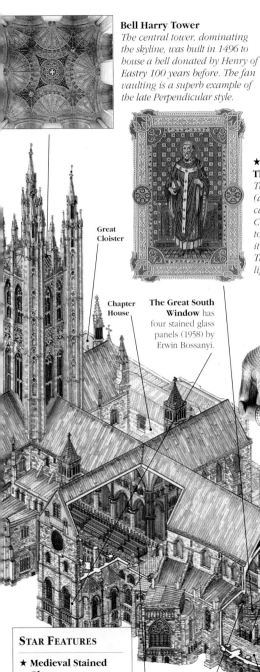

★ Site of the Shrine of St Thomas Becket
This Victorian illustration (anon) portrays Becket's canonization. The Trinity Chapel was built to house his tomb which stood here until it was destroyed in 1538. The spot is now marked by a lighted candle.

Great Cloister

Chapter House

The Great South Window has four stained glass panels (1958) by Erwin Bossanyi.

★ Black Prince's Tomb
This copper effigy is on the tomb of Edward III's son, who died in 1376.

STAR FEATURES

★ Medieval Stained Glass

★ Site of the Shrine of St Thomas Becket

★ Black Prince's Tomb

St Augustine's Chair

The choir, completed in 1184, is one of the longest in England.

Trinity Chapel

The circular Corona Chapel

The keep of Rochester Castle, dominating Rochester and the Medway Valley

Leeds Castle ㉔

Maidstone, Kent. 📞 01622 765400.
🚋 Bearsted then bus. ◯ daily.
⬤ for concerts & 25 Dec. 🎫 ♿ 🚻
🚻 🅿 🆆 www.leeds-castle.co.uk

Sᴜʀʀᴏᴜɴᴅᴇᴅ ʙʏ ᴀ ʟᴀᴋᴇ that reflects the warm buff stone of its crenellated turrets, Leeds is often considered to be the most beautiful castle in England. Begun in the early 12th century, when it was continuously inhabited and its present appearance is a result of centuries of rebuilding and extensions, most recently in the 1930s. Leeds has royal connections going back to 1278, when it was given to Edward I by a courtier seeking favour.

Henry VIII loved the castle and visited it often, escaping from the plague in London. It contains a life-sized bust of Henry from the late 16th century. Leeds passed out of royal ownership when Edward VI gave it to Sir Anthony St Leger in 1552 as a reward for helping to pacify the Irish.

Rochester ㉕

Kent. 🏠 145,000. 🚋 🅿
ℹ️ 95 High Street (01634 843666).

Cʟᴜsᴛᴇʀᴇᴅ ᴀᴛ ᴛʜᴇ ᴍᴏᴜᴛʜ of the River Medway are the towns of Rochester, Chatham and Gillingham, all rich in naval history, but none more

so than Rochester, which occupied a strategic site on the London to Dover road.

England's tallest Norman keep is at **Rochester Castle,** worth climbing for the views over the Medway. The town's medieval history is still visible, with the original city walls – which followed the lines of the Roman fortifications – on view in the High Street, and some well-preserved wall paintings in the **cathedral**, built in 1088.

Eɴᴠɪʀᴏɴs: In Chatham, the **Historic Dockyard** is now a museum of shipbuilding and nautical crafts. **Fort Amherst** nearby was built in 1756 to protect the dockyard and river entrance from attack, and has 1,800 m (5,570 ft) of tunnels to explore that were hewn by Napoleonic prisoners of war.

⚓ Rochester Castle
The Esplanade. 📞 01634 402276.
◯ daily. ⬤ 1 Jan, 24–27, 31 Dec.
🎫 ♿ grounds only. 🚻

🏛 World Naval Base
Dock Rd, Chatham. 📞 01634
823800. ◯ April–Oct: daily; Nov,
Feb–Mar: Wed, Sat, Sun. 🎫 ♿ 📷

⋒ Fort Amherst
Dock Rd, Chatham. 📞 01634
847747. ◯ May–Sep: daily; Oct–Apr:
Wed–Sun ⬤ 24, 25 Dec, 1 Jan. 🎫

Knole ㉖

(NT) Sevenoaks, Kent. 📞 01732
462100. 🚋 Sevenoaks then taxi.
House ◯ Apr–Oct: Wed–Sun (pm),
Good Fri & public hols. **Park** ◯
daily. 🎫 ♿ limited. 🚻 by
arrangement. 🚻 🚻

Tʜɪs ʜᴜɢᴇ ᴛᴜᴅᴏʀ ᴍᴀɴsɪᴏɴ was built in the late 15th century, and was seized by Henry VIII from the Archbishop of Canterbury at the Dissolution (see p50). In 1566 Queen Elizabeth I gave it to her cousin Thomas Sackville. His descendants have lived here ever since, including the writer Vita Sackville-West, (1892–1962). The house is well known for its 17th-century furniture, such as the elaborate bed made for James II. The 405-ha (1,000-acre) park has lovely walks.

Eɴᴠɪʀᴏɴs: A small manor house, **Ightham Mote**, east of Knole, is one of the finest examples of English medieval architecture. Its 14th-century timber-and-stone building

A gladiator, Knole

encloses a central court and is encircled by a moat.

At **Sissinghurst Castle Garden** are gardens created by Vita Sackville-West and her husband Harold Nicolson in the 1930s.

⊞ Ightham Mote
(NT) Ivy Hatch, Sevenoaks. ☎ 01732 810378. ⃝ Apr–end-Oct: Wed–Fri, Sun, Mon & public hols. 🏵 &

❀ Sissinghurst Castle Garden
(NT) Cranbrook. ☎ 01580 710700. ⃝ Apr–mid-Oct: 1–6:30pm Tue–Fri; 10am–5:30pm Sat, Sun, Good Fri. 🏵 & limited. 🎫 🍴

Hever Castle ㉗

Edenbridge, Kent. ☎ 01732 865224. 🚆 Edenbridge. ⃝ Mar–Nov: daily; **Gardens** 11am–6pm; **Castle** noon–6pm. 🏵 & limited. 🎫 🍴 ☑ by arrangement.
W www.hevercastle.co.uk

THIS SMALL, MOATED CASTLE is famous as the 16th-century home of Anne Boleyn, the

CHARLES DICKENS

Charles Dickens (1812–70), a popular writer in his own time, is still widely read today. He was born in Portsmouth but moved to Chatham aged five. As an adult, Dickens lived in London but kept up his Kent connections, taking holidays in Broadstairs, just south of Margate – where he wrote *David Copperfield* – and spending his last years at Gad's Hill, near Rochester. The town celebrates the famous connection with an annual Dickens festival.

The façade of Chartwell, Winston Churchill's home

doomed wife of Henry VIII, executed for adultery. She lived here as a young woman and the king often visited her while staying at Leeds Castle. In 1903 Hever was bought by William Waldorf Astor, who undertook a restoration programme, building a Neo-Tudor village alongside it to accommodate guests and servants. The moat and gatehouse date from around 1270.

ENVIRONS: To the northwest of Hever is **Chartwell**, the family home of Sir Winston Churchill (*see p59*). It remains furnished as it was when he lived here. Some 140 of his paintings are on display.

⊞ Chartwell
(NT) Westerham, Kent. ⓕ 01732 866368. ⃝ Apr–Jun, Sep, Oct: Wed–Sun & public hols; Jul–Aug: Tue–Sun & public hols: 11am–5pm. 🏵 & limited. 🍴 🎫

Royal Tunbridge Wells ㉘

Kent. 🅿 45,000. 🚆 🚌 🎫 *The Old Fish Market, The Pantiles (01892 515675).* ⓢ Wed.

HELPED BY ROYAL patronage, the town became a popular spa in the 17th and 18th centuries after mineral springs were discovered in 1606. The Pantiles – the colonnaded and paved promenade – was laid out in the 1700s.

ENVIRONS: Nearby is a superb example of a medieval manor house, **Penshurst Place**. Built in the 1340s, it has an 18 m (60 ft) high Great Hall.

⊞ Penshurst Place
Tonbridge, Kent. ☎ 01892 870307. ⃝ Apr–Oct: daily; Mar: Sat, Sun: **House** noon–5:30pm; **Gardens** 10:30am–6pm; **Toy Museum** noon–5pm. 🏵 & limited. 🍴 🎫

An early 18th-century astrolabe to measure the stars, Hever Castle garden

EAST ANGLIA

NORFOLK · SUFFOLK · ESSEX · CAMBRIDGESHIRE

THE BULGE OF LAND *between the Thames Estuary and the Wash, flat but far from featureless, sits aside from the main north–south axis through Britain, and for that reason it has succeeded in maintaining and preserving its distinctive architecture, traditions and rural character in both cities and countryside.*

East Anglia's name derives from the Angles, the people from northern Germany who settled here during the 5th and 6th centuries. East Anglians have long been a breed of plain-spoken and independent people. Two prominent East Anglians – Queen Boadicea in the 1st century and Oliver Cromwell in the 17th century – were famous for their stubbornness and their refusal to bow to constituted authority. During the Civil War, East Anglia was Cromwell's most reliable source of support. The hardy people who made a difficult living hunting and fishing in the swampy fens, which were drained in the 17th century, were called the Fen Tigers. After draining, the peaty soil proved ideal for arable farming, and today East Anglia grows about a third of Britain's vegetables. The rotation of crops, heralding Britain's agricultural revolution, was perfected in Norfolk in the 18th century. Many of the region's towns and cities grew prosperous on the agricultural wealth, including Norwich. The sea also plays a prominent role in East Anglian life. Coastal towns and villages support the many fishermen who use the North Sea, rich in herring in former days but now known mainly for flat fish.

In modern times, the area has become a centre of recreational sailing, both off the coast and on the inland waterway system known as the Norfolk Broads. East Anglia is also home to one of Britain's top universities: Cambridge.

Lavender fields in full bloom in July, Heacham, Norfolk

◁ Cley windmill overlooking the sea marshes on the north Norfolk coast

Exploring East Anglia

As you move away from London, you soon reach the countryside immortalized by the painter Constable *(see p190)* and in many ways unchanged since his day, scattered with churches, windmills and medieval agricultural barns. Nature lovers will find it fruitful territory, especially North Norfolk with its bird reserves and seal colonies. Boating enthusiasts, too, are well catered for in this, Britain's driest and sunniest region. The local architecture ranges from a mix of medieval to modern. The distinctive pink-washed cottages in Suffolk, flint cottages in Norfolk and thatched roofs everywhere, are also much in evidence.

Punting on the River Cam in Cambridge

8 NORTH NORFOLK TOUR

7 SANDRINGHAM

6 KING'S LYNN

5

4 SWAFFHAM

1 PETERBOROUGH

Grantham

Leicester

3 GRIMES GRAVES

2 ELY

THETFORD

26 HUNTINGDON

25 ANGLESEY ABBEY

27 CAMBRIDGE

24 NEWMARKET

23 BURY ST EDMUNDS

Bedford, London

22 LAVENHAM

28 AUDLEY END

Bishop's Stortford

21 COGGESHALL

COLCHESTER

30 MALDON

EPPING FOREST

29

London

SOUTHEND-ON-SEA

Thames Estuary

THE WASH

FENS

Norfolk Coast Path

Peddar's Way

Pedlar's Way

KEY

🟫 Motorway

🟫 Major road

🟫 Minor road

🟫 Scenic route

▪ ▪ Scenic path

🟦 River

🌴 Viewpoint

GETTING AROUND

The region's more isolated sights can be very difficult to reach by public transport and, for a few people, car rental may be a cheaper and more efficient method of travelling around. The M11 motorway runs from London to Cambridge. The coast road from Aldeburgh to King's Lynn takes you through some of the best countryside in the area. There are frequent InterCity trains to Norwich, Ipswich and Cambridge although the local trains are more sporadic. There is an international and domestic airport at Norwich.

SEE ALSO

- **Where to Stay** pp547–9

- **Where to Eat** pp584–6

Beach huts on Wells-next-the-Sea beach, north Norfolk

SIGHTS AT A GLANCE

Aldeburgh 🟤16

Anglesey Abbey 🟤25

Audley End 🟤28

Blickling Hall 🟤9

Broads 🟤11

Bury St Edmunds 🟤23

Cambridge pp196–201 🟤27

Coggeshall 🟤21

Colchester 🟤20

Dunwich 🟤15

Ely 🟤2

Epping Forest 🟤29

Fens 🟤5

Framlingham Castle 🟤17

Great Yarmouth 🟤12

Grimes Graves 🟤3

Huntingdon 🟤26

Ipswich 🟤18

King's Lynn 🟤6

Lavenham 🟤22

Lowestoft 🟤13

Maldon 🟤30

Newmarket 🟤24

Norwich 🟤10

Peterborough 🟤1

Sandringham 🟤7

Southwold 🟤14

Swaffham 🟤4

Walks and Tours

Constable Walk 🟤19

North Norfolk Tour 🟤8

0 kilometres 10

0 miles 10

Peterborough ❶

Cambridgeshire. 🏛 *152,000*. 🚄 🚌
ℹ️ *3 Minster Precinct (01733 452336)*. 🛒 *Tue–Sat*.

Peterborough's coat of arms with a Latin inscription: Upon this Rock

Athough one of the oldest settlements in Britain, Peterborough was designated a New Town in 1967 – part of a scheme to shift people from the larger cities – and is now a mix of ancient and modern.

The city centre is dominated by the 12th-century **St Peter's Cathedral** which gave the city its name. The interior of this classic Norman building, with its vast yet simple nave, was badly damaged by Cromwell's troops *(see p52)*, but its unique painted wooden ceiling (1220) has survived intact. Catherine of Aragon, the first wife of Henry VIII, is buried here, although Cromwell's troops also destroyed her tomb.

Environs: The oldest wheel in Britain (10,000 BC) was found preserved in peat at **Flag Fen Bronze Age Excavations**. The site provides a fascinating glimpse into prehistory.

🎋 Flag Fen Bronze Age Excavations

Fourth Drove, Fengate, Peterborough.
📞 *01733 313414*. ⏰ *daily 10am–5pm*. ● *Christmas wk*. 🎫 ♿ 🎁 📷

Ely ❷

Cambridgeshire. 🏛 *14,000*.
🚄 ℹ️ *29 St Mary's St (01353 662062)*. 🛒 *Thu (general), Sat (craft & antiques)*.
W *www.elyeastcambs.co.uk*

Built on a chalk hill, this small city is thought to be named after the eels in the nearby River Ouse. The hill was once an inaccessible island in the then marshy and treacherous Fens *(see p182)*. It was also the last stronghold of Anglo-Saxon resistance, under Hereward the Wake *(see p48)*, who hid in the cathedral until the Normans crossed the Fens in 1071.

Today this small prosperous city, totally dominated by the huge **cathedral**, is the market centre for the rich agricultural area surrounding it.

Grimes Graves ❸

Lynford, Norfolk. 📞 *01842 810656*.
🚄 *Brandon then taxi*. ⏰ *daily*.
● *24–27 Dec*. 🎫 📷 🎁

One of the most important Neolithic sites in England, this was once an extensive complex of flint mines – 366 shafts have been located – dating from before 2000 BC.

Using antlers as pickaxes, Stone Age miners hacked through the soft chalk to extract the hard flint below to make axes, weapons and tools. It is thought that the flint was transported long distances around England on the prehistoric network of paths. You can descend 9 m (30 ft) by ladder into one of the shafts and see the galleries

---

The lantern's glass windows admit light into the dome.

This painted wooden angel *is one of hundreds of bosses that were carved all over the south and north transepts in the 13th and 14th centuries.*

Stained glass museum

The tomb is that of Alan de Walsingham, designer of the unique Octagon.

The Octagon, *made of wood, was built in 1322 when the Norman tower collapsed. Its roof, the lantern, took an extra 24 years to build and weighs 200 tonnes.*

Octagon   **Area of cutaway**

ELY CATHEDRAL

Ely. 📞 *01353 667735*.
⏰ *daily*. ● *special events*. 🎫 ♿ 🍴 🛍 🎁
Begun in 1083, the cathedral took 268 years to complete. It survived the Dissolution *(see p50)* but was closed for 17 years by Cromwell *(see p52)* who lived in Ely for a time.

where the flint was mined. During excavations, unusual chalk models of a fertility goddess *(see p43)* and a phallus were discovered.

ENVIRONS: Nearby, at the centre of the once fertile plain known as the Breckland, is the small market town of **Thetford**.

Once a prosperous trading town, its fortunes dipped in the 16th century, when its priory was destroyed *(see p50)* and the surrounding land deteriorated due to excessive sheep grazing. The area was later planted with pine trees. A mound in the city marks the site of a pre-Norman castle.

The revolutionary writer and philosopher Tom Paine, author of *The Rights of Man*, was born here in 1737.

Oxburgh Hall surrounded by its medieval moat

The huge cathedral spire dominates the flat Fens countryside surrounding Ely.

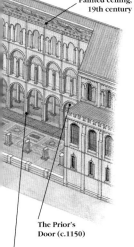

Painted ceiling, 19th century

The Prior's Door (c.1150)

The south aisle has 12 classic Norman arches at its foot, with pointed Early English windows above.

Swaffham ❹

Norfolk. 🚶 6,500. 🚌 🛈 *Apr–Oct: Market Place (01760 722255).* 🛒 *Sat.*

THE BEST-PRESERVED Georgian town in East Anglia and a fashionable resort during the Regency period, Swaffham is at its liveliest on Saturdays when a market is held in the square around the elegant and unusual market cross of 1783. In the centre of the town is the 15th-century **Church of St Peter and St Paul**, with a small spire added to the tower in the 19th century. It has a magnificent Tudor north aisle, said to have been paid for by John Chapman, the Pedlar of Swaffham. He is depicted on the unusual two-sided town sign near the market place. Myth has it that he went to London and met a stranger who told him of hidden treasure at Swaffham. He returned, dug it up and used it to embellish the church, where he is shown in a window.

ENVIRONS: Castle Acre, north of the town, has the remains of a massive Cluniac **priory**. Founded in 1090, its stunning Norman front still stands.

A short drive south is **Oxburgh Hall and Garden**, built by Sir Edmund Bedingfeld in 1482. The hall, entered through a huge 24 m (80 ft) fortified gatehouse, displays the velvet Oxburgh Hangings, embroidered by Mary, Queen of Scots *(see p497)*.

Swaffham town sign

🔒 Castle Acre Priory
Castle Acre. 🗲 01760 755394. ◻ Apr–Oct: daily; Nov–Mar: Wed– Sun. ⬤ 24-26 Dec, Jan 1. 🈲 🚻 limited.

🏛 Oxburgh Hall & Garden
Oxborough. 🗲 01366 328258. ◻ Apr–Oct: Sat–Wed (garden also Nov–Dec: Sat–Sun). 🈲 🚻 limited. 🚻 🛈

BOADICEA AND THE ICENI

When the Romans invaded Britain, the Iceni, the main tribe in East Anglia, joined forces with them to defeat the Catuvellauni, a rival tribe. But the Romans then turned on the Iceni, torturing Queen Boadicea (or Boudicca). In AD 61, she led a revolt against Roman rule: her followers burned down London, Colchester and St Albans. The rebellion was put down and the queen took poison rather than submit. At Cockley Cley, near Swaffham, an Iceni camp has been excavated.

Illustration of Queen Boadicea leading her Iceni followers

A windmill on Wicken Fen

The Fens ❺

Cambridgeshire/Norfolk. ⧨ *Ely.* ⓘ *29 St Mary's St, Ely (01353 662062).*

T HIS IS THE OPEN, flat, fertile expanse that lies between Lincoln, Cambridge, Bedford and King's Lynn. Up until the 17th century it was a swamp, and settlement was possible only on "islands", such as Ely *(see p180)*, raised above their low-lying surroundings.

Through the 17th century, speculators, recognizing the value of the peaty soil for farmland, brought in Dutch experts to drain the fens. However, as the peat dried it contracted, and the fens have slowly been getting lower. Originally pumped by windmills, the area now needs powerful electric pumps to keep it drained.

Nine miles (14 km) from Ely is Wicken Fen, 243 ha (600 acres) of undrained fen providing a habitat for an abundance of water life, wildfowl and wild flowers.

King's Lynn ❻

Norfolk. 🏠 *42,000.* ⧨ 🚌 ⓘ *Purfleet Quay (01553 763044).* ⓐ *Tue, Fri, Sat.*

F ORMERLY BISHOP'S LYNN, its name was changed at the Reformation *(see p50)* to reflect the changing political reality. In the Middle Ages it was one of England's most prosperous ports, shipping grain and wool from the surrounding countryside to Europe. There are still a few warehouses and merchants' houses by the River Ouse surviving from this period. At the north end of the town is **True's Yard**, a relic of the old fishermen's quarter.

Trinity Guildhall, King's Lynn

North Norfolk Coastal Tour ❽

T HIS TOUR TAKES YOU THROUGH some of the most beautiful areas of East Anglia; nearly all of the north Norfolk coast has been designated an Area of Outstanding Natural Beauty. The sea has dictated the character of the area. With continuing deposits of silt, once busy ports are now far inland and the shingle and sand banks that have built up are home to a huge variety of wildlife. Along the coast the sea has taken a different toll and eroded great tracts of land, creating spectacular cliffs.

TIPS FOR DRIVERS

Tour length: 28 miles (45 km). *Stopping-off points:* Holkham Hall makes a pleasant stop for a picnic lunch. There are some good pubs in Wells-next-the-Sea. (See also pp636–7.)

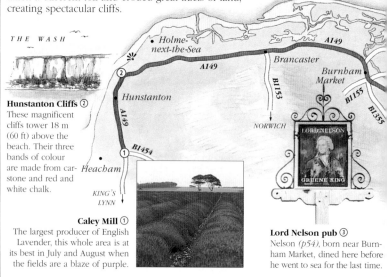

Hunstanton Cliffs ②
These magnificent cliffs tower 18 m (60 ft) above the beach. Their three bands of colour are made from carstone and red and white chalk.

Caley Mill ①
The largest producer of English Lavender, this whole area is at its best in July and August when the fields are a blaze of purple.

Lord Nelson pub ③
Nelson (p54), born near Burnham Market, dined here before he went to sea for the last time.

The **Trinity Guildhall** was built in the 1420s, and among the town regalia on display inside is an early 13th-century sword thought to have been a gift to the town from King John *(see p48)*, who visited the town several times. The last occasion was in 1216. He dined here on his way to the north of England to flee rebellious barons. The next day, while crossing the sea, he lost all his treasure – people have been dredging and diving to try and find it ever since.

On the Market Place is **St Margaret's Church** with work from the 13th-century onwards, including a fine Elizabethan screen.

⛪ Trinity Guildhall
Saturday Market Place. 🕻 *01553 774297.* ⬜ *Easter–Oct: daily; Nov–Easter: Fri–Tue.* ⬤ *24–26 Dec.* 🖼 ⛭

Sandringham House, where the Royal Family spend every Christmas

Sandringham ❼

Norfolk. 🕻 *01553 772675.* 🚌 *from King's Lynn.* ⬜ *Easter–Sep: daily.* ⬤ *three wks Jul–Aug.* 🖼 🖼 🖼 🖼
Ⓦ *www.sandringhamestate.co.uk*

THIS SIZEABLE NORFOLK estate has been in royal hands since 1862 when it was bought by the Prince of Wales, who later became Edward VII. The 18th-century house was elaborately embellished and refurbished by the prince and now retains an appropriately Edwardian atmosphere.

The large stables are now a museum and contain several trophies that relate to hunting, shooting and horse racing – all favourite royal activities. A popular feature is a display of royal motor cars spanning nearly a century. In the park there are scenic nature trails.

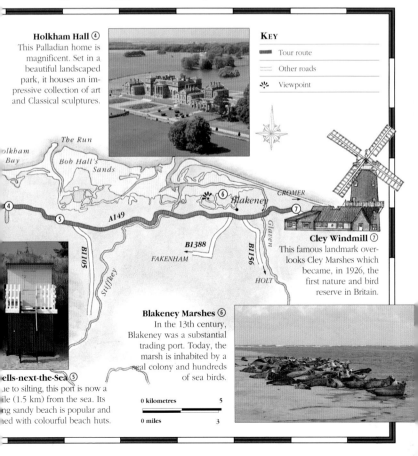

Holkham Hall ④
This Palladian home is magnificent. Set in a beautiful landscaped park, it houses an impressive collection of art and Classical sculptures.

KEY

▬▬ Tour route

═══ Other roads

⚡ Viewpoint

The Run

olkham Bay

Bob Hall's Sands

CROMER

⑥ *Blakeney*

A149

⑦

Cley Windmill ⑦
This famous landmark overlooks Cley Marshes which became, in 1926, the first nature and bird reserve in Britain.

B1388

FAKENHAM

B1105

Stiffkey

B1156

HOLT

Blakeney Marshes ⑥
In the 13th century, Blakeney was a substantial trading port. Today, the marsh is inhabited by a seal colony and hundreds of sea birds.

ells-next-the-Sea ⑤
ue to silting, this port is now a ile (1.5 km) from the sea. Its ng sandy beach is popular and ed with colourful beach huts.

0 kilometres   5

0 miles   3

The symmetrical red-brick façade of the 17th-century Blickling Hall

Blickling Hall ❾

(NT) Aylsham, Norfolk. ☎ *01263 738030.* 🚌 *from Norwich (summer).*
House ⬜ *Apr–Oct: 1–5pm Wed–Sun & public hols; Aug: 1–5pm Tue–Sun.*
Garden ⬜ *Apr–Oct: 10:30am–5:30pm Wed–Sun & public hols; Aug daily.* **Park** ⬜ *daily.* 📷 ♿ 🏪 📷

Approached from the east, its symmetrical Jacobean front framed by trees and flanked by two yew hedges, Blickling Hall offers one of the most impressive vistas of any country house in the area.

Anne Boleyn, Henry VIII's tragic second queen, spent her childhood here, but very little of the original house remains. Most of the present structure dates from 1628, when it was home to James I's Chief Justice Sir Henry Hobart. Later in 1767 the 2nd Earl of Buckinghamshire, John Hobart, celebrated the Boleyn connection with reliefs in the Great Hall depicting Anne and her daughter, Elizabeth I.

The Long Gallery is the most spectacular room to survive from the 1620s. Its ceiling depicts symbolic representations of learning.

The Peter the Great Room marks the 2nd earl's service as ambassador to Russia and was built to display a huge spectacular tapestry (1764) of the tsar on horseback, a gift from Catherine the Great. It also has portraits (1760) of the ambassador and his wife by Gainsborough *(see p149)*.

Norwich ❿

See pp186–7.

The Broads ⓫

Norfolk. 🚆 *Hoveton, Wroxham.* 🚌 *Norwich, then bus.* ℹ️ *Station Rd, Hoveton (01603 782281).* 🌐 *www.broads/authority.gov.uk*

These shallow lakes and waterways south and north-east of Norwich, joined by six rivers – the Bure, Thurne, Ant, Yare, Waveney and Chet – were once thought to have been naturally formed, but in actual fact they are medieval peat diggings which flooded when the water level rose in the 13th century.

During summer the 125 miles (200 km) of open waterways, uninterrupted by locks, teem with thousands of boating enthusiasts, from devotees of pure sail to those who prefer motorboats. You can either hire a boat yourself or take one of the many trips on offer to view the plants and wildlife of the area. Look out for Britain's largest butterfly, the swallowtail. Wroxham, the unofficial capital of the Broads, is the starting point for many of these excursions.

The waterways support substantial beds of strong and durable reeds, much in demand for thatching *(see p29)*. They are cut in winter and carried to shore in the distinctive Broads punts.

For a more detailed look at the origins of the Broads and their varied wildlife, visit the **Broadland Conservation Centre** – a large thatched floating information centre on Ranworth Broad, with displays on all aspects of the area, and a bird-watching gallery.

In the centre of Ranworth is **St Helen's Church** which has a painted medieval screen, a well-preserved 14th-century illuminated manuscript and spectacular views over the entire area from its tower.

🦋 **Broadland Conservation Centre**
Ranworth. ☎ *01603 270479.* ⬜ *Apr–Oct: daily.* ♿ 📷

Sailing boat, Wroxham Broad, Norfolk

Great Yarmouth **⑫**

Norfolk. **89,000.**
Town Hall (01493 846345).
Wed, Fri (in summer), Sat.
www.great-yarmouth.co.uk

HERRING FISHING was once the major industry of this port, with 1,000 boats engaged in it just before World War I. Over-fishing led to a depletion of stocks and, for the port to survive without the herring, it started to earn its living from servicing container ships and the North Sea oil rigs.

It is also the most popular seaside resort on the Norfolk coast and has been since the 19th century, when Dickens *(see p175)* gave it useful publicity by setting part of his novel *David Copperfield* here.

The **Elizabethan House Museum** has a large, eclectic display which illustrates the social history of the area.

In the old part of the town, around South Quay, are a number of charming houses including the 17th-century **Old Merchant's House**. It retains its original patterned plaster ceilings as well as examples of old ironwork

Fishing trawlers at Lowestoft's quays

and architectural fittings from nearby houses, which were destroyed during World War II. The guided tour of the house includes a visit to the adjoining cloister of a 13th-century friary.

⬚ Elizabethan House Museum
4 South Quay. **01493 855746.**
Apr–Oct: daily.
⬚ Old Merchant's House
South Quay. **01493 857900.**
Apr–Oct: daily.

Corn mill at Saxtead Green, near Framlingham

Herringfleet Smock Mill, near Lowestoft

WINDMILLS ON THE FENS AND BROADS

The flat, open countryside and the stiff breezes from the North Sea made windmills an obvious power source for East Anglia well into the 20th century, and today they are an evocative and recurring feature of the landscape. On the Broads and Fens, some were used for drainage, while others, such as that at Saxtead Green, ground corn. On the boggy fens they were not built on hard foundations, so few survived, but elsewhere, especially on the Broads, many have been restored to working order. The seven-storey Berney Arms Windmill is the tallest on the Broads. Thurne Dyke Drainage Mill is the site of an exhibition about the occasionally idiosyncratic mills and their more unusual mechanisms.

Lowestoft **⑬**

Suffolk. **55,000.**
East Point Pavilion, Royal Plain (01502 533600). Tue, Fri, Sat.
www.visit/lowestoft.co.uk

THE MOST EASTERLY TOWN in Britain was long a rival to Great Yarmouth, both as a holiday resort and a fishing port. Its fishing industry has only just survived.

The coming of the railway in the 1040s gave the town an advantage over other resorts, and the solid Victorian and Edwardian boarding houses are evidence of its popularity.

Lowestoft Museum, in a 17th century house, has a good display of the fine porcelain made here in the 18th century, as well as exhibits on local archaeology and domestic life.

ENVIRONS: Somerleyton Hall is built in Jacobean style on the foundations of a smaller mansion. Its gardens are a real delight, and there is a genuinely baffling yew hedge maze.

⬚ Lowestoft Museum
Oulton Broad. **01502 568560.**
Mar (last Mon)–Oct (1st Sun) 10:30am–5pm Mon–Fri, 2–5pm Sat & Sun limited. by arrangement.
⬚ Somerleyton Hall
On B1074. **01502 730224.**
Easter Sun–Sep: Thu, Sun & public hols (Jul–Aug: Tue–Thu, Sun & public hols). by arrangement.

Norwich ⑩

IN THE HEART of the fertile East Anglian countryside, Norwich, one of the best-preserved cities in Britain, is steeped in a relaxed provincial atmosphere. The city was first fortified by the Saxons in the 9th century and still has the irregular street plan of that time. With the arrival of Flemish settlers in the early 12th century and the establishment of a textile industry, the town soon became a prosperous market and was the second city of England until the Industrial Revolution in the 19th century *(see pp56–7)*.

The cobbled street, Elm Hill

Exploring Norwich
The oldest parts of the city are Elm Hill, one of the finest medieval streets in England, and Tombland, the old Saxon market place by the cathedral. Both have well-preserved medieval buildings, which are now incorporated into pleasant areas of small shops.

With a trading history spanning hundreds of years, the colourful market in the city centre is well worth a visit. A good walk meanders around the surviving sections of the 14th-century flint city wall.

🔒 Norwich Cathedral
The Close. ☎ 01603 764385.
◯ *daily.* **Donations.** ♿ 📷 🍴 🚻
This magnificent building was founded in 1096 by Bishop Losinga and built with stone from Caen in France and Barnack.

The precinct originally included a monastery, and the surviving cloister is the most extensive in England. The thin cathedral spire was added in the 15th century, making it, at 96 m (315 ft), the second tallest in England after Salisbury's *(see pp250–51)*. In the majestic nave, soaring Norman pillars

and arches support a 15th-century vaulted roof whose stone bosses, many of which illustrate well-known Bible stories, have recently been beautifully restored.

Easier to appreciate at close hand is the elaborate wood carving in the choir – the canopies over the stalls and the misericords beneath the seats, one showing a small boy being smacked. Not to be missed is the 14th-century Despenser Reredos in St Luke's Chapel. It was hidden for years under a carpenter's table to prevent its destruction by Puritans.

Two gates to the cathedral close survive: **St Ethelbert's**, a 13th-century flint arch, and

One of over a thousand carved bosses in the cathedral cloisters

the **Erpingham Gate** at the west end, built by Sir Thomas Erpingham, who led the triumphant English archers at the Battle of Agincourt in 1415 *(see p49)*.

Beneath the east outer wall is the grave of Edith Cavell, the Norwich-born nurse who was arrested and executed in 1915 by the Germans for helping Allied soldiers escape from occupied Belgium.

🏛 Castle Museum
Castle Meadow. ☎ 01603 493625.
◯ *daily (Sun pm only).* ● *1 Jan, 25, 26 Dec.* 🖥
The brooding keep of this 12th-century castle, refaced in Bath stone in 1834, has been a museum since 1894, when it ended 650 years of service as a prison. The most important Norman feature is a carved door that used to be the main entrance.

Exhibits include significant collections of archaeology, natural history, fine art as

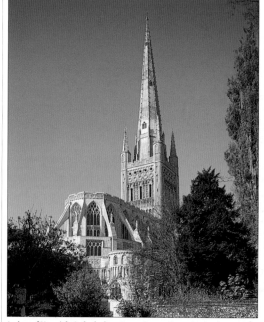

A view of Norwich Cathedral's spire and tower from the southeast

COLMAN'S MUSTARD

It was said of the Colmans that they made their fortune from what diners left on their plate. In 1814 Jeremiah Colman started milling mustard at Norwich because it was at the centre of a fertile plain where mustard was grown. Today at 15 Royal Arcade a shop sells mustard and related items, while a small museum illustrates the history of the company.

A 1950s advertisement for Colman's Mustard

VISITORS' CHECKLIST

Norfolk. 124,000.
Thorpe Road. Surrey St.
Millennium Library (01603 666071). Mon–Sat.

🏛 Strangers' Hall

Charing Cross. 01603 667229.
⬤ for renovation until 2002.
This 14th-century merchant's house gives a glimpse into English domestic life through the ages. The costume display features a unique collection of underwear. The house was lived in by immigrant weavers – the "strangers". It has a fine 15th-century Great Hall.

🏛 The Sainsbury Centre for Visual Arts

University of East Anglia (on B1108).
01603 593199. ⬤ Tue–Sun.
⬤ 23 Dec–2 Jan. by arrangement.
This important art gallery was built in 1978 to house the collection of Robert and Lisa Sainsbury given to the University of East Anglia in 1973.

The collection's strength is in its modern European paintings, including works by Modigliani, Picasso and Bacon, and in its scuptures by Giacometti and Moore. There are also displays of ethnographic art from Africa, the Pacific and the Americas.

The centre, designed by Lord Norman Foster, one of Britain's leading and most innovative architects, was among the first to display its steel structure openly. This style was to be imitated around the world.

well as the world's largest collection of ceramic teapots.

The art gallery is dominated by works from the Norwich School of painters. This group of early 19th century landscape artists painted directly from nature, getting away from the stylized studio landscapes that had been fashionable up to then. Chief among the group were John Crome (1768–1821), whom many compare with Constable (see p190), and John Sell Cotman (1782–1842), known for his watercolours.

There are also regular exhibitions held here which are brought from the Tate Gallery in London.

🔒 Church of St Peter Mancroft

Market Place. 01603 610443.
⬤ 10am–4pm Mon–Fri; 10am–4pm Sat (summer), 10am–1pm (winter); Sun (services only). **Donations**.
This imposing Perpendicular church, built around 1455, so dominates the city centre that many visitors assume it is the cathedral. John Wesley (see p265) wrote of it, "I scarcely ever remember to have seen a more beautiful parish church".

The large windows make the church very light, and the dramatic east window still has most of its 15th-century glass. The roof is unusual in having wooden fan tracery – it is normally in stone – covering the hammerbeam construction. The famous peal of 13 bells rang out in 1588 to celebrate the defeat of the Spanish Armada (see p51) and is still heard every Sunday.

Its name derives from the Latin *magna crofta* (great meadow) which described the area in pre-Norman times.

🏛 Bridewell Museum

Bridewell Alley. 01603 493625.
⬤ 10am–5pm Mon–Sat.
One of the oldest houses in Norwich, this 14th-century flint-faced building was for years used as a jail. It now houses an exhibition of local industries, with displays of old machines, advertisements and reconstructed shops.

🏛 Guildhall

Gaol Hill. 01603 666071.
Above the city's 900-year-old market place is the imposing 15th-century flint and stone Guildhall with its gable of checkered flushwork.

Back of the New Mills (1814) by John Crome of the Norwich School

Purple heather in flower on Dunwich Heath

Southwold ➍

Suffolk. 🚶 *1,400.* 🚆 ➊ *High Street (01502 724729).* 🛒 *Mon, Thu.* Ⓦ *www.southwold.blythweb.co.uk*

THIS PICTURE-POSTCARD seaside resort, with its charming white-washed villas clustered around grassy slopes, has, largely by historical accident, remained unspoiled. The railway line which connected it with London was closed in 1929, which effectively isolated this Georgian town from an influx of day-trippers.

That this was also once a large port can be judged from the size of the 15th-century **St Edmund King and Martyr Church**, worth a visit for the 16th-century painted screens. On

Jack o'the Clock, Southwold

its tower is a small figure dressed in the uniform of a 15th-century soldier and known as Jack o'the Clock. **Southwold Museum** tells the story of the Battle of Sole Bay, which was fought offshore between the English and Dutch navies in 1672.

ENVIRONS: The rail closure in Southwold also cut the link with the pretty village of **Walberswick**, across the creek. By road it is a long detour and the only alternative is a rowing-boat ferry across the harbour. Just inland at Blythburgh, the 15th-century **Holy Trinity Church** dominates the surrounding land. Cromwell's troops *(see p52)* used it as a stable.

In 1944 a US bomber blew up over the church, killing Joseph Kennedy Jr, brother of the future American president.

🏛 **Southwold Museum**
9–11 Victoria St. ◯ *Easter–Oct: 2–4pm daily.* ♿

Dunwich ➎

Suffolk. 🚶 *1,400.*

THIS TINY VILLAGE with a few cottages and the odd fishing boat, is all that remains of a "lost city" consigned to the sea by erosion.

In the 7th century Dunwich was the seat of the powerful East Anglian kings. In the 13th century it was still the biggest port in Suffolk and some 12 churches were constructed during its time of prosperity. But the land was being eroded at about a metre (3 ft) a year, and the last of the original churches collapsed into the sea in 1919.

Dunwich Heath, just to the south, runs down to a sandy beach and is now an important nature reserve. **Minsmere Reserve** has observation hides for watching a huge variety of water dependent birds .

🦅 **Minsmere Reserve**
Westleton. ◖ *01728 648281.* ◯ *Wed–Mon.* ⬤ *25, 26 Dec.* ♿ 📷 💻 🚻

Aldeburgh ➏

Suffolk. 🚶 *2,500.* 🚆 ➊ *High St, Apr–Sep: 01728 453637; Oct–Mar: 01394 382240.*

BEST KNOWN TODAY for the music festivals at Snape Maltings just up the River

Intricate carving on the exterior of the Tudor Moot Hall, Aldeburgh

Alde, Aldeburgh has been a port since Roman times (the Roman area is under water).

Erosion has resulted in the fine Tudor **Moot Hall**, once far inland, now being close to the beach and promenade. Its ground floor, originally the market, is now a museum. The large timbered court room above can only be reached by the original outside staircase.

The **church**, also Tudor, contains a large stained glass window placed in 1979 as a memorial to Benjamin Britten.

⛩ Moot Hall
Market Cross Pl. **[** *01728 452730.* **○** *Jun–Sep: daily (pm only); Oct–Apr: Sat & Sun.* **⊗ ◻**

Framlingham Castle ⓱

Framlingham, Suffolk. **[** *01728 724189.* **☰** *Wickham Market then taxi.* **○** *daily.* **●** *1 Jan, 24–26 Dec.* **⊗ ◻**

PERCHED ON A HILL, the small village of Framlingham has long been an important strategic site, even before the present castle was built in 1190 by the Earl of Norfolk.

Little of the castle from that period survives except the powerful curtain wall and its towers; walk round the top of it for fine views of the town.

Mary Tudor, daughter of Henry VIII, was staying here in 1553 when she heard she was to become queen.

ENVIRONS: To the southeast, on the coast, is the 27 m (90 ft) keep of **Orford Castle**, built for Henry II as a coastal defence at around the same time as Framlingham. It is an early example of an English castle with a 16-sided keep; earlier they were square and later round. A short climb to the top of the castle gives fantastic views.

⋔ Orford Castle
Orford. **[** *01394 450472.* **○** *Apr–Oct: daily; Nov–Mar: Wed–Sun.* **●** *25–26 Dec, 1 Jan.* **⊗ ◻**

Benjamin Britten in Aldeburgh

Ipswich ⓲

Suffolk. **▨** *120,000.* **✈ ☰ ▣** **ℹ** *St Stephen's Lane (01473 258070).* **◓** *Tue, Fri, Sat.* **ⓦ** *www.ipswich.gov.uk*

SUFFOLK'S COUNTY TOWN has a largely modern centre but several buildings remain from earlier times. It rose to prominence after the 13th century as a port for the rich Suffolk wool trade *(see p193)*. Later, with the Industrial Revolution, it began to export coal.

The **Ancient House** in Buttermarket has a superb example of pargeting – the ancient craft of ornamental façade plastering. The town's museum and art gallery,

Christchurch Mansion, is a Tudor house from 1548, where Elizabeth I stayed in 1561. It also boasts the best collection of Constable's paintings out of London *(see p190)*, including four marvellous Suffolk landscapes, as well as pictures by the Suffolk-born painter Gainsborough *(see p149)*.

Ipswich Museum contains replicas of the Mildenhall and Sutton Hoo treasures, the originals being in the British Museum *(see pp108–9)*.

In the centre of the town is **St Margaret's**, a 15th-century church built in flint and stone with a double hammerbeam roof and 17th-century painted ceiling panels. A Tudor gateway of 1527 provides a link with Ipswich's most famous son, Cardinal Wolsey *(see p159)*. He started to build an ecclesiastical college in the town, but fell from royal favour before it was finished.

🏛 Christchurch Mansion
Soane St. **[** *01473 433 554.* **○** *10am–5pm Tue–Sat & public hols; 2:30–4:30pm Sun.* **●** *24–26 Dec, 1 Jan, Good Fri.* **♿** *limited.* **◻ ✦** *by arrangement.*

🏛 Ipswich Museum
High St. **[** *01473 433550.* **○** *Tue–Sat.* **●** *24–26 Dec, 1 Jan, Good Fri.* **◻**

Pargeting on the Ancient House in Ipswich

Constable Walk ⑲

This walk in Constable country follows one of the most picturesque sections of the River Stour. The path followed would have been familiar to the landscape painter John Constable (1776–1837). Constable's father was a wealthy merchant who owned Flatford Mill; the scenery of at least ten of the artist's most important paintings was within view of this much-loved mill. Constable claimed to know and love "every stile and stump, and every lane" around East Bergholt, and the walk encompasses his favourite areas.

The River Stour, used as a backdrop for Constable's *Boatbuilding* (1814)

Tips for Walkers

Starting point: *Car park off Flatford Lane, East Bergholt.*
🛈 **(NT)** *Bridge Cottage Information Centre (01206 298260).*
Getting there: *A12 to Ipswich, then B1070 to East Bergholt, follow signs to Flatford Mill.*
Stopping-off point: *Dedham.*
Length: *3 miles (5 km).*
Difficulty: *Flat trail along riverside footpath with stiles.*

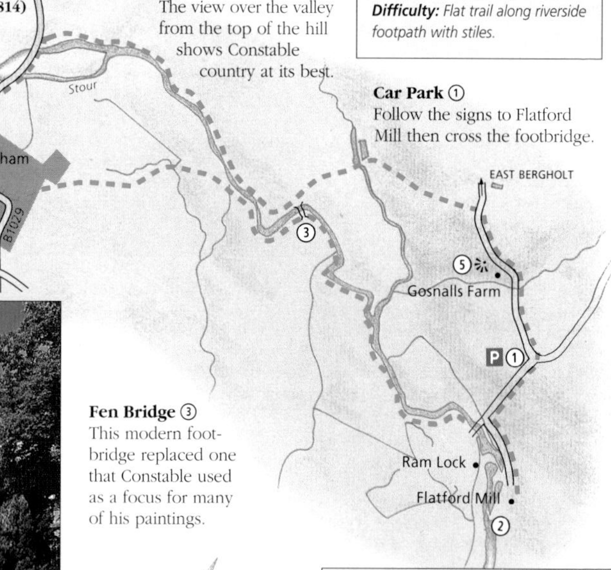

Viewpoint ⑤
The view over the valley from the top of the hill shows Constable country at its best.

Car Park ①
Follow the signs to Flatford Mill then cross the footbridge.

Dedham Mill

Stour

A12

Dedham

④

COLCHESTER

EAST BERGHOLT

③

⑤

Gosnalls Farm

P ①

Fen Bridge ③
This modern foot-bridge replaced one that Constable used as a focus for many of his paintings.

Ram Lock

Flatford Mill

②

Dedham Church ④
The tall church tower appears in many of Constable's pictures including the *View on the Stour near Dedham* (1822).

Key

- ▬ ▬ Route
- ▭▭ B road
- ▭▭ Minor road
- ☀ Viewpoint
- **P** Parking

0 metres   500
0 yards   500

Willy Lott's Cottage ②
This cottage remains much the same as it did when featured in Constable's painting *The Haywain* (see p85).

Colchester ⑳

Essex. 👤 150,000. 🚆 🚍 🚻 Queen St (01206 282920). 🏪 Fri, Sat.

THE OLDEST recorded town in Britain, Colchester was the effective capital of south-east England when the Romans invaded in AD 43, and it was here that the first permanent Roman colony was established.

After Boadicea *(see p181)* burnt the town in AD 60, a 2 mile (3 km) defensive wall was built, 3 m (10 ft) thick and 9 m (30 ft) high, to deter any future attackers. You can still see these walls and the surviving Roman town gate, which is the largest in Britain.

During the Middle Ages Colchester developed into an important weaving centre. In the 16th century, a number of immigrant Flemish weavers settled in an area west of the castle, known as the **Dutch Quarter**, which still retains the original tall houses and steep, narrow streets.

Colchester was besieged for 11 weeks during the Civil War *(see p52)* before being captured by Cromwell's troops.

🏛 Tymperleys

Trinity St. 📞 01206 282943. 🕐 Apr–Oct: daily. ♿ 🚻
Clock-making was an important craft in Colchester, and it is celebrated in this restored half-timbered, 15th-century mansion, also worth visiting for its formal Tudor garden.

🏛 Hollytrees Museum

Castle Park. 📞 01206 282940. 🕐 daily. ♿ 🚻
This elegant Georgian town-house was built in 1719. Now a charming museum of social history, you can experience the day-to-day lives of Colchester people and changing technology during the past 300 years.

🏛 Castle Museum

High St. 📞 01206 282939. 🕐 daily; 11am–5pm Sun. ● 24–27 Dec. ♿ 🚻
This is the oldest and largest Norman keep still standing in England. Twice the size of the White Tower at the Tower of London *(see pp120–21)*, it was built in 1076 on the platform

The Norman keep of the Castle Museum, Colchester

of a Roman temple dedicated to Claudius *(see p44)*, using stones and tiles from other Roman buildings. Today, the museum is packed full of exhibits relating the story of the town from prehistoric times to the Civil War. You can also visit the medieval prison.

🏛 Layer Marney Tower

Off B1022. 📞 01206 330784. 🕐 Apr–Sep: Sun–Fri (pm). ♿ limited. 🎥 by arrangement. 🖼 📷 🚻
This remarkable Tudor gate-house is the tallest in Britain: its pair of six-sided, eight-storey turrets reach to 24 m (80 ft). It was intended to be part of a larger complex but the designer, Sir Henry Marney, died before it was completed. The brickwork and terracotta ornamentation around the roof and windows are models of Tudor craftsmanship. There are fine views of the gardens and deer park from the tower.

❀ Beth Chatto Garden

Elmstead Market. 📞 01206 822007. 🕐 Summer 9am–5pm, winter 9am–4pm; Mar–Oct: Mon–Sat; Nov–Feb: Mon–Fri. ● 24 Dec–6 Jan, public hols. 🎥 📷 🚻
One of Britain's most eminent gardening writers began this experiment in the 1960s to test her belief that it is possible to create a garden in the most adverse conditions. The dry and windy slopes, boggy patches, gravel beds and wooded areas all support an array of plants best suited to that particular environment.

Coggeshall ㉑

Essex. 👤 4,000. 🏪 Thu.

THIS SMALL TOWN has two of the most important and best-preserved medieval and Tudor buildings in the country. Dating from 1140, **Coggeshall Grange Barn** is the oldest surviving timber-framed barn in Europe. Inside is a display of historic farm wagons. The half-timbered merchant's house, **Paycocke's**, was built around 1500 and has a beautifully panelled interior. There is a display of Coggeshall lace.

🏛 Coggeshall Grange Barn

(NT) Grange Hill. 🏠 01376 562226. 🕐 Apr–Oct: Tue, Thu, Sun & public hols (pm). ● Good Fri. 🎥 ♿

🏛 Paycocke's

(NT) West St. 📞 01376 561305. 🕐 Apr–Oct: Tue, Thu, Sun & public hols (pm). ● Good Fri. 🎥 ♿

Beth Chatto Garden, Colchester, in full summer bloom

Lavenham ❷

Suffolk. 🏘 *1,700.* ℹ️ *Lady St (01787 248207).*

OFTEN CONSIDERED the most perfect of all English small towns, Lavenham is a treasure trove of black and white timber-framed houses ranged along streets whose pattern is virtually unchanged from medieval times. For 150 years, between the 14th and 16th centuries, Lavenham was the prosperous centre of the Suffolk wool trade. It still has many outstanding and well-preserved buildings; indeed no less than 300 of the town's buildings are listed, including the magnificent **Little Hall**.

ENVIRONS: **Gainsborough's House**, Sudbury, is a museum on this painter *(see p149).*

🏛 **Little Hall** Market Place. 📞 *01787 247179.* ⏰ *Apr–Oct: Wed, Thu, Sat, Sun & public hols pm only.* ♿
🏛 **Gainsborough's House** Sudbury. 📞 *01787 372958.* ⏰ *Tue–Sun.* ● *some public hols, 25 Dec.* ♿ 📷

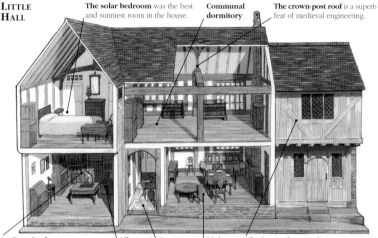

LITTLE HALL

The solar bedroom was the best and sunniest room in the house.

Communal dormitory

The crown-post roof is a superb feat of medieval engineering.

An Egyptian bronze cat represents the Goddess Bastet.

Library

Entrance

Dining room

The herringbone-style timber on the exterior was used often in the 14th century.

Bury St Edmunds ❷

Suffolk. 🏘 *33,000.* 🚉 🚌 ℹ️ *Angel Hill (01284 764667).* 🅿️ *Wed, Sat.* 🌐 *www.stedmundsbury.gov.uk*

ST EDMUND was the last Saxon king of East Anglia, decapitated by Danish raiders in 870. Legend has it that a wolf picked up the severed head – an image that appears in a number of medieval carvings. Edmund was canonized in 900 and buried in Bury, where in 1014 King Canute *(see p157)* built an **abbey** in his honour, the wealthiest in the country, until razed by fire in 1347. The abbey ruins now lie in a garden in the town centre.

Nearby are two large 15th-century churches, built when the wool trade made the town wealthy. **St James's** was designated a cathedral in 1914. The best features of **St Mary's** are the north porch and the hammer-beam roof over the nave. A stone slab in the north-east corner of the church marks the tomb of Mary Tudor *(see p50).*

Illustration of St Edmund

Just below the **market cross** in Cornhill – remodelled by Robert Adam *(see p24)* in 1714 – stands the large 12th-century **Moyse's Hall**, a merchant's house that serves as the town local history museum, displaying archaeology from the area.

ENVIRONS: Three miles (5 km) southwest of Bury is the late 18th-century **Ickworth House**. This eccentric Neo-Classical mansion features an unusual rotunda with a

The 18th-century rotunda of Ickworth House, Bury St Edmunds

domed roof flanked by two huge wings. The art collection includes works by Reynolds and Titian. There are also fine displays of silver, porcelain and sculpture, for example, John Flaxman's (1755–1826) moving *The Fury of Athamas*. The house is set in a large park.

The stallion unit at the National Stud, Newmarket

🏛 **Moyse's Hall**
Cornhill. 📞 *01284 757069.* ◯ *daily.*
● *24–26 Dec, Good Fri.* 📷 ♿ 🏪
🏛 **Ickworth House**
Horringer. 📞 *01284 735270.* ◯
mid-Mar–Oct: Tue, Wed, Fri–Sun;
public hols (pm). 📷 ♿ 🍴 🏪

Newmarket ㉔

Suffolk. 🏘 *17,000.* 🚌 🚗
ℹ *Palace House, Palace St (01638 667200).* 🚌 *Tue, Sat.*

A WALK DOWN the short main street tells you all you need to know about this busy and wealthy little town. The shops sell horse feed and all manner of riding accessories; the clothes on sale are tweeds, jodhpurs and the soft brown hats rarely worn by anyone except racehorse trainers.

Newmarket has been the headquarters of British horse racing since James I decided that its open heaths were ideal for testing the mettle of his fastest steeds against those of his friends. The first ever recorded horse race was held here in 1622. Charles II shared his grandfather's enthusiasm and after the Restoration *(see p53)* would move the whole court to Newmarket, every spring and summer, for the sport – he is the only British king to have ridden a winner.

A horse being exercised on Newmarket Heath

The modern racing industry began to take shape here in the late 18th century. There are now over 2,500 horses in training in and around the town, and two racecourses staging regular race meetings from around April to October *(see p66).* Training stables are occasionally open to the public but you can view the horses being exercised on the heath surrounding the town in the early morning. Tattersall's, the auction house for thoroughbreds, is in the centre of Newmarket.

The **National Stud** can also be visited. You will see the five or six stallions on stud, mares in foal and if you are lucky a newborn foal – most likely in April or May.

The **National Horseracing Museum** tells the history of the sport and contains many offbeat exhibits such as the skeleton of Eclipse, one of the greatest horses ever, unbeaten in 18 races and the ancestor of most of today's fastest performers. It also has a large display of sporting art.

🔵 **National Stud**
Newmarket. 📞 *01638 663464* ◯
Mar–Sep: daily. 📷 ♿ 📷 🏪 🏪
🏛 **National Horseracing Museum**
99 High St, Newmarket. 📞 *01638 667333.* ◯ *Apr–Oct: Tue–Sun.* 📷
♿ 📷 🏪 🏪

St Mary's Church, Stoke-by-Nayland, southeast of Bury St Edmunds

THE RISE AND FALL OF THE WOOL TRADE

Wool was a major English product from the 13th century and by 1310 some ten million fleeces were exported every year. The Black Death *(see p48)*, which swept Britain in 1348, perversely provided a boost for the industry: with labour in short supply, land could not be cultivated and was grassed over for sheep. Around 1350 Edward III decided it was time to establish a home-based cloth industry and encouraged Flemish weavers to come to Britain. Many settled in East Anglia, particularly Suffolk, and their skills helped establish a flourishing trade. This time of prosperity saw the construction of the sumptuous churches, such as the one at Stoke-by-Nayland, that we see today – East Anglia has more than 2,000 churches. The cloth trade here began to decline in the late 16th century with the development of water-powered looms. These were not suited to the area, which never regained its former wealth. Today's visitors are the beneficiaries of this decline, because the wool towns such as Lavenham and Bury St Edmunds never became rich enough to destroy their magnificent Tudor halls and houses and construct new buildings.

The façade of Anglesey Abbey

Anglesey Abbey 25

(NT) Lode, Cambridgeshire. 📞
01223 811200. 🚆 Cambridge then
bus. **House** ◯ Apr–Oct: Wed–Sun;
Garden ◯ Wed–Sun. 🎫 ♿
limited. 🎞 📷 🛈

THE ORIGINAL ABBEY was built
in 1135 for an Augustinian
order. But only the crypt – also
known as the monks' parlour
– with its vaulted ceiling on
marble and stone pillars, survived the Dissolution *(see p50)*.
This was later incorporated
into a manor house whose
treasures include furniture
from many periods and a rare

seascape by Gainsborough
(see p192). The superb garden
was created in the 1930s by
Lord Fairhaven as an ambitious, Classical landscape of
trees, sculptures and borders.

Huntingdon 26

Cambridgeshire. 🏠 18,000. 🚆 🚌
ℹ️ Princes St (01480 388588).
🗓 Wed, Sat.

MORE THAN 300 YEARS
after his death, Oliver
Cromwell *(see p52)* still dominates this small town. Born here
in 1599, a record of his baptism
can be seen in the County
Records Office in Huntingdon.
You can see his name and
traces of ancient graffiti
scrawled all over it which says
"England's plague for five
years". **Cromwell Museum**,
his former school, traces his
life with pictures and mementoes, including his death mask.
Cromwell remains one of
the most disputed figures in
British history. An MP before

he was 30, he quickly became
embroiled in the disputes
between Charles I and Parliament over taxes and religion.
In the Civil War *(see p52)* he
proved an inspired general
and – after refusing the title
of king – was made Lord
Protector in 1653, four years
after the King was beheaded.
But just two years after his
death the monarchy was restored by popular demand,
and his body was taken out
of Westminster Abbey *(see
pp94–5)* to hang on gallows.
There is a 14th-century
bridge across the River Ouse
which links Huntingdon with
Godmanchester, the site of a
Roman settlement.

🏛 **Cromwell Museum**
Grammar School Walk. 📞 01480
375830. ◯ Apr–Oct: Tue–Sun; Nov–
Mar: Tue–Sun (pm only except Sat).
⬤ 24 Dec & public hols. ♿ limited.

Cambridge 27

See pp196–201.

Audley End 28

Saffron Walden, Essex. 📞 01799
522842. 🚆 Audley End then taxi.
◯ Apr–Sep: Wed–Sun & public hols
noon–5pm; Oct: 11am–3pm. 🎫 ♿
limited. 🎞 🎞 🛈 📷

THIS WAS THE largest house
in England when built in
1614 for Thomas Howard,
Lord Treasurer and 1st Earl of
Suffolk. James I joked that
Howard's house was too big
for a king but not for a Lord
Treasurer. Charles II, his grandson, disagreed and bought it
in 1667 as an extra palace; but
he and his successors seldom
went there and in 1701 it was
given back to the Howards,
who demolished two thirds of
it to make it more manageable.
What remains is a Jacobean
mansion, retaining its original
hall and many fine plaster ceilings. Robert Adam *(see p24)*
remodelled most of the interior
in the 1760s and many rooms
have been restored to his original designs. At the same
time, Capability Brown *(see
p23)* landscaped the magnificent 18th-century park.

The Chapel *was completed
in 1772 to a Gothic design.
The furniture was made to
complement the wooden
pillars and vaulting which
are painted to imitate stone.*

Main entrance

The painted window,
built in 1768, represents
the Last Supper.

The Great Hall*,
hung with family
portraits, is the highlight
of the house, with the
massive oak screen and
elaborate hammerbeam
roof surviving in their
Jacobean form.*

Epping Forest ㉙

Essex. 🚃 *Chingford.* 🚇 *Loughton.*
ℹ *High Beach, Loughton (020-8508 0028).*

A S ONE OF THE LARGE open spaces near London, the 2,400 ha (6,000 acre) forest is popular with walkers, just as, centuries ago, it was a favourite hunting ground for kings and courtiers – the word forest denoted an area for hunting.

A depiction of the Battle of Maldon (991) on the *Maldon Embroidery*

Epping Forest contains oaks and beeches up to 400 years old

Henry VIII had a lodge built in 1543 on the edge of the forest. His daughter Elizabeth I, also a keen hunter, often used the lodge and it soon became known as **Queen Elizabeth's Hunting Lodge**.

This three-storey timbered building has been fully renovated and now houses an exhibition explaining the lodge's history and other aspects of the forest's life.

The tracts of open land and woods interspersed with a number of lakes, make an ideal habitat for a variety of plant, bird and animal life: deer roam the northern part, many of a special dark strain introduced by James I. The Corporation of London bought the forest in the mid-19th century to ensure it remained open to the public.

🏛 **Queen Elizabeth's Hunting Lodge**
Rangers Rd, Chingford. 📞 020-8529 6681. 🕐 *Wed–Sun (pm).* ● *24–26 Dec, 1 Jan.* 🏷 🚻 limited. 📷 📷

Maldon ㉚

Essex. 🚶 *15,000* 🚃 *Chelmsford then bus.* ℹ *Coach Lane (01621 856503).* 🅰 *Thu, Sat.*

T HIS DELIGHTFUL old town on the River Blackwater, its High Street lined with shops and inns from the 16th century on, was once an important harbour and is still popular with weekend sailors. One of its main industries is the production of Maldon sea salt, panned in the traditional way.

A fierce battle here in 991, when Viking invaders defeated the Saxon defenders, is told in *The Battle of Maldon,* one of the earliest known Saxon poems. The battle is also celebrated in the *Maldon Embroidery* on display in the **Maeldune Centre**. This 13 m (42 ft) long embroidery, made by locals, depicts the history of Maldon from 991 to 1991.

ENVIRONS: East of Maldon at Bradwell-on-Sea is the sturdy Saxon church of **St Peter's-on-the-Wall**, a simple stone box of a building that stands quite isolated on the shore. It was built in 654, from the stones of a former Roman fort, by St Cedd, who used it as his cathedral. It was fully restored in the 1920s.

🏛 **Maeldune Centre**
High St. 📞 01621 851628. 🕐 *Oct–Mar: Thu–Sat; Apr–Sep: Mon–Sat.* ● *24–26 Dec, 1 Jan.* 🏷

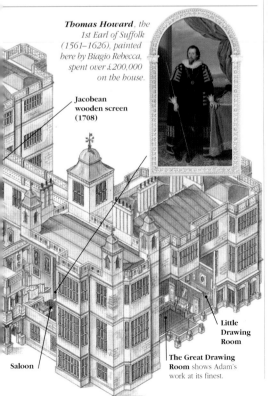

Thomas Howard, the 1st Earl of Suffolk (1561–1626), painted here by Biagio Rebecca, spent over £200,000 on the house.

Jacobean wooden screen (1708)

Saloon

The Great Drawing Room shows Adam's work at its finest.

Little Drawing Room

Street-by-Street: Cambridge 27

C AMBRIDGE HAS BEEN an important town since Roman times as it was sited at the first navigable point on the River Cam. In the 11th century religious orders began to be established in the town and, in 1209, a group of religious scholars broke away from Oxford University *(see pp208–213)* after academic and religious disputes and came here. Student life dominates the city but it is also a thriving market centre serving a rich agricultural region.

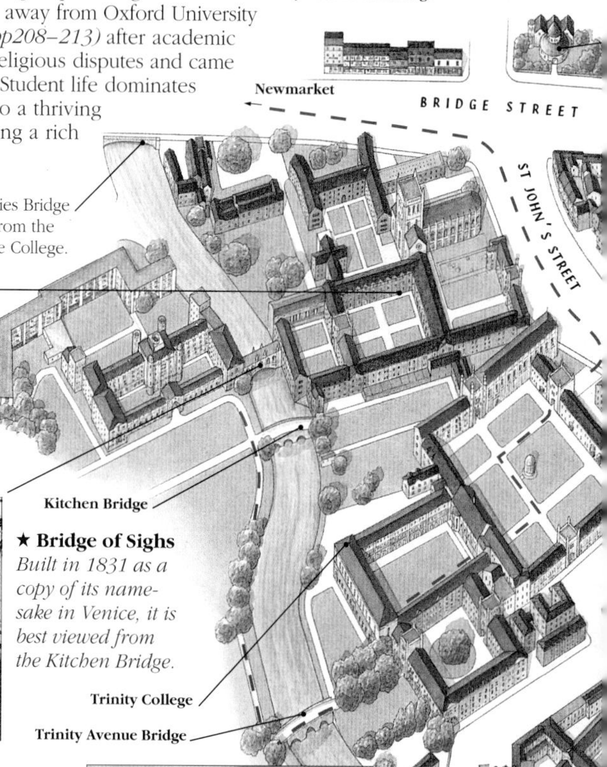

Carving, King's College Chapel

Cyclists in Cambridge

Newmarket

BRIDGE STREET

ST JOHN'S STREET

Magdalene Bridge carries Bridge Street across the Cam from the city centre to Magdalene College.

St John's College has superb Tudor and Jacobean architecture.

Kitchen Bridge

★ Bridge of Sighs
Built in 1831 as a copy of its name-sake in Venice, it is best viewed from the Kitchen Bridge.

Trinity College

Trinity Avenue Bridge

The Backs
This is the name given to the grassy strip lying between the backs of the big colleges and the banks of the Cam – a good spot to enjoy this classic view of King's College Chapel.

KEY

– – – Suggested route

Clare College

Clare Bridge

Grantchester

0 metres		75
0 yards		75

STAR SIGHTS

★ Bridge of Sighs

★ King's College Chapel

Round Church
*The 12th-century
Church of the Holy
Sepulchre has one of
the few round naves in
the country. Its design
is based on the Holy
Sepulchre in Jerusalem.*

Gonville and Caius
(pronounced "keys"),
founded in 1348, is one
of the oldest colleges.

St Mary's Church
*This clock is over the west door
of the university's official church.
Its tower offers fine views.*

VISITORS' CHECKLIST

Cambridgeshire. 🏠 100,000.
✈ Stansted. ✈ Cambridge.
🚆 Station Road. 🚌 Drummer
Street. ℹ Wheeler Street
(01223 322640). 🕐 daily. 🎨
Folk Festival: July; Strawberry
Festival: June.

★ King's College Chapel
*This late medieval masterpiece took
70 years to build (see pp198–9).*

Market square

**Coach
station**

King's College
*Henry VIII, king when
the chapel was com-
pleted in 1515, is
commemorated in
this statue near
the main gate.*

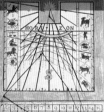

**Queens'
College**
*Its Tudor courts
are among the
university's
finest. This 17th-
century sundial
is over the old
chapel – now a
reading room.*

Corpus Christi College

**To London and
railway station**

Mathematical Bridge
*Linking the two parts of Queens'
College across the Cam, the bridge
was first built without nuts or bolts.*

🏛 Fitzwilliam Museum

Trumpington St. ☎ *01223 332900.*
🔘 *Tue–Sun; public hols.* ⬤ *24 Dec–
1 Jan. Good Fri, May Day.* **Donation.**
♿ *limited.* 📷 *Sun pm.* ▢ ▯

One of Britain's oldest public
museums, this massive Classical building has works of
exceptional quality and rarity,
especially antiquities, ceramics,
paintings and manuscripts.

The core of the collection
was bequeathed in 1816 by
the 7th Viscount Fitzwilliam.
Other gifts have since greatly
added to the exhibits.

Works by Titian (1488–1576)
and the 17th-century Dutch
masters, including Hals, Cuyp
and Hobbema's *Wooded
Landscape* (1686), stand out
among the paintings. French
Impressionist gems include
Monet's *Le Printemps* (1866)
and Renoir's *La Place Clichy*
(1880), while Picasso's *Still
Life* (1923) is notable among
the modern works. Most of
the important British artists
are represented, from
Hogarth in the 18th century
through Constable in the 19th
to Ben Nicholson in the 20th.

The miniatures include the
earliest surviving depiction of
Henry VIII. In the same gallery
are some dazzling illuminated
manuscripts, notably the 15th-
century *Metz Pontifical*, a
sumptuous French liturgical
work produced for a bishop.

The impressive Glaisher
collection of European
earthenware and stoneware
includes a unique display of
English delftware from the
16th and 17th centuries.

Handel's bookcase contains
folios of his work, and nearby
is Keats's original manuscript
for *Ode to a Nightingale* (1819).

**Portrait of Richard James
(c.1740s) by William Hogarth**

Cambridge: King's College

**King's College
Chapel Coat of Arms**

Henry VI founded this college in
1441. Work on the chapel – one
of the most important examples of late
medieval English architecture – began
five years later, and took 70 years to
complete. Henry himself decided that
it should dominate the city and gave
specific instructions about its dimensions: 88 m (289 ft) long, 12 m (40 ft)
wide and 29 m (94 ft) high. The detailed design is
thought to have been by master stonemason Reginald
Ely, although it was altered in later years.

★ Fan Vaulted Ceiling

*This awe-inspiring ceiling,
supported by 22 buttresses,
was built by master stonemason John Wastell in 1515.*

The Fellows' Building was
designed in 1724 by James
Gibbs, as part of an
uncompleted design
for a Great Court.

Henry VI's statue
*This bronze statue of the college's
founder was erected in 1879.*

KING'S COLLEGE CHOIR

When he founded the chapel,
Henry VI stipulated that a choir
of six lay clerks and 16 boy
choristers – educated at the
College school – should sing
daily at services. This still
happens in term time but today
the choir also gives concerts all
over the world. Its broadcast
service of carols has become a
much-loved Christmas tradition.

Choristers in King's College Chapel

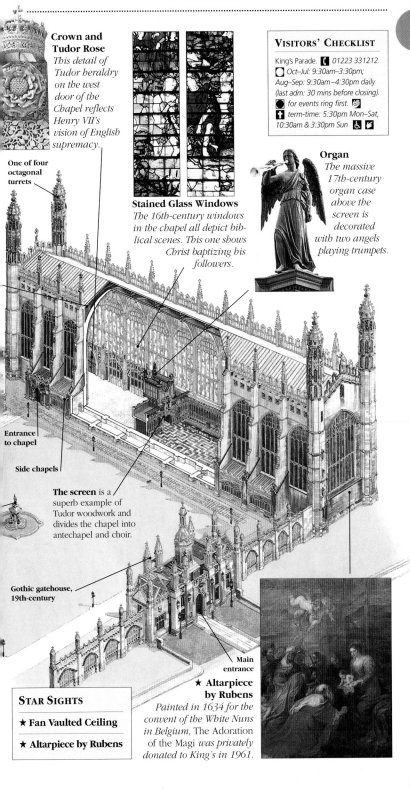

Crown and Tudor Rose
This detail of Tudor heraldry on the west door of the Chapel reflects Henry VII's vision of English supremacy.

Stained Glass Windows
The 16th-century windows in the chapel all depict biblical scenes. This one shows Christ baptizing his followers.

VISITORS' CHECKLIST

King's Parade. ☎ 01223 331212.
◯ Oct–Jul: 9:30am–3:30pm;
Aug–Sep: 9:30am–4:30pm daily
(last adm: 30 mins before closing).
● for events ring first. 🈚
🕈 term-time: 5:30pm Mon–Sat,
10:30am & 3:30pm Sun ♿ ✍

Organ
The massive 17th-century organ case above the screen is decorated with two angels playing trumpets.

One of four octagonal turrets

Entrance to chapel

Side chapels

The screen is a superb example of Tudor woodwork and divides the chapel into antechapel and choir.

Gothic gatehouse, 19th-century

Main entrance

STAR SIGHTS

★ Fan Vaulted Ceiling

★ Altarpiece by Rubens

★ Altarpiece by Rubens
Painted in 1634 for the convent of the White Nuns in Belgium, The Adoration of the Magi was privately donated to King's in 1961.

Exploring Cambridge University

C AMBRIDGE UNIVERSITY HAS 31 COLLEGES *(see pp196–7)*, the oldest being Peterhouse (1284) and the newest being Robinson (1979). Clustered around the city centre, many of the older colleges have peaceful gardens backing onto the River Cam, which are known as the "Backs". The layout of the older colleges, as at Oxford *(see pp212–13)*, derives from their early connections with religious institutions, although few escaped heavy-handed modification in the Victorian era. The college buildings are generally grouped around squares called courts and offer an unrivalled mix of over 600 years of architecture from the late medieval period through Wren's masterpieces and up to the present day.

The nave of the Wren Chapel at Pembroke College

The imposing façade of Emmanuel College

Emmanuel College
Built in 1677 on St Andrew's Street, Sir Christopher Wren's *(see p116)* chapel is the highlight of the college. Some of the intricate interior details, particularly the plaster ceiling and Amigoni's altar rails (1734), are superb. Founded in 1584, the college has a Puritan tradition. One notable graduate was the clergyman John Harvard, who emigrated to America in 1636 and left all his money to the Massachusetts college that now bears his name.

Senate House
King's Parade is the site of this Palladian building, which is used primarily for university ceremonies. It was designed by James Gibbs in 1722 as part of a grand square of university buildings – which was never completed.

Corpus Christi College
Just down from Senate House, this was founded in 1352 by the local trade guilds, anxious to ensure that education was not the sole prerogative of church and nobility. Its Old Court is remarkably well preserved and looks today much as it would have done when built in the 14th century.

The college is connected by a 15th-century gallery of red brick to St Bene't's Church (short for St Benedict's), whose large Saxon tower is the oldest structure in Cambridge.

King's College
See pp198–9.

Pembroke College
The college chapel was the first building completed by Wren *(see p116)*. A formal classical design, it replaced a 14th-century chapel that was turned into a library. The college, just off Trumpington Street, also has fine gardens.

Jesus College
Although founded in 1497, some of its buildings on Jesus Lane are older, as the college took over St Radegond's nunnery, built in the 12th century. There are traces of Norman columns, windows and a well-preserved hammerbeam roof in the college dining hall.

The chapel keeps the core of the original church but the stained glass windows are modern and contain work by William Morris *(see pp206–7)*.

Queens' College
Built in 1446 on Queens' Land, the college was endowed in 1448 by Margaret of Anjou, queen of Henry VI, and again in 1465 by Elizabeth Woodville, queen of Edward IV, which explains the position of the apostrophe. Queens' has a

---

PUNTING ON THE CAM

Punting captures the essence of carefree college days: a student leaning on a long pole, lazily guiding the flat-bottomed river craft along, while others stretch out and relax. Punting is still popular both with students and visitors, who can hire punts from boat-yards along the river – with a chauffeur if required. Punts do sometimes capsize, and novices should prepare for a dip.

Punting by the King's College "Backs"

marvellous collection of Tudor buildings, notably the half-timbered President's Gallery, built in the mid-16th century on top of the brick arches in the charming Cloister Court. The Principal Court is 15th century, as is Erasmus's Tower, named after the Dutch scholar.

Pepys Library in Magdalene College

The college has buildings on both sides of the Cam, linked by the bizarre Mathematical Bridge, built in 1749 to hold together without the use of nuts and bolts – although they have had to be used in subsequent repairs.

Magdalene College
Pronounced "maudlin" – as is the Oxford college *(see p212)* – the college, on Bridge Street, was established in 1482. The diarist Samuel Pepys (1633–1703) was a student here and left his large library to the college on his death. The 12 red-oak bookcases have over 3,000 books. Magdalene was the last all-male Cambridge college and it admitted women students only in 1987.

St John's College
Sited on St John's Street, the imposing turreted brick and stone gatehouse of 1514, with its colourful heraldic symbols, provides a fitting entrance to the second largest Cambridge college and its rich store of 16th- and 17th-century buildings. Its hall, most of it Elizabethan, has portraits of the college's famous alumni, such as the poet William Wordsworth *(see p352)* and the statesman Lord Palmerston. St John's spans the Cam and boasts two bridges, one built in 1712 and the other, the Bridge of Sighs, in 1831, based on its Venetian namesake.

Peterhouse
The first Cambridge college, on Trumpington Street, is also one of the smallest. The hall still has original features from 1286 but its best details are later – a Tudor fireplace which is backed with 19th-century tiles by William Morris *(see pp206–7)*. A gallery connects the college to the 12th-century church of St Mary the Less, which used to be called St Peter's Church – hence the college's name.

William Morris tiles, Peterhouse

VISITORS' CHECKLIST

Cambridge Colleges can usually be visited from 2–5pm daily, but there are no set opening hours. See noticeboards at each college for daily opening times. Some colleges charge admission.

Trinity College
The largest college, situated on Trinity Street, was founded by Henry VIII in 1547 and has a massive court and hall. The entrance gate, with statues of Henry and James I (added later), was built in 1529 for King's Hall, an earlier college incorporated into Trinity. The Great Court features a late Elizabethan fountain – at one time the main water supply. The chapel, built in 1567, has life-size statues of college members, notably Roubiliac's statue of the scientist Isaac Newton (1755).

University Botanic Garden
A delightful place for a leisurely stroll, just off Trumpington Street, as well as an important academic resource, the garden has been on this site since 1846. It has a superb collection of trees and a sensational water garden. The winter garden is one of the finest in the country.

The Bridge of Sighs over the River Cam, linking the buildings of St John's College

THAMES VALLEY

BUCKINGHAMSHIRE · OXFORDSHIRE · BERKSHIRE
BEDFORDSHIRE · HERTFORDSHIRE

THE MIGHTY TIDAL RIVER *on which Britain's capital city was founded has modest origins, meandering from its source in the hills of Gloucestershire through the lush countryside towards London. Almost entirely agricultural land in the 19th century, the Thames Valley maintains its pastoral beauty despite the incursion of modern industry.*

There are ancient royal connections with the area. Windsor Castle has been a residence of kings and queens for more than 900 years, and played a critical role in history in 1215, when King John set out from here to sign the *Magna Carta* at Runnymede on the River Thames. Further north, Queen Anne had Blenheim Palace built for her military commander, the 1st Duke of Marlborough. Elizabeth I spent part of her childhood at Hatfield House, and part of the Tudor palace still stands.

Several towns in this region, most notably Burford in Oxfordshire, developed as coach staging posts on the important trunk routes between London and the West Country. With the introduction of commuter transportation in the early 20th century, much of the area became an extension of suburbia and saw some imaginative experiments in Utopian town planning such as the garden city of Welwyn and the Quaker settlement at Jordons.

Oxford, Thames Valley's principal city, owes its importance to the foundation of Britain's first university there in 1167; many of its colleges are gems of medieval architecture. In the 17th century, a number of battles during the Civil War *(see pp52–3)* were fought around Oxford, which for a time was the headquarters of King Charles I, who was supported by the students. When the royalists were forced to flee Oxford, Cromwell made himself chancellor of the university.

Punting on the River Cherwell, Oxford

◁ **Medieval staircase in Christchurch College, Oxford**

Exploring the Thames Valley

THE PLEASANT COUNTRYSIDE of the Chiltern Hills and of the Thames Valley itself appealed to aristocrats who built stately homes close to London. Many of these are among the grandest in the country, including Hatfield House and Blenheim. Around these great houses grew picturesque villages, with half-timbered buildings and, as you move towards the Cotswolds, houses built in attractive buff-coloured stone. That the area has been inhabited for thousands of years is shown by the number of prehistoric remains, including the most remarkable chalk hillside figure, the White Horse of Uffington.

SIGHTS AT A GLANCE

Walks and Tours

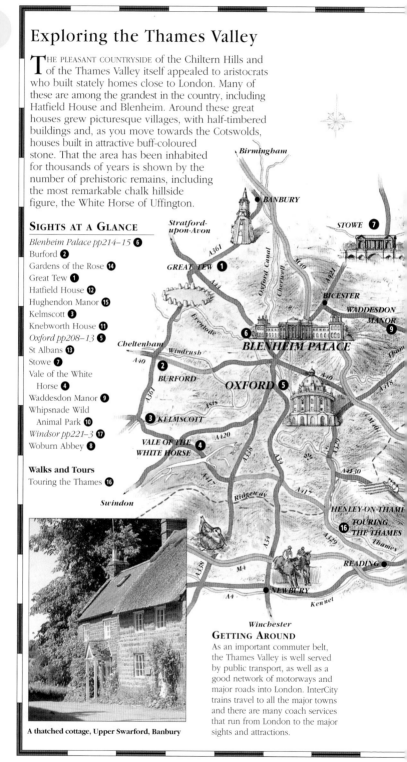

A thatched cottage, Upper Swarford, Banbury

GETTING AROUND

As an important commuter belt, the Thames Valley is well served by public transport, as well as a good network of motorways and major roads into London. InterCity trains travel to all the major towns and there are many coach services that run from London to the major sights and attractions.

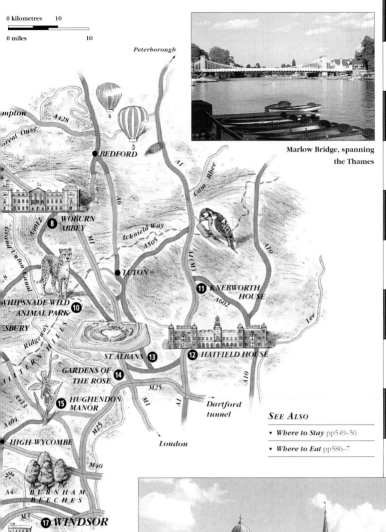

0 kilometres   10

0 miles   10

Peterborough

BEDFORD

8 WOBURN ABBEY

Icknield Way

LUTON

11 KNEBWORTH HOUSE

WHIPSNADE WILD ANIMAL PARK **10**

Ridgeway

ST ALBANS **13**

12 HATFIELD HOUSE

GARDENS OF THE ROSE **14**

15 HUGHENDEN MANOR

M25

Dartford tunnel

HIGH WYCOMBE

London

BURNHAM BEECHES

17 WINDSOR

Marlow Bridge, spanning the Thames

SEE ALSO

- *Where to Stay* pp549–50
- *Where to Eat* pp586–7

KEY

▨	Motorway
▨	Major road
▨	Scenic route
▰▰	Scenic path
〜	River
⚡	Viewpoint

Radcliffe Camera, surrounded by Oxford's spires

Great Tew ❶

Oxfordshire. 🏠 *250.* 🚆 *Oxford then taxi.* ℹ️ *Spiceball Park Rd, Banbury (01295 259855).*

THIS SECLUDED village of ironstone was founded in the 1630s by Lord Falkland for estate workers. It was heavily restored between 1809 and 1811 in the Gothic style then fashionable. Thatched cottages stand in gardens with clipped box hedges, and in the centre of the village is the 17th-century pub, the **Falkland Arms**, which retains its original period atmosphere.

ENVIRONS: Five miles (8 km) west are the **Rollright Stones**, three Bronze Age monuments. They comprise a stone circle of 77 stones, about 30 m (100 ft) in diameter, known as the King's Men; the remains of a burial chamber called the Whispering Knights; and the solitary King Stone. Further north is **Banbury**, well known for its spicy flat cakes and its market cross, immortalized in the nursery rhyme, *Ride a Cock-horse to*

Banbury Cross. The original medieval cross was destroyed but it was replaced in 1859.

The 19th-century Banbury Cross

🍴 **Falkland Arms**
Great Tew. 📞 *01608 683653.* ◯ *daily.* ● *25 Dec.* 🍴

Burford ❷

Oxfordshire. 🏠 *1,000.* ℹ️ *Sheep St (01993 823558).*

A CHARMING SMALL town, Burford has hardly changed from Georgian times, when it was an important coach stop between Oxford and the West Country. Cotswold stone houses, inns and shops, many built in the 16th century, line its main street. **Tolsey Hall** is a Tudor house with an open ground floor where stalls are still set up. The house is located on the corner of Sheep Street, itself a reminder of the importance of the medieval wool trade (*see p193*).

ENVIRONS: Just east of Burford is **Swinbrook**, whose church contains the Fettiplace Monuments, six carved figures from the Tudor and Stuart periods.

Two miles (3 km) beyond are the ruins of **Minster Lovell Hall**, a 15th-century manor house whose unusual dovecote survives intact.

Witney, further west, has a town hall dating from 1730. On its outskirts **Cogges Manor Farm**, founded in the 13th-century, has been restored to its Victorian state and is now a museum of farm life.

🍴 **Minster Lovell Hall & Dovecote**
Minster Lovell. ◯ *daily.*
🍴 **Cogges Manor Farm**
Witney. 📞 *01993 772602.* ◯ *Apr–Oct: Tue–Sun & public hols.* 🔲

Kelmscott ❸

Oxfordshire. 🏠 *100.* ℹ️ *Faringdon (01367 242191).*

THE IMAGINATIVE designer and writer William Morris lived in this pretty Thameside village from 1871 until his death in 1896. He shared his house, the classic Elizabethan **Kelmscott Manor**, with fellow painter Dante Gabriel Rossetti (1828–82), who left after an affair with Morris's wife Jane – the model for many pre-Raphaelite paintings.

Morris and his followers in the Arts and Crafts movement were attracted by the

Cotswold stone houses, Burford, Oxfordshire

The formal entrance of the Elizabethan Kelmscott Manor

medieval feel of the village and several cottages were later built in Morris's memory.

Today Kelmscott Manor has works of art by members of the movement – including some William de Morgan tiles. Morris is buried in the village churchyard, with a tomb designed by Philip Webb.

Two miles (3 km) to the east is **Radcot Bridge**, the oldest bridge still standing over the Thames. Built in 1160 from the local Taynton stone, it was a strategic river crossing, and in 1387 was damaged in a battle between Richard II and his barons. In the 17th and 18th centuries, Taynton stone was shipped from here to London in the building boom.

🏠 **Kelmscott Manor**
Kelmscott. 📞 01367 252486. ◯ Apr–Jun, Sep: Wed, 3rd Sat; Jul–Aug: Wed, 1st & 3rd Sat. 🅿 🚻 limited.

Vale of the White Horse ❹

Oxfordshire. 🚆 Didcot. ℹ 25 Bridge St, Abingdon (01235 522711).

Tʜɪs ʟᴏᴠᴇʟʏ ᴠᴀʟʟᴇʏ gets its name from the huge chalk horse, 100 m (350 ft) from nose to tail, carved into the hillside above Uffington. It is believed to be Britain's oldest hillside carving and has sparked many legends: some say it was cut by the Saxon leader Hengist (whose name means stallion in German), while others believe it has more to do with Alfred the Great, thought to have been born nearby.

It is, however, a great deal older than either of these stories suggest, having been dated at around 3000 BC.

Nearby is the Celtic earth ramparts of the Iron Age hill fort, **Uffington Castle**. A mile (1.5 km) west along the Ridgeway, an ancient trade route,

(see p33), is an even older monument, a large Stone Age burial mound which is known as **Wayland's Smithy**. This is immersed in legends that Sir Walter Scott (see p498) used in his novel *Kenilworth*.

The best view of the horse is to be had from Uffington village which is also worth visiting for the **Tom Brown's School Museum**. This 17th-century school house contains exhibits devoted to the author Thomas Hughes (1822–96). Hughes set the early chapters of his Victorian novel, *Tom Brown's Schooldays*, here. The museum also contains material about excavations on White Horse Hill.

🏛 **Tom Brown's School Museum**
Broad St, Uffington. ℹ 01367 820259. ◯ Easter–Oct: Sat, Sun & public hols (pm). 🅿 🚻 limited.

HILLSIDE CHALK FIGURES

It was the Celts who first saw the potential for creating large-scale artworks on the chalk hills of southern England. Horses – held in high regard by both the Celts and later the Saxons, and the objects of cult worship – were often a favourite subject, but people were also depicted, notably Cerne Abbas, Dorset (see p255) and the Long Man of Wilmington (see p166). The figures may have served as religious symbols or as landmarks by which tribes identified their territory. Many chalk figures have been obliterated, because without any attention they are quickly overrun by grass. Uffington is "scoured", to prevent encroachment by grass, a tradition once accompanied by a fair and other festivities. There was a second flush of hillside carving in the 18th century, especially in Wiltshire. In some cases – for instance at Bratton Castle near Westbury – an 18th-century carving has been superimposed on an ancient one.

Britain's oldest hillside carving, the White Horse of Uffington

Street-by-Street: Oxford ⑤

O XFORD HAS LONG BEEN a strategic point
on the western routes into London – its
name describes its position as a convenient
spot for crossing the river (a ford for oxen).
The city's first scholars, who founded the
university, came from France in 1167. The
development of England's first university
created the spectacular skyline of tall
towers and "dreaming spires".

Old Ashmolean
*Now the Museum
of the History of
Science, this res-
plendent building
was designed in
1683 to show Elias
Ashmole's collec-
tion of curiosities.
The displays were
moved in 1845.*

The Ashmolean Museum
displays one of Britain's
foremost collections of
fine art and antiquities.

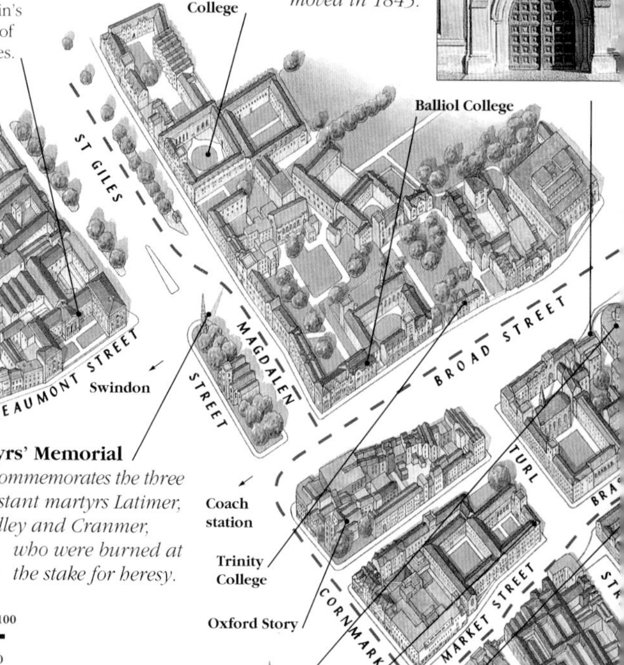

**St John's
College**

Balliol College

ST GILES

MAGDALEN STREET

BEAUMONT STREET   Swindon

BROAD STREET

TURL

BRA

Martyrs' Memorial
*This commemorates the three
Protestant martyrs Latimer,
Ridley and Cranmer,
who were burned at
the stake for heresy.*

**Coach
station**

**Trinity
College**

CORNMARKET STREET

MARKET STREET

ST

Oxford Story

| 0 metres | | 100 |
| 0 yards | | 100 |

**Jesus
College**

**Lincoln
College**

KEY

– – –   Suggested route

**Covered
market**

**Railway
station**

**Lincoln
College
Library**

ST ALD

Museum of Oxford

PERCY BYSSHE SHELLEY

Shelley (1792–1822), one of the
Romantic poets *(see p352)*,
attended University College,
Oxford, but was expelled after
writing the revolutionary
pamphlet *The
Necessity of
Atheism*.
Despite that
disgrace, the
college has
put up a
marble
memorial
to him.

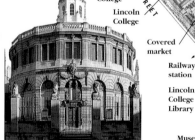

Sheldonian Theatre
*The first building de-
signed by Wren (see
p116) is the scene of
Oxford University's
traditional graduation
ceremonies.*

STAR SIGHTS

★ **Radcliffe Camera**

★ **Christ Church**

★ Radcliffe Camera
This Classical rotunda is Oxford's most distinctive building and is now a reading room of the Bodleian. It was one of the library's original buildings (see p213).

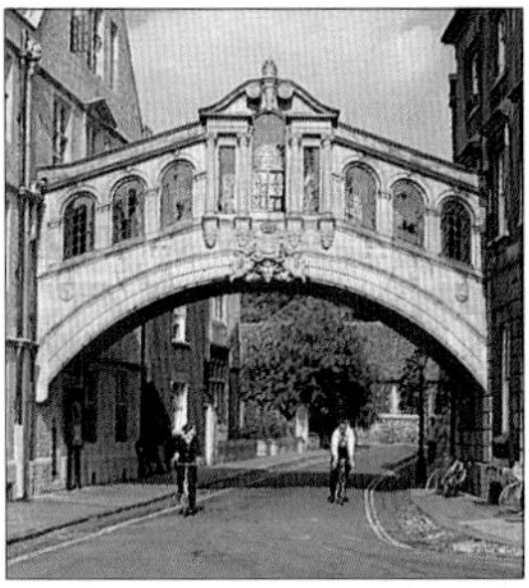

Bridge of Sighs
A copy of the steeply arched bridge in Venice, this picturesque landmark, built in 1914, joins the old and new buildings of Hertford College.

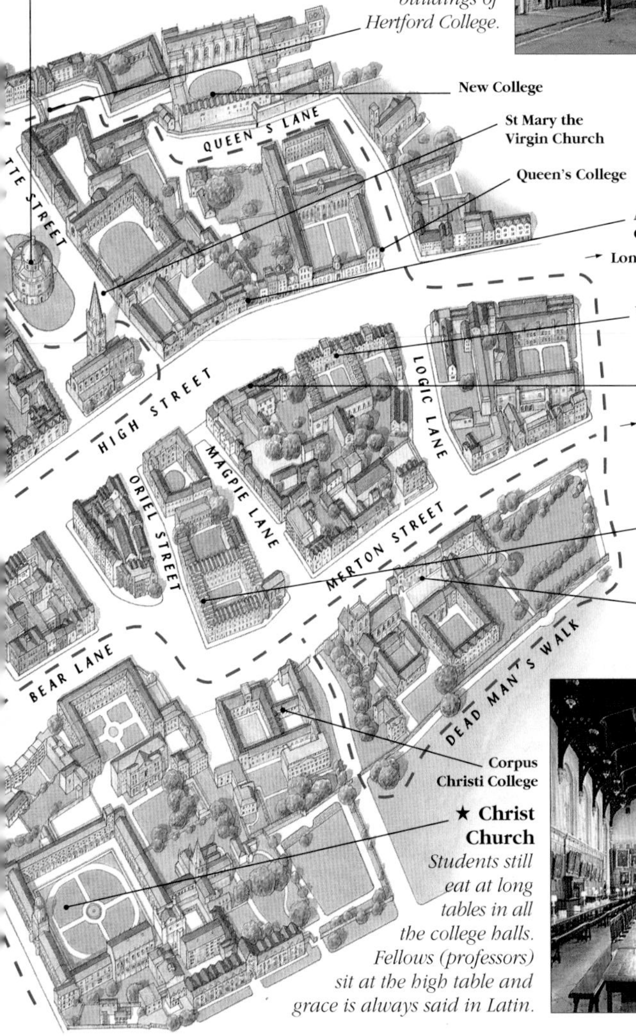

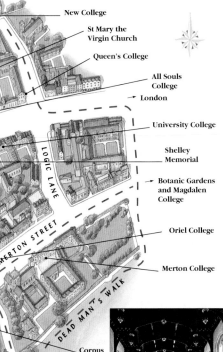

New College
St Mary the Virgin Church
Queen's College
All Souls College
→ London
University College
Shelley Memorial
→ Botanic Gardens and Magdalen College
Oriel College
Merton College
Corpus Christi College

QUEEN'S LANE
HIGH STREET
LOGIC LANE
ORIEL STREET
MAGPIE LANE
MERTON STREET
BEAR LANE
DEAD MAN'S WALK
TTE STREET

★ Christ Church
Students still eat at long tables in all the college halls. Fellows (professors) sit at the high table and grace is always said in Latin.

Exploring Oxford

A bust on the Sheldonian Theatre

OXFORD IS MORE than just a university city; it has one of Britain's most important car factories in the suburb of Cowley. Despite this, Oxford is dominated by institutions related to its huge academic community: like Blackwell's bookshop which has over 20,000 titles in stock. The two rivers, the Cherwell and the Isis (the name given to the Thames as it flows through the city), provide lovely riverside walks, or you can hire a punt and spend an afternoon on the Cherwell.

🏛 Ashmolean Museum

Beaumont St. 📞 01865 278000. ☐ Tue–Sun & public hols. ● 25–28 Dec, 1 Jan, Good Fri. 🚻 📷 Tue, Fri, Sat. 🖥 📱

One of the best museums in Britain outside London, the Ashmolean – the first purpose-built museum in England – was opened in 1683, based on a display known internationally as "The Ark" collected by the two John Tradescants, father and son.

On their many voyages to the Orient and the Americas they collected stuffed animals and tribal artefacts, the like of which had never before been displayed in England. The collection was acquired on their death by the antiquarian Elias Ashmole, who donated it to the university and had a building made for the exhibits on Broad Street – the Old Ashmolean, now the Museum of the History of Science.

During the 19th century part of the Tradescant collection was moved to the University Galleries, a magnificent Neo-Classical building of 1845. This greatly expanded museum is now known as the Ashmolean.

However, what is left of the original curio collection is overshadowed by the other exhibits in the museum, in particular the paintings and drawings. These include Bellini's *St Jerome Reading in a Landscape* (late 15th century); Raphael's *Heads of Two Apostles* (1519); Turner's *Venice: The Grand Canal* (1840); Rembrandt's *Saskia Asleep* (1635); Michelangelo's *Crucifixion* (1557), Picasso's *Blue Roofs* (1901) and a large group of Pre-Raphaelites, including Rossetti, Millais and Holman Hunt. There are also fine Greek and Roman carvings and a collection of stringed musical instruments.

Items of more local interest include a Rowlandson watercolour of Radcliffe Square in about 1790 and the Oxford Crown. This silver coin was minted here during the Civil War in 1644 *(see p52)* when Charles I was based in Oxford, and forms part of the second largest coin collection in Britain. Perhaps the single most important item is the gold enamelled ring known as the Alfred Jewel *(see p47)*, which is over 1,000 years old.

The entrance to the Ashmolean Museum

🌿 Botanic Gardens

Rose Lane. 📞 01865 276920. ☐ daily. ● 25 Dec, Good Fri. 🚻 Apr–Aug. 🚻 📷

Britain's oldest botanic garden was founded in 1621 – one ancient yew tree survives from that period. The ornate entrance gates were designed by Nicholas Stone in 1633 and paid for, like the garden itself, by the Earl of Danby. His statue adorns the gate, along with those of Charles I and Charles II. Though small, the garden is a delightful spot for a stroll, with well-labelled flower beds in the original walled garden and a newer section with a herbaceous border and a rock garden.

The 17th-century Botanic Gardens

🏰 Carfax Tower

Carfax Sq. 📞 01865 792653. ☐ daily. ● 2 Jan, 24 Dec. 🚻 📷 📱

The tower is all that remains of the 14th-century Church of St Martin, demolished in 1896 so that the adjoining road could be widened. Be there to watch the clock strike the quarter hours, and climb to the top for a panoramic view of the city. Carfax was the crossing point of the original north-to-south and east-to-west routes through Oxford and the word comes from the French *quatre voies*, or "four ways".

🎵 Holywell Music Room

Holywell St. ☐ concerts only. 🚻 🚻

This was the first building in Europe designed, in 1752, specifically for public musical performances. Previously, concerts had been held in private houses for invited guests only. Its two splendid chandeliers originally adorned Westminster Hall at the coronation of George IV in 1820, and were given by the king to Wadham College, of which the music room technically forms a part. The room is regularly used for contemporary and classical concerts.

🏛 Museum of Oxford

St Aldate. 01865 815559. Tue–Sun. 25, 26 Dec, 1 Jan.

A well-organized display in the Victorian town hall illustrates the long history of Oxford and its university. Exhibits include a Roman pottery kiln and a town seal from 1191.

The main features are a series of well-reconstructed rooms, including one from an Elizabethan inn and an 18th-century student's room.

🎪 Martyrs' Memorial

This commemorates the three Protestants burned at the stake on Broad Street – Bishops Latimer and Ridley in 1555, and Archbishop Cranmer in 1556. On the accession of Queen Mary in 1553 (see p51), they were committed to the Tower of London, then sent to Oxford to defend their views before the doctors of divinity who, after the hearing, condemned them as heretics.

The memorial was designed in 1843 by George Gilbert Scott and based on the Eleanor crosses erected in 12 English towns by Edward I (1239–1307) to honour his queen.

🏛 Oxford Story

6 Broad St. 01865 728822. daily. 25 Dec. limited.

This audio-visual account of the city's history has a train ride through exhibits which are brought to life with animated, life-size models of major historical characters.

🔒 St Mary the Virgin Church

High St. 01865 279111. daily.

This, the official church of the university, is said to be the most visited parish church in England. The oldest parts date from the early 14th century and include the tower, from the top of which you can enjoy a fine view. Its Congregation House, of the same date, served as the university's first library until the Bodleian was founded in 1488 (see p213). The church is where the three Oxford Martyrs were pronounced heretics in 1555. The architectural highlight of the church is the Baroque south porch, constructed in 1637.

Thomas Cranmer statue, St Mary the Virgin Church

🏛 University Museum and Pitt Rivers Museum

Parks Rd. 01865 272950. daily (pm). 24–26 Dec, Easter Thu–Sat. limited.

Two of Oxford's most interesting museums adjoin each other. The first is a museum of natural history containing relics of dinosaurs as well as a stuffed dodo. This flightless bird has been extinct since the 17th century, but was immortalized by Lewis Carroll (an Oxford mathematics lecturer whose real name was Charles Dodgson) in his book *Alice in Wonderland (see p387)*. The exhibits are housed in a large Victorian building with cast-iron columns which support a glass roof leading to a cavernous interior. This leads into the Pitt Rivers Museum, which has one of the world's most extensive ethnographic collections – masks and tribal totems from Africa and the Far East – and archaeological displays, including exhibits collected by the explorer Captain Cook. An annexe on Banbury Road has an unusual collection of musical instruments, with audio equipment so you can hear them playing.

🎪 Sheldonian Theatre

Broad St. 01865 277299. Mon–Sat. 22 Dec–2 Jan, Easter & public hols. limited.

Completed in 1669, this was the first building designed by Christopher Wren (see p116). It was paid for by Gilbert Sheldon, the Archbishop of Canterbury, as a place to hold university degree ceremonies. The Classical design of the oval building is based on the Theatre of Marcellus in Rome. The octagonal cupola – larger than the original – was built in 1838 and there is a very famous view from its huge Lantern. In the theatre the beautifully painted ceiling depicts the triumph of religion, art and science over envy, hatred and malice.

The impressive frontage of the University Museum and Pitt Rivers Museum

Exploring Oxford University

MANY OF THE 36 COLLEGES which go to make up the university were founded between the 13th and 16th centuries and cluster around the city centre. As scholarship was then the exclusive preserve of the church, the colleges were designed along the lines of monastic buildings but were often surrounded by beautiful gardens. Although most colleges have been altered over the years, many still incorporate a lot of their original features.

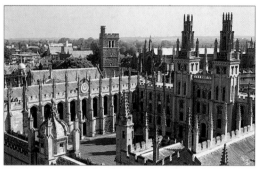

The spectacular view of All Souls College from St Mary's Church

All Souls College

Founded in 1438 on the High Street by Henry VI, the chapel on the college's north side has a classic hammerbeam roof, unusual misericords *(see p327)* on the choir stalls and 15th-century stained glass.

Christ Church College

The best way to view this, the largest of the Oxford colleges, is to approach through the meadows from St Aldate's. Christ Church dates from 1525 when Cardinal Wolsey founded it as an ecclesiastical college to train cardinals. The upper part of the tower in Tom Quad – a rectangular courtyard – was built by Wren *(see p116)* in 1682 and is the largest in the city. When its bell, Great Tom, was hung in 1648, the college had 101 students, which is why the bell is rung 101 times at 9:05pm, to mark the curfew for students (which has not been enforced since 1963). The odd timing is because night falls here five minutes later than at Greenwich *(see p131)*. Christ Church has produced 16 British prime ministers in the last 200 years. Beside the main quad is the 12th-century Christ Church Cathedral, one of the smallest in England.

Lincoln College

One of the best-preserved of the medieval colleges, it was founded in 1427 on Turl Street, and the front quad and façade are 15th century. The hall still has its original roof, including the gap where smoke used to escape. The Jacobean chapel is notable for its stained glass. John Wesley *(see p265)* was at college here and his rooms, now a chapel, can be visited.

Magdalen College

At the end of the High Street is perhaps the most typical and beautiful Oxford college. Its 15th-century quads in contrasting styles are set in a park by the Cherwell, crossed by Magdalen Bridge. Every May Day at 6am, the college choir sings from the top of Magdalen's bell tower (1508) – a 16th-century custom to mark the start of summer.

New College

One of the grandest colleges, it was founded by William of Wykeham in 1379 to educate clergy to replace those killed by the Black Death of 1348 *(see p49)*.

Magdalen Bridge spanning the River Cherwell

Its magnificent chapel on New College Lane, restored in the 19th century, has vigorous 14th-century misericords and El Greco's (1541–1614) famous painting of *St James*.

Queen's College

Most of the college buildings date from the 18th century and represent some of the finest work from that period in Oxford. Its superb library was built in 1695 by Henry Aldrich (1647–1710) The front screen with its bell-topped gatehouse is a feature of the High Street.

STUDENT LIFE

Students belong to individual colleges and usually live in them for the duration of their course. The university gives lectures, sets exams and awards degrees but much of the students' tuition and social life is based around their college. Many university traditions date back hundreds of years, like the graduation ceremonies at the Sheldonian which are still held in Latin.

Graduation at the Sheldonian *(see p210)*

Merton College seen from Christ Church Meadows

St John's College
The impressive frontage on St Giles dates from 1437, when it was founded for Cistercian scholars. The old library has lovely 17th-century bookcases and stained glass, while the Baylie Chapel has a display of 15th-century vestments.

Trinity College
The oldest part of the college on Broad Street, Durham Quad, is named after the earlier college of 1296 which was incorporated into Trinity in 1555. The late 17th-century chapel has a magnificent reredos and wooden screen.

Corpus Christi College
The whole of the charming front quad on Merton Street dates from 1517, when the college was founded. The quad's sundial, topped by a pelican – the college symbol – bears an early 17th-century calendar. The chapel has a rare 16th-century eagle lectern.

Merton College
Off Merton Street, this is the oldest college (1264) in Oxford. Much of its hall dates from then, including a sturdy decorated door. The chapel choir contains allegorical reliefs representing music, arithmetic, rhetoric and grammar. Merton's Mob Quad served as a model for the later colleges.

BODLEIAN LIBRARY
Founded in 1320, the library was expanded in 1426 by Humphrey, Duke of Gloucester (1391–1447) and brother of Henry V, when his collection of manuscripts would not fit into the old library. It was refounded in 1602 by Thomas Bodley, a wealthy scholar, who insisted on strict rules: the keeper was forbidden to marry. The library is one of the six copyright deposit libraries in the country – it is entitled to receive a copy of every book published in Britain.

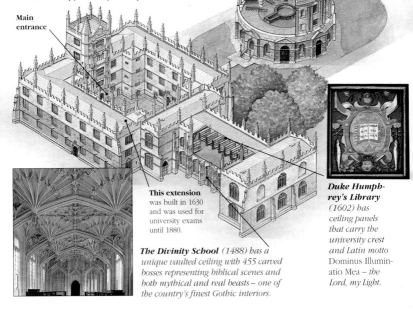

The Radcliffe Camera (1748), a domed Baroque rotunda, was built by James Gibbs as a memorial to the physician Dr John Radcliffe (1650–1714).

Main entrance

This extension was built in 1630 and was used for university exams until 1880.

The Divinity School (1488) has a unique vaulted ceiling with 455 carved bosses representing biblical scenes and both mythical and real beasts – one of the country's finest Gothic interiors.

Duke Humphrey's Library (1602) has ceiling panels that carry the university crest and Latin motto Dominus Illuminatio Mea – the Lord, my Light.

Blenheim Palace ❻

Aᶠᵗᵉʳ ᴊᴏʜɴ ᴄʜᴜʀᴄʜɪʟʟ, the 1st Duke of Marlborough, defeated the French at the Battle of Blenheim in 1704, Queen Anne gave him the Manor of Woodstock and had this palatial house built for him in gratitude. Designed by both Nicholas Hawksmoor and Sir John Vanbrugh *(see p384)*, it is a Baroque masterpiece. It was also the birthplace of Britain's World War II leader, Winston Churchill, in 1874.

★ **Long Library**
This 55 m (183 room was desig by Vanbrugh as picture gallery. portraits include of Queen Anne Sir Godfrey Kne (1646–1723). T stucco on the ceiling is by Isac Mansfield (1725

Winston Churchill and his wife, Clementine

The Grand Bridge was built in 1708. It has a 31 m (101 ft) main span and contains rooms within its structure.

Chapel
The marble monument to the 1st Duke of Marlborough and his family was sculpted by Michael Rysbrack in 1733.

Water Terrace Gardens
These magnificent gardens were laid out in the 1920s by French architect Achille Duchêne in 17th-century style, with detailed patterned beds and fountains.

Sᴛᴀʀ Sɪɢʜᴛs

★ **Long Library**

★ **Saloon**

★ **Park and Gardens**

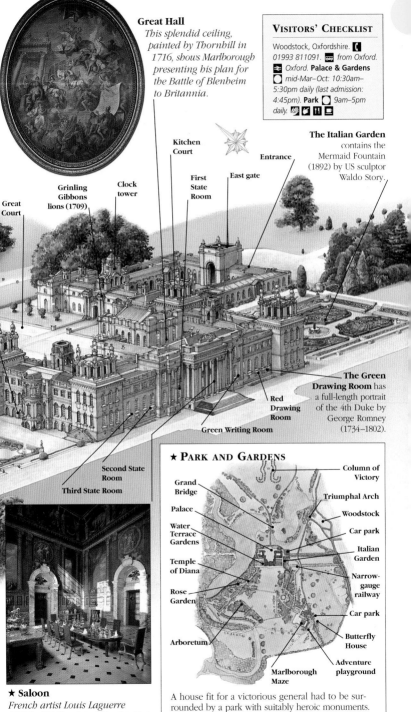

Great Hall
This splendid ceiling, painted by Thornhill in 1716, shows Marlborough presenting his plan for the Battle of Blenheim to Britannia.

The Italian Garden contains the Mermaid Fountain (1892) by US sculptor Waldo Story.

Kitchen Court

Entrance

Clock tower

First State Room

East gate

Grinling Gibbons lions (1709)

Great Court

The Green Drawing Room has a full-length portrait of the 4th Duke by George Romney (1734–1802).

Red Drawing Room

Green Writing Room

Second State Room

Third State Room

★ PARK AND GARDENS

Grand Bridge

Palace

Water Terrace Gardens

Temple of Diana

Rose Garden

Arboretum

Marlborough Maze

Column of Victory

Triumphal Arch

Woodstock

Car park

Italian Garden

Narrow-gauge railway

Car park

Butterfly House

Adventure playground

A house fit for a victorious general had to be surrounded by a park with suitably heroic monuments. They were kept when Capability Brown (*see p22*) re-landscaped the park in 1764 and created the lake.

★ Saloon
French artist Louis Laguerre (1663–1721) painted the detailed scenes on the walls and ceiling of the state dining room.

Canaletto's *Entrance to the Arsenal* (1730) hangs at Woburn Abbey

Stowe ❼

(NT) Buckingham, Buckinghamshire.
☎ 01280 822850. **⊠** Milton
Keynes then bus. **◯** Mar–Oct:
Wed–Sun, public hols. **●** 25 May.
▨ **♿** limited. **▯** **▮**
ⓦ www.nationaltrust.org.uk

THIS IS THE MOST ambitious
and important landscaped
garden in Britain as well as
also being one of the finest
examples of the 18th-century
passion for trying to shape and
improve on nature to make it
conform to fashionable
notions of taste *(see pp22–3)*.

In the space of nearly 100
years the original garden, first
laid out around 1680, was
enlarged and transformed by
the addition of monuments,
Greek and Gothic temples,
grottoes, statues, ornamental
bridges, artificial lakes and
"natural" tree plantings.

Most of the leading designers
and architects of the period
contributed to the design,
including Sir John Vanbrugh,
James Gibbs and Capability
Brown *(see pp22)* who was
head gardener at Stowe for 10
years, at the start of his career.

From 1593 to 1921 the huge
property was owned by the
Temple and Grenville families
– later the Dukes of Buckingham – until the large Palladian house at its centre was
sold and converted into an
elite boys' public school.

The family were soldiers
and politicians in the liberal
tradition, and many of the
buildings and sculptures in
the garden symbolize Utopian
ideals of democracy and freedom. There are temples of
British Worthies, of Ancient
Virtue, the Fane (temple) of

Pastoral Poetry and the
Elysian fields. Some features
deteriorated in the 19th
century and statues were sold.
But a comprehensive restoration programme has meant that
statues have been bought back
and copies made of others.

Woburn Abbey ❽

Woburn, Bedfordshire. **☎** 01525
290666. **⊠** Flitwick then taxi.
◯ 26 Mar–Sep: daily; Jan, Feb, Oct:
Sat, Sun. **●** Nov–Dec. **▨** **♿** ring
first. **▧** by arrangement. **▮** **▯**

THE DUKES OF BEDFORD have
lived here for over 350
years and were among the first
owners of an English stately
home to open their house to
the public some 40 years ago.

The abbey was built in the
mid-18th century on the foundations of a large 12th-century
Cistercian monastery. Its mix
of styles range from Henry
Flitcroft and Henry Holland
(see p24). It is also popular for
its 142 ha (350 acre) safari
park and attractive deer park
with nine species including the

Milu, originally the imperial
herd of China.

Its magnificent state apartments house an important
private art collection with
works by Reynolds (1723–92)
and Canaletto (1697–1768).

Waddesdon Manor ❾

nr Aylesbury, Buckinghamshire. **☎**
01296 653 203. **House ◯** 28 Mar–
4 Nov: 11am–4pm Wed–Sun & Mon
(bank hols only). **Grounds ◯** 28 Feb–
23 Dec: 10am–5pm Wed–Sun & Mon
(bank hols only). **Bachelors' Wing**
◯ 28 Mar–4 Nov: 11am–4pm
Wed–Fri. **▮** **▯**

WADDESDON MANOR was
built between 1874–89
by Baron Ferdinand de
Rothschild and designed by
French architect Gabriel-
Hippolyte Destailleur. The
garden was originally laid
out by French landscape
gardener Elie Lainé.

Built in the style of a French
16th-century chateau, Waddesdon Manor houses one of
the world's finest collections
of French 18th-century decorative art. It also contains
renowned collections of
French furniture, Savonnierie
carpets, Sèvres porcelain and
17th-century paintings.

The garden is renowned for
its seasonal displays and over
the next five years, displays
are being designed by contemporary artists. The design for
2001 was created by fashion
designer Oscar de la Renta.

Wine tasting events are
also hosted in Waddesdon's
comprehensive Wine Cellars.

The 17th-century Palladian bridge over the Octagon Lake in Stowe Park

Hatfield House, one of the largest Jacobean mansions in the country

Whipsnade Wild Animal Park ❿

Nr Dunstable, Bedfordshire.
🕿 01582 872171. 🚌 *Whipsnade.*
(Victoria Station, London: May–Oct.)
◯ *daily.* ⬤ *25 Dec.* 🏷️ ♿ 📷 🛒

THE RURAL BRANCH of London Zoo, this was one of the first zoos to minimize the use of cages, confining animals safely but without constriction.

At 240 ha (600 acres), it is Europe's largest conservation park, with more than 3,000 species. You can drive through some areas or go by steam train. Also popular are the adventure playground and sea lions' underwater display.

Knebworth House ⓫

Knebworth, Hertfordshire.
🕿 01438 812661. 🚊 *Stevenage then taxi.* ◯ *15 Apr–1 May, 27 May–4 Jun, 8 Jul–3 Sep: daily; 6–21 May, 10 Jun–2 Jul, 9 Sep–1 Oct: Sat, Sun & public hols.* ⬤ *18 Jun.* 🏷️ ♿ *limited.* 🏷️ 🛒 🏛️

A NOTABLE TUDOR mansion, with a beautiful Jacobean banqueting hall, Knebworth was overlain with a 19th-century Gothic exterior by Lord Lytton, the head of one of the most colourful families in Victorian England.

His eldest son, the 1st Earl of Lytton, was Viceroy of India, and several exhibits illustrate the Delhi Durbar of 1877, when Queen Victoria became Empress of India.

Hatfield House ⓬

Hatfield, Hertfordshire. 🕿 *01707 287010.* 🚊 *Hatfield.* ◯ *Apr–Sep: Tue–Sun & public hols.* 🏷️ ♿
🍴 🏛️

ONE OF ENGLAND's finest Jacobean houses, it was built between 1607 and 1611 for the powerful statesman Robert Cecil.

Its chief historical interest, though, lies in the surviving wing of the original Tudor Hatfield Palace, where Queen Elizabeth I *(see pp50–51)* spent much of her childhood. She held her first Council of State here when she was crowned in 1558. The palace, which was partly demolished in 1607 to make way for the new house, contains mementoes of her life, including the *Rainbow* portrait painted around 1600 by Isaac Oliver. Visitors can also attend medieval banquets held in its Great Hall.

The house has one of the few 17th-century gardens to survive, laid out by Robert Cecil with help from John Tradescant *(see p210).*

FAMOUS PURITANS

18th-century engraving of John Bunyan

Three major figures connected with the 17th-century Puritan movement are celebrated in the Thames area. John Bunyan (1628–88), who wrote the allegorical tale *The Pilgrim's Progress*, was born at Elstow, near Bedford. A passionate Puritan orator, he was jailed for his beliefs for 17 years. The Bunyan Museum in Bedford is a former site of Puritan worship. William Penn (1644–1718), founder of Pennsylvania in the USA, lived, worshipped and is buried at Jordans, near Beaconsfield. A bit further north at Chalfont St Giles is the cottage where the poet John Milton (1608–74) stayed to escape London's plague. There he completed his greatest work, *Paradise Lost*. The house is now a museum based on his life and works.

William Penn, founder of Pennsylvania

John Milton painted by Pieter van der Plas

St Albans ⑬

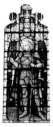

Today a thriving market town and a base for London commuters, St Albans was for centuries at the heart of some of the most stirring events in English history. A regional capital of ancient Britain, it became a major Roman settlement and then a key ecclesiastical centre – so important that during the Wars of the Roses *(see p49)*, two battles were fought for it. In 1455 the Yorkists drove King Henry VI from the town and six years later the Lancastrians retook it.

The martyr St Alban

Exploring St Albans

Part of the appeal of this ancient and fascinating town, little more than an hour's drive from London, is that its 2,000-year history can be traced vividly by visiting a few sites within easy walking distance of one another. There is a large car park within the walls of the Roman city of Verulamium, between the museum and St Michael's Church and across the road from the excavated theatre. From there it is a pleasant lakeside walk across the park, passing more Roman sites, Ye Olde Fighting Cocks inn, the massive cathedral and the historic High Street. Marking the centre of the town, the High Street is lined with several Tudor buildings and a clock tower dating from 1412, from which the curfew bell used to ring at 4am in the morning and 8:30pm at night.

🏛 Verulamium

Just outside the city centre are the walls of Verulamium, one of the first British cities the Romans established after their invasion of Britain in AD 43. Boadicea *(see p181)* razed it

to the ground during her unsuccessful rebellion against the Romans in AD 62, but its position on Watling Street, an important trading route, meant that it was quickly rebuilt on an even larger scale and the city flourished until 410.

🏛 Verulamium Museum

St Michael's. 📞 01727 751810.
⬜ daily. ⚫ 25, 26 Dec. 🎟 ♿
This excellent museum tells the story of the city, but its main attraction is its splendid collection of well-preserved Roman artefacts, notably some breathtaking mosaic floors, including one depicting the head of a sea god, and another of a scallop shell with intricate three-dimensional shading. Other finds included burial urns and lead coffins.

On the basis of excavated plaster fragments, a Roman room has been painstakingly recreated, its walls painted in startlingly bright colours and geometric patterns.

Between here and St Albans Cathedral are a bath house with more mosaics, remnants of the ancient city wall and one of the original gates.

A scallop shell, one of the mosaic floors at the Verulamium Museum

🍺 Ye Olde Fighting Cocks

Abbey Mill Lane. 📞 01727 869152.
⬜ daily. ⚫ 25 Dec.
Believed to be England's oldest surviving pub, Ye Olde Fighting Cocks is certainly, with its

One of the oldest surviving pubs in England

octagonal shape, one of the most unusual. It originated as the medieval dovecote of the old abbey and moved here after the Dissolution *(see p50)*.

🎭 Roman Theatre

St Michael's. 📞 01727 835035.
⬜ daily. ⚫ 25, 26 Dec. 🎟
Just across the road from the museum are the foundations of the open-air theatre, first built around 160 but enlarged several times. It is one of only six known to have been built throughout Roman Britain.

Alongside it are traces of a row of Roman shops and a house, from which many of the museum's treasures – such as a bronze statuette of Venus – were excavated in the 1930s.

🔒 St Michael's Church

St Michael's. 📞 01727 835037.
⬜ Apr–Sep: phone for details. ♿
This church was first founded during the Saxon reign and is built partly with bricks taken from Verulamium, which by then was in decline. Numerous additions have been made since then, including a truly splendid Jacobean pulpit.

The church contains an early 17th-century monument to the Elizabethan statesman and writer Sir Francis Bacon; his father owned nearby Gorhambury, a large Tudor house, now in ruins.

🏛 St Albans Cathedral

Sumpter Yard. 01727 860780. daily. by arrangement.
This outstanding example of medieval architecture has some classic features such as the 13th- and 14th-century wall paintings on the Norman piers.

It was begun in 793, when King Offa of Mercia founded the abbey in honour of St Alban, Britain's first Christian martyr, put to death by the Romans in the third century for sheltering a priest. The oldest parts, which still stand,

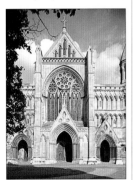

The imposing west side of St Albans Cathedral

were first built in 1077 and are easily recognizable as Norman by the round-headed arches and windows. They form part of the 84 m (276 ft) nave – the longest in England.

The pointed arches further east are Early English (13th century), while the decorated work of the 14th century was added when some of the Norman arches collapsed.

East of the crossing is what remains of St Alban's shrine – a marble pedestal made up of more than 2,000 tiny fragments. Next to it is the tomb of Humphrey, Duke of Gloucester (see p213).

It was also here at the cathedral that the English barons drafted the *Magna Carta* document (see p48), which King John was then forced to sign.

The splendour of the Gardens of the Rose in June

Gardens of the Rose ⓮

Chiswell Green, Hertfordshire. 01727 850461. St Albans then bus. Jun–Sep: 9am–5pm Mon–Sat, 10am–6pm Sun & public hols.

As well as being England's national symbol, the rose is the most popular flower with British gardeners.

The 5 ha (12 acre) garden of the Royal National Rose Society, with over 30,000 plants and 1,700 varieties, is at its peak in late June. The gardens trace the history of the flower as far back as the white rose of York, the red rose of Lancaster (see p49) and the Rosa Mundi – named by Henry II for his mistress Fair Rosamond after she was poisoned by Queen Eleanor in 1177. The nuns who buried Rosamond implied in verse on her tomb that her reputation did not smell of roses.

Hughenden Manor ⓯

High Wycombe, Buckinghamshire. 01494 755565. High Wycombe then bus. Mar: Sat, Sun; Apr–Oct: Wed–Sun & public hols. Good Fri. limited.

The Victorian statesman and novelist Benjamin Disraeli, Prime Minister from 1874 to 1880, lived here for 33 years until his death. Originally a Georgian villa, Disraeli adapted it in 1862 to the Gothic style. Furnished as it was in his day, the house gives an idea of the life of a wealthy Victorian gentleman and shows some portraits of his contemporaries.

GEORGE BERNARD SHAW

Although a controversial playwright and known as a mischievous character, the Irish-born George Bernard Shaw (1856–1950) was a man of settled habits. He lived near St Albans in a house at Ayot St Lawrence, now called Shaw's Corner, for the last 44 years of his life, working until his last weeks in a summer-house at the bottom of his large garden. His plays, combining wit with a powerful political and social message, still seem fresh today. One of the most enduring is *Pygmalion* (1913), on which the musical *My Fair Lady* is based. The house and garden are now a museum of his life and works.

Touring the Thames ⑯

THE THAMES between Pangbourne and Eton is leafy and romantic and best seen by boat. But if time is short, the road keeps close to its bank for much of the way. Swans glide gracefully below ancient bridges, voles dive into the water for cover, and elegant herons stand impassive at the river's edge. Huge beech trees overhang the banks which are lined with fine houses, their gardens sloping to the water. The tranquil scene has inspired painters and writers through the ages as well as operating, until recently, as an important transport link.

Hambledon Mill ⑥
The white weather-boarded mill, which was operational until 1955, is one of the largest on the Thames as well as one of the oldest in origin. There are traces of the original 16th-century mill.

Beale Park ①
The philanthropist Gilbert Beale (1868–1967) created a 10 ha (25 acre) park to preserve this beautiful stretch of river intact and breed endangered birds like owls, ornamental water fowl, pheasants and peacocks.

Henley ⑤
This lovely old river town boasts houses and churches dating from the 15th and 16th centuries and an important regatta, first held 1839 (see p66).

Pangbourne ②
Kenneth Grahame (1859–1932), author of *The Wind in the Willows*, lived here. Pangbourne was used as the setting by artists Ernest Shepard in 1908 and Arthur Rackham in 1951 to illustrate the book.

Sonning Bridge ④
The 18th-century bridge is made up of 11 brick arches of varying width.

TIPS FOR DRIVERS

Tour length: 50 miles (75 km).
Stopping-off points: The picturesque town of Henley has a large number of riverside pubs which will make good stops for lunch. If you are boating you can often moor your boat alongside the river bank. (See also pp636–7.)

Whitchurch Mill ③
This charming village, linked to Pangbourne by a Victorian toll bridge, has a picturesque church and one of the many disused watermills that once harnessed the power of this stretch of river.

Cookham ⑦

This is famous as the home of Stanley Spencer (1891–1959), one of Britain's leading 20th-century artists. His old studio is now a museum containing some of his paintings and equipment, including a sign that warned visitors to leave him alone when he was working. This work, entitled *Swan Upping* (1914–19), recalls a Thames custom.

Cliveden Reach ⑧

The beech trees lining this attractive stretch of river are in the grounds of Cliveden House *(see p148)*.

KEY

▨▨▨ Tour route

══ Other roads

⚜ Viewpoint

0 kilometres   10

0 miles   5

Eton College ⑨

Founded by Henry VI in 1440, Eton is Britain's most famous public school. It has a superb Perpendicular chapel (1441) with a series of English wall paintings (1479–88).

Salter Bros hire boats, moored at Henley

BOATING TOURS

In summer, scheduled river services run between Henley, Windsor, Runnymede and Marlow. Several companies operate from towns along the route. You can hire boats by the hour or the day or, for a longer tour, you can rent cabin cruisers and sleep on board *(see also p641)*. Ring Salter Bros on 01753 865 832 for more information.

Windsor ⓱

Berkshire. 🏠 *30,000.* 🚆
ℹ️ *HighSt (01753 743900).*
🆆 www.windsor.gov.uk

THE TOWN of Windsor is dwarfed by the enormous **castle** *(see p222–3)* on the hill above – appropriately enough because its original purpose was to serve the castle's needs. The town is full of quaint Georgian shops, houses and inns. The most prominent building on the High Street is the **Guildhall** completed by Wren *(see p116)* in 1689. The **Household Cavalry Museum** has an extensive collection of arms and uniforms.

The huge 1,940-ha (4,800-acre) **Windsor Great Park** stretches straight from the castle three miles (5 km) to Snow Hill, where there is a statue of George III.

ENVIRONS: Four miles (7 km) to the southeast is the level grassy meadow known as **Runnymede**. This is one of England's most historic sites, where in 1215 King John was forced by his rebellious barons to sign the *Magna Carta (see p48)*, thereby limiting his royal powers. The dainty memorial pavilion at the top of the meadow was erected in 1957.

🏛 Household Cavalry Museum

St Leonard's Rd. 📞 *01753 755112.* ◻
Mon–Fri. ⬤ *public hols.* **Donation.**

King John signing the *Magna Carta*, Runnymede

Windsor Castle

Henry II rebuilt the castle

The OLDEST CONTINUOUSLY inhabited royal residence in Britain, the castle, originally made of wood, was built by William the Conqueror in 1070 to guard the western approaches to London. He chose the site because it was on high ground and just a day's journey from his base in the Tower of London. Successive monarchs have made alterations that render it a remarkable monument to royalty's changing tastes. King George V's affection for it was shown when he chose Windsor for his family surname in 1917. The castle is a main residence of The Queen and her family who stay here many weekends.

Albert Memorial Chapel
First built in 1240, it was rebuilt in 1485 and finally converted into a memorial for Prince Albert in 1863.

King Henry VIII Gate and main exit

★ St George's Chapel
The architectural highlight of the castle, it was built between 1475 and 1528 and is one of England's outstanding Perpendicular churches. Ten monarchs are buried here.

The Round Tower was first built in wood by William the Conqueror. In 1170 it was rebuilt in stone by Henry II *(see p48)*. It now houses the Royal Archives and Photographic Collection.

Statue of Charles II

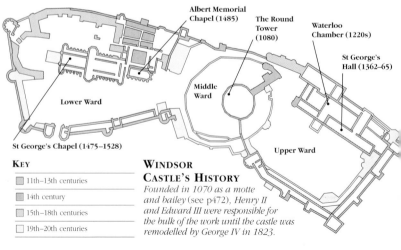

Albert Memorial Chapel (1485)

The Round Tower (1080)

Waterloo Chamber (1220s)

St George's Hall (1362–65)

Middle Ward

Lower Ward

St George's Chapel (1475–1528)

Upper Ward

KEY

- 11th–13th centuries
- 14th century
- 15th–18th centuries
- 19th–20th centuries

WINDSOR CASTLE'S HISTORY
Founded in 1070 as a motte and bailey (see p472), Henry II and Edward III were responsible for the bulk of the work until the castle was remodelled by George IV in 1823.

Royal Collection
*This chalk etching of
Christ by Michelangelo is
part of the Resurrection
series. The great size of
this collection means
that the exhibition is
always changing and
works are often loaned
to other museums.*

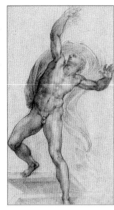

**The Audience
Chamber** is where
the Queen greets
her guests.

**The Queen's
Ballroom**

Queen Mary's Dolls' House was
designed by Sir Edwin Lutyens in
1924. Every item was built on a
1:12 ratio. The wine cellar
contains genuine vintage wine.

Visitors' Checklist

Castle Hill. 01753 869898.
Mar–Oct: 9:45am–5:15pm; Nov–
Feb: 9:45am–4:15pm daily (last
adm 1 hr before closing). 25,
26 Dec, Good Fri. St
Georges Chapel: 5:15pm Mon–Sat,
8:30/10:45/11:45am, 5:15pm Sun.

Waterloo Chamber
*The walls of this banqueting hall, first
built in the 13th century, are lined with
portraits of the leaders who played a
part in Napoleon's defeat (see p55).*

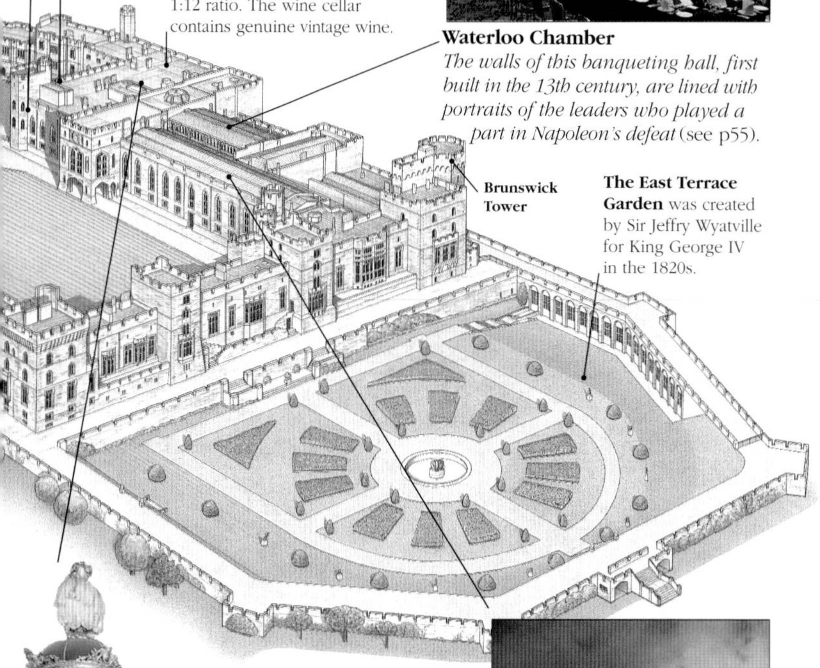

**Brunswick
Tower**

**The East Terrace
Garden** was created
by Sir Jeffry Wyatville
for King George IV
in the 1820s.

★ **State Apartments**
*These rooms contain many treasures,
including this late 18th-century
state bed in the King's State
Bedchamber, made for the
visit in 1855 of Napoleon III.*

STAR SIGHTS

★ **St George's Chapel**

★ **State Apartments**

The Fire of 1992
*A devastating blaze began during
maintenance work on the State
Apartments. St George's Hall was
destroyed but has been rebuilt.*

THE WEST COUNTRY

The West Country at a Glance

THE WEST COUNTRY forms a long peninsula bounded by the Atlantic to the north and the English Channel to the south, tapering down to Land's End, mainland Britain's westernmost point. Whether exploring the great cities and cathedrals, experiencing the awesome solitude of the moors and their prehistoric monuments, or simply enjoying the miles of coastline and mild climate, this region has an enduring appeal for holiday-makers.

Wells (see pp238–9) is a charming town nestling at the foot of the Mendip Hills. It is famous for its exquisite three-towered cathedral with an ornate west façade, featuring an array of statues. Alongside stand the moated Bishop's Palace and the 15th-century Vicar's Close.

Exmoor's (see pp236–7) heather-clad moors and wooded valleys, grazed by wild ponies and red deer, lead down to some of Devon's most dramatic cliffs and seaside coves.

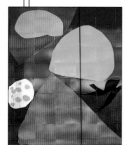

St Ives (see p263) has a branch of the Tate Gallery that shows modern works by artists associated with the area. Patrick Heron's bold coloured glass (1993) is on permanent display.

Devon

DEVON AND CORNWALL
(see pp258–81)

Cornwall

Dartmoor (see pp280–81) is a wilderness of great natural beauty covering an area of 365 sq miles (945 sq km). Stone clapper bridges, picturesque villages and weathered granite tors punctuate the landscape.

◁ **Stunning views of the Lizard Peninsula**

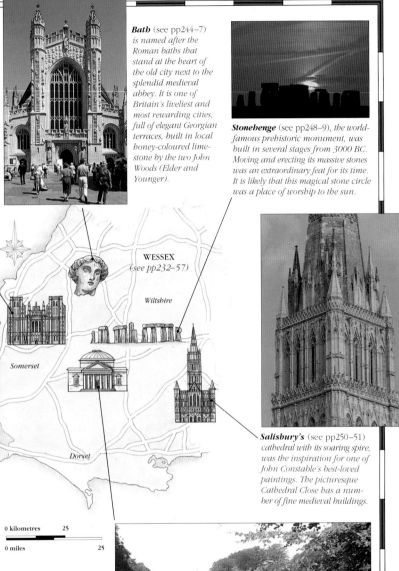

Bath (see pp244–7) is named after the Roman baths that stand at the heart of the old city next to the splendid medieval abbey. It is one of Britain's liveliest and most rewarding cities, full of elegant Georgian terraces, built in local honey-coloured limestone by the two John Woods (Elder and Younger).

Stonehenge (see pp248–9), the world-famous prehistoric monument, was built in several stages from 3000 BC. Moving and erecting its massive stones was an extraordinary feat for its time. It is likely that this magical stone circle was a place of worship to the sun.

WESSEX
(see pp232–57)

Wiltshire

Somerset

Dorset

0 kilometres   25

0 miles   25

Salisbury's (see pp250–51) cathedral with its soaring spire, was the inspiration for one of John Constable's best-loved paintings. The picturesque Cathedral Close has a number of fine medieval buildings.

Stourhead garden (see pp252–3) was inspired by the paintings of Claude and Poussin. Created in the 18th century, the garden is itself a work of art. Contrived vistas, light and shade and a mixture of landscape and gracious buildings, such as the Neo-Classical Pantheon at its centre, are vital to the overall effect.

Coastal Wildlife

THE LONG AND VARIED West Country coastline, ranging from the stark, granite cliffs of Land's End to the pebble-strewn stretch of Chesil Bank, is matched with an equally diverse range of wildlife. Beaches are scattered with colourful shells, while rock pools form miniature marine habitats teeming with life. Caves are used by larger creatures, such as grey seals, and cliffs provide nest sites for birds. In the spring and early summer, an astonishing range of plants grow on the foreshore and cliffs which can be seen at their best from the Southwest Coastal Path (see p32). The plants in turn attract numerous moths and butterflies.

Cliff-tops of Land's End with safe ledges for nesting birds

Chesil Bank is an unusual ridge of pebbles (see p254) stretching 18 miles (29 km) along the Dorset coast. The bank was created by storms and the pebbles increase in size from northwest to southeast due to varying strengths of coastal currents. The bank encloses a lagoon called the Fleet, habitat of the Abbotsbury swans, as well as a large number of wildfowl.

The Painted Lady, often see on cliff-top coastal plants, migrates to Britai in the spring.

High tides wash u driftwood and shel

Cliff-top turf contains many species of wild flowers.

Thrift, in hummocks of honey-scented flowers, is a familiar sight on cliff ledges in spring.

Yellowhammers are to be seen perched on cliff-top bushes.

Marram grass roots help hold back sand against wind erosion.

Grey seals come on land to give birth to their young. They can be spotted on remote beaches.

A BEACHCOMBER'S GUIDE

The best time to observe the natural life of the sea shore is when the tide begins to roll back, before the scavenging seagulls pick up the stranded crab fish and sandhoppers, and the seaweed dries up. Much plant and marine life can be found in the secure habitat provided by rock pools.

COLLECTING SHELLS

Most of the edible molluscs, such as scallops and cockles, are known as bivalves; others, such as whelks and limpets, are known as gastropods.

Great scallop **Common cockle**

Common whelk **Common limpet**

Durdle Door *was formed by waves continually eroding the weaker chalk layers of this cliff (see p256) in Dorset, leaving the stronger oolite to create a striking arch, known in geology as an eyelet.*

Seaweed*, such as bladder wrack, can resemble coral or lichen when in water.*

Rocks are colonized by clusters of barnacles, mussels and limpets.

Oystercatchers *have a distinctive orange beak. They hunt along the shore, feeding on all kinds of shellfish.*

Starfish *can be aggressive predators on shellfish. The light-sensitive tips of their tentacles help them to "see" the way.*

Mussels *are widespread and can be harvested for food.*

Rock pools teem with crabs, mussels, shrimps and plant life.

The Velvet Crab*, often found hiding in seaweed, is covered with fine downy hair all over its shell.*

Grey mullet*, when newly hatched, can often be seen in rock pools.*

West Country Gardens

G ARDENERS HAVE LONG BEEN ATTRACTED to the West Country. Its mild climate is perfect for growing tender and exotic plants, many of which were brought from Asia in the 19th century. As a result, the region has some of England's finest and most varied gardens, covering the whole sweep of garden styles and history *(see pp22–3)*, from the clipped formality of Elizabethan Montacute, to the colourful and crowded cottage-garden style of East Lambrook Manor.

Lanhydrock's (p270) *clipped yews and low box hedges frame a blaze of colourful annuals.*

Trewithen (p267) *is renowned for its rare camellias, rhododendrons and magnolias, grown from seed collected in Asia. The huge garden is at its most impressive in March and June.*

Cotehele (p279) has a lovely lush valley garden.

DEVON AND CORNWALL *(see pp258–8*

Trellisick (p267) has memorable views over the Fal Estuary through shrub-filled woodland.

Glendurgan *(p267)* is a plant-lover's paradise set in a steep, sheltered valley.

Mount Edgcumbe *(p277)* pre-serves its 18th-century French, Italian and English gardens.

Trengwainton (p262) *has a fine stream garden, whose banks are crowded with moisture-loving plants, beneath a lush canopy of New Zealand tree ferns.*

Overbecks (near Salcombe) *enjoys a spectacular site overlooking the Salcombe Estuary. There are secret gardens, terraces and rocky dells.*

CREATIVE GARDENING

Gardens are not simply collections of plants; they rely for much of their appeal on man-made features. Whimsical topiary, ornate architecture, fanciful statuary and mazes help to create an atmosphere of adventure or pure escapism. The many gardens dotted around the West Country offer engaging examples of the vivid imagination of designers.

Mazes *were created in medieval monasteries to teach patience and persistence. This laurel maze at Glendurgan was planted in 1833.*

Fountains and flamboyant statuary have adorned gardens since Roman times. Such eye-catching embellishments add poetic and Classical touches to the design of formal gardens, such as Mount Edgcumbe.

Knightshayes Court (p275) *is designed as a series of formal garden "rooms", planted for scent, colour or seasonal effect.*

East Lambrook Manor *(near South Petherton) is a riot of colours, as old-fashioned cottage plants grow without restraint.*

Stourhead *(see pp252–3)* is a magnificent example of 18th-century landscape gardening.

Athelhampton's *(p255)* gardens make use of fountains, statues, pavilions and columnar yews.

WESSEX
(see pp232–57)

Montacute House *(p254)* has pavilions and a centuries-old yew hedge, and is renowned for its collection of old roses.

0 kilometres   25

0 miles   25

Parnham *(near Beaminster), like many West Country gardens, has several parts devoted to different themes. Here conical yews comple-ment the formality of the stone balustrade; elsewhere there are woodland, kitchen, shade and Mediterranean gardens.*

Many garden buildings *are linked by an element of fantasy; while country houses had to conform to everyday practicalities, the design of many smaller buildings gave more scope for imagination. This fanciful Elizabethan pavilion on the forecourt at Montacute House was first and foremost decora-tive, but sometimes served as a lodging house.*

Topiary *can be traced back to the Greeks. Since that time the sculpting of trees into unusual, often eccentric shapes has been de-veloped over the centuries. The yew topiary of 1920s Knightshayes features a fox being chased by a pack of hounds. The figures form a delightful conceit and come into their own in winter when little else is in leaf.*

WESSEX

WILTSHIRE · SOMERSET · DORSET

THE NATURAL AND DIVERSE BEAUTY *of this predominantly rural region is characterized by rolling hills and charming villages. The area is enriched by a wealth of historical and architectural attractions, ranging from the prehistoric stone circle of Stonehenge to the Roman baths and magnificent Georgian townscape of Bath.*

Vast swathes of bare windswept downland give way to lush river valleys, and the contrast between the two may explain the origin in medieval times of the saying, "as different as chalk and cheese". The chalk and limestone hills provided pasture for sheep whose wool was exported to Europe or turned to cloth in mill towns such as Bradford-on-Avon. Meanwhile the rich cow-grazed pastures of the valleys produced the Cheddar cheese for which the region has become famous.

The area's potential for wealth was first exploited by prehistoric chieftains whose large, mysterious monuments, such as Stonehenge and Maiden Castle, are striking features of the landscape. From this same soil sprang King Arthur *(see p271)* and King Alfred the Great, about whom there are numerous fascinating legends. It was King Arthur who is thought to have led British resistance to the Saxon invasion in the 6th century. The Saxons finally emerged the victors and one of them, King Alfred, first united the West Country into one political unit, called the Kingdom of Wessex *(see p47)*.

Wilton House and Lacock Abbey, both former monasteries, were turned into splendid stately homes during the 16th century, due to the Dissolution of the Monasteries *(see pp50–51)*. Today, their previous wealth can be gauged by the size and grandeur of their storage barns.

Matching the many man-made splendours of the region, Wessex is rich in rare wildlife and plants.

Two visitors enjoying the Elizabethan gardens of Montacute House, Somerset

◁ Eighteenth-century cottages lining Gold Hill, Shaftesbury

Exploring Wessex

FROM THE ROLLING CHALK PLAINS around Stonehenge to the rocky cliffs of Cheddar Gorge and the heather-covered uplands of Exmoor, Wessex is a scenically varied microcosm of England. Reflecting the underlying geology, each part of Wessex contributes its own distinctive architecture, with the Neo-Classically inspired buildings of Bath giving way to the mellow brick and timber of Salisbury and the thatched flint-and-chalk cottages of the Dorset landscape.

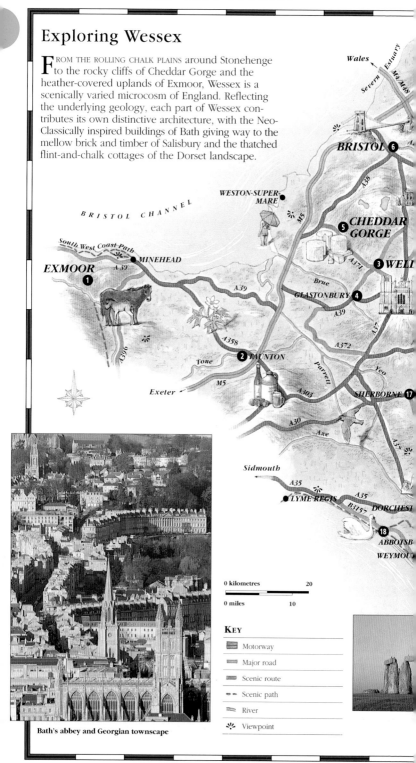

Wales

Severn Estuary

M4/M5

BRISTOL **6**

BRISTOL CHANNEL

WESTON-SUPER-MARE

CHEDDAR GORGE **5**

3 WELLS

South West Coast Path

EXMOOR 1

MINEHEAD

A39

A38

A371

A39

Brue

GLASTONBURY **4**

A39

A358

A396

Tone

2 TAUNTON

M5

Exeter

A358

A37

A303

A372

Parrett

Yeo

SHERBORNE **17**

A30

Axe

Sidmouth

A35

LYME REGIS

A35

B3157

DORCHESTER

18

ABBOTSBURY

WEYMOUTH

| 0 kilometres | | 20 |
| 0 miles | 10 | |

KEY

	Motorway
	Major road
	Scenic route
- -	Scenic path
	River
☀	Viewpoint

Bath's abbey and Georgian townscape

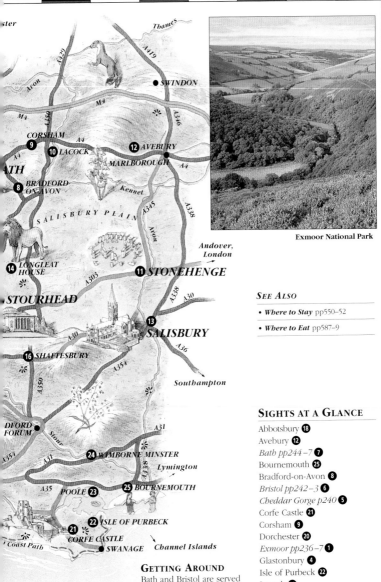

Thames
● SWINDON
● CORSHAM 9
10 LACOCK
12 AVEBURY
MARLBOROUGH
BRADFORD-ON-AVON 8
Kennet
S A L I S B U R Y   P L A I N
Andover, London
14 LONGLEAT HOUSE
STOURHEAD
11 STONEHENGE
13 SALISBURY
16 SHAFTESBURY
Southampton
DFORD FORUM
24 WIMBORNE MINSTER
Lymington
POOLE 23
25 BOURNEMOUTH
22 ISLE OF PURBECK
21 CORFE CASTLE
● SWANAGE
Coast Path
Channel Islands

Exmoor National Park

SEE ALSO

- *Where to Stay* pp550–52
- *Where to Eat* pp587–9

SIGHTS AT A GLANCE

GETTING AROUND

Bath and Bristol are served by fast InterCity trains, other major towns and seaside resorts by regional railways and long-distance bus services. Popular sights such as Stonehenge feature on many tour operators' bus excursions. The rural heart of Wessex, however, has little in the way of public transport and unless you have the time to walk the region's footpaths, you will need a car.

Huge sarsen stones of Stonehenge, dating from around 3000 BC

Exmoor National Park ●

THE MAJESTIC CLIFFS plunging into the Atlantic along Exmoor's northern coast are interrupted by lush, wooded valleys carrying rivers from the high moorland down to sheltered fishing coves. Inland, wild rolling hills are grazed by sturdy Exmoor ponies, horned sheep and the local wild red deer. Buzzards are also a common sight wheeling over the bracken-clad terrain looking for prey. For walkers, Exmoor offers 620 miles (1,000 km) of wonderful footpaths and varied, dramatic scenery, while the tamer perimeters of the park offer less energetic attractions – everything from traditional seaside entertainments to picturesque villages and ancient churches.

Curlew

View east along the Southwest Coast Path

Combe Martin is a pretty setting for the Pack of Cards Inn *(see p272)*.

Parracombe church has a Georgian interior with a complete set of wooden furnishings.

Heddon's Mouth
The River Heddon passes through woodland and meadows down to this attractive point on the coast.

The Valley of Rocks
Gritstone outcrops, eroded into fantastical shapes, characterize this natural gorge.

KEY

i	Tourist information
▬▬	A road
═══	B road
═══	Minor road
- -	Coast path
✻	Viewpoint

Lynmouth
Above the charming fishing village of Lynmouth stands hill-top Lynton. The two villages are connected by a cliff railway (see p274).

Watersmeet
The East Lyn and Hoar Oak Water join together in a tumbling cascade at this spot in the middle of a beautifully wooded valley. There is also a tearoom with a pretty garden.

Culbone church, a mere 10.6 m (35 ft) in length, claims to be Britain's smallest parish church.

VISITORS' CHECKLIST

Somerset/Devon. 🚃 🚌 *Tiverton then bus.* ℹ️ *Fore St, Dulverton (01398 323841).*
Natural History Centre, Malmsmead. 📞 *01643 707624.* ⏰ *mid-May–Sep: 1:30–5pm Wed, Thu; Aug: Tue–Thu.* ♿
Dunster Castle (NT), Dunster. 📞 *01643 821314.* ⏰ *Apr–Oct: Sat–Wed.* ♿

Malmsmead has a Natural History Centre illustrating local wildlife.

Oare's church commemorates the writer RD Blackmore, whose romantic novel *Lorna Doone* (1869) is set in the area.

Porlock
The flower-filled village of Porlock has retained its charm, with steep winding streets, thatched houses and a fascinating old church.

Selworthy is a picturesque village of thatched cottages.

Minehead is a major resort built around a pretty quay. A steam railway runs all the way from here to Bishop's Lydeard.

DUNKERY BEACON
▲ 520 m 1,704 ft

BRENDON HILLS

Exford

WIMBLEBALL LAKE

Dunster has an ancient castle and an unusual octagonal Yarn Market (1609) where local cloth was once sold.

Dulverton

monsbath is a ...od starting point ...r walkers. The ...nies found loc...ly are thought to ...escend from pre...storic ancestors.

xford is a centre for ...ag-hunting, popular ...nce Norman times.

Tarr Steps is an ancient "clapper" bridge built of stone slabs.

Dunkery Beacon
Rising to a height of 520 m (1,700 ft), this is the highest point on Exmoor.

0 kilometres 5
0 miles 3

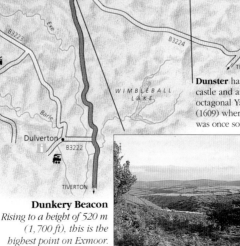

Taunton ②

Somerset. 🏠 77,000. 🚻 🔄
🛈 Paul St (01823 336 344).
🚩 Tue (livestock), Sat.

Taunton lies at the heart of a fertile region famous for its apples and cider, but it was the prosperous wool industry that financed the massive church of **St Mary Magdalene** (1488–1514) with its glorious tower. Taunton's **castle** was the setting for the notorious Bloody Assizes of 1685 when "Hanging" Judge Jeffreys dispensed harsh retribution on the Duke of Monmouth and his followers for an uprising against King James II. The 12th-century building now houses the **Somerset County Museum**, covering local history. A star exhibit is the Roman mosaic from a villa at Low Ham, Somerset, showing the love story of Dido and Aeneas.

Environs: Created in 1903–8, **Hestercombe Garden** is one of Sir Edwin Lutyens' (see p25) and Gertrude Jekyll's (see p23) greatest surviving masterpieces.

🏛 **Somerset County Museum**
Castle Green. 📞 01823 355504. ◯ Tue–Sat & public hols. ● 25, 26 Dec, 1 Jan, Good Fri. 🧾 ♿ ground floor.
♣ **Hestercombe Garden**
Cheddon Fitzpaine. 📞 01823 413923. ◯ daily. 🧾 ▯ ▯

SOMERSET CIDER

Somerset is one of the few English counties where real farmhouse cider, known as "scrumpy", is still made using the traditional methods. Cider once formed part of the farm labourer's wages and local folklore has it that

Scrumpy cider

various unsavoury additives, such as iron nails, were added to give strength. Cider-making can be seen at **Sheppy's** farm, on the A38 near Taunton.

Wells ③

Somerset. 🏠 10,000. 🔄 🛈 Market Place (01749 672552). 🚩 Wed, Sat.

Wells is named after St Andrew's Well, the sacred spring that bubbles up from the ground near the 14th-century **Bishop's Palace**, residence of the Bishop of Bath and Wells. A tranquil market town, Wells is famous for its magnificent cathedral which was begun in the late 1100s. Pennyless Porch, where beggars once received alms, leads from the bustling market place to the calm of the cathedral close. **Wells Museum** has prehistoric finds from nearby Wookey Hole and other caves.

Cathedral clock (1386–92)

Environs: To the northeast of Wells lies the impressive cave complex of **Wookey Hole**, which has an extensive range of popular amusements.

🏛 **Wells Museum**
8 Cathedral Green. 📞 01749 673477. ◯ Easter–Oct: daily; Nov–Easter: Wed–Mon. ● 24–25 Dec. 🧾 ▯
♠ **Wookey Hole**
Off A371. 📞 01749 672243. ◯ daily. 🧾 ▯ ▯ ▯

The West Front features 300 fine medieval statues of kings, knights and saints – many of them life-size.

The Vicars' Close, built in the 14th century for the Vicars' Choir, is one of the oldest complete streets in Europe.

The Chain Gate (1460)

Cloisters

Path leading round the moat

This graceful flight of steps curves up to the octagonal Chapter House which has delicate vaulting dating from 1306. The 32 ribs springing from the central column create a beautiful palm-tree effect.

Glastonbury Abbey, left in ruins in 1539 after the Dissolution

Bishops' tombs circle the chancel. This sumptuous marble tomb, in the south aisle, is that of Bishop Lord Arthur Hervey, who was Bishop of Bath and Wells (1869–94).

The palace moat is home to swans which ring a bell by the gatehouse when they want to be fed. Feeding times are at 11am and 4pm.

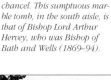

The Bishop's Palace (1230–40)

13th-century ruins of the Great Hall

WELLS CATHEDRAL AND THE BISHOP'S PALACE

The Close. **☎** 01749 674483. ◯ daily. **⛶** limited. **Bishop's Palace** **☎** 01749 678691. ◯ Apr–Oct: Tue–Fri, Sun & public hols (Aug: daily except 1st Sat).

Wells has maintained much of its medieval character with its cathedral, Bishop's Palace and other buildings around the close forming a harmonious group. The most striking features of the cathedral are the west front and the "scissor arches" installed in 1338 to support the tower.

Glastonbury ❹

Somerset. **♟** 9,000. **☐ ✚** Tribunal, High St (01458 832954). **☐** Tue. **W** www.glastonbury.co.uk

SHROUDED in Arthurian myth and rich in mystical association, the town of Glastonbury was once one of the most important destinations for pilgrims in England. Now thousands flock here for the annual rock festival *(see p63)* and for the summer solstice on Midsummer's Day (21 June).

Over the years history and legend have become intertwined, and the monks who founded **Glastonbury Abbey**, around 700, found it profitable to encourage the association between Glastonbury and the mythical "Blessed Isle" known as Avalon – alleged to be the last resting place of King Arthur and the Holy Grail *(see p269)*.

The great abbey was left in ruins after the Dissolution of the Monasteries *(see pp50–51)*. Even so, many magnificent relics survive, including parts of the vast Norman abbey church, the unusual Abbot's Kitchen, with its octagonal roof, and the Victorian farmhouse, now the **Somerset Rural Life Museum**.

Growing in the abbey grounds is a cutting from the famous Glastonbury thorn which is said to have miraculously grown from the staff of St Joseph of Arimathea. According to myth, he was sent around AD 60 to convert England to Christianity. The English hawthorn flowers at Christmas as well as in May.

The **Lake Village Museum** has some interesting finds from the Iron Age settlements that once fringed the marshlands around **Glastonbury Tor**. Seen for miles around, the Tor is a hill crowned by the remains of a 14th-century church.

🏛 Somerset Rural Life Museum
Chilkwell St. **☎** 01458 831197. ◯ Easter–Oct: Tue–Sun; Nov–Easter: Tue–Sat & public hols. **●** 24–26 Dec, 1 Jan, Good Fri. **⛶** limited. **☐** closed winter.

🏛 Lake Village Museum
Tribunal, High St. **☎** 01458 832954. ◯ daily. **●** 25, 26 Dec.

Cheddar Gorge ❺

VISITORS' CHECKLIST

On B3135, Somerset. 🅸
Cheddar Gorge (01934 744071)
🚌 from Wells. 🅿 🚻 🛒
**Cheddar Showcaves, Jacob's
Ladder & Museum** ☎ 01934
742343. ☐ daily. ● 24, 25
Dec. 🎫 🚹 limited. 🛒 🅿
Chewton Cheese Dairy,
Chewton Mendip. ☎ 01761
241666. ☐ Mon–Wed, Fri, Sat.
● 25, 26 Dec, 1 Jan. 🎫 🚹

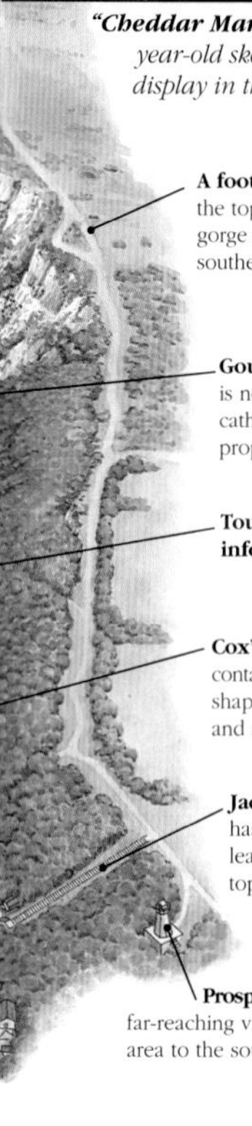

DESCRIBED AS A "deep frightful chasm" by novelist Daniel Defoe in 1724, Cheddar Gorge is a spectacular ravine cut through the Mendip plateau by fast-flowing streams during the glacial phases of the last Ice Age. Cheddar has given its name to a rich cheese which originates from here and is now produced worldwide. The caves in the gorge once provided the perfect environment of constant temperature and high humidity for storing and maturing the cheese.

The Chewton Cheese Dairy
(7 miles or 12 km east along the B3135) has demonstrations of traditional Cheddar cheeses being made by hand (except on Thursdays and Sundays).

"Cheddar Man", *a 9,000-year-old skeleton, is on display in the museum.*

The B3135
road winds round the base of the 3 mile (5 km) gorge.

A footpath follows the top of the gorge on its southern edge.

Gough's Cave is noted for its cathedral-like proportions.

The gorge *is a narrow, winding ravine with limestone rocks rising almost vertically on either side to a height of 120 m (400 ft).*

Tourist information

Cox's Cave contains unusually shaped stalactites and stalagmites.

Jacob's Ladder has 274 steps leading to the top of the gorge.

The rare Cheddar Pink *is among the astonishing range of plant and animal life harboured in the rocks.*

Prospect Tower has far-reaching views over the area to the south and west.

Bristol ⑥

See pp242–3.

Bath ⑦

See pp244–7.

Bradford-on-Avon ⑧

Wiltshire. 🚶 9,500. 🚃 🅸 *Silver St (01225 865797).* 🛒 *Thu.*
🆆 www.bradfordonavon.com

Tᴴɪꜱ ʟᴏᴠᴇʟʏ ᴄᴏᴛꜱᴡᴏʟᴅ-ꜱᴛᴏɴᴇ town with its steep flagged lanes is full of flamboyant houses built by wealthy wool and cloth merchants in the 17th and 18th centuries. One fine Georgian example is **Church House**, on Church Street. A little further along, **St Laurence Church** is a remarkably complete Saxon building founded in 705 *(see p47)*. The

Typical Cotswold-stone architecture in Bradford-on-Avon

church was converted to a school and cottage in the 12th century and was rediscovered in the 19th century when a vicar recognized the characteristic cross-shaped roof.

In the middle of the medieval **Town Bridge** is a small stone cell, built as a chapel in the 13th century but later used as a lock-up for 17th-century vagrants. A short walk away, near converted mill buildings and a stretch of the Kennet and Avon Canal, is the massive 14th-century **Tithe Barn** *(see p28)*.

🏭 **Tithe Barn**
Pound Lane. ◯ *daily.* ● *25, 26 Dec.* ♿

Corsham ⑨

Wiltshire. 🚶 12,000. 🅸 *High St (01249 714660).* 🛒 *Tue.*

Tʜᴇ ꜱᴛʀᴇᴇᴛꜱ of Corsham are lined with stately Georgian houses which make it a delight for connoisseurs of Cotswold-stone architecture. **St Bartholmew's Church** has an elegant spire and a lovely carved alabaster tomb (1960) to the late Lady Methuen, whose family founded Methuen publishers. The family acquired **Corsham Court** in 1745 with its picture gallery and a remarkable collection of Flemish, Italian and English paintings, including works by Van Dyck, Lippi and Reynolds. Peacocks wander through the grounds, adding their colour and elegance to the façade of the Elizabethan mansion.

Peacock in grounds, Corsham Court

🏭 **Corsham Court**
off A4. 🇨 *01249 701610.* ◯ *mid-Mar– Sep: Tue–Sun; Oct–mid-Mar: Sat, Sun (pm).* ● *Dec.* 🅿 ♿ *limited.*

Lacock ⑩

Wiltshire. 🚶 1,000.

Mᴀɪɴᴛᴀɪɴᴇᴅ in its pristine state by the National Trust, with very few modern intrusions, Lacock is a picturesque and delightful village to explore. The meandering River Avon forms the boundary to the north side of the churchyard, while humorous stone figures look down from **St Cyriac Church**. Inside the 15th-century church is the splendid Renaissance-style tomb of Sir William Sharington (1495–1553). He acquired **Lacock Abbey** after the Dissolution of the Monasteries *(see pp50–51)*, but it was a later owner, John Ivory Talbot, who had the buildings remodelled in the

Gothic revival style, in vogue in the early 18th century. The abbey is famous for the window (in the south gallery) from which his descendant William Henry Fox Talbot, an early pioneer of photography, took his first picture in 1835, and for the the sheets of snowdrops which cover the abbey grounds in early spring. A 16th-century barn at the abbey gates has been converted to the **Fox Talbot Museum**, which has displays on his experiments.

Environs: Designed by Robert Adam *(see pp24–5)* in 1769, **Bowood House** includes the laboratory where Joseph Priestley discovered oxygen in 1774, and a rich collection of sculpture, costumes and paintings. Italianate gardens surround the house while the lake-filled grounds, landscaped by Capability Brown *(see p22)*, contain a Doric temple, grotto, cascade and now a large adventure playground.

🏛 **Lacock Abbey**
(NT) Lacock. 🇨 *01249 730227.* ◯ *Apr–Oct: Wed–Mon (pm).* ● *Good Fri.* 🅿 ♿ *limited in house.*
🏛 **Fox Talbot Museum**
(NT) Lacock. 🇨 *01249 730459.* ◯ *Mar–Oct: daily.* ● *Good Fri.* 🅿 ♿
🏭 **Bowood House**
Derry Hill, nr Calne. 🇨 *01249 812102.* ◯ *Apr–Oct: daily.* 🅿 ♿

William Henry Fox Talbot (1800–77)

Bristol **6**

King Brennus, St John's Gate

IT WAS IN 1497 that John Cabot sailed from Bristol on his historic voyage to North America. The city, at the mouth of the Avon, became the main British port for transatlantic trade, pioneering the era of the ocean-going steam liner with the construction of *s.s. Great Britain*. The city flourished as a major trading centre, growing rich on the distribution of wine, tobacco and, in the 17th century, slaves. Because of its docks and aero-engine factories, Bristol was heavily bombed during World War II and the city centre bears witness to the ideas of post-war planners. The docks have been shifted to deeper waters at Avonmouth and the old dock area has been transformed, taking on new life characterized by waterside cafés, shops and art galleries.

Exploring Bristol

The most interesting part of the city lies around Broad, King and Corn streets, known as the Old Quarter. There is a lively covered market, part of which occupies the **Corn Exchange**, built by John Wood the Elder (*see p244*) in 1743. Outside are the famous Bristol Nails, four bronze 16th–17th-century pedestals which Bristol merchants used as tables when paying for goods – hence the expression "to pay on the nail". **St John's Gate**, at the head of Broad Street, has medieval statues of Bristol's two mythical founders, King Brennus and King Benilus. Between Lewins Mead and Colston Street, **Christmas Steps** is a steep lane lined with specialist shops. The **Chapel of the Three Kings** at the top was founded in 1504 and is now adjoined by the Burgundian-style Foster's Almshouses of 1861–83.

A group of buildings around the cobbled King Street include the 17th-century timber-framed **Llandoger Trow** inn. It is

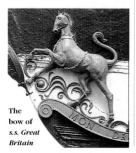

The bow of s.s. Great Britain

***The Two Sisters* (c.1889) by Renoir, City Museum and Art Gallery**

here that Daniel Defoe is said to have met Alexander Selkirk, whose true-life island exile served as the inspiration for Defoe's novel *Robinson Crusoe* (1719). Just up from here is the **Theatre Royal**, a rare survival of a Georgian playhouse, built in 1766.

Not far away the renowned **Arnolfini Gallery** on Narrow Quay is a showcase for contemporary art, drama, dance and cinema. In front, a statue of John Cabot (1425–c.1500) looks wistfully across the old Floating Harbour which is now lined with cafés and bars.

On the Harbourside, **at-Bristol** combines the science centre "Explore-at-Bristol" and the wildlife centre "Wild-screen-at-Bristol."

To the west of the city, the elegant suburbs of **Clifton** revel in ornate Regency crescents, many now used as lodgings or faculties of Bristol University. The impressive

Memorial to William Canynge the Younger (1400–74)

Clifton Suspension Bridge perfectly complements the drama of the steep Avon gorge. Completed in 1864, the bridge is testimony to Brunel's engineering skill. **Bristol Zoo Gardens**, nearby, concentrate on breeding and conserving endangered species.

🔒 St Mary Redcliffe

Redcliffe Way. 【 0117 9291487. ⬜ daily. 🔗 🔗 by arrangement. ◻
Discover the history of Bristol in this magnificent 14th-century church, claimed by Queen Elizabeth I to be "the fairest in England". The church owes much to the generosity of William Canynge the Elder and Younger, both famous mayors of Bristol. Inscriptions on the tombs of merchants and sailors tell of lives devoted to trade in Asia and the West Indies. Look out for the Bristol maze in the north aisle.

🏛 s.s. Great Britain

Gas Ferry Rd. 【 0117 9260680. ⬜ daily. ◼ 24, 25 Dec. 🗓 🔗 limited 🔗 by arrangement. ◻ 🔗
Ⓦ www.ss-great-britain-com
The *s.s. Great Britain*, designed by Isambard Kingdom Brunel, is the world's first large iron passenger ship. Launched in 1843, she travelled 32 times round the world before she was abandoned in the Falkland Islands in 1886. The wreckage was rescued in 1970 and is now being restored in the dock where she was built. The ship is an impressive reminder of the way in which Brunel revolutionized transport.

🏠 Georgian House

7 Great George St. 【 0117 9211362. ⬜ Apr–Oct: Sat–Wed.
Life in a wealthy Bristol merchant's house of the 1790s is illustrated by Adam-style furnishings in the elegant drawing room and by the pots, pans, roasting spits and laundry in the servants' area.

Warehouses overlooking the Floating Harbour

VISITORS' CHECKLIST

Bristol. 400,000. 7 miles (11 km) SW Bristol. Temple Meads. Marlborough St. Wildscreen Walk, Harbourside (0117 926 0767). daily. Harbour Regatta: Jul–Aug; International Balloon Fiesta: Aug; Kite Festival: Sep.

✿ Bristol Industrial Museum

Prince's Wharf. 0117 9251470. Apr–Oct: Sat–Wed; Nov–Mar: Sat–Sun. 25–26 Dec.

The museum's diverse collection of vehicles and models illustrates the astonishing range of products made in Bristol over the last 300 years. Among them are luxurious Bristol cars, the once ubiquitous Bristol bus, the world's first touring caravan and Concorde, represented here by a full-scale model of the pilot's cockpit.

✿ City Museum and Art Gallery

Queen's Rd. 0117 922 3571. daily. 24–25 Dec. limited.

Varied collections include Egyptology, dinosaur fossils, Roman tableware, the largest collection of Chinese glass outside China and a fine collection of European paintings including works by Renoir and Bellini. Bristol artists include Sir Thomas Lawrence and Francis Danby.

⛪ Bristol Cathedral

College Green. 0117 9264879. daily. **Donation.** limited.

Bristol's cathedral took an unusually long time to build. Rapid progress was made between 1298 and 1330, when the wonderfully inventive choir was built; the transepts and tower were finished in 1515, and another 350 years passed before the Victorian architect, GE Street, built the nave.

Humorous and eccentric medieval carving abounds – a small snail crawling across the stone foliage in the antechapel, musical monkeys in the 13th-century Elder Lady Chapel, and a famous set of wooden misericords in the choir.

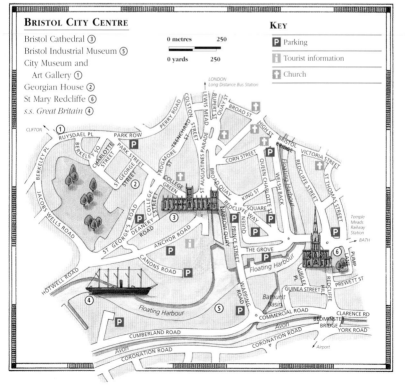

BRISTOL CITY CENTRE

Bristol Cathedral ③
Bristol Industrial Museum ⑤
City Museum and Art Gallery ①
Georgian House ②
St Mary Redcliffe ⑥
s.s. Great Britain ④

KEY

P Parking
i Tourist information
⛪ Church

Street-by-Street: Bath **❼**

BATH OWES ITS MAGNIFICENT Georgian
townscape to the bubbling pool of
water at the heart of the Roman Baths.
The Romans transformed Bath into England's first spa resort and it regained fame
as a spa town in the 18th century. At this
time the two brilliant John Woods (Elder
and Younger), both architects, designed
the city's fine Palladian-style buildings.
Many houses bear plaques recording the
numerous famous
people who have
resided here.

The Circus
*This is a daring
departure from the
typical Georgian
square, by John Wo
the Elder (1705–5*

No. 1 Royal Crescent

No. 17 is where the 18th-
century painter Thomas
Gainsborough lived *(see p149).*

**Assembly Rooms and
Museum of Costume**

★ Royal Crescent
*Hailed the most majestic street in Britain, this graceful
arc of 30 houses (1767–74) is the masterpiece of John
Wood the Younger. West of the Royal Crescent, Royal
Victoria Park (1830) is the city's largest open space.*

KEY

– – –   Suggested route

| 0 metres | 100 |
| 0 yards | 100 |

Jane Austen
(see p148), the
writer, stayed at
No. 13 Queen's
Square on one
of many visits to
Bath in her youth.

Milsom Street and
New Bond Street con-
tain some of Bath's
most elegant shops.

Theatre Royal (1805)

STAR SIGHTS

★ Royal Crescent

★ Roman Baths

★ Bath Abbey

Pump Rooms
*These tearooms once formed the
social hub of the 18th-century spa
community. They contain this
decorative drinking fountain.*

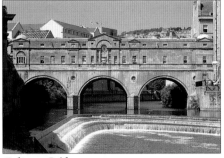

Pulteney Bridge
This charming bridge (1769–74), designed by Robert Adam, is lined with shops and links the centre with the magnificent Great Pulteney Street. Look out for a rare Victorian pillar box on the east bank.

VISITORS' CHECKLIST

Bath. 85,000. Bristol International Airport, 20 miles (32 km) W Bath. Dorchester St. Manvers St. Abbey Chambers, Abbey Church Yard (01225 477101). daily. International Festival: May–Jun.

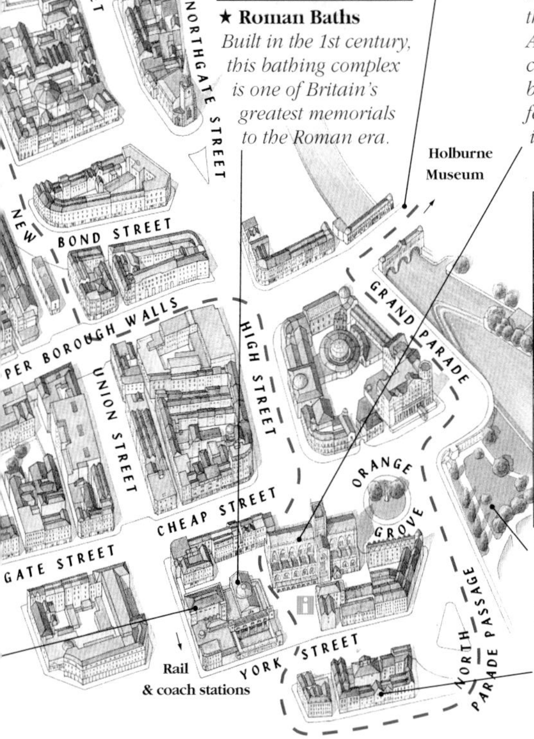

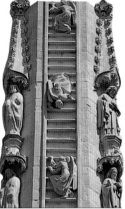

The Building of Bath Museum

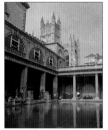

★ Roman Baths
Built in the 1st century, this bathing complex is one of Britain's greatest memorials to the Roman era.

Holburne Museum

Rail & coach stations

★ Bath Abbey
The splendid abbey stands at the heart of the old city in the Abbey Church Yard, a paved courtyard enlivened by buskers. Its unique façade features stone angels climbing Jacob's Ladder to heaven.

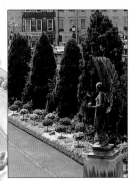

Parade Grounds
Courting couples came to this pretty riverside park for secret liaisons in the 18th century.

Sally Lunn's House (1482) is one of Bath's oldest houses.

Exploring Bath

Piazza cellist

THE BEAUTIFUL AND COMPACT CITY OF BATH is set among the rolling green hills of the Avon valley, and wherever you walk you will enjoy spendid views of the surrounding countryside. The traffic-free heart of this lively city is full of street musicians, museums, cafés and enticing shops, while the elegant honey-coloured Georgian houses, so characteristic of Bath, form an elegant backdrop to city life.

Bath Abbey, at the heart of the old city, begun in 1499

🏠 Bath Abbey

Abbey Churchyard. **☎** 01225 422462. **◯** daily. **●** during services. **Donation.** **⟨⟩** **☐**

This splendid abbey was supposedly designed by divine agency. According to legend, God dictated the form of the church to Bishop Oliver King in a dream; this story has been immortalized in the wonderfully eccentric carvings on the west front. The bishop began work in 1499, rebuilding a church that had been founded in the 8th century. Memorials cover the walls and the varied Georgian inscriptions make fascinating reading. The spacious interior is remarkable for the delicate lace-like fan vaulting of the nave, an addition made by Sir George Gilbert Scott in 1874.

🏛 Assembly Rooms and Museum of Costume

Bennett St. **☎** 01225 477789. **◯** daily. **●** 25, 26 Dec. **⟨⟩** **⟨⟩** **☐**

The Assembly Rooms were built by Wood the Younger in 1769, as a meeting place for the fashionable elite and as an elegant backdrop for many glittering balls. Jane Austen's novel *Northanger Abbey* (1818) describes the atmosphere of gossip and flirtation here.

In the basements, kept dark to preserve the many precious textiles, is a collection of costumes in authentic period settings. The display illustrates changing fashions from the 16th century to the present day.

🏛 No. 1 Royal Crescent

Royal Crescent. **☎** 01225 428 126. **◯** Tue–Sun & public hols. **●** Dec, Jan, Good Fri. **⟨⟩** **☐** **W** www.bath-preservation-trust.org.uk

This museum lets you look inside the first house of Bath's most beautiful terrace, giving a glimpse of what life was like for 18th-century aristocrats, such as the Duke of York, who lived here. The house is furnished down to such details as the dog-powered spit used to roast meat in front of the fire.

🏛 Holburne Museum of Art

Great Pulteney St. **☎** 01225 466669. **◯** daily (Nov–Easter: Tue–Sat, Sun pm). **●** mid-Dec–mid-Feb. **⟨⟩** **⟨⟩**

This historic building is named after William Holburne of Menstrie (1793–1874), whose collections form the nucleus of the museum's impressive display of fine and decorative arts. Paintings can be seen by British artists such as Gainsborough and Stubbs.

ROMAN BATHS MUSEUM

Stall St. **⟨⟩** 01225 477784. **◯** daily. **●** 25, 26 Dec. **⟨⟩** **⟨⟩** limited. **◻** **W** www.romanbaths.co.uk

According to legend, Bath owes its origin to the Celtic King Bladud who discovered the curative properties of its natural hot springs in 860 BC. Cast out from his kingdom as a leper, Bladud cured himself by imitating his swine and rolling in the hot mud at Bath.

In the first century, the Romans built baths around the spring, and a temple dedicated to the goddess Sulis Minerva, who combined the attributes of the Celt water goddess Sulis and the Roman goddess Minerva. Among the museum's Roman relics is a bronze head of the goddess, discovered in 1727. Medieval monks of Bath Abbey also exploited the springs' properties, but it was when Queen Anne visited in 1702–3 that Bath reached its zenith as a fashionable watering place.

Gilded bronze head of Sulis Minerva

🏛 Building of Bath Museum

The Vineyards. 📞 01225 333895. ⏱ Tue–Sun & public hols. ⬤ end-Nov–mid-Feb. 🏷 🚹 limited.

This museum, housed in an old Methodist chapel, is an excellent starting point for exploring the city. It shows how, in the 18th century, Bath was transformed from a medieval wool town into one of Europe's most elegant spas. John Wood and his son designed the Classically inspired stone fronts of the Royal Crescent and the Circus, leaving individual property speculators to develop the houses behind. While the façades speak of harmony and order, the houses behind show the result of rampant individualism, with no two houses alike. The museum looks at every aspect of the buildings, from their construction to a new gallery of Georgian interiors.

🏛 American Museum

Claverton Manor, Claverton Down. 📞 01225 460503. ⏱ Aug: daily (pm); Mar–Oct, mid-Nov–mid-Dec: Tue–Sun (pm). 🏷 🚹 limited. 🖥 🚹

Founded in 1961 in an attempt to deepen mutual understanding between Britain and America, this was the first American museum to be established in this country. Rooms in the 1820 manor house are decorated in many styles, from the first rudimentary dwellings of settlers to opulent 19th-century homes. There are special sections on Shaker furniture, quilts and Native American art, and a replica of George Washington's Mount Vernon garden of 1785.

A 19th-century American Indian weathervane

Elected in 1704 as Master of Ceremonies, "Beau" Nash played a crucial role in transforming Bath into the fashionable centre of Georgian society. During his long career, he devised a never-ending round of games, balls and entertainment (including gambling) that kept the idle rich amused and ensured a constant flow of visitors.

The Great Bath

The open-air Great Bath, which stands at the heart of the Roman spa complex, was not discovered until the 1870s. Leading off this magnificent pool were various bathing chambers which became increasingly sophisticated over the four centuries the Romans were here. The baths fell into ruin, but extensive excavations have revealed the remarkable skill of Roman engineering.

The dome (1897) is based on St Stephen Walbrook church in London (see p115).

Around the edges of the bath are the bases of piers that once supported a barrel-vaulted roof.

York Street

A late 19th-century terrace bears statues of famous Romans such as Julius Caesar.

The sacred spring is enclosed by a reservoir now named the King's Bath.

The water flows from the spring into the corner of the bath at a constant temperature of 46° C (115° F).

The lead-lined bath, steps, column bases and paving stones around the edge all date from Roman times.

Stonehenge ⓫

BUILT IN SEVERAL STAGES from about 3000 BC, Stonehenge is Europe's most famous prehistoric monument. We can only guess at the rituals that took place here, but the alignment of the stones leaves little doubt that the circle is connected with the sun and the passing of the seasons, and that its builders possessed a sophisticated understanding of both arithmetic and astronomy. Despite popular belief, the circle was not built by the Druids, an Iron Age priestly cult that flourished in Britain from around 250 BC – more than 1,000 years after Stonehenge was completed.

Finds from a burial mound near Stonehenge (Devizes Museum)

Stonehenge as it is today

The Heel Stone casts a long shadow straight to the heart of the circle on Midsummer's day.

The Avenue forms a ceremonial approach to the site.

The Slaughter Stone, named by 17th-century antiquarians who believed Stonehenge to be a place of human sacrifice, was in fact one of a pair forming a doorway.

The Outer Bank, dug around 3000 BC, is the oldest part of Stonehenge.

BUILDING OF STONEHENGE

Stonehenge's monumental scale is more impressive given that the only tools available were made of stone, wood and bone. The labour involved in quarrying, transporting and erecting the huge stones was such that its builders must have been able to command immense resources and vast numbers of people. One method is explained below.

RECONSTRUCTION OF STONEHENGE

This illustration shows what Stonehenge probably looked like about 4,000 years ago.

A sarsen stone was moved on rollers and levered into a pit.

With levers supported by timber packing, it was gradually raised.

The stone was then pulled upright by about 200 men hauling on ropes.

The pit round the b[ase] was packed tightly w[ith] stones and chalk.

WILTSHIRE'S OTHER PREHISTORIC SITES

The open countryside of the Salisbury Plain made this area an important centre of prehistoric settlement, and today it is covered in many ancient remains. Ringing the horizon around Stonehenge are scores of circular barrows, or burial mounds, where members of the ruling class were honoured with burial close to the temple site. Ceremonial bronze weapons, jewellery and other finds excavated around Stonehenge and the other prehistoric sites in the area can be seen in the museums at Salisbury *(see pp250–51)* and Devizes.

   Silbury Hill (NT) is Europe's largest prehistoric earthwork,

Silbury Hill

but despite extensive excavations its purpose remains a mystery. Built out of chalk blocks around 2750 BC, the hill covers 2 ha (5 acres) and rises to a height of 40 m (131 ft). Nearby **West Kennet Long Barrow** (NT) is the biggest

The **Sarsen Circle** was erected around 2300 BC and is capped by lintel stones held in place by mortice and tenon joints.

The **Bluestone Circle** was built around 2000 BC out of some 80 slabs quarried in south Wales. It was never completed.

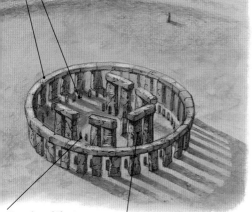

Sarsen stone forming part of the Avebury Stone Circle

VISITORS' CHECKLIST

Off A303, Wiltshire. 01980 624715. Salisbury then No. 3 bus. end-Mar-May: 9:30am–6pm daily; Jun-Aug: 9am–7pm daily; Sep-mid-Oct: 9:30am–6pm daily; end-Oct-mid-Mar: 9:30am–4pm daily. 24–26 Dec, 1 Jan.

Horseshoe of Bluestones

Horseshoe of Sarsen Trilothons

lternate ends
f the lintel were
evered up.

The weight of the lintel was supported by a timber platform.

The lintel was then levered sideways on to the uprights.

chambered tomb in England, with numerous stone-lined "rooms" and a monumental entrance. Built as a communal cemetery around 3250 BC, it was in use for several centuries – old bodies were taken away to make room for newcomers.

Old Sarum is set within the massive ramparts of a 1st-century Romano-British hill fort. The Norman founders of Old Sarum built their own motte and bailey castle inside this ready-made fortification, and the remains of this survive along with the foundations of the huge cathedral of 1075. Above ground nothing remains of the town that once sat within the ramparts. The town's occupants moved to the fertile river valley site that became Salisbury during the early 12th century *(see pp250–51)*.

Old Sarum
Castle Rd. 01722 335398. daily. 24–26 Dec, 1 Jan. limited.

The chambered tomb of West Kennet Long Barrow (c.3250 BC)

Avebury ⑫

Wiltshire. 600. Swindon then bus. Alexander Keiller Museum (01672 539250). W www.english-heritage.org.uk

BUILT AROUND 2500 BC, the **Avebury Stone Circle** (NT) surrounds the village of Avebury and was probably once some form of religious centre. Although the stones used are smaller than those at Stonehenge, the circle itself is wider. Superstitious villagers smashed many of the stones in the 18th century, believing the circle to have been a place of pagan sacrifice.

The original form of the circle is best appreciated by a visit to the excellent **Alexander Keiller Museum** to the west of the site, which illustrates in detail the construction of the circle. There is also a fascinating new exhibition entitled "6,000 Years of Mystery", explaining the changing landscape of Avebury.

St James's Church has a Norman font carved with sea monsters, and a rare 15th-century choir screen.

ENVIRONS: A few minutes drive east, **Marlborough** is an attractive town with a long and broad High Street lined with colonnaded Georgian shops.

Alexander Keiller Museum
(NT) Off High St. 01672 539250. daily. 24–26 Dec, 1 Jan.

Salisbury ⓭

S ALISBURY WAS FOUNDED IN 1220, when the old hill-top
settlement of Old Sarum *(see p249)* was abandoned,
being too arid and windswept, in favour of a new site
among the lush water meadows where the rivers Avon,
Nadder and Bourne meet. Purbeck marble may have
been floated down the Nadder from Chilmark, 12 miles
(20 km) west of Salisbury, for the construction of a new
cathedral which was built mostly in the early 13th
century, over the remarkably short space of 38 years.
Its magnificent landmark spire – the tallest in England –
was an inspired afterthought added in 1280–1310.

**The 15th-century house of John
A'Port, Queen's Street**

alleys fans out from this point
with a number of fine timber-
framed houses. In the large
bustling **Market Place** the
Guildhall is an unusual
cream stone building from
1788–95, used for civic functions. More attractive are the
brick and tile-hung houses on
the north side of the square,
many with Georgian façades
concealing medieval houses.

Bishop's Walk and a sculpture by Elisabeth Frink (1930–93), Cathedral Close

The Cloisters are the largest
in England. They were added
between 1263 and 1284 in
the Decorated style.

Exploring Salisbury

The spacious and tranquil
Close, with its schools,
almshouses and clergy
housing, makes a fine setting
for Salisbury's cathedral.
Among the numerous elegant
buildings here are the
Matrons' College, built in
1682 as a home for clergy
widows, and 13th-century
Malmesbury House with its
splendid Queen Anne façade
(1719), fronted by lovely
wrought-iron gates. Other
buildings of interest include
the 13th-century **Deanery**,
the 15th-century **Wardrobe**,
now a regimental museum,
and the **Cathedral School**,
housed in the 13th-century
Bishop's Palace and famous
for the quality of its choristers.
    Beyond the walls of the
Cathedral Close, Salisbury
developed its chessboard

layout, with areas devoted to
different trades, perpetuated
in street names such as Fish
Row and Butcher Row.
Leaving the Close through
High Street Gate, you
reach the busy High Street
leading to the 13th-
century **Church of St
Thomas**, which has a
lovely carved timber roof
(1450), and a late 15th-
century Doom painting,
showing Christ seated in
judgement and demons
seizing the damned.
Nearby in Silver Street,
Poultry Cross was
built in the 15th
century as a covered
poultry market. An
intricate network of

The Chapter House
displays an original of
the *Magna Carta*. Its
walls have stone friezes
the Old Testament.

**Street signs reflecting trades of
13th-century Salisbury**

The Trinity Chapel
contains the grave of St
Osmund who was bishop of
Old Sarum from 1078–1099.

Bishop Audley's Chantry, a
magnificent 16th-century monument
to the bishop, is one of several small
chapels clustered round the altar.

Choir stalls

🏛 Mompesson House

(NT) The Close. 📞 01722 335659.
🕐 Apr–Oct: noon–5:30pm Sat–Wed.
🎫 ♿ limited. 🚻

Built by a wealthy Wiltshire
family in 1701, the handsomely
furnished rooms of this house
give an indication of
life for the Close's
inhabitants in the 18th
century. The delight-
ful garden, bounded
by the north wall of
the Close, has fine
herbaceous borders.

The graceful spire
soars to a height of
123 m (404 ft).

*The West Front is
decorated by rows of
lavish symbolic figures
and saints in niches.*

A roof tour takes you
up to an external gallery
at the base of the spire
with views of the town
and Old Sarum.

🏛 Salisbury and South Wiltshire Museum

The Close. 📞 01722 332151. 🕐
Mon–Sat (Jul–Aug: Sun pm). 🚫
24–26 Dec. 🎫 ♿ limited. 🚻 📷

In the medieval King's House,
this museum has displays on
early man, Stonehenge and
nearby Old Sarum *(see p249)*.

(see p249)

SALISBURY CATHEDRAL

The Close. 📞 01722 555120. 🕐 daily. **Donation.** ♿ 🚻
The cathedral was mostly built between 1220
and 1258. It is a fine example of the Early
English style of Gothic architecture, typified
by tall, sharply pointed lancet windows, and
it is rare in being almost uniform in style.

The clock dating from
1386 is the oldest work-
ing clock in Europe.

The nave is divided into
ten bays by columns of
polished Purbeck marble.

**Northwest
transept**

**Numerous
windows** add
to the airy
and spacious
atmosphere
of the interior.

VISITORS' CHECKLIST

Wiltshire. 🚗 40,000. 🚉 South
Western Rd. 🚌 Endless St.
ℹ Fish Row (01722 334956).
🏛 Tue, Sat. 🎭 Salisbury Festival:
May; St George's Festival: Apr.

ENVIRONS: The town of Wilton
is renowned for its carpet
industry, founded by the 8th
Earl of Pembroke using French
Huguenot refugee weavers.
The town's ornate **church**
(1844) is a brilliant example
of Neo-Romanesque architecture, incorporating genuine
Roman columns, Flemish
Renaissance woodwork,
German and Dutch stained
glass and Italian mosaics.

Wilton House has been
home to the Earls of Pembroke
since it was converted from a
nunnery after the Dissolution
(see pp50–51). The house,
largely rebuilt by Inigo Jones
in the 17th century, includes
one of the original Tudor
towers, a fine collec-
tion of art and a
landscaped park with
a Palladian bridge
(1737). The two
glories of the house
are the lavish Single
and Double Cube
State Rooms. Both
have magnificently
frescoed ceilings
and gilded stucco
work and were
designed to hang a
series of family por-
traits by Van Dyck.

🏛 Wilton House

Wilton. 📞 01722 746729.
🕐 Easter–Oct: daily. 🎫 ♿ 🍴 📷

**Double Cube room, designed by
Inigo Jones in 1653**

***The Longleat Tree* tapestry (1980) depicting a 400-year history**

Longleat House ⓮

Warminster, Wiltshire. 01985 844400. *Warminster then taxi.* **House** *daily.* **Safari Park** *Apr–Oct.* www.longleat.co.uk

THE ARCHITECTURAL HISTORIAN John Summerson coined the term "prodigy house" to describe the exuberance and grandeur of Elizabethan architecture that is so well represented at Longleat. The house was started in 1540, when John Thynne bought the ruins of a priory on the site of Longleat for the sum of £53. The work he began here was continued by each generation, and over the centuries subsequent owners have added their own touches. These include the Breakfast Room and Lower Dining Room (dating from the 1870s), modelled on the Venetian Ducal Palace, and erotic murals painted by the present owner, the 7th Marquess of Bath. Today, the Great Hall is the only remaining room which belongs to Thynne's time.

In 1949, the 6th Marquess was the first landowner in Britain to open his stately home to the public, in order to fund the maintenance and preservation of the house and its vast estate. The grounds, landscaped by Capability Brown *(see p22)*, were turned into an expansive safari park in 1966, where lions, tigers and other wild animals roam freely. This, along with other commercial additions such as the world's longest maze, the Adventure Castle, and special events, now draw even more visitors than the house.

Stourhead ⓯

STOURHEAD IS AMONG THE FINEST EXAMPLES of 18th-century landscape gardening in Britain *(see pp22–3)*. The garden was begun in the 1740s by Henry Hoare (1705–85), who inherited the estate and transformed it into a breathtaking work of art. Hoare created the lake, surrounding it with rare trees and plants, and Neo-Classical Italianate temples, grottoes and bridges. The Palladian-style house, built by Colen Campbell *(see p24)*, dates from 1724.

Pantheon
Hercules is among the statues of Roman gods housed in the elegant Pantheon (1753).

Gothic Cottage (1806)
Iron Bridge
Turf Bridge
Temple of Flora (1744)

The lake was created from a group of medieval fishponds. Hoare dammed the valley to form a single expanse of water.

★ Temple of Apollo
The Classical temples that dot the garden were all designed by influential architect Henry Flitcroft (1679–1769).

Grotto
Tunnels lead to an artificial cave with a pool and a life-size statue of the guardian of the River Stour, sculpted by John Cheere in 1748.

VISITORS' CHECKLIST

(NT) Stourton, Wiltshire.
☎ 01747 841152. 🖷 0891 335205. 🚌 Gillingham then taxi.
House ◯ Apr–Oct: noon–5:30pm Sat–Wed (last adm: 5pm).
Gardens ◯ 9am–7pm (or dusk if earlier) daily. 🎫 ◎ except in house. ♿ limited. 🛒 🍴 🛍 🚻

★ Stourhead House
Reconstructed after a fire in 1902, the house contains fine Chippendale furniture. The art collection reflects Henry Hoare's Classical tastes and includes The Choice of Hercules *(1637) by Nicolas Poussin.*

Colourful shrubs around the house include fragrant rhododendrons in spring.

Stourton village was incorporated into Hoare's overall design. 🍴 🛍

A walk of 2 miles (3 km) round the lake provides artistically contrived vistas.

The reception contains exhibitions illustrating the story of Stourhead.

Entrance and car park

St Peter's Church
The parish church contains monuments to the Hoare family. The medieval monument nearby was brought from Bristol in 1765.

STAR SIGHTS

★ Temple of Apollo

★ Stourhead House

Shaftesbury ⑯

Dorset. 🏘 7,000. 🅿 ℹ 8 Bell St
(01747 853514). 🛍 Thu.

HILLTOP SHAFTESBURY, with its
cobbled streets and 18th-
century cottages is often used
as a setting for films and TV
commercials to give a flavour
of Old England. Picturesque
Gold Hill is lined on one side
by the wall of the demolished
abbey, founded by King
Alfred in 888. Only the excavated remains of the abbey
church survive, and many
masonry fragments found
in the local history museum.

**The Almshouse (1437) adjoining
the Abbey Church, Sherborne**

Sherborne ⑰

Dorset. 🏘 9,500. 🚆 🅿 ℹ Digby
Rd (01935 815341). 🛍 Thu, Sat.

FEW OTHER TOWNS in Britain
have such a wealth of
unspoilt medieval buildings.
Edward VI (see p41) founded
the famous Sherborne School
in 1550, saving intact the
splendid **Abbey Church**, the
almshouse and other monastic
buildings that might otherwise
have been demolished after
the Dissolution (see pp50–51).
Remains of the first Saxon
church can still be seen in the
abbey's façade, but the most
striking feature is the 15th-
century fan-vaulted ceiling.

Sherborne Castle, built by
Sir Walter Raleigh (see p51) in
1594, is a wonderfully varied
building that anticipates the
flamboyant Jacobean style.
Raleigh also lived briefly in
the early 12th-century **Old
Castle**, which now stands
in ruins, demolished during
the Civil War (see pp52–3).

ENVIRONS: West of Sherborne,
past Yeovil, is the magnificent
Elizabethan **Montacute House**
(see pp230–31), set in 120 ha
(300 acres) of grounds. It is
noted for tapestries and 17th-
century samplers, and for the
Tudor and Jacobean portraits
in the vast Long Gallery.

♣ **Sherborne Castle**
Off A30. 📞 01935 813182.
Castle 🔲 Apr–Oct: Tue, Thu, Sat,
Sun & public hols (pm). **Grounds**
🔲 Thu–Tue. 🏷 🖪 🏛
♣ **Old Castle**
Off A30. 📞 01935 812730.
🔲 Easter–Oct: daily; Nov–Easter: Wed–
Sun. ● 25, 26 Dec, 1 Jan. 🏷 🔲 🏛
🏛 **Montacute House**
(NT) Montacute. 📞 01935 823289.
Grounds 🔲 Apr–Oct: Wed–Mon . 🏛
🍴 🏷

Abbotsbury ⑱

Dorset. 🏘 400. ℹ West St (01305
871130).

THE NAME ABBOTSBURY recalls
the town's 11th-century
Benedictine abbey of which
little but the huge tithe barn,
built around 1400, remains.
Nobody knows when the
Swannery here was founded,
but the earliest record dates
to 1393. Mute swans come to
nest in the breeding season,
attracted by the reed beds
which spread along the Fleet,
a brackish lagoon protected
from the sea by

The Swannery at Abbotsbury

a high ridge of pebbles called
Chesil Bank (see p228). Its
wild atmosphere makes an
appealing contrast to the south
coast resorts, although strong
currents make swimming too
dangerous. **Abbotsbury Sub-
Tropical Gardens** are the
frost-free home to many new
plants, discovered by botanists
travelling in South America
and Asia in the last 30 years.

🦢 **Swannery**
New Barn Rd. 📞 01305 871684.
🔲 Apr–Oct: daily. 🏷 🔲 🖪 🏛
♣ **Abbotsbury Sub-
Tropical Gardens**
Off B3157 📞 01305 871387. 🔲
daily. ● 25, 26 Dec, 1 Jan. 🏷 🔲 🖪

Weymouth ⑲

Dorset. 🏘 62,000. 🚆 🅿 ⛴
ℹ Pavilion Complex, The Esplanade
(01305 785747). 🛍 Thu.
ⓦ www.weymouth.gov.uk

WEYMOUTH'S POPULARITY as
one of Britain's earliest
seaside resorts began in 1789
when George III paid the first
of many summer visits here.
The king's bathing machine

Weymouth Quay, Dorset's south coast

can be seen in the **The Esplanade**, and his statue is a prominent feature on the seafront. Here gracious Georgian terraces and hotels look across to the beautiful expanse of Weymouth Bay. Different in character is the old town around Custom House Quay with its fishing boats and old seamen's inns.

🏛 **The Esplanade**
Hope Sq. 📞 *01305 777622.* ⭕ *daily.* ⚫ *25, 26 Dec, 2 wks in Jan.* 📷

Dorchester ⑳

Dorset. 🏘 *16,000.* 🚇 ℹ️ *Antelope Walk (01305 267992).* 🅿️ *Wed.*

D ORCHESTER, the county town of Dorset, is still recognizably the town that Thomas Hardy used as the background for his novel *The Mayor of Casterbridge* (1886). Here, among the many 17th-century and Georgian houses lining the High Street, is the **Dorset County Museum**, where the original manuscript of the novel is displayed, along with a reconstruction of Hardy's study. There are also finds from Iron Age and Roman sites on the outskirts of the town. **Maumbury Rings** (Weymouth Avenue), is a Roman amphitheatre, originally a Neolithic henge. To the west of the town,

A 55 m (180 ft) giant carved on the chalk hillside, Cerne Abbas (NT)

many Roman graves have been found in a cemetery below the Iron Age hill fort, **Poundbury Camp**.

ENVIRONS: Just southwest of Dorchester, **Maiden Castle** (*see p43*) is a massive, awe-inspiring monument dating from around 100 BC. In AD 43 it was the scene for a battle as the Romans sought to conquer the Iron Age people of southern England.

To the north lies the charming village of **Cerne Abbas** with its magnificent medieval tithe barn and monastic buildings. The huge chalk-cut figure of a giant on the hillside here is a fertility figure thought to represent either the Roman hero-god Hercules or a 2,000-year-old Iron Age warrior.

East of Dorchester are the churches, thatched villages and rolling hills immortalized in Hardy's novels. Picturesque **Bere Regis** is the Kingsbere of *Tess of the D'Urbervilles*, where the tombs of the family whose name inspired the novel may still be seen in the Saxon **church**.

Hardy's Cottage is where the writer was born and **Max Gate** is the house he designed and lived in from 1885 until his death. Hardy's heart is buried along-side his family in the church-

Hardy's statue, Dorchester

yard at **Stinsford** – his body was given a public funeral at Westminster Abbey (*see pp94–5*).

There are beautiful gardens (*see p231*) designed in the 1890s and a magnificent medieval hall at 15th-century **Athelhampton House**.

🏛 **Dorset County Museum**
High West St. 📞 *01305 262735.* ⭕ *Mon–Sat (May–Oct: daily).* ⚫ *25, 26 Dec.* 📷 🍴 ♿ *limited.*
🏚 **Hardy's Cottage**
(NT) Higher Bockhampton.
📞 *01305 262366.* ⭕ *Apr–Oct: Sun–Thu.* 📷 ♿ *garden only.*
🏚 **Max Gate**
(NT) Alington Ave, Dorchester.
📞 *01305 262538.* ⭕ *Apr–Sep: Sun, Mon & Wed (pm).* 📷 ♿ 🚻
🏚 **Athelhampton House**
Athelhampton. 📞 *01305 848363.*
⭕ *Mar–Oct: Sun–Fri.* 📷 ♿ *gardens only.* 📷 🍴 🚻

THOMAS HARDY (1840–1928)

The vibrant, descriptive novels and poems of Thomas Hardy, one of England's best-loved writers, are set against the background of his native Dorset. The Wessex country-side provides a constant and familiar stage against which his characters enact their fate. Vivid accounts of rural life record a key moment in history, when mechanization was about to destroy ancient farming methods, just as the Industrial Revolution had done in the towns a century before (*see pp54–5*). Hardy's power-fully visual style has made novels such as *Tess of the D'Urbervilles* (1891) popular with modern film-makers, and drawn literary pilgrims to the villages and landscapes that inspired his fiction.

Nastassja Kinski in Roman Polanski's film *Tess* (1979)

Corfe Castle ㉑

(NT) Corfe Castle, Dorset. ☎ 01929
481294. ⛟ Wareham then bus.
◻ daily. ⬤ 25, 26 Dec.
▥ ♿ limited. 📷 by arrangement
▣ ◻

THE SPECTACULAR RUINS of
Corfe Castle romantically
crown a jagged pinnacle of
rock above the charming unspoilt village that shares its
name. The castle has dominated the landscape since the
11th century, first as a royal
fortification, then as the dramatic ruins seen today. In
1635 the castle was purchased
by Sir John Bankes, whose
wife and her retainers – mostly
women – courageously held
out against 600 Parliamentary
troops, in a six-week siege
during the Civil War (see
pp52–3). The castle was
eventually taken through trea-
chery and in 1646 Parliament
voted to have it "slighted" –
deliberately blown up to
prevent it being used again.
From the ruins there are far-
reaching views over the Isle of
Purbeck and its coastline.

The ruins of Corfe Castle, dating mainly from Norman times

Isle of Purbeck ㉒

Dorset. ⛟ Wareham. ⛴ Shell Bay.
🛈 Swanage (01929 422885).
ⓦ www.swanage.gov.uk

THE ISLE OF PURBECK, which
is in fact a peninsula, is
the source of the grey shelly
limestone, known as Purbeck
marble, from which the castle
and surrounding houses were
built. The geology changes to
the southwest at **Kimmeridge**,
where the muddy shale is rich
in fossils and recently

discovered oil reserves. The
Isle is fringed with unspoilt
beaches. **Studland Bay** (NT)
– with its white sand and its
sand-dune nature reserve,
rich in birdlife – has been
rated one of Britain's best
beaches. Sheltered **Lulworth
Cove** is almost encircled by
white cliffs and there is a fine
clifftop walk to Durdle Door
(see p229), a natural chalk
arch eroded by the waves.
    The main resort in the area
is **Swanage**, the port where
Purbeck stone was trans-
ported by ship to London, to
be used for everything from
street paving to church building. Unwanted masonry from
demolished buildings was
shipped back and this is how
Swanage got its wonderfully
ornate **Town Hall** façade, designed by Wren around 1668.

Poole ㉓

Dorset. 👥 135,000. ⛟ 🚌 ⛴
🛈 High St (01202 253253).
ⓦ www.pooletourism.com

SITUATED ON ONE of the largest
harbours in the world,
Poole is an ancient, still thriving, seaport. The quay is lined
with old warehouses over-
looking a safe sheltered bay,
popular for water sports. The
Waterfront Museum, partly
housed in 15th-century cellars
on the quay, tells the history
of the port and town. A gallery
also relates how the Boy Scout
Movement was founded by
Robert Baden-Powell after a
trial camp was held on nearby
Brownsea Island in 1907.
Much of this island (reached

Beach adjoining Lulworth Cove, Isle of Purbeck

by boat from the quay) is given over to a woodland nature reserve with a waterfowl and heron sanctuary. Fine views of the Dorset coast add to the island's appeal.

🏛 Waterfront Museum
High St. 📞 01202 262600.
⬜ daily. ⬤ 25, 26 Dec, 1 Jan.

🐾 Brownsea Island
(NT) Poole. 📞 01202 707744.
⬜ Apr–Sep: daily.

Boats in Poole harbour

Wimborne Minster 24

Dorset. 🏠 6,500. 🚉 🛈 29 High St (01202 886116). ⬤ Fri–Sun.
W www.eastdorset.gov.uk

THE FINE COLLEGIATE CHURCH of Wimborne's **Minster** was founded in 705 by Cuthburga, sister of King Ina of Wessex. It fell prey to marauding Danish raiders in the 10th century, and the imposing grey church we see today dates from the refounding by Edward the Confessor (see p49) in 1043. Stonemasons made use of the local Purbeck marble, carving beasts, biblical scenes, and a mass of zig-zag decoration.

The 16th-century **Priest's House Museum** has rooms furnished in the style of different periods.

ENVIRONS: Designed for the Bankes family after the destruction of Corfe Castle, **Kingston Lacy** was acquired by the National Trust in 1981. The estate has always been farmed by traditional methods and is astonishingly rich in

wildlife, rare flowers and butterflies. This quiet, forgotten corner of Dorset is grazed by rare Red Devon cattle and can be explored using paths and "green lanes" that date back to Roman and Saxon times. The fine 17th-century house at the centre of the estate contains an outstanding collection of paintings, including works by Rubens, Velazquez and Titian.

🏛 Priest's House Museum
High St. 📞 01202 882533.
⬜ Apr–Oct: Mon–Sat; Jun–Sep: daily (Sun pm only). limited.

🏰 Kingston Lacy
(NT) on B3082. 📞 01202 883402.
⬜ Apr–Oct: Sun–Wed.
gardens only.

Bournemouth 25

Dorset. 👥 155,000. ✈ 🚉 🚌
🛈 Westover Rd (0906 8020234).
W www.bournemouth.co.uk

BOURNEMOUTH'S POPULARITY as one of England's favourite seaside resorts is due to an almost unbroken sweep of sandy beach, extending from the mouth of Poole Harbour to Hengistbury Head. Most of the seafront is built up, with many large seaside villas and exclusive hotels. To the west there are numerous clifftop parks and gardens, interrupted by beautiful wooded river ravines, known as "chines". The varied and colourful garden of **Compton Acres** was conceived as a museum of many different garden styles.

In central Bournemouth the amusement arcades, casinos, nightclubs and shops cater for the city's many visitors. During the summer, pop groups, TV comedians and the

Marchesa Maria Grimaldi by Sir Peter Paul Rubens (1577–1640), Kingston Lacy

highly regarded Bournemouth Symphony Orchestra perform at the **Winter Gardens Theatre**, off Exeter Road. The **Russell-Cotes Art Gallery and Museum**, housed in a late Victorian villa, has an extensive collection with many fine Oriental and Victorian artefacts.

ENVIRONS: The magnificent **Christchurch Priory**, east of Bournemouth, is 95 m (310 ft) in length – the longest church in England. It was rebuilt between the 13th and 16th centuries and presents a sequence of different styles. The original nave, built around 1093, is an impressive example of Norman architecture, but the highlight is the intricate stone reredos which features a Tree of Jesse, tracing the lineage of Christ. Next to the Priory are the ruins of a Norman **castle**.

Between Bournemouth and Christchurch, **Hengistbury Head** is well worth climbing for grassland flowers, butterflies and sea views, while **Stanpit March**, to the west of Bournemouth, is an excellent spot for viewing herons and other wading birds.

🌿 Compton Acres
Canford Cliffs Rd. 📞 01202 700 778. ⬜ daily.

🏛 Russell-Cotes Art Gallery and Museum
Russell-Cotes Rd. 📞 01202 451800. ⬜ Tue–Sun. ⬤ 25 Dec.

A toy train on the popular seafront at Bournemouth

DEVON AND CORNWALL

DEVON · CORNWALL

MILES OF MAGNIFICENTLY VARIED COASTLINE *dominate this magical corner of Britain. Popular seaside resorts alternate with secluded coves and unspoilt fishing villages rich in maritime history. In contrast there are lush, exotic gardens and the wild terrain of the moorland interior, dotted with tors and historic remains.*

Geographical neighbours, the counties of Devon and Cornwall are very different in character. Celtic Cornwall, with its numerous villages named after early Christian missionaries, is mostly stark and treeless at its centre. In many places it is still scarred by the remains of tin and copper mining that has played an important part in the economy for some 4,000 years. Yet this does not detract from the beauty and variety of the coastline dotted with lighthouses and tiny coves, and penetrated by deep tidal rivers.

Devon, by contrast, is a land of lush pasture divided into a patchwork of tiny fields and threaded with narrow lanes, whose banks support a mass of flowers from the first spring primroses to summer's colourful mixture of campion, foxglove, oxeye daisies and blue cornflowers. The leisurely pace of rural life here, and in Cornwall, contrasts with life in the bustling cities. Exeter with its magnificent cathedral, historic Plymouth, elegant Truro and Elizabethan Totnes are urban centres brimming with life and character.

The spectacular coastline and the mild climate of the region attract families, boating enthusiasts and surfers. For those in search of solitude, the Southwest Coastal Path provides access to the more tranquil areas. There are fishing villages and harbours whose heyday was in the buccaneering age of Drake and Raleigh *(see p51)*, and inland the wild moorland of Bodmin and Dartmoor, which provided inspiration for many romantic tales. Many of these are associated with King Arthur *(see p271)* who, according to legend, was born at Tintagel on Cornwall's dramatically contorted north coast.

Beach huts on the seafront at Paignton, near Torquay

◁ Fishing boats in Port Isaac, on Cornwall's north coast

Exploring Devon and Cornwall

ROMANTIC MOORLAND dominates the inland parts of
Devon and Cornwall, ideal walking country with
few roads and magnificent views stretching for miles.
By contrast the extensive coastline is indented by
hundreds of sheltered river valleys, each one seem-
ingly isolated from the rest of the world – one reason
why Devon and Cornwall can absorb so many visitors
and yet still seem uncrowded. Wise tourists get to
know one small part of Devon or Cornwall intimately,
soaking up the atmosphere of the region, rather than
rushing to see everything in the space of a week.

KEY

▦	Motorway
▬	Major road
▭	Minor road
▰	Scenic route
● ●	Scenic path
▰	River
✹	Viewpoint

SIGHTS AT A GLANCE

AppledNore **16**
Barnstaple **17**
Bideford **15**
Bodmin **11**
Buckfastleigh **23**
Buckland Abbey **26**
Bude **13**
Burgh Island **24**
Clovelly **14**
Cotehele **27**
Dartmoor pp280–81 **29**
Dartmouth **21**
Eden Project pp268–9 **9**
Exeter **19**
Falmouth **6**
Fowey **10**
Helston and the
   Lizard Peninsula **5**
Lynton and Lynmouth **18**
Morwellham Quay **28**
Penzance **3**
Plymouth **25**
St Austell **8**
St Ives **2**
*St Michael's Mount
   pp264–5* **4**
Tintagel **12**
Torbay **20**
Totnes **22**
Truro **7**

Walks and Tours
Penwith Tour **1**

The dramatic cliffs of Land's End, the most
western point of mainland Britain

SEE ALSO

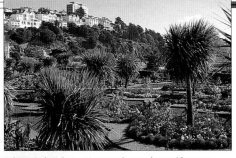

Sub-tropical gardens at Torquay, the popular seaside resort

Getting Around

Large numbers of drivers, many towing caravans (trailers), travel along the M5 motorway and A30 trunk road from mid-July to early September and travel can be slow, especially on Saturdays. Once in Devon and Cornwall, allow ample time if you are travelling by car along the region's narrow and high-banked lanes.

The regular train services, running from Paddington to Penzance, along Brunel's historic Great Western Railway, stop at most major towns. Aside from this, you are dependent on taxis or infrequent local buses.

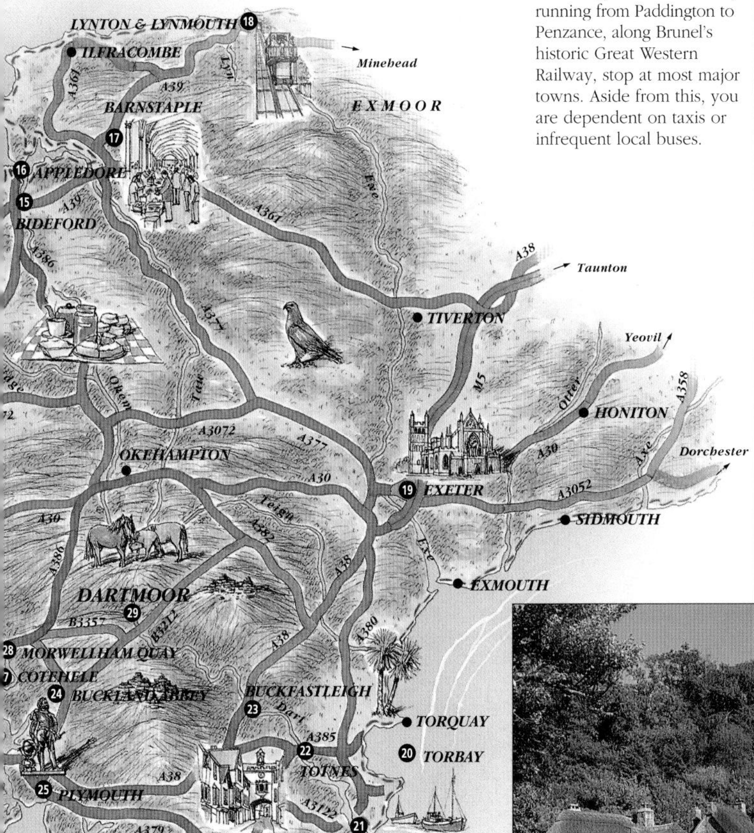

LYNTON & LYNMOUTH 18
ILFRACOMBE
Minehead
EXMOOR
BARNSTAPLE
17
16 APPLEDORE
15 BIDEFORD
Taunton
TIVERTON
Yeovil
HONITON
Dorchester
OKEHAMPTON
19 EXETER
SIDMOUTH
EXMOUTH
DARTMOOR
29
28 MORWELLHAM QUAY
7 COTEHELE
24 BUCKLAND ABBEY
BUCKFASTLEIGH
23
22 TOTNES
TORQUAY
20 TORBAY
25 PLYMOUTH
21 DARTMOUTH
24 BURGH ISLAND
A361
A39
A386
A377
A3072
A30
A38
M5
A358
A3052
A382
A380
A385
A3122
A379
A381
B3357
B3212
Exe
Taw
Okem
Teign
Dart
Otter
Axe
Lyn
0 kilometres 15
0 miles 10

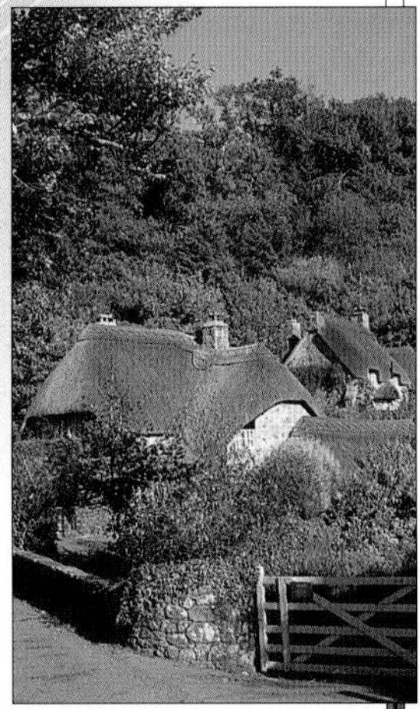

Typical thatched, stone cottages, Buckland-in-the-Moor, Dartmoor

Penwith Tour ●

THIS TOUR PASSES THROUGH a spectacular, remote Cornish landscape, dotted with relics of the tin mining industry, picturesque fishing villages and many prehistoric remains. The magnificent coastline varies between the gentle rolling moorland in the north and the rugged, windswept cliffs that characterize the dramatic south coast. The beauty of the area, combined with the clarity of light, has attracted artists since the late 19th century. Their work can be seen in Newlyn, St Ives and Penzance.

TIPS FOR DRIVERS

Tour length: 31 miles (50 km)
Stopping-off points: There are pubs and cafés in most villages. Sennen Cove makes a pleasant mid-way stop. (See also pp636–7.)

Zennor ①
The carved mermaid in the church here recalls the legend of the mermaid who lured the local squire's son to her ocean lair.

Lanyon Quoit ②
One of many prehistoric monuments, this chambered tomb is visible on the left from the road to Madron.

Botallack Mine ⑧
Derelict enginehouses clinging to the cliffside are a vivid reminder of the region's former industry of tin-mining.

Trengwainton ③
These gardens are noted for their luxuriance (p230).

Land's End ⑦
Britain's most westerly point is noted for its dramatic and wild landscape. A local exhibition reveals its history, geology and wildlife.

Newlyn ④
Cornwall's largest fishing port gave its name to a school of artists founded in the 1880s (p264). Examples of their work can be seen in the art gallery here.

Merry Maidens ⑤
This Bronze Age stone circle is said to be 19 girls turned to stone for dancing on Sunday.

Minack Theatre ⑥
This Ancient Greek-style theatre (1923) overlooks a magical bay of Porthcurno. It forms a magnificent backdrop for productions in summer.

Morvah
St Just
Sennen Cove
Porthcurno
Madron
PENZANCE
Mousehole
Lamorna

B3306
B3318
B3306
A3071
B3306
A30
B3283
B3283
B3315
B3315
B3315
ST IVES

0 kilometres   3
0 miles   2

KEY

▬▬▬ Tour route
═══ Other roads
☀ Viewpoint

St Ives ❷

Cornwall. 👥 *11,000.* 🚢 🅿
ℹ *Street-an-Pol (01736 796297).*

ST IVES is internationally renowned for the **Barbara Hepworth Museum** and the **Tate Gallery** which together celebrate the work of a group of young painters, potters and sculptors who set up a seaside art colony here in the 1920s. The Tate, designed to frame a panoramic view of Porthmeor Beach, reminds visitors of the natural surroundings that inspired the art on display within. The Barbara Hepworth Museum presents the sculptor's work in the house and garden where she lived and worked for many years. The studios are full of sculptors' paraphernalia, while the sub-tropical garden, is laid out as an art gallery.

The Lower Terrace, Tate Gallery

The town of St Ives remains a typical English seaside resort, surrounded by a crescent of golden sands. Popular taste rules in the town's many other art galleries tucked down winding alleys with names such as Teetotal Street, a legacy of the town's Methodist heritage. Many galleries are converted cellars and lofts where fish were once salted and packed. In between are whitewashed cottages with tiny gardens brimming with marigolds, sunflowers and trailing lobelia, their vibrant colours made intense by the unusually clear light that first attracted artists to St Ives.

🏛 Barbara Hepworth Museum

Barnoon Hill. 📞 *01736 796226.*
⏰ *Jul–Aug: daily; Sep–Jun: Tue–Sun & public hols.* ⬤ *24, 25, 26 Dec.* 📷
♿ *by arrangement.*

🏛 Tate Gallery

Porthmeor Beach. 📞 *01736 796226.*
⏰ *Jul–Aug: daily; Sep–Jun: Tue–Sun & public hols.* ⬤ *24, 25, 26 Dec.*
📷 ♿ 🍴 🔲

TWENTIETH-CENTURY ARTISTS OF ST IVES

Ben Nicholson and Barbara Hepworth formed the nucleus of a group of artists that made a major contribution to the development of abstract art in Europe. In the 1920s, St Ives together with Newlyn *(see p262)* became a place for aspiring artists. Among the prolific artists associated with the town are the potter Bernard Leach (1887–1979) and the painter Patrick Heron (1920–99) whose *Coloured Glass Window (see p226)* dominates the Tate Gallery entrance. Much of the art on display at the Tate is abstract and illustrates new responses to the rugged Cornish landscape, the human figure and the ever-changing patterns of sunlight on sea.

Barbara Hepworth (1903–75) was one of the foremost abstract sculptors of her time. Madonna and Child *(1953)* can be seen in the church of St Ia.

John Wells' (b.1907) key interests are in light, curved forms and birds in flight, as revealed in Aspiring Forms *(1950).*

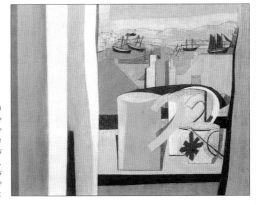

Ben Nicholson's (1894–1982) work shows a change in style from simple scenes, such as the view from his window, to a preoccupation with shapes – as seen in this painting St Ives, Cornwall *(1943–5). Later, his interest moved towards pure geometric blocks of colour.*

Penzance ❸

Cornwall. 🏛 15,000. ⛴ 🅿 ♿
ℹ️ Station Approach (01736 362207).

PENZANCE IS A BUSTLING resort with a climate so mild that palm trees and sub-tropical plants grow happily in the lush **Morrab Gardens**. The town commands fine views of St Michael's Mount and a great sweep of clean sandy beach.

The main road through the town is Market Jew Street, at the top of which stands the magnificent domed Market House (1837), fronted by a statue of Sir Humphrey Davy (1778–1829). Davy, who came from Penzance, invented the miner's safety lamp which detected lethal gases.

Chapel Street is lined with curious buildings, none more striking than the flamboyant **Egyptian House** (1835), with its richly painted façade and lotus bud decoration. Just as curious is **Admiral Benbow Inn** (1696) on the same street, which has a pirate perched on the roof looking out to sea. Opposite is a small **Maritime Museum** displaying items recovered from ancient wrecks. The town's **Museum and Art Gallery** has pictures by the Newlyn School of artists.

ENVIRONS: A short distance south of Penzance, **Newlyn** (see p262) is Cornwall's largest fishing port, which has given its name to the local school of artists founded by Stanhope Forbes (1857–1947). They painted outdoors, aiming to capture the fleeting impressions of wind, sun and sea. Continuing south, the coastal road ends at **Mousehole**

The Egyptian House (1835)

(pronounced Mowzall), a pretty, popular village with a tiny harbour, tiers of cottages and a maze of narrow alleys.

North of Penzance, overlooking the magical Cornish coast, **Chysauster** is a fine example of a Romano-British

St Michael's Mount ❹

(NT) Marazion, Cornwall. 📞 01736 710507. ⛴ from Marazion (Apr–Oct) or on foot at low tide. ◻ Apr–Oct: Mon–Fri; Nov–Mar guided tours only (phone to arrange). 🅿 🚻 🏛

ST MICHAEL'S MOUNT emerges dramatically from the waters of Mount Bay, opposite the small village of Marazion.

According to ancient Roman historians, the mount was the island of Ictis, an important centre for the Cornish tin trade during the Iron Age. It is dedicated to the archangel St Michael who, according to legend, appeared here in 495.

When the Normans conquered England in 1066 (see pp46–7), they were struck by the island's resemblance to their own Mont-St-Michel, whose Benedictine monks were invited to build a small abbey here. The abbey was absorbed into a fortress at the Dissolution of the Monasteries (see pp50–51), when Henry VIII set up a chain of coastal defences to counter an expected attack from France.

In 1659 St Michael's Mount was purchased by Sir John St Aubyn whose descendants subsequently turned the fortress into a magnificent house.

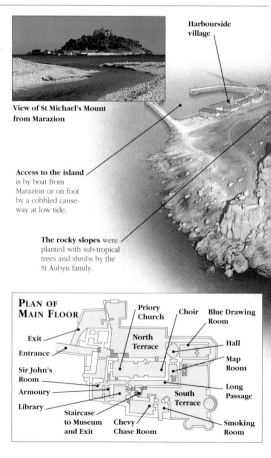

Harbourside village

View of St Michael's Mount from Marazion

Access to the island is by boat from Marazion or on foot by a cobbled causeway at low tide.

The rocky slopes were planted with sub-tropical trees and shrubs by the St Aubyn family.

PLAN OF MAIN FLOOR

- Exit
- Entrance
- Sir John's Room
- Armoury
- Library
- Staircase to Museum and Exit
- Priory Church
- North Terrace
- Choir
- Chevy Chase Room
- South Terrace
- Blue Drawing Room
- Hall
- Map Room
- Long Passage
- Smoking Room

village. The site has remained almost undisturbed since it was abandoned during the 3rd century.

From Penzance, regular boat and helicopter services depart for the **Isles of Scilly**, a beautiful archipelago forming part of the same granite mass as Land's End, Bodmin Moor and Dartmoor. Along with tourism, flower-growing forms the main source of income here.

🏛 Maritime Museum
19 Chapel St. ● *until further notice.* ♿

🏛 Penlee House Gallery and Museum
Morrab Rd. 📞 01736 363625.
● May–Sep: 10am–5pm Mon–Sat;
Oct–Apr: 10:30am–4:30pm Mon–Sat.
● 25–26 Dec, 1 Jan. ♿ 🚻 ▣ 🅿
⌂ **Chysauster**
Off B3311. 📞 07831 757934.
● Apr–Oct: daily. ♿

THE GROWTH OF METHODISM

The hard-working and independent mining and fishing communities of the West Country had little time for the established church, but they were won over by the new Methodist religion, with its emphasis on hymn singing, open-air preaching and regular or "methodical" Bible reading. When John Wesley, the founder of Methodism, made the first of many visits to the area in 1743, sceptical Cornishmen pelted him with stones. His persistence, however, led to many conversions and by 1762 he was preaching to congregations of up to 30,000 people. Simple places of worship were built throughout the county; one favoured spot was the amphitheatre **Gwennap Pit**, at Busveal, south of Redruth. Methodist memorabilia can be seen in the Royal Cornwall Museum in Truro (see p267).

John Wesley (1703–91)

Castle entrance

The South Terrace forms the roof of the large Victorian wing. Beneath it there are five floors of private quarters.

The Blue Drawing Room *was formed from the Lady Chapel in the mid-18th century and is decorated in charming Rococo Gothic style. It contains fine plaster work, furniture and paintings by Gainsborough and Thomas Hudson.*

The Armoury displays sporting weapons and military trophies brought back by the St Aubyn family from various wars.

The Priory Church, *rebuilt in the late 14th century, forms the summit of the island. Beautiful rose windows are found at both ends.*

The Chevy Chase Room *takes its name from a plaster frieze (1641) representing hunting scenes.*

Pinnacles of serpentine rock at Kynance Cove (NT), Lizard Peninsula

Helston and the Lizard Peninsula **5**

Cornwall. 🚌 *from Penzance.* ℹ️ *79 Meneage St (01326 565431).* ☒ *www.helston-online.co.uk/800*

THE ATTRACTIVE TOWN of Helston makes a good base for exploring the windswept coastline of the Lizard Peninsula. The town is famous for its Furry Dance which welcomes spring with dancing through the streets *(see p62);* the **Folk Museum** explains the history of this ancient custom. The Georgian houses and inns of Coinagehall Street are a reminder that Helston was once a thriving stannary town where tin ingots were brought for weighing and stamping before they could be sold. Locally mined tin was brought down river to a harbour at the bottom of this street until access to the sea was blocked in the 13th century by a sand and shingle bar which formed across the estuary. The bar created the freshwater lake, Loe Pool, and there is an attractive walk skirting its wooded shores. In 1880, Helston's trade was taken over by a new harbour created to the east on the River Helford, at Gweek. Today, Gweek is the home of the **National Seal Sanctuary**, where sick and injured seals are nursed back to health before being released again into the sea.

Cornwall's tin mining industry, from Roman to recent times, is covered at the **Poldark Mine** where underground tours reveal the working conditions of miners in the 18th century. Another major attraction is **Flambards Village Theme Park,** with its recreation of a Victorian village and of Britain during the Blitz.

Further south, huge satellite dishes rise from the heathland. The **Goonhilly Earth Station** visitors' centre here explores the world of satellite communications.

Local shops sell souvenirs carved from serpentine, a soft greenish stone which forms the unusual-shaped rocks that rise from the sandy beach at picturesque **Kynance Cove**.

🏛 **Folk Museum**
Market Place, Helston. ℹ️ *01326 564027.* 🕐 *Mon–Sat* ⬤ *Christmas Week* 📷 ♿ 🚻

🐟 **National Seal Sanctuary**
Gweek. ℹ️ *01326 221361.* 🕐 *daily.* ⬤ *25 Dec.* 📷 ♿ 🅿 🚻 🍴

🏛 **Poldark Mine**
Wendron. ℹ️ *01326 573173.* 🕐 *daily.* 📷 🅿 🚻 🍴

🏛 **Flambards Village Theme Park**
Culdrose Manor, Helston. ℹ️ *01326 573404.* 🕐 *Easter– Oct: daily (Apr, May, Sep, Oct phone first).* 📷 ♿ 🍴

🏛 **Goonhilly Earth Station**
Nr Helston, off B3293. ℹ️ *0800 679593.* 🕐 *Apr-Oct: daily.* 📷 ♿ 🅿 🚻

CORNISH SMUGGLERS

In the days before income tax was invented, the main form of government income came from tax on imported luxury goods, such as brandy and perfume. Huge profits were to be made by evading these taxes, which were at their height during the Napoleonic Wars (1780–1815). Remote Cornwall, with its coves and rivers penetrating deep into the mainland, was prime smuggling territory; estimates put the number of people involved, including women and children, at 100,000. Some notorious families resorted to deliberate wrecking, setting up deceptive lights to lure vessels onto the sharp rocks, in the hope of plundering the wreckage.

Falmouth **6**

Cornwall. 🏛 *18,000.* 🚉 🚌 🚕 ℹ️ *28 Killigrew St (01326 312300).* ☒ *www.falmouth-sw-cornwall.co.uk*

FALMOUTH stands at the point where seven rivers flow into a long stretch of water called the **Carrick Roads**. The drowned river valley is so deep that huge ocean-going ships can sail up almost as far as Truro. Numerous creeks are ideal for boating excursions to view the varied scenery and birdlife. Falmouth's sheltered harbour forms the most interesting part of this seaside resort. Its many old houses include the striking **Customs House** and the chimney alongside, known as the "King's Pipe" because it was used for burning contraband tobacco seized from smugglers in the

19th century. **Pendennis Castle** and St Mawes Castle opposite, were built by Henry VIII to protect the entrance of Carrick Roads.

ENVIRONS: To the south, **Glendurgan** *(see p230)* and **Trebah** gardens are both set in sheltered valleys leading down to delightful sandy coves on the River Helford.

Ship's figure-head, Falmouth

♠ **Pendennis Castle**
The Headland. 📞 01326 316594. ◯ daily. ● 24–26 Dec, 1 Jan. 💷 ♿ limited. 🎫 🛒 📷

🌺 **Glendurgan**
(NT) Mawnan Smith. 📞 01872 250906. ◯ Mar–Oct: Tue–Sat & public hols. ● Good Fri. 💷 🛒 📷

🌺 **Trebah**
Mawnan Smith. 📞 01326 250448. ◯ daily. 💷 ♿ 🛒 📷

Truro ⑦

Cornwall. 🏛 18,000. 🚆 🚌
ℹ Boscawen St (01872 274555).
🏪 Wed (cattle), Wed & Sat (farmers' market). 🌐 www.truro.gov.uk

ONCE A market town and port, Truro is now the administrative capital of Cornwall. Truro's many gracious Georgian buildings reflect its prosperity during the tin mining boom of the 1800s. In 1876 the 16th-century parish church was rebuilt to create the first new **cathedral** to be built in England since Wren built St Paul's *(see pp116–17)* in the 17th century. With its central tower, lancet windows and spires, the cathedral is an exuberant building that looks more French than English.

Truro's cobbled streets and alleys lined with craft shops are also a delight to explore. The **Royal Cornwall Museum** provides an excellent introduction to the history of the county with displays on tin mining, Methodism *(see p265)*, and smuggling.

ENVIRONS: On the outskirts of the city lie **Trewithen** and **Trelissick** gardens *(see pp230–31).* The former has a rich collection of Asiatic plants.

🏛 **Royal Cornwall Museum**
River St. 📞 01872 272205. ◯ Mon–Sat. ● public hols. 💷 ♿ 🛒 📷

🌺 **Trewithen**
Grampound Rd. 📞 01726 883647. ◯ Mar–Sep: Mon–Sat (Apr, May: daily). 💷 ♿ 🎫 by arrangement.

🌺 **Trelissick**
(NT) Feock. 📞 01872 862090. ◯ Mar–Oct: daily. 💷 ♿ 🍴 📷

The "Cornish Alps": china-clay spoil tips north of St Austell

St Austell ⑧

Cornwall. 🏛 20,000. 🚆 🚌
ℹ BP Filling Station, Southbourne Rd (01726 76333). 🏪 Fri–Sun.
🌐 www.cornish-riviera.co.uk

THE BUSY INDUSTRIAL town of St Austell is the capital of the local china-clay industry which rose to importance in the 18th century. Clay is still a vital factor in Cornwall's economy; China is the only other place in the world where such quality and quantity of clay can be found. Spoil tips are a prominent feature of the surrounding landscape; on a sunny day they look like snow-covered peaks, meriting the humorous local name the "Cornish Alps".

ENVIRONS: The process of extracting and refining china clay is explained at the **Wheal Martyn Museum**. Trails weave through a clay pit and works that operated from 1878 until the 1920s. The water-wheels and pumps have been restored and the tunnels have been colonized by wildlife.
🏛 **Wheal Martyn Museum**
Carthew. 📞 01726 850362. ◯ Apr–Oct: Sun–Fri; May–Sep: daily. 💷 ♿ limited. 🖥

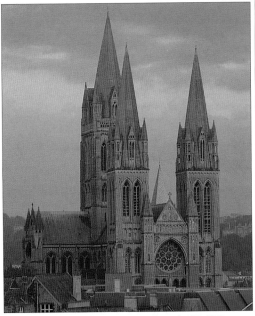

Truro Cathedral, designed by JL Pearson and completed in 1910

Eden Project ❾

BUILT INTO THE WALLS OF an abandoned industrial crater, the Eden Project is a massive greenhouse project where thousands of plants from all over the world are nurtured. Two futuristic conservatories called biomes have been specially designed to mimic the environments of warmer climes: one hot and humid, the other warm and dry. Outside, the walls of the pit have been terraced and planted with species that will thrive in the Cornish climate. Unlike a standard conservatory where plants are set out to be admired as species, the Eden Project seeks to educate by telling the story of plants and habitats. The symbiotic relationship between humans and the natural world is interpreted by storytellers and artists throughout the site.

④ **Tropical South America**
Some plants in Amazonia grow to massive proportions. The giant waterlilies (Victoria cruziana) will stretch to 2m wide.

③ **West Africa**
Tabernanthe Iboga *is central to the African religion Bwiti. Extremely hallucinogenic, it is an integral part of initiation ceremonies.*

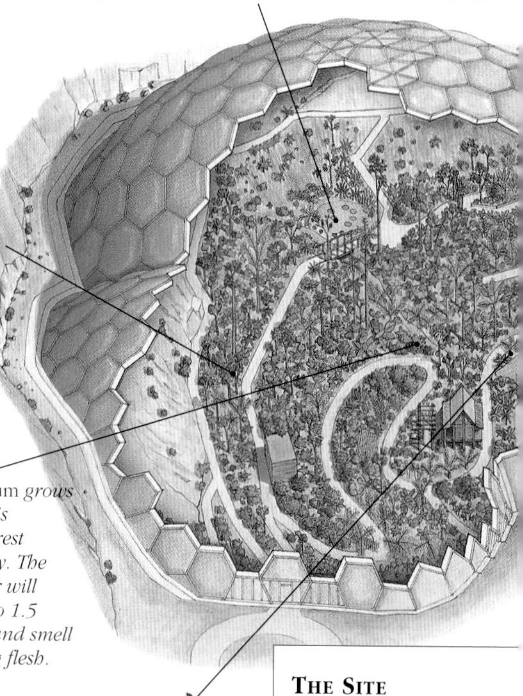

② **Malaysia**
The Titan arum grows within this rainforest display. The flower will grow to 1.5 metres and smell of rotting flesh.

① **Oceanic Islands**
Set apart from the rest of the world, these islands have many fascinating plants. The rare Madagascar Periwinkle (Catharanthus roseus) is thought to help cure leukemia.

THE SITE

Access to the landscape and the biomes is via the Gateway to Eden visitor centre.

Humid Tropics Biome
① Oceanic Islands
② Malaysia
③ West Africa
④ Tropical South America
⑤ Crops and cultivation

Warm Temperate Biome
⑥ The Mediterranean
⑦ South Africa
⑧ California
⑨ Crops and cultivation

VISITORS' CHECKLIST

Bodelva, St. Austell, Cornwall.
📞 01726 811911. 🚃 St Austell.
🚌 dedicated bus service from
St. Austell. 🕐 Mar–Oct: 10am–
6pm daily (last adm 5pm);
Nov–Feb: 10am–4:30pm daily
(last adm 3:30pm). ⬤ 25–26
Dec. 📷 ♿ 🍴 🛍 🎁
Ⓦ www.edenproject.com

Building Eden

Cornwall's declining china clay industry has left behind many abandoned pit mines. The Eden Project makes ingenious use of this industrial landscape. After partly infilling a pit, the massive biomes were nestled into its base and walls.

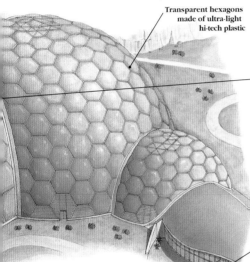

Transparent hexagons made of ultra-light hi-tech plastic

⑤ Crops and cultivation

The coffee plant (Coffea arabica) is one of the many plants on display that are used to manufacture everyday products.

The entrance to both the Humid Tropics and Warm Temperate Biomes is via The Link, where two restaurants are located.

...MID TROPICS BIOME

...vast conservatory houses a lush jungle of 2000 ...s and plants. The dome is high enough to allow ...rainforest trees to grow to their full height.

...side Landscape
...rairie
...Plant for rope and fibre
...Hemp
...teppe
...ea
...Plants and pollinators
...Plants for fuel
...Beer and brewing
...Sunflowers
...Plants in myth and folkore
...Wild Cornwall
...Plants reclamation
...Apples
...Indigo
...Liquorice

㉕ Berries
㉖ Plants and health
㉗ Chilean temperate forest
㉘ Flowerless garden
㉙ Fodder crops

㉚ Plants for tomorrow's industries
㉛ Plants for paper

0 metres 150
0 yards   150

Wetland

Eden Arena

Gateway to Eden

View of Polruan across the estuary from Fowey

Fowey ⑩

Cornwall. 🏯 *2,000.* 🚢 🛈 *4 Custom House Hill (01726 833616).* Ⓦ *www.fowey.com*

FOWEY (pronounced Foy), has been immortalized under the name of Troy Town in the humorous novels of Sir Arthur Quiller-Couch (1863–1944), who lived here in a house called **The Haven**. A resort favoured by many wealthy Londoners with a taste

DAPHNE DU MAURIER

The period romances of Daphne du Maurier (1907–89) are inextricably linked with the wild Cornish landscape where she grew up. *Jamaica Inn* established her reputation in 1936, and with the publication of *Rebecca* two years later she found herself one of the most popular authors of her day. *Rebecca* was made into a film directed by Alfred Hitchcock, starring Joan Fontaine and Lord Laurence Olivier.

for yachting and expensive seafood restaurants, Fowey is the most gentrified of the Cornish seaside towns. The picturesque charm of the flower-filled village is undeniable, with its tangle of tiny steep streets and its views across the estuary to Polruan. The church of **St Fimbarrus** marks the end of the ancient Saint's Way footpath from Padstow – a reminder of the Celtic missionaries who arrived on the shores of Cornwall to convert people to Christianity. Its flower-lined path leads to a majestic porch and carved tower. Inside there are some fine 17th-century memorials to the Rashleigh family whose seat, Menabilly, became Daphne du Maurier's home and featured as Manderley in *Rebecca* (1938).

ENVIRONS: For a closer look at the town of **Polruan** and the ceaseless activity of the harbour there is a number of river trips up the little creeks. At the estuary mouth are the twin towers from which chains were once hung to de-mast invading ships – an effective form of defence.

A fine stretch of coast leads further east to the picturesque fishing villages of **Polperro**, nestling in a narrow green ravine, and neighbouring **Looe**.

Upriver from Fowey is the tranquil town of **Lostwithiel**. Perched on a hill just to the north are the remains of the Norman **Restormel Castle**.

♣ **Restormel Castle**
Lostwithiel. 【 *01208 872687.* ◯ *daily.* ● *24–26 Dec.* 🖾

Bodmin ⑪

Cornwall. 🚊 *Bodmin Parkway.* 🚌 *Bodmin.* 🛈 *Mount Folly Sq, Bodmin (01208 76616).* Ⓦ *www.bodminmoor.co.uk/bodmintic*

BODMIN, CORNWALL'S ancient county town, lies on the sheltered western edge of the great expanse of moorland that shares its name. The history and archaeology of the town and moor is covered by **Bodmin Town Museum**, while **Bodmin Jail**, where public executions took place until 1909, has been turned into a gruesome tourist attraction. The churchyard is watered by the ever-gushing waters of a holy spring, and it was here that St Guron established a Christian cell in the 6th century. The **church** is dedicated to St Petroc, a Welsh missionary who founded a monastery here in the same period, as well as many others in the region. The monastery has disappeared, but the bones of St Petroc remain, housed in a splendid 12th-century ivory casket in the church.

Jamaica Inn, Bodmin Moor

South of Bodmin is the **Lanhydrock** estate. Amid its extensive wooded acres and formal gardens (*see p230*) lies the massive house, rebuilt after a fire in 1881, but retaining some Jacobean features. The labyrinth of corridors and rooms illustrates life in a Victorian manor house and the fine 17th-century plaster ceiling in the Long Gallery depicts scenes from the Bible.

The desolate wilderness of Bodmin Moor is noted for its network of prehistoric field boundaries. The main attraction, however, is the 18th-century **Jamaica Inn**, made famous by Daphne du Maurier's tale of smuggling and romance. Today there is a restaurant and bar based on du Maurier's novel, and a small museum. A 30-minute walk from the Inn is **Dozmary Pool**, reputed to be bottomless until it dried up in 1976.

The ruins of Tintagel Castle on the north coast of Cornwall

According to legend, the dying King Arthur's sword Excalibur was thrown into the pool.

To the east is **Altarnun**. Its spacious 15th-century church of **St Nonna** is known as the "Cathedral of the Moor".

🏛 **Bodmin Town Museum**
Mt Folly Sq, Bodmin. ☎ 01208 77067. ⬜ Easter–Oct: Mon–Sat, Good Fri. ⬤ public hols. ♿ limited.

🏛 **Bodmin Jail**
Berrycombe Rd, Bodmin. ☎ 01208 76292. ⬜ daily. ⬤ 25 Dec. 📷

🏛 **Lanhydrock**
(NT) Bodmin. ☎ 01208 73320.
House ⬜ Apr–Oct: Tue–Sun & public hols. **Gardens** ⬜ daily. 📷

Tintagel ⑫

Cornwall. 🚶 1,700. 🚌 Thu (summer).

THE ROMANTIC and mysterious ruins of **Tintagel Castle**, built around 1240 by Earl Richard of Cornwall, sit high on a hill-top surrounded by crumpled slate cliffs and yawning black caves. Access to the castle is by means of two steep staircases clinging to the cliff-side where pink thrift and purple sea lavender abound.

The earl was persuaded to build in this isolated, wind-swept spot by the popular belief, derived from Geoffrey of Monmouth's fictitious *History of the Kings of Britain*, that this was the birthplace of the legendary King Arthur.

Large quantities of fine eastern Mediterranean pottery dating from around the 5th century have been discovered, indicating that the site was an important trading centre, long before the medieval castle was built. Whoever lived here, perhaps the ancient Kings of Cornwall, could evidently afford a luxurious lifestyle.

A clifftop path leads from the castle to Tintagel's **church** which has Norman and Saxon masonry. In Tintagel village the **Old Post Office** is a rare example of a 14th-century Cornish manor house, restored and furnished with 17th-century oak furniture.

ENVIRONS: A short distance to the east, **Boscastle** is another pretty National Trust village. The River Valency runs down the middle of the main street to the fishing harbour, which is sheltered from the sea by high slate cliffs. Access from the harbour to the sea is via a channel cut through the rocks.

🏰 **Tintagel Castle**
Off High St. ☎ 01840 770328.
⬜ daily. ⬤ 24–26 Dec, 1 Jan. 📷

🏛 **Old Post Office**
(NT) Fore St. ☎ 01840 770024.
⬜ Apr–Oct: daily. 📷

Bude ⑬

Cornwall. 🚶 9,000. ℹ The Crescent car park (01288 354240). 🚌 Fri (summer). 🌐 www.bude.co.uk

WONDERFUL beaches around this area make Bude a popular resort for families. The expanse of clean golden sand that attracts visitors today once made Bude a bustling port. Shelly, lime-rich sand was transported along a canal to inland farms where it was used to neutralize the acidic soil. The canal was abandoned in 1880 but a short stretch survives, providing a haven for birds such as king-fishers and herons.

Kingfisher

KING ARTHUR

Historians think the legendary figure of King Arthur has some basis in historical fact. He was probably a Romano-British chieftain or warrior who led British resistance to the Saxon invasion of the 6th century *(see pp46–7)*. Geoffrey of Monmouth's *History of the Kings of Britain* (1139) introduced Arthur to literature with an account of the many legends connected with him – how he became king by removing the sword Excalibur from a stone, his final battle with the treacherous Mordred, and the story of the Knights of the Round Table *(see p156)*. Other writers, such as Alfred, Lord Tennyson, took up these stories and elaborated on them.

King Arthur, from a 14th-century chronicle by Peter of Langtoft

Clovelly ⑭

Devon. 🚂 350. 🚇 01237 431781.
Town & Visitors' Centre ⬜ daily.
● 25 Dec. ♿ Visitors' Centre.

CLOVELLY has been a noted beauty spot since the novelist Charles Kingsley (1819–75) wrote about it in his stirring story of the Spanish Armada, *Westward Ho!* (1855). Today the whole village is privately owned and has been turned into a tourist attraction, with little sign of the flourishing fishing industry to which it owed its birth. It is a charming, picturesque village with steep cobbled streets rising up the cliff from the harbourside, gaily painted houses and gardens brimming with brightly coloured flowers. There are superb views from the lookout points and fine coastal paths to explore from the tiny quay. The Visitors' Centre offers an introduction to the village.

Hobby Drive is a scenic 3-mile (5-km) approach on foot to the village which runs through woodland along the coast. The road was constructed in 1811–29 to give

Bideford's medieval bridge, 203 m (666 ft) long with 24 arches

employment to local men who had been made redundant at the end of the Napoleonic Wars *(see pp54–5).*

Bideford ⑮

Devon. 🚂 14,000. 🚌 ℹ️ *Victoria Park (01237 477676).* 🚌 *Tue, Sat.*

STRUNG OUT along the boat-filled estuary of the River Torridge, Bideford grew and thrived on importing tobacco from the New World. Some 17th-century merchants' houses survive in Bridgeland Street, including the splendid bay-windowed house at No. 28 (1693). Beyond is Mill Street,

leading to the parish church and the fine medieval bridge. The quay stretches from here to a pleasant park and a statue which commemorates Charles Kingsley, whose novels helped bring visitors to the area in the 19th century.

ENVIRONS: To the west of Bideford, the village **Westward Ho!** was built in the late 19th century and named after Kingsley's popular novel. The development failed and the Victorian villas and hotels are now part of a holiday resort. Rudyard Kipling *(see p149)* was at school here and the hill to the south, known as **Kipling Tors**, was the background for *Stalky & Co* (1899).

Also to the west is **Hartland Abbey**, built as a monastery c.1157, now a family home. Visitors can enjoy a museum, art and antiques collections as well as informal gardens and a woodland walk.

Henry Williamson's *Tarka the Otter* (1927) describes the otters of the **Torridge Valley** and naturalists are hoping to reintroduce otters here. Part of a Tarka Trail has been laid out along the Torridge and bicycles can be hired from the old railway station. The trail passes close to the Royal Horticultural Society's magnificent **Rosemoor Garden**.

Day trips run from Bideford to **Lundy** island, which is abundant in birds and other wildlife.

🌿 **RHS Rosemoor Garden**
Great Torrington. 🚇 *01805 624067.*
⬜ *daily.* ● *25 Dec.* ♿ 🚻 🅿️
🏛 **Hartland Abbey** nr. Bideford.
🚇 *01237 441264.* ⬜ *Apr–Sep: 2–5:30pm Tue (Jul–Aug only), Wed, Thu, Sun, public hols.* ♿ 🅿️

Fishing boats in Clovelly's harbour

Fishermen's cottages, Appledore

Appledore 16

Devon. 3,000.

APPLEDORE'S remote position at the tip of the Torridge Estuary has helped to preserve its charms intact. Busy boatyards line the long riverside quay, which is also the departure point for fishing trips and ferries to the sandy beaches of Braunton Burrows on the opposite shore. Timeworn Regency houses line the main street which runs parallel to the quay, and behind is a network of narrow cobbled lanes with 18th-century fishermen's cottages. Several shops retain their original bow-windows and sell an assortment of crafts, antiques and souvenirs.

Uphill from the quay is the **North Devon Maritime Museum**, with an exhibition on the experiences of Devon emigrants in Australia and models and photographs explaining the work of local shipyards. The tiny **Victorian Schoolroom** which is affiliated to the museum, shows various documentary videos on local trades such as fishing and shipbuilding.

Barnstaple's Pannier Market

North Devon Maritime Museum

Odun Rd. 01237 474852. May–Sep: daily; April, Oct: pm only. limited.

Barnstaple 17

Devon. 33,000. Boutport St (01271 375000). Mon–Sat. www.barnstapletic/visit.org.uk

ALTHOUGTH BARNSTAPLE is an important distribution centre for the whole region, its town centre remains calm due to the exclusion of traffic. The massive glass-roofed **Pannier Market** (1855) has stalls of organic fruit and vegetables, honey and eggs, much of it produced by farmers' wives to supplement their income. Nearby is **St Peter's Church** with its twisted broach spire caused by a lightning strike which warped the timbers in 1810.

On the Strand is a wonderful arcade topped with a statue of Queen Anne, now a small museum. This was built as an exchange where merchants traded the contents of their cargo boats moored on the River Taw alongside. Nearby is the 15th-century bridge and the **Museum of North Devon**, where displays cover local history and the 700-year-old pottery industry, as well as local wildlife, such as the otters that are returning to rivers in the area. The 180-mile (290-km) Tarka Trail circuits around Barnstaple; 35 miles (56 km) of it can be cycled.

Statue of Queen Anne (1708)

ENVIRONS: Just to the west of Barnstaple, **Braunton "Great Field"** covers over 120 ha (300 acres) and is a well-preserved relic of medieval open-field cultivation. Beyond lies **Braunton Burrows**, one of the most extensive wild-dune reserves in Britain. It is a must for plant enthusiasts who would like to spot sea kale, sea holly, sea lavender and horned poppies growing in their natural habitat. The sandy beaches and pounding waves at nearby Croyde and Woolacombe, are favourites among surfing enthusiasts, but there are also calmer areas of warm shallow water and rock pools.

Arlington Court, north of Barnstaple, has a collection of model ships, magnificent perennial borders and a lake. The stables house a collection of horse-drawn vehicles. Carriage rides are available.

Devonshire Cream Teas

Devon people claim all other versions of a cream tea are inferior to their own. The essential ingredient is Devonshire clotted cream which comes from Jersey cattle fed on rich Devon pasture – anything else is second best, or so it is claimed. Spread thickly on freshly baked scones, with lashings of homemade strawberry jam, this makes a seductive, delicious, but fattening, tea-time treat.

A typical cream tea with scones, jam and clotted cream

Museum of North Devon

The Square. 01271 346747. Tue–Sat. 24 Dec–1 Jan. limited.

Arlington Court

(NT) Arlington. 01271 850296. *Apr–Oct: Sun–Fri. limited.*

The village of Lynmouth

Lynton and Lynmouth ⑱

Devon. 🏠 *2,000.* 🚌 ❶ *Town Hall, Lee Rd (015987 52225). See pp236–7.* Ⓦ *www.lynton/lynmouth-tourist.co.uk*

SITUATED AT THE POINT where the East and West Lyn rivers meet the sea, Lynmouth is a picturesque, though rather commercialized, fishing village. The pedestrianized main street, lined with shops selling clotted cream and seaside souvenirs, runs parallel to the Lyn, now made into a canal with high embankments as a precaution against flash floods. One flood devastated the town at the height of the holiday season in 1952. The scars caused by the flood, which was fuelled by heavy rain on Exmoor, are now overgrown by trees in the pretty **Glen Lyn Gorge**, which leads north out of the village. Lynmouth's sister town, Lynton, is a mainly Victorian village perched on the clifftop 130 m (427 ft) above, giving lovely views across the Bristol Channel to the Welsh coast. It can be reached from the harbour front by a cliff railway, by road or by a steep path.

ENVIRONS: Lynmouth makes an excellent starting point for walks on Exmoor. There is a 2 mile (3 km) trail that leads southeast to tranquil **Watersmeet** *(see p237).* On the western edge of Exmoor, **Combe Martin** *(see p236)* lies in a sheltered valley. On the main street, lined with Victorian villas, is the 18th-century Pack of Cards Inn, built by a gambler with 52 windows, for each card in the pack.

Exeter ⑲

EXETER IS DEVON'S CAPITAL, a bustling and lively city with a great deal of character, despite the World War II bombing that destroyed much of its city centre. Built high on a plateau above the River Exe, the city is encircled by substantial sections of Roman and medieval wall, and the street plan has not changed much since the Romans first laid out what is now the High Street. Elsewhere the Cathedral Close forms a pleasant green, and there are cobbled streets and narrow alleys which invite leisurely exploration. For shoppers there is a wide selection of big stores and smaller speciality shops.

Exploring Exeter

The intimate green and the close surrounding Exeter's distinctive cathedral were the setting for Anthony Trollope's novel *He Knew He Was Right* (1869). Full of festive crowds listening to buskers in the summer, the close presents an array of architectural styles. One of the finest buildings here is the Elizabethan **Mol's Coffee House**. Among the other historic buildings that survived World War II are the magnificent **Guildhall** (1330) on the High Street (one of Britain's oldest civic buildings), the opulent **Custom House** (1681) by the quay, and the elegant 18th-century **Rougement House** which stands near the remains of a Norman **castle** built by William the Conqueror *(see pp46–7).*

The port area has been transformed into a tourist attraction with its early 19th-century warehouses converted into craft shops, antique galleries and cafés. Boats can be hired for cruising down the short stretch of canal. The **Quay House Interpretation Centre**

The timber-framed Mol's Coffee House (1596), Cathedral Close

West front and south tower, Cathedral Church of St Peter

(open April–October) has audio-visual and other displays on the history of Exeter.

⛪ Cathedral Church of St Peter

Cathedral Close. 📞 *01392 255573.* ◯ *daily.* ♿ 🍴 🎁
Exeter's cathedral is one of the most gloriously ornamented in Britain. Except for the two Norman towers, the cathedral is mainly 14th century and built in the style aptly known as Decorated because of the swirling geometric patterns of the stone work. The West Front, the largest single collection (66) of medieval figure sculptures in England, includes kings – probably Judah – apostles and prophets. Started in the 14th century, it was completed by 1450. Inside, the splendid Gothic vaulting sweeps from one end of the church to the other, impressive in its uniformity and punctuated by gaily painted ceiling bosses. Among the tombs around the choir is that of Edward II's treasurer, Walter de Stapledon (1261–1326), who was murdered by a mob in London. Stapledon raised much of the money needed to fund the building of this cathedral

Collection of shells and other objects in the library of A La Ronde

VISITORS' CHECKLIST

Devon. 🚗 104,000. ✈ 5 miles
(8 km) east. 🚆 Exeter St David's,
Bonhay Rd; Exeter Central, Queen
St. 🚌 Paris St. 🛈 Paris St
(01392 265700). 🅰 daily. 🎭
Exeter Festival: end Jun–mid-Jul.

and for Exeter College in Oxford *(see pp208–13)*.

🏠 Underground Passages
Roman Gate Passage. 📞 *01392 665 887.* ◯ *Jul–Sep: Mon–Sat; Oct–Jun: Tue–Fri (pm), Sat.* ● *25, 26 Dec, 1 Jan.* 📷 🎫

Under the city centre lie the remains of Exeter's medieval water-supply system. An excellent video and guided tour explain how the stone-lined tunnels were built in the 14th and 15th centuries on a slight gradient to bring in fresh water from springs outside the town.

🏠 St Nicholas Priory
The Mint. 📞 *01392 265858.* ◯ *Easter–Oct.*
Built in the 12th century, this building has retained many original features and rooms. These trace its fascinating history from austere monastic beginnings, through its secular use as a Tudor residence for wealthy merchants, to its 20th-century incarnation as five separate premises occupied by various tradesmen including a bootmaker and an upholsterer.

🏛 Royal Albert Memorial Museum and Art Gallery
Queen St. 📞 *01392 265858.* ◯ *Mon–Sat.* ● *24–26 Dec, 1 Jan, Good Fri.* ♿ 🖥 🎫

This museum has a wonderfully varied collection, including Roman remains, a zoo of stuffed animals, West Country art and a particularly good ethnographic display. Highlights include displays on silverware, watches and clocks.

ENVIRONS: South of Exeter on the A376, the eccentric **A La Ronde** is a 16-sided house built in 1796 by two spinster cousins, who decorated

19th-century head of an Oba, Royal Albert Museum

the interior with shells, feathers and souvenirs gathered while on tour in Europe.

Further east, the unspoilt Regency town of **Sidmouth** lies in a sheltered bay. There is an eclectic array of architecture, the earliest buildings dating from the 1820s when Sidmouth became a popular summer resort. Thatched cottages stand opposite huge Edwardian villas, and elegant terraces line the seafront. In summer the town hosts the famous International Festival of Folk Arts *(see p63)*.

North of Sidmouth lies the magnificent church at **Ottery St Mary**. Built in 1338–42 by Bishop Grandisson, the church is clearly a scaled-down version of Exeter Cathedral, which he also helped build. A memorial in the churchyard wall recalls the fact the poet Coleridge was born in the town in 1772.

Nearby **Honiton** is famous for its extraordinarily intricate and delicate lace, made here since Elizabethan times.

To the north of Exeter, **Killerton** is home to the National Trust's costume collection. Here, displays of bustles and corsets and vivid tableaux illustrate aristocratic fashions from the 18th century to the present day.

Further north near Tiverton, is **Knightshayes Court**, a Victorian Gothic house with fine gardens *(see p230–31)*.

🏛 A La Ronde
(NT) Summer Lane, Exmouth.
📞 *01395 265514.* ◯ *Apr–Oct: Sun–Thu.* 📷 🖥 🎫

🏛 Killerton
(NT) Broadclyst. 📞 *01392 881345.* ● *until May 2003 for restoration.* 📷 ♿ 🖥 🎫

🏠 Knightshayes Court
(NT) Bolham. 📞 *01884 254665.* ◯ *Apr–Sep: Sat–Thu, Good Fri (gardens daily Apr–Oct).* 📷 ♿ *limited.* 🍴 🎫

Mexican dancer at Sidmouth's International Festival of Folk Arts

Torbay ⑳

Torbay. �'🚉 🚌 Torquay, Paignton.
ℹ️ Vaughan Parade, Torquay
(01803 297428).
🌐 www.theenglishriviera.co.uk

THE THREE SEASIDE TOWNS of Torquay, Paignton and Brixham form an almost continuous resort around the great sweep of sandy beach and calm blue waters of Torbay. Because of its mild climate, extensive semi-tropical gardens and exuberant Victorian hotel architecture, this popular coastline has been dubbed the English Riviera. In its heyday, Torbay was patronized by the wealthy, especially during Victorian times. Today, mass entertainment is the theme and there are plenty of attractions of this type, mostly in and around Torquay.

Torre Abbey includes the remains of a monastery founded in 1196 and now serves as an art gallery. There is a magnificent barn in the grounds where prisoners captured from the Spanish Armada of 1588 were once held. **Torquay Museum** nearby covers natural history and archaeology, including finds from **Kents Cavern**, on the outskirts of the town. This is one of England's most important prehistoric sites and the spectacular caves serve as the background for displays on people and animals who lived here up to 350,000 years ago.

The charming miniature town of **Babbacombe Model Village** lies to the north of Torquay, while a mere mile (1.5 km) inland is the lovely little village of **Cockington**. Visitors travel by horse-drawn carriage to view the preserved Tudor manor house, church, thatched cottages and forge.

In Paignton, the celebrated **Paignton Zoo** teaches children about the planet's wildlife, and from here you can take the steam railway – an ideal way to visit Dartmouth.

Continuing south from Paignton, the pretty village of Brixham was once England's most prosperous fishing port.

Bayards Cove, Dartmouth

🏛 **Torre Abbey**
King's Drive, Torquay. ☎ 01803 293593. 🕐 Apr–Oct: daily. 🈸 🅿

🏛 **Torquay Museum**
Babbacombe Rd, Torquay. ☎ 01803 293975. 🕐 daily (Nov–Easter: Mon–Fri). ● Christmas wk, Good Fri. 🈸 🅿

🏛 **Kents Cavern**
Ilsham Rd, Torquay. ☎ 01803 294 059. 🕐 daily. ● 25 Dec. ♿ 🅿

🏛 **Babbacombe Model Village**
Hampton Ave, Torquay. ☎ 01803 328 669. 🕐 daily. ● 25 Dec. 🈸 ♿ 🅿

🐾 **Paignton Zoo**
Totnes Rd, Paignton. ☎ 01803 557 479. 🕐 daily. ● 25 Dec. ♿ ♿

Dartmouth ㉑

Devon. 🏘 5,500. 🚉 ℹ️ Mayors Ave (01803 834224). 🛒 Tue–Fri am.
🌐 www.dartmouth-information.co.uk

SITTING HIGH ON THE CLIFFTOP above the River Dart is the **Royal Naval College**, where British naval officers have trained since 1905. Dartmouth has always been an important port and it was from here that English fleets set sail to join the Second and Third Crusades. Some 18th-century houses adorn the cobbled quay of Bayards Cove, while carved timber buildings line the 17th-century Butterwalk, home to **Dartmouth Museum**. To the south is **Dartmouth Castle** (1388).

🏛 **Dartmouth Museum**
Butterwalk. ☎ 01803 832923. 🕐 Mon–Sat. ● 25 & 26 Dec, 1 Jan. 🈸 🅿

🏰 **Dartmouth Castle**
Castle Rd. ☎ 01803 833588. 🕐 daily (Nov–Easter: Wed–Sun). ● 24–26 Dec, 1 Jan. 🈸 🅿 🅿

Torquay, on the "English Riviera"

Stained glass window in Blessed Sacrament Chapel, Buckfast Abbey

Totnes ㉒

Devon. 🕴 *7,000.* 🚉 🏢 ⬆
ℹ *Coronation Rd (01803 863168).*
🏛 *Tue am (May–Sep), Fri, Sat.*

TOTNES SITS at the highest navigable point on the River Dart with a Norman **castle** perched high on the hill above. Linking the two is the steep High Street, lined with bow-windowed Elizabethan houses. Bridging the street is the **Eastgate**, part of the medieval town wall. Life in the town's heyday is explored in the **Totnes Elizabethan Museum**, which also has a room devoted to the mathematician Charles Babbage (1791–1871) who is regarded as the pioneer of modern computers. There is a medieval **Guildhall**, and a **church** with a delicately carved and gilded rood screen. On Tuesdays in the summer, market stallholders dress in Elizabethan costume.

ENVIRONS: A short walk north of Totnes, **Dartington Hall** has 10 ha (25 acres) of lovely gardens and a world-famous music school where concerts are held in the heavily timbered 14th-century Great Hall.

🔱 **Totnes Castle**
Castle St. 📞 *01803 864406.*
⬜ *Apr–Oct: daily; Nov–Mar: Wed–Sun.* ⚫ *24–26 Dec, 1 Jan.* 🚫
🏛 **Totnes Elizabethan Museum**
Fore St. 📞 *01803 863821.* ⬜
Easter–Oct: Mon–Fri. 🚫 ♿ *limited.*
🎪 **Guildhall**
Rampart Walk. 📞 *01803 862147.*
⬜ *Apr–Oct: Mon–Fri.* 🚫
🌿 **Dartington Hall Gardens**
Dartington Hall Estate. 📞 *01803 862367.* ⬜ *daily.* 🎟 *by appt.*

Buckfastleigh ㉓

Devon. 🕴 *3,300.* 🚉

THIS MARKET TOWN, situated on the edge of Dartmoor *(see p280–81)*, is dominated by **Buckfast Abbey**. The original abbey, founded in Norman times, fell into ruin after the Dissolution of the Monasteries and it was not until 1882 that a small group of French Benedictine monks set up a new abbey here. Work on the present building was

Stallholders in Totnes market

financed by donations and carried out by the monks themselves. The abbey was completed in 1938 and now lies at the heart of a thriving community.

The fine mosaics and modern stained glass window are also the work of the monks.

Nearby is the **Buckfast Butterfly Farm and Otter Sanctuary,** and the **South Devon Steam Railway** terminus where steam trains leave for Totnes.

⛪ **Buckfast Abbey**
Buckfastleigh. 📞 *01364 645500.*
⬜ *daily.* ⚫ *25–27 Dec, Good Fri.* 🍴
🏢 ♿
🦋 **Buckfast Butterfly Farm and Otter Sanctuary**
Buckfastleigh. 📞 *01364 642916.*
⬜ *Easter–Nov: daily.* 🚫 ♿

Burgh Island ㉔

Devon. 🚉 *Plymouth, then taxi.*
ℹ *(01548 810514).*

THE SHORT WALK across the sands at low tide from Bigbury-on-Sea to Burgh Island takes you back to the decadent era of the 1920s and '30s. It was here that the millionaire Archibald Nettlefold built the luxury **Burgh Island Hotel** in 1929. Created in Art Deco style with a natural rock seabathing pool, this was the exclusive retreat of famous figures, such as the Duke of Windsor and writers Agatha Christie and Noel Coward. The restored hotel is worth a visit for the photographs of its heyday and the Art Deco fittings. You can also explore the island and **Pilchard Inn** (1336), reputed to be haunted by the ghost of a smuggler.

The Art Deco style bar in Burgh Island Hotel

Plymouth 🄯

Plymouth. 🅟 250,000. ✈ 🚆 🚌
⛴ 🛈 Island House, The Barbican.
(01752 304849). 🄰 daily.
ⓦ www.plymouth.gov.uk

THE TINY PORT from which
Drake, Raleigh, the Pilgrim
Fathers, Cook and Darwin all
set sail on pioneering voyages
has now grown to a substantial city, much of it boldly
rebuilt after wartime
bombing. Old
Plymouth clusters
around the **Hoe**,
the famous patch of
turf on which Sir
Francis Drake is
said to have calmly
finished his game
of bowls as the
Spanish Armada
approached the port in 1588
(see pp50–51). Today the Hoe
is a pleasant park and parade
ground surrounded by mem-
orials to naval men, including
Drake himself. Alongside is
Charles II's **Royal Citadel**,
built to guard the harbour in

Drake's coat of arms

the 1660s, and the fascinating
Aquarium. A popular attraction is **Plymouth Dome**, a
visitor centre which uses high-
tech display techniques to
explain Plymouth's past and
present, including live satellite
weather pictures and radar
screens for monitoring ships
in the harbour. A short stroll
away, **Mayflower Stone and
Steps** is the spot where the
Pilgrim Fathers set sail for the
New World in
England's third
and successful
attempt at colon-
ization in 1620.

ENVIRONS: A boat
tour of the harbour
is the best way to
see Plymouth's
historic dockyard
complex where warships
have been built since the
Napoleonic Wars *(see pp54–5)*.
There are also splendid views
of the numerous fine gardens,
such as **Mount Edgcumbe
Park** *(see pp230–31)*, scattered around the coastline of

**Mid-18th-century carved wood
chimneypiece, Saltram House**

the Plymouth Sound.
East of the city, the mid-
18th-century **Saltram House**
has two opulent rooms by
Adam *(see pp24–5)*. There are
also portraits by Reynolds who
was born nearby in Plympton.

🏰 **Royal Citadel**
The Hoe. 🄲 01752 775841. 🄰 May–
Sep: daily. 🄯 only. 🄳 🅖 limited.
🐟 **Aquarium**
Ropewalk Coxfide. 🄲 01752
600311. 🄰 daily. 🄯 25 Dec. 🄳 🅖
🏛 **Plymouth Dome**
The Hoe. 🄲 01752 600608. 🄰 call
for times. 🄯 25 Dec. 🄳 🅖 🅟
🌿 **Mount Edgcumbe Park**
Cremyll, Torpoint. 🄲 01752 822236.
🄰 Apr–Sep: Wed–Sun. 🄳 🅖 🅗 🅟
🏰 **Saltram House**
(NT) Plympton. 🄲 01752 336546.
🄰 Apr–Oct: Sun–Thu, Good Fri; Feb–
Mar: Sat & Sun (gardens only).
🄳 🅖 🅗 🅟

Buckland Abbey 🄰

(NT) Yelverton, Devon. 🄲 01822
853607. 🚌 from Yelverton.
🄰 Fri–Wed (Nov–Mar: Sat & Sun
pm). 🄯 25, 26 Dec, Jan–mid Feb.
🄳 🅖 🅗 🅟

FOUNDED BY the Cistercian
monks in 1278, Buckland
Abbey was converted to a
house after the Dissolution of
the Monasteries and became
the home of Drake from
1581–96. Many of the monastic buildings survive in a
garden setting, the most
impressive being the 14th-
century tithe barn *(see p28)*.
Part of the house explains
Drake's life and times through
paintings and memorabilia.

View of Plymouth Harbour from the Hoe

Cotehele ②

(NT) St Dominick, Cornwall.
☎ 01579 351346. ≋ Calstock.
House ◯ Apr–Oct: Sat–Thu & Good
Fri. **Grounds** ◯ daily. 🎫 ♿ limited.

MAGNIFICENT WOODLAND and lush river scenery make Cotehele (pronounced Coteal) one of the most delightful spots on the River Tamar and a rewarding day can be spent exploring the estate. Far from civilization, tucked into its wooded fold in the Cornish countryside, Cotehele has slumbered for 500 years. The main attraction is the house and valley garden at its centre. Built mainly between 1489 and 1520, it is a rare example of a medieval house, set around three courtyards with a magnificent open hall, kitchen, chapel and a warren of private parlours and chambers. The romance of the house is enhanced by colourful terraced gardens to the east, leading via a tunnel into a richly planted valley garden. The path through this garden passes a large domed medieval dovecote and descends to a quay, from where lime and coal were once shipped. There are fine views up and down the winding reed-fringed Tamar and a gallery on the quayside specializes in local arts and crafts. The estate includes a village, riverside quay with a small maritime museum, working mill buildings, ancient lime kilns and workshops complete with 19th-century equipment.

Spanish Armada and British fleets in the English Channel, 1588

SIR FRANCIS DRAKE

Sir Francis Drake (c.1540–1596) was the first Englishman to circumnavigate the globe and he was knighted by Elizabeth I in 1580. Four years later he introduced tobacco and potatoes to England, after bringing home 190 colonists who had tried to establish a settlement in Virginia. To many, however, Drake was no more than an opportunistic rogue, renowned for his exploits as a "privateer", the polite name for a pirate. Catholic Spain was the bitter enemy and Drake further endeared himself to queen and people by his part in the victory over Philip II's Armada *(see pp50–51)*, defeated by bad weather and the buccaneering spirit of the English.

Medieval dovecote in the gardens of Cotehele estate

Morwellham Quay ②

Near Tavistock, Devon. ☎ 01822 832766. ≋ Gunnislake. ◯ daily.
● 23 Dec–1 Jan. 🎫 ♿ limited.
Easter–Oct: 🚻 ▢ 🏠

MORWELLHAM QUAY was a neglected and overgrown industrial site until 1970, when members of a local trust began restoring the abandoned cottages, schoolhouse, farmyards, quay and copper mines to the condition they were in at the turn of the century.

Today, Morwellham Quay is a thriving and rewarding industrial museum, where you can easily spend a whole day partaking in the typical activities of a Victorian village, from preparing the shire horses for a day's work, to riding a tramway deep into a copper mine in the hillside behind the village. The museum is brought to life by characters in costumes, some of whom give demonstrations throughout the day. You can watch, or lend a hand to the

Industrial relics at Morwellham Quay in the Tamar Valley

cooper while he builds a barrel, attend a lesson in the schoolroom, take part in Victorian playground games or dress up in 19th-century hooped skirts, bonnets, top hats or jackets. The staff, who convincingly play the part of villagers, lead you through their lives and impart a huge amount of information about the history of this small copper-mining community.

....

Dartmoor National Park 28

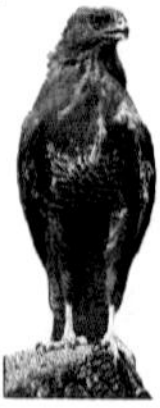

THE WILD AND MIST-SODDEN open moorland of Dartmoor's bleak and isolated heart provided the eerie background for Conan Doyle's thriller, *The Hound of the Baskervilles* (1902). Here at Princetown, surrounded by gaunt weathered outcrops of granite tors, is Britain's most secure prison.

Also dotting the landscape are scores of

Buzzard

prehistoric remains which have survived because of the durability of granite. Elsewhere the mood is very different. Streams tumble through wooded and boulder-strewn ravines forming pretty cascades and waterfalls, and cosy thatched cottages nestle in the sheltered valleys around the margins of the moor offering cream teas and warming fires to weary walkers.

Characteristic moorland near Drewsteignton

Okehampton has the Museum of Dartmoor Life and a ruined 14th-century castle.

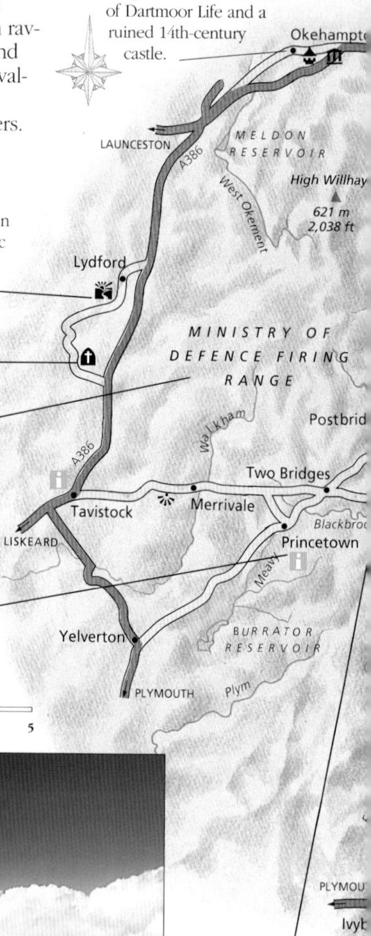

Okehampton

LAUNCESTON

A386

MELDON RESERVOIR

West Okement

High Willhay

621 m 2,038 ft

Lydford Gorge (open Apr–Oct) is a dramatic wooded ravine, leading to a waterfall.

Lydford

MINISTRY OF DEFENCE FIRING RANGE

Walkham

Postbrid

Brentor

This volcanic hill crowned by a tiny church (first built in 1130) is visible for miles.

The Ministry of Defence uses much of this area for training but access is available most days.

A386

Two Bridges

Merrivale

Tavistock

LISKEARD

Blackbroo

Princetown

Meavy

KEY

ℹ	Tourist information
▬▬	A road
▭▭	B road
= =	Minor road
☀	Viewpoint

Main information centre

Yelverton

BURRATOR RESERVOIR

0 kilometres   5

0 miles   5

PLYMOUTH   *Plym*

PLYMOU

Ivyb

Postbridge

Dartmoor's northern moor can be explored from the village of Postbridge. The gently rolling moorland is crossed by many drystone walls.

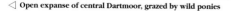

◁ **Open expanse of central Dartmoor, grazed by wild ponies**

Dartmoor Ponies
These small, tough ponies have lived wild on the moor since at least the 10th century.

Grimspound is the impressive site of Bronze Age huts built nearly 4,000 years ago.

Castle Drogo is a magnificent mock-castle built by the architect Sir Edwin Lutyens *(see p25)* in 1910–30.

Becky Falls (open Easter–Nov) offers delightful woodland walks and a viewing platform over the 22 m (72 ft) waterfall.

EXETER
Drewsteignton
Teign
EXETER
Moretonhampstead
Bovey
Manaton A382
EXETER
Bovey Tracey
WORTHY RESERVOIR
Buckland-in-the-Moor A38
ENFORD RESERVOIR
Buckfastleigh
Ashburton
Dart
ON DAM RESERVOIR
A38

Hound Tor
This site includes the substantial remains of a deserted medieval settlement which was inhabited from Saxon times until around 1300.

Bovey Tracey has an extensive woodland reserve.

Haytor Rocks are the most accessible of the many tors.

South Devon Steam Railway

Buckfast Abbey was founded by King Canute *(see p157)* in 1018.

Dartmoor Butterfly and Otter Sanctuary

Dartmeet marks the lovely confluence point of the East and West Dart rivers.

Buckland-in-the-Moor
This is one of the most picturesque thatch-and-granite villages on Dartmoor.

THE
MIDLANDS

The Midlands at a Glance

THE MIDLANDS IS AN AREA that embraces wonderful landscapes and massive industrial
cities. Visitors come to discover the wild beauty
of the rugged Peaks, cruise slowly along the
Midlands canals on gaily painted narrowboats
and explore varied and enchanting gardens.
The area encompasses the full range of
English architecture from mighty cathedrals and humble churches to charming
spa towns, stately homes and country
cottages. There are fascinating industrial
museums, many in picturesque settings.

Cheshire

Staffordsh

Shropshire

Tissington Trail (see
p323) *combines a walk
through scenic Peak
District countryside with
an entertaining insight
into the ancient custom
of well-dressing.*

THE HEART OF ENGLAND
(*see pp290–315*)

Worcestershire

Ironbridge Gorge (see pp300–1) *was the
birthplace of the Industrial Revolution* (see
pp334–5). *Now a World Heritage Centre, the
site is a reminder of the lovely countryside in
which the original factories were located.*

Herefordshire

Gloucestershire

The Cotswolds (see
pp290–91) *are full of
delightful houses built
from local limestone, on
the profits of the medieval
wool trade. Snowshill
Manor* (left) *is situated
near the unspoilt village
of Broadway.*

| 0 kilometres | 25 |
| 0 miles | 25 |

◁ **The front of the half-timbered Lord Leycester Hospital, Warwick**

Chatsworth House (see pp320–21), a magnificent Baroque edifice, is famous for its gorgeous gardens. The "Conservative" Wall, a greenhouse for exotic plants, is pictured above.

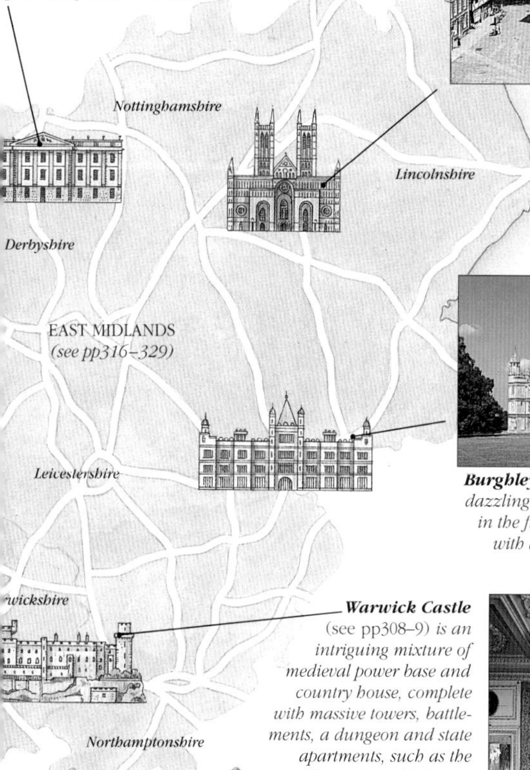

Lincoln Cathedral (see p327), a vast, imposing building, dominates the ancient town. Inside are splendid misericords and the superb 13th-century Angel Choir, which has 30 carved angels.

Nottinghamshire

Lincolnshire

Derbyshire

EAST MIDLANDS
(see pp316–329)

Leicestershire

Burghley House (see pp328–9) is a dazzling landmark for miles around in the flat East Midlands landscape, with architectural motifs from the European Renaissance.

wickshire

Warwick Castle (see pp308–9) is an intriguing mixture of medieval power base and country house, complete with massive towers, battle-ments, a dungeon and state apartments, such as the Queen Anne Bedroom.

Northamptonshire

Stratford-upon-Avon (see pp310–13) has many picturesque houses connected with William Shakespeare's life, some of which are open to visitors. These black and white timber-framed buildings, which abound in the Midlands, are a typical example of Tudor architecture (see pp288–9).

Canals of the Midlands

O NE OF ENGLAND'S FIRST CANALS was built by the 3rd Duke of Bridgewater in 1761 to link the coal mine on his Worsley estate with Manchester's textile factories. This heralded the start of a canal-building boom and by 1805, a 3,000 mile (4,800 km) network of waterways had been dug across the country, linking into the natural river system. Canals provided the cheapest, fastest way of transporting goods, until competition began to arrive from the railways in the 1840s. Cargo transport ended in 1963 but today nearly 2,000 miles (3,200 km) of canals are still navigable, for travellers who wish to take a leisurely cruise on a narrowboat.

The Grand Union Canal (pictured in 1931) is 300 miles (485 km) long and was dug in the 1790s to link London with the Midlands.

Lock-keepers were provided with canalside houses.

Lockside inns cater for narrowboats.

The Farmer's Bridge *is a flight of 13 locks in Birmingham. Locks are used to raise or lower boats from one level of the canal to another. The steeper the gradient, the more locks are needed.*

Heavy V-shaped timber gates close off the lock.

Water pressing against the gate keeps it shut.

The towpath is where horses pulled the canal boats before engines were invented. They were changed periodically for fresh animals.

Narrowboats *have straight sides and flat bottoms and are pointed at both ends. Cargo space took up most of the boat, with a small cabin for the crew. Exteriors were brightly painted.*

MIDLANDS CANAL NETWORK

The industrial Midlands was the birthplace of the English canal system and still has the biggest concentration of navigable waterways.

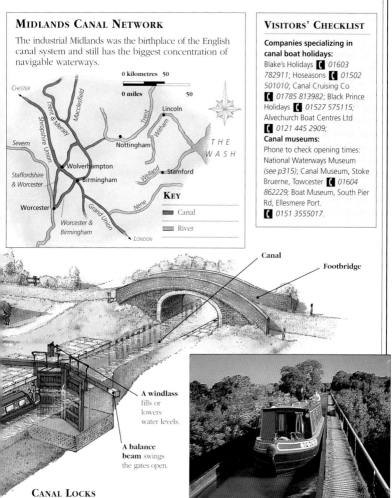

0 kilometres 50

0 miles 50

CHESTER

Trent & Mersey

Macclesfield

Shropshire Union

Severn

Lincoln

Trent

Witham

Nottingham

THE WASH

Staffordshire & Worcester

Wolverhampton

Birmingham

Welland

Stamford

Nene

Worcester

Grand Union

Worcester & Birmingham

LONDON

KEY

▬	Canal
▬	River

VISITORS' CHECKLIST

Companies specializing in canal boat holidays:
Blake's Holidays ☎ 01603 782911; Hoseasons ☎ 01502 501010; Canal Cruising Co ☎ 01785 813982; Black Prince Holidays ☎ 01527 575115; Alvechurch Boat Centres Ltd ☎ 0121 445 2909;
Canal museums:
Phone to check opening times: National Waterways Museum (see p315); Canal Museum, Stoke Bruerne, Towcester ☎ 01604 862229; Boat Museum, South Pier Rd, Ellesmere Port.
☎ 0151 3555017.

Canal

Footbridge

A windlass fills or lowers water levels.

A balance beam swings the gates open.

CANAL LOCKS

Canals used tunnels, embankments and locks for the speedy transportation of goods across country. Locks were used to convey boats up or down hills.

The Edstone Aqueduct, *just north of Stratford-upon-Avon, carries the canal in a cast iron trough. This is supported on brick piers for 180 m (495 ft), over roads and a busy railway line.*

CANAL ART

Canal boat cabins are very small and every inch of space is utilized to make a comfortable home for the occupants. Interiors were enlivened with colourful paintings and attractive decorations.

Furniture was designed to be functional and to brighten up the cramped cabin.

Narrowboats are often decorated with ornamental brass.

Water cans were also painted. The most common designs were roses and castles, with local variations in style.

Tudor Manor Houses

MANY STRIKING MANOR HOUSES were built in central England during the Tudor Age *(see pp50–51)*, a time of relative peace and prosperity. The abolition of the monasteries meant that vast estates were broken up and sold to secular landowners, who built houses to reflect their new status *(see p24)*. In the Midlands, wood was the main building material, and the gentry flaunted their wealth by using timber panelling for flamboyant decorative effect.

The Lucy family arms

The decorative moulding on the south wing was carved during the late 16th century. Ancient motifs, such as vines and trefoils, are combined with the latest imported Italian Renaissance styles.

The rectangular moat was for decoration rather than defence. It surrounds a recreated knot garden (see p22) *that was laid out in 1975 using plants known to have been available in Tudor times.*

The Long Gallery, the last part of the Hall to be built (1580), was used for exercise. It has original murals portraying Destiny *(left)* and Fortune.

Jetties (overhanging upper stories)

TUDOR MANSIONS AND TUDOR REVIVAL

There are many sumptuously decorated Tudor mansions in the Midlands. In the 19th century Tudor Revival architecture became a very popular "Old English" style, intended to invoke family pride and values rooted in the past.

Hardwick Hall in Derbyshire, whose huge kitchen is pictured, is one of the finest Tudor mansions in the country. These buildings are known as "prodigy" houses (see p328) due to their gigantic size.

Charlecote Park, Warwickshire, is a brick mansion built by Sir Thomas Lucy in 1551–59. It was heavily restored in Tudor style in the 19th century, but has a fine original gatehouse. According to legend, the young William Shakespeare (see pp310–13) was caught poaching deer in the park.

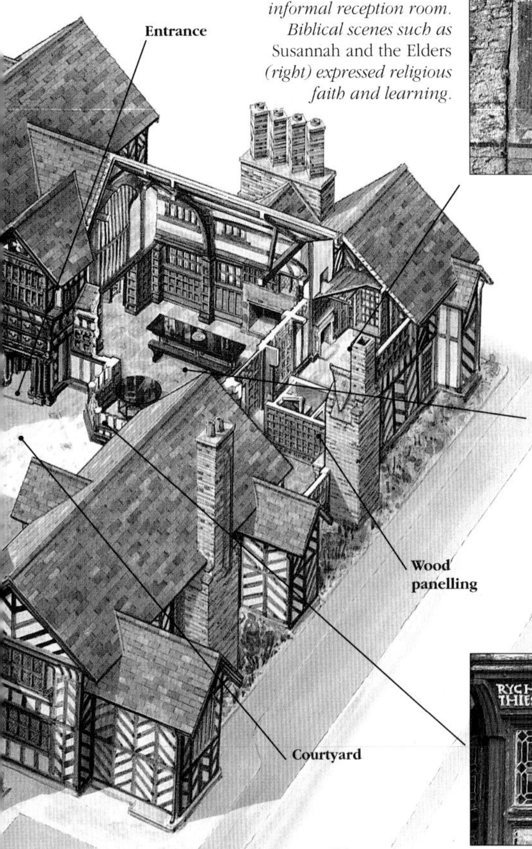

The Parlour *was an informal reception room. Biblical scenes such as Susannah and the Elders (right) expressed religious faith and learning.*

Entrance

The Great Hall *(c.1440) is the oldest part of the house, and in Tudor times was the most important. The open-plan hall was the main communal area for dining and entertainment.*

Wood panelling

Courtyard

LITTLE MORETON HALL

The Moreton family home *(see p297)* was built between 1440 and 1580, from a number of box-shapes, fitted together. Wood panelling and jetties displayed the family's wealth.

The patterned glazing *in the great bay window is typically 16th century: small pieces of locally made glass were cut into diamond shapes and held in place by lead glazing bars.*

Packwood House *in Warwickshire is a timber-framed mid-Tudor house with extensive 17th-century additions. The unusual garden of clipped yew trees dates from the 17th century and is supposed to represent the Sermon on the Mount.*

Moseley Old Hall*, Staffordshire, has a red brick exterior concealing its early 17th-century timber frame. The King's Room is where Charles II hid after the Battle of Worcester (see pp52–3).*

Wightwick Manor*, West Midlands, was built in 1887–93. It is a fine example of Tudor Revival architecture and has superb late 19th-century furniture and decorations.*

Building with Cotswold Stone

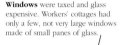

THE COTSWOLDS are a prominent range of limestone hills running over 50 miles (80 km) in a northeasterly direction from Bath *(see p244)*. The thin soils are difficult to plough but ideal for grazing sheep, and the wealth engendered by the medieval wool trade was poured into building majestic churches and opulent town houses. Stone quarried from these hills was used to build London's St Paul's Cathedral *(see pp116–7)*, as well as the villages, barns and manor houses that make the landscape so picturesque.

Dragon, Deerhurst Church

Arlington Row Cottages *in Bibury, a typical Cotswold village, were built in the 17th century for weavers whose looms were set up in the attics.*

Windows were taxed and glass expensive. Workers' cottages had only a few, not very large windows made of small panes of glass.

A drip mould keeps rain off the chimney.

The roof is steeply pitched to carry the weight of the tiles. These were made by master craftsmen who could split blocks of stone into sheets by using natural fault lines.

COTSWOLD STONE COTTAGE
The two-storey Arlington Row Cottages are asymmetrical and built of odd-shaped stones. Small windows and doorways make them quite dark inside.

Timber lintels and doors

Timber framing was cheaper than stone, and was used for the upper rooms in the roof.

VARIATIONS IN STONE
Cotswold stone is warmer-toned in the north, pearly in central areas and light grey in the south. The stone seems to glow with absorbed sunlight. It is a soft stone that is easily carved and can be used for many purposes, from buildings to bridges, headstones and gargoyles.

"Tiddles" *is a cat's gravestone in Fairford churchyard.*

Lower Slaughter *gets its name from the Anglo-Saxon word slough, or muddy place. It has a low stone bridge, over the River Eye.*

COTSWOLD STONE TOWNS AND VILLAGES

The villages and towns on this map are prime examples of places built almost entirely from stone. By the 12th century almost all of the villages in the area were established. Huge deposits of limestone resulted in a wealth of stone buildings. Masons worked from distinctive local designs that were handed down from generation to generation.

① Winchcombe
② Broadway
③ Stow-on-the-Wold
④ Upper and Lower Slaughter
⑤ Bourton-on-the-Water
⑥ Sherborne
⑦ Northleach
⑧ Painswick
⑨ Bibury
⑩ Fairford

Wool merchants' houses were built of fine ashlar (dressed stone) with ornamental cornerstones, doorframes and windows.

The eaves here have a dentil frieze, so-called because it resembles a row of teeth.

STONE GARGOYLES

In Winchcombe's church, 15th-century gargoyles reflect a combination of pagan and Christian beliefs.

Pagan gods warded off pre-Christian evil spirits.

Fertility figures, always important in rural areas, were incorporated into Christian festivals.

Human faces often caricatured local church dignitaries.

Animal gods represented qualities such as strength in pagan times.

COTSWOLD STONE HOUSE

This early Georgian merchant's house in Painswick shows the fully developed Cotswold style, which borrows decorative elements from Classical architecture.

The door frame has a rounded pediment on simple pilasters.

A stone cross (16th century) in Stanton village, near Broadway, is one of many found in the Cotswolds.

Dry-stone walling *is an ancient technique used in the Cotswolds. The stones are held in place without mortar.*

Table-top and "tea caddy", *fine 18th-century tombs, can be found in Painswick churchyard.*

The Cotswold Arms

Bar Snacks
Restaurant
Beer Garden
Morning Coffee

THE HEART OF ENGLAND

CHESHIRE · GLOUCESTERSHIRE · HEREFORDSHIRE
SHROPSHIRE · STAFFORDSHIRE · WARWICKSHIRE · WORCESTERSHIRE

BRITAIN'S GREAT ATTRACTION *is its variety, and nowhere is this more true than at the heart of the country, where the Cotswold hills, enfolding stone cottages and churches, give way to the flat, fertile plains of Warwickshire. Shakespeare country borders on the industrial heart of England, once known as the workshop of the world.*

Coventry, Birmingham, the Potteries and their hinterlands have been manufacturing iron, textiles and ceramics since the 18th century. In the 20th century these industries have declined, and a new type of museum has developed to commemorate the towns' industrial heyday and explain the manufacturing processes which were once taken for granted. Ironbridge Gorge and Quarry Bank Mill, Styal, where the factories are now living museums, are fascinating industrial sites and enjoy beautiful surroundings.

These landscapes may be appreciated from the deck of a narrowboat, making gentle progress along the Midlands canals, to the region on the border with Wales known as the Marches. Here the massive walls of Chester and the castles at Shrewsbury and Ludlow recall the Welsh locked in fierce battle with Norman barons and the Marcher Lords. The Marches are now full of rural communities served by the peaceful market towns of Leominster, Malvern, Ross-on-Wye and Hereford. The cities of Worcester and Gloucester both have modern shopping centres, yet their majestic cathedrals retain the tranquillity of an earlier age.

Cheltenham has Regency terraces, Cirencester a rich legacy of Roman art and Tewkesbury a solid Norman abbey. Finally, there is Stratford-upon-Avon, where William Shakespeare, the Elizabethan dramatist, lived and died.

Leisurely village pastimes, reminiscent of a more tranquil age

◁ **Cotswold stone: an extremely popular building material in the Heart of England**

Exploring the Heart of England

Tᴴᴇ ʜᴇᴀʀᴛ ᴏꜰ ᴇɴɢʟᴀɴᴅ, more than any other
region, takes its character from the landscape.
Picturesque houses, pubs and churches, made
from timber and Cotswold stone, create a harmonic
appearance that delights visitors and adds greatly to
the pleasures of exploration. The area around
Birmingham and Stoke-on-Trent, however – once
the industrial hub of England – contrasts sharply. The
bleak concrete skyline may not appeal, but the area
has a fascinating history that is reflected in the self-
confident Victorian art and architecture, and a series
of award-winning industrial heritage museums.

Arlington Row: stone cottages in the Cotswold village of Bibury

Sɪɢʜᴛꜱ ᴀᴛ ᴀ Gʟᴀɴᴄᴇ

Walks and Tours

Gᴇᴛᴛɪɴɢ Aʀᴏᴜɴᴅ

The Heart of England is easily
reached by train, with InterCity
rail services to Cheltenham,
Worcester, Birmingham, and
Coventry. The M5 and M6
motorways are the major road
routes but are frequently
congested. Long-distance buses
provide regular shuttle services
to Cheltenham and
Birmingham. Travelling within
the region is best done by car.
Rural roads are delightfully
empty, although major
attractions, such as Stratford-
upon-Avon, may be very
crowded during the summer.

Sᴇᴇ Aʟꜱᴏ

• **Where to Stay** pp555–6
• **Where to Eat** pp591–3

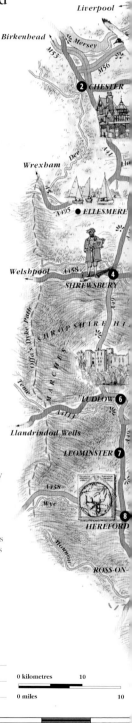

Wigan
Liverpool
Birkenhead
Mersey
M53
M56
❷ CHESTER
Wrexham
Dee
A495 ● ELLESMERE
Welshpool   A458
❹
SHREWSBURY
A49
Offa's Dyke Path
S H R O P S H I R E   H I
M A R C H E S
Trent
LUDLOW ❻
A4113
Llandrindod Wells
LEOMINSTER ❼
A458
Wye
❽
HEREFORD
Monnow
ROSS-ON-

0 kilometres   10
0 miles   10

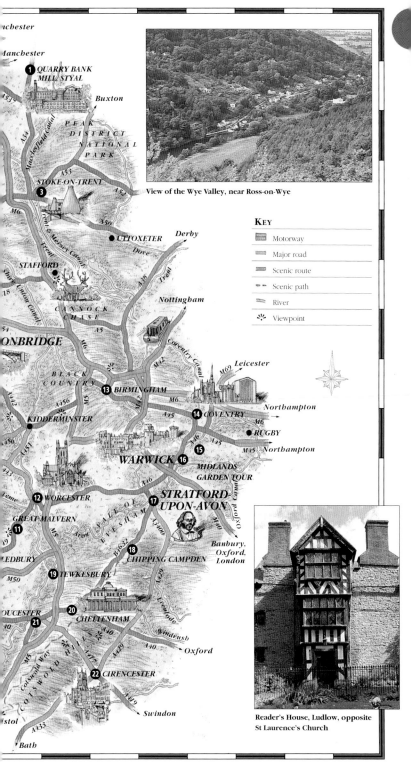

Manchester

Manchester

1 QUARRY BANK MILL, STYAL

Buxton

A537

A34

P E A K
D I S T R I C T
N A T I O N A L
P A R K

Macclesfield Canal

A53

STOKE-ON-TRENT

3

M6

A50

A52

UTTOXETER

Derby

Trent & Mersey Canal

Dove

STAFFORD

A38

Trent

18

Shropshire Union Canal

Staffs & Worcs Canal

C A N N O C K
C H A S E

A5

Nottingham

54

Coventry Canal

ONBRIDGE

M6

A442

B L A C K
C O U N T R Y

M42

13 BIRMINGHAM

M69 *Leicester*

A456

A456

M5

M6

Northampton

KIDDERMINSTER

A435

A45

14 COVENTRY

M6

A443

A451

A435

A46

A45

RUGBY

M45 *Northampton*

15

WARWICK 16

A46

**MIDLANDS
GARDEN TOUR**

Teme

12 WORCESTER

Oxford Canal

**STRATFORD-
UPON-AVON**

17

GREAT MALVERN

V A L E   O F

Aron

E V E S H A M

A3400

M40

11

A449

M5

A4184

*Banbury,
Oxford,
London*

18

CHIPPING CAMPDEN

B632

A429

LEDBURY

19 TEWKESBURY

M50

A38

A46

Leadon

OUCESTER

20

CHELTENHAM

A40

A429

Windrush

21

Oxford

M5

A40

A429

Cotswold Way

22 CIRENCESTER

C O T S W O L D S

A419

A417

istol

A433

Swindon

Bath

View of the Wye Valley, near Ross-on-Wye

KEY

▨ Motorway

▨ Major road

▨ Scenic route

▨ Scenic path

▨ River

☼ Viewpoint

Reader's House, Ludlow, opposite
St Laurence's Church

Quarry Bank Mill, a working reminder of the Industrial Revolution

Quarry Bank Mill, Styal ❶

Cheshire. 🄲 *01625 527468.*
🚆 *Wilmslow then bus.* 🄾 *Apr–Sep: daily; Oct–Mar: Tue–Sun.* ⬤ *23-25 Dec.* 🄶 *limited.* 🍴 🄿
🅆 *www.quarrybankmill.org.uk*

THE HISTORY of the Industrial Revolution *(see pp54–5)* is brought vividly to life at Quarry Bank Mill, an early factory now transformed into a museum. Here, mill master Samuel Greg first used the waters of the Bollin Valley in 1784 to power the water frame, a machine for spinning raw cotton fibres into thread. By the 1840s, the Greg cotton empire was one of the biggest in Britain, and the mill produced bolts of material to be exported all over the world.

Today the massive old mill buildings have been restored to house a living museum of the cotton industry. This dominated the Manchester area for nearly 200 years, but was finally destroyed by foreign competition. The entire process, from the spinning and weaving to the bleaching, printing and dyeing, is shown through a series of reconstructions, demonstrations and hands-on displays.

The weaving shed is full of clattering looms producing textiles. There are fascinating contraptions that demonstrate how water can be used to drive machinery, including an enormous wheel, 50 tons in weight and 7 m (24 ft) high, that is still used daily to provide power for the looms.

The Greg family realized the importance of having a healthy, loyal and stable workforce. A social history exhibition explains how the mill workers were housed in the purpose-built village of Styal, in spacious cottages which had vegetable gardens and toilets. Details of their wages, working conditions and medical facilities are displayed on information boards.

There are guided tours of the nearby **Apprentice House**. Local orphans lived here, and were sent to work up to 12 hours a day at the mill when they were just six or seven years old. Visitors can try the beds in the house and even sample the medicine they were given. Quarry Bank Mill is surrounded by over 115 ha (284 acres) of woodland.

Chester ❷

Cheshire. 🄰 *125,000.* 🚆 🄿
🄸 *Town Hall, Northgate St (01244 402111).* 🄰 *Mon–Sat.*
🅆 *www.chestercc.gov.uk*

FIRST SETTLED BY THE ROMANS *(see pp44–5)*, who established a camp in AD 79 to defend fertile land near the River Dee, the main streets of Chester are now lined with timber buildings. These are the **Chester Rows**, which, with their two tiers of shops and continuous upper gallery, anticipate today's multi-storey shops by several centuries.

Although their oriel windows and decorative timber-work are mostly 19th century, the Rows were first built in the 13th and 14th centuries, and the original structures can be seen in many places. The façade of the 16th-century **Bishop Lloyd's House** in Watergate Street is the most richly carved in Chester. The Rows are at their most varied and attractive where Eastgate Street meets Bridge Street. Here, views of the cathedral and the town walls give the impression of a perfectly preserved medieval city. This illusion is helped by the Town Crier, who calls the hour and announces news in summer from the Cross, a reconstruction of the 15th-century stone crucifix that was destroyed in the Civil War *(see pp52–3)*.

The **Grosvenor Museum**, south of the Cross, explains the town's history. To the north is the **cathedral**. The choir stalls have splendid misericords *(see p327)*, with

Chester's 1897 clocktower

Examples of the intricate carving on Bishop Lloyd's House, a Tudor building in Watergate Street, Chester

The Chester Rows, where shops line the first-floor galleries

scenes including a quarrelling couple. In sharp contrast are the delicate spire-lets on the stall canopies. The cathedral is surrounded on two sides by the **city walls**, originally Roman but rebuilt at intervals. The best stretch is from the cathedral to Eastgate, where a wrought-iron **clock** was erected in 1897. The route to Newgate leads to a **Roman amphitheatre** built in AD 100.

🏛 Grosvenor Museum
Grosvenor St. ☎ 01244 402008.
◯ Mon–Sat, Sun pm. ● 24–26
Dec, 1 Jan, Good Fri. 🅿 🔯
🔒 limited.

⛪ Roman Amphitheatre
Little St John St. ☎ 01244 321616.
◯ daily.

Stoke-on-Trent ❸

Stoke-on-Trent. 🚹 252,000. 🚲 🚌
🚉 Quadrant Rd, Hanley (01782
236000). 🚍 Mon–Sat.
🅦 www.stoke.gov.uk/tourism

FROM THE MID-18TH CENTURY, Staffordshire became a leading centre for mass-produced ceramics. Its fame arose from the fine bone china and porcelain products of Wedgwood, Minton, Doulton and Spode, but the Staffordshire potteries also make a wide range of utilitarian products such as baths, toilets and wall tiles.

In 1910 a group of six towns – Longton, Fenton, Hanley, Burslem, Tunstall and Stoke – merged to form the conurbation of Stoke-on-Trent, also known as the Potteries. Fans of the writer Arnold Bennett (1867–1931) may recognise this area as the "Five Towns", a term he used in a series of novels about the region (Fenton was excluded).

The **Gladstone Pottery Museum** is a Victorian complex of workshops, kilns, galleries and an engine house. There are demonstrations of traditional pottery techniques. The **Potteries Museum and Art Gallery** in Hanley has historic and modern ceramics.

Josiah Wedgwood began his earthenware firm in 1769 and built a workers' village, Etruria. The last surviving steam-powered pottery mill is on display at the **Etruria Industrial Museum**.

ENVIRONS: About 10 miles (16 km) north of Stoke-on-Trent is **Little Moreton Hall** (see pp288–9), a half-timbered early Tudor manor house.

🏛 Gladstone Pottery Museum
Uttoxeter Rd, Longton. ☎ 01782
319232. ◯ daily. ● 24 Dec–2 Jan.
🅿 🔒 🔯 🔯

🏛 Potteries Museum and Art Gallery Bethesda St, Hanley.
☎ 01782 232323. ◯ daily.
● 25 Dec–1 Jan. 🔒 🖥 🔯

🏛 Etruria Industrial Museum
Lower Bedford St, Etruria. ☎ 01782
233144. ◯ Wed–Sun. ● 25 Dec–
1 Jan. 🅿 🔯 by arrangement. 🖥 🔯

🏰 Little Moreton Hall
(NT) Congleton, off A34. ☎ 01260
272018. ◯ Mar–Oct: Wed–Sun &
public hols; Nov–22 Dec: Sat, Sun. 🅿
🔯 🔒 limited. 🍴 🔯

STAFFORDSHIRE POTTERY

An abundance of water, marl, clay and easily mined coal to fire the kilns enabled Staffordshire to develop as a ceramics centre; and local supplies of iron, copper and lead were used for glazing. In the 18th century, pottery became widely accessible and affordable. English bone china, which used powdered animals' bones for strength and translucence, was shipped all over the world, and Josiah Wedgwood (1730–95) introduced simple, durable crockery – though his best known design is the blue jasperware decorated with white Classical themes. Coal-powered bottle kilns fired the clay until the 1950s Clean Air Acts put them out of business. They have been replaced by electric or gas-fired kilns.

Wedgwood candlesticks, 1785

Timber-framed, gabled mansions in Fish Street, Shrewsbury

Shrewsbury ❹

Shropshire. 🚶 96,000. 🚆 🚌
🛈 The Square (01743 281200).
📅 Tue, Wed, Fri, Sat.
🌐 www.shrewsbury.ws

SHREWSBURY is almost an island, enclosed by a great loop of the River Severn. A gaunt **castle** of red sandstone, first built in 1083, guards the entrance to the town, standing on the only section of land not surrounded by the river. Such defences were necessary on the frontier between England and the wilder Marches of Wales, whose inhabitants fiercely defied Saxon and Norman invaders (*see pp 46–7*). The castle, rebuilt over the centuries, now houses the Shropshire Regimental Museum.

In AD 60 the Romans (*see pp44–5*) built the garrison town of *Viroconium*, modern Wroxeter, 5 miles (8 km) east of Shrewsbury. Finds from the excavations are displayed at **Shrewsbury Museum and Art Gallery**, including a decorated silver mirror from the 2nd century and other luxury goods imported by the Roman army.

The town's medieval wealth as a centre of the wool trade is evident in the many timber-framed buildings found along the High Street, Butcher Row,

Roman silver mirror in Rowley's House Museum

and Wyle Cop. Two of the grandest High Street houses, **Ireland's Mansions** and **Owen's Mansions**, are named after Robert Ireland and Richard Owen, the wealthy wool merchants who built them in 1575 and 1570 respectively. Similarly attractive buildings in Fish Street frame a view of the **Prince Rupert Hotel**, which was briefly the headquarters of Charles I's nephew, Rupert, in the English Civil War (*see pp52–3*).

Outside the loop of the river, the **Abbey Church** survives from the medieval monastery. It has a number of interesting memorials, including one to Lieutenant WES Owen MC, better known as the war poet Wilfred Owen (1893–1918), who taught at the local Wyle Cop school and was killed in the last days of World War I.

ENVIRONS: To the south of Shrewsbury, the road to Ludlow passes through the landscapes celebrated in the 1896 poem by AE Housman (1859–1936), *A Shropshire Lad*. Highlights include the bleak moors of **Long Mynd,** with 15 prehistoric barrows, and **Wenlock Edge**, wonderful walking country with glorious, far-reaching views.

♖ **Shrewsbury Castle**
Castle St. 📞 01743 358516.
🕐 Easter–Oct: Tue–Sun; Oct–Mar: phone for details. ● 22 Dec–mid-Feb. ♿ 🅿
🏛 **Shrewsbury Museum and Art Gallery**
Barker St. 📞 01743 361196.
🕐 daily. ● 2 wks over Christmas.
♿ limited. 🅿

Ironbridge Gorge ❺

See pp300–301.

Ludlow ❻

Shropshire. 🚶 9,000. 🚆 🛈 Castle St (01584 875053).

LUDLOW ATTRACTS large numbers of visitors to its splendid castle, but there is much else to see in this town, with its small shops and its lovely Georgian and half-timbered Tudor buildings. Ludlow is an important area of geological research and the **museum**, just off the town centre, has fossils of the oldest known land animals and plants.

The ruined **castle** is sited on cliffs high above the River Teme. Built in 1086, it was damaged in the Civil War (*see pp52–3*) and abandoned in 1689. *Comus*, a court masque using music and drama and a precursor of opera, by John Milton (1608–74) was first performed here in 1634 in the Great Hall. In early summer

The 13th-century south tower and hall of Stokesay Castle, near Ludlow

open-air performances of Shakespeare's plays are held within the castle walls.

Prince Arthur (1486–1502), elder brother of Henry VIII (*see pp50–51*), died at Ludlow Castle. His heart is buried in **St Laurence Church** at the other end of Castle Square, as are the ashes of the poet AE Housman. The east end of the church backs onto the **Bull Ring**, with its ornate timber buildings. Two inns vie for attention across the street: **The Bull**, with its Tudor back yard, and **The Feathers**, with its flamboyant façade, whose name recalls the feathers used in arrow-making, once a local industry.

ENVIRONS: About 5 miles (8 km) north of Ludlow, in a lovely setting, is **Stokesay Castle**, a fortified manor house with a colourful moated garden.

♣ **Ludlow Castle**
The Square. **01584 873355.**
◯ daily. ● 24 Dec–1 Feb. ⧖
& limited. ⬚
🏛 **Ludlow Museum**
Castle St. **01584 873857.**
◯ Apr–Oct: Mon–Sat (Jun–Aug: daily). ⧖ &
♣ **Stokesay Castle**
Craven Arms, A49. **01588 672544.**
◯ Apr–Oct: daily; Nov–Mar: Wed–Sun.
● 24–26 Dec, 1 Jan. ⧖ ⬚ ⬚

Leominster ⓻

Herefordshire. ⛫ 10,000. ▮ ⓘ
Corn Sq (01568 616460). ◷ Fri.
ⓦ www.visitorlinks.com

FARMERS COME TO LEOMINSTER (pronounced "Lemster") from all over this rural region of England to buy supplies. There are two buildings of note in the town, which has been a wool-manufacturing centre for 700 years. In the centre of the town stands the magnificent **Grange Court**, carved with bold and bizarre figures by the carpenter John Abel in 1633. Nearby is the **priory**, whose imposing Norman portal is carved with an equally strange mixture of mythical birds, beasts and serpents. The lions, at least, can be explained: medieval monks believed the name of

A view of Leominster, set on the River Lugg in rolling border country

Leominster was derived from *monasterium leonis*, "the monastery of the lions". In fact, *leonis* probably comes from medieval, rather than Classical Latin, and it means "of the marshes". The aptness of this description can readily be seen in the green lanes around the town, following the lush river valleys that come together at Leominster.

ENVIRONS: To the west of the town, along the River Arrow, are the showcase villages of **Eardisland** and **Pembridge**, with their well-kept gardens and timber-framed houses.

Gatehouse of Stokesay Castle, near Ludlow

Berrington Hall, 3 miles (5 km) north of Leominster, is an 18th-century Neo-Classical house set in grounds designed by Capability Brown. Inside are beautifully preserved ceiling decorations and period furniture, including an original children's nursery.

To the northeast of Leominster is **Tenbury Wells**, which enjoyed a brief popularity as a spa in the 19th century. The River Teme flows through it, full of minnows, trout and other fish and beloved of the composer Sir Edward Elgar (*see p303*), who came to seek inspiration on its banks. The river also feeds **Burford House Gardens**, on the western outskirts of Tenbury Wells, where the water is used to create winding streams, fountains and pools that are rich in a variety of unusual, moisture-loving plants.

♣ **Burford House Gardens**
Tenbury Wells. **01584 810777.**
◯ daily. ● 25–26 Dec, 1 Jan. ⧖ &
⬚ ⬚
🏛 **Berrington Hall**
Berrington. **01568 615721.**
◯ daily. ● 25–26 Dec, 1 Jan. ⧖

Ironbridge Gorge **⑤**

IRONBRIDGE GORGE was one of the most important centres of the Industrial Revolution *(see pp54–5)*. It was here, in 1709, Abraham Darby I (1678–1717) pioneered the use of inexpensive coke, rather than charcoal, to smelt iron ore. The use of iron in bridges, ships and buildings transformed Ironbridge Gorge into one of the world's great iron-making centres. Industrial decline in the 20th century led to the Gorge's decay, although today it has been restored as an exciting complex of industrial archaeology, with several museums strung along the wooded banks of the River Severn.

VISITORS' CHECKLIST

Shropshire. 🚉 2,900. 🚌
Telford then bus. 🛈 01952 433
522. ◻ mid-Apr–Oct: daily; Nov–
mid-Apr: phone for information.
◼ 24, 25 Dec. Some sites closed
Nov–Apr, phone for information.
♿ most sites. 📷 🎞 by
arrangement ◻ 🛈 🍴 🛍
Midsummer Fair: Jun (craft
workshops and demonstrations
all year). List of events available.

Wrought-iron clock (1843) on the roof of the Museum of Iron

MUSEUM OF IRON

THE HISTORY OF IRON and the men who made it is traced in this remarkable museum. Abraham Darby I's discovery of how to smelt iron ore with coke allowed the mass production of iron, paving the way for the rise of large-scale industry. His original blast furnace forms the museum's centrepiece.

One of the museum's themes is the history of the Darby dynasty, a Quaker family who had a great impact on the Coalbrookdale community. The social and working conditions faced by the labourers, who sometimes had to toil for 24 hours at a stretch, are also illustrated.

Ironbridge led the world in industrial innovation, producing the first iron wheels and cylinders for the first steam engine. A restored locomotive and cast-iron statues, many of them

commissioned for the 1851 Great Exhibition *(see pp56–7)*, are among the many Coalbrookdale Company products on display.

One of the Darby family's homes in the nearby village of Coalbrookdale, **Rosehill House**, has been furnished in mid-Victorian style.

MUSEUM OF THE RIVER

THIS PARTLY CASTELLATED, Victorian building was a warehouse for storing products from the ironworks before they were shipped down the River Severn. The warehouse is now home to the Museum of the River, and has displays illustrating the history of the Severn and the development of the water industry.

Until the arrival of the railways in the mid-19th century, the Severn was the main form of transport and communication to and from the Gorge. Sometimes too shallow, at other times in flood, the river was not a particularly reliable means of transportation; by the 1890s river trading had stopped completely. The highlight of the museum is a wonderful 12 m (40 ft) model of the Gorge as it would have appeared in 1796, complete with foundries, cargo boats and growing villages.

Europe **(1860), statue in the Museum of Iron**

JACKFIELD TILE MUSEUM

THERE HAVE BEEN POTTERIES in this area since the 17th century, but it was not until the Victorian passion for decorative tiles that Jackfield became famous. There were two tile-making factories here – Maw and Craven Dunnill – that produced a tremendous variety of tiles from clay mined nearby.

Peacock Panel (1928), one of the tile museum's star attractions

Talented designers created an astonishing range of images. The Jackfield Tile Museum, in the old Craven Dunnill works, has a collection of the decorative floor and wall tiles that were produced here from the 1850s to the 1960s. Visitors can also watch small-scale demonstrations of traditional methods of tile-making in the old factory buildings, including the biscuit kilns and the decoration workshops.

IRONBRIDGE GORGE SIGHTS

Blists Hill Museum ⑥
Coalport China
Museum ⑤
Iron Bridge ③
Jackfield Tile
Museum ④
Museum of Iron ①
Museum of the River ②

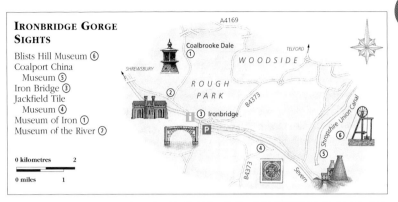

0 kilometres 2

0 miles 1

COALPORT CHINA MUSEUM

In the mid-19th century the Coalport Works was one of the largest porcelain manufacturers in Britain, and its name was synonymous with fine china. The Coalport Company still makes porcelain but has long since moved its operations to Stoke-on-Trent (see p297). Today the china workshops have been converted into a museum, where visitors can watch demonstrations of the various stages of making porcelain, including the skills of pot-throwing, painting and gilding. There is a superb collection of 19th-century china housed in one of the museum's distinctive bottle-shaped kilns.

Coalport China Museum with its bottle-shaped kiln

Nearby is the **Tar Tunnel**, an important source of natural bitumen discovered 110 m (360 ft) underground in the 18th century. It once yielded 20,500 litres (4,500 gal) of tar every week; visitors can still explore part of the tunnel.

THE IRON BRIDGE

Abraham Darby III (grandson of the first man to smelt iron with coke) cast the world's first iron bridge in 1779, revolutionizing building methods in the process. Spanning the Severn, the bridge is a monument to the ironmasters' skills. The toll-house on the south bank charts its construction.

BLISTS HILL MUSEUM

This enormous open-air museum recreates life in Ironbridge Gorge as it was 100 years ago. A group of 19th-century buildings has been reconstructed on the 20 ha (50 acre) site of Blists Hill, an old coal mine that used to supply the ironworks in the Gorge. Here, people in period costume enact roles and perform tasks such as iron forging.

The site has period housing, a church and even a Victorian school. Visitors can change money into old coinage to buy items from the baker or even pay for a drink in the local pub.

The centrepiece of Blists Hill is a complete foundry that still -produces wrought iron. One of the most spectacular sights is the Hay Inclined Plane, which was used to transport canal boats up and down a steep slope. Other attractions include steam engines, a saddlers, a doctors, a chemist, a candlemakers and a sweetshop.

Hereford ⑧

Herefordshire. 🚶 50,000. 🚆 🚗
ℹ️ King St (01432 268430).
🗓️ Wed (cattle, general), Sat (general).
🌐 www.visitorlinks.com

Once the capital of the Saxon kingdom of West Mercia, Hereford is today an attractive town which serves the needs of a primarily rural community. A cattle market is held here every Wednesday, and local produce is sold at the covered market in the town centre. Almost opposite, the timber-framed **Old House** of 1621 is now a museum of local history.

In the **cathedral**, only a short stroll away, interesting features include the Lady Chapel, in richly ornamented Early English style, and the Chained Library, whose 1,500 books are tethered by iron chains to bookcases as a precaution against theft. The best place for an overall view of the cathedral is at the Bishop's Meadow, south of the centre, leading down to the banks of the Wye.

Hereford's many rewarding museums include the **City Museum and Art Gallery**, noted for its Roman mosaics and for watercolours by local artists, and the **Churchill House Museum** of 18th- and 19th-century furniture and costume. Set outside the latter is Roaring Meg, a cannon used in the Civil War (see pp52–3).

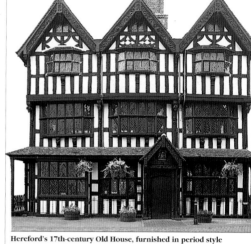

Hereford's 17th-century Old House, furnished in period style

Visitors to the **Cider Museum and King Offa Distillery** can discover the history of traditional cider making. The working distillery where cider brandy is produced can also be visited.

ENVIRONS: During the 12th century, Oliver de Merlemond made a pilgrimage from Hereford to Spain. Impressed by several churches he saw on the way, he brought French masons over to England and introduced their techniques to this area. One result was **Kilpeck Church**, 6 miles (10 km) southwest, covered in lustful figures showing their genitals, and tail-biting dragons. At **Abbey Dore**,

Detail of figures on
Kilpeck Church

4 miles (6 km) west, the Cistercian abbey church is complemented by the serene riverside gardens of **Abbey Dore Court**.

🏚️ **Old House**
High Town. ☎️ 01432 260694.
◯ Apr–Sep: Tue–Sun; Oct–Mar: Tue–Sat; public hols. ● 25, 26 Dec, 1 Jan, Good Fri. ♿ limited. 📷
🏛️ **City Museum and Art Gallery**
Broad St. ☎️ 01432 260692.
◯ Apr–Sep: Tue–Sun; Oct–Mar: Tue–Sat & public hols. ● 25, 26 Dec, 1 Jan, Good Fri. ♿
🏛️ **Churchill House Museum**
Venns Lane. ☎️ 01432 260693.
◯ Apr–Sep: Wed–Fri (pm), Sun (pm). ● Oct–Mar (except by appointment). ♿ limited.
🏛️ **Cider Museum and King Offa Distillery**
Ryelands St. ☎️ 01432 354207.
◯ Apr–Oct: daily; Jan–Mar: Tue–Sun & public hols. ● 25–26 Dec, 1 Jan.
🎫 ♿ limited. 📷 by arrangement.
🍴 📷

MEDIEVAL VIEW

Hereford Cathedral's most celebrated treasure is the *Mappa Mundi*, the Map of the World, drawn in 1290 by a clergyman, Richard of Haldingham. The world is depicted here on Biblical principles: Jerusalem is at the centre, the Garden of Eden figures prominently and monsters inhabit the margins of the world.

Central detail, *Mappa Mundi*

Ross-on-Wye ⑨

Herefordshire. 🚶 10,000. 🚗
ℹ️ Eddie Cross St (01989 562768).
🗓️ Thu, Sat. 🌐 www.ross-on-wye.co.uk

The fine town of Ross sits on a cliff of red sandstone above the water meadows of the River Wye. There are wonderful views over the river from the cliff-top gardens,

The wooded Wye Valley near Ross

given to the town by a local benefactor, John Kyrle (1637–1724). Kyrle was lauded by the poet Alexander Pope (1688–1744) in his *Moral Essays on the Uses of Riches* (1732) for using his wealth in a practical way, and he came to be known as "The Man of Ross". There is a memorial to Kyrle in **St Mary's Church**.

ENVIRONS: From Hereford to Ross, the **Wye Valley Walk** follows 16 miles (26 km) of gentle countryside. From Ross it continues south for 33 miles (54 km), over rocky ground in deep, wooded ravines.

Goodrich Castle, 5 miles (8 km) south of Ross, is a 12th-century red sandstone fort on a rock above the river.

♣ Goodrich Castle
Goodrich. [01600 890538.
○ daily. ● 24–26 Dec, 1 Jan.
& limited. ○ (Apr–Sep only).

Ledbury ⑩

Herefordshire. 🏠 6,500. 🚋 🚌
ℹ 3 Homend (01531 636147).

LEDBURY'S MAIN STREET is lined with timbered houses, including the **Market Hall** which dates from 1655. Church Lane, a cobbled lane running up from the High Street, has lovely 16th-century buildings: the **Heritage Centre** and **Butcher Row House** are both now museums. **St Michael and All Angels Church** has a massive detached bell tower, ornate Early English decoration and a collection of interesting monuments.

Medieval tile from the Priory at Great Malvern

🏛 Heritage Centre
Church Lane. [01531 635680.
○ Easter–Oct: daily. &
🏛 Butcher Row House
Church Lane. ○ Easter–Oct: daily.

Great Malvern and the Malverns ⑪

Worcestershire. 🏠 40,000. 🚋 🚌
ℹ 21 Church St (01684 892289).
🗓 Fri. 🌐 www.malvernhills.gov.uk

THE ANCIENT GRANITE ROCK of the Malvern Hills rises from the plain of the River Severn, its 9 miles (15 km) of glorious scenery visible from afar. Composer Sir Edward Elgar (1857–1934) wrote many of his greatest works here, including the oratorio *The Dream of Gerontius* (1900), inspired by what the diarist John Evelyn (1620–1706) described as "one of the goodliest views in England". Elgar's home was in **Little Malvern**, whose truncated Priory Church of St Giles, set on a steep, wooded hill, lost its nave when the stone was stolen during the Dissolution of the Monasteries (*see pp50–51*). **Great Malvern**, capital of the hills, is graced with 19th-century buildings which look like Swiss sanitoria: patients would stay at institutions such as Doctor Gulley's Water Cure Establishment. The water gushing from the hillside at St Ann's Well, above the town, is bottled and sold throughout Britain.

Malvern's highlight is the **Priory**, with its 15th-century stained-glass windows and medieval misericords. The old monastic fishponds below the church form the lake of the **Winter Gardens**. Here the Festival Theatre hosts performances of Elgar's music and plays by George Bernard Shaw (*see p219*) during the Malvern Festival in late May.

A view of the Malverns range, formed of hard Pre-Cambrian rock

Worcester ⓬

Worcestershire. 🏛 95,000. 🚉
🚌 ℹ️ *High St (01905 722480).*
🅿️ *Mon–Sat.*
🆆 www.cityofworcester.gov.uk

WORCESTER is one of many English cities whose character has been transformed by modern development. The architectural highlight remains the **cathedral**, off College Yard, which suffered a collapsed tower in 1175 and a disastrous fire in 1203, before the present structure was started in the 13th century.

The nave and central tower were completed in the 1370s, after building was severely interrupted by the Black Death, which decimated the labour force *(see pp48–9)*. The most recent and ornate addition was made in 1874, when Sir George Gilbert Scott *(see p451)* designed the High Gothic choir, incorporating 14th-century carved misericords.

There are many interesting tombs, including King John's,

Charles I holding a symbol of the Church on Worcester's Guildhall

a masterpiece of medieval carving, in front of the altar. Prince Arthur, Henry VIII's brother *(see p299)*, who died at the age of 15, is buried in the chantry chapel south of the altar. Underneath, the huge Norman crypt survives from the first cathedral (1084).

From the cathedral cloister, a gate leads to College Green and out into Edgar Street and

its Georgian houses. Here the **Museum of Worcester Porcelain** displays Royal Worcester porcelain dating back to 1751. On the High Street, north of the cathedral, the **Guildhall** of 1723 is adorned with statues of Stuart monarchs, reflecting the city's Royalist allegiances. In Cornmarket is **Ye Olde King Charles House**, in which Prince Charles, later Charles II, hid after the Battle of Worcester in 1651 *(see pp52–3)*.

Some of Worcester's finest timber buildings are found in Friar Street: **Greyfriars**, built around 1480, has been restored in period style. The **Commandery** was originally an 11th-century hospital. It was rebuilt in the 15th century and used by Prince Charles as a base during the Civil War. Now a museum, it has a fine hammerbeam roof.

Elgar's Birthplace was the home of composer Sir Edward Elgar *(see p303)* and contains memorabilia of his life.

🏛 **Museum of Worcester Porcelain**
Severn St. 📞 *01905 23221.*
◯ *daily.* ● *25, 26 Dec, 1 Jan, Easter Sun.* 📷 ♿ ✔️ 🍴 🔓
🏛 **Greyfriars**
(NT) Friar St. 📞 *01905 23571.* ◯
Easter–Oct: Wed, Thu & Mon (public hols only). 📷
🏛 **Commandery**
Sidbury. 📞 *01905 361821.*
◯ *daily (Sun: pm).* ● *25–26 Dec, 1 Jan.* 📷 ♿ 🔓
🏛 **Elgar's Birthplace**
Lower Broadheath. 📞 *01905 333224.*
◯ *daily.* ● *24 Dec–mid-Jan.* 📷 🔓

Birmingham ⓭

Birmingham. 🏛 1,000,000. ✈️
🚉 🚌 ℹ️ *City Arcade (0121 6432514).* 🅿️ *Mon–Sat.*
🆆 www.birmingham.org.uk

BRUM, as it is affectionately known to its inhabitants, grew up as a major centre of the Industrial Revolution in the 19th century. A vast range of manufacturing trades was based in Birmingham and was responsible for the rapid development of grim factories and cramped housing. Since the clearance of several of

Worcester Cathedral, overlooking the River Severn

The Last of England, **Ford Madox Brown, Birmingham Art Gallery**

works by Canaletto (1697–1768).

Birmingham's extensive canal system is now used mainly for leisure boating *(see pp286–7)*, and several former warehouses have been converted into museums and galleries. **Thinktank – the Birmingham Museum of Science and Discovery** celebrates the city's con-tributions to the world of railway engines, aircraft, and the motor trade. The old jewellery quarter has practised its traditional crafts here since the 16th century.

Suburban Birmingham has many attractions, including the **Botanical Gardens** at Edgbaston, and **Cadbury World** at Bournville, where there is a visitor centre dedicated to chocolate (booking ahead is advisable). Bournville village was built in 1890 by the Cadbury brothers for their workers and is a pioneering example of a garden suburb.

these areas after World War II, Birmingham has raised its cultural profile. The city succeeded in enticing Sir Simon Rattle to conduct the City of Birmingham Symphony Orchestra, and persuaded the former Royal Sadler's Wells Ballet (now the Birmingham Royal Ballet) to leave London for the more up-to-date facilities of Birmingham. The **National Exhibition Centre**, 8 miles (13 km) east of the centre, draws thousands of people to its conference, lecture and exhibition halls.

Set away from the massive Bullring shopping centre, Birmingham's 19th-century civic buildings are excellent examples of Neo-Classical architecture. Among them are the **City Museum and Art Gallery**, where the collection includes outstanding works by pre-Raphaelite artists such as Sir Edward Burne-Jones (1833–98), who was born in Birmingham, and Ford Madox Brown (1821–93). The museum also organizes some interesting temporary exhibitions of art, such as

🏛 **City Museum and Art Gallery**
Chamberlain Sq. 📞 0121 303 2834.
🕐 daily (Sun: pm). ⬤ 24–27 Dec, 1–2 Jan. ♿

🏛 **Thinktank**
Millennium Point. 📞 0121 202222.

🌸 **Botanical Gardens**
Westbourne Rd, Edgbaston.
📞 0121 454 1860. 🕐 daily.
⬤ 25 Dec. ♿ 🍴 🎁 📷 by arrangement.

🏛 **Cadbury World**
Linden Rd, Bournville. 📞 0121 4514159. 🕐 Apr–Oct: daily;
Nov–Mar: selected days phone first.
⬤ 23–25, 31 Dec. 📷 ♿

Stately civic office buildings in Victoria Square, Birmingham

Coventry ⑭

Coventry. 🏘 300,000. 🚂 🚌
🛈 Bayley Lane (024 7622 7264).
🛒 Mon–Sat. 🌐 www.coventry.org.uk

A^{S AN ARMAMENTS} centre, Coventry was a prime target for German bombing raids in World War II, and in 1940 the medieval **cathedral** in the city centre was hit. After the war the first totally modern cathedral, designed by Sir Basil Spence (1907–76), was built alongside the ruins.

Epstein's *St Michael Subduing the Devil*, on Coventry Cathedral

Sir Jacob Epstein (1880–1959) added dramatic sculptures, and Graham Sutherland (1903–80) the splendid tapestry, *Christ in Majesty*, on the east wall. Benjamin Britten *(see p189)* composed his *War Requiem* for the rededication ceremony, held on 30 May 1962.

The **Herbert Gallery and Museum** has displays on the 11th-century legend of Lady Godiva, who rode naked through the streets in protest when her husband, the Earl of Mercia, imposed taxes on the town. The city residents remained indoors, except for Peeping Tom, who was struck blind for his curiosity.

🏛 **Herbert Gallery and Museum**
Jordan Well. 📞 024 7683 2381.
🕐 daily (Sun: pm) ⬤ 24–26 Dec, 1 Jan. 💻 📷

Midlands Garden Tour ⑮

Plum tree in blossom

THE CHARMING COTSWOLD stone buildings perfectly complement the lush gardens for which the region is famous. This picturesque route from Warwick to Cheltenham is designed to show every type of garden, from tiny cottage plots, brimming with bell-shaped flowers and hollyhocks, to the deer-filled, landscaped parks of stately homes. The route follows the escarpment of the Cotswold Hills, taking in spectacular scenery and some of the prettiest Midlands villages on the way.

TIPS FOR DRIVERS

Tour length: 35 miles (50 km).
Stopping-off points: Hidcote Manor has excellent lunches and teas; there are refreshments at Kiftsgate Court and Sudeley Castle. Travellers will find a good choice in Broadway, from traditional pubs and tea shops to the de luxe Lygon Arms. (See also pp636–7.)

Cheltenham Imperial Gardens ⑨
These colourful public gardens on the Promenade were laid out in 1817–18 to encourage people to walk from the town to the spa (see p314).

Sudeley Castle ⑧
The restored castle is complemented by box hedges, topiary and an Elizabethan knot garden (see p22). Catherine Parr, Henry VIII's widow, died here in 1548.

Broadway ⑤
Wisteria and cordoned fruit trees cover 17th-century cottages, fronted by immaculate gardens.

Stanway House ⑦
This Jacobean manor has many lovely trees in its grounds and a pyramid above a cascade of water.

Snowshill Manor ⑥
This Cotswold stone manor contains an extraordinary collection, from bicycles to Japanese armour. There are walled gardens and terraces full of *objets d'art* such as the clock (left). The colour blue is a recurrent theme.

arwick Castle ①
he castle's gardens
pp308–9) include
Mound, planted in
edieval style, with
s, oaks, yew trees
and box hedges.

BIRMINGHAM

COVENTRY

WARWICK

LONDON

e Hathaway's Cottage ②
s has a pretty, informal 19th-
ury-style garden *(see p313).*

TER

rd-upon-Avon

BANBURY

CIRENCESTER

BANBURY

OXFORD

Hidcote Manor Gardens ③
Started in the early years of this century, these beautiful gardens pioneered the idea of a garden as a series of outdoor "rooms", enclosed by high yew hedges and planted according to themes.

Kiftsgate Court Garden ④
This charmingly naturalistic garden lies opposite Hidcote Manor. It has many rare and unusual plants on a series of hillside terraces, including the enormous "Kiftsgate" Rose, nearly 30 m (100 ft) high.

KEY

≡≡≡	Motorway
▬▬▬	Tour route
═══	Other roads
⁂	Viewpoint

0 kilometres   5

0 miles   5

Warwick ⑯

Warwickshire. 🏠 *28,000.* 🚉 🚌
ℹ️ *The Courthouse, Jury St (01926 492212).* 🏛 *Sat.* 🅆 *www.warwick-uk.co.uk*

THOUGH WARWICK suffered a major fire in 1694, some spectacular medieval build-ings survived. The **Warwick Doll Museum** in Castle Street (1573) displays rare toys and dolls from all over the world. At the west end of the High Street, a row of medieval guild buildings were transformed in 1571 by the Earl of Leicester (1532–88), who founded the **Lord Leycester Hospital** as a refuge for his old soldiers.

The arcaded **Market Hall** (1670) is part of the Warwick-shire Museum, renowned for its unusual tapestry map of the county, woven in 1558.

In Church Street, to the south of St Mary's Church, is the **Beauchamp Chapel** (1443–64). It is a superb exam-ple of Perpendicular architec-ture and has tombs of the Earls of Warwick. There is a view of **Warwick Castle** *(see pp308–9)* from St Mary's tower.

🏛 **Warwick Doll Museum**
Castle St. 🞖 *01926 495546.*
⭘ *Easter–Oct: daily (Sun: pm); (Nov–Easter: Sat).* 🎟 🞖
🏨 **Lord Leycester Hospital**
High St. 🞖 *01926 491422.* ⭘ *Tue–Sun & public hols.* ⬤ *25 Dec, Good Fri.* **Gardens** ⭘ *same as house but Easter–Sep only.* 🎟 🞖 🦽 *limited.*
🏛 **Market Hall**
Market Place. 🞖 *01926 412500.* ⭘ *Mon–Sat (May–Sep: daily).* ⬤ *25 Dec, 1 Jan.*
🦽 *limited.* 🞖

The Lord Leycester Hospital,
now a home for ex-servicemen

Warwick Castle

Neville family at prayer (c.1460)

WARWICK'S MAGNIFICENT CASTLE is a splendid medieval fortress which is also one of the country's finest stately homes. The original Norman castle was rebuilt in the 14th century, when huge outer walls and towers were added, mainly to display the power of the great feudal magnates, the Beauchamps and the Nevilles, the Earls of Warwick. The castle passed in 1604 to the Greville family who, in the 17th and 18th centuries, transformed it into a great country house. In 1978 the owners of Madame Tussaud's (see p106) bought the castle and set up tableaux of wax figures to illustrate its history.

The Ghost Tower is where the ghost of Sir Fulke Greville, murdered by a servant in 1628, is said to walk.

The Mound has remains of the motte and bailey c (see p472) and the 1 century kee

Royal Weekend Party
The waxwork valet is part of the award-winning exhibition of the Prince of Wales's visit in 1898.

★ Great Hall and State Rooms
Medieval apartments were transformed into the Great Hall and State Rooms. A mark of conspicuous wealth, they display a collection of family treasures from around the world.

Kingmaker Exhibition
Dramatic displays recreate medieval life as "Warwick the Kingmaker", Richard Neville, prepared for battle in the Wars of the Roses .

View of Warwick Castle, south front, by Antonio Canaletto (1697–1768)

VISITORS' CHECKLIST

Castle Lane, Warwick. ☎ 0870 4422000. ◐ Apr–Oct: 10am–6pm daily; Nov–Mar: 10am–5pm daily (last adm: 30 mins before closing). ● 25 Dec. ☑ ◉ ♿ limited. ☑ ❚❚ ▣ ▯

Ramparts and towers, of local grey sandstone, were added in the 14th century to fortify the castle.

Guy's Tower (1393) had lodgings for guests and members of the Earl of Warwick's retinue.

★ Death or Glory, the Armoury
The exhibits include Oliver Cromwell's helmet and a massive 14th-century two-handed sword.

Entrance

Caesar's Tower and dungeon contains a grisly collection of torture instruments.

The Gatehouse is defended by portcullises and "murder holes" through which boiling pitch was dropped onto attackers beneath.

STAR SIGHTS

★ Great Hall and State Rooms

★ Death or Glory

TIMELINE

Shield (1745), Death or Glory

1068 Norman motte and bailey castle built	**1264** Simon de Montfort, champion of Parliament against Henry III, sacks Warwick Castle		**1478** Castle reverts to Crown after murder of Richard Neville's son-in-law	**1893–1910** Visits from future Edward VII

1000	1200	1400	1600	1800

Richard Neville

1356–1401 Present castle built by the Beauchamp family, Earls of Warwick

1449–1471 Richard Neville, Earl of Warwick, plays leading role in Wars of the Roses

1604 James I gives castle to Sir Fulke Greville

1600–1800 Interiors remodelled and gardens landscaped

1642 Royalists imprisoned in the castle

1871 Anthony Salvin (1799–1881) restores Great Hall and State Rooms after fire

Street-by-Street: Stratford-upon-Avon **⑰**

A 1930s jester

Sᴵᴛᴜᴀᴛᴇᴅ ᴏɴ ᴛʜᴇ ᴡᴇꜱᴛ ʙᴀɴᴋ of the River Avon, in the heart of the Midlands, is one of the most famous towns in England. Stratford-upon-Avon dates back to at least Roman times but its appearance today is that of a small Tudor market town, with mellow, half-timbered architecture and tranquil walks beside the tree-fringed Avon. This image belies its popularity as the most visited tourist attraction outside London, with eager hordes flocking to see buildings connected to William Shakespeare or his descendants.

Bancroft Gardens
There is an attractive boat-filled canal basin here and a 15th-century causeway.

★ Shakespeare's Birthplace
This building was almost entirely recon-structed in the 19th century, but in the style of the Tudor original.

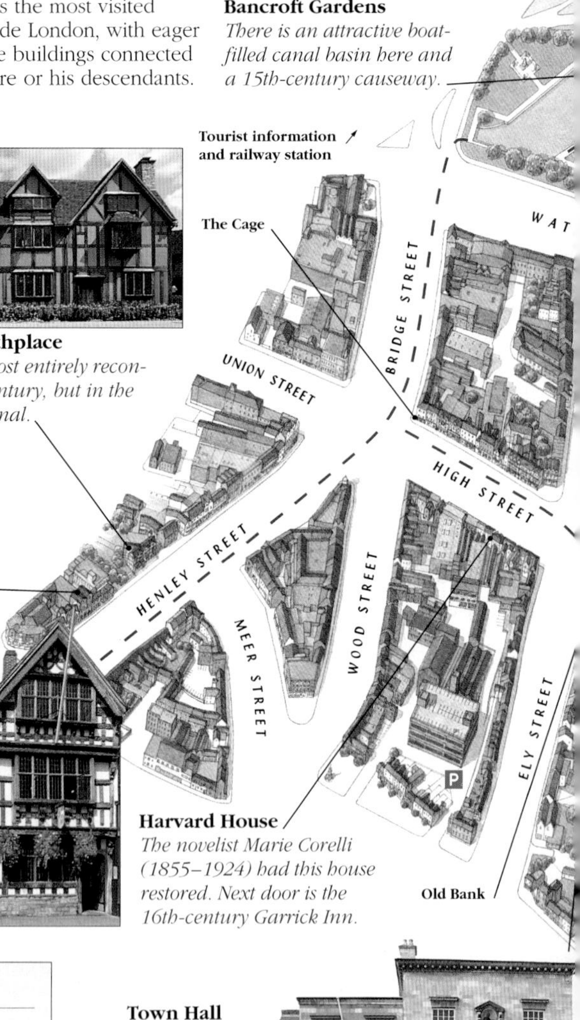

0 metres 100

0 yards 100

Shakespeare Centre

Tourist information and railway station

The Cage

UNION STREET

BRIDGE STREET

W A T

HIGH STREET

HENLEY STREET

MEER STREET

WOOD STREET

ELY STREET

P

Harvard House
The novelist Marie Corelli (1855–1924) had this house restored. Next door is the 16th-century Garrick Inn.

Old Bank

STAR SIGHTS

★ Shakespeare's Birthplace

★ Hall's Croft

★ Holy Trinity Church

Town Hall
Built in 1767, there are traces of 18th-century graffiti on the front of the building saying God Save the King.

Royal Shakespeare Theatre
The highly acclaimed resident theatre company, the RSC, has staged all of Shakespeare's plays since it began in 1961.

VISITORS' CHECKLIST

Warwickshire. 22,000.
20 miles (32 km) NW of
Stratford-upon-Avon. Alcester
Rd. Bridge St. Bridge Foot
(01789 293127); Shakespeare
Centre, Henley St (01789 204016).
Fri. Shakespeare's Birthday:
Apr; Stratford Festival: Jul; Mop
Fair: Oct.

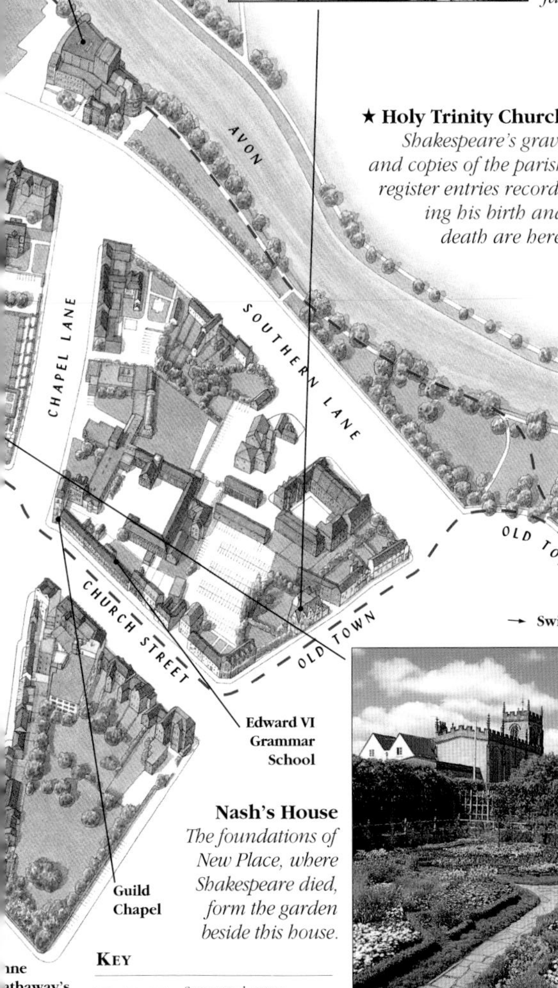

★ Hall's Croft
John Hall, Shakespeare's son-in-law, was a doctor. This delightful house has one room fitted out as a dispensary, with original Jacobean furniture.

★ Holy Trinity Church
Shakespeare's grave and copies of the parish register entries recording his birth and death are here.

AVON

CHAPEL LANE

SOUTHERN LANE

OLD TOWN

CHURCH STREET

OLD TOWN

→ Swindon

Edward VI Grammar School

Nash's House
The foundations of New Place, where Shakespeare died, form the garden beside this house.

Guild Chapel

KEY

ine
athaway's
ttage

- - - Suggested route

Exploring Stratford-upon-Avon

Mosaic of Shakespeare on the beautiful Old Bank (1810)

WILLIAM SHAKESPEARE was born in Stratford-upon-Avon on St George's Day, 23 April 1564. Admirers of his work have been coming to the town since his death in 1616. In 1847 a public appeal successfully raised the money to buy the house in which he was born. As a result Stratford has become a literary shrine to Britain's greatest dramatist. It also has a thriving cultural reputation as the provincial home of the prestigious Royal Shakespeare Company, whose dramas are usually performed in Stratford before playing a second season in London (see p124).

Anne Hathaway's Cottage, home of Shakespeare's wife.

Around Stratford

The centre of Stratford-upon-Avon has many buildings that are connected with William Shakespeare and his descendants. On the High Street corner is the **Cage**, a 15th-century prison. It was converted into a house where Shakespeare's daughter Judith lived, and is now a shop. At the end of the High Street, the **Town Hall** has a statue of Shakespeare on the façade given by David Garrick (1717–79), the actor who in 1769 organized the first Shakespeare festival.

The High Street leads into Chapel Street where the half-timbered **Nash's House** is a museum of local history. It is also the site of **New Place**, where Shakespeare died in 1616, and which is now a herb and knot garden (see p22). In Church Street opposite, the **Guild Chapel** (1496) has a *Last Judgement* painting (c.1500) on the chancel wall. Shakespeare is thought to have attended the **Edward VI Grammar School** (above the former Guildhall) next door.

A left turn into Old Town leads to **Hall's Croft**, home of Shakespeare's daughter Susanna, which displays 16th- and 17th-century medical artefacts. An avenue of lime trees leads to **Holy Trinity Church**, where Shakespeare is buried. A walk along the river follows the Avon to **Bancroft Gardens**, which lies at the junction of the River Avon and the Stratford Canal.

Holy Trinity Church, seen across the River Avon

⌂ Shakespeare's Birthplace

Henley St. 📞 01789 204016. ⬜ daily. ⬤ 23–26 Dec. 🚫 ♿ limited. ▯

Bought for the nation in 1847, when it was a public house, Shakespeare's Birthplace was converted back to Elizabethan style. Objects associated with Shakespeare's father, John, a glovemaker and wool merchant, are on display. The room in which Shakespeare was supposedly born (arbitrarily chosen by Garrick) has a window etched with visitors' autographs, including that of Sir Walter Scott (see p498).

🏛 Harvard House

High St. 📞 *01789 204016.* ⭕ *daily (summer).* ♿ *limited.*

Built in 1596, this ornate house was the home of Katherine Rogers, whose son, John Harvard, emigrated to America and in 1638 left his estate to a new college, later renamed Harvard University. The house contains a Museum of British Pewter and displays relating to John Harvard.

ENVIRONS: No tour of Stratford would be complete without a visit to **Anne Hathaway's Cottage**. Before her marriage to William Shakespeare she lived at Shottery, 1 mile (1.5 km) west of Stratford. Despite fire damage in 1969, the cottage is still impressive, with some original 16th-century furniture. The Hathaway descendants lived here until the early 20th century *(see p307)*.

🏛 Anne Hathaway's Cottage

Cottage Lane. 📞 *01789 292100.* ⭕ *daily.* ⚫ *23–26 Dec, 1 Jan.*

Kenneth Branagh in *Hamlet*

THE ROYAL SHAKESPEARE COMPANY

The Royal Shakespeare Company is renowned for its new interpretations of Shakespeare's work. The company performs at the 1932 Royal Shakespeare Theatre, a windowless brick building adjacent to the Swan Theatre, built in 1986 to a design based on an Elizabethan playhouse. Next to it is a building displaying sets, props and costumes. The RSC also performs at the 150-seat theatre, known as the Other Place, and in London *(see p124)*.

Grevel House, the oldest house in Chipping Campden

Chipping Campden ⑱

Gloucestershire. 👥 *2,000.* ℹ️ *Hollis House, Stow-on-the-Wold (01451 831082).*

THIS PERFECT Cotswold town is kept in pristine condition by the Campden Trust. Set up in 1929, the Trust has kept alive the traditional skills of stonecarving and repair that make Chipping Campden such a unified picture of golden-coloured and lichen-patched stone. Visitors travelling from the northwest along the B4035 first see a group of ruins: the remains of **Campden Manor**, begun around 1613 by Sir Baptist Hicks, 1st Viscount Campden. The manor was burned by Royalist troops to stop it being sequestered by Parliament at the end of the Civil War *(see pp52–3)*, but the almshouses opposite the gateway were spared. They were designed in the form of the letter "I" (which is Latin for "J"), a symbol of the owner's loyalty to King James I.

The town's **Church of St James**, one of the finest in the Cotswolds, was built in the 15th century, financed by merchants who bought wool from Cotswold farmers and exported it at a high profit. Inside the church there are many elaborate tombs, and a magnificent brass dedicated to William Grevel, describing him as "the flower of the wool merchants of England". He built **Grevel House** (c.1380) in the High Street, the oldest in a fine row of buildings, which is distinguished by a double-storey bay window.

Viscount Campden donated the **Market Hall** in 1627. His contemporary, Robert Dover, founded in 1612 the "Cotswold Olimpicks", long before the modern Olympic Games had been established. The 1612 version included such painful events as the shin-kicking contest. It still takes place on the first Friday after each Spring Bank Holiday, followed by a torchlit procession into town ready for the Scuttlebrook Wake Fair on the next day. The setting for the games is a spectacular natural hollow on **Dover's Hill** above the town, worth climbing on a clear day for the marvellous views over the Vale of Evesham.

The 17th-century Market Hall in Chipping Campden

Tewkesbury's abbey church overlooks the town, crowded onto the bank of the River Severn

Tewkesbury **⑲**

Gloucestershire. 🏠 *11,000.*
ℹ️ *Barton St (01684 295027).*
🚲 *Wed, Sat.*
🌐 *www.tewkesburybc.com*

THIS LOVELY TOWN sits on the confluence of the rivers Severn and Avon. It has one of England's finest Norman abbey churches, **St Mary the Virgin**, which locals saved during the Dissolution of the Monasteries *(see p50)* by paying Henry VIII £453. Around the church, with its bulky tower and Norman façade, timbered buildings are crammed within the bend of the river. Warehouses are a reminder of past wealth, and Borough Mill on Quay Street, the only mill left harnessed to the river's energy, still grinds corn.

ENVIRONS: Boat trips can be taken from the river to **Upton-on-Severn**'s riverside pubs, 6 miles (10 km) north.

Cheltenham **⑳**

Gloucestershire. 🏠 *107,000.* 🚆
🚌 ℹ️ *77 Promenade (01242 522878).* 🚲 *Sun.*
🌐 *www.visitcheltenham.gov.uk*

CHELTENHAM'S REPUTATION for elegance was first gained in the late 18th century, when high society flocked to the spa town to "take the waters", following the example set by George III *(see pp54–5)*. Many gracious terraced houses were built, in a Neo-Classical style, along broad avenues. These survive around the Queen's Hotel, near **Montpellier**, a lovely Regency arcade lined with craft and antique shops, and in the **Promenade**, with its smart department stores and couturiers. A more modern atmosphere prevails in the newly built Regency Arcade, where the star attraction is the 1987 **clock** by Kit Williams: visit on the hour to see fish blowing bubbles over the onlookers' heads. The **Museum and Art Gallery** is worth a visit to see its unusual collection of furniture and other crafts made by members of the influential Arts and Crafts Movement *(see p25)*, whose strict principles of utilitarian design were laid down by William Morris *(see p206)*.

Pump Room detail, Cheltenham

The **Pitville Pump Room** (1825–30), modelled on the Greek Temple of Ilissos in Athens, is frequently used for performances during the town's renowned annual festivals of music (July) and literature (October).

The event that really attracts the crowds, though, is the Cheltenham Gold Cup – the premier event of the National Hunt season – held in March *(see p66)*.

🏛 **Museum and Art Gallery**
Clarence St. 📞 *01242 237431.*
🕐 *daily.* ⬤ *25 Dec, 1 Jan & public hols.* 📷 🚻 ♿ ✏️ *by arrangement.*

🎭 **Pitville Pump Room**
Pitville Park. 📞 *01242 523852.*
🕐 *Phone for details.* ⬤ *25, 26 Dec, 1 Jan & for functions.*

Fantasy clock, by Kit Williams, in Cheltenham's Regency Arcade

Gloucester Cathedral's nave

Gloucester ㉑

Gloucestershire. 🏙 *110,000.* 🚆 🚌
ℹ️ *28 Southgate St (01452 421188).*
🚹 *Wed, Sat.* 🌐 *www.visit-glos.org.uk*

GLOUCESTER has played a prominent role in the history of England. It was here that William the Conqueror ordered a vast survey of all the land in his kingdom, to be recorded in the Domesday Book of 1086 *(see p48).*

The city was popular with the Norman monarchs and in 1216 Henry III was crowned in its magnificent **cathedral**. The solid, dignified nave was begun in 1089. Edward II *(see p425),* who was murdered in 1327 at Berkeley Castle, 14 miles (22 km) to the south-west, is buried in a tomb near the high altar. Many pilgrims came to honour Edward's tomb, leaving behind generous donations, and Abbot Thoky was able to begin rebuilding in 1331. The result was the wonderful east window and the cloisters, where the fan vault was developed and then copied in other churches all over the country.

The impressive buildings around the cathedral include College Court, with its **Beatrix Potter Exhibition** in the house used by the children's author *(see p353)* for her illustrations of the story of the *Tailor of Gloucester.* A museum complex has been created in the **Gloucester Docks**, part of which is still a port, linked to the Bristol Channel by the Gloucester and Sharpness Canal (opened in 1827). In the old port, the

National Waterways Museum relates the history of canals, and the fascinating **Robert Opie Collection – Museum of Advertising and Packaging** looks at the promotion of household goods from 1880s.

🏛 **Beatrix Potter Exhibition**
College Court. 📞 *01452 422856.*
⏰ *Mon–Sat.* ⚫ *public hols.* ♿ 🚻
🏛 **National Waterways Museum**
Llanthony Warehouse, Gloucester Docks. 📞 *01452 318054.* ⏰ *daily.*
⚫ *25 Dec.* ♿ 🚻 📷
🏛 **Robert Opie Collection**
Albert Warehouse, Gloucester Docks.
📞 *01452 302309.* ⏰ *Mar–Sep: daily; Oct–Feb: Tue–Sun.* ⚫ *25, 26 Dec.*
♿ 🚻 📷

Cirencester ㉒

Gloucestershire. 🏙 *20,000.* 🚌
ℹ️ *Market Place (01285 654180).*
🚹 *Mon, Tue (cattle) & Fri.*

KNOWN AS THE CAPITAL of the Cotswolds, Cirencester has as its focus a market place where cheese, fish and flowers are sold every Monday and Friday. Overlooking the market is the **Church of St John Baptist**, whose "wineglass" pulpit (1515) is one of the few pre-Reformation pulpits to survive in England. To the west, **Cirencester Park** was laid out by the 1st Earl of Bathurst from 1714, with help from the poet Alexander Pope *(see*

p303). The mansion is surrounded by a massive yew hedge, claimed to be the tallest in the world. Clustering round the park entrance are the 17th- and 18th-century wool merchants' houses of Cecily Hill, built in grand Italianate style. Much humbler Cotswold houses are to be found in Coxwell Street, and underlying this is a Roman town, evidence of which emerges whenever the ground is dug.

The **Corinium Museum** (*Corinium* was the Latin name) features excavated objects in a series of tableaux illustrating life in a Roman household.

🌿 **Cirencester Park**
Cirencester Park. 📞 *01285 653135.*
⏰ *daily.* ♿
🏛 **Corinium Museum**
Park St. 📞 *01285 655611.*
⏰ *daily (Sun pm only).* ⚫ *25 Dec, 1 Jan.* ♿ 🚻 📷

Cirencester's fine parish church, one of the largest in England

---

ART AND NATURE IN THE ROMAN WORLD

Cirencester was an important centre of mosaic production in Roman days. Fine examples of the local style are shown in the Corinium Museum and mosaics range from Classical subjects, such as Orpheus taming lions and tigers with the music of his lyre, to the naturalistic depiction of a hare. At

Chedworth Roman Villa, 8 miles (13 km) north, mosaics are inspired by real life. In the *Four Seasons* mosaic, *Winter* shows a peasant, dressed in a woollen hood and a wind-blown cloak, clutching a recently caught hare in one hand and a branch for fuel in the other.

Hare mosaic, Corinium Museum

EAST MIDLANDS

....

DERBYSHIRE · LEICESTERSHIRE · LINCOLNSHIRE
NORTHAMPTONSHIRE · NOTTINGHAMSHIRE

THREE VERY DIFFERENT KINDS OF LANDSCAPE *greet visitors to the East Midlands. In the west, wild moors rise to the craggy heights of the Peak District. These give way to the low-lying plain and the massive industrial towns at the region's heart. In the east, hills and limestone villages stretch to a long, flat seaboard.*

The East Midlands owes much of its character to a conjunction of the pastoral with the urban. The spa resorts, historical villages and stately homes coexist within a landscape shaped by industrialization. Throughout the region there are swathes of scenic countryside – and grimy industrial cities.

The area has been settled since prehistoric times. The Romans mined lead and salt, and they built a large network of roads and fortresses. Anglo-Saxon and Viking influence is found in many of the place names. During the Middle Ages profits from the wool industry enabled the development of towns such as Lincoln, which still has many fine old buildings. The East Midlands was the scene of ferocious battles during the Wars of the Roses and the Civil War, and insurgents in the Jacobite Rebellion reached as far as Derby.

In the west of the region is the Peak District, Britain's first National Park. Created in 1951, it draws crowds in search of the wild beauty of the heather-covered moors, or the wooded dales of the River Dove. The peaks are very popular with rock climbers and hikers.

The eastern edge of the Peaks descends through stone-walled meadows to sheltered valleys. The Roman spa of Buxton adds a final note of elegance before the flatlands of Derbyshire, Leicestershire and Nottinghamshire are reached. An area of coal mines and factories since the late 18th century, the landscape is set to be transformed over the next century into a new national forest.

Well-dressing dance, an ancient custom at Stoney Middleton in the Peak District

◁ **West front of Chatsworth House, a superb Baroque stately home in the Peak District**

Exploring the East Midlands

T HE EAST MIDLANDS is a popular tourist destination, easily accessible by road, but best explored on foot. Numerous well-marked trails pass through the Peak District National Park. There are superb country houses at Chatsworth and Burghley and the impressive historic towns of Lincoln and Stamford to discover.

SIGHTS AT A GLANCE

Burghley pp328–9 ❽
Buxton ❶
Chatsworth pp320–21 ❷
Lincoln pp326–7 ❼
Matlock Bath ❸
Northampton ❿
Nottingham ❻
Stamford ❾

Walks and Tours

Peak District Tour ❺
Tissington Trail ❹

GETTING AROUND

The M6, M1 and A1 are the principal road routes to the East Midlands, but they are subject to frequent delays because of the volume of traffic they carry. It can be faster and more interesting to find cross-country routes to the region, for example through the attractive countryside and villages around Stamford and Northampton. Roads in the Peak District become very congested during the summer and an early start to the day is advisable. Lincoln and Stamford are well served by fast InterCity trains from London. Rail services in the Peak District are far more limited, but local lines run as far as Matlock and Buxton.

KEY

▦	Motorway
▭	Major road
▬	Scenic route
▬▬	Scenic path
▭	River
⁂	Viewpoint

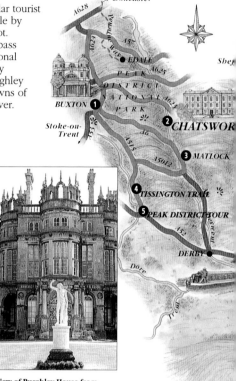

View of Burghley House from the north courtyard

SEE ALSO

- **Where to Stay** pp558–59
- **Where to Eat** pp593–95

Peak District countryside seen from the Tissington Trail

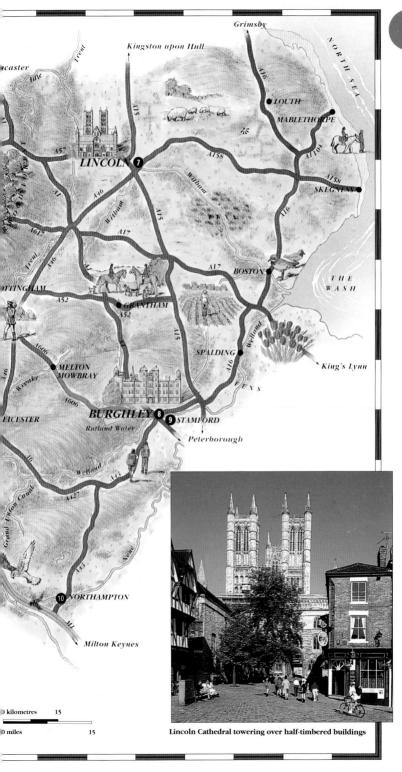

Lincoln Cathedral towering over half-timbered buildings

0 kilometres 15

0 miles 15

Buxton Opera House, a late 19th-century building restored in 1979

Buxton ❶

Derbyshire. 🏠 20,000. 🚌 🚉
ℹ️ *The Crescent (01298 25106).*
📅 *Tue, Sat.* 🌐 *www.highpeak.gov.uk*

Buxton was developed as a spa town by the 5th Duke of Devonshire during the late 18th century. It has many fine Neo-Classical buildings, including the **Devonshire Royal Hospital** (1790), originally stables, at the entrance to the town. The **Crescent** was built (1780–90) to rival Bath's Royal Crescent (*see p244*).

At its southwest end, the tourist information office is housed in the former town baths. Here, a spring where water surges from the ground at a rate of 7,000 litres (1,540 gallons) an hour can be seen. Buxton water is bottled and sold commercially but there is a public fountain at **St Ann's Well**, opposite.

Steep gardens known as the Slopes lead from the Crescent to the small, award-winning **Museum and Art Gallery**, with geological and archaeological displays. Behind the Crescent, overlooking the Pavilion Gardens, is the striking 19th-century iron and glass **Pavilion**, and the splendidly restored **Opera House**, where a Music and Arts Festival is held in summer.

🏛 **Buxton Museum and Art Gallery**
Terrace Rd. 📞 *01298 24658.*
🕐 *Easter–Sep: Tue–Sun (Oct–Easter: Tue–Sat).* ⏺ *25 Dec–2 Jan.* 📷 ♿ 🚹
🎪 **Pavilion**
St John's Rd. 📞 *01298 23114.*
🕐 *daily.* ⏺ *25 Dec.* ♿ 🍴 🛍 🚹

Chatsworth House and Gardens ❷

CHATSWORTH IS ONE of Britain's most impressive stately homes. Between 1687 and 1707, the 4th Earl of Devonshire replaced the old Tudor mansion with this Baroque palace. The house has beautiful gardens, landscaped in the 1760s by Capability Brown (*see p22*) and developed by the head gardener, Joseph Paxton (*see pp56–7*), in the mid-19th century.

First house built in 1552 by Bess of Hardwick

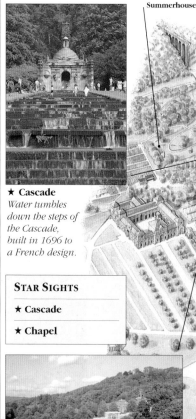

Summerhouse

Round ponds, known as the Spectacles

★ **Cascade**
Water tumbles down the steps of the Cascade, built in 1696 to a French design.

> **STAR SIGHTS**
>
> ★ **Cascade**
> ───────────
> ★ **Chapel**

Garden entrance

House entrance

Paxton's "Conservative" Wall
This iron-and-glass conservatory wall was designed in 1848 by Joseph Paxton, the creator of Chatsworth's Great Conservatory (now demolished).

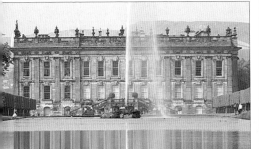

South front and canal pond with Emperor fountain

Maze: site of Paxton's Great Conservatory

Rhododendron Walk

Grotto

★ Chapel
The chapel (1693) is resplendent with art and marble.

War Horse
This sculpture (1991) is by Elisabeth Frink.

Canal pond

Sea-horse fountain

State Rooms
The rooms have fine interiors and superb art, such as this trompe l'oeil by Jan van der Vaart (1651–1727).

Matlock ❸

Derbyshire. 🏘 *23,000.* 🚆
ℹ️ *Crown Square (01629 583388).*
🌐 *www.derbyshiredales.gov.uk*

M ATLOCK WAS DEVELOPED as a spa from the 1780s. Interesting buildings include the massive structure (1853) on the hill above the town, built as a hydrotherapy centre but now council offices. On the hill opposite is the mock-Gothic **Riber Castle**.

From Matlock, the A6 winds through the outstandingly beautiful **Derwent Gorge** to **Matlock Bath**. Here, cable cars ascend to the **Heights of Abraham** pleasure park, with caves, nature trail and extensive views. Lead-mining is the subject of the **Peak District Mining Museum**, and visitors can inspect the old **Temple Mine** nearby. **Arkwright's Mill** (1771), the world's first water-powered cotton-spinning mill, is at the southern end of the gorge *(see p325)*.

🎪 **Heights of Abraham**
On A6. 📞 *01629 582365.*
◯ *Easter–Oct: daily; phone first at other times.* 📷 ♿ *limited.*
🏛 **Peak District Mining Museum**
The Pavilion, off A6. 📞 *01629 583834.* ◯ *daily.* ● *25 Dec.* 📷
♿ 🅿️
⛏ **Temple Mine**
Temple Rd, off A6. 📞 *01629 583834.* ◯ *daily (winter: by arrangement).*
● *25 Dec.* 📷
⛏ **Arkwright's Mill**
Mill Lane, Cromford. 📞 *01629 824297.* ◯ *daily.* ● *25 Dec.* ♿ 🅿️

Cable cars taking visitors to the Heights of Abraham

Tissington Trail ❹

See p323.

Peak District Tour ❺

See pp324–5.

Nottingham ❻

Nottinghamshire. 🏘 *283,000.*
🚆 🖼 ℹ️ *Smithy Row (0115 9155330).* 🛍 *daily.*
🌐 *www.profilenottingham.co.uk*

T HE NAME OF NOTTINGHAM often conjures up the image of the evil Sheriff, adversary of Robin Hood. **Nottingham Castle** stands on a rock riddled with underground passages. The castle houses a museum, with displays on the city's history, and what was Britain's first municipal art gallery, featuring works by Sir Stanley Spencer (1891–1959) and Dante Gabriel Rossetti (1828–82). At the foot of the castle, Britain's oldest tavern, the **Trip to Jerusalem** (1189), is still in business. Its name may refer to the 12th- and 13th-century crusades, but much of it is 17th-century.

There are several museums near the castle, ranging from the **Tales of Robin Hood**, which tells the story of the outlaw, to the **Museum of Costume and Textiles**, explaining Nottingham's role as a leading centre for embroidery, lace-making, tapestries and knitted textiles.

ENVIRONS: Stately homes within a few miles of Nottingham include the Neo-Classical **Kedleston Hall** *(see pp24–5)*. "Bess of Hardwick", Countess of Shrewbury *(see p320)*, built the spectacular **Hardwick Hall** *(see p288)*.

♠ **Nottingham Castle and Museum**
Castle Rd. 📞 *0115 9153700.* ◯ *daily.* ● *Nov–Feb: Fri; 25, 26 Dec, 1 Jan.* 📷 *Sat, Sun & public hols.* 🅿️
♿ 🅿️
🏛 **Tales of Robin Hood**
30–38 Maid Marion Way. 📞 *0115 9483284.* ◯ *daily.* ● *24–26 Dec.*
📷 ♿ 🅿️ 🅿️
🏛 **Museum of Costume and Textiles**
51 Castle Gate. 📞 *0115 9153500.* ◯ *Wed–Sun.* ● *24 Dec–1 Jan.* 🅿️
🏛 **Kedleston Hall**
(NT) off A38. 📞 *01332 842191.* ◯ *Apr–Oct: Sat–Wed (pm).* 📷 🅿️
🍴 ♿
🏛 **Hardwick Hall**
(NT) off A617. 📞 *01246 850430.* ◯ *Apr–Oct: Wed, Thu, Sat, Sun & public hols.* 📷 ♿ *limited.* 🍴 🅿️

ROBIN HOOD OF SHERWOOD FOREST

England's most colourful folk hero was a legendary swordsman, whose adventures are depicted in numerous films and stories. He lived in Sherwood Forest, near Nottingham, with a band of "merry men", robbing the rich to give to the poor. As part of an ancient oral tradition, Robin Hood figured mainly in ballads; the first written records of his exploits date from the 15th century. Today historians think that he was not one person, but a composite of many outlaws who refused to conform to medieval feudal constraints.

Victorian depiction of Friar Tuck and Robin Hood

Tissington Trail ⁴

Tʜᴇ ꜰᴜʟʟ-ʟᴇɴɢᴛʜ Tissington Trail runs for 13 miles (22 km), from the village of Ashbourne to Parsley Hay, where it meets the High Peak Trail. This is a short version, taking an easy route along a dismantled railway line around Tissington village and providing good views of the beautiful White Peak countryside. The Derbyshire custom of well-dressing is thought to have originated in pre-Christian times. It was revived in the early 17th century, when the Tissington village wells were decorated in thanksgiving for deliverance from the plague, in the belief that the fresh water had had a medicinal effect. Well-dressing is still an important event in the Peakland calendar, and can be seen in other villages where the water supplies are prone to dry up.

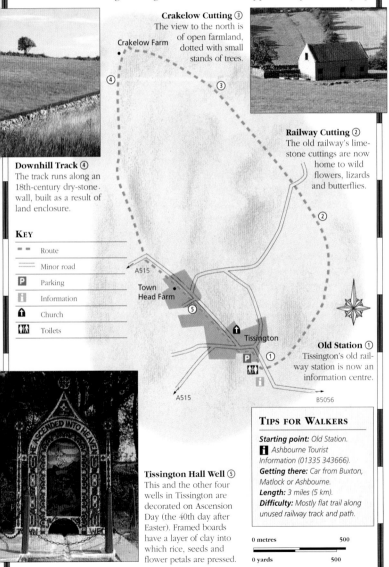

Crakelow Cutting ③
The view to the north is of open farmland, dotted with small stands of trees.

Crakelow Farm

Railway Cutting ②
The old railway's limestone cuttings are now home to wild flowers, lizards and butterflies.

Downhill Track ④
The track runs along an 18th-century dry-stone wall, built as a result of land enclosure.

KEY

- -	Route
====	Minor road
P	Parking
ℹ	Information
⌖	Church
🚻	Toilets

A515

Town Head Farm

Tissington

Old Station ①
Tissington's old railway station is now an information centre.

A515

B5056

Tissington Hall Well ⑤
This and the other four wells in Tissington are decorated on Ascension Day (the 40th day after Easter). Framed boards have a layer of clay into which rice, seeds and flower petals are pressed.

TIPS FOR WALKERS

Starting point: Old Station.
ℹ Ashbourne Tourist Information (01335 343666).
Getting there: Car from Buxton, Matlock or Ashbourne.
Length: 3 miles (5 km).
Difficulty: Mostly flat trail along unused railway track and path.

0 metres	500
0 yards	500

Peak District Tour ⑤

Detail, Buxton Opera House

THE PEAK DISTRICT'S natural beauty and sheep-grazed crags contrast with the factories of nearby valley towns. Designated Britain's first National Park in 1951, the area has two distinct types of landscape. In the south are the gently rolling hills of the limestone White Peak. To the north, west and east are the wild, heather-clad moorlands of the Dark Peak peat bogs, superimposed on millstone grit.

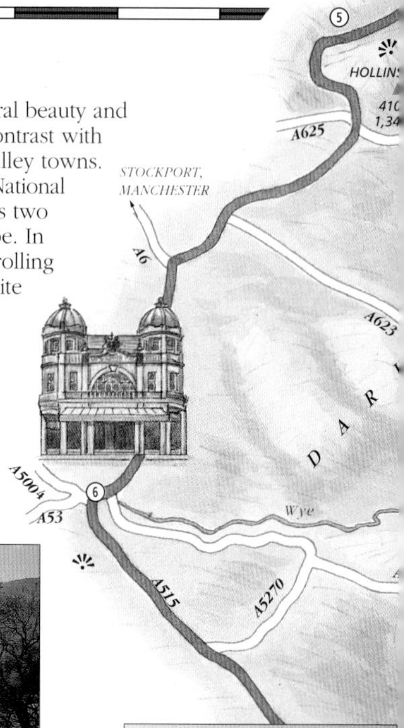

STOCKPORT, MANCHESTER

Edale ⑤

The high, dangerous peaks of scenic Edale mark the starting point of the 256 mile (412 km) Pennine Way footpath *(see p32)*.

Buxton ⑥

This lovely spa town's opera house *(see p320)* is known as the "theatre in the hills" because of its magnificent setting.

TIPS FOR DRIVERS

Tour length: *40 miles (60 km).*
Stopping-off points: *There are refreshments at Crich National Tramway Museum and Arkwright's Mill in Cromford. Eyam has good old-fashioned tea shops. The Nag's Head in Edale is a charming Tudor inn. Buxton has many pubs and cafés. (See also pp636–7.)*

Arbor Low ⑦

This stone circle, known as the "Stonehenge of the North", dates from around 2000 BC and consists of 46 recumbent stones enclosed by a ditch.

KEY

▬▬▬	Tour route
═══	Other roads
☀	Viewpoint

Dovedale ⑧

Popular Dovedale is the prettiest of the Peak District's river valleys, with its stepping stones, thickly wooded slopes and wind-sculpted rocks. Izaac Walton (1593–1683), author of *The Compleat Angler*, used to fish here.

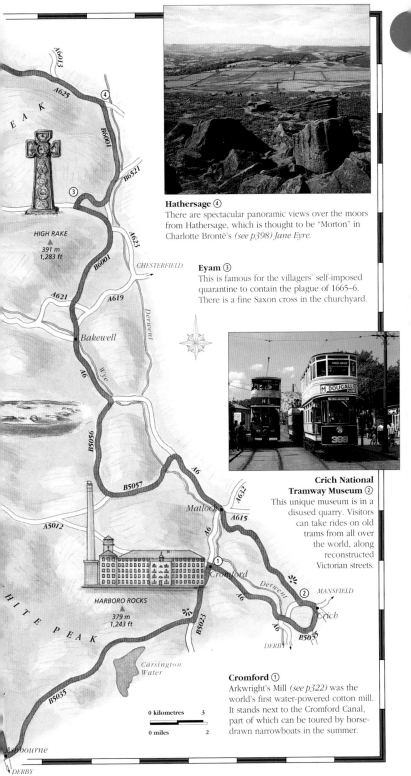

Hathersage ④
There are spectacular panoramic views over the moors from Hathersage, which is thought to be "Morton" in Charlotte Brontë's *(see p398) Jane Eyre.*

Eyam ③
This is famous for the villagers' self-imposed quarantine to contain the plague of 1665–6. There is a fine Saxon cross in the churchyard.

Crich National Tramway Museum ②
This unique museum is in a disused quarry. Visitors can take rides on old trams from all over the world, along reconstructed Victorian streets.

Cromford ①
Arkwright's Mill *(see p322)* was the world's first water-powered cotton mill. It stands next to the Cromford Canal, part of which can be toured by horse-drawn narrowboats in the summer.

HIGH RAKE
391 m
1,283 ft

HARBORO ROCKS
379 m
1,243 ft

Bakewell

Matlock

Cromford

Crich

MANSFIELD

CHESTERFIELD

Carsington Water

0 kilometres 3

0 miles 2

Ashbourne

DERBY

Street-by-Street: Lincoln ❼

Carving in Angel Choir

Sᴜʀʀᴏᴜɴᴅᴇᴅ ʙʏ the flat landscape of the Fens, Lincoln rises dramatically on a cliff above the River Witham, the three towers of its massive cathedral visible from afar. The Romans *(see pp44–5)* founded the first fortress here in AD 50. By the time of the Norman Conquest *(see p47)*, Lincoln was one of the most important cities in England (after London, Winchester and York). The city's wealth was due to its strategic importance for the export of wool from the Lincolnshire Wolds to Europe. Lincoln has managed to retain much of its historic character. Many remarkable medieval buildings have survived, most of which are along the aptly named Steep Hill, leading to the cathedral.

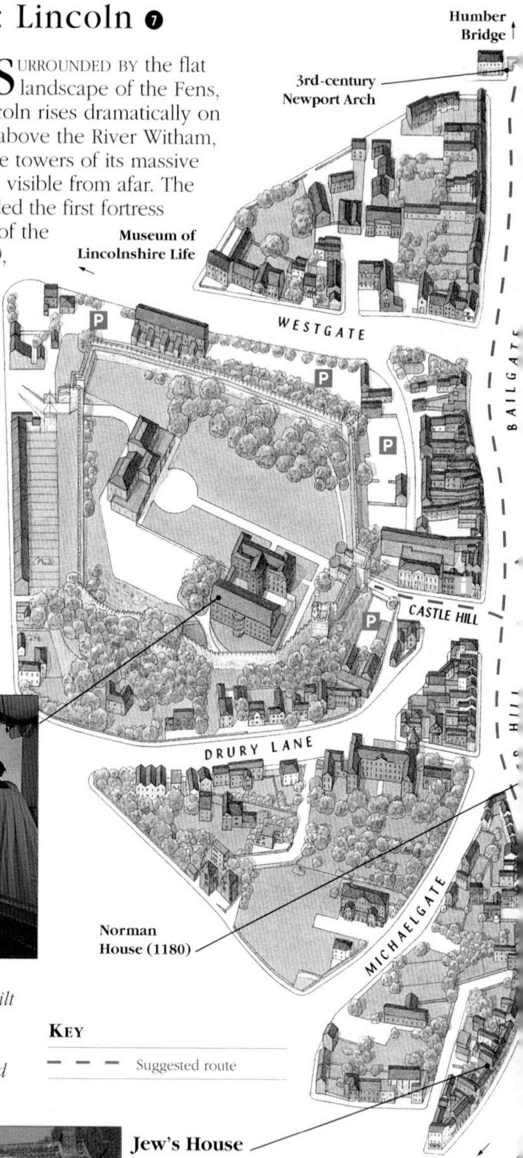

Humber Bridge ↑

3rd-century Newport Arch

Museum of Lincolnshire Life

WESTGATE

BAILGATE

CASTLE HILL

STEEP HILL

DRURY LANE

MICHAELGATE

Norman House (1180)

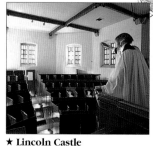

★ Lincoln Castle
The early Norman castle, rebuilt at intervals, acted as the city prison from 1787–1878. The chapel's coffin-like pews served to remind felons of their fate.

Kᴇʏ

— — — Suggested route

Jew's House
Lincoln had a large medieval Jewish community. This mid-12th-century stone house, one of the oldest of its kind, was owned by a Jewish merchant.

15th-century Stonebow Gate and railway station

| 0 metres | | 100 |
| 0 yards | | 100 |

Sᴛᴀʀ Sɪɢʜᴛs

★ **Lincoln Castle**

★ **Lincoln Cathedral**

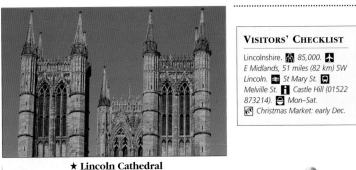

VISITORS' CHECKLIST

Lincolnshire. 🏛 85,000. ✈
E Midlands, 51 miles (82 km) SW
Lincoln. 🚇 St Mary St. 🚌
Melville St. 🛈 Castle Hill (01522
873214). 🖉 Mon–Sat.
🎄 Christmas Market: early Dec.

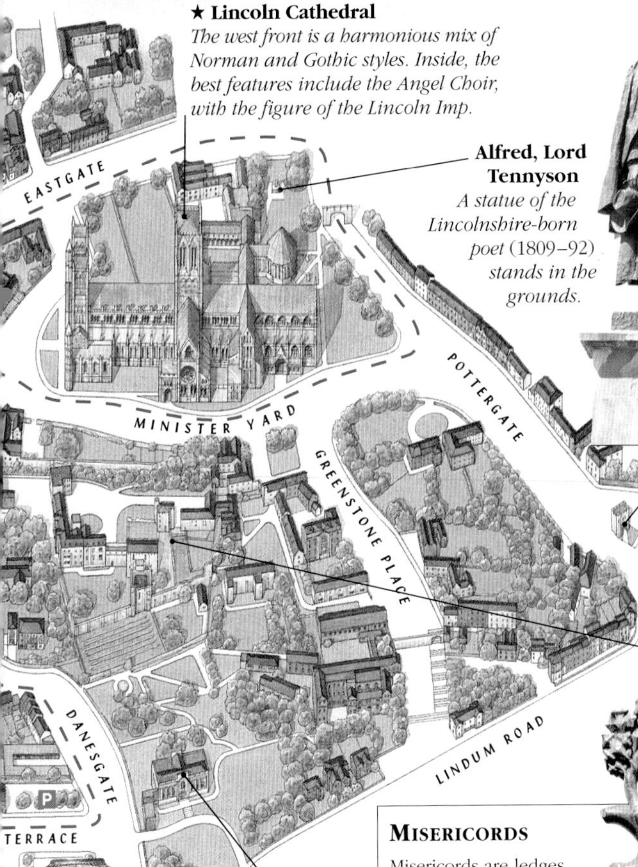

★ Lincoln Cathedral
*The west front is a harmonious mix of
Norman and Gothic styles. Inside, the
best features include the Angel Choir,
with the figure of the Lincoln Imp.*

EASTGATE

MINISTER YARD

GREENSTONE PLACE

POTTERGATE

DANESGATE

TERRACE

LINDUM ROAD

**Alfred, Lord
Tennyson**
*A statue of the
Lincolnshire-born
poet (1809–92)
stands in the
grounds.*

**The 14th-century
Pottergate Arch**

Arboretum

**Ruins of
Bishop's Palace**

**Coach
station**

Usher Art Gallery
*This is packed with
clocks, ceramics,
and silver. There
are paintings
by Peter de
Wint (1784–
1849) and
JMW Turner
(see p93).*

MISERICORDS

Misericords are ledges
that project from the
underside of the hinged
seat of a choir stall, which
provide support while standing.
Lincoln Cathedral's
misericords in the early
Perpendicular-style canopied
choir stalls are some of the best
in England. The wide variety of
subjects includes parables, fables,
myths, biblical scenes and irrev-
erent images from daily life.

**St Francis
of Assisi**

One of a pair of lions

Burghley House ⓑ

Portrait of Sir Isaac Newton, Billiard Room

WILLIAM CECIL, 1ST LORD BURGHLEY (1520–98) was Queen Elizabeth I's adviser and confidant for 40 years. He built the wonderfully dramatic Burghley House in 1560–87, probably designing it himself. The roof line bristles with stone pyramids, chimneys disguised as Classical columns and towers shaped like pepper pots. The busy skyline only resolves itself into a symmetrical pattern when viewed from the west, where a lime tree stands, one of many planted by Capability Brown *(see p22)* when the surrounding deer park was landscaped in 1760. Burghley's interior is lavishly decorated with Italian paintings of Greek gods enacting their dramas across the walls and ceiling.

★ Old Kitchen
Gleaming copper pans hang from the walls of the fan-vaulted kitchen, little altered since the Tudor period.

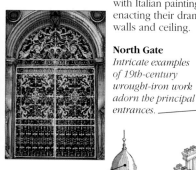

North Gate
Intricate examples of 19th-century wrought-iron work adorn the principal entrances.

The Billiard Room
has many fine portraits inset in oak panelling.

Cupolas were very fashionable details, inspired by European Renaissance architecture.

A chimney has been disguised as a Classical column.

Mullioned windows were added in 1683 when glass became less expensive.

The Gatehouse, with its side turrets, is a typical feature of the "prodigy" houses of the Tudor era *(see p288)*.

West Front
Featuring the Burghley crest, the West Front was finished in 1577 and formed the original main entrance.

STAR SIGHTS

★ **Old Kitchen**

★ **Heaven Room**

★ **Hell Staircase**

VISITORS' CHECKLIST

Off A1 SE of Stamford, Lincolnshire.
01780 752451. Stamford.
Apr–mid-Oct: 11am–4:30pm daily. one day Sep (for horse trials). limited.

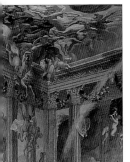

★ Heaven Room
Gods tumble from the sky, and satyrs and nymphs play on the walls and ceiling in this masterpiece by Antonio Verrio (1639–1707).

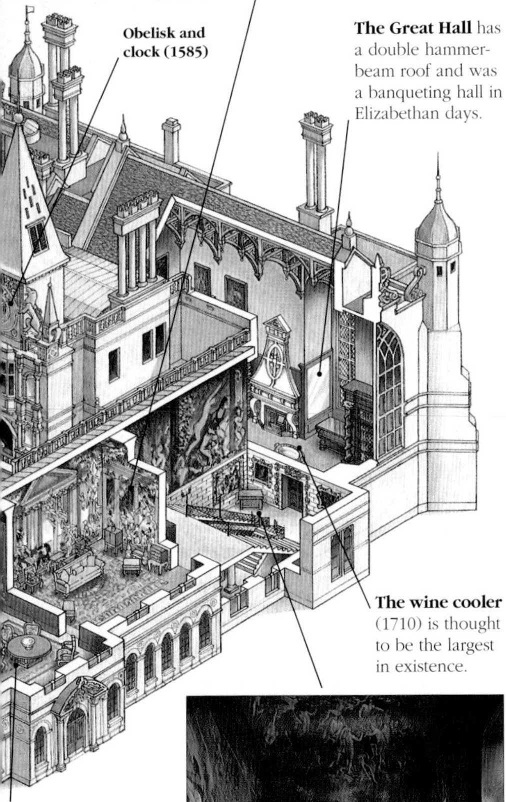

Obelisk and clock (1585)

The Great Hall has a double hammer-beam roof and was a banqueting hall in Elizabethan days.

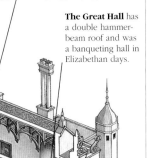

The wine cooler (1710) is thought to be the largest in existence.

The Fourth George Room, one of a suite, is panelled in oak stained with ale.

★ Hell Staircase
Verrio painted the ceiling to show Hell as the mouth of a cat crammed with tormented sinners. The staircase, of local stone, was installed in 1786.

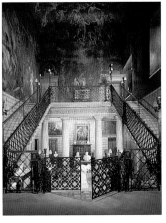

Stamford 9

Lincolnshire. *18,000.*
27 St Mary's St (01780 755611).
Fri. www.skdc.com

STAMFORD is a showpiece town, famous for its many churches and its Georgian townhouses. Stamford retains a medieval street plan, with a warren of winding streets and cobbled alleys.

The spires of the medieval churches (five survive of the original 11) give Stamford the air of a miniature Oxford.

Barn Hill, leading up from All Saints Church, is the best place for a view of Stamford's Georgian architecture in all its variety. Below it is Broad Street, where the **Stamford Museum** covers the history of the town. By far the most popular exhibit is a waxwork of Britain's fattest man, Daniel Lambert, who was 336 kg (53 stone) and died while attending Stamford Races in 1809.

Stamford Museum
Broad St. *01780 766317.*
Apr–Sep: daily. (Sun: pm); Oct–Mar: Mon–Sat. *25, 26 Dec.*
limited.

Northampton 10

Northamptonshire. *187,000.*
St Giles Square (01604 622677). *Tue–Sat (Thu: antiques).*
www.northampton.gov.uk

THIS MARKET TOWN was once a centre for shoe-making, and the **Central Museum and Art Gallery** holds the world's largest collection of footwear. One of many fine old buildings is the Victorian Gothic **Guildhall**. Six miles west of the town is **Althorp House**, family home of Diana Princess of Wales. Visitors can tour the house, grounds, and see her island resting place.

Central Museum and Art Gallery
Guildhall Rd. *01604 238548.*
daily (Sun: pm). *25, 26 Dec.*

Althorp House
Great Brington (off A428). *0870 1679000.* *Jul–Aug daily.*
www.althorp.com

THE NORTH
COUNTRY

The North Country at a Glance

RUGGED COASTLINES, spectacular walks and climbs, magnificent stately homes and breathtaking cathedrals all have their place in the north of England, with its dramatic history of Roman rule, Saxon invasion, Viking attacks and border skirmishes. Reminders of the industrial revolution are found in towns such as Halifax, Liverpool and Manchester, and peace and inspiration in the dramatic scenery of the Lake District, with its awe-inspiring mountains and waters.

Hadrian's Wall (see pp408–9), *built around 120 to protect Roman Britain from the Picts to the north, cuts through rugged Northumberland National Park scenery.*

NORTHUMB
(see pp400–4

Northumbe

Durl

The Lake District (see pp340–57) *is a combination of superb peaks, tumbling rivers and falls and shimmering lakes such as Wast Water.*

Cumbria

Yorkshire Dales National Park (see pp370–72) *creates a delightful environment for walking and touring the farming landscape, scattered with attractive villages such as Thwaite, in Swaledale.*

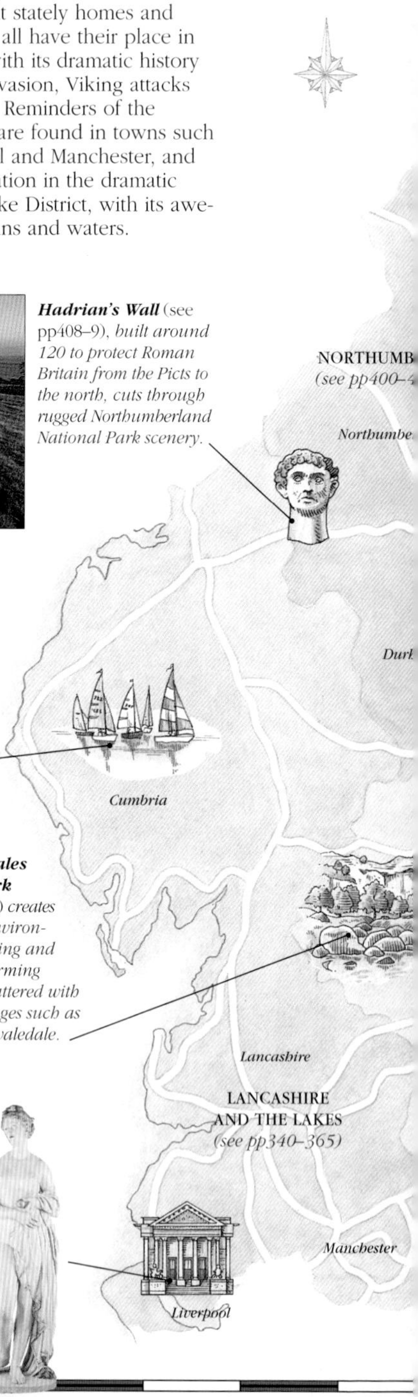

Lancashire

LANCASHIRE AND THE LAKES
(see pp340–365)

The Walker Art Gallery (see pp364–5) *in Liverpool is one of the jewels in the artistic crown of the north, with an internationally renowned collection ranging from Old Masters to modern art. Sculpture includes John Gibson's* Tinted Venus *(c.1851–6).*

Manchester

Liverpool

◁ **The 11th-century Alnwick Castle, Alnwick, Northumberland, from across the River Aln**

Durham Cathedral (see pp414–5), *a striking Norman structure with an innovative southern choir aisle and fine stained glass, has towered over the city of Durham since 995.*

Fountains Abbey (see pp376–7), *one of the finest religious buildings in the north, was founded in the 12th century by monks who desired simplicity and austerity. Later the abbey became extremely wealthy.*

Castle Howard (see pp384–5), *a triumph of Baroque architecture, offers many magnificent settings, including this Museum Room (1805–10), designed by CH Tatham.*

Cleveland

North Yorkshire

ORKSHIRE
ND THE
IUMBER
REGION
(pp366–399)

Leeds

East Riding of Yorkshire

York (see pp390–95) *is a city of historical treasures, ranging from the medieval to Georgian. Its magnificent minster has a large collection of stained glass and the medieval city walls are well preserved. Other sights include churches, narrow alleyways and notable museums.*

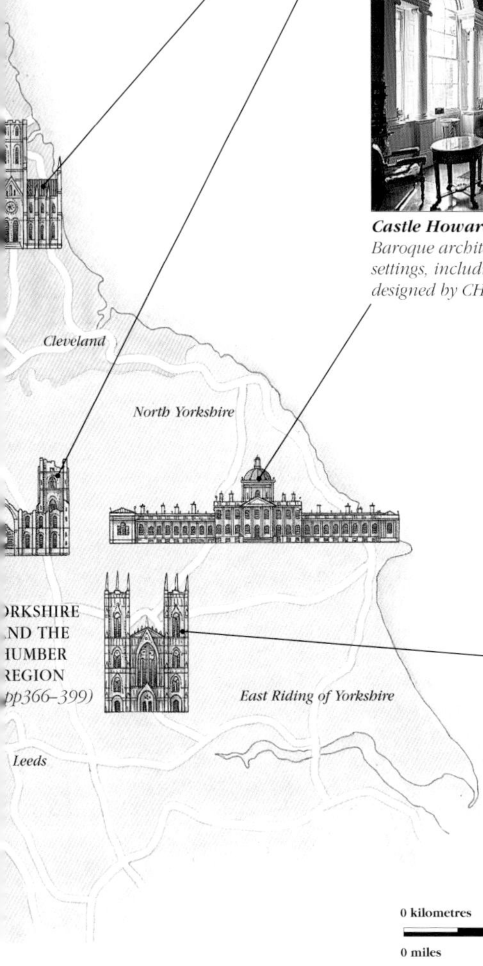

0 kilometres   25

0 miles   25

The Industrial Revolution in the North

THE FACE OF NORTHERN ENGLAND in the 19th century was dramatically altered by the development of the coal mining, textile and shipbuilding industries. Lancashire, Northumberland and the West Riding *(see p367)* of Yorkshire all experienced population growth and migration to cities. The hardships of urban life were partly relieved by the actions of several wealthy industrial philanthropists, but many people lived in extremely deprived conditions. Although most traditional industries have now declined sharply or disappeared as demand has moved elsewhere, a growing tourist industry has developed in many of the former industrial centres.

Back-to-backs or colliers' rows, such as these houses at Easington, were provided by colliery owners from the 1800s onwards. They comprised two small rooms for cooking and sleeping, and an outside toilet

1815 Sir Humphrey Davy invented a safety oil lamp for miners. Light shone through a cylindrical gauze sheet which prevented the heat of the flame igniting methane gas in the mine. Thousands of miners benefited from this device.

Coal mining was a family industry in the North of England with women and children working alongside the men.

1750		1800
PRE-STEAM		**STEAM AGE**
1750		1800

1781 Leeds–Liverpool Canal opened. The building of canals facilitated the movement of raw materials and finished products, and aided the process of mechanization immeasurably.

1830 Liverpool Manchester r opened, connecting the biggest cities of London. Within a mor railway carried passe

Halifax's Piece Hall (see p399), restored in 1976, is the most impressive surviving example of industrial architecture in northern England. It is the only complete 18th-century cloth market building in Yorkshire. Merchants sold measures of cloth known as "pieces" from rooms lining the cloisters inside.

Hebden Bridge (see p398), a typical West Riding textile mill town jammed into the narrow Calder Valley, typifies a pattern of workers' houses surrounding a central mill. The town benefited from its position when the Rochdale Canal (1804) and then the railway (1841) took advantage of this relatively low-level route over the Pennines.

Saltaire (see p397) *was a model village built by the wealthy cloth merchant and mill-owner Sir Titus Salt (1803–76), for the benefit of his workers. Seen here in the 1870s, it included houses and facilities such as shops, gardens and sportsfields, with almshouses, a hospital, school and chapel. A disciplinarian, Salt banned alcohol and pubs from Saltaire.*

***George Hudson** (1800–71) built the first railway station in York (see p394) in 1840–42. In the 1840s he owned more than a quarter of the railways in Britain and was known as the "railway king".*

1842 Coal Mines Act prevented women and children from working in harsh conditions in the mines.

***Port Sunlight** (see p365) was founded by William Hesketh Lever (1851–1925) to provide housing for workers at his Sunlight soap factory. Between 1889 and 1914 he built 800 cottages. Amenities included a pool.*

Strikes to improve working conditions were common. Violence flared in July 1893 when colliery owners locked miners out of their pits and stopped their pay after the Miners' Federation resisted a 25 per cent wage cut. Over 300,000 men struggled without pay until November, when work resumed at the old rate.

1850		1900
FULL MECHANIZATION		
1850		1900

***Power loom weaving** transforms the textile industry while creating unemployment among skilled hand loom weavers. By the 1850s, the West Riding had 30,000 power looms, used in cotton and woollen mills. Of 79,000 workers, over half were to be found in Bradford alone.*

***Furness dry dock** was built in the 1890s when the shipbuilding industry moved north, in search of cheap labour and materials. Barrow-in-Furness, Glasgow (see pp502–5) and Tyne and Wear (see p410) were the new centres.*

***Joseph Rowntree** (1836–1925) founded his chocolate factory in York in 1892, having formerly worked with George Cadbury. As Quakers, the Rowntrees believed in the social welfare of their workers (establishing a model village in 1904), and, with Terry's confectionary (1767), they made a vast contribution to York's prosperity. Today, Nestlé Rowntree is the world's largest chocolate factory and York is Britain's chocolate capital.*

North Country Abbeys

NORTHERN ENGLAND has some of the finest and best preserved religious houses in Europe. Centres of prayer, learning and power in the Middle Ages, the larger of these were designated abbeys and were governed by an abbot. Most were located in rural areas, considered appropriate for a spiritual and contemplative life. Viking raiders had destroyed many Anglo-Saxon religious houses in the 8th and 9th centuries *(see pp46–7)* and it was not until William the Conqueror founded the Benedictine Selby Abbey in 1069 that monastic life revived in the north. New orders, Augustinians in particular, arrived from the Continent and by 1500 Yorkshire had 83 monasteries.

Cistercian monk

Ruins of St Mary's Abbey today

The Liberty of St Mary was the name given to the land around the abbey, almost a city within a city. Here, the abbot had his own market, fair, prison and gallows – all exempt from the city authorities.

ST MARY'S ABBEY

Founded in York in 1086, this Benedictine abbey was one of the wealthiest in Britain. Its involvement in the wool trade in York and the granting of royal and papal privileges and land led to a relaxing of standards by the early 12th century. The abbot was even allowed to dress in the same style as a bishop, and was raised by the pope to the status of a "mitred abbot". As a result, 13 monks left in 1132, to found Fountains Abbey *(see pp376–7)*.

Gatehouse and St Olave's church

Interval tower

Water tower

Hospitium or guest house

MONASTERIES AND LOCAL LIFE

As one of the wealthiest landowning sections of society, the monasteries played a vital role in the local economy. They provided employment, particularly in agriculture, and dominated the wool trade, England's largest export during the Middle Ages. By 1387 two thirds of all wool exported from England passed through St Mary's Abbey, the largest wool trader in York .

Cistercian monks tilling their land

WHERE TO SEE ABBEYS TODAY

Fountains Abbey *(see pp376–7)*, founded by Benedictine monks and later taken over by Cistercians, is the most famous of the numerous abbeys in the region. Rievaulx *(see p379)*, Byland *(see p378)* and Furness *(see p356)* were all founded by the Cistercians, and Furness became the second wealthiest Cistercian house in England after Fountains. Whitby Abbey *(see p382)*, sacked by the Vikings, was later rebuilt by the Benedictine order. Northumberland is famous for its early Anglo-Saxon monasteries, such as Ripon, Lastingham and Lindisfarne *(see pp404–5)*.

Mount Grace Priory *(see p380), founded in 1398, is the best-preserved Carthusian house in England. The former individual gardens and cells of each monk are still clearly visible.*

THE DISSOLUTION OF THE MONASTERIES (1536–40)

By the early 16th century, the monasteries owned one-sixth of all English land and their annual income were four times that of the Crown. Henry VIII ordered the closure of all religious houses in 1536, acquiring their wealth in the process. His attempt at dissolution provoked a large uprising of Catholic northerners led by Robert Aske later that year. The rebellion failed and Aske and others were executed for conspiracy. The dissolution continued under Thomas Cromwell, who became known as "the hammer of the monks".

Thomas Cromwell (c.1485–1549)

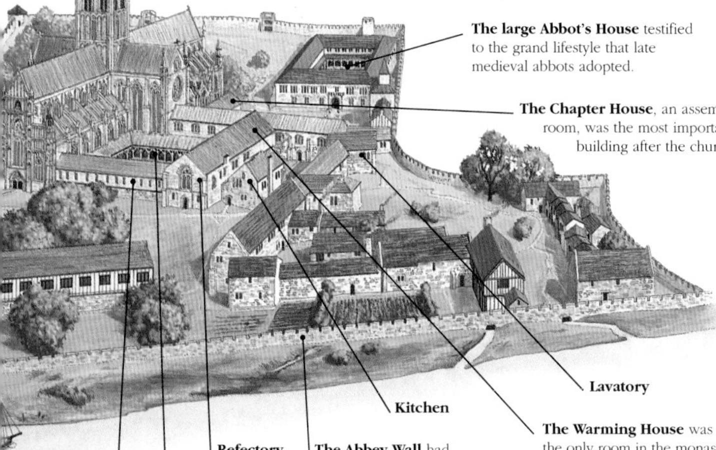

The large Abbot's House testified to the grand lifestyle that late medieval abbots adopted.

The Chapter House, an assembly room, was the most important building after the church.

Lavatory

Kitchen

The Warming House was the only room in the monastery, apart from the kitchen, which had a fire.

Refectory

The Abbey Wall had battlements added in 1318 to protect it against raids by Scottish armies.

Common parlour

Cloister

Kirkham Priory, an Augustinian foundation of the 1120s, enjoys a tranquil setting on the banks of the River Derwent, near Malton. The finest feature of the ruined site is the 13th-century gatehouse which leads into the priory complex.

Kirkstall Abbey was founded in 1152 by monks from Fountains Abbey. The well-preserved ruins of this Cistercian house near Leeds include the church, the late-Norman chapter house and the abbot's lodging. This evening view was painted by Thomas Girtin (1775–1802).

...sby Abbey lies beside the River Swale, outside the pretty market town of Richmond. Among the ...mains of this Premonstratensian ...house, founded in 1155, are the ...h-century refectory and sleeping ...rters and 14th-century gatehouse.

The Geology of the Lake District

Piece of Lake District slate

THE LAKE DISTRICT contains some of England's most spectacular scenery. Concentrated in just 900 sq miles (231 sq km) are the highest peaks, deepest valleys and longest lakes in the country. Today's landscape has changed little since the end of the Ice Age 10,000 years ago, the last major event in Britain's geological history. But the glaciated hills which were revealed by the retreating ice were once part of a vast mountain-chain whose remains can also be found in North America. The mountains were first raised by the gradual fusion of two ancient landmasses which, for millions of years, formed a single continent. Eventually the continent broke into two, forming Europe and America, separated by the widening Atlantic Ocean.

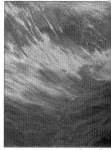

Honister Pass, with its distinctive U-shape, is an example of a glaciated valley, once completely filled with ice.

GEOLOGICAL HISTORY

The oldest rock formed as sediment under an ocean called Iapetus. Some 450 million years ago, Earth's internal movements made two continents collide, and the ocean disappear.

1 *The collision buckled the former sea bed into a mountain range. Magma rose from Earth's mantle, altered the sediments and cooled into volcanic rock.*

2 *In the Ice Age, glaciers slowly excavated huge rock basins in the mountainsides, dragging debris to the valley floor. Frost sculpted the summits.*

3 *The glaciers retreated 10,000 years ago, their meltwaters forming lakes in valleys dammed by debris. As the climate improved, plants colonized the fells.*

RADIATING LAKES

The diversity of lakeland scenery owes much to its geology: hard volcanic rocks in the central lakes give rise to rugged hills, while soft slates to the north produce a more rounded topography. The lakes form a radial pattern, spreading out from a central volcanic rock zone.

Scafell Pike is the highest peak in England. One of the three Scafell Pikes, its two neighbours are Broad Crag and Ill Crag.

▲ Great Gable

▲ Old Man of Coniston

Coniston Water

Wast Water is the deepest of the lakes. Its southeastern cliffs are streaked with granite scree – the debris formed each year as rock shattered by the winter frost tumbles down during the spring thaw.

MAN ON THE MOUNTAIN

The sheltered valley floors with their benign climate and fertile soils are ideal for settlement. Farmhouses, dry-stone walls, pasture and sheep pens are an integral part of the landscape. Higher up, the absence of trees and bracken are the result of wind and a cooler climate. Old mine workings and tracks are the relics of once-flourishing industries.

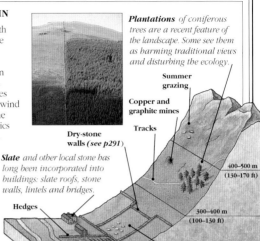

Plantations of coniferous trees are a recent feature of the landscape. Some see them as harming traditional views and disturbing the ecology.

Summer grazing

Copper and graphite mines

Tracks

400–500 m (130–170 ft)

300–400 m (100–130 ft)

Dry-stone walls (see p291)

Slate and other local stone has long been incorporated into buildings: slate roofs, stone walls, lintels and bridges.

Hedges

Sheep pens for winter grazing

▲ Blencathra

▲ Helvellyn

Ullswater

High Street

Windermere

Skiddaw is composed of slate, formed when the muddy sediment of the ancient ocean floor was altered by extreme pressure.

Striding Edge is a long, twisting ridge which leads to the summit of Helvellyn. It was sharpened by the widening of the valleys on either side caused by the build up of glaciers.

The Langdale Pikes are remnants of the volcanic activity which once erupted in the area. They are made of hard igneous rocks, known as Borrowdale Volcanics. Unlike the Skiddaw Slates, they have not eroded smoothly, so they leave a craggy skyline.

MERSEYSIDE
MARITIME
MUSEUM

LANCASHIRE AND THE LAKES

CUMBRIA · LANCASHIRE

T HE LANDSCAPE PAINTER *John Constable (1776–1837) declared that the Lake District, now visited by 18 million people annually, had "the finest scenery that ever was". The Normans built many religious houses here, and William II created estates for English barons. Today, the National Trust is its most important landowner.*

Within the 30 mile (45 km) radius of the Lake District lies an astonishing number of fells and lakes. Today, all looks peaceful, but from the Roman occupation to the Middle Ages, the northwest was a turbulent area, as successive kings and rulers fought over the territory. Historians can revel in the various Celtic monuments, Roman remains, stately homes and monastic ruins. Although the scenery is paramount, there are many outdoor activities as well as spectator sports, such as Cumbrian wrestling, and wildlife to observe.

Lancashire's portfolio of tourist attractions includes the fine county town of Lancaster, bright Blackpool with its autumn illuminations and fairground attractions, and the peaceful seaside beaches to the south. Inland, the most appealing regions are the Forest of Bowland, a sparse expanse of heathery grouse moor, and the picturesque Ribble Valley.

Further south still are the industrial conurbations of Manchester and Merseyside, where the attractions are more urban. There are many fine Victorian buildings in Manchester, where the industrial quarter of Castlefield has been revitalized. Liverpool, with its restored Albert Dock, is best known as the seaport city of the Beatles. It has a lively club scene and is increasingly used as a film location. Both cities have good art galleries and museums.

Jetty at Grasmere, one of the most popular regions of the Lake District

◁ Restored Albert Dock, lining the River Mersey in Liverpool

Exploring Lancashire and the Lakes

T HE LAKE DISTRICT'S natural scenery outweighs
any of its man-made attractions. Its natural
features are the result of geological upheavals
over millennia *(see pp338–9)*, and four of its
peaks are higher than 1,000 m (3,300 ft).
Human influences have left their mark
too: the main activities are quarrying,
mining, farming and tourism.

The Lakes are most crowded in
summer when activities include
lake trips and hill-walking. The best
bases are Keswick and Ambleside,
while there are also good hotels on
the shores of Windermere and
Ullswater and in the Cartmel area.

Lancashire's Forest of Bowland is
an attractive place to explore on foot,
with picturesque villages. Further
south, Manchester and Liverpool have
excellent museums and galleries.

Canoeing, a popular sporting pastime, at Derwent
Water in the Northern Fells and Lakes area

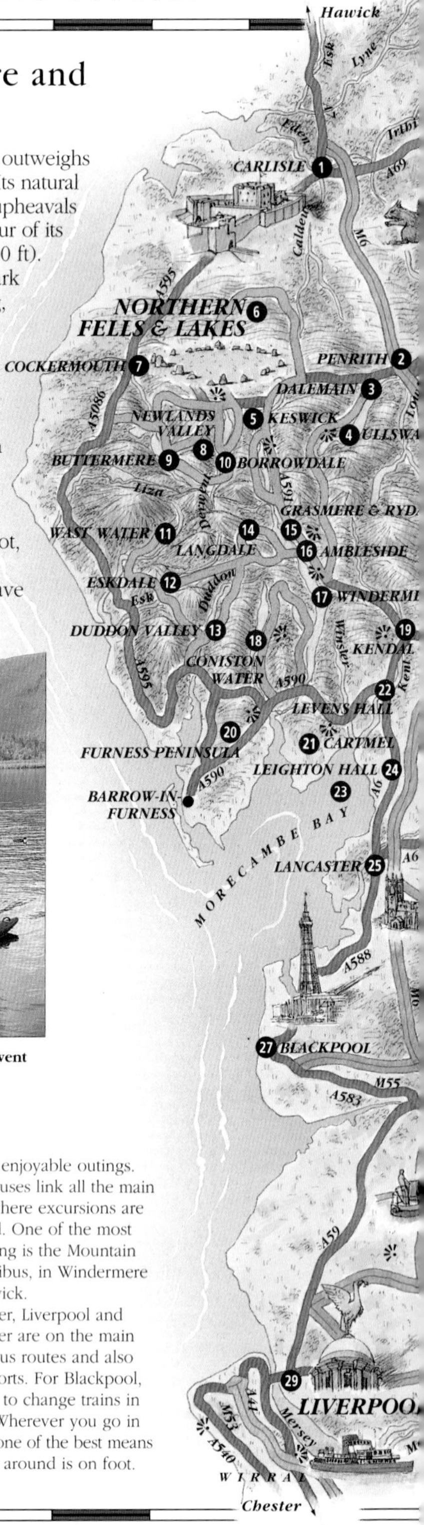

GETTING AROUND

For many, the first glimpse of
the Lake District is from the
M6 near Shap Fell, but the A6
is a more dramatic route. You
can reach Windermere by
train, but you need to change
at Oxenholme, on the main
InterCity route from Euston to
Carlisle. Penrith also has rail
services and bus links into the
Lakes. L'al Ratty, the miniature
railway up Eskdale, and the
Lakeside & Haverthwaite
railway, which connects with
the steamers on Windermere,

make for enjoyable outings.
Regular buses link all the main
centres where excursions are
organized. One of the most
enterprising is the Mountain
Goat minibus, in Windermere
and Keswick.

Lancaster, Liverpool and
Manchester are on the main
rail and bus routes and also
have airports. For Blackpool,
you need to change trains in
Preston. Wherever you go in
the area, one of the best means
of getting around is on foot.

View over Crummock Water, north of Buttermere, one of the quieter Western Lakes

SIGHTS AT A GLANCE

Ambleside 16
Blackpool 27
Borrowdale 10
Buttermere 9
Carlisle 1
Cartmel 21
Cockermouth 7
Coniston Water 18
Dalemain 3
Duddon Valley 13
Eskdale 12
Furness Peninsula 20
Grasmere and Rydal 15
Kendal 19
Keswick 5
Lancaster 25
Langdale 14
Leighton Hall 24
Levens Hall 22
Liverpool pp362–5 29
Manchester pp360–61 28
Morecambe Bay 23
Newlands Valley 8
Northern Fells and Lakes pp346–7 6
Penrith 2
Ribble Valley 26
Ullswater 4
Wast Water 11
Windermere 17

KEY

▬ Motorway
▬ Major road
▬ Scenic route
- - Scenic path
▬ River
☼ Viewpoint

0 kilometres 20

0 miles 10

SEE ALSO

• *Where to Stay* pp559–61

• *Where to Eat* pp595–7

Preserved docks and Liver Building, Liverpool

Carlisle ❶

Cumbria. 🏘 102,000. ☒ 🚆 🚍
ℹ️ *The Old Town Hall, Green Market
(01228 625600).* 🖊 www.historic-
carlisle.org.uk

DUE TO ITS proximity to the
Scottish border, this city
has long been a defensive site.
Known as Luguvalium
by the Romans, it was
an outpost of Hadrian's
Wall *(see pp408–9).*
Carlisle was sacked and
pillaged repeatedly
by the Danes, the
Normans and border
raiders, and suffered
damage as a Royalist
stronghold under
Cromwell *(see p52).*
Today, Carlisle is the
capital of Cumbria. In its
centre are the timber-
framed Guildhall and
market cross, and forti-
fications still exist around
its West Walls, drum-
towered gates and its
Norman **castle**. The
castle tower has a small
museum devoted to the
King's Own Border Regi-
ment. The cathedral,
originally an Augustinian
priory, dates from 1122.
One of its features is a
decorative east window.
Carlisle's **Tullie House
Museum** imaginatively
recreates the city's past

**Saxon iron sword in the
Tullie House Museum**

with sections on Roman
history and Cumbrian wildlife.
Nearby lie the evocative ruins
of **Lanercost Priory** (c.1166).

♣ **Carlisle Castle**
Castle Way. 🎫 *01228 591922.* ◯
daily. ● *24–26 Dec, 1 Jan.* 🏷 ♿
limited. 🚻 ✔

🏛 **Tullie House Museum**
Castle St. 🎫 *01228 534781.* ◯ *daily
(Sun: pm).* ● *25, 26 Dec.* 🏷 ♿

♠ **Lanercost Priory**
Nr Brampton. 🎫 *016977 3030.*
◯ *Apr–Oct: daily.* 🏷 ♿ *limited.* 🚻

Penrith ❷

Cumbria. 🏘 15,000. ℹ️ *Robinson's
School, Middlegate (01768 867466).*
🚍 *Tue, Sat.* 🖊 www.visiteden.co.uk

TIMEWARP SHOPFRONTS on the
market square and a 14th-
century **castle** of sandstone
are Penrith's main attractions.
There are some strange hog-
back stones in St Andrew's
churchyard, allegedly a giant's

Façade of Hutton-in-the-Forest with medieval tower on the right

grave, and the 285 m (937 ft)
Beacon provides stunning
views of distant fells.

ENVIRONS: Just northeast of
Penrith at Little Salkeld is one
of the area's most notable
ancient monuments, a Bronze
Age circle (with 66 tall
stones) known as **Long Meg
and her Daughters**. Six
miles (9 km) northwest of
Penrith lies **Hutton-in-the-
Forest**. The oldest part of this
house is the 13th-century
tower, built to withstand Scots
raiders. Inside is a magnificent
Italianate staircase, a sumptuously panelled 17th-century
Long Gallery, a delicately
stuccoed Cupid Room dating
from the 1740s, and several
Victorian rooms. Outside, you
can walk around the walled
garden and topiary terraces, or
explore the woods.

♣ **Penrith Castle**
Ullswater Rd. ◯ *daily.* ♿ *in grounds.*

🏯 **Hutton-in-the-Forest**
Off B5305. 🎫 *017684 84449.*
House ◯ *Easter–Sep: Thu, Fri, Sun &
public hols (pm).* **Grounds** ◯ *Sun–
Fri.* ● *25 Dec.* 🏷 ♿ *limited.*
🚍 🚻

Dalemain ❸

Penrith, Cumbria. 🎫 *017684 86450.*
🚆 🚍 *Penrith then taxi.* ◯ *Apr–
Sep: Sun–Thu.* 🏷 ♿ *limited.* 🚻 🚍

A SEEMLY GEORGIAN façade
gives this fine house near
Ullswater the impression of
architectural unity, but hides
a greatly altered medieval and
Elizabethan structure with a
maze of rambling passages.
Public rooms include a superb
Chinese drawing room with
hand-painted wallpaper, and

TRADITIONAL CUMBRIAN SPORTS

Cumberland wrestling is one of the most interesting sports to
watch in the summer months. The combatants, often clad in
longjohns and embroidered velvet pants, clasp one another
in an armlock and attempt to topple each other over. Technique and good balance outweigh physical force. Other traditional Lakeland sports include fell-racing, a gruelling test of
speed and stamina up and down local peaks at ankle-
breaking speed. Hound-trailing is also a popular sport in
which specially bred
hounds follow an
aniseed trail over the
hills. Sheep-dog trials,
steam fairs, flower
shows and gymkhanas
take place in summer.
The Egremont Crab
Fair in September
holds events such as
greasy-pole climbing.

Cumberland wrestlers

Sheep resting at Glenridding, on the southwest shore of Ullswater

a panelled 18th-century drawing room. Several small museums occupy various outbuildings, and the gardens contain a fine collection of fragrant shrub roses and a huge silver fir.

Sumptuous Chinese drawing room at Dalemain

Ullswater ❹

Cumbria. Penrith. Main car park, Glenridding, Penrith (017684 82414).

OFTEN CONSIDERED the most beautiful of all Cumbria's lakes, Ullswater stretches from gentle farmland near Penrith to dramatic hills and crags at its southern end. The main western shore road can be very busy. In summer, two restored Victorian steamers ply regularly from Pooley Bridge to Glenridding. One of the best walks crosses the eastern shore from Glenridding to Hallin Fell and the moorland of Martindale. The western side passes Gowbarrow, where Wordsworth's immortalized "host of golden daffodils" bloom in spring *(see p352)*.

Keswick ❺

Cumbria. 5,000. Moot Hall, Market Sq (017687 72645). www.keswicktic@lake-district.gov.uk

POPULAR AS A tourist venue since the advent of the railway in Victorian times, Keswick now has guest houses, a summer repertory theatre, outdoor equipment shops and a serious parking problem in high season. Its most striking central building is the **Moot Hall**, dating from 1813, now used as the tourist office. The town prospered on wool and leather until, in Tudor times, deposits of graphite were discovered. Mining then took over as the main industry and Keswick became an important centre for pencil manufacture. In World War II, hollow pencils were made to hide espionage maps on thin paper. The factory includes the **Pencil Museum** with interesting audiovisual shows. Among the many fine exhibits at the **Keswick Museum and Art Gallery** are the original manuscripts of Lakeland writers, musical stones and many other curiosities.

To the east of the town lies the ancient stone circle of Castlerigg, thought to be older than Stonehenge.

Pencil Museum
Carding Mill Lane. 017687 73626. daily. 25, 26 Dec, 1 Jan.

Keswick Museum and Art Gallery
Fitz Park, Station Rd. 017687 73263. Easter–Oct: daily.

Outdoor equipment shop in Keswick

Northern Fells and Lakes ⑥

MANY VISITORS praise this northern area of the Lake District National Park for its scenery and geological interest *(see pp338–9)*. It is ideal walking country, and nearby Derwent Water, Thirlmere and Bassenthwaite provide endless scenic views, rambles and opportunities for watersports. Large areas surrounding the regional centre of Keswick *(see p345)* are accessible only on foot, particularly the huge mass of hills known as Back of Skiddaw – located between Skiddaw and Caldbeck – or the Helvellyn range, east of Thirlmere.

The rare red squirrel, native to the area

The Whinlatter Pass is an easy route from Keswick to the foreste Lorton Vale. It gives a good view of Bassenthwaite Lake and a glimpse of Grisedale Pike.

Bassenthwaite is best vie from the east shore. The road passes through Dod Wood at the foot of Skidd

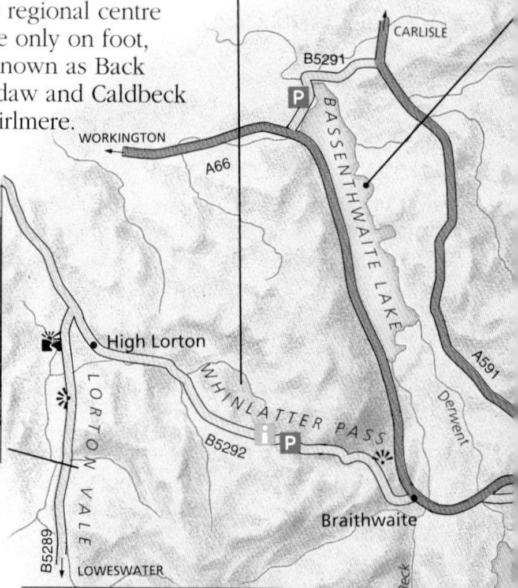

Lorton Vale
The lush, green farmland south of Cockermouth creates a marked contrast with the more rugged mountain landscapes of the central Lake District. In the village of Low Lorton is the private manor house of Lorton Hall, dating from the 15th century.

Derwent Water
Surrounded by woodland slopes and fells, this attractive oval lake is dotted with tiny islands. One of these was inhabited by St Herbert, a disciple of St Cuthbert (see p405), who lived there as a hermit until 687. A boat from Keswick provides a lake excursion.

THE MAJOR PEAKS

The Lake District hills are the highest in England. Although they seem small by Alpine or world standards, the scale of the surrounding terrain makes them look extremely grand. Some of the most important peaks are shown on the following pages. Each peak is regarded as having its own personality. This section shows the Skiddaw fells, which are north of Keswick.

Blencathra
Skiddaw
Grisedale Pike
Grasmoor
Knott Rigg
Helvellyn
Great Gable
High Street
West Water
Screes
Scafell
Hard Knott
The Old Man
of Coniston

KEY

⬛ From ① Blencathra to ② Cockermouth *(see opposite)*

⬛ From ③ Grisedale Pike to ④ the Old Man of Coniston *(see pp348–9)*

⬛ From ⑤ the Old Man of Coniston to ⑥ Windermere and Tarn Crag *(see pp350–51)*

— National Park boundary

VISITORS' CHECKLIST

Keswick, Cumbria. 🚉 Keswick.
🛈 Market Square, Keswick. ☎
017687 72645. **(NT) Castlerigg
Stone Circle** ◯ daily.

Skiddaw

*At 931 m (3,054 ft) Skiddaw is England's
fourth highest peak. Its rounded shape
makes it a manageable two-hour walk for
anyone reasonably fit.*

Blencathra, also
known as Saddleback
because of its twin
peaks (868 m; 2,847 ft),
is a challenging climb,
especially in winter.

St John's in the Vale

*This valley contains Castle
Rock for climbers, and its
old legends were used by
Sir Walter Scott (see
p498) in The Bridal
of Triermain. Lakeland
poet John Richardson is
buried in the churchyard.*

KEY

🛈	Information
▬▬	Major road
▭▭	Minor road
☀	Viewpoint

Thirlmere
was created
as a reservoir
to serve
Manchester
in 1879.

Castlerigg Stone Circle

*Described by Keats (see p129) as "a dismal
cirque of Druid stones upon a forlorn
moor", these ancient stones overlook
Skiddaw, Helvellyn and Crag Hill.*

| 0 kilometres | 5 |
| 0 miles | 3 |

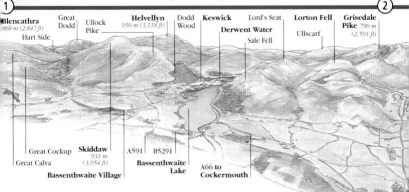

Blencathra
(868 m (2,847 ft))
Hart Side
Great
Dodd
Great Cockup
Great Calva
Ullock
Pike
Skiddaw
931 m
(3,054 ft)
Helvellyn
950 m (3,118 ft)
A591
B5291
Bassenthwaite
Lake
Bassenthwaite Village
Dodd
Wood
Keswick
Derwent Water
Sale Fell
A66 to
Cockermouth
Lord's Seat
Ullscarf
Lorton Fell
Grisedale
Pike 790 m
(2,591 ft)

Crummock Water, one of the quieter "western lakes"

Cockermouth ❼

Cumbria. 🏘 8,000. 🚆 Workington.
🚌 🛈 Town Hall, Market St (01900
822634). 🚌 Mon.

COLOURWASHED TERRACES and restored workers' cottages beside the river are especially attractive in the busy market town of Cockermouth, which dates from the 12th century. The place not to miss is the handsome **Wordsworth House**, in the Main Street, where the poet was born *(see p352)*. This fine Georgian building still contains a few of the family's possessions, and is furnished in the style of the late 18th century. Wordsworth mentions the attractive terraced garden, which overlooks the River Derwent, in his *Prelude*. The local parish church contains a Wordsworth memorial window. Cockermouth **castle** is partly ruined but still inhabited and not open to the public. The town also has small museums of printing, toys and a mineral collection, and an art gallery. The **Jennings Brewery**, founded in 1828, invites visitors for tours and tastings.

Kitchen, with an old range and tiled floor, at Wordsworth House

🏛 **Wordsworth House**
(NT) Main St. 📞 *01900 824805.*
⏰ *Apr–May, Sep, Oct: Mon–Fri, public hols (incl Sat), Jun–Aug: Mon–Sat.*
🔅 ♿ *gardens.* 📷 🚻
🍺 **Jennings Brewery**
Castle Brewery. 📞 *01900 821011.*
⏰ *Apr–Oct: daily.* 📷 🚻

Newlands Valley ❽

Cumbria. 🚆 Workington then bus. 🚌
Cockermouth. 🛈 Town Hall, Market
St, Cockermouth (01900 822634).

FROM THE gently wooded shores of Derwent Water, the Newlands Valley runs through a scattering of farms towards rugged heights of 335 m (1,100 ft) at the top of the pass, where steps lead to the waterfall, Moss Force. Grisedale Pike, Grasmoor and Knott Rigg all provide excellent fell walks, passing through bracken-covered land grazed by hardy sheep. Local mineral deposits of copper, graphite, lead and even small amounts of gold and silver were extensively mined here from Elizabethan times onwards. **Little Town** was used as a setting by Beatrix Potter *(see p353)* in *The Tale of Mrs Tiggywinkle*.

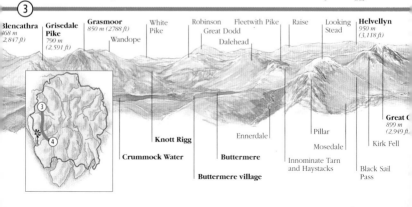

③

| Blencathra 868 m 2,847 ft) | Grisedale Pike 790 m (2,591 ft) | Grasmoor 850 m (2788 ft) Wandope | White Pike | Robinson Great Dodd Dalehead | Fleetwith Pike | Raise | Looking Stead | Helvellyn 950 m (3,118 ft) |

Knott Rigg

Crummock Water

Ennerdale

Buttermere

Buttermere village

Pillar

Mosedale

Innominate Tarn and Haystacks

Black Sail Pass

Great ○ 899 m (2,949 ft.

Kirk Fell

Buttermere **9**

Cumbria. 🚉 *Workington then bus.* 🚌 *Cockermouth.* 🛈 *Town Hall, Market St, Cockermouth (01900 822634).*

INTERLINKING WITH Crummock Water and Loweswater, Buttermere and its surroundings contain some of the most appealing countryside in the region. Often known as the "western lakes", the three are remote enough not to become too crowded. Buttermere is a jewel amid grand fells: High Stile, Red Pike and Haystacks. Here the ashes of the celebrated hill-walker and author of fell-walking books, AW Wainwright, are scattered.

The village of Buttermere, with its handful of houses and a couple of inns, is a popular starting point for walks round all three lakes. Loweswater is hardest to reach and therefore the quietest, surrounded by woods and gentle hills. Nearby Scale Force is the highest waterfall in the Lake District, plunging 36 m (120 ft).

Verdant valley of Borrowdale, a favourite with artists

Borrowdale **10**

Cumbria. 🚉 *Workington.* 🚌 *Cockermouth.* 🛈 *Town Hall, Market St, Cockermouth (01900 822634).*

THIS ROMANTIC VALLEY, subject of a myriad sketches and watercolours before photography stole the scene, lies beside the densely wooded shores of Derwent Water under towering crags. It is a popular trip from Keswick and a great variety of walks is possible along the valley.

The tiny hamlet of **Grange** is one of the prettiest spots, where the valley narrows dramatically to form the "Jaws of Borrowdale". Nearby Castle Crag has superb views.

From Grange you can complete the circuit of Derwent Water along the western shore, or move southwards to the more open farmland around Seatoller. As you head south by road, look out for a National Trust sign *(see p25)* to the **Bowder Stone**, a delicately poised block weighing nearly 2,000 tonnes, which may have fallen from the crags above or been deposited by a glacier millions of years ago.

Two attractive hamlets in Borrowdale are **Rosthwaite** and **Stonethwaite**. Also worth a detour, preferably on foot, is Watendlath village, off a side road near the famous beauty spot of **Ashness Bridge**.

WALKING IN THE LAKE DISTRICT

Two long-distance footpaths pass through the Lake District's most spectacular scenery. The 70 mile (110 km) Cumbrian Way runs from Carlisle to Ulverston via Keswick and Coniston. The western section of the Coast-to-Coast Walk *(see pp32–3)* passes through this area. There are hundreds of shorter walks along lake shores, nature trails or following more challenging uphill routes. Walkers should stick to paths to avoid erosion, and check weather conditions at National Park information centres.

Typical Lake District stile over dry-stone wall

---

④

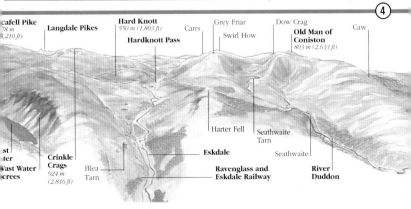

Scafell Pike
978 m
(3,210 ft)

Langdale Pikes

Hard Knott
550 m (1,803 ft)

Hardknott Pass

Carrs

Grey Friar

Swirl How

Dow Crag

Old Man of Coniston
803 m (2,633 ft)

Caw

st
ter

Crinkle Crags
924 m
(2,816 ft)

Blea Tarn

Harter Fell

Seathwaite Tarn

Seathwaite

Eskdale

ast Water
crees

Ravenglass and Eskdale Railway

River Duddon

Convivial Wasdale Head Inn *(see p561)* at Wasdale Head

Wast Water ⓫

Cumbria. 🚇 *Whitehaven.* 🅸 *12 Main St, Egremont (01946 820693).*

A SILENT REFLECTION of truly awesome surroundings, black, brooding **Wast Water** is a mysterious, evocative lake. The road from Nether Wasdale continues along its northwest side. Along its eastern flank loom walls of sheer scree over 600 m (2,000 ft) high. Beneath them the water looks inky black, whatever the weather, plunging an icy 80 m (260 ft) from the waterline to the bottom to form England's deepest lake. You can walk along the screes, but it is an uncomfortable and dangerous scramble. Boating on the lake is banned for conservation reasons, but fishing permits are available from the nearby National Trust camp site.

At **Wasdale Head** lies one of Britain's grandest views: the austere pyramid of **Great Gable**, centrepiece of a fine mountain composition, with the huge forms of Scafell and **Scafell Pike**. The scenery is utterly unspoilt, and the only buildings lie at the far end of the lake: an inn and a tiny church commemorating fallen climbers. Here the road ends, and you must turn back or take to your feet, following signs for Black Sail Pass and Ennerdale, or walk up the grand fells ahead. Wasdale's irresistible backdrop was the inspiration of the first serious British mountaineers, who flocked here during the 19th century, insouciantly clad in tweed jackets, carrying little more than a length of rope slung over their shoulders.

Eskdale ⓬

Cumbria. 🚇 *Ravenglass then narrow-gauge railway to Eskdale (Easter–Oct: daily; Dec–Feb: Sat, Sun).* 🅸 *12 Main St, Egremont (01946 820693).*

THE PASTORAL DELIGHTS of Eskdale are best encountered over the gruelling **Hardknott Pass**, which is the most taxing drive in the Lake District, with steep gradients. You can pause at the 393-m (1,291-ft) summit to explore the Roman **Hardknott Fort** or enjoy the lovely view. As you descend into Eskdale, rhodo-dendrons and pines flourish in a landscape of small ham-lets, narrow lanes and gentle farmland. The main settlements below are the attractive village of Boot and coastal Ravenglass, both with old **corn mills**.

Just south of Ravenglass is the impressive **Muncaster Castle**, the richly furnished home of the Pennington fam-ily. Another way to enjoy the scenery is to take the miniature railway (La'l Ratty) from Ravenglass to Dalegarth.

🏭 **Eskdale Mill**
Boot. 🄲 *019467 23335.* ⬤ *Apr–Sep: Tue–Sun, public hols.* 🄼 🄳 🄸
🏭 **Muncaster Mill**
Ravenglass. 🄲 *01229 717232.* ⬤ *Apr–Oct: daily.* 🄼 🄿
🄳 *limited.*
🏰 **Muncaster Castle**
Ravenglass. 🄲 *01229 717614.*
Castle ⬤ *mid-Mar–mid-Nov: Sun–Fri (pm) & public hols.* **Garden** ⬤ *daily.*
🄼 🄳 *ground floor only.* 🄿 🄸

Remains of the Roman Hardknott Fort, Eskdale

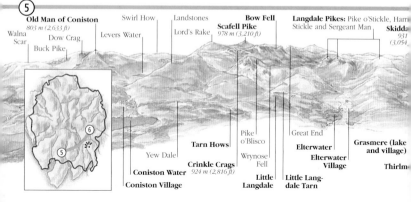

⑤

Old Man of Coniston
803 m (2,633 ft)

Walna Scar   Dow Crag   Levers Water   Swirl How   Landstones   Lord's Rake   **Scafell Pike**
978 m (3,210 ft)   **Bow Fell**   **Langdale Pikes:** Pike o'Stickle, Harri
Stickle and Sergeant Man   **Skidda**
931 (3,054

Buck Pike

Yew Dale   **Tarn Hows**   Pike o'Blisco   Great End   Elterwater   **Grasmere (lake and village)**

Coniston Water   *924 m (2,816 ft)*   **Crinkle Crags**   Wrynose Fell   Elterwater Village   Thirlm

Coniston Village   Little Langdale   Little Lang-dale Tarn

Autumnal view of Seathwaite, in the Duddon Valley, a popular centre for walkers and climbers

Duddon Valley ⑬

Cumbria. 🚉 *Ulverston.* 🛈 *Ruskin Ave, Coniston (015394 41533).*

Aɪꜱᴏ ᴋɴᴏᴡɴ as Dunnerdale, this picturesque tract of countryside inspired 35 of Wordsworth's sonnets *(see p352)*. The prettiest stretch lies between Ulpha and Cockley Beck. In autumn the colours of heather moors and a light sprinkling of birch trees are particularly beautiful. Stepping stones and bridges span the river at intervals, the most charming being Birk's Bridge, near Seathwaite. At the southern end of the valley, where the River Duddon meets the sea at Duddon Sands, is

Broughton-in-Furness, a pretty village of 18th-century houses, with an 11th-century church. Note the old stocks, and the stone slabs used for fish on market day in the main square.

Langdale ⑭

Cumbria. 🚉 *Windermere.* 🛈 *Central Buildings, Market Cross, Ambleside (015394 32582).*

Sᴛʀᴇᴛᴄʜɪɴɢ ꜰʀᴏᴍ Skelwith Bridge, where the Brathay surges powerfully over waterfalls, to the summits of Great Langdale is the two-pronged Langdale Valley. Walkers and climbers throng here to take on **Pavey Ark, Pike o'Stickle,**

Crinkle Crags and **Bow Fell**. The local mountain rescue teams are the busiest in Britain.

Great Langdale is the more spectacular valley and it is often crowded, but quieter **Little Langdale** has many attractions too. It is worth completing the circuit back to Ambleside via the southern route, stopping at Blea Tarn. Reedy **Elterwater** is a picturesque spot, once a site of the gunpowder industry. Wrynose Pass, west of Little Langdale, climbs to 390 m (1,281 ft), a warm-up for Hardknott Pass further on. At its top is Three Shires Stone, marking the former boundary of the old counties of Cumberland, Westmorland and Lancashire.

⑥

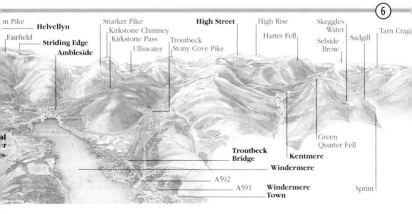

Rydal Water, one of the major attractions of the Lake District

Ambleside ⑯

Cumbria. 🏠 *3,400.* 🚃 **i** *Central Buildings, Market Cross (015394 32582).* 🚌 *Wed.* W *www.amblesideonline.co.uk*

AMBLESIDE has good road connections to all parts of the Lakes and is an attractive base, especially for walkers and climbers. Mainly Victorian in character, it has a good range of outdoor clothing, crafts and specialist food shops. An enterprising little cinema and a summer classical music festival add life in the evenings. Sights in town are small-scale: the remnants of the Roman fort of Galava, AD 79, Stock Ghyll Force waterfall and **Bridge House**, now a National Trust information centre.

ENVIRONS: Within easy reach are the wooded Rothay valley, the **Kirkstone Galleries** at Skelwith Bridge, with their unusual souvenirs and furnishings. At nearby Troutbeck is the restored farmhouse of **Townend**, dating from 1626,

The tiny Bridge House over Stock Beck in Ambleside

Grasmere and Rydal ⑮

Cumbria. **Grasmere** 🏠 *700.* **Rydal** 🏠 *100.* 🚃 *Grasmere.* **i** *Redbank Rd, Grasmere (015394 35245).* W *www.lake-district.gov.uk*

THE POET William Wordsworth lived in both these pretty villages on the shores of two sparkling lakes. Fairfield, Nab Scar and Loughrigg Fell rise steeply above their reedy shores and offer good opportunities for walking. Grasmere is now a sizable settlement and the famous Grasmere sports *(see p344)* attract large crowds every August.

The Wordsworth family is buried in St Oswald's Church, and crowds flock to the annual ceremony of strewing the church's earth floor with fresh rushes. Most visitors head for **Dove Cottage**, where the poet spent his most creative years. The museum in the barn behind includes such artefacts as the great man's socks. The Wordsworths moved to a larger house, **Rydal Mount**, in

Rydal in 1813 and lived here until 1850. The grounds have waterfalls and a summerhouse. Dora's Field nearby is a blaze of daffodils in spring and Fairfield Horseshoe offers an energetic, challenging walk.

🏛 Dove Cottage and the Wordsworth Museum
Off A591 nr Grasmere. **(** *015394 35544.* 🕐 *daily.* ● *24–26 Dec, mid-Jan–mid-Feb.* ▨ & ✔ ▣ ⋒
🏛 Rydal Mount
Rydal. **(** *015394 33002.* 🕐 *Mar–Oct: daily; Nov–Feb: Wed–Mon.* ● *25 Dec, three wks in Jan.* ▨ & *limited.* ⋒

WILLIAM WORDSWORTH (1770-1850)

Best known of the Romantic poets, Wordsworth was born in the Lake District and spent most of his life there. After school in Hawkshead and a period at Cambridge, a legacy enabled him to pursue his literary career. He settled at Dove Cottage with his sister Dorothy and in 1802 married an old school friend, Mary Hutchinson. They lived simply, walking, bringing up their children and receiving visits from poets such as Coleridge and de Quincey. Wordsworth's prose works include one of the earliest guidebooks to the Lake District.

BEATRIX POTTER AND THE LAKE DISTRICT

Although best known for her children's stories with characters such as Peter Rabbit and Jemima Puddle-duck, which she also illustrated, Beatrix Potter (1866–1943) became a champion of conservation in the Lake District after moving there in 1906. She married William Heelis, devoted herself to farming, and was an expert on Herdwick sheep. To conserve her beloved countryside, she donated land to the National Trust.

Cover illustration of *Jemima Puddleduck* (1908)

whose interior gives an insight into Lakeland domestic life.

🏛 **Kirkstone Galleries**
Skelwith Bridge. 📞 015394 34002. ◻ *daily.* ⬤ *24–26 Dec.* ▢ ♿ *limited.*

🏛 **Townend**
(NT) Troutbeck, Windermere. 📞 015394 32628. ◻ *Apr–Oct: Tue–Fri, Sun & public hols.* 📷

Windermere ⓱

Cumbria. 🚉 *Station Precinct.* 🅿 *Victoria St.* 🈯 *Victoria St (015394 46499) or Glebe Rd, Bowness-on-Windermere (015394 42895).*

At over 10 miles (16 km) long, this dramatic watery expanse is England's largest mere. Industrial magnates built mansions around its shores long before the railway arrived. Stately **Brockhole**, now a national park visitor centre, was one such grand

estate. When the railway reached Windermere in 1847, it enabled crowds of workers to visit the area on day trips.

Today, a year-round car ferry service connects the lake's east and west shores (it runs between Ferry Nab and Ferry House), and summer steamers link Lakeside, Bowness and Ambleside on the north-south axis. Belle Isle, a wooded island on which a unique round house stands, is one of the lake's most attractive features, but landing is not permitted. **Fell Foot Park** is at the south end of the lake, and there are good walks on the northwest shore. A quite stunning viewpoint is Orrest Head 238 m (784 ft) northeast of Windermere town.

ENVIRONS: Bowness-on-Windermere, on the east shore, is a hugely popular centre. Many of its buildings display Victorian details, and

St Martin's Church dates back to the 15th century. The **Windermere Steamboat Museum** has a collection of superbly restored craft, and one of these, *Swallow*, makes regular lake trips. The **World of Beatrix Potter** recreates her characters in an exhibition, and a film tells her life story.

Beatrix Potter wrote many of her books at **Hill Top**, the 17th-century farmhouse at Near Sawrey, northwest of Windermere. Hill Top is furnished with many of Potter's possessions, and left as it was in her lifetime. The **Beatrix Potter Gallery** in Hawkshead holds annual exhibitions of her manuscripts and illustrations.

🚩 **Brockhole Visitor Centre**
On A591. 📞 015394 46601. ◻ *Apr–Oct: daily.* ♿ ▢ 🈯

🌳 **Fell Foot Park**
(NT) Newby Bridge. 📞 015395 31273. ◻ *daily.* ♿ ▢

🏛 **Windermere Steamboat Museum**
Rayrigg Rd, Windermere. 📞 015394 45565. ◻ *late Mar–Oct: daily.* 📷 ▢ 🈯 ♿

🏛 **World of Beatrix Potter**
The Old Laundry, Crag Brow. 📞 015394 88444. ◻ *daily.* ⬤ *25 Dec, last three wks in Jan.* 📷 ♿ ▢ 🈯

🏚 **Hill Top**
(NT) Near Sawrey, Ambleside. 📞 015394 36269. ◻ *Apr–Oct: Sat–Wed.* 📷 🈯

🏛 **Beatrix Potter Gallery**
(NT) The Square, Hawkshead. 📞 015394 36355. ◻ *Apr–Oct: Sun–Thu.* 📷 🈯

Boats moored along the shore at Ambleside, the north end of Windermere

Peaceful Coniston Water, the setting of Arthur Ransome's novel, *Swallows and Amazons* (1930)

Coniston Water ⑱

Cumbria. 🚆 *Windermere then bus.* 🚌 *Ambleside then bus.* ℹ️ *Coniston car park, Ruskin Ave (015394 41533).* 🅦 www.coniston-net.com

FOR THE FINEST VIEW of this stretch of water just outside the Lake District, you need to climb. The 19th-century art critic, writer and philosopher John Ruskin, had a fine view from his house, **Brantwood**, where his paintings and memorabilia can be seen today. Contemporary art exhibitions and events take place throughout the year.

An enjoyable excursion is the summer lake trip from Coniston Pier on the National Trust steam yacht, *Gondola*, calling at Brantwood. Coniston was also the scene of Donald Campbell's fatal attempt on the world water speed record in 1967. The green slate village of Coniston, once a centre for copper-mining, now caters for local walkers.

Also interesting is the traffic-free village of **Hawkshead** to the northwest, with its quaint alleyways and timber-framed houses. To the south is the vast Grizedale Forest, dotted with woodland sculptures.

Just north of Coniston Water is the man-made **Tarn Hows**, a landscaped tarn surrounded by woods. There is a pleasant climb up the 803 m (2,635 ft) Old Man of Coniston.

🏛 **Brantwood**
Off B5285, nr Coniston. 📞 *015394 41396.* ⭕ *mid-Mar–mid-Nov: daily; mid-Nov–mid-Mar: Wed–Sun.* ⬤ *25, 26 Dec.* 🈺 ♿ *limited.* 🍴 🖥 🛍

Kendal ⑲

Cumbria. 🏙 *26,000.* 🚆 ℹ️ *Town Hall, Highgate (01539 725758).* 🚌 *Mon–Sat.*

A BUSY MARKET TOWN, Kendal is the administrative centre of the region and the southern gateway to the Lake District. Built in grey limestone, it has an arts centre, the **Brewery**, and a central area which is best enjoyed on foot. **Abbot Hall**,

Kendal mint cake, the famous lakeland energy-booster for walkers

built in 1759, has paintings by Turner and Romney as well as Gillows furniture *(see p358).* In addition, the hall's stable block contains the **Museum of Lakeland Life**, with occasional lively workshops demonstrating local crafts and trades. There are dioramas of geology and wildlife in the **Museum of Natural History and Archaeology**. About 3 miles (5 km) south of the town is

14th-century **Sizergh Castle**, with a fortified tower, carved fireplaces and a lovely garden.

🏛 **Abbot Hall Art Gallery and Museum of Lakeland Life**
Kendal. 📞 *01539 722464.* ⭕ *mid-Feb–20 Dec: daily.* 🈺 *gallery.* 📷 *by arrangement.* 🖥 🛍
🏛 **Kendal Museum of Natural History and Archaeology**
Station Rd. 📞 *01539 721374.* ⭕ *mid-Feb–20 Dec: Mon–Sat.* 🈺 ♿ *limited.* 🛍
⚓ **Sizergh Castle**
(NT) off A591 & A590. 📞 *015395 60070.* ⭕ *Apr–Oct: Sun–Thu.* 🈺 ♿ *grounds only.* 🖥 🛍

Furness Peninsula ⑳

Cumbria. 🚆 🚌 *Barrow-in-Furness.* ℹ️ *28 Duke St, Barrow-in-Furness (01229 894784).*

B ARROW-IN-FURNESS *(see p335)* is the peninsula's main town. Its **Dock Museum**, cleverly built over a Victorian dock where ships were repaired, traces the history of Barrow using lively displays, including an old schooner, *Emily Barratt*.

Ruins of the red sandstone walls of **Furness Abbey** remain in the wooded Vale of Deadly Nightshade, with a small exhibition of monastic life. The historic town of Ulverston received its charter in 1280. **Ulverston Heritage**

◁ **The attractive woodland of Thirlmere, under the shadow of Helvellyn**

Centre charts its development from market town to port. Stan Laurel, of Laurel and Hardy fame, was born here in 1890. His memorabilia **museum** has a cinema.

🏛 Dock Museum
North Rd, Barrow-in-Furness. **📞** 01229 894444. ⭘ Apr–Oct: Tue–Sun; Nov–Mar: Wed–Sun (Sat, Sun: pm); public hols. ⬤ 25, 26 Dec, 1 Jan. 🖥 🅿 ♿

⛪ Furness Abbey
Vale of Deadly Nightshade. **📞** 01229 823420. ⭘ Easter–Sep: daily; Oct–Easter: Wed–Sun. ⬤ 24–26 Dec, 1 Jan. 🖥 ♿ limited. 🅿

🏛 Ulverston Heritage Centre
Lower Brook St. **📞** 01229 580820. ⭘ Apr–Dec: Mon–Sat; Jan–Mar: Mon, Tue, Thu–Sat. ⬤ 25, 26 Dec, 1 Jan. 🖥 🅿 ♿ limited.

🏛 Laurel and Hardy Museum
Upper Brook St, Ulverston. **📞** 01229 582292. ⭘ daily. ⬤ 25 Dec; Jan. 🖥 ♿

Staircase at Holker Hall

Cartmel ㉑

Cumbria. 🚶 700. 🛈 Victoria Hall, Main St, Grange-over-Sands (015395 34026).

THE HIGHLIGHT of this pretty village is its 12th-century **priory**, one of the finest Cumbrian churches. Little remains of the original priory except the pretty gatehouse in the village centre. The restored church has an attractive east window, a stone-carved 14th-century tomb, and beautiful misericords.

Cartmel also boasts a small racecourse. The village has given its name to its surroundings, a hilly district of green farmland with mixed woodland and limestone scars.

One of the main local attractions is **Holker Hall**, former residence of the Dukes of Devonshire. Inside are lavishly furnished rooms, with fine marble fireplaces, and a superb oak staircase. Outside are stunning gardens and a deer park.

🏰 Holker Hall
Cark-in-Cartmel. **📞** 015395 58328. ⭘ Apr–Oct: Sun–Fri. 🖥 ♿ limited. 🖼 by arrangement. 🅿 🅿

Levens Hall ㉒

Nr Kendal, Cumbria. **📞** 015395 60321. 🚌 from Kendal or Lancaster. ⭘ Apr–mid-Oct: Sun–Thu. ♿ gardens only. 🖥 🅿 **W** www.levenshall.co.uk

THE OUTSTANDING attraction of this Elizabethan mansion is its topiary, but the house itself has much to offer. Built around a 13th-century tower, it contains a fine collection of Jacobean furniture and watercolours by Peter de Wint (1784–1849). Also of note are the ornate ceilings, Charles II dining chairs, the earliest example of English patchwork and the gilded hearts on the drainpipes.

The yew and box topiary was designed in 1694 by French horticulturist Guillaume Beaumont.

The 18th-century Turret Clock has a single hand, a common design of the period.

Main entrance

Box hedges were a common component of geometrically designed gardens of this period.

Over 300 years old, the garden's box-edged beds are filled with colourful herbaceous displays.

The complex topiary, shaped into cones, spirals and pyramids, is kept in shape by gardeners. Some specimens are 6 m (20 ft) high.

Morecambe Bay, looking northwest towards Barrow-in-Furness

Morecambe Bay ㉓

Lancashire. ☒ *Morecambe.*
☒ *Heysham (to Isle of Man).* ☐
Central Promenade (01524 582808).
☒ *www.lancaster.gov.uk*

THE BEST WAY to explore
Morecambe Bay is by train
from Ulverston to Arnside. The
track follows a series of low
viaducts across a huge expanse
of glistening tidal flats where
thousands of wading birds
feed and breed. The bay is
one of the most important
bird reserves in Britain. On
the Cumbrian side, retirement
homes have expanded the
sedate Victorian resort of
Grange-over-Sands, which
grew up after the arrival of
the railway in 1857. Its best
feature is its natural setting.
Nearby, **Hampsfield Fell**
and **Humphrey Head Point**
give fine views along the bay.

Leighton Hall ㉔

Carnforth, Lancashire. ☎ 01524
734474. ☒ to Yealand Conyers
(from Lancaster). ☐ May–Sep:
Tue–Fri, Sun. ● special events. ☒
☒ ground floor only. ☒ only. ☒ ☒

LEIGHTON HALL'S estate dates
back to the 13th century,
but most of the building is
19th-century, including its
Neo-Gothic façade. It is
owned by the Gillow family, of
the Lancastrian furniture business, whose products are
now prized antiques. Excellent pieces can be seen here,
including a ladies' work-box

inlaid with biblical scenes. In
the afternoon the hall's large
collection of birds of prey
display their aerial prowess.

Lancaster ㉕

Lancashire. ☒ 45,000. ☒
☒ ☐ Castle Hill (01524
32878). ☒ Mon–Sat. ☒
www.lancaster.gov.uk

THIS COUNTY TOWN
of Lancashire is
tiny compared to
Liverpool or
Manchester
(now counties
in their own
right), but it
has a long history. The Romans
named it after their camp over
the River Lune. Originally a
defensive site, it developed

into a prosperous port largely
on the proceeds of the slave
trade. Today, its university and
cultural life still thrive. The
Norman **Lancaster Castle** was
expanded in the 14th and 16th
centuries. It has been a crown
court and a prison since the
13th century. The Shire Hall is
decorated with 600 heraldic
shields. Some fragments from
Hadrian's Tower (which has a
collection of torture instruments) are 2,000 years old.
    The nearby priory church
of **St Mary** is on Castle Hill.
Its main features include a
Saxon doorway and carved
14th-century choir stalls. There
is an outstanding museum of
furniture in the 17th-century
Judge's Lodgings, while the
Maritime Museum, in the
Georgian custom house
on St George's Quay,
contains displays on the
port's history. The **City
Museum**, based in the
old town hall, concen-
trates on the history of
Lancaster.
    The splendid **Lune
Aqueduct** carries the
canal over the
River Lune on
five wide arches.
Other attractions
are found in
**Williamson
Park**, site of

**Tawny eagle at
Leighton Hall**

the 1907 Ashton Memorial.
This folly was built by the
local linoleum magnate and
politician, Lord Ashton.

CROSSING THE SANDS

Morecambe Bay sands are very dangerous. Travellers used to
cut across the bay at low tide to shorten the long trail around
the Kent estuary. Many perished as they were caught by
rising tides or quicksand, and sea fogs hid the paths. Locals
who knew the bay became guides, and today you can travel
with a guide from Kents Bank to Hest Bank near Arnside.

The High Sheriff of Lancaster Crossing Morecambe Sands (anon)

There are fine views from the top of this 67 m (220 ft) domed structure. Opposite is the tropical butterfly house, and the pavilion café.

Façade of Lancaster's Judge's Lodgings, now a museum

♣ **Lancaster Castle**
Castle Parade. ☎ 01524 64998. ◯ mid-Mar–mid-Dec: daily. 📷 only but limited when court is in session. 📷 🏠

🏛 **Judge's Lodgings**
Church St. ☎ 01524 32808. ◯ Easter–31 Oct: Mon–Sat (pm). ● Nov–Good Fri. 📷 🏠

🏛 **Maritime Museum**
Custom House, St George's Quay. ☎ 01524 64637. ◯ daily (Nov–Easter: pm). ● 24–26, 31 Dec, 1 Jan. 📷 ♿ 🖥 🏠

🏛 **City Museum**
Market Sq. ☎ 01524 64637. ◯ Mon–Sat. ● 24 Dec–2 Jan. ♿ 🏠

♣ **Williamson Park**
Wyresdale Rd. ☎ 01524 33318. ◯ daily. ● 25–26 Dec, 1 Jan. 📷 ♿ limited. 🖥 🏠

Ribble Valley 26

Lancashire. 🚉 Clitheroe. 🎫 Market Place, Clitheroe (01200 425566). ⛺ Tue, Thu, Sat. �🌐 www.ribblevalley.gov.uk

CLITHEROE, A SMALL market town with a hilltop castle, is a good centre for exploring the Ribble Valley's rivers and old villages, such as Slaidburn. Ribchester has a **Roman Museum**, and there is a ruined **Cistercian abbey** at Whalley. East is 560 m (1,830 ft) Pendle Hill with a Bronze Age burial mound at its peak.

THE WITCHES OF PENDLE

In 1612, ten women were convicted of witchcraft at Lancaster Castle. The evidence against them was mostly based on the revelations of a small child who implicated them in satanic rituals. Many of the accused came from two peasant families, reduced to penury by a feud, who roamed the countryside begging, and cursing those who refused to oblige. Several of the women confessed to their crimes, but they were coerced, deranged or had indeed dabbled in the "black arts" is impossible to assess.

Mother Chattox, a Pendle "witch"

🏛 **Roman Museum**
Ribchester. ☎ 01254 878261. ◯ daily (Sat, Sun: pm). ● 24, 25 Dec, 1 Jan. 📷 ♿ 🖥 🏠 by arrangement.

🏠 **Whalley Abbey**
Whalley. ☎ 01254 828400. ◯ daily. ● 24 Dec–2 Jan. 📷 ♿ 🖥 🏠

Blackpool 27

Lancashire. 🏘 150,000. ✈ 🚤 🚌 🎫 Clifton St (01253 478222). �🌐 www.blackpooltourism com

BRITISH HOLIDAY patterns have changed in the past few decades, and Blackpool is no longer the apogee of seaside entertainmen, but it remains a unique experience. A wall of amusement arcades, piers, bingo halls and fast-food stalls stretch behind the sands. Trams run along the promenade. At night, entertainers strut their stuff under the bright lights. The town attracts thousands of visitors during September and October when the Illuminations trace the skeleton of the 158 m (518 ft) Blackpool Tower. Blackpool's resort life dates back to the 18th century, but it burst into prominence when the railway first arrived in 1840, bringing Lancastrian workers to their holiday resort.

Blackpool Tower, painted gold for its centenary in 1994

Manchester ❷❽

Sign for the John Rylands Library

Mᴀɴᴄʜᴇsᴛᴇʀ's ʜɪsᴛᴏʀʏ dates back to Roman times, when, in AD 79, Agricola's legions set up a base camp called Mancunium on the site of the present city. It rose to prominence in the late 18th century, when Richard Arkwright's steam-powered spinning machines introduced the brave new world of cotton processing. By 1830, the first railway linked Manchester and Liverpool, and in 1894 the Manchester Ship Canal opened, allowing cargo vessels 36 miles (55 km) inland. Confident civic buildings sprang up from the proceeds of cotton wealth, but these were in stark contrast to the overcrowded slums of the millworkers. Social discontent led writers, politicians and reformers to espouse liberal or radical causes. One result was the foundation in 1821 of the forthright local newspaper, the *Manchester Guardian*, a forerunner of today's *Guardian*. The city was the first to introduce massive slum clearance and smoke-less zones during the 1950s.

Exploring Manchester

Manchester is a fine, compact city with much to see in its central areas. It has a lively club scene and many ethnic restaurants. The restoration of the tram system has helped to ease the pressures of urban transport. The mills and docks have left a huge architectural heritage. Among the fine 19th-century buildings are the **John Rylands Library**, now part of the university, the **Town Hall**, the **Royal Exchange**, now a theatre and restaurant, and the **Free Trade Hall**. **Castlefield**, once a dere-lict industrial site, has been regenerated as a thriving leisure area.

The G-Mex Exhibition and Event Centre, once the central railway station

MANCHESTER CITY CENTRE

Air and Space Gallery ③
Castlefield ②
Manchester Art Galleries ⑨
Free Trade Hall ⑤
G-Mex Centre ④
John Rylands Library ⑥
Museum of Science and
Industry in Manchester ①
Royal Exchange ⑦
Town Hall ⑧

KEY

🚌 Bus station
🚐 Coach station
🚋 Tram
— Tramline

🚆 Train station
🅿 Parking
ℹ Tourist information
✝ Church

0 metres   250
0 yards   250

Trafford Road Bridge on the Manchester Ship Canal

VISITORS' CHECKLIST

Manchester. 🕇 2.5 million. ✈
Off M56 11 miles (18 km) S
Manchester. 🚆 Oxford Road,
Victoria, Piccadilly. 🚌 Chorlton St.
🛈 Lloyd St (0161 234 3157). 🚲
daily. 🎦 Manchester Festival: Oct.

🏛 Museum of Science and Industry in Manchester

Liverpool Rd. 【 *0161 832 2244.*
◯ *daily.* ● *24–26 Dec.* 🎨 ♿ ▯
Part of the Castlefield Urban Heritage Park and one of the largest science museums in the world, the spirit of scientific enterprise and industrial might of Manchester's heyday is conveyed here. Among the best sections are the Power Hall, a collection of working steam engines, the Electricity Gallery, tracing the history of domestic power, and an exhibition on the Liverpool and Manchester Railway. Planes that made flying history are displayed in the Air Space Hall.

🏛 Manchester Art Galleries

Mosley St & Princess St. 【 *0161 234 5000.* ● *until summer 2002 for major refurbishment.*
The porticoed building which Sir Charles Barry (1795–1860) designed in 1824, contains an excellent collection of British art, notably Pre-Raphaelites such as Holman Hunt and Dante Gabriel Rossetti. Early Italian, Flemish and French Schools are also represented. It has a fine collection of silver, ceramics and glass.

🏞 G-Mex Centre

Windmill St. 【 *0161 834 2700.* ◯
During exhibitions ring for details.
● *25 Dec.* ♿ ▯
The former central railway station, closed in 1969, is now a huge exhibition and conference centre. It has more than 9,290 sq m (100,000 sq ft) of pillarless floor space in which to host major concerts

and shows, and looks particularly dramatic when lit up at night.

🏞 Manchester Ship Canal

This magnificent engineering feat was inaugurated by Queen Victoria in May 1894. It was designed to bring deep sea shipping from Eastham on the Mersey into the heart of the city, at Salford Quays, 36 miles (58 km) inland. Three thousand ships still use the canal every year, and the docks at the head of the canal are being restored.

Jacob Epstein's *Genesis* (1930–1) in Whitworth Art Gallery

🏛 The Lowry

Water St. 【 *0161 876 2000.*
◯ *daily.* ♿ ▯ ▯
This spectacular new gallery at Salford Quays is home to two theatres, art galleries and ArtWorks, an interactive area that encourages creative innovation. It also houses the world's largest collection of works by Salford-born artist LS Lowry, famous for his industrial landscapes.

🏛 Whitworth Art Gallery

University of Manchester, Oxford Rd. 【 *0161 275 7450.*
◯ *daily (Sun: pm).* ● *23 Dec–10 Jan, Good Fri.*
▯ ▯ ♿
This fine red-brick building, named after the Manchester machine tool manufacturer and engineer, Sir Joseph Whitworth, houses a superb collection of contemporary art, textiles and prints. Jacob Epstein's *Genesis* nude occupies the entrance, but the Turner *(see p93)* watercolours are more universally appreciated. Japanese woodcuts and some examples of wallpaper-making are an extra bonus.

THE PETERLOO MASSACRE

In 1819, the working conditions of Manchester's factory workers were so bad that social tensions reached breaking point. On 16 August, 50,000 people assembled in St Peter's Field to protest at the oppressive Corn Laws. Initially peaceful, the mood darkened and the poorly trained mounted

G Cruikshank's *Peterloo Massacre* cartoon

troops panicked, charging the crowd with their sabres. Eleven were killed and many wounded. The incident was called Peterloo (the Battle of Waterloo had taken place in 1815). Reforms such as the Factory Act came in that year.

Liverpool ⑳

Traces of settlement on Merseyside date back to the 1st century. In 1207 "Livpul", a fishing village, was granted a charter by King John. The population was only 1,000 in Stuart times, but during the 17th and 18th centuries Liverpool's westerly seaboard gave it a leading edge in the lucrative Caribbean slave trade. The first docks opened in 1715 and eventually stretched 7 miles (11 km) along the Mersey. Liverpool's first ocean steamer set out from here in 1840, and would-be emigrants to the New World poured into the city from Europe, including a flood of Irish refugees from the potato famine. Many settled permanently in Liverpool and a large, mixed community developed. Today, the port handles even greater volumes of cargoes than in the 1950s and 1960s, but container ships use Bootle docks. Despite economic and social problems, the irrepressible "Scouse" or Liverpudlian spirit re-emerged in the Swinging Sixties, when four local lads stormed the pop scene. Many people still visit Liverpool to pay homage to the Beatles, but the city is also known for its orchestra, the Liverpool Philharmonic, its sport (football and the Grand National) steeplechase) and its universities.

Liver Bird on the Royal Liver Building

Victorian ironwork, restored and polished, at Albert Dock

Exploring Liverpool

Liverpool's waterfront by the Pier Head, guarded by the mythical Liver Birds (a pair of cormorants with seaweed in their beaks) on the Royal Liver Building, is one of the most easily recognized in Britain. Nearby are the famous ferry terminal across the River Mersey and the revitalized

LIVERPOOL CITY CENTRE

Beatles Story ⑤
Cavern Quarter ①
Liverpool Museum ②
Merseyside Maritime Museum ⑦
Metropolitan Cathedral ④

Museum of Liverpool Life ⑧
Royal Liver Building ⑨
Tate Gallery Liverpool ⑥
Town Hall ⑩
Walker Art Gallery pp364–5 ③

KEY

🚌 Bus station
🚉 British Rail station
⛴ Ferry terminal
🅿 Parking
ℹ Tourist information
✝ Church

0 metres 250
0 yards 250

docklands. Other attractions include top-class museums and fine galleries, such as the Walker Art Gallery *(see pp364–5)*. Its wealth of interesting architecture includes some of Britain's finest Neo-Classical buildings in the city centre, and two cathedrals.

Albert Dock

🎫 *0151 708 8854.* ⏰ *daily.* ⬤ *25–26 Dec, 1Jan.* 🎟 *some attractions.* ♿
There are five warehouses surrounding Albert Dock, all designed by Jesse Hartley in 1846. By the early 1900s the docks had become less important and had closed by 1972. After a decade of dereliction, these Grade I listed buildings *(see p617)* were restored in a development that includes museums, galleries, shops, restaurants, bars and businesses.

Ship's bell in the Maritime Museum

Albert Dock quay beside the River Mersey

🏛 Merseyside Maritime Museum

Albert Dock. 🎫 *0151 478 4499.* ⏰ *daily.* ⬤ *23–26 Dec, 1 Jan.* ♿ *not Piermaster's House or basement.* 🈺 🈺
Devoted to the history of the Port of Liverpool, this large complex has good sections on shipbuilding and the Cunard and White Star liners as well as a Transatlantic Slavery gallery. The area on the Battle of the Atlantic in World War II includes models and charts. Another gallery deals with emigration to the New World. The Customs and Excise section reveals the world of smuggling in all its modern forms. Across the quayside is the rebuilt Piermaster's House and the Cooperage.

🏛 Museum of Liverpool Life

Mann Island. 🎫 *0151 478 4080.* ⏰ *daily.* ⬤ *24–26 Dec, 1 Jan.* ♿ 🈺
Many aspects of Liverpool culture converge here. Exhibits cover the history of Liverpool, its people and their contribution to international life. The *City Soldier's* gallery explores life in the King's Regiment in times of war and peace. Other interactive exhibits and accounts of daily life tell stories of sporting and political events from the 1800s to the present day.

VISITORS' CHECKLIST

Liverpool. 🅿 *450,000.* ✈ *7 miles (11 km) SE Liverpool.* 🚆 *Lime St.* 🚌 *Norton St.* ⛴ *from Pier Head to the Wirral, also sightseeing trips; to Isle of Man & N Ireland.* 🛈 *Queens Sq (09066 806886).* 🛒 *Sun (heritage market).* 🎭 *Liverpool Show: May; River Festival: Jun; Beatles Festival: Aug.*

🏛 Beatles Story

Britannia Volts. 🎫 *0151 709 1963.* ⏰ *daily.* ⬤ *25, 26 Dec.* 🎟 ♿ 🈺
In a walk-through exhibition, this museum records the history of The Beatles' meteoric rise to fame, from their first record, *Love Me Do*, through Beatlemania to their last live appearance together in 1969, and their eventual break-up. The hits that mesmerized a generation can be heard.

🏛 Tate Gallery Liverpool

Albert Dock. 🎫 *0151 702 7400.* ⏰ *Tue–Sun, public hols.* ⬤ *Mon; 24–26 Dec.* 🎟 *for some exhibitions.* ♿ 🎫 *by arrangement.* 🈺 🈺
The northern Tate houses one of the best selections of contemporary art outside London. Marked by bright blue and orange panels, the gallery was converted from an old warehouse by contemporary architect James Stirling. It opened in 1988 as the London Tate's first outstation. Three spacious floors provide an ideal setting for the changing exhibitions housed here.

THE BEATLES

Liverpool has produced many good bands and a host of singers, comedians and entertainers before and since the 1960s. But the Beatles – John Lennon, Paul McCartney, George Harrison and Ringo Starr – were the most sensational, and locations associated with the band, however tenuous, are revered as shrines in Liverpool. Bus and walking tours trace the hallowed ground of the Salvation Army home at *Strawberry Fields* and *Penny Lane* (both outside the city centre), as well as the boys' old homes. The most visited site is Mathew Street, near Moorfields Station, where the Cavern Club first throbbed to the Mersey Beat. The original site is now a shopping arcade, but the bricks have been used to create a replica. Nearby are statues of the Beatles and *Eleanor Rigby*.

Liverpool: Walker Art Gallery

Italian dish (c.1500)

Fᴏᴜɴᴅᴇᴅ ɪɴ 1873 by Sir Andrew Barclay Walker, a local brewer and Mayor of Liverpool, this gallery houses one of the finest art collections in the North. Paintings range from early Italian and Flemish works to Rubens, Rembrandt, Poussin, and French Impressionists such as Degas' *Woman Ironing* (c.1890). Among the strong collection of British artists from the 18th century onward are works by Millais and Turner and Gainsborough's *Countess of Sefton* (1769). There is 20th-century art by Hockney and Sickert, and the sculpture collection includes works by Henry Moore.

Seashells (1870)
Albert Moore paint female figures base on antique statues. Influenced by Whistler (see p505), he adopted subtle shading.

15

14

5

13

7

12

Interior at Paddington
(1951) Lucian Freud's friend Harry Diamond posed for six months for this picture, intended by the artist to "make the human being uncomfortable".

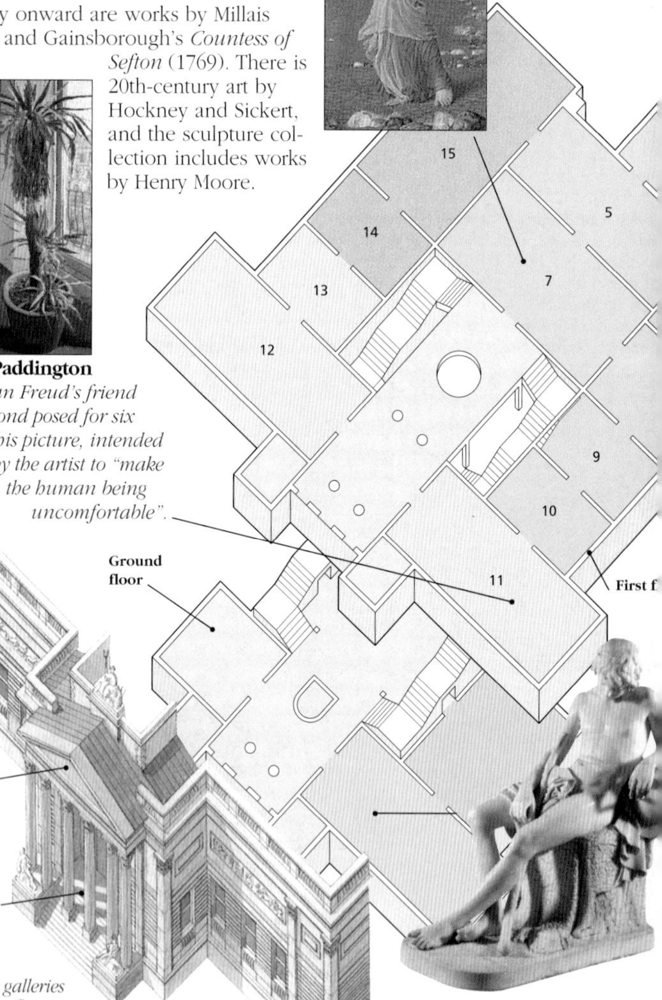

9

10

11

First f

Ground floor

Façade was designed by HH Vale and Cornelius Sherlock.

Main entrance

Gᴀʟʟᴇʀʏ Gᴜɪᴅᴇ
*All the picture galleries are on the first floor.
Rooms 1–2 house medieval and Renaissance paintings; Room 3 has 17th-century Dutch, French, Italian and Spanish art. British 18th- and 19th-century works are in Rooms 4–6 and 12–15. Modern art is in Rooms 9 and 11, and Room 10 has Impressionists and Post-Impressionists.*

Sleeping Shepherd (1835)
The greatest British Neo-Classic sculptor of the mid-19th century John Gibson (1790–1866), used traditional colours to give his statuary a smooth appearance.

VISITORS' CHECKLIST

William Brown St, Liverpool.
🛈 0151 478 4199. 🚇 Lime St.
🚌 to Empire Theatre or Lime St.
🕐 10am–5pm Mon–Sat; noon–
5pm Sun. ⬤ 23–26 Dec, 1 Jan.
♿ 📷 by arrangement. 📷

The 7th-century Kingston Brooch in Liverpool Museum

🏛 Liverpool Museum

William Brown St. 🛈 0151 478 4399.
🕐 daily (Sun: pm). ⬤ 24–26 Dec,
1 Jan. ♿ 📷 📷
Five floors of exhibits in this
excellent museum include
hands-on galleries, a Treasure
House and a Discovery
Centre, allowing close contact
with rarely seen treasures.
The Bug House shows the
world from an insect's point
of view.

⛪ Anglican Cathedral

St James' Mount. 🛈 0151 709
6271. 🕐 daily (Sun: pm). ♿ 📷 📷
Although Gothic in style, this
building was only completed
in 1978. The largest Anglican
cathedral in the world is a fine
red sandstone edifice designed
by Sir Giles Gilbert Scott. The
foundation stone was laid
in 1904 by Edward VII, but
dogged by two world wars,
building work dragged on to
modified designs. The aisles
are built as tunnels through
the walls. Note the stained
glass, high altar and sumptuous embroidery collection.

⛪ Metropolitan Cathedral of Christ the King

Mount Pleasant. 🛈 0151 709 9222.
🕐 daily. **Donation.** ♿ 📷
Liverpool's Roman Catholic
cathedral rejected traditional
forms in favour of a striking
modern design. Early plans,
drawn up by Pugin and later
by Lutyens (see p25) in the
1930s, proved too expensive.
The final version, brainchild of
Sir Frederick Gibberd and
built from 1962–7, is a circular
building surmounted by a
stylized crown of thorns 88 m
(290 ft) high. It is irreverently
known as "Paddy's Wigwam"
by non-Catholics (a reference
to Liverpool's large Irish
population). Inside, the stained

glass lantern, designed by John
Piper and Patrick Reyntiens,
floods the circular nave with
diffused blueish light. A tour
around the inner walls reveals
many sculptures and a fine
bronze of Christ by Elisabeth
Frink (1930–94) on the altar.

ENVIRONS: A spectacular richly
timbered building dating from
1490, **Speke Hall** lies 6 miles
(10 km) east of Liverpool's
centre, surrounded by lovely
grounds. The oldest parts of
the hall enclose a cobbled
courtyard dominated by two
yew trees, Adam and Eve. The
16th-century hiding places for
persecuted priests still remain.

Birkenhead on the Wirral
peninsula has been linked to
Liverpool by ferry for over
800 years. Now, road and rail
tunnels supplement access.
The Norman Priory is still in
use on Sundays, and stately
Hamilton Square was designed
from 1825–44 by J Gillespie
Graham, one of the architects
of Edinburgh's New Town.

On the Wirral side of the
Mersey is **Port Sunlight
Village** (see p335), a Victorian
garden village built by
successful and enlightened
soap manufacturer William
Hesketh Lever for the benefit
of his factory workers.

🚊 Speke Hall

(NT) The Walk, Speke. 🛈 0151 427
7231. 🕐 Apr–Oct: Wed–Sun (pm);
Nov–mid-Dec: Sat, Sun (pm); public
hols. 📷 ♿ limited. 📷 📷

🚊 Port Sunlight Village & Heritage Centre

95 Greendale Rd, Port Sunlight, Wirral.
🛈 0151 644 6466. 🕐 Apr–Oct:
10am–4pm; Nov–Mar: 11am–4pm
daily. ⬤ Christmas wk. 📷 📷
♿ 📷

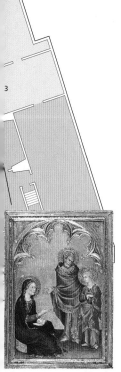

Christ Discovered in the Temple (1342)
Simone Martini's Holy
Family conveys emotional
tension through highly
expressive body language.

KEY TO FLOORPLAN

☐ 13th–17th-century European

☐ 18th–19th-century British,
Pre-Raphaelites and Victorian

☐ Impressionist/Post-Impressionist

☐ 20th-century British

☐ Sculpture gallery

☐ Craft and design gallery

☐ Contemporary

☐ Temporary exhibitions

☐ Non-exhibition space

Entrance to the half-timbered manor house of Speke Hall

YORKSHIRE AND THE HUMBER REGION

NORTH YORKSHIRE · EAST RIDING OF YORKSHIRE

*W*ITH THE HISTORIC CITY *of York at its heart, this is an area of picturesque moorland and valleys. To the north lie the Yorkshire Dales and the North York Moors; eastwards, a coastline of beaches; and southwards, a landscape of lush meadows.*

Yorkshire was originally made up of three separate counties, formerly known as "Ridings". Today it covers over 5,000 sq miles (12,950 sq km). The northeast section has dramatic limestone scenery that was carved by glaciers in the Ice Age. Farming was the original livelihood, and the dry-stone walls weaving up precipitous scars and fells were used to divide the land. Imposed on this were the industries of the 19th century; blackened mill chimneys and crumbling viaducts are as much a part of the scenery as the grand houses of those who profited from them.

Close to the Humber, the landscape is very different, dominated historically by the now flagging fishing industry, and geographically by lush, sprawling meadows. Its coastline is exceptional, and further north are the attractions of wide, sandy beaches and bustling harbour towns. Yet it is the contrasting landscapes that make the area so appealing, ranging from the bleak moorland of the Brontë novels to the ragged cliff coast around Whitby, and the flat expanse of Sunk Island.

The city of York, where Roman and Viking relics exist side by side, is second only to London in the number of visitors that tread its streets. Indeed the historical centre of York is the region's foremost attraction. Those in search of a real taste of Yorkshire, however, should head for the countryside. In addition to excellent touring routes, a network of rewarding walking paths range from mellow ambles along the Cleveland Way to rocky scrambles over the Pennine Way at Pen-y-Ghent.

Lobster pots on the quayside at the picturesque fishing port of Whitby

◁ **The peaceful valley of Rosedale, North York Moors**

Exploring Yorkshire and the Humber Region

Yorkshire covers a wide area, once made up of three counties or "Ridings". Until the arrival of railways, mining and the wool industry in the 19th century, the county was a farming area. Dry-stone walls dividing fields still pepper the northern part of the county, alongside 19th-century mill chimneys and country houses. Among the many abbeys are Rievaulx and the magnificent Fountains. The medieval city of York is a major attraction, as are Yorkshire's beaches. The Humber region is characterized by the softer, rolling countryside of the Wolds, and its nature reserves attract enormous quantities of birds.

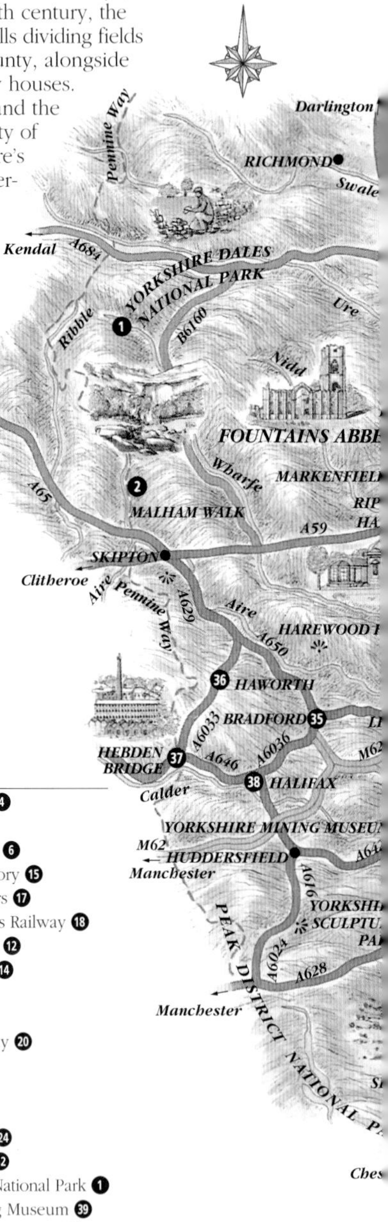

Rosedale village in the North York Moors

SIGHTS AT A GLANCE

Darlington

RICHMOND

Swale

Kendal

A684

YORKSHIRE DALES
NATIONAL PARK

Ribble

1

B6160

Ure

Nidd

FOUNTAINS ABBEY

Wharfe

MARKENFIELD

2

MALHAM WALK

RIP
HA

A59

A65

SKIPTON

Clitheroe

Aire Pennine Way

A629

Aire

A650

HAREWOOD H

36 HAWORTH

A6033

BRADFORD **35**

LI

HEBDEN
BRIDGE **37**

A646

A6036

M62

Calder

38 HALIFAX

YORKSHIRE MINING MUSEUM

M62

HUDDERSFIELD

A64

Manchester

A616

YORKSHI
SCULPTU
PA

PEAK DISTRICT NATIONAL PA

A6024

A628

Manchester

Ches

S

Section of Lendal Bridge (1863)
crossing the Ouse in York

Middlesbrough

MOUNT
GRACE
PRIORY **15**
Cleveland Way

NORTH YORK
MOORS
NATIONAL PARK

WHITBY **19** ROBIN
HOOD'S
BAY **20**

Esk

A169

A171

NORTH YORK
MOORS **17** **18**

NORTH YORK
MOORS RAILWAY

HUTTON-LE-
HOLE **16**

A170

Seven

RIEVAULX ABBEY **14**

13 HELMSLEY

Derwent

21

SCARBOROUGH

RIVAULX ABBEY

BYLAND
ABBEY

9

10

COXWOLD **11**

12 NUNNINGTON HALL

A170 Hertford

A165

CASTLE
HOWARD

Rye

22 **23** EDEN CAMP

A64

BEMPTON &
FLAMBOROUGH HEAD
26

Ouse

A19

Derwent

WHARRAM PERCY **24**

A166

BURTON AGNES **25**

A166

A164

A165

N
O
R
T
H

S
E
A

KNARESBOROUGH

Nidd

A59

32 YORK

A64

Ouse

A1079

BEVERLEY **27**

A164

A165

28 BURTON CONSTABLE

A63

A63

Aire

M62

KINGSTON UPON HULL **29**

Hull

B1238

A63

M62

Trent

Don

M18

M180

A15

SUNK
ISLAND

Humber

A180

HOLDERNESS
&SPURN
HEAD **30**

DONCASTER

M18

A1(M)

GRIMSBY **31**

A16

A15

Newark-on-
Trent

M1

Nottingham

0 kilometres   15

0 miles   10

KEY

Motorway

Major road

Minor road

Scenic route

Scenic path

River

Viewpoint

GETTING AROUND

The area is served by the A1, the M1,
the M62 and the A59. InterCity trains
run to major cities such as York and
Leeds, and there are train or coach
(bus) links between many towns and
hamlets. The Yorkshire Dales and
North York Moors national parks are
good for walkers and cyclists can enjoy
rides around York and the river Humber.

Yorkshire Dales National Park ➊

THE YORKSHIRE DALES is a farming landscape, formed from three principle dales, Swaledale, Wharfedale and Wensleydale, and a number of small ones, such as Deepdale. Glaciation in the Ice Age helped carve out these steep-sided valleys, and this scenery contrasts with the high moorlands. However, 12 centuries of settlement have altered the landscape in the form of cottages, castles and villages which create a delightful environment for walking. A national park since 1954, the area provides recreation while serving local community needs.

Monk's Wynd – one of Richmond's narrow, winding streets

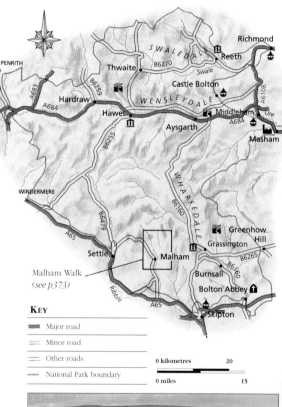

KEY

▮▮▮▮	Major road
≈≈≈	Minor road
≈≈≈	Other roads
━━	National Park boundary

Malham Walk
(see p.373)

0 kilometres   20

0 miles   15

Exploring Swaledale

Swaledale's prosperity was founded largely on wool, and it is famous for its herd of sheep that graze on the wild higher slopes in the harshest weather. The fast-moving river Swale that gives the northernmost dale its name travels from bleak moorland down magnificent waterfalls into the richly wooded lower slopes, passing through the village of Reeth and the town of Richmond.

♠ Richmond Castle

Tower Street. **[** 01748 822493.
⭘ *daily.* ⬤ 25 Dec. ◪ & *limited.*
Swaledale's main point of entry is the medieval market town of Richmond, which has the largest cobbled marketplace in England. Alan Rufus, the Norman 1st Earl of Richmond, began building the castle in 1071, and some of the masonry on the curtain walls probably dates from that time. It has a fine Norman keep, 30 m (100 ft) high with walls 3.3 m (11 ft) thick. An 11th-century arch leads into a courtyard containing Scolland's Hall (1080), one of England's oldest buildings.

Richmond's marketplace was once the castle's outer bailey. Its quaint, narrow streets gave rise to the song, *The Lass of Richmond Hill* (1787), written by Leonard McNally for his wife, Frances I'Anson, who was brought up in Hill House, on Richmond Hill. Turner (*see*

The green, rolling landscape of Deepdale, near Dent

p93) depicted the town many times. The Georgian Theatre (1788), which was restored in 1962, is the only one of its age still surviving.

🏛 Swaledale Folk Museum
Reeth Green. 📞 *01748 884373.*
◯ *Easter–Oct: daily.* 🅿
Reeth, a town that became known as the centre of the lead-mining industry and helped bring prosperity to the region, houses this museum in a former Methodist Sunday school (1830). Included in it are mining and wool-making artifacts (wool from the hardy Swaledale sheep was another mainstay of the economy) and brass band memorabilia.

🗻 Buttertubs
Near Thwaite, on the B6270 Hawes road, are a series of potholes that streams fall into. These became known as the Buttertubs when farmers going to market lowered their butter into the holes to keep it cool.

Buttertubs, near Thwaite

Exploring Wensleydale
The largest of the Yorkshire dales, Wensleydale is famous for its cheese and more recently for James Herriot's books and the television series, *All Creatures Great and Small.* It is easy walking country for anyone seeking an alternative to major moorland hikes.

🏛 Dales Countryside Museum
Station Yard, Hawes. 📞 *01969 667450.* ◯ *daily.* 🅿 🅖
In a former railway goods warehouse in Hawes, capital of Upper Wensleydale, is a

Barrels at the Theakston Brewery

fascinating museum, filled with items from life and industry in the 18th- and 19th-century Upper Dales. This includes cheese- and butter-making equipment. Wensleydale cheese was created by monks at nearby Jervaulx Abbey. There is also a rope-making works a short walk away.

Hawes itself is the highest market town in England, at 259 m (850 ft) above sea level. It is a thriving centre where thousands of sheep and cattle are auctioned each summer.

🗻 Hardraw Force
At the tiny village of Hardraw, nearby, is England's tallest single-drop waterfall, with no outcrops to interrupt its 29 m (96 ft) fall. It became famous in Victorian times when the daredevil Blondin walked across it on a tightrope. Today, you can walk right under this fine waterfall, against the rock face, and look through the stream without getting wet.

🗻 Aysgarth Waterfalls
An old packhorse bridge gives a clear view of the point at which the previously placid River Ure suddenly begins to plunge in foaming torrents over wide limestone shelves. Turner painted the impressive lower falls in 1817.

🏛 Theakston Brewery
Masham. 📞 *01765 689057.*
◯ *Apr–Oct: daily; Nov: Wed, Sat, Sun.* 🔴 *mid-Dec–Mar.* 🅖
🅖 *limited.* 🅿 🅖
The pretty town of Masham is the home of Theakston brewery, creator of the potent ale Old Peculier. The history of this local family brewery from its origin in 1827 is on

VISITORS' CHECKLIST

North Yorkshire. 🚆 *Skipton.*
🅸 *National Park Centre, Grassington (01756 752774).*

display in the visitors' centre. Masham village itself has an attractive square once used for sheep fairs, surrounded by 17th- and 18th-century houses. There is a medieval church.

♟ Bolton Castle
Castle Bolton, nr Leyburn. 📞 *01969 623981.* ◯ *daily.* 🔴 *25 Dec.* 🅖
🅿 🅸 🅖 *to gardens.*
Situated in the village of Castle Bolton, this castle was built in 1379 by the 1st Lord Scrope, Chancellor of England. It was used as a fortress from 1568 to 1569 when Mary, Queen of Scots *(see p497)* was held prisoner here by Elizabeth I *(see pp50– 51).* Three of the castle's towers are at their original height of 30 m (100 ft).

♟ Middleham Castle
Middleham, nr Leyburn. 📞 *01969 623899.* ◯ *Jan–Mar: 10am–4pm Wed–Sun; Apr–Sep: 10am–6pm daily; Oct: 10am–5pm daily; Nov–Dec: 10am– 4pm daily.* 🔴 *24–26 Dec.* 🅖 🅖 🅿
Owned by Richard Neville, Earl of Warwick, it was built in 1170. The castle is better known as home to Richard III *(see p49)* when he was made Lord of the North. It was once one of the strongest fortresses in the north but became uninhabited during the 15th century, when many of its stones were used for nearby buildings. The keep provides a fine view of the landscape.

Remains of Middleham Castle, once residence of Richard III

Extensive ruins of Bolton Priory, dating from 1154

Exploring Wharfedale

This dale is characterized by gritstone moorland, contrasting with quiet market towns along meandering sections of river. Many consider Grassington a central point for exploring Wharfedale, but the showpiece villages of Burnsall, overlooked by a 506 m (1,661 ft) fell, and Buckden, 701 m (2,302 ft), near Buckden Pike, also make excellent bases.

Nearby are the Three Peaks of Whernside, 736 m (2,416 ft), Ingleborough, 724 m (2,376 ft) and Pen-y-Ghent 694 m (2,278 ft). They are known for their potholes and tough terrain, but this does not deter keen walkers from attempting to climb them all in one day. If you sign in at the Pen-y-Ghent café at Horton-in-Ribblesdale, at the centre of the Three Peaks, and complete the 20 mile (32 km) course, reaching the summit of all three peaks in less than 12 hours, you can qualify for membership of the Three Peaks of Yorkshire Club.

🔒 Burnsall

St Wilfrid's, Burnsall. 📞 *01756 720232.* ◯ *daily.* ♿
Preserved in St Wilfrid's church graveyard are the original village stocks, gravestones from Viking times and a headstone carved in memory of the Dawson family by sculptor Eric Gill (1882–1940). The village has a five-arched bridge and hosts Britain's oldest fell race every August.

🏛 Upper Wharfedale Museum

The Square, Grassington.
◯ *Apr–Sep: daily (pm); Oct–Mar: Sat & Sun (pm).* 🈺 ♿ *limited.*
This folk museum is set in two 18th-century lead miners' cottages. Its exhibits illustrate the domestic and working history of the area, including farming and lead mining.

🔒 Bolton Priory

Bolton Abbey, nr Skipton. 📞 *01756 710238.* ◯ *daily.* ♿
One of the most beautiful areas of Wharfedale is around the village of Bolton Abbey, set in an estate owned by the Dukes of Devonshire. While preserving its astounding beauty, its managers have incorporated over 30 miles (46 km) of footpaths, many suitable for the disabled and young families.

The ruins of Bolton Priory, established by Augustinian canons in 1154 on the site of a Saxon manor, are extensive. They include a church, chapter house, cloister and prior's lodging. These all demonstrate the wealth accumulated by the canons from the sale of wool from their flocks of sheep. The priory nave is still used as a parish church. Another attraction of the estate is the "Strid", a point where the River Wharfe surges spectacularly through a gorge, foaming yellow and gouging holes out of the rocks.

📷 Stump Cross Caverns

Greenhow Hill, Pateley Bridge.
📞 *01756 752780 or 01423 711042.*
◯ *Apr– Oct: daily; Nov–Mar: Sat & Sun (26 Dec–1 Jan daily); ring in winter as may be closed due to bad weather.* ● *25 Dec.* 🈺 🖥 🚻
These caves were formed over a period of half a million years: trickles of underground water formed intertwining passages and carved them into fantastic shapes and sizes. Sealed off in the last Ice Age, the caves were only discovered in the 1850s when lead miners sank a mine shaft into the caverns.

♣ Skipton Castle

High St. 📞 *01756 792442.* ◯ *daily (Sun: pm).* ● *25 Dec.* 🈺 🖥 🚻
The market town of Skipton is still one of the largest auctioning and stockraising centres in the north. Its 11th-century castle was almost entirely rebuilt by Robert de Clifford in the 14th century. Beautiful Conduit Court was added by Henry, Lord Clifford, in Henry VIII's reign. The central yew tree was planted by Lady Anne Clifford in 1659 to mark restoration work to the castle after Civil War damage.

Conduit Court (1495) and yew tree at Skipton Castle

Malham Walk ②

THE MALHAM AREA, shaped by glacial erosion 10,000 years ago, has one of Great Britain's most dramatic limestone landscapes. The walk from Malham village can take over four hours if you pause to enjoy the viewpoints and take a detour to Gordale Scar. Those who are short of time tend to go only as far as Malham Cove. This vast natural amphitheatre, formed by a huge geological tear, is like a giant boot-heel mark in the landscape. Above lie the deep crevices of Malham Lings, where rare flora such as hart's-tongue flourishes. Unusual plants grow in the lime-rich Malham Tarn, said to have provided inspiration for Charles Kingsley's *The Water Babies* (1863). Coot and mallard visit the tarn in summer and tufted duck in winter.

Sandpiper at Malham Tarn

Where the path meets the road ⑤
From here, you can catch a bus back to Malham village.

🏠 Malham Tarn House

Malham Tarn ④
Yorkshire's second-largest lake lies 305 m (1,000 ft) above sea level in a designated nature reserve.

Malham Lings ③
This fine limestone pavement was formed when Ice Age meltwater seeped into cracks in the rock, then froze and expanded.

Gordale Scar ⑥
Guarded by steep limestone cliffs, this deep gorge was created by meltwater from Ice Age glaciers.

Malham Cove ②
The black streak in the centre of this 76 m (250 ft) cove is the site of a former waterfall.

SKIPTON

KEY

- ▪▪ Walk route
- ══ Minor road
- ⚡ Viewpoint
- 🅿 Parking
- ℹ Tourist information
- 🚻 Toilets

Malham ①
An attractive riverside village, it has an information centre with details of drives and walks.

0 kilometres	1

| 0 miles | ½ |

TIPS FOR WALKERS

Starting point: Malham.
Getting there: Leave M65 at Junction 14 and take A56 to Skipton, then follow signs to Malham which is off A65.
Length: 7 miles (11 km).
Difficulty: Malham Cove is steep but the Tarn area is flatter.

A 1920s poster advertising the spa town of Harrogate

Harrogate ❸

North Yorkshire. 🏃 69,000. ☎ 🚌
🛈 Assembly Rooms, Crescent Rd
(01423 537300). 🗓 Mon–Sat.
🖥 www.harrogate.gov.uk

BETWEEN 1880 and World War I, Harrogate was the north's leading spa town, with nearly 90 medicinal springs. It was ideal for aristocrats who, after a tiring London season, were able to stop for a health cure before journeying on to grouse-shooting in Scotland.

Today, Harrogate's main attractions are its spa town atmosphere, fine architecture, public gardens and its convenience as a centre for visiting North Yorkshire and the Dales.

The naturally welling spa waters may not currently be in use, but you can still go for a Turkish bath in one of the country's most attractive steam rooms. The entrance at the side of the Royal Bath

Assembly Rooms (1897) is unassuming, but once inside, the century-old **Harrogate Turkish Baths** are a visual feast of tiled Victoriana.

The town's spa history is recorded in the **Royal Pump Room Museum**. At the turn of the century, the waters were thought to be rich in iron early in the day. So, between 7am and 9am the 1842 octagonal building would have been filled with rich and fashionable people drinking glasses of water. Poorer people could take water from the pump outside. Today you can sample the waters and enjoy the museum's exhibits, including a Penny Farthing bicycle.

Harrogate is also known for the rainbow-coloured flowerbeds in **The Stray**, a common space to the south of the town centre, and for the ornamental **Harlow Car Gardens**, owned by the Northern Horticultural Society. Visitors can enjoy the

delicious cakes at **Betty's Café Tea Rooms** (see p598).

🏛 **Harrogate Turkish Baths**
Assembly Rooms, Crescent Rd. ☎ 01423 556746. 🗓 **Men**: Mon, Wed & Fri: (pm); Sat. **Women**: Mon (am); Tue & Thu: (pm); Fri (am); Sun. **Mixed** (in costume): Tue (am); (couples only in costume): Fri (eve); Sun (eve). ⬤ public hols (except Good Friday). 🎫

🏛 **Royal Pump Room Museum**
Crown Pl. ☎ 01423 556188. 🗓 daily. ⬤ 24–26 Dec, 1 Jan. 🎫 ♿ 🚻

🏛 **Betty's Café Tea Rooms**
1 Parliament St. ☎ 01423 502746. 🗓 daily. ⬤ 25–26 Dec, 1 Jan.

🌿 **Harlow Car Gardens**
Crag Lane. ☎ 01423 565418. 🗓 daily. 🎫 ♿ 🍴 🛍

Knaresborough ❹

North Yorkshire. 🏃 14,000. ☎ 🚌 from Harrogate. 🛈 9 Castle Courtyard, Market Place (01423 866886). 🛒 Wed.

PERCHED PRECIPITOUSLY above the River Nidd is one of England's oldest towns, mentioned in the Domesday Book of 1086 (see p48). Its historic streets – which link the church, John of Gaunt's ruined castle, and the market place with the river – are now lined with fine 18th-century houses.

Nearby is **Mother Shipton's Cave**, reputedly England's oldest tourist attraction. It first went on show in 1630 as the birthplace of Ursula Southeil, a famous local prophetess. Today, people can view the

Mother Shipton's cave, with objects encased in limestone

Tudor gatehouse and moat at Markenfield Hall

effect the well near her cave has on objects hung below the dripping surface. Almost any item, from umbrellas to soft toys, will become encased in limestone within a few weeks.

Mother Shipton's Cave

Prophesy House, High Bridge.
01423 864600. ☐ daily. ● 25 Dec. 🌀 ☤ limited. ☑ ☐ ☐

Ripley ❺

North Yorkshire. ⚐ 150. 🚌 from Harrogate or Ripon.

SINCE THE 1320s, when the first generation of the Ingilby family lived in an early incarnation of **Ripley Castle**, the village has been made up almost exclusively of castle employees. The influence of one 19th-century Ingilby had the most visual impact. In the 1820s, Sir William Amcotts Ingilby was so entranced by a village in Alsace Lorraine that he created a similar one in French Gothic style, complete with an *Hotel de Ville*. Present-day Ripley has a cobbled market square, and quaint cottages line the streets. The churchyard has a medieval cross with niches for kneeling at the base.

Ripley Castle, with its 15th-century gatehouse, was where Oliver Cromwell *(see p52)* stayed following the Battle of Marston Moor. The 28th generation of Ingilbys live here, and it is open for tours. The attractive grounds contain two lakes and a deer park, as well as more formal gardens.

♠ Ripley Castle

Ripley. ◀ 01423 770152. ☐ Sep–May: Tue, Thu–Sun; Jun–Aug: daily. ● 25 Dec. 🌀 ☤ ☑ ☐ ☐

Markenfield Hall ❻

Nr Markenfield, North Yorkshire.
🛈 01765 604625. 🚌 from Harrogate or Ripon. ● until further notice.

A MOATED MANOR house dating from the 14th century, Markenfield Hall is not sign-posted and open only in the summer. To find it you need to drive 3 miles (5 km) south of Ripon, and turn up a farm track marked with a bridleway sign (Hell Wath Lane). On one side of the drawbridge, between the moat and the manor walls, is the farmer's vegetable patch. Once inside the L-shaped house, note the great banqueting hall, chapel and kitchen fireplace.

The Markenfields were one of the powerful northern families to oppose Henry VIII and the Dissolution of the Monasteries *(see p337)*. It was from their manor house that an army set off in 1569 in an unsuccessful attempt to remove Elizabeth I from the throne and replace her with the Catholic Mary, Queen of Scots.

Fountains Abbey ❼

See pp376–7.

Ripon ❽

North Yorkshire. ⚐ 14,000. 🚌 from Harrogate. 🛈 Minster Rd (01765 604625). 🏛 Thu.

RIPON, A CHARMING small city, is best known for the cathedral and "the watch", which has been announced since the Middle Ages by the Wakeman. In return for protecting Ripon citizens, he would charge an annual toll of two pence per household. Today, a man still blows a horn in the Market Square each evening at 9pm, and every Thursday a handbell is rung to open the market.

The **Cathedral of St Peter and St Wilfrid** is built above a 7th-century Saxon crypt. At less than 3 m (10 ft) high and just over 2 m (7 ft) wide, it is held to be the oldest complete crypt in England. The cathedral is known for its collection of misericords *(see p327)*, which include both pagan and Old Testament examples. The architectural historian Sir Nikolaus Pevsner (1902–83) considered the cathedral's West Front the finest in England.

Ripon's **Prison and Police Museum**, housed in the 1686 "House of Correction", looks at the history of the police and, in its first floor cells, the conditions in Victorian prisons.

🏛 Prison and Police Museum

St Marygate. ◀ 01765 690799. ☐ Apr–Oct: daily. ● Nov–Mar. 🌀 ☤ limited.

Ripon's Wakeman, blowing his horn in the Market Square

Fountains Abbey **7**

Nestling in the wooded valley of the River Skell are the extensive sandstone ruins of Fountains Abbey and the outstanding water garden of Studley Royal. Fountains Abbey was founded by Benedictine monks in 1132 and taken over by Cistercians three years later. By the mid-12th century it had become the wealthiest abbey in Britain, though it fell into ruin during the Dissolution (*see p50*). In 1720, John Aislabie, the MP for Ripon and Chancellor of the Exchequer, developed the land and forest of the abbey ruins. He began work, continued by his son William, on the famous water garden, the statuary and Classical temples in the grounds. This makes a dramatic contrast to the simplicity of the abbey.

Fountains Hall
Built by Sir Stephen Proctor around 1611, with stones from the abbey ruins, its design is attributed to architect Robert Smythson. It included a great hall with a minstrels' gallery and an entrance flanked by Classical columns.

THE ABBEY

The abbey buildings were designed to reflect the Cistercians' desire for simplicity and austerity. The abbey frequently dispensed charity to the poor and the sick, as well as travellers.

The Chapel of Nine Altars at the east end of the church was built from 1203 to 1247. It is ornate, compared to the rest of the abbey, with an 18 m (60 ft) high window complemented by another at the western end of the nave.

Chapter house

Cloister

Cellarium (storehouse)

Kitchen

Abbot's house

Monks' infirmary hall

Refectory

Lay brothers' infirmary

Lay brothers' refectory

The undercroft, supported by 19 pillars, with vaulting 90 m (300 ft) long, was used for storing fleeces which the abbey monks sold to Venetian and Florentine merchants.

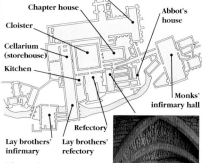

To Visitor Centre and car park

River Skell

Paths leading to the estate park

★ **Abbey**
This was built by using stones taken from the Skell valley.

STAR SIGHTS

★ **Abbey**

★ **Temple of Piety**

St Mary's Church
This sumptuous Victorian Gothic church was built by architect William Burges in 1871–8. Inside, the choir stalls are decorated with multi-coloured carved parrots.

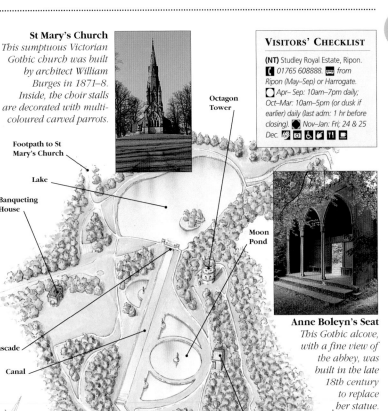

Footpath to St Mary's Church

Lake

Banqueting House

Octagon Tower

Moon Pond

Cascade

Canal

VISITORS' CHECKLIST

(NT) Studley Royal Estate, Ripon.
☎ 01765 608888. ⛟ from Ripon (May–Sep) or Harrogate.
🕐 Apr–Sep: 10am–7pm daily; Oct–Mar: 10am–5pm (or dusk if earlier) daily (last adm: 1 hr before closing). ● Nov–Jan: Fri; 24 & 25 Dec. 🚫 📷 👥 📮 🍴 🛍

Anne Boleyn's Seat
This Gothic alcove, with a fine view of the abbey, was built in the late 18th century to replace her statue.

Temple of Fame
The columns of this domed building are made of hollow timber but look like sandstone.

★ Temple of Piety
This garden house was originally dedicated to Hercules. It was renamed as a symbol of filial piety by William Aislabie after his father's death in 1742.

The 19th-century white horse, seen on one of the walks around Sutton Bank

Sutton Bank ⑨

North Yorkshire. ⬛ *Thirsk.* ⓘ *Sutton Bank (01845 597426).*

Nᴏᴛᴏʀɪᴏᴜs ᴀᴍᴏɴɢ motorists for its 1 in 4 gradient, which climbs for about 107 m (350 ft), Sutton Bank itself is well known for its panoramic views. On a clear day you can see from the Vale of York to the Peak District *(see pp324–5)*. William and his sister Dorothy Wordsworth stopped here to admire the vista in 1802, on their way to visit his future wife, Mary Hutchinson, at

Brompton. Apart from Sutton Bank, where you can walk round the white horse, the area is less wild than the coastal side, and suitable for children.

Byland Abbey ⑩

Coxwold, York. ⓒ *01347 868614.* 🚌 *from York or Helmsley.* ⬛ *Thirsk.* ○ *Apr–Oct: daily.* ● *Nov–Mar.* 🅿 ♿ *limited.*

Tʜɪs ᴄɪsᴛᴇʀᴄɪᴀɴ monastery was founded in 1177 by monks from Furness Abbey in Cumbria. It featured what was

then the largest Cistercian church in Britain, 100 m (328 ft) long and 41 m (135 ft) wide across the transepts. The layout of the entire monastery, including extensive cloisters and the west front of the church, is still visible, as is the green and yellow glazed tile floor. Fine workmanship is shown in carved stone details and in the capitals, kept in the small museum.

In 1322 the Battle of Byland was fought nearby, and King Edward II *(see p40)* narrowly escaped capture when the invading Scottish army learned that he was dining with the Abbot. In his hurry to escape, the king had to leave many treasures behind, which were looted by the invading soldiers.

Coxwold ⑪

North Yorkshire. 🏠 *160.* ⓘ *23 Kirkgate, Thirsk (01845 522755).* 🆆 *www.hambleton.gov.uk*

Sɪᴛᴜᴀᴛᴇᴅ ᴊᴜsᴛ inside the bounds of the North York Moors National Park *(see p381)*, this charming village nestles at the foot of the Howardian Hills. Its pretty houses are built from local stone, and the 15th-century church has some fine Georgian

Shandy Hall, home of author Laurence Sterne, now a museum

box pews and an impressive octagonal tower. But Coxwold is best known as the home of the author Laurence Sterne (1713–68), whose writings include *Tristram Shandy* and *A Sentimental Journey*.

Sterne moved here in 1760 as the church curate. He rented a rambling house that he named **Shandy Hall** after a Yorkshire expression meaning eccentric. Originally built as a timber-framed, open-halled house in the 15th century, it was modernized in the 17th century and Sterne later added a façade. His grave lies beside the porch at Coxwold's church.

🏠 Shandy Hall

Coxwold. 📞 *01347 868465*.
🕐 *May–Sep: Wed & Sun (pm).*
♿ *limited.* **Gardens** 🕐 *Sun–Fri.*

Nunnington Hall ⑫

(NT) Nunnington, York. 📞 *01439 748283*. 🚌 *Malton, then bus or taxi.* 🕐 *Apr–May, Sep–Oct: Wed–Sun (pm); Jun–Aug: Tue–Sun, public hols (pm).* 📷 ♿ *ground floor.*

S ET IN ALLURING surroundings, this 17th-century manor house is a combination of architectural styles, including features from the Elizabethan and Stuart periods. Both inside and outside, a notable architectural feature is the use of the broken pediment (the upper arch is left unjoined).

Nunnington Hall was a family home until 1952, when Mrs Ronald Fife donated it to the National Trust. A striking

The miniature Queen Anne drawing room at Nunnington Hall

feature is the panelling in the Oak Hall. Formerly painted, it extends over the three-arched screen to the Great Staircase. Nunnington's collection of 22 miniature furnished period rooms is popular with visitors.

A mid-16th-century tenant Dr Robert Huickes, physician to Henry VIII *(see p50 – 51)*, is best known for advising Elizabeth I that she should not, at the age of 32, consider having any children.

Helmsley ⑬

North Yorkshire. 🚶 *2,000.* 🚌 *from Malton.* ℹ️ *Town Hall, Market Place (01439 770173).* 🚐 *Fri.* 🌐 *www.ryesdale.gov.uk/tourism*

T HIS PRETTY MARKET TOWN is noted for its **castle**, now an imposing ruin. Built from 1186 to 1227, its main function and strength as a fortress is illustrated by the remaining keep, tower and curtain walls. The original D-shaped keep had one part blasted away in the Civil War *(see p52)*, but remains the

dominant feature. The castle was so impregnable that there were few attempts to force entry. However, in 1644, after holding out for a three-month seige against Sir Thomas Fairfax, the Parliamentary general, the castle was finally taken.

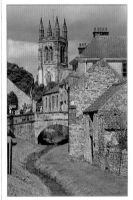

Helmsley church tower

Rievaulx Abbey ⑭

Nr Helmsley, North Yorkshire. 📞 *01439 798228*. 🚌 *Thirsk, then bus or taxi.* 🕐 *daily.* ⬤ *24–26 Dec, 1 Jan.* 📷 ♿ *limited.*

R IEVAULX IS PERHAPS the finest abbey in the area, partly due to its dramatic setting in the steep wooded valley of the River Rye and partly to its extensive remains. It is almost entirely surrounded by steep banks that form natural barriers from the outside world. Monks of the French Cistercian order from Clairvaux founded this, their first major monastery in Britain, in 1132. The main buildings, which include the Cistercian nave, were finished before 1200. The layout of the chapel, kitchens and infirmary give an idea of monastic life.

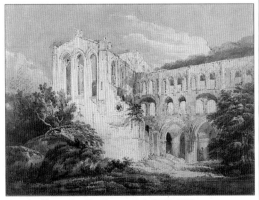

Rievaulx Abbey, painted by Thomas Girtin (1775–1802)

Mount Grace Priory ruins, with farm and mansion in foreground

Mount Grace Priory **⑮**

(NT) Northallerton, North Yorkshire. 01609 883494. ☎ Northallerton then bus. ☐ Apr–Oct: daily; Nov–Mar: Wed–Sun. ● 24–26 Dec, 1 Jan. ☐ grounds & shop only. ☐

FOUNDED BY Thomas Holland, Duke of Surrey, and in use from 1398 until 1539, this is the best-preserved Carthusian or charterhouse monastery *(see pp336–7)* in England. The monks, just 20 of them at the beginning, took a vow of silence and lived in solitary cells, each with his own garden and an angled hatch so that he would not even see the person serving his food. They only met at matins, vespers and feast-day services. Attempts at escape by those who could not endure the rigour of the rules were punished by imprisonment.

The ruins of the priory include the former prison, gatehouse and outer court, barns, guesthouses, cells and the church. The 14th-century church, the best-preserved section of the site, is particularly small, as it was only rarely used by the community. A cell has been reconstructed to give an impression of monastic life.

Hutton-le-Hole **⑯**

North Yorkshire. 🅰 400. ☎ Malton then bus. ℹ The Ropery, Pickering (01751 473791).

THIS PICTURESQUE VILLAGE is characterized by a spacious green, grazed by roaming sheep, and surrounded by houses, an inn and shops. Lengths of white wood, replacing stone bridges, span the moorland stream. Its cottages, some with date panels over the doors, are made from limestone, with red pantiled roofs. In the village centre is the excellent **Ryedale Folk Museum**,

Wheelwright's workshop at Ryedale Folk Museum

which records the lifestyle of an agricultural community by means of Romano-British artifacts and reconstructed buildings.

🏛 **Ryedale Folk Museum**
Hutton-le-Hole. 01751 417367. ☐ mid-Mar–mid-Nov: daily. ☐ ☐

North York Moors Tour **⑰**

See p381.

North York Moors Railway **⑱**

Pickering & Grosmont, North Yorkshire. 01947 895359. ☐ mid-Mar–Oct: daily; some weekends in Nov & Dec. ☐ ☐ ☐ ☐

DESIGNED in 1831 by George Stephenson as a route along the North York Moors and links with the Esk Valley, Pickering and Whitby *(see p382)*, this railway was considered an engineering miracle. Due to budget constraints, Stephenson was not able to build a tunnel, so had to lay the route down the mile-long (1.5 km) incline between Beck Hole and Goathland. The area around Fen Bog had to be stabilized using timber, heather, brushwood and fleeces so that a causeway could be built over it. A horse was used to pull a coach along the track at 10 miles (16 km) per hour. After horsepower came steam, and for almost 130 years the railway linked Whitby to the rest of the country. In the early 1960s the line was closed but in 1967, a group of locals began a campaign to relaunch it, and in 1973 it was officially reopened. Today, the 18 mile (29 km) line runs from Pickering via Levisham, Newtondale Halt and Goathland before stopping at Grosmont, through the scenic heart of the North York Moors.

North York Moors ⑰

The area between Cleveland, the Vale of York and the Vale of Pickering is known as the North York Moors National Park. The landscape consists of bleakly beautiful moors interspersed with lush green valleys. Agriculture is still the main source of income here as it has been for centuries, and until the advent of coal, the communities' local source of fuel was turf. In the 19th century, the geology of the area created extractive industries which included ironstone, lime, coal and building stone.

Farndale
During springtime, this area is famous for the beauty and profusion of its daffodils.

Mallyan Spout
A footpath leads to this waterfall from Goathland.

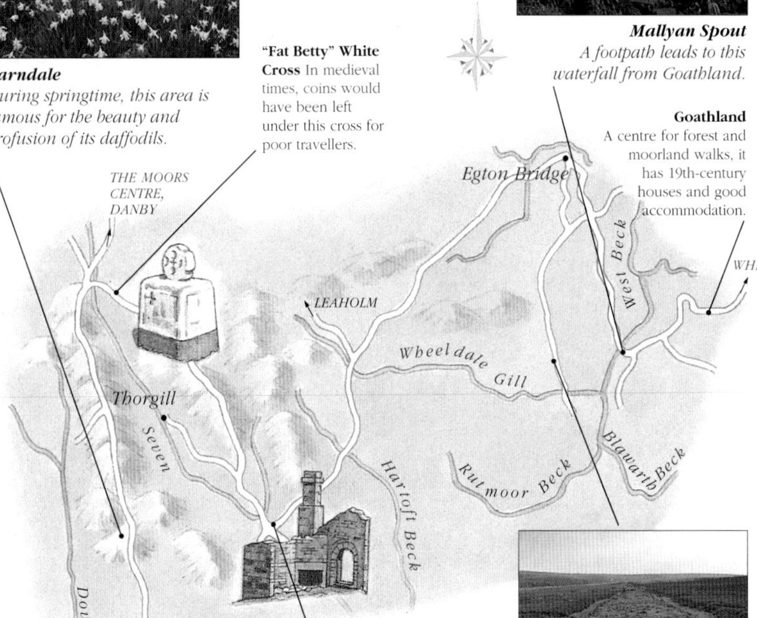

"Fat Betty" White Cross In medieval times, coins would have been left under this cross for poor travellers.

THE MOORS CENTRE, DANBY

Egton Bridge

Goathland
A centre for forest and moorland walks, it has 19th-century houses and good accommodation.

WHITBY

LEAHOLM

West Beck

Wheeldale Gill

Thorgill

Seven

Hartoft Beck

Rutmoor Beck

Blawarth Beck

Dove

Rosedale
After the discovery of ironstone in 1856, this pretty valley became a busy mining centre. Remains of the iron kilns can still be seen.

Hutton-le-Hole
This lovely village has an excellent museum with displays on local crafts and customs.

Spaunton

0 kilometres 2
0 miles 2

Lastingham
Lastingham's church, dating from 1078, has a Norman crypt with stone carving.

Wade's Causeway
This road was built by the Roman army around AD 80, from sandstone slabs laid over a ridge of gravel and sand. It is said that a giant called Wade built the road as a footpath for his wife.

VISITORS' CHECKLIST

North Yorkshire. 🚆 *Pickering.*
🚌 *Pickering.* **Moorsbus**
📞 01439 770567
🛈 Eastgate, Pickering (01751 473791) Helmsley (Fri); Thirsk (Mon & Sat).

KEY

☆ Viewpoint

Whitby ⑲

Jet comb (c.1870)

W HITBY'S KNOWN HISTORY dates back to the 7th century, when a Saxon monastery was founded on the site of today's famous 13th-century abbey ruins. In the 18th and early 19th centuries it became an industrial port and shipbuilding town, as well as a whaling centre. In the Victorian era, the red-roofed cottages at the foot of the east cliff were filled with workshops crafting jet into jewellery and ornaments. Today, the tourist shops that have replaced them sell antique-crafted examples of the distinctive black gem.

VISITORS' CHECKLIST

North Yorkshire. 🏘 13,500.
🚉 Teeside, 50 miles (80 km)
NW Whitby. 🚌 Station Sq. 🔲
Langborne Rd (01947 602674).
🔺 Tue, Sat. 🎪 Whitby Festival:
Jun; Angling Festival: Jul; Lifeboat Day: 29 Aug; Folk Week:
19–25 Aug; Whitby Regatta:
Aug; Captain Cook Festival: Oct.

Exploring Whitby

Whitby is divided into two by the estuary of the River Esk. The Old Town, with its pretty cobbled streets and pastel-hued houses, huddles round the harbour. High above it is St Mary's Church with a wood interior reputedly fitted by ships' carpenters. The ruins of the 13th-century Whitby Abbey, nearby, are still used as a landmark by mariners. From them you get a fine view over the still-busy harbour, strewn with colourful nets. A pleasant place for a stroll, the harbour is overlooked by an imposing bronze clifftop statue of the explorer Captain James Cook (1728–79), who was apprenticed as a teenager to a Whitby shipping firm.

Lobster pots lining the quayside of Whitby's quaint harbour

Medieval arches above the nave of Whitby Abbey

⛪ Whitby Abbey

Abbey Lane. 【 01947 603568.
🔲 daily. 🌑 24–26 Dec. 🎟 🔲
The monastery that Abbess Hilda founded in 657 for men and women was sacked by Vikings in 870. At the end of the 11th century it was rebuilt as a Benedictine Abbey. The present ruins date mainly from 13th-century rebuilding.

⛪ St Mary's Parish Church

East Cliff. 【 01947 603421. 🔲 daily.
Stuart and Georgian alterations to this Norman church have left a mixture of twisted wood columns and maze-like 18th-century box pews. The 1778 triple-decker pulpit has rather avant-garde decor – ear-trumpets used by a Victorian rector's deaf wife.

🏛 Captain Cook Memorial Museum

Grape Lane. 【 01947 601900.
🔲 Mar: Sat & Sun; Apr–Oct: daily.
🎟 🔲
The young James Cook slept in the attic of this 17th-century harbourside house when he was apprenticed nearby. The museum has displays of period furniture in the style described in Cook's inventories and also watercolours by artists who travelled on his voyages.

🏛 Whitby Museum and Pannett Art Gallery

Pannett Park. 【 01947 602908.
🔲 May–Sep: daily; Oct– Apr:
Tue–Sun. 🌑 Sun: am; 24 Dec–2 Jan.
🎟 museum. 🅖 limited. 🔲
The Pannett park grounds, museum and gallery were a gift of Whitby solicitor, Robert Pannett (1834–1920), to house his art collection. Among the museum's treasures are objects illustrating local history, such as jet jewellery, and Captain Cook artefacts.

🏛 Museum of Victorian Whitby

Sandgate. 【 01947 601221.
🔲 daily. 🌑 25 Dec. 🎟
Among the exhibits on Victorian life in Whitby are the animated wheel-house of a whaling ship and a unique collection of miniature room settings.

⛪ Caedmon's Cross

East Cliff. 【 01947 603421.
On the path side of the abbey's clifftop graveyard is the cross of Caedmon, an illiterate labourer who worked at the abbey in the 7th century. He had a vision that inspired him to compose cantos of Anglo-Saxon religious verse still sung today.

Cross of Caedmon (1898)

Robin Hood's Bay ㉒

North Yorkshire. 🚶 *1,400.* 🚆 🚌
Whitby. ℹ️ *Langbourne Rd, Whitby
(01947 602674).* 🌐 www.ycc.org.uk

LEGEND HAS IT that Robin Hood (*see p322*) kept his boats here in case he needed to make a quick getaway. The village has a history as a smugglers' haven, and many houses have ingenious hiding places for contraband beneath the floor and behind the walls. The cobbled main street is so steep that visitors need to leave their vehicles in the car park. In the village centre, attractive, narrow streets full of colour-washed stone cottages huddle around a quaint quay. There is a rocky beach with rock pools for children to play in. At low tide, the pleasant walk south to Boggle Hole takes 15 minutes, but you need to keep an eye on the tides.

Cobbled alley in the Bay Town area of Robin Hood's Bay

The fishing port and town of Scarborough nestling round the harbour

Scarborough ㉑

North Yorkshire. 🚶 *54,000.* 🚆 🚌
ℹ️ *Pavilion House, Valley Bridge Rd
(01723 373333).* 🛒 *Mon–Sat.*
🌐 www.scarborough.gov.uk

THE HISTORY OF Scarborough as a resort can be traced back to 1626, when it became known as a spa. In the Industrial Revolution (*see pp334–5*) it was nicknamed "the Queen of the Watering Places", but the post-World War II trend for holidays abroad has meant fewer visitors. The town has two beaches; the South Bay amusement arcades contrast with the quieter North Bay.

Playwright Alan Ayckbourn premiers his work at the Joseph Rowntree theatre, and Anne Brontë (*see p398*) is buried in St Mary's Church.

Bronze and Iron Age relics have been found on the site of **Scarborough Castle**, and **Wood End Museum** exhibits local geology and history. The **Rotunda** (1828–9) was one of Britain's first purpose-built museums. Works by local artist Atkinson Grimshaw (1836–93) hang in **Scarborough Art Gallery**. The **Sea-Life and Marine Sanctuary**'s baby seals are its main attraction.

⚓ **Scarborough Castle**
Castle Rd. ☎️ *01723 372451.*
🕐 *Apr–Oct daily; Nov–Mar:
Wed–Sun.* ⬛ *24–26 Dec.* 🎫 ♿ 🚻
🏛 **Wood End Museum**
The Crescent. ☎️ *01723 367326.*
🕐 *May–mid-Oct: Tue–Sun; mid-
Oct–Apr: Wed, Sat, Sun & public hols.*
⬛ *25, 26 Dec, 1 Jan.* 🎫 🚻
🏛 **Rotunda Museum**
Vernon Rd. ☎️ *01723 374839.*
🕐 *May–mid-Oct: Tue–Sun; mid-
Oct–Apr: Tue, Sat, Sun & public hols.*
⬛ *25, 26 Dec, 1 Jan.* 🎫 🚻
🏛 **Scarborough Art Gallery**
The Crescent. ☎️ *01723 374753.*
🕐 *May–mid-Oct: Tue–Sun; mid-
Oct–Apr: Thu, Fri, Sat & public hols.*
⬛ *25, 26 Dec, 1 Jan.* 🎫 🖥 🚻
🐟 **Sea-Life and Marine Sanctuary**
Scalby Mills Rd. ☎️ *01723 376125.*
🕐 *daily.* ⬛ *25 Dec.* 🎫 ♿ 🖥 🚻

THE GROWING POPULARITY OF SWIMMING

During the 18th century, sea-bathing came to be regarded as a healthy pastime, and from 1735 onwards men and women, on separate stretches of the coast, could be taken out into the sea in bathing huts, or "machines". In the 18th century, bathing was segregated although nudity was permitted. The Victorians brought in fully clothed bathing, and 19th-century workers from Britain's industrial heartlands used the new steam trains to visit the coast for their holidays. At this time, British seaside resorts such as Blackpool (*see p359*) and Scarborough expanded to meet the new demand.

A Victorian bathing hut on wheels

Castle Howard ㉒

Pillar detail in the Great Hall, carved by Samuel Carpenter

STILL OWNED and lived in by the Howard family, Castle Howard was created by Charles, 3rd Earl of Carlisle. When he came to his title in 1692, he commissioned Sir John Vanbrugh, a man of dramatic ideas but with no previous architectural experience, to design a palace for him. Vanbrugh's grand designs of 1699 were put into practice by architect Nicholas Hawksmoor *(see p24)* and the main body of the house was completed by 1712. The West Wing was built in 1753–9, using a design by Thomas Robinson, son-in-law of the 3rd Earl. Castle Howard was used as the location for the television version of Evelyn Waugh's novel *Brideshead Revisited* (1945).

Temple of the Four Winds
Vanbrugh's last work, designed in 1724, has a dome and four Ionic porticoes. Situated in the grounds at the end of the terrace, it is typical of an 18th-century "landscape building".

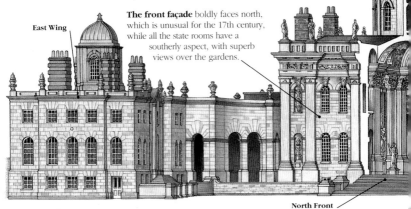

East Wing

The front façade boldly faces north, which is unusual for the 17th century, while all the state rooms have a southerly aspect, with superb views over the gardens.

North Front

★ Great Hall
Rising 20 m (66 ft), from its 515 sq m (5,500 sq ft) floor to the dome, the Great Hall has columns by Samuel Carpenter (1660–1713), wall paintings by Pellegrini and a circular gallery.

SIR JOHN VANBRUGH

Vanbrugh (1664–1726) trained as a soldier, but became better known as a playwright, architect and member of the Whig nobility. He collaborated with Hawksmoor over the design of Blenheim Palace, but his bold architectural vision, later greatly admired, was mocked by the establishment. He died while working on the garden buildings and grounds of Castle Howard.

Chapel Stained Glass

Admiral Edward Howard, Lord Lanerton, altered the chapel in 1870–75. The windows were designed by Edward Burne-Jones and William Morris.

Bust of the 7th Earl

JH Foley sculpted this head and shoulders portrait, which stands at the top of the Grand Staircase in the West Wing, in 1870.

★ Long Gallery

The Howard lineage is illustrated here by a large number of portraits, including works by Lely and Van Dyck.

West Wing

Tourist entrance

Antique Passage

Antiquities collected in the 18th and 19th centuries by the various earls of Carlisle are on display here. The plethora of mythical figures and gods reflects contemporary interest in Classical civilizations.

Museum Room

Furniture here includes Regency chairs, Persian rugs and this 17th-century cabinet.

STAR SIGHTS

★ Great Hall

★ Long Gallery

Eden Camp ❷❸

Malton, North Yorkshire. 📞 *01653 697777.* 🚆 *Malton then taxi.*
⬤ *mid-Jan–late Dec: daily.* 🅿️
♿ 🏪 🚻

THIS IS AN UNUSUAL, award-winning theme museum which pays tribute to the British people during World War II. Italian and German prisoners of war were kept at Eden Camp between 1939 and 1948. Today, some original huts built by Italian prisoners in 1942 are used as a museum, with period tableaux and a soundtrack. Each hut adopts a theme to take the visitor through civilian life in war-time, from Chamberlain's radio announcement of the outbreak of hostilities to the coming of peace. Visitors, including schoolchildren and nostalgic veterans, can see the Doodle-bug V-1 bomb which crashed outside the Officers' Mess, take tea in the canteen or experience a night in the Blitz. A tour can last for several hours.

British and American flags by the sign for Eden Camp

Wharram Percy ❷❹

North Yorkshire. 📞 *0191 2611585 (English Heritage).* 🚆 *Malton, then taxi.* ⬤ *daily.*

THIS IS ONE of England's most important medieval village sites. Recent excavations have unearthed evidence of a 30-household community, with two manors, and the remains of a medieval church. There is also a millpond which has beautiful wild flowers in late spring. Wharram Percy is set in a pretty valley, sign-posted off the B1248 from Burdale, in the heart of the green, rolling Wolds. It is about 20 minutes' walk from the car park, and makes an ideal picnic stop.

Alabaster carving on the chimney-piece at Burton Agnes

Burton Agnes ❷❺

Nr Driffield, East Yorkshire. 📞 *01262 490324.* 🚆 *Driffield, then bus.* ⬤ *Apr–Oct: daily.* 🅿️ ♿ *limited in house.*

OF ALL the grand houses in the triangle between Hull, York and Scarborough, Burton Agnes Hall is a firm favourite. This is partly because the attractive, red-brick Elizabethan mansion has such a homely atmosphere. One of the first portraits you see in the Small Hall is of Anne Griffith, whose father, Sir Henry, built the house. There is a monument to him in the local church.

Burton Agnes has remained in the hands of the original family and has changed little since it was built, between 1598 and 1610. You enter it by the turreted gatehouse, and the entrance hall has a fine Elizabethan alabaster chimney piece. The massive oak stair-case is an impressive example of Elizabethan woodcarving.

In the library is a collection of Impressionist and Post-Impressionist art, pleasantly out of character with the rest of the house, including works by André Derain, Renoir and Augustus John. The extensive grounds include a purpose-built play area for children.

Bempton and Flamborough Head ❷❻

East Yorkshire. 🧍 *4,300.* 🚆 *Bempton.* 🚌 *Bridlington.* ℹ️ *25 Prince St, Bridlington (01262 673474).* 🌐 *www.bridlington.net*

BEMPTON, which consists of 5 miles (8 km) of steep chalk cliffs between Speeton and Flamborough Head, is the largest seabird-breeding colony in England, and is famous for its puffins. The ledges and fissures provide ideal nest-sites for more

Nesting gannet on the chalk cliffs at Bempton

than 100,000 pairs of birds. Today, eight different species, including skinny black shags and kittiwakes, thrive on the Grade 1 listed *(see p617)* Bempton cliffs. Bempton is the only mainland site for goose-sized gannets, well known for their dramatic fishing techniques. May, June and July are the best bird-watching months.

The spectacular cliffs are best seen from the north side of the Flamborough Head peninsula.

Beverley ㉗

East Riding of Yorkshire. 30,000. 34 Butcher Row (01482 867430). Sat. www.inbeverley.co.uk

THE HISTORY of Beverley dates back to the 8th century, when Old Beverley served as a retreat for John, later Bishop of York, who was canonized for his healing powers. Over the centuries Beverley grew as a medieval sanctuary town. Like York, it is an attractive combination of both medieval and Georgian buildings.

The best way to enter Beverley is through the last of five town gates, the castellated North Bar that allowed the medieval inhabitants in and out of the town's surrounding walls. It was rebuilt in 1409–10.

The skyline is dominated by the twin towers of the magnificent **minster**. This was co-founded in 937 by Athelstan, King of Wessex, in place of the church that John of Beverley had chosen as his final resting place in 721. The decorated nave is the earliest surviving building work which dates back to the early 1300s. It is particularly famous for its 16th-century choir stalls and 68 misericords *(see p327)*.

The minster contains many early detailed stone carvings, including a set of four from about 1308 that illustrate figures with ailments such as toothache and lumbago. On the north side of the altar is the richly carved 14th-century Gothic Percy tomb, thought to be that of Lady Idoine Percy, who died in 1365. Also on the north side is the Fridstol, or Peace Chair, said to date from 924-39, the time of Athelstan. Anyone who sat on it would then be granted 30 days' sanctuary.

Minstrel Pillar in St Mary's Church

Within the North Bar, **St Mary's Church** has a 13th-century chancel and houses Britain's largest number of medieval stone carvings of musical instruments. The brightly painted 16th-century Minstrel Pillar is particularly notable. Painted on the panelled chancel ceiling are portraits of monarchs after 1445. On the richly sculpted doorway of St Michael's Chapel is the grinning pilgrim rabbit said to have inspired Lewis Carroll's White Rabbit in *Alice in Wonderland.*

The inspiration for Lewis Carroll's White Rabbit, St Mary's Church

Southeast of the minster, the **Museum of Army Transport** contains over 100 exhibits of army vehicles. A Saturday market takes place near here.

Museum of Army Transport
Flemingate. 01482 860445. daily. 24–26 Dec.

Beverley Minster, one of Europe's finest examples of Gothic architecture

Burton Constable ㉘

Nr Hull, East Yorkshire. 📞 01964
562400. 🚆 Hull then taxi. 🕐 Easter–
Oct: Sat–Thu. 📷 ♿ 📷 🖥

T HE CONSTABLE FAMILY have
been leading landowners
since the 13th century, and
have lived at Burton Constable
since work began on it in
1570. It is an Elizabethan
house, altered in the 18th
century by Thomas Lightholer,
Thomas Atkinson and James
Wyatt. Today, its 30 rooms
include Georgian and
Victorian interiors. Burton
Constable has a fine
collection of Chippendale
furniture and family portraits
dating from the 16th century.
Most of the collections of
prints, textiles and drawings
belong to Leeds City Art
Galleries. The family still lives
in the south wing.

**The Princes' Dock in Kingston
upon Hull's restored docks area**

Kingston upon Hull ㉙

Kingston upon Hull. 🏠 270,000.
🚆 🚌 ♿ 🚢 Paragon St. (01482
223559). 🚃 Tue, Fri, Sat.
🌐 www.hullcc.gov.uk

T HERE IS A LOT MORE to Hull
than the heritage of a
thriving fishing industry. The
restored town centre docks
are attractive, and Hull's Old
Town, laid out in medieval
times, is all cobbled, winding
streets and quaintly askew
red-brick houses. You can
follow the Fish Trail, a path
of inlaid metal fishes on the
city's pavements that illustrates
the many different varieties
that have been landed in Hull,
from anchovy to shark. In

Painting of Burton Constable (c.1690) by an anonymous artist

Victoria Square is the
Maritime Museum. Built in
1871 as the offices of the Hull
Dock Company, it traces the
city's maritime history. Among
its exhibits are an ornate whale-
bone and vertebrae bench and
a display of complicated rope
knots such as the Eye Splice
and the Midshipman's Hitch.

An imposing Elizabethan
building, **Hands on History**,
explores Hull's story through
a collection of some of its
families' artefacts.

In the heart of the Old Town,
on a street that often reeks of
salty sea air, is the **William
Wilberforce House**, one of
the surviving examples of the
High Street's brick merchants'
dwellings. Its first-floor oak-
panelled rooms date from the
17th century, but most of the
house is dedicated to the

Wilberforce family, whose
connection began in 1732
with the grandfather of the
abolitionist. Among the more
gruesome museum exhibits
are iron ankle fetters for slaves.
A fine Victorian doll collection
strikes a lighter note.

Nearby is the **Streetlife
Transport Museum**, Hull's
most popular and noisiest
museum, loved by children. It
features Britain's oldest
tramcar, a simulated mailcoach
ride, amd breathtaking period
street scenes.

🏛 **Maritime Museum**
Queen Victoria Sq. 📞 01482
613903. 🕐 daily (Sun: pm). ●
23–27 Dec, 1 Jan, Good Fri, ♿ 📷
🏛 **Hands on History**
South Churchside. 📞 01482 613952.
🕐 weekends and school holidays. ●
23–27 Dec, 1 Jan, Good Fri. ♿ 📷

WILLIAM WILBERFORCE (1758–1833)

William Wilberforce, born in Hull to a merchant family, was
a natural orator. After studying Classics at Cambridge, he
entered politics and in 1784 gave one of his first public
addresses in York. The
audience was captivated,
and Wilberforce realized
the potential of his powers
of persuasion. From 1785
onwards, adopted by the
Pitt government as spokes-
man for the abolition of
slavery, he conducted a
determined and conscien-
tious campaign. But his
speeches won him enemies,
and in 1792, threats from a
slave-importer meant that
he needed a constant
armed guard. In 1807 his
bill to abolish the lucrative
slave trade became law.

**A 19th-century engraving of
Wilberforce by J Jenkins**

🏛 **William Wilberforce House**

High St, Hull. ☎ *01482 613921.* ◯ *daily (Sun: pm).* ● *24–27 Dec, 1 Jan, Good Fri.* ♿ *limited.* 📷

🏛 **Streetlife Transport Museum**

High St, Hull. ☎ *01482 613902.* ◯ *Mon–Sat, Sun pm.* ● *25–26 Dec, 1 Jan.* ♿ 📷

Holderness and Spurn Head ㉚

East Riding of Yorkshire. 🚆 *Hull (Paragon St) then bus.* ℹ *120 Newbegin, Hornsea (01964 536404).*

Tʜɪs ᴄᴜʀɪᴏᴜs ꜰʟᴀᴛ ᴀʀᴇᴀ east of Hull, with straight roads and delicately waving fields of oats and barley, in many ways resembles Holland, except that its mills are derelict. Beaches stretch for 30 miles (46 km) along the coastline. The main resort towns are **Withernsea** and **Hornsea**, well known for its pottery.

The Holderness landscape only exists because of erosion higher up the coast. The sea continues to wash down tiny bits of rock which accumulate. Around 1560, this began to form a sandbank, and by 1669 it had become large enough to be colonized as Sonke Sand. The last bits of silting mud and debris joined the island to the mainland as recently as the 1830s. Today, you can drive through the eerie, lush wilderness of Sunk Island on the way east to Spurn Head. This is located at the tip of the Spurn Peninsula,

a 3.5 mile (6 km) spit of land that has also built up as the result of coastal erosion elsewhere. Flora, fauna and birdlife have been protected here by the Yorkshire Wildlife Trust since 1960. Walking here gives the eerie feeling that the land could be eroded from under your feet at any time. A surprise discovery at the end of Spurn Head is a tiny community of pilots and lifeboat crew, constantly on call to guide ships into Hull harbour, or help cope with disasters.

Fishing boat at Grimsby's National Fishing Heritage Centre

Grimsby ㉛

North East Lincolnshire. 👥 *92,000.* 🚆 🚌 ℹ *Heritage Sq (01472 323111).* 🛒 *Tue, Thu, Fri, Sat.*

Pᴇʀᴄʜᴇᴅ at the mouth of the River Humber, Grimsby was founded in the Middle Ages by a Danish fisherman

by the name of Grim, and rose to prominence in the 19th century as one of the world's largest fishing ports. Its first dock was opened in 1800 and, with the arrival of the railways, the town secured the means of transporting its catch all over the country. Even though the traditional fishing industry had declined by the 1970s, dock area redevelopment has ensured that Grimsby's unique heritage is retained.

This is best demonstrated by the award-winning **National Fishing Heritage Centre**, a museum that recreates the industry in its 1950s heyday, capturing the atmosphere of the period. Visitors sign on as crew members on a trawler and, by means of a variety of vivid interactive displays, travel from the back streets of Grimsby to the Arctic fishing grounds. On the way, they can experience the roll of the ship, the smell of the fish and the heat of the engine. The tour can be finished off with a guided viewing of the restored 1950s trawler, the *Ross Tiger*.

Other attractions in Grimsby include an International Jazz Festival every July, a restored Victorian shopping street called Abbeygate, a market, a wide selection of restaurants, and the nearby seaside resorts of Cleethorpes, Mablethorpe and Skegness.

🏛 **National Fishing Heritage Centre**

Heritage Sq, Alexandra Dock. ☎ *01472 323345.* ◯ *Sat–Thu.* ● *25, 26 Dec, 1 Jan.* 📷 ♿ 🎦 🖥

Isolated lighthouse at Spurn Head, at the tip of Spurn Peninsula

Street-by-Street: York ⑫

Monk Bar coat of arms

The City of York has retained so much of its medieval structure that walking into its centre is like entering a living museum. Many of the ancient timbered houses, perched on narrow, winding streets, such as the Shambles, are protected by a conservation order. Cars are banned from the centre, so there are always student bikes bouncing over cobbled streets. Its strategic position led to its development as a railway centre in the 19th century.

★ York Minster
England's largest medieval church was begun in 1220 (see pp392).

Stonegate
The medieval red devil is a feature of this street, built over a Roman road.

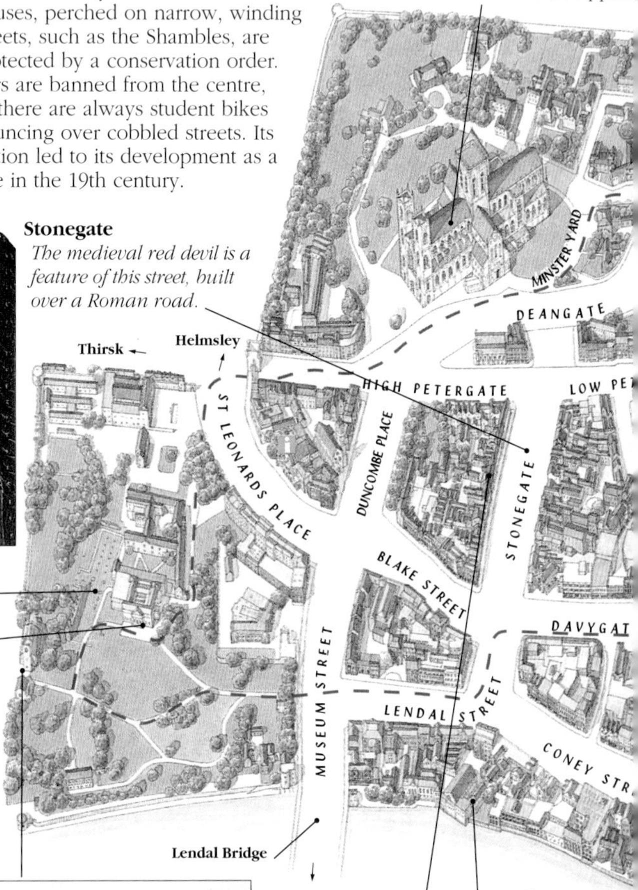

Thirsk ← Helmsley

St Mary's Abbey

Yorkshire Museum
contains a fine collection of fossils, discovered at Whitby in the 19th century.

Lendal Bridge

Railway station, coach station, National Railway Museum, and Leeds

Ye Old Starre Inne is one of the oldest pubs in York.

St Olave's Church
The 11th-century church, next to the gatehouse of St Mary's Abbey (see p336), was founded by the Earl of Northumbria in memory of St Olaf, King of Norway. To the left is the Chapel of St Mary on the Walls.

Guildhall
This two-headed medieval roof boss is on the 15th-century Guildhall, situated beside the River Ouse and restored after bomb damage during World War II.

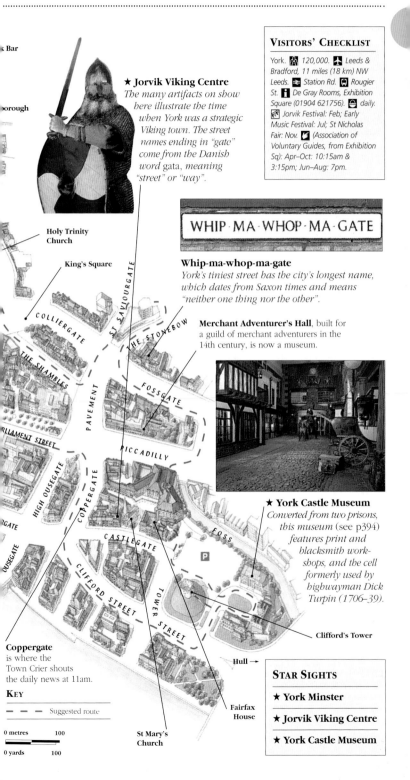

★ Jorvik Viking Centre
*The many artifacts on show
here illustrate the time
when York was a strategic
Viking town. The street
names ending in "gate"
come from the Danish
word* gata, *meaning
"street" or "way".*

VISITORS' CHECKLIST

York. 120,000. Leeds &
Bradford, 11 miles (18 km) NW
Leeds. Station Rd. Rougier
St. De Gray Rooms, Exhibition
Square (01904 621756). daily.
Jorvik Festival: Feb; Early
Music Festival: Jul; St Nicholas
Fair: Nov. (Association of
Voluntary Guides, from Exhibition
Sq): Apr–Oct: 10:15am &
3:15pm; Jun–Aug: 7pm.

**Holy Trinity
Church**

King's Square

WHIP · MA · WHOP · MA · GATE

Whip-ma-whop-ma-gate
*York's tiniest street has the city's longest name,
which dates from Saxon times and means
"neither one thing nor the other".*

Merchant Adventurer's Hall, built for
a guild of merchant adventurers in the
14th century, is now a museum.

COLLIERGATE

ST SAVIOURGATE

THE STONEBOW

THE SHAMBLES

PAVEMENT

FOSSGATE

PARLIAMENT STREET

PICCADILLY

HIGH OUSEGATE

COPPERGATE

FOSS

CASTLEGATE

CLIFFORD STREET

TOWER STREET

★ York Castle Museum
*Converted from two prisons,
this museum (see p394)
features print and
blacksmith work-
shops, and the cell
formerly used by
highwayman Dick
Turpin (1706–39).*

Clifford's Tower

Coppergate
is where the
Town Crier shouts
the daily news at 11am.

KEY

– – – Suggested route

0 metres   100
0 yards   100

Hull →

**Fairfax
House**

**St Mary's
Church**

STAR SIGHTS

★ **York Minster**

★ **Jorvik Viking Centre**

★ **York Castle Museum**

York Minster

THE LARGEST Gothic church north of the Alps, York Minster is 158 m (519 ft) long and 76 m (249 ft) wide across the transepts, and houses the largest collection of medieval stained glass in Britain (see p395). The word "minster" usually means a church served by monks, but priests always served at York. The first minster began as a wooden chapel used to baptize King Edwin of Northumbria in 627. There have been several cathedrals on or near the site, including an 11th-century Norman structure. The present minster was begun in 1220 and completed 250 years later. In July 1984, the south transept roof was destroyed by fire. Restoration cost £2.25 million.

Central sunflower in rose window

Central Tower
Reconstructed in 1420–65 (after partial collapse in 1407), from a design by the master stonemason William Colchester, its geometrical roof design has a central lantern.

Lady Chapel

The Choir has a vaulted entrance with a 15th-century boss of the Assumption of the Virgin.

Exit in south transept

The 16th-century rose window

★ **Choir Screen**
Sited between the choir and the nave, this 15th-century stone screen depicts kings of England from William I to Henry VI, and has a canopy of angels.

The Nave, built 1291, was severely damaged by fire 1840. Rebuilding costs were heavy but it was re-opened with a new peal of bells in 184

★ **Chapter House**
A Latin inscription near the entrance of the wooden-vaulted Chapter House (1260–85) reads: "As the rose is the flower of flowers, so this is the house of houses".

Timbered interior of the Merchant Adventurers' Hall

The western towers, with their
15th-century decorative panelling
and elaborate pinnacles, contrast
with the simpler design of the
north transept. The southwest
tower is the minster belfry.

🏰 Monk Bar

This is one of York's finest original medieval gates, situated
at the end of Goodramgate. It
is vaulted on three floors, and
the portcullis still works. In
the Middle Ages, the rooms
above it were rented out, and
it was a prison in the 16th
century. Its decorative details
include men holding stones
ready to drop on intruders.

🏛 Museum of Automata

9 Tower St. 🌑 until further notice.
The history of mechanically
moving objects, from simple
articulated figurines of ancient
civilizations to more modern
20th-century artworks, is
charted in this museum.
Automata too fragile for
frequent operation, such as
the acrobats and clowns in
the French Gallery,
which date from the
1820s, are brought
to life using a
video wall.

🏰 Clifford's Tower

Clifford's St. 📞 01904 646940.
⏱ daily. 🌑 24–26 Dec, 1 Jan.
📷 🏪
Sited on top of a mound that
William the Conqueror built
for his original wooden castle,
destroyed by fire during anti-
Jewish riots in 1190, Clifford's
Tower dates from the 13th
century. Built by Henry III,
it was named after the de
Clifford family, who were
constables of the castle.

🏛 ARC

St Saviourgate. 📞 01904 654324.
⏱ Mon–Sat (Sat: pm). 🌑 mid-Dec–
5 Jan, Good Fri. 📷 🏪
Housed in a restored medieval
church off the Shambles, the
ARC is a centre for exploring
archaeology. Visitors become
archaeological detectives
and can discover how
archaeologists have pieced
together clues from the past
to unravel the history of the
Viking age in York.

🏰 Merchant
Adventurers' Hall

Fossgate. 📞 01904 654818. ⏱
Easter–Sep: daily; Oct–Easter: Mon–Sat.
🌑 24 Dec–3 Jan. 📷 ♿ limited.
Built by the York Merchants'
Guild, which controlled the
northern cloth trade in the
15th–17th centuries, this building has fine timberwork. The
Great Hall is probably the best
example of its kind in Europe.
Among its paintings is an un-
attributed 17th-century copy of
Van Dyck's portrait of Charles
I's queen, Henrietta Maria.
Below the Great Hall is the
hospital, which was used by
the guild until 1900, and a
private chapel.

Great west door

Great west window
(see p395)

**One of the mechanical toys on
show at the Museum of Automata**

Exploring York

THE APPEAL OF YORK is its many layers of history. A medieval city constructed on top of a Roman one, it was first built in AD 71, when it became capital of the northern province and was known as Eboracum. It was here that Constantine the Great was made emperor in 306, and reorganized Britain into four provinces. A hundred years later, the Roman army had withdrawn. Eboracum was renamed Eoforwic, under the Saxons, and then became a Christian stronghold. The Danish street names are the reminder that it was a Viking centre from 867, and one of Europe's chief trading bases. Between 1100 and 1500 it was England's second city. The glory of York is the minster *(see pp392–3)*. The city also boasts 18 medieval churches, 3 mile long (4.8 km) medieval city walls, elegant Jacobean and Georgian architecture and fine museums.

Grand staircase and fine plaster ceiling at Fairfax House

The Middleham Jewel, Yorkshire Museum

🏛 York Castle Museum

The Eye of York. **🛈** 01904 653611. ◯ daily. ● 25, 26 Dec, 1 Jan. 📷 ♿ ground floor only. 🚻 📷

Housed in two 18th-century prisons, the museum has a fine folk collection, started by Dr John Kirk of the market town of Pickering. Opened in 1938, its period displays include a Jacobean dining room, a moorland cottage, and a 1950s front room. It also contains an exhibition on the traditions of birth, marriages and death in Britain from 1700 to 2000.

The most famous exhibits include the reconstructed Victorian street of Kirkgate, complete with shopfronts and model carriage horse; and the Anglo Saxon York Helmet, discovered in 1982.

🛐 York Minster

See pp392–3.

🏛 Jorvik, The Viking City

Coppergate. **🛈** 01904 643211. ◯ daily. ● 25 Dec. 📷 ♿ ring first. 🚻

This popular centre is built on the site of the original Viking settlement which archaeologists uncovered at Coppergate. It is most famous for recreating the smells of Viking York. A dynamic vision of 10th-century York combines with 21st-century technology to transform archaeological evidence and bring the hub of the Viking world to life.

🏛 Yorkshire Museum and St Mary's Abbey

Museum Gardens. **🛈** 01904 551800. ◯ daily. ● 25, 26 Dec, 1 Jan. 📷 ♿

Yorkshire Museum was in the news when it purchased the 15th-century Middleham Jewel for £2.5 million, one of the finest pieces of English Gothic jewellery found this century. Other exhibits include 2nd-century Roman mosaics and an Anglo-Saxon silver gilt bowl.

St Mary's Abbey *(see p336)* in the riverside grounds is where the medieval York Mystery Plays are set every three years.

🏛 Fairfax House

Castlegate. **🛈** 01904 655543. ◯ daily (Sun: pm, Fri: booked tour only). ● 23–26 Dec, 6 Jan–20 Feb. 📷 📷 ♿ limited. 📷

From 1755 to 1762 Viscount Fairfax built this fine Georgian town house for his daughter, Anne. The house was designed by John Carr *(see p24)*, and restored in the 1980s. Between 1920 and 1965 it was a cinema and dancehall. Today, visitors can see the bedroom of Anne Fairfax (1725– 93), and a fine collection of 18th-century furniture, porcelain and clocks.

🏛 National Railway Museum

Leeman Rd. **🛈** 01904 621261. ◯ daily. ● 24–26 Dec. 📷 ♿ 🚻 📷

The world's largest railway museum and the 2001 European Museum of the Year, covers nearly 200 years of history using a variety of visual aids. Visitors can try wheel-tapping and shunting in the interactive gallery, or find out what made Stephenson's *Rocket* so successful. Exhibits include uniforms, rolling stock from 1797 onward and Queen Victoria's Royal Train carriage, as well as the very latest rail innovations.

Reproduction of an engine and 1830s first-class carriage (left) in York's National Railway Museum

The Stained Glass of York Minster

YORK MINSTER houses the largest collection of medieval stained glass in Britain, some of it dating from the late 12th century. The glass was generally coloured during production, using metal oxides to produce the desired colour, then worked on by craftsmen on site. When a design had been produced, the glass was first cut, then trimmed to shape. Details

Window detail

were painted on, using iron oxide-based paint which was fused to the glass by firing in a kiln. Individual pieces were then leaded together to form the finished window.

Part of the fascination of the minster glass is its variety of subject matter. Some windows were paid for by lay donors who specified a particular subject, others reflect ecclesiastical patronage.

Miracle of St Nicholas (late 12th century) was put in the nave over 100 years after it was made. It shows a Jew's conversion.

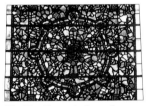

The Five Sisters in the north transept are the largest examples of grisaille glass in Britain. This popular 13th-century technique involved creating fine patterning on clear glass and decorating it with black enamel.

St John the Evangelist, in part of the Great West Window (c.1338), is holding an eagle, itself an example of stickwork, where paint is scraped off to reveal clear glass.

Noah's Ark with its distinct boat-like shape is easily identified in the Great East Window.

The Great East Window (1405-8), the size of a tennis court, is the largest area of medieval painted glass in the world. The Dean and Chapter paid master glazier John Thornton four shillings a week for this celebration of the Creation.

Edward III is a fine example of the 14th-century "soft" style of painting, achieved by stippling the paint.

Walter Skirlaw, whose bishopric was revoked in favour of Richard Scrope, donated this window on its completion in 1408.

Harewood House 33

Leeds. 0113 2181010. Leeds then bus. Mar–Oct: daily. by arrangement.
www.harewood.org

DESIGNED BY John Carr in 1759, Harewood House is the Yorkshire home of the Earl and Countess of Harewood.

The grand Palladian exterior is impressive, with interiors created by Robert Adam and an unrivalled collection of 18th-century furniture made specifically for Harewood by Yorkshire-born Thomas Chippendale (1711–79). There is a collection of paintings by Italian and English artists, including Reynolds and Gainsborough, and two watercolour rooms. The grounds by Capability Brown (see p23) include the **Harewood Bird Garden**, which has exotic species and a breeding programme of certain endangered varieties.

Bali starling, one of Harewood's rare birds

Leeds 34

Leeds. 750,000. Leeds City Station (0113 2425242). Mon–Sat. www.leeds.gov.uk

THE THIRD LARGEST of Britain's provincial cities, Leeds was at its most prosperous during the Victorian period. The most impressive legacy from this era is a series of ornate, covered shopping arcades. Also of note is the **Town Hall**, designed by Cuthbert Brodrick and opened by Queen Victoria in 1858.

Today, although Leeds is primarily an industrial city, it also offers a thriving cultural scene. Productions at **The Grand** by Opera North, one of Britain's top operatic companies, are of a high quality.

The **City Art Gallery** has an impressive collection of British 20th-century art and fine examples of Victorian paintings including works by local artist Atkinson Grimshaw (1836–93). Among the late 19th-century

French art are works by Signac, Courbet and Sisley. The Henry Moore Institute, added in 1993, is devoted to the research, study and display of sculpture of all periods. It comprises a reading room, study centre, library and video gallery, as well as galleries and an archive of material on and by Moore and other sculptural pioneers.

The **Armley Mills Museum**, in a 19th-century woollen mill, explores the industrial heritage of Leeds. Filled with original equipment, recorded sounds and models in 19th-century workers' clothes, it traces the history of the ready-to-wear industry.

A striking waterfront development by the River Aire has attracted two museums. The **Royal Armouries Museum**, from the Tower of London, tells the story of arms and armour around the world in battle, sport, self-defence and fashion, using live demonstrations, film, music and poetry. The **Thackray Medical Museum**, the largest of its kind in Europe, is a fascinating interactive display of medical advances, from a re-created vision of Victorian slum life to modern-day medical challenges.

Leeds has two sights that are especially suitable for children. **Tropical World**

The County Arcade, one of Leeds' restored shopping arcades

features crystal pools, a rainforest house, butterflies and tropical fish. There is also a farm and a Rare Breeds centre in the grounds of the Tudor-Jacobean **Temple Newsam House**, which has a collection of Chippendale furniture.

City Art Gallery
The Headrow. 0113 2478248. daily (Sun: pm). 25, 26 Dec, 1 Jan & public hols.

Armley Mills Museum
Canal Rd, Armley. 0113 2637861. Tue–Sun (Sun: pm); public hols. 24–26 Dec, 1 Jan.

Royal Armouries
Armouries Drive. 0113 2201999. daily. 24, 25 Dec.

Thackray Medical Museum
Beckett St. 0113 2457084. daily. 24–26, 31 Dec, 1 Jan.

Tropical World
Canal Gdns, Princes Ave. 0113 2661850. daily. 25, 26 Dec.

Temple Newsam House
Off A63. 0113 2647321. closed until further notice.

Working loom at the Armley Mills Museum in Leeds

The Other Side (1990–93) by David Hockney at Bradford's 1853 Gallery in Saltaire

Bradford ③⑤

Bradford. 492,000. City Hall, Centurion Square (01274 753678). Mon–Sat.
www.bradford.gov.uk

IN THE 16TH CENTURY, Bradford was a thriving market town, and the opening of its canal in 1774 boosted trade.

By 1850, it was the world's capital for worsted (fabric made from closely twisted wool). Many of the city's well-preserved civic and industrial buildings date from this period, such as the Wool Exchange on Market Street. In the 1800s a number of German textile manufacturers settled in what is now called Little Germany. Their houses are characterized by decorative stone carvings that illustrated the wealth and standing of the occupants.

Daguerreotype camera by Giroux (1839)

The **National Museum of Photography, Film and Television**, founded in 1983, explores the technology and art of these media. There is a television section called TV Heaven, where visitors can ask to watch their favourite programme. They are also encouraged to see themselves read the news on TV. The giant IMAX screen uses the world's largest film format. Film subjects include journeys into space, CyberWorld and The Human Body.

The **Colour Museum** traces dyeing and textile printing from ancient Egypt to the present day. Hands-on elements include taking charge of computerized technology to test the colour of a material. **Bradford Industrial Museum** is housed in an original spinning mill. As well as seeing and hearing all the mill machinery, you can ride on a horse-drawn tram. Saltaire, a Victorian industrial village *(see p335)*, is on the outskirts of the city. Built by Sir Titus Salt for his Salts Mill workers, it was completed in 1873. The **1853 Gallery** has the world's largest collection of works by David Hockney, born in Bradford.

National Museum of Photography, Film and Television
Pictureville. 01274 202030. daily (school hols); Tue–Sun (school term times); public holidays. 24–26 Dec.

Colour Museum
1 Providence St. 01274 390955. Tue–Sat. Christmas period.

Bradford Industrial Museum
Moorside Mills, Moorside Rd. 01274 631756. Tue–Sat, Sun (pm), public hols. 25, 26 Dec.

1853 Gallery
Salts Mill, Victoria Rd. 01274 531163. daily. 25–26 Dec, 1 Jan.

BRADFORD'S INDIAN COMMUNITY

Immigrants from the Indian subcontinent originally came to Bradford in the 1950s to work in the mills, but with the decline of the textile industry many began small businesses. By the mid-1970s there were 1,400 such enterprises in the area. Almost one fifth were in the food sector, born out of simple cafés catering for mill-workers whose families were far away. As Indian food became more popular, these restaurants thrived, and today there are over 200 serving the highly spiced dishes of the Indian subcontinent.

Balti in a Bradford restaurant

Haworth Parsonage, home to the Brontë family, now a museum

Haworth ㊱

Bradford. 🏠 *5,000.*
🚉 *Keighley.* 🛈 *2–4 West Lane
(01535 642329).*

THE SETTING OF HAWORTH, in
bleak Pennine moorland
dotted with farmsteads, has
changed little since it was
home to the Brontë family. The
village boomed in the 1840s,
when there were more than
1,200 hand-looms in operation,
but is more famous today for
the Brontë connection.

You can visit the **Brontë
Parsonage Museum**, home
from 1820–61 to novelists
Charlotte, Emily and Anne,
their brother Branwell and
their father, the
Reverend Patrick
Brontë. Built in
1778–9, the house
remains decorated
as it was during
the 1850s. Eleven
rooms, including
the children's study
and Charlotte's
room, display letters,
manuscripts, books, furniture
and personal treasures.

Also evocative of the Brontë
sisters' novels are the walks the
family enjoyed, for which stout
boots are advised, among them
the **Brontë Falls** and **Brontë
Bridge**. Nearby is the **Brontë
Seat**, a chair-shaped stone.

In summer, the nostalgic
Victorian **Keighley and Worth
Valley Railway** runs through
Haworth. It stops at Oakworth
station, where parts of The

Railway Children were filmed.
At the end of the line is the
Railway Museum at Oxenhope.

**🏛 Brontë Parsonage
Museum**

Church St. 📞 *01535 642323.*
🕐 *daily.* ⬤ *24–27 Dec, mid-Jan–
early Feb.* 🈲 🅿 ♿ *limited.*

Hebden Bridge ㊲

Calderdale. 🏠 *12,500.* 🚉 🛈 *1
Bridgegate (01422 843831).* 🛒 *Thu.*
Ⓦ *www.hebdenbridge.co.uk*

HEBDEN BRIDGE is a delightful
South Pennines former
mill town, surrounded by
steep hills
and former
19th-century
mills. The
houses
seem to
defy grav-
ity as they
cling to
the valley
sides. Due
to the
gradient,
one house
is made
from two bottom floors and the
top two floors form another
unit. To separate ownership of
these "flying freeholds", an Act
of Parliament was devised.

There is a superb view of
Hebden Bridge from nearby
Heptonstall, where the poet
Sylvia Plath (1932–63) is
buried. The village contains a
Wesleyan chapel (1764).

**Charlotte Brontë's
childhood story book,
for her sister, Anne**

Halifax ㊳

Calderdale. 🏠 *88,000.* 🚉 🅿 🛈
Piece Hall (01422 368725).
🛒 *Thu–Sat.*

HALIFAX'S HISTORY has been
influenced by textiles
since the Middle Ages, but
today's visual reminders date
mainly from the 19th century.
The town inspired William
Blake's vision of "dark Satanic
mills" in his poem *Jerusalem*
(1820). The wool trade helped
to make the Pennines into
Britain's industrial backbone.

Until the mid-15th century
cloth production was modest,
but vital enough to inspire
the 11th-century Gibbet Law,
which stated that anyone
caught stealing cloth could be
hanged. There is a replica of
the gibbet used for decapita-
tion at the bottom of Gibbet
Street. Many of Halifax's 18th-

CHARLOTTE BRONTË

During a harsh, motherless
childhood, Charlotte (1816–
55) and her sisters, Emily
and Anne, retreated into
fictional worlds of their
own, writing poems and
stories. As adults, they had
to work as governesses or
teachers, but still published
a poetry collection in 1846.
Only two copies were sold,
but in the following year
Charlotte had great success
with *Jane Eyre*, which
became a best seller. After
the deaths of her siblings
in 1848–9 Charlotte turned
to the solitude of writing
and published her last
novel, *Villette*, in 1852. She
married the Reverend
Arthur Bell Nicholls, her
father's curate, in 1854, but
died shortly afterwards.

Children playing on the Giant Mouth at Halifax's Eureka! museum

and 19th-century buildings owe their existence to wealthy cloth traders. Sir Charles Barry (1795–1860), architect of the Houses of Parliament, was commissioned by the Crossley family to design the Town Hall. They also paid for the landscaping of the People's Park by the creator of the Crystal Palace, Sir Joseph Paxton (1801–65). Thomas Bradley's 18th-century **Piece Hall** was where wool merchants once sold their pieces of cloth, trading in one of the hall's 315 "Merchants' Rooms". It has a massive Italianate courtyard built by the town's wool merchants and now beautifully restored. Today, Halifax's market takes place here.

Eureka! is a museum designed for children, with "learning adventures" on exhibits such as the Giant Mouth Machine and the Wall of Water. **Shibden Hall Museum** is a fine period house, parts of which date to the 15th century. It reflects the prosperous home life of a 17th–18th-century landowner. Its 17th-century Pennine barn is filled with horse-drawn vehicles. In the cobbled courtyard there are 19th-century workshops.

ENVIRONS: The nearby village of **Sowerby Bridge** was an important textile centre from the Middle Ages to the 1960s – the first mill in Yorkshire was erected here in 1778. The village takes its name from a stone bridge over the River Calder erected in the 16th century. Today visitors come to enjoy the scenic canals.

🏛 Eureka!
Discovery Rd. **🎫** 01426 983191.
🎫 01422 330069 for group bookings & exhibition information.
◯ daily. ⬤ 24–26 Dec. 🖼 ♿
🏛 Shibden Hall Museum
Listers Rd. **🎫** 01422 352246.
◯ daily (Sun: pm). ⬤ 24 Dec–2 Jan. 🖼 ▯ ▯

Yorkshire Mining Museum ③⑨

Wakefield. **🎫** 01924 848806.
🚌 Wakefield then bus. ◯ daily.
⬤ 24–26 Dec, 1 Jan. 🖼 ♿ ✓

HOUSED IN THE old Caphouse Colliery, this museum gives visitors the chance to go into a real mine shaft: warm clothing is advised. An underground tour takes you 137 m (450 ft) down, equipped with a hat and a miner's lamp. You can enter some of the narrow seams and see exhibits such as life-size working models. Other displays depict mining methods and conditions from 1820 to the present day.

Yorkshire Sculpture Park ④⓪

Wakefield. **🎫** 01924 830302.
🚌 Wakefield then bus. ◯ daily.
⬤ 24–25, 29–31 Dec. ♿ ▯ ▯

THIS IS ONE of Europe's leading open-air galleries situated in 45 ha (110 acres) of beautiful 18th-century parkland. Each year a programme of large temporary exhibitions of sculpture by international artists is organized alongside the existing collection, which includes work by Barbara Hepworth, Sol LeWitt and Mimmo Paladino. Henry Moore (1898-1986), the Park's first patron, believed that daylight and sun were necessary to appreciate sculpture. Bretton Country Park features his largest European collection.

Large Two Forms (1966–9) by Henry Moore in Bretton Country Park

NORTHUMBRIA

NORTHUMBERLAND · COUNTY DURHAM

E NGLAND'S NORTHEAST *extremity is a tapestry of moorland, ruins, castles, cathedrals and huddled villages. With Northumberland National Park and Kielder Water reservoir to the north, a rugged eastern coastline, and the cities of Newcastle and Durham to the south, the area combines a dramatic history with abundant natural beauty.*

The empty peaceful hills, elusive wildlife and panoramic vistas of Northumberland National Park belie the area's turbulent past. Warring Scots and English, skirmishing tribes, cattle drovers and whisky smugglers have all left traces on ancient routes through the Cheviot Hills. Slicing through the southern edge of the park is the famous reminder of the Romans' 400-year occupation of Britain, Hadrian's Wall, the northern boundary of their empire.

Conflict between Scots and English continued for 1,000 years after the Romans departed, and even after the 1603 union between the two crowns. A chain of massive crenellated medieval castles punctuates the coastline, while other forts that once defended the northern flank of England along the River Tweed lie mostly in ruins. Seventh-century Northumbria was the cradle of Christianity under St Aidan, but this was sharply countered by Viking violence from 793 onward, as the Scandinavian invaders raided the monasteries. But a reverence for Northumbrian saints is in the local psyche, and St Cuthbert and the Venerable Bede are both buried in Durham Cathedral. The influence of the Industrial Revolution, concentrated around the mouths of the rivers Tyne, Wear and Tees, made Newcastle upon Tyne the north's main centre for coal mining and shipbuilding. Today, the city is famous for its "industrial heritage" attractions and urban regeneration schemes.

Section of Hadrian's Wall, built by the Romans in about 120, looking east from Cawfields

◁ **The towers of Durham Cathedral, rising above the River Wear**

Eyem[...]

Exploring Northumbria

H ISTORIC SITES ARE PLENTIFUL along Northumbria's coast. South of Berwick-upon-Tweed, a causeway leads to the ruined priory and castle on Lindisfarne, and there are major castles at Bamburgh, Alnwick and Warkworth. The hinterland is a region of wide open spaces, with wilderness in the Northumberland National Park, and fascinating Roman remains of Hadrian's Wall at Housesteads and elsewhere. The glorious city of Durham is dominated by its castle and cathedral, and Newcastle upon Tyne has a lively nightlife.

SIGHTS AT A GLANCE

Alnwick Castle **5**
Bamburgh **4**
Barnard Castle **17**
Beamish Open Air Museum **13**
Berwick-upon-Tweed **1**
Cheviot Hills **8**
Corbridge **10**
Durham pp414–15 **14**
Farne Islands **3**
Hadrian's Wall pp408–409 **11**
Hexham **9**
Kielder Water **7**
Lindisfarne **2**
Middleton-in-Teesdale **16**
Newcastle upon Tyne **12**
Warkworth Castle **6**

Walks and Tours
North Pennines Tour **15**

SEE ALSO

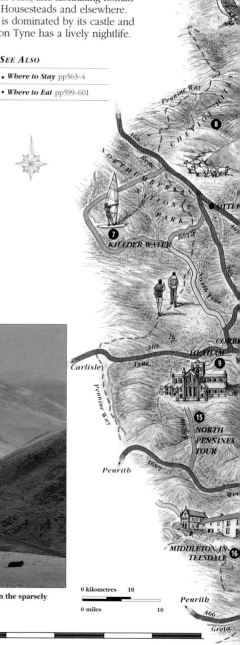

Kelso

Pennine Way

CHEVIOT HILLS **8**

NORTHUMBERLAND NATIONAL PARK

OTTE[...]

7 KIELDER WATER

Carlisle

A69

Tyne

Pennine Way

9 HEXHAM

CORB[...]

15 NORTH PENNINES TOUR

Penrith

A689

We[...]

16 MIDDLETON-IN-TEESDALE

Penrith

A66

Gret[...]

The wilderness of Upper Coquetdale in the sparsely populated Cheviot Hills

| 0 kilometres | 10 |
| 0 miles | 10 |

The rugged coastline of Northumberland, with Bamburgh Castle in the distance

GETTING AROUND

North of Newcastle, the A1068 meets the A1 linking the sights of the Northumbrian coast, and continuing on to Scotland. Two spectacular inland routes, the A696 and the A68, merge near Otterburn to skirt the Northumberland National Park. A mainline railway links Durham, Newcastle and Berwick, but a car is necessary to explore Northumbria comprehensively.

KEY

	Motorway
	Major road
	Minor road
	Scenic route
– –	Scenic path
	River
☀	Viewpoint

Map labels:

FARNE ②
FARNE ISLANDS ③
④
BAMBURGH
ALNWICK CASTLE ⑤
WARKWORTH CASTLE ⑥
Wansbeck
HADRIAN'S WALL
WHITLEY BAY
NEWCASTLE UPON TYNE ⑫
BEAMISH OPEN AIR MUSEUM ⑬
SUNDERLAND
DURHAM ⑭
BISHOP AUCKLAND
HARTLEPOOL
MIDDLESBROUGH
Cleveland Way
Whitby
BARNARD CASTLE
DARLINGTON
NORTH YORK MOORS NATIONAL PARK
Richmond
Northallerton
NORTH SEA

Guildhall, Newcastle upon Tyne

View over Berwick-upon-Tweed's three bridges

Berwick-upon-Tweed ❶

Northumberland. 🚶 *13,000.*
🚆 🛈 *106 Mary Gate (01289 330733).* 🛒 *Wed, Sat.*
ⓦ *www.berwickonline.org.uk*

BETWEEN THE 12th and 15th centuries Berwick-upon-Tweed changed hands 14 times in the wars between the Scots and English. Its position, at the mouth of the river which divides the two nations, made the town strategically vital.

The English finally gained permanent control in 1482 and maintained Berwick as a fortified garrison. Ramparts dating from 1555, 1.5 miles (2.5 km) long and 7 m (23 ft) thick, offer superb views over the Tweed. Within the 18th-century barracks are the **King's Own Scottish Borderers Regimental Museum**, an **art**

gallery, and **By Beat of Drum**, charting the history of British infantrymen.

🏛 **King's Own Scottish Borderers Regimental Museum**

The Barracks. 📞 *01289 307427.*
◯ *Mon–Sat.* ● *22 Dec–3 Jan, public hols.* 🖼 🛈

Lindisfarne ❷

Northumberland. 🚆 *Berwick-upon-Tweed then bus.* 🛈 *The Maltings, Eastern Lane, Berwick-upon-Tweed (01289 330733).*

TWICE DAILY a long, narrow neck of land sinks under the North Sea tide for five hours, separating Lindisfarne, or Holy Island, from the coast. At low tide, visitors stream over the causeway to the island made famous by St Aidan, St Cuthbert and the Lindisfarne

gospels. Nothing remains of the Celtic monks' monastery, finally abandoned in 875 after successive Viking attacks, but the magnificent arches of the 11th-century **Lindisfarne Priory** are still visible.

After 1540, stones from the priory were used to build **Lindisfarne Castle**, which was restored and made into a private home by Sir Edwin Lutyens *(see p25)* in 1903. It includes an attractive walled garden created by Gertrude Jekyll *(see p23)*.

♣ **Lindisfarne Castle**

(NT) Holy Island. 📞 *01289 389244.*
◯ *Apr–Oct: Sat–Thu & Good Fri (pm).* 🖼

Farne Islands ❸

(NT) Northumberland. 🚢 *from Seahouses.* 🛈 *106 Mary Gate, Berwick-upon-Tweed (01289 330733).*

THERE ARE BETWEEN 15 and 28 Farne Islands off the coast from Bamburgh, some of them periodically covered by sea. The highest is around 31 m (100 ft) above sea level. Nature wardens and lighthouse keepers share them with seals, puffins and other seabirds.

Boat tours depart from **Seahouses** harbour and can only land on Staple and Inner Farne, site of St Cuthbert's 14th-century chapel.

Lindisfarne Castle (1540), the main landmark on the island of Lindisfarne

Celtic Christianity

THE IRISH MONK St Aidan arrived in Northumbria in 635 from the island of Iona, off western Scotland, to evangelize the north of England. He founded the monastery on the island of Lindisfarne, and it became one of the most important centres for Christianity in England. This and other monastic communities thrived in Northumbria, becoming rich in scholarship, although the monks lived simply. It also emerged as a place of pilgrimage after miracles were reported at the shrine of St Cuthbert, Lindisfarne's most famous bishop. But the monks' pacifism made them defenceless against 9th-century Viking raids.

St Cuthbert on a sea voyage

St Aidan's Monastery was added to over the centuries to become Lindisfarne Priory. This 8th-century relic with interlaced animal decorations is from a cross at the site.

The Venerable Bede (673–735), the most brilliant early medieval scholar, was a monk at the monastery of St Paul in Jarrow. He wrote The Ecclesiastical History of the English People in 731.

St Aidan (600–651), an Irish missionary, founded a monastery at Lindisfarne and became Bishop of Northumbria in 635. This 1960 sculpture of him, by Kathleen Parbury, is in Lindisfarne Priory grounds.

St Cuthbert (635–87) was the monk and miracle worker most revered of all. He lived as a hermit on Inner Farne (a chapel was built there in his memory) and later became Bishop of Lindisfarne.

Lindisfarne Priory was built by Benedictines in the 11th century, on the site of St Aidan's earlier monastery.

THE LINDISFARNE GOSPELS

This book of richly illustrated portrayals of Gospel stories is one of the masterpieces of the "Northumbrian Renaissance" which left a permanent mark on Christian art and history-writing. The work was carried out by monks at Lindisfarne under the direction of Bishop Eadfrith, around 700. Monks managed to save the book and carried it with them when they fled from Lindisfarne in 875 after suffering repeated Viking raids. Other treasures were plundered.

Elaborately decorated initial to the *Gospel of St Matthew* (c.725)

Illustration of Grace Darling from the 1881 edition of *Sunday at Home*

Bamburgh **4**

Northumberland. 🏛 *1,100.*
🚉 *Berwick.* ℹ *106 Mary Gate, Berwick-upon-Tweed (01289 330733).*

DUE TO NORTHUMBRIA'S history of hostility against the Scots, there are more strongholds and castles here than in any other part of England. Most were built from the 11th to the 15th centuries by local warlords, as was Bamburgh's red sandstone **castle**. Its coastal position had been fortified since prehistoric times, but the first major stronghold was built in 550 by a Saxon chieftain, Ida the Flamebearer.

In its heyday between 1095 and 1464, Bamburgh was the royal castle that was used by the Northumbrian kings for coronations. By the end of the Middle Ages it had fallen into obscurity, then in 1894 it was bought by Newcastle arms tycoon Lord Armstrong, who restored it. Works of art are exhibited in the cavernous Great Hall, and there are suits of armour and medieval artifacts in the basement.

Bamburgh's other main attraction is the tiny **Grace Darling Museum** which celebrates the bravery of the 23-year-old, who, in 1838, rowed through tempestuous seas with her father, the keeper of the Longstone lighthouse, to rescue nine people from the wrecked *Forfarshire* steamboat.

Carrara marble fireplace (1840) at Alnwick Castle

⚓ **Bamburgh Castle**
Bamburgh. (*01668 214515.*
⭘ *Apr–Oct: daily.* 🎫 ⭑ ▢
🏛 **Grace Darling Museum**
Radcliffe Rd. (*01668 214465.*
⭘ *Easter–Oct: daily.* ⭑

Alnwick Castle **5**

Alnwick, Northumberland. (*01665 510777.* 🚉 🚌 *Alnmouth.*
⭘ *April–Oct: daily.* 🎫 ⭑ *limited.*

DOMINATING THE MARKET town on the River Aln is another great fortress, Alnwick Castle. Described by the Victorians as the "Windsor of the north", it is the main seat of the Duke of Northumberland, whose family, the Percys, have lived here since 1309. This border stronghold has survived many battles, but now peacefully dominates the pretty market town of Alnwick, overlooking landscape designed by Capability Brown. The stern medieval exterior belies the fine treasure house within, furnished in palatial Renaissance style with an exquisite collection of Meissen china and paintings by Titian, Van Dyck and Canaletto. The Postern Tower contains a collection of early British and Roman relics. The **Regimental Museum of Royal Northumberland Fusiliers** is in the Abbot's Tower. Among other attractions are the Percy State coach, the dungeon, the gun terrace and superb countryside views.

Warkworth Castle **6**

Warkworth, nr Amble. (*01665 711423.* ⭘ *daily.* ● *24–26 Dec, 1 Jan.* 🎫 ⭑ *limited.* ▢

WARKWORTH CASTLE sits on a green hill overlooking the River Coquet. It was one of the Percy family homes. Shakespeare's *Henry IV* features the castle in the scenes between the Earl of Northumberland and his son, Harry Hotspur.

Much of the present-day castle remains date from the 14th century. The unusual turreted, cross-shaped keep, which was also added in the 14th century, is a central feature of the castle tour.

Warkworth Castle reflected in the River Coquet

Kielder Water **7**

Yarrow Moor, Falstone, Hexham.
(*01434 240398.* ⭘ *daily.* ●
24–26 Dec, 1, 2 Jan. ⭑

ONE OF THE top attractions of Northumberland, Kielder Water lies close to the Scottish border, surrounded by spectacular scenery. With a perimeter of 27 miles (44 km), it is Europe's largest man-made lake, and offers facilities for sailing, windsurfing, canoeing, water-skiing and fishing. In summer, the cruiser *Osprey* departs from Leaplish on trips around the lake. The Kielder Water Exhibition, next to the Tower Knowe Visitor Centre, depicts the history of the valley from the Ice Age to the present day.

Cheviot Hills ❽

THESE BARE, LONELY MOORS, smoothed into rounded humps by Ice Age glaciers, form a natural border with Scotland. Walkers and outdoor enthusiasts find a near-wilderness unmatched anywhere else in England. This remotest extremity of the Northumberland National Park nevertheless has a long and vivid history. Roman legions, warring Scots and English border raiders, cattle drovers and whisky smugglers have all left traces along the ancient routes and tracks they carved out here.

The Cheviots' isolated burns and streams are among the last habitats in England for the shy, elusive otter.

Chew Green Camp, which to the Romans was ad fines, or, "towards the last place", has fine views from the remaining fortified earthworks.

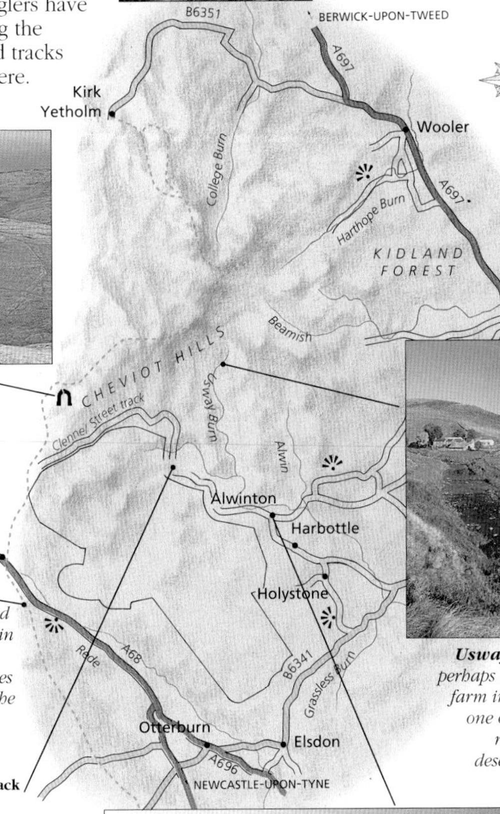

The Pennine Way starts in Derbyshire and ends at Kirk Yetholm in Scotland. The final stage (shown here) goes past Byrness, crosses the Cheviots and traces the Scottish border.

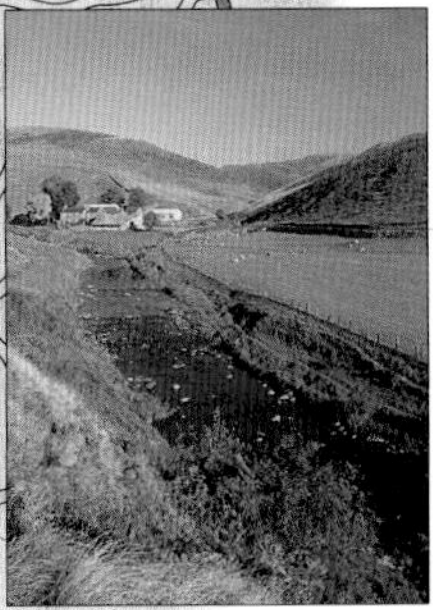

Uswayford Farm track

KEY

▨▨▨ A roads

▨▨ B roads

═ Minor roads

--- Pennine Way

🔆 Viewpoint

0 kilometres 5

0 miles 5

Uswayford Farm, is perhaps the most remote farm in England, and one of the hardest to reach. It is set in deserted moorland.

Alwinton, a tiny village built mainly from grey stone, is situated beside the River Coquet. It is an access point for many fine walks in the area, and the wild landscape is deserted except for sheep.

Hexham ❾

Northumberland. 🏛 *14,000.* ⬛
🚉 🛈 *Wentworth Car Park
(01434 652220).* 🗓 *Tue.*
🌐 *www.hadrianswallcountry.org*

THE BUSY MARKET TOWN of Hexham was established in the 7th century, growing up around the church and monastery built by St Wilfrid, but the Vikings sacked and looted it in 876. In 1114, Augustinians began work on a priory and abbey on the original church ruins to create **Hexham Abbey**, which still towers over the market square. The Saxon crypt, built partly with stones from the former Roman fort at Corbridge, is all

**Ancient stone carvings at
Hexham Abbey**

that remains of St Wilfrid's Church. The south transept has a 12th-century night stair: stone steps leading from the dormitory. In the chancel is the Frith Stool, a Saxon throne in the centre of a circle which protected fugitives.

Medieval streets, many with Georgian and Victorian shopfronts, spread out from the market square, The 15th-century Moot Hall was once a council chamber and the old gaol (jail) contains a **museum** of border history.

Hadrian's Wall ⓫

ON THE ORDERS of Emperor Hadrian, work began in AD 120 on a 73 mile (117 km) wall to be erected across northern England, to mark and defend the northern limits of the British province and the northwest border of the Roman Empire. Troops were stationed at milecastles along the wall, and large turrets, later forts, were built at 5 mile (8 km) intervals. The wall, now the responsibility of English Heritage, was abandoned in 383 as the Roman Empire crumbled, but much of it remains.

Vindolanda is the site of several forts. The first timber fort dated from AD 90 and a stone fort was not built until th[e] 2nd century. The museum has a collec-tion of Roman writing tablets providi[ng] details of food, clothes and work.

**Location of
Hadrian's Wall**

Great Chesters Fort was built facing east to guard Caw Gap, but there are few remains today. To the south and east of the fort are traces of a civil settle-ment and a bathhouse.

Carvoran Fort is probably pre-Hadrianic. Little of the fort survives, but the Roman Army museum nearby covers the wall's history.

Housesteads Set[tle]ment includes th[e] remains of terrace[d] shops or taverns.

Cawfields, 2 m[iles] (3 km) north of Haltwhistle, is th[e] access point to o[ne] of the highest an[d] most rugged sect[ions] of the wall. To th[e] east, the remain[s of] a milecastle sit o[n] Whin Sill crag.

Emperor Hadrian (76–138) came to Britain in 120 to order a stronger defence system. Coins were often cast to record emperors' visits, such as this bronze sestertius. Until 1971, the penny was abbreviated to d, short for denarius, a Roman coin.

**The parson's 14th-century forti-
fied tower house at Corbridge**

🔒 **Hexham Abbey**
Market Place. 📞 *01434 602031.*
⭕ *daily.* ♿

🏛 **Border History Museum**
Old Gaol, nr Hallgate. 📞 *01434
652349.* ⭕ *Apr–Oct: daily; Nov,
Feb, Mar: Sat, Mon, Tue.* 📷 📹 🛈

Corbridge ⑩

Northumberland. 👥 *4,000.* 🚉
🛈 *Hill St (01434 652220).*

T**HIS QUIET TOWN** conceals a
few historic buildings
constructed with stones from
the Roman garrison town of
nearby Corstopitum. Among
these are the thickset Saxon
tower of St Andrew's Church
and the 14th-century fortified
tower house built to protect
the local clergyman. Excavations of Corstopitum, now
known as **Corbridge Roman
Site and Museum**, have
exposed earlier forts, a well-
preserved granary, temples,
fountains and an aqueduct.

🏛 **Corbridge Roman Site
and Museum**
📞 *01434 632349.* ⭕ *Apr–Oct:
daily; Nov–Mar: Wed–Sun.* ⚫ *24–26
Dec,1 Jan.* 📷 ♿ *limited.* 🛈 📹

THE WALL COAST-TO-COAST

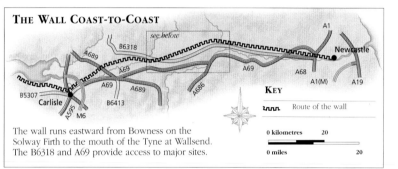

see below

A1

B6318

A689

A69

A69

A689

B6413

B5307

Carlisle

A595

M6

A69

A686

A69

A68

A1(M)

A19

Newcastle

KEY

〰〰〰 Route of the wall

0 kilometres   20

0 miles   20

The wall runs eastward from Bowness on the
Solway Firth to the mouth of the Tyne at Wallsend.
The B6318 and A69 provide access to major sites.

Carrawburgh Fort, a 500-man
garrison, guarded the Newbrough
Burn and North Tyndale approaches.

Limestone Corner Milecastle is
sited at the northernmost part of
the wall and has magnificent views
of the Cheviot Hills (*see p407*).

*Sewingshields Milecastle, with
magnificent views west to Housesteads,
is one of the best places for walking.
This reconstruction shows the layout
of a Roman milecastle on the wall.*

Chesters Fort was a
bridgehead over the
North Tyne. In the
museum are altars, sculp-
tures and inscriptions.

Chesters Bridge crossed the
Tyne. The original Hadrianic
bridge was rebuilt in 207. The
remains of this second bridge
abutment can still be seen.

***Housesteads Fort** is the best-
preserved site on the wall, with
fine views over the countryside.
The excavated remains include
the commanding officer's house
and a Roman hospital.*

0 metres   500

0 yards   500

Newcastle upon Tyne ⓬

Newcastle upon Tyne. 🚶 *273,000.*
✈ 🚊 🚌 🚊 ⓘ *132 Granger St
(0191 2610610).* 🚢 *Sun.*
W www.newcastle.gov.uk

NEWCASTLE OWES ITS NAME to its Norman **castle** which was founded in 1080 by Robert Curthose, the eldest son of William the Conqueror (*see p47*). The Romans had bridged the Tyne and built a fort on the site 1,000 years earlier. During the Middle Ages it was still a fortress town guarding the mouth of the river and was used as a base for English campaigns against the Scots. From the Middle Ages, the city flourished as a coal mining and exporting centre. It was known in the 19th century for engineering, steel production and later as the world's foremost shipyard. The city's industrial base has declined in recent years, but "Geordies", as inhabitants of the city are known, have refocused their civic pride on the ultra-modern Metro Centre shopping mall at Gateshead, some 4 miles (6 km) southwest of the city, and Newcastle United soccer team. The city's lively night scene includes clubs, pubs, theatres and ethnic restaurants. The visible trappings of its past are reflected in the magnificent Tyne Bridge and in Benjamin Green's monument commemorating Earl Grey. The grand façades of city centre thoroughfares, such as Grey Street, also reflect this former prosperity. Many buildings on the quayside are being restored.

Bridges crossing the Tyne at Newcastle

♣ The Castle
St Nicholas St. 📞 *0191 232 7938.* ⏰ *daily.* ● *25–26 Dec, 1 Jan, Good Fri.* 🖼 🚫 🎫 *(parties).*
Curthose's original wooden "new castle" was rebuilt in stone in

Beamish Open Air Museum ⓭

Tram symbol

THIS GIANT OPEN AIR MUSEUM, spread over 120 ha (300 acres) of County Durham, recreates an authentic picture of family, working and community life in the northeast before World War I. It has a typical High Street, a colliery village, a disused mine, a school, chapel and farm, all with guides in period costume. A restored tramline serves the different parts of the museum, which carefully avoids romanticizing the past.

Home Farm recreates the atmosphere of an old-fashioned farmyard. Rare breeds of cattle and sheep, more common before the advent of mass breeding, can be seen.

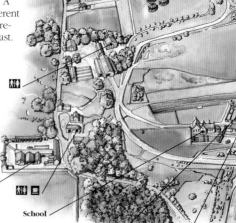

The station has locomotives, coaches, freight trucks, a platform, a signal box and a wrought-iron footbridge. The station and its vicinity is closed for redevelopment until 2003.

School

Miners' houses were tiny, oil-lit dwellings, backing onto vegetable plots and owned by the colliery.

Chapel

the 12th century. Only the thickset, crenellated keep remains intact with two suites of royal apartments. A series of staircases spiral up to the renovated battlements, from where there are fine views over the city and the Tyne. The castle also has a restored Norman chapel (c.1168–78), Great Hall and garrison room.

♦ St Nicholas Cathedral
St Nicholas Sq. ☎ 0191 2321939.
◯ daily. ♿

This is one of Britain's tiniest cathedrals, there are remnants inside of the original 11th-century Norman church on which the present 14th- and 15th-century structure was founded. Its most striking feature is its ornate "lantern tower" – half tower, half spire – of which there are only three others in Britain. First built in 1448, it was rebuilt in 1608, then repaired during the 18th and 19th centuries.

Reredos of the Northumbrian saints in St Nicholas Cathedral

🚇 Bessie Surtees' House
41–44 Sandhill. ☎ 0191 2611585.
◯ Mon–Fri. ● 25 Dec–2 Jan, public hols. 🏠 ♿

The story of beautiful, wealthy Bessie, who lived here before eloping with penniless John Scott, later Lord Chancellor of

England, is the romantic tale behind these half-timbered 16th- and 17th-century houses. The window through which Bessie escaped now has a blue glass pane. These buildings also throw light on mercantile life in the quayside district.

🚇 Tyne Bridge
Newcastle–Gateshead.
☎ 0191 2328520. ◯ daily. ♿

Opened by King George V in 1928, this two-pin steel arch was the longest of its type in Britain with a span of 162 m (531 ft). Designed by Mott, Hay and Anderson, it soon became the city's most potent symbol.

🚇 Earl Grey's Monument
Grey St. ☎ 0191 2328520.
Benjamin Green created this memorial to the 2nd Earl Grey, Liberal Prime Minister from 1830 to 1834 and responsible for the Great Reform Bill. The statue was crafted by Edward H Baily.

The High Street *has a sweet shop, newspaper office, solicitor, dentist and music teacher. There is also a pub.*

VISITORS' CHECKLIST

Beamish, County Durham. ☎ 0191 370 4000. 🚉 🚌 Durham, then bus. ◯ Apr–Oct: 10am–5pm daily (last adm 3pm); Nov–Mar: High Street only 10am–4pm Tue–Thu, Sat, Sun. ● 10–31 Dec, 1 Jan, Good Fri. 📷 🚻 🎁

The Co-op *stocked everything a family needed at the turn of the century. A full range of foods available in 1913 is displayed.*

Pockerley Manor farm

Steam Winding Engine

Mahogany Drift mine, *a tunnel driven into coal seams near the surface, was here long before the museum and was worked from the 1850s to 1958. Visitors are given guided tours to underground pits.*

Entrance

P

Houses built by the London Lead Company in Middleton-in-Teesdale

Durham ⑭

See pp414–5.

North Pennines Tour ⑮

See p413.

Cotherstone cheese, a speciality of the Middleton-in-Teesdale area

Middleton-in-Teesdale ⑯

County Durham. 🏛 *1,100.* 🚆 *Darlington.* ❱ *10 Market Place (01833 641001).*

CLINGING TO A HILLSIDE amid wild Pennine scenery on the River Tees is this old lead mining town. Many of its rows of grey stone cottages were built by the London Lead Company, a paternalistic, Quaker-run organization who influenced every corner of its employees' daily lives.

The company began mining in 1753, and soon it virtually owned the town. Workers were expected to observe strict temperance, send their children to Sunday school and conform to the many company maxims. Today, mining has all but ceased in Teesdale, with Middleton standing as a monument to the 18th-century idea of the "company town". The offices of the London Lead Company can still be seen, as well as Nonconformist chapels from the era and a memorial fountain made of iron.

The crumbly Cotherstone cow's milk cheese, a speciality of the surrounding dales, is available in the shops.

Barnard Castle ⑰

County Durham. 🏛 *5,000.* 🚆 *Darlington.* ❱ *Woodleigh, Flatts Rd (01833 690909).* 🛒 *Wed.*

BARNARD CASTLE, known in the area as "Barney", is a little town full of character, with old shopfronts and a cobbled market overlooked by the ruins of the Norman castle from which it takes its name. The original Barnard Castle was built around 1125–40 by Bernard Balliol, ancestor of the founder of Balliol College, Oxford *(see p208)*, to guard a river crossing point. Later, the market town grew up around the fortification.

Today, Barnard Castle is known for the extraordinary French-style château to the east of the town, surrounded by acres of formal gardens. Started in 1860 by the local aristocrat John Bowes and his French wife Josephine, an artist and actress, it was never a private residence, but always intended as a museum and public monument. The château finally opened in 1892, by which time the couple were both dead. Nevertheless, the **Bowes Museum** stands as a monument to his wealth and her extravagance.

The museum houses a strong collection of Spanish art which includes El Greco's *The Tears of St Peter*, dating from the 1580s, and Goya's *Don Juan Meléndez Váldez*, painted in 1797. Clocks, porcelain, furniture, musical instruments, toys and tapestries are among its treasures, with a mechanical silver swan as a showpiece.

🏛 **Bowes Museum**
Barnard Castle. 📞 *01833 690606.* 🕐 *daily.* ● *25, 26 Dec, 1 Jan.* 🚫 &. ⬜ 🎥 🎦 *(summer).*

The Bowes Museum, a French-style château near Barnard Castle

North Pennines Tour ⑮

STARTING JUST TO THE SOUTH of Hadrian's Wall, this tour explores the South Tyne Valley, and Upper Weardale. It crosses one of England's wildest and most remote tracts of moorland, then heads north again. The high ground is mainly blanketed with heather, dotted with sheep or criss-crossed with dry-stone

Sheep grazing on the moors

walls, a feature of this region. Harriers and other birds hover above, and streams tumble into valleys of tightly huddled villages.

Celts, Romans and other settlers have left imprints on the North Pennines. The wealth of the area was based on lead mining and stone quarrying which has long co-existed with farming.

Haltwhistle ①
In the Church of the Holy Cross is the tombstone of John Ridley, brother of Protestant martyr, Nicholas Ridley, burnt at the stake in 1555 (see p211).

Haydon Bridge ③
There are some delightful walks near this spa town where the painter John Martin was born in 1789. Nearby Langley Castle is worth a visit.

Hexham ④
A pretty old town (see p408), Hexham has a fine abbey.

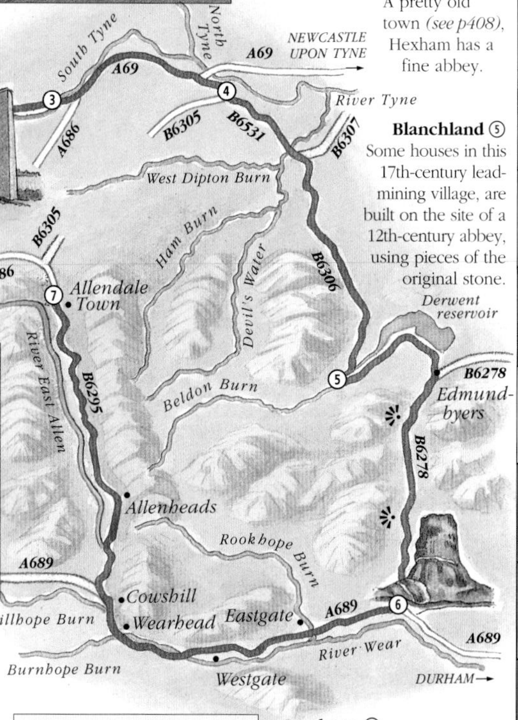

Bardon Mill ②
To the north is the Roman fort and civilian settlement of Vindolanda (see p408).

Blanchland ⑤
Some houses in this 17th-century lead-mining village, are built on the site of a 12th-century abbey, using pieces of the original stone.

Allendale ⑦
With its capital at Allendale Town, this is an area of spectacular scenery, with many walking and trout fishing opportunities.

Stanhope ⑥
An 18th-century castle overlooks the market square. The giant stump of a fossilized tree, said to be 250 million years old, guards the graveyard.

KEY

▨▨▨ Tour route

═══ Other roads

🔆 Viewpoint

TIPS FOR DRIVERS

Length: 50 miles (80 km)
Stopping-off points: Several pubs in Stanhope serve bar meals, and the Durham Dales Centre provides teas all year round. Horsley Hall Hotel at Eastgate serves meals all day. (See also pp636–7.)

0 kilometres 5

0 miles 5

Map labels: CARLISLE, A69, NEWCASTLE UPON TYNE, River Tyne, South Tyne, North Tyne, A686, B6305, B6531, B6307, West Dipton Burn, Ham Burn, Allendale Town, Devil's Water, B6306, Derwent reservoir, River East Allen, B6295, Beldon Burn, B6278, Edmund-byers, Allenheads, Rookhope Burn, A689, Cowshill, Killhope Burn, Wearhead, Eastgate, A689, Westgate, River Wear, Burnhope Burn, DURHAM

Durham ⑭

Cathedral Sanctuary knocker

THE CITY OF DURHAM was built on Island Hill or "Dunholm" in 995. This rocky peninsula, which defies the course of the River Wear's route to the sea, was chosen as the last resting place for the remains of St Cuthbert. The relics of the Venerable Bede were brought to the site 27 years later, adding to its attraction for pilgrims. Durham Cathedral was treated by architects as an experiment for geometric patterning, while the Castle served as the Episcopal Palace until 1832, when Bishop William van Mildert gave it up and surrendered part of his income to found Britain's third university. The 23 ha (57 acre) peninsula has many footpaths, views and fine buildings.

★ Cathedral
Built from 1093 to 1274, it is a striking Norman structure.

Old Fulling Mill, a largely 18th-century building, houses a museum of archaeology.

Prebend's footbridge was built in 1777. Two sculptures by Colin Winbourne are situated at the "island" end.

College Green

Monastic kitchen

Church of St Mary the Less

College gatehouse

South Bailey

St Cuthbert's Tomb

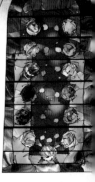

"Our Daily Bread" Window
This modern stained glass window in the north nave aisle was donated in 1984 by a local department store.

Galilee Chapel
Architects began work on the exotic Galilee Chapel in 1170, drawing inspiration from the Great Mosque of Cordoba in Andalusia. It was altered by Bishop Langley (d.1437) whose tomb is by the west door.

STAR SIGHTS

★ Cathedral

★ Castle

★ **Castle**
Begun in 1072, the castle is a fine Norman fortress. The keep, sited on a mound, is now part of the university.

Town Hall (1851)

St Nicholas' Church (1857)

Tunstal's Chapel
Situated at the end of the Tunstal's Gallery, the castle chapel was built c.1542. Its fine woodwork includes this unicorn misericord (see p327).

University buildings
were built by Bishop John Cosin in the 17th century.

Castle Gatehouse
Traces of Norman stonework can be seen in the outer arch, while the sturdy walls and upper floors are 18th century, rebuilt in a style dubbed "gothick" by detractors.

CATHEDRAL ARCHITECTURE

The vast dimensions of the 900-year-old columns, piers and vaults, and the inventive giant lozenge and chevron, trellis and dogtooth patterns carved into the stone columns, are the main innovative features of Durham Cathedral. It is believed that 11th- and 12th-century architects such as Bishop Ranulph Flambard tried to unify all parts of the structure. This can be seen in the south aisle of the nave below.

Ribbed vaults,
criss-crossing above the nave, are now common in church ceilings. One of the major achievements of Gothic architecture, they were first built at Durham.

The lozenge *shape is a pattern from prehistoric carving, but never before seen in a cathedral.*

Chevron patterns
on some of the piers in the nave are evidence of Moorish influence.

h of St e Bow

ngsgate bridge, ilt from 3, leads o North Bailey.

ace een

WALES

Wales at a Glance

Wales is a country of outstanding natural beauty with varied landscapes. Visitors come to climb dramatic mountain peaks, go walking in the forests, fish in the broad rivers and enjoy the miles of unspoilt coastline. The country's many seaside resorts have long been popular with English holidaymakers. As well as outdoor pursuits there is the vibrancy of Welsh culture, with its strong Celtic roots, to be experienced. Finally there are many fine castles, ruined abbeys, mansions and cities full of magnificent architecture.

Beaumaris Castle *was intended to be a key part of Edward I's "iron ring" to contain the rebellious Welsh (see p422). Begun in 1295 but never completed, the castle (see p424) has a sophisticated defence structure that is unparalleled in Wales.*

Portmeirion (see pp440–41) *is a private village whose astonishing buildings seem rather incongruous in the Welsh landscape. The village was created by the architect Sir Clough Williams-Ellis to fulfill a personal ambition. Some of the buildings are assembled from pieces of architecture taken from sites around the country.*

St David *is the smallest city in Britain. The cathedral (see pp450–51) is the largest in Wales, and its nave is noted for its carved oak roof and beautiful rood screen. Next to the cathedral is the medieval Bishop's Palace, now a ruin.*

◁ **Caernarfon's colourful quayside marina**

Llanberis and Snowdon
(see p437) *is an area
famous for dangerous, high
peaks, long popular with
climbers. Mount Snowdon's
summit is most easily
reached from Llanberis. Its
Welsh name, Yr Wyddfa
Fawr, means "great tomb"
and it is the legendary
burial place of a giant slain
by King Arthur (see p271).*

Flintshire

*onwy
lwyn*   *Denbighshire*

NORTH WALES
(see pp426–41)

Wrexham

Conwy Castle *guards one of the
best-preserved medieval fortified
towns in Britain (see pp432–3).
Built by Edward I, the castle
was besieged and came close
to surrender in 1294. It was
taken by Owain Glyndŵr's
supporters in 1401.*

Powys

OUTH AND MID-WALES
(see pp442–61)

The Brecon Beacons *(see pp454–5) is a national park,
a lovely area of mountains, forest and moorland in South
Wales, which is a favourite with walkers and naturalists.
Pen-y-Fan is one of the principal summits.*

Cardiff Castle's
*(see pp458–9) Clock
Tower is just one of
many 19th-century
additions by the
eccentric but gifted
architect William
Burges. His flamboy-
ant style still delights
and amazes visitors.*

Monmouthshire

iff Swansea & Environs

0 kilometres   25

0 miles   25

A PORTRAIT OF WALES

L ONG POPULAR WITH BRITISH HOLIDAYMAKERS, *the many charms of Wales are now becoming better known internationally. They include spectacular scenery and a vibrant culture specializing in male-voice choirs, poetry and a passionate love of team sports. Governed from Westminster since 1536, Wales has its own distinct Celtic identity and in 1999 finally gained partial devolution.*

Much of the Welsh landmass is covered by the Cambrian Mountain range, which effectively acts as a barrier from England. Wales is warmed by the Gulf Stream and has a mild climate, with more rain than most of Britain. The land is unsuitable for arable farming, but sheep and cattle thrive; the drove roads, along which sheep used to be driven across the hills to England, are now popular walking trails. It is partly because of the rugged terrain that the Welsh have managed to maintain their separate identity and their ancient language.

One of Wales's splendid National Parks

Welsh is an expansive, musical language, spoken by only one-fifth of the 2.7 million inhabitants, but in parts of North Wales it is still the main language of conversation. There is an official bilingual policy: road signs are in Welsh and English, even in areas where Welsh is little spoken. Welsh

place names intrigue visitors being made up of native words that describe features of the landscape or ancient buildings. Examples include *Aber* (river mouth), *Afon* (river), *Fach* (little), *Llan* (church) *Llyn* (lake) and *Nant* (valley).

Wales was conquered by the Romans, but not by the Saxons. The land and the people therefore retained Celtic patterns of settlement and husbandry for six centuries before the Norman Conquest in 1066. This allowed time for the development of a distinctive Welsh nation whose homogeneity continues to this day.

The early Norman kings subjugated the Welsh by appointing "Marcher Lords" to control areas bordering England. A string

Rugby: the popular Welsh sport

of massive castles provides evidence of the turbulent years when Welsh insurrection was a constant threat. It was not until 1535 that Wales formally became part of Britain, and today it is governed from Westminster, with a cabinet minister responsible for its affairs.

Religious non-conformism and radical politics are deeply rooted in Welsh consciousness. Saint David converted the country to Christianity in the 6th century. Methodism, chapel and teetotalism became firmly entrenched in

Mountain sheep: a familiar sight in rural Wales

A *gorsedd* (assembly) of bards at the eisteddfod

of music derives from the ancient bards: minstrels and poets, who may have been associated with the Druids. Bardic tales of quasi-historical figures and magic were part of the oral tradition of the Dark Ages. They were first written down in the 14th century as the *Mabinogion,* which has inspired Welsh poets up to the 20th century's Dylan Thomas. The male-voice choirs found in many towns, villages and factories, particularly in the industrial south, express the Welsh musical heritage. Choirs compete in eisteddfods: festivals that celebrate Welsh culture.

the Welsh psyche during the 19th century. Even today some pubs stay closed on Sundays (alcohol is not sold at all in the Llŷn Peninsula). A long-standing oral tradition in Wales has produced many outstanding public speakers, politicians and actors. Welsh labour leaders have played important roles in the British trade union movement and the development of socialism.

Welsh heritage is steeped in song, music, poetry and legend rather than handicrafts, although one notable exception is the carved Welsh lovespoon – a craft recently revived. The well-known Welsh love

Welsh lovespoon

In the 19th century, the opening of the South Wales coalfield in Mid-Glamorgan – for a time the biggest in the world – led to an industrial boom, with mass migration from the countryside to the iron and steelworks. This prosperity was not to last: apart from a brief respite in World War II, the coal industry has been in terminal decline for decades, causing severe economic hardship. Today tourism is being promoted in the hope that the wealth generated, by outdoor activities in particular, will be able to take "King Coal's" place.

Conwy's picturesque, medieval walled town, fronted by a colourful harbour

The History of Wales

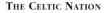

WALES HAS BEEN SETTLED since prehistoric times, its history shaped by many factors, from invasion to industrialization. The Romans set up bases in the mountainous terrain, but it was effectively a separate Celtic nation when Offa's Dyke was built as the border with England in 770. Centuries of cross-border raids and military campaigns followed before England and Wales were formally united by the Act of Union in 1535. The rugged northwest, the former stronghold of the Welsh princes, remains the heartland of Welsh language and culture.

St David, patron saint of Wales

Owain Glyndŵr, heroic leader of Welsh opposition to English rule

THE CELTIC NATION

Ornamental Iron Age bronze plaque from Anglesey

WALES WAS SETTLED by waves of migrants in prehistoric times. By the Iron Age (see p42), Celtic farmers had established hillforts and their religion, Druidism. From the 1st century AD, until the legions withdrew around 400, the Romans built fortresses and roads, and mined lead, silver and gold. During the next 200 years, Wales was converted to Christianity by missionaries from Europe. St David (see pp450–51), the Welsh patron saint, is said to have turned the leek into a national symbol. He persuaded soldiers to wear leeks in their hats to distinguish themselves from Saxons during a 6th-century skirmish.

The Saxons (see pp46–7) failed to conquer Wales, and in 770 the Saxon King Offa built a defensive earthwork along the unconquered territory (see p447). Beyond Offa's Dyke the people called themselves *Y Cymry* (fellow countrymen) and the land *Cymru*. The Saxons called the land "Wales" from the Old English *wealas*, meaning foreigners. It was divided into kingdoms of which the main ones were Gwynedd in the north, Powys in the centre and Dyfed in the south. There were strong trade, cultural and linguistic links between each.

MARCHER LORDS

THE NORMAN INVASION of 1066 (see p47) did not reach Wales, but the border territory ("the Marches") was given by William the Conqueror to three powerful barons based at Shrewsbury, Hereford and Chester. These Marcher Lords made many incursions into Wales and controlled most of the lowlands. But the Welsh

Edward I designating his son Prince of Wales in 1301

princes held the mountainous northwest and exploited English weaknesses. Under Llywelyn the Great (d.1240), North Wales was almost completely independent; in 1267 his grandson, Llywelyn the Last, was acknowledged as Prince of Wales by Henry III.

In 1272 Edward I came to the English throne. He built fortresses and embarked on a military campaign to conquer Wales. In 1283 Llywelyn was killed in a skirmish, a shattering blow for the Welsh. Edward introduced English law and proclaimed his son Prince of Wales (see p430).

OWAIN GLYNDŴR'S REBELLION

WELSH RESENTMENT against the Marcher Lords led to rebellion. In 1400 Owain Glyndŵr (c.1350–1416), a descendant of the Welsh princes, laid waste to English-dominated towns and castles. Declaring himself Prince of Wales, he found Celtic allies in Scotland, Ireland, France and Northumbria. In 1404 Glyndŵr captured Harlech and Cardiff, and formed a parliament in Machynlleth (see p448). In 1408 the French made a truce with the English king, Henry IV. The rebellion then failed and Glyndŵr went into hiding until his death.

UNION WITH ENGLAND

WALES SUFFERED greatly during the Wars of the Roses *(see p49)* as Yorkists and Lancastrians tried to gain control of the strategically important Welsh castles. The wars ended in 1485, and the Welshman Henry Tudor, born in Pembroke, became Henry VII. The Act of Union in 1535 and other laws abolished the Marcher Lordships, giving Wales parliamentary representation in London instead. English practices replaced inheritance customs and English became the language of the courts and administration. The Welsh language survived, partly helped by the church and by Dr William Morgan's translation of the Bible in 1588.

Vernacular Bible, which helped to keep the Welsh language alive

INDUSTRY AND RADICAL POLITICS

THE INDUSTRIALIZATION of south and east Wales began with the development of open-cast coal mining near Wrexham and Merthyr Tydfil in the 1760s. Convenient ports and the arrival of the railways helped the process. By the second half of the 19th century open-cast mines had been superseded by deep pits in the Rhondda Valley.

Living and working conditions were poor for industrial and agricultural workers. A series of "Rebecca Riots" in

Miners from South Wales pictured in 1910

South Wales between 1839 and 1843, involving tenant farmers (dressed as women) protesting about tithes and rents, was forcibly suppressed. The Chartists, trade unions and the Liberal Party had much Welsh support.

The rise of Methodism *(see p265)* roughly paralleled the growth of industry: 80 per cent of the population was Methodist by 1851. The Welsh language persisted, despite attempts by the British government to discourage its use, which included punishing children caught speaking it.

WALES TODAY

IN THE 20TH CENTURY the Welsh, for the first time, became a power in British politics. David Lloyd George, although not born in Wales, grew up there and was the first British Prime Minister to come from a Welsh family. Aneurin Bevan, a miner's son who became a Labour Cabinet Minister, helped create the National Health Service *(see p59).*

Welsh nationalism continued to grow: in 1926 Plaid Cymru, the Welsh Nationalist Party, was formed. In 1955 Cardiff

was recognized as the capital of Wales *(see p456)* and four years later the ancient symbol of the red dragon became the emblem on Wales' new flag. Plaid Cymru won two parliamentary seats at Westminster in 1974, and in a 1998 referendum the Welsh espoused limited home rule.

The Welsh language has declined: whereas half the population could speak it in 1901, the figure was down to 21 per cent 70 years later. The 1967 Welsh Language Act gave it protection by making Welsh compulsory in schools and the television channel S4C (Sianel 4 Cymru), formed in 1982, broadcasts many programmes in Welsh.

From the 1960s the steel and coal industries declined, creating mass unemployment. This has been only partly alleviated by the emergence of new, high-tech industries, and by the recent growth in tourism and higher education.

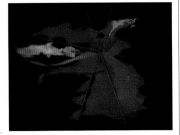
The logo of S4C, Wales's own television station

Castles of Wales

A French 15th-century painting of Conwy Castle

W ALES IS RICH in romantic medieval castles. Soon after the Battle of Hastings, in 1066 *(see p47)*, the Normans turned their attentions to Wales. They built earth and timber fortifications, later replaced by stone castles, initiating a building programme that was pursued by the Welsh princes and invading forces. Construction reached its peak during the reign of Edward I *(see p422).* As the need for security lessened in the later Middle Ages, some castles became stately homes.

The north gatehouse was planned to be 18 m (60 ft) high, providing lavish royal accommodation, but its top storey was never built.

The inner ward was lined with a hall, granary, kitchens and stables.

Rounded towers, with fewer blind spots than square ones, gave better protection.

Arrow slit

BEAUMARIS CASTLE

The last of Edward I's Welsh castles *(see p430),* this perfectly symmetrical, concentric design was intended to combine impregnable defence with comfort. Invaders would face many obstacles before reaching the inner ward.

Moat

Curtain wall

WHERE TO SEE WELSH CASTLES

In addition to Beaumaris, in North Wales there are medieval forts at Caernarfon *(see p430),* Conwy *(see p432)* and Harlech *(see p440).* Edward I also built Denbigh, Flint (near Chester) and Rhuddlan (near Rhyll). In South and mid-Wales, Caerphilly (near Cardiff), Kidwelly (near Carmarthen) and Pembroke were built between the 11th and 13th centuries. Spectacular sites are occupied by Cilgerran (near Cardigan), Criccieth (near Porthmadog) and Carreg Cennen *(see p454).* Chirk Castle, near Llangollen, is a good example of a fortress that has since become a stately home.

Caerphilly, *6 miles (10 km) north of Cardiff, is a huge castle with concentric stone and water defences that cover 12 ha (30 acres).*

Harlech Castle (see p440) *is noted for its massive gatehouse, twin towers and the fortified stairway to the sea. It was the headquarters of the Welsh resistance leader Owain Glyndŵr (see p422) from 1404–8.*

CASTELL-Ŷ-BERE

This native Welsh castle at the foot of Cader Idris *(see p440)* was founded by Llywelyn the Great in 1221 *(see p422)*, to secure internal borders rather than to resist the English.

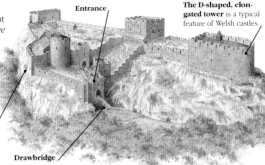

Entrance

The D-shaped, elongated tower is a typical feature of Welsh castles.

The castle's construction follows the shape of the rock. The curtain walls are too low and insubstantial to be of much practical use.

Drawbridge

Chapel Tower has a [be]autiful medieval chapel.

The protected dock, on a channel that originally led to the sea, received supplies during sieges.

[in]**ner wall**, with an [passage], was higher [the] curtain wall to [it] simultaneous firing.

Twin-towered gatehouse

Edward I (see p422) *was the warrior king whose castles played a key role in the subjugation of the Welsh people.*

EDWARD I AND MASTER JAMES OF ST GEORGE

In 1278 Edward I brought over from Savoy a master stonemason who became a great military architect, James of St George. Responsible for planning and building at least 12 of Edward's fine Welsh castles, James was paid well and liberally pensioned off, indicating the esteem in which he was held by the king.

A plan of Caernarfon Castle illustrates how its position, on a promontory surrounded by water, has determined the building's shape and defence.

Caernarfon Castle (see p430), birthplace of the ill-fated Edward II (see p315), was intended to be the official royal residence in North Wales, and has palatial private apartments.

Castell Coch was restored in Neo-Gothic style by Lord Bute and William Burges (see p458). Mock-castles were built by many Victorian industrialists.

Conwy Castle (see p433), like many other castles, required forced labour on a massive scale for its construction.

NORTH WALES

ABERCONWY & COLWYN · ANGLESEY · CAERNARFONSHIRE &
MERIONETHSHIRE · DENBIGHSHIRE · FLINTSHIRE · WREXHAM

THE NORTH WALES LANDSCAPE *has a dramatic quality reflected in its history. In prehistoric times, Anglesey was a stronghold of the religious elite known as the Druids. Roman and Norman invasions concentrated on the coast, leaving the mountains to the Welsh. These wild areas are the centre of Welsh language and culture.*

Defence and conquest have been constant themes in Welsh history. North Wales was the scene of ferocious battles between the Welsh princes and Anglo-Norman monarchs determined to establish English rule. The string of formidable castles which still stand in North Wales are as much a testament to Welsh resistance as to the wealth and strength of the invaders. Several massive fortresses, including Beaumaris, Caernarfon and Harlech, almost surround the rugged high country of Snowdonia, an area that even today maintains an untamed quality.

Sheep and cattle farming are the basis of the rural economy here, though there are also large areas of forestry. Along the coast, tourism is a major activity. Llandudno, a purpose-built Victorian resort, popularized the sandy northern coastline in the 19th century. The area continues to attract large numbers of visitors, though major development is confined to the narrow coastal strip that lies between Prestatyn and Llandudno, leaving the island of Anglesey and the remote Llŷn Peninsula largely untouched.

The Llŷn Peninsula remains one of the strongholds of the Welsh language, along with rather isolated inland communities, such as Dolgellau and Bala.

No part of North Wales can truly be called industrial, though there are still remnants of the once-prosperous slate industry in Snowdonia, where the stark, grey quarries provide a striking contrast to the natural beauty of the surrounding mountains. At the foot of Snowdon (the highest mountain in Wales), the villages of Beddgelert, Betws-y-Coed and Llanberis are popular bases for walkers who come to enjoy the spectacular views and striking beauty of this remote region.

Caernarfon Castle, one of the forbidding fortresses built by Edward I

◁ **The River Dee at Llangollen, still an area of unspoilt natural beauty**

Exploring North Wales

THE DOMINANT FEATURE of North Wales is Snowdon, the highest mountain in Wales. Snowdonia National Park extends dramatically from the Snowdon massif south beyond Dolgellau, with thickly wooded valleys, mountain lakes, moors and estuaries. To the east are the softer Clwydian Hills, and unspoilt coastlines can be enjoyed on Anglesey and the beautiful Llŷn Peninsula.

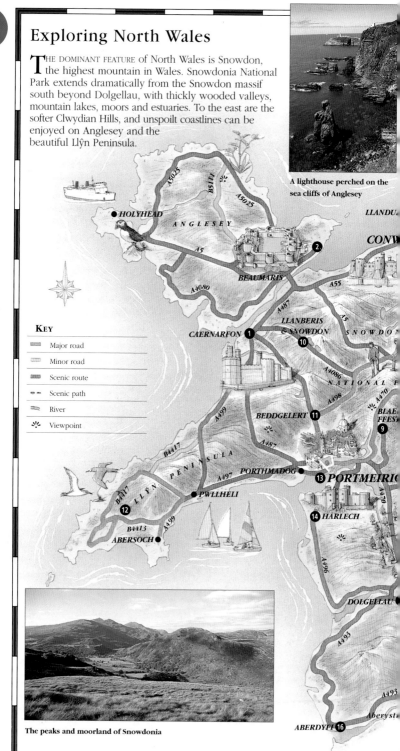

A lighthouse perched on the sea cliffs of Anglesey

KEY

▨	Major road
▨	Minor road
▨	Scenic route
➳	Scenic path
▬	River
☀	Viewpoint

HOLYHEAD

ANGLESEY

A5025
B5111
A5025
A5
A4080

BEAUMARIS

LLANDU.

CONW

A55

CAERNARFON ①

LLANBERIS & SNOWDON
⑩

SNOWDON

A55

A487

A4086

A498

NATIONAL P

A470

BLAE
FFEST
⑨

BEDDGELERT ⑪

A487

A4212
B4391

LLŶN PENINSULA
B4417
A497
PORTHMADOG
⑬ PORTMEIRIO

A499
PWLLHELI
⑭ HARLECH

A4413
A499
ABERSOCH
⑫
A470

DOLGELLAU

A493

A493
A497

ABERDYFI ⑯
Aberysta

The peaks and moorland of Snowdonia

GETTING AROUND

The main route into North Wales from the northwest of England is the A55, a good dual carriageway which bypasses several places that used to be traffic bottlenecks, including Conwy. The other main route through the region is the A5 Shrewsbury to Holyhead road, which follows a trail through the mountains pioneered by the 19th-century engineer Thomas Telford *(see p433)*. Rail services run along the coast to Holyhead, connecting with ferries across the Irish Sea to Dublin and Dun Laoghaire. Scenic branch lines travel from Llandudno Junction to Blaenau Ffestiniog (via Betws-y-Coed) and along the southern Llŷn Peninsula.

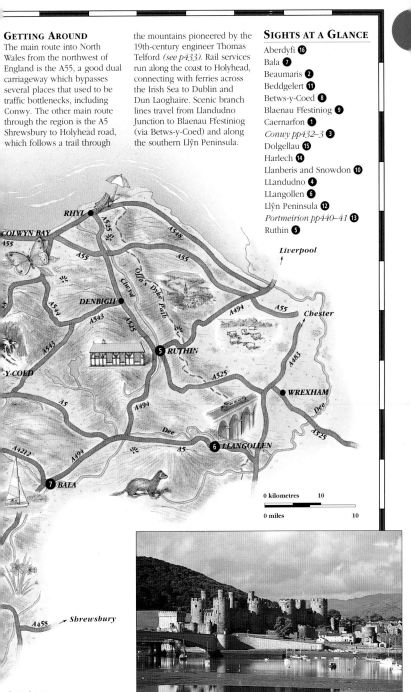

RHYL

COLWYN BAY

A55

A525

A548

A55

A55

Offa's Dyke Path

Clwyd

DENBIGH

A543

A525

🔵 RUTHIN

A494

Liverpool ↑

A55

Chester →

A483

A525

A5

A494

A525

Dee

🔵 LLANGOLLEN

WREXHAM

Dee

A525

-Y-COED

A5

A4212

A494

A5

7️⃣ BALA

0 kilometres   10

0 miles   10

A458 → Shrewsbury

SEE ALSO

• *Where to Stay* pp564–565

• *Where to Eat* pp601–602

The imposing castle built at Conwy by Edward I in the 13th century

Caernarfon Castle, built by Edward I as a symbol of his power over the conquered Welsh

Caernarfon ●

Caernarfonshire & Merionethshire
(Gwynedd). 🏛 *10,000.* 🚌
ℹ Castle St (01286 672232). 🚇 Sat.
ⓦ www.gwynedd.gov.uk

ONE OF THE MOST FAMOUS
castles in Wales looms
over this busy town. Both
were created after Edward I's
defeat of the last native Welsh
prince, Llywelyn ap Gruffydd
(Llywelyn the Last) in 1283
(see p422). The town walls
merge with modern streets that
spread beyond the medieval
centre to a market square.

Overlooking the town and
its harbour, **Caernarfon**

THE INVESTITURE

In 1301 the future Edward
II became the first English
Prince of Wales *(see p422)*,
a title since held by the
British monarch's eldest
son. In 1969 the invest-
iture in Caernarfon Castle
of Prince Charles *(above)*
as Prince of Wales drew
500 million TV viewers.

Castle *(see p425)*, with its
polygonal towers, was built
as a seat of government for
North Wales. Caernarfon was
a thriving port in the 19th
century, and during this
period the castle ruins were
restored by the architect
Anthony Salvin. Displays in
the castle include the Royal
Welch Fusiliers Museum, and
exhibitions tracing the history
of the Princes of Wales and
exploring the theme "Chieftains and Princes".

On the hill above the town
are the ruins of **Segontium**,
a Roman fort built in about
AD 78. Local legend claims that
the first Christian Emperor of
Rome, Constantine the Great,
was born here in 280.

♙ **Caernarfon Castle**
Y Maes. 🚇 *01286 677617.* ◻ *daily.*
● *24–26 Dec, 1 Jan.* 🎫 📷 *phone
for details.*

𝘯 **Segontium**
Beddgelert Rd. 🚇 *01286 675625.*
◻ *daily (Sun: pm).* ● *24, 26 Dec, 1
Jan.* 🎫 🚻 *limited.*

Beaumaris ●

Anglesey (Gwynedd). 🏛 *2,000.* 🚇
ℹ Llanfair PG, Station Site, Holyhead
Rd, Anglesey (01248 713177).
ⓦ www.anglesey.gov.uk

HANDSOME GEORGIAN and
Victorian architecture
gives Beaumaris the air of a
resort on England's southern
coast. The buildings reflect
this sailing centre's past role
as Anglesey's chief port, before
the island was linked to the
mainland by the road and

railway bridges built across
the Menai Strait in the 19th
century. This was the site of
Edward I's last, and possibly
greatest, **castle** *(see p424)*,
which was built to command
this important ferrying point
to the mainland of Wales.

Ye Olde Bull's Head inn,
on Castle Street, was built in
1617. Its celebrated literary
patrons have included Dr
Samuel Johnson (1709–84)
and Victorian novelist Charles
Dickens *(see p175)*.

The town's **Courthouse**,
was built in 1614 and the
recently restored 1829 **Gaol**
preserves its soundproofed
punishment room and a huge
treadmill for prisoners. Two
public hangings took place
here. Richard Rowlands, the
last victim, protested his inno-
cence and cursed the church
clock as he was led to the
gallows, declaring that its four
faces would never show the
same times again. It failed to
show consistent times until it
had an overhaul in 1980.

Beaumaris's award-winning
Museum of Childhood contains a collection of toys from
the 19th and 20th centuries.

♙ **Beaumaris Castle**
Castle St. 🚇 *01248 810361.* ◻
daily. ● *24–26 Dec, 1 Jan.* 🎫 🚻
🏛 **Courthouse**
Castle. 🚇 *01248 810921.* ◻ *Apr–
Sep: daily.* 🎫 🚻
🏛 **Gaol**
Bunkers Hill. 🚇 *01248 810921.*
◻ *Apr–Sep: daily.* 🎫 🚻 *limited.*
🏛 **Museum of Childhood**
Castle St. 🚇 *01248 712498.* ◻
*2 wks before Easter–Nov: daily (Sun:
pm).* 🎫 🚻 🚻 *limited.*

ALICE IN WONDERLAND

The Gogarth Abbey Hotel, Llandudno, was the summer home of the Liddells. Their friend, Charles Dodgson (1832–98), would entertain young Alice Liddell with stories of characters such as the White Rabbit and the Mad Hatter. As Lewis Carroll, Dodgson wrote his magical tales in *Alice's Adventures in Wonderland* (1865) and *Through the Looking-Glass* (1871).

Arthur Rackham's illustration (1907) of *Alice in Wonderland*

🏛 **The Alice in Wonderland Centre**

Trinity Sq. 📞 *01492 860082.* ⭕ *Easter–Oct: daily; Nov–Easter: Mon–Sat.* ⬤ *25–26 Dec, 1 Jan.* 📷 ♿ 📷📷

🔨 **Great Orme Copper Mines**

Off A55. 📞 *01492 870447.* ⭕ *Feb–Oct: daily.* 📷 ♿ *limited.* 📷 🚻

Ruthin ❺

Denbighshire (Clwyd). 👥 *5,000.* 🚉 ℹ️ Craft Centre, Park Rd *(01824 703992).* 🛍 *1st Tue of every month; Thu (indoor).* 🌐 *www.borderlands.co.uk*

RUTHIN'S LONG-STANDING prosperity as a market town is reflected in its fine half-timbered medieval buildings. These include the National Westminster and Barclays banks in St Peter's Square. The former was a 15th-century courthouse and prison, the latter the home of Thomas Exmewe, Lord Mayor of London in 1517–18. **Maen Huail** ("Huail's stone"), a boulder outside Barclays, is said to be where King Arthur *(see p271)* beheaded Huail, his rival in a love affair.

St Peter's Church, on the edge of St Peter's Square, was founded in 1310 and has a Tudor oak roof in the north aisle, with 500 carved panels. Next to the Castle Hotel is the 17th-century **Myddleton Arms** pub, whose seven unusual, Dutch-style, dormer windows are known locally as the "eyes of Ruthin".

Conwy ❸

See pp432–3.

Llandudno ❹

Gwynedd. 👥 *19,000.* 🚉 🚌 ℹ️ *1–2 Chapel St (01492 876413).* 🛍 *Mon–Sat.*

Llandudno's crescent-shaped bay

LLANDUDNO retains much of the holiday spirit of the 19th century, when the new railways brought crowds to the coast. Its **pier**, more than 700 m (2,295 ft) long, and its canopied walkways recall the heyday of seaside holidays. The town is proud of its association with the author Lewis Carroll. **The Alice in Wonderland Centre** is a grotto decorated with life-sized scenes from his books.

Llandudno's cheerful seaside atmosphere owes much to a strong sense of its Victorian roots – unlike many British seaside towns, which embraced the flashing lights and funfairs of the 20th century. To take full advantage of its sweeping beach, Llandudno was laid out between its two headlands, Great Orme's Head and Little Orme's Head.

Great Orme's Head, now a Country Park and Nature Reserve, rises to 207 m (680 ft) and has a long history. In the Bronze Age copper was mined here; the **copper mines** and their excavations are open to the public. The **church** on the headland was built from timber in the 6th century by St Tudno, rebuilt in stone in the 13th century, restored in 1855 and is still in use. Local history and wildlife can be traced in an information centre on the summit.

There are two effortless ways to reach the summit: on the **Great Orme Tramway**, one of only three cable-hauled street tramways in the world (the others are in San Francisco and Lisbon), or by the **Llandudno Cable Car**. Both operate only in summer.

The "eyes of Ruthin", an unusual feature in Welsh architecture

Street-by-Street: Conwy ❸

Conwy is one of Britain's most underrated historic towns. Until the early 1990s it was famous as a traffic bottleneck, but thanks to a town bypass, its concentration of architectural riches – unparalleled in Wales – can now be appreciated. The castle dominates: a brooding, intimidating monument built by Edward I *(see p424)*. But Conwy is set apart from other medieval towns by its amazingly well-preserved town walls. Fortified with 21 towers and three gateways, the walls form an almost unbroken shield around the old town.

Smallest House
This fisherman's cottage on the quayside, just over 3 m (10 ft) high, is said to be the smallest house in Britain.

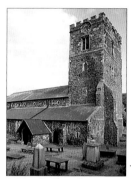

St Mary's Church
This medieval church, on the site of a 12th-century Cistercian abbey, is set in peaceful grounds.

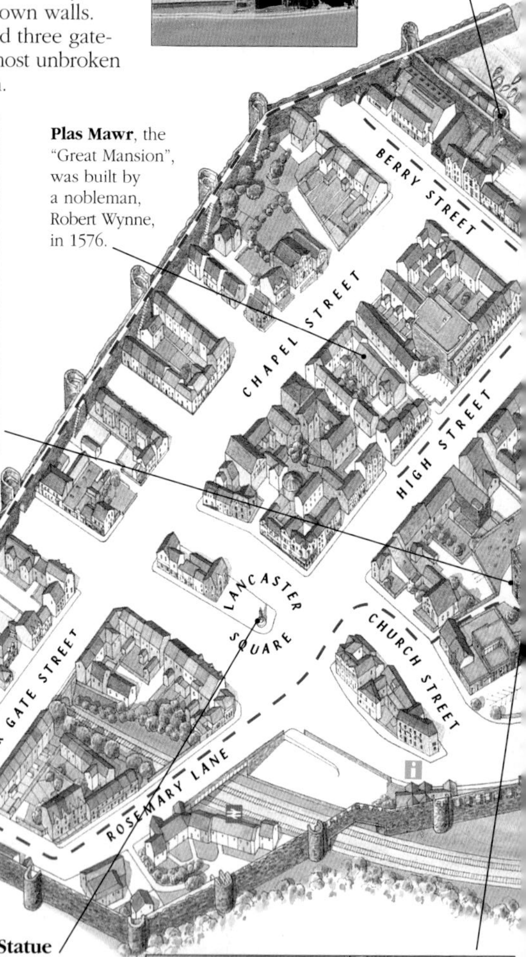

Plas Mawr, the "Great Mansion", was built by a nobleman, Robert Wynne, in 1576.

Bangor

BERRY STREET

CHAPEL STREET

HIGH STREET

UPPER GATE STREET

LANCASTER SQUARE

CHURCH STREET

ROSEMARY LANE

Upper Gate

Llywelyn's Statue
Llywelyn the Great (see p422) was arguably Wales's most successful medieval leader.

Aberconwy House
This restored 14th-century house was once the home of a wealthy merchant.

THOMAS TELFORD

Thomas Telford (1757–1834) was the gifted Scottish engineer responsible for many of Britain's roads, bridges and canals. The Menai Bridge (*see p430*), the Pontcysyllte Aqueduct (*see p436*) and Conwy Bridge are his outstanding works in Wales. Telford's graceful bridge at Conwy has aesthetic as well as practical qualities. Completed in 1826 across the mouth of the Conwy estuary, it was designed in a castellated style to blend with the castle. Before the bridge's construction the estuary could only be crossed by ferry.

VISITORS' CHECKLIST

Conwy. 🏘 8,000. 🚆 Conwy.
ℹ 01492 592248. 🎪 Conwy
Festival: Jul. **Aberconwy House**
🕻 01492 592246. ◯ Wed–
Mon. ◯ Nov–Mar. 🚫 **Conwy
Castle** 🕻 01492 592358.
◯ daily. ● 25, 26 Dec, 1 Jan.
🚫 🏠 **Smallest House**
◯ Apr–Oct: daily. 🚫

★ Town Walls
These remarkably well-preserved medieval walls are 1,280 m (4,200 ft) long and over 9 m (30 ft) high.

Telford's bridge

Railway bridge

Entrance to castle

KEY

– – – Suggested route

STAR SIGHTS

★ Town Walls

★ Conwy Castle

★ Conwy Castle
This atmospheric watercolour, Conwy Castle *(c.1770), is by the Nottingham artist Paul Sandby.*

Pontcysyllte Aqueduct, built in 1795–1805, carrying the Llangollen Canal

Llangollen ❻

Denbighshire. 🏛 5,000. 🚊 ⓘ
Town Hall, Castle St (01978 860828).
🚋 *Tue.* Ⓦ *www.llangollen.org.uk*

BEST KNOWN for its annual eisteddfod (festival), this pretty town sits on the River Dee, which is spanned by a 14th-century bridge. The town became notorious in the 18th century, when two eccentric Irishwomen, Lady Eleanor Butler and Sarah Ponsonby, the "Ladies of Llangollen", set up house together in the half-timbered **Plas Newydd**. Their unconventional dress and literary enthusiasms attracted such celebrities as the Duke of Wellington *(see p148)* and William Wordsworth *(see p352)*. The ruins of a 13th-century castle, **Castell Dinas Brân**, occupy the summit of a hill overlooking the house.

ENVIRONS: Boats on the **Llangollen Canal** sail from Wharf Hill in summer and cross the spectacular 300 m (1,000 ft) long Pontcysyllte Aqueduct, built by Thomas Telford *(see p433)*.

🏛 **Plas Newydd**
Hill St. 📞 *01978 861314.*
◯ *Easter–Oct: daily.* 🏷 🚻 *limited.*

Bala ❼

Gwynedd. 🏛 2,000. 🚌 *from Llangollen.* ⓘ *Penllyn, Pensarn Rd (01678 521021).*

BALA LAKE, Wales's largest natural lake, lies between the Aran and Arenig mountains at the fringes of Snowdonia

National Park. It is popular for water-sports and boasts a unique fish called a *gwyniad*, which is related to the salmon.

The little grey-stone town of Bala is a Welsh-speaking community, its houses strung out along a single street at the eastern end of the lake. Thomas Charles (1755–1814), a Methodist church leader, once lived here. A plaque on his former home recalls Mary Jones who, in 1800, walked 28 miles (42 km) barefoot from Abergynolwyn to buy a bible. This prompted Charles to establish the Bible Society, to provide cheap bibles to the working class.

The narrow-gauge **Bala Lake Railway** follows the lake shore from Llanuwchllyn, 4 miles (6 km) southwest.

Betws-y-Coed ❽

Conwy. 🏛 600. 🚆 ⓘ *The Old Stables (01690 710426).*

THIS VILLAGE near the peaks of Snowdonia has been a hill-walking centre since the 19th century. To the west are

the **Swallow Falls**, where the River Llugwy flows through a wooded glen. The bizarre **Tŷ Hyll** ("Ugly House"), is a *tŷ unnos* ("one-night house"); traditionally, houses erected between dusk and dawn on common land were entitled to freehold rights, and the owner could enclose land as far as he could throw an axe from the door.

To the east is **Waterloo Bridge**, built by the talented engineer Thomas Telford to celebrate the famous victory against Napoleon.

🏛 **Tŷ Hyll**
Capel Curig. 📞 *01690 720287.*
◯ *Easter–Sep: daily.* 🏷 🚻 *limited.*

The ornate Waterloo Bridge, built in 1815 after the famous battle

◁ **The picturesque village of Beddgelert in Snowdonia National Park**

A view of the Snowdonia countryside from Llanberis Pass, the most popular route to Snowdon's peak

Blaenau Ffestiniog ❾

Gwynedd. 🏠 5,500. 🚆
🚌 Betws-y-Coed (01690 710426).
♦ Tue (Jun–Sep).

BLAENAU FFESTINIOG, once the slate capital of North Wales, sits among mountains riddled with quarries. The **Llechwedd Slate Caverns**, overlooking Blaenau, opened to visitors in the early 1970s, marking a new role for the declining industrial town. The electric Miners' Tramway takes passengers on a tour into the original caverns.

On the Deep Mine tour, visitors descend on Britain's steepest passenger incline railway to the underground chambers, while sound effects recreate the atmosphere of a working quarry. The dangers included landfalls and floods, as well as the more gradual threat of slate dust breathed into the lungs.

There are slate-splitting demonstrations on the surface, a quarryman's cottage and a re-creation of a Victorian village to illustrate the cramped and basic living conditions endured by workers between the 1880s and 1945.

The popular narrow-gauge **Ffestiniog Railway** (see pp438–9) runs from Blaenau to Porthmadog.

🏛 Llechwedd Slate Caverns
Off A470. 📞 01766 830306.
⬜ daily. ⬤ 25, 26 Dec, 1 Jan. 🚫
♿ except the Deep Mine. 🅿 🎁

Llanberis and Snowdon ❿

Gwynedd. 🏠 2,100. 🚌 High St, Llanberis (01286 870765).
ⓦ www.gwynedd.gov.uk

SNOWDON, which at 1,085 m (3,560 ft) is the highest peak in Wales, is the main focus of the vast Snowdonia National Park, whose scenery ranges from this rugged mountain country to moors and sandy beaches.

The easiest route to Snowdon's summit begins in Llanberis: the 5 mile (8 km) **Llanberis Track**. From Llanberis Pass, the Miners' Track (once used by copper miners) and the Pyg Track are alternative paths. Walkers should beware of sudden weather changes and dress accordingly. The narrow-gauge **Snowdon Mountain Railway**, which opened in 1896, is an easier option.

Llanberis was a major 19th-century slate town, with grey terraces hewn into the hills. Other attractions are the 13th-century shell of **Dolbadarn Castle**, and, above Lake Peris, the **Electric Mountain**, which has tours of Europe's biggest hydro-electric pumped storage station.

♦ Dolbadarn Castle
Off A4086 nr Llanberis. 📞 01286 870765. ⬜ daily.
🚌 Electric Mountain
Llanberis. 📞 01286 870636. ⬜ Jan–Easter: Thu–Sun; Easter–23 Dec: daily. ⬤ 24 Dec– 1st wk in Jan. 🚫
♿ 🅿 🅿 🎁 by arrangement.

BRITAIN'S CENTRE OF SLATE

Welsh slates provided roofing material for Britain's new towns in the 19th century. In 1898, the slate industry employed nearly 17,000 men, a quarter of whom worked at Blaenau Ffestiniog. Foreign competition and new materials later took their toll. Quarries such as Gloddfa Ganol and Llechwedd in Blaenau Ffestiniog now survive on the tourist trade.

The dying art of slate-splitting

The village of Beddgelert, set among the mountains of Snowdonia

Beddgelert ⑪

Gwynedd. 🏔 *500.* ℹ *High St, Porthmadog (01766 512981).*
🌐 *www.gwynedd.gov.uk*

BEDDGELERT enjoys a spectacular location among some of Snowdonia's most dramatic landscapes. The village sits on the confluence of the Glaslyn and Colwyn rivers at the approach to two mountain passes: the beautiful Nant Gwynant Pass, which leads to Snowdonia's highest reaches, and the Aberglaslyn Pass, a narrow wooded gorge which acts as a gateway to the sea.

Business was given a boost by Dafydd Pritchard, the landlord of the Royal Goat Hotel, who in the early 19th century adapted an old Welsh legend to associate it with Beddgelert. Llywelyn the Great *(see p422)* is said to have left his faithful hound Gelert to guard his infant son while he went hunting. He returned to find the cradle overturned and Gelert covered in blood. Thinking the dog had savaged his son, Llywellyn slaughtered Gelert, but then discovered the boy, unharmed, under the cradle. Nearby was the corpse of a wolf, which Gelert had killed to protect the child. To support the tale, Pritchard created **Gelert's Grave** (*bedd Gelert* in Welsh) by the River Glaslyn, a mound of stones a short walk south of the village.

ENVIRONS: There are many fine walks in the area: one leads south to the Aberglaslyn Pass and along a disused part of the Welsh Highland Railway. The **Sygun Copper Mine**, 1 mile (1.5 km) northeast of Beddgelert, offers self-guided tours of caverns recreating the life of Victorian miners.

🔨 Sygun Copper Mine
On A498. ☎ *01766 890595/510100.* ☐ *Mar–Nov: daily.* ● *24, 25 Dec.* 📷 ♿ *limited.* 🎧 *(audio/visual).*

Ffestiniog Railway

Engine plaque

THE FFESTINIOG narrow-gauge railway takes a scenic 14 mile (22 km) route from Porthmadog Harbour to the mountains and the slate town of Blaenau Ffestiniog *(see p437)*. Designed to carry slate from the quarries to the quay, the railway replaced a horse-drawn tramway constructed in 1836, operating on a 60 cm (2 ft) gauge. After closure in 1946, it was reconstructed by volunteers and re-opened in sections from 1955–82.

Steam traction *trains were first used on the Ffestiniog Railway in 1863. There are some diesel engines but most trains on the route are still steam-hauled.*

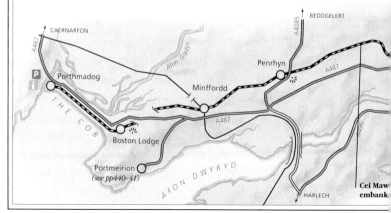

Llŷn Peninsula ⑫

Gwynedd. ✈ 🚉 Pwllheli.
⛴ Aberdaron to Bardsey Island.
ℹ Min-y-don, Station Sq, Pwllheli
(01758 613000).
Ⓦ www.nwt.co.uk

This 24 MILE (38 km) finger of land points southwest from Snowdonia into the Irish Sea. Although it has popular beaches, notably at Pwllheli, Criccieth, Abersoch and Nefyn, the coast's overriding feature is its untamed beauty. Views are at their most dramatic in the far west and along the mountain-backed northern shores.

The windy headland of **Braich-y-Pwll**, to the west of Aberdaron, looks out towards Bardsey Island, the "Isle of 20,000 Saints". This became a place of pilgrimage in the 6th century, when a monastery was founded here. Some of the saints are said to be buried in the churchyard of the ruined 13th-century **St Mary's Abbey**. Close by is **Porth Oer**, a small bay also known as "Whistling Sands" (the sand is meant to squeak, or whistle, underfoot).

East of Aberdaron is the 4 mile (6.5 km) bay of **Porth Neigwl**, known in English as Hell's Mouth, the scene of many shipwrecks due to the bay's treacherous currents. Hidden in sheltered grounds above Porth Neigwl bay, 1 mile (1.5 km) northeast of Aberdaron, is **Plas-yn-Rhiw**, a small, medieval manor house with Tudor and Georgian additions and lovely gardens.

The former quarrying village and "ghost town" of **Llithfaen**, tucked away below the sheer cliffs of the mountainous north coast, is now a centre for Welsh language studies.

🏠 **Plas-yn-Rhiw**
(NT) off B4413. 【 01758 780219.
🕐 Apr–mid-May: Thu–Mon; mid-May–Sep: Wed–Mon. 🚫 ♿ limited.

Llithfaen village, now a language centre, on the Llŷn Peninsula

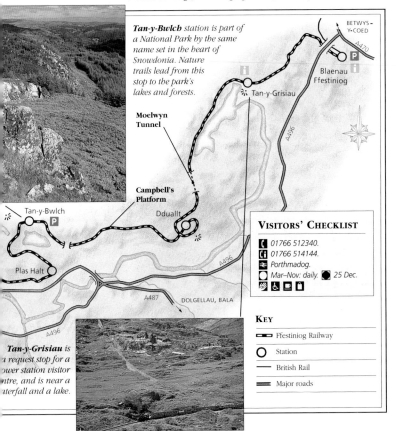

Tan-y-Bwlch station is part of a National Park by the same name set in the heart of Snowdonia. Nature trails lead from this stop to the park's lakes and forests.

Moelwyn Tunnel

Campbell's Platform

Tan-y-Bwlch

Plas Halt

Dduallt

Tan-y-Grisiau

Blaenau Ffestiniog

BETWYS-Y-COED

Tan-y-Grisiau is a request stop for a power station visitor centre, and is near a waterfall and a lake.

VISITORS' CHECKLIST

【 01766 512340.
🎫 01766 514144.
🚉 Porthmadog.
🕐 Mar–Nov: daily. ⬤ 25 Dec.
🚫 ♿ 🚻 🅿

KEY

▬▬ Ffestiniog Railway
⭕ Station
— British Rail
══ Major roads

Portmeirion ⑬

Gwynedd. 📞 01766 770000.
🚉 Minffordd. ⬜ daily. ⬛ 25 Dec.
🅿️ ♿ limited. 🔲 🏪 ✓

T HIS BIZARRE ITALIANATE village
on a private peninsula at
the top of Cardigan Bay was
created by Welsh architect Sir
Clough Williams-Ellis
(1883–1978). He fulfilled a
childhood dream by building
a village "to my own fancy on
my own chosen site". About
50 buildings surround a
central piazza, in styles
from Oriental to
Gothic. Visitors
can stay at the
luxurious hotel
or in one of the
charming village
cottages.
Portmeirion has
been an atmo-
spheric location
for many films
and television
programmes,
including the
popular 1960s
television series
The Prisoner.

**Sir Clough
Williams-Ellis at
Portmeirion**

Hercules *is a life-size 19th-
century copper statue near
the Town Hall, where a 17th-
century ceiling, rescued from
a demolished mansion,
depicts his legend.*

Fountain Cottage is
where Noel Coward
(1899–1973) wrote
Blithe Spirit.

The **Amis
Reunis** is a
stone replica
of a boat that
sank in the bay

Swimming
pool

*The Portmeirion Hotel
has many exotic interiors: the
furniture in the Jaipur Bar
comes from Rajasthan, India.*

Harlech ⑭

Gwynedd. 👥 1,300. 🚉 🛈 High St
(01766 780658). 🔄 Sun (summer).
🌐 www.gwynedd.gov.uk

T HIS SMALL TOWN with fine
beaches is dominated by
Harlech Castle, a medieval
fortress (see p424) built by
Edward I between 1283 and
1289. The castle sits on a precipitous crag, with superb
views of Tremadog Bay and

the Llŷn Peninsula to the west,
and Snowdonia to the north.
When the castle was built, the
sea reached a fortified stairway
cut into the cliff, so that supplies could arrive by ship, but
now the sea has receded. A
towering gatehouse protects
the inner ward, enclosed by
walls and four round towers.
   Despite its defences, Harlech
Castle fell to Owain Glyndŵr
(see p422) in 1404, and served
as his court until its recapture

four years later. The song Men
of Harlech is thought to have
been inspired by the castle's
heroic resistance during an
eight-year siege in the Wars
of the Roses (see p49).

♠ **Harlech Castle**
Castle Sq. 📞 01766 780552.
⬜ daily. ⬛ 24–26 Dec, 1 Jan. 🅿️ 🏪

Dolgellau ⑮

Gwynedd. 👥 2,650. 🛈 Eldon Sq
(01341 422888). 🔄 Fri (livestock).
🌐 www.gwynedd.gov.uk

T HE DARK LOCAL STONE gives
a stern, solid look to this
market town, where the Welsh
language and customs are still
very strong. It lies in the long
shadow of the 892 m (2,927 ft)
mountain of Cader Idris where,
according to legend, anyone
who spends a night on its
summit will awake a poet or a
a madman – or not at all.
   Dolgellau was gripped by
gold fever in the 19th century,
when high-quality gold was

Harlech Castle's strategic site overlooking mountains and sea

The Triumphal Arch is the main entrance to Portmeirion village.

Central Piazza

Lodge

Campanile

Royal Dolphin Cottage

Bristol Colonnade

Viewing platform

The Pantheon was built in 1958, but lack of funds meant that the dome was originally made from plywood instead of copper and painted green. The Pantheon's unusual façade is formed by the upper half of a music room fireplace by Norman Shaw (see p25).

***The Ship Shop** sells Portmeirion's famous flowered pottery.*

Dolgellau's grey-stone buildings, dwarfed by the mountain scenery

discovered in the Mawddach Valley nearby. The deposits were not large enough to sustain an intensive mining industry for long. Nevertheless, up until 1999, small amounts were mined and crafted locally into fine jewellery.

Dolgellau is a good centre for walking, whether you wish to take gentle strolls through beautiful leafy countryside or strenuous hikes across extreme terrain with dramatic mountain views. The lovely **Cregennen lakes** are set high in the hills above the thickly wooded **Mawddach Estuary** to the northwest; north are the harsh, bleak **Rhinog moors**, one of Wales's last true wildernesses.

Aberdyfi ⑯

Gwynedd. 900. Wharf Gardens (01654 767321). W
www.gwynedd.gov.uk

PERCHED ON THE MOUTH of the Dyfi Estuary, this little harbour resort and sailing centre makes the most of its splendid but rather confined location, its houses occupying every yard of a narrow strip of land between mountain and sea. In the 19th century, local slate was exported from here, and between the 1830s and the 1860s about 100 ships were built in the port. *The Bells of Aberdovey*, a song by Charles Dibdin for his opera *Liberty Hall* (1785), tells the legend of Cantref-y-Gwaelod, thought to have been located here, which was protected from the sea by dykes. One stormy night, the sluice gates were left open by Prince Seithenyn, when he was drunk, and the land was lost beneath the waves. The submerged church bells are said to peal under the water to this day.

Neat Georgian houses by the sea, Aberdyfi

SOUTH AND MID-WALES

....

CARDIFF, SWANSEA & ENVIRONS · CARDIGANSHIRE
CARMARTHENSHIRE · MONMOUTHSHIRE · POWYS · PEMBROKESHIRE

*S*OUTH AND MID-WALES *are less homogeneous regions than North Wales. Most of the population lives in the southeast corner. To the west is Pembrokeshire, the loveliest stretch of Welsh coastline. To the north the industrial valleys give way to the wide hills of the Brecon Beacons and the rural heartlands of central Wales.*

South Wales's coastal strip has been settled for many centuries. There are prehistoric sites in the Vale of Glamorgan and Pembrokeshire. The Romans established a major base at Caerleon, and the Normans built castles all the way from Chepstow to Pembroke. In the 18th and 19th centuries, coal mines and ironworks opened in the valleys of South Wales, attracting immigrants from all over Europe. Close communities developed here, focused on the coal trade, which turned Cardiff from a sleepy coastal town into the world's busiest coal-exporting port.

The declining coal industry has again changed the face of this area: slag heaps have become green hills, and the valley towns struggle to find alternative forms of employment. Coal mines such as Blaenafon's Big Pit are now tourist attractions; today, many of the tour guides taking visitors underground are ex-miners, who can offer a first-hand glimpse of the hard life found in mining communities before the pits closed.

The southern boundary of the Brecon Beacons National Park marks the beginning of rural Wales. With a population sparser than anywhere in England, this is an area of small country towns, hill-sheep farms, forestry plantations and spectacular man-made lakes.

The number of Welsh-speakers increases and the sense of Welsh culture becomes stronger as you travel further from the border with England, with the exception of an English enclave in south Pembrokeshire.

The changing face of the coal industry: former miners take visitors down the Big Pit in Blaenafon

◁ **Magnificent coastal scenery near St David's, Pembrokeshire**

Exploring South and Mid-Wales

MAGNIFICENT COASTAL SCENERY marks the Pembrokeshire Coast National Park and cliff-backed Gower Peninsula, while Cardigan Bay and Carmarthen Bay offer quieter beaches. Walkers can enjoy grassy uplands in the Brecon Beacons and gentler country in the leafy Wye Valley. Urban life is concentrated in the southeast of Wales, where old mining towns line the valleys north of Cardiff, the capital.

GETTING AROUND

The M4 motorway is the major route into Wales from the south of England, and there are good road links west of Swansea running to the coast. The A483 and A488 give access to mid-Wales from the Midlands. Frequent rail services connect London with Swansea, Cardiff and the ferry port of Fishguard.

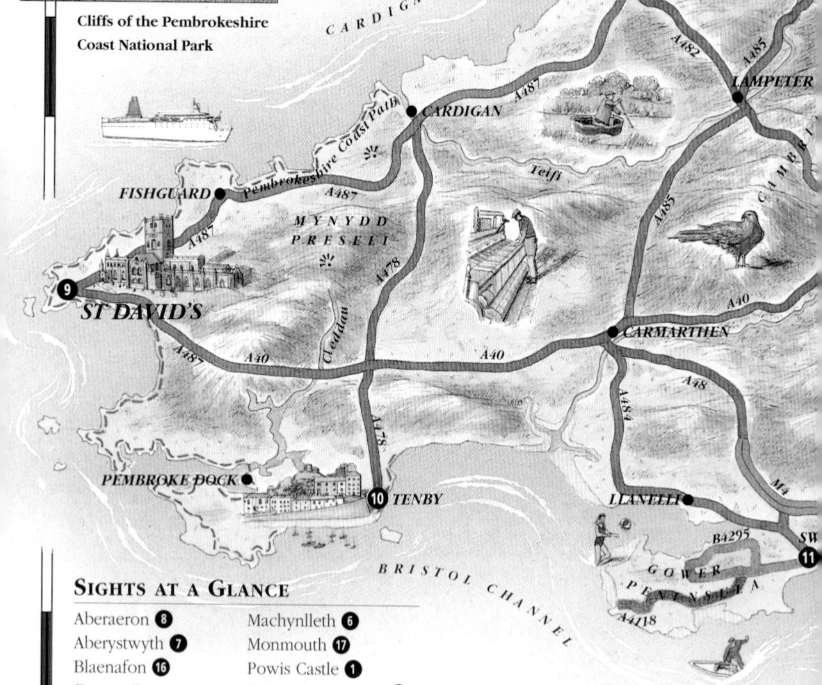

**Cliffs of the Pembrokeshire
Coast National Park**

SIGHTS AT A GLANCE

SEE ALSO

MACHYNLL

ABERYSTWYTH ⑦   Rheidol

⑧ ABERAERON

LAMPETER

CARDIGAN BAY

CARDIGAN

Teifi

FISHGUARD

MYNYDD
PRESELI

⑨
ST DAVID'S

CARMARTHEN

A40

A48

PEMBROKE DOCK

⑩ TENBY   LLANELLI

⑪

BRISTOL CHANNEL   GOWER
PENINSULA

SW

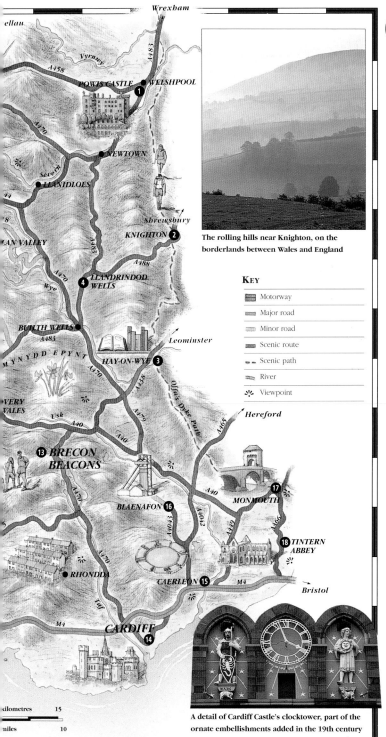

ellau

Vyrnwy

A458

A483

POWIS CASTLE • WELSHPOOL
1

A470

• NEWTOWN

Severn

• LLANIDLOES

A44

A8

Shrewsbury

KNIGHTON 2

LAN VALLEY

A488

A470 A483

Wye

4 LLANDRINDOD WELLS

BUILTH WELLS •

A483

Leominster

MYNYDD EPYNT

HAY-ON-WYE 3

A470 A458 Offa's Dyke Path

VERY VALES

Usk A40 A479 A465

Hereford

13 BRECON BEACONS

A470

A40

A40

BLAENAFON 16

A4042

A40 A449

17 MONMOUTH

A4043

A466

RHONDDA •

CAERLEON 15

18 TINTERN ABBEY

A4061

M4

Bristol

M4

CARDIFF

14

The rolling hills near Knighton, on the
borderlands between Wales and England

KEY

▨	Motorway
▨	Major road
▨	Minor road
▨	Scenic route
▫▫	Scenic path
▨	River
☀	Viewpoint

kilometres 15

miles 10

A detail of Cardiff Castle's clocktower, part of the
ornate embellishments added in the 19th century

Italianate terraces and formal gardens at Powis Castle, adding a Mediterranean air to the Welsh borderlands

Powis Castle ❶

(NT) Welshpool, Powys. *01938 557018.* ⚡ *Welshpool then bus.* ⬛ *Apr–Jun & Sep–Oct: Wed–Sun; Jul–Aug: Tue–Sun & public hols.* 🎟 ⬛ *limited.* 📷 📖

POWIS CASTLE – the spelling is an archaic version of "Powys" – has outgrown its military roots. Despite its sham battlements and dominant site, 1 mile (1.6 km) to the southwest of the town of Welshpool, this red-stone building has served as a country mansion for centuries. It began life in the 13th century as a fortress, built by the princes of Powys to control the border with England.

The castle is entered through one of few surviving medieval features: a gateway, built in 1283 by Owain de la Pole. The gate is flanked by two round towers with arrow slits and portcullis slots.

The castle's lavish interiors soon banish all thoughts of war. A **Dining Room**, decorated with fine 17th-century panelling and family portraits, was originally designed as the castle's Great

Hall. The **Great Staircase**, added in the late 17th century and elaborately decorated with carved fruit and flowers, leads to the main apartments: an early 19th-century library, the panelled **Oak Drawing Room** and the Elizabethan **Long Gallery**, where ornate plasterwork on the fireplace and ceiling date from the 1590s. In the **Blue Drawing Room** there are three 18th-century Brussels tapestries.

The Herbert family bought the property in 1587 and were proud of their Royalist connections; the panelling in

The richly carved 17th-century Great Staircase

the **State Bedroom** bears the royal monogram. Powis Castle was defended for Charles I in the Civil War *(see pp52–3),* but fell to Parliament in 1644. The 3rd Baron Powis, a supporter of James II, had to flee the country when William and Mary took the throne in 1688 *(see pp52–3).*

The castle's **Clive Museum** has an exhibition concerning "Clive of India" (1725–74), the general and statesman who helped strengthen British control in India in the mid-18th century. The family's link with Powis Castle was established by the 2nd Lord Clive, who married into the Herbert family and became the Earl of Powis in 1804.

The gardens at Powis are among the best-known in Britain, with their series of elegant Italianate terraces, adorned with statues, niches, balustrades and hanging gardens, all stepped into the steep hillside beneath the castle walls. Created between 1688 and 1722, these are the only formal gardens of this period in Britain that are still kept in their original form *(see pp22–3).*

Knighton ❷

Powys. 🏠 *2,800.* 🚉 **ⓘ** *West St (01547 528753).* 🛒 *Thu.*
Ⓦ *www.offasdyke.demon.co.uk*

Knighton's Welsh name, Tref y Clawdd ("The Town on the Dyke"), reflects its status as the only original settlement on **Offa's Dyke**. In the 8th century, King Offa of Mercia (central and southern England) constructed a ditch and bank to mark out his territory, and to enable the enforcement of a Saxon law: "Neither shall a Welshman cross into English land without the appointed man from the other side, who should meet him at the bank and bring him back again without any offence being committed." Some of the best-preserved sections of the 6 m (20 ft) high earthwork lie in the hills around Knighton. The Offa's Dyke Footpath runs for 177 miles (285 km) along the border between England and Wales.

Knighton is set on a steep hill, sloping upwards from **St Edward's Church** (1877) with its medieval tower, to the summit, where a castle once stood. The main street leads via the market square, marked by a 19th-century clock tower, along **The Narrows**, a Tudor street with little shops. **The Old House** on Broad Street is a medieval "cruck" house (curved timbers form a frame to support the roof), with a hole in the ceiling instead of a chimney.

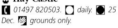
Knighton's clock

Hay-on-Wye ❸

Powys. 🏠 *1,300.* **ⓘ** *Oxford Rd (01497 820144).* 🛒 *Thu.*
Ⓦ *www.hay-on-wye.co.uk*

Book-lovers from all over the world come to this quiet border town in the Black Mountains. Hay-on-Wye has over 25 second-hand book-shops stocking millions of titles, and in early summer hosts a prestigious Festival of Literature. The town's love affair with books began when a bookshop was opened in the 1960s by Richard Booth, who claims the (fictitious) title of King of Independent Hay and lives in **Hay Castle**, a 17th-century mansion in the grounds of the original 13th-century castle. Hay's oldest inn, the 16th-century **Three Tuns** on Bridge Street, is still functioning and has an attractive half-timbered façade.

Environs: Hay sits on the approach to the Black Mountains and is surrounded by rolling hills. To the south are the heights of Hay Bluff and the Vale of Ewyas, where the 12th-century ruins of **Llanthony Priory** *(see p455)* retain fine pointed arches.

⛪ **Hay Castle**
☎ *01497 820503.* ⬜ *daily.* ⬤ *25 Dec.* 📷 *grounds only.*

Llandrindod Wells ❹

Powys. 🏠 *5,000.* 🚉 **ⓘ** *Memorial Gardens (01597 822600).* 🛒 *Fri.*
Ⓦ *www.visitllandrindod.co.uk*

Llandrindod is a perfect example of a Victorian town, with canopied streets, delicate wrought ironwork, gabled villas and ornamental parklands. This purpose-built spa town became Wales's

One of Hay-on-Wye's bookshops

premier inland resort of the 19th century. Its sulphur and magnesium spring waters were taken to treat skin complaints and a range of other ailments.

The town now makes every effort to preserve its Victorian character, with a boating lake and the well-tended **Rock Park Gardens**. The **Heritage Centre** houses a heritage exhibition and a restored 19th-century **Pump Room** is now a restaurant and is the focus of the summer Victorian Festival, when residents don period costume and cars are banned from the town centre.

The **Radnorshire Museum** traces the town's past as one of a string of 19th-century Welsh spas which included Builth, Llangammarch and **Llanwrtyd** (now a pony trekking centre).

🏛 **Heritage Centre**
Rock Park. ☎ *01597 829267.* ⬜ *Mon–Fri.* ⬤ *Christmas week.* ♿ **ⓘ**

🏛 **Radnorshire Museum**
Memorial Gardens. ☎ *01597 824513.* ⬜ *Tue–Sat & public hols.* ⬤ *Christmas week.* 📷 ♿ *limited.*

Victorian architecture on Spa Road, Llandrindod Wells

Craig Goch, one of the original chain of Elan Valley reservoirs

Elan Valley ❺

Powys. 🚆 *Llandrindod.*
ℹ *Rhayader (01597 810898).*
🌐 www.elanvalley.org.uk

A STRING OF SPECTACULAR reservoirs, the first of the country's man-made lakes, has made this one of Wales's most famous valleys. **Caban Coch**, **Garreg Ddu**, **Pen-y-Garreg** and **Craig Goch**, were created between 1892 and 1903 to supply water to Birmingham, 73 miles (117 km) away. They form a chain of lakes about 9 miles (14 km) long, holding 50 billion litres (13 billion gallons) of water. Victorian engineers selected these high moorlands on the Cambrian Mountains, for their high annual rainfall of 1,780 mm (70 inches). The choice created bitter controversy and resentment: more than 100 people had to move from the valley that was flooded in order to create Caban Coch.

Unlike their more utilitarian modern counterparts, these dams were built during an era when decoration was seen as an integral part of any design. Finished in dressed stone, they have an air of grandeur which is lacking in the huge **Claerwen** reservoir, a stark addition built during the early 1950s to double the lakes' capacity. Contained by a 355 m (1,165 ft) dam, it lies 4 miles (6 km) along the B4518 that runs through Elan Valley and offers magnificent views.

The remote moorlands and woodlands surrounding the lakes are an important habitat

for wildlife; the red kite can often be seen here. The **Elan Valley Visitors' Centre**, beside the Caban Coch dam, describes the construction of the lakes, as well as the valley's own natural history. **Elan Village**, set beside the centre, is an unusual example of a model workers' village, built during the 1900s to house the waterworks staff. Outside the centre is a statue of the poet Percy Bysshe Shelley *(see p208)*, who stayed in the valley at the mansion of Nantgwyllt in 1810 with his wife, Harriet. The house now lies underneath the waters of Caban Coch, along with the rest of the old village. Among the buildings submerged were the village school and a church.

The trail from Machynlleth to Devil's Bridge, near Aberystwyth

Machynlleth ❻

Powys. 👥 *2,200.* 🚆 ℹ *Canolfan Owain Glyndŵr (01654 702401).* 🅰 *Wed.*

HALF-TIMBERED BUILDINGS and Georgian façades appear among the grey-stone houses in Machynlleth. It was here that Owain Glyndŵr, Wales's last native leader *(see p422)*, held a parliament in 1404. The restored **Parliament House** has displays on his life and a brass-rubbing centre.

The ornate **Clock Tower**, in the middle of Maengwyn Street, was erected in 1874 by the Marquess of Londonderry to mark the coming of age of his heir, Lord Castlereagh. The Marquess lived in **Plas Machynlleth**, a 17th-century house in parkland off the main street, which is now a centre of Celtic heritage and culture.

ENVIRONS: In an old slate quarry 2.5 miles (4 km) to the north, a "village of the future" is run by the **Centre for Alternative Technology**. A water-balanced cliff railway takes summer visitors to view low-energy houses and organic gardens, to see how to make the best of Earth's resources.

Parliament House sign, Machynlleth

🏛 **Parliament House**
Maengwyn St. 📞 *01654 702827.*
🕐 *Easter–Sep: Mon–Sat.* ♿ ℹ
🏛 **Centre for Alternative Technology** On A487. 📞 *01654 702400.* 🕐 *daily.* ● *24–26 Dec, first 2 weeks Jan.* 🎫 🚻 ♿

Aberystwyth ❼

Ceredigion. 👥 *11,000.* 🚆 🚌 ℹ *Terrace Rd (01970 612125).* 🌐 www.ceredigion.gov.uk

THIS SEASIDE AND UNIVERSITY town claims to be the cultural capital of mid-Wales. By the standards of this rural area, "Aber" is a big place, its population increased for much of the year by students.

To Victorian travellers, Aberystwyth was the "Biarritz

of Wales". There have been no great changes along the promenade, with its gabled hotels, since the 19th century. **Constitution Hill**, a steep outcrop at the northern end, can be scaled in summer on the electric **Cliff Railway**, built in 1896. At the top, in a *camera obscura*, a lens

Buskers on Aberystwyth's seafront

projects views of the town. The ruined **Aberystwyth Castle** (1277) is located south of the promenade. In the town centre, the **Ceredigion Museum**, set in a former music hall, traces the history of the town.

To the northeast of the town centre, **The National Library of Wales**, next to Aberystwyth University, has a valuable collection of ancient Welsh manuscripts.

SAVIN'S HOTEL

When the Cambrian Railway opened in 1864, businessman Thomas Savin put £80,000 into building a new hotel in Aberystwyth for package tourists. The scheme made him bankrupt, but the seafront building, complete with mock-Gothic tower, was bought by campaigners attempting to establish a Welsh university. The "college by the sea" opened in 1872, and is now the Theological College.

Mosaics on the college tower

ENVIRONS: During the summer the narrow-gauge Vale of Rheidol Railway runs 12 miles (19 km) to **Devil's Bridge**, where a dramatic series of waterfalls plunges through a wooded ravine and a steep trail leads to the valley floor.

🏛 **Ceredigion Museum**
Terrace Rd. 📞 01970 633088.
⬜ Mon–Sat. ⬤ 25 Dec–2 Jan,
Good Fri. 🚻

Aberaeron ❽

Ceredigion. 👥 1,500.
🚉 Aberystwyth, then bus. 🅸 The
Quay (01545 570602).
🆆 www.ceredigion.gov.uk

ABERAERON'S HARBOUR, lined with Georgian houses, became a trading port and shipbuilding centre in the early 19th century. Its orderly streets were laid out in pre-railway days, when the ports along Cardigan Bay enjoyed considerable wealth. The last boat was built here in 1994 and its harbour is now full of holiday sailors. The harbour can be crossed via a wooden footbridge.

On the quayside, the popular Honey Bee Ice Cream Parlour serves world-renowned ice creams to a loyal clientele. There is also a centre of local crafts in the town, Clos Pengarreg.

Rows of brightly painted Georgian houses lining the purpose-built harbour at Aberaeron

St Davids ❾

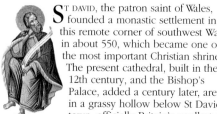

ST DAVID, the patron saint of Wales, founded a monastic settlement in this remote corner of southwest Wales in about 550, which became one of the most important Christian shrines. The present cathedral, built in the 12th century, and the Bishop's Palace, added a century later, are set in a grassy hollow below St Davids town, officially Britain's smallest city. The date of St David's death, 1 March, is commemorated throughout Wales.

Icon of Elijah, south transept

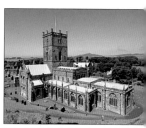

St David's Cathedral, the largest in Wales

The Private Chapel was a late 14th-century addition, built, like the rest of the palace, over a series of vaults.

★ Great Hall
The open arcade and decorated parapet were added by Bishop Gower (1328–47) to unify different sections of the palace.

Entrance

BISHOP'S PALACE
The bishop's residence, built between 1280–1350 and now in ruins, had lavish private apartments.

Palace latrines

Typical medieval window

Rose window

The Bishop's Hall, smaller than the Great Hall, may have been reserved for private use.

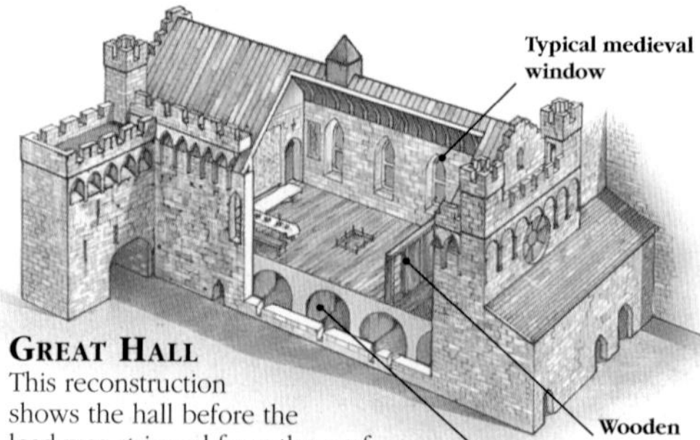

GREAT HALL
This reconstruction shows the hall before the lead was stripped from the roof. Bishop Barlow, St David's first Protestant bishop (1536–48), is thought to have been responsible for the lead's removal.

Wooden screen

Vault

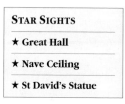

STAR SIGHTS

★ **Great Hall**

★ **Nave Ceiling**

★ **St David's Statue**

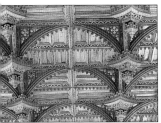

★ **Nave Ceiling**
The roof of the nave is lowered and hidden by an early 16th-century oak ceiling. A beautiful 14th-century rood screen divides the nave from the choir.

VISITORS' CHECKLIST

Cathedral Close, St Davids. 📞 01437 720202. 🚉 Haverfordwest then bus. 🕐 9am–6pm daily (Sat, Sun: pm). ✝ 7:30am, 8am, 6pm, Mon–Sat; 8am, 9:30am, 11:15am, 6pm Sun. 🚻 📷

Stained Glass Window
In the nave's west end, eight panels, produced in the 1950s, radiate from a central window showing the dove of peace.

CATHEDRAL
St David was one of the founders of the 6th-century monastic movement, so this was an important site of pilgrimage. Three visits here equalled one to Jerusalem.

St Mary's College Chapel

Bishop Vaughan's Chapel has a fine fan-vaulted early Tudor roof.

Entrance

Tower Lantern Ceiling
The medieval roof was decorated with episcopal insignia when restored in the 1870s by Sir George Gilbert Scott.

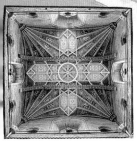

Sixteenth-Century Choir Stalls
The royal coat of arms on one of the carved choir stalls shows that the sovereign is a member of St David's Chapter. There are some interesting misericords (see p327) in these stalls.

★ **St David's Statue**
A statue of the saint is placed near the shrine. Thought to symbolize the Holy Spirit, a dove is said to have landed on David's shoulder as he spoke to a gathering of bishops.

Tenby ⑩

Pembrokeshire (Dyfed). 🚶 5,000.
🚌 🅿 🚲 🛈 *The Croft (01834 842402).*

TENBY HAS SUCCESSFULLY trodden the fine line between over-commercialization and popularity, refusing to submit its historic character to the garish excesses of some seaside towns. Georgian houses overlook its handsome harbour, which is backed by a well-preserved medieval clifftop town of narrow streets and passages. The old town was defended by a headland fortress, now ruined, flanked by two wide beaches and a ring of 13th-century walls. These survive to their full height in places, along with a fortified gateway, the **Five Arches**.

The three-storeyed **Tudor Merchant's House** is a 15th-century relic of Tenby's highly prosperous seafaring days, with original fireplaces and chimneys. There are regular boat trips from the harbour to **Caldey Island**, 3 miles (5 km) offshore, home of a perfume-making monastic community.

🏛 **Tudor Merchant's House**
(NT) Quay Hill. 📞 01834 842279.
◯ Apr–Sep: Thu–Tue; Oct: Thu, Fri, Sun–Tue (Sun: pm). ● Nov–Mar.
🅿 for pre-booked parties.

A partly medieval restaurant next to the Tudor Merchant's House

Swansea and the Gower Peninsula ⑪

Swansea. 🚶 250,000. 🚌 🅿 🚲
🛈 Plymouth St (01792 468321). ⊖
Mon–Sat. 🆆 www.want2getaway.net

SWANSEA, WALES'S SECOND CITY, is set along a wide, curving bay. The city centre was rebuilt after heavy bombing in World War II but, despite the modern buildings, a traditional Welsh atmosphere prevails. This is particularly noticeable in the excellent food market, full of Welsh delicacies such as laverbread *(see p36)* and locally caught cockles.

The award-winning **Maritime Quarter** redevelopment has transformed the old docklands. In an old warehouse on the waterfront, the **Maritime and Industrial Museum** has displays on the city's copper and tin-plate industries, and on the first passenger-carrying railway in the world, the horse-drawn Mumbles Railway, opened in 1807.

Swansea's most celebrated son, the poet Dylan Thomas

A statue of copper magnate John Henry Vivian (1779–1855) overlooks the marina. The Vivians, a leading Swansea family, founded the **Glynn Vivian Art Gallery**, which has exquisite Swansea pottery and porcelain. Archaeology and Welsh history feature at the **Swansea Museum**, the oldest museum in Wales.

The poet Dylan Thomas (1914–53), whose statue overlooks the Maritime Quarter, spent his childhood in the city's suburbs. **Cwmdonkin Park** was the scene of an early poem, *The Hunchback in the Park*, and its water garden has a memorial stone quoting from his *Fern Hill*.

Swansea's austere **Guildhall** (1934) has a surprisingly rich interior. The huge panels, by Sir Frank Brangwyn (1867–1956), on the theme of the British Empire, were originally

Picturesque fishermen's cottages at the Mumbles seaside resort

painted for the House of Lords.

Swansea Bay leads to the **Mumbles**, a popular watersports centre at the gateway to the 18 mile long (29 km) Gower Peninsula, which in 1956 was the first part of Britain to be declared an Area of Outstanding Natural Beauty. A string of sheltered, south-facing bays leads to Oxwich and Port-Eynon beaches.

Rhossili's enormous beach leads to north Gower and a coastline of low-lying burrows, salt marshlands and cockle beds. The peninsula is littered with ancient sites such as **Parc Le Breose**, a prehistoric burial chamber.

Near Camarthen is the **National Botanic Garden of Wales**, with formal gardens centred on The Great Glasshouse which contains a Mediterranean ecosystem.

🏛 **Maritime and Industrial Museum**
Museum Sq. 📞 01792 650351.
◯ Tue–Sun & public hols. ● 25, 26 Dec, 1 Jan. ♿ 🅿 🛈

🏛 **Glynn Vivian Art Gallery**
Alexandra Rd. 📞 01792 655006.
◯ Tue–Sun & public hols. ● 23–26 Dec, 1 Jan. ♿ limited. 🛈 🅿 by arrangement.

🏛 **Swansea Museum**
Victoria Rd. 📞 01792 653763.
◯ Tue–Sun & public hols. ● 25, 26 Dec, 1 Jan. ♿ limited. 🛈

🏛 **Guildhall**
St Helen's Rd. 📞 01792 636000. ◯ Mon–Fri. ● public hols. ♿

🌸 **National Botanic Garden of Wales**
Middleton Hall, Llanarthne.
📞 01558 668768. ◯ daily.
♿ 🛈 🍴 ✏ 🅿 🛈

Wild Wales Tour ⑫

THIS TOUR WEAVES ACROSS the Cambrian Mountains' windswept moors, green hills and high, deserted plateaux. New roads have been laid to the massive Llyn Brianne Reservoir, north of Llandovery, and the old drover's road across to Tregaron has a tarmac surface. But the area is still essentially a "wild Wales" of hidden hamlets, isolated farmsteads, brooding highlands and traditional, quiet market towns.

Llanidloes ⑥
The town was a centre of religious and social unrest in the 17th and 18th centuries (*see p423*). There is a rare example of a free-standing Tudor market hall. The medieval church was restored in the late 19th century.

B4518   A470

Devil's Bridge ④
This is a popular, romantic beauty spot with waterfalls, rocks, wooded glades and an ancient stone bridge – built by the Devil, according to legend.

ABERYSTWYTH

Llangurig   B4518

A44

Elan Valley ⑤
This is an area of lakes and important wildlife habitats (*see p448*).

Strata Florida ③
This famous ruined abbey was an important political, religious and educational centre during the Middle Ages.

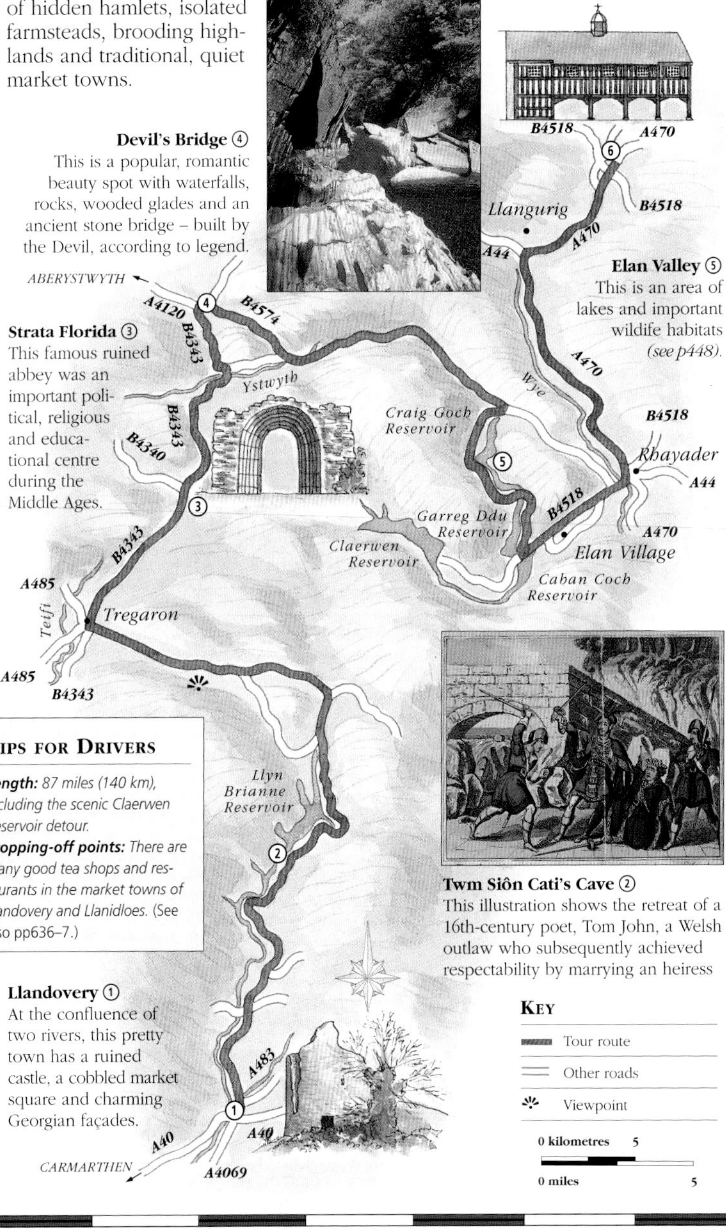

Ystwyth

Craig Goch Reservoir

Wye

B4518

Rhayader   A44

Garreg Ddu Reservoir

Claerwen Reservoir

B4518

A470
Elan Village

Caban Coch Reservoir

A485

Teifi

Tregaron

A485

B4343

TIPS FOR DRIVERS

Length: 87 miles (140 km), including the scenic Claerwen Reservoir detour.
Stopping-off points: There are many good tea shops and restaurants in the market towns of Llandovery and Llanidloes. (See also pp636–7.)

Llyn Brianne Reservoir

Twm Siôn Cati's Cave ②
This illustration shows the retreat of a 16th-century poet, Tom John, a Welsh outlaw who subsequently achieved respectability by marrying an heiress

Llandovery ①
At the confluence of two rivers, this pretty town has a ruined castle, a cobbled market square and charming Georgian façades.

CARMARTHEN

A40   A40

A483

A4069

KEY

▬▬▬	Tour route
═══	Other roads
☀	Viewpoint

0 kilometres   5

0 miles   5

Brecon Beacons ⓭

Trekking in the Beacons

T HE BRECON BEACONS National Park covers 519 sq miles (1,345 sq km) from the Wales–England border almost all the way to Swansea. There are four mountain ranges within the park: the Black Mountain (to the west), Fforest Fawr, the Brecon Beacons and the Black Mountains (to the east). Much of the area consists of high, open country with smooth, grassy slopes on a bedrock of red sandstone. The park's southern rim has limestone crags, wooded gorges, waterfalls and caves. Visitors can enjoy many outdoor pursuits, from fishing in the numerous reservoirs to pony trekking, caving and walking.

Llyn y Fan Fach
This remote, myth-laden glacial lake is a 4 mile (6.5 km) walk from Llanddeusant.

The Black Mountain, a largely unex-plored wilderness of knife-edged ridges and high, empty moorland, fills the western corner of the National Park.

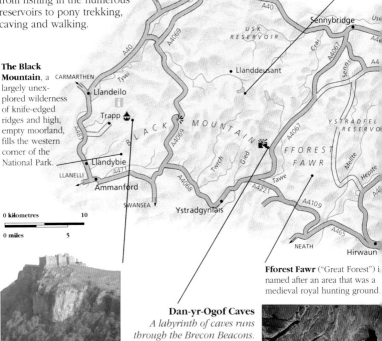

0 kilometres   10

0 miles   5

Carreg Cennen Castle
Spectacularly sited, the ruined medieval fortress of Carreg Cennen (see p424) stands on a sheer limestone cliff near the village of Trapp.

Fforest Fawr ("Great Forest") i named after an area that was a medieval royal hunting ground.

Dan-yr-Ogof Caves
A labyrinth of caves runs through the Brecon Beacons. Guided tours of two large caves are offered here.

KEY

▬▬	A road
▭▭	B road
═══	Minor road
– –	Footpath
☀	Viewpoint

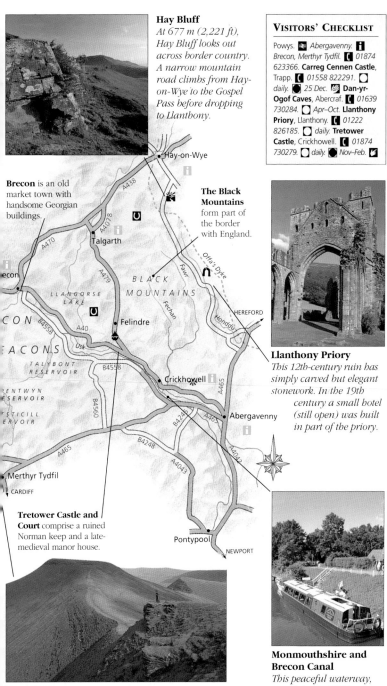

Hay Bluff
*At 677 m (2,221 ft),
Hay Bluff looks out
across border country.
A narrow mountain
road climbs from Hay-
on-Wye to the Gospel
Pass before dropping
to Llanthony.*

VISITORS' CHECKLIST

Powys. ✈ *Abergavenny.* 🚌
Brecon, Merthyr Tydfil. **ℹ** *01874
623366.* **Carreg Cennen Castle,**
Trapp. **ℹ** *01558 822291.* ◯
daily. ● *25 Dec.* ♨ **Dan-yr-
Ogof Caves,** Abercraf. **ℹ** *01639
730284.* ◯ *Apr–Oct.* **Llanthony
Priory,** Llanthony. **ℹ** *01222
826185.* ◯ *daily.* **Tretower
Castle,** Crickhowell. **ℹ** *01874
730279.* ◯ *daily.* ● *Nov–Feb.* ✍

Brecon is an old
market town with
handsome Georgian
buildings.

**The Black
Mountains**
form part of
the border
with England.

Llanthony Priory
*This 12th-century ruin has
simply carved but elegant
stonework. In the 19th
century a small hotel
(still open) was built
in part of the priory.*

**Tretower Castle and
Court** comprise a ruined
Norman keep and a late-
medieval manor house.

**Monmouthshire and
Brecon Canal**
*This peaceful waterway,
completed in 1812, was
once used to transport raw
materials between Brecon
and Newport. It is now
popular with leisure boats.*

Pen y Fan
*At 886 m (2,907 ft), Pen y Fan is the highest point in
South Wales. Its distinctive, flat-topped summit, once
a Bronze Age burial ground (see p42), can be reached
by footpaths from Storey Arms on the A470.*

Cardiff ⓮

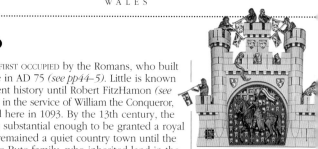

CARDIFF WAS FIRST OCCUPIED by the Romans, who built
a fort here in AD 75 *(see pp44–5)*. Little is known
of its subsequent history until Robert FitzHamon *(see
p458)*, a knight in the service of William the Conqueror,
was given land here in 1093. By the 13th century, the
settlement was substantial enough to be granted a royal
charter, but it remained a quiet country town until the
1830s when the Bute family, who inherited land in the
area, began to develop it as a port. By 1913 this was
the world's busiest coal-exporting port, profiting from
rail links with the South Wales mines. Its wealth paid
for grandiose architecture, while the docklands became
a raucous boom-town. Cardiff was confirmed as the
first Welsh capital in 1955, by which time demand for
coal was falling and the docks were in decline. The city
is now dedicated to commerce and administration, and
is being transformed by urban renewal programmes.

**Fireplace detail in the Banqueting
Hall, Cardiff Castle *(see pp458–9)***

**City Hall's dome, adorned with a
dragon, the emblem of Wales**

Exploring Cardiff
Cardiff is a city with two focal
points. The centre, laid out
with Victorian and Edwardian
streets and gardens, is the first
of these. There is a Neo-Gothic
castle and Neo-Classical civic
buildings, as well as indoor
shopping malls and a 19th-
century **covered market**.
Canopied arcades, lined with
shops, lead off the main
streets, the oldest being the
Royal Arcade of 1856. The
Millennium Stadium (on
the site of Cardiff Arms Park,
the first home of Welsh
rugby) opened in 1999 with
the Rugby World Cup, and is
open for tours every day.
To the south of the centre,
the docklands are now being
transformed into the second
focal point by the creation of
a marina and waterfront. A
new Cardiff is taking shape,
especially around the Inner
Harbour area. The **Pier Head
Building**, constructed on

Cardiff Bay in 1896 for the
Cardiff Railway Company, is a
reminder of the city's heyday.
Its intricate decoration and
terracotta detail was partly
influenced by the red Mogul
buildings of India. Another
attraction in the area is
National Techniquest, a
hands-on science museum.
The wooden **Norwegian
Church** on Waterfront Park
was first erected in 1868 for
Norwegian sailors bringing
wooden props for use in the
coal pits of the South Wales
valleys. Once surrounded by
warehouses, it was taken
apart and rebuilt during the
dockland development. The
Cardiff Bay Visitor Centre,

near the Pier Head Building,
has displays on the various
building projects that are
uniting the civic centre with
the maritime district.

♦ Cardiff Castle
See pp458–9.

▦ City Hall and Civic Centre
Cathays Park. **[** 029-2087 1102.
○ *Mon–Fri.* **●** *public hols.* **&**
Cardiff's civic centre of Neo-
Classical buildings in white
Portland stone is set among
parks and avenues around
Alexandra Gardens. The City
Hall (1905), one of its first
buildings, is dominated by its
60 m (200 ft) dome and clock
tower. Members of the public
can visit the first-floor Marble
Hall, which is furnished with
Siena marble columns and
statues of Welsh heroes,
among them St David, Wales's
patron saint *(see pp450–51)*.
The Crown Building, at the
northern end of the complex,

The Pier Head Building overlooking the redeveloped area of Cardiff Bay

now houses the Welsh Office, which is responsible for all Welsh government affairs.

🏛 National Museum of Wales

Cathays Park. 📞 029-2039 7951. ⏰ Tue–Sun & public hols. ⬤ 24, 25 Dec. ♿🅿️📷📹 by arrangement.

Opened in 1927, the museum occupies an impressive civic building with a colonnaded portico, guarded by a statue of David Lloyd George *(see p423)*. Displays include a magnificent collection of Impressionist art by Renoir, Monet and Van Gogh, donated after World War II by two local sisters Gwendoline and Margaret Davies.

🏛 Crafts in the Bay

52 Bute St. 📞 029-2048 4611. ⏰ daily. ⬤ 25, 26 Dec, 1 Jan. ♿🅿️

An extensive new crafts centre, organized by the Makers' Guild in Wales, opened here in March 1996.

The building now houses a wide variety of craft displays and demonstrations, including textile weaving and ceramic making.

As well as the permanent displays, there are frequently changing exhibitions on crafts-related themes. Visitors are free to browse around the centre or take part in any of the workshops which are regularly set up by the guild.

Statue of Welsh politician David Lloyd George

ENVIRONS: Established during the 1940s at St Fagans, on the western edge of the city, the open-air **Museum of Welsh Life** was one of the first of its kind. Buildings from all over Wales, including workers' terraced cottages, farmhouses, a tollhouse, a row of shops, a chapel and an old schoolhouse have been carefully reconstructed within the 40 ha (100 acre) parklands, along with a recreated Celtic village. There is also a Tudor mansion

which can be visited, boasting its own beautiful gardens in the grounds.

Llandaff Cathedral lies in a deep, grassy hollow beside the River Taf at Llandaff – a pretty "village suburb" which is 2 miles (3 km) northwest of the city centre. The cathedral was first a medieval building, occupying the site of a 6th-century monastic community.

Restored after suffering severe bomb damage during World War II, it was eventually reopened in 1957 with the addition of Sir Jacob Epstein's huge, stark statue, *Christus*, which is mounted on a concrete arch.

🏛 Museum of Welsh Life

St Fagans. 📞 029-2057 3500. ⏰ daily. ⬤ 24, 25 Dec. ♿🅿️🍴

CARDIFF TOWN CENTRE

Cardiff Castle pp458–9 ③
City Hall & Civic Centre ②
Covered market ⑤
Crafts in the Bay ⑥
Millennium Stadium ④
National Museum of Wales ①
Crafts in the Bay ⑤
National Techniquest ⑦
Norwegian Church ⑨
Pier Head Building ⑧

0 metres   500
0 yards   500

KEY

🚌 Coach station
🚈 Railway station
🅿️ Parking
ℹ Tourist information
✝ Church

Cardiff Castle

CARDIFF CASTLE BEGAN LIFE as a Roman fort, whose remains are separated from later work by a band of red stone. A keep was built within the Roman ruins in the 12th century. Over the following 700 years, the castle passed to several powerful families and eventually to John Stuart, the Earl of Bute, in 1766. His great-grandson, the 3rd Marquess of Bute, employed the "eccentric genius", architect William Burges, who created an ornate mansion between 1867 and 1881, rich in medieval images and romantic detail.

Arab Room
The gilded ceiling, with Islamic marble and lapis lazuli decorations, was produced by Arab craftsmen in 1881.

Herbert Tower

Animal Wall
A lion and other creatures guard the wall to the south of the castle. They were added between 1885 and 1930.

★ **Summer Smoking Room**
This was part of a complete bachelor suite in the Clock Tower, that also included a Winter Smoking Room.

Clock Tower

Main entrance to apartments

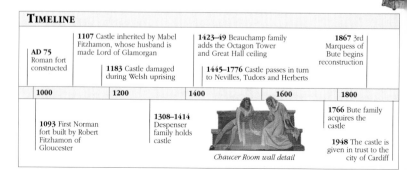

TIMELINE

AD 75 Roman fort constructed	**1107** Castle inherited by Mabel Fitzhamon, whose husband is made Lord of Glamorgan	**1423–49** Beauchamp family adds the Octagon Tower and Great Hall ceiling		**1867** 3rd Marquess of Bute begins reconstruction
	1183 Castle damaged during Welsh uprising	**1445–1776** Castle passes in turn to Nevilles, Tudors and Herberts		
1000	**1200**	**1400**	**1600**	**1800**
1093 First Norman fort built by Robert Fitzhamon of Gloucester	**1308–1414** Despenser family holds castle		*Chaucer Room wall detail*	**1766** Bute family acquires the castle **1948** The castle is given in trust to the city of Cardiff

VISITORS' CHECKLIST

Castle St, Cardiff. 029-2087
8100. Mar–Oct: 9:30am–
6pm daily; Nov–Feb: 9:30am–
4:30pm daily. 24–26 Dec, 1
Jan. grounds only.

★ **Banqueting Hall**
The design and decoration of
this room depicts the castle's
history, making impressively
ingenious use of the murals
and castellated fireplace.

The Octagon Tower, also
called the Beauchamp
Tower, is the setting for
Burges's Chaucer Room,
decorated with themes
from the *Canterbury
Tales (see p172).*

★ **Roof Garden**
Using tiles, shrubs and
a central fountain,
Burges aimed to create
a Mediterranean feel
in this indoor garden,
turning it into the
crowning glory of the
castle's apartments.

**The Bute
Tower** had
a suite of
private rooms
added in 1873,
including a
dining room,
bedroom and
sitting room.

★ **Library**
Carved figures representing ancient characters
of Greek, Assyrian, Hebrew and Egyptian
alphabets decorate the library's chimneypiece.

STAR SIGHTS

★ **Banqueting Hall**

★ **Library**

★ **Summer Smoking
Room**

★ **Roof Garden**

Remains of Caerleon's amphitheatre, built in the 2nd century

Caerleon 🕒

Newport (Gwent). 🚶 11,000.
🚪 5 High St (01633 422656).
🌐 www.caerleon.net

TOGETHER WITH YORK *(see pp390–91)* and Chester *(see pp296–7)*, Caerleon was one of only three fortress settlements in Britain built for the Romans' elite legionary troops. From AD 74 Caerleon *(Isca* to the Romans, after the River Usk, which flows beside the town) was home to the 2nd Augustan Legion, which had been sent to Wales to crush the native Silures tribe. The remains of their base now lie between the modern town and the river.

An altar at Caerleon's Legionary Museum

The excavations at Caerleon are of great social and military significance. The Romans built not just a fortress for their crack 5,500-strong infantry division but a complete town to service their needs, including a stone amphitheatre. Judging by the results of the excavation work carried out since the archaeologist Sir Mortimer Wheeler unearthed the amphitheatre in 1926, Caerleon is one of the largest and most important Roman military sites in Europe. The defences enclosed an area of 20 ha (50 acres), with 64 rows of barracks, arranged in pairs, a hospital, and a bath-house complex.

Outside the settlement, the amphitheatre's large stone foundations have survived in an excellent state of preservation. Six thousand spectators could enjoy the blood sports and gladiators' combat.

More impressive still is the fortress baths complex, which opened to the public in the mid-1980s. The baths were designed to bring all the home comforts to an army posted to barbaric Britain. The Roman troops could take a dip in the open-air swimming pool, play sports in the exercise yard or covered hall, or enjoy a series of hot and cold baths.

Nearby are the foundations of the only Roman legionary barracks on view in Europe. The many excavated artifacts, including a collection of engraved gemstones, are displayed at the **Roman Legionary Museum**.

🏛 Roman Legionary Museum
High St. 📞 01633 423134. ⏰ Mon–Sat, Sun (pm). ● 24–26 Dec, 1 Jan. 🖼 ♿ 🚻

Big Pit Mining Museum, reminder of a vanished industrial society

Blaenafon 🕒

Torfaen. 🚶 6,000. 🚪 Blaenafon Ironworks, North St. 📞 01495 792615. 🌐 www.blaenafon.ws

COMMERCIAL COAL-MINING has now all but ceased in the South Wales valleys – an area which only 100 years ago was gripped by the search for its "black gold". Though coal is no longer produced at **Big Pit** in Blaenafon, the **Mining Museum** provides a vivid reminder of this tough industry. The Big Pit closed as a working mine in 1980, and opened three years later as a museum. Visitors follow a marked-out route around the mine's surface workings to the miners' baths, the blacksmith's forge, the workshops and the engine house. There is also a replica of an underground gallery, where mining methods are explained. But the climax of any visit to Big Pit is beneath the ground. Kitted out with helmets, lamps and safety batteries, visitors descend by cage 90 m (300 ft) down the mineshaft and then are guided by ex-miners on a tour of the underground workings and pit ponies' stables.

Blaenafon also has remains of the iron-smelting industry. Across the valley from Big Pit stand the 18th-century smelting furnaces and workers' cottages that were once part of the **Blaenafon Ironworks**, and which are now a museum.

🏛 Big Pit Mining Museum
Blaenafon. 📞 01495 790311. ⏰ mid-Feb–Nov: daily. 🖼 ♿ phone first. 🚻 🖼 🚻
🏛 Blaenafon Ironworks
North St. 📞 01495 792615. ⏰ Apr–Oct: daily. 🖼

Monmouth 🕒

Monmouthshire (Gwent). 🚶 10,000. 🚌 🚪 Shire Hall (01600 713899). 🛍 Fri, Sat. 🌐 www.visitwyevalley.com

THIS MARKET TOWN, which sits at the confluence of the Wye and Monnow rivers, has many historical associations. The 11th-century castle, behind Agincourt Square, is in ruins but the **Regimental Museum**,

Monnow Bridge in Monmouth, once a watchtower and jail

Tintern Abbey 🔞

Monmouthshire (Gwent). 📞 *01291 689251.* 🚆 *Chepstow then bus.* 🕐 *daily.* ⬤ *24–26 Dec, 1 Jan.* 🎫 ♿ 🏠

EVER SINCE THE 18th century, travellers have been enchanted by Tintern's setting in the steep and wooded Wye Valley and by the majestic ruins of its abbey. Poets were often inspired by the scene. Wordsworth's sonnet, *Lines composed a few miles above Tintern Abbey*, embodied his romantic view of landscape:

once again
Do I behold these steep and
* lofty cliffs,*
That on a wild, secluded
* scene impress*
Thoughts of more deep
* seclusion*

The abbey was founded in 1131 by Cistercian monks, who cultivated the surrounding lands (now forest), and developed it as an influential religious centre. By the 14th century this was the richest abbey in Wales, but along with other monasteries it was dissolved in 1536 by Henry VIII *(see p50)*. Its skeletal ruins are now roofless and exposed, the soaring arches and windows giving them a poignant grace and beauty.

beside it, remains open to the public. The castle was the birthplace of Henry V *(see p49)* in 1387. A statue of Henry stands in the square, along with that of Charles Stewart Rolls (born at nearby Hendre), co-founder of the Rolls-Royce car manufacturers, who died in a flying accident in 1910.

Lord Horatio Nelson *(see p54)*, the famous admiral, visited Monmouth in 1802. An excellent collection of Nelson memorabilia, gathered by Lady Llangattock, mother of Charles Rolls, is displayed at the **Nelson Museum**.

Monmouth was the county town of the old Monmouthshire. The wealth of elegant Georgian buildings, including the elaborate **Shire Hall**,

which dominates Agincourt Square, reflect its former status. The most famous architectural feature in Monmouth is **Monnow Bridge**, a narrow 13th-century gateway on its western approach, thought to be the only surviving fortified bridge gate in Britain.

For a lovely view over the town, climb the Kymin, a 256 m (840 ft) hill crowned by a **Naval Temple** built in 1801.

🏛 Monmouth Castle and Regimental Museum
The Castle. 📞 *01600 772175.* 🕐 *Apr–Oct: daily (pm); Nov–Mar: Sat & Sun (pm).* ⬤ *25 Dec.* ♿

🏛 Nelson Museum
Priory St. 📞 *01600 713519.* 🕐 *daily (Sun: pm).* ⬤ *24–26 Dec, 1 Jan.* 🎫 ♿ 🏠

Tintern Abbey in the Wye Valley, in the past a thriving centre of religion and learning, now a romantic ruin

SCOTLAND

Scotland at a Glance

STRETCHING from the rich farmlands of the Borders to a chain of isles only a few degrees south of the Arctic Circle, the Scottish landscape has a diversity without parallel in Britain. As you travel northwest from Edinburgh, the land becomes more mountainous and its archaeological treasures more numerous. In the far northwest, Scotland's earliest relics stand upon the oldest rock on Earth.

Western Isles

Skye (see pp520–21), *renowned for its dramatic scenery, has one of Scotland's most striking coastlines. On the east coast, a stream plunges over Kilt Rock, a cliff of hexagonal basalt columns named after its likeness to an item of Scottish national dress.*

THE HIGHLAN
AND ISLANI
(see pp510

Argyll and Bute

Clyde Valley

Ayrs

The Trossachs (see pp480–81) *are a beautiful range of hills straddling the border between the Highlands and the Lowlands. At their heart, the forested slopes of Ben Venue rise above the still waters of Loch Achray.*

Culzean Castle (see pp508–9) *stands on a cliff's edge on the Firth of Clyde, amid an extensive country park. One of the jewels of the Lowlands, Culzean is a magnificent showcase of work by the Scottish-born architect, Robert Adam (see p24).*

◁ **Loch Lomond, the Lowlands**

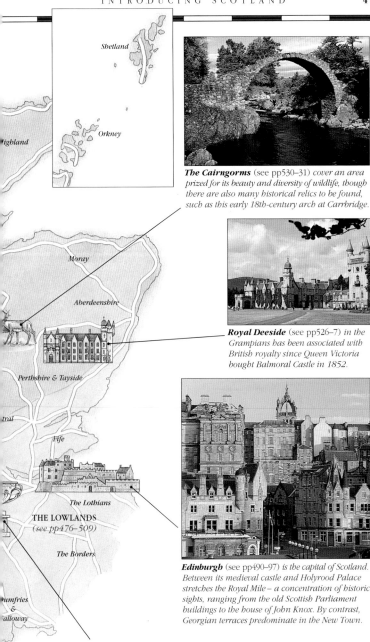

Shetland

Orkney

ighland

Moray

Aberdeenshire

Perthshire & Tayside

ral

Fife

The Lothians

THE LOWLANDS
(see pp476–509)

The Borders

*umfries
&
alloway*

The Cairngorms *(see pp530–31) cover an area prized for its beauty and diversity of wildlife, though there are also many historical relics to be found, such as this early 18th-century arch at Carrbridge.*

Royal Deeside *(see pp526–7) in the Grampians has been associated with British royalty since Queen Victoria bought Balmoral Castle in 1852.*

Edinburgh *(see pp490–97) is the capital of Scotland. Between its medieval castle and Holyrood Palace stretches the Royal Mile – a concentration of historic sights, ranging from the old Scottish Parliament buildings to the house of John Knox. By contrast, Georgian terraces predominate in the New Town.*

The Burrell Collection *(see pp506–7), on the southern outskirts of Glasgow, is a museum of some of the city's greatest art treasures. It is housed in a spacious, glass building opened in 1983.*

0 kilometres	50
0 miles	50

A PORTRAIT OF SCOTLAND

*F*ROM THE GRASSY HILLS *of the Borders to the desolate Cuillin Ridge of Skye, the landscape of Scotland is breathtaking in its variety. Lonely glens, sparkling lochs and ever-changing skies give the land a challenging character, which is reflected in the qualities of the Scottish people. Tough and self-reliant, they have produced some of Britain's finest soldiers, its boldest explorers and most astute industrialists.*

The Scots are proud of their separate identity and their own systems of law and education and, in 1998, voted overwhelmingly for their own parliament. Many Scots welcomed this as a long-awaited reversal of the Act of Union that united the English and Scottish parliaments in

A hammer-thrower at the Braemar Games

1707. But despite their national pride, they are not a homogeneous people, the main division is between traditionally Gaelic-speaking Highlanders, and the Lowlanders who spoke Scots, a form of Middle English which is now extinct. Today, though Gaelic survives (chiefly in the Western Isles), most people speak regional dialects or richly accented English. Many Scottish surnames derive from Gaelic: the prefix "mac" means "son of". A Norse heritage can be found in the far north, where Shetlanders welcome the annual return of the sun during the Viking fire festival, Up Helly Aa.

In the 16th century, a suspicion of authority and dislike of excessive flamboyance attracted many Scots to the Presbyterian church with its absence of bishops and its stress on simple worship. The Presbyterian Church of Scotland was established in 1689, though a substantial Catholic minority remained which today predominates in the crofting (small-scale farming) communities of the Western Isles. Now sparsely populated, the Isles preserve a rural culture that once dominated the Highlands, a region that is the source of much that is distinctively Scottish. The clan system originated there, along with the tartans, the bagpipes and such unique sports as tossing the caber – a large tree trunk. Highland sports, along with traditional dances, are still performed at annual games *(see p64).*

Edinburgh bagpiper

Resourcefulness has always been a prominent Scottish virtue, and Scotland has produced a disproportionately high number of Britain's geniuses. James Watt designed the first effective steam engine to power the Industrial Revolution, while Adam Smith became the 18th century's most influential economist. In the 19th century, James Simpson discovered the anaesthetic qualities of

The Viking festival, Up Helly Aa, in Lerwick, Shetland

A traditional stone croft on the Isle of Lewis

With some of the harshest weather conditions in Europe it is perhaps less surprising that Scotland has bred numerous great explorers, the most famous being Robert Scott (of the Antarctic) and African missionary David Livingstone. There is also a strong intellectual and literary tradition, from the 18th-century philosopher David Hume, through novelists Sir Walter Scott and Robert Louis Stevenson, to the poetry of Robert Burns. Today Scotland hosts a variety of arts festivals, such as Edinburgh's.

chloroform, James Young developed the world's first oil refinery and Alexander Bell revolutionized communications by inventing the telephone. The 20th century saw one of the greatest advances in medicine with the discovery of penicillin by Alexander Fleming.

The Scots are also known for being shrewd businessmen, and have always been prominent in finance: both the Bank of England and the Royal Bank of France were founded by Scots, while Andrew Carnegie created one of 19th century-America's biggest business empires.

Detail of Edinburgh's Festival Fringe office

With a population density only one-fifth of England and Wales, Scotland has vast tracts of untenanted land which offer numerous outdoor pleasures. It is richly stocked with game, and the opening of the grouse season on 12 August is a highlight on the social calendar. Fishing and hill-walking are popular and in winter thousands flock to the Cairngorms and Glencoe for skiing. Though the weather may be harsher than elsewhere, the Scots will claim that the air is purer – and that enjoying rugged conditions is what distinguishes them from their soft southern neighbours.

The blue waters of Loch Achray in the heart of the Trossachs, north of Glasgow

The History of Scotland

Bonnie Prince Charlie, by G Dupré

SINCE THE ROMAN INVASION of Britain, Scotland's history has been characterized by its resistance to foreign domination. The Romans never conquered the area, and when the Scots extended their kingdom to its present boundary in 1018, a long era of conflict began with England. After many wars, the Scots finally accepted union with the "auld enemy": first with the union of crowns, and then with the Union of Parliament in 1707. In 1999 the inauguration of the Scottish Parliament was a dramatic change.

An elaborately carved Pictish stone at Aberlemno, Angus

EARLY HISTORY

THERE IS MUCH EVIDENCE in Scotland of important prehistoric population centres, particularly in the Western Isles, which were peopled mostly by Picts who originally came from the Continent. By the time Roman Governor Julius Agricola invaded in AD 81, there were at least 17 independent tribes, including the Britons in the southwest, for him to contend with.

The Romans reached north to the Forth and Clyde valleys, but the Highlands deterred them from going further. By 120, they had retreated to the line where the Emperor Hadrian had built his wall to keep the Picts at bay (not far from today's border). By 163 the Romans had retreated south for the last time. The Celtic influence began when

"Scots" arrived from Ireland in the 6th century, bringing the Gaelic language with them.

The Picts and Scots united under Kenneth McAlpin in 843, but the Britons remained separate until 1018, when they became part of the Scottish kingdom.

THE ENGLISH CLAIM

THE NORMAN KINGS regarded Scotland as part of their territory but seldom pursued the claim. William the Lion of Scotland recognized English sovereignty by the Treaty of Falaise (1174), though English control never spread to the northwest. In 1296 William Wallace, supported by French (the start of the Auld Alliance, which lasted two centuries), began the long war of independence. During this bitter conflict, Edward I seized the sacred Stone of Destiny from Scone *(see p484)*, and took it to Westminister Abbey. The war lasted for more than 100 years. Its great hero was Robert the Bruce, who defeated the English in 1314 at Bannockburn. The English held the upper hand after that, even though the Scots would not accept their rule.

John Kn[...] statue Edinbu[...]

THE ROAD TO UNION

THE SEEDS OF UNION between the crowns were sown in 1503 when James IV of Scotland married Margaret Tudor, daughter of Henry VII. When her brother, Henry VIII, came to the throne, James sought to assert independence but was defeated and killed at Flodden Field in 1513. His granddaughter, Mary, Queen of Scots *(see p497)*, married the French Dauphin in order to cement the Auld Alliance and gain assistance in her claim to

Bruce in Single Combat at Bannockburn (1906) by John Hassall the throne of her English cousin, Elizabeth I. She had support from the Catholics wanting to see an end to Protestantism in England and Scotland. However, fiery preacher John Knox won support for the Protestants and established the Presbyterian Church in 1560. Mary's Catholicism led to the loss of her Scottish throne in 1568, and her subsequent flight to England, following defeat at Langside. Finally, after nearly 20 years of imprisonment she was executed for treason by Elizabeth in 1587.

The factories on Clydeside, once creators of the world's greatest ships

UNION AND REBELLION

ON ELIZABETH I's death in 1603, Mary's son, James VI of Scotland, succeeded to the English throne and became James I, king of both countries. Thus the crowns were united, though it was 100 years before the formal Union of Parliaments in 1707. During that time, religious differences within the country

Articles of Union between England and Scotland, 1707

reached boiling point. There were riots when the Catholic-influenced Charles I restored bishops to the Church of Scotland and authorized the printing of a new prayer book. This culminated in the signing, in Edinburgh in 1638, of the National Covenant, a document that condemned all Catholic doctrines. Though the Covenanters were suppressed, the Protestant William of Orange took over the English throne in 1688 and the crown passed out of Scottish hands.

In 1745, Bonnie Prince Charlie *(see p521)*, descended from the Stuart kings, tried to seize the throne from the Hanoverian George II. He

marched far into England, but was driven back and defeated at Culloden field *(see p523)* in 1746.

INDUSTRIALIZATION AND SOCIAL CHANGE

IN THE LATE 18TH AND 19th centuries, technological progress transformed Scotland from a nation of crofters to an industrial powerhouse. In the notorious Highland Clearances *(see p517)*, from the 1780s on, landowners ejected tenants from their smallholdings and gave the land over to sheep and other livestock. The first ironworks was established in 1760 and was soon followed by coal mining, steel production and shipbuilding on the Clyde. Canals were cut, railways and bridges built.

A strong socialist movement developed as workers sought to improve their conditions. Keir Hardie, an Ayrshire coal miner, in 1892 became the first socialist elected to parliament, and in 1893 founded the Independent Labour Party. The most enduring symbol of this time is the spectacular Forth rail bridge *(see p488)*.

SCOTLAND TODAY

ALTHOUGH THE STATUS of the country appeared to have been settled in 1707, a strong nationalist sentiment remained

and was heightened by the Depression of the 1920s and '30s which had severe effects on the heavily industrialized Clydeside. This was when the Scottish National Party formed, advocating self-rule. The Nationalists asserted themselves in 1950 by stealing the Stone of Scone from Westminister Abbey.

The discovery of North Sea oil in 1970 encouraged a nationalist revival and, in 1979, the Government promised to establish a separate assembly if 40 per cent of the Scottish electorate endorsed the plan in a referendum. This figure was finally surpassed in 1998, and the Scottish Parliament was duly inaugurated in 1999.

A North Sea oil rig, helping to provide prosperity in the 1970s

Clans and Tartans

T HE CLAN SYSTEM, by which Highland society was
divided into tribal groups led by autocratic chiefs,
can be traced to the 12th century, when clans were
already known to wear the chequered wool cloth
later called tartan. All members of the clan
bore the name of their chief, but not all
were related by blood. Though they had
noble codes of hospitality, the clansmen
had to be warriors to protect their herds, as
can be seen from their mottoes. After the
Battle of Culloden (see p523), all the clan
lands were forfeited to the Crown, and the
wearing of tartan was
banned for nearly
100 years.

The Mackays, *also
known as the Clan
Morgan, won lasting
renown during the
Thirty Years War.*

The MacLeods *are
of Norse heri-
tage. The clan
chief still lives
in Dunvegan
Castle, Skye
(see p520).*

The Mackenzies
*received much of
the lands of Kintail
(see p516) from
David II in 1362.*

The MacDonalds
*were the most power-
ful of all the clans,
holding the title of
Lords of the Isles.*

CLAN CHIEF

The chief was the clan's patriarch, judge
and leader in war, commanding absolute
loyalty from his clansmen who gave military service in return for his protection.
The chief sum-
moned his clan
to do battle by
sending a run-
ner across his
land bearing a
burning cross.

Bonnet
with eagle
feathers,
clan crest
and plant
badge.

Dirk

Sporran,
or pouch,
made of
badger's
skin.

**Feileadh-
mor**, or
"great plaid"
(the early
kilt), wrap-
ped around
waist and
shoulder.

**Basket-
hilted
sword**

The Campbells
*were a widely
feared clan who
fought the Jacobites
in 1746 (see p523).*

The Black Watch, *raised in 1729
to keep peace in the Highlands, was
one of the Highland regiments in
which the wearing of tartan survived. After 1746, civilians were
punished by exile for up to seven
years for wearing tartan.*

The Sinclairs *came from France in the 11th century and became Earls of Caithness in 1455.*

George IV, *dressed as a Highlander, visited Edinburgh in 1822, the year of the tartan revival. Many tartan "setts" (patterns) date from this time, as the original ones were lost.*

The Frazers *came to Britain from France with William the Conqueror (see p47) in 1066.*

The Gordons *were famously good soldiers; the clan motto is "by courage, not by craft".*

The Stuarts *were Scotland's royal dynasty. Their motto was "no one harms me with impunity".*

The Douglas *clan were prominent in Scottish history, though their origin is unknown.*

CLAN TERRITORIES

The territories of 10 prominent clans are marked here with their clan crests. Dress tartans tend to be colourful, while hunting tartans are darker.

PLANT BADGES

Each clan had a plant associated with its territory. It was worn on the bonnet, especially on the day of battle.

Scots pine was worn by the MacGregors of Argyll.

Rowan berries were worn by the Clan Malcolm.

Ivy was worn by the Clan Gordon of Aberdeenshire.

Spear thistle, now a national symbol, was a Stuart badge.

Cotton grass was worn by the Clan Henderson.

HIGHLAND CLANS TODAY

Once the daily dress of the clansmen, the kilt is now largely reserved for formal occasions. The one-piece *feileadh-mor* has been replaced by the *feileadh-beag*, or "small plaid", made from approximately 7 m (23 ft) of material with a double apron fastened at the front with a silver pin. Though they exist now only in name, the clans are still a strong source of pride for Scots, and many still live in areas traditionally belonging to their clans. Many visitors to Britain can trace their Scots ancestry *(see p27)* to the Highlands.

Modern Highland formal dress

Evolution of the Scottish Castle

THERE ARE FEW more romantic sights in the British Isles
than a Scottish castle on an island or at a lochside. These
formidable retreats, often in remote settings, were essential
all over the Highlands, where incursions and strife between
the clans were common. From the earliest Pictish *brochs (see
p42)* and Norman-influenced motte and bailey castles, the
distinctively Scottish tower-house evolved, first appearing in
the 14th century. By the mid-17th century fashion had
become more important than defence, and there followed a
period in which numerous huge Scottish palaces were built.

**Detail of the Baroque
façade, Drumlanrig**

MOTTE AND BAILEY

These castles first appeared in the
12th century. They stood atop two
adjacent mounds enclosed by a wall,
or palisade, and defensive ditches.
The higher mound, or motte, was
the most strongly defended as it
held the keep and chief's house.
The lower bailey was where the
people lived. Of these
castles little more
than earthworks
remain today.

**Keep, with chief's house,
lookout and main defence**

**All that remains today of Duffus
Castle, Morayshire**

*Duffus Castle,
(c.1150), was atypically
made of stone rather than
wood. Its fine defensive position
dominates the surrounding
flatlands north of Elgin.*

**Bailey enclosing
dwellings and
storehouses**

**Motte of earth or rock, some-
times partially man-made**

EARLY TOWER-HOUSE

Designed to deter local attacks
rather than a major assault, the first
tower-houses appeared in the 13th
century, though their design lived
on for 400 years. They were built
initially on a rectangular plan,
with a single tower divided into
three or four floors. The walls
were unadorned, with few windows. Defensive structures were
on top, and extra space was
made by building adjoining
towers. Extensions were made as
vertically as possible, to minimize
the area open to attack.

Crenellated parapet for sentries

**Featureless, straight
walls with arrow slits
for windows**

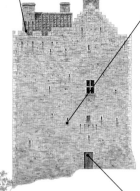

**Claypotts Castle (c.1570)
with uniquely projecting
garrets above its towers**

**Small, inconspicuous
doorway**

**Braemar Castle (c.1630), a con-
glomeration of extended towers**

*Neidpath Castle, standing
upon a steep rocky crag above the
River Tweed, is an L-shaped tower-
house dating from the late 14th century.
Once a stronghold for Charles II, its
walls still bear damage from a siege
conducted by Oliver Cromwell (see p52).*

LATER TOWER-HOUSE

Though the requirements of defence were being replaced by those of comfort, the style of the early tower-house remained popular. By the 17th century, wings for accommodation were being added around the original tower (often creating a courtyard). The battlements and turrets were kept more for decorative than defensive reasons.

Drum Castle *(see p527)*, a 13th-century keep with a mansion house extension from 1619

Priest's room with secret access

The original 15th-century tower-house

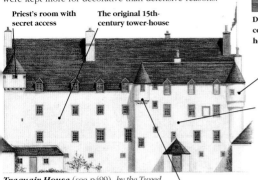

Round angle tower, containing stairway

A 16th-century horizontal extension

Traquair House (see p499), *by the Tweed, is reputedly the oldest continuously inhabited house in Scotland. The largely unadorned, roughcast exterior dates to the 16th century, when a series of extensions were built around the original 15th-century tower-house.*

Decorative, corbelled turret

Blair Castle *(see p529)*, incorporating a medieval tower

CLASSICAL PALACE

By the 18th century, the defensive imperative had passed and castles were built in the manner of country houses, rejecting the vertical tower-house in favour of a horizontal plan (though the building of imitation fortified buildings continued into the 19th century with the mock-Baronial trend). Outside influences came from all over Europe, including Renaissance and Gothic revivals, and echoes of French châteaux.

Dunrobin Castle (c.1840), Sutherland

Larger windows due to a lesser need for defence.

Balustrades instead of battlements

Decorative cupola

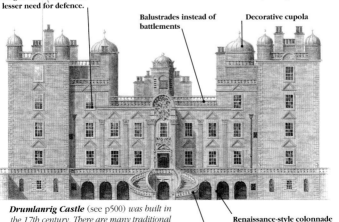

Drumlanrig Castle (see p500) *was built in the 17th century. There are many traditional Scots aspects as well as such Renaissance features as the decorated stairway and façade.*

Renaissance-style colonnade

Baroque horseshoe stairway

Scottish Food and Drink

Porridge *is a breakfast of oats, boiled in water and milk, with salt or sugar.*

THE SCOTTISH LARDER is generous in meat and fish, which are usually served simply, without heavy sauces. Grouse and deer range the hills, Aberdeen Angus beef is world famous, and the rivers are renowned for their salmon and trout. With Scotland's cold, wet climate and shallow soil, wheat was grown less than oats, which are still present in traditional Scottish foods, such as porridge and oatcakes (rather than bread) and, of course, haggis.

Kippers, *eaten at breakfast, are fresh herring split down the back, salted and cured by smoking over a fire.*

Poached salmon *tastes best when cooked whole in a bouillon of water, wine and vegetables, during which its deep red flesh turns a delicate pink. Salmon are caught in all Scotland's rivers.*

Scotch broth *is a light, thin soup based on neck of mutton, to which pearl barley and vegetables are added.*

Venison *is allowed to hang for ten days before being seasoned with mixed spices, wine and vinegar, and then roasted.*

Haggis, *served boiled with swedes, or "neeps", and potatoes, is spiced sheep's innards, here mixed with oatmeal.*

MARMALADE

Marmalade was created in Dundee *(see p485)* in the 1700s after a rash purchase left grocer James Keiller with a large cargo of bitter Seville oranges. He was unable to re-sell them, so his wife Janet added them to a preserve. Word soon spread about her delicious creation which now appears on breakfast tables throughout the world.

Dundee cake *is a rich, sweet cake made of dried fruits and spices topped with almonds.*

Bonnet

Shortbread   Bonchester

Scottish oatcakes *are flat biscuits of fine oatmeal which accompany sweets or savouries. Hard Bonnet and soft Bonchester are popular among the Scottish cheeses.*

Traditional orange   **Grapefruit and ginger**

How Whisky is Made

Traditionally made from just barley, yeast and stream water, Scottish whisky (from the Gaelic *usquebaugh*, or the "water of life") takes a little over three weeks to produce, though it must be given at least three years to mature. Maturation usually takes place in oak casks, often in barrels previously used for sherry. The art of blending was pioneered in Edinburgh in the 1860s.

Barley grass

1 Malting is the first stage. Barley grain is soaked in water and spread on the malting floor. With regular turning the grain germinates, producing a "green malt". Germination stimulates the production of enzymes which turn the starches into fermentable sugars.

2 Drying of the barley halts germination after 12 days of malting. This is done over a peat fire in a pagoda-shaped malt-kiln. The peat-smoke gives flavour to the malt and eventually to the mature whisky. The malt is gleaned of germinated roots and then milled.

3 Mashing of the ground malt, or "grist", occurs in a large vat, or "mash tun", which holds a vast quantity of hot water. The malt is soaked and begins to dissolve, producing a sugary solution called "wort", which is then extracted for fermentation.

4 Fermentation occurs when yeast is added to the cooled wort in wooden vats, or "washbacks". The mixture is stirred for hours as the yeast turns the sugar into alcohol, producing a clear liquid called "wash".

5 Distillation involves boiling the wash twice so that the alcohol vaporizes and condenses. In copper "pot stills", the wash is distilled – first in the "wash still", then in the "spirit still". Now purified, with an alcohol content of 57 per cent, the result is young whisky.

Traditional drinking vessels, or *quaichs*, made of silver

6 Maturation is the final process. The whisky mellows in oak casks for a legal minimum of three years. Premium brands give the whisky a 10- to 15-year maturation, though some are given up to 50 years.

Blended whiskies are made from a mixture of up to 50 different single malts.

Single malts vary according to regional differences in the peat and stream water used.

THE LOWLANDS

CLYDE VALLEY · CENTRAL SCOTLAND · FIFE · THE LOTHIANS
AYRSHIRE · DUMFRIES AND GALLOWAY · THE BORDERS

S OUTHEAST *of the Highland boundary fault line lies a part of Scotland very different in character from its northern neighbour. If the Highlands embody the romance of Scotland, the Lowlands have traditionally been her powerhouse. Lowlanders have always prospered in agriculture and, more recently, in industry and commerce.*

Being the region of Scotland closest to the English border, the Lowlands inevitably became the crucible of Scottish history. For centuries after the Romans built the Antonine Wall *(see p44)* across the Forth–Clyde isthmus, the area was engulfed in conflict. The Borders are scattered with the castles of a territory in uneasy proximity to rapacious neighbours, and the ramparts of Stirling Castle overlook no fewer than seven different battlefields fought over in the cause of independence.

The ruins of medieval abbeys, such as Melrose, also bear witness to the dangers of living on the invasion route from England, though the woollen trade founded by their monks still flourishes in Peebles and Hawick.

North of the Borders lies Edinburgh, the cultural and administrative capital of Scotland. With its Georgian squares dominated by a medieval castle, it is one of Europe's most elegant cities. While the 18th and 19th centuries saw a great flowering of the arts in Edinburgh, the city of Glasgow became a merchant city second only to London. Fuelled by James Watt's development of the steam engine in the 1840s, Glasgow became the cradle of Scotland's Industrial Revolution, which created a prosperous cotton industry and launched the world's greatest ships.

Both cities retain this dynamism today: Edinburgh annually hosts the world's largest arts festival, and Glasgow is acclaimed as a model of industrial renaissance.

A juggler performing at the annual arts extravaganza, the Edinburgh Festival

◁ Glamis Castle, 12 miles (19 km) north of Dundee, with its typically Scottish turreted exterior

Exploring the Lowlands

THE LOWLANDS are traditionally all the land south of the fault line stretching northeast from Loch Lomond to Stonehaven. Confusingly, they include plenty of wild upland country. The region illustrates best the diversity of Scotland's magnificent scenery. The wooded valleys and winding rivers of the borders give way to the stern hills of the Cheviots and Lammermuirs. Lively fishing villages cling to the rocky east coast, while the Clyde coast and its islands are dotted with cheerful holiday towns. Inland lies the Trossachs, a romantic area of mountain, loch and woodland east of Loch Lomond that is a magnet for walkers *(see pp32–3)* and well within reach of Glasgow.

Loch Katrine seen from the Trossachs

SEE ALSO

- **Where to Stay** pp568-70

- **Where to Eat** pp604-6

Fort William

TROSSACHS **1**

DOUNE CASTLE **3**

West Highland Way

Loch Lomond

Forth

STIRLING **2**

NEWTON

A886

B836

A8003

A84

COLINTRAIVE A8

KAMES

A809

A82

A80

M9

Firth of Clyde

24 *GLASGOW*

M74

M8

A78

A77

NEW LANARK

Isle of Arran

ARDROSSAN

A70

A70

PRESTWICK

30 *BURNS COTTAGE*

A76

25 *SAN Nit*

29 *CULZEAN CASTLE*

DRUMLANRIG CASTL

A77

A75

A713

A75

27 *THREAVE CASTLE*

STRANRAER

A747

WHITHORN **28**

KEY

- Motorway
- Major road
- Scenic route
- - - Long-distance footpath
- River
- ☆ Viewpoint

GETTING AROUND

Access to the Lowlands is made easy from the south by the M74 to Glasgow or A702 to Edinburgh which connect the region to the M6 in England. Other motorways lead to Edinburgh, Glasgow, Stirling and Perth, north of which A roads lead to the Highlands. Glasgow, Edinburgh and Prestwick have international airports. Ferries from Ardrossan provide access to the Isle of Arran.

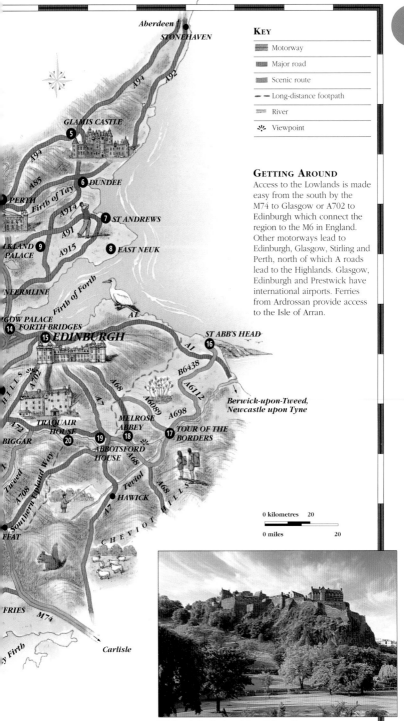

Edinburgh Castle viewed from Princes Street

The Trossachs ❶

Golden eagle

COMBINING THE RUGGEDNESS of the Grampians with the pastoral tranquillity of the Borders, this beautiful region of craggy hills and sparkling lochs is the colourful meeting place of the Lowlands and Highlands. Home to a wide variety of wildlife, including the golden eagle, peregrine falcon, red deer and the wildcat, the Trossachs have inspired numerous writers, including Sir Walter Scott (see p498) who made the area the setting for several of his novels. It was the home of Scotland's folk hero, Rob Roy, who was so well known that, in his own lifetime, he was fictionalized in *The Highland Rogue* (1723), a novel attributed to Daniel Defoe.

Loch Katrine
The setting of Walter Scott's of the Lake (1 *this freshwater loch can be explored on the Victorian stea Sir Walter Scot which cruises f the Trossachs F*

FORT WILLIAM

Inveruglas

LOCH ARKLET

B829

A82

Tarbet

BEN LOMOND
▲
974 m
3,196 ft

Kinlo

BEN UIRD
▲
596 m
1,955 ft

B83

Loch Lomond
Britain's largest freshwater lake was immortalized in a ballad composed by a local Jacobite soldier, dying far from home. He laments that though he will return home before his companions who travel on the high road, he will be doing so on the low road (of death).

Luss

LOCH
LOMOND

Baln

A81

The West Highland Way
provides a good footpath through the area.

Luss
With its exceptionally picturesque cottages, Luss is one of the prettiest villages in the Lowlands. Surrounded by grassy hills, it occupies one of the most scenic parts of Loch Lomond's western shore.

KEY

🚩	Tourist information
▬▬	A road
▭▭	B road
⋯⋯	Minor road
– –	Footpath
❋	Viewpoint

Balloch

GLASGOW

0 kilometres   5

0 miles   5

Inchmahome Priory
Mary, Queen of Scots (see p497) was hidden in this island priory to escape the armies of Henry VIII (see p498).

VISITORS' CHECKLIST

Stirling. 🚌 Stirling. 🚂 Callander.
🛈 Rob Roy & Trossachs Visitor Centre, Ancaster Sq, Callander (01877 330342). ⬛ Mar–Dec. **Inchmahome Priory**, off A81, nr Aberfoyle. 🕿 0131 668 8800. ⬛ Apr–Sep: 9:30am–6:30pm daily. 🅿 🚻 limited. **ss Sir Walter Scott**: ring Visitor Centre.

Balquhidder ☖
PERTH

LOCH VOIL

Rob Roy's grave

TROSSACHS

LOCH LUBNAIG

BEN LEDI
878 m
2,881 ft

A84

Callander

Brig O'Turk

A821

LOCH VENNACHAR

A81

MENTEITH HILLS

Aberfoyle

A81

A873

LAKE OF MENTEITH

Goodie Water

STIRLING

A811 STIRLING

Arnprior

A811

Balfron

Killearn

Callander
With its Rob Roy and Trossachs Visitor Centre, Callander is the most popular town from which to explore the Trossachs.

ROB ROY (1671–1734)

Robert MacGregor, known as Rob Roy (Red Robert) from the colour of his hair, grew up as a herdsman near Loch Arklet. After a series of harsh winters, he took to raiding richer Lowland properties to feed his clan, and was declared an outlaw by the Duke of Montrose who then burned his house to the ground. After this, Rob's Jacobite *(see p523)* sympathies became inflamed by his desire to avenge the crime. Plundering the duke's lands and repeatedly escaping from prison earned him a reputation similar to England's Robin Hood *(see p322)*. He was pardoned in 1725 and spent his last years freely in Balquhidder, where he is buried.

The Duke's Pass, between Callander and Aberfoyle, affords some of the finest views in the area.

Queen Elizabeth Forest Park
There are woodland walks through this vast tract of countryside, home to black grouse and red deer, between Loch Lomond and Aberfoyle.

The 17th-century town house of the Dukes of Argyll, Stirling

Stirling ❷

Stirling. 🏠 28,000. 🚉 🅿
ℹ 41 Dunbarton Rd (01786 475019).
🌐 www.scottish.heartlands.org

SITUATED BETWEEN the Ochil Hills and the Campsie Fells, Stirling grew up around its castle, historically one of Scotland's most important fortresses. Below the castle the Old Town is still protected by the original 16th-century walls, built to keep Mary Queen of Scots safe from Henry VIII. The medieval **Church of the Holy Rude**, on Castle Wynd, where the infant James VI was crowned in 1567, has one of Scotland's few surviving hammerbeam oak roofs. The ornate façade of **Mar's Wark** is all that remains of a grand palace which, though never completed, was commissioned in 1570 by the 1st Earl of Mar. It was destroyed by the Jacobites (see p523) in 1746. Opposite stands the beautiful 17th-century town house of the Dukes of Argyll.

ENVIRONS: Two miles (3 km) south, the **Bannockburn Heritage Centre** stands by the field where Robert the Bruce defeated the English (see p468). After the battle, he dismantled the castle so it would not fall back into English hands. A bronze equestrian statue commemorates the man who is an icon of Scottish independence.

🏠 **Bannockburn Heritage Centre**
(NTS) Glasgow Rd. 📞 01786 812664. 🅾 Apr–Sep: 10am–5:30pm daily; Oct–Mar: 11am–4:30pm daily. 🌑 24 Dec–Feb. 🈲 ♿

Stirling Castle

RISING HIGH on a rocky crag, this magnificent castle, which dominated Scottish history for centuries, now remains one of the finest examples of Renaissance architecture in Scotland. Legend says that King Arthur (see p271) wrested the original castle from the Saxons, but there is no evidence of a castle before 1124. The present building dates from the 15th and 16th centuries and was last defended, against the Jacobites (see p523), in 1746. From 1881 to 1964 the castle was a depot for recruits into the Argyll and Sutherland Highlanders, though now it serves no military function.

Gargoyle on castle wall

Robert the Bruce
In the esplanade, this modern statue shows Robert the Bruce sheathing his sword after the Battle of Bannockburn in 1314.

Prince's Tower

Forework

Entrance

Stirling Castle in the Time of the Stuarts, painted by Johannes Vorsterman (1643–99)

★ **Palace**
The otherwise sparse interiors of the royal apartments contain the Stirling Heads. These Renaissance roundels depict 38 figures, thought to be contemporary members of the royal court.

VISITORS' CHECKLIST

Castle Wynd, Stirling. 01786 450000. Apr–Sep: 9:30am–6pm daily; Oct–Mar: 9:30am–5pm daily (last adm: 45 mins before closing). 25–26 Dec, 1–2 Jan. except museum. limited.
W www.historic-scotland.gov.uk

The King's Old Building houses the Regimental Museum of the Argyll and Sutherland Highlanders.

★ **Chapel Royal**
Seventeenth-century frescoes by Valentine Jenkins adorn the chapel, reconstructed in 1594.

Nether Bailey

STAR SIGHTS

★ **Palace**

★ **Chapel Royal**

The Great Hall, built in 1500, has been restored to its former splendour.

The Elphinstone Tower was made into a gun platform in 1714.

Grand Battery
Seven guns stand on this parapet, built in 1708 during a strengthening of defences following the revolution of 1688 (see p53).

STIRLING BATTLES

At the highest navigable point of the Forth and holding the pass to the Highlands, Stirling occupied a key position in Scotland's struggles for independence. Seven battlefields can be seen from the castle; the 67 m (220 ft) Wallace Monument at Abbey Craig recalls William Wallace's defeat of the English at Stirling Bridge in 1297, foreshadowing Bruce's victory in 1314 *(see p468).*

The Victorian Wallace Monument

Perth seen from the east across the Tay

Doune Castle ❸

Doune, Stirling. ▐ *01786 841742.*
🚆 🚌 *Stirling then bus.* ⭕
Apr–Sep: 9:30am–6pm, daily;
Oct–Mar: 9:30am–4pm, Sat–Thu.
⭕ *21 Dec–8 Jan.* 📷 ♿ *limited.*

BUILT AS THE residence of
Robert, Duke of Albany,
in the 14th century, **Doune
Castle** was a Stuart stronghold
until it fell into ruin in the 18th
century. Now fully restored, it
is one of the most complete
castles of its time and offers a
unique insight into the medieval royal household.

The Gatehouse, once a self-
sufficient residence, leads
through to the central courtyard from which the Great
Hall can be entered. Complete
with its reconstructed open-
timber roof, minstrels' gallery
and central fireplace, the
Hall adjoins the Lord's Hall
and Private Room with its
original privy and well-hatch.
A number of private stairs and
narrow passages illustrate the
ingenious means by which the
royal family tried to protect
itself during times of danger.

Perth ❹

Perthshire. 🏛 *45,000.* 🚆 🚌
ℹ *45 High St (01738 450600).*
🌐 *www.perthshire.co.uk*

ONCE THE CAPITAL of medieval Scotland, Perth's rich
heritage is reflected in many of
its buildings. It was in the
Church of Saint John,
founded in 1126, that John
Knox *(see p469)* delivered
many of his fiery sermons. The
Victorianized **Fair Maid's
House**, on North Port, is one
of the oldest houses in town
(c.1600) and was the fictional
home of the heroine of Sir
Walter Scott's *(see p498) The
Fair Maid of Perth* (1828).

In **Balhousie Castle**, the
Museum of the Black Watch
commemorates the first
Highland regiment, while the
Art Gallery and Museum has
displays on local industry and
exhibitions of Scottish painting.

ENVIRONS: Two miles (3 km)
north of Perth, the Gothic
mansion of **Scone Palace**
stands on the site of an abbey
destroyed in 1559. Between
the 9th and 13th centuries,
Scone guarded the sacred
Stone of Destiny *(see
pp468–9)*, now kept in
Edinburgh Castle *(see pp492-
3)*. Some of Mary, Queen of
Scots' *(see p497)* embroideries
are on display within.

⚜ **Balhousie Castle**
RHQ Black Watch, Hay St. ▐ *0131
310 8530.* ⭕ *May–Sep: 10am–
4:30pm, Mon–Sat; Oct–Apr: 10am–
3:30pm, Mon–Fri.* ⭕ *23 Dec–6 Jan.*
🏛 **Art Gallery and Museum**
78 George St. ▐ *01738 632488.*
⭕ *10am–5pm Mon–Sat.*
⚜ **Scone Palace**
A93 to Braemar. ▐ *01738 552300.*
⭕ *Good Fri–mid-Oct:
10:30am–5:30pm daily.* 📷 ♿

Glamis Castle ❺

Forfar, Angus. ▐ *01307 840242.*
🚆 🚌 *Dundee then bus.*
⭕ *Apr–Oct: 10:30am–5:30pm daily.*
📷 ♿ *grounds.* 🎞

WITH THE pinnacled fairy-
tale outline of a Loire
chateau, the imposing medieval tower-house of **Glamis**

Glamis Castle with statues of James VI (left) and Charles I (right)

Castle began as a royal hunting lodge in the 11th-century but underwent extensive reconstruction in the 17th century. It was the childhood home of Queen Elizabeth the Queen Mother, and her former bedroom can be seen with a youthful portrait by Henri de Laszlo (1878–1956).

Many rooms are open to the public, including Duncan's Hall, the oldest in the castle and Shakespeare's setting for the king's murder in *Macbeth*. Together, the rooms present an array of china, paintings, tapestries and furniture spanning five centuries. In the grounds stand a pair of wrought-iron gates made for the Queen Mother on her 80th birthday in 1980.

View of St Andrews over the ruins of the cathedral

Dundee ❻

Dundee City. 150,000. ✈ ⇥
🚉 🛈 *7–21 Castle Street (01382 527527)*. 🎭 *Tue, Fri–Sun.*
W *www.angusanddundee.co.uk*

FAMOUS FOR ITS cake, marmalade and the DC Thomson publishing empire (creators of children's magazines *Beano* and *Dandy*), **Dundee** was also a major ship-building centre in the 18th and 19th centuries, a period which can be atmospherically recreated with a trip to the Victoria Docks.

HMS Unicorn, built in 1824, is the oldest British-built warship still afloat and is still fitted as it was on its last voyage. Berthed at Riverside is the royal research ship **Discovery**, built here in 1901 for the first

of Captain Scott's voyages to the Antarctic. Housed in a Victorian Gothic building, the **McManus Galleries** provide a glimpse of Dundee's industrial heritage, as well as exhibitions covering archaeology and Victorian art. The **Howff Burial Ground**, near City Square, has intriguing Victorian tombstones.

🏛 HMS Unicorn
Victoria Docks.
📞 *01382 200900.*
🕐 *10am–5pm daily.*
● *late Dec–early Jan.*
🅿 👤 *limited.*
🏛 Discovery
Discovery Point. 📞 *01382 201245.* 🕐 *Apr–Oct: 10am–5pm; Nov–Mar:10am–4pm, Sun pm.*
● *25 Dec, 1, 2 Jan.* 🅿
👤 📷 *by appointment.*
🏛 McManus Galleries
Albert Sq. 📞 *01382 432020.* 🕐 *10am–5pm daily (7pm Thu, 12:30–4pm Sun).* ● *25, 26 Dec, 1–3 Jan.* 👤

St Mary's College insignia, St Andrews University

St Andrews ❼

Fife. 🏠 *14,000.* ⇥ *Leuchars.*
🚉 *Dundee.* 🛈 *70 Market St (01334 472021).* W *www.standrews.co.uk*

SCOTLAND'S OLDEST UNIVERSITY town and one-time ecclesiastical capital, **St Andrews** is now a shrine to golfers from all over the world *(see below)*. Its three main streets and numerous cobbled alleys, full of crooked housefronts, dignified university buildings and medieval churches, converge on the venerable ruins of the 12th-century **cathedral**. Once the largest in Scotland, the cathedral was later pillaged for stones to build the town. **St Andrew's Castle** was built for the bishops of the town in 1200. The dungeon can still be seen. The city's golf courses to the west are each open for a modest fee. The **British Golf Museum**, tells how the city's Royal and Ancient Golf Club became the ruling arbiter of the game.

⚜ St Andrew's Castle
The Scores. 📞 *01334 477196.* 🕐 *Apr–Sep: 9:30–6pm; Oct–Mar: 9:30–4pm daily.* ● *25, 26 Dec, 1, 2 Jan.*
🅿 👤
🏛 British Golf Museum
Bruce Embankment. 📞 *01334 478880.* 🕐 *Easter–mid-Oct: 9:30am–5:30pm daily; mid-Oct–Easter: 11am–3pm Thu–Mon.* 🅿 👤

THE ANCIENT GAME OF GOLF

Scotland's national game was pioneered on the sandy links around St Andrews. The earliest record dates from 1457, when golf was banned by James II on the grounds that it was interfering with his subjects' archery practice.

Mary, Queen of Scots *(see p497)* enjoyed the game and was berated in 1568 for playing straight after the murder of her husband Darnley.

Mary, Queen of Scots at St Andrews in 1563

The central courtyard of Falkland Palace, bordered by rose bushes

East Neuk ➑

Fife. 🚆 Leuchars. 🚌 Glenrothes & Leuchars. 🅸 70 Market Street, St Andrews (01334 472021).

A STRING of pretty fishing villages scatters the shoreline of the **East Neuk** (the eastern "corner") of Fife, stretching from Earlsferry to Fife Ness. Much of Scotland's medieval trade with Europe passed through these ports, a connection reflected in the Flemish-inspired crow-stepped gables of many of the cottages. Although the herring industry has declined and the area is now a peaceful holiday centre, the sea still dominates village life. Until the 1980s, fishing boats were built at St Monans, a charming town of narrow twisting streets, while Pittenweem is the base for the East Neuk fishing fleet.

The town is also known for **St Fillan's Cave**, the retreat of a 9th-century hermit whose relic was used to bless the army of Robert the Bruce (see p468) before the Battle of Bannockburn. A church stands among the cobbled lanes and colourful cottages of Crail; the stone by the church gate is said to have been hurled to the mainland from the Isle of May by the Devil.

Several 16th- to 19th-century buildings in the village of Anstruther contain the **Scottish Fisheries Museum** which tells the area's history with the aid of interiors, boats and displays on whaling. From the village you can also embark for the nature reserve on the **Isle of May** which teems with seabirds and grey seals. The statue of Alexander Selkirk in Lower Largo recalls the local boy whose adventures inspired Daniel Defoe's *Robinson Crusoe* (1719). Disagreeing with his captain, he was dumped on a desert island for four years.

🏛 **Scottish Fisheries Museum**
Harbour Head, St Ayles, Anstruther.
🅲 01333 310628. ⏱ 10am–5:30pm daily. ⬤ 25–26 Dec, 1, 2 Jan. 🅿 ♿ 📷

Falkland Palace ➒

(NTS) Falkland, Fife. 🅲 01337 857397. 🚆 🚌 Ladybank, Kirkcaldy, then bus. ⏱ Apr–Oct: 11am-5:30pm daily (Sun: pm). 📷

T HIS STUNNING Renaissance palace was designed as a hunting lodge of the Stuart kings. Although its construction was begun by James IV in 1500, most of the work was carried out by his son, James V (see p496), in the 1530s. Under the influence of his two French wives he employed French workmen to redecorate the façade of the East Range with dormers, buttresses and medallions, and to build the beautifully proportioned South Range. The palace fell into ruin during the years of the Commonwealth (see p52) and was occupied briefly by Rob Roy (see p481) in 1715.

After buying the estates in 1887, the 3rd Marquess of Bute became the Palace Keeper and restored it. The richly panelled interiors are filled with superb furniture and contemporary portraits of the Stuart monarchs. The royal tennis court was built in 1539 for James V, and is the oldest in Britain.

Dunfermline ➓

Fife. 🚶 45,000. 🚆 🚌 🅸 13–15 Maygate (01383 720999).

S COTLAND'S CAPITAL until 1603, Dunfermline is dominated by the ruins of the 12th-century abbey and palace which recall its royal past. The town first came to prominence in the 11th century as the seat of King Malcolm III, who founded a priory on the present site of the **Abbey Church**. With its Norman nave and 19th-century choir, the church contains the tombs of 22 Scottish kings and queens, including Robert the Bruce (see p468).

The ruins of the **palace**, where Malcolm married his queen, Margaret, soar over the beautiful gardens of Pittencrieff Park. Dunfermline's most famous son, philanthropist Andrew Carnegie (1835–1919), had been forbidden entrance

---

THE PALACE KEEPER

Due to the size of the royal household and the necessity for the king to be itinerant, the office of Keeper was created by the medieval kings who required custodians to maintain and replenish the resources of their many palaces while they were away. Now redundant, it was a hereditary title and gave the custodian permanent and often luxurious lodgings.

James VI's bed in the Keeper's Bedroom, Falkland Palace

The 12th-century Norman nave of
Dunfermline Abbey Church

to the park as a boy, though
after making his fortune he
bought the entire Pittencrieff
estate and gave it to the people
of Dunfermline. He was born
in the town, though moved
with his family to Pennsylvania
in his teens. There, he made
a vast fortune in the iron and
steel industry, becoming one
of the wealthiest men in the
world, and donating some
$350 million for the benefit of
mankind. The **Carnegie
Birthplace Museum** is still
furnished as it was when he
lived there, and tells the story
of his meteoric career and ·
many charitable donations.

**⌂ Carnegie Birthplace
Museum**
Moodie St. **[** 01383 724302.
○ Apr–Oct: daily. **●** 25, 26 Dec,
1, 2 Jan. **[⋯] [♿]**

Culross ⓫

Fife. **[🏠]** 450. **[🚂]** Dunfermline.
[🚌] Dunfermline. **[ℹ]** National Trust,
The Palace (01383 880359).
○ Apr–Sep: 11am–5pm daily. **[⋯] [♿]**
limited.

A N IMPORTANT religious
centre in the 6th century,
the town of Culross is said to
have been the birthplace of St
Mungo in 514. Now a beautifully preserved 16th- and
17th-century village, Culross
prospered in the 16th century
with the growth of its coal and
salt industries, most notably
under the genius of Sir George
Bruce. Descended from the
family of Robert the Bruce
(see p468), Sir George took
charge of the Culross colliery
in 1575 and created a
drainage system called the
"Egyptian Wheel" which
cleared a mile-long (1.5 km)
mine beneath the River Forth.
During its subsequent decline Culross stood unchanged
for over 150 years. The
National Trust for Scotland
began restoring the town in
1932 and now provides a
guided tour. This starts at the
Visitors' Centre, housed in
the one-time village prison.
Built in 1577, Bruce's **palace**
has the crow-stepped gables,
decorated windows and red
pantiles typical of the period.
The interior retains its original
early 17th-century painted
ceilings. Crossing the Square,
past the **Oldest House**,

dating from 1577, head for
the **Town House** to the west.
Behind it, a cobbled street
known as the Back Causeway
(with its raised section for
nobility) leads to the turreted
Study, built in 1610 as a house
for the Bishop of Dunblane.
The main room is open to
visitors and should be seen for
its original Norwegian ceiling.
Continuing northwards to the
ruined abbey, fine church and
Abbey House, don't miss the
Dutch-gabled **House with
the Evil Eyes**.

The 17th-century Study, with its
decorated ceiling, Culross

Linlithgow
Palace ⓬

Linlithgow, West Lothian. **[** 01506
842896. **[🚂] [🚌] [ℹ] ○** Apr–Sep:
9:30am–6:30pm daily; Oct–Mar:
9:30am–4:30pm Mon–Sat, 2–4:30pm
Sun. **●** 25, 26 Dec, 1, 2 Jan.
[⋯] [♿] limited.

O N THE EDGE of Linlithgow
Loch stands the former
royal palace of **Linlithgow**.
Today's remains are mostly of
the building commissioned by
James I in 1425, though some
sections date from the 14th
century. The scale of the
building is demonstrated by
the 28 m (94 ft) long Great
Hall, with its huge fireplace
and windows. The restored
fountain in the courtyard was a
wedding present in 1538 from
James V to his wife, Mary of
Guise. His daughter, Mary,
Queen of Scots (see p497),
was born here in 1542.
The adjacent **Church of St
Michael** is Scotland's largest
pre-Reformation church.

The 16th-century palace of industrialist George Bruce, Culross

Hopetoun House ⑬

West Lothian. 📞 *0131 331 2451.*
🚃 *Dalmeny then taxi.* 🕐 *mid-Apr–Sep: 10am-5:30pm daily.* 🎦 ♿ *limited.* ▨

A N EXTENSIVE PARKLAND by the Firth of Forth, designed in the style of Versailles, is the setting for one of Scotland's finest stately homes. The original house was built by 1707; it was later absorbed into William Adam's grand extension. The dignified, horseshoe-shaped plan and lavish interior plasterwork represent Neo-Classical 18th-century architecture at its finest. The red and yellow drawing rooms, with their Rococo plasterwork and highly ornate mantelpieces, are particularly impressive. The Marquess of Linlithgow, whose family still occupies part of the house, is a descendant of the 1st Earl of Hopetoun, for whom the house was built.

A wooden panel above the main stair, depicting Hopetoun House

Forth Bridges ⑭

Edinburgh. 🚃 🚉 *Dalmeny, Inverkeithing.*

T HE SMALL TOWN of South Queensferry is dominated by the two great bridges that span the mile (1.6 km) across the River Forth to North Queensferry. The spectacular rail bridge, the first major steel-built bridge in the world, was opened in 1890 and remains one of the greatest engineer-

The shattered crags and cliffs of St Abb's Head

ing achievements of the late Victorian era. Its massive cantilevered sections are held together by more than 8 million rivets, and the painted area adds up to some 55 ha (135 acres). The saying "it's like painting the Forth Bridge" has become a byword for non-stop, repetitive endeavour. It was the rail bridge that inspired *The Bridge* (1986) by the writer Iain Banks.

The neighbouring road bridge was the largest suspension bridge outside the USA when it was opened in 1964, a distinction now held by the Humber Bridge in England. The two bridges make an impressive contrast, best seen from South Queensferry promenade. The town received its name from the 11th-century Queen Margaret *(see p493)*, who used the ferry here on her journeys between Edinburgh and the royal palace at Dunfermline *(see p487)*.

Edinburgh ⑮

See pp490–97.

St Abb's Head ⑯

Scottish Borders. 🚃 *Berwick-upon-Tweed.* 🚌 *from Edinburgh.*

T HE JAGGED CLIFFS of St Abb's Head, rising 91 m (300 ft) from the North Sea near the southeastern tip of Scotland, offer a spectacular view of thousands of seabirds wheeling and diving below. This 80 ha (200 acre) nature reserve is an important site for cliff-nesting sea birds and becomes, during the May to June breeding season, the home of more than 50,000 birds, including fulmars, guillemots, kittiwakes and puffins that throng the headland near the fishing village of St Abbs. The village has one of the few unspoiled working harbours on Britain's east coast. A clifftop trail begins at the **Visitors' Centre**, where displays include identification boards and a touch table where young visitors can get to grips with wings and feathers.

🏛 Visitors' Centre
St Abb's Head. 📞 *018907 71443.*
🕐 *Easter–Oct: 10am-5pm daily.* ▨

The huge, cantilevered Forth Rail Bridge, seen from South Queensferry

A Tour of the Borders ⑰

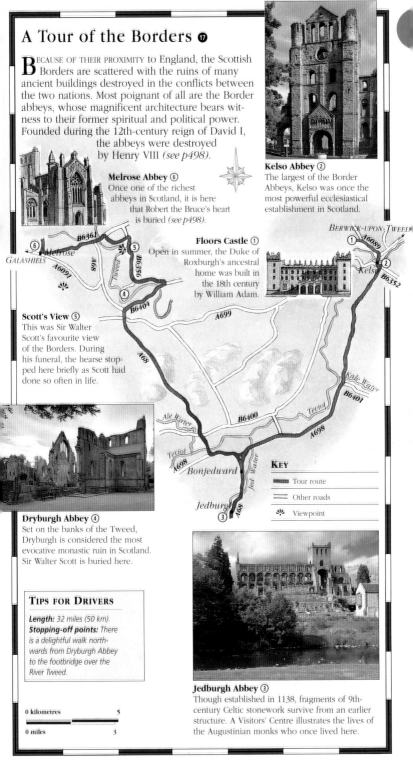

BECAUSE OF THEIR PROXIMITY to England, the Scottish Borders are scattered with the ruins of many ancient buildings destroyed in the conflicts between the two nations. Most poignant of all are the Border abbeys, whose magnificent architecture bears witness to their former spiritual and political power. Founded during the 12th-century reign of David I, the abbeys were destroyed by Henry VIII *(see p498)*.

Melrose Abbey ⑥
Once one of the richest abbeys in Scotland, it is here that Robert the Bruce's heart is buried *(see p498)*.

Kelso Abbey ②
The largest of the Border Abbeys, Kelso was once the most powerful ecclesiastical establishment in Scotland.

Floors Castle ①
Open in summer, the Duke of Roxburgh's ancestral home was built in the 18th century by William Adam.

Scott's View ⑤
This was Sir Walter Scott's favourite view of the Borders. During his funeral, the hearse stopped here briefly as Scott had done so often in life.

Dryburgh Abbey ④
Set on the banks of the Tweed, Dryburgh is considered the most evocative monastic ruin in Scotland. Sir Walter Scott is buried here.

TIPS FOR DRIVERS

Length: 32 miles (50 km).
Stopping-off points: There is a delightful walk northwards from Dryburgh Abbey to the footbridge over the River Tweed.

KEY

━━━ Tour route
═══ Other roads
※ Viewpoint

0 kilometres   5
0 miles   3

Jedburgh Abbey ③
Though established in 1138, fragments of 9th-century Celtic stonework survive from an earlier structure. A Visitors' Centre illustrates the lives of the Augustinian monks who once lived here.

Edinburgh 15

WITH ITS STRIKING medieval and Georgian districts, overlooked by the extinct volcano of Arthur's Seat and, to the north-east, Calton Hill, Edinburgh is widely regarded as one of Europe's most handsome capitals. The city is famous for the arts (it was once known as "the Athens of the North"), a pre-eminence reflected in its hosting every year of Britain's largest arts extravaganza, the Edinburgh Festival *(see p495)*. Its museums and galleries display the riches of many cultures.

Royal Scots soldiers from the castle

The doorway of the Georgian House, 7 Charlotte Square

Exploring Edinburgh

Edinburgh falls into two main sightseeing areas, divided by Princes Street, the city's most famous thoroughfare and commercial centre. The Old Town straddles the ridge between the castle and the Palace of Holyrood, with most of the city's medieval history clustered in the alleys of the Grassmarket and Royal Mile areas. The New Town, to the north, evolved after 1767 when wealthy merchants expanded the city beyond its medieval walls. This district contains Britain's finest concentration of Georgian architecture.

🏛 National Gallery of Scotland

The Mound. 📞 *0131 556 8921.*
🕐 *10am–5pm Mon–Sat, noon–5pm Sun.* ● *25, 26. Dec, 1, 2 Jan, May Day.* ⚫ 🚹 *by appointment.*
One of Scotland's finest art galleries, the National Gallery of Scotland is worth visiting for its 15th- to 19th-century British and European paintings alone, though plenty more can

be found to delight the art-lover. Ranks of paintings hang on deep red walls behind a profusion of statues and other works. Highlights among the Scottish works include portraits by Allan Ramsay and Henry Raeburn, such as his *Reverend Robert Walker Skating on Duddingston Loch* (c.1800). The Early German collection includes Gerard David's almost comic-strip treatment of the *Three Legends of Saint Nicholas* (c.1500). Works by Raphael, Titian and Tintoretto accompany southern European paintings such as Velazquez's *An Old Woman Cooking Eggs* (1620) and the entire room devoted to *The Seven Sacraments* (c.1640) by Nicholas Poussin. Flemish painters represented include Rembrandt, Van Dyck and Rubens while, among the British, important works by Reynolds, Ramsay and Gainsborough can be seen.

Raeburn's *Rev. Robert Walker Skating on Duddingston Loch*

🚻 Georgian House

7 Charlotte Sq. 📞 *0131 226 3318.*
🕐 *Apr–Oct: daily.* 🎟 ⚫ *limited.*
In the heart of the New Town, Charlotte Square is a superb example of Georgian architecture, its north side, built in the 1790s, being a masterwork by the architect Robert Adam *(see pp24–25)*. The Georgian House at No. 7 has been furnished and repainted in its original 18th-century colours which provide a memorable introduction to the elegance of wealthy New Town life. The dining room table is arranged with Sheffield plate, Wedgwood china and mid-18th-century glasses, while the chairs are mainly Edinburgh "brander backs". The drawing room, arranged with chairs around the perimeter, is in stately contrast to the intimacy of the parlour with its Staffordshire and Spode china services.

The view from Duncan's Monument on Calton Hill, looking west towards the castle

🏛 National Gallery of Modern Art & Dean Gallery

Belford Rd. ☎ 0131 556 8921. ⬜ 10am-5pm Mon-Sat, noon-5pm Sun. ⬤ 25, 26 Dec, 1, 2 Jan. ♿

Situated in extensive grounds to the northwest of the city centre, a classical 19th-century school is home to this gallery. Most European and American 20th-century greats are represented here, from Vuillard and Picasso, to Magritte and Lichtenstein. Work by John Bellany can be found among the Scottish painters. Sculpture by Henry Moore is on display in the garden.

Medieval chessmen, Museum of Scotland

Lichtenstein's *In the Car*, National Gallery of Modern Art

🏛 Museum of Scotland

Chambers St. ☎ 0131 225 7534. ⬜ 10am-5pm Mon-Sat, noon-5pm Sun. ⬤ 25 Dec. 🖼 except children. *Includes entry to the Royal Museum (see p497).* ♿ 🔲 🚻 ❚❙

This purpose-built museum houses the Scottish Collections of the National Museums of Scotland. Exhibitions tell the story of Scotland, the land and its people, dating from its geological beginnings right up to the constitutionally exciting events of today..

Key exhibits include the famous medieval *Lewis Chessmen*; *Pictish Chains*, known as Scotland's earliest crown jewels; the *Ellesmere* railway locomotive and icons of the 20th century selected both by famous Scots and the public. Children's guidebooks and activities are available.

VISITORS' CHECKLIST

Edinburgh. 🏠 420,000. ✈ 8 miles (13 km) W Edinburgh. 🚆 North Bridge (Waverley Station). 🚌 St Andrew Sq. 🛈 3 Princes St (0131 473 3800). 📅 Edinburgh International: Aug; Military Tattoo: Aug; Fringe: Aug. 🌐 www.edinburgh.org

🏛 Scottish National Portrait Gallery

1 Queen St. ☎ 0131 556 8921. ⬜ 10am-5pm Mon-Sat, noon-5pm Sun. ⬤ 25, 26 Dec, 1, 2 Jan. ♿ 📷 *by appointment.*

The National Portrait Gallery contains a rich and informative exhibition on the royal house of Stuart, explaining the turbulent history of 12 generations of Scottish monarchs from Robert the Bruce *(see p468)* to Queen Anne. Memorabilia from many reigns include Mary, Queen of Scots' *(see p497)* jewellery and a silver travelling canteen abandoned by Bonnie Prince Charlie *(see p521)* at Culloden *(see p523)*. The upper gallery has portraits of famous Scots, including Robert Burns *(see p501)* by Alexander Nasmyth.

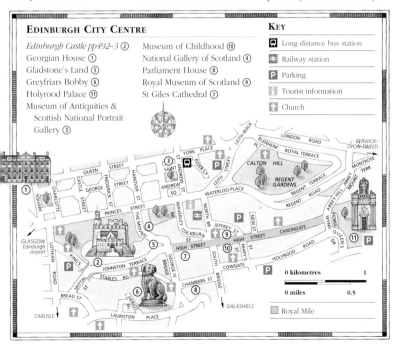

EDINBURGH CITY CENTRE

Edinburgh Castle pp492–3 ②
Georgian House ①
Gladstone's Land ⑤
Greyfriars Bobby ⑥
Holyrood Palace ⑪
Museum of Antiquities & Scottish National Portrait Gallery ③

Museum of Childhood ⑩
National Gallery of Scotland ④
Parliament House ⑧
Royal Museum of Scotland ⑨
St Giles Cathedral ⑦

KEY

🚌 Long-distance bus station
🚆 Railway station
🅿 Parking
🛈 Tourist information
✝ Church

0 kilometres 1
0 miles 0.5

◻ Royal Mile

Edinburgh Castle

Beam support in the Great Hall

STANDING UPON the basalt core of an extinct volcano, Edinburgh Castle is an assemblage of buildings dating from the 12th to the 20th centuries, reflecting its changing role as fortress, royal palace, military garrison and state prison. Though there is evidence of Bronze Age occupation of the site, the original fortress was built by the 6th-century Northumbrian King Edwin, from whom the city takes its name. The castle was a favourite royal residence until the Union of Crowns *(see p469)* in 1603, after which the king resided in England. After the Union of Parliaments in 1707, the Scottish regalia were walled up in the Palace for over a hundred years. The castle is now the zealous possessor of the so-called Stone of Destiny, a relic of ancient Scottish kings which was seized by the English and not returned until 1996.

Scottish Crown
Now on display in the palace, the Crown was restyled by James V of Scotland in 1540.

Military Prison

Governor's House
Complete with Flemish-style crow-stepped gables, this building was constructed for the governor in 1742 and now serves as the Officers' Mess for the castle garrison.

Old Back Parade

Vaults
This French graffiti, dating from 1780, recalls the many prisoners who were held in the vaults during the wars with France in the 18th and 19th centuries.

MONS MEG

Now kept in the castle vaults, the siege gun (or *bombard*) Mons Meg was made in Belgium in 1449 for the Duke of Burgundy, who gave it to his nephew, James II of Scotland. It was used by James against the Douglas family in their stronghold of Threave Castle *(see p501)* in 1455, and later by James IV against Norham Castle in England. After exploding during a salute to the Duke of York in 1682, it was kept in the Tower of London until it was returned to Edinburgh in 1829, at Sir Walter Scott's request.

STAR SIGHTS
★ Great Hall
★ Palace

VISITORS' CHECKLIST

Castle Hill. ☎ *0131 225 9846*.
◯ *Apr–Oct: 9:30am–6pm daily;
Nov–Mar: 9:30am–5pm daily (last
adm: 45 mins before closing).*
● *25, 26 Dec, 1, 2 Jan.* 📷

Argyle Battery
This fortified wall commands a spectacular northern view of the city's New Town.

★ **Palace**
Mary, Queen of Scots (see p497) *gave birth to James VI in this 15th-century palace, where the Scottish regalia are on display.*

Entrance

Royal Mile →

The Esplanade is the location of the Military Tattoo *(see p495).*

The Half Moon Battery was built in the 1570s as a platform for the artillery defending the northeastern wing of the castle.

St Margaret's Chapel
This stained glass window depicts Malcolm III's saintly queen, to whom the chapel is dedicated. Probably built by her son, David I, in the early 12th century, the chapel is the castle's oldest existing building.

★ **Great Hall**
With its restored open-timber roof, the Hall dates from the 15th century and was the meeting place of the Scottish parliament until 1639.

Exploring the Royal Mile: Castlehill to High Street

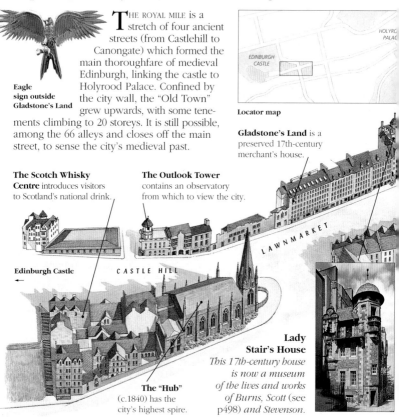

THE ROYAL MILE is a stretch of four ancient streets (from Castlehill to Canongate) which formed the main thoroughfare of medieval Edinburgh, linking the castle to Holyrood Palace. Confined by the city wall, the "Old Town" grew upwards, with some tenements climbing to 20 storeys. It is still possible, among the 66 alleys and closes off the main street, to sense the city's medieval past.

Eagle sign outside Gladstone's Land

EDINBURGH CASTLE

HOLYROOD PALACE

Locator map

Gladstone's Land is a preserved 17th-century merchant's house.

The Scotch Whisky Centre introduces visitors to Scotland's national drink.

The Outlook Tower contains an observatory from which to view the city.

LAWNMARKET

Edinburgh Castle

CASTLE HILL

Lady Stair's House
This 17th-century house is now a museum of the lives and works of Burns, Scott (see p498) and Stevenson.

The "Hub" (c.1840) has the city's highest spire.

🏛 Gladstone's Land

(NTS) 477B Lawnmarket. **▌** *0131 2265856.* **◯** *Apr–Oct: 10am–5pm Mon–Sat, 2–5pm Sun* 🚫

This 17th-century merchant's house, recently restored, provides a window on life in a typical Old Town house before overcrowding drove the rich to the Georgian New Town. "Lands", as they were known, were tall, narrow buildings erected on small plots of land. The six-storey Gladstone's Land was named after Thomas Gledstanes, the merchant who built it in 1617. The house still has the original arcade booths on the street front and a painted ceiling with fine Scandinavian floral designs. Though extravagantly furnished, it also contains items which are a reminder of the less salubrious side of the old city, such as wooden overshoes which had to be worn in the dirty streets. A chest in the beautiful Painted Chamber is said to have been given by a Dutch sea captain to a Scottish merchant who saved him from a shipwreck. A similar house, Morocco Land, can be found on Canongate *(see p497).*

🏛 Parliament House

Parliament Sq, High St. **▌** *0131 2252595.* **◯** *9am–5pm Mon–Fri.* **◐** *public hols.* **♿** *limited.*

This majestic, Italianate building was constructed in the 1630s for the Scottish parliament. Parliament House has been home to the Court of Session and the High Court since the Union of Parliaments *(see p469)* in 1707. It is well worth seeing, as much for the spectacle of its many gowned and wigged advocates as for the stained-glass window in its Great Hall, commemorating the inauguration of the Court of Session by James V, in 1532.

The bedroom of Gladstone's Land

The Signet Library has one of the city's most lavish interiors. Visits can be made after a written application.

St Giles Cathedral
A bagpiping angel can be found on the arched entrance to the Chapel of the Thistle.

The City Chambers were designed by John Adam in the 1750s.

BANK STREET

HIGH STREET

GEORGE IV BRIDGE

Rib-vaulting in the Thistle Chapel, St Giles Cathedral

Charles II Statue

The Heart of Midlothian is an arrangite of granite cobblestones on the former site of the city jail.

Parliament House was built in 1639. The Scottish parliament convened here from 1640 until 1707.

🏛 St Giles Cathedral

Royal Mile. ☎ 0131 2259442.
🕐 9am–7pm Mon–Sat, 1–5pm Sun.
● 25, 26 Dec, 1 Jan.

Properly known as the High Kirk (church) of Edinburgh, it is ironic that St Giles is popularly known as a cathedral. Though it was twice the seat of a bishop in the 17th century, it was from here that John Knox *(see p469)* directed the Scottish Reformation with its emphasis on individual worship freed from the authority of bishops. A tablet marks the place where Jenny Geddes, a stallholder from a local market, scored a victory for the Covenanters *(see p469)* by hurling her stool at a preacher reading from an English prayer book in 1637.

The Gothic exterior is dominated by a 15th-century tower, the only part to escape heavy renovation in the 19th century.

Inside, the impressive Thistle Chapel can be seen, with its elaborate rib-vaulted roof and carved heraldic canopies. The chapel honours the knights, past and present, of the Order of the Thistle. The carved royal pew in the Preston Aisle is used by the Queen when she stays in Edinburgh.

EDINBURGH FESTIVAL

Every year, for three weeks in late summer *(see p63)*, Edinburgh hosts one of the world's most important arts festivals, with every available space (from theatres to street corners) overflowing with international artists and performers. It has been held in Edinburgh since 1947 and brings together the best in contemporary theatre, music, dance and opera. The alternative Festival Fringe, with some 600 companies involved, balances the classic productions with a host of innovative performances. The most popular event is the Edinburgh Tattoo, held on the Castle Esplanade – a spectacle of Scottish infantry battalions marching to pipe bands from all over the world.

Street performer from the Edinburgh Festival Fringe

Exploring the Royal Mile: High Street to Canongate

THE SECOND SECTION of the Royal Mile passes two monuments to the Reformation: John Knox's House and the Tron Kirk. The latter is named after a medieval *tron* (weighing beam) that stood nearby. The Canongate was once an independent district, owned by the canons of the Abbey of Holyrood, and sections of its south side have been excellently restored. Beyond Morocco's Land, the road stretches for the final half-mile (800 m) to Holyrood Palace.

Locator map

HIGH STREET

SOUTH BRIDGE STREET

The Mercat Cross marks the city centre. It was here that Bonnie Prince Charlie *(see p521)* was proclaimed king in 1745.

The Tron Kirk was built in 1630 for the Presbyterians who left St Giles Cathedral when it came under the Bishop of Edinburgh's control.

🏛 Museum of Childhood

42 High St. 📞 *0131 529 4142.*
⬜ *10am–5pm Mon–Sat (daily during Festival).* ⚫ *25–27 Dec.* ♿ *limited.*
This lovely museum is not merely a toy collection but a magical insight into childhood, with all its joys and trials. Founded in 1955 by a city councillor, Patrick Murray (who claimed to enjoy eating children for breakfast), it was the first museum in the world to be devoted to the history and theme of childhood. The collection includes medicines, school books and prams as well as galleries full of old-fashioned toys. With its nickelodeon, antique slot machines

An 1880 automaton of the Man on the Moon, Museum of Childhood

The entrance to Holyrood Palace, seen from the west

and the general enthusiasm of visitors, this has been called the world's noisiest museum.

♛ Holyrood Palace

East end of Royal Mile. 📞 *0131 556 1096.* ⬜ *9:30am–4:45pm daily.* ⚫ *phone first for seasonal closures.* 📷 ♿ *limited.*
Now the Queen's official Scottish residence, Holyrood Palace is named after the "rood", or cross, which King David I is said to have seen between the antlers of a stag he was hunting here in 1128.
The present palace was built in 1529 to accommodate James V *(see p487)* and his French wife, Mary of Guise, though it was remodelled in

the 1670s for Charles II. The Royal Apartments (including the Throne Room and Royal Dining Room) are used for investitures and banquets whenever the Queen visits the palace, though they are otherwise open to the public. A chamber in the James V tower is associated with the unhappy reign of Mary, Queen of Scots. It was here, in 1566, that she saw the murder of her trusted Italian secretary, David Rizzio, by her jealous husband, Lord Darnley. She had married Darnley a year earlier in Holyrood chapel.
Bonnie Prince Charlie held court here in 1745 in the Jacobite *(see p523)* rising.

John Knox's House

Dating from 1490, the oldest house in the city was the home of John Knox (see p469) in the 1560s. He is said to have died in an upstairs room. Open daily, it contains relics of his life.

Morocco Land is a reproduction of a 17th-century tenement house. It takes its name from the statue of a Moor which adorns the entrance.

→ **Holyrood Palace**

CANONGATE

Museum of Childhood

Though created as a museum for adults by a city councillor who was known to dislike children, this lively musem now attracts flocks of young visitors.

MUSEUM OF CHILDHOOD

Moubray House was to be the signing place of the Treaty of Union in 1707 *(see p469)*, until a mob forced the authorities to retreat to another venue.

🏛 Royal Museum of Scotland

Chambers St. ☎ 0131 225 7534. ◐ 10am–5pm Mon–Sat, noon–5pm Sun. ● 25 Dec. ♿ except children. *Includes entry to the Scottish collections of the Museum of Scotland (see p491).* ♿ 🚻 📷 🏛

This elegant museum, purpose-built in 1861, houses the National Museum of Scotland's international collections. Exhibits include examples from the applied arts and sciences. The Main Hall's fine collection of Asian sculpture includes a beautiful 13th-century statue of the Hindu goddess Parvati. European Art from 1200 to 1800 is on the first floor, while the second

Parvati, at the Royal Museum of Scotland

floor exhibits rare scientific instruments. Geological specimens and Eastern decorative arts are on the top floor.

🚻 Greyfriars Bobby

On an old drinking fountain near the gateway to Greyfriars Church stands the statue of a little Skye terrier. This commemorates the dog who, for 14 years, guarded the grave of his master, John Gray, who died in 1858. The people of Edinburgh fed him until his death in 1872. He was also granted citizenship to prevent him being destroyed as a stray.

MARY, QUEEN OF SCOTS (1542–87)

Born only days before the death of her father, James V, the young Queen Mary spent her childhood in France, after escaping Henry VIII's invasion of Scotland *(see p498)*. A devout Catholic, she married the French Dauphin, and made claims on the English throne. This alarmed Protestants throughout England and Scotland, and when she returned as a widow to Holyrood, aged 18, she was harangued for her faith by John Knox *(see p469)*. In 1567 she was accused of murdering her second husband, Lord Darnley. Two months later, when she married the Earl of Bothwell (also implicated in the murder), rebellion ensued. She lost her crown and fled to England where she was held prisoner for 20 years, before being charged with treason and beheaded at Fotheringhay.

The ruins of Melrose Abbey, viewed from the southwest

Melrose Abbey ⑱

Abbey Street, Melrose, Scottish Borders. 📞 01896 822562. ☐ 10am–4:30pm daily. ● 25, 26 Dec, 1, 2 Jan. 🖼 ♿ limited.

THE ROSE-PINK RUINS of one of the most beautiful of the border abbeys *(see p489)* bear testimony to the hazards of standing in the path of successive English invasions. Built by David I in 1136 for Cistercian monks from Yorkshire, and also to replace a 7th-century monastery, Melrose was repeatedly ransacked by English armies, notably in 1322 and 1385. The final blow, from which none of the abbeys recovered, came in 1545 during Henry VIII's destructive

Scottish policy known as the "Rough Wooing". This resulted from the failure of the Scots to ratify a marriage treaty between Henry VIII's son and the infant Mary, Queen of Scots *(see p497)*. What remains of the abbey are the outlines of cloisters, the kitchen and other monastic buildings and the shell of the abbey church with its soaring east window and profusion of medieval carvings. The rich decorations of the south exterior wall include a gargoyle shaped like a pig playing the bagpipes, and several animated figures, including a cook with his ladle.

An embalmed heart, found here in 1920, is probably that of Robert the Bruce *(see p468)*, who had decreed that

his heart be taken on a crusade to the Holy Land. It was returned to Melrose after its bearer, Sir James Douglas *(see p501)*, was killed in Spain.

Abbotsford House ⑲

Galashiels, Scottish Borders. 📞 01896 752043. 🚌 from Galashiels. ☐ mid-Mar–May & Oct: 10am–5pm daily (Sun: 2–5pm); Jun–Sep: daily. 🖼 ♿ limited. 🖥 W www.melrose. bordernet.co.uk/abbotsford

FEW HOUSES bear the stamp of their creator so intimately as Abbotsford House, the home of Sir Walter Scott for the last 20 years of his life. He bought a farm here in 1811, known as Clarteyhole ("dirty hole" in Scots), though he soon renamed it Abbotsford, after the monks of Melrose Abbey who used to cross the River Tweed nearby. He later demolished the house to make way for the turreted building we see today, funded by the sales of his novels.

Scott's library contains more than 9,000 rare books and his collections of historic relics reflect his passion for the heroic past. An extensive collection of arms and armour includes Rob Roy's broadsword *(see p481)*. Stuart mementoes include a crucifix that belonged to Mary, Queen of Scots and a lock of Bonnie Prince Charlie's *(see p521)* hair. The small study in which he wrote his *Waverley* novels can be visited as can the room, overlooking the river, in which he died in 1832.

The Great Hall at Abbotsford, adorned with arms and armour

SIR WALTER SCOTT

Sir Walter Scott (1771–1832) was born in Edinburgh and trained as a lawyer. He is best remembered as a major champion and literary figure of Scotland, whose poems and novels (most famously his *Waverley* series) created enduring images of a heroic wilderness filled with the romance of the clans. His orchestration, in 1822, of the state visit of George IV to Edinburgh *(see p471)* was an extravaganza of Highland culture that helped re-establish tartan as the national dress of Scotland. He served as Clerk of the Court in Edinburgh's Parliament House *(see p494)* and for 30 years was Sheriff of Selkirk in the Scottish Borders, which he loved. He put the Trossachs *(see pp480–81)* firmly on the map with the publication of the *Lady of the Lake* (1810). His final years were spent writing to pay off a £114,000 debt following the failure of his publisher in 1827. He died with his debts paid, and was buried at Dryburgh Abbey *(see p489)*.

Traquair House ⑳

Peebles, Scottish Borders. 〖 01896
830 323. 🚌 from Peebles. ◯
Easter–Oct: noon–5:30pm; Jul–Aug:
10:30am–5:30pm daily 🅰 🅱
limited. 🆆 www.traquair.co.uk

A S SCOTLAND'S OLDEST continuously inhabited house,
Traquair has deep roots in
Scottish religious and political
history, stretching back over
900 years. Evolving from a
fortified tower to a stout-
walled 17th-century
mansion (see
p473), the house
was a Catholic
Stuart stronghold for
500 years. Mary,
Queen of Scots (see
p497) was among the
many monarchs to have
stayed here and her bed
is covered by a counter-
pane which she made.
Family letters and
engraved Jacobite
(see p523) drinking
glasses are among
relics recalling the
period of the
Highland rebellions.

**Mary, Queen of
Scots' crucifix,
Traquair House**

After a vow made
by the 5th Earl, Traquair's
Bear Gates (the "Steekit
Yetts"), which closed after
Bonnie Prince Charlie's (see
p521) visit in 1745, will not
reopen until a Stuart reas-
cends the throne. A secret
stairway leads to the Priest's
Room which attests to the
problems faced by Catholic
families until Catholicism was
legalized in 1829. Traquair
House Ale is still produced in
the 18th-century brewhouse.

Biggar ㉑

Clyde Valley. 🕴 2,000. 🚩 High St
(01899 221066).

T HIS TYPICAL Lowland market town has a number of
museums worth visiting.
The **Gladstone Court
Museum** boasts a recon-
structed Victorian street
complete with a milliner's,
printer's and a village library,
while the grimy days of the
town's industrial past are
recalled at the **Gasworks
Museum**, with its collection
of engines, gaslights and
appliances. Established in
1839 and preserved in
the 1970s, the Biggar
Gasworks is the only
remaining rural gas-
works in Scotland.

🏛 **Gladstone Court
Museum**
Northback Rd. 〖 01899 221050.
◯ Apr–Oct: 10am–5pm daily (Sun:
2–5pm). 🅰 🅱
🏛 **Gasworks Museum**
Gasworks Rd. 〖 01899 221070.
◯ Jun–Sep: 2–5pm daily.

Pentland Hills ㉒

The Lothians. 🚆 Edinburgh, then
bus. 🚩 Regional Park Headquarters,
Biggar Rd, Edinburgh (0131 4453383).

T HE PENTLAND HILLS, stretching for 16 miles (26 km)
southwest of Edinburgh, offer
some of the best hill-walking
country in the Lowlands.
Leisurely walkers can saunter
along the many signposted
footpaths, while the more
adventurous can take the
chairlift at the Hillend dry ski
slope to reach the higher
ground leading to the 493 m
(1,617 ft) hill of Allermuir. Even
more ambitious is the classic
scenic route along the ridge
from Caerketton to West Kip.
　To the east of the A703,
in the lee of the Pentlands,
stands the exquisite and
ornate 15th-century **Rosslyn
Chapel**. It was originally
intended as a church, but
after the death of its founder,
William Sinclair, it was used
as a burial ground for his
descendants. The delicately
wreathed Apprentice Pillar
recalls the legend of the
apprentice carver who was
killed by the master stonemason in a fit of jealousy at
his pupil's superior skill.

🚩 **Rosslyn Chapel**
Roslin. 〖 0131 4402159.
◯ 10am–4pm daily. 🅰 🅱

Details of the decorated vaulting in Rosslyn Chapel

The Classical 18th-century tenements of New Lanark on the banks of the Clyde

New Lanark ㉓

Clyde Valley. 🏔 150. 🚆 🚌 Lanark.
ℹ Horsemarket, Ladyacre Rd
(01555 661661). 🚌 Mon.
🌐 www.seeglasgow.com

Sᴵᴛᴜᴀᴛᴇᴅ ʙʏ ᴛʜᴇ falls of the
River Clyde, the village of
New Lanark was founded in
1785 by the industrial entre-
preneur David Dale. Ideally

DAVID LIVINGSTONE

Scotland's great missionary
doctor and explorer was
born in Blantyre where he
began working life as a
mill boy at the age of ten.
Livingstone (1813–73)
made three epic journeys
across Africa, from 1840,
promoting "commerce and
Christianity". He became
the first European to see
Victoria Falls and died in
1873 while searching for
the source of the Nile. He
is buried in Westminster
Abbey (see pp94–5).

located for the working of its
water-driven mills, the village
had become Britain's largest
cotton producer by 1800.
Dale and his successor, Robert
Owen, were philanthropists
whose reforms proved that
commercial success need not
undermine the wellbeing of
the workforce. Now a museum,
New Lanark is a window on to
working life in the early 19th
century. The **New Millennium
Experience** provides a
special-effects ride through
time, from the life of a mill girl
in 1820 to the 23rd century.

Eɴᴠɪʀᴏɴs: 15 miles (24 km)
north, Blantyre has a memorial to the famous Scottish
explorer David Livingstone.

🏛 New Millennium
Experience
New Lanark Visitor Centre. 📞 01555
661345. 🕐 11am–5pm daily. ⬤ 25
Dec, 1 Jan. 🅿 🛗 🎫 by appt.

Glasgow ㉔

See pp502–7.

Sanquhar ㉕

Dumfries & Galloway. 🏔 2,500. 🚆
🚌 ℹ 64 Whitesands, Dumfries
(01387 253862).

Nᴏᴡ ᴏꜰ ᴄʜɪᴇꜰʟʏ historic
interest, the town of
Sanquhar was famous in the
history of the Covenanters

(see p469). In the 1680s, two
declarations opposing the rule
of bishops were pinned to the
Mercat Cross, the site of which
is now marked by a granite
obelisk. The first protest was
led by a local teacher, Richard
Cameron, whose followers
became the Cameronian regiment. The Georgian **Tolbooth**
was designed by William
Adam (see p534) in 1735 and
houses a local interest museum
and tourist centre. The Post
Office, opened in 1763, is the
oldest in Britain, predating
the mail coach service.

Drumlanrig
Castle ㉖

Thornhill, Dumfries & Galloway. 📞
01848 330248. 🚆 🚌 Dumfries,
then bus. 🕐 May–Aug: 11am–4pm
Mon–Sat, noon–4pm Sun. 🅿 🛗

Rɪsɪɴɢ sQᴜᴀʀᴇʟʏ from a
grassy platform, the
massive fortress-palace of
Drumlanrig (see p473) was
built from pink sandstone
between 1679 and 1691 on the
site of a 15th-century Douglas

**The Baroque front steps and
doorway of Drumlanrig Castle**

stronghold. A formidable multi-turreted exterior contains a priceless collection of art treasures as well as such Jacobite relics as Bonnie Prince Charlie's camp kettle and sash. Hanging within oak-panelled rooms are paintings by da Vinci, Holbein and Rembrandt. The emblem of a crowned and winged heart, shown throughout the castle, recalls Sir James, the "Black Douglas", who bore Robert the Bruce's *(see p468)* heart while on crusade to fulfil a vow made by the king. After being mortally wounded he threw the heart at his enemies with the words "forward brave heart!"

The sturdy island fortress of Threave Castle on the Dee

Threave Castle ⓐ

(NTS) Castle Douglas, Dumfries & Galloway. █ 01556 502611. ▨ *Dumfries.* ◯ *Apr–Sep: 9:30am–6:30pm daily.* ▨

THIS MENACING GIANT of a tower, a 14th-century Black Douglas *(see above)* stronghold standing on an island in the Dee, commands the most complete medieval riverside harbour in Scotland. Douglas's struggles against the early Stewart kings culminated in his surrender here after a two-month siege in 1455 – but only after James II had brought the cannon Mons Meg *(see p492)* to batter the castle. Threave was dismantled after Protestant Covenanters *(see p469)* defeated its Catholic defenders in 1640. Inside the

tower, only the shell of the kitchen, great hall and domestic levels remains. Over the 15th-century doorway is the "gallows knob", a reminder of when the owners are said to have boasted that it never lacked its noose. Access to the castle is by rowing boat.

Whithorn ⓐ

Dumfries & Galloway. ▨ *1,000.* ▨ *Stranraer.* ▨ ▯ *Dashwood Sq, Newton Stewart (01671 402431).* ▨ www.dumfriesandgalloway.co.uk

THE EARLIEST SITE of continuous Christian worship in Scotland, Whithorn (meaning white house) takes its name from the white chapel built here by St Ninian in 397. Though nothing remains of his chapel, a guided tour of the archaeological dig reveals evidence of Northumbrian, Viking and Scottish settlements ranging from the 5th to the 19th centuries. A visitors' centre, **Whithorn: Cradle of Christianity**, provides information on the excavations and contains a collection of carved stones. One, dedicated to Latinus, dates to 450, making it Scotland's earliest Christian monument.

🏛 Whithorn: Cradle of Christianity
The Whithorn Trust, 45–47 George St. █ 01988 500508. ◯ *Apr–Oct: 10:30am–5pm daily.* ▨ ▨ ▨

Culzean Castle ⓐ

See pp508–9.

Robert Burns surrounded by his creations, by an unknown artist

Burns Cottage ⓐ

Alloway, South Ayrshire. █ 01292 443700. ▨ *Ayr, then bus.* ◯ *10am–4pm daily.* ● *25, 26 Dec, 1, 2 Jan.* ▨ ▨ ▨ *by appointment.* ▨ www.robertburns.org

ROBERT BURNS (1759–96), Scotland's favourite poet, was born and spent his first seven years in this small thatched cottage in Alloway. Built by his father, the cottage still contains much of its original furniture. There is also a small museum next door displaying many of Burns' manuscripts along with some early editions of his works. Much of his poem *Tam o' Shanter* (1790) is set in Alloway, which commemorates him with a huge monument on the outskirts of the village.

Burns became a celebrity following the publication in 1786 of the Kilmarnock Edition of his poems. He died at the age of 37 from heart disease. Scots everywhere gather to celebrate Burns Night *(see p65)* on his birthday, 25 January.

SCOTTISH TEXTILES
Weaving in the Scottish Borders goes back to the Middle Ages, when monks from Flanders established a thriving woollen trade with the Continent. Cotton became an important source of wealth in the Clyde Valley during the 19th century, when handloom weaving was overtaken by power-driven mills. The popular Paisley patterns were based on Indian designs.

A colourful pattern from Paisley

Glasgow ㉔

The coat of arms of Glasgow city

Though its Celtic name, *Glas cu*, means "dear green place", Glasgow is more often associated with its industrial past, and once enjoyed the title of Second City of the Empire (after London). Glasgow's architectural standing, as Scotland's finest Victorian city, reflects its era of prosperity, when ironworks, cotton mills and ship-building were fuelled by Lanarkshire coal. The Science Centre now sits on the Clyde's revitalized south bank. Glasgow rivals Edinburgh *(see pp490–97)* in the arts, with galleries such as the Kelvingrove and the Burrell Collection *(see pp506–7).*

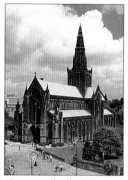

Glasgow's medieval cathedral viewed from the southwest

Exploring Glasgow

With some relics of its grimy industrial past and glossy new image, modern Glasgow is a city of contrasts. The deprived area of the East End, with its busy weekend market, "the Barras", stands by the restored 18th-century Merchant City and Victorian George Square. The more affluent West End pros-pered in the 19th century as a retreat for wealthy merchants escaping the heavily industri-alized Clydeside, and it is here that Glasgow's chief galleries and museums can be found.

South of the river, the Govan and Gorbals districts give way to the Pollok Country Park, site of the Burrell Collection. An underground network provides easy travel around the city.

🏛 Glasgow Cathedral

Cathedral Square. **🔹** 0141 5526891 **◯** Easter–Oct: 9:30am–6pm Mon–Sat, 2–5pm Sun; Nov–Easter: 9:30am–4pm Mon–Sat, 2–4pm Sun. **ᴅ**
As one of the only cathedrals to escape destruction during the Scottish Reformation *(see pp468–9)* – by adapting itself to Protestant worship – this is

a rare example of an almost complete 13th-century church. It was built on the site of a chapel founded by the city's patron saint, St Mungo, a 6th-century bishop of Strathclyde. According to legend, Mungo placed the body of a holy man named Fergus on a cart yoked to two wild bulls, telling them to take it to the place ordained by God. In the "dear green place" at which the bulls stopped he built his church. Because of its sloping site, the cathedral is on two levels.

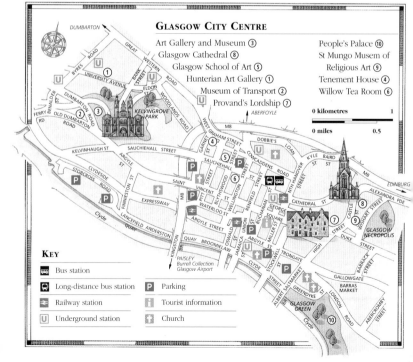

GLASGOW CITY CENTRE

Art Gallery and Museum ③
Glasgow Cathedral ⑧
Glasgow School of Art ⑤
Hunterian Art Gallery ①
Museum of Transport ②
Provand's Lordship ⑦
People's Palace ⑩
St Mungo Musem of Religious Art ⑨
Tenement House ④
Willow Tea Room ⑥

KEY

🚌 Bus station
🚍 Long-distance bus station
🚉 Railway station
Ⓤ Underground station
P Parking
ℹ Tourist information
✝ Church

Situated in the cathedral precinct, this new museum is a world first. The main exhibition illustrates religious themes with superb artifacts, including a 19th-century dancing Shiva and an Islamic painting entitled the *Attributes of Divine Perfection* (1986) by Ahmed Moustafa. An exhibition on religion in Glasgow throws light on the life of the missionary David Livingstone *(see p500)*. Recently moved from the Kelvingrove Art Gallery and Museum *(see p505)*, Salvador Dalí's powerful work *Christ of St John of the Cross* (1951) is now here. Outside you can visit Britain's only permanent Zen Buddhist garden.

Dalí's *Christ of St John of the Cross* at the St Mungo Museum of Religious Life and Art

VISITORS' CHECKLIST

City of Glasgow.  735,000.
Argyle St (Glasgow Central). Buchanan St.
11 George Square (0141 2044400). Sat, Sun.
Mayfest : May; Jazz Festival: July.

The preserved Edwardian kitchen of the Tenement House

The crypt contains the tomb of St Mungo, surrounded by an intricate forest of columns springing up to end in delicately carved rib-vaulting. The Blackadder Aisle, reputed to have been built over a cemetery blessed by St Ninian *(see p501)*, has a ceiling thick with decorative bosses.

St Mungo Museum of Religious Life and Art

2 Castle St. ☎ 0141 5532557. ◯ 10am–5pm daily. ● 25, 26 Dec, 1 Jan. ♿ 📷 by appointment.

Tenement House

(NTS) 145 Buccleuch St.
☎ 0141 3330183. ◯ Mar–Oct: 2–5pm daily. 📷 📷 by appointment.
Less a museum than a time capsule, the Tenement House is an almost undisturbed record of life in a modest Glasgow flat in a tenement estate during the early 20th century. Glasgow owed much of its vitality and neighbourliness to tenement life, though many of these Victorian and Edwardian apartments were to earn a bad name for poverty

and overcrowding, and many have now been pulled down. The Tenement House was first owned by Miss Agnes Toward who lived here from 1911 until 1965. It remained largely unaltered and, since Agnes threw very little away, it is now a treasure-trove of social history. The parlour, previously used only on formal occasions, has afternoon tea laid out on a white lace cloth. The kitchen, with its coal-fired range and box bed, is filled with the tools of a vanished era such as a goffering iron for crisping waffles, a washboard and a stone hot-water bottle.

Agnes's lavender water and medicines are still in the bathroom, as though she had stepped out for a minute 70 years ago, and forgotten to return home.

The Kelvingrove Art Gallery and the Glasgow University buildings, viewed from the south

Glasgow's medieval house, Provand's Lordship

🏵 Provand's Lordship

3 Castle St. [C] 0141 2872699.
[○] 10am–5pm daily (11am Fri & Sun).

Now a museum, Provand's Lordship was built as a canon's house in 1471, and is the city's oldest surviving house. Its low ceilings and austere wooden furnishings create a vivid impression of life in a wealthy 15th-century household. It is thought that Mary, Queen of Scots (see p497)

may have stayed here when she made a visit to Glasgow in 1566 to see her cousin and husband, Lord Darnley.

🏵 Willow Tea Room

217 Sauchiehall St. [C] 0141 332 0521. [○] 9am–5pm Mon–Sat, Sun 1–5pm. [●] public hols, 2 Jan.

This is the sole survivor of a series of delightfully frivolous tea rooms created by Charles Rennie Mackintosh at the turn of the century for the celebrated restaurateur Miss Kate Cranston. Everything from the high-backed chairs to the tables and cutlery was of his own design. In particular, the 1904 Room de Luxe sparkles with eccentricity: striking mauve and silver furniture, coloured glass and a flamboyant leaded door create a remarkable venue in which to enjoy afternoon tea.

Mackintosh's interior of the Willow Tea Room

🏛 Museum of Transport

1 Bunhouse Rd. [C] 0141 2872000.
[○] 10am–5pm Mon–Thu, Sat, 11am–5pm Fri, Sun. [●] 25, 26 Dec, 1 Jan.
[♿] [✉]

Housed in Kelvin Hall, this imaginative museum conveys the optimism and vigour of the city's industrial heyday. Model ships and ranks of gleaming Scottish-built steam engines, cars and motorcycles recall the 19th and early 20th centuries, when Glasgow's supremacy in shipbuilding, trade and manufacturing made her the "second city" of the British Empire. Old Glasgow can be seen through fascinating footage of the town in the cinema and through a reconstruction of a 1938 street, with Art Deco shop fronts, a cinema and an Underground station.

The Museum of Transport's reconstructed 1938 street, with Underground station

⛪ Glasgow Necropolis

Cathedral Sq. [C] 0141 5526891.
[○] daily. [♿] limited.

Behind the cathedral, the reformer John Knox (see p469) surveys the city from his Doric pillar overlooking a Victorian cemetery. It is filled with crumbling monuments to the dead of Glasgow's wealthy merchant families.

CHARLES RENNIE MACKINTOSH

A Mackintosh floral design

Glasgow's most celebrated designer, Charles Rennie Mackintosh (1868–1928), entered Glasgow School of Art at 16. After his first big break with the Willow Tea Room, he became a leading figure in the Art Nouveau movement, developing a unique style that borrowed from Gothic and Scottish Baronial designs. He believed a building should be a fully integrated work of art, creating furniture and fittings that complemented the overall construction. Nowhere is this total design better seen than in the Glasgow School of Art, which he designed in 1896. Unrecognized in his lifetime, Mackintosh's work is now widely imitated. Its characteristic straight lines and flowing detail are the hallmark of early 20th-century Glasgow style, in all fields of design from textiles to architecture.

🏛 People's Palace

Glasgow Green. **[** *0141 5540223.*
🕐 *10am–5pm Mon–Thu, Sat, 11am–*
5pm Fri, Sun. ● *25, 26 Dec, 1 Jan.* &

This Victorian sandstone
structure was purpose-built in
1898 as a cultural museum for
the people of Glasgow's East
End. It houses everything from
temperance tracts to trade-
union banners, suffragette
posters to comedian Billy
Connolly's banana-shaped
boots, providing a social history of the city from the 12th
to the 20th century. A superb
conservatory at the back contains an exotic winter garden.

🏛 Glasgow School of Art

167 Renfrew St. **[** *0141 3534526.*
🕐 *by appointment only.*
🗷 & *limited.* W *www.gsa.ac.uk*

Widely considered to be
Charles Rennie Mackintosh's
greatest architectural work,
the Glasgow School of Art
was built between 1897 and
1909 to a design he submitted
in a competition. It was built
in two periods due to financial
constraints. The later, western
wing displays a softer design
than the more severe eastern
half, built only a few years
earlier and compared by a
contemporary critic to a prison.

A student guide takes you
through the building to the
Furniture Gallery, Board
Room and the Library, the
latter a masterpiece of spatial
composition. Each room is an
exercise in contrasts between
height, light and shade with
innovative details echoing the
architectural themes of the
structure. How much of the
school can be viewed depends
on curricular requirements at
the time of visiting.

🏛 Hunterian Art Gallery

82 Hillhead St. **[** *0141 3305431.*
🕐 *9:30am-5pm Mon–Sat.* ● *24
Dec–5 Jan & public hols.* & *limited.*

Built to house a number of
paintings bequeathed to
Glasgow University by ex-
student and physician Dr
William Hunter (1718–83), the
Hunterian Art Gallery contains
Scotland's largest print collec-
tion and works by major
European artists stretching
back to the 16th century. A
collection of work by Charles
Mackintosh is supplemented

George Henry's *Japanese Lady with a Fan* (1894), Art Gallery and Museum

by a complete reconstruction
of No. 6 Florentine Terrace,
where he lived from 1906 to
1914. A major collection of
19th- and 20th-century Scottish
art includes work by William
McTaggart (1835–1910), but
by far the gallery's most famous collection is of work by
the Paris-trained American
painter, James McNeill
Whistler (1834–1903).

Whistler's *Sketch for Annabel Lee*
(c.1869), Hunterian Art Gallery

🏛 Kelvingrove Art Gallery and Museum

Argyle St, Kelvingrove. **[** *0141 287
2699.* 🕐 *10am–5pm Mon–Thu &
Sat, 11am–5pm Fri & Sun.*
● *25, 26 Dec, 1, 2 Jan.* & 🗷
W *www.glasgow.gov.uk*

An imposing red sandstone
building, Scotland's most
popular gallery houses a magnificent art collection. Best
known for its 17th-century
Dutch and 19th-century French
paintings, the collection began
as the gift of a Glasgow coach-
builder who died in 1854,
leaving works by Botticelli,
Giorgione and Rembrandt.
Prominent among Continental
artists are Degas, Millet and
Monet, while in the Scottish
Gallery, the famous *Massacre
of Glencoe (see p529)* by
James Hamilton (1853–94)
can be seen alongside works
by the Glasgow Boys.

Other exhibitions cover
ceramics, silver, armour and
Scottish geology. The archaeological display has a replica
of the Antonine Wall *(see p44).*

The Georgian Pollok House, viewed from the south

Pollok House ⑰

(NTS) 2060 Pollokshaws Rd. ☎ *(0141) 616 6410.* ○ *Apr–Oct: 10am–5pm daily, Nov–Mar: 11am–4pm daily.* 📷 *Apr–Oct only.*

Pollok house is Glasgow's finest 18th-century domestic building and contains one of Britain's best collections of Spanish paintings. The Neo-Classical central block was finished in 1750, the sobriety of its exterior contrasting with the exuberant plasterwork within. The Maxwells have lived at Pollok since the mid-13th century, but the male line ended with Sir John Maxwell, who added the grand entrance hall in the 1890s and designed most of the terraced gardens and parkland beyond.

Hanging above the family silver, porcelain, hand-painted Chinese wallpaper and Jacobean glass, the Stirling Pollok paintings are strong on British and Dutch schools, including William Blake's *Sir Geoffrey Chaucer and the Nine and Twenty Pilgrims* (1745) as well as William Hogarth's portrait of James Thomson, who wrote the words to *Rule Britannia*.

Spanish 16th- to 19th-century art predominates: El Greco's *Lady in a Fur Wrap* (1541) hangs in the library, while the drawing room contains works by Francisco de Goya and Esteban Murillo. In 1966 Anne Maxwell Macdonald gave the house and 146 ha (361 acres) of parkland to the City of Glasgow. The park provides the site for the city's fascinating Burrell Collection.

Burrell Collection ⑱

Given to the city in 1944 by Sir William Burrell (1861–1958), a wealthy shipping owner, this internationally acclaimed collection is the star of Glasgow's renaissance, with objects of major importance in numerous fields of interest. The building housing these pieces was purpose-built in 1983. When the sun shines in, the stained glass blazes with colour, while the shaded tapestries seem a part of the surrounding woodland.

Figure of a Lohan
This sculpture of Buddha's disciple dates from the Ming Dynasty (1484).

Hutton Castle Drawing Room
This is a reconstruction of the Drawing Room at Burrell's own home – the 16th-century Hutton Castle, near Berwick-upon-Tweed. The Hall and Dining Room can also be seen nearby.

Bull's Head
Dating from the 7th century BC, this bronze head from Turkey was once part of a cauldron handle.

Hornby Portal
This detail shows the arch's heraldic display. The 14th-century portal comes from Hornby Castle in Yorkshire.

Main entrance

Star Exhibits

★ **Stained Glass**

★ **Tapestries**

Rembrandt van Rijn
This self-portrait, signed and dated 1632, has pride of place among the Dutch paintings hanging in the 17th- and 18th-century room.

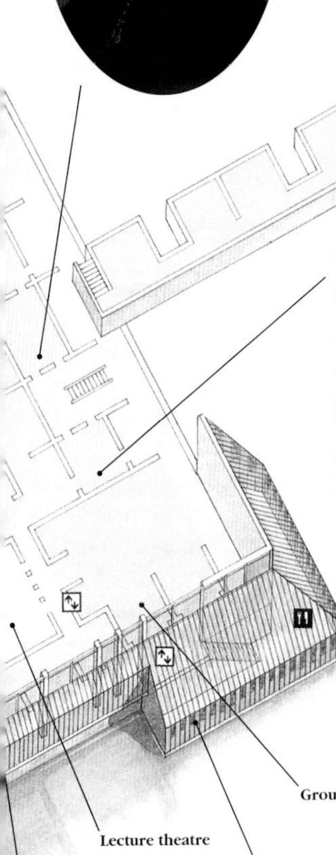

VISITORS' CHECKLIST

2060 Pollokshaws Rd, Glasgow.
☎ (0141) 287 2550. ➾ Pollokshaws West. 🚌 45, 47, 48, 57 from Glasgow. ◷ 10am–5pm Mon–Thu, Sat, 11am–5pm Fri, Sun. 🍴 🛒 🚫 📷 🎥 ♿ 🎁 🏧

Mezzanine floor

GALLERY GUIDE
Except for a mezzanine-floor display of paintings, the exhibitions are on the ground floor. Right of the entrance hall, rooms are devoted to tapestries, stained glass and sculpture, while ancient civilizations, Oriental art and the period galleries are ahead.

KEY TO FLOORPLAN

☐ Ancient civilizations

☐ Oriental art

☐ Medieval and post-medieval European art, stained glass and tapestries

☐ Period galleries

☐ Hutton Castle Rooms

☐ Paintings and drawings

☐ Temporary exhibition area

Matthijs Maris
This popular Dutch painter's ethereal style appealed to late 19th-century tastes. The Sisters (1875) is one of over 50 Maris works acquired by Burrell.

Ground floor

Lecture theatre

★ Stained Glass
A man warming himself before a fire is one of many secular themes illustrated in the stained-glass display. This 15th-century piece once decorated a church in Suffolk.

★ Tapestries
Scenes from the Life of Christ and of the Virgin *(c.1450), a Swiss work in wool, is one of many tapestries on show.*

Culzean Castle 🏰

Robert Adam by George Willison

S TANDING ON A CLIFF'S EDGE in an extensive parkland estate, the 16th-century keep of Culzean (pronounced Cullayn), home of the Earls of Cassillis, was remodelled between 1777 and 1792 by the Neo-Classical architect Robert Adam *(see p24)*. Restored in the 1970s, it is now a major showcase of his later work. The grounds became Scotland's first public country park in 1969 and, with farming flourishing alongside ornamental gardens, they reflect both the leisure and everyday activities of a great country estate.

View of Culzean Castle (c.1815), by Nasmyth

Lord Cassillis' Rooms contain typical mid-18th-century furnishings, including a gentleman's wardrobe of the 1740s.

A PLAN OF CULZEAN CASTLE

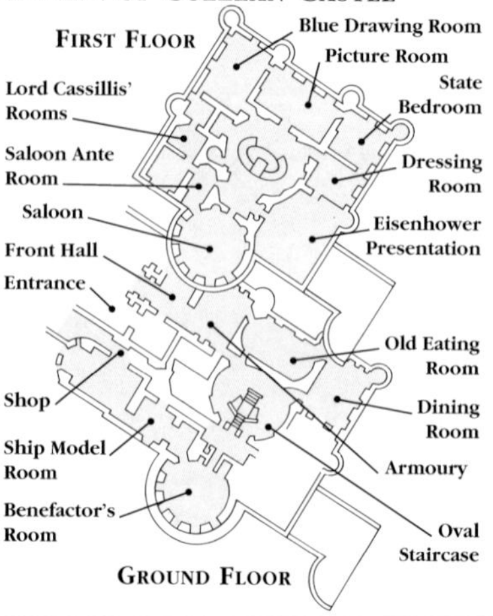

FIRST FLOOR

Blue Drawing Room
Picture Room
State Bedroom
Lord Cassillis' Rooms
Saloon Ante Room
Dressing Room
Saloon
Eisenhower Presentation
Front Hall
Entrance
Old Eating Room
Shop
Dining Room
Ship Model Room
Armoury
Benefactor's Room
Oval Staircase

GROUND FLOOR

The clock tower, fronted by the circular carriageway, was originally the family coach house and stables. The clock was added in the 19th century, and today the buildings are used for residential and educational purposes.

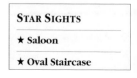

STAR SIGHTS
★ Saloon
★ Oval Staircase

Armoury
On the walls are the bayonet blades and flintlock pistols issued to the West Lowland Fencible Regiment when Napoleon threatened to invade in the early 1800s.

The Eisenhower Presentation honours the general who was given the top floor of Culzean in gratitude for his role in World War II.

VISITORS' CHECKLIST

(NTS) 4 miles (6 km) West of Maybole. 📞 *01655 884400.* 🚌 *Ayr, then bus.* **Castle** ☐ *Apr– Oct: 10am–5:30pm daily (last adm: 5pm).* **Grounds** ☐ *dawn until dusk daily.* ♿ 🅿 🛒 🍴 🚻

Fountain Court
This sunken garden is a good place to begin a tour of the grounds to the east.

Carriageway

★ Saloon
With its restored 18th-century colour scheme and Louis XVI chairs, this elegant saloon perches on the cliff's edge 46 m (150 ft) above the Firth of Clyde. The carpet is a copy of the one designed by Adam.

★ Oval Staircase
Illuminated by an overarching skylight, the staircase, with its Ionic and Corinthian pillars, is considered one of Adam's finest achievements.

THE HIGHLANDS AND ISLANDS

ABERDEENSHIRE · MORAY · ARGYLL & BUTE · PERTH & KINROSS
SHETLAND · ORKNEY · WESTERN ISLES · HIGHLANDS · ANGUS

MOST OF THE STOCK IMAGES *of Scottishness – clans and tartans, whisky and porridge, bagpipes and heather – originate in the Highlands and enrich the popular picture of Scotland as a whole. But for many centuries the Gaelic-speaking, cattle-raising Highlanders had little in common with their southern neighbours.*

Clues to the non-Celtic ancestors of the Highlanders lie scattered across the Highlands and Islands in the form of stone circles, brochs and cairns some over 5,000 years old. By the end of the 6th century, the Gaelic-speaking Celts had arrived from Ireland, along with St Columba who taught Christianity. Its fusion with Viking culture in the 8th and 9th centuries produced St Magnus Cathedral in the Orkney Isles.

For over 1,000 years, Celtic Highland society was founded on a clan system, built on family ties to create loyal groups dependent on a feudal chief.

However, the clans were systematically broken up by England after 1746, following the defeat of the Jacobite attempt on the British crown, led by Bonnie Prince Charlie *(see p521)*. A more romantic vision of the Highlands started in the early 19th century. Its creation was largely due to Sir Walter Scott, whose novels and poetry depicted the majesty and grandeur of a country previously considered merely poverty-stricken and barbaric. Another great popularizer was Queen Victoria, whose passion for Balmoral helped to establish the trend for acquiring Highland sporting estates. But behind the sentimentality lay harsh economic realities that drove generations of Highlanders to seek a new life overseas.

Today, over half the inhabitants of the Highlands and Islands still live in communities of less than 1,000. Oil and tourism have supplemented fishing and whisky as the main businesses and population figures are rising.

A wintry dawn over the Cairngorms, the home of Britain's only herd of reindeer

◁ **The stunningly sited castle of Eilean Donan, Loch Duich in Glen Shiel**

Exploring the Highlands and Islands

To the north and west of Stirling (the historic gateway to the Highlands) lie the magnificent mountains and glens, fretted coastlines and lonely isles that are the epitome of Scottish scenery. Inverness, the Highland capital, makes a good starting point for exploring Loch Ness and the Cairngorms, while Fort William holds the key to Ben Nevis. Inland from Aberdeen lie Royal Deeside and the Spey Valley whisky heartland. The romantic Hebrides can be reached by ferry from Oban or Ullapool.

0 kilometres   25

0 miles   25

Highland cattle grazing on the Isle of Skye

See Also

- **Where to Stay** pp570–73
- **Where to Eat** pp606–7

Getting Around

There are no motorways in the region, though travel by car is made easy by a good system of A roads. Single-track roads predominate on the isles, which are served by a ferry network and a new bridge to Skye. The rail link ends to the west at Kyle of Lochalsh and to the north at Wick and Thurso. There are regular flights from London to Inverness, Aberdeen and Wick.

JOHN O' GROATS 3

WICK

DORNOCH 8

STRATHPEFFER 10 **BLACK ISLE**

ELGIN 16

FORT GEORGE 14

CAWDOR CASTLE 15

CULLODEN 13

INVERNESS 12

LOCH NESS

CAIRNGORMS 23

ABERDEEN 17

ROYAL DEESIDE TOUR 18

BLAIR CASTLE 22

KILLIECRANKIE WALK 21

PITLOCHRY 20

South Esk

DUNKELD 19

Dundee

Stirling **Perth**

Inset map labels:

SHETLAND 1

LERWICK

ORKNEY 2

KIRKWALL

JOHN O' GROATS 3

0 kilometres 50

0 miles 25

KEY

▬▬	Major road
▬▬	Scenic route
- ▬	Scenic path
▬▬	River
☀	Viewpoint

Colour-washed houses at the harbour of Tobermory, Mull

SIGHTS AT A GLANCE

Shetland ①

Shetland. 🏃 23,000. ✈ ⛴ from Aberdeen and Stromness on mainland Orkney. ℹ Lerwick (01595 693434). 🌐 www.shetland-tourism.co.uk

LYING SIX DEGREES SOUTH of the Arctic Circle, the rugged Shetland islands are Britain's most northerly region and were, with Orkney, part of the kingdom of Norway until 1469. In the main town of Lerwick, this Norse heritage is remembered during the ancient midwinter festival Up Helly Aa *(see p466)*, in which costumed revellers set fire to a replica Viking longship. Also in the town, the **Shetland Museum** tells the story of a people dependent on the sea, right up to modern times with the discovery of North Sea oil and gas in the 1970s.

One of Shetland's greatest treasures is the Iron Age tower, **Mousa Broch**, which can be visited on its isle by boat from Sandwick. There is more ancient history at Jarlshof where a museum explains the sprawling sea-front ruins which span 3,000 years.

A boat from Lerwick sails to the isle of Noss where grey seals bask beneath sandstone cliffs crowded with Shetland's seabirds – a spectacle best seen between May and June.

🏛 **Shetland Museum**
The Hillhead, Lerwick. 📞 01595 695057. 🕐 10am–5pm Mon–Sat. ⬤ 23–26 Dec, 1, 2 Jan, local hols. ♿

Orkney ②

Orkney. 🏃 19,800. ✈ ⛴ from John o'Groats (summer only), Scrabster, Aberdeen. ℹ Broad St, Kirkwall (01856 872856). 🌐 www.orkney.com

THE FERTILE ISLES of Orkney are remarkable for the wealth of prehistoric monuments which place them among Europe's most treasured archaeological sites. In the town of Kirkwall, the sandstone **St Magnus Cathedral** stands amid a charming core of narrow streets. Its many interesting tombs include that of its 12th-century patron saint. Nearby, the early 17th-century

---

THE SHETLAND SEABIRD ISLES

As seabirds spend most of their time away from land, nesting is a vulnerable period in their lives. The security provided by the inaccessible cliffs at such sites as Noss and Hermaness on Unst finds favour with thousands of migrant and local birds.

Puffin

Great Skua

Fulmar

Black Guillemot

Razorbills

Herring Gull

Earl's Palace is widely held to be one of Scotland's finest Renaissance buildings. To the west of Kirkwall lies Britain's most impressive chambered tomb, the cairn of **Maes Howe**. Dating from 2000 BC, the tomb has runic graffiti on its walls believed to have been left by Norsemen returning from the crusades in 1150.

Nearby, the great **Standing Stones of Stenness** may have been associated with Maes Howe rituals, though these still remain a mystery. Further west, on a bleak heath, stands the Bronze Age **Ring of Brodgar**.

Another archaeological treasure can be found in the Bay of Skail – the complete Stone Age village of **Skara Brae**. It was unearthed by a storm in 1850, after lying buried for 4,500 years. Further south, the town of Stromness was a vital

The Norman façade of the St Magnus Cathedral, Orkney

centre of Scotland's herring industry in the 18th century. Its story is told in the local museum, while the **Pier Arts Centre** displays work by British artists and holds regular exhibitions of international art.

🏛 **Earl's Palace**
Palace Rd, Kirkwall. 📞 0131 668 8800. 🕐 Apr–Sep: 9:30am–6:30pm daily. 🎫 ♿ limited.

🏛 **Pier Arts Centre**
Victoria St, Stromness. 📞 01856 850209. 🕐 10:30am–5pm Tue–Sat. ⬤ 24 Dec–10 Jan. ♿ limited.

John o'Groats ③

Highland. 🏃 500. ✈ 🚌 🚗 Wick ⛴ May–Sep: John o'Groats to Burwick, Orkney. ℹ John o'Groats (01955 611373).

SOME 876 miles (1,409 km) north from Land's End, Britain's most northeasterly mainland village faces Orkney, 8 miles (13 km) across the turbulent Pentland Firth. The village takes its name from a 15th-century Dutchman John de Groot, who, to avoid accusations of favouritism, is said to have built an octagonal house here with one door for each of his eight heirs. The spectacular cliffs and rock stacks of Duncansby Head lie a few miles further east.

Western Isles

WESTERN SCOTLAND ENDS with this remote chain of islands, made of some of the oldest rock on Earth. Almost treeless landscapes are divided by countless waterways, the western, windward coasts edged by miles of white sandy beaches. For centuries, the eastern shores, composed largely of peat bogs, have provided the islanders with fuel. Man has been here for 6,000 years, living off the sea and the thin turf, though such monuments as an abandoned Norwegian whaling station on Harris attest to the difficulties in commercializing the islanders' traditional skills. Gaelic, part of an enduring culture, is widely spoken.

The Black House Museum, a traditional croft on Lewis

The monumental Standing Stones of Callanish in northern Lewis

Lewis and Harris

Western Isles. 🏔 22,000. ✈ Stornoway. ⛴ Uig (Skye), Ullapool, Kyle of Lochalsh. 🛈 26 Cromwell St, Stornoway (01851 703088). **Black House Museum** 📞 01851 710395. ⭘ Mon–Sat. ⬤ public hols. ♿ ▣

Forming the largest landmass of the Western Isles, Lewis and Harris are a single island, though Gaelic dialects differ between the two areas. From the administrative centre of **Stornoway**, with its bustling harbour and colourful house fronts, the ancient **Standing Stones of Callanish** are only 16 miles (26 km) to the west. Just off the road on the way to Callanish are the ruins of **Carloway Broch**, a Pictish (*see p468*) tower over 2,000 years old. The more recent past can be explored at Arnol's **Black House Museum** – a showcase of crofting life as it was until only 50 years ago.

South of the rolling peat moors of Lewis, a range of mountains marks the border with Harris, which one enters as one passes Aline Lodge at the head of Loch Seaforth. Only a little less spectacular than the "Munros" (peaks over 914 m; 3,000 ft) of the mainland and the Isle of Skye

(*see pp520–21*), the mountains of Harris are a paradise for the hillwalker and, from their summits on a clear day, the distant Isle of St Kilda can be seen 50 miles (80 km) to the west.

The ferry port of Tarbert stands on a slim isthmus separating North and South Harris. The tourist office provides addresses for local weavers of the tough Harris Tweed. Some still use plants to make their dyes.

From the port of Leverburgh, close to the southern tip of Harris, a ferry can be taken to the isle of North Uist, where a causeway has been built to Berneray.

The Uists, Benbecula and Barra

Western Isles. 🏔 7,200. ✈ Barra, Benbecula. ⛴ From Uig (Skye), Oban & Mallaig. 🚇 ⛴ Oban, Mallaig, Kyle of Lochalsh. 🛈 26 Cromwell St, Stornoway, Lewis (01851 703088).

After the dramatic scenery of Harris, the lower-lying, largely waterlogged southern isles may seem an anticlimax, though they nurture secrets well worth discovering. Long, white, sandy beaches fringe the Atlantic coast, edged with one of Scotland's natural treasures: the lime-rich soil known as *machair*. During the summer months, the soil is covered with wild flowers, the fragrance of which can be smelled far out to sea.

From **Lochmaddy**, North Uist's main village, the A867 crosses 3 miles (5 km) of causeway to Benbecula, the isle from which the brave Flora MacDonald smuggled Bonnie Prince Charlie (*see p521*) to Skye. Another causeway leads to South Uist, with its golden beaches renowned as a National Scenic Area. From Lochboisdale, a ferry sails to the tiny isle of Barra. The ferry docks in Castlebay, affording an unforgettable view of **Kisimul Castle**, the ancestral stronghold of the MacNeils of Barra.

The remote and sandy shores of South Uist

The western side of the Five Sisters of Kintail, seen from above Loch Duich

Skye **❺**

See pp520–1.

The Five Sisters **❻**

Skye & Lochalsh. ⟲ *Kyle of Lochalsh.* ⬚ *Glenshiel.* ⓘ *Bayfield House, Bayfield Lane, Portree, Isle of Skye (01478 612137).*

DOMINATING one of Scotland's most haunting regions, the awesome summits of the Five Sisters of Kintail rear into view at the northern end of Loch Cluanie as the A87 enters Glen Shiel. The **Visitor Centre** at Morvich offers ranger-led excursions in the summer. Further west, the road passes **Eilean Donan Castle**, connected by a bridge. A Jacobite *(see p523)* stronghold, it was destroyed in 1719 by English warships. In the 19th century it was restored and now contains Jacobite relics.

♠ **Eilean Donan Castle**
Off A87, nr Dornie. ⓒ *01599 555202.* ◯ *Apr–Oct: 10am–5pm daily.* 📷

Wester Ross **❼**

Ross & Cromarty. ⟲ *Achnasheen, Strathcarron.* ⓘ *Gairloch (01445 712130).*

LEAVING LOCH CARRON to the south, the A890 suddenly enters the northern Highlands and the great wilderness of Wester Ross. The Torridon

Estate includes some of the oldest mountains on Earth (Torridonian rock is over 600 million years old), and is home to red deer, wild cats and wild goats. Peregrine falcons and golden eagles nest in the towering sandstone mass of Liathach, above the village of Torridon with its breathtaking views over Applecross to Skye. The **Torridon Countryside Centre** provides guided walks in season and essential information on the natural history of the region.

To the north, the A832 cuts through the Beinn Eighe National Nature Reserve in which remnants of the ancient Caledonian pine forest still stand on the banks and isles of Loch Maree.

Along the coast, exotic gardens thrive in the warming currents of the Gulf Stream, most impressive being **Inverewe Garden** created in 1862 by Osgood Mackenzie (1842–1922). May and June are the months to see the display of

Typical Torridonian mountian scenery in the Wester Ross

rhododendrons and azaleas; July and August for the herbaceous borders.

🏛 **Torridon Countryside Centre**
(NTS) Torridon. ⓒ *01445 791221.* ◯ *May–Sep: 10am–5pm Mon–Sat, 2–5pm Sun.* 📷 ♿
♣ **Inverewe Garden**
(NTS) off A832, nr Poolewe. ⓒ *01445 781200.* ◯ *mid-Mar–Oct: 9:30am–dusk daily.* 📷 ♿

Dornoch **❽**

Sutherland. 🏔 *2,200.* ⟲ *Golspie, Tain.* ⓘ *The Square, Dornoch (01862 810400).*

WITH ITS FIRST-CLASS golf course and extensive sandy beaches, **Dornoch** is a popular holiday resort, though it has retained a peaceful atmosphere. Now the parish church, the medieval cathedral was all but destroyed in a clan dispute in 1570; it was finally restored in the 1920s for its 700th anniversary. A stone at the beach end of River Street marks the place where Janet Horne, the last woman to be tried in Scotland for witchcraft, was executed in 1722.

ENVIRONS: Twelve miles (19 km) northeast of Dornoch is the stately Victorianized pile of **Dunrobin Castle**, magnificently situated in a great park with formal gardens overlooking the sea. Since the 13th century, this has been the seat of the Earls of Sutherland.

Many of its rooms are open to visitors. A steam-powered fire engine is among the miscellany of objects on display.

South of Dornoch stands the town of **Tain**. Though patronized by medieval kings as a place of pilgrimage, it became an administrative centre of the Highland Clearances. All is explained in the heritage centre, **Tain Through Time**.

⚓ **Dunrobin Castle**
Nr Golspie. **(** 01408 633177.
🕐 Apr–mid-Oct: 10:30am–4:30pm, noon–4:30pm Sun. 📷
🏛 **Tain Through Time**
Tower St. **(** 01862 894089.
🕐 Apr–Oct: 10am–5pm Mon–Sat, 2–5pm Sun; Nov–Mar: by appointment only. 📷 ♿

The serene cathedral precinct in the town of Dornoch

Strathpeffer ❾

Ross & Cromarty. 🏔 1,400. 🚆 Dingwall. 🚌 Inverness. 🛈 North Kessock (01463 731505).

Sᴛᴀɴᴅɪɴɢ 5 miles (8 km) east of the Falls of Rogie, the popular town of Strathpeffer still has the refined charm for which it was well known in Victorian times, when it flourished as a spa and health resort. The town's grand hotels and gracious layout recall the days when European royalty flocked to the chalybeate- and sulphur-laden springs, which were believed to help tuberculosis. The water can still be sampled at the **Water Tasting Pavilion**.

🚰 **Water Tasting Pavilion**
The Square. 🕐 Easter–Oct: 9am–5pm daily.

The shores of the Black Isle in the Moray Firth

The Black Isle ❿

Ross & Cromarty. 🚆 🚌 Inverness.
🛈 North Kessock (01463 731505).

Tʜᴏᴜɢʜ ᴛʜᴇ ᴅʀɪʟʟɪɴɢ platforms in the Cromarty Firth are reminders of how oil has changed the local economy, the peninsula of the Black Isle is still largely composed of farmland and fishing villages. The town of **Cromarty** was an important port in the 18th century, with thriving rope and lace industries. Many of its merchant houses still stand; the award-winning museum in the **Cromarty Courthouse** provides heritage tours of the town. The thatched **Hugh Miller's Cottage** is a museum to the theologian and geologist Hugh Miller (1802–56), who was born here.
Fortrose boasts a ruined 14th-century cathedral, while a stone on Chanonry Point commemorates the Brahan Seer, a 17th-century prophet burnt alive in a tar barrel by the Countess of Seaforth after he foresaw her husband's infidelity. For local archaeology, visit **Groam House Museum** in Rosemarkie.

🏛 **Cromarty Courthouse**
Church St, Cromarty. **(** 01381 600418. 🕐 Apr–Oct: 10am–5pm daily; Nov–Mar: noon–4pm daily. ⬤ 23 Dec–25 Feb. 📷
🏚 **Hugh Miller's Cottage**
(NTS) Church St, Cromarty. **(** 01381 600245. 🕐 May–Sep: 11am–5pm daily (Sun: 2–5pm). 📷 ♿ limited.
🏛 **Groam House Museum**
High St, Rosemarkie. **(** 01381 620961. 🕐 May–Sep: 10am–5pm daily (Sun: 2–4:30pm); Oct–Apr: Sat & Sun (pm). 📷 ♿ ground floor only.

Tʜᴇ Hɪɢʜʟᴀɴᴅ Cʟᴇᴀʀᴀɴᴄᴇs

During the heyday of the clan system (see p470) tenants paid their clan chiefs rent for their land in the form of military service. However, with the decline of the clan system after the Battle of Culloden (see p523) and the coming of sheep from the borders, landowners were able to command a financial rent their tenants were unable to afford and the land was bought up by Lowland and English farmers. In what became known as "the year of the sheep" (1792), thousands of tenants were evicted to make way for sheep. Many emigrated to Australia, America and Canada. Ruins of their crofts can still be seen in Sutherland and Wester Ross.

The Last of the Clan **(1865) by Thomas Faed**

Isle of Skye ❸⑥

**Otter by the coast
at Kylerhea**

THE LARGEST of the Inner Hebrides, Skye can be reached by the bridge linking Kyle of Lochalsh and Kyleakin. A turbulent geological history has given the island some of Britain's most varied and dramatic scenery. From the rugged volcanic plateau of northern Skye to the ice-sculpted peaks of the Cuillins, the island is divided by numerous sea lochs, leaving the traveller never more than 8 km (5 miles) from the sea. Limestone grasslands predominate in the south, where the hillsides, home of sheep and cattle, are scattered with the ruins of crofts abandoned during the Clearances *(see p517)*. Historically, Skye is best known for its association with Bonnie Prince Charlie.

Skeabost has the ruins of a chapel which is associated with St Columba. Medieval tombstones can be found in the graveyard.

Grave of Flora MacDonald

WESTERN ISLE

LOCH SNIZORT

• Lusta

B886

• Milovaig

A850

B884

ℹ️ Dunvegan

A863

S

0 kilometres   10

0 miles   5

Portnalong

▲ Talisker

B8009

Dunvegan Castle
For over seven centuries, Dunvegan Castle has been the seat of the chiefs of the Clan Mac-Leod. It contains the Fairy Flag, a fabled piece of magical silk treasured for its protection.

The Talisker distillery produces one of the best Highland malts, often described as "the lava of the Cuillins".

Cuillins
Britain's finest mountain range is within walking distance of Sligachan, and in summer a boat sails from Elgol to the desolate inner sanctuary of Loch Coruisk. As he fled across the surrounding moorland, Bonnie Prince Charlie is said to have claimed: "even the Devil shall not follow me here!"

KEY

ℹ️	Tourist information
▰▰	Major road
▱▱	Minor road
═	Narrow lane
❋	Viewpoint

◁ **Dawn over the desolate tablelands of northern Skye, viewed from the Quiraing**

Quiraing
A series of landslides has exposed the roots of this volcanic plateau, revealing a fantastic terrain of spikes and towers. They are easily explored off the Uig to Staffin road.

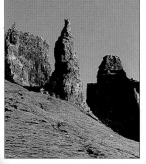

VISITORS' CHECKLIST

The Highlands. 10,000. *Kyle of Lochalsh.* *Portree.* *from Mallaig or Glenelg.* *Bayfield House, Portree (01478) 612137.* www.host.co.uk
Dunvegan Castle, *Dunvegan.* *(01470) 521206.* *daily.* *limited.* **Armadale Castle**, *Armadale.* *(01471) 844227.* *Apr–Oct: daily (gardens open all year).*
Talisker Distillery, *Carbost.* *(01478) 614308.* *Jul–Sep: Mon–Sat.* *limited.*

Staffin
SOUND OF RAASAY
RAASAY
A855
B883
Sconser
SCALPAY
Luib
A87
Broadford
Kilchrist
Kyleakin
A87
KYLE OF LOCHALSH
B8083
Kylerhea
LOCH EISHORT
A851
Armadale
MALLAIG

Kilt Rock

The Storr
The erosion of this basalt plateau has created the Old Man of Storr, a monolith rising to 49 m (160 ft) by the Portree road.

Portree
With its colourful harbour, Portree (meaning "port of the king") is Skye's metropolis. It received its name after a visit by James V in 1540.

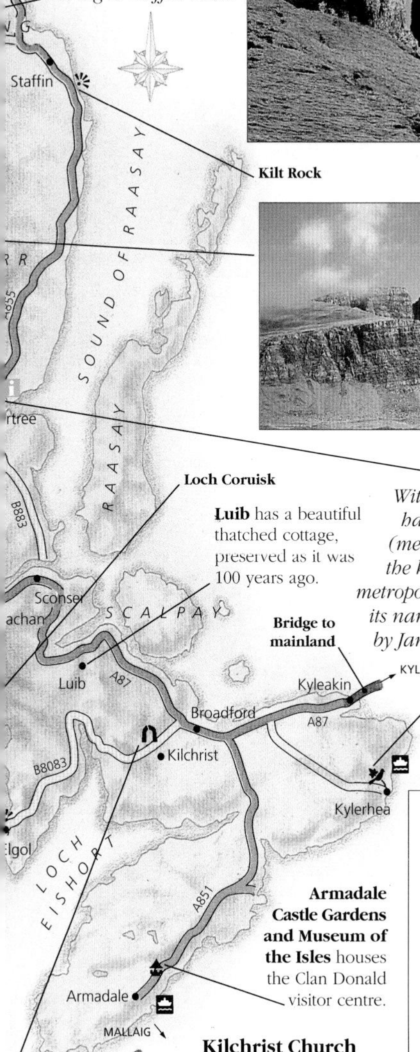

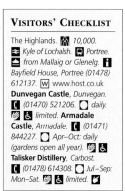

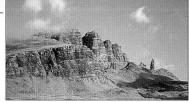

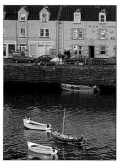

Loch Coruisk

Luib has a beautiful thatched cottage, preserved as it was 100 years ago.

Bridge to mainland

Otters can be seen from the haven in Kylerhea.

Armadale Castle Gardens and Museum of the Isles houses the Clan Donald visitor centre.

Kilchrist Church
This ruined pre-Reformation church's last service was held in 1843. It once served Skye's most populated areas, though the surrounding moors are now deserted.

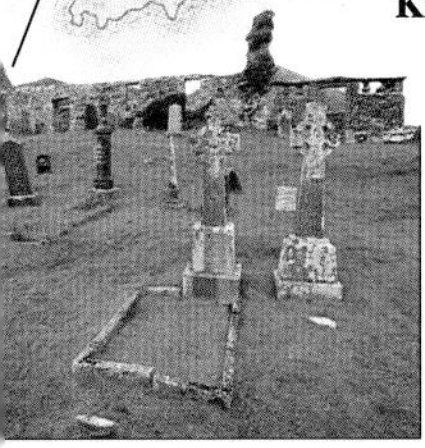

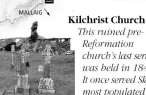

BONNIE PRINCE CHARLIE

The last of the Stuart claimants to the Crown, Charles Edward Stuart (1720–88), came to Scotland from France in 1745 to win the throne. After marching as far as Derby, his army was driven back to Culloden where it was defeated. Hounded for five months through the Highlands, he escaped to Skye, disguised as the maidservant of a woman called Flora MacDonald, from Uist. From the mainland, he sailed to France in September 1746, and died in Rome. Flora was buried in 1790 at Kilmuir, on Skye, wrapped in a sheet taken from the bed of the "bonnie" (handsome) prince.

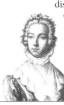

The prince, disguised as a maidservant

The ruins of Urquhart Castle on the western shore of Loch Ness

Loch Ness ⓫

Inverness. ⚅ 🏠 *Inverness.*
ℹ *Castle Wynd, Inverness (01463 234353).*

AT 24 MILES (39 km) long, one mile (1.5 km) at its widest and up to 305 m (1,000 ft) deep, **Loch Ness** fills the northern half of the Great Glen fault from Fort William to Inverness. It is joined to lochs Oich and Lochy by the 22 mile (35 km) Caledonian Canal, designed by Thomas Telford *(see p433).* On the western shore, the A82 passes the ruins of the 16th-century **Urquhart Castle**, which was blown up by government supporters in 1692 to prevent it falling into Jacobite hands. A short distance to the west, **The Official Loch Ness Exhibition Centre** provides a wealth of audio-visual information.

♣ Urquhart Castle
Nr Drumnadrochit. 📞
01456 450551. ⏱
Easter–Oct: 9:30am–6pm; Nov–Easter: 9:30am–4pm daily. ⬤
25, 26 Dec, 1, 2 Jan. 📷

🏛 The Official Loch Ness Exhibition Centre
Drumnadrochit. 📞 *01456 450573.* ⏱ *Apr–May: 9am–6pm; Jun–Oct: 9am–8pm; Nov–Mar: 10am–4pm daily.* ⬤ *25 Dec.* 📷 ♿

THE LOCH NESS MONSTER

First sighted by St Columba in the 6th century, "Nessie" has attracted increasing attention since ambiguous photographs were taken in the 1930s. Though serious investigation is often undermined by hoaxers, sonar techniques continue to yield enigmatic results: plesiosaurs, giant eels and too much whisky are the most popular explanations. Nessie appears to have a close relative in the waters of Loch Morar *(see p532).*

Inverness ⓬

Highland. 🏔 60,000. ⚅ 🏠
ℹ *Castle Wynd (01463 234353).*
🅦 *www.host.co.uk*

AS THE HIGHLAND capital, Inverness makes an ideal base from which to explore the surrounding countryside. The Victorian castle dominates the town centre, the oldest buildings of which are found in nearby Church Street. Today the castle is used as law courts. The **Inverness Museum and Art Gallery** provides a good introduction to the history of the Highlands with exhibits including a lock of Bonnie Prince Charlie's *(see p521)* hair and a fine collection of Inverness silver. The **Scottish Kiltmaker Visitor Centre** explores the history and tradition of Scottish kilts as well as workshops, while those in search of tartans and knitwear should visit the **James Pringle Weavers of Inverness**. **Jacobite Cruises** runs regular summer cruises along the Caledonian Canal and on to Loch Ness. The unfolding scenery makes this a most pleasant and tranquil way to spend a sunny afternoon.

Kilt maker with royal Stuart tartan

🏛 Museum and Art Gallery
Castle Wynd. 📞 *01463 237114.* ⏱ *9am–5pm Mon–Sat.* ⬤ *25, 26 Dec, 1, 2 Jan.* ♿

🏠 James Pringle Weavers of Inverness
Holm Woollen Mill, Dores Rd. 📞 *01463 223311.* ⏱ *9am–5pm Mon–Sat, 11am–4pm Sun.* ⬤ *25 Dec, 1 Jan.* ♿

🏛 Scottish Kiltmaker Visitor Centre
Huntly St. 📞 *01463 222781.* ⏱ *9am–5pm daily.* ⬤ *25 Dec, 1 Jan.* 📷

Jacobite Cruises
Glenurquhart Road. 📞 *01463 233999.* ⏱ *Easter–Oct: daily.* 📷 ♿

Culloden ⑬

(NTS) Inverness. 🚻 🏛 *Inverness.*

A DESOLATE STRETCH of moorland, Culloden looks much as it did on 16 April 1746, the date of the last battle to be fought on British soil *(see p469)*. Here the Jacobite cause, with Bonnie Prince Charlie's *(see p521)* leadership, finally perished under the onslaught of Hanoverian troops led by the Duke of Cumberland. All is explained, with audiovisual displays, in the excellent **NTS Visitor Centre**.

ENVIRONS: Signposted for a mile (1.5 km) or so east are the outstanding Neolithic burial sites, the **Clava Cairns**.

🛈 **NTS Visitor Centre**
On the B9006 east of Inverness.
☎ 01463 790607. ⬤ Apr–Oct:
9am–6pm; Nov–Mar: 10am–4pm
daily. ⬤ Jan. 🏛 🖋 ♿

Fort George ⑭

Inverness. ☎ 01667 462777.
🚻 🏛 Inverness, Nairn. ⬤ 9:30am–
6:30pm Mon–Sat, 2–5pm Sun.
⬤ 25, 26 Dec, 1, 2 Jan. 🏛 🖋 ♿
🌐 www.historicscotland.co.uk

O NE OF THE FINEST works of European military architecture, Fort George stands on a windswept promontory jutting into the Moray Firth, ideally located to suppress the Highlands. Completed in 1769, the fort was built after the Jacobite risings to discourage further rebellion in the Highlands and has remained a military garrison ever since.

(see p53)

THE JACOBITE MOVEMENT

The first Jacobites (mainly Catholic Highlanders) were the supporters of James II of England (James VII of Scotland) who was deposed by the "Glorious Revolution" of 1688 *(see p53)*. With the Protestant William of Orange on the throne, the Jacobites' desire to restore the Stuart monarchy led to the uprisings of 1715 and 1745. The first, in support of James VIII, the "Old Pretender", ended

James II, by Samuel Cooper (1609–72)

at the Battle of Sheriffmuir (1715). The failure of the second uprising, with the defeat at Culloden, saw the end of Jacobite hopes and led to the end of the clan system and the suppression of Highland culture for over a century *(see p471)*.

The drawbridge on the eastern side of Cawdor Castle

The Fort houses the **Regimental Museum** of the Queen's Own Highlanders, and some of its barrack rooms reconstruct the conditions of the common soldiers stationed here more than 200 years ago. The **Grand Magazine** contains an outstanding collection of arms and military equipment. The battlements also make an excellent place from which to watch dolphins in the Moray Firth.

Cawdor Castle ⑮

On B9090 (off A96). ☎ 01667
404615. 🚻 Nairn, then bus.
🚌 from Inverness. ⬤ May–mid-Oct:
10am–5pm daily. 🖋 ♿ gardens &
ground floor only.
🌐 www.cawdorcastle.com

W ITH ITS TURRETED central tower, moat and drawbridge, Cawdor Castle is one of the most romantic stately homes in the Highlands. Though the castle is famed for being the 11th-century home of Shakespeare's *(see p310)* Macbeth and the scene of his murder of King Duncan, it is not historically proven that either came here.

An ancient holly tree preserved in the vaults is said to be the one under which, in 1372, Thane William's donkey, laden with gold, stopped for a rest during its master's search for a place to build a fortress. According to legend, this was how the site for the castle was chosen. Now, after 600 years of continuous occupation (it is still the home of the Thanes of Cawdor) the house is a treasury of family history, containing a number of rare tapestries and portraits by the 18th-century painters Joshua Reynolds (1723–92) and George Romney (1734–1802). Furniture in the Pink Bedroom and Woodcock Room includes work by Chippendale and Sheraton. In the Old Kitchen, the huge Victorian cooking range stands as a shrine to below-stairs drudgery. The grounds provide nature trails and a nine-hole golf course.

A contemporary picture, *The Battle of Culloden* (1746), by D Campbell

Elgin ⓰

Moray. 🅐 25,000. 🚉 🚏
ℹ️ 17 High St, Moray (01343 542666).

WITH ITS COBBLED market-
place and crooked lanes,
the popular holiday centre of
Elgin still retains much of its
medieval layout. The 13th-
century **cathedral** ruins next
to King Street are all that
remain of one of Scotland's
architectural triumphs, the
design of its tiered windows
reminiscent of the cathedral at
St Andrews (*see p485*). Once
known as the Lantern of the
North, the cathedral was
severely damaged in 1390 by
the Wolf of Badenoch (the son
of Robert II) in revenge for
his excommunication by the
Bishop of Moray. Even worse
damage came in 1576 when
the Regent Moray ordered the
stripping of its lead roofing.
Among its outstanding re-
mains is a Pictish cross-slab in
the nave, and a basin in a

**Details of the central tower of
Elgin Cathedral**

corner where one of Elgin's
benefactors, Andrew
Anderson, was kept as a
baby by his homeless mother.
As well as local history, the
Elgin Museum has anthropo-
logical and geological displays,
while the **Moray Motor
Museum** has over 40 vehicles.

🏛 **Elgin Museum**
1 High St. 📞 01343 543675.
🕐 Easter–Oct: 10am–5pm daily
(Sun: pm). 🚫 ♿
🏛 **Moray Motor Museum**
Bridge St, Bishopmill. 📞 01343
544933. 🕐 Easter–Oct: 11am–5pm
daily. 🚫 ♿

Aberdeen ⓱

SCOTLAND'S THIRD LARGEST CITY and Europe's offshore
oil capital, Aberdeen has prospered since the discovery of petroleum in the North Sea in 1970. The sea bed
has now yielded 50 oilfields. Widely known as the Granite
City, its rugged outlines are softened by sumptuous
year-round floral displays in its public parks and gardens,
the Duthie Park Winter Gardens being the largest indoor
garden in Europe. The harbour, now primarily supporting
offshore oil activities, is at its best early in the morning
during the auctions at Scotland's largest fish market.

The spires of Aberdeen, rising behind the city harbour

Exploring Aberdeen
The city centre flanks the mile-
long (1.5 km) Union Street
ending to the east at the Mercat
Cross. The cross stands by
Castlegate, the one-time site
of the city castle, now only a
marketplace. From here the
cobbled Shiprow winds southwest and passes Provost Ross's
House (*see p526*) on its way to
the harbour with its fish market. A bus can be taken a mile
(1.5 km) north of the centre to
Old Aberdeen which, with its
medieval streets and wynds,
has the peaceful character of
a separate village. Driving is
restricted in some streets.

🏫 King's College
College Bounds, Old Aberdeen.
📞 01224 273702. 🕐 10am–5pm
Mon-Sat, noon–5pm Sun. ● 24
Dec–3 Jan. ♿
Founded in 1495 as the city's
first university, the college
now has a Visitor Centre. The
inter-denominational chapel,
in the past consecutively
Catholic and Protestant, has a
lantern tower rebuilt after a
storm in 1633. Stained-glass
windows by Douglas Strachan
add a contemporary touch to
the interior which contains a
1540 pulpit, later carved with
heads of Stuart monarchs.

🛐 St Andrew's Cathedral
King St. 📞 01224 640290.
🕐 May–Sep: 10am–4pm Mon–Sat.
♿ 🎫 by appointment.
The Mother Church of the
Episcopal Communion in
America, St Andrew's has a
memorial to Samuel Seabury,
the first Episcopalian bishop
in the United States, who was
consecrated in Aberdeen in
1784. Coats of arms adorn the
ceiling above the north and
south aisles, contrasting col-
ourfully with the white walls
and pillars. They represent
the American States and local
Jacobite (*see p523*) families.

**The elegant lantern tower of the
chapel at King's College**

PROVOST SKENE'S HOUSE

Guestrow. ☎ 01224 641086. ◯ 10am–5pm Mon–Sat, 1–4pm Sun.
● 25, 26, 31 Dec–2 Jan. ⧉ W www.agm.co.uk

Once the home of Sir George Skene, a 17th-century provost
(mayor) of Aberdeen, the house was built in 1545. Inside, period
rooms span 200 years of design. The Duke of Cumberland
stayed here before the Battle of Culloden *(see p523)*.

VISITORS' CHECKLIST

City of Aberdeen. 👥 220,000.
✈ 8 miles (13 km) NW Aberdeen.
🚌 🚍 Guild St. ℹ Broad St
(01224 632727). 🗓 Thu, Fri, Sat.

The 18th-century Parlour,
with its walnut harpsichord and
covered chairs by the fire, was
the informal room in which the
family would have tea.

The Regency Room typifies
early 19th-century elegance. A
harp dating from 1820 stands
by a Grecian-style sofa and a
French writing table.

The Painted Gallery has
one of Scotland's most important cycles of religious art. The
panels are early 17th century,
though the artist is unknown.

The 17th-century Great Hall
contains heavy oak dining
furniture. Provost Skene's
wood-carved coat of arms
hangs above the fireplace.

The Georgian Dining Room,
with its Classical design, was
the main formal room in the
16th century and still has its
original flagstone floor.

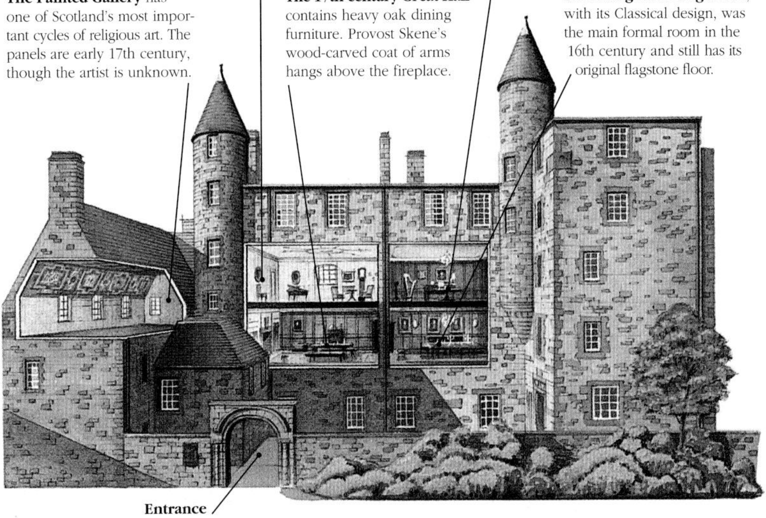

Entrance

ABERDEEN CITY CENTRE

Aberdeen Art Gallery ①
St Andrew's Cathedral ⑤
Fish Market ⑧
Marischal College ④
Maritime Museum ⑦
Mercat Cross ⑥
Provost Skene's
House ③
St Nicholas
Kirk ②

KEY

🚍 Long-distance bus station
🚆 Railway station
⚓ Ferry service
🅿 Parking
ℹ Tourist information
✝ Church

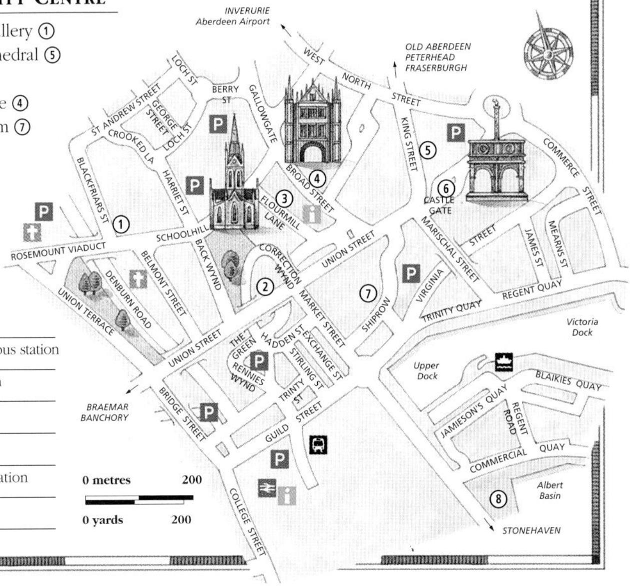

0 metres 200
0 yards 200

🏛 Art Gallery

Schoolhill. ☎ 01224 523700.
🕐 10am–5pm Mon–Sat, 2–5pm Sun.
● 25 Dec–2 Jan. ♿
🌐 www.aberdeen.net-uk

Housed in a Neo-Classical building, purpose-built in 1884, the Art Gallery has a wide range of exhibitions, with an emphasis on contemporary work. A fine collection of Aberdonian silver can be found among the decorative arts on the ground floor, and is the subject of a video presentation.
A permanent collection of 18th–20th-century fine art features such names as Toulouse-Lautrec, Reynolds and Zoffany. Several of the works were bequeathed in 1900 by a local granite merchant, Alex Macdonald. He commissioned many of

Aberdonian silver in the Art Gallery

the paintings in the Macdonald Room, which displays 92 self-portraits by British artists. Occasional poetry-readings, music recitals and films are on offer.

🔒 St Nicholas Kirk

Union St. 🕐 May–Sep: 10am–4pm
daily; Oct–Apr: Mon–Fri (am). ♿

Founded in the 12th century, St Nicholas is Scotland's largest parish church. Though the present structure dates from 1752, many relics of earlier times can be seen inside.
After being damaged during the Reformation, the interior was divided into two. A chapel in the East Church contains iron rings used to secure witches in the 17th century, while in the West Church there are some embroidered panels attributed to one Mary Jameson (1597–1644).

🏛 Maritime Museum

Shiprow. ☎ 01224 337700.
🕐 10am–5pm Mon–Sat, 11am–5pm
Sun. ● 25 Dec, 1, 2, 3 Jan. ♿

Overlooking the harbour is Provost Ross's House, which dates back to 1593 and is one of the oldest residential buildings in the town. This museum traces the history of Aberdeen's long seafaring tradition. Exhibitions include shipwrecks, rescues, shipbuilding and the many oil installations off Scotland's east coast.

🔒 St Machar's Cathedral

The Chanonry. 🕐 9am–5pm daily. ♿

Dominating Old Aberdeen, the 15th-century edifice of St Machar's is the oldest granite building in the city. The stonework of one arch even dates as far back back as the 14th century. The impressive nave now serves as a parish church and its magnificent oak ceiling is adorned with the coats of arms of 48 popes, emperors and princes of Christendom.

Royal Deeside Tour ⑱

SINCE QUEEN VICTORIA's purchase of the Balmoral estate in 1852, Deeside has been best known as the summer home of the British Royal Family, though it has been associated with royalty since the time of Robert the Bruce *(see p468)*. The route follows the Dee, formerly a prolific salmon river, through some magnificent Grampian scenery.

Muir of Dinnet Nature Reserve ④
An information centre on the A97 provides an excellent place from which to explore this beautiful mixed woodland area, formed by the retreating glaciers of the last Ice Age.

Balmoral ⑥
Bought by Queen Victoria for 30,000 guineas in 1852, after its owner choked to death on a fishbone, the castle was rebuilt in the Scottish Baronial style at Prince Albert's request.

Ballater ⑤
The old railway town of Ballater has royal warrants on many of its shop fronts. It grew as a 19th-century spa town, its waters reputedly providing a cure for tuberculosis.

Dunkeld ⓳

Perth & Kinross. 🏘 2,200. 🚊 Birnam.
🚍 🛈 The Cross (01350 727688).

Sɪᴛᴜᴀᴛᴇᴅ by the River Tay, this ancient and charming village was all but destroyed in the Battle of Dunkeld, a Jacobite (see p523) defeat, in 1689. The **Little Houses** lining Cathedral Street were the first to be rebuilt, and remain fine examples of imaginative restoration. The sad ruins of the 14th-century **cathedral** enjoy an idyllic setting on shady lawns beside the Tay, against a backdrop of steep and wooded hills. The choir is used as the parish church and its north wall contains a Leper's Squint: a little hole through which lepers could see the altar during mass. It was while on holiday in the Dunkeld countryside that Beatrix Potter (see p353) found the location for her Peter Rabbit stories.

The ruins of Dunkeld Cathedral

Pitlochry ⓴

Perth & Kinross. 🏘 2,500. 🚊 🚍
🛈 22 Atholl Rd (01796 472215).
ⓦ www.pitlochry.org.uk

Sᴜʀʀᴏᴜɴᴅᴇᴅ by the pine-forested hills, Pitlochry became famous after Queen Victoria (see p56) described it as one of the finest resorts in Europe. In early summer, salmon swim up the ladder built into the Power Station Dam, on their way to spawning grounds upriver. The **Power Station Visitor Centre** outlines the hydro-electric scheme which harnesses the waters of the River Tummel. The home of Bell's whisky, the **Blair Atholl Distillery**, gives an insight into whisky making (see p475) and is open for tours. The **Festival Theatre**, one of Scotland's most famous, puts on a summer season when the programme changes daily.

🛈 **Power Station Visitor Centre**
Port-na-Craig. 🕻 01796 473152.
◯ late Mar–Oct: 10am–5:30pm daily. 🈳 🇬
🎭 **Festival Theatre**
Port-na-Craig. 🕻 01796 472680.
◯ mid-May–Oct: daily. 🈳 🚻 🇬
🏭 **Blair Atholl Distillery**
Perth Rd. 🕻 01796 472234.
◯ Easter–Sep: 9am–4:30pm daily (Sun: pm); Oct–Easter: Mon–Fri.
● 22 Dec–3 Jan. 🈳 🚻 limited. 🇬

TIPS FOR DRIVERS

Length: 69 miles (111 km).
Stopping-off points: Crathes Castle café. ◯ May–Sep: daily; Tor-na-Collie Hotel, Banchory for Scottish meals. (See also pp636–7)

Drum Castle ①
This impressive 13th-century keep was granted by Robert the Bruce to his standard bearer in 1323, in gratitude for his services.

Banchory ③
Local lavender is a popular attraction here. From the 18th-century Brig o' Feugh, salmon can be seen.

Crathes Castle and Gardens ②
This is the family home of the Burnetts, who were made Royal Foresters of Drum by Robert the Bruce. Along with the title, he gave Alexander Burnett the ivory Horn of Leys which is still on display.

PETERHEAD
A96
ABERDEEN
A93
A96
A980
A93
Peterculter ①
Dee
Crathes ②
③ B9077
A90
STONEHAVEN
B974

0 kilometres 5
0 miles 4

KEY

▬▬▬ Tour route
══ Other roads
☼ Viewpoint

Killiecrankie Walk ㉑

IN AN AREA famous for its scenery and historical connections, this circular walk offers typical Highland views. The route is fairly flat, though ringed by mountains, and follows the River Garry south to Loch Faskally, meandering through a wooded gorge, passing the Soldier's Leap and a Victorian viaduct. There are several ideal picnic spots along the way. Returning along the River Tummel, the walk crosses one of Queen Victoria's favourite Highland areas, before doubling back along the rivers to complete the circuit.

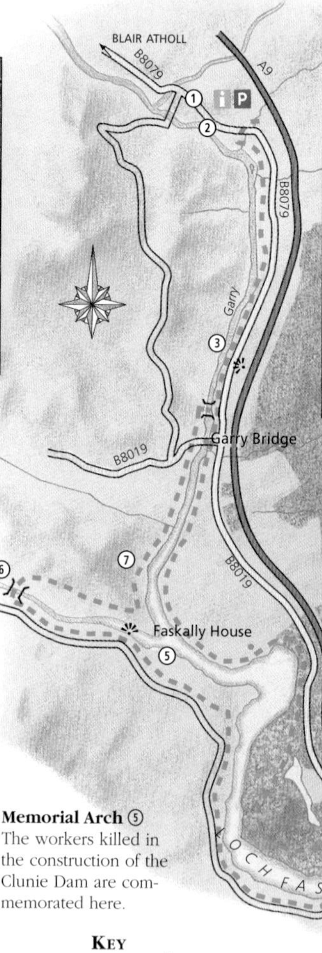

BLAIR ATHOLL

Killiecrankie ①
A Visitor Centre provides information on the Battle of Killiecrankie, fought in 1689.

Linn of Tummel ⑦
The path passes a pool beneath the Falls of Tummel and leads through a beautiful forest trail.

Coronation Bridge ⑥
Spanning the River Tummel, this footbridge was built in 1860 in honour of George IV.

Garry Bridge

Faskally House

Soldier's Leap ②
The English soldier Donald Macbean leapt over the river here to avoid capture by Jacobites during the 1689 battle.

TUMMEL FOREST PARK

Killiecrankie Pass ③
A 17th-century military road built by General Wade follows the gorge.

Memorial Arch ⑤
The workers killed in the construction of the Clunie Dam are commemorated here.

LOCH FASKALLY

PITLOCHRY

KEY

▪ ▪	Route
▨▨▨	Major road
▨▨▨	B road
═══	Minor road
⁂	Viewpoint
P	Parking
i	Visitor Centre

Clunie Foot Bridge ④
This bridge crosses the artificial Loch Faskally, created by the damming of the River Tummel for hydro-electric power in the 1950s.

0 kilometres — 1

0 miles — 0.5

TIPS FOR WALKERS

Starting point: NTS Visitor Centre Killiecrankie. [phone] 01796 473233.
Getting there: Bus from Pitlochry or Aberfeldy.
Length: 6 miles (10 km).
Difficulty: Very easy.

The Three Sisters, Glencoe, in late autumn

Blair Castle ㉒

Blair Atholl, Perthshire. ☎ 01796 481207. 🚆 Blair Atholl. ◯ Apr–Oct: 10am–6pm daily. 🅿 ♿ limited. 🆆 www.blair-castle.co.uk

Tʜɪs ʀᴀᴍʙʟɪɴɢ, turreted castle has been altered and extended so often in its 700-year history that it now provides a unique insight into the history of Highland aristocratic life. The 18th-century wing, with its draughty Victorian passages hung with antlers, has a display containing the gloves and pipe of Bonnie Prince Charlie (*see p521*) who spent two days here gathering Jacobite (*see p523*) support. Family portraits cover 300 years and include paintings by such masters as Johann Zoffany and Sir Peter Lely. Sir Edwin Landseer's priceless *Death of a Stag in Glen Tilt* (1850) was painted nearby. In 1844 Queen Victoria visited the castle and conferred on its owners, the Dukes of Atholl, the distinction of being allowed to maintain a private army. The Atholl Highlanders still flourish.

The Cairngorms ㉓

See pp530–31.

Glencoe ㉔

Highland. 🚆 Fort William. 🚌 Glencoe. 🅸 Cameron Sq, Fort William (01397 703781).

Rᴇɴᴏᴡɴᴇᴅ for its awesome scenery and savage history, Glencoe was compared by Dickens to "a burial ground of a race of giants". The precipitous cliffs of Buachaille Etive Mor and the knife-edged ridge of Aonach Eagach (both over 900 m; 3,000 ft) present a formidable challenge even to experienced mountaineers.

Against a dark backdrop of craggy peaks and the tumbling River Coe, the Glen offers superb hill-walking in the summer. Stout footwear, waterproofs and attention to safety warnings are essential. Details of routes, ranging from the easy half-hour between the **NTS Visitor Centre** and Signal Rock (from which the signal was given to commence the massacre) to a stiff 6 mile (10 km) haul up the Devil's Staircase can be had from the Visitor Centre. Guided walks are offered in summer by the NTS Ranger service.

🅸 **NTS Visitor Centre**
Ballachulish. ☎ 01855 811307. ◯ Mar–Oct: 10am–5pm daily. 🅿 ♿

Tʜᴇ Mᴀssᴀᴄʀᴇ ᴏғ Glᴇɴᴄᴏᴇ

In 1692, the chief of the Glencoe MacDonalds was five days late in registering an oath of submission to William III, giving the government an excuse to root out a nest of Jacobite (*p523*) supporters. For ten days 130 soldiers, captained by Robert Campbell, were hospitably entertained by the unsuspecting MacDonalds. At dawn on 13 February, in a terrible breach of trust, the soldiers fell on their hosts, killing some 38 MacDonalds. Many more died in their wintry mountain hideouts. The massacre, unsurprisingly, became a political scandal, though there were to be no official reprimands for three years.

Detail of *The Massacre of Glencoe* by James Hamilton

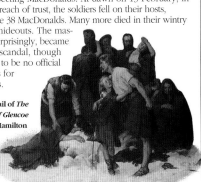

The Cairngorms ㉒

Wild goat

Rising to a height of 1,309 m (4,296 ft), the Cairngorm mountains form the highest landmass in Britain. Cairn Gorm itself is the site of one of Britain's first ski centres. A weather station at the mountain's summit provides regular reports, essential in an area known for sudden changes of weather. Walkers should be sure to follow the mountain code without fail. The chairlift that climbs Cairn Gorm affords superb views over the Spey Valley. Many estates in the valley have centres which introduce the visitor to Highland land use.

Strathspey Steam Railway
This track between Aviemore and Boat of Garten dates from 1863.

Aviemore, the commercial centre of the Cairngorms, provides buses to the ski area 13 km (8 miles) away.

Kincraig Highland Wildlife Park
Driving through this park, the visitor can see bison alongside bears, wolves and wild boar. All of these animals were once common in the Highlands.

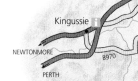

INVERNESS
A 938　Carrbridge
B9153
Boat of Garten
Aviemore
Coylur
Beanaidh
LOCH AN EILEIN
A9　B9152　Spey
Kincraig
LOCH INSH
Feshie
Kingussie
NEWTONMORE
B970
Tolvah
PERTH
BRAERIA
1,295 m
(4,248 f
LOCH EINICH

0 kilometres　　5
0 miles　　　　5

The Cairngorms by Aviemore

Rothiemurchus Estate
Highland cattle can be seen among many other creatures at Rothiemurchus. A visitor centre provides guided walks and illustrates life on a Highland estate.

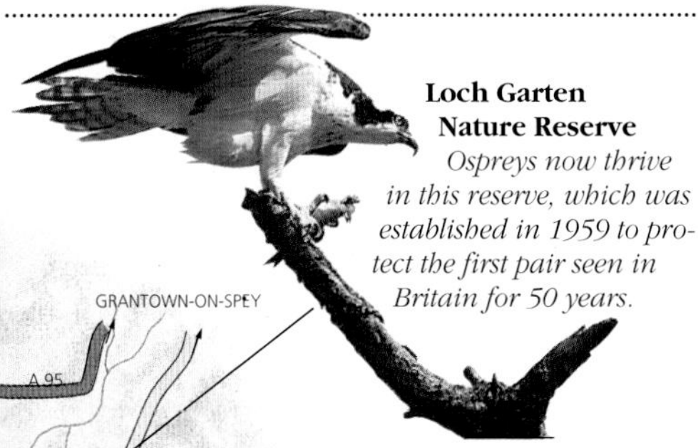

Loch Garten Nature Reserve
Ospreys now thrive in this reserve, which was established in 1959 to protect the first pair seen in Britain for 50 years.

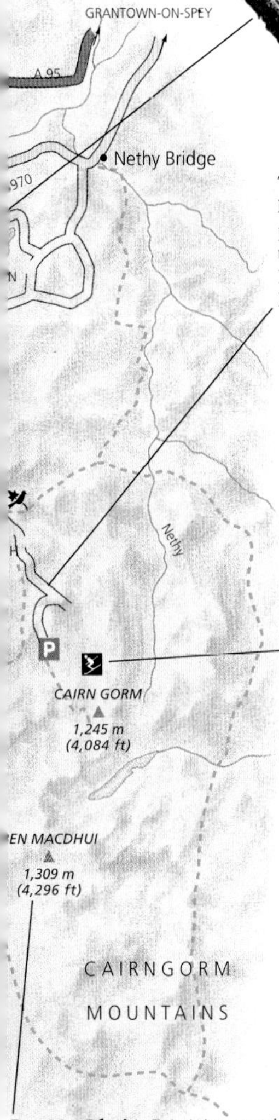

GRANTOWN-ON-SPEY
A 95
Nethy Bridge
970
N
Nethy
H
P
CAIRN GORM
1,245 m
(4,084 ft)
EN MACDHUI
1,309 m
(4,296 ft)
CAIRNGORM MOUNTAINS

The Cairngorm Reindeer Centre provides walks in the hills among Britain's only herd of reindeer.

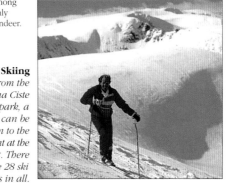

Skiing
From the Coire na Ciste car park, a chairlift can be taken to the restaurant at the summit. There are 28 ski runs in all.

Ben MacDhui is Britain's second highest peak, after Ben Nevis.

KEY

- Tourist information
- Major road
- Minor road
- Narrow lane
- Footpath
- Viewpoint

VISITORS' CHECKLIST

The Highlands. Aviemore. Grampian Rd, Aviemore (01479) 810363. **Cairngorm Reindeer Centre**, *Loch Morlich.* (01479) 861228. daily. **Kincraig Highland Wildlife Park** (01540) 651270. daily (weather permitting). **Rothiemurchus Visitor Centre,** *near Aviemore.* (01479) 810858. daily. **Loch Garten Nature Reserve** (01479) 831694. daily. **Skiing** (01479) 861261.

FLORA OF THE CAIRNGORMS

With mixed woodland at their base and the summits forming a sub-polar plateau, the Cairngorms present a huge variety of flora. Ancient Caledonian pines (once common in the area) survive in Abernethy Forest, while arctic flowers flourish in the heights.

1,200 m
(3,950 ft)
1,000 m
(3,300 ft)
800 m
(2,650 ft)
600 m
(2,000 ft)
400 m
(1,300 ft)
200 m
(650 ft)
0 m
(0 ft)

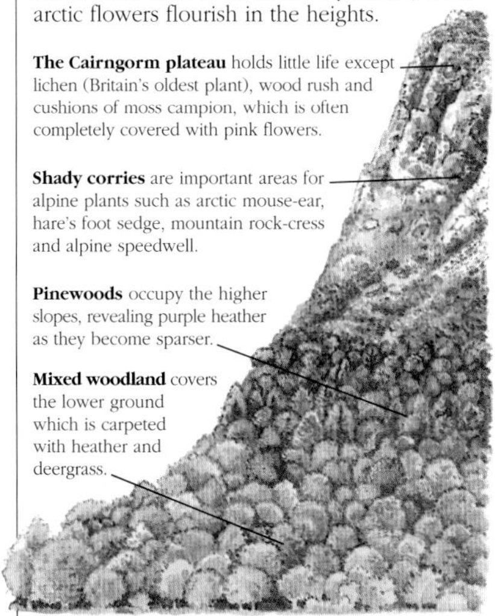

The Cairngorm plateau holds little life except lichen (Britain's oldest plant), wood rush and cushions of moss campion, which is often completely covered with pink flowers.

Shady corries are important areas for alpine plants such as arctic mouse-ear, hare's foot sedge, mountain rock-cress and alpine speedwell.

Pinewoods occupy the higher slopes, revealing purple heather as they become sparser.

Mixed woodland covers the lower ground which is carpeted with heather and deergrass.

An idealized section of the Cairngorm plateau

Road to the Isles Tour ㉕

THIS SCENIC ROUTE goes past vast mountain-corridors, breathtaking beaches of white sand and tiny villages, to the town of Mallaig, one of the ferry ports for the isles of Skye, Rum and Eigg. As well as the stunning scenery, the area is steeped in Jacobite history *(see p523)*.

TIPS FOR DRIVERS

Tour length: 45 miles (72 km).
Stopping-off points: Glenfinnan NTS Visitors' Centre (01397 722 250) explains the Jacobite risings and serves refreshments; the Arisaig House Hotel has excellent Scottish food. (See also pp636–7.)

Mallaig ⑦
The Road to the Isles ends at Mallaig, an active little fishing port with a very good harbour and one of the ferry links to Skye *(see pp520-21)*.

Morar ⑥
The road continues through Morar, an area renowned for its white sands, and Loch Morar, rumoured to be the home of a 12 m (40 ft) monster known as Morag.

Prince's Cairn ⑤
Crossing the Ardnish Peninsula to Loch Nan Uamh, a cairn marks the spot from which Bonnie Prince Charlie finally left Scotland for France in 174(

Oban ㉖

Argyll & Bute. 8,500. 🚆 🚍 ⛴
ℹ Argyll Sq (01631 563122).
🅦 www.scottish-heartlands.org

LOCATED ON the Firth of Lorne and commanding a magnificent view of the Argyll coast, the bustling port of Oban is a popular destination for travellers on their way to Mull and the Western Isles *(see p515)*.

Dominating the skyline is McCaig's Tower, an unfinished Victorian imitation of the Colosseum in Rome. It is worth making the 10-minute climb from the town centre for the sea views alone. Attractions in the town include working centres for glass, pottery and whisky; the Oban distillery produces one of the country's finest malt whiskies *(see p475)*. The **Oban Seal and Marine Centre** rescues injured and orphaned seals and has displays of underwater life. A busy harbour shelters car ferries going to

Barra and South Uist, Mull, Tiree and Colonsay islands.

🏛 **Oban Seal and Marine Centre**
Barcaldine. 📞 01631 720386.
🕐 daily. 🈲 ♿

Mull ㉗

Argyll & Bute. 2,800. ⛴ from Oban, Kilchoan, Lochaline. ℹ Main Street, Tobermory (01688 302182).

MOST ROADS on this easily accessible Hebridean island follow the sharply

indented rocky coastline, affording wonderful sea views. From Craignure, the Mull and West Highland Railway serves the baronial **Torosay Castle**. A pathway through its gardens is lined with statues, while inside, 19th-century furniture and paintings can be found. On a promontory to the east lies **Duart Castle**, home of the chief of Clan Maclean. Visitors can see the Banqueting Hall and State Rooms in the 13th-century keep. Its dungeons once held prisoners from a Spanish Armada galleon sunk by a Donald Maclean in 1588.

Looking out to sea across Tobermory Bay, Mull

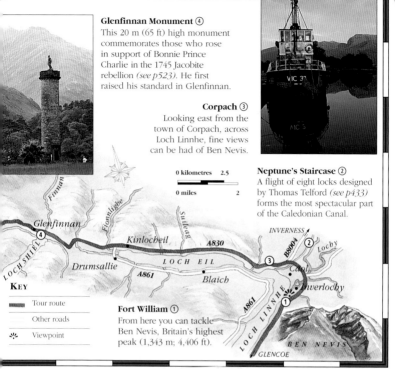

Glenfinnan Monument ④
This 20 m (65 ft) high monument commemorates those who rose in support of Bonnie Prince Charlie in the 1745 Jacobite rebellion *(see p523)*. He first raised his standard in Glenfinnan.

Corpach ③
Looking east from the town of Corpach, across Loch Linnhe, fine views can be had of Ben Nevis.

Neptune's Staircase ②
A flight of eight locks designed by Thomas Telford *(see p433)* forms the most spectacular part of the Caledonian Canal.

0 kilometres   2.5

0 miles   2

KEY

▬▬▬	Tour route
▬▬▬	Other roads
☀	Viewpoint

Fort William ①
From here you can tackle Ben Nevis, Britain's highest peak (1,343 m; 4,406 ft).

ENVIRONS: From Fionnphort, a ferry goes to **Iona**, where St Columba *(see p511)* began his mission in Scotland in 563. North of Iona, the Isle of Staffa should be visited for its magnificent **Fingal's Cave**.

⛪ **Torosay Castle**
Off A849, Nr Craignure. [01680 812421. **Castle** ☐ Easter–mid-Oct: 10:30am–5:30pm daily. **Gardens** ☐ 10:30am–dusk daily. ♿ ⬤ gardens only. ☐ for groups.

⛪ **Duart Castle**
Off A849, nr Craignure. [01680 812309. ☐ May–mid-Oct: 10:30am–6pm daily. ♿

Loch Awe ㉘

Argyll & Bute. ⛴ ☐ Dalmally.
🛈 Inveraray (01499 302063).

ONE OF the longest of Scotland's freshwater lochs, Loch Awe fills a 25 mile (40 km) glen in the south-western Highlands. A short drive east of the village of Lochawe leads to the lochside

The ruins of Kilchurn Castle on the shore of Loch Awe

remains of **Kilchurn Castle**, which was abandoned after being struck by lightning in the 18th century. Dwarfing the castle is the huge bulk of Ben Cruachan, whose summit can be reached by the narrow Pass of Brander, in which Robert the Bruce *(see p468)* fought the Clan MacDougal in 1308. From the A85, a tunnel leads to the cavernous Cruachan Power Station.

Near the village of Taynuilt the preserved Lorn Furnace at Bonawe is a reminder of the iron-smelting industry that caused the destruction of much of the area's woodland in the 18th and 19th centuries.

Marked prehistoric cairns are found off the A816 between Kilmartin and Dunadd. The latter boasts a 6th-century hill fort from which the Stone of Destiny *(see p468)* originated.

Inveraray Castle ㉙

Inveraray, Argyll & Bute. 🚉 *Arrochar,*
then bus. 📞 *01499 302203.*
⭕ *Apr–Jun, Sep–Oct: Sat–Thu;*
Jul–Aug: daily 10am–5:45pm
(Sun: pm). 🅿️ ♿ *limited.* ✉️
Ⓦ *www.inveraray-castle.com*

The pinnacled, Gothic exterior of Inveraray Castle

THIS MULTI-TURRETED mock
Gothic palace is the family
home of the powerful Clan
Campbell who have been the
Dukes of Argyll since 1701.
Built in 1745 by architects
Roger Morris and William
Adam on the ruins of a 15th-
century castle, the conical
towers were added later, after
a fire in 1877. Magnificent
interiors, designed by Robert
Mylne in the 1770s, form a
backdrop to a huge collection
of Oriental and European
porcelain and Regency furniture and portraits by Ramsay,
Gainsborough and Raeburn.
The Armoury Hall features a
display of weaponry collected
by the Campbells to fight the
Jacobites *(see p523).* In the
stables, the Combined Operations Museum commemorates
the allied troops who trained
here during World War II.

Auchindrain Museum ㉚

Inveraray, Argyll & Bute. 📞 *01499*
500235. 🚌 *Inveraray, then bus.*
⭕ *Apr–Sep: 10am–5pm daily.*
🅿️ ♿ *limited.*

THE FIRST OPEN-AIR museum
in Scotland, Auchindrain
illuminates the working lives
of the kind of farming community that was typical of the
Highlands until the late 19th
century. Originally a town-
ship of some 20 thatched
buildings, the site was com-
munally farmed by its tenants until the last one retired
in 1962. Visitors can wander
through the build-
ings, many of
which combine

living space, kitchen and
cattle shed under one roof.
Some of them are furnished
with box beds and old rush
lamps. The homes of Auch-
indrain are a quite fascinating
memorial to the time before
the transition from subsis-
tence to commercial farming.

**An old hay turner at the
Auchindrain Museum**

Crarae Gardens ㉛

Crarae, Argyll & Bute. 📞 *01546*
886614 (Apr–Oct) or 01546 886388
(Nov–Mar). 🚌 *Inveraray, then bus.*
⭕ *Easter–Oct: 9am–6pm; Nov–Easter:*
10am–dusk daily. 🅿️ ♿ *limited.*
Ⓦ *www.crarae-gardens.org*

CONSIDERED the most
beguiling of the many
gardens of the West High-
lands, the **Crarae Gardens**
were created in the 1920s by
Lady Grace Campbell. She
was the aunt of explorer
Reginald Farrer, whose specimens from Tibet were the
beginnings of a collection of
exotic plants. The gardens are

nourished by the warmth of
the Gulf Stream and the high
rainfall of the region. Although
there are many unusual
Himalayan rhododendrons
flourishing here, the gardens
are also home to exotic plants
from Tasmania, New Zealand
and the USA. Plant collectors
still contribute to the gardens
which are best seen in spring
and early summer, against the
blue waters of Loch Fyne.

Jura ㉜

Argyll & Bute. 🚶 *250.* ⛴️ *from*
Kennacraig to Islay, then Islay to Jura.
ℹ️ *Bowmore (01496 810254).*

BARREN, MOUNTAINOUS and
overrun by red deer, the
isle of Jura has only one road
which connects the single
village of Craighouse to the
Islay ferry. Though walking is
restricted during the stalking
(deer hunting) season between August and October,
the island offers superb hill-
walking, especially on the
slopes of the three main peaks,
known as the Paps of Jura.
The tallest of these is Beinn
An Oir at 784 m (2571 ft). Beyond the northern tip of the isle
are the notorious whirlpools
of Corryvreckan. The novelist
George Orwell (who came to
the island to write his final
novel, *1984)* nearly lost his
life here in 1946 when he fell
into the water. A legend tells

Lagavulin distillery, producer of one Scotland's finest malts, on Islay

Mist crowning the Paps of Jura, seen at sunset across the Sound of Islay

of Prince Breackan who, to win the hand of a princess, tried to keep his boat anchored in the whirlpool for three days, held by ropes made of hemp, wool and maidens' hair. The Prince drowned when a single rope, containing the hair of a girl who had been untrue, finally broke.

Islay ③③

Argyll & Bute. 🕌 3,500. ⛴ from Kennacraig. 🅸 The Square, Bowmore (01496 810254). ⓦ www.isle-of-islay.com

THE MOST SOUTHERLY of the Western Isles, Islay (pronounced 'Eyeluh') is the home of respected Highland single malt whiskies Lagavulin and Laphroaig. Most of the island's distilleries produce heavily peated malts with a distinctive tang of the sea. The Georgian village of Bowmore has the island's oldest distillery and a circular church designed to minimize the Devil's possible lurking-places. The **Museum of Islay Life** in Port Charlotte contains fascinating information on social and natural history. Seven miles (11 km) east of Port Ellen stands the Kildalton Cross. A block of local green stone adorned with Old Testament scenes, it is one of the most impressive 8th-

century Celtic crosses in Britain. Worth a visit for its archaeological and historical interest is the medieval stronghold of the Lords of the Isles, **Finlaggan**, under excavation. Islay's beaches support a variety of bird life, some of which can be observed at the RSPB reserve at Gruinart.

🏛 Museum of Islay Life
Port Charlotte. 📞 01496 850358. ⓞ Easter–Oct: 10am–5pm Mon–Sat, 1–4pm Sun. 🦽 ⓺

Kintyre ③④

Argyll & Bute. 🕌 8,000. ⛴ Oban. 🚌 Campbeltown. 🅸 MacKinnon House, The Pier, Campbeltown (01586 552056).

ALONG, NARROW PENINSULA stretching far south of Glasgow, Kintyre has superb views across to the islands of Gigha, Islay and Jura. The 9 mile (14 km) Crinan Canal,

opened in 1801, is a delightful inland waterway, its 15 locks bustling with pleasure craft in the summer. The town of Tarbert (meaning "isthmus" in Gaelic) takes its name from the neck on which it stands, which is narrow enough to drag a boat across between Loch Fyne and West Loch Tarbert. This feat was first achieved by the Viking King Magnus Barfud who, in 1198, was granted by treaty as much land as he could sail around. Travelling south past Campbeltown, the B842 ends at the headland known as the Mull of Kintyre, which was made famous when former Beatle Paul McCartney commercialized a traditional pipe tune of the same name. Westward lies the isle of Rathlin, where Robert the Bruce *(see p468)* learned patience in his struggles against the English by watching a spider weaving a web in a cave.

Fishing boats and yachts moored at Tarbert harbour, Kintyre

TRAVELLERS' NEEDS

WHERE TO STAY 538–573

WHERE TO EAT 574–611

WHERE TO STAY

HE RANGE OF HOTELS and accommodation available in Britain is extensive, and whatever your budget you should find something to suit you. Various types of accommodation are described over the next four pages, and the hotel listings section *(see pp542–573)* includes over 350 of the best places to stay, from luxurious country-house hotels to cosy guesthouses. This selection has been made on the basis that it represents excellence and good value.

Hilton doorman, London

The confusing rating systems for hotel classification operated by the various tourist authorities in Great Britain is also demystified. Information is included on self-catering holidays which are becoming increasingly popular, particularly for those on a shoestring budget, with young children, or both. We have also added some introductory information on Britain's many camp sites and caravan parks which can provide an adventurous, reasonably priced alternative to bricks and mortar.

COUNTRY-HOUSE HOTELS

THE PECULIARLY BRITISH concept of the country-house hotel has gone from strength to strength over the last 15 years. The term has been somewhat liberally used by unscrupulous hoteliers where some cursory redecoration, gas log-fires and reproduction furniture allowed for the word "country-house" to be added to the new hotel brochure. However, the genuine article is not hard to spot: the buildings are invariably of some architectural value, and filled with antiques and fine furnishings. Often they are situated in extensive grounds. Comfort and luxury are guaranteed – as well as a high tariff. Some country-houses are run by resident owner-proprietors such as Chedington Court *(see p551)* while others may be owned by hotel chains such as Historic House Hotels.

CORPORATE HOTELS AND HOTEL CHAINS

OFTEN AT THE TOP END of the market are the large corporate hotels such as the Sheraton group which provide every imaginable comfort and facility, nearly always including an excellent restaurant, swimming pool and a leisure and fitness centre. Though they tend to lack individuality and atmosphere, they make up for this in creature comforts.

Major hotel chains such as Forte Crest are to be found in all the larger cities. Prices can be high, but are often quoted for the room rather than per person. They do not always include breakfast, so check before you book. Sometimes chain hotels will offer special weekend rates for tourists who book in advance, though weekdays can often see them full with business travellers and conference delegates.

Atholl Palace Hotel *(see p572)*

CLASSIC HOTELS AND COACHING INNS

IN THE MIDDLE PRICE range there are traditional hotels. They are often family-run and rely on a regular clientele, sometimes they can be a little uninspiring but usually offer reasonable comfort and decor. In towns you may also find small, privately-run modern hotels offering good value.

Coaching inns, such as the Swan in Suffolk *(see p548)* can be found all over England and Wales. They used to be staging points for people journeying by horse and carriage, where horses would be rested and travellers refreshed and given lodging. They are generally attractive historic buildings. Often they are the town's focal point, usually decorated traditionally, with a reliable restaurant and a friendly atmosphere.

Buckland Manor *(see p555)*, Worcestershire

◁ **The 11th-century ruins of Corfe Castle, Dorset**

The Swan, Suffolk *(see p548)*, a converted coaching inn

BED-AND-BREAKFASTS AND GUEST HOUSES

BED-AND-BREAKFAST hotels, or B&Bs as they are more commonly known, dominate the lower price range, and such guesthouses and farmhouses can be found all over Britain. They are often family-owned and offer basic, no-frills accommodation, usually with a choice of English or Continental breakfast included in the price of the room.

B&Bs don't normally accept traveller's cheques or credit cards; payment is preferred in cash or personal cheque (with a cheque guarantee card). Many tourist boards publish a *Bed & Breakfast Touring Map* which gives details of places they have inspected.

WOLSEY LODGES

WOLSEY LODGES are a group of privately owned, very comfortable houses, mainly in the country, which offer hospitality. They are named after Cardinal Wolsey who travelled around the country in the 16th century expecting the highest standards from his hosts.

Food is an important feature of your stay, and dinner is often along the lines of a dinner party; everyone eats around one table, along with the host and hostess. You feel as though you are staying in a familiar home rather than an impersonal hotel.

The aim is to make visitors feel like welcome guests rather than paying clients. Prices vary from £20 to £45 per person for a double room with bathroom and a full breakfast. Brochures can be obtained from local tourist offices or the Wolsey Lodge office *(see Directory p541)*.

HOTEL CLASSIFICATIONS

ONE USEFUL GUIDE to follow when making your hotel selection is the British Tourist Authority's crown classification system. Over 17,000 hotels, guesthouses, motels, inns, B&Bs and farmhouses take part in the system. The classification gradings range from "listed" (the lowest category) to "five crowns".

An annual inspection is carried out by the local tourist board to ensure standards are maintained. The number of crowns given is related to the range of facilities and services offered but a lower classification does not imply lower standards. This is where the BTA's "quality gradings" system comes in. These grade places, but on criteria such as warmth of welcome and comfort of furnishings. The four levels of ratings are termed "approved", "commended", "highly commended" and "de luxe". Thus you may come across a de luxe B&B which has only one crown – this means that while its facilities are limited they are nevertheless of a very high standard.

HIDDEN EXTRAS

TIPPING is not usually expected in Britain, and is becoming rare except in the most exclusive hotels, or on occasions when you have been particularly impressed with the quality of service.

One of the most expensive extras on all hotel bills can be the telephone. Hotels will usually charge a higher tariff for calls made from your room – check the rate before you launch into lengthy conversations – it may well be worth buying a phonecard and using the telephone in the hotel lobby instead.

Hintlesham Hall, Suffolk *(see p548)*

PRICES AND BOOKING

HOTEL RATES are normally quoted per room and are inclusive of VAT and service charge; if single rooms are not available the supplement charged on a double room is generally quite substantial. Top-of-the-range hotels could cost you anything over £200 a night and may not even include breakfast.

An average hotel in London will cost about £70 to £150 for two persons including bathroom and breakfast. Outside London expect to pay from £50 to £90 for facilities that will be of a similar standard.

Bed-and-breakfast accommodation (out of London) depends on the time of year and ranges from about £12.50 to £30 per person, per night.

The elegant hallway of the Gore Hotel in London (see p542)

A guesthouse (also outside London) would start at about £20 per person for one night. Farmhouse lodgings nearly always include a substantial dinner, so for full board you are likely to pay between £19 to £30 per person per night.

Some hotels ask for a deposit in advance when a written or telephone booking is made. This can sometimes be as a request for your credit card number – the amount will be charged to you regardless of whether you show up or not. Acceptance of a booking by telephone, in writing or by fax constitutes a legally binding contract in Britain, but if you cancel a booking as early as possible, you may not necessarily have to pay the full amount.

The folly of Doyden Castle, Cornwall, now a National Trust holiday cottage

SELF-CATERING

FOR THOSE WHO prefer to stay in one place and be independent, or have young children and a limited budget, self-catering is an excellent option. There are many places all around the country, and of all types, from luxury apartments and log cabins to beautifully converted barns or mills. Local tourist offices have the most comprehensive and up-to-date lists (they can also provide a booking service).

The **British Tourist Authority** classifies self-catering accommodation in a system similar to its hotel ratings. Those which have been inspected are then given a "key rating". One to five keys are awarded – this is dependent on the range of facilities and equipment on offer, and similar to the hotel system *(see p539)*, they can also be further rated on four gradings of commendation and quality.

Roadside signboard for bed-and-breakfast

In Scotland, the classification uses crowns and follows the same criteria as the quality gradings in England.

Unlike Scotland and England, the Welsh authorities combine their classifications into one: dragons reflect the overall quality of the accommodation, the number of facilities and also their standard.

The **Landmark Trust** is a self-catering organization that has saved many buildings of interest, and then made them available to the public to rent on a weekend or weekly basis. Book ahead.

The **National Trust** *(see p25)* has a self-catering section which offers interesting historic buildings for rent.

CARAVANNING, CAMPING AND MOTOR HOMES

THERE IS A good choice of camp sites and caravan (RV) parks throughout Britain, normally open from Easter to October. During the peak summer months, parks fill up quickly, so book in advance. In England, the tourist offices listed can be contacted during the summer to check on availability. International caravan and camping signs indicate many park locations on the main roads. The BTA publishes a fairly comprehensive list called *Camping and Caravan Parks in Britain*. Two clubs – the **Caravan Club**, and the **Camping and Caravanning Club** – publish guides listing their parks, and it may be worthwhile becoming a member. Both clubs operate their own grading system. A typical camping or caravan pitch will cost approximately £6 to £10 per night.

An alternative to a tent or caravan is to rent a motor home, which gives you great freedom to explore at your own pace and to stay almost anywhere. They are usually comfortable and very well equipped. The BTA guide *Britain:Vehicle Hire* provides full details of motor-home rental. Expect to pay between between £500 and £800 per week for a luxury six-berth vehicle which can even include a generator, microwave and television. Motor home companies can arrange for you to pick up your vehicle direct from the airport or ferry terminal. Most camping and caravan sites in Britain welcome motor home drivers.

Campsite, Ogwen Valley, Snowdonia

DISABLED TRAVELLERS

DISABLED TRAVELLERS should look out for the "Tourism for All" symbol which indicates properties that have satisfied specific accessibility requirements. **RADAR**, the Royal Association for Disability and Rehabilitation, publishes *Holidays in the British Isles: A Guide for Disabled People*

annually and it is available by mail order from their offices or from major UK book shops. Contact RADAR for any advice on travelling in Britain. We have indicated in our hotel listings those which have facilities for the disabled.

The facilities that are provided for disabled caravanners and campers are generally of a better standard on the newer, more modern sites. Both the Camping and Caravanning Club and the Caravan Club can give you details of all their sites that are

accessible to wheelchairs and have washing and toilet facilities for the disabled.

The **Scottish Tourist Board** has access information included in all its major accommodation and sightseeing guides. The **Disability Scotland Information Service** is another invaluable source of information, who produce a free directory for visitors to north of the border.

Information on all aspects of accommodation and travel for visitors with disabilities is available from **Holiday Care**.

DIRECTORY

HOTELS

Best Western
Amy Johnson Way,
Clifton Moor,
York, YO30 4GP.
☎ 01904 695400.

Edwardian Hotels
140 Bath Road,
Hayes, Middlesex
UB3 5AW.
☎ 020-8759 6311.

Forte
Oak Court, Dudley Road,
Brierly Hill, W. Midlands
DY5 1GL.
☎ 0345 404040.

**Historic House
Hotels**
Bishopthorpe Road,
York YO2 1QB.
☎ 01904 641241.

Sheraton
Piccadilly,
London W1Y 8BX.
☎ 020-7499 6321.

Wolsey Lodges
9 Market Place,
Hadleigh, Ipswich,
Suffolk, IP7 5DL.
☎ 01473 822058.

CARAVANNING, CAMPING AND MOTOR HOMES

Caravan Club
East Grinstead House,
London Road,
East Grinstead,
West Sussex
RH19 1UA.
☎ 01342 326944.

**Camping and
Caravanning
Club**
Westwood Way, Coventry,
West Midlands, CV4 8JH.
☎ 02476 694995.

Tilshead Caravans
Oakley Corner Garage,
Stockbridge Road,
Lopcombe, Salisbury,
Wiltshire, SP5 1BS.
☎ 01980 863636.

SELF-CATERING

**BTA (Self-Catering
Holiday Homes)**
Thames Tower,
Black's Road,
London W6 9EL
(no phone enquiries).

Landmark Trust
Shottesbrooke, Maidenhead, Berkshire SL6 3SW.
☎ 01628 825925.

**National Trust
(Holiday Bookings)**
PO Box 536, Melksham,
Wiltshire SN12 8SX.
☎ 01225 791199.

**National Trust for
Scotland**
28 Charlotte Square,
Edinburgh EH2 4ET.
☎ 0131 243 9300.
Ⓦ www.hts.org.uk

**Snowdonia Tourist
Services**
High Street, Porthmadog,
Gwynedd LL49 9PG
☎ 01766 513829

DISABLED TRAVELLERS

**Disability Scotland
Information
Service**
Princes House,
5 Shandwick Place,
Edinburgh
EH2 4RG.
☎ 0131-668 2487.

Holiday Care
2nd floor, Imperial
Buildings, Victoria Road,
Horley, Surrey RH6 7PZ.
☎ 01293 774535.

RADAR
Unit 12, City Forum,
250 City Road, London
EC1V 8AF.
☎ 020-7250 3222.

**Scottish Tourist
Board**
23 Ravelston Terrace,
Edinburgh EH4 3EU.
☎ 0131 332 2433.

Choosing a Hotel

THE HOTELS in this guide have been selected across a wide price range for their excellent facilities and locations. Many also have a recommended restaurant. The chart lists the hotels by region, starting with London; colour-coded thumb tabs indicate the regions covered on each page. For restaurant listings, see pp574–607.

	CREDIT CARDS	RESTAURANT	CHILDREN WELCOME	GARDEN/TERRACE	NUMBER OF ROOMS
LONDON					
PADDINGTON: *Delemere*. **Map 2 E1.** W www.delemerehotels.com ££ 130 Sussex Gardens W2. 020 7706 3344. FAX 020 7262 1863. A well-managed welcoming hotel that stands out in a street packed with budget accommodation. Bedrooms are small but tidy.	AE DC MC V	▓			38
PADDINGTON: *Mornington*. **Map 2 E1.** W www.mornington.se/ £££ 12 Lancaster Gate, W2. 020 7262 7061. FAX 020 7706 1028. Cool bedrooms contrast with the masculine clubbiness of the bar at this Swedish hotel which offers *Smorgasbord* buffet breakfasts.	AE DC MC V		●		66
PADDINGTON: *Hempel*. **Map 2 E1.** W www.the-hempel.co.uk £££££ 31 Craven Hill Gardens, W2. 020 7298 9000. FAX 020 7402 4666. Edwardian building that is grand and family-run. The third-generation Gorings keep immaculate standards; superb restaurant. There is also a book-lined library.	AE DC MC V	▓	●		47
NOTTING HILL: *Abbey Court*. **Map 1 B2.** £££ 20 Pembridge Gardens, W2. 020 7221 7518. FAX 020 7720 0858. Quiet rooms furnished with books and personal touches mark this Victorian townhouse near Notting Hill Gate.	AE DC MC V		●	▓	22
NOTTING HILL: *Portobello*. **Map 1 A2.** ££££ 21 Stanley Gardens, W11. 020 7727 2777. FAX 020 7792 9641. Eccentric place that has an exotic, sophisticated decor – a mix of Victorian and Edwardian periods. Rooms range from tiny to lavish. ● *24 Dec–2 Jan.*	AE MC V	▓	●		24
NOTTING HILL: *Westbourne*. **Map 1 A2.** ££££ 165 Westbourne Grove, W11. 020 7243 6008. FAX 020 7229 7201. W www.zoohotels.com The mood of this streamlined hang-out in the heart of Notting Hill is chic and contemporary. Many original works of art.	AE DC MC V	▓	●		20
NOTTING HILL: *Halcyon*. **Map 1 A3.** W www.thehalcyon.com £££££ 81 Holland Park, W11. 020 7727 7288. FAX 020 7229 8516. This romantic hideaway in elegant Holland Park is the last word in luxury exuding classic charm at every turn.	AE DC MC V	▓	●		42
KENSINGTON: *Abbey House*. **Map 1 C3.** W www.abbeyhousekensington.com £ 11 Vicarage Gate, W8. 020 7727 2594. Once a Victorian family home, now a no-frills bed-and-breakfast. Rooms though spacious are simply furnished without *en suite* bathrooms.			●		16
KENSINGTON: *Kensington House*. **Map 2 D5.** £££ 15–16 Prince of Wales Terrace, W8. 020 7937 2345. FAX 020 7368 6700. This smart, newly opened townhouse hotel combines period interest with understated contemporary style.	AE DC MC V	▓	●		41
KENSINGTON: *Gore*. **Map 2 D5.** W www.gorehotel.com ££££ 189 Queen's Gate, SW7. 020 7584 6601. FAX 020 7589 8127. This idiosyncratic Victorian hotel is over a pair of chic restaurants. Bedrooms vary from tiny singles to Tudor fantasies with their own minstrels' galleries. Charming service. ● *22–27 Dec.*	AE DC MC V	▓	●		53
KNIGHTSBRIDGE: *Beaufort*. **Map 5 A3.** ££££ 33 Beaufort Gardens, SW3. 020 7584 5252. FAX 020 7589 2834. An aristocratic hideaway in a quiet square with beautifully decorated rooms. Room service and free health club membership.	AE DC MC V	▓	●		28
KNIGHTSBRIDGE: *Basil Street*. **Map 5 A3.** W www.thebasil.com £££££ 23 Basil Street, SW3. 020 7581 3311. FAX 020 7581 3693. An enduringly popular hotel just off Sloane Street. It has a long history and lots of personality. Its brasserie-wine bar is superb and very good value for this expensive area.	AE DC MC V	▓	●		80

Price categories for a standard double room per night, inclusive of breakfast, service charges and any additional taxes such as VAT:
£ under £50
££ £50–£100
£££ £100–£150
££££ £150–£200
£££££ £200 plus.

RESTAURANT
Hotel restaurant or dining room usually open to non-residents unless otherwise stated.

CHILDREN WELCOME
Child cots available. Some hotel restaurants have children's portions and high-chairs.

GARDEN/TERRACE
Hotels with a garden, courtyard or terrace, often providing tables for eating outside.

CREDIT CARDS
Indicates which credit cards are accepted: *AE* American Express; *DC* Diners Club; *MC* Master Card/Access; *V* Visa.

	CREDIT CARDS	RESTAURANT	CHILDREN WELCOME	GARDEN/TERRACE	NUMBER OF ROOMS
KNIGHTSBRIDGE: *Halkin.* Map 5 A3. W www.halkin.co.uk **£££££** 5 Halkin Street, SW1. 020 7333 1000. FAX 020 7333 1100. Sophisticated Italian design with Oriental touches combined with Stefano Cavallini's understated restaurant overlooking a courtyard garden makes this hotel a startling experience.	AE DC MC V	■	●	■	41
SOUTH KENSINGTON: *Five Sumner Place.* Map 2 E5. **£££** 5 Sumner Place, SW7. 020 7584 7586. W www.sumnerplace.com A small hotel with a quiet, courteous welcome and good facilities. Breakfast is served with complimentary newspapers.	AE JCB MC V				15
SOUTH KENSINGTON: *Blakes.* Map 2 E5. W www.blakeshotel.co.uk **£££££** 33 Roland Gardens, SW7. 020 7370 6701. FAX 020 7373 0442. Opulent hotel, each room a fantasy of natural materials and antiques. Secluded gardens and an Oriental-style restaurant.	AE JCB MC V	■	■	■	50
VICTORIA: *Morgan House.* Map 5 B4. W www.morganhouse.co.uk **£** 120 Ebury Street, SW1. 020 7730 2384. FAX 020 7730 8442. This stylish budget B&B in a Georgian terrace has light, modern decor; just three rooms have private bathrooms.	MC V		●		11
VICTORIA: *Windermere.* Map 5 C4. **££** 142–144 Warwick Way, SW1. 020 7834 5163. FAX 020 7630 8831. Inexpensive, friendly hotel, ten minutes' walk from Victoria Station. Lovely breakfast room which doubles as a dining room. Light, clean bedrooms. Helpful service.	AE MC V	■	●		22
VICTORIA: *Tophams Belgravia.* Map 5 B4. W www.tophams.co.uk **£££** 28 Ebury St, SW1. 020 7730 8147. FAX 020 7823 5966. Several adjacent townhouses make up this classy hotel. Family heirlooms deck cosy public rooms. ● 23 Dec–3 Jan.	AE DC MC V		●		39
VICTORIA: *Goring.* Map 5 B4. **£££££** Beeston Place, SW1. 020 7396 9000. FAX 020 7834 4393. Fine Belgravia hotel with elegant furnishings and a warm welcome. Immaculate gardens make a pleasant backdrop.	AE DC MC V	■	●	■	75
WESTMINSTER: *Dolphin Square.* Map 6 D5. **£££** Chichester St, SW1. 020 7834 3800. FAX 020 7798 8735. A smart complex of suites and studios near the Tate Britain. Facilities include gardens, sports courts, a swimming pool, a shopping mall, a Gary Rhodes restaurant and a brasserie.	AE DC MC V	■	●	■	148
ST JAMES'S: *22 Jermyn Street.* Map 6 D1. W www.22jermyn.com **£££££** 22 Jermyn St, SW1. 020 7734 2353. FAX 020 7734 9750. A luxurious complex of suites and studios with round-the-clock service, a video library and use of the nearby health club.	AE DC MC V		●		18
MAYFAIR: *Chesterfield.* Map 6 D1. **££££** 35 Charles St, W1. 020 7491 2622. FAX 020 7491 4793. This quiet, well-kept place near Berkeley Square is decked with fruit and flowers, bedrooms are deluxe and staff welcoming.	AE DC MC V	■	●		110
MAYFAIR: *Brown's.* Map 6 D1. W www.brownshotel.com **£££££** Albemarle St, W1. 020 7493 6020. FAX 020 7493 9381. A long-established and highly traditional hotel which rambles through 11 townhouses and offers classic bedrooms.	AE DC MC V	■	●		118
OXFORD STREET & SOHO: *Edward Lear.* Map 3 5A. **££** 28–30 Seymour St, W1. 020 7402 5401. FAX 020 7706 3766. Clean, simple bed-and-breakfast, once the home of the author Edward Lear. Single travellers and families are made very welcome.	MC V		●		31

Price categories for a standard double room per night, inclusive of breakfast, service charges and any additional taxes such as VAT:
£ under £50
££ £50–£100
£££ £100–£150
££££ £150–£200
£££££ £200 plus.

RESTAURANT
Hotel restaurant or dining room usually open to non-residents unless otherwise stated.

CHILDREN WELCOME
Child cots available. Some hotel restaurants have children's portions and high-chairs.

GARDEN/TERRACE
Hotels with a garden, courtyard or terrace, often providing tables for eating outside.

CREDIT CARDS
Indicates which credit cards are accepted: *AE* American Express; *DC* Diners Club; *MC* Master Card/Access; *V* Visa.

	CREDIT CARDS	RESTAURANT	CHILDREN WELCOME	GARDEN/TERRACE	NUMBER OF ROOMS
OXFORD STREET & SOHO: *Durrants*. Map 3 A4. £££ George St, W1. 020 7935 8131. FAX 020 7487 3510. Georgian hotel that still has the feel of the old coaching inn it once was. The look is of old leather and wood. Bedrooms are unfussy.	AE MC V	■	●		92
OXFORD STREET & SOHO: *Hazlitt's*. Map 3 A4. ££££ 6 Frith St, W1. 020 7434 1771. FAX 020 7439 1524. W www.hazlittshotel.com Three 18th-century houses in the heart of Soho make a peaceful bolthole, for artistic temperaments of many kinds. The interior is furnished with Victorian antiques with mod cons unobtrusively incorporated.	AE MC V				23
OXFORD STREET & SOHO: *Sanderson*. Map 3 A4. £££££ 50 Berners St, W1. 020 7300 1400. FAX 020 7300 1401. One of London's sleekest hotels. Decor is truly eye-catching with courtyard, fountains and voguish bedrooms.	AE MC V	■	●	■	150
BLOOMSBURY: *Generator*. Map 4 D3. £ 37 Tavistock Place, WC1. 020 7388 7666. FAX 020 7388 7644. Somewhere between sci-fi and industrial chic, this youth-orientated hostel provides budget solutions for impecunious travellers.	MC V	■	●		200
BLOOMSBURY: *Academy*. Map 4 D3. £££ 21 Gower St, WC1. 020 7631 4115. FAX 020 7636 3442. Five Georgian townhouses near the heart of London University. Inside, the ambience is sophisticated without excess.	AE DC MC V	■			49
BLOOMSBURY: *Charlotte Street*. Map 4 E4. £££££ 15 Charlotte St, W1. 020 7806 2000. FAX 020 7806 2002. The "Bloomsbury" theme incorporates original period art in the spacious. public areas, while bedrooms run to mini-TV screens in the granite bathrooms and exemplary high-tech facilities.	AE DC MC V	■	●	■	52
COVENT GARDEN & STRAND: *Covent Garden*. Map 4 F6. £££££ Monmouth St, WC2. 020 7806 1000. FAX 020 7806 1100. W www.firmdale.com A discreet but theatrical hotel on one of Covent Garden's most interesting streets. A tour-de-force of dramatic interior design.	AE MC V	■	●		58
COVENT GARDEN & STRAND: *One Aldwych*. Map 4 F6. £££££ Aldwych, WC2. 020 7300 1000. FAX 020 7300 1001. W www.onealdwych.co.uk Filled with contemporary works of art, every inch of this hotel is imaginative, with well-thought out rooms. Underwater classical music plays in the swimming pool.	AE DC MC V	■	●		105
COVENT GARDEN & STRAND: *Savoy*. Map 4 F6. £££££ Strand, WC2. 020 7836 4343. FAX 020 7872 8901. W www.savoy-group.co.uk Flamboyant Art Deco hotel with glorious waterfront views, combining period character with modern comforts.	AE DC MC V	■	●	■	207
REGENTS PARK & MARYLEBONE: *Dorset Square*. Map 3 A3. ££££ 39–40 Dorset Sq, NW1. 020 7723 7874. FAX 020 7724 3328. W www.firmdale.com Beautifully restored Regency building with antiques, overlooking an 18th-century square. Rooms have distinct characters, service is friendly.	AE MC V	■	●		38
WATERLOO & SOUTHWARK: *Novotel Waterloo*. Map 6 F3. £££ 113 Lambeth Rd, SE1. 020 7793 5730. FAX 020 7793 0202. Good for families – two children stay free when they share parents' rooms. Front rooms have views of Lambeth Palace and Westminster.	AE DC MC V	■	●		187
WATERLOO & SOUTHWARK: *County Inn Travel Inn Capital*. Map 6 F3. £ Belvedere Rd, SE1. 020 7902 1600. FAX 020 7902 1619. W www.travelinn.co.uk Excellent value in the old GLC building near the London Eye. Practical and spacious rooms and central location. Book in advance.	AE DC MC V	■			313

CITY: *Novotel Tower Bridge.*   £££
10 Pepys St, EC3. 020 7265 6000. FAX 020 7265 6060. W www.novotel.com
This newly opened chain hotel in a fascinating part of London has well-equipped pleasing bedrooms. Good value for families. 🛏 🔧 💤
AE DC MC V   203

CITY: *Great Eastern.*   £££££
Liverpool St, EC2. 020 7618 5010. FAX 020 7618 5011.
A restoration of Liverpool Street's grand railway hotel with smart restaurants and elegant bedrooms. 🛏 🔧 💤
AE DC MC   267

CITY: *Rookery*   £££££
Cowcross St, EC1. 020 7336 0931. FAX 020 7336 0932.
Lovingly restored B&B in several 18th-century cottages near Smithfield market.
All rooms have handsome period furnishings. 🛏 💤
AE DC MC V   33

CANARY WHARF: *Four Seasons Canary Wharf*   £££££
46 Westferry Circus, E14. 020 7510 1999. FAX 020 7510 1998.
A stunning complex with superb waterfront views and facilities. The Holmes
Place leisure centre is just next door. 🛏 🔧 💤
AE DC MC V   139

HAMPSTEAD: *La Gaffe*   ££
107–111 Heath St, NW3. 020 7435 8965. FAX 020 7794 7592. W www.lagaffe.co.uk
A cheerful, family-run Italian restaurant-with-rooms, in the heart of Hampstead
village. Bedrooms are simple but pretty. 🛏 💤
AE MC V   18

THE DOWNS AND CHANNEL COAST

ASHFORD: *Bettman's Oast*   ££
Hareplain Rd, Beddenden, Ashford, Kent, TN27 8LJ. & FAX 01580 291463.
Set within ten acres of Kentish countryside, this hotel was once an oast house
(where hops or malt are dried) and barn. The spacious rooms are oak-beamed
and pine-furnished, with relaxing, rural views. 🛏 P
MC V   2

BATTLE: *Powdermills* W www.powdermills.co.uk   £££
Powdermill Lane, Battle, E Sussex TN33 0SP.
01424 775511. FAX 01424 774540.
Surrounded by parkland that includes a fishing lake, this hotel has
very comfortable rooms and an attractive restaurant. 🛏 P 🏊 🔧
AE DC MC V   35

BRIGHTON: *Dove*   ££
18 Regency Square, Brighton BN1 2FG.
01273 779222. FAX 01273 746912.
Only a few minutes' walk to the sea, this family-run Regency house has
modern pristine bedrooms. Service is efficient and friendly. 🛏
AE DC MC V   9

BRIGHTON: *Topps*   £££
17 Regency Square, Brighton BN1 2FG.
01273 729334. FAX 01273 203679.
This smart hotel is a pair of beautifully furnished Regency town houses.
Most bedrooms have gas-coal fires and large bathrooms. 🛏 🔧
AE DC MC V   15

CANTERBURY: *Thanington* W www.thaningtonhotel.co.uk   ££
140 Wincheap, Canterbury, Kent CT1 3RY. 01227 453227. FAX 01227 453225.
Only minutes from the town centre, this smart Georgian house offering
bed-and-breakfast is immaculately kept throughout. 25 Dec. 🛏 P 🏊
AE DC MC V   15

CUCKFIELD: *Ockenden Manor* W www.itshotels.co.uk   £££
Ockenden Lane, Cuckfield, W Sussex RH17 5LD. 01444 416111. FAX 01444 415549.
A 16th-century manor with lovely gardens and views of the South Downs.
Extremely comfortable with a good restaurant. 🛏 P
AE DC MC V   22

DOVER: *Number One Guesthouse* W www.number1guesthouse.co.uk   £
1 Castle St, Dover, Kent CT16 1QH. 01304 202001. FAX 01304 214078
Immaculate B&B overlooked by Dover Castle, only minutes to the
Channel Tunnel and ferry. Breakfast in your room.
25 Dec, 1 Jan. 🛏 P
   4

FLETCHLING: *Griffin* W www.thegriffin.co.uk   ££
Fletchling, nr Uckfield, E Sussex TN22 3SS. 01825 722890. FAX 01825 722810.
An oak-panelled and beamed 16th-century inn on the village
high street. Beautiful views and excellent restaurant. Bedrooms in the converted
barn have four-poster beds. *(See also p608.)* 🛏 💤 P 🔧
AE DC MC V   8

<table>
<tr><td colspan="2">

Price categories for a standard double room per night, inclusive of breakfast, service charges and any additional taxes such as VAT:
£ under £50
££ £50–£100
£££ £100–£150
££££ £150–£200
£££££ £200 plus.

</td><td colspan="2">

RESTAURANT
Hotel restaurant or dining room usually open to non-residents unless otherwise stated.
CHILDREN WELCOME
Child cots available. Some hotel restaurants have children's portions and high-chairs.
GARDEN/TERRACE
Hotels with a garden, courtyard or terrace, often providing tables for eating outside.
CREDIT CARDS
Indicates which credit cards are accepted: *AE* American Express; *DC* Diners Club; *MC* Master Card/Access; *V* Visa.

</td></tr>
</table>

	CREDIT CARDS	RESTAURANT	CHILDREN WELCOME	GARDEN/TERRACE	NUMBER OF ROOMS
HAYLING ISLAND: *Cockle Warren Cottage* **££** 36 Seafront, Hayling Island, Hants PO11 9HL. ☎ 023 92464961. FAX 023 92464838. Across the road from the sea, this modern hotel has a conservatory restaurant. Bedrooms are small but pleasant. ● 24–26 Dec. 🖼 🔳 P 🌊	MC V	▪		▪	6
HOLMBURY ST MARY: *Bulmer Farm* **£** Holmbury St Mary, Dorking, Surrey RH5 6LG. ☎ 01306 730210. The grounds of this 17th-century farmhouse have an 1-ha (2-acre) lake, which is a haven for birds and other wildlife. Good local pubs. 🖼 🔳 P				▪	8
HORDLE: *Gordleton Mill* **££** Silver St, Hordle, Lymington, Hants SO41 6DJ. ☎ 01590 682219. FAX 01590 683073. Attractive 17th-century mill house on the River Avon with large garden. Luxurious bedrooms and a fine restaurant. 🖼 🔳 P	AE MC V	▪		▪	9
MAIDSTONE: *Chilston Park Hotel* W www.macdonaldhotel.co.uk **£££** Sandway, Lenham, Kent ME17 2BE. ☎ 01622 859803. FAX 01622 858588. A romantic 16th-century country mansion, grade 1 listed, set in 250 acres of open parkland. The hotel has beautiful views over the lake and the surrounding area. 🖼 🔳 24 🔳 P	AE DC MC V	▪	●	▪	53
MIDHURST: *Angel* W www.hshotels.co.uk **£££** North St, Midhurst, W Sussex GU29 9DN. ☎ 01730 812421. FAX 01730 815928. Smartly modernized 16th-century coaching inn, in the centre of this historic village. Both restaurant and brasserie are excellent. 🖼 24 P	AE DC MC V	▪	●	▪	28
NEW MILTON: *Chewton Glen* W www.chewton.glen.com **£££££** Christchurch Rd, New Milton, Hants BH25 6QS. ☎ 01425 275341. FAX 01425 272310. Luxury country house hotel on the edge of the New Forest, with excellent leisure facilities and a justly acclaimed restaurant. 🖼 🔳 🔳 P	AE DC MC V	▪		▪	62
RINGWOOD: *Moortown Lodge* W www.moortownlodge.co.uk **££** 244 Christchurch Rd, Ringwood, Hants BH24 3AS. ☎ 01425 471404. FAX 01425 476052. Simple but attractive hotel with comfortable rooms. Good value and atmospheric restaurant. ● 25 Dec–mid-Jan. 🖼 P	AE MC V	▪	●		6
RYE: *Jeake's House* W www.jeakeshouse.com **££** Mermaid St, Rye, E Sussex TN31 7ET. ☎ 01797 222828. FAX 01797 222623. A 17th-century house in one of the prettiest cobbled streets in Rye. Comfortable, well-decorated rooms. Lots of choice at breakfast. 🖼 P	MC V				12
RYE: *Old Vicarage* W www.oldvicaragerye.co.uk **££** 66 Church Square, Rye, E Sussex TN31 7HF. ☎ 01797 222119. FAX 01797 227466. Very attractive pink 18th-century house in the heart of historic Rye. Comfortable, pretty rooms and delicious breakfasts. 🖼 🔳 P			●	▪	5
ST MARGARET'S-AT-CLIFFE: *Wallett's Court* W www.wallettscourt.com **££** West Cliffe, St Margaret's-at-Cliffe, Dover, Kent CT15 6EW. ☎ 01304 852424. FAX 01304 853430. @ wallettscourt@compuserve.com Well-positioned for Dover, this family-run 17th-century manor house is comfortably old-fashioned with a good restaurant. 🖼 P 🌊	AE DC MC V	▪	●	▪	16
SEAVIEW: *Seaview* W www.seaviewhotel.co.uk **££** High St, Seaview, Isle of Wight PO34 5EX. ☎ 01983 612711. FAX 01983 613729. The hotel has great views of the sea from some of the bedrooms and the sitting room. A choice of two bars to unwind in. Pets allowed. ● 24–27 Dec. 🖼 P 24	AE DC MC V	▪	●	▪	16
SEVENOAKS: *Royal Oak Hotel* **££** High St, Sevenoaks, Kent TN13 1HY. ☎ 01732 455109. FAX 01732 740187. Individually decorated rooms in a 17th-century coaching inn and modern annexe. Situated just opposite Knole House. 🖼 P	AE DC MC V	▪	●	▪	37

UCKFIELD: *Hooke Hall* [W] www.johansens.com　　££　AE MC V　● ■ 10
250 High St, Uckfield, E Sussex TN22 1EN. [C] *01825 761578.* [FAX] *01825 768025.*
This Queen Anne house offers a very high standard of comfort.
Restaurant specializes in Italian cooking. ● *24 Dec–2 Jan.* [icons] P

VENTNOR: *Royal* [W] www.royalhoteliow.co.uk　　£££　AE DC MC V　■ ● ■ 55
Belgrave Rd, Ventnor, Isle of Wight PO38 1JJ. [C] *01983 852186.* [FAX] *01983 855395.*
Once an annexe to Osborne House, this grand Victorian hotel has
flamboyant public rooms and a conservatory with views of the garden and sea.
Rooms are spacious and smart. ● *26 Dec–2 Jan.* [icons] P

WICKHAM: *Old House Hotel and Brasserie*　　££　AE MC V　■ ● ■ 9
The Square, Wickham, Hants PO17 5JG. [C] *01329 833049.* [FAX] *01329 833672.*
Set among listed buildings, this 18th-century hotel has simple yet
stylish decor and excellent food. ● *26 Dec–1 Jan.* [icons] P

WINCHESTER: *Wykeham Arms*　　££　AE DC MC V　■ ■ 13
75 Kingsgate St, Winchester, Hants SO23 9PE. [C] *01962 853834.* [FAX] *01962 854411.*
One of the oldest pubs in the town with its original charm intact. The bars
are lit by low lights and log fires. Cosy bedrooms. ● *25 Dec.* [icons] P

EAST ANGLIA

BLAKENEY: *White Horse*　　££　AE MC V　■ ● ■ 10
4 High St, Blakeney, Holt, Norf NR25 7AL. [C] *01263 740574,* [FAX] *01263 741303.*
A friendly pub in the centre of this attractive coastal village. Restaurant
in a converted coach house. Pleasant bedrooms. ● *2–17 Jan.* [icons] P

BROXTED: *Whitehall* [W] www.whitehallhotel.co.uk　　£££　AE DC MC V　■ ● ■ 26
Broxted, nr Stansted Airport, Essex CM6 2BZ. [C] *01279 850603.* [FAX] *01279 850385.*
Useful for the airport, this Elizabethan manor has large bedrooms.
Excellent restaurant. ● *25–30 Dec.* [icons] P

BURNHAM MARKET: *Hoste Arms* [W] www.thehostearm.co.uk　　££　MC V　■ ● ■ 28
The Green, Burnham Market, Kings Lynn, Norf PE31 8HD.
[C] *01328 738257.* [FAX] *01328 730103.* [@] thehostearms@compuserve.com
A popular inn facing the green, with bars and a choice of restaurants.
Decor throughout is attractive. Good-sized bedrooms. [icons] P

CAMBRIDGE: *Lensfield Hotel* [W] www.lensfieldhotel.co.uk　　££　AE DC MC V　■ ● ■ 36
53 Lensfield Rd, Cambridge, Cambs CB2 1EN. [C] *01223 355017.* [FAX] *01223 312022.*
Conveniently located within walking distance of the city centre, with a
restaurant serving English, French and Greek cuisine. ● *20 Dec–5 Jan.* [icons] P

CAMBRIDGE: *Sorrento Hotel* [W] www.sorrentohotel.com　　££　AE DC MC V　■ ● 30
196 Cherry Hinton Rd, Cambridge, Cambs CB1 7AN.
[C] *01223 243533.* [FAX] *01223 213463.*
Attractive family-run hotel, boasting an excellent restaurant. [icons] P

CAMPSEA ASHE: *Old Rectory*　　££　AE DC MC V　■ ■ 7
Campsea Ashe, nr Woodbridge, Suff IP13 0PU. [C] & [FAX] *01728 746524.*
A part-Georgian, part-Tudor creeper-clad rectory. In summer, dinner is in the
conservatory overlooking the gardens. ● *23 Dec–mid-Jan; 10–31 Mar.* [icons] P

CAWSTON: *Grey Gables*　　£££　　● ■ 8
Norwich Rd, Cawston, Norwich, Norf NR10 4EY. [C] & [FAX] *01603 871259.*
An former rectory set in a large garden (with tennis court) and vineyard.
It is available from between £800–£2,000 per week, self-catering. [icons] P

CLEY-NEXT-THE-SEA: *Cley Mill* [W] www.smoothhound.co.uk/hotel/cleymill　　££　MC V　■ 8
Cley-next-the-sea, Holt, Norf NR25 7NN. [C] & [FAX] *01263 740209.*
Converted 18th-century windmill makes for an unusual hotel. Charming
rooms with views across the marshes. Evening meal on request. [icons] P

DEDHAM: *Dedham Hall* [W] www.dedhamhall.demon.co.uk　　££　MC V　■ ● ■ 16
Brook St, Dedham, Essex CO7 6AD. [C] *01206 323027.* [FAX] *01206 323293.*
A 15th-century cottage with an annexe of bedrooms. Comfy sitting
rooms with log fires and games. Good home cooking. ● *2 weeks Jan.* [icons] P

EYE: *Cornwallis Arms* [W] www.thecornwall...　　££　MC V　■ ■ 16
Brome, Eye, Suff IP23 8AJ. [C] *01379 870326.* [FAX] *01379 870051.*
Dating back to 1561, this hotel is based within a Grade 2 listed building. The
20-acregrounds contain some of the finest examples of topiary in Britain. [icons] P

Price categories for a standard double room per night, inclusive of breakfast, service charges and any additional taxes such as VAT:
£ under £50
££ £50–£100
£££ £100–£150
££££ £150–£200
£££££ £200 plus.

RESTAURANT
Hotel restaurant or dining room usually open to non-residents unless otherwise stated.

CHILDREN WELCOME
Child cots available. Some hotel restaurants have children's portions and high-chairs.

GARDEN/TERRACE
Hotels with a garden, courtyard or terrace, often providing tables for eating outside.

CREDIT CARDS
Indicates which credit cards are accepted: *AE* American Express; *DC* Diners Club; *MC* Master Card/Access; *V* Visa.

	CREDIT CARDS	RESTAURANT	CHILDREN WELCOME	GARDEN/TERRACE	NUMBER OF ROOMS
GREAT DUNMOW: *Starr* W www.zynet.co.uk/menu/starr £££ Market Place, Great Dunmow, Essex CM6 1AX. 01371 874321. FAX 01371 876337. Originally a pub, the 500-year-old Starr is now a restaurant-with-rooms. Warm and welcoming. ● *1st week Jan.*	AE MC DC V	■	●		8
GREAT SNORING: *Old Rectory* W www.norfolkcountryhouse.co.uk £££ Barsham Rd, Great Snoring, Fakenham, Norf NR21 0HP. 01328 820597. FAX 01328 820048. @ greatsnoringoldrectory@compuserve.com Close to Walsingham, this hotel makes a perfect base for exploring this part of Norfolk. Homely comfort in a peaceful setting. ● *24–27 Dec.*	AE DC MC V	■		■	6
GRIMSTON: *Congham Hall* W www.conghamhallhotel.co.uk £££ Grimston, Kings Lynn, Norf PE32 1AH. 01485 600250. FAX 01485 601191. A fine Georgian house with a restaurant that uses vegetables and herbs from its garden. Guests are expected to change for dinner.	AE DC MC V	■		■	14
HINTLESHAM: *Hintlesham Hall* W www.hintlesham-hall.co.uk £££ George St, Hintlesham, nr Ipswich, Suff IP8 3NS. 01473 652334. FAX 01473 652463. With a fine symmetrical Georgian frontage, this sophisticated hotel has a range of room styles. *(See also p585.)*	AE DC MC V	■	●	■	33
HORDON-ON-THE-HILL: *Hill House* W www.bell-inn.co.uk ££ High Road, Hordon-on-the-Hill, Essex SS17 8LD. 01375 642463. FAX 01375 361611. @ bell-inn@sdn.co.uk Bedrooms are well decorated with good bathrooms. Guests can eat at the Bell down the road. Excellent value. ● *25–31 Dec.*	AE MC V	■		■	16
LAVENHAM: *Angel* W www.lavenham.co.uk/angel ££ Market Pl, Lavenham, Suff CO10 9QZ. 01787 247388. FAX 01787 248344. Friendly, unpretentious 600-year-old inn. Great atmosphere with a rustic feel. Lots of beams. Bedrooms are clean and cheerful.	AE MC V	■	●	■	8
LAVENHAM: *Swan* W www.heritagehotels.com £££££ High St, Lavenham, Sudbury, Suff CO10 9QA. 01787 247477. FAX 01787 248286. In this historical village, the Swan dates back to the 14th century: full of cosy corners. Well-decorated panelled bedrooms.	AE DC MC V	■			51
LONG MELFORD: *The Black Lion* ££ The Green, Long Melford, Suff CO10 9DN. 01787 312356. FAX 01787 374557. Very popular, friendly place overlooking the green. Unpretentious and bright with lots of books, games and childrens' toys. Good food.	AE MC V	■	●	■	10
LONG MELFORD: *Bull* W www.oldenglish.co.uk £££ Hall St, Long Melford, Suff CO10 9JG. 01787 378494. FAX 01787 880307. The centrally placed Bull is a reliable base for the area. The pretty village of Long Melford is famous for antique shops.	AE DC MC V	■	●	■	25
MORSTON: *Morston Hall* W www.morstonhall.com £££ Morston, Holt, Norf NR25 7AA. 01263 741041. FAX 01263 740419. Comfort and delicious food on this beautiful stretch of the north Norfolk coast. Price includes four-course dinner. Pets allowed. ● *Jan.*	AE MC V	■	●		6
ROCHFORD: *Renouf* W www.hotelrenouf.fsnet.co.uk ££ Bradley Way, Rochford, Essex SS4 1BU. 01702 541334. FAX 01702 549563. A modern, efficiently run, comfortable hotel. Extremely good French restaurant. Excellent value and high standards. ● *26–30 Dec.*	AE DC MC V	■	●	■	23
SOUTHWOLD: *Crown* @ crownreception/adnams@adnams.co.uk ££ High St, Southwold, Suff IP18 6DP. 01502 722275. FAX 01502 727263. Friendly atmosphere with wooden floors and armchairs in the bars. Excellent food. Old-fashioned bedrooms: good value. ● *2 wk Jan.*	AE DC MC V	■	●		14

SOUTHWOLD: *Swan* @ swan.hotel@adnams.co.uk £££ AE DC MC V | 43
Market Pl, Southwold, Suff IP18 6EG. (01502 722186. FAX 01502 724800.
A smart family hotel. The dinner menu is traditionally English. Bedrooms
are decorated to a high standard with all the trimmings. 🛁 24 & P

STOKE-BY-NAYLAND: *Angel* ££ MC V | 6
Stoke-by-Nayland, nr Colchester, Essex CO6 4SA.
(01206 263245. FAX 01206 263373.
In the heart of the village, the Angel is immediately welcoming. Homely rooms
and excellent food. Bars buzz with activity. ● 25–26 Dec, 1 Jan. 🛁 🎐 & P

SWAFFHAM: *Strattons* w www.strattons-hotel.co.uk £££ AE MC V | 6
4 Ash Close, Swaffham, Norf PE37 7NH. (01760 723845. FAX 01760 720458.
Elegance and panache evident in this small but special hotel. Bedrooms
are luxurious but the atmosphere is relaxed. ● 24–26 Dec. 🛁 🎐 P

THORNHAM: *The Lifeboat* w www.lifeboatinn.co.uk ££ MC V | 13
Ship Lane, Thornham, Norf PE36 6LT. (01485 512236. FAX 01485 512323.
Attractive pub overlooking the marshes. Rooms are of a high standard.
The pub is traditional, but the restaurant is sophisticated. 🛁 🎐 P

WELLS-NEXT-THE-SEA: *Lifeboat Inn* £ | 6
Station Rd, Wells-next-the-Sea, Norf NR23 1EA. (01328 710288.
Centrally located in one of the oldest buildings in town and only two minutes'
walk from the quayside. ● 24–25 Dec. 🛁 🎐 P

THAMES VALLEY

BLEDLOW: *Cross Lanes Cottage* ££ | 3
West Lane, Bledlow, Bucks P27 9PF. (01844 345339. FAX 01844 274165.
The Cross Lanes is a pretty 16th century cottage with a typically English
country garden, set within a small conservation village. The staff are very
friendly, and insist upon guests making themselves at home. 🛁 🎐 24 P

BURFORD: *Burford House* w www.burford-house.co.uk £££ AE MC V | 7
High St, Burford, Oxon OX18 4QA (01993 823151. FAX 01993 823240.
In a touristy village, this 15th-century house offers B&B, lunches and high teas.
Residents escape to their lounge and luxurious bedrooms. ● 24, 25 Dec. 🛁 🎐

CHADLINGTON: *Chadlington House* w www.chadlingtonhouse.com ££ MC V | 10
Chadlington, Oxon OX7 3LZ. (& FAX 01608 676437.
An unpretentious, long-established hotel which is hired by groups for exclusive
use. A mixture of old-fashioned and modern furnishings. Good service. 🛁 P

CLANFIELD: *Plough* £££ AE DC MC V | 12
Bourton Rd, Clanfield, Oxon OX18 2RB. (01367 810222. FAX 01367 810596.
Very attractive Cotswold-stone village inn. Popular throughout the year,
with a great atmosphere in the bar. Comfortable bedrooms. 🛁 🎐 P

HENLEY-ON-THAMES: *Red Lion* w www.redlionhenley.co.uk £££ AE MC V | 26
Hart St, Henley-on-Thames, Oxon RG9 2AR. (01491 572161. FAX 01491 410039.
A 14th-century coaching inn on the river. A major refurbishing programme
was completed in 1998. All rooms are furnished with antiques. 🛁 24 P

HUNGERFORD: *Marshgate Cottage* w www.marshgate.co.uk £ MC V | 10
Marsh Lane, Hungerford, Newbury RG17 0QX.
(01488 682307. FAX 01488 685475. @ reservations@henley.co.uk
Small family hotel about a mile from the centre of Hungerford. The dining room
serves good food with a European emphasis, but only to groups. 🛁 P &

HURLEY: *Ye Olde Bell* w www.jarvis.co.uk ££££ AE DC MC V | 47
High St, Hurley, Nr. Maidenhead, Berks SL6 5LX. (01628 825881. FAX 01628 825939.
Dating back to the 12th century and said to be England's oldest inn.
Bedrooms and the public rooms retain the house's character. 🛁 24 P

KELMSCOTT: *The Plough* ££ MC V | 8
Kelmscott, Lechlade, Oxon GL7 3HG. (01367 253543. FAX 01367 252514.
A pretty inn in an unspoilt village on the Thames. The furnishings are naturally
William Morris as his former home, Kelmscott Manor, is nearby. 🛁 🎐 P

MARLOW BOTTOM: *Holly Tree House* ££ AE MC V | 5
Burford Close, Marlow Bottom, Bucks SL7 3NE. (01628 891110. FAX 01628 481278.
An efficient, modern B&B with plenty of facilities and good breakfasts.
Near the centre of Marlow but in a rural setting. 🛁 🎐 P 🏊

Price categories for a standard double room per night, inclusive of breakfast, service charges and any additional taxes such as VAT:
£ under £50
££ £50–£100
£££ £100–£150
££££ £150–£200
£££££ £200 plus.

RESTAURANT
Hotel restaurant or dining room usually open to non-residents unless otherwise stated.

CHILDREN WELCOME
Child cots available. Some hotel restaurants have children's portions and high-chairs.

GARDEN/TERRACE
Hotels with a garden, courtyard or terrace, often providing tables for eating outside.

CREDIT CARDS
Indicates which credit cards are accepted: *AE* American Express; *DC* Diners Club; *MC* Master Card/Access; *V* Visa.

	Credit Cards	Restaurant	Children Welcome	Garden/Terrace	Number of Rooms
MOULSFORD ON THAMES: *Beetle and Wedge* £££ Ferry Lane, Moulsford on Thames, Oxon OX10 9JF. 01491 651381. FAX 01491 651376. An exceptionally appealing hotel on the banks of the Thames. Friendly and efficient service, excellent food and pleasant bedrooms.	AE DC MC V	■	●	■	10
NORTH NEWINGTON: *La Madonette Country Guest House* ££ North Newington, Banbury, Oxon OX15 6AA. 01295 730212. FAX 01295 730363. lamadonett@aol.com A former mill-house, this is a very attractive B&B. In a rural setting, yet close to Banbury. A good-value base for exploring the area.	DC MC V		●	■	5
OXFORD: *Cotswold House* W www.house363.freeserve.co.uk ££ 363 Banbury Rd, Oxford OX2 7PL. 01865 310558. FAX 01865 310558. A small, friendly guesthouse two miles from the city centre on a main residential road.	MC V		●		7
OXFORD: *Old Parsonage* W www.oxford-hotelrestaurant.co.uk ££££ 1 Banbury Rd, Oxford OX2 6NN. 01865 310210. FAX 01865 311262. Very comfortable hotel. Relaxed atmosphere in an excellent spot for sightseeing of the city and outlying countryside. ● 23–28 Dec.	AE DC MC V	■		■	30
SHIPTON-UNDER-WYCHWOOD: *Shaven Crown* ££ Shipton-under-Wychwood, Oxon OX7 6BA. 01993 830330. FAX 01993 832136. Beautiful old inn dating back to 1350.	AE MC V	■	●	■	9
SPARSHOLT: *Star* ££ Watery Lane, Sparsholt, nr Wantage, Oxon OX12 9PL. & FAX 01235 751539. A stone-flagged inn in a tiny village. The bar is popular with walkers and the racing fraternity. Bedrooms are in a separate building.	MC V	■		■	8
STEEPLE ASTON: *Westfield Farm Motel* ££ The Fenway, Steeple Aston, Oxon OX6 3SS. 01869 340591. FAX 01869 347594. A very warm welcome awaits guests, who stay in newly refurbished, converted stables and milking parlour. Evening meals provided.	AE DC MC V	■	●	■	9
UFFINGTON: *Craven* W www.thecraven.co.uk £ Uffington, Oxon SN7 7RD. 013678 241846. Attractive 17th-century B&B in a thatched cottage with one room in an annexe. Dinner round the kitchen table.	AE MC V	■		■	5
WARE: *Hanbury Manor* W www.marriot.com £££ Ware, Herts SG12 0SD. 01920 487722. FAX 01920 487692. Luxury hotel with golf course, health club and swimming pool. An ideal place to relax and unwind.	AE DC MC V	■	●	■	161
WELWYN GARDEN CITY: *Tewin Bury Farmhouse* W www.tewinbury.co.uk ££ Tewin, nr Welwyn Garden City, Herts AL6 0JB. 01438 717793. FAX 01438 840440. Efficient, friendly operation set in farmland. Most bedrooms and the rustic-style restaurant are in converted outbuildings. ● 24 Dec–2 Jan.	AE MC V	■	●	■	29
YARNTON: *Eltham Villa Guest House* £ 148 Woodstock Rd, Yarnton, Oxon OX5 1PW. & FAX 01865 376037. A modest, modern and well-kept B&B with breakfast room and small guest lounge. ● 23–1st week Jan.	MC V		●		6

WESSEX

	Credit Cards	Restaurant	Children Welcome	Garden/Terrace	Number of Rooms
BARWICK: *Little Barwick House* £ Barwick Village, nr Yeovil, Som BA22 9TD. 01935 423902. FAX 01935 420908. Attractive restaurant-with-rooms near the centre of Barwick. Extremely friendly, relaxed atmosphere. Cosy bedrooms and good food.	AE DC MC V	■		■	6

BATH: *Cheriton House* w www.cheritonhouse.co.uk £££
9 Upper Oldfield Park, Bath, BA2 3JX. 01225 429862. FAX 01225 428403.
Reasonably priced B&B about ten minutes' walk from the town centre.
Simple, unfussy decor in the sitting room and bedrooms. — AE DC MC V — 9

BATH: *Paradise House* w www.paradise-house.co.uk £££
86–88 Holloway, Bath, BA2 4PX. 01225 317723. FAX 01225 482005.
An attractive house within easy walking distance of Bath's centre.
Extremely well-decorated with a relaxed atmosphere. — AE DC MC V — 11

BATH: *Sydney Gardens* w sydneygardens.co.uk £££
Sydney Rd, Bath, BA2 6NT. 01225 464818. FAX 01225 484347.
Italianate Victorian villa just outside Bath offering B&B. A delight to
stay in. High standards of comfort and service. 24 Dec–31 Jan. — AE MC V — 6

BATH: *Queensberry* w www.bathqueenberry.com £££££
Russell Street, Bath, BA1 2QF. 01225 447928. FAX 01225 446065.
Four 18th-century terraced houses form a smart hotel in the heart of
Bath. Fine rooms decorated with style. 24–29 Dec. — MC V — 29

BATHFORD: *Eagle House* w www.eaglehouse.co.uk £££
Church St, Bathford, Som BA17RS. 01225 859946. FAX 01225 859430.
Beautiful Georgian house situated in this village only three miles (5 km)
from Bath. Large, light and airy rooms. 20–30 Dec. — MC V — 10

BRADFORD-ON-AVON: *Bradford Old Windmill* £££
4 Masons Lane, Bradford-on-Avon, Wilts BA15 1QN.
01225 866842. FAX 01225 866648.
This converted windmill is unique. The cosy circular rooms make this a
memorable place to stay at. Efficient service with a smile. Jan–Feb. — AE MC V — 3

BRADFORD-ON-AVON: *Priory Steps* £££
Newtown, Bradford-on-Avon, Wilts BA15 1NQ.
01225 862230. FAX 01225 866248.
A fine lodge where guests are treated like family. Dinner is eaten round
the communal table and must be ordered in advance. — MC V — 5

BRISTOL: *Berkely Square Hotel* w www.clifftonhotels.com £££
15 Berkely Square, Cliffton, Bristol BS8 1HB.
0117 925 4000. FAX 0117 925 2970. @ berkelysquare@bestwestern.co.uk
A smart and comfortable town house, with a stylish cocktail bar and restaurant
in the basement. The hotel is cheaper at weekends. — AE DC MC V — 42

CALNE: *Chilvester House* £££
Calne, Wilts SN11 0LP. 01249 813981. FAX 01249 814217.
An elegant but hospitable Victorian country house easy to find just off the A4
near Chippenham. This Wolsey Lodge has excellent home cooking. — AE DC MC V — 3

CRUDWELL: *Old Rectory Hotel* w www.oldrectorycrudwell.co.uk £££££
Crudwell, nr Malmesbury, Wilts SN16 9EP. 01666 577194. FAX 01666 577853.
This 17th-century former rectory is now a beautiful restaurant-with-
rooms, with a relaxed atmosphere and excellent food. — AE DC MC V — 15

DULVERTON: *Ashwick House* w www.ashwickhouse.co.uk £££
Dulverton, Som TA22 9QD. & FAX 01398 323868.
Lovely Edwardian house on the edge of Exmoor overlooking tranquil grounds
on the banks of the River Barle. Well-equipped rooms. — MC V — 6

EVERSHOT: *Summer Lodge* w www.summerlodgehotel.com £££££££
Evershot, Dorset DT2 0JR. 01935 83424. FAX 01935 83005.
One of the country's most attractive hotels, designed by the author Thomas
Hardy. Always full of beautiful flowers. Pretty bedrooms. Extensive wine
list in the restaurant. Croquet and tennis available. — AE DC MC V — 18

HINTON CHARTERHOUSE: *Homewood Park* w www.homewoodpark.com £££££
Hinton Charterhouse, NE Som BA3 6BB. 01225 723731. FAX 01225 723820.
A stylish Georgian house in large well-kept gardens. An attractive alternative
to staying in Bath. Very good restaurant. Tennis and croquet. — AE DC MC V — 19

LOWER BROCKHAMPTON: *Yalbury Cottage* @ yarlbury.cottage@virgin.com £££
Lower Brockhampton, Dorset DT2 8PZ. 01305 262382. FAX 01305 266412.
B&B in a delightful, 300-year-old thatched cottage opposite Thomas
Hardy's school. Evening meals are also provided. Jan. — MC V — 8

For key to symbols see bookmark

		CREDIT CARDS	RESTAURANT	CHILDREN WELCOME	GARDEN/TERRACE	NUMBER OF ROOMS
MINEHEAD: *Exmoor House Hotel*	£		■	●	■	4

Chapel St, Exford, Minehead, Som TA24 7PU. **(** 01643 831304.
A small, family-run business with a friendly atmosphere. Set in the centre of the moor, overlooking the village green and surrounding countryside. 🖥 **P**

NETTLETON: *Fosse Farmhouse* W www.fossefarmhouse.8m.com	£££	AE MC V	■	●	■	6

Nettleton Shrub, Nettleton, nr Chippenham, Wilts SN14 7NJ.
(01249 782286. **FAX** 01249 783066. **@** caroncooper@compuserve.com
Charming small country hotel built of Cotswold stone. There's also a tea-room and antique shop. A hotel with lots of originality. 🖥 **P**

PIDDLETRENTHIDE: *Poachers Inn* W www.thepoachersinn.co.uk	££	MC V	■	●	■	18

Piddletrenthide, Dorset DT2 7QX. **(** 01300 348358. **FAX** 01300 348153.
This whitewashed inn offers good value for money and the spacious bedrooms have recently been refurbished. There is a heated outdoor swimming pool making it ideal for families. ● 24–26 Dec. 🖥 **P** 🏊

SHIPHAM: *Daneswood House* W www.daneswoodhotel.co.uk	££	AE DC MC V	■	●	■	17

Cuck Hill, Shipham, nr Winscombe, Som BS25 1RD. **(** 01934 843145. **FAX** 01934 843824.
Imposing Edwardian hotel with hospitable owners and good food. Rooms in the main house have great character. Modern styling in the new wing. 🖥 📶 **P**

SIMONSBATH: *Simonsbath House*	££	MC V	■		■	7

Simonsbath, Exmoor, Som TA24 7SH. **(** 01643 831259. **FAX** 01643 831557.
A 300-year-old family-run hotel in the heart of Exmoor. Cosy and welcoming. Creaky floors make the place atmospheric. 🖥 **P**

SOMERTON: *Lynch Country House* W www.thelynchcountryhouse.co.uk	££	AE DC MC V		●	■	5/7

Somerton, Som TA11 7PD. **(** 01458 272316. **FAX** 01458 272590.
Bright, friendly Georgian house with comfortable bedrooms. There are five rooms in winter, and seven in summer. ● Dec–Jan. 🖥 📶 **P**

TAUNTON: *Castle* W www.the-castle-hotel.com	£££	AE DC MC V	■	●	■	44

Castle Green, Taunton, Som TA1 1NF. **(** 01823 272671. **FAX** 01823 336066.
Magnificent castle clad in wisteria: a local landmark. The building dates back to Norman times. *(See also p589.)* 🖥 🔲 **24** **P**

TROWBRIDGE: *Old Manor* W www.oldmanorhotel.com	£££	AE DC MC V	■		■	18

Trowle, Trowbridge, Wilts BA14 9BL. **(** 01225 777393. **FAX** 01225 765443.
Most rooms are in the converted buildings across the courtyard. The homely sitting rooms are in the farmhouse. ● 25–26 Dec. 🖥 **P**

VELLOW: *Curdon Mill* W www.curdonmill.com	££	MC V	■		■	6

Vellow, Williton, Som TA4 4LS. **(** 01984 656522. **FAX** 01984 656197.
This converted water mill offers neat bedrooms and a sitting room. You can also enjoy a delicious dinner. ● 25–26 Dec. 🖥 📶 **P** 🏊

WEST BEXINGTON: *Manor*	££	AE DC MC V	■	●	■	13

West Bexington, Dorchester, Dorset DT2 9DF. **(** 01308 897616. **FAX** 01308 897035.
A warm welcome is assured at the Manor, only minutes from Chesil Beach. Inviting residents' lounge with views of the sea. 🖥 **P** **24**

WHITEPARISH: *Newton Farmhouse* W www.newtonfarmhouse.co.uk	£			●	■	8

Southampton Rd, Whiteparish, Salisbury, Wilts SP5 2QL. **(** & **FAX** 01794 884416.
This 16th-century B&B offers six four-poster beds, and evening meals (by arrangement) with vegetables and fruit from the lovely garden. 🖥 📶 **P** 🏊

DEVON AND CORNWALL

ASHBURTON: *Holne Chase* W www.holne-chase.co.uk	£££	MC V	■	●	■	17

2 Bridges Rd, Ashburton, Devon TQ13 7NS. **(** 01364 631471. **FAX** 01364 631453.
Comfortable, informal country hotel in a peaceful position. Large grounds, including a stretch of the River Dart for fishing guests. 🖥 **P**

BARNSTAPLE: *Lynwood House* W www.lynwoodhouse.co.uk £££
Bishops Tawton Rd, Barnstaple, Devon EX32 9EF.
[01271 343695. FAX 01271 379340.
Adequate, well-planned bedrooms have everything you need, though
Lynwood's emphasis is on its excellent restaurant. 🛏 24 P

AE
MC
V

5

BISHOPS TAWTON: *Downrew House* W www.downrew.co.uk £££
Bishops Tawton, nr Barnstaple, Devon EX32 ODY. [& FAX 01271 346673.
A tranquil, family-run hotel surrounded by meadows and gardens. Comfort and
personal service rather than style. Plenty of sports. 🛏 P 🏊

AE
MC
V

12

BISHOPS TAWTON: *Halmpstone Manor* W www.halmpstonemanor.co.uk £££
Bishops Tawton, Barnstaple, Devon EX32 OEA.
[01271 830321. FAX 01271 830826. @ reservations@halmpstonemanor.co.uk
Converted farmhouse in a peaceful setting, run with great style. Lovely
panelled dining room and huge bedrooms. ● Jan. 🛏 P

AE
DC
MC
V

5

BOTALLACK: *Manor Farm* £
Botallack, St Just, nr Penzance, Corn TR19 7QG. [01736 788525.
This comfortable 300-year-old house offers B&B only, but there's good
pub food to be found in the village. Substantial breakfasts. 🛏 P

3

BOVEY TRACEY: *Edgemoor* W www.edgemoor.co.uk £££
Haytor Rd, Bovey Tracey, Devon TQ13 9LE.
[01626 832466. FAX 01626 834760.
A 19th-century ivy-clad hotel close to Dartmoor National Park. Efficiently
run with attractive public rooms and bedrooms. ● 27 Dec–3 Jan. 🛏 P

AE
MC
V

15

BRANSCOMBE: *Bulstone Hotel* W www.best-hotel-co.uk/bulstone £
Higher Bulstone, Branscombe, Sidmouth, Devon EX12 3BL. [& FAX 0129 7680 446.
Excellent facilities for families. Suites with parents' and children's rooms, parents'
kitchen, baby-sitting, a playroom and outdoor play area. 🍽 all rooms. P

11

CHAGFORD: *Mill End* @ millendhotel@talk21.com £££££
Sandy Park, Chagford, Devon TQ13 8JN. [01647 432282. FAX 01647 433106.
Well-run, converted flour mill in a lovely setting. Cosy sitting rooms and a
restaurant offering exceptionally good food. ● Jan. 🛏 P

AE
MC
V

17

CULLOMPTON: *Manor House* £££
Fore St, Cullompton, Devon EX15 1JL. [01884 32281. FAX 01884 38344.
Pristine town hotel only minutes from the A5. Built in the 17th century
and faithfully restored, it has elegance and charm. 🛏 P

MC
V

10

DARTMOUTH: *Royal Castle* W www.royalcastle.co.uk £££££
11 The Quay, Dartmouth, Devon TQ6 9PS. [01803 833033. FAX 01803 835445.
Popular, 300-year-old coaching inn on the quay. Bar food with a smarter
restaurant upstairs. Great views from some bedrooms. 🛏 24 P

AE
MC
V

25

DITTISHAM: *Fingals Hotel* W www.fingals.com.co.uk £££
Dittisham, Dartmouth, Devon TQ6 OJA. [01803 722398. FAX 01803 722401.
Highly individual hotel mixing a warm welcome with informality and comfort.
Tennis and croquet available. ● 2 Jan–end Mar. 🛏 P 🏊

AE
MC
V

11

DODDISCOMBSLEIGH: *Nobody Inn* @ inn.nobody@virgin.net £££
Doddiscombsleigh, nr Exeter EX6 7PS. [01647 252394. FAX 01647 252978.
A 16th-century inn, close to Dartmoor National Park. Extremely popular;
additional bedrooms located in a nearby house. *(See also p590.)*
● 24–26 Dec. 🛏 P

MC
V

7

DREWSTEIGNTON: *Hunts Tor* £££
Drewsteignton, Devon EX6 6QW. [01647 281228.
Interesting 17th- and 18th-century building with an Edwardian interior.
Extremely good set dinner served by arrangement. ● Dec–Jan. 🛏

3

EAST PORTLEMOUTH: *Gara Rock* W www.gara.co.uk £
East Portlemouth, nr Salcombe, Devon TQ8 8PH.
[01548 842342. FAX 01548 843033.
Ex-Admiralty coastguard station in a wonderful setting on the cliff-top. Lacking
style, but good facilities. A hotel for all the family. ● mid-Dec–mid-Feb. 🛏 P 🏊

MC
V

23

FOWEY: *Marina* W www.themarinahotel.co.uk £££
The Esplanade, Fowey, Corn PL23 1HY. [01726 833315. FAX 01726 832779.
Compact, neat hotel with efficient service overlooking the Fowey Estuary. A good
base for exploring east Cornwall's fishing villages. 🛏

AE
DC
MC
V

13

<table>
<tr><td colspan="2">

Price categories for a standard double room per night, inclusive of breakfast, service charges and any additional taxes such as VAT:

£ under £50
££ £50–£100
£££ £100–£150
££££ £150–£200
£££££ £200 plus.

</td><td colspan="3">

RESTAURANT
Hotel restaurant or dining room usually open to non-residents unless otherwise stated.

CHILDREN WELCOME
Child cots available. Some hotel restaurants have children's portions and high-chairs.

GARDEN/TERRACE
Hotels with a garden, courtyard or terrace, often providing tables for eating outside.

CREDIT CARDS
Indicates which credit cards are accepted: *AE* American Express; *DC* Diners Club; *MC* Master Card/Access; *V* Visa.

</td></tr>
</table>

	CREDIT CARDS	RESTAURANT	CHILDREN WELCOME	GARDEN/TERRACE	NUMBER OF ROOMS
HELSTON: *Tregaddra Farm* W www.tregaddra.freeserve.co.uk Cury, Cross Lanes, Helston, Corn TR12 7BB. 📞 & FAX *01326 240235*. Two bedrooms have balconies and one a four-poster on this working farm B&B. There is a tennis court and evening meals are provided. 🔲 ⚡ P 🛏	£		●	●	5
LYDFORD: *Castle Inn* W www.smoothhounddirectory.co.uk/lydford Lydford, Okehampton, Devon EX20 4BH. 📞 *01822 820242*. FAX *01822 820454*. Very appealing pink-washed inn. Jolly, convivial atmosphere in the bar and restaurant. Food imaginative and delicious. 🔲 P	££	MC V	■	●	■	9
MEVAGISSEY: *Kerryanna Country House* W www.kerryanna.co.uk Treleaven Farm, Mevagissey, Cornwall PL26 6RZ. 📞 & FAX *01726 843558*. This modern house offers stylish B&B and home-cooked evening meals. There is a games barn and a putting green. ● *Oct–Easter.* 🔲 P 🛏	£	MC V		●	■	6
MITHIAN: *Rose-in-Vale Hotel* W www.rose-in-vale-hotel.co.uk Mithian, St Agnes, Corn TR5 0QD. 📞 *01872 552202*. FAX *01872 552700*. Once the home of a tin-mine owner, this Georgian house is now efficiently run as a country-house hotel. ● *Jan–Feb.* 🔲 P 🛏	££	MC V	■	●	■	18
NORTH BOVEY: *Blackaller* W www.blackaller.co.uk North Bovey, Moreton Hampstead, Devon TQ13 8QY. 📞 *01647 440322*. Delightful and individual converted woollen mill. Full of interesting antiques and curios, it is an extremely relaxing, comfortable place to stay at and a good base for the area. ● *Jan–Feb.* 🔲 ⚡ P	££		■		■	5
PADSTOW: *St Petroc's House* W www.rickstein.com Riverside, Padstow, Corn PL28 8BY. 📞 *01841 532700*. FAX *01841 533344*. St Petroc's is just round the corner from the Seafood Restaurant *(see p590)*, with charming rooms, a reading room, bar and bistro. ● *15–27 Dec.* 🔲 P	££	MC V	■	●	■	13
PENZANCE: *Abbey* W www.abbey-hotel.co.uk Abbey St, Penzance, Corn TR18 4AR. 📞 *01736 366906*. FAX *01736 351163*. A blue-painted, Gothic exterior and an original interior give this comfortable hotel a Bohemian feel. An exceptional place. ● *25, 26 Dec.* 🔲 P	£££	AE MC V	■	●	■	7
ST IVES: *Garrack* W www.garrack.com Burthallan Lane, St Ives, Corn TR26 3AA. 📞 *01736 796199*. FAX *01736 798955*. A family-run hotel above St Ives, within easy reach of the centre. The standard of decor in the bedrooms varies. 🔲 P 🛏	£££	AE DC MC V	■	●	■	18
ST KEYNE: *Well House* W www.wellhouse.co.uk St Keyne, Liskeard, Corn PL14 4RN. 📞 *01579 342001*. FAX *01579 343891*. Stylish, small hotel in an attractive Victorian building with a well-kept garden. The food is flawless as are the comfort and service. Tennis available. 🔲 P 🛏	£££	MC V	■	●	■	9
SALCOMBE: *South Sands Hotel* W www.southsandshotel.com South Sands, Salcombe, Devon TQ8 8LL. 📞 *01548 843741*. FAX *01548 842112*. Relaxing, family-friendly hotel right by a small beach overlooking Salcombe's picturesque waterfront – best enjoyed from the nautically themed terrace bar. Large indoor pool and playroom for children. 🔲 P 🛏	££	AE MC V	■	●	■	30
SIDMOUTH: *Riviera* W www.hotelriviera.co.uk The Esplanade, Sidmouth, Devon EX10 8AY. 📞 *01395 515201*. FAX *01395 577775*. Smart, efficient hotel, part of a fine Regency terrace on the sea front in this pretty seaside town. Strongly co-ordinated decor in public rooms and bedrooms. Helpful staff. ● *Jan–early Feb.* 🔲 🛗 24 P 🚻	£££	AE DC MC V	■	●	■	27
TAVERSTOCK: *The Horn of Plenty* W www.thehornofplenty.co.uk Gulworthy, Taverstock, Devon, PL19 8JD 📞 & FAX *01822 832528*. A 200-year old building with high ceilings and cornices. Surrounded by nearly five acres of gardens. *(See p590)* ● *23–27 Dec.* 🔲 24 ⚡ P	£££	AE MC V	■	●	■	10

VERYAN: *Nare Hotel* w www.narehotel.co.uk — £££££ — MC V — 40
Carne Beach, Veryan, Truro, Corn TR2 5PF.
☎ 01872 501279. FAX 01872 501856.
A modern hotel, with a Victorian-style interior. Most rooms have exceptional
views looking straight out to sea. There is also a gym. 🛏 24 P ≋ 🖕

WIDEGATES: *Coombe Farm* — ££ — AE DC MC V — 9
Widegates, nr Looe, Corn PL13 1QN. ☎ 01503 240223. FAX 01503 240895.
Comfortable, friendly place in a peaceful spot. Lovely views down the valley
to the sea. Facilities include a games room, bar and croquet. 🛏 P ≋ 🖕

THE HEART OF ENGLAND

ALTON: *Alton Towers* w www.altontowers.com — £££ — AE MC V — 175
Alton, Stoke-on-Trent, Staffs ST10 4DB. ☎ 01538 704600. FAX 01538 704657.
Family-orientated hotel very close to the theme park. The Secret Garden restaurant
and Pirate's Lagoon pool cater to children. ● 24–30 Dec. 🛏 ♠ ✂ 🖕 P

BIBURY: *Bibury Court* w www.biburycourt.co.uk — £££ — AE DC MC V — 18
Bibury, nr Cirencester, Glos GL7 5NT.
Jacobean country house. Old-fashioned in parts, but a very relaxing,
friendly place to stay at. Tranquil setting. 🛏 P

BIRMINGHAM: *Asquith House* w www.to-let.birmingham.com — ££ — MC V — 10
19 Portland Rd, Edgbaston, Birmingham B16 9HN.
☎ 0121 454 5282. FAX 0121 456 4668.
Close to the centre of Birmingham, this ivy-clad Victorian house
is immaculate; decor is in keeping with the period. ● 25 Dec–2 Jan. 🛏 P

BIRMINGHAM: *Copperfield House* w www.copperfieldhousehotel.co.uk — ££ — AE MC V — 17
60 Upland Rd, Selly Park, Birmingham B29 7JS.
☎ 0121 472 8344. FAX 0121 415 5655.
Town-house hotel just over two miles from the city centre. Rooms
vary in standard and size, some have been refurbished. Small attractive
restaurant serving good food. ● 21 Dec–2 Jan. 🛏 P 🖕

BIRMINGHAM: *Marriot Hotel* w www.marriott.com/marriot/bhxbh — £££ — AE DC MC V — 98
12 Hagley Rd, Five Ways, Birmingham B16 8SJ. ☎ 0121 452 1144. FAX 0121 456 3442.
Elegant, Edwardian-style hotel, complete with an Egyptian-themed leisure
centre with a gym. Cocktail bar, and two restaurants. 🛏 ♠ 24 P ≋

BLEDINGTON: *King's Head Inn* w www.smoothhound.co.uk — ££ — AE MC V — 12
The Green, Bledington, nr Kingham, Oxon OX7 6HD.
☎ 01608 658 365. FAX 01608 658902.
This delightful 15th-century inn is on a quiet village green. The restaurant
specializes in local game. ● 25–26 Dec. 🛏 ✂ P 🖕

BLOCKLEY: *Lower Brook House* w www.lowerbrookhouse.co.uk — ££ — MC V — 7
Lower St, Blockley, Moreton-in-Marsh, Glos GL56 9DS. ☎ & FAX 01386 700286
In one of the Cotswolds' prettiest villages, this creeper-covered stone cottage is
the stuff of postcards. Add to this the generous hostess who cooks like a dream
and you have the perfect stay. 🛏 ✂ P

BROAD CAMPDEN: *Malt House* w www.malthouse.co.uk — ££ — AE MC V — 8
Broad Campden, Glos GL55 6UU. ☎ 01386 840295. FAX 01386 841334.
Pretty 17th-century cottage with a lovely garden, a charming place
furnished with antiques throughout. Very good food. ● 24–28 Dec. 🛏 P

BROADWAY: *Lygon Arms* w www.the-lygon-arms.co.uk — £££ — AE DC MC V — 69
Broadway, Worcs WR12 7DU. ☎ 01386 852255. FAX 01386 858611.
Situated in a beautiful Cotswold village, this is one of Britain's oldest
and most celebrated inns. The period rooms are filled with antiques,
and the stunning Great Hall (now the restaurant) comes complete with
a 17th century minstrels' gallery and a heraldic freize. 🛏 24 P ≋

BUCKLAND: *Buckland Manor* w www.bucklandmanor.com — £££££ — AE DC MC V — 13
Buckland, nr Broadway, Worcs WR12 7LY. ☎ 01386 852626. FAX 01386 853557.
Lovely 13th-century manor house. A luxury hotel that has managed to
keep its original charm intact and provide high standards. 🛏 P ≋

CHIPPING CAMPDEN: *Cotswold House* w www.cotswoldhouse.com — £££ — AE MC V — 15
Chipping Campden, Glos GL55 6AN. ☎ 01386 840330. FAX 01386 840310.
A 17th-century house which is an extremely smart, stylish hotel.
Exceptional bedrooms and a choice of restaurants. 🛏 P

For key to symbols see bookmark

Price categories for a standard double room per night, inclusive of breakfast, service charges and any additional taxes such as VAT:
£ under £50
££ £50–£100
£££ £100–£150
££££ £150–£200
£££££ £200 plus.

RESTAURANT
Hotel restaurant or dining room usually open to non-residents unless otherwise stated.

CHILDREN WELCOME
Child cots available. Some hotel restaurants have children's portions and high-chairs.

GARDEN/TERRACE
Hotels with a garden, courtyard or terrace, often providing tables for eating outside.

CREDIT CARDS
Indicates which credit cards are accepted: AE American Express; DC Diners Club; MC Master Card/Access; V Visa.

	Credit Cards	Restaurant	Children Welcome	Garden/Terrace	Number of Rooms
CORSE LAWN: *Corse Lawn House* w www.corselawnhousehotel.com £££ Corse Lawn, Glos GL19 4LZ. 01452 780771. FAX 01452 780840. Elegant Queen Anne house on the edge of the village. Outstanding bedrooms, formal but relaxed dining room and a lower-priced bistro. ● 24–26 Dec.	AE DC MC V	■	●	■	19
EATON BISHOP: *Ancient Camp* ££ Ruckhall, Eaton Bishop, Hereford HR2 9QX. 01981 250449. FAX 01981 251581. Welcoming inn with spectacular view of the River Wye. Bedrooms are simple but pleasing. The bar-restaurant is stylishly rustic and the food uses lots of local produce. ● early Jan.	MC V	■		■	5
EVESHAM: *Evesham Hotel* w www.eveshamhotel.com ££ Coopers Lane, off Waterside, Evesham, Worcs WR11 6DA. 01386 765566. FAX 01386 765443. @ reception@eveshamhotel.com Highly original family hotel that will appeal especially to those with children. Everything has been thought of to keep all ages amused. ● 25–26 Dec.	AE DC MC V	■	●	■	40
GREAT RISSINGTON: *Lamb Inn* w www.thelamb-inn.com ££ Great Rissington, Cheltenham, Glos GL54 2LP. 01451 820388. FAX 01451 820724. A most attractive, 300-year-old village inn built of Cotswold stone. Food served in the bar and the rustic-style restaurant.	AE MC V	■		■	14
HANWOOD: *White House* w www.whitehousehanwood.freeserve.co.uk £ Hanwood, Shrewsbury, Shrops SY5 8LP. & FAX 01743 860414. Attractive hotel just south of Shrewsbury. A well-restored 16th-century building with beautiful antique furniture. Good value. Bar for guests only.		■		■	6
HARVINGTON: *Mill at Harvington* ££££ Anchor Lane, Harvington, Evesham, Worcs WR11 5NR. & FAX 01386 870688. Appealing hotel consisting of a Georgian house and a converted mill alongside it. The River Avon passes through the grounds. Excellent restaurant with efficient staff. ● 24–26 Dec.	AE DC MC V	■		■	21
IRONBRIDGE: *Severn Lodge* w www.severnlodge.com ££ New Rd, Ironbridge, Shrops TF8 7AS. 01952 432148. Comfortable, up-market B&B in a quiet spot but only a few minutes' walk from the centre of Ironbridge. Delicious breakfasts. ● Dec.				■	3
KEMERTON: *Upper Court* ££ Kemerton, Tewkesbury, Glos GL20 7HY. 01386 725351. FAX 01386 725472. Idyllic Georgian manor of Cotswold stone in beautiful gardens. Convivial four-course dinners served around a single long table. ● 24–25 Dec.	AE MC V			■	6
KENILWORTH: *Castle Laurels* @ moores22@aol.com ££ 22 Castle Rd, Kenilworth, Warw CV8 1NG. 01926 856179. FAX 01926 854954. Victorian house on main road opposite the ruins of Kenilworth Castle, minutes from town centre. Well kept. ● 20 Dec – 2 Jan.	DC MC V			■	11
LITTLE MALVERN: *Holdfast Cottage* w www.holdfast-cottage.co.uk ££ Marlbank Rd, Little Malvern, Worcs WR13 6NA. 01684 310288. FAX 01684 311117. Small, wisteria-covered hotel, originally 17th century with Victorian additions. Public rooms and bedrooms are well decorated. ● 2–16 Jan.	MC V	■	●	■	8
LUDLOW: *Number Twenty-Eight* w www.no28.co.uk ££ 28 Lower Broad St, Ludlow, Shrops SY8 1PQ. 01584 876996. FAX 01584 876860. A warm welcome awaits at this listed town house of great charm and character. Conveniently located only a few minutes' walk from the town centre.	MC V		●	■	9
MARKET DRAYTON: *Goldstone Hall* w www.goldstonehall.com ££ Market Drayton, Shrops TF9 2NA. 01630 661202. FAX 01630 661585. Rural country-house hotel in a rural setting. Open fires in the public rooms in winter and well-appointed bedrooms.	AE DC MC V	■	●	■	8

OAKAMOOR: *Ribden Farm* [W] www.ribden.fsnet.co.uk
Nr Oakamoor, Stoke-on-Trent ST10 3BW. [C] & [FAX] 01538 702830.
A 1740s farmhouse set in moorland and just a five-minute drive from
Alton Towers. B&B with modernised, well-equipped rooms. ● *Nov–Mar.* 🖶 P
£ | MC V | | ● | ■ | 5

OAKMERE: *Nunsmere Hall* [W] www.nunsmere.co.uk
Tarporley Rd, Oakmere, nr Northwich, Ches CW8 2ES.
[C] 01606 889100. [FAX] 01606 889055. [@] nunsmere@aol.com
Huge Edwardian house with vast lake. Stylish and unstuffy. Delicious
food in the excellent restaurant. 🖶 📶 24 P 🔥
££££ | AE DC MC V | ■ | ● | ■ | 36

PAINSWICK: *Painswick* [W] www.painswickhotel.com
Kemps Lane, Painswick, Glos GL6 6YB. [C] 01452 812160. [FAX] 01452 814059.
A hotel in the heart of the Cotswolds off a main road. Set in peaceful
grounds. Civilized and stylish throughout with a good bar. 🖶 P
£££ | AE MC V | ■ | ● | ■ | 19

STANSHOPE: *Stanshope Hall* [W] www.stanshope.net
Stanshope, nr Ashbourne, Staffs DE6 2AD. [C] 01335 310278. [FAX] 01335 310470.
Historic building on a hill with good views. Highly original with snug
public rooms and bedrooms painted by local artists. ● *24–26 Dec.* 🖶 P
££ | DC MC V | | ● | ■ | 3

STOW-ON-THE-WOLD: *Wyck Hill House* [W] www.wyckhill.com
Burford Rd, Stow-on-the-Wold, Glos GL54 1HY. [C] 01451 831936. [FAX] 01451 832243.
Manor house with superb views over Windrush Valley. Cheaper rooms
in the courtyard. Good food in the formal restaurant. 🖶 📶 24 P 🔥
££££ | AE DC MC V | ■ | ● | ■ | 32

STRATFORD-UPON-AVON: *Caterham House*
58–59 Rother St, Stratford-upon-Avon, Warw CV37 6LT.
[C] 01789 267309. [FAX] 01789 414836.
Centrally placed B&B made from two Georgian houses. Very attractive
inside and out. Comfortable, stylish and well run. ● *24–25 Dec.* P 🖶
££ | MC V | | ● | ■ | 13

ULLINGSWICK: *Steppes Country House* [W] www.steppeshotel.co.uk
Ullingswick, nr Hereford HR1 3JG. [C] 01432 820424. [FAX] 01432 820042.
Restored 400-year-old former farmhouse that is elegant and charming.
A comfortable base from which to explore the area. ● *Dec–Jan.* 🖶 📶 P
££ | MC V | | | ■ | 6

WATERHOUSES: *Old Beams*
Leek Rd, Waterhouses, Staffs ST10 3HW. [C] 01538 308254. [FAX] 01538 308157.
A well-established family-run restaurant-with-rooms on the fringes of the Peak
District. The 18th-century beamed restaurant has a Michelin star.
● *Jan.* 🖶 📶 P 🔥
££ | | ■ | ● | ■ | 5

WEM: *Soulton Hall* [W] www.soultonhall.fsbusiness.co.uk
Wem, Shrewsbury, Shrops SY4 5RS. [C] 01939 232786. [FAX] 01939 234097
Ancient manor farm surrounded by oakwoods and a river. Exposed beams
and Tudor brickwork add an air of distinction. 🖶 P
££ | DC MC V | ■ | ● | ■ | 4

WESTON-UNDER-REDCASTLE: *Citadel* [W] www.citadel2000.freeserve.co.uk
Weston-under-Redcastle, nr Shrewsbury, Shrops SY4 5JY. [C] & [FAX] 01630 685204.
Unusual castellated house built in the early 19th century. ● *Nov–Mar.* 🖶 P
££ | MC V | | ● | ■ | 3

WILMCOTE: *Pear Tree Cottage* [W] www.peartreecot.co.uk
Church Rd, Wilmcote, Stratford-upon-Avon, Warw CV37 9UX.
[C] 01789 205889. [FAX] 01789 262862.
Charming part-Elizabethan cottage. B&B only, but kitchens for the use of
guests. Furnished with antiques. Pretty gardens. ● *24 Dec–31 Jan.* P 🔥
££ | | | | ■ | 7

WOOLSTASTON: *Rectory Farm*
Woolstaston, Leebotwood, nr Church Stretton, Shrops SY6 6NN. [C] 01694 751306.
Convivial atmosphere in attractive, half-timbered farmhouse with garden
and fields. Cosy sitting rooms and large bedrooms. ● *mid-Dec–mid-Jan.* 🖶 P
£ | | | | ■ | 2

WORFIELD: *Old Vicarage Hotel* [W] www.oldvicarageworfield.com
Worfield, Bridgnorth, Shrops WV15 5JZ. [C] 01746 716497. [FAX] 01746 716552.
Imposing Edwardian vicarage with friendly owners. Pristine decoration.
Comfortable rooms with views of the garden and meadows. 🖶 P 🔥
£££ | AE DC MC V | ■ | ● | ■ | 14

EAST MIDLANDS

ASWARBY: *Tally Ho Inn*
Aswarby, Sleaford, Lincs NG34 8SA. [C] 01529 455205. [FAX] 01529 455773.
Historic roadside inn between Lincoln and Peterborough, offering good pub
fare and pretty bedrooms with beamed ceilings and chintzy decor. 🖶 P
£ | MC V | ■ | | ■ | 6

For key to symbols see bookmark

Price categories for a standard double room per night, inclusive of breakfast, service charges and any additional taxes such as VAT:
ⓔ under £50
ⓔⓔ £50–£100
ⓔⓔⓔ £100–£150
ⓔⓔⓔⓔ £150–£200
ⓔⓔⓔⓔⓔ £200 plus.

RESTAURANT
Hotel restaurant or dining room usually open to non-residents unless otherwise stated.
CHILDREN WELCOME
Child cots available. Some hotel restaurants have children's portions and high-chairs.
GARDEN/TERRACE
Hotels with a garden, courtyard or terrace, often providing tables for eating outside.
CREDIT CARDS
Indicates which credit cards are accepted: AE American Express; DC Diners Club; MC Master Card/Access; V Visa.

	CREDIT CARDS	RESTAURANT	CHILDREN WELCOME	GARDEN/TERRACE	NUMBER OF ROOMS
BASLOW: *Cavendish* @ info@cavendish-hotel.net — ⓔⓔⓔ Baslow, Derbs DE45 1SP. 📞 01246 582311. FAX 01246 582312. Very attractive roadside hotel surrounded by the Chatsworth estate. Well-appointed, civilized atmosphere and decorated to a high standard. 🚗 P ♿	AE DC MC V	▦	●	▦	24
CASTLE ASHBY: *Falcon* — ⓔⓔ Castle Ashby, Northnts NN7 1LF. 📞 01604 696200. FAX 01604 696673. Attractive 16th-century stone inn with a warm atmosphere and friendly owners. Good-quality furnishings in the comfortable rooms. Bar serves real ales. 🚗 P	AE MC V	▦	●	▦	16
CHEDDLETON: *Brook House Farm* — ⓔ Brook House Lane, Cheddleton, Leek, Staffs ST13 7DF. 📞 & FAX 01538 360296. B&B accommodation is in spacious bedrooms in the farmhouse and a converted cowshed around a courtyard on this 150-year-old working dairy farm. 🚗 ⚡ P		▦	●	▦	5
EAST BARKWITH: *Bodkin Lodge* — ⓔⓔ Torrington Lane, East Barkwith, Mkt Rasen, Lincs LN8 5RY. 📞 01673 858249. Lovely house in a peaceful location and with excellent views. Large, bright rooms are tasteful and very pleasant. ● 25 Dec – 2 Jan 🚗 P ♿				▦	2
EMPINGHAM: *White Horse* W www.the-white-horse.co.uk — ⓔⓔ Main St, Empingham, Rutland LE15 8PS. 📞 01780 460221. FAX 01780 460521. Delightful rooms either in the original 17th-century country inn or in the attractively converted stable block. The bar food is good and there is also a bistro. 🚗 ⚡ P ♿	AE DC MC V	▦	●	▦	13
GLOSSOP: *Wind in the Willows* W www.windinthewillows.co.uk — ⓔⓔ Derbyshire Level, Glossop, Derbs SK13 1PT. 📞 01457 868001. FAX 01457 853354. Efficiently run Victorian house overlooking the Peak District National Park and ideally situated as a base for exploring this part of the country. The restaurant is for guests only. Golf course nearby. 🚗 P	AE DC MC V	▦	●	▦	12
HATHERSAGE: *Highlow Hall* — ⓔⓔ Highlow, Hathersage, Hope Valley, Derbs S32 1AX. 📞 & FAX 01433 650393. Imposing 16th-century hall in the heart of the Peak District. Inside, it is comfy and unpretentious. Friendly management. 🚗 ⚡ P	MC V			▦	3
ISLEY WALTON: *Donington Park Farmhouse Hotel* — ⓔⓔ Melbourne Rd, Isley Walton, nr Castle Donington, Leic DE74 2RN. 📞 01332 862409. FAX 01332 862364. @ info@parkfarmhouse.co.uk Easy-going atmosphere and great hospitality in this 17th-century farmhouse. Cosy lounge and bar and neat bedrooms. 🚗 P ♿	AE DC MC V	▦	●	▦	15
LANGAR: *Langar Hall* W www.langarhall.com — ⓔⓔⓔ Langar, nr Nottingham NG13 9HG. 📞 01949 860559. FAX 01949 861045. Attractive 19th-century country house built of pale stone. Inside, it is full of antiques. Charming hostess and welcoming atmosphere. 🚗 P	AE DC MC V	▦	●	▦	12
LINCOLN: *D'Isney Place* W www.d'isneyplacehotel.co.uk — ⓔⓔ Eastgate, Lincoln, Lincs LN2 4AA. 📞 01522 538881. FAX 01522 511321. Smart, elegant B&B in the heart of Lincoln. Close to the cathedral. No lounge, but the bedrooms more than compensate. 🚗 24 P	AE DC MC V		●		17
LINCOLN: *Minster Lodge Hotel* W www.minsterlodge.com — ⓔⓔ 3 Church Lane, Lincoln, Lincs LN2 1QJ. 📞 FAX 01522 513220. Conveniently located close to the historic quarter, within two minutes' walk of the cathedral and surrounded by restaurants. 🚗 ⚡ P	AE MC V		●		6
LINCOLN: *White Hart* W www.heritage-hotel.com — ⓔⓔⓔ Bailgate, Lincoln, Lincs LN1 3AR. 📞 01522 526222. FAX 01522 531798. This lovely coaching inn, next to the castle walls, is a smart, well-run hotel that has been receiving guests for over 600 years. 🚗 ⬆ 24 P	AE DC MC V	▦	●	▦	48

MATLOCK BATH: *Hodgkinson's* W www.hodgkinson-hotel.co.uk   ££
150 South Parade, Matlock Bath, Derbs DE4 3NR. 01629 582170.
Hotel-restaurant, lovingly restored. Individually decorated and furnished
bedrooms. Delicious food served in restaurant. ● 25–26 Dec.
AE MC V — 7

PAULERSPURY: *Vine House*   ££
100 High St, Paulerspury, Northnts NN12 7NA. 01327 811267. FAX 01327 811309.
An accomplished restaurant-with-rooms in an attractive 18th-century cottage of
golden ironstone. Bedrooms are furnished with antiques, old clocks and china,
and there is a pretty garden. ● Dec–Jan.
MC V — 6

REDMILE: *Peacock Farm Guest House* W www.peacock-farm.co.uk   ££
Redmile, Vale of Belvoir, Leic NG13 0GQ. 01949 842475. FAX 01949 843127.
Warm welcome in a rambling, extended farmhouse. Good atmosphere
and reasonable comfort. Children made welcome.
AE MC V — 8

SHOTTLE: *Dannah Farm Country Guest House* W www.dannah.co.uk   ££
Bowmans Lane, Shottle, Belper, Derbs DE56 2DR. 01773 550273. FAX 01773 550590.
This lovely Georgian farmhouse on a working farm offers B&B and
home-cooked evening meals by arrangement. ● 25–26 Dec.
MC V — 8

STAMFORD: *The George of Stamford* W www.georgehotelofstamford.com   £££
71 St Martins, Stamford, Lincs PE9 2LB. 01780 750750. FAX 01780 750701.
Splendid 16th-century coaching inn, cosily furnished with a courtyard garden.
Wide choice of meals and the bedrooms are individually designed.
AE DC MC V — 47

STAPLEFORD: *Stapleford Park* W www.stapleford.co.uk   ££££
Stapleford, Melton Mowbray, Leic LE14 2EF. 01572 787 522. FAX 01572 787651.
Huge Jacobean and Neo-Classical country-house hotel. A luxurious, easy-
going place to stay at, with riding, shooting and fishing.
AE DC MC V — 51

UPPINGHAM: *Lake Isle*   ££
16 High St East, Uppingham, Rutland LE15 9PZ. & FAX 01572 822951.
Individually decorated bedrooms in a rustic-style restaurant-with-rooms.
Excellent cooking and a relaxed, convivial atmosphere.
AE DC MC V — 12

LANCASHIRE AND THE LAKES

AMBLESIDE: *Chapel House* W www.chapelhousehotel.co.uk   ££
Kirkstone Rd, Ambleside, Cumbria LA22 9DZ. & 015394 33143.
A few minutes' steep walk up from the main street to this friendly
guesthouse. Small, cottagey bedrooms. ● Jan–Feb.
— 10

AMBLESIDE: *Wateredge* W www.wateredgeinn.co.uk   ££
Waterhead, Ambleside, Cumbria LA22 0EP. 015394 32332. FAX 015394 31878.
On the shores of Windermere, with panoramic views from the sitting
room. New suites in the annexe.
AE DC MC V — 20

APPLEBY-IN-WESTMORLAND: *Royal Oak* W www.royaloak.co.uk   ££
Bongate, Appleby-in-Westmorland, Cumbria CA16 6UN. 017683 51463. FAX 017683 52300.
A very atmospheric place to stay at: the inn dates back to the 1100s and is
near the castle. The restaurant's cuisine is modern British.
AE DC MC V — 9

BASSENTHWAITE: *Ravenstone Lodge* W www.ravenstonelodge.co.uk   ££
Bassenthwaite, Keswick, Cumbria CA12 4QG. & FAX 017687 76629.
This attractive B&B has wonderful views across the fields to Bassenthwaite
Lake. Charming owners make guests feel very welcome.
MC V — 9

BASSENTHWAITE LAKE: *Pheasant Inn* W www.the-pheasant.co.uk   £££
Bassenthwaite Lake, Cockermouth, Cumbria CA13 9YE.
017687 76234. FAX 017687 76002.
A lovely old country inn next to the lakeside with a choice of cosy sitting
rooms. Unfussy bedrooms with modern bathrooms. ● 24–25 Dec.
MC V — 17

BEACON EDGE: *Roundthorn Country House*   ££
Beacon Edge, Penrith, Cumbria CA11 8SJ. 01768 863952. FAX 01768 864100.
An elegant Georgian house set in landscaped gardens on the edge of the
Beacon, with panoramic views of the surrounding area. Light snacks
are served on request in the evenings. Full bar.
AE MC V — 10

BOWNESS-ON-WINDERMERE: *Laurel Cottage* W www.laurelcottage-bnb.co.uk   £
St Martin's Sq, Kendal Rd, Bowness-on-Windermere, Cumbria LA23 3EF.
& FAX 015394 45594. Rooms in the old cottage, or in the more spacious Victorian
part of the house, which was once a grammar school. B&B only.
— 13

For key to symbols see bookmark

<table>
<tr><td colspan="2">

Price categories for a standard double room per night, inclusive of breakfast, service charges and any additional taxes such as VAT:

£ under £50
££ £50–£100
£££ £100–£150
££££ £150–£200
£££££ £200 plus.

</td></tr>
</table>

RESTAURANT
Hotel restaurant or dining room usually open to non-residents unless otherwise stated.

CHILDREN WELCOME
Child cots available. Some hotel restaurants have children's portions and high-chairs.

GARDEN/TERRACE
Hotels with a garden, courtyard or terrace, often providing tables for eating outside.

CREDIT CARDS
Indicates which credit cards are accepted: *AE* American Express; *DC* Diners Club; *MC* Master Card/Access; *V* Visa.

	CREDIT CARDS	RESTAURANT	CHILDREN WELCOME	GARDEN/TERRACE	NUMBER OF ROOMS
BOWNESS-ON-WINDERMERE: *Linthwaite House* **££££** Crook Rd, Bowness-on-Windermere, Cumbria LA23 3JA. 015394 88600. FAX 015394 88601. @ admin@linthwaite.com Stylish and comfortable Edwardian hotel in a stunning location overlooking the lake. Outside lakeview terrace; fishing, croquet and bike hire.	AE DC MC V	■	●	■	26
BUTTERMERE: *Fish Hotel* W www.fishhotel.com **££** Buttermere, nr Cockermouth, Cumbria CA13 9XA. 017687 70253. FAX 017687 70287. Most rooms have a lake view in this former coaching inn in a secluded hamlet. Good bar menu in the evenings. ● Jan.	MC V	■	●	■	12
CARLISLE: *Beeches* **£** Wood St, Carlisle, Cumbria CA1 2SF. 01228 511962. Pretty, pink-washed Georgian cottage with typical English garden. Bedrooms attractively decorated. Dinner on request.				■	3
CARTMEL: *Aynsome Manor* @ info@aynsomemanorhotel.co.uk **£££** Cartmel, nr Grange-over-Sands, Cumbria LA11 6HH. 015395 36653. FAX 015395 36016. Traditional country-house hotel – very cosy. There are great views from most rooms over the peaceful vale of Cartmel. Rates include dinner. ● Jan.	AE MC V	■		■	12
CARTMEL FELL: *Lightwood* W www.lightwoodguesthouse.co.uk **£** Cartmel Fell, Cumbria LA11 6NP. 015395 31454. A 17th-century farmhouse in a peaceful location. Some pretty, cottage-style bedrooms in converted outbuildings. B&B only. ● 24–25 Dec.	MC V		●	■	6
CLAPPERSGATE: *Nanny Brow* W www.nannybrow.co.uk **£££** Clappersgate, Ambleside, Cumbria LA22 9NF. 015394 32036. FAX 015394 32450. Well-run, comfortable hotel close to Ambleside, set in lovely grounds. Lots of facilities and an excellent restaurant.	AE DC MC V	■	●	■	16
COWAN BRIDGE: *Hipping Hall* **££** Cowan Bridge, Kirkby Lonsdale, Carnforth, Lancs LA6 2JJ. 015242 71187. FAX 015242 72452 An elegant 15th-century country house with antique-furnished rooms and an eyecatching Great Hall dining room. ● mid Nov–Easter.	AE MC V	■		■	6
ELTERWATER: *Britannia Inn* W www.britinn.co.uk **££** Elterwater, Cumbria LA22 9HP. 015394 37210. FAX 015394 37311. Set on the village green, this busy little 16th-century inn offers nine rooms in the house and four in the annexe above the post office and village shop. Dinners and cream teas are served in the pub's dining area. ● 24–26 Dec.	AE MC V	■	●	■	13
GRANGE-IN-BORROWDALE: *Borrowdale Gates* **££** Grange-in-Borrowdale, Keswick, Cumbria CA12 5UQ. 017687 77204. FAX 017687 77254. W www.borrowdalegates.com Traditionally furnished, comfortable hotel, well off the beaten track. Great views from the huge picture windows. ● Jan.	AE MC V	■		■	29
GRASMERE: *Thistle Grasmere* W www.grasmere@thistle.co.uk **££** Keswick Rd, Grasmere, Cumbria LA22 9PR. 015394 35666. FAX 015394 35565. A lovely Edwardian building with tastefully modernized facilities. The setting, right next to the lake, is fabulous. Games room and bar.	AE DC MC V	■	●		72
GRASMERE: *White Moss House* W www.whitemoss.com **££** Rydal Water, Grasmere, Cumbria LA22 9SE. 015394 35295. This 18th-century, creeper-covered house has an outstanding reputation for its food, but is also a civilized, comfortable place to stay at. ● Dec.	MC V	■			8
LITTLE SINGLETON: *Mains Hall* W www.mainshall.co.uk **££** Little Singleton, Blackpool FY6 7LE. 01253 885130. FAX 01253 894132. George IV stayed in this historic house, which has lovely grounds and good views over the River Wyre.	AE DC MC V	■	●	■	12

MANCHESTER: *Crowne Plaza* W www.crowneplaza.com £££££ | AE DC MC V | 303
Peter St, Manchester M60 2DS. ☎ 0161 236 3333. FAX 0161 932 4100.
Located in the heart of the city, this venerable hotel dates back to
Victorian times. Facilites include a gym and pool.

MUNGRISDALE: *Mill Hotel* £££ | | 9
Mungrisdale, Penrith, Cumbria CA11 0XR. ☎ 017687 79659. FAX 017687 79155.
Lovely setting for this former mill cottage. Simple, immaculate bedrooms and
cosy public rooms. Exceptional food. Rates include dinner. ● Dec–Feb.

SEATOLLER: *Seatoller House* W www.seatollerhouse.co.uk ££ | MC V | 9
Seatoller, Borrowdale, Keswick, Cumbria CA12 5XN. ☎ 017687 77218. FAX 017687 77189.
Charming guesthouse with friendly, relaxed hosts. It is an ideal walking
base and very good value. Excellent set dinners at 7pm. ● Dec–Feb.

TROUTBECK: *Mortal Man* @ d-mortalman@btinternet.com ££ | AE MC V | 12
Troutbeck, Windermere, Cumbria LA23 1PL. ☎ 015394 33193. FAX 015394 31261.
There are wonderful views to Windermere from this 300-year-old inn.
A mixture of beamed rooms and Victoriana.

WASDALE HEAD: *Wasdale Head Inn* W www.wasdale.com ££ | AE MC V | 9
Wasdale Head, Gosforth, Cumbria CA20 1EX.
☎ 019467 26229. FAX 019467 26334.
Archetypal walkers' pub. Largely Victorian, serving traditional beers and
wholesome food. Simple, unadorned bedrooms and studios.

WATERMILLOCK: *Old Church* W www.oldchurch.co.uk ££ | AE MC V | 10
Watermillock, Penrith, Cumbria CA11 0JN. ☎ 017684 86204. FAX 017684 86368.
On the shores of Ullswater, this stylish and comfortable country-house
hotel is one of the best in the area. ● Nov–Mar.

WATER YEAT: *Water Yeat Country Guest House* ££ | | 5
Water Yeat, nr Ulverston, Cumbria LA12 8DJ. ☎ & FAX 01229 885306.
Charming 17th-century farmhouse in a lovely setting, run with great style and
flair. Attractive bedrooms and imaginative cooking. ● Dec–mid-Feb.

WHITEWELL: *Inn at Whitewell* ££ | AE DC MC V | 17
Whitewell, Forest of Bowland, Clitheroe, Lancs BB7 3AT.
☎ 01200 448222. FAX 01200 448298.
Special pub with sophistication and a relaxed atmosphere. Comfortable
well-equipped bedrooms.

WINDERMERE: *Cedar Manor* W www.cedarmanor.co.uk ££ | MC V | 12
Ambleside Rd, Windermere, Cumbria LA23 1AX.
☎ 015394 43192. FAX 015394 45970. @ cedarmanor@fsbdial.co.uk
This charming small hotel offers a warm welcome and comfortable rooms.
The imaginative cooking is recommended. ● 21–27 Dec, 7–31 Jan.

WINDERMERE: *Holbeck Ghyll* W www.holbeck-ghyll.co.uk £££ | AE DC MC V | 20
Holbeck Lane, Windermere, Cumbria LA23 1LU.
☎ 015394 32375. FAX 015394 34743. @ accommodation@holback-ghyll.co.uk
Imposing Victorian house in a superb position with views over the lake
to the mountains. Very attentive courteous service. Gym and sauna.

WITHERSLACK: *Old Vicarage* W www.oldvicarage.com £££ | AE MC V | 15
Witherslack, nr Grange-over-Sands, Cumbria LA11 6RS.
☎ 015395 52381. FAX 015395 52373. @ hotel@old-vic.demon.co.uk
Informal country-house hotel situated at the end of a leafy country
lane. A perfect place to escape the crowds on the tourist trail.

YORKSHIRE AND THE HUMBER REGION

HARROGATE: *Balmoral* W www.balmoralhotel.co.uk £££ | AE MC V | 19
16 Franklin Mount, Harrogate, N Yorks HG1 5EJ. ☎ 01423 508208. FAX 01423 530652.
A central hotel with quirky, eccentric decor. Bedrooms are flamboyantly
furnished, and the menu is international in flavour.

HAWORTH: *Weavers* W www.weaverssmallhotel.com ££ | AE DC MC V | 3
15 West Lane, Haworth, Bradford BD22 8DU. ☎ 01535 643822. FAX 01535 644832.
Three traditional cottages make up this restaurant-with-rooms in the
village where the Brontë sisters grew up. Delicious, wholesome
food, efficient service and pleasant bedrooms. ● 26 Dec–7 Jan.

For key to symbols see bookmark

RESTAURANT
Hotel restaurant or dining room usually open to non-residents unless otherwise stated.

CHILDREN WELCOME
Child cots available. Some hotel restaurants have children's portions and high-chairs.

GARDEN/TERRACE
Hotels with a garden, courtyard or terrace, often providing tables for eating outside.

CREDIT CARDS
Indicates which credit cards are accepted: *AE* American Express; *DC* Diners Club; *MC* Master Card/Access; *V* Visa.

	Price	Credit Cards	Restaurant	Children Welcome	Garden/Terrace	Number of Rooms
HOLDSWORTH: *Holdsworth House* w www.holdsworthhouse.co.uk Holdsworth, Halifax, Calderdale HX2 9TG. 01422 240024. FAX 01422 245174. Extremely pretty, Jacobean house near Halifax, with most of the decor in keeping with the period. Excellent food. ● 24–31 Dec. 🔒 P	£££	AE DC MC V	■	●	■	40
HUDDERSFIELD: *Lodge* 48 Birkby Lodge Rd, Birkby, Huddersfield, Kirklees HD2 2BG. 01484 431001. FAX 01484 421590. On the outskirts of Huddersfield in a residential street, this is an agreeable, well-maintained hotel. Very good restaurant. ● 24–31 Dec. 🔒 P 🔱	££	AE MC V	■	●	■	12
HUNMANBY: *Wrangham House* 10 Stonegate, Hunmanby, nr Filey, N Yorks YO14 0NS. 01723 891333. FAX 01723 892973 @ mervynpoulter@line1.net Former vicarage with 17th-century origins. Tastefully decorated, with a relaxed, hospitable atmosphere. 🔒 P 🔱	££	AE MC V	■	●	■	13
ILKLEY: *Rombalds* @ reception@rombalds.demon.co.uk West View, Wells Rd, Ilkley, Bradford LS29 9JG. 01943 603201. FAX 01943 816586. Family-run hotel that maintains consistently good standards. Overlooking both the town and beautiful Ilkley Moor. The views are outstanding. Extremely good restaurant. 🔒 P	££	AE DC MC V	■	●	■	16
LASTINGHAM: *Lastingham Grange* w www.lastinghamgrange.co.uk Lastingham, York YO6 6TH. 01751 417345. Family-run hotel with a traditional, homely feel. Well-situated for exploring the historic city of York and the county of Yorkshire. Quiet and peaceful and set in large grounds. ● Dec–Feb. 🔒 P	£££	AE DC V	■	●	■	12
LEEDS: *42 The Calls* w www.42thecalls.co.uk 42 The Calls, Leeds LS2 7EW. 01132 440099. FAX 01132 344100. Very chic, stylish city hotel with a quiet, informal atmosphere. Good brasserie and well-equipped bedrooms. ● 24–27 Dec. 🔒 ⬆ 24 P 🔱	£££	AE DC MC V		●		41
MARKINGTON: *Hob Green* w www.hobgreen.com Markington, Harrogate, N Yorks HG3 3PJ. 01423 770031. FAX 01423 771589. @ hobgreen.hotel@virgin.net Family-run, family-atmosphere hotel just outside Markington. Lovely grounds including a superb croquet lawn and public rooms. 🔒 P	££	AE DC MC V	■	●	■	12
MASHAM: *King's Head* w www.mashamshire/kingshead.com Market Place, Masham, N Yorks HG4 4EF. 01765 689295. FAX 01765 689070. Friendly and traditional inn situated in a brewery town. An excellent selection of local beers in the bar. 🔒 P	££	AE DC MC V	■	●	■	10
MIDDLEHAM: *Miller's House* w www.hotelwensleydale.com Middleham, Wensleydale, N Yorks DL8 4NR. 01969 622630. FAX 01969 623570. Just off the market place in this attractive village – an excellent base for exploring the area. Immaculate throughout. ● Jan–Feb. 🔒 ✂ P	££	MC V	■		■	7
RICHMOND: *Whashton Springs Farm* w www.whashtonsprings.co.uk Richmond, N Yorks DL11 7JS. 01748 822884. FAX 01748 826285. B&B in an elegant Georgian farmhouse on a working farm three miles from Richmond. Some rooms in converted buildings around a well-kept courtyard. ● mid-Dec–end Jan. 🔒 ✂ P	££	MC V			■	8
RIPON: *Mallard Grange* Aldfield, nr Fountains Abbey, Ripon. N Yorks HG4 3BE. 01765 620242. A rambling 16th-century farmhouse brimming with character and charm. The emphasis here is on quality and comfort – the extremely hospitable owners see the same visitors return here year after year. ● 24 Dec–2 Jan. 🔒 P	££				■	4

ROSEDALE ABBEY: *White Horse Farm* [W] www.whitehorsefarmhotel.co.uk £££
Rosedale Abbey, nr Pickering, N Yorks YO18 8SE.
01751 417239. FAX 01751 417781.
Unpretentious hotel overlooking the village – an inn since 1702. Full
of charm and character. A warm welcome is assured.
AE DC MC V · 15

SEDBUSK: *Stonehouse* [W] www.stonehousehotel.com £££
Sedbusk, nr Hawes, Wensleydale, N Yorks DL8 3PT.
01969 667571. FAX 01969 667720. @ daleshotel@aol.com
Attractive stone house built in 1908 and surrounded by old-fashioned
English gardens. Family-run, with a relaxed atmosphere. ● Jan.
MC V · 22

STOKESLEY: *Chapters* £££
27 High St, Stokesley, Middlesbrough TS9 5AD 01642 711888. FAX 01642 713387.
Restored 18th-century coaching inn in the town centre with an excellent
restaurant and comfortable bedrooms. ● 25 Dec.
AE DC MC V · 13

WALKINGTON: *Manor House* [W] www.the-manor-house.co.uk £££
Northlands, Walkington, nr Beverley, E Yorks HU17 8RT.
01482 881645. FAX 01482 866501.
Civilized and comfortable hotel in a lovely location in the heart of
the Wolds. Lovely, light rooms and delicious food.
MC V · 7

WEST WITTON: *Wensleydale Heiffer* [W] www.wensleydale@heiffer.co.uk £££
West Witton, Wensleydale, N Yorks DL8 4LS. 01969 622322. FAX 01969 624183.
A classic Dales pub, recently refurbished in bold colour schemes. Extensive
dining space with lively menus, and pretty rooms.
AE DC MC VC · 14

WINTERINGHAM: *Winteringham Fields* [W] www.winteringhamfields.com £££
Winteringham, Scunthorpe, North Lincs DN15 9PF. 01724 733096. FAX 01724 733898.
A 400-year-old farmhouse, now a popular restaurant-with-rooms.
Comfortable bedrooms. ● Mon, 1st week Aug, 24 Dec–8 Jan.
AE MC V · 10

YORK: *Holmwood House* [W] www.holmwoodhousehotel.co.uk £££
114 Holgate Rd, York YO2 4BB. 01904 626183. FAX 01904 670899.
Exceptional B&B about 15 minutes' walk from the centre of the city. Very
comfortable. Delicious breakfasts and charming owners.
MC V · 14

YORK: *Middlethorpe Hall* [W] www.middlethorpe.com £££££
Bishopthorpe Rd, York YO23 1GB.
01904 641241. FAX 01904 620176. @ reception@middlethorpe.com
Superbly restored and beautifully furnished manor just outside York. Top
class standards and service. Facilities include spa and sauna.
MC V · 30

NORTHUMBRIA

BAMBURGH: *Burton Hall* £
Bamburgh, Northum NE69 7AR. 01668 214213. FAX 01668 214538.
B&B on a working farm just three fields away from the sea with a glorious
view of the Farne Islands. ● Dec–Easter.
· 9

BELLINGHAM: *Westfield Guest House* [W] www.westfield-house.net £££
Bellingham, Northum NE48 2DP.
01434 220340. FAX 01434 220694. @ westfield.house@virgin.net
Cosy and welcoming guesthouse in a very attractive rural position. Peace
and quiet are assured in simple rooms. Dinner on request.
MC V · 5

BERWICK-UPON-TWEED: *Dervaig Guest House* £
1 North Rd, Berwick-upon-Tweed, Northum TD15 2AN. 01289 307378.
Just north of the town centre, this Victorian guesthouse has a beautiful
secluded garden and a general air of tranquillity.
· 5

BERWICK-UPON-TWEED: *Old Vicarage* £
Church Rd, Tweedmouth, Berwick-upon-Tweed, Northum TD15 2AN. 01289 306909.
A few minutes' walk from this 19th-century former vicarage and you
will find yourself right in the centre of town. Cosiness, comfort
and hospitable management. ● 25 Dec–2 Jan.
· 7

BLANCHLAND: *Lord Crewe Arms* £££
Blanchland, nr Consett, Durham DH8 9SP.
01434 675251. FAX 01434 675337. @ lord@crewearms.freeserve.co.uk
This historic coaching inn at the centre of the village has a convivial
atmosphere, and is very popular both with locals and visitors.
AE DC MC V · 19

For key to symbols see bookmark

Price categories for a standard double room per night, inclusive of breakfast, service charges and any additional taxes such as VAT:
£ under £50
££ £50–£100
£££ £100–£150
££££ £150–£200
£££££ £200 plus.

RESTAURANT
Hotel restaurant or dining room usually open to non-residents unless otherwise stated.
CHILDREN WELCOME
Child cots available. Some hotel restaurants have children's portions and high-chairs.
GARDEN/TERRACE
Hotels with a garden, courtyard or terrace, often providing tables for eating outside.
CREDIT CARDS
Indicates which credit cards are accepted: *AE* American Express; *DC* Diners Club; *MC* Master Card/Access; *V* Visa.

	Credit Cards	Restaurant	Children Welcome	Garden/Terrace	Number of Rooms
CROOKHAM: *The Coach House* w www.coachhousecrookham.com ££ Crookham, Cornhill-on-Tweed, Northum TD12 4TD 01890 820293. FAX 01890 820284 The original coach house is now an airy sitting room with high rafters and a huge fireplace. Lots of rustic character; good country cooking. ● *Nov–Easter.*	V	■	●	■	9
DURHAM: *Georgian Town House* ££ 10 Crossgate, Durham DH1 4PS. & FAX 0191 3868070. Lovely Georgian house in the heart of the city, decorated with great flair and imagination. Bright bedrooms and good breakfasts. ● *24 Dec–2 Jan.*				■	7
HEXHAM: *East Peterel Field Farm* ££ Yarridge Rd, Hexham, Northum NE46 2LT. 01434 607209. FAX 01434 601753. Classy accommodation on a working stud farm, with lovely peaceful views. The owner is a Cordon Bleu chef, so work up an appetite.		■	●	■	3
LONGHORSLEY: *Linden Hall* w www.lindenhall.co.uk £££ Longhorsley, Morpeth, Northum NE65 8XF. 01670 500000. FAX 01670 500001. Surrounded by 400 acres of parkland, this fine Georgian house has become a grand hotel and health spa. Sports include tennis and golf.	AE DC MC V	■	●	■	50
NEWCASTLE: *Waterside* w www.watersidehotel.com ££ 48–52 Sandhill, Quayside, Newcastle NE1 3JF. 0191 2300111. FAX 0191 2301615. Smart hotel on the city's quayside. Neat and new, it has well-furnished bedrooms and a good Italian restaurant. ● *25–26 Dec.*	AE DC MC V	■			36
ROMALDKIRK: *Rose and Crown* w www.rose-and-crown.co.uk ££ Romaldkirk, Barnard Castle, Durham DL12 9EB. 01833 650213. FAX 01833 650828. Popular inn on the village green. Well-equipped bedrooms, and a choice of bar food, or meals in the wood-panelled restaurant. ● *25–26 Dec.*	MC V	■	●	■	12

NORTH WALES

	Credit Cards	Restaurant	Children Welcome	Garden/Terrace	Number of Rooms
ABERDYFI: *Penhelig Arms* @ penheligarms@saqnet.co.uk ££ Aberdyfi, Gwynedd LL35 0LT. 01654 767215. FAX 01654 767690. All but one of the bedrooms in this whitewashed inn have a sea view. It has been refurbished and is smart and comfortable. *(See also p601.)* ● *25–26 Dec.*	MC V	■	●	■	14
ABERSOCH: *Porth Tocyn* w www.porth-tocynhotel.co.uk ££ Abersoch, Gwynedd LL53 7BU. 01758 713303. FAX 01758 713538. Very cosy hotel. Children are particularly welcome but there's still peace and quiet. There is a tennis court. *(See also p601.)* ● *Nov–23 March.*	MC V	■	●	■	17
BEDDGELERT: *Sygun Fawr Country House* w www.sygunfawr.co.uk ££ Beddgelert, Gwynedd LL55 4NE. & FAX 01766 890258. Old hotel with its original beams but with light, pretty bedrooms. Very well placed for climbing and walking in Snowdonia. Guest-only bar. ● *Jan.*	MC V	■	●	■	9
BENLLECH: *Bryn Meirion* ££ Amlwch Rd, Benllech, Anglesey LL74 8SR. 01248 853118. Superb views over Redwarf Bay from this modern guesthouse. Many of the rooms have been adapted for the disabled.	MC V	■	■	■	7
BRYNSIENCYN: *Bodlawen* £ Brynsiencyn, Anglesey LL61 6TQ. 01248 430379. Expect a warm welcome and exceptional views of Snowdon at this farmhouse on the Menai Straits. B&B only. ● *24, 25 Dec.*	MC V		●	■	3
CAPEL GARMON: *Tan-y-Foel* w www.tyfhotel.co.uk ££ Capel Garmon, Betws-y-Coed, Conwy LL26 0RE. 01690 710507. FAX 01690 710681. Converted farmhouse with guest sitting rooms and individual bedrooms. Situated in a beautifully secluded spot near Snowdonia.	AE DC MC V	■			7

CRICCIETH: *Mynydd Ednyfed* £££ · AE MC V · 9
Caernarfon Rd, Criccieth, Gwynedd LL52 0PH. ☎ 01766 523269.
Over 400 years old, this hotel has charm and character, together with all the modern conveniences, including a gym. Lovely views to the sea. 🛏 P

LLANABER: *Llwyndu Farmhouse* w www.llwyndu-farmhouse.co.uk £££ · MC V · 7
Llanaber, nr Barmouth, Gwynedd LL42 1RR. ☎ 01341 280144. FAX 01341 281236.
B&B and evening meal in a 1590s listed building. The atmosphere is friendly and the rooms are modern – some with four-posters. 🛏 P

LLANDRILLO: *Tyddyn Llan* w www.tyddynllan.co.uk £££ · AE DC MC V · 10
Llandrillo, nr Corwen, Denbigh LL21 0ST. ☎ 01490 440264. FAX 01490 440414.
Relaxed place to stay at. Stylish with lovely decor and furnishings; each bedroom individually decorated. (See also p602.) 🛏 P

LLANDUDNO: *St Tudno Hotel and Restaurant* w www.st-tudno.co.uk £££ · AE DC MC V · 20
Promenade, Llandudno LL30 2LP. ☎ 01492 874411. FAX 01492 860407.
Regulars return time and again to this Victorian house on the seafront. Charming and friendly. Bedrooms vary in size. 🛏 P

LLANFAIR DRYFFYN CLWYD: *Eyarth Station* £ · MC V · 6
Llanfair Dryffyn Clwyd, Denbigh LL15 2EE. ☎ 01824 703643. FAX 01824 707464.
Friendly B&B with evening meals. The house was once a railway station. A swimming pool is now where the tracks were. Pets allowed. 🛏 P

LLANGOLLEN: *Gales* @ gales@llangollen.oyt.uk £££ · AE MC V · 15
18 Bridge St, Llangollen, Denbigh LL20 8PF. ☎ 01978 860089. FAX 01978 861313.
Variety of sizes and styles of rooms. Relaxed atmosphere in the wine bar. Lively during the International Eisteddfod (see p436). ● 24 Dec–2 Jan. 🛏 P

LLANSANFFRAID GLAN CONWY: *Old Rectory* £££ · MC V · 6
Llansanffraid Glan Conwy, nr Conwy, Conwy LL28 5LF.
☎ 01492 580611 FAX 01492 584555. w www.oldrectorycountryhouse.co.uk
Stunning views over the Conwy Estuary and an intimate atmosphere. Tastefully decorated rooms and Michelin-starred cuisine. ● Dec–Jan. 🛏 P

LLECHWEDD: *Berthlwyd Hall* £££ · AE DC MC V · 9
Llechwedd, Conwy LL32 8DQ. ☎ 01492 592409. FAX 01492 572290.
Victorian mansion that has many of its original features. Residents' lounge in keeping with the period. Very good French cooking. 🛏 P

NANTGWYNANT: *Pen-y-Gwryd* £ · 16
Nantgwynant, Gwynedd LL55 4NT. ☎ 01286 870211.
Spartan accommodation and simple food in a bleak, remote spot in Snowdonia but beautiful. Generous hospitality. ● Nov–Dec, mid-Jan–end Feb. P

PORTMEIRION: *Portmeirion* w www.portmeirion-village.com ££££ · AE DC MC V · 40
Portmeirion, Gwynedd LL48 6ET. ☎ 01766 770228. FAX 01766 771331.
It is a unique experience staying in this Mediterranean-style village (see pp440–1). The hotel itself is no disappointment. ● 25 Dec. 🛏 P

TALSARNAU: *Maes-Y-Neuadd* w www.neuadd.com £££ · AE DC MC V · 16
Talsarnau, nr Harlech, Gwynedd LL47 6YA. ☎ 01766 780200. FAX 01766 780211.
Part of this grey-stone house dates back to the 14th century. Beautifully restored, affording great comfort, with spectacular gardens and good food. 🛏 P

TALYLLYN: *Minffordd* w www.minffordd.com ££ · MC V · 6
Talyllyn, Twyn, Gwynedd LL36 9AJ. ☎ 01654 761665. FAX 01654 761517.
This simple whitewashed building is a marvellous place to stay at. A dramatic location. ● Dec–Feb. 🛏 P

SOUTH AND MID-WALES

ABERGAVENNY: *Llanwenarth House* ££ · 5
Govilon, Abergavenny, Monmouthshire NP7 9SF. ☎ 01873 830289. FAX 01873 832199.
A historic country-house hotel that has an intimate atmosphere and a strong emphasis on personal service. Home cooking most nights. ● mid-Jan–Feb. 🛏 P

BERRIEW: *Lion* ££ · AE DC MC V · 7
Berriew, nr Welshpool, Powys SY21 8PQ. ☎ 01686 640452. FAX 01686 640604.
Friendly pub in the centre of the village. Great atmosphere and imaginative food. The bedrooms are quite grand. 🛏 P

For key to symbols see bookmark

Price categories for a standard double room per night, inclusive of breakfast, service charges and any additional taxes such as VAT:
£ under £50
££ £50–£100
£££ £100–£150
££££ £150–£200
£££££ £200 plus.

RESTAURANT
Hotel restaurant or dining room usually open to non-residents unless otherwise stated.

CHILDREN WELCOME
Child cots available. Some hotel restaurants have children's portions and high-chairs.

GARDEN/TERRACE
Hotels with a garden, courtyard or terrace, often providing tables for eating outside.

CREDIT CARDS
Indicates which credit cards are accepted: *AE* American Express; *DC* Diners Club; *MC* Master Card/Access; *V* Visa.

	CREDIT CARDS	RESTAURANT	CHILDREN WELCOME	GARDEN/TERRACE	NUMBER OF ROOMS
BUILTH WELLS: *Dollynwydd* £ Builth Wells, Powys LD2 3RZ. (01982 553660. FAX 01982 553660. Simple, charming farmhouse dating from the 17th century. Home-grown produce and eggs from resident hens provide generous evening meals and breakfasts. **P**				■	4
DRUIDSTONE HAVEN: *Druidstone* w www.druidstone.co.uk ££ Druidstone Haven, nr Haverfordwest, Pembroke SA62 3NE. (01437 781221. Ideal for families, with a beach nearby, large grounds for children to explore and music evenings. Guests have access to the bar. ● mid-Nov–mid-Dec. **P**	AE MC V	■	●	■	9
EGLWYSFACH: *Ynyshir Hall* w www.ynyshir-hall.co.uk £££ Eglwysfach, Machynlleth, Powys SY20 8TA. (01654 781209. FAX 01654 781366. An elegant part-Georgian country house run with style and panache. The restaurant serves modern British cuisine, using local produce. ● 4–28 Jan. **P**	AE DC MC	■	V	■	10
FISHGUARD: *Manor House* w www.smoothhound.co.uk £ Main St, Fishguard, Pembroke SA65 9HG. (FAX 01348 873260. Good value, family-run hotel overlooking the harbour. ● Nov, 25 Dec.	MC V	■		■	6
FISHGUARD: *Three Main Street* ££ 3 Main St, Fishguard, Pembroke SA65 9HG. (01348 874275. FAX 01348 874017. Informal but stylishly decorated restaurant, coffee shop and guesthouse. It has great charm, pristine bedrooms and delicious food. ● Feb. **P**		■	●		3
GLYNARTHEN: *Penbontbren Farm* ££ Glynarthen, Ceredig SA44 6PE. (01239 810248. FAX 01239 811129. A converted traditional Welsh farm, this is a taste of rural Wales. The stone outbuildings have been converted into bedrooms. ● 25–26 Dec. **P**	AE DC MC V	■	●	■	10
HAVERFORDWEST: *Foxdale* w www.foxdale.guest.co.uk £ Glebe Lane, Marloes, Haverfordwest, Pembroke SA62 3AY. (01646 636243. Family-run, good-value guesthouse on the cliff path, close to the island of Skomer, famous for its puffins. A must for any ornithologist. ● end Dec–end Jan. **P**				■	3
LLANDEILO: *Cawdor Arms* w www.cawdor-arms.co.uk ££ 72 Rhosmaen St, Llandeilo, Camarthen SA19 6EN. (01558 823500. FAX 01558 822399. A wisteria-covered verandah fronts this 17th-century coaching inn in the town centre. The interior is traditionally furnished. ● 1st wk Jan. **P**	AE DC MC V	■	●		17
LLANDEGLEY: *Ffaldau Country House* w www.ffaldau.co.uk £ Llandegley, Llandrindod Wells, Powys LD1 5UD. (01597 851421. Very attractive, comfortable, mullion-windowed hospitable guesthouse in this picturesque part of Wales. Evening meals by arrangement. **P**	MC V			■	3
LLANGAMMARCH WELLS: *Lake Country House* £££ Llangammarch Wells, Powys LD4 4BS. (01591 620202. FAX 01591 620457. An impressive Edwardian country house, stylishly decorated with elegant public rooms and luxurious bedrooms. **P**	AE DC MC V	■		■	19
LLANGATTOCK: *Ty Cresco Hotel* w www.wiz.to/tycreso.co.uk ££ The Dardy, Llangattock, Crickhowell, Powys NP8 1PU. (& FAX 01873 810573. A very peaceful place to stay at with an excellent Welsh table d'hôte menu. Nearly all the bedrooms have beautiful views. **P**	AE MC V	■	●	■	8
LLANWDDYN: *Lake Vyrnwy* w www.lakevyrnwy.com £££ Llanwddyn, Powys SY10 0LY. (01691 870692. FAX 01691 870259. Ex-hunting lodge on the edge of Lake Vyrnwy – the location is stunning. Panoramic views across the water from the restaurant. **P**	DC MC V	■	●	■	35
LLANWRTYD WELLS: *Carlton House* w www.carltonrestaurant.co.uk ££ Llanwrtyd Wells, Powys LD5 4RA. (& FAX 01591 610248. Very well run, good-value guesthouse with well-furnished rooms. Beautifully prepared, well-presented dinners, served with homeliness. ● 10–27 Dec.	AE MC V	■		■	7

MILEBROOK: *Milebrook House* W www.milebrookhouse.co.uk   ££   AE MC V   10
Milebrook, Knighton, Powys LD7 1LT. 01547 528632. FAX 01547 520509.
A relaxed atmosphere in this attractively decorated house in the Teme
Valley. Bedrooms are spacious and the food is delicious.

NEWPORT: *Cnapan* W www.online-holidays.net/cnapan   ££   MC V   5
East St, Newport, Pembroke SA42 0SY. 01239 820575. FAX 01239 820878.
The quiet seaside resort of Newport and the Nevern estuary make an attractive
backdrop to this cheerful, family-run hotel.

PENALLY: *Penally Abbey* W www.penally-abbey.com   ££   AE MC V   12
Penally, nr Tenby, Pembroke SA70 7PY. 01834 843033. FAX 01834 844714.
Gothic-style architecture adds romance to this Victorian country house near
overlooing the lovely Tenby coast. Grand but friendly, with richly furnished,
individually styled rooms.

PORTHKERRY: *Egerton Grey Country House* W www.egertongrey.co.uk   ££   AE DC MC V   10
Porthkerry, nr Cardiff CF62 3BZ. 01446 711666. FAX 01446 711690.
Part-Victorian, part-Edwardian house close to Cardiff airport, though its
size and location make it seem a million miles away. It combines both
comfort and sophistication. Excellent food.

REYNOLDSTON: *Fairyhill Country House* W www.fairyhill.net   £££   AE MC V   8
Reynoldston, Gower, Swansea SA3 1BS.
01792 390139. FAX 01792 391358.
Stylish and civilized country-house hotel surrounded by woodland
on the Gower Peninsula. Restful and relaxing.

SPITTAL: *Lower Haythog* W www.www.lowerhaythogfarm.co.uk   £   6
Spittal, Haverfordwest, Pembroke SA62 5QL. & FAX 01437 731279.
This dairy, beef and sheep farm offers B&B in the old, historic farmhouse
surrounded by landscaped gardens. Excellent evening meals.

ST BRIDES WENTLOOGE: *West Usk Lighthouse*   ££   AE DC MC V   4
Lighthouse Rd, St Brides Wentlooge, Newport NP1 9SF.
01633 810126. W www.westusklighthouse.co.uk
This former lighthouse is a unique place to stay at. Pleasant owners and an
easygoing atmosphere. Some rooms have a four-poster bed. ● 26 Dec.

SEION LLANDDEINIOLEN: *Tyn Rhos Country House* W www.tynrhos.co.uk   ££   AE MC V   14
Seion Llanddeiniolen, Caernarfon, Gwyn LL55 3AE. 01248 670489. FAX 01248 670079.
Stylishly decorated hotel with a civilized air. Good food in the
restaurant. Excellent hospitality. ● 23–30 Dec.

THREE COCKS: *Three Cocks* W www.threecockshotel.com   ££   MC V   7
Three Cocks, nr Brecon, Powys LD3 0SL. & FAX 01497 847215.
Small and friendly roadside coaching inn offering good food. Unfussy
decor and furnishings with light, airy bedrooms. ● Dec–Feb.

TINTERN: *Parva Farmhouse* W www.hoteltintern.co.uk   ££   AE MC V   9
Tintern, Monmouth NP6 6SQ. 01291 689411. FAX 01291 689557.
Converted farmhouse on the banks of the Wye, immaculately neat both
inside and out. Only minutes from the ruins of Tintern Abbey.

WELSH HOOK: *Stone Hall*   ££   AE DC MC V   5
Welsh Hook, Haverfordwest, Pembroke SA62 5NS.
01348 840212. FAX 013481 840815.
Part-14th century and set in lovely grounds, this is a welcoming hotel
with comfy rooms and very good French cooking.

WHITEBROOK: *Crown* W www.crown@whitebrook.com   ££   AE DC MC V   10
Whitebrook, Monmouth NP25 4TX.
01600 860254. FAX 01600 860607. @ thecrown@whitebrook.demon.co.uk
Set just back from the road up in the wooded hills above the Wye
Valley, this is a fairly informal restaurant-with-rooms. High-quality
French cooking and reasonable bedrooms. ● 2–16 Jan.

THE LOWLANDS

ABERDOUR: *Hawkcraig House*   ££   2
Hawkcraig Point, Aberdour, Fife KY3 0TZ. 01383 860335.
Staying in this small, whitewashed, old ferryman's house is a pleasant
experience. Lovely setting and friendly owners. ● Oct–April.

For key to symbols see bookmark

Price categories for a standard double room per night, inclusive of breakfast, service charges and any additional taxes such as VAT: £ under £50 ££ £50–£100 £££ £100–£150 ££££ £150–£200 £££££ £200 plus.	**RESTAURANT** Hotel restaurant or dining room usually open to non-residents unless otherwise stated. **CHILDREN WELCOME** Child cots available. Some hotel restaurants have children's portions and high-chairs. **GARDEN/TERRACE** Hotels with a garden, courtyard or terrace, often providing tables for eating outside. **CREDIT CARDS** Indicates which credit cards are accepted: *AE* American Express; *DC* Diners Club; *MC* Master Card/Access; *V* Visa.			

	CREDIT CARDS	RESTAURANT	CHILDREN WELCOME	GARDEN/TERRACE	NUMBER OF ROOMS
AUCHENCAIRN: *Balcary Bay Hotel* **£££** Auchencairn, Castle Douglas, D & G D67 1Q2. **(01556 640217. FAX** 01556 640272. Family-run hotel in an excellent position on the shores of Balcary Bay. Quality of service is shown by the fact that many visitors return here year after year. Friendly and traditional. ● *mid-Nov–Feb.* 🛏 **P**	AE MC V	■	●	■	21
AUCHTERARDER: *Auchterarder House* **££££** Auchterarder, Perth & Kin PH3 1DZ. **(01764 663646. FAX** 01764 662939. A fine Victorian Baronial-style house; the rooms have royal proportions but the ambience is relaxed and cosy. Very good food. 🛏 TV 24 **P** ⅙	AE DC MC V	■		■	15
BIGGAR: *Shieldhill House* @ enquiries@shieldhill.co.uk **£££** Quothquan, nr Biggar, S Lanark ML12 6NA. **(01899 220035. FAX** 01899 221092. Delightful hotel in a building whose origins go back to the 12th century. Elegant public rooms and spacious bedrooms. 🛏 **P**	MC V	■		■	16
CALLANDER: *Roman Camp Country House* **£££** Callander, Stirling FK17 8BG. **(01877 330003. FAX** 01877 331533. Set in extensive gardens, near the centre of town, this is a peaceful, charming retreat with a unique atmosphere. 🛏 TV ≈ **P** ⅙	AE DC MC V	■	●	■	14
CARDROSS: *Kirkton House* @ info@kirktonhouse.co.uk **££** Darleith Rd, Cardross, Argyll & Bute G82 5EZ. **(01389 841951. FAX** 01389 841868. Fabulous views over the Clyde from this farmhouse guesthouse providing good home cooking in comfortable, rustic-style surroundings. 🛏 TV **P** ⅙	AE DC MC V	■	●	■	6
DENNY: *The Topps Farm* w www.thetopps.com **£** Fintry Rd B818, Denny, Falkirk FK6 5JF. **(01324 822471. FAX** 01324 823099. The modern farmhouse of this sheep and goat farm offers comfortable rooms and a restaurant also open to non-residents. 🛏 TV ≈ **P** ⅙	MC V	■	●	■	8
DUNFERMLINE: *Clarke Cottage* @ clarkecottage@ukonline.co.uk **£** 139 Halbeath Rd, Dunfermline, Fife KY11 4LA. **(01383 735935.** A comfortable B&B in a Victorian house with bedrooms furnished in pine. Breakfasts are served in the conservatory. 🛏 **P** ⅙			●		9
EDINBURGH: *Duthus Lodge* w www.edinburghguesthouse.com **££** 5 West Coates, Edinburgh EH12 5JG. **(0131 337 6876. FAX** 0131 313 2264. Splendid detached family-run establishment in tastefully decorated surroundings. Ideal base for exploring Edinburgh's attractions. Close to Murrayfield Stadium and the conference centre. 🛏 TV ≈ **P**	DC MC V		●	■	7
EDINBURGH: *Melvin House Hotel* @ reservation@melvinhouse.demon.co.uk **££** 3 Rothesay Terrace, Edinburgh EH3 7RY. **(0131 225 5084. FAX** 0131 226 5085. Situated within easy walking distance of Princes Street, this fine example of Victorian architecture has a galleried library and elegant public rooms. 🛏 ⬆	AE DC MC V	■	●		22
EDINBURGH: *Channings* w www.channings.co.uk **£££££** South Learmonth Gardens, Edinburgh EH4 1EZ. **(0131 315 2226. FAX** 0131 332 9631. @ reserve@channings.co.uk Close to the city centre, this hotel consists of five converted Edwardian houses. Smart and very well kept but still homely. 🛏 24 **P**	AE DC MC V	■	●		46
GLASGOW: *Babbity Bowster* **££** 16–18 Blackfriars St, Glasgow G1 1PE. **(0141 552 5055. FAX** 0141 552 7774. Unusual hotel with immense character. Behind the finely restored Adam façade are a few simple, neat bedrooms. 🛏 **P**	AE MC V	■	●	■	6
GLASGOW: *Malmaison* w wwwmalmaison.com **££** 278 West George St, Glasgow G2 4LL. **(0141 572 1000. FAX** 0141 572 1002 Beautifully decorated rooms, all with satellite TV and CD players, provide a stylish stay. The brasserie serves Mediterranean cuisine. 🛏 ⬆ ≈ 24 ⅙	AE DC MC V	■	●		72

GLASGOW: *Town House* [w] www.thetownhouseglasgow.com
4 Hughenden Terrace, Glasgow G12 9XR. [0141 357 0862. FAX 0141 339 9605.
Expertly restored Victorian house, where you are assured a friendly
welcome. Bedrooms have grand proportions.
££ | MC V | 10

GLASGOW: *One Devonshire Gardens*
1 Devonshire Gardens, Glasgow G12 OUX. [0141 339 2001. FAX 0141 337 1663.
The ultimate smart town-hotel. Lavish furnishings and stylish decor.
First class service. Excellent restaurant. (See also p605.)
££££ | AE DC MC V | 27

INNERLEITHEN: *Traquair Arms Hotel* [@] traquairarms@scotsborders.co.uk
Traquair Rd, Innerleithen, Borders EH44 6PD. [01896 830229. FAX 01896 830260.
An old coaching inn known for its good-value meals. It also has a tea
room offering home baking.
££ | AE DC MC V | 10

IRVINE: *Annfield House Hotel*
6 Castle St, Irvine, Ayrshire KA12 8RJ.
[01294 278903. FAX 01294 278904.
Overlooking the River Irvine, this comfortable hotel offers a country house
ambience, only a few minutes from the centre of town.
££ | AE DC MC V | 9

JEDBURGH: *Hundalee House* [@] sheila.whittaker@btinternet.com
Jedburgh, Roxburgh, Borders TD8 6PA. [& FAX 01835 863011.
Well-presented B&B in an attractive 18th-century house. Set in large
gardens; guests are assured privacy and seclusion. ● Nov–Mar.
£ | | 5

KIRKCUDBRIGHT: *Gladstone House* [@] sue@gladstonehouse.freeserve.co.uk
48 High St, Kirkcudbright, D & G DG6 4JX. [& FAX 01557 331734.
Exceptional bed-and-breakfast hotel in this appealing town. Decorated
with taste, it is an attractive and civilized place to stay.
££ | MC V | 3

MARKINCH: *Balbirnie House* [@] balbirnie@breathemail.net
Balbirnie Park, Markinch, Fife KY7 6NE. [01592 610066. FAX 01592 610529.
Surrounded by extensive parkland, this Georgian mansion has an outstanding
setting. It is unashamedly luxurious, yet both informal and unstuffy.
££££ | AE DC MC V | 30

MELROSE: *Burts Hotel* [w] www.burtshotel.co.uk
Market Square, Melrose, Borders TD6 9PN.
[01896 822285. FAX 01896 822870. [@] burtshotel@aol.com
A smart, family-run hotel with a friendly atmosphere in the centre of this
small town. The breakfasts are excellent.
££ | AE DC MC V | 20

MOFFAT: *Beechwood Country House*
Harthope Pl, Moffat, D & G DG10 9RS. [01683 220210. FAX 01683 220889.
Friendly and efficient family-run hotel. Perched on a hill and surrounded
by trees. Simple decor and carefree atmosphere. ● Jan–mid-Feb.
££ | AE MC V | 7

MUIRFIELD: *Greywalls* [w] www.greywalls.co.uk
Muirfield, Gullane, E Lothn EH31 2EG. [01620 842144. FAX 01620 842241.
This place is a delight. Lovely rooms, great vistas and extreme comfort.
Excellent Scottish hospitality. ● mid-Oct–mid-Apr.
££££ | AE DC MC V | 23

PEEBLES: *Cringletie House* [@] enquiries@cringletie.com
Peebles, Borders EH45 8PL. [01721 730233. FAX 01721 730244.
Comfortable, reliable hotel set in large grounds that has an excellent
restaurant and relaxed atmosphere.
£££ | AE MC V | 14

PORTPATRICK: *Crown*
North Crescent, Portpatrick, Stranraer DG9 8SX. [01776 810261. FAX 01776 810551.
Popular pub-hotel overlooking the harbour. Bedrooms are spotless,
bright and neat. Food is served in the traditional bar and the smart
conservatory restaurant.
££ | AE MC V | 12

STRACHUR: *Creggans Inn* [@] info@creggans-inn.co.uk
Strachur, Argyll & Bute PA27 8BX. [01369 860279. FAX 01369 860637.
Convivial inn in a superb spot overlooking Loch Fyne. Pretty bedrooms.
Excellent food, particularly seafood, in the formal restaurant or at the bar.
£££ | MC V | 14

TROON: *Piersland House* [w] www.piersland.co.uk
Craigend Rd, Troon, S Ayrshire KA10 6HD. [01292 314747. FAX 01292 315613.
An appealing mock-Tudor house close to the championship golf course.
Each suite in a cottage annexe has its own sitting room.
£££ | MC V | 28

<table>
<tr><td colspan="2">

Price categories for a standard double room per night, inclusive of breakfast, service charges and any additional taxes such as VAT:
£ under £50
££ £50–£100
£££ £100–£150
££££ £150–£200
£££££ £200 plus.

</td><td colspan="4">

RESTAURANT
Hotel restaurant or dining room usually open to non-residents unless otherwise stated.

CHILDREN WELCOME
Child cots available. Some hotel restaurants have children's portions and high-chairs.

GARDEN/TERRACE
Hotels with a garden, courtyard or terrace, often providing tables for eating outside.

CREDIT CARDS
Indicates which credit cards are accepted: AE American Express; DC Diners Club; MC Master Card/Access; V Visa.

</td><td>CREDIT CARDS</td><td>RESTAURANT</td><td>CHILDREN WELCOME</td><td>GARDEN/TERRACE</td><td>NUMBER OF ROOMS</td></tr>
</table>

WALKERBURN: *Tweed Valley Country House* ££
Walkerburn, nr Peebles, Tweeddale, Borders EH43 6AA.
☎ 01896 870636. **FAX** 01896 870639. @ tweedvalley@scotlandhotel.co.uk
Family hotel with an emphasis on relaxation and comfort, close to the village and River Tweed. A lovely location which reflects and complements the warmth of the service. 🔒 24 P
AE MC V · ■ ● ■ · 8

THE HIGHLANDS AND ISLANDS

ACHILTIBUIE: *Summer Isles* @ summerisleshotel@aol.com £££
Achiltibuie, nr Ullapool, Ross & Cromarty, Highland IV26 2YG.
☎ 01854 622282. **FAX** 01854 622251.
Special hotel that meets all expectations. Well-appointed rooms and superb restaurant. Breathtaking views of the Summer Isles. ● mid-Oct–Easter. 🔒 P
MC V · ■ ■ · 15

ARISAIG: *Arisaig House* **W** www.arisaighouse.co.uk £££££
Beasdale, nr Arisaig, Highland PH39 4NR.
☎ 01687 450622. **FAX** 01687 450626. @ arisaighse@aol.com
Dour exterior gives no indication of the bright, cheerful interior and the charming and courteous staff. Smart, stylish public rooms and pleasant bedrooms. Pretty gardens and a wonderful restaurant. ● Dec–Feb. 🔒 ⚡ P
MC V · ■ · ■ 12

BALLATER: *Balgonie Country House* £££
Braemar Place, Ballater, Aberdeenshire AB35 5RQ.
☎ & **FAX** 013397 55482. @ balgonie@lineone.net
Family-run country-house hotel on the outskirts of Ballater. Excellent fare favours Scottish cuisine, and the wonderful hospitality favours any guest who likes home-from-home comforts. ● Jan–mid-Feb. 🔒 P
AE DC MC V · ■ · ■ 9

BALLINDALLOCH: *Delnashaugh Inn* £££
Ballindalloch, Moray AB37 9AS. ☎ 01807 500255. **FAX** 01807 500389.
Overlooking the River Avon in the Spey valley, this hotel makes a perfect base for exploring the area, and is lovely to return to after a day's sightseeing. Room rate includes dinner, and the food is especially good. 🔒 P ♿
MC V · ■ ● · 9

BALQUHIDDER: *Monachyle Mhor Farmhouse* **W** www.monachylemohr.com ££
Balquhidder, Lochearnhead, Stirling FK19 8PQ.
☎ 01877 384622. **FAX** 01877 384305.
Set in extensive grounds overlooking Loch Voil, this hotel combines friendliness and high standards. Excellent restaurant, cosy bar. 🔒 ⚡ P ♿
MC V · ■ · ■ 10

BLAIRGOWRIE: *Kinloch House* **W** www.kinlochhouse.com ££££
Nr Blairgowrie, Perthshire PH10 6SG. ☎ 01250 884237. **FAX** 01250 884333.
A handsome Baronial house, this hotel's emphasis is on country pursuits. Wonderful, relaxed surroundings. The restaurant is recommended, and the hotel has recently opened a health and fitness centre. ● last 2 wks Dec. 🔒 ⚡ P ♿
AE DC MC V · ■ · ■ 20

BRAE: *Busta House* @ reservations@bustahouse.com ££
Busta, Brae, Shetland ZE2 9QN. ☎ 01806 522506. **FAX** 01806 522588.
Civilized, family-run hotel. Beside its own little harbour, this early 18th-century house offers a relaxed and comfortable stay. 🔒 P
AE DC MC V · ■ ● ■ · 20

BRAEMAR: *Callater Lodge Hotel* **W** www.hotel-braemar.co.uk ££
9 Glenshee Rd, Braemar, Aberdeenshire AB35 5YQ. ☎ 013397 41275. **FAX** 013397 41345.
This small, friendly, family-run hotel is near the village centre. Most of the rooms in the Victorian house are spacious. Request evening meals in advance. Vegetarian, gluten-free and other special diets are catered for. 🔒 ⚡ P
MC V · ■ · ■ 7

CRINAN: *Crinan Hotel* **W** www.crinanhotel.com £££££
Crinan, Lochgilphead, Argyll & Bute PA31 8SR. ☎ 01546 830261. **FAX** 01546 830292
Hotel in a superb position on the harbour where the Sound of Jura meets Loch Crinan. The service is excellent, but a visit is worth it for the stunning views alone. 🔒 ⬆ ⚡ P ♿
AE MC V · ■ ● ■ · 22

CROMARTY: *Royal* @ royerom@cali.co.uk £££
Marine Terrace, Cromarty, Highland IV11 8YN. ☎ 01381 600217. FAX 01381 600813.
There are beautiful views overlooking the Firth of Cromarty from
this friendly, unpretentious hotel. The well-decorated bedrooms
are comfortable and spotless. ⊟ P

AE MC V	▨	●	▨		10

DUNOON: *Enmore* W www.enmorehotel.co.uk £££
Marine Parade, Dunoon, Argyll & Bute PA23 8HH. ☎ 01369 702230. FAX 01369 702148.
Very well-kept family hotel on the seafront. Cheerful and friendly,
with very obliging, courteous service. ⊟ P

AE MC V	▨	●	▨		10

ELGIN: *Mansion House And Country Club* @ reception@mhelgin.co.uk £££
The Haugh, Elgin, Moray IV30 1AW. ☎ 01343 548811. FAX 01343 547916.
Imposing Victorian mansion which also has a leisure and country club.
Welcoming and unpretentious – a real treat, and good value. ⊟ 24 P ≋

AE DC MC V	▨	●	▨		23

FORT WILLIAM: *Ashburn House* W www.scotland2000.com/ashburn ££
Achintore Rd, Fort William PH6 6RQ. ☎ 01397 706000. FAX 01397 702024.
Sitting quietly on the shore of Loch Linnhe yet only five minutes walk from the
town centre, this hotel provides an ideal base for touring. ● Dec–Jan. ⊟ ⚡ P

AE MC V		●	▨		7

GRANTOWN-ON-SPEY: *Culdearn House* W www.culdearn.com £££
Woodlands Terrace, Grantown-on-Spey, Moray PH26 3JU.
☎ 01479 872106. FAX 01479 873641. @ culdearn@globalnet.co.uk
Traditionally decorated Victorian villa with friendly owners. Highland dancing
displays are put on occasionally. Rate includes dinner. ● Nov–Feb. ⊟ P

AE DC MC V			▨		9

HEREBOSH: *Dunorin House Hotel* W www.dunorin.com ££
Dunvegan, Isle of Skye, Highland IV55 8GZ.
☎ & FAX 01470 521488. @ stay@dunorin.freeserve.co.uk
Enjoying outstanding views of the Cuillin mountains, this family-run hotel has a
comfortable, relaxing atmosphere and an excellent menu. ● Nov–Mar. ⊟ ⚡ P

MC V	▨	●	▨		10

INVERNESS: *Dunain Park* W www.dunainparkhotel.co.uk ££££
Inverness, Highland IV3 6JN. ☎ 01463 230512. FAX 01463 224532.
Surrounded by a large garden and close to Inverness, this hotel is
a convenient and peaceful base for the area. Pleasant staff and
comfortable standards. ⊟ ⚡ P ≋ ⅛

AE MC V	▨		▨		13

ISLE OF HARRIS: *Ardvourlie Castle* £££
Aird Amhulaidh, Isle of Harris, W Isles HS3 3AB.
☎ 01859 502307. FAX 01859 502348
Victorian hunting lodge on the shores of Loch Seaforth. Original features
include working gas and oil lamps. The highly praised restaurant offers
local fare; dinner is included in the price of the room. ● Nov–Mar. ⊟ P

	▨	●	▨		4

ISLE OF HARRIS: *Scarista House* W www.scaristahouse.com £££
Isle of Harris, Highland HS3 3HX. ☎ 01859 550238. FAX 01859 550277.
This Georgian manse provides an extremely agreeable retreat. Set in a
wonderfully remote spot overlooking a beach. Delicious food. ⊟ P ⚡

MC V	▨		▨		5

ISLE OF IONA: *Argyll Hotel* @ reception@argyllhoteliona.co.uk ££
Isle of Iona, Argyll & Bute PA76 6SJ. ☎ 01681 700334. FAX 01681 700510.
Unpretentious, friendly hotel on this very special island. Simple,
unfussy style. Ask for a bedroom facing the sea for the most
wonderful views. ● Nov–Mar. ⊟

MC V	▨	●	▨		15

ISLE OF MULL: *Druimard Country House* W www.druimard.co.uk £££
Dervaig, by Tobermory, Isle of Mull PA75 6QW. ☎ & FAX 01688 400345.
Overlooking the River Bellart, this beautifully restored Victorian country house
offers every comfort including an award-winning restaurant. Boat trips
can be organised and Mull Little Theatre is in the grounds. ● Nov–Mar. ⊟ 24 P

AE V	▨	●	▨		7

ISLE ORNSAY: *Hotel Eilean Iarmain* W www.eileaniarmain.co.uk £££
Sleat, Isle of Skye, Highland IV43 8QR. ☎ 01471 833332. FAX 01471 833275.
Traditional 19th-century seaside inn with a Gaelic feel. Wonderful
views from the comfy bedrooms and public rooms. ⊟ ⚡ P

AE MC V	▨	●	▨		16

KENTALLEN OF APPIN: *Ardsheal House* @ info@ardsheal.co.uk ££
Kentallen of Appin, Argyll & Bute PA38 4BX.
☎ 01631 740227. FAX 01631 740342.
Set above the shores of Loch Linnhe, with stunning views. Very hospitable.
Bedrooms and public rooms are well furnished. ● mid-Dec–mid-Jan.
⊟ P

AE MC V	▨	●	▨		9

For key to symbols see bookmark

<table>
<tr><td colspan="6">

Price categories for a standard double room per night, inclusive of breakfast, service charges and any additional taxes such as VAT:
£ under £50
££ £50–£100
£££ £100–£150
££££ £150–£200
£££££ £200 plus.

</td></tr>
</table>

RESTAURANT
Hotel restaurant or dining room usually open to non-residents unless otherwise stated.

CHILDREN WELCOME
Child cots available. Some hotel restaurants have children's portions and high-chairs.

GARDEN/TERRACE
Hotels with a garden, courtyard or terrace, often providing tables for eating outside.

CREDIT CARDS
Indicates which credit cards are accepted: *AE* American Express; *DC* Diners Club; *MC* Master Card/Access; *V* Visa.

	CREDIT CARDS	RESTAURANT	CHILDREN WELCOME	GARDEN/TERRACE	NUMBER OF ROOMS
KILDRUMMY: *Kildrummy Castle Hotel* **£££** Kildrummy, nr Alford, Gordon, Moray AB33 8RA. 📞 019755 71288. FAX 019755 71345. Large, rather stately Victorian castellated building set in lovely gardens overlooking a 13th-century castle ruin. The superb interior decoration is every bit as stimulating as the surroundings. ● *Jan.* 🔧 P	AE MC V	■	●	■	16
KINGUSSIE: *The Cross* @ relax@TheCross.co.uk **££££** Tweed Mill Brae, Kingussie PH21 1TC. 📞 01540 661166. FAX 01540 661080 Built as a water-powered tweed mill in the 19th century, this renovated building still maintains its original character. The individually-styled rooms are comfortable. Award-winning restaurant. ● *Dec & Jan.* 🔧 ⚡ P ♿	MC V	■	●	■	9
KIRKWALL: *Foveran* @ foveranhotel@aol.com **££** St Ola, Kirkwall, Orkney KW15 1SF. 📞 01856 872389. FAX 01856 876430. Modern hotel with great views over Scapa Flow and the South Isles. Comfortable rooms and a good restaurant. 🔧 24 P	MC V	■			8
KYLESKU: *Newton Lodge* **££** Kylesku, Highland IV27 4HW. 📞 01971 502070. @ newtonlge@aol.com A friendly, family-run B&B. Evening meals might include fish caught by the owner in his own fishing boat. Rooms are modern and comfortable and many guests return each year. ● *Nov–Mar.* 🔧 TV ⚡ P	MC V	■			7
LARGS: *Brisbane House* W www.maksu-group.co.uk **££** 14 Greenock Rd, Esplanade, Largs, N Ayrshire KA30 8NF. 📞 01475 687200. FAX 01475 676295. Attractive 18th-century house completely modernized to make it smart and stylish. Some of the rooms look over the Firth of Clyde, so they are the ones to ask for. 🔧 24 P	AE DC MC V	■	●	■	23
LEDAIG: *Isle of Eriska* @ office@eriska-hotel.co.uk **£££££** Ledaig, nr Oban, Argyll & Bute PA37 1SD. 📞 01631 720371. FAX 01631 720531. Situated on its very own island, this grand, 19th-century Baronial hall has charming rooms. Service in the dining room is formal in the evenings; an air of comforting tradition pervades. ● *Jan–mid-Feb.* 🔧 24 P ♒ ♿	AE MC V	■	●	■	17
MUIR OF ORD: *The Dower House* @ info@thedowerhouse.co.uk **£££** Highfield, Muir of Ord, Highland IV6 7XN. 📞 & FAX 01463 870090. Extremely agreeable small hotel that is attractively decorated. Pleasing bedrooms and a first-rate restaurant. 🔧 24 ⚡ P ♿	MC V	■	●	■	5
NAIRN: *Clifton House* @ macintyre@clara.net **£££** Nairn, Highland IV12 4HW. 📞 01667 453119. FAX 01667 452836. Individual town-hotel, decorated and furnished with style, flair and unremitting good taste. The restaurant comes highly recommended. ● *Dec–Jan.* 🔧 P	AE DC MC V	■			12
OBAN: *Knipoch Hotel* @ reception@knipochhotel.co.uk **£££** Kilninver, nr Oban, Argyll & Bute PA34 4QT. 📞 01852 316251. FAX 01852 316249. Panoramic views across Loch Feochan from this restored 16th-century house which has an impressively atmospheric historical feel. Pristine bedrooms and charming service. ● *Dec–Feb.* 🔧 P	AE DC MC V	■	●	■	17
OLD MELDRUM: *The Redgarth* @ redgarth1@aol.com **££** Kirk Brae, Old Meldrum, Aberdeenshire AB51 0DJ. 📞 01651 872353. Enjoying magnificent views over Bennachie and the surrounding area, this hotel offers cask-conditioned ales as a speciality. 🔧 ⚡ P	AE DC MC V	■		■	3
PITLOCHRY: *Atholl Palace* W www.athollpalace.com **££** Pitlochry, Perthshire PH16 5LY. 📞 01796 472400. FAX 01796 473036. Huge and grandiose hotel, though somewhat overbearing, this is an excellent example of Scottish Baronial architecture. Vast rooms with various styles of decor and furnishings. 🔧 P ♒ ♿	AE DC MC V	■	●	■	76

PLOCKTON: *Plockton Hotel* W www.plocktonhotel.co.uk   £££
41 Harbour St, Plockton, Highland IV52 8TN. ◖ *01599 544274.* FAX *01599 544475.*
A popular and very friendly little village inn right on the palm tree-lined
seafront. The bar and restaurant are popular with locals and visitors.
Fresh, local seafood is usually on the menu. 🖶 ♿
MC V — 14

PORT APPIN: *The Airds Hotel* W www.airds-hotel.com   ££££
Port Appin, Appin, Argyll & Bute PA38 4DF.
◖ *01631 730236.* FAX *01631 730535.* @ airds@airds-hotel.com
A former ferry inn with a modest whitewashed exterior. Inside, it is smart
and comfortable. Very good restaurant. *(See also p607.)* 🖶 P
MC V — 12

PORTREE: *Viewfield House* @ info@viewfieldhouse.com   ££
Portree, Isle of Skye, Highland IV51 9EU. ◖ *01478 612217.* FAX *01478 613517.*
Guests are made very welcome in this rambling 200-year-old family
house where everyone dines together. ● *mid-Oct–mid-Apr.* 🖶 P ♿
MC V — 13

SHIELDAIG: *Tigh-an-Eilean* @ tighaneileanhotel@shieldaig.fsnet.co.uk   £££
Shieldaig, nr Strathcarron, Highland IV54 8XN. ◖ *01520 755251.* FAX *01520 755321.*
On the banks of Loch Shieldaig, this is one of the best small hotels in
Scotland. Very comfortable, with charming owners and a high standard
of both food and service. ● *mid-Oct–Easter.* 🖶 P
MC V — 11

THURSO: *Forss House* @ jamie@forsshouse.co.uk   ££
Thurso, Caithness, Highland KW14 7XY. ◖ *01847 861201.* FAX *01847 861301.*
Welcoming hotel on the wilds of the northern coast. Imposing on the
outside, but inside it is comfortable and cheerful. 🖶 ⚡ P ♿
AE MC V — 10

TIMSGARRY: *Baile Na Cille* @ randjgollin@compuserve.com   ££
Timsgarry, Isle of Lewis, Highland HS2 9JD. ◖ *01851 672242.* FAX *01851 672241.*
Very easy-going, friendly hotel in an amazing location at the end of a
long beach. A perfect place to get away from it all. ● *mid-Oct–Mar.* 🖶 ⚡ P
MC V — 12

TORLUNDY: *Inverlochy Castle* W www.inverlochy.co.uk   £££££
Torlundy, Fort William, Highland PH33 6SN.
◖ *01397 702177.* FAX *01397 702953.* @ info@inverlochy.co.uk
Superbly run country-house hotel. Elegant rooms with beautiful furniture
and high ceilings. Luxurious bedrooms. ● *Jan–Feb.* 🖶 24 P
AE MC V — 17

ULLAPOOL: *Morefield Hotel*   £
North Rd, Ullapool, Highland IV26 2PQ. ◖ *01854 612161.* FAX *01854 612171.*
The bedrooms have recently been refurbished and a conservatory added.
If you enjoy seafood, this is the place to stay – it has an excellent restaurant
using the best catches from local boats. 🖶 P
MC V — 10

ULLAPOOL: *Ceilidh Place*   ££
14 West Argyle St, Ullapool, Highland IV26 2TY.
◖ *01854 612103.* FAX *01854 612886.* @ reservations@ceilidh.demon.co.uk
Lots going on here – musical evenings and exhibitions. There is also a
café and bookshop. Residents can escape the hurly-burly to their own
peaceful sitting room. 🖶 ⚡ P ♿
MC V — 13

ULLAPOOL: *Altnaharrie Inn*   £££££
Ullapool, Highland IV26 2SS. ◖ *01854 633230.*
Reached by boat from Ullapool, this hotel will guarantee you tranquil
panoramic views. Staying here is a special experience. Good food, but
expensive. No smoking allowed. *(See also p607.)* 🖶 ⚡ P
AE MC V — 8

WALLS: *Burrastow House* @ burr.hs.hotel@zetnet.co.uk   ££££
Walls, Shetland ZE2 9PD. ◖ *01595 809307.* FAX *01595 809213.*
In a very remote part of western Shetland, this is a wonderful
place to escape to for absolute calm and tranquillity. Comfort is not
sacrificed and the food is delicious. ● *Jan–Easter.* 🖶 P ♿
AE MC V — 5

WEST LAROCH: *Lyn-Leven Guesthouse* @ lynleven@amserve.net   £
West Laroch, Ballachulish, Highland PH49 4JP. ◖ *01855 811392.* FAX *01855 811600.*
A well-kept, modern guesthouse close to Glencoe and overlooking Loch
Leven with bedrooms all on the ground floor. There is good, plain home
cooking for the evening meal. ● *Dec 25, 26.* 🖶 P
MC V — 8

WHITEBRIDGE: *Knockie Lodge* @ info@knockielodge.co.uk   £££
Whitebridge, Inverness, Highland IV1 2UP. ◖ *01456 486276.* FAX *01456 486389.*
Outstanding setting for this former hunting lodge above Loch Nan Lann.
Nothing for miles – enjoy the good food undisturbed. ● *Nov–Apr.* 🖶 P
DC MC V — 10

For key to symbols see bookmark

WHERE TO EAT

BRITISH FOOD need strike no terrors to the visiting gourmet's heart; the UK's restaurant scene has moved far from its once dismal reputation. This is partly due to an influx of foreign chefs and cooking styles; you can now sample a wide range of international cuisine throughout Britain, with the greatest choice in London and the other major cities. Home-grown restaurateurs have risen to the challenge of redeeming British food too, and our indigenous cooking (once thought to consist only of fish and chips, overcooked vegetables, meat pies and

Michelin Man at Bibendum, London

lumpy custard) has improved out of all recognition in the last decade. You can now also eat extremely well in Britain whatever your budget – and at most times of day in the towns. Much less elaborate, but well-prepared, affordable food is making a mark in all types of brasseries, restaurants and cafés throughout the country; more modern approaches combine fresh produce and dietary common sense with influences from around the world. The restaurant listings *(see pp578–607)* feature some of the very best places as well as those with a steady track record.

WHAT'S ON THE MENU?

THE CHOICE seems endless in large cities, particularly London. Cuisines from all over the world are represented, as well as their infinite variations – Thai and Tex-Mex, Turkish and Tuscan, Tandoori, Bhel Poori and Balti. There are many more unusual styles of cooking such as Hungarian, Polish, Caribbean and Pacific Rim. French and Italian restaurants are still highly regarded, offering everything from pastries and espresso coffee to the highest standards of *haute cuisine*. Outside the major cities the food scene is more limited, but most towns will have at least a couple of Italian,

Indian and Chinese restaurants. The vague term "modern-international cuisine" adopted by many restaurants disguises a diverse rag-bag of styles. The spectrum ranges from French to Asian recipes, loosely characterized by the imaginative use of fresh, high-quality ingredients, which are cooked simply with imaginative seasonings.

Nostalgic yearnings for British food have produced a revival of hearty traditional dishes such as steak and kidney pie and treacle pudding *(see p37)*, though "Modern British" cooking adopts a lighter more innovative approach to old-fashioned stodge. The distinctions between this and Modern

International food are starting to blur, which is mostly a change for the better as young chefs apply Oriental and Mediterranean flavours to home-grown ingredients.

BREAKFAST

IT USED TO BE SAID that the best way to enjoy British food was to eat breakfast three times a day. Traditional British breakfast starts with cereal and milk followed by bacon, eggs and tomato, perhaps with fried black pudding *(see p37)* in the North and Scotland. It is finished off with toast and marmalade washed down with tea. Or you can just have black coffee and fruit juice, with a croissant or two (known as Continental breakfast in hotels). The price of breakfast is often included in hotel tariffs in Britain.

LUNCH

MANY RESTAURANTS offer light lunches at fixed prices, sometimes of only two courses (choose either a starter or a dessert). The most popular lunchtime foods are sandwiches, salads, baked potatoes with fillings and ploughman's lunches, the latter found mainly in pubs. A traditional Sunday lunch of roast chicken, lamb or beef is served in some pubs and restaurants.

The Gay Hussar, London, a top Hungarian restaurant *(see p578)*

AFTERNOON TEA

No visitor should miss the experience of a proper English afternoon tea, which rivals breakfast as the most enjoyable meal of the day (see p34). Some of the most palatial teas are offered by country-house and top London hotels such as the Ritz or Browns. The area that is best known for its classic "cream teas" is the West Country (see p271); these always include scones, spread with clotted cream, butter and jam. Wales, Scotland, Yorkshire and the Lake District also offer tasty teas with regional variations; in the North Country a slice of apple pie or fruit cake is served hot with a piece of North Yorkshire Wensleydale cheese on top.

An afternoon tea including sandwiches, cakes and scones

DINNER

At dinner time, the grander restaurants and hotels offer elaborately staged meals, sometimes billed as five or six courses (though one may be simply a sorbet, or coffee with *petits fours*). Dessert is often followed by cheese and crackers. Confusingly, in the North of England and Scotland "lunch" can be called "dinner" and "dinner" may be called "tea".

Generally, you can choose to take your dinner before 6pm or after 9pm only in larger towns, where there is a broad choice of ethnic restaurants, bars and all-day brasseries, which often have long opening hours.

Leith Docks in Edinburgh, a centre of good pubs, bars and restaurants

PLACES TO EAT

Eating venues are extremely varied, with brasseries, bistros, wine bars, tearooms, *tapas* bars and theatre cafés now competing with the more conventional cafés and restaurants. Many pubs also now serve excellent bar food at often reasonable prices (see p608–11).

BRASSERIES, BISTROS AND CAFÉS

French-style café-brasseries are now popular in Britain. Sometimes they stay open all day, serving coffee, snacks and fairly simple dishes along with a selection of beers and wines. Alcoholic drinks, however, may only be available at certain times of day. The atmosphere is usually young and urbane, with decor to match. Drinks such as imported bottled beers, exotic spirits or cocktails may be fairly expensive.

The interior of the Tate Gallery café, St Ives, Cornwall (see p591)

Wine bars are similar to brasseries, but with a better selection of wines, which may include English varieties (see pp146–47). Some bars have a good range of ciders and real ales as well (see p34). Bistros are another French import, serving full meals at lunch and dinner time with less formality and more moderate prices than you would expect at a restaurant. You should expect to pay anything from £12 to £30 for a standard three-course meal in a bistro.

RESTAURANTS-WITH-ROOMS AND HOTELS

Restaurants-with-rooms are a new breed of small establishments with only a handful of bedrooms and usually excellent food. They tend to be expensive and are usually in a rural location.

Many hotel restaurants happily serve non-residents. They tend to be expensive, but the best can be unparalleled. Hotels serving a high standard of food are also included in the hotel listings.

RESTAURANT ETIQUETTE

As a rule of thumb, the more expensive the restaurant, the more formal the dress code – though few restaurants nowadays will expect men to wear a shirt and tie. If you are not sure, ring first.

Some establishments do not allow smoking at all, while others now have separate sections or tables for people who wish to smoke.

Raymond Blanc's Le Manoir Aux Quat'Saisons *(see p586)*, one of Britain's most acclaimed restaurants-with-rooms

ALCOHOL

BRITAIN'S LAWS concerning the sale of alcohol, the "licensing laws", were once among the most restrictive in Europe. Now they are more relaxed, but some establishments may still only serve alcohol at set times with food. Some unlicensed restaurants operate a "Bring Your Own" policy. A corkage fee is often charged. The Scottish laws are different to the rest of Britain, most apparent in the later closing times of pubs.

VEGETARIAN FOOD

BRITAIN IS AHEAD of many of its European counterparts in providing vegetarian alternatives to meat dishes. A few of our selections serve only vegetarian meals, but most cater for carnivores as well. Vegetarians who want a wider choice should seek out South Indian, Chinese and other ethnic restaurants which have a tradition of vegetarian cuisine.

FAST FOOD

FAST FOOD comes much cheaper, usually well under £10. Apart from the numerous individually owned fish and chip shops, there are many fast food chains in Britain, such as McDonald's, Burger King, Pizza Hut and

KFC. Sandwich bars are very popular, and are often good value; some also have seating. Budget cafés, nicknamed "greasy spoons", serve simple, inexpensive food, often in the form of endless variations of the breakfast fry-up (see p36).

Betty's Café in Harrogate *(see p598)*

BOOKING AHEAD

IT IS ALWAYS SAFER to book a table first before making a special journey to a restaurant; city restaurants can be very busy and some of the more renowned establishments can be fully booked a month in advance. If you cannot keep a reservation, you should ring up and cancel. A lot of restaurants operate on knife-edge profit margins, and customers not turning up can threaten their livelihood.

CHECKING THE BILL

ALL RESTAURANTS are required by law to display their current prices outside the door. These amounts include Value Added Tax (VAT), currently at 17.5 per cent. Service and cover charges (if any) are also specified. So you should have a rough idea of what a meal may cost beforehand.

Wine is always pricey in Britain, and extras like coffee or bottled water can be disproportionately expensive.

Service charges (usually between 10 per cent and 15 per cent) are sometimes automatically added to your bill. If you feel that the service has been poor, you are entitled to subtract this service charge. If no service charge has been added, you are expected to add 10 to 15 per cent to the bill, but it is your decision.

Some restaurants may leave the "total" box of credit card slips blank, hoping customers will add something extra to the service charge. Another growing trend is for smart restaurants to boost their sagging profit margins with a "cover charge" for flowers, bread and butter, etc. Live entertainment may also be costed. The majority of restaurants accept credit cards, or cheques with a guarantee card, but pubs and cafés expect cash – do not rely on plastic.

MEALTIMES

BREAKFAST IS A MOVEABLE feast. It may be as early as 6:30am in a city business hotel (most hoteliers will make special arrangements if you have a plane to catch or some other reason for checking out early) or as late as 10:30am in relaxed country house establishments. Few hoteliers relish cooking bacon and eggs that late, however, and some insist you are up and about by 9:00 sharp if you want anything to eat. But you can find breakfast all day long in some urban restaurants. The American concept of Sunday "brunch" (a leisurely halfway house between breakfast and lunch) is becoming increasingly popular in some hotels, restaurants and cafés.

Lunch in pubs and restaurants is usually served between 12:30pm and 2:30pm. Try to arrive in time to order the main course before 1:30pm, or you may find choice restricted and service peremptory. Most tourist areas have plenty of cafés, fast-food diners and coffee bars where you can have a snack at any time of day. During peak hours there may be a minimum charge.

If you are lucky enough to be in one of the places where you can get a traditional afternoon tea, it is usually served between 3pm and 5pm.

Dinner is usually served from 7pm until 10pm; some places, especially ethnic restaurants, stay open later. In guest houses or small hotels, dinner may be served at a specific time (sometimes uncomfortably early).

CHILDREN

THE CONTINENTAL NORM of dining out *en famille* is steadily becoming more acceptable in Britain, and visiting a restaurant may no longer entail endless searches for a baby-sitter. Many places welcome junior diners, and some actively encourage families, at least during the

L'Artiste Musculé wine bar-bistro (see p578), London

Ice cream parlour sign

day or early evening. Formal restaurants sometimes cultivate a more adult ambience at dinner time, and some impose age limits. If you want to take young children to a restaurant, check when you book. Italian, Spanish, Indian, fast-food restaurants and ice cream parlours nearly always welcome children, and sometimes provide special menus or high chairs for them. Even traditional English pubs, which were once a strictly adult preserve, are now relaxing their rules to accommodate families and may even provide special rooms or play areas.

The places that welcome children are indicated in the pubs guide *(see pp608–11)*. The restaurant listings also indicate which establishments cater for children's needs.

DISABLED ACCESS

AS IN MOST WALKS of life, restaurant facilities in Britain could be better for disabled visitors, but things are gradually improving. Modern premises usually take account of mobility problems, but it's always best to check first if you have special needs.

PICNICS

EATING OUTSIDE is becoming more popular in Britain, though it is more likely that you will find tables outside pubs in the form of a beer garden, than outside restaurants. One inexpensive option is to make up your own picnic; most towns have good delicatessens and bakeries where you can collect provisions, and in Britain you do not usually have to worry about shops closing at mid-day as they often do on the Continent.

Look out for street markets to pick up fresh fruit and local cheeses at bargain prices. Department stores like Marks & Spencer and supermarkets such as Sainsbury's and Tesco often sell an excellent range of prepacked sandwiches and snacks; large towns usually have several sandwich bars to choose from. Your hotel or guest house may also be able to provide a packed lunch. Ask for it the night before.

An option for a chillier day is a hot takeaway meal; fish and chips with salt and vinegar all wrapped in paper is not only a British cliché but also a national institution.

Eating alfresco at Grasmere in the Lake District

Choosing a Restaurant

THE RESTAURANTS in this guide have been selected across a wide range of price categories for their good value, exceptional food and interesting location. This chart lists the restaurants by region, starting with London. Use the colour-coded thumb tabs, which indicate the regions covered on each page, to guide you to the relevant sections of the chart.

	CREDIT CARDS	CHILDREN WELCOME	FIXED-PRICE MENU	VEGETARIAN	OUTDOOR TABLES

LONDON

BAYSWATER & PADDINGTON: *40 Degrees at Veronicas.* **Map** 2 D2. £££
3 Hereford Rd, W2. 020 7229 5079.
Specializing in regional, historical and Modern British cuisine. Choice of dining room includes Victorian style and a modern room with leather tablecloths. 🍷

	AE MC	●	■		

NOTTING HILL: *Mandola* **Map** 1 C1. ££
139-143 Westbourne Grove W11. 020-7229 4734.
Sudanese cuisine, including a seven salad starter, in a "Khartoum" setting.

	MC V	●		●	

NOTTING HILL: *Bali Sugar* **Map** 1 B1. ££££
33a All Saint's Road, W11. 020-7221 4477.
A split-level, cleverly converted terraced house, tastefully decorated. Sashimi of seabream is a taste of what to expect, with weekend brunch a highlight. 🍴 🍷

	AE DC MC V		■	●	■

KENSINGTON: *Sticky Fingers* **Map** 2 D2. ££
1a Phillimore Gdns, W8. 020-7938 5338.
With plenty of Rolling Stones memorabilia creating a distinctive atmosphere, the menu includes a range of American staples like great burgers.

	AE MC V	●			

KENSINGTON: *Kensington Place* **Map** 1 C4. £££
201-209 Kensington Church St W8. 020-7727 3184.
Minimalist venue attracting a vibrant, dedicated crowd. Progressive Modern International cuisine includes chicken and goat's cheese mousse with olives. 🍷

	AE DC MC V	●	■	●	

KENSINGTON: *Wódka* **Map** 1 C4. £££
12 St Alban's Grove W8. 020-7937 6513
A mixture of classic and modern Polish food (blini with smoked salmon, roast duck), served in a modern but friendly setting. Great range of vodkas. 🍷

	AE DC MC V		■	●	

KENSINGTON: *Bombay Brasserie* **Map** 2 D5. ££££
Courtfield Close, Courtfield Rd SW7. 020-7370 4040
Acclaimed restaurant with an impressive colonial atmosphere, including conservatory, cocktail bar and pianist. Bombay and regional cuisine. 🍴 🍷

	AE DC MC V			●	

KNIGHTSBRIDGE & VICTORIA: *Boisdale* **Map** 5 B4. ££££
15 Eccleston St, SW1. 020-7730 6922.
Traditional and Modern British with Scottish specialities such as haggis and salmon, served in a traditional, clubby atmosphere. 🍷

	AE DC MC V	●	■	●	

KNIGHTSBRIDGE & VICTORIA: *The Fifth Floor* **Map** 5 A2. ££££
Fifth Floor, Harvey Nichols, 109-125 Knightsbridge, SW1. 020 7235 5250.
At the top of London's most fashionable department store, Modern British food in a contemporary setting. Also a café, sushi counter and foodmarket. 🍴 🍷

	AE MC V		■	●	

KNIGHTSBRIDGE & VICTORIA: *L'Incontro* **Map** 5 B4. ££££
87 Pimlico Rd, SW1. 020-7730 5062.
Wonderful Italian dishes with a leaning towards Venetian cuisine: seabass with balsamic vinegar and risotto with radicchio, served in an elegant Italianate setting.

	DC MC V				

KNIGHTSBRIDGE & VICTORIA: *Rhodes in the Square* **Map** 6 D5. ££££
Dolphin Sq, Chichester St, SW1. 020 7798 6767
Inspired Modern British dishes (red wine beef lasagne with a chestnut mushroom cream sauce), served amid an Art Deco setting. ● *Sun–Mon.* 🍴 🍷

	AE DC MC V		■	●	

KNIGHTSBRIDGE & VICTORIA: *Zafferano* **Map** 5 B3. ££££
15 Lowndes St SW1. 020-7235 5800.
One of London's finest Modern Italian restaurants, with white truffle dishes among the numerous specialities. The wine list includes grappa. 🍷

	AE DC MC V	●	■	●	

KNIGHTSBRIDGE & VICTORIA: *Café Fish* **Map** 5 B4. £££££
36-40 Rupert St SW1. 020-7287 8989
A classic French approach is applied to the fish and seafood, with favourites including fish and chips and seafood platter. 🍴 🍷

	AE DC MC V	●	■	●	

	CREDIT CARDS	CHILDREN WELCOME	FIXED-PRICE MENU	VEGETARIAN	OUTDOOR TABLES

Price categories include a three-course meal for one, half a bottle of house wine, and all unavoidable extra charges such as cover, service, VAT:
£ under £15
££ £15–£25
£££ £25–£35
££££ £35–£50
£££££ over £50.

CHILDREN WELCOME
Restaurants which offer smaller portions and high-chairs for children. Special menus sometimes available.
FIXED-PRICE MENU
A good value fixed-price meal, at lunch, dinner or both, usually of three courses.
VEGETARIAN
Vegetarian specialities served, sometimes for both starters and main courses.
CREDIT CARDS
Indicates which credit cards are accepted: *AE* American Express; *DC* Diners Club; *MC* Master Card/Access; *V* Visa.

KNIGHTSBRIDGE & VICTORIA: *La Tante Claire* **Map** 5 C4. **£££££** The Berkeley Hotel, Wilton Place SW1. 📞 020-7823 2003 Elegant restaurant, run by master-chef Pierre Koffman, who is renowned for Gascon cuisine served par excellence. ⬤ *Sun.*	AE DC MC V	●	▣	●	
CHELSEA & FULHAM: *Bibendum* **£££** 1st Floor, Michelin House, 81 Fulham Rd, SW3. 📞 020 7581 5187. A retro-chic showcase for Modern French cuisine, including bistro dishes, game and offal. The ground floor features an Oyster Bar and separate café. 🍴 ▯	AE MC V	●	▣	●	
CHELSEA & FULHAM: *Bluebird* **£££** The King's Road Gastrodome, 350 King's Rd SW3. 📞 020-7559 1000. Inspired conversion of a 1923 garage, renovating the original mix of Classical Neo-Georgian and Art Deco elements. Game and crustacea a speciality.	AE DC MC V	●	▣	●	
CHELSEA & FULHAM: *Chutney Mary* **£££** 535, Kings Rd SW10. 📞 020-7351 3113 An Indian term for women crossing two cultures, "Chutney Mary" serves a delicious blend of Indian and Western cuisine. Attractive colonial Raj decor. 🍴	AE DC MC V		▣	●	
CHELSEA & FULHAM: *Aubergine* **£££££** 11 Park Walk SW10. 📞 020-7352 3449. Provençale decor, charming service and faultless cuisine: salad of quail, foie gras, sweetbreads and truffle dressing. ⬤ *Sun, 19 Dec–6 Jan, 2 wks Aug.* ▯	AE DC MC V		▣		
PICCADILLY & MAYFAIR: *Sofra* **Map** 2 D2. **£** 18 Shepherd St W1. 📞 020-7493 3320 One of London's best-value chains of Turkish restaurants. 🍴	MC V	●	▣	●	▣
PICCADILLY & MAYFAIR: *Carluccio's* **Map** 3 B5. **££** 3-5 Barrett St, St Christopher's Pl, W1. 📞 020-7935 5927 Authentic Italian dishes available throughout the day, including soup and pasta, with a shop stocking Carluccio's range of Italian foodstuffs.	AE MC V	●		●	
PICCADILLY & MAYFAIR: *L'Artiste Musclé* **Map** 5 C1. **££** 1 Shepherds Mkt, W1. 📞 020-7493 6150 French bistro cuisine: boeuf Bourguignon, Toulouse sausage, in a classic bistro setting, with pavement tables overlooking Shepherd Market.	AE DC MC V			●	▣
PICCADILLY & MAYFAIR: *Chor Bizarre* **Map** 5 C1. **£££** 16 Albermarle St W1. 📞 020-7629 9802 Amid numerous Indian antiques (all for sale), the menu has a Kashmiri focus, such as *gostaba* (minced lamb with cardamom and yogurt). 🍴 ▯	AE MC V	●	▣	●	
PICCADILLY & MAYFAIR: *Green's Restaurant & Oyster Bar* **Map** 5 C1. **£££** 36 Duke St St James's, SW1. 📞 020-7930 4366. Classic English "gentleman's club" decor, with banquettes and booths, serving a range of British classics, with fish and oysters a particular feature. ▯	AE DC MC V	●	▣	●	
PICCADILLY & MAYFAIR: *Hard Rock Café* **Map** 5 B1. **£££** 150 Old Park Lane W1. 📞 020-7629 0382. No reservations means queues, but the reward is classic American fare (great burgers and a daily changing special) amid music videos and memorabilia. 🍴	AE MC V	●		●	▣
PICCADILLY & MAYFAIR: *Veeraswamy* **Map** 3 C5. **£££** Mezzanine Floor, Victory House, 99 Regent St W1. 📞 020-7734 1401 London's oldest Indian (established 1927) it is also one of the most modern. Inspiring, original and authentic Indian dishes, with great service. 🍴	AE DC MC V		▣	●	
PICCADILLY & MAYFAIR: *Criterion Brasserie* **Map** 6 D1. **££££** Piccadilly Circus W1. 📞 020-7930 0488. Stunning, historic interiors culminate in a glittering neo-Byzantine mosaic ceiling. French dishes with Mediterranean influences. ▯	AE DC MC V	●	▣	●	

For key to symbols see bookmark

Price categories include a three-course meal for one, half a bottle of house wine, and all unavoidable extra charges such as cover, service, VAT:
£ under £15
££ £15–£25
£££ £25–£35
££££ £35–£50
£££££ over £50.

CHILDREN WELCOME
Restaurants which offer smaller portions and high-chairs for children. Special menus sometimes available.

FIXED-PRICE MENU
A good value fixed-price meal, at lunch, dinner or both, usually of three courses.

VEGETARIAN
Vegetarian specialities served, sometimes for both starters and main courses.

CREDIT CARDS
Indicates which credit cards are accepted: *AE* American Express; *DC* Diners Club; *MC* Master Card/Access; *V* Visa.

		CREDIT CARDS	CHILDREN WELCOME	FIXED-PRICE MENU	VEGETARIAN	OUTDOOR TABLES

PICCADILLY & MAYFAIR: *Momo* **Map** 5 C1. ££££
25 Heddon St, W1. 020-7434 4040
Housed within a wonderful "antique Moroccan palace", the cuisine is North African, balancing tradition with a more modern approach.
Credit cards: AE MC V — Fixed-Price Menu, Vegetarian

PICCADILLY & MAYFAIR: *Quaglino's* **Map** 5 C1. ££££
16 Bury St, SW1. 020-7930 6767.
Modern British brasserie, thriving on Conran design. Classic dishes include calves' liver and bacon, roast guinea fowl with buttered spinach and almonds.
Credit cards: AE DC MC — Fixed-Price Menu, Vegetarian

PICCADILLY & MAYFAIR: *The Sugar Club* **Map** 5 C1. ££££
21 Warwick St W1. 020-7437 7776.
Pacific Rim cuisine, served in a streamlined setting: spicy kangaroo salad with mint, peanuts and lime chilli dressing, and plenty of New World wines.
Credit cards: AE MC V — Vegetarian

PICCADILLY & MAYFAIR: *Chez Nico* **Map** 5 B1. £££££
90 Park Lane W1. 020-7409 1290.
Superstar chef Nico Ladenis has in traded his three Michelin stars, but his classical French gastronomic artistry remains at a culinary peak. ● *Sun.*
Credit cards: AE DC MC V — Children Welcome, Fixed-Price Menu, Vegetarian

PICCADILLY & MAYFAIR: *Le Gavroche* **Map** 5 C1. £££££
43 Upper Brook St W1. 020-7408 0881
Superlative modern and classical French cuisine (lobster mousse with caviar and champagne sauce) in a sophisticated setting. Smart bar for aperitifs and lounge for coffee and cigars. ● *Sat–Sun.*
Credit cards: AE DC MC V — Fixed-Price Menu, Vegetarian

PICCADILLY & MAYFAIR: *The Grill Room* **Map** 2 D2. £££££
The Dorchester Hotel, Park La, W1. 020-7317 6336
Traditional British cuisine (home smoked breast of Norfolk duck with pimento and onion compote), a separate vegetarian menu. Opulent decor
Credit cards: AE MC V — Children Welcome, Vegetarian

PICCADILLY & MAYFAIR: *Nobu* **Map** 5 B1. £££££
19 Old Park Lane, W1. 020-7447 4747.
Views over Hyde Park and great staff serve sensational Japanese, South American fusion cuisine, with black cod in miso a signature dish.
Credit cards: AE DC MC V — Children Welcome, Fixed-Price Menu, Vegetarian

REGENT'S PARK & MARYLEBONE: *Stephen Bull* **Map** 3 B4. £££
5-7 Blandford St W1. 020-7486 9696.
Stylishly modern, streamlined but colourful venue, offering a daily changing menu of Modern British fine dining (crusted cod with swede purée). ● *Sun.*
Credit cards: AE DC MC V — Vegetarian

SOHO: *Yo! Sushi* **Map** 4 E5. £
52-53 Poland St, W1. 020-7287 0443.
Sushi, sashimi, salads, soups and noodles pass by on a conveyor belt, in this modern, minimalist setting. Yo! Below bar in the basement.
Credit cards: AE DC MC V — Children Welcome, Vegetarian

SOHO: *Mildred's* **Map** 4 E5. ££
58 Greek St W1. 020-7494 1634.
Global vegetarian cuisine accompanied by an all-organic wine list. ● *Sun.*
— Vegetarian, Outdoor Tables

SOHO: *Alastair Little* **Map** 4 E5. £££
49 Frith St W1. 020-7734 5183.
Modern International cooking with a distinct Italian accent: Tuscan fish casserole, grilled seabass with flageolet and lemon minestra. ● *Sun.*
Credit cards: AE MC V — Children Welcome, Fixed-Price Menu, Vegetarian

SOHO: *The Gay Hussar* **Map** 4 E5. £££
2 Greek St W1. 020-7437 0973
Bohemian library setting serving various politicians, media and literary figures: chilled wild cherry soup, Transylvanian stuffed cabbage. ● *Sun.*
Credit cards: AE DC MC V — Fixed-Price Menu, Vegetarian

SOHO: *Mezzo* **Map** 4 E5. £££
100 Wardour St W1. 020-7314 4000.
A Soho landmark, housed in an elegant, mirrored basement, modern European dishes such as bruschetta of goat's cheese, fig and San Daniele ham.
Credit cards: AE DC MC V — Fixed-Price Menu, Vegetarian

Soho: *Sri Siam* **Map** 4 E5. £££ — AE DC MC V
16 Old Compton St W1. 020-7434 3544.
This stylish restaurant is a perfect place for your first taste of Thai food; the heat is toned down, but the flavours aren't: seafood dishes, as well as satay and curries.

Covent Garden & Strand: *Belgo Centraal* **Map** 4 F5. £ — AE DC MC V
50 Earlham St WC2. 020-7813 2233
An industrial lift takes you down to this modern, monastic basement with refectory seating and booths. Belgian mussel pots and platters a speciality.

Covent Garden & Strand: *Bertorelli's* **Map** 4 F5.. ££ — AE DC MC V
44a Floral St WC2. 020-7836 3969
Modern Italian cuisine with traditional favourites, including pizza, pasta, meat and fish dishes. Relaxed and inviting decor. ● *Sun.* 🍴 🍷

Covent Garden & Strand: *Chez Gerard* **Map** 4 F5.. £££ — AE MC V
Opera Terrace, The Market, Covent Garden Piazza, WC2. 020-7379 0666.
A French selection encompasses grills, fish and vegetarian dishes, while renowned for classic Parisian *steak frites*. Terrace overlooking the piazza. 🍴 🍷

Covent Garden & Strand: *Simpson's-in-the-Strand* **Map** 4 F5. £££ — AE DC MC V
100 Strand WC2. Map 13 C2. 020-7836 9112
For a truly traditional English experience, with Victorian interiors, the menu includes a superb traditional breakfast. A smart cocktail bar is ideal for aperitifs.

Covent Garden & Strand: *The Ivy* **Map** 4 F5. ££££ — AE DC MC V
1 West St WC2. 020-7836 4751.
An institution of the theatre district, this celebrity haven features artworks and stained glass windows. Crispy duck salad and fish cakes are classics. 🍷

Covent Garden & Strand: *Orso* **Map** 4 F5. £££ — AE MC V
27 Wellington St WC2. 020-7240 5269
A media, theatre-goers rendezvous, with soft teracotta walls, white linen tablecloths and and Italianate pictures, serving Italian regional cuisine. 🍴 🍷

Covent Garden & Strand: *Rules* **Map** 4 F5. ££££ — AE DC MC V
35 Maiden La WC2. 020-7836 5314.
London's oldest surviving restaurant serving traditional British fare since 1798. Dishes include Dover sole, rib of beef, game, amid Edwardian decor. 🍴

Bloomsbury & Fitzrovia: *Wagamama* **Map** 4 E4. £ — AE DC MC V
4 Streatham St WC1. 020-7323 9223
Modern refectory-style, within a spacious, bustling basement, serving various types of noodles. Queues may look daunting, but are also fast-moving. 🍴

Bloomsbury & Fitzrovia: *Hakkasan* **Map** 4 D4. £££ — AE DC MC V
8 Hanway Pl, W1. 020-7927 7000
Dim sum is served all day, changing to à la carte for dinner, with the lounge bar also serving snacks in the evening. Modern ethnic decor. 🍷

Bloomsbury & Fitzrovia: *Villandry* **Map** 3 C4 £££ — AE DC MC V
Great Portland St, W1. 020-7631 3131.
Chic and thoroughly comprehensive Euro-deli and grocery store with a stylish modern restaurant. The bar has a separate all-day menu. 🍴

Spitalfields & Clerkenwell: *Quality Chop House* £££ — MC V
94 Farringdon Road EC1. 020-7837 5093.
Beautiful Victorian diner with its original 1869 fittings. Sausage and mash, and salmon fish cakes are appealing staples. 🍴

Spitalfields & Clerkenwell: *Maison Novelli* £££££ — AE DC MC V
29 Clerkenwell Green EC1. 020-7251 6606
Jean-Christophe Novelli's background is *haute cuisine*, and it shows in his modern French cuisine; the chocolate plate dessert is legendary. ● *Sun.* 🍴

City & Southbank: *Wine Wharf at Vinopolis* **Map** 8 D4. £ — AE MC V
Storey Street, Borough Market, SE1. 020-7940 8335
Graze on tapas-type dishes including salads and cheeses, or tackle the fuller menu, within this converted Victorian warehouse. Great choice of wines. 🍷

City & Southbank: *Club Gascon* **Map** 7 C2. £££ — AE MC V
57 West Smithfield, EC1. 020 796 0699.
Regional cuisine from southwest France, with foie gras, truffle and seafood dishes a speciality. Also served tapas-style in the bar. ● *Sun.* 🍷

For key to symbols see bookmark

Price categories include a three-course meal for one, half a bottle of house wine, and all unavoidable extra charges such as cover, service, VAT:
£ under £15
££ £15–£25
£££ £25–£35
££££ £35–£50
£££££ over £50.

CHILDREN WELCOME
Restaurants which offer smaller portions and high-chairs for children. Special menus sometimes available.

FIXED-PRICE MENU
A good value fixed-price meal, at lunch, dinner or both, usually of three courses.

VEGETARIAN
Vegetarian specialities served, sometimes for both starters and main courses.

CREDIT CARDS
Indicates which credit cards are accepted: *AE* American Express; *DC* Diners Club; *MC* Master Card/Access; *V* Visa.

	Credit Cards	Children Welcome	Fixed-Price Menu	Vegetarian	Outdoor Tables
CITY & SOUTHBANK: *The Tate Britain Restaurant* **Map** 7 C3. £££ Tate Britain, Millbank, SE1. 020-7887 8825. Modern English cuisine, and over 300 wines to choose from. Witty, whimsical murals by Rex Whistler date from 1925 and provide an enchanting setting.	AE DC MC V		▨	●	
CITY & SOUTHBANK: *Livebait* **Map** 7 B4. ££££ 43 The Cut SE1. 020-7928 7211 Retaining the original Victorian ceramic tiles, mirrors and chrome, the fish and shellfish repertoire includes traditional fish and chips. ● *Sun.*	AE DC MC V	●		●	
CITY & SOUTHBANK: *The Oxo Tower* **Map** 7 B3. ££££ Oxo Tower Wharf, Barge House St, SE1. 020 7803 3888. Set on the eighth floor of this landmark 1930s building, with stunning views along the Thames. Exemplary Modern British cuisine.	AE MC V		▨	●	▨
CITY & SOUTHBANK: *Le Pont de la Tour* **Map** 8 F4. £££££ Butlers Wharf SE1. 020-7403 8403 Riverside marvel with great views, a separate crustacea bar, pianist nightly, and French cuisine with Euro-Mediterranean influences. Decor is classic Conran.	AE DC MC V	●		●	▨
FURTHER AFIELD: *River Café* £££££ Thames Wharf Studios, Rainville Rd W6. 020-7381 8824 A modern style that also provides river views, serving interpretations of traditional Italian cuisine such as chargrilled squid with chilli and rocket.	AE DC MC V	●		●	▨

THE DOWNS AND CHANNEL COAST

	Credit Cards	Children Welcome	Fixed-Price Menu	Vegetarian	Outdoor Tables
AMBERLEY: *Queen's Room, Amberley Castle* ££££ On B2139, Amberley, W Sussex. 01798 831992. @ info@amberleycastle.co.uk A romantic medieval fortress provides a dramatic backdrop for "castle cuisine", a mix of ancient and Modern British recipes.	AE DC MC V		▨	●	
BOUGHTON LEES: *Eastwall Manor* @ eastwell@btinternet.com £££££ Eastwell Park, Boughton Lees, nr Ashford, Kent. 01233 219955. A grand parkland setting graces this dynamic hotel restaurant where the service is formal but friendly.	AE DC MC V	●	▨	●	▨
BRIGHTON: *Food for Friends* £ 17–18 Prince Albert St, Brighton. 01273 202310. @ simon@foodies.freeserve.co.uk This vegetarian wholefood café in the Lanes offers friendly service, generous helpings and imaginative cooking amid pine and pot plants. ● *25–26 Dec.*	DC MC V	●		●	
BRIGHTON: *Black Chapati* ££ 12 Circus Parade, New England Rd, Brighton. 01273 699011. Adventurous and eclectic "Indian" cooking fizzes with original ideas in a stark café setting just outside the town centre. The service is efficient, and the atmosphere friendly and welcoming. ● *Sun–Mon.*	AE MC V			●	
BRIGHTON: *Terre à Terre* £££ 71 East St, Brighton. 01273 729051. Close to the pavilion, pier and the Lanes, this vegetarian retaurant has an imaginative international menu. ● *Mon L.*	AE DC MC V	●		●	
BROCKENHURST: *Simply Poussin* £££ The Courtyard, Brookley Rd, Brockenhurst, Hants. 01590 623063. New Forest produce such as venison and wild pork appears on the menu in robust provincial French-style fare. ● *Sun & Mon.*	MC V		▨		▨
CUCKMERE: *Golden Galleon* ££ Exceat Bridge, Cuckmere Haven, E Sussex. 01323 892247. This pub-restaurant has its own brewery and smokery; try the home-smoked salmon and duck breast. Conservatory and terrace with sea views. ● *Sun D winter.*	MC V	●		●	▨

EAST GRINSTEAD: *Gravetye Manor* £££££ MC V
Vowels Lane, East Grinstead, W Sussex. 📞 01342 810567. @ gravetye@relaischateaux.fr
Classic food is served in this plush Elizabethan mansion, a luxury
hotel in gorgeous grounds. 🍴 🍷

EDENBRIDGE: *Honours Mill* £££ MC V
87 High St, Edenbridge, Kent. 📞 01732 866757.
Mind your head: the beams are low. Well-tried French classics are
daringly adapted in this quiet, friendly restaurant. ● *Sat L, Sun D, Mon.* 🍷

EMSWORTH: *36 on the Quay* ££££ AE DC MC V
47 South St, Emsworth, Hants. 📞 01243 375592.
Stylish smugglers' inn by the waterfront. Food is innovative but disciplined. Local
fish features on the menu. ● *Sat L, Sun, Mon L, bank hols (except Good Fri).* 🍴 ♿ 🍷

FERNHURST: *King's Arms* ££ MC V
Midhurst Road, Fernhurst, Surrey. 📞 01428 652005.
The accomplished modern-British cooking always includes fish dishes, the chef's
speciality, at this 17th-century country dining pub. ● *Sun D, 25 Dec, 1 Jan.* ♿ 🍷

HAMPTON HILL: *Monsieur Max* ££££ AE DC MC V
133 High St, Hampton Hill, Middx. 📞 020 8979 5546. @ monsmax@aol.com
First-class ingredients and proficient cooking are all part of the package of this
Michelin-starred French restaurant. ● *Sat & Mon L.* ♿ 🍷

HASTINGS: *Rösers* @ gerald@rosers.co.uk ££££ AE DC MC V
64 Eversfield Pl, St Leonards, Hastings, E Sussex. 📞 01424 712218.
Freshness is the watchword here: sausages and bread are made on the
premises. With the sea so close, fish is a speciality. ● *Sat L, Sun, Mon.* ♿ 🍷

HAYWARDS HEATH: *Jeremy's at Borde Hill* £££ AE MC V
Balcombe Rd, Haywards Heath, W. Sussex. 📞 01444 441102.
Vivaciously modern European cooking produces memorable results
in this civilized modern interior overlooking a walled garden. ● *Sun D, Mon.* ♿ 🍴

HURSTBOURNE TARRANT: *Esseborne Manor* £££ AE DC MC V
On A343, N of Hurstbourne Tarrant, Hants. 📞 01264 736444.
Well-flavoured and sophisticated English country cooking is offered in
this stylish Victorian manor-house hotel. Good-value set lunch. ♿ 🍴 🍷

JEVINGTON: *Hungry Monk* £££ MC V
Between Polegate and Alfriston, E Sussex. 📞 01323 482178.
This restaurant's popularity rests partly on its 15th-century setting and on
innovative food. Its most famous creation is banoffi pie. ● *Mon–Sat L.* 🍴 🍷

NEW MILTON: *Marryat, Chewton Glen* £££££ AE DC MC V
Christchurch Rd, New Milton, Hants. 📞 01425 275341. @ pcrome@chewtonglen.com
A gastronomic shrine in a tranquil New Forest country-house hotel.
The conservatory restaurant overlooks lovely gardens. ♿ 🍴 🍷

RICHMOND: *Nightingales* @ dining@petershamhotel.co.uk ££££ AE DC MC V
Petersham Hotel, Nightingale Lane, Richmond upon Thames, Surrey. 📞 020 8940 7471.
A superb Thames view adds to the pleasure of mostly traditional
English cooking at this Victorian hotel. ● *Sun D.* 🍷 ♿

RIPLEY: *Michels'* ££££ AE MC V
High St, Ripley, Surrey. 📞 01483 224777.
Ambitious menus change with the seasons. Picturesque setting. In summer
you can have drinks in a walled garden. ● *Sat L, Sun D, Mon.*

ROMSEY: *Old Manor House* £££ AE MC V
21 Palmerston St, Romsey, Hants. 📞 01794 517353.
Italianate influences enhance ingredients including venison and home-
made salami in this brick-and-timber Tudor building. ● *Sun D, Mon.* 🍷

RYE: *Landgate Bistro* ££ AE DC MC V
5–6 Landgate, Rye, E Sussex. 📞 01797 222829.
Local produce like Romney Marsh lamb or freshly caught fish figures
imaginatively in this pleasant cottage-style restaurant. ● *Sun, Mon.* ♿ 🍴

STORRINGTON: *Fleur de Sel* £££ AE MC V
Manleys Hill, Storrington, W Sussex. 📞 01903 742331.
French cooking at this cottage restaurant where
service is calm and efficient. ● *Sat L, Sun D, Mon.* 🍷 ♿

For key to symbols see bookmark

Price categories include a three-course meal for one, half a bottle of house wine, and all unavoidable extra charges such as cover, service, VAT:
£ under £15
££ £15–£25
£££ £25–£35
££££ £35–£50
£££££ over £50.

CHILDREN WELCOME
Restaurants which offer smaller portions and high-chairs for children. Special menus sometimes available.

FIXED-PRICE MENU
A good value fixed-price meal, at lunch, dinner or both, usually of three courses.

VEGETARIAN
Vegetarian specialities served, sometimes for both starters and main courses.

CREDIT CARDS
Indicates which credit cards are accepted: *AE* American Express; *DC* Diners Club; *MC* Master Card/Access; *V* Visa.

	CREDIT CARDS	CHILDREN WELCOME	FIXED-PRICE MENU	VEGETARIAN	OUTDOOR TABLES

TUNBRIDGE WELLS: *Sankeys* **££**
39 Mount Ephraim, Tunbridge Wells, Kent. (*01892 511422.*
A smart restaurant offering seafood from all parts of Britain, from Scotland to Cornwall. There is also an informal bar serving food. ● *Sun.*

AE DC MC V	●		●	▨

TUNBRIDGE WELLS: *Thackeray's House* **£££**
85 London Rd, Tunbridge Wells, Kent. (*01892 511921.*
The novelist's home is now a double-decker restaurant and wine bar where local produce is given a Gallic touch. ● *Sun, Mon.*

MC V	●	▨	●	▨

WHITSTABLE: *Whitstable Oyster Fishery Co* **£££**
Royal Native Oyster Stores, Whitstable, Kent. (*01227 276856.*
The name suggests what it does best, but other fishy things appear on the menu in this Victorian building by the harbour. ● *Sun D (winter), Mon.*

AE DC MC V	●		●	▨

WICKHAM: *Old House* **££££**
The Square, Wickham, Hants. (*01329 833049.* @ *enq@theoldhousehotel.co.uk*
British/European-inspired food with exotic touches, served in the timber-framed former stable-block of a Georgian house. ● *Mon L, Sun D.*

AE MC V	●	▨	●	▨

EAST ANGLIA

ALDEBURGH: *Regatta* **££**
171–173 High St, Aldeburgh, Suff. (*01728 452011.*
Seafaring decor reflects the fish specialities which are always cooked with care. Sometimes there's local game on the menu. The ingredients are always top quality, and the service is friendly. ● *Sun D, Mon–Wed L.*

AE MC V	●	▨	●	

BURNHAM MARKET: *Fishes'* **££**
Market Pl, Burnham Market, Norf. (*01328 738588.*
Located on the 18th-century village green, this restaurant provides reliable fish specialities: the best of the catch at fair prices. Try potted shrimps or something from the smokehouse. ● *Sun D, Mon.*

AE DC MC V	●	▨		

BURY ST EDMUNDS: *Maison Bleu* **££**
31 Churchgate St, Bury St Edmunds, Suff. (*01284 760623.*
Straightforward seafood fresh from the market. There's a huge menu and good white wines. Can get very busy. ● *Sun–Mon.*

AE MC V	●	▨	●	

CAMBRIDGE: *Restaurant Twenty-two* **£££**
22 Chesterton Rd, Cambs. (*01223 351880.*
Courteous service complements pleasingly inventive food in Victorian setting. Three-course menus change every month. ● *Tue–Sat L, Sun, Mon.*

AE DC MC V		▨	●	

CAMBRIDGE: *Midsummer House* **£££££**
Midsummer Common, Cambs. (*01223 369299.*
An intimate restaurant serving fixed-price menus of great complexity. Puddings are luscious and elaborate. ● *Sun–Mon.*

AE MC V		▨	●	▨

COLCHESTER: *Warehouse Brasserie* **££**
12A Chapel St North, Colchester, Essex. (*01206 765656.*
A popular restaurant with an emphasis on fish and vegetarian dishes. Lots of local produce; some light main courses. ● *Sun–Mon.*

MC V	●	▨	●	

DEDHAM: *Le Talbooth* @ *itreception@talbooth.co.uk* **££££**
Gun Hill, Dedham, nr Colchester, Essex. (*01206 323150.*
Standards stay high at this long-established Tudor restaurant by the River Stour. Creative cooking that is popular with locals and visitors alike.

AE DC MC V	●	▨	●	▨

DISS: *Weaver's Wine Bar* **££**
Market Hill, Diss, Norf. (*01379 642411.*
A charming timbered setting for a cheerful, ad hoc restaurant.
● *Sat L, Sun, Mon L, public hols.*

AE DC MC V	●	▨	●	

ELY: *Old Fire Engine House* £££ | MC V
25 St Mary's St, Ely, Cambs. 01353 662582.
Local produce inspires hearty British cooking in the old fire station
by the cathedral. Friendly, unfussy atmosphere.

ERPINGHAM: *Ark* £££
The Street, Erpingham, Norf. 01263 761535.
The relaxing, informal atmosphere at this old brick cottage complements the
hearty and wholesome country fare. Tue–Sat L, Mon & Tue (Oct–Easter).

FRESSINGFIELD: *Fox and Goose* ££ | MC V
On B1116, Fressingfield, Suff. 01379 586247.
This remote country pub serves a wide range of inventive British and
international dishes. Children are welcomed.

HARWICH: *Pier at Harwich* £££ | AE DC MC V
The Quay, Harwich, Essex. 01255 241212.
A bustling harbourside stop-over with nautical decor and excellent fish
served with chips. Comfortable rooms are also available.

HINTLESHAM: *Hintlesham Hall* ££££ | AE DC MC V
On A1071, Hintlesham, Suff. 01473 652268.
Presentation is the key to success at this hotel west of Ipswich.
Excellent cheese-board. (See also p548.) Sat L.

HUNTINGDON: *Old Bridge* £££ | AE DC MC V
1 High St, Huntingdon, Cambs. 01480 424300. @ oldbridge@huntsbridge.co.uk
A handsome riverside inn with an airy restaurant proffering British and
Mediterranean fare, and splendid English cheeses. Good teas too.

ICKLINGHAM: *Red Lion* ££ | MC V
The Street, Icklingham, Suff. 01638 717802.
Attractive, 16th-century inn with exposed beams and log fires. Choose from the
wide range of seafood, or try game dishes such as wild boar. 25 Dec.

KING'S LYNN: *Rococo* ££££ | AE DC MC V
11 Saturday Market Pl, King's Lynn, Norf. 01553 771483. @ rococorest@aol.com
Local produce is served with panache in a cheerful yellow dining room.
Try Norfolk shrimps or specially reared duck. Sun, Mon L.

NORWICH: *Adlard's* ££££ | AE MC V
79 Upper St Giles St, Norwich, Norf. 01603 633522.
A deceptively elegant setting belies high-quality cooking of great
flair. The cuisine is mostly classical French. Sun, Mon L.

ORFORD: *Butley Orford Oysterage* ££ | MC V
Market Hill, The Square, Orford, Woodbridge, Suff. 01394 450277.
Café-restaurant with its own smokehouse and oyster-beds. Enjoy a
snack or meal in a delightful Suffolk village. Sun–Thu D.

SNAPE: *Plough and Snail* ££ | AE DC MC V
Snape Maltings Riverside Centre, Snape, Suff. 01728 688413.
Sprats and other local fish are the specialities at this popular pub with
restaurant – part of a concert hall/craft shop/art gallery complex.

SWAFFHAM: *Stratton House* £££ | MC V
4 Ash Close, Swaffham, Norf. 01760 723845.
Lady Hamilton once stayed in this 18th-century house which is now a hotel.
The changing menu includes some inventive dishes. L, 25–26 Dec.

THORPE MARKET: *Green Farm Restaurant* ££ | AE DC MC V
North Walsham Road, Thorpe Market, Norf. 01263 833602. @ grfarmh.aol.com
This restaurant in a 16th-century farmhouse has an excellent reputation for top-class
dishes made from fresh local ingredients. Try the crab, sea trout or venison.

WEST MERSEA: *The Blackwater Restaurant* ££ | MC V
20–22 Church Rd, West Mersea, Essex. 01206 383338.
An popular favourite in the Essex marshes. Inventive fish dishes
prepared in a European style. Comfortable rooms. Mon L.

WOODBRIDGE: *Captain's Table* ££ | MC V
3 Quay Street, Woodbridge, Suff. 01394 383145.
Set in a 16th-century building, this restaurant presents an eclectic British and
European menu cooked with flair. Sun D, Mon.

For key to symbols see bookmark

Price categories include a
three-course meal for one, half
a bottle of house wine, and all
unavoidable extra charges such
as cover, service, VAT:
£ under £15
££ £15-£25
£££ £25-£35
££££ £35-£50
£££££ over £50.

CHILDREN WELCOME
Restaurants which offer smaller portions and high-chairs
for children. Special menus sometimes available.
FIXED-PRICE MENU
A good value fixed-price meal, at lunch, dinner or both,
usually of three courses.
VEGETARIAN
Vegetarian specialities served, sometimes for both starters
and main courses.
CREDIT CARDS
Indicates which credit cards are accepted: *AE* American
Express; *DC* Diners Club; *MC* Master Card/Access; *V* Visa.

	CREDIT CARDS	CHILDREN WELCOME	FIXED-PRICE MENU	VEGETARIAN	OUTDOOR TABLES
THAMES VALLEY					
BRAY: *Waterside Inn* @ waterside@relaischateaux.fr £££££ Ferry Rd, Bray, Windsor & Maidenhead. 01628 620691. Renowned pillar of French classic cuisine in an idyllic riverside setting. The set lunches are excellent. *Mon, Tue L.*	AE DC MC V	●	■	●	
CHINNOR: *Sir Charles Napier* £££ Spriggs Alley, nr Chinnor, Oxon. 01494 483011. Service is informal, but the food is good in this Chiltern pub-restaurant. The garden has eccentric sculptures. *Sun D, Mon.*	AE MC V	●	■	●	■
COOKHAM: *Alfonso's* ££ 19–21 Station Hill Parade, Cookham, Windsor & Maidenhead. 01628 525775. Intimate, family-run restaurant full of friendly enthusiasm and Iberian specialities such as Serrano ham and lambs' kidneys in sherry. Some excellent Rioja wines are available. *Sat L, Sun.*	AE DC MC V	●	■	●	■
DINTON: *La Chouette* ££££ Westlington Green, Dinton, Bucks. 01296 747422. Belgian gastronomic flair in this beautiful 16th-century building. The *patron* also offers live jazz and Trappist beers. *Sat L, Sun.*	MC V	●	■		■
EASINGTON: *Mole & Chicken* ££ Easington Terrace, Chilton Rd, Bucks. 01844 208387. Adventurous cooking is the hallmark of this friendly and efficient restaurant. Specialities include duckling in orange sauce.	AE MC V	●	■	●	
GODSTOW: *Trout* £ Godstow, Wolvercote, Oxon. 01865 302071. A trout stream runs past this charming creeper-covered medieval pub north of Oxford. Peacocks strut outside; inside, it is always civilized.	MC V	●			■
GORING: *Leatherne Bottel* ££££ On B4009, Goring, Oxon. 01491 872667. @ leathernebottel@aol.com A glorious riverside setting accounts for the popularity of this relaxing place. Fresh local ingredients are presented with Pacific Rim touches. *Sun D.*	AE MC V		■	●	■
GREAT MILTON: *Le Manoir aux Quat'Saisons* £££££ Church Rd, Great Milton, Oxon. 01844 278881. @ lemanoir@blanc.co.uk Raymond Blanc's gastronomic pleasure palace is a rural idyll. The superb food is fresh, inventive and fully flavoured. A memorable experience, though not cheap.	AE DC MC V	●	■	●	■
GREAT MISSENDEN: *La Petite Auberge* ££££ 107 High St, Great Missenden, Bucks. 01494 865370. An intimate restaurant producing reliable provincial French cooking. Service is efficient but unobtrusive. *L, Sun, public hols.*	DC MC V	●			
HADDENHAM: *Green Dragon* £££ 8 Church Way, Haddenham, Bucks. 01844 291403. A village dining pub with very varied British food such as scallops. The big dining rooms are open to the bar. *Sun D.*	AE MC V			●	■
KINTBURY: *Dundas Arms* £££ 53 Station Rd, Kintbury, Newbury. 01488 658263. @ info@dundasarms.co.uk This old riverside pub serves an appetizing range of bar snacks and traditional dishes, competently prepared. *Sun, Mon D.*	AE MC V	●		●	■
LONG CRENDON: *Angel Inn* £££ Bicester Rd, Long Crendon, Bucks. 01844 208268. Antique, listed 16th-century inn offering fresh fish, blackboard specials, mouth-watering puddings and good-value wines. *Sun D.*	MC V	●	■	●	■

MELBOURN: *Pink Geranium* @ lawrence@pinkgeranium.co.uk   £££££ — AE MC V
Station Rd, Melbourn, nr Royston, Herts. ☎ 01763 260215.
Assured cooking is served in this pretty thatched cottage by the church.
The atmosphere is welcoming, the decor pink. ● *Sun D, Mon.* & *limited* ⚡ ☽

MOULSFORD: *Beetle and Wedge*   £££ — AE DC MC V
Ferry Lane, Moulsford, Oxon. ☎ 01491 651381.
On the Thames in the heart of *Wind in the Willows* country. Eat in the
informal Boathouse or sophisticated dining room. & ⚡ ☵

OXFORD: *Nosebag*   £ — MC V
6–8 St Michael's St, Oxford. ☎ 01865 721033.
Excellent salads, soups and imaginative light dishes are served to queues
of hungry students on the upper floor of a quaint building. ● *Mon D.* ⚡

OXFORD: *Al-Shami*   ££ — MC V
25 Walton Crescent, Oxford. ☎ 01865 310066.
This bustling Lebanese restaurant serves *falafel, tabouleh, ful medames*
and other favourites, with authentic desserts to follow. & ☽

OXFORD: *Browns*   ££ — MC V
5–11 Woodstock Rd, Oxford. ☎ 01865 511995. @ browns.oxford@bass.com
A lively, informal restaurant serving a tempting range of snacks and fuller
meals amid bentwood furnishings and potted plants. ● *25, 26 Dec.* & ☽

OXFORD: *Cherwell Boathouse*   ££ — AE DC MC V
Bardwell Rd, Oxford. ☎ 01865 552746.
A romantic punting spot on the River Cherwell. The fixed-price menus
are Mediterranean with a twist. ● *Sun D.* & ⚡ ☵

SHINFIELD: *L'Ortolan* @ lortolan@shinfield3.freeserve.co.uk   £££££ — AE DC MC V
Old Vicarage, Church Lane, Shinfield, Reading. ☎ 0118 9883783.
L'Ortolan is one of Britain's best restaurants. The setting is charming,
though the modern French and British dishes are very pricey. Set menus
represent better value. ● *Sun D, Mon.* ⚡

SPEEN: *Old Plow*   £££ — AE MC V
Flowers Bottom, Speen, Bucks. ☎ 01494 488300.
An informal bistro in a picturesque former pub. Much is home-made,
and all of it is fresh. ● *Sat L, Sun D, Mon.* & *limited.* ⚡ ☵

STONOR: *Stonor Arms*   £££ — AE MC V
On B480, Stonor, Oxon. ☎ 01491 638345. @ stonorarms.hotel@virgin.net
A restaurant near Henley-on-Thames. Good local produce is cooked with
flair then served in the conservatory. & ⚡ ☵

STREATLEY: *Swan Diplomat*   ££££ — AE DC MC V
High St, Streatley, Berks. ☎ 01491 878800. @ sales@swan-diplomat.co.uk
A Thames-side business hotel serving expert if conservative food in a
delightful setting. ● *Sat L.* & ☵

WINDSOR: *Al Fassia*   ££ — AE DC MC V
27 St Leonards Rd, Windsor, Berks. ☎ 01753 855370
Highly sought after Moroccan restaurant with traditional North African decor. Try
filo parcels of chicken and almonds, or the lamb tagine. ● *Sun.* & ⚡ ☵

WOBURN: *Paris House*   ££££ — AE DC MC V
Woburn Park, Woburn, Beds. ☎ 01525 290692. @ gail@parishouse.co.uk
French classics star at this smart mock-Tudor building in the grounds
of Woburn Abbey. Try the hot raspberry soufflé. ● *Sun D, Mon, Feb.*

WOBURN SANDS: *Spooners*   ££ — AE DC MC V
61 High St, Woburn Sands, Milton Keynes, Bucks. ☎ 01908 584385.
This Victorian terraced house makes an agreeable place for a light lunch
or a substantial meal in the evenings. The steaks are especially tasty.
Warm, friendly atmosphere. ● *Sun, Mon.* & ⚡

WESSEX

AVEBURY: *The Circle Restaurant*   £ — MC V
Avebury, Wilts. ☎ 01672 539514
Wholefood fans rave about the dishes at this self-service vegetarian
restaurant beside the ancient stone circle. Some lovely soups and
British cheeses on the menu. ● *Evenings.* & ⚡

Price categories include a three-course meal for one, half a bottle of house wine, and all unavoidable extra charges such as cover, service, VAT:
ⓔ under £15
ⓔⓔ £15-£25
ⓔⓔⓔ £25-£35
ⓔⓔⓔⓔ £35-£50
ⓔⓔⓔⓔⓔ over £50.

CHILDREN WELCOME
Restaurants which offer smaller portions and high-chairs for children. Special menus sometimes available.

FIXED-PRICE MENU
A good value fixed-price meal, at lunch, dinner or both, usually of three courses.

VEGETARIAN
Vegetarian specialities served, sometimes for both starters and main courses.

CREDIT CARDS
Indicates which credit cards are accepted: AE American Express; DC Diners Club; MC Master Card/Access; V Visa.

	CREDIT CARDS	CHILDREN WELCOME	FIXED-PRICE MENU	VEGETARIAN	OUTDOOR TABLES
BARWICK: *Little Barwick House* ⓔⓔⓔ Off A37, Barwick, Som. 01935 423902. Non-residents can dine at this Georgian dower-house hotel. The quality of the local ingredients underpins the menu. *(See p551.)* 🔲 ♿	AE MC V	●	▣	●	
BATH: *Hole in the Wall* ⓔⓔⓔ 16 George St, Bath, B & NE Som. 01225 425242. The new management has made dynamic changes in this famous cellar. Sample modern British cooking at its best. ● *Sun, public hols.* 🔲 🌙 ♟	AE MC V		▣	●	
BATH: *Moon and Sixpence* ⓔⓔⓔ 6A Broad St, Bath, B & NE Som. 01225 460962. This popular bistro and wine bar serves inexpensive lunchtime dishes and good-value dinners. The downstairs conservatory is particularly pleasant in summer. ● *26 Dec.* 🌙 ♟	AE MC V	●	▣	●	
BATH: *Priory* ⓔⓔⓔⓔⓔ Weston Rd, Bath, B & NE Som. 01225 331922. @ bathprioryhotel@compuserve.com This palatial but relaxing country-house hotel in lovely gardens offers French and English cooking in a variety of themed rooms. ♿ 🔲 ♟	AE DC MC V	●	▣	●	▣
BEAMINSTER: *Bridge House* ⓔⓔⓔ 3 Prout Bridge, Beaminster, Dorset. 01308 862200. @ enquiries@bridge-house.co.uk This ancient clergy house dishes up old favourites and inventive adaptations in a civilized setting. Good-value rooms. ● *27–1 Jan.* 🔲 ♿ ♟	AE DC MC V		▣	●	▣
BOURNEMOUTH: *Chez Fred* ⓔ 10 Seamoor Rd, Westbourne, Bournemouth. 01202 761023. Fred's fish and chips and wicked puddings, such as treacle sponge, are his claim to fame. The service is friendly, the atmosphere lively. ● *Sun L.* ♿ 🔲	MC V	●		●	
BRADFORD-ON-AVON: *Woolley Grange* ⓔⓔⓔⓔ Woolley Green, Bradford-on-Avon, Wilts. 01225 864705. A delightful Jacobean country-house hotel with everything from children's chicken nuggets to enterprising international cuisine. The atmosphere is informal, and the service excellent. ♿ 🔲 ♟	DC MC V	●	▣	●	▣
BRISTOL: *Markwicks* ⓔⓔⓔ 43 Corn Street, Bristol. 01179 262658. French and Mediterranean influences combine in the delicious creations on offer in the basement of a bank building. The fish dishes are good, as is the choice of desserts. ● *Sat L, Sun, 25 Dec–2 Jan, Easter week, last 2 weeks Aug.* ♟	AE DC MC V	●	▣	●	
BRISTOL: *Harveys* ⓔⓔⓔⓔ 12 Denmark St, Bristol. 01179 275034. The 13th-century cellars of Bristol's famous wine-shipper are the setting for this sophisticated restaurant. ● *Sat L, Sun, public hols.* 🔲 ♟	AE DC MC V			●	
CLEVEDON: *Junior Poon* ⓔⓔⓔ 16 Hill Rd, Clevedon, Som. 01275 341900. A relaxed Peking and Szechuan restaurant and wine bar, set in a Grade II listed Georgian building. Try the tiger prawns in garlic butter sauce. ● *Sun.* ♿	AE MC V	●	▣	●	
COLERNE: *Lucknam Park* ⓔⓔⓔⓔⓔ Off A420, Colerne, Wilts. 01225 742777. @ sales@lucknampark.co.uk A luxurious country-house hotel offering suitably posh cooking. The atmosphere is discreet and formal. Men are required to wear a jacket and tie. A memorable experience. ● *Mon–Sat L.* ♿ 🔲 ♟	AE DC MC V		▣	●	▣
LACOCK: *At the Sign of the Angel* ⓔⓔⓔ 6 Church St, Lacock, Wilts. 01249 730230. The 14th-century hotel with low beams, wood panelling and open fires serves superb traditional British fare, including steak and kidney pie. ● *Mon L.* ♿ ♟	AE DC MC V	●		●	▣

....

MAIDEN NEWTON: *Le Petit Canard*   **£££**   MC V
Dorchester Rd, Maiden Newton, Dorset. **(** *01300 320536.*
Modern British dishes prepared using fresh local produce
feature in this candlelit restaurant. ● *Tue–Sat L, Sun, Mon.* ✂

MONTACUTE: *The King's Arms Inn*   **££**   AE MC V
Off A303 nr Martock, Som. **(** *01935 822513.*
This 16th-century inn houses the award-winning Abbey Room, offering
superb modern British cuisine in cosy surroundings. ♿ ✂ ♟

SALISBURY: *Aprés LXIX Bar & Bistro*   **£**   AE DC MC V
69 New St, Salisbury, Wilts. **(** *01722 333355.*
Right next to the cathedral, this bar and bistro combines casual dining with an
adjoining, more formal restaurant. Modern British cooking. ● *Sun.* ♿ ✂ ♟

SALISBURY: *Harpers*   **££**   AE DC MC V
6–7 Ox Row, Market Place, Salisbury, Wilts. **(** *01722 333118.*
Light, friendly, first-floor restaurant offers unpretentious roasts, casseroles
as well as daily specials. Worth a visit for the wonderful views over
historic Salisbury. ● *Sun (Oct–May).* ✂ ♟

SHAFTSBURY: *La Fleur de Lys*   **£££**   AE DC MC V
25 Salisbury St, Shaftsbury, Dorset. **(** *01747 853717.* **@** lafleurdelys@fsbdial.co.uk
This unobtrusive place (a wood panelled loft conversion above a stable block)
conceals some accomplished cooking. ● *Sun D, 2 weeks Jan.* ✂ ♟

SHEPTON MALLET: *Bowlish House*   **£££**   MC V
Wells Rd, Shepton Mallet, Som. **(** *01749 342022.*
A Georgian merchant's house with peaceful gardens. Dinner is a relaxed,
unstuffy experience. Modern British and French cuisine. ● *Mon & Sun L.* ✂ ♟

STON EASTON: *Ston Easton Park*   **££££**   AE DC MC V
On A37, Ston Easton, Som. **(** *01761 241631.* **@** stoneastonpark@stoneaston.co.uk
Straightforward menus characterize this splendid country-house hotel.
The modern European cookery justifies the expense. An experience
that will not be a disappointment. ♿ ✂ ♟

STURMINSTER NEWTON: *Plumber Manor*   **£££**   AE DC MC V
Hazelbury Bryan Rd, Sturminster Newton, Dorset. **(** *01258 472507.*
Oil paintings adorn this hotel dining room, but they won't distract from the
food. The fish is superb, and the desserts are very tempting. ● *Mon–Sat L.* ♿ ✂

TAUNTON: *Castle*   **£££**   AE DC MC V
Castle Green, Taunton, Som. **(** *01823 272671.* **@** reception@thecastlehotel.com
A dignified but unostentatious wisteria-clad hotel makes a fine setting
for consistently excellent modern British fare. *(See also p552.)* ♿ ✂ ▶ ♟

WARMINSTER: *Bishopstrow House*   **££££**   AE DC MC V
On B3414, Warminster, Wilts. **(** *01985 212312.* **@** enquiries@bishopstrow.co.uk
Light lunches and dinners in the elegant Georgian surroundings
of this country-house hotel. Try the impressive cheeseboard. ✂

WEST BAY: *Riverside*   **££**   MC V
Off A35 nr Bridport, Dorset. **(** *01308 422011.*
Fish is the mainstay of this long-established restaurant, but there's a good
selection of casual snacks. Book ahead. ● *Sun D, Mon, Dec–mid-Feb.* ♿ ✂

WEST BEXINGTON: *Manor*   **££**   AE DC MC V
Beach Rd, West Bexington, Dorset. **(** *01308 897785.*
A delightful range of bar and restaurant food in an old stone inn with nice
guestrooms and a garden for children. Close to Chesil Beach. ● *25 Dec D.* ♿ ✂

DEVON AND CORNWALL

AVONWICK: *Avon Inn*   **££**   MC V
Avonwick, nr South Brent, Devon. **(** *01364 73475.*
A dining pub on the banks of the Avon. The restaurant has an Italian
chef, so expect lots of delicious Italian dishes. ● *Sun.* ♟ ♿

BARNSTAPLE: *Lynwood House*   **£££**   AE MC V
Bishops Tawton Rd, Barnstaple, Devon. **(** *01271 343695.* **@** info@lynwoodhouse.co.uk
Family-run Victorian house hotel offering real home cooking. Good
fish soup and seafood dishes. Comfy rooms. ♿ ✂ ♟

For key to symbols see bookmark

Price categories include a three-course meal for one, half a bottle of house wine, and all unavoidable extra charges such as cover, service, VAT:
£ under £15
££ £15–£25
£££ £25–£35
££££ £35–£50
£££££ over £50.

CHILDREN WELCOME
Restaurants which offer smaller portions and high-chairs for children. Special menus sometimes available.

FIXED-PRICE MENU
A good value fixed-price meal, at lunch, dinner or both, usually of three courses.

VEGETARIAN
Vegetarian specialities served, sometimes for both starters and main courses.

CREDIT CARDS
Indicates which credit cards are accepted: *AE* American Express; *DC* Diners Club; *MC* Master Card/Access; *V* Visa.

	Credit Cards	Children Welcome	Fixed-Price Menu	Vegetarian	Outdoor Tables
CHAGFORD: *Gidleigh Park* £££££ Chagford, Devon. 01647 432367. @ gidleighpark@gidleigh.co.uk Imaginative details mark out from the crowd this first-class country-house hotel and restaurant. Pricey, a place for special occasions.	MC V		▓	●	
CHAGFORD: *22 Mill Street* ££££ 22 Mill St, Chagford, Devon. 01647 432244. Exquisite Modern European cooking, such as crab lasagne or seabass roasted with pickled ginger and basil. ● *Wed–Sat L, 2 weeks Jan, last week May.*	MC V		▓	●	
DARTINGTON: *Cott Inn* ££ Dartington, Devon. 01803 863777. A restaurant-with-rooms in a 14th-century inn. Good British home cooking with a daily changing menu and a nice garden.	AE MC V			●	▓
DARTMOUTH: *Carved Angel* ££££ 2 South Embankment, Dartmouth, Devon. 01803 832465. One of Britain's best restaurants occupies a quayside Tudor building. The menu features local salmon and shellfish, and in winter makes use of local game, like wild duck. ● *Sun D, Mon, 24–25 Dec.*	AE MC V	●	▓	●	
DODDISCOMBSLEIGH: *Nobody Inn* ££ Doddiscombsleigh, nr Exeter, Devon. 01647 252394. @ inn.nobody@virgin.net The traditional, beamed restaurant in this dining pub has a stunning wine list and an amazing choice of local cheeses. *(See also p553.)*	AE MC V			●	▓
EXETER: *Lamb's* £££ 15 Lower North St, Exeter, Devon. 01392 254269. Influences ranging from Mediterranean to Moroccan can be tasted at this welcoming restaurant. ● *Sat L, Sun, Mon.*	AE MC V	●	▓	●	▓
EXETER: *Thai Orchid* £££ 5 Cathedral Yard, Exeter, Devon. 01392 214215. Authentic Thai cuisine is expertly served within a 15th-century listed building which originally housed the stonemasons working on the cathedral. Fresh orchids on every table add to the elegance. ● *Sun, 25–26 Dec, 1 Jan.*	MC V	●	▓	●	
KINGSBRIDGE: *Queen Anne, Buckland-Tout-Saints* £££ Goveton, Kingsbridge, Devon. 01548 853055. @ buckland@tout-saints.co.uk Refined cuisine served in a handsome Queen Anne house in lovely grounds. British produce is cooked with Gallic finesse. ● *15 Jan–5 Feb.*	MC V	●	▓	●	
LEWDOWN: *Lewtrenchard Manor* ££££ Off A30, Lewdown, Devon. 01566 783256. @ s&j@lewtrenchard.co.uk This Elizabethan manor-house hotel with mouthwatering fixed-price menus makes a gloriously romantic retreat.	AE DC MC V		▓		
LIFTON: *Arundell Arms* £££ Off A30, Lifton, Devon. 01566 784666. @ ArundellArms@btinternet.com An attractive sporting inn in a peaceful village. Local fish and game appear on the fixed-price menus. Bar snacks are also available for lunch and dinner. Convivial atmosphere.	AE DC MC V	●	▓	●	
LYNMOUTH: *The Rising Sun* £££ Harbourside, Lynmouth, Devon. 01598 753223. @ risingsunlynmouth@easynet.co.uk Fish is unloaded almost on the doorstep of this 14th-century smugglers' haunt, but it excels in cooking other things as well.	AE DC MC V			●	
PADSTOW: *Seafood Restaurant* £££££ Riverside, Padstow, Corn. 01841 532700. @ seafoodpadstow@cs.com A favourite with fish-lovers, this restaurant has a wonderful harbourside location. Stylish accommodation and plainer, but good, food in sister hotel-restaurant St Petroc's House. *(See also p554.)* ● *18–26 & 31 Dec.*	MC V		▓	●	

PENZANCE: *Harris's* £££ AE MC V
46 New St, Penzance, Corn. 01736 364408.
Game, when in season, and locally farmed meat are a match for the fish dishes.
The lunch menu is good value. ● *Sun L (Sun D in winter), Mon (winter).* ✦ ♟

POLPERRO: *Kitchen* ££ MC V
The Coombes, Polperro, Corn. 01503 272780.
A tiny restaurant that is established as a sound choice for the tourists
who flock to Polperro in summer. ● *L, mid-Oct–Mar.* ✦

PORT ISAAC: *Slipway* ££ AE MC V
Harbour Front, Port Isaac, Corn. 01208 880264. @ slipwayhotel@portisaac.com
In season, this 16th-century chandlery offers a perfect sample of
North Cornwall's fishy fare. ● *ring to check.* ✦ ♟

PORTREATH: *Tabb's* ££ MC V
Tregea Terrace, Portreath, Corn. 01209 842488.
A small restaurant in an old forge. Everything on the deliciously eclectic menu
is home-made. ● *Mon–Sat L, 26 Dec, 1 Jan.* ✦ ♟ ✦

ST IVES: *Tate St Ives Coffee Shop and Restaurant* ££
Porthmeor Beach, St Ives, Corn. 01736 791122.
Admire the views from this art-gallery brasserie while tucking into wholefood
dishes made with fresh local produce, including fish and shellfish.
● *D, Mon (winter).* ✦ ✦

ST IVES: *Russets* £££ AE MC V
18A Fore St, St Ives, Corn TR26 1AB. 01736 794700.
This seafood restaurant in St Ives main thoroughfare is casual, laid-back
and yet surprisingly lively. Local artists' work hangs from the walls. ● *L* ✦ ✦

TAVERSTOCK: *The Horn of Plenty* ££££ AE MC V
Gulworthy, Taverstock, Devon PL19 8JD. & FAX 01822 832528.
A 200-year-old building set in almost five acres of gardens. TV
cook Peter Gorton is head chef. *(See also p553.)* ● *Mon L, 23–26 Dec.* ✦ ♟ ✦

TREBURLEY: *Springer Spaniel* ££ MC V
Treburley, nr Launceston, Cornwall. 01579 370424.
A friendly dining pub with an attractive, beamed restaurant. The menu
changes frequently, reflecting the owners' desire to use local produce,
including home-grown vegetables and salads. ✦ ✦

TORQUAY: *Mulberry Room* ££
1 Scarborough Rd, Torquay, Torbay. 01803 213639.
This friendly restaurant offers snacks and delicious lunches (dinners on Fri
to Sun). Try the bread and cakes. ● *Mon, Tue.* ✦ ✦

TOTNES: *Willow* £
87 High St, Totnes, Devon. 01803 862605.
Vegetarian specialities from around the globe, including Mexican, Indian,
Caribbean and Italian, make this place cosmopolitan and eclectic. Warm
welcoming atmosphere. ● *Sun, Mon D, Tues D.* ○ *Thurs D (summer only).* ✦ ♟ ✦

VIRGINSTOW: *Percy's at Coombeshead* £££ AE DC MC V
Virginstow, Devon EX21 5EA. 01409 211236. FAX 01409 211275.
Modern British food is the fare of this very rural restaurant, situated some 9 miles
from Launceston in the midst of a 130 acre estate. ✦ ♟ ✦

THE HEART OF ENGLAND

ABBERLEY: *Brooke Room, The Elms* ££££ AE DC MC V
Stockton Rd, Abberley, Worcs. 01299 896666.
Traditional and more daring choices are the bill of fare at this elegant
Queen Anne mansion. Lovely decor and rooms. ✦ ✦ ♟

BIRMINGHAM: *Chung Ying Garden* £££ AE DC MC V
17 Thorp St, Birmingham. 0121 6666622.
A flamboyant Cantonese food palace offering a giant range of specialities,
including *dim sum.* ✦ ▶

BISHOP'S TACHBROOK: *Mallory Court* ££££ AE MC V
Off B4087 nr Leamington Spa, Warw. 01926 330214. @ mallorycourt@mallory.co.uk
Classic French and British cuisine weighs in at a hefty price at this manor-
house hotel, but the results are impressive. Beautiful gardens. ✦ ✦ ♟

Price categories include a three-course meal for one, half a bottle of house wine, and all unavoidable extra charges such as cover, service, VAT:
£ under £15
££ £15–£25
£££ £25–£35
££££ £35–£50
£££££ over £50.

CHILDREN WELCOME
Restaurants which offer smaller portions and high-chairs for children. Special menus sometimes available.
FIXED-PRICE MENU
A good value fixed-price meal, at lunch, dinner or both, usually of three courses.
VEGETARIAN
Vegetarian specialities served, sometimes for both starters and main courses.
CREDIT CARDS
Indicates which credit cards are accepted: *AE* American Express; *DC* Diners Club; *MC* Master Card/Access; *V* Visa.

	CREDIT CARDS	CHILDREN WELCOME	FIXED-PRICE MENU	VEGETARIAN	OUTDOOR TABLES
BRIMFIELD: *The Roebuck Inn* £££ Brimfield, Here. 01584 711230. A deceptively simple setting (a village pub) and a relaxed atmosphere conceal highly sophisticated British cooking.	MC V	●	●	●	●
BROADWAY: *Collin House* @ collin.house@virgin.net ££ Along A44, 2nd turning right, Broadway, Worcs. 01386 858354. This modest Cotswold country house welcomes non-residents. Light lunches are on offer in the bar; an imaginative *carte* in the dining room. 24–29 Dec.	MC V			●	
BURTON UPON TRENT: *Dovecliff Hall* £££ Dovecliff Rd, Stretton, Burton upon Trent, Staffs. 01283 531818. A Georgian country house in extensive grounds by the River Dove. An elegant setting. Modern British food. Sat L, Sun D, Mon L, bank hols.	AE MC V		●	●	
CHELTENHAM: *Le Champignon Sauvage* £££ 24 Suffolk Rd, Cheltenham, Glos. 01242 573449. Gallic dishes with startling ingredient combinations: sardine and *tapenade* (olive and anchovy paste), rabbit and black pudding. A delight to the palate. Sun, Mon, 24 Dec–3 Jan, 2 weeks in June.	AE DC MC V	●	●		
COVENTRY: *Ryton Organic Gardens Restaurant* ££ Henry Doubleday Research Assoc., Ryton Organic Gardens, off A45. 024 76303517. Set within 10 acres of organic display gardens, this is a recommended organic restaurant. Offering meat, fish, vegetarian and vegan meals, many of the vegetables are grown on site. D, 25, 26 Dec, 2 Jan.	MC V	●		●	●
CHESTER: *Francs* ££ 14 Cupping St, Chester, Ches. 01244 317952. An ever-popular brasserie where French rock beats out over tasty *plats du jour*. Sundays are family days and under-10s eat free. Book ahead.	AE MC V	●		●	
DORRINGTON: *Country Friends* ££££ On A49 nr Shrewsbury, Shrops. 01743 718707. Simple, reliable English cooking in a pleasant mock-Tudor setting. Fixed-price menu available. Log fires burn in winter. Sun, Mon, Tue.	MC V	●	●	●	
KENILWORTH: *Restaurant Bosquet* ££££ 97A Warwick Rd, Kenilworth, Warw. 01926 852463. This Victorian house offers serious classic French food with rich sauces and fresh seasonal produce. Sat L, Sun, Mon.	AE MC V	●	●		
LEAMINGTON SPA: *Piccolino's Pizzeria* £ 9 Spencer St, Leamington Spa, Warw. 01926 422988. A jovial family-owned place serving home-cooked Italian favourites – pizza and pasta, of course, and other dishes at inexpensive prices.	MC V	●		●	
LEAMINGTON SPA: *Flynns* ££ 14 The Parade, Leamington Spa, Warw. 01926 421620. There is live jazz 1930s-style in this relaxed brasserie concealed behind a cake shop. Stylish decor.	AE MC V	●	●	●	
LOWER SLAUGHTER: *Lower Slaughter Manor* £££££ Off A429, Lower Slaughter, Glos. 01451 820456. @ lowsmanor@aol.com Renowned restaurant in a beautiful Cotswolds manor. The menu is based on French and British classics, modernized by the latest influences from all over the globe. Highly recommended.	AE MC V		●	●	
LUDLOW: *Unicorn Inn* ££ 66 Corve St, Ludlow, Shrops. 01584 873555. The emphasis is on local produce in the restaurant of this 17th-century, black-and-white, beamed inn. The home-made puddings are good.	AE MC V	●	●	●	●

MALVERN WELLS: *Croque-en-Bouche* £££
221 Wells Rd, Malvern Wells, Worcs. 01684 565612. @ mail@croque-en-bouche.co.uk
A dedicated couple both manage the restaurant and do all the cooking here.
The results are distinctive and varied international dishes. ● Sun–Wed.
○ D only. & ⚡ ☰
Cards: MC V

MIDDLEWICH: *Tempters* ££
11 Wheelock St, Middlewich, Ches. 01606 835175.
A split-level wine bar with wooden tables. Daily specials are chalked on
the blackboard; lighter fare such as sandwiches available at lunchtime.
● Sun, Mon, Tue & Wed L. & ☰
Cards: MC V

MORETON-IN-MARSH: *Marsh Goose* ££££
High St, Moreton-in-Marsh, Glos. 01608 653500.
A relaxing place with a maze of small rooms. Menus feature French and
British country cooking. ● Sun D, Mon, Tue L. & ⚡ ☰
Cards: AE DC MC V

PRESTBURY: *White House* £££
The Village, Prestbury, Ches. 01625 829376. @ stay@cheshire-white-house.com
The smart and elegant decor matches the up-market cosmopolitan food
here. There's a conservatory for warm summer evenings. Attractive rooms.
● Sun D, Mon L. ⚡
Cards: AE DC MC V

ROSS-ON-WYE: *Meader's* £
1 Copse Cross St, Ross-on-Wye, Here. 01989 562803.
Friendly Hungarian business; you can sample authentic goulash and
galuska (dumplings) without breaking the bank. ● Sun, Mon. ⚡
Cards: MC V

ROSS-ON-WYE: *Le Faison D'Oré* £££
52 Edde Cross St, Ross-on-Wye, Here. 01989 565751.
A cheerful, homely restaurant in a former 17th-century tavern offers
honest, robust food, and personal service. ● Sun, Mon. & ⚡ ☰
Cards: AE DC MC V

STRATFORD-UPON-AVON: *Opposition* ££
13 Sheep St, Stratford-upon-Avon, Warw. 01789 269980.
A bustling bistro offering simple pre-theatre suppers. The day's specials
are chalked on blackboards. ● Sun L. ▶ (Fri–Sat).
Cards: MC V

STRATFORD-UPON-AVON: *Russons* ££
8 Church St, Stratford-upon-Avon, Warw. 01789 268822.
This rustic 17th-century setting fits the Shakespearian location. A varied menu
with pre-theatre dinners available and varied inexpensive meals.
● Sun, Mon. ⚡
Cards: AE MC V

TETBURY: *Gumstool* ££
Calcot Manor, Tetbury, Gloucs. 01666 890391.
The dining area and bar are combined in this popular gastro dining pub.
The eclectic menu ranges·from local beer sausages to roasted
Mediterranean vegetables. &
Cards: AE DC MC V

WATERHOUSES: *Old Beams* ££££
Leek Road, Waterhouses, Staffs. 01538 308254.
French-style, classically based cooking from a restaurant-with-rooms
near Alton Towers. Good wines by the glass. ● Mon. & ⚡ ☰
Cards: AE DC MC V

EAST MIDLANDS

BAKEWELL: *Renaissance* £££
Bath St, Bakewell, Derbs. 01629 812687.
French-style cuisine enjoyed in this traditionally beamed house. Despite
lavish ingredients, (truffles and *foie gras*), the prices are reasonable.
● Sun D, Mon, 1–15 Jan, early Aug. & ⚡ ☰
Cards: MC V

BASLOW: *Fischer's at Baslow* ££££
Baslow Hall, Calver Rd, Baslow, Derbs. 01246 583259.
Whether you eat in the smart dining room or more casually at the
adjoining Café Max, the cooking is top notch. Handy for Chatsworth.
& ⚡ ☰
Cards: AE DC MC V

BECKINGHAM: *Black Swan* ££
Hillside, Beckingham, Lincs. 01636 626474.
This 17th-century coaching inn is a mite cramped, but it is intimate; the
quality of the modern British dishes is high and the service is always
friendly and efficient. ● Mon, Sun D. & ⚡
Cards: MC V

For key to symbols see bookmark

Price categories include a three-course meal for one, half a bottle of house wine, and all unavoidable extra charges such as cover, service, VAT:
£ under £15
££ £15-£25
£££ £25-£35
££££ £35-£50
£££££ over £50.

CHILDREN WELCOME
Restaurants which offer smaller portions and high-chairs for children. Special menus sometimes available.
FIXED-PRICE MENU
A good value fixed-price meal, at lunch, dinner or both, usually of three courses.
VEGETARIAN
Vegetarian specialities served, sometimes for both starters and main courses.
CREDIT CARDS
Indicates which credit cards are accepted: *AE* American Express; *DC* Diners Club; *MC* Master Card/Access; *V* Visa.

	CREDIT CARDS	CHILDREN WELCOME	FIXED-PRICE MENU	VEGETARIAN	OUTDOOR TABLES
BIRCH VALE: *Waltzing Weasel* £££	AE MC V	●	▨	●	▨
BOTTESFORD: *Paul's Contemporary Cuisine* ££	MC V	●	▨	●	▨
BURTON ON THE WOLDS: *Langs* ££	MC V	●	▨	●	▨
CASTLETON: *Castle Inn* ££	AE MC V	●		●	▨
COLSTON BASSETT: *Martins Arms* £££	MC V	●			▨
EMPINGHAM: *White Horse* ££	AE DC MC V	●			▨
GAUNTON NEWARK: *Gaunton Beck* £££	AE DC MC V	●	▨	●	▨
HAMBLETON: *Hambleton Hall* ££££	MC V	●	▨	●	
KEYSTON: *The Pheasant Inn* ££	AE DC MC V	●		●	▨
LEICESTER: *Bobby's* ££	MC V	●	▨	●	
LEICESTER: *Case* £££	AE DC MC V	●		●	
LINCOLN: *Wig and Mitre* ££	AE DC MC V	●	▨	●	

BIRCH VALE: *Waltzing Weasel* £££
New Mills Rd, Birch Vale, High Peak, Derbs. (01663 743402. @ w-weasel@zen.co.uk
Hearty English fare (roasts, chops, game pie and Stilton) is served, accompanied by panoramic views of Kinder Scout. Attractive rooms. ♿ 🔆

BOTTESFORD: *Paul's Contemporary Cuisine* ££
1 Market St, Bottesford, Leics. (01949 842375. @ pauls@primeuk.net
Local supplies of game in season is one reason for this bistro's success; attractive beamed decor is another. ● *Sun D, Mon.* 🔆

BURTON ON THE WOLDS: *Langs* ££
147 Melton Rd, Burton on the Wolds, Leics. (01509 880980.
Smartly furnished barn conversion offering inventive dishes and startling arrays of classic treatments of fish and meat. ● *Sun D, Mon.* ♿ 🍷 🔆

CASTLETON: *Castle Inn* ££
Castle St, Castleton, Derbs. (01433 620578.
Relaxing pub restaurant in the heart of the Peak District. Traditional British food with Mediterranean influences served in an oak-beamed room. 🔆 ♿ 🍷

COLSTON BASSETT: *Martins Arms* £££
School Lane, Colston Bassett, Notts. (01949 81361.
Situated in a former farmhouse, this traditional English pub includes a comfortable dining room that serves much more than standard pub fare. The cooking is in the modern British style. ● *Sun D, 25 Dec.* ◗

EMPINGHAM: *White Horse* ££
Empingham, Rutland. (01780 460221.
This delightful, 17th-century stone-built courthouse now holds a bar and bistro. It also serves morning croissants and afternoon teas. ♿ 🔆 🍷

GAUNTON NEWARK: *Gaunton Beck* £££
Main St, Gaunton Newark, Notts. (01636 636793.
An eclectic menu of French, British and Moroccan dishes are served in this 1750s beamed building. Nice patio in summer. 🔆 ♿ 🍷

HAMBLETON: *Hambleton Hall* ££££
Off A606 nr Oakham, Rutland. (01572 756991. @ hotel@hambletonhall.com
Splendid views over Rutland Water are a good start to the menu of ornate concoctions with lobsters and *foie gras*. Such memorable feasts don't come cheap. Smart accommodation. ♿ 🔆 🍷

KEYSTON: *The Pheasant Inn* ££
Off A14, Keyston, Northnts. (01832 710241.
Book a table in the dining room or eat informally in this delightful thatched inn. An eclectic, modern menu makes good use of game items; the home-made ices are delicious. ♿ 🔆 🍷

LEICESTER: *Bobby's* ££
154–156 Belgrave Rd, Leicester. (0116 2660106.
Vegetarian Gujarati and South Indian dishes make an interesting, good-value treat. The combinations of freshly ground spices make this place unique. Unlicensed, so bring your own alcohol. ● *Mon.* ♿ 🔆 ◗

LEICESTER: *Case* £££
4–6 Hotel St, Leicester. (01162 517675.
Stylish, light restaurant serving Modern European dishes such as home-made pigeon faggots with red currant sauce. ● *Sun, 24–27 Dec, 1–2 Jan.* 🍷 🔆

LINCOLN: *Wig and Mitre* ££
29 Steep Hill, Lincoln. (01522 535190.
This operates on similar lines to its sibling, Welford Place. French and British dishes. Diners appreciate its flexibility and long opening hours. 🔆 ◗

LINCOLN: *Jew's House* £££ | AE DC MC V
15 The Strait, Lincoln. [01522 524851.
A fascinating old building close to the cathedral, serving food à la
française. Wonderful, calorific hand-made chocolates. ● *Sun, Mon.* ⚡

NEWARK: *Gannets Café* £
35 Castlegate, Newark, Notts. [01636 702066.
A cheery ground-floor café by the castle with a garden extension and an
upstairs bistro. It is plain, simple and affordable. The staff are very friendly
and the atmosphere is bohemian. ● *D, 25–26 Dec, 1 Jan.* ⚡

NOTTINGHAM: *Saagar* ££ | AE MC V
473 Mansfield Rd, Sherwood, Nottingham. [0115 9622014.
North "Indian" cookery from the Punjab, Kashmir and Pakistan. Menus
change frequently and new recipes spice up the choice. ● *Sun L.* ⚡ D

NOTTINGHAM: *Sonny's* ££ | AE MC V
3 Carlton St, Hockley, Nottingham. [0115 9473041.
Blend of simple snack-bar and restaurant offering roasted peppers or
pan-fried monkfish. The atmosphere is laid-back and fashionable. ⚡ D

PAULERSPURY: *Vine House* £££ | MC V
100 High St, Paulerspury, Northnts. [01327 811267.
Seventeenth-century house just off the A5. Unusual ingredients, modern
British influences and informal, pleasant rooms. ● *Sat L, Sun, Mon–Wed L.* ⚡ D

PLUMTREE: *Perkins Restaurant* ££ | AE DC MC V
Old Railway Station, Plumtree, Notts. [0115 9373695.
This bistro serves a mix of British game and fish with French sauces.
Good bar snacks. ● *Sun D, Mon.* ⚡

REDMILE: *Peacock* ££ | MC V
Church Corner, Redmile, Leics. [01949 842554.
An excellent dining pub offering a changing menu of modern and traditional
British and European dishes. Menu changes regularly. ⚡

RIDGEWAY: *Old Vicarage* ££££ | AE MC V
Ridgeway Moor, Ridgeway, Derbs. [0114 2475814. @ eat@theoldvicarage.co.uk
High-quality meat, vegetables and fresh herbs produce insistent flavours
at this stone-built Victorian house. A conservatory bistro offers cheaper
menus, and there are plenty of vegetarian choices. ● *Sun D, Mon.* ⚡ D ♟

ROADE: *Roade House* @ reservations@roadehousehotel.demon.co.uk ££ | AE MC V
16 High St, Roade, Northnts. [01604 863372.
This family business offers imaginative British cooking. Most dishes
have complex sauces. Game features during winter. ● *Sat L, Sun D, Mon.* ⚡

STOKE BRUERNE: *Bruerne's Lock* £££ | AE MC V
5 The Canalside, Stoke Bruerne, Northnts. [01604 863654. @ bruernelock@aol.com
A fast-evolving modern British restaurant by the side of the Grand
Union Canal. Personal service is the keynote. ● *Sat L, Sun D, Mon.* ⚡

STRETTON: *Ram Jam Inn* ££ | AE MC V
Great North Rd, Stretton, Leic. [01780 410776. @ rji@ratnet.co.uk
This roadside haven has provided hospitality since 1750. Hearty snacks and
freshly prepared hot dishes are served all day, every day. ● *25 Dec.* ⚡ D

WINTERINGHAM: *Winteringham Fields* ££££ | AE MC V
Winteringham, N Lincs. [01724 733096.
Superlative Modern British cooking is served in this hotel, in a setting
of carefully achieved, opulent Victoriana. *(See also p563.)* ● *Sun, Mon.* ⚡ ♟

LANCASHIRE AND THE LAKES

AMBLESIDE: *Sheila's Cottage* ££ | MC V
The Slack, Ambleside, Cumbria. [015394 33079.
Tasty baking takes place in this converted stable-block cottage. A range
of tea breads and cakes supplements savoury dishes such as Cumbrian
sugar-baked ham or Flookburgh shrimps. ● *Wed D, Nov–Easter.* ⚡

AMBLESIDE: *Zeffirelli's* ££ | MC V
Compston Rd, Ambleside, Cumbria. [015394 33845.
An unusual enterprise combining shops, café, a cinema and a trendily
decorated pizzeria serving pizzas, salads and pasta. ● *Mon–Fri L.* ⚡

		CREDIT CARDS	**CHILDREN WELCOME**	**FIXED-PRICE MENU**	**VEGETARIAN**	**OUTDOOR TABLES**

Price categories include a three-course meal for one, half a bottle of house wine, and all unavoidable extra charges such as cover, service, VAT:
£ under £15
££ £15–£25
£££ £25–£35
££££ £35–£50
£££££ over £50.

CHILDREN WELCOME
Restaurants which offer smaller portions and high-chairs for children. Special menus sometimes available.
FIXED-PRICE MENU
A good value fixed-price meal, at lunch, dinner or both, usually of three courses.
VEGETARIAN
Vegetarian specialities served, sometimes for both starters and main courses.
CREDIT CARDS
Indicates which credit cards are accepted: *AE* American Express; *DC* Diners Club; *MC* Master Card/Access; *V* Visa.

	CREDIT CARDS	CHILDREN WELCOME	FIXED-PRICE MENU	VEGETARIAN	OUTDOOR TABLES
AMBLESIDE: *Rothay Manor* @ hotel@rothaymanor.co.uk £££ Rothay Bridge, Ambleside, Cumbria. 015394 33605. This elegant Regency hotel mainly serves traditional English dishes. Lunch and splendid teas are excellent value.	AE DC MC V	●	▣	●	
APPLETHWAITE: *Underscar Manor* ££££ Off A66 nr Keswick, Cumbria. 017687 75000. A sumptuous Italianate house in peaceful gardens sets the scene for ambitious food. Beautifully decorated rooms make a romantic retreat.	AE MC V		▣	●	▣
BLACKPOOL: *September Brasserie* £££ 15–17 Queen St, Blackpool. 01253 623282. @ pat.wood@cyberscape.net Amid the flotsam of Blackpool's eateries, this brasserie is a beacon of hope. It produces some highly innovative robust dishes. ● *Mon, Sun.*	AE DC MC V	●	▣		
BOWNESS-ON-WINDERMERE: *Porthole Eating House* £££ 3 Ash St, Bowness-on-Windermere, Cumbria. 015394 42793. Summer crowds fail to jade this Italian restaurant. It maintains its pleasing simplicity of style and provides good value. ● *Sat L, Tue, mid-Dec–mid-Feb.*	AE DC MC V	●		●	▣
BRAITHWAITE: *Ivy House* £££ Off A66 nr Keswick, Cumbria. 017687 78338. @ stay@ivy-house.co.uk This Georgian hotel is in the centre of the village. Striking decor. Dinners have panache. Comfortable accommodation. ● *Jan.*	AE DC MC V		▣	●	
CARTMEL: *Uplands* £££ Haggs Lane, Cartmel, Cumbria. 015395 36248. @ uplands@kencomp.net This peaceful hotel sets excellent-value lunches of local produce; the views towards Morecambe Bay are delightful. A place to come back to, year after year. ● *Mon, Tue & Wed L.*	AE MC V		▣		
CLITHEROE: *Auctioneer* ££ New Market St, Clitheroe, Lancs. 01200 427153. Themed menus change regularly in this cottagey place, it might be Tuscany one week, Loire Valley the next. ● *Sun D, Mon, Tue L.*	AE MC V	●	▣	●	
COCKERMOUTH: *Quince and Medlar* ££ 13 Castlegate, Cockermouth, Cumbria. 01900 823579. Adventurous vegetarian cooking in a modest house near the castle. The award-winning menu is well worth sampling. ● *L, Sun, Mon.*	MC V			●	
CROSTHWAITE: *Punch Bowl Inn* @ enquiries@punchbowl.fsnet.co.uk ££ Crosthwaite, nr Kendal, Cumbria. 01539 568237. People come from miles around to eat at this 17th-century coaching inn. There is a choice of several rooms to lunch or dine in. The menu is eclectic and special diets are cheerfully catered for. ● *25 Dec, 26 Dec D, 1 Jan D.*	MC V	●	▣	●	▣
GRASMERE: *White Moss House* ££££ On A591 at Rydal Water, Cumbria. 01539 435295. @ sue@whitemoss.com Classy set dinners are served unpompously in this comfortable country-house hotel. A traditional setting and attentive service in a house that once belonged to William Wordsworth. ● *L, Sun.*	MC V	●	▣		
KENDAL: *Moon* ££ 129 Highgate, Kendal, Cumbria. 01539 729254. A creative bistro with many vegetarian specialities. The style is pleasantly informal, but ingredients are always up to the mark. ● *L, Mon.*	MC V	●		●	
LANGHO: *Northcote Manor* @ admin@ncotemanor.com £££££ On A59 nr Blackburn, Blackb with Darwen. 01254 240555. Nigel Howarth cooks with regional flair including several Lancashire specialities. Also more gastronomic dishes served in the evenings. Highly recommended food and wine.	AE DC MC V	●	▣	●	

LIVERPOOL: *60 Hope St* ££££ MC V
60 Hope St, Liverpool. **(** 0151 707 6060. **FAX** 0151 707 6016
Spread over three floors of a Georgian building, the modern interior is both
relaxed and vibrant. Quality service, superb food. ● Sun D, Mon. 🌙 🍷

LIVERPOOL: *Becher's Brook* ££££ AE DC MC V
29A Hope St, Liverpool. **(** 0151 707 0005.
A classy restaurant in a Georgian listed building in the city centre. The
seasonally changing menu is modern international. ● Sat L, Sun, public hols. 🍴 🍷

LONGRIDGE: *Paul Heathcote's* ££££ AE DC MC V
104–106 Higher Rd, Longridge, Lancs. **(** 01772 784969. **@** longridge@heathcotes.co.uk
The relaxed style of this British restaurant is deceptive, as the food is prepared
with slick technique and innovative talent. ● Mon, Tue, Sat L. ♿ 🍴

MANCHESTER: *Siam Orchid* ££ AE MC V
54 Portland St, Manchester. **(** 0161 236 1388.
Manchester's best Thai restaurant has a great range of dishes, including many
vegetarian choices. There are also influences from other parts of south-east
Asia. Beware the fiery sauces; quell them with Singha beer. ● Sat L, Sun L. 🌙

MANCHESTER: *Moss Nook* ££££ AE MC V
B5166 nr airport, Manchester. **(** 0161 437 4778.
Moss Nook offers a superb presentation of gastronomic medleys. Try the
vast *menu surprise*, or one of the many desserts. ● Sat L, Sun, Mon.

MELMERBY: *Village Bakery* £ DC MC V
On A686 nr Penrith, Cumbria. **(** 01768 881515.
An 18th-century barn is the setting for this shop and eaterie. Organic
and vegetarian meals are available all day. ● D. ♿ 🍴

NEAR SAWREY: *Ees Wyke* ££ AE
On B52 nr Hawkshead, Cumbria. **(** 015394 36393.
The views towards Esthwaite Water are one attraction; charming hosts
and excellent, good-value dinners are others. This is a place that you will
not forget in a hurry. ● L, Jan–Feb. 🍴

POULTON-LE-FYLDE: *River House* ££££ MC V
Skippool Creek, Thornton-le-Fylde, Lancs. **(** 01253 883497.
This restaurant-with-rooms prides itself on its details (cheeses,
teas and *petits fours*) being as good as the main courses. ● Sun. 🍷

SADDLEWORTH: *The Old Bell Inn Hotel* ££ AE MC V
Huddersfield Rd, Delph, Oldham. **(** 01457 870130.
A seasonally changing menu is offered in the main restaurant,
with informal meals and snacks served in the bar. 🍴

ULLSWATER: *Sharrow Bay* ££££ MC V
Nr Pooley Bridge, Ullswater, Cumbria. **(** 017684 86301. **@** enquiries@sharrow-bay.com
This is one of Britain's greatest country-house hotels. Mealtimes
are a gastronomic blowout – even the teas at Sharrow Bay are a
banquet. ● Dec–Feb. ♿ 🍴 🍷

WATERMILLOCK: *Rampsbeck Country House Hotel* ££££ MC V
On A592 nr Pooley Bridge, Cumbria. **(** 017684 86442.
Rampsbeck's dining room occupies a fine stretch of lakeshore, but
the modern British food is ambitious enough to hold the attention
and the service is pleasant. Book for lunch. ● 4 Jan–mid-Feb. 🍴 🍷

WHITEWELL: *Inn at Whitewell* £££ AE DC MC V
Whitewell, Forest of Bowland, Clitheroe, Lancs. **(** 01200 448222.
Full of atmosphere and very friendly, this old coaching inn's restaurant
offers an above-average menu of predominantly English dishes. 🍷

WINDERMERE: *Miller Howe* ££££ AE DC MC V
Rayrigg Rd, Windermere, Cumbria. **(** 015394 42536. **@** lakeview@millerhouse.com
This restaurant is also a beautiful hotel, and the elaborate and theatrical
dishes are the main reason for visiting. ● 6–25 Jan. 🍴 🌙 🍷

WITHERSLACK: *Old Vicarage* £££ AE DC MC V
Church Rd, Witherslack, Cumbria. **(** 015395 52381.
This idyllic country-house hotel serves dinner at 8pm, a mouthwatering
affair using Cumberland produce. Book ahead. ● Mon–Sat L. 🍴 🍷 ♿

For key to symbols see bookmark

CHILDREN WELCOME
Restaurants which offer smaller portions and high-chairs for children. Special menus sometimes available.

FIXED-PRICE MENU
A good value fixed-price meal, at lunch, dinner or both, usually of three courses.

VEGETARIAN
Vegetarian specialities served, sometimes for both starters and main courses.

CREDIT CARDS
Indicates which credit cards are accepted: *AE* American Express; *DC* Diners Club; *MC* Master Card/Access; *V* Visa.

YORKSHIRE AND THE HUMBER REGION

	CREDIT CARDS	CHILDREN WELCOME	FIXED-PRICE MENU	VEGETARIAN	OUTDOOR TABLES
ASENBY: *Crab and Lobster* ££££ Off A168 nr Thirsk, N Yorks. 01845 577286. @ reservations@crabandlobster.co.uk A great seafood pub just off the A1. Blackboards reflect the unpredictability of fresh catches. The place hums with activity. Rooms available.	AE MC V		■	●	■
BOLTON ABBEY: *Devonshire Arms Country House Hotel* £££££ On A59 nr Ilkley, N Yorks. 01756 710441. @ sales@thedevonshirearms.co.uk A luxurious country-house hotel. All types flock to enjoy the smart restaurant, excellent bar snacks and luscious teas. ● *Mon–Sat L.*	AE DC MC V	●	■	●	
BRADFORD: *Bombay Brasserie* £ Simes St, Bradford. 01274 737564. This up-market Indian restaurant specializes in Balti fish and vegetarian dishes, although the menu offers plenty of variety for all. Tandooris are an especially strong point. ● *Sat L.*	MC V	●	■	●	
BRADFORD: *Guide Post Hotel* £££ Common Rd, Low Moor, Bradford BD12 0ST. 01274 607866. The location of this restaurant may not be ideal – a warehouse district surrounds the building – but it is definitely worth a visit for the quality of the English and continental food and for the service. ● *Sat L, Sun D.*	AE DC MC V	●		●	
BREARTON: *The Malt Shovel* £ Brearton, N Yorks. 01423 862929. Varied blackboard menu featuring British, European and Oriental influences, served in a 16th-century beamed pub. ● *Mon, Sun D, 25–26 Dec.*		●		●	■
ELLAND: *Relish International Dinner & Bar* ££ 7 Town Hall Buildings, Elland, Calderdale. 01422 378833. Food from around the world, including Tex-Mex, pizzas, pasta, chicken tikka Peking crispy duck pancakes, as reflected in the name. The desserts are pure indulgence. ● *Mon, Tue–Thu L.*	AE MC V	●		●	
HARROGATE: *Betty's* ££ 1 Parliament St, Harrogate, N Yorks. 01423 502746. Betty's serves breakfasts, lunches and dinners as well as an eye-popping range of cakes, teas and coffees, all in a refined atmosphere of Edwardian living. ● *25, 26 Dec, 1 Jan.*	MC V	●		●	
HARROGATE: *Drum and Monkey* ££ 5 Montpellier Gardens, Harrogate, N Yorks. 01423 502650. A town-centre pub now achieving a more elevated status as a smart seafood wine bar and restaurant. It's fish or nothing here. ● *Sun.* limited.	MC V	●			
HAWORTH: *Weaver's* ££ 15 West Lane, Haworth, Bradford. 01535 643822. Hearty Yorkshire home cooking is given a modern accent at Weaver's, to the delight of hungry pilgrims seeking sustenance after tramping Heathcliff's moors. ● *Sun, Mon.*	AE DC MC V	●	■	●	
HEADINGLEY: *Bryan's* £ 9 Weetwood Lane, Headingley, Leeds. 0113 2785679. A traditional fish and chip restaurant of the best Yorkshire sort. Beef dripping and fresh fish are the secrets behind perfect results. Traditional, delicious desserts like treacle pudding round off the meal.	MC V	●	■	●	
HETTON: *Angel Inn* ££ Off B6265 nr Skipton, N Yorks. 01756 730263. This convivial beamed restaurant is more than a village pub, but the bar and brasserie food stay down to earth. ● *D.*	AE MC V	●	■	●	

ILKLEY: *Box Tree* £££worth
35–37 Church St, Ilkley, Bradford. 01943 608484. info@theboxtree.co.uk
Cuisine is definitely haute in this 18th-century farmhouse, recently
revitalized by a new and creative chef. Desserts and cheeses do
not disappoint. ● *Sun D, Mon.* 丸 ⚞ ▶
AE MC V

KNARESBOROUGH: *Carriages Wine Bar* ££
89 High St, Knaresborough, N Yorks. 01423 867041.
The Australian owner and chef serves mainly Pacific Rim cuisine
in summer and French and Mediterranean food in winter. A lovely
garden overlooks the quiet, pretty railway station and the viaduct
over the Nidd Gorge. ● *Mon.* ⏣ 丸 *limited.*
MC V

LEEDS: *Brasserie Forty-four* £££
44 The Calls, Leeds. 0113 2343232.
This waterfront warehouse complex combines bright, sophisticated
cooking with stylish accommodation. The lively atmosphere
makes this a fun night out. Especially pleasant in summer.
● *Sat L, Sun.* ▶ 丸
AE DC MC V

LEEDS: *Haley's* £££
Shire Oak Rd, Headingley, Leeds. 0113 2784446. sales@haleys.co.uk
A peaceful Victorian hotel in the university district produces
Anglo-French cuisine with exquisite presentation. Light, modern
bedrooms. ● *L.* ⚞ 丸 *limited.*
AE DC MC V

LIVERSEDGE: *Lillibet's Pub* £
64 Leeds Rd, Liversedge, Kirklees. 01924 404911.
This neat stone house offers dinner spanning three courses
with equal flair, mixing traditional and new ideas. 丸
AE MC V

RIPLEY: *Boar's Head* ££
Ripley Castle Estate, Ripley, N Yorks. 01423 771888.
This coaching inn provides luxury accommodation and fine dining as well as a
bistro. Fine wines and a great selection of ales. 丸 ⏣ ⚞
AE DC MC V

SHEFFIELD: *Greenhead House* £££
84 Burncross Rd, Chapeltown, Sheffield. 0114 2469004.
Four-course menus give a taste of France in the smart
dining room of this stone house. Home-made soups
a speciality. ● *Sun–Tue, Wed L, Sat L.* ⚞ 丸 ⏣
AE MC V

WATH IN NIDDERDALE: *Sportsman's Arms* ££
Wath in Nidderdale, Pateley Bridge, nr Harrogate, N Yorks. 01423 711306.
This restaurant-with-rooms also has a bar, but it is the well-cooked food
that attracts customers. Local produce features strongly on the menu. ⚞ 丸
MC V

WHITBY: *Magpie Café* £
14 Pier Rd, Whitby, N Yorks. 01947 602058.
This house by the harbour serves superlative fish and chips
with good cheer. Don't miss the diverse and unusual puddings.
● *Jan–early-Feb.* ⚞
MC V

YORK: *Little Betty's* ££
46 Stonegate, York. 01904 622865.
A wide range of Yorkshire and Swiss specialities, home-made cakes
and light lunches are served in this medieval building. ⚞
MC V

YORK: *Melton's* £££
7 Scarcroft Rd, York. 01904 634341.
This small restaurant in a Victorian terrace is good value and welcoming,
serving varied Anglo-French food. ● *Sun D, Mon L.* 丸 *limited.* ⚞ ⏣
MC V

NORTHUMBRIA

BELFORD: *The Blue Bell Hotel* ££
Market Place, Belford, Northum. 01668 213543.
The walled gardens of this old coaching inn shelter a profusion of organic
produce, complementing local meat and fish on seasonally changing menus. ⚞
AE MC V

CONSETT: *Pavilion* ££
Iveston, Consett, Durham. 01207 503388.
Bustling Cantonese restaurant serving generous helpings from an extensive
Chinese menu. Friendly atmosphere and good value. 丸
AE DC MC V

For key to symbols see bookmark

Price categories include a three-course meal for one, half a bottle of house wine, and all unavoidable extra charges such as cover, service, VAT:
£ under £15
££ £15-£25
£££ £25-£35
££££ £35-£50
£££££ over £50.

CHILDREN WELCOME
Restaurants which offer smaller portions and high-chairs for children. Special menus sometimes available.
FIXED-PRICE MENU
A good value fixed-price meal, at lunch, dinner or both, usually of three courses.
VEGETARIAN
Vegetarian specialities served, sometimes for both starters and main courses.
CREDIT CARDS
Indicates which credit cards are accepted: *AE* American Express; *DC* Diners Club; *MC* Master Card/Access; *V* Visa.

	CREDIT CARDS	CHILDREN WELCOME	FIXED-PRICE MENU	VEGETARIAN	OUTDOOR TABLES
DARLINGTON: *Cottage Thai* £££ 94–96 Parkgate, Darlington, Durham. (01325 361717. Handy for the station and theatre, this simple place offers Thai classics like *tom yum* soups, and red and green curries. ✂ ❱	AE MC V	●		●	
DURHAM: *Bistro 21* ££ Aykley Heads House, Aykley Heads, Durham. (0191 3844354. Eclectic modern cooking with menus that include enough variety to satisfy just about any taste. Relaxed atmosphere. ● *Sun, 25 Dec, bank hols.* ✂ ⎅ ♟	AE DC MC V	●	▨	●	▨
EAST BOLDON: *Forsters* £££ 2 St Bedes, Station Rd, East Boldon, S Tynes. (0191 5190929. A family enterprise run on classic British lines, welcoming and unpretentious but with plenty of sparkle. The food is never disappointing. ● *Sun, Mon, Tue–Sat L.* ✂ ♟	AE DC MC V		▨	●	▨
GATESHEAD: *Fumi* ££ 248 Durham Rd, Gateshead. (0191 4771152. A Japanese outpost offering plenty of fresh *sushi, tempura* and noodle soup dishes. Service is courteous. ● *L, Mon.* ❱	MC V			●	
GATESHEAD: *Eslington Villa* £££ On A6127, Low Fell, Gateshead. (0191 4876017. Reliable classic cooking figures in this attractive, graciously furnished hotel. Guests are greeted with bonhomie. ● *Sat L, Sun D.* ✂ ⎅ ♟	AE DC MC V	●	▨	●	
HAYDON BRIDGE: *General Havelock Inn* ££ Radcliffe Rd, Haydon Bridge, Northum. (01434 684376. Good food at sensible prices, both for the evening four-course menu and the lunchtime specials. Gardens run down to the River Tyne. ● *Mon, Sun D.* ✂ ⎅	DC MC V	●	▨	●	
HEXHAM: *The Valley Connection 301* £££ 19 Market Pl, Hexham, Northum. (01434 601234. Luxurious interior and top-quality Indian cuisine using unusual herbs and spices. Good views of St Wilfred's Abbey, floodlit at night. ● *Mon, 25 Dec.* ✂ ⎅	MC V			●	
NEWCASTLE UPON TYNE: *Café 21* £££ 19–21 Queen St, Princes Wharf, Quayside, Newcastle upon Tyne. (0191 2220755. Much more than just a café, this is a warm, welcoming bistro with a cosy feel. The menu is written up on the blackboard and changes on a daily basis. Unruffled service. ● *Sat L, Sun, Mon.* ⎅ ❱ ♟ ✂	AE DC MC V	●	▨	●	
NEWCASTLE UPON TYNE: *Treacle Moon* £££ 5–7 The Side, Newcastle upon Tyne. (0191 2325537. Fresh local meat, game and exotic fish feature in this brasserie. Modern-international cuisine gives flavour and colour. A laid-back atmosphere with jazz in the background. ● *Sat L, Sun, Mon.* ✂ ⎅ *limited.* ♟	AE MC V	●	▨	●	
NEWCASTLE UPON TYNE: *Fisherman's Lodge* £££££ Jesmond Dene, Jesmond, Newcastle upon Tyne. (0191 2813281. Situated in the centre of Jesmond Dene park, serving excellent food of the highest quality. Fish is a speciality. ● *Sun, 25, 26 Dec, bank hols.* ✂ ⎅	AE MC V	●	●	●	▨
ROMALDKIRK: *Rose and Crown* £££ On B6277 nr Barnard Castle, Durham. (01833 650213. This handsome coaching inn offers a splendid mix of pub with good-value bar meals and undaunting restaurant. Well worth making a detour for. Good selection of ales. ● *24, 26 Dec.* ✂ ⎅	MC V	●	▨	●	●
SEATON BURN: *Horton Grange* ££££ Off A1 at Stannington, Northum. (01661 860686. @ andrew@horton-grange.co.uk This pleasant stone farmhouse hotel offers local English produce. Decor and cooking are sophisticated, light and elegant. ● *L, Sun.* ✂ ⎅ ♟	AE MC V		▨	●	

STOKESLEY: *Chapters*   £££   AE DC MC V
27 High St, Stokesley, N Yorks. 01642 711888.
A successful duo of informal bistro and more serious dining room.
Cooking is French with global cross-currents. ● *Sun, 25 Dec, 1 Jan.*

NORTH WALES

ABERDYFI: *Penhelig Arms*   £££   MC V
Aberdyfi, Gwynedd. 01654 767215.
Freshly caught fish features strongly on the menu at this hotel-restaurant
right by the sea. *(See also p564.)* ● *25, 26 Dec.*

ABERSOCH: *Porth Tocyn*   £££   MC V
Abersoch, Gwynedd. 01758 713303. @ porthtocyn.hotel@virgin.net
Few fail to be charmed by this coastal hotel. There are light alternatives
to the menu on offer. *(See also p564.)* ● *Nov–wk before Easter.*

ABERSOCH: *Riverside Hotel*   £££   AE MC V
On A499 nr Pwllheli, Gwynedd. 01758 712419.
Morning coffee, light lunches and afternoon teas are served in the lounge and
garden. Restaurant evening meals ooze with Mediterranean charm.

CAPEL COCH: *Tre-Ysgawen Hall*   £££   AE MC V
On B5111 nr Llangefni, Anglesey. 01248 750750.
A firm classical cuisine tailors the modern French cooking at this
massive country-house hotel. Service is courteous and attentive.

COLWYN BAY: *Café Niçoise*   £££   AE MC V
124 Abergele Rd, Colwyn Bay, Conwy. 01492 531555.
This French-style bistro comes complete with jazz and blues and Parisian
scenes. Modern European cooking inspires the menus. ● *Mon L, Tue L, Sun.*

CONWY: *Old Rectory*   ££££   MC V
Llanrwst Rd, Llansanffraid Glan, nr Conwy. 01492 580611.
Great care is lavished on the four-course dinners here. Inside, there
are many paintings and antiques. ● *30 Nov–1 Feb.*

DEGANWY: *Paysanne*   £££   MC V
Station Rd, Deganwy, Conwy. 01492 5820/9.
This bustling Gallic bistro serves daily specials and three-course provincial dinners.
Special dietary needs catered for by arrangement. ● *L, Sun, Mon.*

DOLGELLAU: *Dylanwad Da*   ££
2 Ffôs-y-Felin, Dolgellau, Gwynedd. 01341 422870.
Bright little neighbourhood bistro serving Welsh lamb and port, plum and ginger
pie. Open dinner only. ○ *Thu–Sat, Tues–Sat/Sun in summer.* ● *Feb–mid-Mar.*

EYTON: *Plassey Restaurant*   ££   AE DC MC V
Eyton, nr Wrexham. 01978 780905.
Set amid a complex of Edwardian farm buildings and craft workshops,
Plassey offers good bar snacks and blackboard specials. Slow-roasted
Welsh lamb is a delicious speciality. ● *Mon (except public hols).*

GLANWYDDEN: *Queen's Head*   ££   MC V
Off B5115 nr Llandudno Junction, Conwy. 01492 546570.
Popular country pub offering Welsh lamb, local mussels and soups.
Traditional puddings also appear on a long list of sweets.

HARLECH: *Castle Cottage*   £££   MC V
Pen Llech, Harlech, Gwynedd. 01766 780479.
Despite modern extensions, this is one of the oldest buildings in Harlech.
Menus have Welsh and English elements. Fresh local produce gives the
dishes an authentic flavour. Bedrooms available. ● *L, Feb.*

LLANARMON DYFFRYN CEIRIOG: *West Arms Hotel*   ££   MC V
Llanarmon Dyffryn Ceiriog, nr Llangollen, Denbighs.
01691 600665. @ gowestarms@aol.com
Superb cooking and excellent presentation await at this restaurant in an idyllic
16th-century inn. The local fish dishes are especially good. ● *L.*

LLANBERIS: *Y Bistro*   £££   MC V
43–45 High St, Llanberis, Gwynedd. 01286 871278. @ ybistro@fsbdial.co.uk
Hungry walkers flock to this restaurant at the foot of the Snowdon
railway. A good range of hearty main courses. ● *L, Sun.*

For key to symbols see bookmark

Price categories include a three-course meal for one, half a bottle of house wine, and all unavoidable extra charges such as cover, service, VAT:
£ under £15
££ £15-£25
£££ £25-£35
££££ £35-£50
£££££ over £50.

CHILDREN WELCOME
Restaurants which offer smaller portions and high-chairs for children. Special menus sometimes available.

FIXED-PRICE MENU
A good value fixed-price meal, at lunch, dinner or both, usually of three courses.

VEGETARIAN
Vegetarian specialities served, sometimes for both starters and main courses.

CREDIT CARDS
Indicates which credit cards are accepted: *AE* American Express; *DC* Diners Club; *MC* Master Card/Access; *V* Visa.

	Price	Credit Cards	Children Welcome	Fixed-Price Menu	Vegetarian	Outdoor Tables
LLANDRILLO: *Tyddyn Llan* On B4401 nr Corwen, Denbigh. [01490 440264. This Georgian farmhouse hotel produces distinctive, high-quality cooking using local ingredients such as Welsh Black beef and fish *(See also p565.)*. ● *Mon L.* & ⚡	£££	AE DC MC V	●	▪	●	▪
LLANDUDNO: *Richard's* 7 Church Walks, Llandudno, Conwy. [01492 877924. This bistro in a Victorian town house is deservedly popular. The menu has plenty of options. ● *L, Sun–Mon, 25–26 Dec.*	£££	AE DC MC V	●		●	
LLANDUDNO: *Martin's Restaurant with Rooms* 11 Mostyn Avenue, Craig-y-don, LLandudno, Conwy. [01492 870070. FAX *01492 876661* Gourmet, country-house style cuisine is served in this Edwardian villa. The four en-suite rooms are named Mahogany, Pine and Oak. ● *Sun–Mon, 2 wks Jan.*	££££	AE DC MC V	●	▪	●	▪
LLANGOLLEN: *Gales* 18 Bridge St, Llangollen, Denbighs. [01978 860089. @ richard@galesofllangollen.co.uk A wine bar, restaurant and guesthouse. Food is served in a panelled bar with church pews; bedrooms are furnished with antiques. ● *Sun, 25 Dec–2 Jan* & 🍷	££	AE DC MC V	●		●	
MENAI BRIDGE: *Jodie's* Telford Rd, Menai Bridge, Anglesey. [01248 714864. Wine-bar food is served in a conservatory and garden overlooking the Menai Bridge. Also serves vegetarian dishes. & ⚡	£	MC V			●	▪
NORTHOP: *Soughton Hall* Off A5119, Northop, Flint. [01352 840811. Grand cooking matches this hotel's palatial setting: an 18th-century bishop's palace in parkland. Service and dress are formal. ● *L.* ⚡ 🍷	£££	AE MC V		▪	●	▪
PWLLHELI: *Plas Bodegroes* Nefyn Rd, Pwllheli, Gwynedd. [01758 612363. @ gunna@bodegroes.co.uk This elegant Georgian country house takes full advantage of excellent local ingredients to produce accomplished British cooking for its three-course dinners. Fish especially good. ● *L (except Sun), Mon, Dec–Feb.* 🍷 ⚡ &	£££	MC V	●	▪	●	▪

SOUTH AND MID-WALES

	Price	Credit Cards	Children Welcome	Fixed-Price Menu	Vegetarian	Outdoor Tables
ABERAERON: *Hive on the Quay* Cadwgan Pl, Aberaeron, Cered. [01545 570445. Honey is the speciality at this summertime café, which serves wholesome teas and lunches (dinners too, in high summer) in a homely setting of stripped pine and lots of pot plants. ● *mid-Sep–May.* ⚡ &	££	MC V	●		●	▪
BRECHFA: *Ty Mawr* Brechfa, Carmarthen. [01267 202332. @ tymawr@tymawrcountryhotel.co.uk Small, rural hotel with good home baking. Local produce is treated to international flourishes. Reservation only. & ⚡	£££	MC V	●	▪		
CARDIFF: *La Brasserie/Champers/Le Monde* 60 St Mary St, Cardiff. [029 20372164. Bustling complex of French brasserie (fish and grills), tapas bar and pub-like fish restaurant with friendly atmosphere and good wines. ● *Sun L.* & ⬤	££	AE DC MC V	●	▪	●	▪
CARDIFF: *Woods Brasserie* Pilotage Building, Stuart St, Cardiff. [029 20492400. Minimalist but comfortable, serving Modern British food, with an emphasis on fish and Welsh chicken and pork. ● *Sun D, Mon, 25–26 Dec, 31–1 Jan.* &	£££	AE DC MC V	●	▪	●	▪
CLYTHA: *Clytha Arms* Nr Abergavenny, Monmouth. [01873 840206. Country pub where France and Wales meet in fare such as laverbread *(see p36)* or oysters with leeks. ● *Sun D, Mon D (except parties, by arrangement).* ⚡	£££	AE DC MC V	●	▪	●	▪

COWBRIDGE: *Off the Beeton Track*   £££
1 Town Hall Sq, Cowbridge, V of Glam. (01446 773599.
Home-baked cakes, simple lunches and afternoon teas as well as Sunday
roast lunches. Sauces are a strong point. ● Mon. 🍴 &

| | AE DC MC V | ● | | ● | ▣ |

CRICKHOWELL: *Nantyffin Cider Mill Inn*   £££
Brecon Rd, Crickhowell, Powys. (01873 810775. @ nantyffin@aol.com
This unpretentious, 16th-century stone-built inn proffers Modern British
and European dishes, plus local game and seafood. ● Mon. & 🍴

| | AE MC V | ● | | ● | ▣ |

DRUID HAVEN: *Druidstone Hotel*   £££
Druid Haven, Broad Haven, Pembroke. (01437 781221.
This informal family hotel combines local produce with international spices. Set
in vast grounds with clifftop views. ● Sun L, (phone for winter opening hours). & 🍴

| | AE MC V | ● | | ● | ▣ |

FISHGUARD: *Three Main Street*   ££££
3 Main St, Fishguard, Pembroke. (01348 874275.
In a Georgian building overlooking the harbour the Modern British menu may include
crab soufflé and roast breast of guinea fowl. ● Sun–Mon, Feb, 2 weeks end Nov.

| | | ● | ▣ | | |

LAMPHEY: *Dial Inn*   £££
The Ridgeway, Lamphey, Pembroke. (01646 672426.
Hearty fare such as steak and kidney pie with oysters keeps the
customers happy. Fish and vegetarian choices too. ● 25 Dec. & 🍴

| | AE MC V | ● | | ● | ▣ |

LLANDEWI SKIRRID: *Walnut Tree Inn*   ££££
On B4521 nr Abergavenny, Monmouth. (01873 852797.
This popular, informal bistro offers a vast selection of eclectic food,
unpretentiously served but carefully prepared. ● Sun, Mon. &

| | MC V | ● | | ● | ▣ |

LLYSWEN: *Griffin Inn*   £££
On A470, Llyswen, Powys. (01874 754241.
Shooting and fishing are the attractions in the Wye Valley, home of this
15th-century inn; the fare reflects this. Rooms available. ● Sun D. & 🍴

| | AE DC MC V | ● | | ● | ▣ |

MUMBLES: *L'Amuse*   ££££
93 Newton Rd, Mumbles. (01792 366006. **FAX** 01792 368090.
Authentic French cuisine is the style of fare here, with pig's trotters a speciality.
A regular clientele returns again and again. ● Mon, 24 Dec–26 Jan. &

| | AE DC MC V | ● | | ● | |

NANTGAREDIG: *Four Seasons, Cwmtwrch Farm*   ££££
On B4310, Carmarthen. (01267 290238. @ jen4seas@aol.com
Local produce receives honest farmhouse treatment in this family-run
restaurant. Welsh lamb and smoked salmon feature prominently. ● Sun, Mon.

| | MC V | ● | ▣ | ● | |

NEWPORT: *Cnapan*   ££££
East St, Newport, Pembroke. (01239 820575.
This Georgian restaurant-with-rooms is open all day for coffee and tea. Lunch
and dinner include Welsh specialities. ● Tue, Jan–Feb. & 🍴

| | MC V | ● | | ● | ▣ |

PONTFAEN: *Tregynon Country Farmhouse*   £££
Off B4313, Gwaun Valley, Newport. (01239 820531. @ tregynon@online-holidays.net
The food here is delicious and carefully considered (home-smoked bacon
and wholefoods). Best to book. ● L, Sun, Thu, Wed (winter). 🍴

| | MC V | | ▣ | | ▣ |

PORTHGAIN: *Harbour Lights*   ££££
Porthgain, nr St David's, Pembroke. (01348 831549. @ harblights@aol.com
This old seaside cottage offers generous local fare with fresh herbs, local seafood
and lots of laverbread (see p36). Opening times are seasonal. ● Mon, Tues. & 🍴

| | MC V | | ▣ | ● | ▣ |

ST DAVID'S: *Morgan's Brasserie*   ££££
20 Nun St, St David's, Pembroke. (01437 720508. @ ceri@morgbras.freeserve.co.uk
Fish is the main attraction at this family-run brasserie. Local beef and
cheeses also feature. ● Jan & Feb: daily; Mar: Sun–Tue; Nov & Dec: Mon–Thu. & 🍴

| | AE MC V | ● | | ● | |

SWANSEA: *La Braseria*   £££
28 Wind St, Swansea. (01792 469683.
This Spanish restaurant is especially popular at lunchtime for good-value
set lunches garnished with chips, salads and garlic bread. ● Sun. & ▶

| | AE DC MC V | | ▣ | ● | |

TRELLECH: *Village Green Brasserie*   £££
Trellech, nr Monmouth. (01600 860119.
Eclectic cuisine from around the world in this 400-year-old former
priory. Fixed-priced meals only for Sunday lunch. & 🍴

| | MC V | ● | ▣ | ● | ▣ |

For key to symbols see bookmark

<table>
<tr><td colspan="6">

Price categories include a three-course meal for one, half a bottle of house wine, and all unavoidable extra charges such as cover, service, VAT:
(£) under £15
(£)(£) £15–£25
(£)(£)(£) £25–£35
(£)(£)(£)(£) £35–£50
(£)(£)(£)(£)(£) over £50.

</td></tr>
</table>

CHILDREN WELCOME
Restaurants which offer smaller portions and high-chairs for children. Special menus sometimes available.

FIXED-PRICE MENU
A good value fixed-price meal, at lunch, dinner or both, usually of three courses.

VEGETARIAN
Vegetarian specialities served, sometimes for both starters and main courses.

CREDIT CARDS
Indicates which credit cards are accepted: *AE* American Express; *DC* Diners Club; *MC* Master Card/Access; *V* Visa.

	CREDIT CARDS	CHILDREN WELCOME	FIXED-PRICE MENU	VEGETARIAN	OUTDOOR TABLES
WELSH HOOK: *Stone Hall* **(£)(£)** Off A40 nr Wolf's Castle, Pembroke. **[** 01348 840212. French cooking with unusual touches reigns in this hotel-restaurant in wooded grounds. ● *L.* ♿	AE DC MC V	●	■	●	
WHITEBROOK: *Crown at Whitebrook* **(£)(£)(£)(£)** Whitebrook, nr Monmouth, Monmouth. **[** 01600 860254. This 17th-century outpost of provincial France can be found deep in the Wye Valley; it is now run as a restaurant-with-rooms. ● *Sun D, Mon L, Christmas & New Year.* ⚑ ♟	AE DC MC V		■	●	
<div align="center">**THE LOWLANDS**</div>					
ANSTRUTHER: *Cellar* **(£)(£)(£)(£)** 24 East Green, Anstruther, Fife. **[** 01333 310378. One of this fishing port's oldest buildings. Only top-quality produce is used; fresh seafood dominates the menu. ● *Nov–Mar: Sun, Mon; 24–28 Dec.* ⚑ ♟	AE MC V		■	●	
AYR: *Fouters Bistro* **(£)(£)** 2A Academy St, Ayr, S Ayrshire. **[** 01292 261391. Lively bistro in a vaulted basement. Ingredients are Scottish, cooking mostly provincial-French, with vegetarian dishes. ● *Sun, Mon.* ▶	AE DC MC V	●	■	●	
CANONBIE: *Riverside Inn* **(£)(£)** On A7 nr border, Dumfries & Galloway. **[** 013873 71512. Consistently good cooking ensures the popularity of this 17th-century inn overlooking the Esk. You can eat in the bar or restaurant. ⚑ ♟	MC V	●		●	■
CUPAR: *Ostlers Close* **(£)(£)(£)** Bonnygate, Cupar, Fife. **[** 01334 655574. Fish plays a large part in the menus at this tiny place, but plenty of meat or game dishes get expert French treatment too. Wild mushrooms are one of their delicious specialities. ● *Sun, Mon, Tue–Thu L.* ♿ *limited* ♟	AE MC V	●		●	
DIRLETON: *Open Arms Hotel* **(£)(£)(£)** Dirleton, E Lothian. **[** 01620 850241. On the edge of the village green overlooking the 13th-century castle the well-established hotel-restaurant enjoys a deserved reputation for good food. Choice between formal restaurant or the brasserie. ♿ ⚑ ♟	MC V	●	■	●	■
EDINBURGH: *Henderson's* **(£)** 94 Hanover St, Edinburgh. **[** 0131 2252131. This institution has a wide range of vegetarian specialities. Cakes and unusual cheeses accompany filling salads and hot dishes. ⚑ ▶	AE MC V			●	
EDINBURGH: *The Lost Sock Diner* **(£)** 11 East London St, Edinburgh. **[** 0131 5576097. This eatery is one of the best in the area. Interesting menu, including New York tortilla "wraps". Breakfast served until 4pm. ♿ ⚑ ♟		●	■		
EDINBURGH: *Susie's Diner* **(£)** 53 West Nicolson St, Edinburgh. **[** 0131 6678729. A friendly wholefood vegetarian café centrally located near Edinburgh University. Good-quality ingredients, impeccably flavoured. ♿		●		●	■
EDINBURGH: *Kalpna* **(£)(£)** 2–3 St Patrick Sq, Edinburgh. **[** 0131 6679890. Indian vegetarian cookery in a calming environment near the university. Flavours are mild and service variable. ● *Sat L, Sun.* ⚑ ▶	MC V	●	■	●	
EDINBURGH: *Daniel's* **(£)(£)** 88 Commercial St, Leith, Edinburgh. **[** 0131 5535933. One of the best of the new conservatory restaurants, situated opposite the Scottish Office. Serves hearty Alsace cuisine. ♿ ⚑ ♟	MC V	●	■	●	

EDINBURGH: *Atrium & Blue Bar Café* £££ · AE MC V
10 Cambridge St, Edinburgh. 0131 2288882.
An ultra-stylish interior by the Traverse Theatre complements the light,
simple, but exciting cooking here. This is the cutting edge of Modern
British cookery; Mediterranean influences dominate. ● *Sat L, Sun.* ⓰ ❱ ❚

EDINBURGH: *Vintners Rooms* £££ · AE MC V
87 Giles St, Leith, Edinburgh. 0131 5546767.
This unusual candlelit restaurant is housed in a wine warehouse. Both
cooking and service are admirably unpretentious. Light lunches are
served in the wine bar. ● *Sun, last week Dec, first week Jan.* ⓰ ❚

EDINBURGH: *Waterfront Wine Bar* £££ · MC V
1C Dock Place, Leith, Edinburgh. 0131 5547427.
Best of the Leith waterfront bar-restaurants with a cosy bar, excellent wine list,
and conservatory restaurant serving modish fare. ● *25 & 26 Dec.* ⓰ ❚

EDINBURGH: *Martin's* ££££ · AE DC MC V
70 Rose St, North Lane, Edinburgh. 0131 2253106.
City-centre premises attract business folk and shoppers for a range of
imaginative, contemporary Scottish cooking. ● *Sun, Mon.* ❚

GLASGOW: *The Buttery* ££££ · AE DC MC V
652 Argyle St, Glasgow. 0141 2218188.
Attractive turn-of-the-century pub converted into an elegant dining room.
Simpler food is served downstairs in the Belfry. ● *Sat L, Sun, 25 Dec, 1 Jan.* ❱

GLASGOW: *Ubiquitous Chip* ££££ · AE DC MC V
12 Ashton Lane, Glasgow. 0141 3345007.
The lighthearted individuality suggested by the name reveals itself most
in the upstairs bistro. The food throughout is good, with well-rehearsed
and hugely varied treatments of Scottish fare. ⓰ ❱ ❚

GLASGOW: *Camerons, Glasgow Hilton* ££££ · AE DC MC V
1 William St, Glasgow. 0141 2045511.
This is theme-park Scotland, but both food and service are beyond
reproach at this business hotel and restaurant. ● *Sat L, Sun.* ⓰ ❱

GLASGOW: *One Devonshire Gardens* ££££ · AE DC MC V
1 Devonshire Gardens, Glasgow. 0141 3392001.
French and British inspiration at this sumptuous hotel-restaurant.
The atmosphere is pleasantly relaxed. *(See also p569.)* ● *Sat L.* ❚ ❱

LARGS: *Nardini's* ££ · AE DC MC V
The Esplanade, Largs, N Ayrshire. 01475 674555.
A splendid Art Deco interior sets the scene of this seafront lounge café.
Breakfasts, cakes, Italian and British dishes are served all day. This is
the perfect place in which to sit back, read the paper and relax. ⓰ ❚ ❱

LINLITHGOW: *Champany Inn* ££££ · AE DC MC V
Champany, nr Linlithgow, W Lothian. 01506 834532.
Wines spring to the fore here, but the food is good too, whether a perfect
Angus steak, or more ornate dishes with sauces. ● *Sat L, Sun.* ⓰ ❚

MOFFAT: *Well View* £££ · AE MC V
Ballplay Rd, Moffat, Dumfries & Galloway. 01683 220184.
Modern French cooking with some Scottish elements is served in this family-run
hotel. Peaceful atmosphere. No children under five at night. ● *Sat L.* ❚

PORTPATRICK: *Knockinaam Lodge* ££££ · AE DC MC V
Off A77 nr Portpatrick, Dumfries & Galloway. 01776 810471.
An idyllic location overlooking the sea. Cooking is smart, French and
modern, with casseroles and fish. ⓰ ❚

ST ANDREWS: *Brambles* ££ · MC V
5 College St, St Andrews, Fife. 01334 475380.
Popular self-service café specializing in wholefood and vegetarian recipes,
though meat and fish also appear. Cakes are freshly baked on the premises. ❚

ST ANDREWS: *The Peat Inn* ££££ · AE DC MC V
On B940 nr St Andrews, Fife. 01334 840206.
Highly accomplished modern cooking with regional produce and
seasonal vegetables has established this fine hotel-restaurant as one of the
best in Britain. Lunch is a bargain. ● *Sun, Mon.* ⓰ ❚ ❚

For key to symbols see bookmark

		CREDIT CARDS	CHILDREN WELCOME	FIXED-PRICE MENU	VEGETARIAN	OUTDOOR TABLES

Price categories include a three-course meal for one, half a bottle of house wine, and all unavoidable extra charges such as cover, service, VAT:
£ under £15
££ £15-£25
£££ £25-£35
££££ £35-£50
£££££ over £50.

CHILDREN WELCOME
Restaurants which offer smaller portions and high-chairs for children. Special menus sometimes available.
FIXED-PRICE MENU
A good value fixed-price meal, at lunch, dinner or both, usually of three courses.
VEGETARIAN
Vegetarian specialities served, sometimes for both starters and main courses.
CREDIT CARDS
Indicates which credit cards are accepted: *AE* American Express; *DC* Diners Club; *MC* Master Card/Access; *V* Visa.

SWINTON: *Wheatsheaf* ££ MC V
Main St, Swinton, Borders. (01890 860257.
This country inn offers imaginative cooking served in a traditional dining room or conservatory. Bedrooms available. ● *Mon.* 🛦 ⚡

TROON: *Highgrove House* £££ AE MC V
Old Loans Rd, Troon, S Ayrshire. (01292 312511.
Watery prospects over the Firth of Clyde accompany informal meals from a wide-ranging menu in this retired sea-captain's house. Bedrooms available.

THE HIGHLANDS AND ISLANDS

ABERDEEN: *The Silver Darling* £££ AE DC MC V
Pocra Quay, Footdee, North Pier, Aberdeen. (01224 576229.
Located on the noth side of Aberdeen Harbour, this restaurant offers superb seafood, which varies with the daily catch.
● *Sat L, Sun, 24 Dec–mid-Jan.* 🍷

ABERFOYLE: *Braeval Old Mill* £££ MC V
On A81 nr Aberfoyle, Stirling. (01877 382711.
Set four-course dinners offer dishes of carefully prepared local meat, game and fish, followed by tempting desserts. ● *Tue–Sat L, Sun D, Mon.* 🛦 🍷

ALEXANDRIA: *Georgian Room, Cameron House* £££££ AE DC MC V
Off A82, Loch Lomond, Alexandria, W Dunbar. (01389 755565.
This large, comfortable hotel caters for the well-heeled leisure market of fishing and golf. The food is attractive and rich. ● *Mon.* ⚡

ALYTH: *Drumnacree House* ££ MC V
St Ninian's Rd, Alyth, Perthshire. (01828 632194.
The smokehouse and garden provide produce for a mixed bag of cooking styles used with great enthusiasm and flair. An eclectic range of original ideas to tempt any palate. ● *Mon.* 🛦 ⚡

AUCHMITHIE: *But 'n' Ben* ££ MC V
Off A92 nr Arbroath, Angus. (01241 877223.
Twin cottages in a working fishing village. The day's catch figures at lunch and dinner, and there are splendid high teas.
● *Tue.* 🛦 ⚡

BALLATER: *Green Inn* £££ AE DC MC V
9 Victoria Rd, Ballater, Aberdeenshire. (013397 55701.
Scottish produce is given the full works at this refurbished former pub. Service is friendly and informed. Rooms available.
● *L, 2 wks in Oct, 25–27 Dec.* 🛦 ⚡

BALLATER: *Darroch Learg* ££££ AE DC MC V
Braemar Rd, Ballater, Aberdeenshire. (013397 55443.
A Victorian shooting lodge. The fare is local, the cooking modern Scottish using a wide range of ingredients.
● *23–27 Dec, 10 Jan–1 Feb.* 🛦 ⚡ 🍷

CAIRNDOW: *Loch Fyne Oyster Bar* ££ DC MC V
Clachan Farm, Ardkinglas, Cairndow, Argyll & Bute. (01499 600236.
This splendid place offers a warm welcome with platters of shellfish, overlooking the lochside oyster beds. 🛦 ⚡

COLBOST BY DUNVEGAN: *The Three Chimneys* £££ AE MC V
Colbost, nr Dunvegan, Isle of Skye. (01470 511258. FAX 01470 511358
Situated a few miles from Dunvegan, on the western shore of Loch Dunvegan. Once a stone-built crofters cottage, this award-winning restaurant offers seafood and game lovingly prepared with fresh local ingredients. The atmosphere is peaceful and relaxed. Accommodation is also available. ● *Feb.* 🛦 ⚡ 🍷

DUNKELD: *Kinnaird* £££££ MC V
Kinnaird Estate, off B898 nr Dunkeld, Perthshire. 01796 482440.
This estate hotel produces ornate food of great originality.
Lunch is more affordable. ● *Jan–Feb: Mon, Tues, Wed.* & ⚡ ▯

FORT WILLIAM: *Crannog Seafood Restaurant* ££ MC V
Town Pier, Fort William, Highland. 01397 705589.
Nothing detracts from the simple pleasure of eating exquisitely fresh
seafood overlooking a panoramic loch view. Helpings are generous.
The atmosphere is warm and welcoming, and the service efficient. & ⚡ ▶

INVERNESS: *Culloden House* ££££ AE DC MC V
Off A96 at Culloden, Highland. 01463 790461.
The food is Scottish country-house style, with sauces, jellies, sorbets and
mousses interspersing hearty meat, game and fish dishes. Rooms available. ⚡

KILBERRY: *Kilberry Inn* ££ MC V
Kilberry by Tarbert, Argyll & Bute. 01880 770223.
This low, white croft (former post office, now pub) in a quiet coastal village
serves traditional British farmhouse cooking. Accommodation is also
available. ● *Mon (except public hols).* ⚡

KILLIECRANKIE: *The Killiecrankie Hotel* £££ MC V
Off A9 nr Pitlochry, Perthshire. 01796 473220.
Excellent bar meals supplement more ambitious dinnertime fare in this
attractive hotel. It's hearty stuff, with a few Oriental dishes. & *limited* ⚡

KINCLAVEN: *Ballathie House* ££££ AE DC MC V
Off B9099 nr Stanley, Perthshire. 01250 883268.
A warm, hearty hotel in a huge estate on the Tay. The restaurant
serves appropriate fare like venison and, of course, salmon. & ⚡

KINCRAIG: *The Boathouse Restaurant* £ MC V
Loch Insh, Kincraig, Invernesshire, Highland. 01540 651272.
Food is served all day at this log-cabin restaurant – fresh fish, haggis or steak.
Snacks are also available. A bar and a gift shop can also be found here. & ⚡

KYLE OF LOCHALSH: *Seagreen Restaurant and Book Shop* ££ MC V
Plockton Rd, Kyle of Lochalsh, Highland. 01599 534388.
All-day counter service offering snacks or casseroles, with waitress service
in the evenings. A pleasant vegetarian and fish menu that even the
most hardened meat-eater will enjoy. ● *Jan–early Apr.* & ⚡

KYLESKU: *Kylesku Hotel* ££ MC V
On A894 by Lairg, Highland. 01971 502231.
Lochs and mountains provide a splendid backdrop to this hotel. The
repertoire is limited, but fresh fish is always a good option. ⚡

OBAN: *Knipoch Hotel* ££££ AE DC MC V
On A816 nr Oban, Argyll & Bute. 01852 316251.
Dinners range from three to five courses. Huge arrays of vegetables
and flamboyant puddings are features. ● *mid-Dec–Feb.* ⚡ ▯

PERTH: *Let's Eat* £££ AE MC V
77 Kinnoull St, Perth. 01738 643377.
Local ingredients – fish, game, beef and lamb – are the mainstay of the modern
cooking here. ● *Sun, Mon, 25–26 Dec, 1–2 Jan, 2 weeks mid-Jan, 2 weeks mid-Jul.* &

PORT APPIN: *The Airds Hotel* ££££ MC V
Port Appin, Appin, Argyll & Bute. 01631 730236.
This hotel restaurant has a fine waterfront location and cheerful interior
to complement the splendidly flavoured dinners. *(See also p573.)* ⚡ ▯

ST MARGARET'S HOPE: *The Creel Restaurant* £££ MC V
Front Rd, St Margaret's Hope, S. Ronaldsay, Orkney. 01856 831311.
Excellent, honest cooking. Seafood predominates, but you might try the
seaweed-fed lamb. ● *Jan–Feb, 2 weeks mid-Oct.* &

ULLAPOOL: *Altnaharrie Inn* £££££ MC AE V
Ullapool, Highland. 01854 633230.
Set dinners stretch to five courses, with fresh fish straight from boat
or creel. Cooking is modern but not over-trendy. Wild ingredients from
field and hedgerow add interest. Dining here is a real pleasure.
(See also p573.) ● *early Nov–Easter.* ▯ ⚡ ▯

For key to symbols see bookmark

British Pubs

No tour of britain could be complete without some exploration of its public houses *(see pp34–5)*. These are a great social institution, descendants of centuries of hostelries, ale-houses and stagecoach halts. Some have colourful histories or fascinating contents, and still occupy a central role in the community, staging quiz games and folk dancing. Many of those listed below are lovely buildings, or have attractive settings. Most serve a variety of beers, spirits and wine by the glass.

A "free house" is independent and will stock several leading regional beers, but most pubs are "tied" – this means that they are owned by a brewery and only stock that brewery's selection.

Many pubs offer additional attractions such as live music and beer gardens with picnic tables. Traditional pub food is often served at lunchtime, and increasingly food is served in the evenings too. Traditional pub games take many forms, including cribbage, shove ha'penny, skittles, dominoes and darts.

LONDON

Bloomsbury: *Lamb*
94 Lamb's Conduit St, WC1.
Unspoilt Victorian pub with cut-glass "snob screens" and theatrical photographs. Small courtyard at the rear.

City: *Black Friar*
174 Queen Victoria St, EC4.
Eccentric inside and out, with intriguing Art Nouveau decor. Attentive service.

City: *Olde Cheshire Cheese*
Wine Office Court, Fleet St EC4.
Authentic 17th-century inn haunted by the shades of Johnson, Pope and Dickens. Restored to its plain, bareboarded glory with open fires in winter.

Hammersmith: *Dove*
19 Upper Mall, W6.
One of the most attractive of West London's riverside pubs, where you can watch rowing crews from the terrace. Very crowded in fine weather.

Hampstead: *Spaniards Inn*
Spaniards Lane, NW3.
Famous Hampstead landmark dating from the 18th century, once part of a tollgate. Attractive garden.

Kensington: *Windsor Castle*
114 Campden Hill Rd, W8.
A civilized Georgian inn with traditional oak furnishings and open fires. The walled garden attracts well-heeled, youngish crowds in summer. Hearty English food.

Southwark: *George Inn*
77 Borough High St, SE1.
Quaint coaching inn with unique galleried courtyard, now owned by the National Trust *(see p25)*. Rooms ramble upstairs and downstairs, and the overspill sits outside. Morris men and Globe Players may be seen at times.

THE DOWNS AND CHANNEL COAST

Alciston: *Rose Cottage*
Off A27 nr Lewes, Sussex.
Charming, creeper-covered cottage inn decorated with rustic bygones. Limited room inside.

Alfriston: *Star*
Alfriston, Sussex.
This quaint old inn, once a pilgrim hostel, is now a smart hotel but is full of character.

Chale: *Wight Mouse Inn*
On B3399, Chale, Isle of Wight.
Cheerful, family-oriented inn with large gardens. Bric-a-brac dangles from the ceilings.

Fletchling: *Griffin*
Off A272, Fletchling, Sussex.
Sophisticated but very laid-back country inn with a 1930s air, which serves imaginative food. Attractive accommodation.

Rye: *Mermaid*
Mermaid St, Rye, Sussex.
Famous historic building in a steep cobbled street, full of panelling, frescoes and antiques.

Smarden: *Bell*
Off A274, Smarden, Kent.
An ancient brick-and-beam pub among orchards. Traditional games, inglenook fireplaces and flagstone floors *(see p546)*.

Walliswood: *Scarlett Arms*
Off A29 nr Ewhurst, Surrey.
Workers' cottages converted into a relaxing pub with beams, log fires and trestle tables.

Winchester: *Wykeham Arms*
75 Kingsgate St, Winchester, Hants.
Classy, idiosyncratic town centre pub/hotel with fascinating decor. Excellent food, wine and accommodation *(see p547)*.

EAST ANGLIA

Cambridge: *Boathouse*
14 Chesterton Rd, Cambridge.
One of the best of Cambridge's waterside pubs, overlooking Jesus Green. For entertainment in summer, sit and watch barges and punts glide past; oars hang in the bars.

Holywell: *Olde Ferry Boat*
Off A1123 at Needingworth, Cambs.
The Great Ouse reaches almost to the door of this picturesque thatched pub. Inside it is comfortably modernized, with cosy bedrooms. Wide range of food, and a resident ghost called Juliette.

Littlebury: *Queens Head Inn*
High St, Littlebury, Essex.
This Tudor village pub has kept plenty of its original character. It offers outstanding real ales and food in a welcoming atmosphere.

Snape: *Golden Key*
Priory Lane, Snape, Suffolk.
Pretty gardens, stylish interior and appetizing food are a draw at this inn. Very popular during the Aldeburgh Festival *(see p63)*.

Snettisham: *Rose & Crown*
Off A149 nr Heacham, Norfolk.
Former coaching inn with three attractive bars and plenty of room for children to play in the garden.

Southwold: *Crown*
High Street, Southwold, Suffolk.
Popular seaside haunt with nautical decor and oak panelling. Excellent food and Adnam beers *(see p548)*.

STIFFKEY: *Red Lion*
On A149, Norfolk.
Traditional English pub with open
fires in winter and the garden
overlooking the Stiffkey River on
the North Norfolk Coastal Path.

TILLINGHAM: *Cap & Feathers*
South St, Tillingham, Essex.
Smoked meat and fish are on offer
at this 15th-century pub near the
salt marshes. It plays a central role
in village life.

THAMES VALLEY

BARLEY: *Fox & Hounds*
High St, Barley, Herts.
Look for the tall chimney and the
hunting scene sign. Both food and
real ales are excellent. Disabled
visitors welcome.

BROOM: *Cock*
23 High St, Broom, Bedfordshire.
Charming 17th-century inn called
"the pub with no bar" (place your
orders at the hatch, and the beer
comes straight from the cellar
casks).

BURFORD: *Lamb*
Sheep St, Burford, Oxon.
This picture-postcard Cotswolds
inn has roses round the door and
mullioned windows. Food is good,
as is the service and atmosphere.

FAWLEY: *Walnut Tree*
Off B4155 nr Henley, Buckinghamshire.
A splendid base for enjoying the
Chilterns. You can even hitch
your horse up in the car park.

GREAT TEW: *Falkland Arms*
Off B4022 nr Chipping Norton, Oxon.
This partly thatched and creeper-
covered inn is in an idyllic corner
of rural England. It is delightfully
straightforward and simply decorated, with mugs and jugs and
gleaming horsebrasses.

OXFORD: *Turf Tavern*
Bath Pl, St Helen's Passage, Oxford.
Tiny pub in the heart of the old
collegiate quarter gives you an
idea of cloistered quadrangles. Sit
outside in fine weather.

WATTON-ON-STONE:
George & Dragon
High St, Watton-on-Stone, Herts.
Attractive pink building dating
back to 1603. Smart but also welcoming; plenty of locals use it, and
there are newspapers to read.

WEST ILSLEY: *Harrow*
Off A34 nr Newbury, Berkshire.
A stylish, white, tiled inn by the
village pond, catering for walkers
and racing folk. Up-market food.

WESSEX

ABBOTSBURY: *Ilchester Arms*
Market St, Abbotsbury, Dorset.
The pub is a main feature of this
honey-coloured village near Chesil
Beach. Warm, rambling rooms are
smartly done up with prints. The
restaurant has a conservatory
extension.

BATHFORD: *Crown*
2 Bathford Hill, Bathford, Avon.
This hilly village has enjoyed its
namesake hostelry since its 18th-
century heyday. Now it is stylish
inside, with ambitious food.

CROSCOMBE: *Bull Terrier*
On A371 nr Wells, Somerset.
One of Somerset's oldest pubs
(originally a priory), this inn is
much loved for good food, and
has welcoming service. Try the
Bull Terrier best bitter, and the walk
to the Bishop's Palace at Wells.

FORD: *White Hart*
On A420 nr Chippenham, Wiltshire.
A delightful trout-stream setting
adds a lot to this lovely 16th-
century pub-hotel. It is very
popular in summer. Good walks
nearby.

NORTON ST PHILIP: *George*
On A366, Somerset.
This famous old pub sheltered the
Duke of Monmouth before the
Battle of Sedgemoor. It is a
splendid half-timbered building
with good food and an ancient
galleried courtyard.

SALISBURY: *Haunch of Venison*
1 Minster St, Salisbury, Wiltshire.
Once the church house for St
Thomas's, this ancient pub dates
back 650 years. The severed,
mummified hand of an 18th-
century card-player is on display
among more cheerful clutter in its
genuinely antique interior.

STANTON WICK:
Carpenters Arms
Off A368, Avon.
A row of pretty converted miners'
cottages contain this welcoming
place with log fires. Excellent food
and occasional live music are
major attractions.

DEVON AND
CORNWALL

BROADHEMBURY: *Drewe Arms*
Off A373, Devon.
Fresh fish is one reason to come
to this thatched village pub, but
the West Country ales, garden and
atmosphere add to its appeal.

DARTMOUTH: *Cherub*
13 High St, Dartmouth, Devon.
Dartmouth's oldest building,
dating from 1380 and once a
wool-merchant's house. Local fish
prominent on the menu.

KNOWSTONE: *Masons Arms*
Off A361 nr South Molton, Devon.
One of Devon's favourite inns,
with plenty of local life and welcoming hosts. The rustic decor
includes farm tools. The big
fireplace has a bread oven.
Good bar food.

LYDFORD: *Castle Inn*
Off A386, Devon.
Pretty, pink-washed Tudor inn by
a ruined castle and scenic river
gorge. Staff are friendly, food is
imaginative, and there's lots of
historic interest. Good value rooms
(see p554).

MYLOR BRIDGE: *Pandora*
Off A39 nr Penryn, Cornwall.
Medieval thatched pub by the
waterside. Popular with boating
folk and crowded in summer.
Bags of atmosphere.

PORT ISAAC:
Port Gaverne Inn
Off B3314 nr Pendoggett, Cornwall.
Gorgeous seafront setting. A 17th-
century building with slate floors,
panelling and maritime decor.
Excellent wine list. Good rooms
available.

TREGADILLETT: *Eliot Arms*
Off A30 nr Launceston, Cornwall.
Cluttered with horsebrasses, old
postcards, prints, books and china,
and a curious collection of clocks.

THE HEART OF
ENGLAND

ALDERMINSTER: *Bell*
On A34 nr Stratford-upon-Avon,
Warwickshire.
Coaching inn conveniently near
Stratford. A civilized place to stop
for a meal with well-kept beers.
Good wines too.

For key to symbols see back flap

BICKLEY MOSS:
Cholmondeley Arms
On A49, Cholmondeley, Cheshire.
Food draws the crowds to this
Victorian school room pub near
the castle grounds. Lots of period
interest inside. 🚶 🍴 🏠

BLOCKLEY: *Crown*
High St, Blockley, Gloucestershire.
Smart Elizabethan pub in a
gorgeous Cotswolds village. The
food and courtyard gardens are
a great draw. 🍴 🏠

BRETFORTON: *Fleece*
The Cross, Bretforton,
Hereford & Worcester.
Astonishing medieval house
owned by the National Trust, first
licensed in 1848. A living museum
of rural antiquities such as dough-
proving tables and cheese moulds.
Food is simple, but beers are
excellent. Lots of community
gatherings for Morris dancing.
🚶 🍴 🏠 🥾

CAULDON: *Yew Tree*
Off A523 nr Ashbourne, Staffs.
An extraordinary collection of
musical machines is on display
(working polyphones, pianolas,
symphonions), along with many
other fascinating bygones. The
interior is homely, with battered
furnishings and traditional pub
games. Simple snacks and beers.
🚶 🥾 🎵

TUTBURY: *Dog & Partridge*
On A50 nr Burton-on-Trent, Staffs.
Imposing Tudor coaching inn,
agreeably modernized into bars
and family-oriented eating areas.
Pleasant service. 🚶 🍴 🏠 🎵 🥾

WENLOCK EDGE:
Wenlock Edge Inn
Hilltop, Much Wenlock, Shropshire.
There's a wood-burning stove and
friendly bar owner; Monday night
is story night. Good walks nearby
and rooms available. 🚶 🍴 🏠

BIRCHOVER: *Druid Inn*
Main St, Birchover, Derbyshire.
Creeper-covered village pub with
a large menu of good fresh food.
Excellent walking centre with Row
Tor Rocks (allegedly a place of
Druid rituals) and Stanton Moor
nearby. 🚶 🍴 🏠

FOTHERINGHAY: *Falcon*
Main St, Fotheringhay, Northants.
A splendid pub, now modernized
to serve a range of excellent food.
The public bar keeps its original
character and local clientele.
🚶 🍴 🏠 🥾

GLOOSTON: *Old Barn*
Andrews Lane, Glooston, Leicestershire.
Sixteenth-century inn with
tastefully renovated interior and
several cosy rooms. Better-than-
average food and hand-pumped
ales. Rooms available. 🚶 🍴 🏠

MONSAL HEAD:
Monsal Head Hotel
On B6465, Derbyshire.
Former stable block with horsy
decor. Magnificent view of the
steep Wye valley from the hotel
lounge; good walks all round.
🚶 🍴 🏠 🥾

NOTTINGHAM:
Olde Trip to Jerusalem
Brewhouse Yard, Nottingham.
Unique pub built into sandstone
caverns once used as a meeting
place for crusaders. One of the
oldest in Britain. 🍴 🏠 🥾

STAMFORD: *George*
71 High St, Stamford, Lincolnshire.
Splendid old coaching inn with
vestiges of a Norman pilgrim hos-
pice. Now very elegant, it offers
an excellent range of food with
Italian wines. Pretty cobbled courtyard and croquet lawn. 🚶 🍴 🏠

UPTON: *Cross Keys*
Main St, Upton, Nottinghamshire.
Beamed pub with hanging baskets
and pictures. Good bar food with
fresh fish. The restaurant is in the
old dovecote. 🚶 🍴 🏠 🥾 🎵

CARTMEL FELL: *Mason's Arms*
Off A5074 at Bowland Bridge sign,
Cumbria.
Lively, characterful pub with an
immense range of bottled beers,
real ales, cider and country wines.
Good walks nearby. 🚶 🍴 🏠 🥾

ELTERWATER: *Britannia Inn*
Off A593 nr Ambleside, Cumbria.
Unadorned rustic interior and
open fires in the Langdale valley.
An excellent walking or touring
base with rooms. 🚶 🍴 🏠 🥾

GARSTANG: *Th'Owd Tithebarn*
Off Church St, Garstang, Lancashire.
A converted barn by the canal
with rustic decor. You may see
Morris dancing here. 🚶 🍴

LANGDALE:
Old Dungeon Ghyll
On B5343, Langdale, Cumbria.
Dramatic setting by the waterfall
in the Langdale Pikes. A walking
and climbing base with rooms,
plain but cosy. 🚶 🍴 🏠 🥾 🎵

LIVERPOOL: *Philharmonic*
36 Hope St, Liverpool.
One of the most characterful
Merseyside haunts, a Victorian
setting with plasterwork, stained
glass and mahogany. 🍴

MANCHESTER: *Lass o' Gowrie*
36 Charles St, Manchester.
Popular student dive with a gaslit
bar and its own brewery in the
cellar. Lively at weekends. 🚶 🍴

NEAR SAWREY:
Tower Bank Arms
B5285, Near Sawrey, Cumbria.
This pretty village is a mecca for
Beatrix Potter fans. The pub backs
on to her house, Hill Top. Well-
preserved interior. 🚶 🍴 🏠 🥾

ASKRIGG: *Kings Arms*
Off A684 nr Bainbridge, N Yorks.
The rustic interior is used as the
set in a TV series. Good bar food,
wines and beers are other reasons
to find it. 🚶 🍴 🏠

COXWOLD: *Fauconberg Arms*
Coxwold, N Yorks.
"Olde worlde" pub with antique
oak settles and Windsor armchairs
to sit on, and plenty of beer, wine,
and good food. 🚶 🍴 🏠 🥾

FLAMBOROUGH: *Seabirds*
On B1255, Flamborough, Humbs.
The white chalk cliffs nearby are a
marvellous place for birdwatching.
Interesting interior. The fish is the
highlight of the menu. 🚶 🍴 🏠

GOATHLAND: *Mallyan Spout*
Off A169, Goathland, N Yorks.
Traditional moorland inn with a
relaxing air and good food. The
open fires make it popular with
walkers. Good rooms. 🚶 🍴 🏠

HULL: *Olde White Harte*
Off 25 Silver St, Hull, Humbs.
This ancient tavern lies behind a
modern "White Hart". The interior
sports inglenook fireplaces and
copper-topped bar. 🚶 🍴 🏠 🥾

LOW CATTON: *Gold Cup*
Off A166 at Stamford Bridge, Humbs.
The farm animals around add an
authentic touch to this rural pub
with comfortable, relaxing bars
and good food. 🚶 🏠 🍴 🥾

MOULTON: *Black Bull*
Off A1 nr Scotch Corner, N Yorks.
This pleasant old place puts
masses of energy into the food,
bar snacks and good wines. The
atmosphere is upmarket. 🍴 🏠

NORTHUMBRIA

BLANCHLAND: *Lord Crewe Arms*
Blanchland, Northumb.
Moorland inn with priests' holes, 13th-century fireplaces and ghosts. Popular with walkers; good food and rooms *(see p563)*. 🚶 🍴 🛏 🚲

CRASTER: *Jolly Fisherman*
Off B1339 nr Alnwick, Northumb.
Unassuming local pub with beautiful sea views. Home-made crab soup and kipper pâté are a speciality. Excellent cliff-top walks. 🚶 🍴 🛏 🚲

GRETA BRIDGE: *Morritt Arms*
Off A66 nr Scotch Corner, Co Durham.
A fine stone coaching inn with a splendid, spacious interior with oak settles. Attractive riverside setting. 🚶 🍴 🛏 🚲

NEW YORK: *Shiremoor House Farm*
Off A191, New York, Tyne & Wear.
A skilful conversion from some derelict farm buildings, it is now comfortable and stylish. Has interesting food, and families welcome. 🚶 🍴 🛏 🚲

NEWCASTLE UPON TYNE: *Crown Posada*
31 The Side, Newcastle upon Tyne.
A Victorian pub with an ornate interior of gilt mirrors and stained glass. It is a city pub for drinkers, so no children are allowed.

SEAHOUSES: *Olde Ship*
On B1340, Seahouses, Northumb.
Maritime curiosities festoon this harbour-front inn. From the window you can see the Farne Islands. Good coastal walks. 🚶 🍴 🛏

NORTH WALES

BEAUMARIS: *Olde Bulls Head*
Castle St, Beaumaris, Anglesey.
A 500-year-old building with fascinating details inside including a 17th-century water clock, cutlasses and a witch's ducking stool. 🚶 🍴 🚲

BODFARI: *Dinorben Arms*
Off A541, Bodfari, Denbighshire.
Hillside pub with excellent bar food, lots of whiskies and a pleasant range of terraces for admiring the views. 🚶 🍴 🛏 🚲

CAPEL CURIG: *Bryn Tyrch Hotel*
On A5 nr Betws-y-Coed, A & C.
Popular with walkers and climbers exploring the Snowdonia National Park. Serves vegetarian bar food. 🚶 🍴 🛏 🚲

GLANWYDDEN: *Queen's Head*
Off B5115, The Glanwydden, A & C.
Excellent pub food is a major draw at this village pub. It can get crowded in season. 🚶 🍴 🛏

MAENTWROG: *Grapes*
On A496, Maentwrog, A & C.
Coaching inn with lovely views and a walled garden. Much of the furniture was salvaged from disused chapels. 🚶 🍴 🛏

SOUTH AND MID-WALES

ABERYSTWYTH: *Halfway Inn*
On A4120, Pisgah, Cardiganshire.
Rheidol Valley pub where you can tap your ale from the cask. Events include sheep-shearing contests. Comfy rooms. 🚶 🍴 🛏 🚲 🎵

CRICKHOWELL: *Bear*
Brecon Rd, Crickhowell, Powys.
Old inn with splendid food and excellent range of drinks. Period features and interesting decor. Bedrooms available. 🚶 🍴 🛏

EAST ABERTHAW: *Blue Anchor*
On B4265, East Aberthaw, V of Glam.
Charming thatched pub with low-ceilinged, intimate warren-like rooms and open fires. Estuary walks. 🚶 🍴 🛏 🚲

HAY-ON-WYE: *Old Black Lion*
26 Lion St, Hay-on-Wye, Powys.
A 13th-century inn with ambitious restaurant food. Lots of local sporting activities (fishing, riding, golf), plus bookshops. 🚶 🍴 🛏

NEVERN: *Trewern Arms*
On B4582, Nevern, Pembrokeshire.
Appealing riverside inn in a pretty village. The slate-floored bar is crammed with agricultural and domestic bygones. 🚶 🍴 🛏 🚲

PENALLT: *Boat Inn*
Long Lane, Penallt, Monmouthshire.
A mecca for music and ale right on the border; drinks are served in Wales. Disused railway cycle tracks and canoeing. 🚶 🍴 🛏 🎵

THE LOWLANDS

EDINBURGH: *Bow Bar*
80 West Bow, Edinburgh.
Bar of mahogany and mirrorglass, with malts and real ales. No children, games or music.

EDINBURGH: *Cafe Royal Circle Bar*
West Register St, Edinburgh.
Refurbished in Victorian style – tiled portraits of Scottish worthies, leather seating and chandeliers. Scottish ales and simple food.

ELIE: *Ship Inn*
The Harbour, Elie, Fife.
Atmospheric quayside pub with nautical decor and attractive views. Summer barbecues are a feature. 🚶 🍴 🛏

GLASGOW: *Horseshoe*
17–19 Drury St, Glasgow.
Busy Victorian pub with a long bar and plenty of period features. Good value bar snacks. Karaoke in the evenings. 🚶 🍴 🎵 🚲

ISLE OF WHITHORN: *Steam Packet*
Isle of Whithorn, Dumfries & Galloway.
Superb setting on a lovely harbour scene. Pleasant eating areas and real ales. Boat trips from the harbour. 🚶 🍴 🛏 🎵

THE HIGHLANDS AND ISLANDS

APPLECROSS: *Applecross Inn*
Shore St, Applecross, Wester Ross, Highland.
Spectacularly located beyond Britain's highest mountain pass, this pub overlooks Skye. Local seafood is served, and there is music some evenings. 🚶 🍴 🛏 🚲 🎵

DUNDEE: *Fishermans Tavern*
12 Fort St, Broughty Ferry, Tayside.
Award-winning real ales and lots of malts too. Good seafront and Tay rail bridge views. Rooms available. 🚶 🍴 🛏 🚲 🎵

ISLE OF SKYE: *Tigh Osda Eilean Iarmain*
Off A851, Isle Ornsay, Isle of Skye.
Welcoming hotel bar. Lots of malts and good bar food. Gorgeous setting. 🚶 🍴 🎵

LOCH LOMOND: *The Byre Inn*
A821, Brig o'Turk, Central.
This used to be a cowshed. Now it's a comfortable place on the edge of a forest park, with excellent food. 🚶 🍴 🛏

PORTSOY: *The Shore Inn*
The Old Harbour, Portsoy, Banffshire.
A 300-year-old seafaring inn nestling in a picturesque harbour. Traditional cask ale and a real open fire. 🚶 🍴 🚲 🎵

ULLAPOOL: *Ferry Boat*
Shore St, Ullapool, Highland.
Good whiskies and bar lunches, and fine views over the harbour. A two-roomed bar with a coal fire and big windows. 🚶 🍴 🎵

For key to symbols see back flap

SURVIVAL
GUIDE

PRACTICAL INFORMATION

ILLIONS ANNUALLY seek out what the British often take for granted – the country's ancient history, colourful pageantry, and spectacularly varied countryside. The range of facilities on offer to visitors in Britain has expanded and improved considerably over the last few years. To enjoy Britain fully it is best to know something about the nuts and bolts of British life: when to visit, how to get around, where to find information and what to do if things go wrong. Whether

A mounted sentry, London

or not you find Britain an expensive country will depend a lot on the exchange rate between the pound and your own currency. Prices vary within Britain; regional differences in some items are very noticeable. London, not surprisingly, is the most expensive. The knock-on effect extends to most of southern England, Britain's most affluent region. Entertainment, food, hotels, transport and consumer items in shops are generally cheaper in other parts of the country.

Weymouth beach, Dorset, on a busy public holiday weekend

WHEN TO VISIT

BRITAIN'S TEMPERATE maritime climate does not produce many temperature extremes *(see p68)*. There are many fine days but it is impossible to predict rain or shine reliably in any season. Weather patterns shift constantly, and the climate can differ widely in places only a short distance apart. The southeast is generally drier than elsewhere. But wherever you are going be sure to pack a mix of warm and cool clothes and an umbrella. Always get an up-to-date weather forecast before you set off on foot to remote mountain areas or moorland. Walkers can be surprised by the weather, and the Mountain Rescue services are often called out due to

A sign for the Mountain Rescue

unexpectedly severe conditions. Weather reports are given on television and radio, in newspapers, or by phone services *(see p637)*.

Britain's towns and cities are all-year destinations, but many attractions open only between Easter and October. Some hotels are crammed at Christmas and New Year. The main family holiday months, July and August, and public holidays *(see p65)* are always busy. Spring and autumn offer a compromise between some good weather and a relative lack of crowds. The information at the beginning of each attraction listed in this guide gives opening days.

INSURANCE

IT IS SENSIBLE to take out travel insurance to cover cancellation or curtailment of your holiday, theft or loss of money and possessions, and the cost of any medical treatment *(see p620)*. It is better to arrange this in advance, although you can organize it once on your trip if necessary. If your country has a reciprocal medical arrangement with Britain (for example Australia, New Zealand and the EU), you can obtain free treatment under the National Health Service, but there are a number of forms to fill in. Certain benefits covered by medical insurance will not be included. North American and

Canadian health plans or student identity cards may give you some protection against costs, but check the small print. If you want to drive a car in Britain, it is illegal to drive without third-party insurance and it is advisable to take out fully comprehensive insurance.

ADVANCE BOOKING

OUT OF SEASON, you should have few problems booking accommodation or transport at short notice, but in the high season, if you have set your heart on a popular West End show, luxury hotel, well-known restaurant, or specific flight or tour, always try to book ahead. Contact the **British Tourist Authority** (BTA) in your country, or a travel agent for advice and information.

TOURIST INFORMATION

TOURIST INFORMATION is available in many towns and public places, including airports, main rail and coach stations and at some places of historical interest. These bureaus will be able to help you on almost anything in their area. Look out for the tourist information symbol, which can indicate anything from a large and busy central

The most common English tourist information sign

◁ **Fishing boats in Scarborough port, North Yorkshire**

office to a simple kiosk or even an information board in a parking area.

Free leaflets are generally offered but a charge may be made for more detailed maps and booklets. Most tourist offices can suggest guided walks, places of interest and nearly all will reserve accommodation for you on request. During the busy holiday periods it is worth asking about the *Book-a-bed-ahead* scheme to places you intend to visit. Tourist office addresses and phone numbers are listed wherever possible in this guide. The **BTA's** monthly magazine *In Britain*, which is available from tourist offices, contains articles about worthwhile places to visit and also includes a useful events diary.

BTA's magazine

DISABLED TRAVELLERS

THE FACILITIES on offer for disabled visitors to Britain are steadily improving: recently designed or newly renovated buildings and public spaces now offer lifts and ramps for wheelchair access (information given in the headings for each entry in this book); specially designed toilets; grab rails, and for the hearing impaired, earphones. Given advance notice, British Rail *(see p638)*, ferry or bus

staff will help any disabled passengers. Ask a travel agent about the Disabled Persons Railcard, which entitles you to discounted rail fares. Many banks, theatres and museums can now provide aids for the visually or hearing impaired. Specialist tour operators, such as **Holiday Care Service**, cater for the physically handicapped visitor. If renting a car, Hertz offers hand-controlled vehicles for hire without any extra cost *(see p637)*. For permission to use any of the disabled parking spaces, you need to display a special sign in your car. For more general information contact **RADAR** or **Mobility International**.

One of the best series for disabled travellers is *Access* by Pauline Hephaistos, published by Survey Projects. You could also try *Holidays in the British Isles: a Guide for Disabled People* (RADAR), and *The World Wheelchair Traveller* by Ann Tyrrell and Susan Abbott (AA).

RADAR
☎ 020-7250 3222.

Mobility International
North America
☎ (503) 343 1284.

Holiday Care Service
☎ 01293 774 535.

DIRECTORY

INTERNATIONAL TOURIST INFORMATION

BTA Australia
210 Clarence St, 4th Floor,
Sydney, NSW 2000.
☎ 02/ 267 4555.

BTA Canada
111 Avenue Rd, Suite 450,
Toronto, Ontario
M5R 3J8.
☎ 905 405 1720.

BTA Ireland
18 College Green,
Dublin 2
☎ 01 670 8000.

REGIONAL TOURIST BOARDS

Britain
☎ 020-8846 9000.

Cumbria
☎ 01539 444444.

East of England
☎ 01473 822922.

The Heart of England
☎ 01905 763436.

London
☎ 020-7932 2000.

Northumbria
☎ 0191 375 3000.

Northwest
☎ 01942 821222.

Scotland
☎ 0131 332 2433.

Southeast
☎ 01892 540766.

Southern
☎ 02380 625400.

Wales
☎ 01222 499 909.

West Country
☎ 01392 360050.

Yorkshire and the Humber region
☎ 01904 707961.

Lorna Doone Cottage and National Trust Information Centre, Somerset

A visit to HMS Victory *(p155)*

TRAVELLING WITH CHILDREN

BRITAIN IS NOT the easiest or most welcoming place for young children, but things are slowly changing.

Peak holiday times – Easter, July and August – and school holidays have most to offer in the way of entertainment for children. Many places have something child-centred going on at Christmas too, particularly pantomimes. Discounts for children, or family tickets, are now widely available for travel, theatre shows and other entertainments.

Choose accommodation that welcomes children, or opt for self-catering solutions with hard-wearing furnishings and room in which to run around. Many hotels now provide baby-sitting or baby-listening services, and may offer reductions or free accommodation for very young children *(see pp536–73)*.

Restaurants are becoming less child-phobic than they used to be and many now provide highchairs and special child menus *(see pp574–607)*. Italian eateries are often the most friendly and informal, but even the British pub, once resolutely child-free, is now relenting with beer gardens and family rooms. Under-18s are not permitted near the bars and must not buy or consume alcohol. The annual publication *Family Welcome* (HarperCollins) is available from newsagents and lists those places where children are made welcome.

PUBLIC TOILETS

ALTHOUGH MANY older-style supervised public toilets still exist, these have largely been replaced by the modern free-standing, coin-operated "Superloos". Young children should never use these toilets on their own.

STUDENT TRAVELLERS

FULL-TIME STUDENTS who have an International Student Identity Card (ISIC), are often entitled to discounts on things like travel, sports facilities and entrance fees. North American students can also get medical cover but it may be very basic *(see p620)*. If you don't have an ISIC, they are available from **STA Travel**, or the **National Union of Students**.

An **International Youth Hostel Federation** card enables you to stay in Britain's hundreds of youth hostels. Inexpensive accommodation is also available (out of term) at many of the university halls of residence – such as the **University of London** – a good way of staying in city centres on a tight

Great British Heritage Pass

budget. If you are exploring the wilder regions of Britain, sleeping quarters can be found in camping barns (dormitory-style bunkhouses) which, though spartan, cost very little. For information on working in Britain, contact **BUNAC**.

BUSINESS HOURS

MANY BUSINESSES and shops are closed on Sundays, though trading is now legal. Monday to Friday hours are generally 9 or 10am to 5 or 5:30pm, but shop hours can vary, with late shopping one evening a week, lunch-time or even half-day closing – usually a Wednesday.

Museums in London often open later at weekends but those outside the capital may have more inflexible hours, sometimes closing during the morning, or for one day a week – often on Mondays.

On public holidays, known as bank holidays in Britain, banks, offices, most shops, restaurants and attractions will generally close.

ADMISSION CHARGES

THESE VARY WIDELY from a nominal 50p to over £10 for the popular attractions, although moves are afoot to make more museums free to enter. Museums now combine entertainment with education, and are livelier than they ever used to be. Alongside this move, however, is a corresponding rise in admission charges. But reductions are often available for groups, senior citizens, children or students (proof of identity will be required). North American citizens may buy

The privately owned, admission-charging, Hever Castle *(see p175)*

A Cotswold church, one of hundreds of parish churches open to the public free of charge

a Great British Heritage Pass, which gives access to over 600 sights, available from travel agents and British Airways offices *(see p634).* A few local authority museums and art galleries are free, but donations are always welcome, and are sometimes requested in ways that are hard to refuse. Other sights are in private hands, run either as a commercial venture or on a charitable basis, and in some cases, even as a personal hobby. Stately homes open to the public may still belong to the gentry who have lived there for centuries; a charge is made to defray the enormous costs of upkeep. Many of these beautiful houses have added safari parks or garden centres to encourage and attract more visitors, such as Woburn Abbey *(see p216).*

Britain's thousands of small parish churches are among the country's greatest architectural treasures. None of the churches charge an entrance fee, although some, sadly, are locked because of vandalism.

Increasingly, many of the great cathedrals expect a donation from visitors who are not attending services.

Information leaflets, National Trust

ENGLISH HERITAGE AND THE NATIONAL TRUST

MANY OF BRITAIN'S historic buildings, parks, gardens, and vast tracts of countryside and coastline are cared for by **English Heritage** (EH), the **National Trust** (NT) or the **National Trust for Scotland** (NTS). We identify NT and NTS properties at the beginning of each entry. Entrance fees are often high, so if you wish to visit several stately homes it may be worth taking out annual membership, which allows free access thereafter to any NT or NTS property (remember many are closed in winter).

Many of the NT's properties are "listed". These are buildings or sites that are recognized as having special architectural or historical interest and therefore fully protected from alterations and demolition.

ENGLISH HERITAGE

The sign and symbol of English Heritage

USEFUL PUBLICATIONS

BOTH THE REGIONAL and national tourist boards produce comprehensive lists of local attractions and registered accommodation. For route planning, excellent, clear, large-format motoring atlases are produced by the RAC and AA *(see p636)*. For rural exploration, *Ordinance Survey* maps are ideal.

MEDIA

BRITISH NATIONAL newspapers fall into two categories: broadsheets – quality papers, such as *The Times* or *The Guardian* – and tabloids, heavy on gossip, such as *The Sun* or *The Daily Mirror*.

The Sunday newspapers are more expensive than dailies but are packed with supplements of all kinds, including sections on the arts, motoring, restaurants, entertainment, travel, listings and reviews.

Specialist periodicals are available from newsagents on just about every topic from hamster-keeping to hi-fi. For a more in-depth analysis of current events buy *The Economist, New Statesman & Society* or *The Spectator,* while *Private Eye* cocks a satirical snook at public figures. There are a few foreign magazines and newspapers available in large towns, often at main railway stations, but mostly in London. One of the most popular is the *International Herald Tribune,* which is available on the day of issue.

Television is undergoing an upheaval in Britain as satellite and cable networks invade the airwaves. Still more influential,

Some of Britain's national newspapers

A local newsagent and sub-post office at Arisaig, Scotland

however, is the state-run BBC (British Broadcasting Corporation), which operates two TV channels and maintains its reputation for producing some of the best television in the world without commercial breaks. The BBC's three commercial rivals are ITV, Channel Four and Channel 5, the first tending toward popular soap operas and gameshows, Channel Four catering for more minority tastes (art films and offbeat documentaries), and the last relying heavily on US imports and TV movies.

There are also regional variations throughout Britain. The BBC has a number of radio stations, ranging from pop music (Radio One) to the middlebrow Radio Four. There are many local commercial radio stations.

Full TV and radio schedules are listed in daily newspapers and several listings magazines; one of the best is the *Radio Times,* a weekly publication found in most newsagents.

SMOKING

IT IS NOW forbidden to smoke in many public places in Britain. These include most public transport systems, taxis, some British Rail stations, theatres and cinemas. The exception to the anti-smoking trend is pubs. ASH (Action on Smoking and Health) can give you advice on smoke-free venues (020-7935 3519).

WORKING RESTRICTIONS

RESIDENTS OF THE EU can work in Britain with no permit, while Commonwealth citizens under the age of 27 may work part-time for up to two years in the UK. North American students can get a blue card through their university, which enables them to work for up to six months – get this before arrival in Britain. BUNAC *(see p617)* is a student club which will organize exchange schemes for students to work abroad.

ELECTRICITY

THE VOLTAGE IN Britain is 220/240 AC, 50 Hz. Electrical plugs have three square pins and take fuses of 3, 5 and 13 amps. Visitors will need an adaptor for North American or continental appliances which have been bought from home, such as portable computers, hairdriers and tape recorders. Most hotels will have two-pronged European-style sockets for shavers only.

Standard British three-pin plug

Clock, the Old Royal Observatory, Greenwich *(see p131)*

TIME

BRITAIN IS ON Greenwich Mean Time (GMT) during the winter months, five hours ahead of Eastern Standard Time and ten hours behind Sydney. From the middle of March to October, the clocks go forward one hour to British Summer Time (equivalent to Central European Time). To check the correct time, you can dial 123 to contact the Speaking Clock service.

CUSTOMS AND IMMIGRATION

A VALID PASSPORT is needed to enter Britain. Visitors from the European Union (EU), the United States, Canada, New Zealand and Australia do not require visas to enter the country. Nor are inoculations or vaccinations necessary. When you arrive at any British air or seaport you will find separate queues at immigration control – one for European Union nationals, and several others for everyone else. As a result of Britain's membership of the European Union, anyone who arrives in Britain from a member country can pass through a blue channel – but random checks are still being made to detect entry of any prohibited goods, particularly drugs, indecent material and weapons. Never, under any circumstances, carry luggage or parcels through customs for someone else.

Highland malt

Travellers entering from outside the EU still have to pass through customs channels. Go through the green channel if you have nothing to declare over the customs allowances for overseas visitors, and the red channel if you have goods to declare. If you are unsure of importation restrictions go through the red channel.

Limits on the quantities of alcohol are: two litres of still table wine plus one litre of alcoholic drink over 22 per cent vol or two litres of alcoholic drink not over 22 per cent vol; for tobacco products the limits are: 200 cigarettes or 50 cigars. You are allowed up to £145 worth of other goods

Green and red customs channels at Heathrow airport (see p634)

including gifts, souvenirs, cider and beer. No live animals may be imported into the UK without a permit as Britain is still free of rabies. Any animals found will be impounded and may be destroyed. Non-EU residents can obtain a VAT refund on goods bought in Britain (see p626).

HM Customs and Excise

Thomas Paine House, Angel Square, Torrens St, London EC1.
📞 020-7865 3000.
Contact for information regarding import or export restrictions.

The mosque in Regent's Park (see p105), London

RELIGIOUS ORGANIZATIONS

Baptist
London Baptist Association, 235 Shaftsbury Avenue, London WC2.
📞 020-8980 6818.

Buddhist
Buddhist Society, 58 Eccleston Sq, London SW1.
📞 020-7834 5858.

Church of England
Great Smith St, London SW1.
📞 020-7898 1000.

Evangelical Alliance
Whitefield Hse, 186 Kennington Park Rd, London SE11.
📞 020-7207 2100.

Jewish
Liberal Jewish Synagogue, 28 St John's Wood Rd, London NW8.
📞 020-7286 5181.

United Synagogue (Orthodox), Adler House, 135 High Rd, North Finchley, London, N12.
📞 020-8343 8989.

Moslem
Islamic Cultural Centre, 146 Park Rd, London NW8.
📞 020-7724 3363.

Quakers
Friends Hse, 173 Euston Rd, London NW1.
📞 020-7663 1000.

Roman Catholic
Westminster Cathedral, Victoria St, London SW1.
📞 020-7798 9055.

EMBASSIES AND CONSULATES

Australian High Commission
Australia Hse, the Strand, London WC2.
📞 020-7379 4334.

Canadian High Commission
Macdonald Hse, 1 Grosvenor Sq, London W1.
📞 020-7258 6600.

New Zealand High Commission
New Zealand Hse, 80 Haymarket, London SW1.
📞 020-7930 8422.

United States Embassy
24 Grosvenor Sq, London W1.
📞 020-7499 9000.

CONVERSION CHART

Britain is officially metricated in line with the rest of Europe, but imperial measures are still in common usage, including road distances (measured in miles). Imperial pints and gallons are 20 per cent larger than US measures.

Imperial to metric
1 inch = 2.5 centimetres
1 foot = 30 centimetres
1 mile = 1.6 kilometres
1 ounce = 28 grams
1 pound = 454 grams
1 pint = 0.6 litres
1 gallon = 4.6 litres

Metric to imperial
1 millimetre = 0.04 inch
1 centimetre = 0.4 inch
1 metre = 3 feet 3 inches
1 kilometre = 0.6 mile
1 gram = 0.04 ounce
1 kilogram = 2.2 pounds

Personal Security and Health

BRITAIN IS A DENSELY POPULATED COUNTRY which, like any other, has its share of social problems. However, it is very unlikely that you will come across any violence. If you do encounter difficulties, never hesitate to contact the police for help. Britain's National Health Service can be relied upon for both emergency and routine treatment. However, you may have to pay if your country has no reciprocal arrangement with Britain.

HOSPITALS AND MEDICAL TREATMENT

ALL VISITORS to Britain are strongly advised to take out medical insurance against the cost of any emergency hospital care, repatriation and specialists' fees, especially for those visitors from outside the European Union (EU). Emergency medical treatment in a British National Health Service (NHS) casualty ward is free, but any kind of additional medical care could prove very expensive.

Residents of the European Union and nationals of some other Commonwealth and European countries are entitled to free medical treatment under the NHS, though the process is bureaucratic. Before travelling, you should obtain a form confirming that your country of origin has adequate reciprocal health arrangements with Britain. But some treatments are not covered and repatriation is not included, so medical insurance is preferable.

If you need to see a dentist while staying in Britain, you will have to pay. The cost varies, depending on your entitlement to NHS treatment, and whether you can find an NHS dentist to treat you. Emergency dental treatment is available in some hospitals, but if you would prefer a private dentist, try looking in the *Yellow Pages (see p622)*.

PHARMACISTS

YOU CAN BUY a wide range of proprietary medicines without prescription from chemists in Britain. Boots is the best-known and largest supplier, with branches in most towns. Many medicines, however, are only available with a doctor's prescription, which you must take to a dispensing chemist or pharmacist. If you are likely to need drugs, either bring your own or get your doctor to write out the generic name of the drug (as opposed to the brand name). If you are entitled to an NHS prescription, you will be charged a standard rate; without

Pharmacy sign

this entitlement you will be charged the full cost of the drug. Remember to ask for a receipt for any insurance claim.

Some pharmacies are open until midnight; for emergencies contact the local hospital. Doctors' surgeries are normally open mornings and early evenings. You can turn up at a hospital casualty department any time. In an emergency, dial 999 for an ambulance.

CRIME

BRITAIN IS NOT a dangerous place for visitors, and it is most unlikely that your stay will be blighted by crime. Practical advice to help you avoid loss or injury is given below. Due to past terrorist attacks, there are occasional security alerts, especially on the Underground, but these are mainly false alarms often due to people accidentally leaving a bag or parcel lying around. Always co-operate with the authorities if your bag has to be searched or if you are asked to evacuate a building.

SUITABLE PRECAUTIONS

TAKE GOOD CARE of your belongings at all times. Make sure your possessions are adequately insured before you arrive. Never leave them unattended in public places.

Keep your valuables well concealed, especially in crowds. In cinemas or theatres, keep handbags on your lap, not on the floor. It is always advisable not to carry too much cash or jewellery with you; leave it in your hotel safe instead. Pickpockets love crowded places like bustling markets, busy shops and all modes of transport during rush-hour.

Female police constable   Traffic police officer   Male police constable

If you are travelling alone at night try and avoid deserted and poorly lit buildings and places such as back streets and car parks. By far the safest way of carrying large amounts of cash around is in traveller's cheques *(see p625)*.

Begging is an increasingly common sight in many British cities, and foreign visitors are frequent targets for hard-luck stories. Requests for money are usually polite; but any abuse should be reported to the police immediately.

WOMEN TRAVELLING ALONE

IT IS NOT UNUSUAL in Great Britain for women to travel unaccompanied, or visit a bar or restaurant with a group of female friends. Nor is it especially dangerous, but caution is advisable in deserted places, especially after dark. Try to avoid using public transport when there is just one other passenger or a group of young men. Summon a licensed taxi *(see p642)* rather than walk through a lonely area at night, especially if you do not know the district very well.

Legally, you cannot carry any offensive weapons around with you in Britain, even for self-defence. This include knives, coshes, guns or teargas, however, personal alarm systems are allowed.

POLICE

THE SIGHT of a traditional British bobby patrolling the streets in a tall hat is now less common than the police patrol car, sometimes with wailing sirens and flashing lights. But the old-fashioned police constable does still exist, particularly in rural areas and in crowded city centres, and continues to be courteous, approachable and helpful.

Unlike in many countries, the police force in Great Britain do not carry guns. If you are lost, the advice to

Police car

Ambulance

Fire engine

ask a policeman or woman still applies. Traffic wardens may also be able to help you with directions.

In a crisis, dial 999 to get the police, fire and ambulance services which are on call 24-hours a day. Calls are free from any public or private phone, but they should only be made in real emergencies. Along the coastal areas of Great Britain this number will also put you in touch with Britain's voluntary coastguard rescue service, the Royal National Lifeboat Institute.

Royal National Lifeboat Institute logo

LOST PROPERTY

IF YOU ARE UNLUCKY enough to lose anything or have anything stolen, go straight to the nearest police station and make a report your loss. If you plan to make a claim on your insurance for any theft, you will need a written report from the local police. All of the main bus or rail stations have lost property offices. Don't leave your valuables on display in your room: hotels usually disclaim all responsibility for valuables not kept in their safe.

CRISIS INFORMATION

Police, Fire and Ambulance services
999. Calls are free (24-hour phoneline).

Accident and Emergency Departments
For your nearest Accident and Emergency unit check in phone directory or contact the police.

Childline
0800 1111. Calls are free for children in need of any help (24-hour phoneline).

Emergency Dental Care
020-7837 3646 (24-hour phoneline).

Rape Crisis Centre
020-7837 1600 (24-hour phoneline).

Samaritans
0845 7909090 (24-hour phoneline for all emotional problems). Look in local telephone directory for nearest branch.

HELPLINES

Alcoholics Anonymous
0845 7697555.

Disabled Helplines
The Disability Helpline.
01302 310123.
Disabled Living Foundation.
020-7289 6111.

Late-opening Chemists
Contact your local police station or hospital for a list.

Lost Property
Contact your local police station.

National Helpline for Drugs
0800 776600.

National Helpline for the Blind
Royal National Institute for the Blind
020-7388 1266.

National Helpline for the Deaf
0808 6080123.

Pregnancy Advice
0345 304030.

Victim Support
0845 3030900 (local offices listed in phone book).

Communications

Modern BT phone box

WITH CONTINUOUSLY IMPROVING telecommunication systems and the spread of e-mail, staying in contact and making plans while travelling has never been easier. The telephone system in Britain is efficient and inexpensive. Charges depend on when, where and for how long you talk. The cheapest time to call is between 6pm and 8am Monday to Friday, and throughout the weekend. Local calls made on public payphones, however, are charged at a fixed rate per minute.

PAYPHONES

YOU CAN PAY for a payphone using coins or a card. Payphones accept 10p, 20p, 50p and £1 pieces, while newer phones also accept £2 coins. The minimum cost of a call is 20p. If you expect a call to be short, use 10p or 20p pieces, as payphones only return unused coins. You may find a phone card more convenient than coins. BT (formerly British Telecom) issues prepaid phone cards for use in BT phone boxes in denominations of up to £20. The BT PhonecardPlus can be used at any phone, including home phones and mobiles. Either slide it into a card phone or call the access number printed on the back and follow the voice prompt.

TELEPHONE DIRECTORIES

DIRECTORIES, SUCH as *Yellow Pages* and *Thomson Local*, list local businesses and services. They can be found at local Post Office branches, libraries and often at your hotel.

USING A CARD PHONE

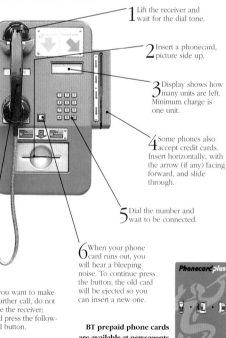

1 Lift the receiver and wait for the dial tone.

2 Insert a phonecard, picture side up.

3 Display shows how many units are left. Minimum charge is one unit.

4 Some phones also accept credit cards. Insert horizontally, with the arrow (if any) facing forward, and slide through.

5 Dial the number and wait to be connected.

6 When your phone card runs out, you will hear a bleeping noise. To continue press the button; the old card will be ejected so you can insert a new one.

7 If you want to make a further call, do not replace the receiver; instead press the follow-on call button.

BT prepaid phone cards are available at newsagents and Post Office outlets

ACCESSING THE INTERNET

MOST CITIES AND towns now have some form of public access to computers and the Internet. Free Internet access is often available at main library branches, although you may have to book a time slot. Internet cafés usually charge by the minute for computer use. Charges tend to build up quickly, especially when including the cost of printed pages. EasyEverything, a chain of massive Internet cafés, has branches in many cities including Edinburgh (58 Rose Street) and London (7 Strand). Internet access is very cheap and is most reasonable during off-peak times.

24-hour Internet access at the Europe-wide chain EasyEverything

Sending a Letter

Red and gold Post Office logo

BESIDES MAIN POST OFFICE branches that offer all the mail services available, there are many Post Office outlets in newsagents, grocery stores and general information centres, particularly in more isolated areas. In many villages the Post Office outlet is also the only shop. Post Office branches are usually open from 9am to 5:30pm Monday to Friday, and until 12:30pm on Saturday. Post boxes – in all shapes and sizes but always red – are found throughout cities, towns and villages.

A Cotswold Post Office outlet

POSTAL SERVICES

STAMPS CAN BE BOUGHT at many outlets, including supermarkets and petrol stations. Hotels often have post boxes at their reception. When writing to a British address always include the postcode, which can be obtained from either the **Royal Mail** enquiry line or website. Letters and postcards can be sent either first or second class within the UK. First-class service is more expensive but quicker, with most letters reaching their destination the following day (except Sunday); second-class mail takes a day or two longer.

Royal Mail
0845 7740740.
www.royalmail.com

POSTE RESTANTE

LARGE URBAN Post Office branches have a *poste restante* service where letters can be sent for collection. To use the service be sure to print the surname (last name) clearly so it will be filed correctly. Send it to *Poste Restante* followed by the address of the Post Office branch. To collect your post you will have to show your passport or other form of identification. Post will be kept for one month. London's main Post Office branch is in William IV Street, WC2. The American Express office at 6 Haymarket, London (see p86) has a *poste restante* service for customers.

POST BOXES

THESE MAY BE either free-standing "pillar boxes" or wall safes, both painted bright red. Some pillar boxes have separate slots, one for overseas and first-class mail, another for second-class mail.

Collections are usually made several times a day during weekdays (less often on Saturdays and Sundays); times are marked on the box.

A rural mailbox, embedded in a stone wall

MAILING ABROAD

Pillar box

AIR LETTERS go by Royal Mail's fast airmail service anywhere in the world and cost the same regardless of destination. On average, it usually takes three days for them to reach cities in Europe, and four to six days for destinations elsewhere. Sending post overseas by surface mail may be more economical, but it can take anywhere up to eight weeks for it to reach its final destination. Royal Mail offers an express airmail service called **Swiftair**. Available from all Post Office branches, mail goes on the first available flight to the country of destination. **Parcelforce Worldwide** offers courier-style services to most international destinations and is comparable in price to **DHL**, **Crossflight**, **Expressair** or **UPS**.

Crossflight
01753 776000.

DHL
08701 100300.

Expressair
020-8897 6568.

Parcelforce Worldwide
0800 224466.

Swiftair
08457 740740.

UPS
08457 877877.

All air letters are 1st class

1st-class stamp   2nd-class stamp

Greetings stamps featuring characters from children's fiction

Banking and Local Currency

VISITORS TO BRITAIN usually find that the high-street banks offer them the best rates of exchange. However, if you do find yourself having to use one of the hundreds of privately-owned bureaux de change that are found at nearly every major airport, rail station and tourist area, care should be taken to check the commission and minimum charges before completing any transaction. Traveller's cheques are by far the safest method of bringing currency to Britain with you.

Lloyds bank with bureau de change facilities

BUREAUX DE CHANGE

SMALL PRIVATE bureaux de change may be more conveniently located and open when banks are closed. But rates of exchange can vary considerably and commission charges can be high, so it may be worth looking around.

The reputable firms such as **Exchange International**, **Thomas Cook**, **American Express** and **Chequepoint** usually offer good exchange facilities and have branches throughout Britain.

British Banks
All these high street banks have branches in most of Britain's towns and cities. Most will also offer exchange facilities, but proof of identity may be required.

BANKS

BANKS GENERALLY offer the best rates of exchange for visitors, though commissions may vary considerably.

Every large town and city in Britain will have a branch of at least one of these five high-street clearing banks – **Barclays**, **Lloyds TSB**, **HSBC**, **National Westminster**, and the **Royal Bank of Scotland**. Many banks have a cash machine from which you can obtain money with a credit card and your personal identification number (PIN); arrange this before you leave home. Some of the most modern machines have easy-to-read computerized instructions in several languages. American Express cards may be used in 24-hour Lloyds and Royal Bank of Scotland cash machines. Once again you will need a PIN number to access your personal account. There is a 2 per cent handling charge for each transaction that you make. If you run out of funds, another way to get money is

Barclays Bank logo

HSBC Bank logo

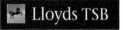

Lloyds TSB Bank logo

National Westminster logo

Royal Bank of Scotland logo

to contact your own bank and ask them to wire the cash to the nearest British bank. You can also ask branches of Thomas Cook or American Express to do this for you. North American visitors can get cash dispatched through **Western Union** to a bank or post office. Take along your passport to claim the money.

Banking hours vary, but the minimum opening times are 9:30am to 3:30pm, Monday to Friday. Many will stay open longer, especially in cities, and some open Saturday mornings. All banks close on Public Holidays *(see p65)*.

CREDIT CARDS

CREDIT AND STORE cards are widely accepted throughout Britain, and you will definitely need a credit card in order to rent a car and usually for hotel bookings. But many smaller shops, markets, guesthouses and cafés may not accept them, so it is always wise to check in advance. Cards that are accepted are usually displayed on the windows of the establishment. The main card used throughout Britain is Visa, but other credit cards include Diners Club, American Express, Access and Mastercard.

You can get cash advances with a credit card (up to your credit limit) at any bank and ATM (cash dispenser) displaying the appropriate card sign. You will be charged the credit card company's interest rate for obtaining cash, which will appear on your statement with the amount advanced when you return home.

Exchange International
℃ *020-7630 1107.*

Thomas Cook
℃ *020-7408 4179.*

American Express
℃ *020-7834 5555.*

Chequepoint
℃ *020-7373 0111.*

Western Union
℃ *0800 833 833.*

CURRENCY AND TRAVELLER'S CHEQUES

BRITAIN'S CURRENCY is the pound sterling (£), which is divided into 100 pence (p). There are no exchange controls in Britain, so you may bring in and take out as much cash as you like. Scotland has its own notes, which, though legal tender throughout Britain, are not always accepted in England and Wales. Traveller's cheques are the safest alternative to carrying large amounts of cash.

A Scottish one pound (£1) bank note

Always keep the receipts from your traveller's cheques separately from the cheques themselves because it makes it easier to obtain a refund if your cheques are lost or stolen. Some high-street banks issue traveller's cheques free of commission to their account holders, but the normal rate is about 1 per cent. When changing money ask for some smaller notes, as these are easier to use.

Bank Notes
English notes are produced in denominations of £5, £10, £20, and £50. Always get small denominations as some shops may refuse the larger notes.

£50 note

£20 note

£10 note

£5 note

Coinage
Coins currently in use are £1, 50p, 20p, 10p, 5p, 2p and 1p (shown here at actual sizes). There are also a few £2 coins in circulation, issued to commemorate special occasions.

2 pounds (£2)   **1 pound (£1)**   **50 pence (50p)**   **20 pence (20p)**

10 pence (10p)   **5 pence (5p)**   **2 pence (2p)**   **1 penny (1p)**

Shopping in Britain

WHILE THE WEST END OF LONDON *(see pp122–3)* is undeniably Britain's most exciting place to shop, many regional centres offer nearly as wide a range of goods. Moreover regional shopping can be less stressful, less expensive, and remarkably varied, with craft studios, farm shops, street markets and factory showrooms adding to the enjoyment of bargain-hunting. Britain is famous for its country clothing: wool, waxed cotton and tweed are all popular along with classic prints such as Liberty or Laura Ashley and tartan. Other particularly British goods include antiques, floral soaps and scents, porcelain, glass and local crafts.

Antiques stall at Bermondsey Market

SHOPPING HOURS

IN GENERAL, you can assume most shops in Britain will open during the week from 9am or 10am, and they will close after 5pm or 6pm. Hours on Saturdays may be shorter. Few town centre shops open on Sundays, unless it is near Christmas. Some stores open late for one evening a week – Thursday in London's West End – while village shops may close at lunch-time, or for one afternoon each week. Market days vary from town to town; some markets *(see pp122–3)* are held on Sundays.

HOW TO PAY

MOST LARGE SHOPS all over the UK will accept well-known credit cards such as Access and VISA. Charge cards such as American Express or Diners Club are acceptable in some places, but Marks & Spencer, markets and some small shops will not take credit cards. Traveller's cheques can

be used in larger stores, though exchange rates for non-sterling cheques may be poor. Take your passport with you for identification. Few places will accept cheques drawn on foreign banks. Cash is still the most popular way to pay for small purchases.

RIGHTS AND REFUNDS

IF SOMETHING YOU BUY is defective, you are entitled to a refund, provided you have kept your receipt as proof of purchase and return the goods in the same condition as when you bought them, and preferably in the same packaging. This may not always apply to sale goods clearly marked as seconds, imperfect, or shopsoiled. Inspect these carefully before you buy. You do not have to accept a credit note in place of a cash refund.

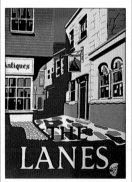

Sign for the Lanes, Brighton *(see p161)*

ANNUAL SALES

TRADITIONALLY, sales take place during January, and in June and July, when nearly every shop cuts prices to get rid of slow-selling or imperfect stock. But you may well find special offers at any time of the year. Some shops begin their winter sales just before Christmas. Department stores and fashion houses have some excellent bargains for keen shoppers; one of the most prestigious sales is at Harrod's *(see p99)*, where queues will usually form long before opening time.

VAT AND TAX-FREE SHOPPING

VALUE ADDED TAX (VAT) is charged on most goods and services sold in Britain – exceptions include food, books and children's clothes. It is usually included in the advertised price. Visitors from outside the European Union who stay less than three months may claim this tax back. Take your passport with you whenever you go

Vivienne Westwood's designer label

shopping. You must complete a form in the shop when you buy your goods and give a copy to the customs authorities when you leave the country. You may have to show your goods as proof of purchase. If you arrange to have the goods shipped from the store, the VAT should be deducted before you pay.

OUT-OF-TOWN SHOPPING CENTRES

THESE LARGE COMPLEXES, built along the lines of North American malls, are rapidly increasing around Britain. The advantages of car access and easy, cheap parking are undeniable, and most centres are accessible by public transport too. The centres usually feature clusters of popular high street stores, with many services on offer such as toilets, cafés, crèches, restaurants and cinemas.

A traditional shop front in Stonegate, York (see p390)

DEPARTMENT STORES

A FEW BIG DEPARTMENT stores, such as Harrod's, are only found in London, but others have provincial branches. John Lewis, for example, has shops in 22 locations. It sells a huge range of fabrics, clothing and household items, combining quality service with good value. Marks & Spencer, with 303 branches through Britain, is even more of a household name, famed for its good-value clothing and pre-prepared food. Debenhams and British Home Stores (BhS) are other well-known general stores with inexpensive clothing and home furnishings. Habitat is a reputable supplier of modern furniture. The sizes of all these stores, and the range of stock they carry, will differ from region to region.

Local Teesdale cheeses

CLOTHES SHOPS

O NCE AGAIN, London has the widest range, from *haute couture* to cheap and cheerful items ready-made. Shopping for clothing in the regions, however, can often be less tiring. Many towns popular with tourists – Oxford, Bath and York for instance – have independently owned clothes shops where you receive a more personal service. Or you could try one of the chain stores in any high street such as Principles or Next for smart, reasonably priced clothes, and Top Shop and Miss Selfridge for younger and cheaper fashions.

SUPERMARKETS AND FOODSHOPS

S UPERMARKETS are a good way to shop for food. The range and quality of items in stock is usually excellent. Several large chains compete for market share and as a result prices are generally lower than smaller shops. Sainsbury, Tesco, Asda, Safeway and Waitrose are some of the national names. However, the smaller town-centre shops such as local bakeries, greengrocers or farm shops, may give you a more interesting choice of fresh regional produce, and more personal service.

SOUVENIR, GIFT AND MUSEUM SHOPS

B UYING PRESENTS is a must for most travellers. Most reputable large stores can arrange freight of high-value

The Mustard Shop (see p187), Norwich

items. If you want to buy things you can carry back in your suitcase, the choice is wide. You can buy attractive, well-made, portable craft items all over the country, especially in areas tourists are likely to visit. For slightly more unusual presents, have a look in museum shops and the gifts available in National Trust (see p25) and English Heritage properties.

SECONDHAND AND ANTIQUE SHOPS

B RITAIN'S LONG HISTORY means there are many interesting artifacts to be found. A visit to any of Britain's stately homes will reveal a national passion for antiques. Most towns will have an antique or bric-a-brac (miscellaneous second-hand items) shop or two. Look for auctions – tourist information centres (see pp614–15) can help you to locate them. You may like to visit a jumble or car boot sale in the hope of picking up a bargain.

Book stall, Hay-on-Wye, Wales (see p447)

MARKETS

L ARGE TOWNS AND CITIES usually have a central covered market which operates most weekdays, selling everything from fresh produce to pots and pans. The information under each town entry in this guide lists market days. Many towns hold weekly markets in the main square. While you browse among the stalls, look out for local fresh produce and the jams and cakes of the Women's Institute stalls.

Entertainment in Britain

LONDON IS WITHOUT DOUBT the entertainment capital of Britain (see pp124–7), but many regional theatres, opera houses and concert halls have varied programmes. Edinburgh, Manchester, Birmingham, Leeds and Bristol in particular have a lot to offer and there are a number of summer arts festivals around the country such as those at Bath and Cheltenham (see pp62–3). Ticket prices are often cheaper outside the capital.

Punch and Judy show

SOURCES OF INFORMATION

IN LONDON, check the listings magazines, such as *Time Out*, or the *Evening Standard*, London's evening newspaper. All of the quality broadsheet newspapers (see p618) provide comprehensive arts reviews and listings of the cultural events and shows throughout the country, with the largest sections at the weekends. Local newspapers, libraries, or tourist offices (see p617) can supply details of regional events. Specialist magazines such as *NME* or *Melody Maker* give up-to-date news of the pop music scene and are available from any newsagent.

THEATRES

BRITAIN HAS AN enduring theatrical tradition dating back to Shakespeare (see pp310–13) and beyond. All over the country, amateurs and professionals tread the boards in purpose-built auditoriums, pubs, clubs and village halls. Productions and performance standards are generally high, and British actors have an international reputation.

London is the place to enjoy theatre at its most varied and glamorous (see p124). The West End alone has more than 50 theatres (see p125) ranging from elaborate Edwardian, upholstered in red plush, to exciting modern buildings such as the National Theatre on the South Bank in London.

In Stratford-upon-Avon, the Royal Shakespeare Company presents a year-round programme of Shakespeare, as well as avant-garde and experimental plays. Bristol also has a long dramatic tradition, the Theatre Royal (see p242) being the oldest working theatre in Britain. Some of the best productions outside the capital can be found at the West Yorkshire Theatre in Leeds, the Royal Exchange in Manchester (see p360) and the Traverse in Edinburgh.

Street entertainer

Open-air theatre ranges from the free street entertainment that is to be found in many city centres, to student performances on the grounds of Cambridge or Oxford colleges or a production at Cornwall's spectacular clifftop amphitheatre, the Minack Theatre (see p262). Every fourth year, York also stages a series of open-air medieval mystery plays called the York Cycle. Perhaps the liveliest theatrical tradition in Britain is the Edinburgh Festival (see p495). Seaside resorts put on summer programmes of lighthearted entertainment, traditionally stand-up comedy.

Ticket availability varies from show to show. You may be able to buy a ticket at the door, especially for a mid-week matinee, but for the more popular West End shows tickets may have to be booked weeks or even months in advance. You can book through agencies and some travel agents, and most hotels will organize theatre tickets for you. Booking fees are often charged. Beware of tickets offered by touts (see p67) – these may be counterfeit. There are no age restrictions in Britain's theatres. It is left to your discretion to decide whether a show is suitable for children.

MUSIC

A DIVERSE musical repertoire can be found in a variety of venues. Church choral music is a great national tradition and many churches and cathedrals host concerts. London, Manchester, Birmingham, Liverpool, Bristol and Bournemouth all have their own excellent orchestras.

Rock, jazz, folk and country-and-western concerts are staged periodically in pubs, clubs and sometimes in outdoor auditoria. Wales has a strong musical tradition which you will come across in many Welsh pubs; northern England is renowned for its booming brass and silver bands; and Scotland, of course, has its famous bag-pipers (see p466).

The Buxton Opera House, the Midlands

The multiplex Warner West End cinema, Leicester Square, London

CINEMAS

THE LATEST FILMS can be seen in any large town. Check the local papers or the tourist office to find out what is on.

Cinemas are having a revival, with luxurious multi-screen cinemas taking over from the local, single-screen cinemas. In larger cities a more diverse range of films is often on offer including more foreign-language productions. These tend to be shown at arts or repertory cinemas. Mainstream English-speaking films are usually shown by the big chains. Age limits apply to certain films. Young children are allowed to see any feature film which is graded with a U (universal) or PG (parental guidance) certificate. Cinema prices vary widely; some are cheaper at off-peak times, such as Mondays or afternoons. For new releases it is advisable to book in advance.

CLUBS

MOST CITIES have some sort of club scene, though London has the most famous venues (see p124). These may feature live music, discos, or DJ or dance performances. Some insist on dress codes or

members only, and most have doormen, or "bouncer". Apart from the major cities, Brighton and Bristol have lively clubs.

DANCE

THIS COVERS a multitude of activities: everything from classical ballet and acid-house parties to traditional English Morris dancing or the Scottish Highland fling, which you may come upon in pubs and villages around the country.

Dance halls are rarer than they were, but ballroom dancing is alive and well. Other dance events you may find are ceilidhs (pronounced kaylee), which is Celtic dancing and music; May Balls often held at universities (invitation only); dinner or tea dances and square dancing.

Birmingham is home to the Birmingham Royal Ballet and is the best place to see performances outside London. Avant-garde contemporary dance is also performed.

GAY

MOST LARGE communities will have some gay meeting places, mostly bars and clubs. You can find out about them from publications such as the free *Pink Paper* or *Gay Times* on sale in some newsagents, and in gay bars and clubs. London's gay life is centred around Soho (see p82) with its many European-style cafés and bars. Outside London, the most active gay scenes are in Manchester and Brighton. Gay Pride is the largest free outdoor festival in Europe.

Three revellers, Gay Pride Festival

CHILDREN

LONDON OFFERS children a positive goldmine of fun, excitement and adventure, though it can be expensive. From the traditional sights to something more unusual such as a discovery centre, London has a wide range of activities,

many interactive, to interest children of all ages. Kidsline, open from 4pm to 6pm, is a London listings service for children (tel 020-7222 8070).

Outside London, activities for children range from nature trails to fun fairs. Your local tourist office or the local library will have information on things to do with children.

Pirate Ship, Chessington World of Adventures, Surrey

THEME PARKS

THEME PARKS in Britain are enjoyed by children of all ages. Alton Towers has conventional rides plus a motor museum, all set in spectacular gardens. Chessington World of Adventures is a huge complex south of London. Based on a zoo, it now includes nine themed areas, such as Calamity Canyon, Transylvania and Circus World. Thorpe Park, in Surrey, is a large watery theme park full of scale model buildings, exciting roller-coaster rides and a peaceful pet farm. Legoland, the latest park, opened in March 1996.

Alton Towers
Alton, Staffordshire.
[01538 702200.

Chessington World of Adventures
Leatherhead Rd, Chessington, Surrey.
[0870 4447777.

Legoland
Winkfield Rd, Windsor, Berkshire.
[0990 040404.

Thorpe Park
Staines Rd, Chertsey, Surrey.
[01932 569393.

Specialist Holidays and Outdoor Activities

BRITAIN OFFERS MANY special interest holidays or courses where you can learn a new sport or skill, practise an activity you enjoy, or simply have fun and meet people. If you prefer less structured activities, there is a variety of sports you can participate in, from walking in Britain's national parks to sailing on the many waterways and skiing in Scotland, or exploring the country on horseback. Another option is volunteer work on a nature or bird reserve, or an archaeological dig or conservation project.

Horse riding on a country bridleway *(see p33)*

SPECIALIST HOLIDAYS

A GREAT ADVANTAGE to these holidays is that you can attend the courses alone but without feeling too solitary. There are hundreds of options: any kind of sport – boating, golf, skiing, riding, tennis; arts and crafts such as painting, pottery, calligraphy, jewellery-making; and educational courses on everything from Shakespeare to ecology.

The English and Scottish Tourist Boards *(see p615)* have lists and pamphlets on some of these activities, and can tell you who to contact for more information. Look out for their publication, **Activity Holidays** (Jarrold), available from some bookshops.

You can book direct with the organizers, or through a travel agent. Introductory courses generally provide you with all the equipment you need plus accommodation and sometimes transport.

Courses are available at all levels of expertise, for all ages. If you are fit and interested in the countryside, you may like to work on a conservation project for a few days. It can be hard work but worthwhile. Contact the tourist board.

WALKING AND CYCLING

WALKING ALLOWS YOU to experience at first hand the spectacular variety of the British landscape, by yourself or with a club. There is a network of long-distance footpaths and shorter trail routes all over Britain *(see pp32–3)*.

Cyclists may use designated cycle routes and bridleways *(see p643)* and the quieter rural roads can be a delight. Choose a flat or hilly one depending on your energy and fitness. Be sure to take spare parts with you.

GOLF AND TENNIS

THERE ARE ABOUT 2,000 golf courses in Britain and many clubs welcome visiting players. Weekends are usually busy. Specialist operators will book packages for you. Green fees vary widely; many clubs offer temporary membership.

You will find tennis courts in every town and many hotels and some clubs offer temporary membership, but courts in summer are in demand. The **Lawn Tennis Association** can provide more information.

Sailing, Cardigan Bay, Welsh coast

BOATING AND SAILING

MESSING ABOUT IN BOATS is a British obsession. You can sail at many places – the Isle of Wight and the south coast are full of pleasure craft. Inland, the network of rivers, lakes and canals can offer a calmer sort of pleasure. Canal-cruising is very popular *(see p641)* and the Norfolk Broads *(see p184)* provides one of the best inland boating experiences (the **Broads Authority** will provide information). Elsewhere, the Thames and the canals slice through lovely landscape. The Lake District *(see pp340–57)* is another area which is popular with boating enthusiasts.

OTHER WATER SPORTS

WITH SO MUCH coastline, Britain is a place for enjoying the water, even if temperatures are low. The best areas for surfing are the

Walkers and rock climbers, Yorkshire Dales National Park *(see pp370–71)*

West Country and South Wales. Windsurfing is also popular, both on the coast and on lakes. Tuition and equipment hire are available at many resorts, and several also offer water-skiing facilities. Most towns and resorts have public swimming pools, many with water tunnels, slides and wave machines. Scuba diving is popular around rocky parts of the West Country.

FISHING

Fishing in the sea and on rivers is Britain's biggest participation sport. Regulations are very strict, so check for

details of rod licences, close seasons and other restrictions at tourist offices or tackle shops. You may have to join a club, or buy a temporary permit. The best game fishing (salmon and trout) is in the West Country, the Northeast, Wales and Scotland.

SPECTATOR SPORTS

Football (soccer) is a passion for a large section of the population. League fixtures are held at many large towns once or twice a week in the season. If you want to see a game, ask at the local tourist office, or check the local papers. Rugby Football also has a good following and games are played in cities such as London, Cardiff and Edinburgh. Cricket is the English national game, and matches are played from April to September on village greens throughout the land. Both flat-racing and steeplechasing are very popular and betting is big business. You can find details of race meetings in most national newspapers.

Paragliding over the South Downs *(see p167)*

ADVENTURE SPORTS

Adventure sports are well-catered for and popular. Among the options are rock-climbing and mountaineering; aeronautical sports and gliding; ice-skating in many major cities and horse riding throughout the country. Although expensive, it is also possible to try go-karting. Facilities for skiing are limited in the UK but there are winter sports facilities at Scottish resorts such as the Cairngorms.

Solitary sea fisherman, England's southeast coast

DIRECTORY

Aircraft Owners and Pilots Association
50A Cambridge St, London SW1V.
(020-7834 5631.

Association of Pleasure Craft Operators
Parkland House, Audley Ave, Newport, Shropshire TF10.
(01952 813572.

Association of British Riding Schools
Queens Chambers, 38–40 Queen Street, Penzance, Cornwall TR18.
(01736 369440.

British Activity Holiday Association
22 Green Lane, Hersham, Surrey KT12.
(01932 252994.

British Hang-Gliding and Para-gliding Association

The Old School Room, Loughborough Rd, Leicester LE4.
(0116 2611322.

British Mountaineering Council
177–179 Burton Rd, Manchester M20.
(0161 445 4747.

British Surfing Association
Champions Yd, Penzance, Cornwall TR18.
(01736 360250.

British Water Ski Federation
390 City Rd, London EC1V.
(020-7833 2855.

British Trust for Conservation Volunteers
80 York Way, London N1.
(020-7278 4293.

British Waterways
Willow Grange, Church Rd, Watford, Herts WD1.
(01923 226422.

Broads Authority
18 Colegate, Norwich, Norfolk NR3.
(01603 610734.

English Golf Union
National Golf Centre, The Broadway, Woodhall Spa, Lincs LN10.
(01526 354500.

Football Association
16 Lancaster Gate, London W2.
(020-7262 4542.

Lawn Tennis Association
Queen's Club, West Kensington, London W14.
(020-7381 7111.

National Feder-ation of Anglers
Halliday Hse, Egginton Junction. Derbyshire DE65.
(01283 734735.

National Cricket Association
Lord's Cricket Ground, St John's Wood, NW8.
(020-7432 1200.

Environment Agency
Rio House, Waterside Drive, Aztec West, Almondsbury BS12.
(01454 624411.

Outward Bound
Watermillock, Nr Penrith, Cumbria CA11.
(0990 134227.

Racecourse Association
Winkfield Rd, Ascot, Berks SL5.
(01344 25912.

Royal Yachting Association
RYA Hse, Romsey Rd, Eastleigh, Hants SO5.
(01703 627400.

Rugby Football Union
Rugby Rd, Twickenham, Middx TW1.
(020-8892 2000.

Ski Club of Great Britain
The White House, 57–63 Church Rd, London SW1.
(020-8410 2000.

TRAVEL INFORMATION

AS IT IS AN international gateway for air and sea traffic, travelling to Britain poses few problems. By air, travellers have a very large choice of carriers serving North America, Australasia and Europe. Bus travel is a cheap, albeit rather slow, form of transport from Europe, while travelling by train has been transformed with the advent of the Channel Tunnel – three hours from Paris to London. Travelling

British Airways' supersonic passenger plane, Concorde

within Britain itself is fairly easy. There is an extensive network of roads to all parts of the country and hiring a car is often the best way of travelling around. The InterCity rail network is very efficient and the network to the smaller towns, especially around London, is good. Travelling by coach is the cheapest option; the bus network serves most areas but can be slow. If time is short, air travel is possible but expensive.

Passenger concourse, Waterloo Station, London

TRAVELLING AROUND BRITAIN

CHOOSING THE BEST way to travel around Britain depends very much on where and when you want to go, although the quickest and most convenient methods are generally the most expensive.

Distances between any two points within mainland Britain are relatively small (at least by American or Australian standards) so air travel usually makes sense only between the extremes, such as London to Edinburgh. For shorter journeys, the time spent getting to and from airports often outweighs any savings in actual travelling time. Rail services are the best alternative if you want to visit Britain's major cities, though fares, especially at peak times, can be quite expensive. If you plan to do much travelling within Britain, a rail pass can be very good value. You can buy a pass before you arrive in the UK as several schemes cater for overseas visitors *(see p638)*.

Bus networks cover a wide number of UK destinations, and are cheaper than trains, but take longer and may be less comfortable. Taxis are available at all major bus or rail stations to take you to your hotel; without a car you will avoid the stress of driving in congested city centres.

If you plan a more flexible touring holiday, hiring your own car is more feasible than relying on public transport. Car rental can be arranged at all major airports, large railway stations and city centre outlets. To get the best deals, book from abroad. Small local firms often undercut the large operators in price, but may not be as reliable or convenient.

For detailed exploration of smaller areas such as Britain's National Parks or popular

regions like the Lake District *(see pp346–59)* you may prefer more leisurely transportation offered by bike, horse or narrowboat. Sometimes there are picturesque local options like a rowing-boat ferry, such as the one between Southwold and Walberswick on the Blyth Estuary *(see p189)*. There are also larger car ferries which travel to Britain's islands.

Rowing-boat ferry on the River Blyth, Southwold, Suffolk

CHANNEL TUNNEL

This historic landlink between Britain and France opened for business in late 1994 and closed one of the "missing links" in the European transport system. The sleek new rolling-stock is high-tech and very comfortable, producing an experience more akin to air travel than rail. Passengers on buses and cars get onto a freight train run by **Eurotunnel** which takes 35 minutes to travel between Calais and Folkestone.

Eurotunnel logo

For those travelling by rail there are about 40 scheduled **Eurostar** services, operated by the French, Belgian and British. They run between Brussels, Paris and London and there is no need to change at either end of the tunnel. There are two passenger tunnels – and one service tunnel – which lie 25–45 m (82–147 ft) below the sea bed. All the tunnels are made of concrete and iron, and are 31 miles (50 km) long.

Arriving by Sea, Rail and Bus

IF YOU ARE travelling from Europe by foot, car, coach or rail you will have to cross the English Channel or North Sea either by ferry or the Channel Tunnel. Ferry services operate to a huge number of ports on the European mainland and have good link-ups with international buses, with services from most European cities to Britain. The Channel Tunnel has meant there is now a non-stop rail link between Britain and Europe. Prices between the ferries and the tunnel services remain very competitive.

Ferry arriving at Dover

FERRY SERVICES FROM EUROPE

A COMPLEX NETWORK of ferry services operate between over a dozen British ports with around 20 car and passenger ferry services that travel regularly across the Channel and North Sea routes to many ports in northern and southern Europe *(see pp10–15)*.

Because of the number of areas they reach, ferries can be more convenient for those in cars or on foot than the Channel Tunnel. Fares vary greatly according to the season, time of travel and duration of stay. The shortest crossings are not always the cheapest: you pay for the speed of the journey.

CROSSING TIMES

CROSSING TIMES VARY from just over an hour on the shortest routes to a full 24 hours on services from Spain and Scandinavia. If you take an overnight sailing, you may have to pay extra for sleeping accommodation, but it is often worth booking a cabin on the longer trips to avoid feeling exhausted when you arrive. Fast hovercraft services

between Dover, Boulogne and Calais are run by **Hoverspeed**, while a **Seacat** (catamaran) service crosses between Folkestone and Boulogne. These are the fastest routes across the Channel, taking just over half an hour, and all these craft can carry vehicles. The crossings lack the dip and sway of a conventional ship, and so may be less painful for poor sailors.

SEAPORT BUREAUCRACY

THOSE VISITORS from outside the European Union should allow plenty of time for immigration control and customs clearance at British seaports *(see p619)*. You are not allowed to bring pets into Britain because of rabies.

A hovercraft crossing the English Channel

INTERNATIONAL BUS TRAVEL

ALTHOUGH BUS TRAVEL is comparably cheaper than other methods of travel, it is not the most comfortable way of travelling across Europe. But if you have a lot of spare time and want to stop off en route it can be convenient. Once you have paid for your ticket you will not have to pay again to use the ferry or the Channel Tunnel.

INTERNATIONAL RAIL TRAVEL

WITH THE ADVENT of the Channel Tunnel, there is now access to the French high-speed rail network, and from there to the rest of the European rail network. Rail travel can be an efficient, comfortable and fast way of travelling across Europe to Britain – in France trains reach speeds of up to 185 mph (300 kmph). The cost is comparable to flying, although it is much more convenient.

DIRECTORY

FERRIES, RAIL AND COACH TRAVEL

Brittany Ferries
0990 360 360.

P&O Portsmouth
0870 2424999.

P&O/Stena Line
0870 6000600.

Stena Line
0990 707070.

Hoverspeed/Seacat
0870 5240241.

European Rail Travel
0990 848 848 (for info).

International Coach Travel
020-7730 3466.

EUROTUNNEL

Eurostar
0990 186186 (for foot & rail passengers).

Eurotunnel/Le Shuttle
0990 353535 (for cars & coach travel).

Arriving by Air

BRITAIN HAS ABOUT 130 licensed airports but only a handful of these are equipped for long-haul traffic. The largest is London's Heathrow, the world's busiest international airport and one of Europe's central routing points for international air travel. It is served by most of the world's leading airlines with direct flights from nearly all the major cities. The other major international airports include Gatwick, Stansted, Manchester, Glasgow, Newcastle, Birmingham and Edinburgh. Smaller airports such as London City, Bristol, Norwich and Cardiff have daily flights to European destinations.

Platform sign for express railway service to London

which flies to Western Europe.

The main American airlines offering scheduled services to Britain include **Delta**, **US Air** and **American Airlines**. From Canada, the main carriers are **Canadian Airlines** and **Air Canada**. From Australasia, the national carriers **Qantas** and **Air New Zealand** vie with many Far Eastern rivals.

Britain imposes an airport tax on all departing passengers – currently £10 for domestic and EC routes, and £20 for non-EC and long-haul flights.

A British Airways 747 jet at Heathrow Airport

BRITISH AIRPORTS

THE MAJORITY of Britain's largest and best known airports are run by the British Airports Authority – the rest are owned by a local authority or are in private hands. All BAA airports offer up-to-date facilities, including 24-hour banking, shops, cafés, hotels and restaurants. Security is strict at all British airports and it is important never to leave baggage unattended.

If you are starting your visit in London, flights to Gatwick, Heathrow or Stansted are equally convenient. But if you plan to visit northern England, there are an increasing number of flights going to Birmingham,

Newcastle and Manchester, while for Scotland you can fly to Glasgow or Edinburgh.

Heathrow has four terminals and some others have two. Before you fly, check with the airport from which terminal your flight leaves.

During severe weather conditions in the winter months, your flight may be diverted to another airport. If this happens, the airline will organize transportation back to your original destination.

British Airways has flights to nearly all the world's important destinations. Other British international airlines include **Virgin Atlantic**, with routes to the USA and the Far East, and **British Midland**,

TRANSPORT FROM THE AIRPORT

BRITAIN'S INTERNATIONAL airports lie some way from city centres, but transport to

Arrival terminal at Heathrow Airport

AIRPORT	INFORMATION	DISTANCE TO CITY CENTRE	TAXI FARE TO CITY CENTRE	PUBLIC TRANSPORT TO CITY CENTRE
Heathrow	08700 000123	14 miles (23 km)	£25–30	Rail: 15 min Tube: 40 min
Gatwick	01293 535353	28 miles (45 km)	£40–45	Rail: 30 min Bus: 70 min
Stansted	08700 000303	37 miles (60 km)	£45–50	Rail: 45 min Bus: 75 min
Manchester	0161 4893000	10 miles (16 km)	£10–12	Rail: 15 min Bus: 30 min
Birmingham	0121 7675511	8 miles (13 km)	£12–15	Bus: 30 min
Newcastle	0191 2860966	5 miles (8 km)	£7–10	Metro: 20 min Bus: 20 min
Glasgow	0141 8871111	8 miles (13 km)	£12–15	Bus: 20 min
Edinburgh	0131 3331000	8 miles (13 km)	£12–15	Bus: 20 min

and from them is efficient. Every airport has taxis and these are the most convenient form of door-to-door travel, but they are also expensive and can be slow if there is traffic congestion – very likely if you travel in the rush hour *(see p636)*. This can also be a problem with taking a coach or bus, although they are a lot cheaper than taxis.

Heathrow and Newcastle are both linked to the centre of the city by the Underground *(see p643)*. These are efficient, quick and cheap. Manchester, Stansted, Gatwick and Heathrow *(see p638)* have regular express trains which are not too expensive and are a reliable method for travelling into the heart of the city.

National Express Coaches *(see p640)* provide direct connections from major airports to many British destinations. They have a regular service between Gatwick and Heathrow.

CHOOSING A TICKET

FINDING THE RIGHT FLIGHT at the right price can be difficult. Promotional fares do come up and it is always worth checking with the airlines direct. Cheap deals are often available from package operators and are advertised in newspapers and travel magazines. Students and under 26s, senior citizens and regular or business travellers may be able to obtain a discount through student travel agencies. Children and babies also travel at cheaper rates.

A modern Forte Crest hotel at Gatwick Airport

AIR FARES

FARES TO BRITAIN are usually seasonal, the highest being from June to September. The best deals are available from November to April, excluding the Christmas period – if you want to travel then, be sure to book well in advance.

APEX (Advance Purchase Excursion) fares are often the best value, though they must be booked up to a month ahead, and are subject to restrictions. Charter flights offer even cheaper seats, but are not usually flexible.

If you choose a discount fare, always buy from a reputable operator, and do not part with cash until you have seen your ticket and ensure your seat has been confirmed.

Packages may be worth considering, even if you enjoy independent travel, as sometimes car rental or rail travel is included. This can be cheaper than arranging it yourself when you have arrived in Britain.

TRAVELLING WITHIN BRITAIN BY AIR

Britain's size means that internal air travel only makes sense over longish distances, where it can save a great deal of time – for example, London to Scotland, or to one of the many offshore islands. Air fares can be expensive, but if you book well ahead, fares can be up to three times cheaper than if you just turn up at the airport – although you are still always guaranteed a seat. The British Airways shuttle flights that operate between London and cities such as Glasgow, Edinburgh and Manchester are extremely popular with business travellers. At peak times of the day, flights leave every hour, while at other times there is usually a flight every two hours. Bad weather can cause delays or diversions during the winter months. Even on domestic flights, security is stringent, and you should never leave your bags unattended.

Award-winning exterior of Stansted Airport

Travelling Around by Car

THE MOST STARTLING difference for most foreign motorists is that in Britain you drive on the left, with corresponding adjustments at roundabouts and junctions. Distances are measured in miles. Once you adapt, rural Britain is an enjoyable place to drive, though traffic density in towns and at busy holiday times can cause long delays – public holiday weekends near the south coast can be particularly horrendous. An extensive network of toll-free motorways and trunk roads has now cut travelling time to most parts of the country.

WHAT YOU NEED

TO DRIVE IN BRITAIN you need a current driving licence with an international driving permit if required. In any vehicle you drive you must carry proof of ownership or a rental agreement, plus any insurance documents.

ROADS IN BRITAIN

PEAK RUSH-HOUR traffic can last from 8–9:30am and 5–6:30pm on weekdays in the cities; at these times traffic can grind to a halt. In the country a good touring map is essential; the AA or RAC motoring atlases are fairly straightforward to use. For exploration of more rural areas, the Ordnance Survey series is the best. On all road maps B roads are secondary roads and A roads, often dual carriageways, are main routes. B routes are often less congested and more enjoyable to use. Rural areas

A motorway sign in miles

are crisscrossed by a web of tiny lanes. Motorways are marked with M followed by their identifying number.

ROAD SIGNS

SIGNS are now generally standardized in line with Europe. Directional signs are colour-coded: blue for motorways, green for major routes and white for minor routes. Signposting in Britain is not consistent and city suburbs can be confusing. Brown signs indicate places of interest. Advisory or warning signs are usually triangles in red and white, with easy-to-understand pictograms. Watch for electronic notices on motorways that warn of road works, accidents or patches of fog. Level crossings, found at rail lines, often have automatic barriers. If the lights are flashing red it means a train is coming and you must stop. The *UK Highway Code Manual* – available from most good bookshops – is an up-to-date guide to all the current British driving regulations and traffic signs.

RULES OF THE ROAD

SPEED LIMITS are 30–40 mph (50–65 kmph) in built-up areas and 70 mph (110 kmph) on motorways or dual carriageways – look out for speed signs on other roads. It is compulsory to wear seat-belts in Britain. Drink-driving penalties are severe – see the *UK Highway Code Manual* for legal limits.

No stopping	Speed limit applies
No entry	No right-turn allowed
Railway level crossing	Give way to all vehicles
One-way traffic	Gradient of a road

PARKING

THIS IS THE BANE of the British motorist's life. Parking meters operate during working hours (usually 8am–6:30pm Mon–Sat); keep a supply of coins for them. Some cities have "park and ride" schemes, where you can take a bus from an out-of-city car park into the centre. Other towns have a "disc" parking scheme; ask the tourist office or a local newsagent for a disc to mark your arrival time. Many car parks operate on a pay-and-display system. Avoid double yellow lines at all times; single lines mean you can park in the evenings and at weekends but check carefully. Traffic wardens wear distinctive uniforms and will not hesitate to ticket, clamp or tow your car away. If in any doubt, find a car park *(see pp642–3)*. Outside urban areas and popular tourist zones, parking is not such a problem. Look out for the letter P: this indicates legal parking spaces.

Sign for a car park

The A30 dual carriageway going through Cornwall

PETROL

NORTH AMERICAN visitors may find fuel (gas) very expensive in Britain. Large supermarkets often have the cheapest petrol; look out for branches of Tesco or Sainsbury with petrol stations. Motorway service areas are generally more expensive. Petrol is sold in three grades: diesel, LRP (lead replacement petrol) and unleaded. Most modern cars in Britain use unleaded petrol – any vehicle you hire will probably do so. Unleaded and diesel are cheaper than LRP. Most petrol stations in Britain are self-service but instructions at pumps are easy to follow.

BREAKDOWN SERVICES

BRITAIN'S MAJOR motoring organizations, the **AA** (Automobile Association) and the **RAC** (Royal Automobile Club), provide a comprehensive 24-hour breakdown service, as well as many other motoring services. Both offer reciprocal assistance for members of overseas motoring organizations – before arrival check with your own group to see if you are covered. You can contact the AA or RAC from the roadside SOS phones found on motorways. **Green Flag** is the other major rescue service in Britain, which can sometimes be quicker and cheaper since it makes greater use of local garages.

Most car hire agencies have their own cover, and their charges include membership of either the AA, the RAC or Green Flag while you are driving. Be sure to ask the rental company for the service's emergency number.

Even if you are not a member of an affiliated organization you can still call out a rescue service, although it will be expensive. Always follow the advice given on your insurance policy or rental agreement. If you have an accident that involves injury or another vehicle, call the police as soon as possible *(see p621)*.

RAC and AA logos

A small rural petrol station in Goathland, North Yorkshire

CAR HIRE

HIRING A CAR in Britain can be expensive. One of the most competitive national companies is **Hire For Lower**, but small local firms may undercut even these rates. Many companies prefer you to leave a credit card number; otherwise you may have to part with a substantial cash deposit. You need your driving licence and a passport when you hire. Most companies will not hire to novice drivers, and set age limits (usually 21–70). Automatic cars are fairly scarce. If you are touring Britain for three weeks or more, you may find a leasing arrangement cheaper than hiring. Remember to add VAT and insurance costs when you check hire rates.

HITCHHIKING

HITCHHIKING is a common practice in Britain, and you are likely to thumb a long-distance lift if you stand near a busy exit road junction. In rural or walking areas like the Lake District, tired hikers may well be offered a lift. It is illegal to hitch on motorways or their approach roads. As anywhere, there is a risk in hitchhiking alone, especially for a woman. Lift-sharing is now a common practice. The small-ads magazine *Loot* (sold in newsagents in London, Manchester and Bristol) has a large section for lift-seekers.

DIRECTORY

BREAKDOWN

AA
(0800 887 766.

Green Flag
(0800 400 600.

RAC
(0800 828 282.

CAR HIRE

Avis
(0990-900 500.

Budget
(0800 181 181.

Europcar/British Car Rental
(0345 222 525.

Hertz
(0870 8448844.

Hire For Lower
(020-7287 6000.

National Car Rentals
(0990 365 365.

GENERAL INFORMATION

AA Road Watch
(09003 401100.

AA Disabled Line
(0800 262050.

Emergency Calls
(999.

Weathercall
(*Britain area by area:* 0891 500401.

Travelling Around by Rail

BRITAIN HAS a privatized rail network which covers the whole of the country. It is divided into regional sections which serve over 2,500 stations throughout Britain. The system is generally efficient and reliable with quiet, modernized rolling stock, particularly on the InterCity services. Travelling across the country, rather than out of London, may involve a number of changes as most lines radiate from London, which has seven major terminals. There is now a rail link with Continental Europe, from Waterloo rail terminal in London through the Channel Tunnel *(see p632)*.

InterCity train speeding through countryside

TICKETS

LARGE TRAVEL AGENTS and all railway stations sell rail tickets. First-class tickets cost about one-third more than standard fares, and generally return fares are cheaper than two singles.

Allow plenty of time to buy your ticket and always ask about any special offers or reduced fares. There are four types of discounted fares for adults. Apex tickets are available in limited numbers on some long-distance Inter-City routes and have to be booked at least a week in advance. SuperApex fares have to be purchased 14 days in advance and again are available in limited numbers on a few InterCity services. Savers can be used at week-ends and on most weekday trains outside rush hours. Finally, Supersavers cannot be used on Fridays, or any peak-hour service to, from or through London.

Ticket offices in rural areas may close at weekends, but small branch lines have a conductor on board who sells tickets. Otherwise buy a ticket beforehand as inspectors can levy on-the-spot fines if you do not have a valid ticket. Many stations have automatic ticket machines.

RAIL PASSES

IF YOU PLAN to do much train travelling around Britain, buy a rail pass. These can be bought from many agents abroad, such as **Rail Europe** or **CIE Tours International**. An All Line Rail Rover gives adults unlimited travel throughout England, Scotland and Wales for 7 or 14 days. Children under 16 travel half price, or a Family Rail Card is available. It can be used for up to four adults and four children. Discounts are also available for 16- to 25-year-olds or full-time students attending a UK educational establishment with a Young Person's Rail Card. For those over the age of 60, the Senior Rail Card entitles you to a one-third price discount on most fares. There are special passes for London transport and a pass that covers London, Oxford, Canterbury and Brighton. Children of 5–15 years pay half fare; the under-5s travel free. Family tickets are also available. Disabled travellers qualify for many discounts. Keep a passport-sized photo handy for buying passes. If you have a pass, make sure you always show it when you buy a ticket.

GENERAL TIPS

BRITAIN'S FASTEST and most comfortable trains are those on the InterCity routes. These are very popular services and get booked up quickly. It is always advisable to reserve your seat in advance, especially if you want to travel at peak times such as Friday evenings. InterCity trains have dining cars, air-conditioning and are fast, travelling to Edinburgh from London, for example, in just over four hours.

For those arriving at Heathrow Airport and travelling into London *(see pp634–5)*, an alternative to the Underground *(see p643)* is the fast train to Paddington Station. Unlike the tube service, this operates 24 hours a day. Trains run frequently from 9am until midnight and then every hour between midnight and 5.30am, and every half hour thereafter until 9am.

Rail terminal, Liverpool Lime Street Station

Porters are rare on British stations, although trolleys are often available for passengers to help themselves. If you are disabled and need help, contact the relevant train company before you travel. A yellow line above a train window indicates a first class compartment. You cannot use these without paying the full fare, even if the train is full. Check which section of the train to join as they sometimes split through the journey and proceed to different destinations. Trains stop for only a minute at each station, so be ready to get on and off. Some stations are a little way from town centres, but are well signposted and nearly always on a bus route. Sunday trains and public holiday services are often a lot slower than normal.

SCENIC TRAIN RIDES

As MOTOR TRANSPORT made many rural railways redundant in the mid-20th century, picturesque sections of track, as well as many old steam engines, were rescued and restored to working order by enthusiasts. These services are often privately run: the local tourist office, railway station ticket office or travel agents will provide you with information. Most of the lines are short – around 20 miles (32 km) – but cover some of the prettiest parts of the country and are one of the best ways to enjoy its spectacular scenery. Lines include: the South Devon Steam Railway *(see p275);* the Ffestiniog Railway *(see pp438–9)* in North Wales; the

North York Moors Railway *(see p380);* the Strathspey Steam Railway in the Cairngorm Mountains of the Scottish Highlands *(see p530)* and the La'l Ratty Railway in Cumbria *(see p350).*

A reconditioned steam train, North Yorkshire

InterCity Rail Map

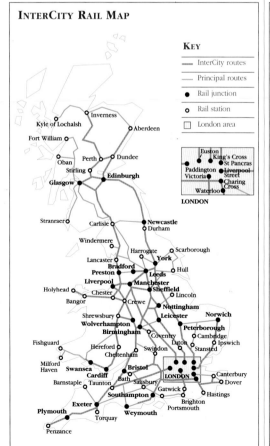

KEY

— InterCity routes
— Principal routes
● Rail junction
○ Rail station
□ London area

LONDON

Euston
King's Cross
St Pancras
Paddington
Victoria
Liverpool Street
Charing Cross
Waterloo

Travelling around by Coach

IN BRITAIN, coaches refer to the long-distance express buses and those used for sightseeing excursions. What the British refer to as buses, however, covers those vehicles that operate on regular routes with scheduled stops around or between villages, towns and cities. Many coach services duplicate rail routes, but are generally cheaper. Journey times, however, are longer and much less predictable on crowded roads. Modern coaches are comfortable, sometimes with refreshments, toilets and entertainment – in the form of feature films – on board. Some city to city routes, especially at weekends, are so popular that it is a good idea to buy a reserved journey ticket, which guarantees you a seat.

A coach tour, the Royal Mile, Edinburgh

NATIONAL COACH NETWORK

THERE ARE A LOT OF regional coach companies, but by far the largest British coach operator is **National Express** with a nationwide network of over 1,000 destinations (see pp12–15). On the more popular routes – particularly on Friday evenings – it is best to book ahead. National Express offers two levels of service; the faster of the two is the *Rapide* service which has a host or hostess and catering facilities.

A Britexpass card

Discounts are available for full-time students or anyone under 25. Senior citizens also qualify for a Discount Coach Card (30 per cent reduction). Britexpass cards lasting 30 days and Tourist Trail Passes are also available for those planning to cover many destinations in a limited period.

You can buy these from most coach travel agents in North America – via **British Travel Associates** – or while in the UK, at the major international airports, **Victoria Coach Station** and most large travel agents. The other coach operator is **Scottish Citylink**, with regular services between London, the North and Scotland. Some services run direct from Heathrow or Gatwick airports. Allow plenty of time to buy your ticket before boarding. Luggage is stowed in the vehicle hold.

British Travel Associates
(800 327 6097 (in North America).

National Express
(0990 808080.

Scottish Citylink
(0990 505050.

Victoria Coach Station
(020-7730 3466.

COACH TOURS

DOZENS OF COACH TOURS are available in the UK, for all interests, age groups and destinations. Some include a tour guide. They may last anything from a couple of hours to two weeks or more, touring coast or countryside and visiting places of interest. Some are highly structured, organizing every last photo opportunity or cup of tea; others leave you to sightsee or shop at your own pace. You can opt for a prearranged route, or commission your own itinerary for a group.

Coach tours are popular, but may leave you feeling somewhat herded. Groups always travel at the pace of their slowest member, which can mean a lot of waiting. But at the same time all the stress of organizing a similar trip for yourself is taken away. Some coach operators will pick up passengers from their hotels and then drop them back.

Any large town will have a selection of coach companies. Check the local *Yellow Pages* (see p622), or ask your hotel or the local tourist office. You can also book coach trips direct from overseas through a specialist travel agent.

Seaside resorts and tourist sites are destinations for many day trips, especially in high season. In some of the more popular rural areas, such as the Lake District, special small buses operate for ease of movement. You can book

A *Rapide* coach, Victoria Coach Station, London

these in advance, or just turn up before the coach leaves, although the tour is likely to be fully booked, especially in high season. The local tourist information point or travel agent will be able to tell you where these trips leave from, the cost and may even sell you tickets. It is customary to tip the guide after your tour.

REGIONAL BUSES

R EGIONAL BUS SERVICES are run by a large number of companies, some private and some operated by local authorities. Less economic services to remote rural areas tend to be sporadic and expensive, with some buses running just once a week and many isolated villages having no service at all. Only a few rural buses are equipped for wheelchairs.

As a general rule, you can assume that the further you get from a city, the fewer the buses and the more expensive the fare. It is therefore unwise to rely on local buses for transport, and if you want to see a lot of the country, renting a car is a better option. But if you do have the time, local buses can be a pleasant and often sociable way of travelling around Britain's lovely countryside.

Most buses run with just one operator – the driver. All drivers prefer you to have the correct fare, so always have a selection of low denomination coins handy. Some routes do not operate on Sundays and public holidays, and those that do are much reduced.

Always check your routes, schedules and fares at the local tourist office or bus station before you depart on a bus. This will prevent your being stranded somewhere with no return transport.

The Trossach Trundler exploring the Trossachs, Scotland

Travelling Britain's Coasts and Waterways

B RITAIN HAS THOUSANDS OF MILES of inland waterways and hundreds of islands scattered along its coastline. Cruising along a canal in the beautiful Midlands countryside or travelling on one of the small local ferries to a remote Scottish island are both wonderful experiences. Canal boats can be hired and scores of ferries run between Britain's offshore islands.

A barge on the Welsh Backs, Bristol, Avon

CANALS

A S INDUSTRIAL PRODUCTION grew in the 18th century, it became vital to find a cheap and effective way of transporting heavy loads. Canals fulfilled this need and a huge network was built, linking most industrial areas in the north and sea ports.

The arrival of the railways and their immediate success for freight made most canals redundant, but there are still some 2,000 miles (3,200 km) left, most in the old industrial heartland of the Midlands.

Today these canals lure the travellers who are content to cruise on old-fashioned, slow narrowboats, taking their time to enjoy the wildlife, the views and the canalside inns, originally built to satisfy the bargees' thirsts and to supply stabling for the horses that pulled the barges. These canal holidays can be very relaxing if you have the time.

If you wish to hire a narrowboat, you can book with a specialist travel firm or contact **British Waterways**.

British Waterways
🄲 01442 235400.

LOCAL FERRIES

B RITAIN'S LOCAL FERRIES can offer anything from a tenminute river journey to a seven-hour sea cruise.

Many of Scotland's ferries are operated by **Caledonian MacBrayne**. They sail to lots of different destinations, such as the Isle of Skye to the Kyle of Lochalsh, or the five-hour journey from Oban to Lochboisdale in the Western Isles. They offer a variety of different ticket types, from unlimited rover tickets for a specific period of time, to island-hop passes or all-inclusive coach tour and ferry tickets. Not all the island ferries take cars.

A car ferry travelling from Oban to Lochboisdale

River ferries make an interesting alternative to the more usual forms of transport. The ferry across the Mersey, between the cities of Liverpool and Birkenhead, is still used by many people commuting to work. London's river trips, such as the one that runs from Westminster to Tower Bridge (see p118), offer a different perspective on the city and make a change from tubes, buses and cars. Local tourist information centres can give you information about ferries in their area.

Caledonian MacBrayne
🄲 01475 650100.

Travelling within Cities

URBAN PUBLIC TRANSPORT in Britain is efficient and can be fun – children love London's double-decker buses. Fares are good value, bearing in mind that you avoid the expense and difficulty of parking a car. Most of the larger cities have good bus services. London, Newcastle and Glasgow also have an underground system, while Manchester and Blackpool have trams. Taxis are available at every railway station and at ranks near hotels and city centres. The best way to see many cities is on foot, but whatever transport you choose, try to avoid the rush hours from 8am to 9:30am, and 4:30pm to 6:30pm.

Local buses travelling along Princes Street, Edinburgh

LOCAL BUSES

THE DEREGULATION of bus services has led to a complex system with many buses often duplicating services on the busiest routes. On most buses you pay the driver as you enter. They will not always accept notes so keep a selection of coins handy. Credit cards and cheques are not accepted. The fare depends on the distance you travel. If you are exploring a city by bus, a daily pass is a good idea. Many of the larger cities have daily or weekly passes that can be used on all public transport in that city; these can often be bought from newsagents. Check with the tourist office for schedules and fares. All-night services are only available in major cities, from about 11pm until early morning. You cannot use a day pass on these.

A London double-decker bus

In London night buses are prefixed with the letter N and all of them pass through Trafalgar Square.

Be on your guard when travelling home alone late at night, when there may be few other passengers aboard.

Bus designs have become more innovative in the last few years. The old "big red bus" with a conductor still exists in London, but has been joined by a plethora of modern vehicles of all shapes, colours and sizes, with automatic doors and comfortable interiors. Many are small single-deckers, able to weave in and out of traffic more easily.

Many cities have bus lanes, intended to bypass car traffic jams during the rush hours. These can be effective but your journey could still take a long time. Schedules are hard to keep to, so regard timetables as advisory. At some stops, called request stops, the driver will not halt unless you signal that you want to get on or off. If you want to board, raise your arm as the bus approaches the stop; if you want to get off, ring the bell once before your stop.

Destinations are shown on the front of buses. If you are not sure which stop you need, ask the driver or conductor to alert you and stay on the lower deck. Always keep your ticket until the end of the journey in case an inspector boards, who can impose an on-the-spot fine if you are without a valid ticket. Stops can often be quite a long distance apart.

DRIVING IN CITIES

TO PREVENT CONGESTION in city centres, parking is strictly controlled, and even minor infringements can result in heavy fines or your vehicle being clamped or towed away. You will have to pay a hefty fine to have it released. Always be sure to check the parking regulations carefully on the meters and signs before leaving your vehicle. If you are not sure how long you are likely to stay, try to find a car park where you will be charged as you leave. Many visitors prefer not to drive in British cities but there is nothing daunting about it if you obey the rules (*see p636*).

A traditional parking meter

TAXIS

IN LARGE TOWNS there are plenty of taxis to be found at taxi ranks and train stations. Some operate by radio so you have to phone. The local *Yellow Pages (see p622)*, pubs, restaurants and hotels will all have a list of taxi numbers. Prices are usually controlled, but competition is fierce and many firms undercut licensed taxis. Always ask the price before you start your journey if there is no taxi meter. If you are not sure of the correct fare ask the local tourist information point.

Licensed taxi drivers undergo strict tests and all licensed cabs must carry a "For Hire" sign, which is lit up whenever they are free. Care is needed if you use unlicensed minicabs – some may be mechanically unsound or even uninsured.

An illegally parked car immobilized by a wheel clamp

Do not accept an unbooked minicab ride in the street. The famous London black cabs are almost as much of an institution as the big red bus. These are the safest cabs to use in London as all the drivers are licensed and they are forbidden to drive their cab with damaged bodywork. They also know where they are going. Even these are changing, however, and you will see cabs of many colours, many covered with advertising. The newer cab designs are equipped to carry wheelchairs. If a cab stops for you in London, it must by law take you anywhere within a radius of 6 miles (10 km) so long it is

One of London's black cabs

within the Metropolitan Police District. This includes most of London and Heathrow Airport.

All licensed cabs will have meters that start ticking as soon as the driver accepts your custom. The fare will increase minute by minute or for each 311 m (1,020 ft) travelled. Surcharges are added for each piece of luggage, each extra passenger or unsocial hours. Most drivers expect a tip of between 10 and 15 per cent of the fare. If you have a complaint, note the serial number found in the back of the cab.

GUIDED BUS TOURS

IN MOST MAJOR tourist cities, sightseeing bus tours are available. Weather permitting, a good way to see the cities is from a traditional open-topped double-decker bus. Private tours can be arranged with many companies. Contact the tourist information centre.

TRAMS

AFTER A LONG ABSENCE (apart from a few nostalgic remnants in Blackpool) trams are making a comeback in clean, energy efficient and more modern guises. One of the best tram schemes in Britain is Manchester's Metrolink.

LONDON UNDERGROUND

THE UNDERGROUND in London, known as the tube, is one of the largest systems of its kind in the world. It has over 270 stations, each of which are clearly marked with the London Underground logo. The only other cities to have an underground system are Glasgow and Newcastle, but both are small. London tube trains run every day, except Christmas Day, from about 5:30am until just after midnight, but some of the outlying sections have a less frequent service. Fewer trains run on Sundays.

The 11 tube lines are colour-coded and maps called *Journey Planners* are posted at every station, while maps of the central section are displayed in each train. Most tube journeys between central destinations in London can be completed with only one or two changes of train. Smoking is not permitted on the Underground.

Newcastle's tube system is limited to the city centre but Glasgow's skirts around the centre. Both are clean and efficient, running the same hours as London's.

A tram along Blackpool's famous promenade

WALKING IN CITIES

ONCE YOU GET USED to traffic on the left, Britain's cities can be safely and enjoyably explored on foot.

There are two types of pedestrian crossing: striped zebra crossings and push-button crossings at traffic lights. At a zebra crossing traffic should stop for you, but at push-button crossings cars will not stop until the lights change in your favour. Look for instructions written on the road; these will tell you from which direction you can expect the traffic to come. More and more cities and towns are creating traffic-free zones in the city centre for pedestrians.

A London Underground sign outside a station

CYCLING

Cycling is a popular pastime in Britain. Even in the smallest town there is usually somewhere you can hire bikes. Whether you cycle in towns or the countryside, a helmet is recommended. Cyclists may not use motorways or their approach roads, nor can they ride on pavements, footpaths or pedestrianized zones. Many city roads have cycle lanes and their own traffic lights. You can take a bike on most trains for a charge. Never leave your bike unlocked.

Cycling under the Bridge of Sighs, Oxford

General Index

Acknowledgments

DORLING KINDERSLEY would like to thank the following people whose contributions and assistance have made the preparation of this book possible.

MAIN CONTRIBUTOR

Michael Leapman was born in London in 1938 and has been a professional journalist since he was 20. He has worked for most British national newspapers and now writes about travel and other subjects for several publications, among them *The Independent, Independent on Sunday, The Economist* and *Country Life.* He has written 11 books, including the award-winning *Companion Guide to New York* (1983, revised 1995) and *Eyewitness Travel Guide to London.* In 1989 he edited the widely praised *Book of London.*

ADDITIONAL CONTRIBUTORS

Paul Cleves, James Henderson, Lucy Juckes, John Lax, Marcus Ramshaw.

ADDITIONAL ILLUSTRATIONS

Christian Hook, Gilly Newman, Paul Weston.

DESIGN AND EDITORIAL

MANAGING EDITOR Georgina Matthews
SENIOR ART EDITOR Sally Ann Hibbard
DEPUTY EDITORIAL DIRECTOR Douglas Amrine
DEPUTY ART DIRECTOR Gaye Allen
PRODUCTION David Proffit
PICTURE RESEARCH Ellen Root
DTP DESIGNER Ingrid Vienings
MAP CO-ORDINATORS Michael Ellis, David Pugh
RESEARCHER Pippa Leahy
Eliza Armstrong, Sam Atkinson, Moerida Belton, Josie Barnard, Hilary Bird, Louise Boulton, Roger Bullen, Deborah Clapson, Elspeth Collier, Gary Cross, Cooling Brown Partnership, Guy Dimond, Danny Farnham, Joy Fitzsimmons, Fay Franklin, Ed Freeman, Charlie Hawkings, Martin Hendry, Andrew Heritage, Paul Hines, Annette Jacobs, Gail Jones, Steve Knowlden, Nic Kynaston, Esther Labi, Pippa Leahy, James Mills Hicks, Rebecca Milner, Elaine Monaghan, Marianne Petrou, Chez Picthall, Clare Pierotti, Andrea Powell, Mark Rawley, Jake Reimann, Carolyn Ryden, David Roberts, Alison Stace, Hugh Thompson.

ADDITIONAL PHOTOGRAPHY

Max Alexander, Peter Anderson, Steve Bere, Deni Bown, June Buck, Michael Dent, Philip Dowell, Mike Dunning, Chris Dyer, Andrew Einsiedel, Philip Enticknap, Jane Ewart, DK Studio/Steve Gorton, Frank Greenaway, Stephen Hayward, John Heseltine, Ed Ironside, Dave King, Neil Mersh, Robert O'Dea, Stephen Oliver, Vincent Oliver, Roger Phillips, Karl Shone, Chris Stevens, Jim Stevenson, Clive Streeter, Harry Taylor, David Ward, Mathew Ward, Alan Williams, Stephen Wooster, Nick Wright, Colin Yeates.

PHOTOGRAPHIC AND ARTWORK REFERENCE

Christopher Woodward of the Building of Bath Museum, Franz Karl Freiherr von Linden, NRSC Air Photo Group, The Oxford Mail and Times and Mark and Jane Rees.

PHOTOGRAPHY PERMISSIONS

DORLING KINDERSLEY would like to thank the following for their assistance and kind permission to photograph at their establishments: Banqueting House (Crown copyright by kind permission of Historic Royal Palaces); Cabinet War Rooms; Paul Highnam at English Heritage; Dean and Chapter Exeter Cathedral; Gatwick Airport Ltd; Heathrow Airport Ltd; Thomas Woods at Historic Scotland; Provost and Scholars Kings College; Cambridge; London Transport Museum; Madame Tussaud's; National Museums and Galleries of Wales (Museum of Welsh Life); Diana Lanham and Gayle Mault at the National Trust; Peter Reekie and Isla Roberts at the National Trust for Scotland; Provost Skene House; Saint Bartholmew the Great; Saint James's Church; London

St Paul's Cathderal; Masters and Wardens of the Worshipful Company of Skinners; Provost and Chapter of Southwark Cathderal; HM Tower of London; Dean and Chapter of Westminster; Dean and Chapter of Worcetser Cathedral and all the other churches, museums, hotels, restaurants, shops, galleries and sights too numerous to thank individually.

PICTURE CREDITS

t = top; tl = top left; tlc = top left centre; tc = top centre; tr = top right; cla = centre left above; ca = centre above; cra = centre right above; cl = centre left; c = centre; cr = centre right; clb = centre left below; cb = centre below; crb = centre right below; bl = bottom left; b = bottom; bc = bottom centre; bcl = bottom centre left; br = bottom right; d = detail.

Works of art have been reproduced with the permission of the following copyright holders: © ADAGP, Paris and DACS, London 1995: 157t; © Alan Bowness, Hepworth Estate 263bl; © DACS, London 1995: 93c; © Patrick Heron 1995 all rights reserved DACS: 226ch; © D Hockney: 1970–1 93tr, 1990–3 397t; © Estate of Stanley Spencer 1995 all rights reserved DACS 221t; © Angela Verren-Taunt 1995 all rights reserved DACS: 263br.

The work of Henry Moore, *Large Two Forms,* 1966, illustrated on page 399b has been reproduced by permission of the Henry Moore Foundation.

The publisher would like to thank the following individuals, companies and picture libraries for permission to reproduce their photographs:

ABBOT HALL ART GALLERY AND MUSEUM, Kendal: 358b(d); ABERDEEN ART GALLERIES 526t; ABERDEEN AND GRAMPIAN TOURIST BOARD 465ca; ACTION PLUS: 67t; 466t; Steve Bardens 66bl, 420c; David Davies 67cr; Glynn Kirk 66tl; Peter Tarry 66cla, 67bl; Printed by kind permission of MOHAMED AL FAYED: 99t; AMERICAN MUSEUM, Bath: 247tl; ANCIENT ART AND ARCHITECTURE COLLECTION: 42cb, 44ca, 44clb, 45ca, 45clb, 46bl, 46br, 48crb, 51ca, 218tl, 221br, 425t; APEX PHOTO AGENCY: Nick Gregory 269tl; THE ARCHIVE & BUSINESS RECORDS CENTRE, University of Glasgow: 469t; T & R ANNAN AND SONS: 502b(d); ASHMOLEAN MUSEUM, OXFORD: 47t; MUSEUM OF AUTOMATA, YORK: 393b.

BARNABY'S PICTURE LIBRARY: 60tr; BEAMISH OPEN AIR MUSEUM: 410c, 401b, 411ca, 411cb, 411b; BRIDGEMAN ART LIBRARY, LONDON AND NEW YORK: Agnew and Sons, London 309t; Museum of Antiquities, Newcastle upon Tyne 44tl; Apsley House, The Wellington Museum, London 26tl; Bibliotheque Nationale, Paris *Neville Book of Hours* 308t(d); Birmingham City Museums and Gallery 305t; Bonham's, London, *Portrait of Lord Nelson with Santa Cruz Beyond,* Lemuel Francis Abbot 54cb(d); Bradford Art Galleries and Museums 49clb; City of Bristol Museums and Art Galleries 242c; British Library, London, *Pictures and Arms of English Kings and Knights* 41t(d), 39t(d), *The Kings of England from Brutus to Henry* 26bl(d), *Stowe manuscript* 40tl(d), *Liber Legum Antiquorum Regum* 46t(d), *Calendar Anglo-Saxon Miscellany* 44–7t(d), 46–7c(d), 46–7b(d), *Decrees of Kings of Anglo-Saxon and Norman England* 47clb, 49bl(d), *Portrait of Chaucer,* Thomas Occleve 49br(d), *Portrait of Shakespeare,* Droeshurt 51bl(d), *Historia Anglorum* 40bl(d), 222tl(d), *Chronicle of Peter of Langtoft* 271b(d), *Lives and Miracles of St Cuthbert* 405tl(d), 405cl(d), 405cr(d), *Lindisfarne Gospels* 405br(d), *Commendatio Lamentabilis intransitu Edward IV* 422b(d), *Histoire du Roy d'Angleterre Richard II* 424t(d), 523b; Christies, London 431t; Claydon House, Bucks, *Florence Nightingale,* Sir William Blake Richmond 148t; Department of Environment, London 48tr; City of Edinburgh Museums and Galleries, *Chief of Scottish Clan,* Eugene Deveria 470bl(d); Fitzwilliam Museum, University of Cambridge, *George IV as Prince Regent,* Richard Cosway 165cb, 198bl, *Flemish Book of Hours* 336tl(d); Giraudon/Musee de la

Tapisserie, with special authorization of the city of Bayeux 47b,167b; Guildhall Library, Corporation of London, *The Great Fire*, Marcus Willemsz Doornik 53bl(d), *Bubbler's Melody* 54br(d), *Triumph of Steam and Electricity*, The Illustrated London News 57t(d), *Great Exhibition, The transept from Dickenson's Comprehensive Pictures* 56–7, *A Balloon View of London as seen from Hampstead* 107c(d); Harrogate Museum and Art Gallery, North Yorkshire 374t; Holburne Museum and Crafts Study Centre, Bath 53t; Imperial War Museum, *London Field Marshall Montgomery*, J Worsley 27cbr(d); Kedleston Hall, Derbyshire 24br; King Street Galleries, London, *Bonnie Prince Charlie*, G Dupré 468tl; Lambeth Palace Library, London, *St Alban's Chronicle* 49t; Lever Brothers Ltd, Cheshire 335cra; Lincolnshire County Council, Usher Gallery, Lincoln, *Portrait of Mrs Fitzherbert after Richard Cosway* 165b; London Library, *The Barge Tower from Ackermann's World in miniature*, F Scoberl 55t; Manchester City Art Galleries 361b; David Messum Gallery, London 433b; National Army Museum, London, *Bunker's Hill*, R Simkin 54ca; National Gallery, London, *Mrs Siddons the Actress*, Thomas Gainsborough 54t(d), 149ca; National Museet, Copenhagen 46ca; Phillips, the International Fine Art Auctioneers, *James I*, John the Elder Decritz 52b(d); Private Collections: 8–9, 26ca(d), 34tl, 48–9, 55cla, 55bl, 56clb, Vanity Fair 57br, 149t, *Ellesmere Manuscript* 174b(d), *Armada: map of the Spanish and British Fleets*, Robert Adam 279t, 382t, 408b; Royal Geographical Society, London 149cb(d); Royal Holloway & Bedford New College, the *Princes Edward and Richard in the Tower*, Sir John Everett Millais 121b; Smith Art Gallery and Museum, Stirling 482b; Tate Gallery, London: 56crb, 223t; Thyssen-Bornemisza Collection, Lugo Casta, *King Henry VIII*, Hans Holbein the Younger 50b(d); Victoria and Albert Museum, London 24t(d), 56b, 99c, 190t, 337cr, 379b, *Miniature of Mary Queen of Scots*, by a follower of Francois Clouet 497br, 523t(d); Walker Art Gallery, Liverpool 364c; Westminster Abbey, London, *Henry VII Tomb effigy*, Pietro Torrigiano 26br(d), 40bc(d); The Trustees of the Weston Park Foundation, *Portrait of Richard III*, Italian School 49cla(d); Christopher Wood Gallery, London, *High Life Below Stairs*, Charles Hunt 25c(d); reproduced with permission of the BRITISH AIRWAYS: Adrian Meredith Photography 632t; BFI LONDON IMAX CINEMA WATERLOO: Richard Holttum 125c; BRITISH LIBRARY BOARD: *Cotton Faustina BVII folio 85* 49cb, 109cl; © THE BRITISH MUSEUM: 42cr, 43cb, 73tl, 83c, 105, 108–9 all except 109t and 109bl; © THE BRONTE SOCIETY: 398 all; BURTON CONSTABLE FOUNDATION: Dr David Connell 388t.

CADOGEN MANAGEMENT: 86b; CADW – Welsh Historic Monuments (Crown Copyright), 460t; CAMERA PRESS: Cecil Beaton 94bl; CARDIFF CITY COUNCIL: 458tr, 459t, 459c; FKB CARLSON: 35bcl; CASTLE HOWARD ESTATE LTD: 385tl; COLIN DE CHAIRE: 183c; TRUSTEES OF THE CHATSWORTH SETTLEMENT: 320b, 321b; MUSEUM OF CHILDHOOD, Edinburgh: 496b; BRUCE . COLEMAN LTD: 31br; Stephen Bond 280b; Jane Burton 31cra; Mark N. Boulton 31cl; Patrick Clement 30clb; Peter Evans 530tl; Paul van Gaalen 236tl; Sir Jeremy Grayson 31bl; Harald Lange 30bc; Gordon Langsbury 531t; George McCarthy 30t, 31bl, 228b, 271br; Paul Meitz 514clb; Dr. Eckart Pott 30bl, 514t; Hans Reinhard 30cb, 31tc, 280t, 480tl; Dr Frieder Sauer 520t; N Schwiatz 31clb; Kim Taylor 31tl, 514cra; Konrad Wothe 514ca; JOE CORNISH: 389b; courtesy of the CORPORATION OF LONDON: 115b; DOUG CORRANCE: 471b; JOHN CROOK: 157b.

EASYEVERYTHING: James Hamilton 622br; 1805 CLUB: 27t; 1853 GALLERY, Bradford 397t; ENGLISH HERITAGE: 132b, 194c, 194b, 195b, 234–5b, 249b, 336br, 337b, 380t, 405tr, 405c; Avebury Museum 42ca; Devizes Museum 42br, drawing by Frank Gardiner 409br; Salisbury Museum 42t, 42bl; Skyscan Balloon Photography 43t, 248b; 380t; 409bl; ENGLISH LIFE PUBLICATIONS LTD, Derby: 328tl, 328tr, 329t, 329b; ET ARCHIVE: 41tc, 41cr, 52cb, 53clb, 58crb, 148b; Bodleian Library, Oxford 48crb; British Library, London 48tl, 48ca; Devizes Museum 42cl, 43b, 248c; Garrick Club 422tl(d); Imperial War Museum, London 58clb(d), 59br;

Labour Party Archives 60br; London Museum 43cla; Magdalene College 50ca; National Maritime Museum, London 39b; Stoke Museum Staffordshire Polytechnic 41bc, 52tl; Victoria & Albert Museum, London 50t(d); EUREKA!: 399t; MARY EVANS PICTURE LIBRARY: 9 inset, 34tr, 40br, 41tl, 41cl, 41bl, 41br, 44bl, 44br, 46cb, 47cla, 51t, 51cb, 51br, 53crb, 54bl, 55br, 56tl, 58ca, 59ca, 59clb, 59crb, 81cb, 106t, 107t, 119b, 143 inset, 148cb, 149b, 173c, 175c, 181b, 192c, 208bl, 214tl, 217c, 217bl, 217br, 220bl, 225 inset, 265t, 283 inset, 322b, 335t, 335cla, 359tr, 406t, 433tl, 468b, 485b, 498bl, 500b, 501t, 521b, 613 inset. CHRIS FAIRCLOUGH: 281b, 338b, 640b; PAUL FELIX: 220c; FFOTOGRAFF © Charles Aithie: 421t; FISHBOURNE ROMAN VILLA: 45t; LOUIS FLOOD: 470br; FOREIGN AND BRITISH BIBLE SOCIETY: Cambridge University Library 423c; FOTOMAS INDEX: 107caa. GARDEN PICTURE LIBRARY: J S Sira 23crt; John Glover 23rb; Steven Wooster 22–23t; GLASGOW MUSEUMS: Burrell Collection 507ca, 506–7 all except 506tl; Art Gallery & Museum, Kelvingrove 505t, 517b, 529b(d); Saint Mungo Museum of Religious Life and Art 503tl; Museum of Transport 504cr; JOHN GLOVER: 62cr, 146cb, 191b; THE GORE HOTEL, London: 540c.

SONIA HALLIDAY AND LAURA LUSHINGTON ARCHIVE: 395t; ROBERT HARDING PICTURE LIBRARY: 168t, 534t; Jan Baldwin 273b; M H Black 274t; Teresa Black 621cb; Nigel Blythe 632ca; L Bond 323b; Michael Botham 32br; C Bowman 629c; Lesley Burridge 290tr; Martyn F Chillman 291bc; Philip Craven 103t, 186b, 311b; Nigel Francis 205b, 635b; Robert Francis 66–7; Paul Freestone 212b; Brian Harrison 515b; Van der Hars 524t; Michael Jenner 45b, 515c; Norma Joseph 65b; Christopher Nicholson 239t; B O'Connor 33ca; Jenny Pate 147bc; Rainbird Collection 47crb; Roy Rainsford 33b, 154t, 284b, 324cr, 356t, 372t, 461b; Walter Rawling 21t; Hugh Routledge 2–3; Peter Scholey 285t; Michael Short 291br; James Strachen 370b; Julia K Thorne 472bl; Adina Tovy 61tl, 472br; Andy Williams 165t, 220br, 332c, 418t, 510; Adam Woolfitt 20t, 20c, 44tr, 45crb, 246b, 258, 273ca, 291bl, 425bl, 454tl, 530tr; HAREWOOD HOUSE: 396c; PAUL HARRIS: 32t, 62cl, 287bl(d), 324b, 353b, 612–3, 630c, 630b; HARROGATE INTERNATIONAL CENTRE: 375b; HEATHROW AIRPORT LTD: 619b; Crown copyright is reproduced with the permission of the Controller of HMSO: 73br, 120bl, 120br, 121tl; CATHEDRAL CHURCH OF THE BLESSED VIRGIN MARY AND ST ETHELBERT IN HEREFORD: 302b; HERTFORDSHIRE COUNTY COUNCIL: Bob Norris 58–9; JOHN HESELTINE: 74t, 104, 109t, 110, 236tr, 236c, 455tl; HISTORIC ROYAL PALACES (Crown Copyright): 22l, 159 all; HISTORIC SCOTLAND (Crown Copyright): 483c, 492tr, 492c; PETER HOLLINGS: 334bl; NEIL HOLMES: 244b(d), 246c, 272t, 359b, 415tl, 415tr, 437b, 643t; ANGELO HORNAK LIBRARY: 392tl, 392bl, 392br, 395br; Reproduced by permission of the CLERK OF RECORDS, HOUSE OF LORDS: 469c; DAVID MARTIN HUGHES: 142–3, 150; HULTON-DEUTSCH COLLECTION: 22c, 22tr, 27cl, 27cr, 53cla, 54c, 56c, 57cb, 58tl 58tr, 58b, 59t, 60ca, 60bl, 148ca, 155c, 219b, 286t, 334c, 335crb, 336bl, 363b, 383b, 384br, 423t, 481b, 508tl, 522b; HUNTERIAN ART GALLERY: 505b; HUTCHISON LIBRARY: Catherine Blacky 34cb; Bernard Gerad 467t; HUTTON IN THE FOREST: Lady Inglewood 344t.

THE IMAGE BANK, London: Derek Berwin538t; David Gould 343b; Romilly Lockyer 74bl; Colin Molyneux 455bl; Stockphotos/Steve Allen360c, Trevor Wood 272b; Simon Wilkinson 166b; IMAGES COLOUR LIBRARY: 30cla, 43c, 207b, 220t, 235t, 236bl, 237b, 322t, 324cl, 325t, 339c, 638t, 638b; Horizon/Robert Estall 424c; Landscape Only 33cb, 234, 351, 425br; IRONBRIDGE MUSEUM: 301b. JARROLD PUBLISHERS: 198br, 215t(d), 290bl; MICHAEL JENNER: 290t, 326b, 514b; JORVIK VIKING CENTRE, York: 391t. ROYAL BOTANIC GARDENS, Kew: 76ca.

FRANK LANE PICTURE AGENCY: 386b(d); W Broadhurst 240b; Michael Callan 228crb; ANDREW LAWSON: 23c, 23cb, 230br, 231tl, 231tr, 231br; LEEDS CASTLE ENTERPRISES: 151b; LEIGHTON HOUSE, Royal Borough of Kensington: 128br; published by kind permission DEAN AND CHAPTER OF LINCOLN 326t, 327cb, 327bl; LINCOLNSHIRE COUNTY COUNCIL: USHER GALLERY, Lincoln: c 1820 by William Ilbery 327bl; LLANGOLEN INTERNATIONAL MUSICAL EISTEDDFOD 436c; LONDON AMBULANCE SERVICE: 621ca;

London Film Festival: 62t; London Transport Museum: 82t; Longleat House: 252t.

Madame Tussauds: 106b; Maldom Millenium Trust: 195t; Mansell Collection, London: 27clb, 40tr, 52ca, 55cb, 247tr, 309bl, 335clb, 388b; Nick Meers: 18t, 224–5; Metropolitan Police Service: 621t; Archie Miles: 226ca; Simon Miles: 338tr; Minack Theatre: Murray King 262b; Mirror Syndication International: 76b, 89b, 112; BTA/Juilian Nieman 34ca; Philip Russell 354–5; Museum of London: 44crb, 113t. National Fishing Heritage Centre, Grimsby: 389t; National Gallery, London: 73tr, 84–5 all; National Gallery Of Scotland: *The Reverend Walker Skating on Duddington Loch*, Sir Henry Raeburn 490c(d); National Library of Wales: 422tr, 425c(d), 453b; National Museum Of Film And Television, Bradford: 397c; Board of Trustees of the National Museums and Galleries on Merseyside: Liverpool Museum 365t; Maritime Museum 363t; Walker Art Gallery 332b, 364tl, 364tr, 364b, 365c; National Museums Of Scotland: 491t, 497bl; National Museum of Wales: 422c; By courtesy of the National Portrait Gallery, London: *First Earl of Essex*, Hans Peter Holbein 337t(d); National Tramway Museum, Crich: 325c; National Trust Photographic Library: *Bess of Hardwick (Elizabeth, Countess of Shrewsbury)*, Anon 320tl(d); Mathew Antrobus 288br, 376cl, 377bl; Oliver Benn 25br, 264c, 279bl, 376b; John Bethell 265c, 265bl, 265br, 289t; Nick Carter 241b; Joe Cornish 442; Prudence Cumming 253c; Martin Dohrn 50crb; Andreas Von Einsidedel 25bl, 288cb, 289ca; Roy Fox 257t; Geoffry Frosh 275t; Jerry Harpur 230t, 230bl; Derek Harris 230clb, 253t; Nadia MacKenzie 24cl; Nick Meers 252b, 253b, 306b, 615b; Rob Motheson 278t; Cressida Pemberton Piggot 540t; Ian Shaw 446t; Richard Surman 289br, 348b; Rupert Truman 289br, 365b; Andy Tryner 288bl; Charlie Waite 377t; Jeremy Whitaker 289bc, 379t, 446b; Mike Williams 288ca, 377c; George Wright 230crlb, 278c; National Trust For Scotland: 464b, 486b, 487c, 494b, 508tr, 509tl, 509tr, 509br; Glyn Satterley 503tr; Lindsey Robertson 509bl; National Waterways Museum at Gloucester: 287bc, 287br; NHPA: Martin Garwood 381ca; Daniel Heuclin 268la; Nature Photographers: Andrew Cleave 228cla; E A James 31cla, 346t; Hugh Miles 407t; Owen Newman 31ca; William Paton 514crb; Paul Sterry 30crb, 30br, 31cb, 31crb, 220c, 241t, 373t, 514cla; Roger Tidman 183b; Network Photographers: Laurie Sparham 466b; New Shakespeare Theatre Co: 125t; Norfolk Museums Service: Norwich Castle Museum 187b; Oxford Scientific Films: Okapia 268lb.

'PA' News Photo Library: John Stillwell 61 cr. Palace Theatre Archive: 124c; Photos Horticultural: 147tlc, 147cra, 147cb, 147crb, 230ca, 231c; Pictures: 632t; Planet Earth Pictures: David Phillips 23crca; Popperfoto: 27br, 59bl, 60clb, 60crb, 61bl, 88tl, 146tr, 189t, 270cl, 430b; AFP/Eric Feferber 61br; SG Forester 67br; Port Merion Ltd: 440tl; Press Association: Martin Keene 62b; Public Record Office (Crown Copyright): 48b.

Rob Reichenfeld: 160t, 161c, 161b, 286b, 626b, 631t; Rex Features Ltd: 27ca, 41tr, 60tl, 61bc, 222c, 223br; Barry Beattie 245cl; Peter Brooke 27bc, 624br; Nils Jorgensen 26c, 629t, 636c; Eileen Kleinman 629br; Hazel Murray 61tr; Tess, Renn-Burrill Productions 255b; Brian Rasic 63t; Nick Rogers

61tc; Tim Rooke 64cr, 66tr; Sipa/Chesnot 27bl; Today 21c; Richard Young 60tl; The Ritz, London: 83t; Royal Academy Of Arts, London: 86ca; Royal Collection © 1995 Her Majesty Queen Elizabeth II: *The Family of Henry VIII*, Anon 38(d), 87c, 88tr, 88bl, 89t, 222tr, 223tl(d), 223tr, 223bl, *George IV, in full Highland dress*, Sir David Wilkie 471t; David Cripps 89c; John Freeman 88br; Royal College Of Music, London: 98c; Royal Pavilion, Art Gallery and Museums, Brighton: 164c, 164bl, 164br, 165cl, 165cr; Royal Shakespeare Theatre Company: Donald Cooper 313cc(d).

St. Alban's Museums: Verulamium Museum 218b; Sartaj Balti House: Clare Carnegie 397b; Scottish National Gallery of Modern Art: Roy Lichtenstein In the Car 493c; Scottish National Portrait Gallery: on loan from the collection of the Earl of Roseberry, *Execution of Charles I*, Unknown Artist 52–3; S4C (Channel 4 Wales): 423b; Sidmouth Folk Festival: Derek Brooks 275b; Skyscan Balloon Photography: 248t; John Snocken: 23cr, 23ra; Southbank Press Office: 126t; Sporting Pictures: 66cra, 66bc, 66br, 67cl, 344b; Still Moving Pictures: Doug Corrance 534b; Wade Cooper 469b; Derek Laird 468c; Robert Lees 65t; STB 530br, 531c, Paisley Museum 501b, Paul Tomkins 515tr; SJ Whitehorn 481t; Tony Stone Images: 34–5, 536–7; Rex A.Butcher 83c; Richard Elliott 64b; Rob Talbot 339ca; David Woodfall 426. Tate Britain, London: 73bl, 93 all except c and tl, 263c, 263bl, 263br, 93c with kind permission of the Henry Moore Foundation; Rob Talbot: 339cb; Tuille House Museum, Carlisle: 344c. Courtesy of the Board of Trustees of the Victoria And Albert Musuem, London: 72b, 100–101 all except 100t.

Charlie Waite: 535t; © Wales Tourist Board: 419c, 420b, 424–5, 454br, 455tr, 455br; Roger Vitos 454tl, 454bl; The Wallace Collection, London: 106cb; David Ward: 511b, 529t; Frederick Warne & Co: 353t(d); Courtesy of the Trustees of The Wedgwood Museum, Barlaston, Staffordshire, England: 297b; Jeremy Whitaker: 214tr, 214c, 215b; Whitbread Plc: 34bl; Whitworth Art Gallery, University of Manchester: courtesy of Granada Television Arts Foundation 361c; Christopher Wilson: 390bl; Wilton House Trust: 251b; Winchester Cathedral: 157t; Woburn Abbey – by kind permission of the Marquess of Tavistock and Trustees of the Bedford Estate: 50–1, 216t; Timothy Woodcock Photolibrary: 5b; Photo © Woodmansterne, Watford, UK: Jeremy Marks 116t, 117t.

York Castle Museum: 391cb; Dean & Chapter York Minster: 395cla, 395ca, 395cl; Peter Gibson 395cra, 395cr, 395cl; Jim Korshaw 392tr; Reproduced by couresty of the Yorkshire Museum: 394c; Yorkshire Sculpture Park: Jerry Hardman Jones 399b. Zefa: 64t, 126b, 249t, 255t, 472c, 627t, 634c, 636bl; Bob Croxford 63cr; Weir 183t.

Cover: All special photography except Robert Harding Picture Library/Rosehaven Ltd: front top. Front Endpaper: All special photography except Robert Harding Picture Library/Andy Williams tl, Adam Woolfitt bl; David Martin Hughes brl; National Trust Photographic Library/Joe Cornish clc; Tony Stone Images/David Woodfall cl. Back Endpaper: All special photography except John Heseltine tl, br.

DORLING KINDERSLEY SPECIAL EDITIONS

Dorling Kindersley books can be purchased in bulk quantities at discounted prices for use in promotions or as premiums. We are also able to offer special editions and personalized jackets, corporate imprints, and excerpts from all of our books, tailored specifically to meet your own needs.

To find out more, please contact:
(in the United Kingdom) – Special Sales,
Dorling Kindersley Limited,
80 Strand, London WC2R 0RL;

(in the United States) – Special Markets Dept.,
Dorling Kindersley Publishing, Inc.,
95 Madison Avenue, New York, NY 10016.

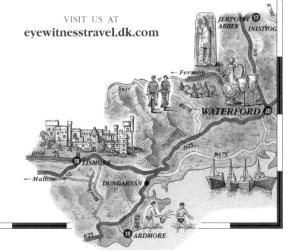

Central London

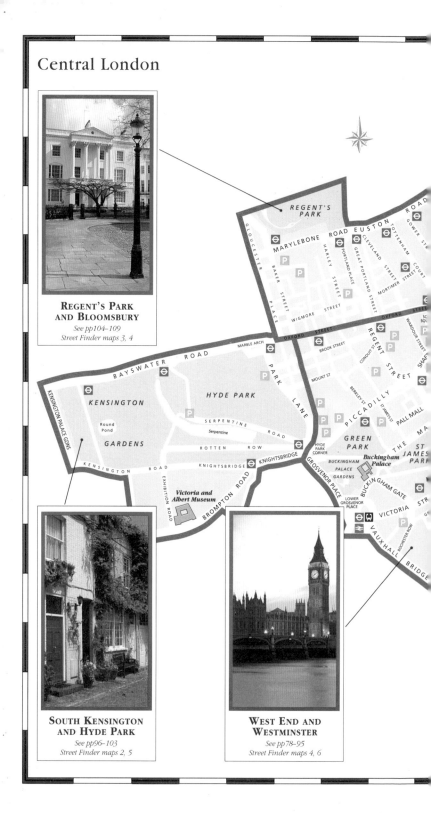

**REGENT'S PARK
AND BLOOMSBURY**
See pp104–109
Street Finder maps 3, 4

REGENT'S
PARK

MARYLEBONE ROAD EUSTON ROAD

GLOUCESTER PLACE
BAKER STREET
HARLEY STREET
PORTLAND PLACE
GREAT PORTLAND STREET
CLEVELAND STREET
MORTIMER STREET
TOTTENHAM COURT ROAD
GOWER STREET

WIGMORE STREET

OXFORD STREET

OXFORD STREET
WARDOUR STREET

REGENT STREET

BROOK STREET

CONDUIT STREET

BAYSWATER ROAD

MARBLE ARCH

PARK LANE

MOUNT ST

BERKELEY ST
ST JAMES ST

PICCADILLY

SHAFT

PALL MALL

**SOUTH KENSINGTON
AND HYDE PARK**
See pp96–103
Street Finder maps 2, 5

KENSINGTON PALACE GDNS

KENSINGTON
GARDENS

Round
Pond

KENSINGTON ROAD

HYDE PARK

SERPENTINE ROAD

Serpentine

ROTTEN ROW

KNIGHTSBRIDGE

BROMPTON ROAD

EXHIBITION ROAD

*Victoria and
Albert Museum*

HYDE PARK CORNER

GREEN
PARK

THE MA

ST
JAMES
PARK

BUCKINGHAM
PALACE
GARDENS

*Buckingham
Palace*

BUCKINGHAM GATE

GROSVENOR PLACE

LOWER
GROSVENOR
PLACE

VICTORIA

ROCHESTER ROW

VAUXHALL BRIDGE

STR

G

**WEST END AND
WESTMINSTER**
See pp78–95
Street Finder maps 4, 6